THE OXFORD HAN

ROMAN SCULPTURE

THE OXFORD HANDBOOK OF

ROMAN SCULPTURE

Edited by

ELISE A. FRIEDLAND

and

MELANIE GRUNOW SOBOCINSKI

with

ELAINE K. GAZDA

OXFORD
UNIVERSITY PRESS

OXFORD
UNIVERSITY PRESS

Oxford University Press is a department of the University of Oxford. It furthers the University's objective of excellence in research, scholarship, and education by publishing worldwide. Oxford is a registered trade mark of Oxford University Press in the UK and certain other countries.

Published in the United States of America by Oxford University Press
198 Madison Avenue, New York, NY 10016, United States of America.

First issued as an Oxford University Press paperback, 2018

CIP data is on file at the Library of Congress
ISBN 978–0–19–992182–9 (hardcover); 978–0–19–088700–1 (paperback)

Dedicated to the memory of Natalie B. Kampen and Miranda Marvin,
two prominent specialists of Roman sculpture,
who had agreed to write chapters for this *Handbook*,
but who passed away while the volume was in preparation.

Contents

PART IV SPATIAL AND SOCIAL CONTEXTS

PART V REGIONS AND PROVINCES

PART VI VIEWING AND RECEPTION

Acknowledgments

We would like to thank Stefan Vranka at Oxford University Press for his interest in and support of this volume, as well as Sarah Pirovitz at OUP and Eric Cline of The George Washington University for their assistance and encouragement throughout. We also thank Lea Stirling and Ellen Perry for their comments and input on the initial proposal and their continued input during the planning and editing of the volume. Peter Stewart and Elizabeth Fisher also made helpful suggestions during the planning phases. We especially thank all of the contributors for the prompt submission of their essays, images, and image permission letters; their diligence enabled the timely production of this volume. We are grateful to the many professionals at museums and other institutions who facilitated granting of permissions and publication of images. In addition, many of the authors wish to thank colleagues (for input on their contributions and various other modes of assistance) and institutions (for access to materials and financial support); however, as space did not permit individual acknowledgements following each essay, we take this opportunity to thank all those who had a hand in supporting our contributors' efforts for this volume. For assisting with indexing the volume, we thank Alison Rittershaus. Finally, we would like to offer special thanks to our families for their patience and encouragement: Elise, especially to Andrew M. Smith II and Eleanor Abigail Friedland; and Melanie, to Gregg, Elizabeth, and Margaret Sobocinski.

List of Contributors

Mark B. Abbe, University of Georgia

Anna Anguissola, Università di Pisa

François Baratte, Université Paris-Sorbonne, UMR 8167 "Orient et Méditerranée"

Elizabeth Bartman, Independent Scholar

Kimberly Cassibry, Wellesley College

Nathalie de Chaisemartin, Université Paris-Sorbonne, UMR 8167 "Orient et Méditerranée"

Amanda Claridge, Royal Holloway, University of London

Eve D'Ambra, Vassar College

Adi Erlich, University of Haifa

Björn C. Ewald, University of Toronto

Elise A. Friedland, The George Washington University

Bernard Frischer, Indiana University

Mark D. Fullerton, Ohio State University

Eleonora Gasparini, La Sapienza–Università di Roma

Elaine K. Gazda, University of Michigan

Nancy T. de Grummond, Florida State University

Alicia Jiménez, Duke University

Barbara Kellum, Smith College

Troels Myrup Kristensen, Aarhus University

Brenda Longfellow, University of Iowa

Hima Mallampati Gleason, Independent Scholar

Carol C. Mattusch, George Mason University

Matthew M. McCarty, University of British Columbia

Eric M. Moormann, Radboud Universiteit Nijmegen

Diana Y. Ng, University of Michigan–Dearborn

Patrizio Pensabene, La Sapienza–Università di Roma

Ellen E. Perry, College of the Holy Cross

Lauren Hackworth Petersen, University of Delaware

Jerry Podany, J. Paul Getty Museum

Jessica Powers, San Antonio Museum of Art

Christina Riggs, University of East Anglia

Isabel Rodà, UAB (Universitat Autònoma de Barcelona)-ICAC (Institut Català d'Arqueologia Clàssica)

Ben Russell, University of Edinburgh

Josephine Shaya, The College of Wooster

Melanie Grunow Sobocinski, Independent Scholar

Michael Squire, King's College London

Mary C. Sturgeon, University of North Carolina, Chapel Hill

Molly Swetnam-Burland, The College of William and Mary

Lori-Ann Touchette, Independent Scholar

Jennifer Trimble, Stanford University

Francesca Tronchin, Independent Scholar

Steven L. Tuck, Miami University, Ohio

Eric R. Varner, Emory University

Thomas M. Weber-Karyotakis, German-Jordanian University Amman

Christian Witschel, Universität Heidelberg

Elizabeth Wolfram Thill, Indiana University–Purdue University Indianapolis

Susan Wood, Oakland University

INTRODUCTION

ELISE A. FRIEDLAND AND
MELANIE GRUNOW SOBOCINSKI

Rationale and Goals

In the past two decades, the field of Roman sculptural studies has advanced dramatically. Well-established methods of stylistic, iconographic, and technical analysis have been enriched by new theoretical thinking, additional scientific approaches, attempts to move beyond the confines of dualistic categories, a heightened focus on settings and contexts, and an expanding corpus. This *Handbook* reflects these developments and at the same time presents a critical look at the state of the field of Roman sculptural studies. It offers the apparatus necessary for students and scholars to pursue their study of Roman sculpture and provides a platform for future research.

The study of Roman sculpture has been an essential part of the disciplines of art history and classical studies since their emergence in the eighteenth century. From Johann Joachim Winckelmann's 1764 *History of the Art of Antiquity* to the cast galleries of Europe and then of early America, Roman sculpture (with ideal statuary often seen as a proxy for no-longer-extant Greek originals) served as one of the primary forms of material culture that gave scholars access to the ancient world. Since the early nineteenth century, specialists have studied Roman sculptures in their artistic, architectural, and cultural contexts, cataloging and categorizing ideal sculpture, monumental reliefs, public honorific sculptures, portraits, sarcophagi, funerary reliefs, figurines, and other less common sculptural types. From methodologies such as *Kopienkritik* to social readings of plebian and patrician art and beyond, scholars have returned repeatedly to Roman sculpture to answer a variety of questions about Roman art, society, and history. Indeed, the field of Roman sculptural studies encompasses not only the full chronological range of the Roman world and its expansive geography, but also a variety of artistic media (e.g., bronze, various stones, coroplastic), formats (freestanding and relief), sizes, and functions. Moreover, because sculptures populated both the urban and private realms in numbers that are unparalleled today and because these sculptures were essential to communicating political, religious, and social messages, statuary provides an invaluable entrée into Roman society.

Exciting new theories, methods, and evidence have transformed the specialized literature on Roman sculpture in recent decades. Diana E. E. Kleiner's heavily illustrated textbook *Roman Sculpture* (1992) remains a masterful chronological presentation of the best-known and most representative examples of various periods, genres, and styles, and Patrick Schollmeyer's *Römische Plastik: Eine Einführung* (2005) provides a synthesis in German; however, since the publication of Kleiner's textbook, no overview of the topic has appeared in English beyond those in volumes on Roman art as a whole. Thus, this *Handbook* seeks to fill the gap between such introductory textbooks (which often do not reveal the critical apparatus to the user) and the highly focused professional literature. Here, readers will find a compendium of new technical, scientific, literary, and theoretical approaches to the study of Roman sculpture (including discussions of their advantages and disadvantages). This *Handbook* aspires to synthesize current approaches to studying this central medium of Roman art and to situate Roman sculpture within the larger fields of art history, classical archaeology, and Roman studies.

Scope and Organization

Chronologically, this volume includes material from the early republican period through late antiquity (c. 500 BC to AD 500), just after the fall of the western Roman Empire. Geographically, the *Handbook* considers sculpture in Rome and in regions dominated by the Roman Empire, including Italy, Gaul, Spain, the Northern European provinces, North Africa, Greece, Asia Minor, Egypt, and the Near East. Part V focuses on specific areas of the empire, but essays throughout the volume consider geographic variation in the production, display, and meaning of sculpture.

Essays in this *Handbook* discuss historiography, pertinent theories, conceptual approaches, and methodologies. However, the detailed treatment of iconography is beyond the scope of this volume, since the whole gamut of ancient iconography appears in Roman sculpture. Individual essays explore correlations between genre and iconography and germane examples of particular iconographies. For more detailed treatments of iconography, we encourage readers to consult specialist studies on the iconographic topic of interest. The volumes of the *Lexicon Iconographicum Mythologiae Classicae* (*LIMC*) as well as those of the *Thesaurus Cultus et Rituum Antiquorum* (*ThesCRA*) are excellent resources.

The *Handbook* begins with part I, "Collecting, Conservation, and Display," a section that in some ways comes "last" chronologically but first in considering how the sculptures we encounter came to be in their current state. The essays in this section explore key moments of historiography and the multiple contexts in which Roman sculpture has been analyzed and exhibited: the early history of collecting statuary in both premodern

Europe and early America and its impact on the field of Roman sculptural studies (1.1, Bartman; and 1.3, Mallampati Gleason); the role of eighteenth- and nineteenth-century restoration and modern derestoration and conservation (1.2, Podany); issues of modern museum display (1.4, Powers); and the use and interpretive possibilities of emerging technologies for scanning and three-dimensional digital reconstruction of sculptures and their contexts (1.5, Frischer).

All studies of Roman sculpture are rooted in the individual object as the basic unit of analysis. Part II of this *Handbook*, "Production and Distribution," therefore addresses aspects of analysis imbedded in the materiality of objects, reviews our current knowledge concerning the production of major sculptural media, and presents our growing arsenal of technical and scientific approaches. The first three essays focus on marble (white and colored): the location, ownership and administration, and scientific differentiation of marble quarries (2.1, Pensabene and Gasparini); the carving techniques, workshops, and artisans who sculpted marble (2.2, Claridge); and the techniques and meaning of the frequent recarving and reuse of marble statues, and portraits in particular (2.3, Varner). Though bronze sculptures are less frequently preserved, bronze was indeed the other major sculptural medium of the Roman world. The essay on bronzes (2.4, Mattusch) reviews the technical, stylistic, and literary evidence for this important medium. Terracotta figurines and statuettes also played a vital role in Roman society, as the essay on the coroplastic arts argues (2.5, Erlich). These mass-produced and inexpensive objects were accessible to a wide range of social classes, including women, children, and the poor. An essay on polychromy added to white and colored marble as well as bronze (2.6, Abbe) demonstrates the critical role of this often-neglected final stage of sculptural production and highlights recently developed nondestructive techniques for detecting traces of color even on apparently over-cleaned surfaces in "a new micro-stratigraphic surface archaeology of ancient sculpture." Part II closes with recent work on the shipping, transport, and distribution of Roman sculpture (2.7, Russell), which illuminates questions related to supply, demand, and the empire-wide art market.

Part III of the *Handbook*, "Styles and Genres," maintains the focus on materiality. The essays explore both the major genres and styles of Roman sculpture and the challenges to those categories posed by traditionally marginalized bodies of material and by methodologically vigorous re-evaluation of familiar sculptures. The first essay in this section (3.1, Fullerton) assesses the centrality of style as an analytic category in Roman sculptural studies and points out the limitations of style as a chronological indicator. Also addressed by essays in this section are the ways in which Roman artists adapted earlier artistic traditions—Etruscan (3.2, de Grummond), Greek (3.3, Anguissola; and 3.6, Touchette), and Egyptian (3.7, Swetnam-Burland)—for new audiences through practices such as emulation and eclecticism. Other essays focus on the taxonomic categories of ideal sculpture (3.3, Anguissola), portraiture (3.4, Wood), and monumental reliefs (3.5, Sobocinski and Wolfram Thill), as well as the changes and continuities in the "sculpture habit" during the final centuries of the Roman Empire (3.8, Witschel).

Part IV, "Spatial and Social Contexts," highlights the important trend of studying the settings and functions of Roman sculpture and the critical role sculpture played in the political, social, and religious realms of ancient society. The section begins with a look at the physical and spatial contexts of sculpture as displayed in antiquity by examining sculpture in the public, urban landscapes of the Roman world (4.1, Longfellow). Sacred environments featuring sculptures—cult, votive, and other—offer the opportunity to explore the relationships not only between sanctuary sculpture and civic dedications but also between religious statues and ritual, demonstrating the complexity of the surviving evidence and the nuances involved in interpreting it (4.2, McCarty). An essay that examines the display of sculpture in the domestic realm (4.3, Gazda) calls attention to immersive environments that include not only sculptures but also other artistic media that are often visually or thematically linked. Funerary sculpture can transcend the categories of "public" and "private" and offers much evidence for self-expression (4.4, Ewald). Four final essays in this section explore the epigraphic evidence for the patronage of statuary (4.5, Tuck), imperial messages and their reception (4.6, Kellum), the patronage and representation of non-elites (4.7, Petersen), and issues of gender and sexuality (4.8, D'Ambra and Tronchin).

Part V of this book, "Regions and Provinces," focuses on differences in the production, display, and role of sculpture in a number of territories of the Roman Empire, including Northern Gaul, Germany, and Britain (5.1, Cassibry); Hispaniae and Narbonensis (5.2, Jiménez and Rodà); North Africa (5.3, Baratte and Chaisemartin); Greece (5.4, Sturgeon); Asia Minor (5.5, Ng); Egypt (5.6, Riggs); and the Near East (5.7, Weber). These essays address not only the realities of the sculptural environments in the various regions, but also how sculpture expressed responses to Roman imperialism in material, style, subject matter, display context, patronage, messages, and more. This section also connects Roman sculptural studies to broader debates in Roman studies, such as those surrounding "Romanization" and identity.

The final section of the book, part VI, "Viewing and Reception," examines the multiple bodies of evidence that reveal ways in which the ancients themselves conceived of, perceived, and interacted with statues. The first essay examines the literary evidence for how Romans conceived of and evaluated sculpture by highlighting the diversity of responses—from Cicero's notions of the importance of appropriateness of the subjects of statuary for its setting, to Pliny the Elder's emphasis on the history of sculpture, to Quintilian's relating of art criticism to rhetorical theory (6.1, Squire). These ancient "theories" of Roman sculpture are balanced by an introduction to modern reception theory as applied to Roman statuary (6.2, Trimble). The remainder of the volume addresses the ancient viewing and reception of sculpture by considering tangible sculptural remains, beginning with an essay on Roman "museums" or purposeful public and private collections and displays of sculpture in antiquity (6.3, Shaya). Another essay presents insights into the role of statuary in the Roman world gleaned from depictions of sculpture in other media (6.4, Moormann). The volume concludes with two essays that concern human interactions with statues. One (6.5, Perry) discusses the relations of humans with statues that leave no discernable trace, such as touching, bathing, clothing, feeding, and carrying (as with religious statues) or seeking asylum at, urinating near, or removing from display (as with imperial portraits). The other (6.6, Kristensen) explores sculpture breaking, or iconoclasm—often the result of *damnatio memoriae* or religious conflict—and the insights that this aggressive form of human engagement with statues can offer on the social history of Roman sculpture, especially when interpreted through recent theories of cultural memory. Thus the volume ends in some ways where it began, with a call not only to examine the original contexts for which statuary was created, but to be mindful of the full cultural biographies of Roman statues.

Highlights and Debates

Several issues, particular sculptural monuments, and specific display contexts are discussed by multiple contributors and therefore merit special consideration. We highlight just a few here. Throughout the volume individual authors have presented the historiography of their particular subfields; among these, Tonio Hölscher's work, most completely spelled out in *The Language of Images in Roman Art* ([1987] 2004), should be noted as one of the transformational theories of Roman art for the current generation of scholars. Our authors refer repeatedly to and in many cases depend on Hölscher's theory of a semantics of Roman art in their examination of such widely-ranging topics as the relationship between Greek and Roman sculpture, non-elite sculpture, the sculpture of Roman Greece, and ancient reception (see essays 3.1, Fullerton; 3.3, Anguissola; 3.5, Sobocinski and Wolfram Thill; 4.6, Kellum; 4.7, Petersen; 5.4, Sturgeon; 6.1, Squire; and 6.2, Trimble). Special mention should also be made of Jennifer Trimble's essay (6.2), which in part responds to one major contribution to the historiography of Roman art (Smith 2002), a subject upon which much has been published (e.g., Brendel [1953] 1979; Donohue and Fullerton 2003; Kampen 2003; Elsner 2004).

One of the prominent debates in the field—occurring both at the level of practice and in theory—regards the usefulness of style as a category of chronological analysis. Those delving deeper into theory tend to avoid style as a signifier of chronology (note the especially strong positions on this subject of Fullerton [3.1], Touchette [3.6], and Wood [3.4]), instead following the lead of Hölscher in treating style as primarily a carrier of meaning, on a par with iconography itself. Yet as sculpture specialists and archaeologists, we all face the knotty problem of how to propose a date for a sculpture based only on internal (i.e., stylistic) evidence. In this volume, Susan Wood states that "stylistic analysis. . . is rarely useful for determining dates of Roman sculpture." Yet much of past and indeed current archaeological practice and publication reflects the opposite position: in the scholarship we encounter sculptures dated to within a quarter century based on drapery styles, hairstyles, or facial emulations; or we note the avoidance of "undatable" objects in our historically driven textbooks (e.g., D. E. E. Kleiner 1992; F. S. Kleiner 2007). In contrast to those by Mark Fullerton, Lori-Ann Touchette, and Wood, the essays by Adi Erlich (2.5) on terracottas and Diana Ng (5.5) on sculpture in Asia Minor both assert the usefulness of stylistic criteria for dating as part of our toolkit; and other essays simply present dates based solely on style as unproblematic. Even as publications present more examples of stylistic composites—or "eclecticism," as Touchette explains—and the chronological conundrums they represent, the weight of historical practice and the perceived utility of style for sorting sculptures, even if only as a means to classify the previously unpublished sculpture of a region or new excavation, suggest that the practice will persist. And to some extent, as several of our authors point out, stylistic analysis is a valid methodological starting point, though as others argue, it is an interpretive tool that should be wielded with care and full knowledge of its limitations (Smith 2011; see also essay 3.5, Sobocinski and Wolfram Thill).

The essays in this volume also make it clear that analyzing the Greek impact on Roman sculpture and its centrality to the elite Roman conception of art continues to be a fruitful avenue of investigation, and indeed, Anna Anguissola explores the intricate nuances of this topic in detail (3.3). Some contributors point out ways that freestanding mythological and heroic statuary was often viewed by the Romans as the "understood" norm of sculpture: for example, Michael Squire points out that Cicero "strove to decorate [his] villa *à la grecque*" (6.1), and Eric Moormann observes that "*opera nobilia* (famous works of art of Greek origin, Plin. *HN* 36.39) are the most frequently adopted motif in two-dimensional art" (6.4). Although it is clear that *Kopienkritik* has not vanished as an analytical tool, we should not see these and similar statements as a return to the outmoded view that "Roman art is a copy of Greek"; instead, it is in the creative synthesis and forging of novel forms and interpretations, which reference earlier cultural traditions throughout the empire ("stylistic eclecticism"), that Roman sculpture is at its most interesting. For instance, Touchette (3.6) concentrates on the Roman repurposing of archaic Greek styles and archaic Etruscan materials to signify sanctity. Particularly thought-provoking here is Molly Swetnam-Burland's essay on Egyptian-style monuments (3.7), which examines a parallel case to the Roman integration of Greek art, investigating the range of ways in which connections to Egypt could be expressed—from the importation of Egyptian antiquities and the use of Egyptian materials, to the emulation (with varying degrees of fidelity) of Egyptian styles and iconography, creating a wholly Roman hybrid with new meanings. Throughout part V, Regions and Provinces, the individual essays discuss further instances of synthesis between local traditions and Roman influences. They move beyond asking what was "derivative" about Roman or provincial sculpture to explore how Romans throughout the empire expressed their identity, social and financial standing, and religious and cultural concerns (among others) through hybridity.

Several statues or sculptural groups and particular display contexts emerge as frequently cited examples, employed by contributors to make a variety of points. For example, especially prominent are the portrait of Plancia Magna from one of the niches in a wall near to the city gate that she renovated in her home town of Perge (Asia Minor; see essays 3.4, Wood; 4.1, Longfellow; 4.5, Tuck; 4.6, Kellum; and 5.5, Ng), the sculptural display at Herculaneum's Villa of the Papyri (see essays 2.4, Mattusch; 3.3, Anguissola; 3.6, Touchette; 4.3, Gazda; and 6.1, Squire), and the monument of the Augustales at Misenum on the Bay of Naples (see essays 3.4, Wood; 4.2, McCarty; 4.5, Tuck; 4.6, Kellum; and 6.5, Perry). Certainly, these finds are all exceptional: Plancia Magna for the window onto female patronage and public honor; the Villa of the Papyri for the incredible preservation of a (largely) complete domestic sculptural display *in situ* (though as Gazda cautions, the record of findspots is problematic, and much of the villa remains unexcavated); and the monument of the Augustales at Misenum for its example of patronage by freedmen and the transmission of and response to imperial messages. But the reliance on these examples attests to something more: the importance of the preservation of broader contexts of sculpture—epigraphic context, to understand the role of statuary in political and social dialogues between local elite, their city's population, and the imperial house (see essay 4.5, Tuck, on "sculptural dialogue"); architectural context, to reconstruct modes of display and programmatic messages of sculpture (see essay 4.1, Longfellow); and archaeological context, to reveal the cumulative nature of sculptural displays and the reuse of statuary over time (see essay 6.6, Kristensen).

Future Directions

While the essays in this volume provide a survey of the current state of Roman sculptural studies, they also highlight many areas that are ripe for future exploration. We summarize some of those here and point readers to the online edition of this *Handbook*, which will allow for both the updating of current essays and the addition of new chapters covering topics that could not be treated here.

Exciting developments in emergent technologies have the potential to transform our understanding of sculptures, through new information about the surfaces of objects (traces of pigment especially), the origins of materials (geological and chemical analyses of marbles and bronzes), the volumetrics of objects (three-dimensional digital scanning, allowing the testing of hypotheses about recarving, for example), and the appearance and context of items (3-D digital models exploring various reconstructions of color scheme, positioning, surrounding architecture, and sightlines, among others). It is clear that the field will advance dramatically in the coming years thanks to these and other developing techniques.

Much remains to be done on material of all media, genres, and contexts from the Roman provinces. Certainly work will continue on the documentation of unpublished or understudied material and newly discovered sculptures and sculptural groups, and as many of the essays in part V note, deeper analyses await the publications of regional corpora (some of which are currently underway; see also the *Corpus Signorum Imperii Romani* [*CSIR*]). It is also in the provinces where debates such as the use of metropolitan styles as chronological indicators can be fruitfully explored. As some of the authors demonstrate by their comparisons of trends within their regions and among provinces, there are also opportunities to relate provincial sculpture to its broader regional, provincial, and empire-wide contexts. Here, the International Colloquia on Roman Provincial Art, which have been expanding in both scope and attendance, should be noted as important settings that support such interprovincial analyses. Continued study of the provincial material will offer an art historical perspective on broader debates in the field of classical studies, such as those about Roman imperialism, "Romanization," and identity. The complexity of the material and the great variety of its historical, cultural, and political contexts make the study of provincial sculpture particularly rewarding.

Several authors here have argued that dichotomies (Hellenizing/Italic; core/periphery; high quality/low quality; local/Roman; slave/free; elite/non-elite; male/female) unnecessarily simplify a complex human picture and that pluralistic models are more effective. While binary models may continue to be created—and resisted—over the next few decades, the contributions to this volume make clear that exploring and complicating dichotomies offer significant opportunities to advance scholarship in every area of Roman sculptural studies.

Finally, one area not explicitly addressed as the topic of any essay in this *Handbook*, but implicit in many and prevalent in contemporary media, is the need to understand Roman sculpture in terms of cultural heritage. The richness of many of the detailed studies included in this volume depends on access to vulnerable contextual information and calls attention to the damage done in cases of illegal excavation and looting (see essay 3.4, Wood). Scholars need to be aware of policies established by international agencies (e.g., the 1970 UNESCO Convention: the Convention on Cultural Property Implementation and the 1995 UNIDROIT Convention on Stolen or Illegally Exported Cultural Objects) and by professional organizations (such as the Archaeological Institute of America's Code of Ethics and Code of Professional Standards). We must also recognize that cultural heritage is increasingly a point of international political negotiation. Roman sculptures, as long-prized pieces of cultural heritage, could very well play a role in cultural diplomacy, negotiations between nation-states conducted surrounding issues of heritage but as a platform to deepening economic and political connections. As part of the call to take into account the full biographies of objects noted in the final essay of this volume, scholars will want to be mindful of the emerging role of all cultural heritage—Roman statues included—as currency in diplomatic negotiation (Luke and Kersel 2012).

It is our hope that this *Handbook* brings together the current state of knowledge and methods of study—and thereby enhances the potential for future advancement—of the field of Roman sculptural studies, while simultaneously providing a rich resource for students and scholars.

Notes Regarding the Text

All abbreviations are from the *American Journal of Archaeology's* (*AJA*) "AJA Abbreviations" (http://www.ajaonline.org/submissions/abbreviations) or the *Oxford Classical Dictionary*, 4th edition (2012, edited by S. Hornblower, A. Spawforth, and E. Eidinow; Oxford: Oxford University Press). Unless otherwise noted, all translations are the authors'.

Bibliography

Archaeological Institute of America. 1997. "Code of Ethics." http://www.archaeological.org/news/advocacy/130.

Archaeological Institute of America. 1997. "Code of Professional Standards." http://www.archaeological.org/news/advocacy/132.

Brendel, O. J. (1953) 1979. *Prolegomena to the Study of Roman Art*. New Haven: Yale University Press.

Donohue, A. A., and M. D. Fullerton, eds. 2003. *Ancient Art and Its Historiography*. Cambridge: Cambridge University Press.

Elsner, J. 2004. "Foreword." In Hölscher (1987) 2004, xv–xxxi.

Fondation pour le Lexicon Iconographicum Mythologiae Classicae. 1981–2009. *LIMC: Lexicon Iconographicum Mythologiae Classicae*. 20 vols. Zürich: Artemis. http://www.limcnet.org/LIMCLink/LIMC/tabid/198/Default.aspx.

Fondation pour le Lexicon Iconographicum Mythologiae Classicae (LIMC). 2004–2011. *ThesCRA: Thesaurus Cultus et Rituum Antiquorum*. 6 vols. Los Angeles: J. Paul Getty Museum. http//:www.limcnet.org/ThesCRALink/ThesCRA/tabid/230/Default.aspx.

Hölscher, T. (1987) 2004. *The Language of Images in Roman Art*. Translated by A. Snodgrass and A. Künzl-Snodgrass. Cambridge: Cambridge University Press. Originally published as *Römische Bildsprache als semantisches System*.

Kampen, N. B. 2003. "On Writing Histories of Roman Art." *ArtB* 85(2): 371–86.

Kleiner, D. E. E. 1992. *Roman Sculpture*. New Haven: Yale University Press.

Kleiner, F. S. 2007. *A History of Roman Art*. Victoria: Thomson/Wadsworth.

Luke, C., and M. M. Kersel. 2012. *U.S. Cultural Diplomacy and Archaeology: Soft Power, Hard Heritage*. New York: Routledge.

Smith, R. R. R. 2002. "The Use of Images: Visual History and Ancient History." In *Classics in Progress: Essays on Ancient Greece and Rome*, edited by T. P. Wiseman, 59–102. Oxford: Oxford University Press.

———. 2011. "Marble Workshops at Aphrodisias." In *Roman Sculpture in Asia Minor*, edited by F. D'Andria and I. Romeo, 62–76. JRA Supplement 80. Portsmouth, RI: Journal of Roman Archaeology.

Schollmeyer, P. 2005. *Römische Plastik: Eine Einführung*. Darmstadt: Wissenschaftliche Buchgesellschaft.

Winckelmann, J. J. [1764] 2006. *History of the Art of Antiquity*. Translated by H. Mallgrave. Los Angeles: Getty Publications. Originally published as *Geschichte der Künst des Ältertums*.

PART I

COLLECTING, CONSERVATION, AND DISPLAY

CHAPTER 1.1

COLLECTING IN PREMODERN EUROPE

ELIZABETH BARTMAN

Introduction

For much of the premodern period, the collecting of ancient sculpture was synonymous with the collecting of art. Although frequently—and erroneously—thought to be Greek (Marvin 2008), the ancient sculpture that was then collected was actually Roman (by which I mean created by artists working for Roman patrons). This brief survey will examine the major collections formed between the fifteenth and the late nineteenth centuries, a span that stretches the definition of premodern somewhat in order to highlight an important late episode in the history of collecting. Over the course of these years the practice of collecting changed radically; consistent throughout, however, are two elements singled out by Paula Findlen as at the core of a collection: possession and display (Findlen 1994, 3). According to Findlen, possession leads to knowledge, and display leads to honor and reputation. In distinguishing a collection, intentionality is key; an assemblage of works left undisturbed in their original place of display—for example, the Julio-Claudian portraits from the theater at Velleia and now in Parma—does not qualify as a collection. Contrary to the modern view, it is not always the aesthetic character of the works that made them prized; as we will see, some works were revered for their symbolic or ideological connotations rather than their aesthetic value. Except in isolated cases, a statue's provenance was rarely a factor in collecting.

As we would expect, in view of their centuries-long prestige, most ancient statues found in the premodern era have had a succession of owners since their first discovery. Barely a single collection of the many formed during the sixteenth century survived intact into the seventeenth; likewise most of those formed in the seventeenth century were broken up in the subsequent era, victims not so much of changing tastes as of changing family fortunes. Statues were uncovered by archaeology and less scientific digging; repaired, restored, and even faked; bought, sold, and traded; and acquired through donation, bequest, and coercion (Salerno 1970; Haskell and Penny 1981; Pietrangeli 1993; Gasparri 1994). Consequently, the narrative of collecting is a rich one, in which we can observe a series of changes occurring approximately each century in response to shifting intellectual currents.

Notwithstanding the evolution in the practice of collecting, the hierarchy of genres established early on tended to prevail through the centuries: at the top were three-dimensional statues of real or fictive persons—especially prized when depicted nude—followed by sarcophagi and other reliefs, altars, and decorative works such as masks, vases, or table legs. Large-scale reliefs depicting historical subjects—the genre we call "historical reliefs"—also occupied a privileged position, although they were extremely difficult to obtain (see essay 3.5, Sobocinski and Wolfram Thill). Similarly, large-scale bronzes, while esteemed, were so rare as barely to figure in the premodern collection; for the most part, their counterparts in the format of small-scale statuettes were not publicly displayed; kept in cabinets or in the intimate confines of the Renaissance *studiolo*, these miniature works actually may have had a personal value for their owners higher than the larger pieces. Historically, however, large-scale marbles have predominated in the most important collections, and they will be the focus of this essay. Few examples of nonmetropolitan or provincial art were collected in the premodern era.

A Late Fourteenth-Century Collection at the Lateran

Assembled at a time when many ancient statues were considered idols with demonic powers, the Lateran bronzes, a late fourteenth-century collection, stand out as an anomaly (Pietrangeli 1964; Buddensieg 1969). During the Middle Ages, several bronzes believed to be ancient—Marcus Aurelius on Horseback, the Spinario, the Capitoline Wolf, and a colossal head of Constantine—were brought together at the Lateran. Some have dismissed this group as a collection, although its deliberate and self-conscious "curating"—all the statues are bronze and, at least until recently, regarded as ancient (Carruba 2006)—would seem to qualify it as such. That this ensemble was formed on land belonging to the Church underscores the complex relationship that the papacy had toward Rome's antique past. While many religious authorities endorsed iconoclasm against "pagan" survivals, others had a more beneficent view. An obsessive (and to some, irreligious) collector, Pope Pius II fell into the latter camp. When he transferred the bronzes to the Capitoline in 1471, his successor Sixtus IV staged a public-relations coup; not only could he claim to divest the Church of pagan works, but he also paid homage to the public in bestowing upon it works deemed more appropriate to the nascent municipal collection. Marcus Aurelius and the Capitoline Wolf in particular had symbolic value as images of Rome's glorious—and pagan—past. Their transfer to the Capitoline catapulted them to fame, both as unimpeachable works of artistic quality and as souvenirs of Rome itself; thus we see artists such as Pier Jacopo Alari de Bonacolsi (better known as "Antico") making exquisite miniature replicas of these celebrated statues in bronze and gold for such patrons as the Marchesa Isabella d'Este of Mantua.

The Fifteenth and Sixteenth Centuries: Renaissance Italy and Europe

By the 1500s, throughout Europe ancient statues had shed any lingering maledictory potential to become paragons of beauty, elegance, and refined taste. Italian humanists and writers such as Francesco Petrarch (1304–1374) may have taken the lead in embracing this new attitude, but aristocratic circles and even the papal court quickly followed. For the noble elite with the means to collect, ancient statues were a vehicle by which to claim a direct connection with the past, and statues on display in one's house helped convey the notion (sometimes fictive) of a long and distinguished family genealogy. That these collections were a significant phenomenon can be seen from their publication by Ulisse Aldrovandi (1556), Antoine Lafrérey (1567), and others in books whose very conception as compendia emphasized the cultural novelty of the collection.

As the primary source of Roman sculpture, Italy inevitably played host to many major collections in the fifteenth and sixteenth centuries. Nearly a hundred are documented for Rome alone, a statistic hardly surprising in that the former imperial capital was *fons et origo* of both statues and statue collections; indeed the major collections displayed elsewhere—in Florence (Lorenzo de' Medici), Mantua (Isabella d'Este), and Venice (Domenico Grimani)—were largely formed in Rome (Maugeri 2001; Christian 2010, 164–5). Collections outside Italy, like that of the painter Peter Paul Rubens at Antwerp or of King Albert of Bavaria at Munich, played a less significant historical role (Weski and Frosien-Leinz 1987). At Rome, aristocratic families such as the del Bufalo, Piccolomini, Sassi, and della Valle displayed works in their palace courtyards and gardens. Today dispersed, their holdings can be reconstructed through archival documents and drawings by contemporary artists such as Maartin Van Heemskerck (figure 1.1.1); although some illustrations convey a sense of picturesque ruin, in fact many of these collections seem to have been carefully arranged with regard to scale, symmetry, and architectural setting.

In a sense, the most celebrated collection of the age—that of the Belvedere Court in the papal palace (figure 1.1.2; Winner, Andreae, and Pietrangeli 1998)—was a typical early Renaissance collection writ large through works that were more spectacular and architecture that was more monumental than its contemporaries. Begun by Pope Julius II in 1503, the Belvedere statue court quickly came to house the most celebrated sculptures of the time, notably the Apollo (assuming the epithet "Belvedere") and the Laocoön. The subject matter of the latter, along with a statue of Venus (Venus Felix), was

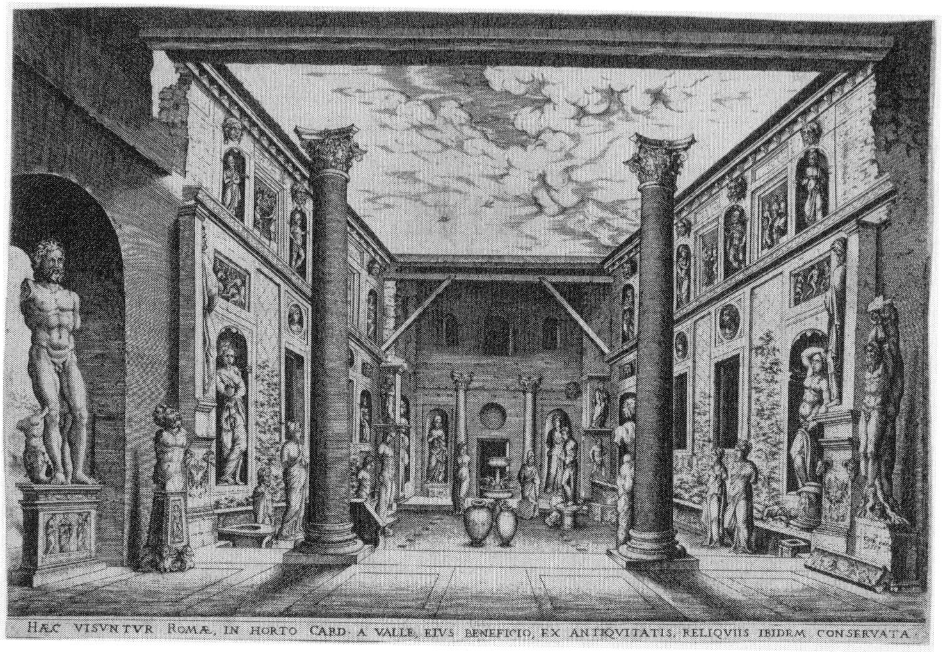

FIGURE 1.1.1 Hanging garden of Cardinal Andrea della Valle. Drawing attributed to Maartin Van Heemskerck. c. 1532–7.

seen as Vergilian in theme and part of a self-conscious attempt by Julius II to suggest descent from Julius Caesar. Conceived as a garden with numerous trees, the courtyard was a *locus amoenus* (literally a "pleasant place") that evoked Vergilian pastoral settings and ideally stimulated viewers—of which there were many—to poetry and other elevated intellectual pursuits. In the Belvedere as well as in other collections throughout Italy, ancient statues connected patrons and viewers with the past but also inspired them to artistic creativity.

The Vatican's holdings are among the few that remained intact over the centuries. Indeed, by the end of the sixteenth century almost all the leading sculpture collections had been broken up and sold to the small circle of wealthy and politically powerful cardinals and popes who emerged as Rome's dominant collectors. The Cesi, Farnese, Mattei, and Medici belong to this new breed; their extraordinary social position and purchase of older collections (for example, in 1584 the Medici bought the della Valle collection in its entirety) endowed collecting with a new elite (even princely) and rarified status.

Among the best documented, the Farnese collection formed throughout the fifteenth century exemplifies the trends as well as the sometimes ruthless methods by which statues were acquired (Riebesell 1989; 2010). Giulio Sangallo's architectural plans for Cardinal Alessandro Farnese's palace did not include antiquities, but the situation changed upon the cardinal's elevation to the papacy in 1534 as Paul III. During his reign, the Farnese had access to recent discoveries like the Province Reliefs from the

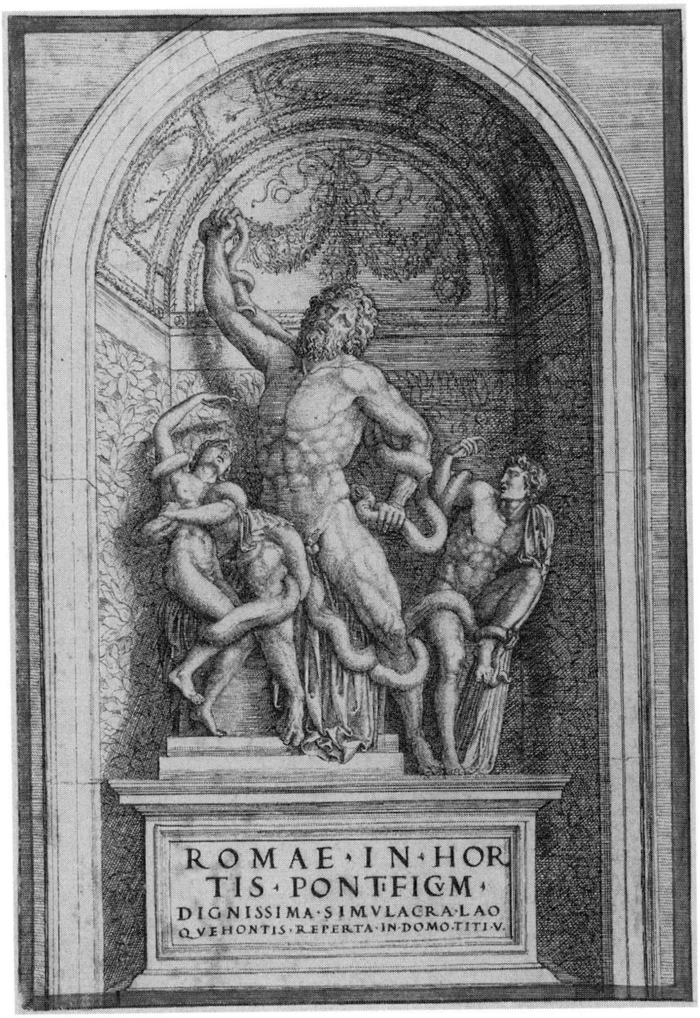

FIGURE 1.1.2 Laocoön in Belvedere Courtyard. Drawing by Francesco de Hollande. Mid-sixteenth century.

Hadrianeum in Rome, as well as finds made on Farnese properties in and outside of Rome. Unearthed at the Baths of Caracalla between 1545 and 1546, colossal and stunning works such as the Weary Hercules (henceforth called "Farnese"), the Dirce group, and the famous portrait bust of Commodus were placed in the *cortile* of the Palazzo Farnese in an arrangement not dissimilar to that of earlier Renaissance palaces. There were 258 statues listed in the seventeenth-century inventory, most of which were transferred to Naples in 1738 and are now in the Museo Archeologico Nazionale di Napoli (Gasparri 2007).

Gradually, however, some statues migrated indoors as part of the Farnese's self-congratulatory celebration of Rome and the family's position. The Farnese was one of the first palaces with statues displayed on the *piano nobile* (main floor). The installation of antiquities in the statue niches of the new gallery painted by the brothers Agostino and Annibale Caracci in 1601 (figure 1.1.3, see color insert) proclaimed the prestige of the antique: it was ancient not modern statues that the Farnese saw fit to place in the architectural niches that, along with the *trompe l'oeil* architecture and richly painted figures, conveyed the "Loves of the Gods" to spectacular effect. Creating a syncopated rhythm of life-size marble on the two long sides of the 20 m gallery, the Farnese installation pioneered the so-called "Long Gallery" mode of statue display that would enjoy popularity for the next three centuries.

The Seventeenth Century

Seventeenth-century Rome witnessed the continued near-monopoly in collecting by powerful "cardinal nephews," such as Cardinals Maffeo Barberini (Faun, Togatus, Juno) and Camillo Pamphili. Scipio Borghese, nephew of Paul V, bought prize works for his new villa on the Pincio, including the Gladiator, Sleeping Hermaphrodite, Centaur with Cupid, and Silenus with Infant Dionysus (Kalveram 1995; Coliva et al. 2011). Ludovico Ludovisi collected during the reign of his uncle Gregory XV and installed the Dying Gaul, Battle Sarcophagus, Peplophoros, San Ildefonso Group (figure 6.1.2), and other works in his (now-destroyed) Esquiline Villa (Palma 1983). To this day, many of these works bear the names of their original owners (e.g., the Barberini Faun now in the Glyptothek, Munich). Such nomenclature accompanied the canonization of select ancient works, promoted by the contemporary art critic Giovan Pietro Bellori in his *Nota delli musei* ([1664] 1976; Borea and Gasparri 2000) and other writings. In the early decades of the seventeenth century, the Marchese Vincenzo Giustiniani, a rich banker, also emerged as a collector, amassing some 1200 statues for display in various properties. Like his papal colleagues, he used his statuary collection as a means of promoting himself and his noble family (Gallottini 1998; Fusconi 2001). Both a lavish illustrated catalogue published in 1631 (figure 1.1.4) and his placement of the family coat of arms on all statue bases trumpeted the Giustiniani *magnificenza*.

As the expectations for statues as status-enhancers for their collectors rose, they tended to be installed in ever more formal settings, appropriate for their higher status. This preference gave rise to the practice of restoration, as formal architectural settings outfitted with niches and colonnades required whole statues rather than fragments. Although restoration reached its technical apex later in the eighteenth century (see essay 1.2, Podany), the involvement of major sculptors such as Gianlorenzo Bernini and Alessandro Algardi in the seventeenth century underscored the worth of ancient statues as models of emulation, which also encouraged the continued desirability of ancient statues among collectors. Gianlorenzo Bernini's *Ares* for the Ludovisi clan and Nicholas Cordier's *Zingarella* for the Borghese, if different in the degree to which they left the ancient parts intact, underscore that collectors wanted complete images even if the process of restoration compromised their authenticity as antiquities.

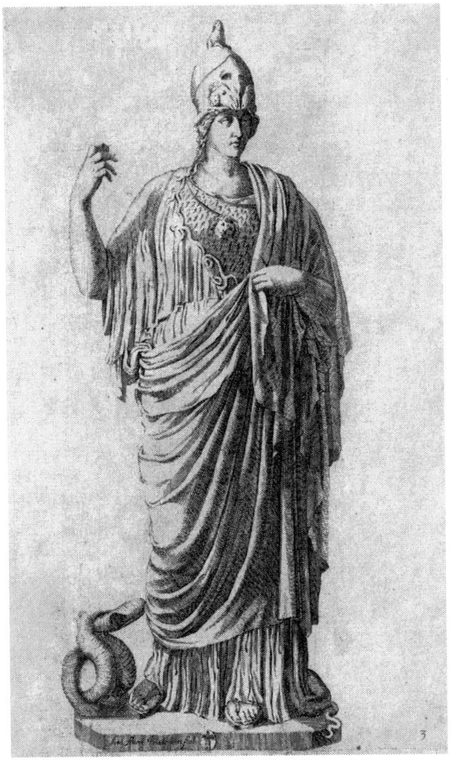

FIGURE 1.1.4 Engraving showing Athena Giustiniani, from *Galleria Givstiniana del marchese Vincenzo Givstiniani*, pl. 3. 1631.

In the sixteenth and seventeenth centuries many collectors began to diversify by acquiring rare and precious natural objects such as gemstones, shells, and animal specimens, creating *Wunderkammern* or "cabinets of curiosities"; at Rome, that of the Jesuit Athanasius Kircher won international renown, while those of Ulisse Adrovandi at Bologna, the Elector Augustus of Saxony at Dresden, and Ole Worm in Copenhagen were also significant (Lugli 1990; Fearrington 2013). In contrast to the highly competitive nature of collecting ancient marbles, the ethos among cabinet proprietors was one of sharing and swapping for the common advancement of knowledge. Although a celebrated engraving showing Kircher's museum at the Collegio Romano depicts a long gallery with statues on pedestals (De Sepi 1678, fig. 20), statues in fact did not play a major role in these cabinets, which focused on the rare, the precious, and the exotic. That some statues (figure 1.1.5) were included in these encyclopedic assemblages, however, speaks to sculpture's potential for illuminating the classical past in a collection that was conceived as the "theater of the world" (Bruni 2001; Paris 2001). For Kircher, ancient statues depicting "idols" (Isis, Diana, Jupiter) and "heroes" (Cicero, Seneca, Agrippina, Hercules) were of interest not so much for their aesthetic virtues as for their insights into the religion and daily life of the Romans. The budding taxonomies applied to the scientific exempla, moreover,

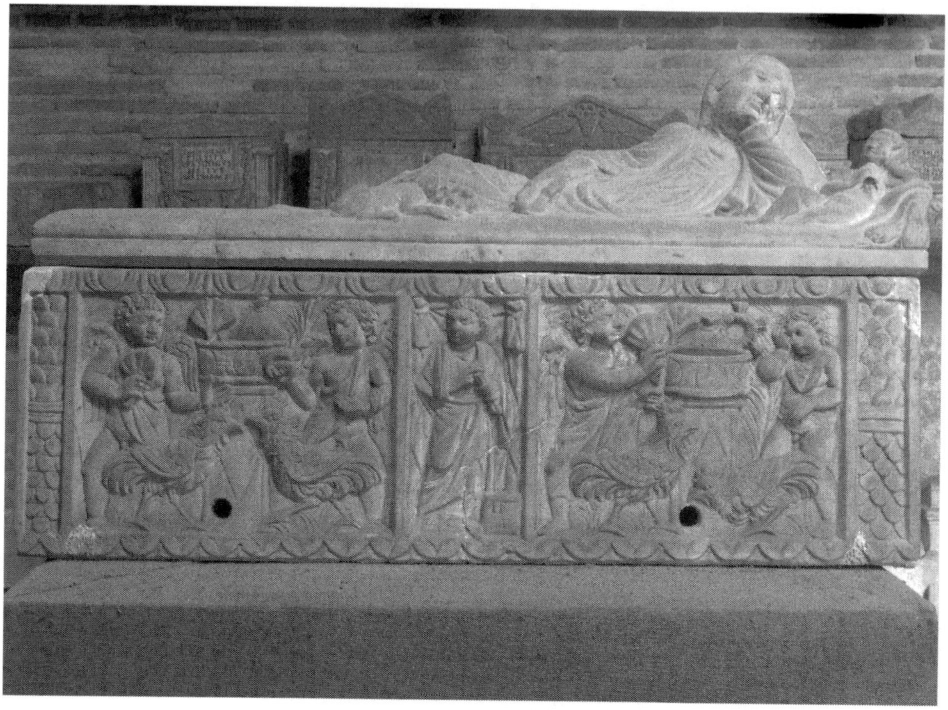

FIGURE 1.1.5 Child's sarcophagus from Museum Kircheranum. Rome, Museo Nazionale Romano, Terme di Diocleziano, inv. no. 65200.

were a harbinger of the more scientific approach toward categorizing ancient statuary that would be more fully developed in the next century—and indeed in the Kircher collection as well, when its new patron Clement XI in the early eighteenth century embraced the age of archaeology (Findlen 2001).

Archaeology figured as well in the formation of one of the first collections outside Italy, that of Thomas Howard, 2nd Earl of Arundel. Sent abroad in 1612 for health reasons, Howard visited Rome the next year and undertook systematic excavations that revealed portrait statues, among other works. His later purchases through agents in the Greek East have tended to attract modern attention, but many of the Roman works he acquired in Italy form the core of the Ashmolean Museum at Oxford today, to which they were given by family bequest circa 1667 (Haynes 1968; Vickers 2006). Later in the seventeenth century, Christina, Queen of Sweden, avidly collected—she was one of the few women to do so. Her most celebrated acquisition, a cycle of Muses found in the late fifteenth century at Hadrian's Villa, was sold along with other works to the Odescalchi in 1692, who in turn sold them to the king of Spain in 1724 (Schröder 2004). Their history underscores a fundamental tenet of marble collecting: many pieces gained value from their association with royalty and titled nobility, and virtually nothing went "out of fashion" so as to become unsalable.

The Eighteenth Century

With the rise of the neoclassical movement in the eighteenth century making ancient statuary a desirable element of interior decor, an international cadre of buyers—primarily British, French, Poles, Swedes, and Russians on the Grand Tour—made collecting an increasingly competitive practice. While many purchased from the old collections of aristocratic families in economic decline, the increased demand fueled excavation around Rome, as well as restoration to salvage otherwise unwanted fragments. Cardinal Alessandro Albani (1692–1779) represents the rare Roman who formed a collection (more precisely, three collections) during this period. A discerning connoisseur who employed Johann Joachim Winckelmann as his librarian, the cardinal excavated at many sites around Rome, amassing hundreds of statues. Albani sold his first collection in 1728 to Frederick Augustus II, elector of Saxony and king of Poland, who installed it in his palace in Dresden; parts of Albani's second collection were purchased for the new Capitoline Museum in 1733; his third and final collection—minus some 300 marbles seized by Napoleon and never returned—remains *in situ* at the villa he constructed on the Via Salaria. A rare example of an eighteenth-century installation of ancient sculptures—its mirrored walls were a novelty—the villa included such important works as a bronze Apollo Sauroctonos, the so-called Torlonia Girl, and a relief of Antinous (Collier 1987; Bol 1989).

As the well-connected papal nephew at the center of a network of diggers, dealers, and restorers, Albani would have played a role, even if only indirectly, in the formation of virtually all other collections made during his lifetime. Most of these were made by foreigners: Englishmen such as William Petty-Fitzmaurice, Earl of Shelbourne, bought for Lansdowne House at London (Amazon, Hercules, Sandal-binder), and Charles Wyndham, Earl of Egremont, for Petworth (Michaelis 1882; Raeder 2000); Swedes such as King Gustav III purchased sculptures, as did his cousin Catherine the Great of Russia, who launched her collection in circa 1787 by buying *en bloc* that of Lyde Browne of Wimbledon. All of these collectors mixed works from Roman aristocratic collections with newly excavated works from Rome and its environs; the English in particular aimed to recreate the ancient Roman lifestyle of leisure (*otium*) at the country houses they styled as ancient "villas."

At the same time as thousands of statues departed Rome for foreign shores, papal authorities in Rome began to acknowledge the value of these works as part of the city's history and cultural heritage. This realization lies at the heart of the creation of two museums: the Museo Capitolino and the Museo Pio-Clementino at the Vatican. Although founded by Pope Clement XII in 1733, the Capitoline was intended to display works of special significance to Rome itself, hence its possession of bronzes such as the Lateran She-Wolf, the bust of Brutus, the Dying Gaul, and many historical reliefs. Even if not technically the first "public" museum, as it is often credited to be, undoubtedly the Capitoline was conceived as a municipal collection, both legally and spiritually (Pietrangeli 1964; Cagiano de Azevedo 1964).

Likewise, the suite of rooms known collectively today as the Museo Pio-Clementino, after the founding Popes Clement XIV (1769–74) and Pius VI (1775–99), aimed to provide a suitably magnificent home for hundreds of works that would otherwise have been exported by foreign buyers. Among the early efforts to curtail export was the acquisition of the prize pieces of the Mattei collection (including the eponymous Amazon) in 1770. As a papal territory, Rome and the antiquities it harbored belonged by law to the pope, and by the eighteenth century no pope had to be persuaded of the aesthetic or monetary value of ancient marbles. Indeed, particular statues or ensembles could be pressed into service to advance papal ideologies (so the Muses cycle in the Sala delle Muse): with their huge proportions and lavish decorations, these new public spaces presented the popes as inheritors of Rome's imperial age (Pietrangeli 1993; Collins 2004).

The quality of the works in the Pio-Clementino varies widely—many of the most important Roman sculptures to survive belong to the collection (including the tufa sarcophagus of L. Cornelius Scipio Barbatus, porphyry sarcophagi of Constantina and Helena, colossal Antinous, and colossal gilt bronze Hercules), but there are numerous less significant works as well. Further rooms added in the nineteenth and twentieth centuries, known collectively today as the Museo Chiaramonti (1805–07), Braccio Nuovo (1822), and the Museo Gregoriano Profano (1970), now house spectacular works such as the full-length portrait of Augustus from Prima Porta, the Cancelleria reliefs, and the tomb reliefs of the Haterii.

Another eighteenth- to nineteenth-century collection intended to glorify regnant power was that formed by Charles Bourbon and his son Ferdinand for the Kingdom of Naples and the Two Sicilies. Shaped by inheritance (in 1738, the celebrated Farnese collection of sculptures discussed above), as well as active excavation on royal land that included the buried Vesuvian cities of Pompeii and Herculaneum, the collection of the Real Museo Borbonico (now the Museo Archeologico Nazionale di Napoli) was continuously expanded through the nineteenth century to include significant local finds such as the bronze Julio-Claudian portraits from the "Basilica" at Herculaneum and hundreds of bronze and marble statues from the suburban Villa of the Papyri (Mattusch 2005; see essays 2.4, Mattusch; and 6.1, Squire).

Later Dispersals

In 1794, hundreds of statues, including such masterpieces as the Apollo Belvedere, left Rome for Paris under the terms of the Treaty of Tolentino negotiated by Napoleon. Although most were returned in 1815, enough remained in Paris to form the core of the Greek and Roman collections of the Louvre, the huge encyclopedic museum envisioned by Napoleon as testament to France's power and national identity (Martinez 2004). At about the same time, Napoleon's brother-in-law Prince Camillo Borghese ceded permanently hundreds of statues, among them the so-called Gladiator, Sleeping Hermaphrodite, and famed bust of Lucius Verus. These joined works such as the Artemis of Versailles and the Venus of Arles that had once belonged to Louis XIV (though part of his collection was installed at Versailles; Maral and Milovanovic 2012) and Cardinals Mazarin and Richelieu, important collectors in the seventeenth century. Palatial in its dimensions, the new Louvre displayed works in opulent but old-fashioned settings such as the Grand Gallery, an architecturally repetitive "long gallery" over 100 m in length. Along with Egyptian antiquities acquired in Napoleon's campaigns, the many classical marbles established the Louvre as one of the world's leading collections and the French as imperial in their archaeological endeavors.

Imperialist ideologies, expressed through excavation and encyclopedism, also drove the foundation of archaeological collections in Berlin, London, and other European capitals (Gaehtgens 1996; Jenkins 1992). To fill his new Glyptothek in Munich, Prince Ludwig of Bavaria bought hundreds of Albani marbles that had been taken by Napoleon to Paris; on a trip to Italy in 1804–5 Prince Ludwig also acquired the celebrated Barberini Faun. In comparison to imposing monuments collected and displayed by later generations, such as the Ishtar Gate from Babylon, the reliefs of the Great Altar of Zeus at Pergamon, or the reliefs from the Temple at Bassae, the holdings of Roman statuary in many of these newly created museums may seem unprepossessing, but the images depicting emperors and other historical personages offered visual paradigms for contemporary leaders such as the German Kaiser or English nobility. With their often lifelike dimensions and physiognomies, the many portraits in these two collections made antiquity approachable and seemingly pre-European; we may single out Berlin's exceptional portraits of Antinous, Hadrian, and Sabina, and the British Museum's basalt Germanicus, bust of Clytie, and funerary relief of the Antistii. At the core of the British Museum's Roman sculpture collection are marbles such as the Venus from Campo Iemini, purchased from the heirs of Charles Townley; Britain's most celebrated connoisseur during the eighteenth century, Townley epitomized the Grand Tour collector whose purchase of hundreds of Roman statues helped establish neoclassicism as a defining element of modern British collecting and culture.

Toward the end of the nineteenth century, Carl Jacobsen, owner of the Carlsberg Brewery in Copenhagen and already a collector of contemporary painting, hired Wolfgang Helbig as his agent in Rome to acquire ancient marbles (Moltesen 2012). Over the course of nearly thirty years, Carl Jacobsen purchased—both legally and illegally—nearly 1000 works through Helbig for what was to become the Ny Carlsberg Glyptotek (figure 1.1.6). Among them were portraits and sarcophagi from the tomb of the Licinii, an Artemis and Iphigenia group from the Horti Sallustiani, and a basalt statue of Agrippina. Like the Grand Tour buyers of a century earlier, Helbig benefitted from the financial straits of old Roman families such as the Borghese and Sciarra, and also from new excavations occasioned by the construction boom in postunification Rome. A "prince of business" like the American Henry Clay Frick, Jacobsen created his museum out of a sense of civic duty and pride. Although not entirely altruistic—after all, it still bears his name—Carl Jacobsen's benefaction introduced the notion of the arts as a public benefit, a thoroughly modern sentiment.

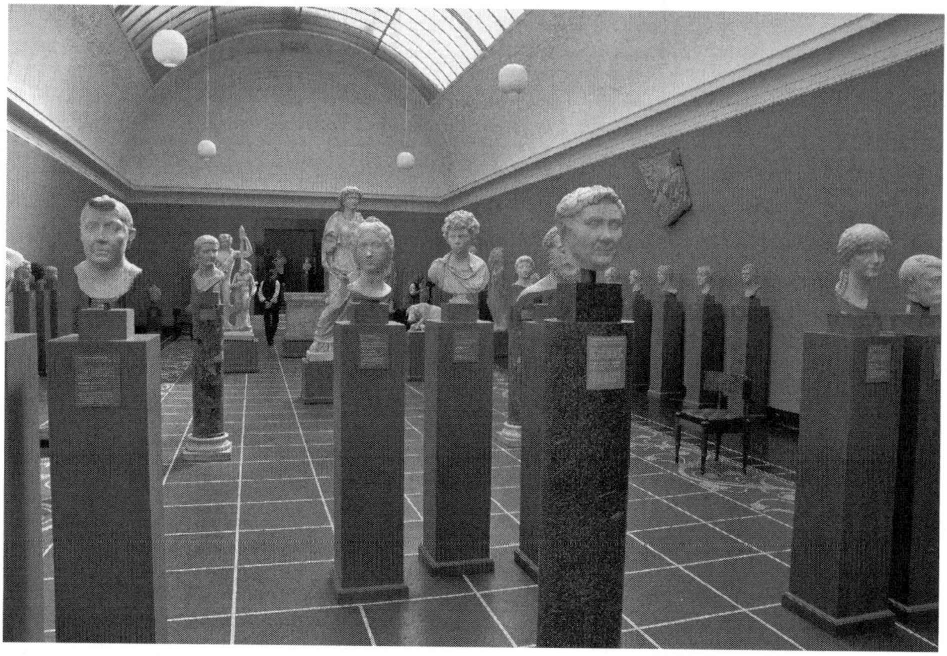

FIGURE 1.1.6 View of the Roman portrait gallery, Ny Carlsberg Glyptotek, Copenhagen.

Conclusion

Brief as it is, this survey is meant to introduce the reader to the major premodern collections of ancient Roman statuary. By highlighting the dominant trends in collecting during nearly five centuries, it aims as well to encourage readers to consider a statue's postantique afterlife when investigating a work of sculpture. Rather than being a marginalized topic, ownership history is critical to understanding a work of art from the past: a statue's owner (or those in his or her employ) makes decisions about its restoration, display, and labeling. In turn, these elements influence its interpretation and, beyond that, the discipline of classical scholarship of which the study of ancient Roman sculpture is a small yet vital part.

Bibliography

Aldrovandi, U. 1556. *Delle statue antiche che per tutta Roma, in diversi luoghi et case particolari si veggono, raccolte e descritte*. Venice: Apresso Giordano Ziletti.

Bellori, G. P. (1664) 1976. *Nota delli musei, librerie, galerie, et ornamenti di statue e pitture ne' palazzi, nelle case, e ne' giardini di Roma*. Facsimile edition, with preface and commentary by E. Zocca. Rome: Istituto nazionale di archeologia e storia dell'arte.

Bol, P., ed. 1989. *Forschungen zur Villa Albani: Katalog der antiken Bildwerke*. Vol. 1, *Bildwerke im Treppenaufgang und im Piano nobile des Casino*. Berlin: Mann.

Borea, E., and C. Gasparri, eds. 2000. *L'idea del bello: Viaggio per Roma nel Seicento con Giovan Pietro Bellori*. Rome: De Luca.

Bruni, S. 2001. "Il museo Kircheriano e il Museo Nazionale Romano." In *Athanasius Kircher: Il museo del mondo*, edited by E. Lo Sardo, 335–42. Rome: De Luca.

Buddensieg, T. 1969. "Zum Statuensprogramm im Kapitolsplan Pauls III." *ZfK* 32: 177–228.

Cagiano de Azevedo, M. 1964. "Le sculture antiche." *Capitolium* 39: 213–18.

Carruba, A. M. 2006. *La Lupa Capitolina: Un bronzo medievale*. Rome: De Luca.

Christian, K. W. 2010. *Empire without End: Antiquities Collections in Renaissance Rome, c. 1350–1527*. New Haven: Yale University Press.

Coliva, A., M.-L. Fabréga-Dubert, J.-L. Martinez, and M. Minozzi, eds. 2011. *I Borghese e l'antico*. Milan: Skira.

Collier, W. 1987. "The Villa of Cardinal Alessandro Albani, Hon. F.S.A." *AntJ* 67: 338–47.

Collins, J. 2004. *Papacy and Politics in Eighteenth-Century Rome: Pius VI and the Arts*. Cambridge: Cambridge University Press.

De Sepi, G. 1678. *Romani collegi Societatis Jesu Musaeum celeberrimum*. Amsterdam: Janssonio-Waebergiana.

Fearrington, F. 2013. *Rooms of Wonder from Wunderkammer to Museum, 1599–1899*. New York: Grolier Club.

Findlen, P. 1994. *Possessing Nature: Museums, Collecting, and Scientific Culture in Early Modern Italy*. Berkeley: University of California Press.

———. 2001. "Science, History, and Erudition: Athanasius Kircher's Museum at the Collegio Romano." In *The Great Art of Knowing: The Baroque Encyclopedia of Athanasius Kircher*, edited by D. Stolzenberg, 17–26. Stanford: Stanford University Press.

Fusconi, G., ed. 2001. *I Giustiniani e l'antico*. Rome: "L'Erma" di Bretschneider.

Gaehtgens, T. 1996. "The Museum Island in Berlin." In *The Formation of National Collections of Art and Archaeology*, edited by G. Wright, 53–77. Hanover: National Gallery of Art, Washington, DC.

Gallottini, A. 1998. *Le sculture della collezione Giustiniani*. Vol. 1, *Documenti*. Rome: "L'Erma" di Bretschneider.

Gasparri, C. 1994. "Collezioni archeologiche." *EAA* Supplement 2, vol. 2: 192–225.

Gasparri, C., ed. 2007. *Le sculture farnese: Storia e documenti*. Naples: Electa.

Haskell, F., and N. Penny. 1981. *Taste and the Antique: The Lure of Classical Sculpture, 1500–1900*. New Haven: Yale University Press.

Haynes, D. 1968. "The Arundel Marbles." *Archaeology* 21: 85–91, 206–211.

Jenkins, I. 1992. *Archaeologists and Aesthetes: In the Sculpture Galleries of the British Museum, 1800–1939*. London: British Museum.

Kalveram, K. 1995. *Die Antikensammlung des Kardinals Scipione Borghese*. Worms: Wernersche Verlagsgesellschaft.

Lafrérey, A. 1567. *Speculum Romae magnificentiae*. Rome.

Lugli, A. 1990. *Naturalia et Mirabilia: Il collezionismo enciclopedico nelle Wunderkammern d'Europa*. 2nd ed. Milan: Mazzotta.

Maral, A., and N. Milovanovic, eds. 2012. *Versailles et l'antique*. Paris: Artlys.

Martinez, J.-L., ed. 2004. *Les antiques du Louvre: Une histoire du goût d'Henri IV à Napoléon Ier*. Paris: Fayard.

Marvin, M. 2008. *The Language of the Muses: The Dialogue between Roman and Greek Sculpture.* Los Angeles: J. Paul Getty Museum.
Mattusch, C. C. 2005. *The Villa dei Papiri at Herculaneum: Life and Afterlife of a Sculpture Collection.* Los Angeles: J. Paul Getty Museum.
Maugeri, M. 2001. "Il trasferimento a Firenze della collezione antiquaria di Villa Medici." *Mitteilungen des Kunsthistorischen Instituts in Florenz* 44: 306–33.
Michaelis, A. 1882. *Ancient Marbles in Great Britain.* Cambridge: Cambridge University Press.
Moltesen, M. 2012. *Perfect Partners: The Collaboration between Carl Jacobsen and His Agent in Rome, Wolfgang Helbig, in the Formation of the Ny Carlsberg Glyptotek,* 1887–1914. Copenhagen: Ny Carlsberg Glyptotek.
Palma, B. 1983. *I Marmi Ludovisi: Storia della collezione.* Vol. 1, pt. 4 of *Museo Nazionale Romano: Le Sculture,* edited by A. Giuliano. Rome: De Luca.
Paris, R. 2001. "Antichità romane per il luogo d'arte e delle meraviglie." In *Athanasius Kircher: Il museo del mondo,* edited by E. Lo Sardo, 327–34. Rome: De Luca.
Pietrangeli, C. 1964. "La formazione delle raccolte." *Capitolium* 39: 209–12.
———. 1993. *The Vatican Museums: Five Centuries of History.* Translated by P. Spring. Rome: Edizioni Quasar; Biblioteca Apostolica Vaticana.
Raeder, J. 2000. *Die antiken Skulpturen in Petworth House (West Sussex).* Mainz: Philipp von Zabern.
Riebesell, C. 1989. *Die Sammlung des Kardinal Alessandro Farnese: Ein "studio" für Künstler und Gelehrte.* Weinheim: VCA, Acta Humaniora.
———. 2010. "L'ideologia politica Farnese: Creazione dell'identità culturale attraverso l'antico." In *Palazzo Farnèse dalle collezioni rinascimentali ad Ambasciata di Francia,* edited by F. Buranelli, 62–71. Florence: Giunti.
Salerno, L. 1970. "Collezioni archeologiche (Collezioni dal Rinascimento al sec. XVIII)." *EAA* Supplement: 242–59.
Schröder, S. F. 2004. *Katalog der antiken Skulpturen des Museo del Prado in Madrid.* Vol. 2, *Idealplastik.* Mainz: Philipp von Zabern.
Vickers, M. 2006. *The Arundel and Pomfret Marbles.* Oxford: Ashmolean Museum.
Weski, E., and H. Frosien-Leinz. 1987. *Das Antiquarium der Münchner Residenz.* Munich: Hirmer.
Winner, M., B. Andreae, and C. Pietrangeli, eds. 1998. *Il Cortile delle Statue: Der Statuenhof des Belvedere im Vatikan.* Mainz: Philipp von Zabern.

CHAPTER 1.2

CONSERVATION AND RESTORATION

JERRY PODANY

Introduction

Perhaps it is in human nature to feel a sense of melancholy combined with awe when we gaze upon ruins. Ancient fragments have, by chance or design, survived the passing centuries far beyond our own options for longevity. Curiosity brings us to wonder how they might have once looked, who made them, and for what purpose. And we ask: "Can any of this be retrieved?"

The reception of the fragment is a complex issue. Our respect for historic evidence and our desire to preserve it, whether for knowledge or as a romantic illusion, allow us to engage with broken remains. But when the fragment is recognizably part of the human form, our engagement often shifts to disgust. What Seymour Howard (2003, 30) calls "empathic discomfort" triggers the desire to heal scars, to restore. Such complexities are woven throughout the history of restoration. Two approaches, one to preserve *as is* and the other to restore *as we think it might have been*, often overlap and complement each other, and are equally often at odds. This duality makes it challenging to trace the evolution of restoration to conservation. One approach regards the remains of antiquity as decorative embellishments or romantic stage settings. Another sees them as basic raw materials to continue an ideal. And yet another approach perceives these objects as evidence for historicism's restraint in support of authenticity. By tracing these parallel tracks it is also possible to trace how restoration—and its more contemporary and expansive counterpart, conservation—have responded (and now respond) to cultural shifts, contemporary fashions, and the dynamic world around us.

Restoration approaches have changed over time and have directly influenced our knowledge and perception of antiquity. Changes and additions to ancient sculptures, almost always resulting in permanent alterations, reflect shifting tastes and evolving knowledge. Jessica Hughes has called restored sculptures "multi-authored, hybrid creations . . . remodeled according to later cultural contexts and art historical trends" (Hughes 2011, 2). Even political and religious zeal add to the mix in which the classical past is only one of the influences shaping the hybrid's form and future. Contemporary theory in heritage conservation now requires that we consider all the values of an object, including the historical value accreted to the object by its dynamic and multilayered progression through time, which includes recent restorations.

Restoration in the Past

To consider how we might approach the conservation of a Roman sculpture today, we must begin with the question of whether the sculpture is a recent archaeological discovery or has been previously restored. Why that makes a difference can be best understood by first considering a brief review of how ancient sculpture was dealt with in the past.

Secrecy, misleading claims, lack of documentation, and the repeated replacement of earlier restorations all make tracing the history of restoration challenging. Much of the evidence has been lost. However, the evolving path of restoration can be clarified through the examination of drawings, diaries, invoices, edicts, and, of course, the sculptures themselves, as well as the countless restoration segments removed but not destroyed.

From Antiquity to the Renaissance: Raw Material and Homage

Reverence for artistic patrimony was evident in the maintenance of ancient objects well before the Renaissance. One can find early critical reviews of restoration, as in the opinions of Pliny the Elder in 25 BC, who noted how a painting was ruined through a botched cleaning effort: "He [Aristides] also painted . . . the Tragedian and a Child, in the Temple of Apollo, a picture which has lost its beauty, owing to the lack of skill of the painter to whom Marcus Junius as Praetor entrusted the cleaning of it" (Plin. *HN* 35.36, trans. Rackham). We must assume, given the volume of sculpture in the Roman Empire, that restoration was a fully formed industry. As early as the first century AD, Cassius Dio (60.5) complained about the density of sculpture in Rome and referred to it as ὄχλος, a crowd or mob. By the third century AD the number of statues in Rome has been estimated at over 500,000 among a population of 1.5 million, a ratio of one sculpture for every three citizens (Barr 2008, 44).

Throughout late antiquity and into the early medieval period, architectural and sculptural fragments were often used as raw material for building and decorative projects. Although lacking the prestige of textual remains, these sculptural fragments were valued for their symbolic connection to the once-great Roman Empire, and, for this reason, they were sometimes protected. Theodoric's removal of architectural fragments from ruined sites to be built into new structures, for example, clearly has a dimension of preservation as well as politics (Brenk 1987). One might also consider the Roman Senate's declaration in 1162 that made it a capital offense to damage the Column of Trajan.

With the rediscovery of antiquity in the Renaissance came an expansive growth in collecting. At his death in 1637, Vincenzo Giustiniani left a collection of some 1,800 sculptures (Raggio 2005, 197). The growing incorporation of ancient artifacts as decorative elements in palaces and palazzi, often to enhance the status of wealthy individuals, began a division between those fragments that were treated as exceptional works of art and those that were used as raw material.

The restoration of these collected objects increasingly became the norm in the sixteenth century. Their physical destiny depended directly on their degree of *grazia* (or grace), defined as the perceived, sometimes assumed, visual rhythm and movement of the object. In describing Lorenzetto's arrangement of ancient fragments and sculptures in Cardinal Andrea della Valle's courtyard around 1525, Vasari wrote:

> Within the courtyard he [Lorenzetto] arranged columns, antique bases and capitals, and distributed around the basement piles of ancient fragments [carved with] stories. On an upper storey, beneath some of the larger niches, he made another frieze made up of antique fragments; above these he placed statues—also antique and of marble—which, although they were not intact, some headless or missing an arm and some with no legs at all, that is all missing some portion, he never the less managed the whole thing very well, having had excellent sculptors replace all the missing parts. And this is why other gentlemen, following this example, had many antiquities restored. And it is true, these antiquities have much more grace when restored in this manner, than have those imperfect trunks, or those limbs—headless or in some other respect defective or incomplete. (Vasari [1568] 1912, 5: 55)

In judging the fragment as defective and resolving this by completion, Lorenzetto undertook the first systematic restoration of ancient sculpture.

Even at this early date, however, the two discordant paths of restoration and conservation were present. A few ancient fragments were recognized in the Renaissance as having *grazia* even in their incomplete state (though not because of it, which was a later Romantic consideration). The Belvedere Torso, known since the 1430s, which influenced artists from Michelangelo to today, is one of the best-known examples.

Expressions of dissatisfaction with poor restoration also continued, sometimes to the point of suggesting, as Vasari did, that "it would be better at times to reserve the work of excellent masters half ruined, than to have them retouched by those who are less able" (quoted in Conti 2007, 39). Nonetheless it was the *grazia* and *disegno* (design) of ancient fragments that the restorers of the sixteenth century desired to enhance, reinstate, and sometimes invent. Today's interpretive restraint was lacking, and little consideration was given to the fragments as historical documents. Fragments represented an opportunity to continue an ideal in the form of what Seymour Howard (2003, 31) called a "circumspect homage" to antiquity, even though the *ideal* changed many times due to fashion, knowledge, and evidence.

That "circumspect homage" helps us understand why, when the mannerist artist Benvenuto Cellini was presented with a fragmented ancient torso, he exclaimed that the artist called upon him to serve. He did so from 1548 to 1550 by creating a wholly new and invented object that depicted a young Ganymede with an eagle, now in the Museo Nazionale del Bargello, Florence. It must be understood that those viewing the sculpture at that time recognized the Ganymede as Cellini's creation and not as a retrieval of the fragment's previous form. Cellini's homage was, in effect, a partnership between the restorer and the viewer.

Seventeenth through Eighteenth Centuries: Invention and the Sciences

By the early seventeenth century, restoration gained a degree of legitimacy through a close link to antiquarianism. Even though the President of Antiquities for Rome, Monsignor Francesco Bianchini, felt that restorations should be restricted to drawings, in some form or another restoration had become indispensible to collecting, displaying, and understanding ancient sculpture. Restorers sought to assure not only the proper figural pose and proportions but also a connection to ancient mythology and history. Restoration was both a physical and an intellectual activity, no longer simple reconstruction but rather a vehicle for presentation and comment. Orfeo Boselli, in his *Osservationi della Scultura Antica (1642–1663)*, noted that the ability to do restoration well was an activity for an enquiring mind and not as simplistic as many might assume (quoted in Weil 1967, 86).

At this time two distinct reasons existed for collecting ancient sculptures, which determined the approach taken by the restorer. The objects viewed as true works of art and exhibited in loggias with other masterpieces (usually paintings), were restored in an interpretive way. In contrast, those sculptural fragments destined to be incorporated into the general decor and gardens of palazzi were restored with less care and more license. In such cases pastiches abounded, and Boselli was highly critical of these creations (though he himself had done such work), likening the results to "monsters described in Horace's *Ars Poetica*" (quoted in Weil 1967, 86).

An over-life-size marble figure discovered in the early eighteenth century, missing its head, right arm, and parts of the feet, illustrates how most restorers of the period harmonized their restorations with the ancient fragments. By 1704, the fragment had already been restored and illustrated in the *Raccolta di Statue Antiche e Moderne* by Paolo Alessandro Maffei and Domenico de Rossi (figure 1.2.1). Known first in the house of Carlo Carioli, it soon became part of the Albani collection. By providing the fragment with a helmeted head, right arm, and staff, the first restorer presented the object as Alexander the Great. It is understandable that the remains of an imposing sculpture of high quality would be interpreted as a significant ruler, and portraits of Alexander the Great had been known since the Renaissance from Hellenistic coins. Curiously,

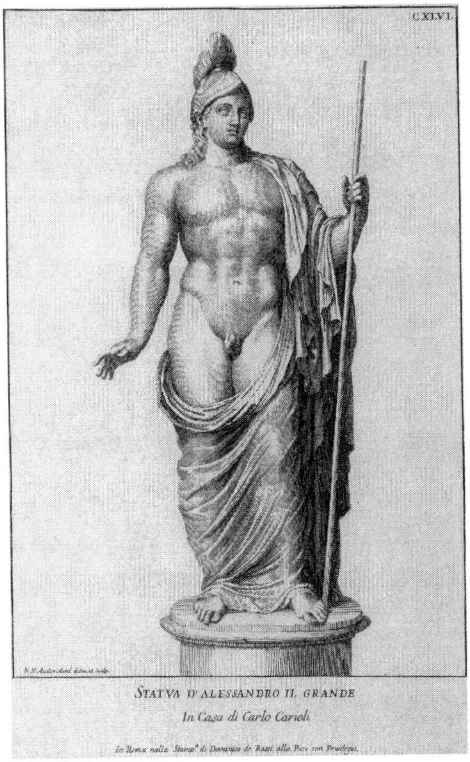

FIGURE 1.2.1 Engraving of a statue of a god restored as Alexander the Great, 1704, Robert van Audenaerde (Belgian, 1663–1743), 18 3/4 × 14 9/16 in. (Maffei and de Rossi 1704).

however, the missing head had been replaced with one from an ancient portrayal of the warrior goddess Athena. This reused head was combined with an invented helmet, presenting the fragment's new identity. After the statue entered the Saxony princely collections in Dresden, it was illustrated again by R. Leplat in 1733, with an added fig leaf and spear-end rather than staff.

A robust antiquities trade existed in Rome at this time and provided perfect conditions for such completions. The Grand Tour made it possible for those of means to acquire the finest antiquities, and those purchases created a restoration industry within Italy with attendant brokers, middlemen, advisors, investors, laborers, and, of course, scoundrels. The eighteenth century also saw the birth of archaeology and a further expansion of collections, which ultimately led to the formation of public museums such as the Palazzo Nuovo in 1734, the British Museum in 1753, the Uffizi in 1765, and the Louvre in 1793. These public institutions promoted the idea of antiquities as more than decorative objects and nurtured a more restrained attitude toward restoration. Museums added to their responsibilities the stewardship and preservation of ancient sculpture. In 1770, for example, Gaspare Sibilla was appointed the first official restorer of ancient sculpture for the Museo Capitolino and the Vatican Palaces and Gardens. His shop and staff were located within the Museo Pio-Clementino and, as such, defined an important new aspect of museum practice.

Johann Joachim Winckelmann, through his 1764 work *Geschichte der Künst des Ältertums* (*History of the Art of Antiquity*), revealed that the majority of objects in collections were Roman copies of Greek originals and noted that they had been compromised by restorers. Winckelmann held that the mistakes of connoisseurs were often due to undiscovered restorations, and he encouraged detailed recording.

Restorations fell further under suspicion as they proved inaccurate when compared to the growing variety of artifacts and fragments being uncovered following the mid-eighteenth century discoveries at Herculaneum and Pompeii. But ancient fragments were also seen to have a didactic value and were restored with that in mind. Antoine-Chrysostome Quatremère de Quincy, for example, praised the full restoration of the Aegina pediment figures, for which Bertel Thorvaldsen (1770–1844) had created new elements in the "ancient style" to complete the fragmented group (Quatremère de Quincy 1818, 82).

Although antiquarian interests and Winckelmann's insights changed the underlying dictates of restoration in the eighteenth century, the deceit necessary for the practice continued in one form or another until the nineteenth century, particularly for private collections. In 1787, the restorer Vincenzo Pacetti needed an Apollo figure for a temple commissioned by Marcantonio Borghese. None being at hand, he set about reworking an ancient sculpture of Pan for the purpose.

Such guises were particularly attractive to British collectors. Viccy Coltman's study of British neoclassicism between 1760 and 1800 describes how fragments of sculptures were patched together for invention, like blank canvases (Coltman 2006). Indeed, many of the Roman mythological figures in English country houses owe their identities to eighteenth-century restorers.

As a result one sees again the two approaches continuing on parallel paths, propelled by different interests: the collector, who preferred perfection and so encouraged restoration and invention, and the museum collections, whose curators were more inclined toward an academic balance between the didactic and the documentary. In most cases, restorers served both interests. But the published philosophies of prominent restorers of the time were not necessarily applied in their workshops. There is a stark contrast between Winckelmann's attempts to categorize "style" systematically and the restorer's work to assemble unrelated fragments into invented objects serving the desires of those willing to pay the price. Indeed, one of those restorers was both befriended and admired by Winckelmann: Bartolomeo Cavaceppi.

Ennio Quirino Visconti noted that Cavaceppi "introduced an improved manner to restorations, he adapted marbles which were completely disfigured by their condition, restored the missing parts without removing any of the original, introducing a new, more correct and truer method by which to return monuments to their antique splendor" (quoted in Conti 2007, 228). While this may be true, when compared to the inventive freedom employed by earlier restorers, Visconti's own words reveal the desire to "return" the objects to their perceived earlier "splendor." The goal remained full restoration, which, in the hands of Cavaceppi and his apprentices, quite often included invention.

Cavaceppi employed a number of clever techniques to fool the viewer's eye and camouflage additions. Despite Visconti's words, Cavaceppi would in fact often dramatically cut back the broken areas of ancient marble fragments, so that the joints between the fragments and his additions would be located at strategic areas, such as drapery folds, and would be further disguised. He left the ancient segments unpolished and textured his restorations to create an illusion of authenticity. False breaks were often chiseled into the surfaces of both ancient segments and additions to further confuse the viewer.

Cavaceppi seems to have been successful in two quite distinct worlds: that of private collections and that of public museums. In 1744, he was hired by the first director of the Museo Capitolino to restore the fragments of an antique red marble faun. By 1746, he had added the missing sections of the faun in such a manner that, even today, close examination of the striations and inclusions in the dark-red marble is necessary to delineate his work from the ancient parts.

By his death Cavaceppi had amassed over 1,000 ancient marble fragments, along with many engraved gems, coins, terracotta models, plaster casts, and molds. It is no wonder that his studio was called the "Museo Cavaceppi." But he was not unusual in this. Vincenzo Pacetti also sought raw material from archaeological sites for his restorations and creations, particularly from the excavations of Hadrian's Villa at Tivoli and in the collections of wealthy families in Rome. Such material was abundant in the late eighteenth century. For example, the marble feet, hands, and other sculpture fragments, recovered from the Pantanello ("little swamp" or "bog" in Italian) at Hadrian's Villa and then purchased by Pacetti, were surely intended for future restorations (Ramage 1999, 83).

In comparison with earlier restorers, however, both Cavaceppi and Pacetti were seen to be applying rigorous antiquarianism. Certainly Cavaceppi wanted to appear to be in line with the latest philosophical thinking and Winckelmann's support suggests that he was successful in this.

As progress was being made toward historical accuracy, propelled by the discovery of new archaeological evidence and resulting advances in scholarship, the demand for the removal and replacement of earlier restorations grew. Indeed the idea that restoration was wholly unnecessary took on significant importance as illustrated famously by the insistence of the renowned neoclassical sculptor Antonio Canova (1757–1822) that the fragments of the Parthenon frieze sculptures at the British Museum not be restored. Yet at exactly the same time, Thorvaldsen was praised for his imitative, in-the-style completion of the Aegina pedimental sculptures. Canova made no objection to Thorvaldsen's work, since he saw these pieces as having a didactic purpose rather than as perfect artistic exemplars in the category of the Parthenon figures.

All of this made the life of the restorer complex and somewhat schizophrenic. In 1787, Carlo Albacini had left the torso of the Psyche of Capua unrestored (though interestingly its broken surfaces had been cut smooth in preparation for restorations). So as not to mislead future scholars, no restoration was to be done unless it could be fully justifiable. And yet when Albacini was called upon to restore a Discobolus fragment found in Tivoli around 1791 (now in the British Museum), he added an incorrectly placed head that did not belong.

The Nineteenth through Twentieth Centuries: Science and Compromise

The first decades of the nineteenth century were pivotal for the shift from restoration toward less intervention. In 1820, the Pacca Edict restricted the export of artistic treasures from Rome, and at that time members of the German philological school combined their knowledge of ancient texts and Roman sculpture to seek better understanding of Greek originals. For them, previous restorations were obstructions that should be removed. The distrust of restoration emerged in Britain through the Society of Dilettanti, whose members expressed an interest in authenticity and exactness in recording condition. Just as at the Royal Society of London, which was at the leading edge of science and accurate observation, measurement was all-important. In *Specimens of Ancient Sculpture, Egyptian, Etruscan, Greek and Roman: Selected from Different Collections in Great Britain* (begun in 1799 and published in 1809), many of the engravings clearly illustrated restorations. In a publication of a marble bust in the collection of Lord Egremont, Richard Payne Knight, who championed the *Specimens* project and felt that restorations constituted fraud, commented: "The head . . . is now mounted upon a cumbrous modern bust, from which we have delivered it in print, and from which we could wish to see it delivered in the gallery" (quoted in Redford 2008, 147). Clearly support of derestoration was on the horizon.

The previously mentioned fragment restored as Alexander the Great (figure 1.2.1) reflects these changes in attitude. The object was illustrated in an 1804 catalogue of the Dresden collections of antiquities by Wilhelm Gottlieb Becker with the right arm and spear shaft gone and the joint in the middle of the torso clearly delineated (figure 1.2.2). Although the head remained in place, the sculpture was now referred to as Bacchus, reflecting a more accurate interpretation of the body type.

Although this new treatment was partial, it illustrates the direction being espoused by the Italian architect Camillo Boito, who promoted, as part of "scientific restoration," the recognition of objects as both artistic and historic documents (Boito [1883] 2003). In his "Prima Carta del Restauro," Boito encouraged the removal of all restorations in the treatment of buildings and monuments. A full circle had been scribed in which restoration, once the way to heal disfigurement, was now avoided and seen as the source of disfigurement.

In nineteenth-century Rome debates about restoration focused predominantly on monuments and reflected a desire to codify rules for practice. The results had a significant impact on the treatment of ancient sculpture. In 1807, Raffaello Stern stabilized the side of the Roman Colosseum, reflecting a respect for the fabric of the ruin through his

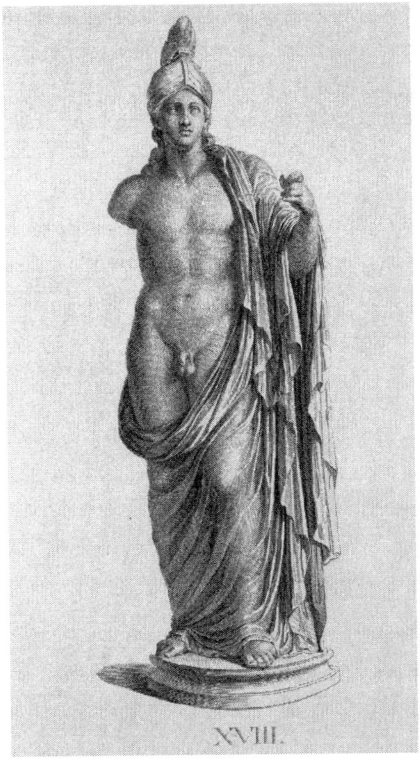

FIGURE 1.2.2 Engraving of a statue of a god restored as Alexander the Great, 1804, after Schubert (German, active 1700s), 15 7/8 × 12 1/16 in. (Becker 1804, pl. 18).

choice of materials and the functional form of the addition. In 1819–21 the restoration of the Arch of Titus, started by Stern and completed by Giuseppe Valadier, not only integrated a different material from the original, but also simplified that new material to be distinguishable from the ancient parts. This approach soon found its way into the collections of Rome, such as the Villa Giulia and the Capitoline Museum, where Baroque restorations, following Boito's advice, were being removed and then replaced by flat, monochromatic, and sometimes recessed infills. Though some may see these works as the first "purist" restorations, they were not. That distinction belongs to the Egyptian red granite obelisk of Montecitorio, which Giovanni Antinori restored between 1789 and 1792. Pope Pius VI should be credited with this exemplary instance of forward thinking, since he required that the additions be of plain stone with a flat surface and devoid of any invented hieroglyphs (common in the earlier restorations of other obelisks around Rome) so as to distinguish clearly the new work from the original parts (Collins 2000).

Romanticism in the mid-nineteenth century came to view the fragment as an embodiment of purity and a source of melancholic loss. Sculptures that, despite inaccuracies of restoration, had gone unassailed for centuries and had served as touchstones for developing art historical thought, were now reduced to the preferred (and assumed) pure state of the fragment.

By the end of the nineteenth century the practice of derestoration flared into a kind of iconoclastic rage fed by the antiquarians' search for truth, the insistence on material proof born from positivism, and the prominence of romanticism. Sculptures were stripped of previous restorations, often leaving behind no more than amputated forms. In their resulting state, these could no longer accurately represent the ancient fragment, given that they had been extensively recut and that their surfaces had been dramatically reduced through polishing during the restoration process. These were permanent changes that could not be altered, and the narratives presented by these amputated forms were less archaeological than medical.

Despite this rush toward purity, compromises could be found. In a mid-nineteenth-century photograph by Hermann Krone, made before the reinstallation of the galleries at the Dresden Albertinum (figure 1.2.3), the Alexander of figures 1.2.1 and 1.2.2 has been physically re-restored as a statue of Antinous in the guise of Bacchus. The work was carried out by Emil Cauer the Elder between 1829 and 1832. This time the transformation had been achieved by introducing a poor-quality plaster

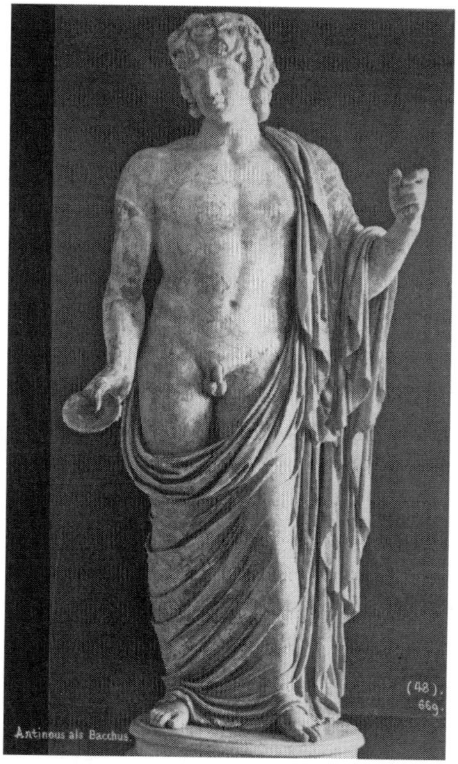

FIGURE 1.2.3 Photograph of Antinous as Bacchus, 1885–8, by Hermann Krone. The eighteenth-century restorations had been removed by Emil Cauer the Elder sometime between 1829 and 1832, and a crude plaster head of Antinous has been attached, as well as a restored marble arm holding an offering vessel.

interpretation of a portrait of Antinous and a marble restoration of the right arm, holding an offering vessel.

At the closing of the nineteenth century, restoration gave way to responsible stewardship. In 1863, Giovanni Battista Cavalcaselle, inspector of museums in Florence, emphasized conservation and stability over restoration. He encouraged restorers to carry out experiments of completion and interpretation on copies of the originals and advised that any additions to original fragments should be made easily distinguishable and neutral (Conti 2007, 327–44).

In preparation of the new Albertinum Museum in Dresden, the Alexander sculpture, now Antinous/Bacchus, was again altered sometime between 1888 and 1894 (figure 1.2.4). The director of the Skulpturensammlung, Georg Treu, undertook an experiment using the guidelines of Cavalcaselle. He modified Cauer's restoration by substituting the previous plaster head with a plaster cast taken from an ancient bust of Antinous as Bacchus in the British Museum (inv. no. 1899). Treu altered the inclination and rotation of the head to achieve a convincing placement. The well-recognized image of Antinous

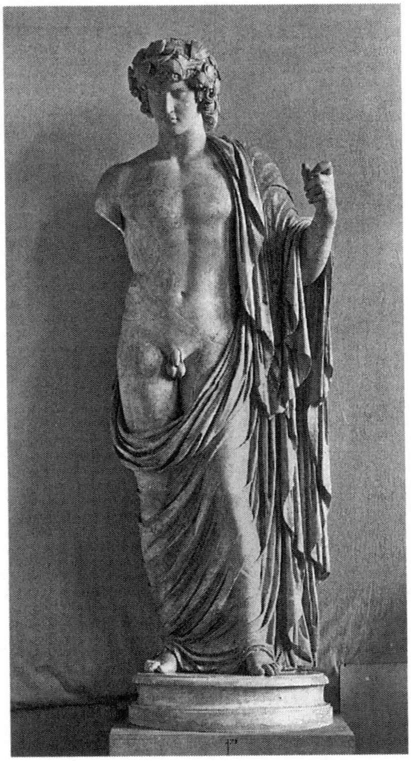

FIGURE 1.2.4 Early twentieth-century photograph depicting the re-restoration carried out between 1888 and 1894 by Georg Treu, director of the Skulpturensammlung, Staatliche Kunstsammlungen Dresden. A plaster cast of a bust of Antinous in the guise of Bacchus from the collection of the British Museum was altered to fit the statue. All other restorations have been removed.

acted like the addition of an attribute to assign an identity to the ancient fragment. Adhering to the new views on restoration, Treu also removed the restored right arm added by Cauer only a few decades earlier.

The Twentieth Century: Restoration Becomes Conservation

At the beginning of the twentieth century, the restorer/craftsman was becoming the "conservator," and studios were becoming scientific "laboratories." The late nineteenth-century art historian Alois Riegl, who outlined a variety of values that a monument might retain, gave far greater importance to the object as a witness to history than previously ascribed. The objects were now primary documents to be read and to be preserved with a range of values all worth attention (Jokilehto 1999, 215).

Derestoration continued well into the twentieth century. For example, although part of the appeal of the Giustiniani marbles in New York's Metropolitan Museum of Art lay in their restorations, curator Giesela M. A. Richter had most of the baroque restorations removed in 1939. Her decision was meant to reflect contemporary trends and to allow more direct study of the pieces for her *Catalog of Greek Sculptures* (Raggio 2005, 201).

Even as late as the 1970s, restorations that had defined certain ancient sculptures for generations were systematically removed. The Lansdowne Herakles, for example, was stripped of its eighteenth-century additions in the spirit of modern archaeological inquiry (Podany 2003, 19). But this process revealed that the eighteenth-century restorer, most likely Albacini, had done much more than replace missing limbs. He had reworked much of the surface, resulting in ancient segments that were similar to, but not exactly the same as, those existing when the figure was first found. This example demonstrated that the objective spirit of "scientific" investigation, resulting in the uncovering of a pure fragment, unpolluted by previous interventions, was clearly an illusion. And so in 1996 the restorations were again put back, in recognition not only of their historic importance but also of the permanent changes that had occurred to the ancient fragments. Didactic labeling now reveals what was ancient and what was restored.

In the twentieth century, the parallel paths of restoration and conservation once again emerged as a debate between aesthetics (art) and objective interpretations of observable fact (science). The assumed objective distance of science came up short at the beginning of the twentieth century when Riegel's "historic value" turned out to be, in part, a visually subjective preference, fully susceptible to the tropes of Romanticism. The artistic message and visual intent, which had previously been minimized somewhat by the art historian's and archaeologist's overwhelming interest in materiality, once again vied for the viewer's attention.

In 1963, Cesare Brandi reintroduced aesthetic concerns into the discipline of restoration/conservation. In his book *Teoria del Restauro*, he gave artistic components primacy over the material aspects of the object. The visual unity of the object became a leading concern, and to combine objectivity with this aesthetic concern, conservators achieved a clear visual distinction of the modern interventions from the original fabric through gestalt principles of perception. But these minimalist fills, whether monochromatic or blended with short strokes of color, had their beginnings in the mid-nineteenth century in the work of Valadier and Stern and even earlier with the demands of Pope Pius VI concerning the restoration of the obelisk of Montecitorio.

The Power of the Restorer

The complex way in which restoration developed and then evolved into conservation is more than a mere historic note. The various approaches have had a powerful influence on both the viewers and the objects. The results of the two paths have influenced how we value past restorations and understand their relationships to the ancient fragments. Decisions to keep or remove these additions, like decisions to carry out an intervention, must be carefully considered: what might be gained and lost, both at the time of the intervention and well into the future? Some restorations have become so iconic that an intense reluctance has formed around the question of their alteration. The sixteenth- to eighteenth-century restorations of the Laocoön group (figure 1.1.2) provide an example. The history of the group is well rehearsed in modern literature, and a summary suffices to set the stage for considering the power of the restorer/conservator.

Well known after its discovery in 1506, the Laocoön group was restored several times between the 1520s and 1727. Laocoön's missing arm was recreated in drawings, replicas, wax, terracotta, and then finally marble. Although the proposed position of the arm was suspected to be incorrect from the very beginning, it was accepted, because it completed a preferred composition. Even Winckelmann observed that the more likely position of the original arm, bent back over the head, would have detracted from the work's beauty. He thus knowingly gave his approval to an incorrect restoration and revealed a clear preference for a compositional taste born of his era. In 1906, the ancient arm was found and its position coincided with the earliest proposed reconstruction. Nonetheless, four decades passed before it replaced the eighteenth-century restoration (figure 1.5.2). It is likely that the iconic status of the group strongly influenced the delay, irrespective of the archaeological evidence. There can be no clearer evidence of the power of the restorer. Even today, questions remain. A compelling case can be made that early restorers incorrectly placed one figure and that it should be rotated and repositioned (Howard 1989); however, doing so would undo the frontal formality and "classical planigraphic" composition so popular in the sixteenth century and so long-known. It is not clear whether this repositioning will be implemented (see essay 1.5, Frischer). One is reminded of the fragment of an ancient torso restored as a statue of Alexander the Great now in Dresden and illustrated above (figures 1.2.1–2): at some point it became clear that the object did not represent Alexander, and surely it was obvious that the marble head, although ancient, did not belong, nor was it even a male head; yet, the incorrect head was left in place for almost 125 years. The decision and actions of a restorer or conservator continue to have ramifications for the perception of an object long after these actions might have proven to be mistaken or fallen into disfavor.

Conservators today not only face the challenges of stabilizing new finds arriving from the field or new additions being made to museum collections, but also must assure that the surviving evidence—both on the surface and contained in the fabric of the sculpture—is fully recorded and protected. Conservation professionals are dedicated to the preservation of as many of the values presented by the object as possible, but this may require a delicate balance between protection and accessibility, stabilization and nonintervention. Whatever must be done must also be well reasoned, allowing for as little permanent change to the object as possible, and must assure, to a reasonable degree, ease of removal of any added parts or treatment materials. Such "reversibility" is essential since each generation perceives the past differently and has the capacity to alter the surviving material evidence to meet the viewers' tastes and presumptions. We are no different.

Today: Converging Paths

There has never been any lack of wonder when something that has lain buried for centuries comes to light again. The object carries with it a promise of "filling in" parts of the past no longer available to us, of bringing us closer to another time. These artifacts are primary documents brimming with information, and we need only learn to read them. Today, the respect for the amount of information such objects hold is magnified by the knowledge we bring to them and by the analytical power that we have at our command. There is no doubt that even stronger lenses for reading will be developed in the future. Because of this, conservators in the twenty-first century tread lightly when treating ancient material. Conservators recognize that chemical and physical evidence is contained in the accretions or alteration layers and that the patina provides evidence of age and the passing of time (see essay 2.6, Abbe). In a world where physical authenticity is continually assailed by the availability of convincing alternative realities, such proof is an anchor for the actualities of the past.

We are likely today to leave a fragmented sculpture just as it was found. Computer modeling, like Cavalcaselle's plaster copies, offers us a myriad of noninvasive alternatives to view how something might have looked without having to impose a direct and permanent change on the object itself (see essay 1.5, Frischer). We have less need to restore and greater appreciation for the effects of time. That is not to say that fragments that belong together should not be reassembled, nor that encrustations that hide the form of an object, its decorative surface, or subtle inscriptions, should not be reduced. These actions can be undertaken with prudence and skill to reveal both evidence and subtleties with a resulting gain of essential information. Today the hybridity of the ancient sculpture comes from the combination of the object as historic document and as a work of art. We find in these two ingredients the familiar paths that we have been following for centuries. But today the conservator seeks to balance the paths, which appear to be converging into a single direction.

To this end, the Dresden Antinous in the guise of Bacchus (figures 1.2.3–4) now stands as an assembly of surviving ancient fragments with the previous restorations documented but not attached (figure 1.2.5). Reportedly an accident during the return of the sculpture to Dresden after the Second World War left the object once again fragmentary, and a recent 2008 re-restoration allowed scholars and conservators to consider how best to present the fragment in the twenty-first century. It was decided not to incorporate the plaster head added by Treu (missing since the war) but to present only what ancient fragments remained. Where necessary, infills unify the object but are clearly discernible as modern additions. The figure is labeled "statue of a god, possibly Antinous," informing the viewer that there is still much to learn.

Eugène Viollet-le-Duc, a French architect and theorist of the nineteenth century, once described restoration as bringing a building to a state in which it may never have

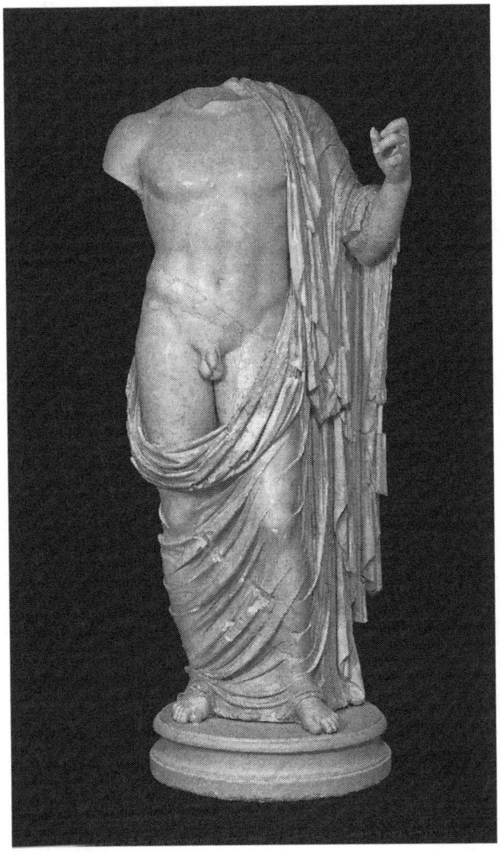

FIGURE 1.2.5 Statue of a god (Roman, AD 100–200) in the collection of the Skulpturensammlung, Staatliche Kunstsammlungen in Dresden after the most recent conservation treatment.

existed (Viollet-le-Duc [1854] 1990, 195). Irrespective of how minimal the treatment of an ancient object is, this statement proves true if taken literally. Whether an object is broken or reassembled, left with accreted dirt on its surface or cleaned, minimally repaired or fully restored, the inevitable result is a new state, one in which it has never existed before. The conservator's aim therefore is to manage change and assure accessibility while protecting the original fabric, intent, and evidence of age.

Modern technology has contributed significantly to our preservation efforts. We no longer need the welder's torch or the foundry's molten metal to assemble the fragments of an ancient bronze. Today's adhesives are sufficiently strong to avoid the holes in ancient fabric that would once have been needed for the screws and bolts securing fragments to an iron armature. Modern high-strength alloys provide structural support and stability with less disturbance of the ancient fabric. Lasers and microscopes provide tools to assure that necessary cleaning will not harm either ancient surface or preserved evidence. In short, we have little excuse to do harm and every opportunity to expand our knowledge while preserving our past.

We have come to accept the change and loss that accompany the passage of time. And we see the fragment as perhaps something greater, or at least with broader meaning, than the whole. The conservator's attention is now placed on treatments that stabilize the object and assure future accessibility. In all, this seems to be both a wise and productive path forward, since we know that Orfeo Boselli, a sculptor and restorer of the seventeenth century, was wrong when, in describing his joining technique, he wrote: "Place two good clamps with melted lead, and beat them in, and thus secure it for eternity" (quoted in Weil 1967, 96). Dynamic fashions and tastes guide the world of restoration and the efforts of conservation. We are committed to pass on what we find, enhanced by greater knowledge, not diminished by permanent and unwanted changes.

Bibliography

Barr, S. M. 2008. "Making Something out of Next to Nothing: Bartolomeo Cavaceppi and the Major Restorations of Myron's Discobolus." PhD diss., University of Arizona.

Becker, W. G. 1804. *Augusteum; ou, description des monuments antiques qui se trouvent à Dresde*. Leipzig: C. A. Hempel.

Boito, C. (1883) 2003. "Prima Carta del Restauro." Resolution Adopted by the Congresso degli Ingegneri et Architetti Italiani in Rome. In *Carte, risoluzioni e documenti per la conservazione ed il restauro, Siena, Marzo 2003*, edited by R. Della Monica and T. A. Hermanès. Siena: CERR. CD-ROM.

Brandi, C. 1963. *Teoria del restauro*. Rome: Edizioni di storia e letteratura.

Brenk, B. 1987. "Spolia from Constantine to Charlemagne: Aesthetics versus Ideology." In "Studies on Art and Archaeology in Honor of Ernst Kitzinger on His Seventy-Fifth Birthday," edited by W. Tronzo and I. Lavin, special issue, *DOP* 41: 103–9.

Collins, J. 2000. "Obelisks as Artifacts in Early Modern Rome: Collecting the Ultimate Antiques." In "Viewing Antiquity: The Grand Tour, Antiquarianism and Collecting," edited by C. Paul and L. Marchesano, special issue, *Ricerche di Storia dell'arte* 72: 49–68.

Coltman, V. 2006. *Fabricating the Antique: Neoclassicism in Britain, 1760–1800*. Chicago: University of Chicago Press.

Conti, A. 2007. *History of the Restoration and Conservation of Works of Art*. Translated by H. Glanville. London: Elsevier.

Grossman, J. B., J. Podany, and M. True, eds. 2003. *History of Restoration of Ancient Stone Sculpture*. Los Angeles: J. Paul Getty Museum.

Howard, S. 1989. "Laocoon Rerestored." *AJA* 93: 417–22.

———. 2003. "Restoration and the Antique Model." In Grossman, Podany, and True 2003, 25–44.

Hughes, J. 2011. "The Myth of Return: Restoration as Reception in Eighteenth-Century Rome." *Classical Receptions Journal* 3(1): 1–28.

Jokilehto, J. 1999. *A History of Architectural Conservation*. Oxford: Butterworth-Heinemann.

Maffei, P. A., and D. de Rossi. 1704. *Raccolta di statue antiche e moderne data in luce sotto i gloriosi auspici della Santità di N. S. Papa Clemente XI*. Rome: Stamperia alla Pace.

Pliny the Elder. 1980. *The Natural History*. Vol. 9. Translated by H. Rackham. Loeb Classical Library. Cambridge: Harvard University Press.

Podany, J. 2003. "Lessons from the Past." In Grossman, Podany, and True 2003, 13–24.

Quatremère de Quincy, A.-C. 1818. *Lettres escrites de Londres à Rome et addressèes à M. Canova sur les Marbres d'Elgin à Athènes*. Letter 4. Paris: n.p.

Raggio, O. 2005. "A Giustiniani Bacchus and François Duquesnoy." *MMAJ* 40: 197–210.

Ramage, N. H. 1999. "The Pacetti Papers and the Restoration of Ancient Sculpture in the 18th Century." In *Von der Schönheit Weissen Marmors: Zum 200. Todestag Bartolomeo Cavaceppis*, edited by T. Weiss and A. Dostert, 79–83. Mainz: Philipp von Zabern.

Redford, B. 2008. *Dilettanti: The Antic and the Antique in Eighteenth-Century England*. Los Angeles: J. Paul Getty Museum.

Vasari, G. (1568) 1912. *Lives of the Most Eminent Painters, Sculptors, and Architects*. Translated by G. du C. De Vere. London: Macmillan. Originally published as *Le Vite de' più eccellenti pittori, scultori, ed architettori*. Florence: I Giunti.

Viollet-le-Duc, E.-E. (1854) 1990. *The Foundations of Architecture*. Translated by K. D. Whitehead. New York: George Braziller.

Weil, P. D. 1967. "Contributions toward a History of Sculpture Techniques: I. Orfeo Boselli on the Restoration of Antique Sculptures." *Studies in Conservation* 12(1): 81–101.

CHAPTER 1.3

COLLECTING IN EARLY AMERICA

HIMA MALLAMPATI GLEASON

Introduction

Discussing the importance of ancient art, C. C. Perkins, a founder of the Museum of Fine Arts, Boston, wrote that both a scholar and the "man of general culture" could learn from the "masterpieces of ancient art, which are exponents of national thought and development, guides to historical knowledge, and verifiers of history" (1871, 51). The acquisition of these "masterpieces of ancient art," specifically sculpture, has a long and varied history in America, and responses to these objects reveal much about the historical identity and ideological concerns of Americans. This essay considers collecting of classical sculpture from the mid-eighteenth century until 1917, the date of the War Revenue Act, which permitted income tax deductions for donations to nonprofits, thereby significantly altering patterns of acquisition in America.

The focus here is primarily on institutional collecting of sculpture rather than on personal collecting, with the understanding that the behavior of individual collectors often shaped institutional practices. Indeed, classical art collections owned by individuals in early America have received far less scholarly attention than those in Europe perhaps because of their smaller scale and, arguably, their differences in quality. American individual collecting activity, however, mirrored that of institutions. In the colonial period, there were a few small collections, though some, like those of Joseph Allen Smith of South Carolina, were more ambitious. During the post-Revolutionary War period, a heightened classicism emerged in the new country, which began to assert its political and cultural connections to the democratic traditions of Athens and republican Rome. Other periods of avid collecting of classical objects took place immediately following the Civil War, when the country struggled with adopting a new national identity, and during the Gilded Age with its greater emphasis on artistic genius. As Elizabeth Bartman discusses in this volume (see essay 1.1), individual collecting in Europe was often associated with promoting one's noble status and lineage, but in early America, the motivations for collecting (both by individuals and institutions) were less to assert genealogical connections among elites and more to affirm educational, political, and cultural ties to the classical past.

American institutional collectors often concentrated on the acquisition of casts of classical sculpture rather than original objects, but the rationale for why these objects were acquired and how they were displayed altered during the late eighteenth through the twentieth centuries. Even with these changes, however, institutional acquisitions of both casts and ancient sculpture were ways to create and reframe narratives of the past and also to solidify new narratives of the cultural and political connection between contemporary American society and ancient traditions. In certain venues, especially those that were publicly accessible, these classical images were thought to serve as powerful transformative mechanisms for reshaping how Americans conceived of beauty, understood the power of technology, and applied methods of innovation.

Unlike in the United States, Roman sculpture was part of the material fabric of contemporary life in European countries because of its presence in extant architectural structures and on archaeological sites. This absence of the archaeological record from the American landscape undercut Americans' physical and, in turn, cultural connections to the classical past, but this lack of immediate access to the ancient world could be willfully ignored thanks to the prominent presence of classical objects within American institutions. As will be discussed in further detail, America's geographical conditions affected the import and the physical movement of statuary but also influenced the types, scale, and medium of sculpture brought to the United States. Furthermore, sociopolitical considerations, finances, reliance on private rather than governmental aid, concepts of education, and legal restrictions all played varying roles in how institutional collectors acquired classical material.

This essay begins with a brief discussion of the collecting of classical sculpture in mid-eighteenth century America followed by a lengthier analysis of the collection of casts in post-Revolutionary America until the 1870s. In this later section, I examine collecting in art academies, for-profit museums, universities, and libraries and use specific examples, such as the collection of the University of Michigan and the Athenaeum in Boston, in order to provide more details of collecting ventures. The subsequent section considers collecting strategies at large-scale nonprofit museums, with a particular focus on the Museum of Fine Arts, Boston, from the 1870s until 1917. Here, I explore how Italian export and ownership laws, American tariffs, authenticity, and changing opinions on the role of museums spurred on the collection of ancient artifacts rather than casts of statuary. The essay concludes with a discussion about the multiple purposes and uses of casts and ancient statuary in early American society.

Collecting in Colonial America and "Cast Culture"

From 1734, Boston was home to one of the earliest publicly accessible displays of casts of classical statuary in the British American colonies. The painter John Smibert opened a studio there with an array of engravings, reproductions of European paintings, and classical casts, some of which he had acquired in the hopes of educating students in painting courses for a failed college in Bermuda (McNutt 1990, 159; Saunders 1995, 100). Casts, which were generally made of plaster of Paris, but sometimes terracotta or bronze, were fabricated by cast-makers from molds of ancient statuary or from other casts. Collectors could acquire casts from various European cast-making workshops that sold canonical images of classical art, some of which were run by European museums; only much later were casts available from cast-makers in America (Frieze 1876a, 443–4; Connor 1989, 214; Haskell and Penny [1981] 2006).

As the casts in Smibert's studio illustrate, from early in American history some collectors used imagery of classical statuary as sources of artistic inspiration, to foster aesthetic appreciation, and to train artists. Casts were valuable in instructing artists and tradespeople because of the uniformity in their color, which was free from the incrustations and soil deposits found on ancient statuary, and because casts highlighted the objects' form over other considerations (Bury 1991, 123). For example, later painters, including Charles Willson Peale and John Singleton Copley, sketched the casts in Smibert's studio, which his heirs maintained and kept open to the public even after Smibert's death in 1752 (Wittlin 1970, 116). Nonartists could also visit the studio, which was in the same building as Smibert's painting shop. The lifelike qualities of the casts impressed audiences with one visitor describing a cast of the Venus de Medici as "the breathing Statue" and a bust of Homer as "the living Bust" (quoted in McNutt 1990, 159). In early colonial America, however, most cast collections were not on public display but maintained behind closed doors. As discussed below, the explosive growth of cast collecting in institutional venues occurred following the Revolutionary War.

Post-Revolutionary America: 1790–1870s

In post-revolutionary America until the decade following the Civil War, art academies, libraries, and universities often acquired classical statuary to broaden awareness of European cultural heritage, to encourage interest in and study of classical civilization, to advance civic pride, to refine taste, to inspire technological innovation or improvement, and to train young artists. Although there were multiple purposes for classical imagery, two main trends stood out in this period, namely the use of ancient statuary and casts to educate the viewing public and to train new artists and designers. These two distinct purposes both relied on visual inspection and access to a variety of specimens for analysis. Casts afforded audiences the opportunity to perambulate, measure, and touch replicas of ancient statuary, a practice not possible with other types of classical imagery found in engravings, prints, or (later) lantern slides. In this period, casts became important sources of visual data and permitted contact with ancient statuary in foreign museums and still *in situ* on monuments; when displayed together, they also offered a visual presentation or compendium of classical statuary. The multiple benefits provided by casts made them prevalent among various types of institutions.

Classical Statuary in Art Academies

Art academies were popular early venues to showcase classical imagery in the United States. In 1795, one of the visitors to Smibert's studio, Charles Willson Peale, opened his own short-lived art school in Philadelphia with a borrowed plaster cast of the Venus de Medici, which he showed only upon request (McNutt 1990, 161; Kurtz 2000, 126). Nine years later, Peale displayed Joseph Allen Smith's collection of classical casts in his American Museum in Philadelphia (McNutt 1990, 162). By 1805, the Pennsylvania Academy of Fine Arts in Philadelphia, which Peale and others had helped to establish, showcased Smith's collection. When a fire destroyed much of the academy's cast collection in 1845, its trustees replaced these objects with other casts, which the institution continued to acquire throughout the latter half of the nineteenth century (Stone 1987, 26).

In the early decades of the nineteenth century, other cities also established fine arts academies that formed cast collections for their members. At New York's American Academy of Fine Arts, portions of a subscription service of fifty dollars received from seventy-nine New Yorkers were used to acquire casts of the Apollo Belvedere, the Laocoön, and the Dying Gaul from the cast-making workshop at the Louvre (Miller 1969, 92). Some members of New York's Academy and local artists soon became disenchanted with the purchase of casts. In 1831, some of the local artists criticized the academy director's attempt to raise a subscription to acquire copies of the Parthenon Marbles and urged the institution to buy contemporary American artwork, create a building fund, or promote another educational endeavor (Miller 1969, 100). As evidenced in this example, the tension between using funds for purchasing casts and for other purposes recurs throughout the nineteenth century and was a controversial issue for later museums.

During the early nineteenth century, many art academies, confronted by the problematic aspects of exhibiting nude statuary in their institutions, addressed whether women should be permitted access to this imagery, and if so, whether gendered segregation of viewing this material was a viable method for adhering to social customs.

In some institutions, special viewing times were set aside for female audiences (Burt 1977, 42; Haskell and Penny [1981] 2006, 91). Describing her visit to the cast gallery at the Pennsylvania Academy of Fine Arts in 1830, Frances Trollope, an English entrepreneur and author of the *Domestic Manners of Americans*, commented on the academy's defaced casts, scarred by crude graffiti, and suggested that individuals were less likely to touch and vandalize statuary in the presence of the other gender. Commenting on the fingerprints and fig leaves, Trollope wrote, "I never felt my delicacy shocked at the Louvre, but I was strongly tempted to resent as an affront the hint I received that I might steal a glance at what was deemed indecent" (quoted in McNutt 1990, 164). According to Trollope, segregated viewing perpetuated the notion that nude classical imagery was lewd and pornographic. Until 1820, concerns about affronting public sensibilities were the primary reason why New York's Academy rarely exhibited its casts of nude figures (male or female) and stored these objects in crates (Swan 1940, 138). The subsequent wider-scale display of casts and the public's exposure to classical imagery in a number of institutional settings altered public mores regarding how and to whom classical sculpture would be shown.

Classical Statuary in For-Profit Museums

The growth and popularity of for-profit museums during the early through mid-nineteenth century, including Peale's American Museum and later P. T. Barnum's American Museum in New York City and Moses Kimball's Boston Museum and Gallery of Fine Arts, fostered increased public contact with classical imagery. These "dime museums," which charged a dime or a quarter for access, exposed people from a wide array of professions and socioeconomic backgrounds to classical civilization. A guidebook to Barnum's American Museum described the entrepreneur's Roman urns as especially appealing to the "lovers of antiquity and those who are curious in the Customs of other countries" (1850, 21). In Boston, Moses Kimball's collection contained a display of Greek statuary, and at least one of these statues was subsequently deposited in the Museum of Fine Arts, Boston (Cummings 1902, 336). The collection of this material by for-profit institutions, which relied heavily on visitor attendance rates for their survival, suggests that classical material appealed to their audiences.

Classical Statuary in University Museums

Particularly from the mid-nineteenth until the early twentieth centuries, universities and colleges became large consumers of classical casts, which were acquired by funds from faculty members, administrators, local members of the community, alumni, and even graduating students (Mallampati 2010, 95–121). During this period, Cornell University, the University of Missouri, the University of Illinois, Brown University, Columbia University, Dartmouth College, Harvard University, Mount Holyoke College,

Ohio State University, Princeton University, Yale University, and the University of Michigan all amassed sizable cast collections (Dyson 1998, 140; Wallach 1998, 46; Dyson 2010, 561–3). Faculty relied on casts for lectures, for their function as powerful, tangible links between classical languages taught in the classroom and modern understandings of classical culture, and for reinforcing the study and appreciation of the artistic and literary achievements of ancient communities. Indeed, some professors collected classical statuary and replicas in response to educational reforms that sought to limit the influence of classical education within the university.

At the University of Michigan, Professor Henry Frieze of the Latin Department spearheaded the opening of the Museum of Art and Antiquities in 1856 with a collection of plaster casts, terracotta statuary, and architectural fragments, intending to create a "classical museum in the University" that could display "specimens of Ancient art illustrative of the classics" (Proceedings of the Board of Regents, March 29, 1855, Bentley Historical Library, University of Michigan). Frieze argued that the display of ancient art was fundamental to the development of cultural unity, economic growth, and industrial trade, and to the education of university students and (more broadly) the entire citizenry. Particularly by the 1870s, such nationalist commentary on the importance of collecting and displaying classical artifacts probably reflected efforts to assert a united national identity following the Civil War. Frieze argued that "the improvement of the national taste" was an incentive to create museums with classical collections (Frieze 1876a, 436). According to Frieze, the creation of a national taste would also promote industrial advancement by encouraging the growth of "national industries" and new technologies inspired by classical imagery (Frieze 1876a, 435–6). Today, we are skeptical that a singular national taste is even possible, and we see many problematic biases in the canon Frieze sought to perpetuate, based as it was upon earlier European precedents (Haskell and Penny [1981] 2006).

Cost was an important consideration for many university museums, and the reasonable price of casts allowed even those institutions with limited financial resources the opportunity to acquire and showcase classical objects (Frieze 1876a, 443–4). Advocating for the collection of casts of statuary because of their large scale, wide availability, inexpensive price, and status as facsimiles of the most famous ancient statuary, Frieze wrote that "even more perfect than copies in marble could be made, and for all the purposes of art quite as valuable as the originals, can readily be obtained at an average cost of $25" (Frieze 1876b, 3).

Like his contemporaries, Frieze believed that how and where casts were exhibited was of crucial importance for educating viewers. From 1883 until 1910, many of the classical casts at Michigan were displayed alongside modern artworks, such as Randolph Rogers's *Nydia, the Blind Flower Girl of Pompeii*, reinforcing the notion that classical material was not to be viewed in isolation but rather as a significant source of inspiration for modern artistic creations (figure 1.3.1). Many other cast collections, however, were arranged in chronological sequence, enabling the study of the stylistic development of classical artwork and providing a context for the ancient authors that faculty taught in their language classes. Whether casts were showcased alongside modern artwork or in a

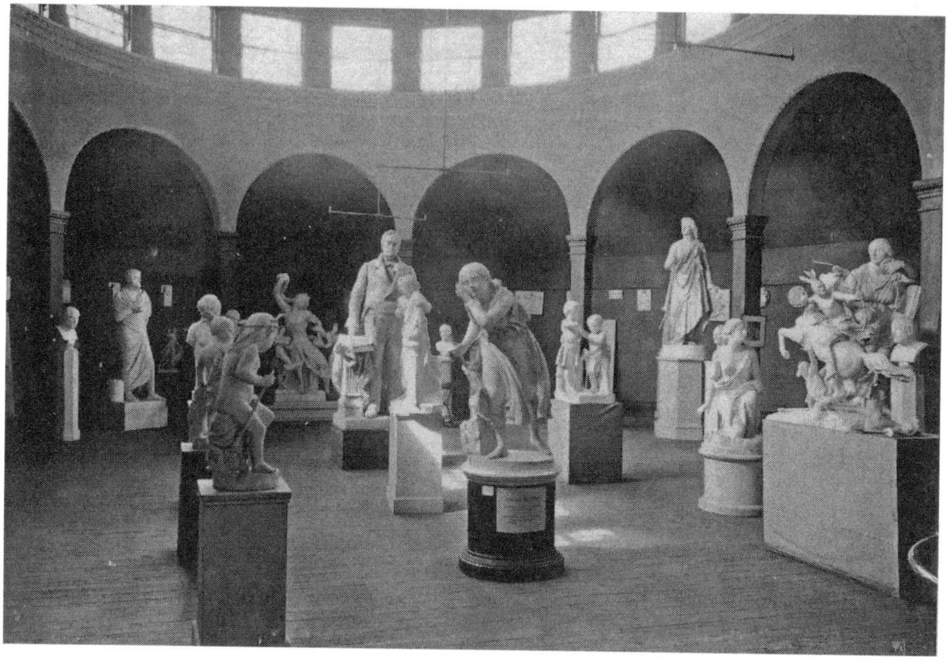

FIGURE 1.3.1 Cast Gallery in the Old Library at the University of Michigan, c. 1900.

chronological framework, their display in universities became a unifying and emblematic visual symbol for the educated.

Classical Statuary in Libraries

The significant role of casts in education was a prominent reason for their display in libraries. For example, the Boston Athenaeum, a member-supported private library founded in 1807, began to acquire casts of classical statuary in the early nineteenth century. In the *Memoir of the Boston Athenaeum*, published in 1807, the library's officers wrote that a display of artwork would aid in the "correction and refinement of taste" (quoted in Swan 1940, 3). By 1823, however, the Athenaeum's trustees were asserting that a public display of art would also enhance Boston's reputation, increase visitors' personal enjoyment, encourage financial growth, and raise visitor attendance to the Athenaeum (Athenaeum Committee Appointed to Solicit Subscriptions, March 6, 1823, quoted in Swan 1940, 8). Initially, the Athenaeum's classical casts were not exhibited in the public gallery (accessible to women), but displayed in the Library alongside the stacks of books and in other private rooms open only to men. The display of classical casts alongside books reinforced the notion that educational inspiration could be derived from the objects of the classical past and also that classical imagery was directly associated with educational aims. By 1839, the cast collection had outgrown the space available in the

Athenaeum Library complex and some casts were put on display in the public gallery (Swan 1940, 139–40).

The classical casts offered different learning opportunities for viewers than the Athenaeum's painting collection. "The study of the antique," observed Franklin Dexter, a trustee of the Athenaeum, "is the very alphabet of art" (letter to the trustees of the Athenaeum, 1833, quoted in Swan 1940, 139). This "alphabet of art" and its comprehensive nature fit well with the letters and other books in the library. Franklin continued that the casts were the preferred method of study because they offered "the *only* practicable method of learning the perfect proportion for the human figure; for those proportions cannot be elsewhere found without opportunities for that study." The Athenaeum's collection included not only famous works, such as the Laocoön, the Apollo Belvedere, the Venus de Medici, the Capitoline Venus, the Discobolus, the Barberini Faun, and Demosthenes, but also a few original classical sculptures including a marble bas-relief of a horse from Herculaneum (Swan 1940, 134–5, 137, 157–8). By 1866, the Athenaeum's trustees, overwhelmed by the large number of casts and the limited space at the Athenaeum, had decided to establish a "separate Institution, for the Fine Arts" to house many of the casts (C. Storrow, Standing Committee of the Athenaeum Report, March 1866, quoted in Swan 1940, 173). This institution became the Museum of Fine Arts (MFA), Boston (figure 1.3.2).

The Emergence of Nonprofit Museums: 1870s to 1917

From the late 1860s and early 1870s to 1917, the growth of large-scale nonprofit museums, such as the MFA, Boston, drastically altered the type, scope, and scale of classical statuary that was acquired and displayed in the United States. From the mid-1870s on, these institutions, which relied much more heavily than the smaller-scale for-profit institutions on private monetary and in-kind donations, slowly began to turn away from collecting casts and began to acquire more ancient classical statuary. Reasons for this change included developing legal restrictions on both sides of the Atlantic, America's changing educational needs, and the increased sale of existing collections.

Italian Export and Ownership Laws

The changes to Italian laws over the course of the nineteenth and early twentieth centuries, the complex nature of these laws, and American interest in Italian classical artifacts all provoked great discussion and debate in the American press. In fact, some of the best primary sources on this topic are newspaper articles from the period. The *New York Times*, for example, has a wealth of information on American collecting activity

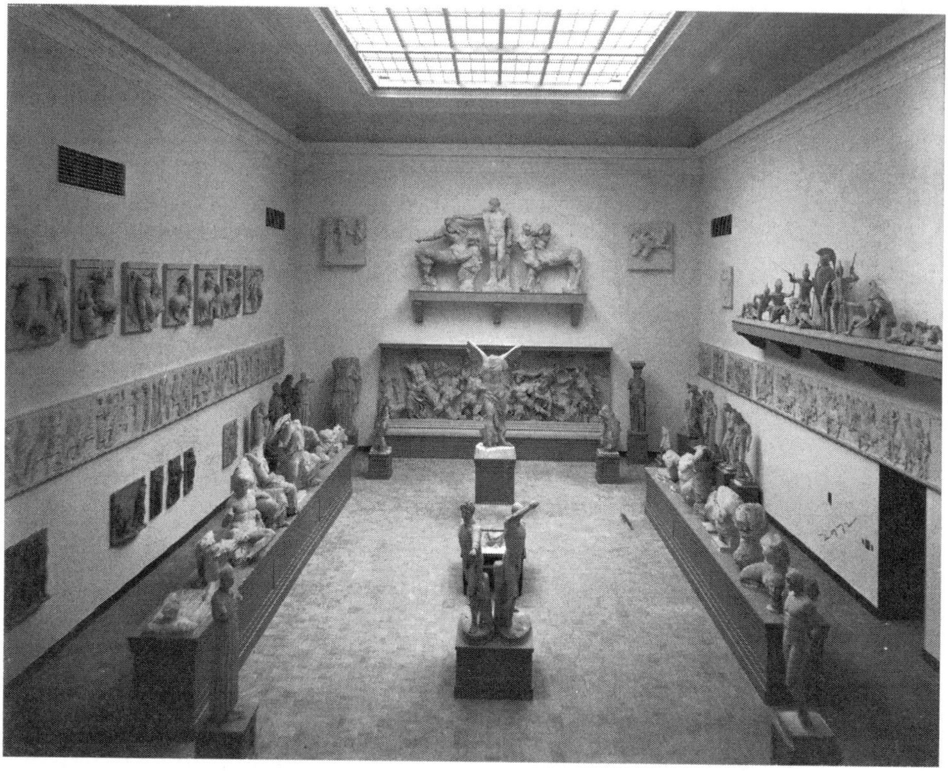

FIGURE 1.3.2 Court of Classical Casts, Museum of Fine Arts, Boston, c. 1910.

especially at the turn of the nineteenth and twentieth centuries. During the course of the nineteenth century, a number of Italian states enacted legal restrictions to ensure that antiquities would remain within state borders ("Art Treasures for Sale," *New York Times*, May 28, 1879, 2). For example, the Pacca Edict of April 7, 1820, attempted to stem the sale of ancient artifacts in Rome after the Napoleonic plunder and prohibited the export of art and antiquities without the approval of the papal government (see essay 1.2, Podany). In 1902, a new nationwide antiquities legislation vested ownership in newly found artifacts with the Italian state but permitted private ownership of objects that had been owned prior to the law's implementation ("Italy's New Law on Antiquities," *New York Times*, June 28, 1903, 6). The motivations for these export and ownership laws were numerous and included a desire to protect ancient artifacts from looting, to preserve the current architectural landscape by restricting the recycling of ancient materials for new buildings, and to uphold the interests and needs of specific social classes. Moreover, a renewed interest in classical studies invested ancient artifacts with educational and financial value (Guerzoni 1997, 112, 115).

During the late nineteenth and early twentieth centuries, American journalists wrote extensively about the effects of Italian cultural patrimony laws on American collecting activity and presented arguments resonant of contemporary debates about the collection of classical artifacts. Opponents of these foreign laws, including the art critic and collector James Jackson Jarves, argued that Italy was squandering its economic opportunities with burdensome legal restrictions that hindered American collecting, because sales of classical material could generate incredible revenue for Italy (Jarves 1879, 3; "Impeding Progress in Art," *New York Times*, November 8, 1879, 2). Likewise, others asserted that Italian museums were already filled with duplicates of materials that "have no value to Italy, but will be bought abroad for round prices" ("Italy's New Law on Antiquities," *New York Times*, June 28, 1903, 6). Yet, others recognized that these laws were enacted to preserve cultural materials for Italian citizens, but that ancient objects could have profound consequences for the development of American museums ("The Tariff on Works of Art," *New York Times*, February 28, 1902, 9).

Dealers' letters showcase their efforts to secure statuary for museums and fret about the effect of Italian legislation on American interests. Edward P. Warren, a dealer for the MFA, Boston, wrote that acquiring complete sculptures was challenging, because they appeared more rarely on the market and thus were much more difficult to "extract from Rome" (E. P. Warren, letter to Fairbanks, June 20, 1917, Edward P. Warren Box, E. P. Warren 1914–1917 file, MFA Archives). To evade various legal restrictions, Warren occasionally asked officials at the MFA not to display a recent acquisition until a set period of time had elapsed, and in other instances he noted that if an object were displayed, he would refrain from informing the MFA of its provenience for a predetermined period of time (E. P. Warren: letter to General Loring, November 11, 1895; letter to Brimmer, January 8, 1896, Edward P. Warren Box, E. P. Warren 1894–1898 file, MFA Archives; letter to E. Robinson, June 26, 1903, Warren folders, Art of the Ancient World Department, E. P. Warren 1903–1904 file, MFA Archives). In at least one instance concerning a bronze statuette, Warren concedes, "bronzes were just what we had to smuggle in, disguising their cost by covering them with other things which cost less" (E. P. Warren, letter to Fairbanks, April 12, 1912, Edward P. Warren Box, E. P. Warren 1899–1913 file, MFA Archives). Although Warren does not discuss to which locations these bronzes were smuggled or even where they originated, his admission regarding obscuring the monetary value of objects indicates his role in subverting export restrictions or customs' duties and tariffs in his acquisitions.

American Tariffs

Tariffs affected the prices of objects and the size of museum collections, but public discussions about tariffs also played an important role in debates about casts, the purpose of museum education, and the public's reconsideration of the value of original objects. The American tariff imposed specific fees on private collectors for importing objects based on the material, age, size, and whether the object was part of a collection (*In Re Marquand*, 55 F. 642 [2nd Cir. 1893], *Goodwin et al. v. US*, 66 F 739 [SDNY 1895], and *U.S. v. Sixty-Five Terracotta Vases*, 18 F. 508 [SDNY 1883]). From 1816 on, however, educational institutions, such as universities and nonprofit museums, did not pay tariffs on antiquities or casts of materials under the rationale that objects imported to further community interests provided by these organizations should not be subject to taxation (*Benziger v. United States*, 192 U.S. 38 [1904]). Critics of the tariffs, including some museum officials and collectors, however, argued that these duties restricted the number of artifacts entering the country through private hands, thereby reducing the number of in-kind donations to museums (Jarves 1880, 2; Marquand 1883, 5; Lane 1908). This argument assumed that greater personal collecting of objects would lead to increased donations to American museums.

Public debates regarding tariffs took place concurrently with American museums' shift toward acquiring original materials rather than casts. Responding to public criticism about the application of the tariff on artwork and its negative consequences for museum donations, Congress passed a new tariff act (the Payne-Aldrich Tariff Act) in 1909, later amended in 1913. The Payne-Aldrich Act freely admitted paintings over twenty years old and all antiquities over one hundred years old. Furthermore, changes to the tax laws in 1917 under the War Revenue Act permitted individuals to deduct the fair market value of donations of artwork to museums from their federal income tax. With fewer financial impediments via tariffs to acquiring artifacts and, following the War Revenue Act of 1917, increased incentives to donate material to collections, private collecting of original material swelled and in turn the donation of ancient objects to museums blossomed. There were exceptions to this trend, however. At the Museum of Fine Arts, Boston, for example, these American laws had a negligible effect on the museum's activities, because a significant percentage of the MFA's classical statuary had been acquired before the implementation of these two American laws (Mallampati 2010, 161–225).

Authenticity in Museums

In addition to changing laws that encouraged the importation of ancient artworks and their subsequent donation to museums, changing theoretical attitudes about the educational and societal value of ancient materials, the related changes to the art market, and shifting views on the function of museums and their displays resulted in increased acquisition of ancient objects by museums and universities. Emerging ideals of originality and authenticity played a significant role in the abandonment of casts in favor of ancient sculpture (Beard 1993, 22). For example, in 1912, the Director of the MFA, Boston, A. Fairbanks, a historian of Greek art, wrote that "casts became mere plaster without a soul and we recognized the magic of the craftsman's hands, the beauty of texture and the nobility of form" of ancient objects ("The Museum of Fine Arts," *Boston Sun*, September 14, 1912, quoted in Harris 1962, 559–60). Fairbanks stressed the importance of artistic creativity and believed that the ancient material object housed a touch of artistic genius that could not be found in casts.

The uniformity of "national taste" promised by the familiar canon of the most famous works became a disadvantage. Now, the exclusive display of original artifacts offered benefits to museums. Exhibiting casts alongside original artifacts could distract visitors and compromise the properties of original material (where the emphasis on artistic creativity and uniqueness are paramount) and diminish any value based on the aura of original material (M. Prichard, letter to S. Warren and trustees, November 1, 1904, quoted in Whitehill 1970, 202; Benjamin [1936] 1968). Moreover, a museum's possession of an original artifact triggered personalized and unique experiences with specific ancient objects not found in any other institution (Handler 1986, 4; Hein 2000, 71). Encouraging such experiences with original objects permitted museums to distinguish themselves and their collections from other institutions and enabled museums to foster a distinct relationship with their visitors. Finally, a unique collection conferred status upon a museum and permitted institutions desperate for funding to define their roles and clarify their distinguishing attributes, while competing with other charities for philanthropic aid.

Museums and Education

Early commentators, such C. C. Perkins, a founder of the Museum of Fine Arts, Boston, remarked that the intent behind institutions such as the MFA was not to cultivate the education of a few but rather to benefit "all classes of the community" (Perkins 1871, 50). In particular, sculpture, rather than other forms of classical art such as coins and vases, was viewed by some museum officials, such as M. Brimmer, the president of the Museum of Fine Arts, Boston, as having the most public appeal and in turn the ability to capture public interest in the museum (M. Brimmer, letter to E. Warren, July 24, 1895, Edward P. Warren Box, E. P. Warren 1894–1898 file, MFA Archives). The emphasis, however, on how classical sculpture could serve in education, what education meant, and how this education could assist the community changed in the late nineteenth and early twentieth centuries.

In nonprofit museums, education could serve many functions, including elevating public taste (thereby functioning as a method of social engineering), teaching about the history and processes of artistic creation, entertaining, enlightening, and inspiring creativity (Smolensky 1986, 764). Where the emphasis of the museum would lie on this educational spectrum and which objects could best be used to accomplish museums' purposes were discussed at length by a number of museum staff members. For the larger museums that sought to educate the masses, classical images, both casts and ancient artifacts, were efficacious tools in fostering aesthetic appreciation and informing the public about material creation and ancient history.

In the late nineteenth century, the rationales for acquiring casts rather than ancient artifacts in the large museums were similar to those offered by Frieze, namely casts' low cost, high availability, comprehensive representation of subjects and artists, educational value, and freedom from export restrictions and legal burdens (Comfort 1870, 507–8;

Report of the Committee on the Museum, Fall 1883, quoted in Whitehill 1970, 61; J. Elliot Cabot, Report of the Committee on the Museum, 1886, quoted in Whitehill 1970, 31; Boston MFA 1883). A collection of casts was a safer hedge than acquiring original artifacts, wrote J. Elliot Cabot, a Trustee of the MFA, in 1886, because there was no danger in "wasting our money through mistakes of" judgment (J. Elliot Cabot, Report of the Committee on the Museum, 1886, quoted in Whitehill 1970, 31). Whether Cabot feared wasting money on forgeries or on original artifacts whose educational or financial value dropped at a subsequent period, his proposition was that casts afforded more safeguards against the vagaries of the market.

By the turn of the nineteenth and twentieth centuries, some staff members at the MFA and dealers argued that the market offered the best opportunities for acquisitions of new masterpieces of classical statuary, which in turn, offered museums the possibility of differentiating themselves (M. Prichard letter to S. Warren and trustees, November 1, 1904, quoted in Whitehill 1970, 201). The dealer E. P. Warren suggested that with his aid the MFA would become a "summa artistic [venue] of the best qualities of Greek art, boasting its fine specimens in each branch of sculpture, its few masterpieces" (E. P. Warren, Address to the Trustees of the MFA, November 13, 1900, Edward P. Warren Box, MFA Archives). Influenced by a focus on connoisseurship, some staff members at the MFA argued that the primary purpose of the art museum was not to engage in pedagogy, but rather to foster and maintain aesthetic taste in the community (Gilman 1904, 213, 217; Whitehill 1970, 183; Wallach 1998, 50, 56). This taste could not be found in the mechanically reproduced casts, which MFA staff member M. Prichard referred to as "engines of education," but rather in authentic ancient artworks that were the "objects of inspiration" (M. Prichard letter to S. Warren and Trustees, Nov. 1, 1904, quoted in Whitehill 1970, 202). Here the museum's primary functional value lay in its ability to inspire appreciation, and the museum's role as refined tastemaker became paramount through its display of ancient sculpture.

Many casts were deaccessioned to clear precious floor and storage space for ancient statuary. At the MFA, Boston, the trustees gave some of the casts to local schools in Massachusetts, and museum staff members destroyed others with sledgehammers (Whitehill 1970, 437; G. Chase [Acting Curator of Classical Art at the MFA], letter to G. Aarons of the Samuel Adams School, November 5, 1947, Art of the Ancient World Department, Correspondence A 1941–1950, MFA Archives). Large museums' abandonment of casts, once valued and esteemed tools for societal advancement, and their turn to amassing collections of original antiquities—in this period primarily statuary—had profound consequences for public conceptions of museums, originality, and education.

Conclusion

In the early United States, the acquisition and display of classical statuary and casts reinforced American political and social beliefs and asserted American cultural connections with classical civilization. The ownership of casts of statuary and later of original ancient sculptures, therefore, was a visual expression of American identity and interests, or at least the identity and interests espoused by some Americans. Casts offered a democratization of ancient culture both through their ease of production that afforded low-cost alternatives to ancient statuary and through the manner of their consumption. Casts permitted those familiar and unfamiliar with classical civilization the opportunity to gaze at and receive the benefits of canonical classical imagery. Supporters of casts asserted that this interaction could transform and enlighten the masses. Under this view, the legacy of ancient Greece and Rome was envisioned as the keystone of American culture. Classical civilization, however, was not a cultural history shared by or even recognized by all of the inhabitants of and immigrants to the United States. Unlike casts, original pieces of ancient sculpture enabled American museums and universities to distinguish themselves from their European counterparts. An emphasis on artistic genius in museums prioritized the ancient object but also underscored museums' roles as tastemakers, astute connoisseurs, and disseminators of unique visual knowledge in American society.

Bibliography

Barnum's American Museum. 1850. *Barnum's American Museum Illustrated Guide Book.* http://lostmuseum.cuny.edu/archives/guidecover.htm.

Beard, M. 1993. "Casts and Cast-Offs: The Origins of the Museum of Classical Archaeology." *PCPS* 39: 1–29.

Benjamin, W. (1936) 1968. "The Work of Art in the Age of Mechanical Reproduction." In *Illuminations*, edited by H. Arendt, 219–53. New York: Schocken.

Boston Museum of Fine Arts (MFA). 1883. "Special Report on the Increase of the Collections." In *Eighth Annual Report of the Trustees of the Museum of Fine Arts, for the Year Ending Dec. 31, 1883*, 10. Boston: Alfred Mudge and Son.

Burt, N. 1977. *Palaces for the People.* Boston: Little, Brown.

Bury, M. 1991. "Introduction: Plaster and Marble: The Classical and Neo-Classical Portrait Bust." *Journal of the History of Collections* 3(2): 121–4.

Comfort, G. 1870. "Art Museums in America." *Old and New* 1: 503–12.

Cummings, C. Oct. 1902. "Moses Kimball." *New England Historical and Genealogical Register* 56: 335–40.

Connor, P. 1989. "Cast-Collecting in the Nineteenth Century." In *Rediscovering Hellenism: The Hellenic Inheritance and the English Imagination*, edited by G. W. Clarke, 187–235. New York: Cambridge University Press.

Dyson, S. L. 1998. *Ancient Marbles to American Shores: Classical Archaeology in the United States.* Philadelphia: University of Pennsylvania Press.

———. 2010. "Cast Collecting in the United States." In *Plaster Casts: Making, Collecting and Displaying from Classical Antiquity to the Present*, edited by R. Fredericksen and E. Marchand, 557–76. New York: Walter de Gruyter.

Frieze, H. S. 1876a. "Art Museums and Their Connection with Public Libraries." In *Public Libraries in the United States of America: Their History, Condition, and Management. Special*

Report: Part I, U.S. Bureau of Education, 434–44. Washington, DC: Government Printing Office.

———. 1876b. *Catalogue of the Museum of Art and History in the University of Michigan*. Ann Arbor: University of Michigan.

Gilman, B. I. 1904. "One of the Distinctive Purpose of Museums of Art." *Museums Journal* 3(7): 213–24.

Guerzoni, G. 1997. "Cultural Heritage and Preservation Policies: Notes on the History of the Italian Case." In *Economic Perspectives on Cultural Heritage*, edited by M. Hutter and I. Rizzo, 107–132. New York: St. Martin's.

Handler, R. 1986. "Authenticity." *Anthropology Today* 2(1): 2–4.

Harris, N. 1962. "The Gilded Age Revisited: Boston and the Museum Movement." *American Quarterly* 14(4): 545–66.

Haskell, F., and N. Penny. (1981) 2006. *Taste and the Antique: The Lure of Classical Sculpture, 1500–1900*. New Haven: Yale University Press.

Hein, H. S. 2000. *The Museum in Transition: A Philosophical Perspective*. Washington, DC: Smithsonian Free Press.

Jarves, J. J. 1879. "Art Treasures of Italy: A Proposed Exhibition in Florence." *New York Times*, July 30, 3.

———. 1880. "A Blow at American Art: Discouraging Effect of Our Customs Duties." *New York Times*, September 25, 2.

Kurtz, D. 2000. *The Reception of Classical Art in Britain: An Oxford Story of Plaster Casts from the Antique*. BAR-BS 308. Oxford: Archaeopress.

Lane, G. M. 1908. "Statement of Mr. Gardiner M. Lane, President of the Boston Museum of Fine Arts." *Tariff Hearings before the Committee on Ways and Means of the House of Representatives*, November 27, 60th Congress: 2611–12.

Mallampati, H. 2010. "Acquiring Antiquity: The Classical Collections at the University of Michigan and the Museum of Fine Arts, Boston, ca. 1850–1925." PhD diss., University of Michigan.

Marquand, H. 1883. "Are Pictures Luxuries?" *New World*, April 22, 5.

McNutt, J. K. 1990. "Plaster Casts after Antique Sculpture: Their Role in the Elevation of Public Taste and in American Art Instruction." *Studies in Art Education* 31(3): 158–67.

Miller, L. 1969. *Patrons and Patriotism: The Encouragement of the Fine Arts in the United States, 1790–1860*. Chicago: University of Chicago Press.

Perkins, C. C. 1871. "Art Education in America." *Journal of Social Science: Transactions of the American Association* 3: 37–57.

Saunders, R. H. 1995. *John Smibert: Colonial America's First Portrait Painter*. New Haven: Yale University Press.

Smolensky, E. 1986. "Municipal Financing the U.S. Fine Arts Museum: A Historical Rationale." *Journal of Economic History* 46(3): 757–68.

Stone, C. 1987. "Antique Casts in America." *Sculpture Review* 36: 26–7, 31, 33.

Swan. M. 1940. *The Athenaeum Gallery, 1827–1873: The Boston Athenaeum as an Early Patron of Art*. Boston: Boston Athenaeum.

Wallach, A. 1998. *Exhibiting Contradiction*. Amherst, MA: University of Massachusetts Press.

Whitehill, W. M. 1970. *Museum of Fine Arts, Boston: A Centennial History*. Vol. 1. Cambridge, MA: Belknap Press.

Wittlin, A. 1970. *Museums: In Search of a Usable Future*. Cambridge, MA: MIT Press.

CHAPTER 1.4

CURRENT TRENDS IN MUSEUM DISPLAY

JESSICA POWERS

INTRODUCTION

THOUGH students, scholars, and the lay public alike most frequently encounter Roman sculptures in museums, until recently little scholarly attention had been devoted to how museums present this material, apart from occasional notes in the introduction to collection catalogs. In the past few decades, several factors have combined to increase significantly the interest in this subject. New methodological developments in each of the disciplines of art history, classics, and archaeology have called for greater awareness of the position of the observer and of the inherent biases of the modern age that affect how we perceive and respond to past cultures and their material remains. As part of a broader interest in the modern reception of the classical past, scholars have become more conscious—and critical—of the role of museums in determining how visitors encounter the works on display (e.g., Dyson 1998; Kampen 2003; Newhouse 2005; Scott 2006; Bilsel 2012). At the same time, the restitution of Greek, Roman, and Etruscan objects from several museums in the United States to the governments of Italy, Greece, and Turkey and legal proceedings against dealers and curators allegedly involved in the illicit trade in antiquities have focused attention on how museums, particularly those in the United States, handle ancient material.

The reinstallation of many collections since the 1990s has given further impetus to a public conversation about how Roman art and artifacts are displayed in museums. These include the reorganization of part of the Museo Nazionale Romano's immense collection in the Palazzo Massimo and Palazzo Altemps in Rome, the opening of new galleries in the Capitoline Museums, the reinstallation of the Farnese sculptures in the Museo Archeologico Nazionale in Naples and of the Roman galleries at the Metropolitan Museum of Art in New York, the reopening of the Getty Villa in Malibu and of the Altes Museum and the Neues Museum in Berlin, the reinstallation of the Ny Carlsberg

Glyptotek in Copenhagen, the refurbished Roman galleries in the Museum of Fine Arts, Boston, and the planned reorganization of the Roman galleries at the Louvre, as well as reinstallations of smaller collections in Baltimore, Chicago, Cleveland, Detroit, Frankfurt, Kassel, and San Antonio, and at university museums in Oxford, Cambridge (both England and Massachusetts), Philadelphia, New Haven, Providence, and Ann Arbor, to name only a few. In addition to extensive coverage by the news media and cultural magazines and websites, these openings have received attention from the scholarly community, for example in the new museum reviews feature of the *American Journal of Archaeology* (Cohen 2008) and in several (unpublished) conferences in both North America and Europe.

In this essay I comment on what I see as the major themes and issues reflected in recent installations of permanent collections, as well as the goals and impediments that have shaped them, with particular attention to the relationship between academic scholarship on Roman sculpture and museum displays. Although they tend to consume much effort on the part of museums and their staffs, temporary exhibitions are not my focus here. Unlike many who have contributed to the evaluation and critique of museum practices in recent years, I write from the position of a curator, a museum "insider." The observations I share here are based largely on my own experience working in several American museums and as a visitor to others throughout the United States and Europe. Other perspectives on the display of Roman art and artifacts in present-day museums include Giuliani (2000), Borromeo and Goulet (2001), Zanker (2003), Borbein (2004), Swain (2007), Rudolph (2008), and Barbanera (2008; 2013), as well as Siapkas and Sjögren (2013), which addresses several of the issues mentioned here at greater length, but unfortunately reached me only after this essay was essentially complete.

Organizing Principles

The place of Roman sculpture collections within their respective museums—not just physically, but conceptually as well—ultimately underlies how they are displayed. The wide variety of museums now housing Roman sculptures makes it difficult to speak of these institutions in general. They range from encyclopedic museums with collections representing many of the world's cultures to site museums focused on the material remains of a specific place or region, from art museums to those emphasizing archaeology and history. They also include state-sponsored, privately-supported, and university museums. Factors such as a particular museum's history and mission and the priorities of its leadership and external funders all affect the allocation of gallery space. Although these internal considerations often are not readily apparent to the ordinary museum-goer, they can have a considerable impact on how a collection is presented. The changing fate of the Metropolitan Museum's Roman Court, from gallery to restaurant and back to gallery, is but one example of such forces at work (Picón 2007). More worrisome has been the elimination of curatorial positions dedicated to ancient art at several museums and the incorporation of important Greek and Roman collections into other departments, as has happened, for example, at the Detroit Institute of Arts and the Toledo Museum of Art. The display of sculptures is also naturally shaped by the scope of the individual museum's collection. Whether the collection was acquired centuries ago or in living memory, the decisions, interests, and preferences of the collectors and curators by whom it was formed will continue to affect current and future installations, in terms of what issues can be addressed and what stories can be told (see essays 1.1, Bartman; and 1.3, Mallampati Gleason).

In most cases, sculptures are but one element of a museum's Roman collection, which frequently belongs in turn to a curatorial department that also encompasses Greek, Etruscan, and sometimes Egyptian and ancient Near Eastern material. Following long-standing divisions within the discipline of classical archaeology, these collections have traditionally been organized by typology or chronology or a combination of the two. In many nineteenth- and early twentieth-century installations, typological considerations led to the display of Greek and Roman sculptures in stone and large-scale bronzes separately from smaller works, such as bronze and terracotta figures, glass, ceramics, and household furnishings and utensils. A handful of museums today, particularly those with exceptionally large sculpture collections, like the Vatican and Capitoline Museums, the Louvre, the Ny Carlsberg Glyptotek, and the Munich Glyptothek, maintain suites of galleries dedicated exclusively to Roman sculptures. Recent installations reflect in a variety of ways changing scholarly attitudes to these disciplinary boundaries. One result has been a conscious effort to integrate sculptures with Roman art in other media. Such is the case in the Altes Museum in Berlin, where the Roman collection was reinstalled in 2010 (Scholl and Maischberger 2010). Once displayed with Greek sculptures in the Pergamon Museum, the Roman sculptures have been reorganized in several galleries on the upper floor of the Altes Museum. Portraits in marble and bronze, for example, can now be compared with those on cameos and coins on view in cases nearby. In another gallery, sculptures depicting mythological and genre subjects accompany bronze vessels from Boscoreale, the Hildesheim silver treasure, and a group of glass vessels to evoke the accouterments of a Roman villa. Such installations—other examples include the new galleries at the Metropolitan Museum as well as the Getty Villa—convey something of the breadth of Roman visual culture and enable comparison of popular subjects and compositions across different media.

Unlike archaic and classical Greek sculpture, which lends itself to chronological installation on the grounds of general scholarly agreement over the course of its stylistic development, Roman sculpture fits this model less readily. While imperial and private portraits, and to a lesser extent sarcophagi and other funerary sculptures, can be arranged relatively easily in approximate chronological order (see essays 3.4, Wood; and 4.4, Ewald), sculptures of mythological figures pose more challenges to precise dating and thus are difficult to incorporate in a chronological installation. This division is reinforced by the long-established scholarly practices of studying Roman sculpture by genre and of associating Roman mythological sculptures closely with Greek precedents, a challenging issue to which I return below. As a result in many installations the

Roman portraits are organized by date with sarcophagi sometimes interspersed among the later portraits, while mythological sculptures are displayed separately. Variations on this approach can be seen, among other examples, in the recent installations at the Metropolitan Museum, the Ny Carlsberg Glyptotek, and the Altes Museum.

In recent years, however, many both within and without museums have questioned the effectiveness of organizing museum installations by chronological periods (e.g., Moltesen 2007; Blythe and Palley 2011). Arranging works by date has long been seen as a way to emphasize stylistic developments and to provide structure, particularly for visitors who may have little prior knowledge of (art) history, but many museum professionals have come to recognize that the minutiae of stylistic change are not especially engaging for most museum-goers. And chronological installations allow little flexibility, since they make sense only if visitors follow a fixed linear path through the galleries. Rethinking this approach in relation to art of all periods, not just classical antiquity, has led to a shift away from chronology toward installations organized around thematic narratives. Among antiquities collections, perhaps the most celebrated thematic installation is that of the Getty Villa, which reopened in 2006 (Moltesen 2007). Here Greek, South Italian, Etruscan, and Roman works are shown together in individual galleries according to broad themes such as "Gods and Goddesses," "Dionysos and the Theater," "Women and Children in Antiquity," and so on, an arrangement that suits the villa's layout, with many small- to medium-size galleries opening off the central courtyard (figure 1.4.1). While these groupings may prove more accessible to museum-goers than an installation

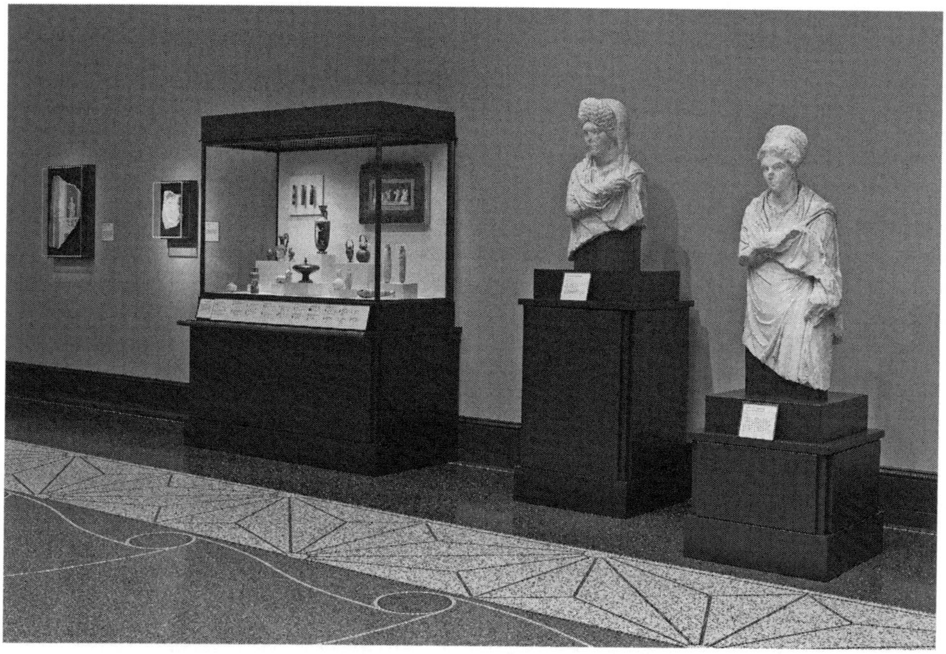

FIGURE 1.4.1 Two Roman portraits of women displayed near Greek and Roman perfume vessels in the "Women and Children in Antiquity" gallery of the Getty Villa, Malibu.

based on art-historical criteria, their wide-ranging nature risks obscuring significant differences among the cultures and periods represented. Another approach to a thematic installation has been taken by the Ashmolean Museum, which opened a substantial expansion in 2009 (James 2010). The new installation is guided by an overarching theme of cross-cultural exchange. On each of three floors dedicated to antiquity, the medieval period, and the early modern era, an introductory gallery emphasizes the trade routes that connected far-flung lands. Among the antiquities galleries, carefully arranged lines of sight and double-sided cases encourage visitors to make connections between neighboring cultures, linking the Roman material both to Greece and to India.

Responding to increased interest in how objects were used and displayed in antiquity, some installations—not only in site museums but also in those with larger collections from diverse sources—organize objects around various ancient contexts. Often this approach takes the form of sections devoted to the tomb or the villa as general settings for sculptures and other objects. Judicious use of photomurals, such as photos of the Vigna Codini columbarium that accompany recent installations of funerary sculptures in the Metropolitan Museum and the Fitzwilliam Museum, can help to convey a sense of ancient contexts. In a few instances, ancient settings have actually been recreated within the museum, as with the reconstruction of the now-submerged nymphaeum off Punta Epitaffio to house its famous sculptures in the archaeological museum in Baiae (Miniero 2000). In other museums, elements of the exhibition design evoke the ancient setting: at the University of Pennsylvania Museum, for example, a mural depicting Lake Nemi and its surroundings serves as a backdrop for sculptures from the sanctuary of Diana. Similarly, the Walters Art Museum's remarkable group of sarcophagi have been installed in a compact, darkened room to call to mind the tomb on the Via Salaria where they were found (Bartman 2004). In less dramatic installations the connections are made clear through labels and text panels, as in the galleries of the Capitoline Museums now dedicated to sculptures from the *horti* of Rome (Fentress 2007) and, on a smaller scale, the installation as a group of the portraits from the Tomb of the Licinii within the early imperial portrait gallery of the Ny Carlsberg Glyptotek (Bartman and Nagy 2007).

Many museums have combined several of these approaches to suit the demands of space and the strengths of their collections. And the sculptures themselves invite a certain fluidity: a female portrait bust, for example, might be effectively displayed with portraits, with images of women, with household utensils and decor, or with funerary material. The 2008 reinstallation of the San Antonio Museum of Art's Roman sculptures, which I curated, reflects these challenges and opportunities (Powers 2008). Located in a large, square gallery that can be entered or exited on only one side and thus precludes any single path for visitors, the new installation places mythological sculptures, loosely grouped by subject, at the center of the room. The surrounding quadrants, anchored by large works, each have a different theme: pre-Roman Italy; daily life, incorporating glass and silver; portraits, arranged chronologically and displayed alongside a selection of coins; and funerary sculpture, uniting works from Roman Italy and the provinces. On a similar scale, the 2010 reinstallation of the Fitzwilliam Museum's Greek and Roman gallery features a chronological installation animated by engaging label panels that emphasize the people connected with such objects, from artisans and ancient consumers to modern archaeologists and collectors (Burn 2012).

Whatever the overarching aims of the installation, practical considerations invariably intrude in its execution. Many of the museums housing Roman sculptures are now a century old or more, and the existing buildings may limit (or render very costly) opportunities to adjust the configuration of gallery spaces. This problem is particularly acute for museums that occupy buildings originally constructed to serve entirely different purposes, such as ornate royal palaces (Louvre) and noble residences (Palazzo Altemps; De Angelis d'Ossat and Capodiferro 2011), where the rich decor threatens to overwhelm the collections on display. Other examples include the Museo Nazionale Romano's ancient baths turned into cloisters and repurposed industrial structures such as the Capitoline Museums' satellite space in the Centrale Montemartini power station (Bertoletti, Cima, and Talamo 2007). The San Antonio Museum of Art occupies a nineteenth-century brewery, with the Roman gallery in what had been the vast boiler room (Powers and Johnston 2012). The exposed original walls of pale brick presented environmental problems and created a distracting backdrop for the similarly colored marble sculptures; a newly added skin wall serves both as a barrier to the elements and as a more subtle background (figure 1.4.2). In new and old construction alike, building codes, accessibility requirements, and the need to facilitate the flow of visitors through galleries may limit the placement of statues. The considerable weight of marble, with

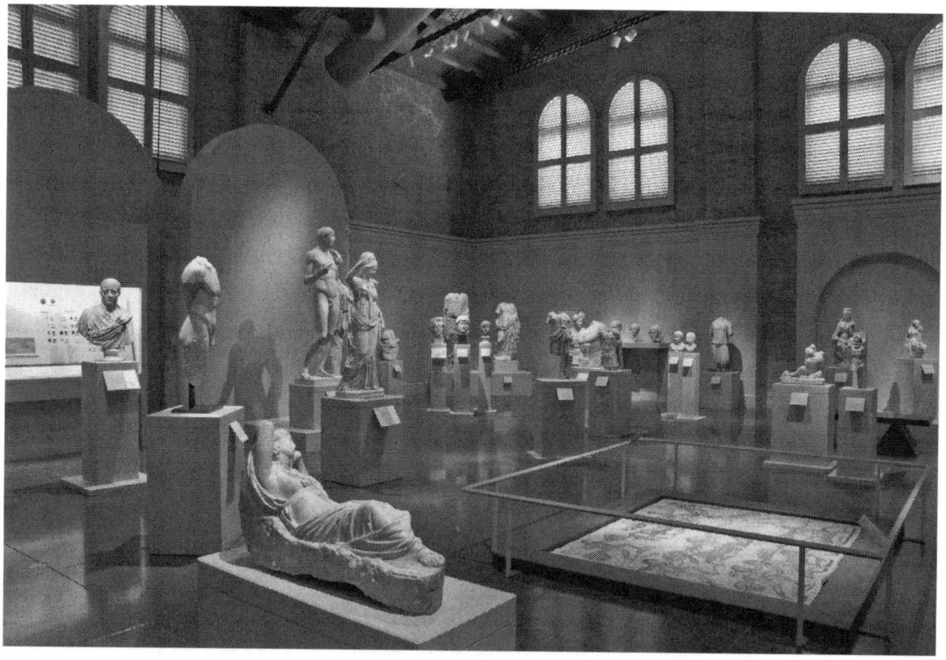

FIGURE 1.4.2 The Roman gallery in the San Antonio Museum of Art after reinstallation in 2008. Photography by Peggy Tenison.

life-size statues weighing as much as 2,000 pounds (900 kg) or more, restricts sculpture installations to the ground floor of many museums or to reinforced areas of upper floors.

Addressing the Audience

In recent decades museums have come under pressure from a variety of directions to increase attendance, and as a result there has been a growing desire to understand the interests and motivations of both visitors and nonvisitors. Much recent work in the burgeoning field of museum studies seeks to explain visitors and their needs to those who work in museums (e.g., Falk 2009; Pitman and Hirzy 2010). Many institutions have attempted in varying degrees to adapt the museum "experience" to meet the desires of visitors and thereby increase attendance. Gallery installations, once the domain of the curator and museum director, are now shaped by many voices, including not only conservators and preparators, but also exhibition designers and museum educators, especially in American and British museums. The final appearance of an installation thus reflects a process of collaboration among coworkers with vastly different backgrounds and priorities.

Elements of exhibition design contribute greatly to drawing museum visitors into galleries and helping them engage readily and comfortably with the objects on display. Effective design strives for layouts that are both intellectually meaningful and aesthetically pleasing. Placing particularly significant or interesting works, especially those featured in museum publications and websites, along sight lines leading between galleries helps guide visitors through the building, and because of their size and presence, sculptures often perform this role effectively in antiquities galleries. The bronze head of Augustus from Meroë, for example, with its startling inlaid eyes, serves as a focal point at the entrance to the British Museum's Roman Empire gallery (MacGregor 2010, 221–6; Francis, Slack, and Edwards 2011; see essay 5.6, Riggs). Many recent sculpture installations reflect an effort to display freestanding statues in the round as much as possible—a great boon to the curious and to anyone interested in hairstyles or carving techniques—even though doing so takes up more space than placing them against a wall and thus limits the number of works that can be displayed. The overall tendency has been to decrease the crowding of galleries by displaying fewer objects, but giving more attention, in the form of informative labels and appropriate lighting, to those on view. A number of recent installations of Greek and Roman sculpture make use of filtered natural light, in addition to artificial light, to improve visibility of the ancient stone surfaces. And new installations increasingly reflect greater attention to visitors' physical comfort by allowing space for seating in the gallery.

How to communicate effectively to museum visitors, in their thousands and millions, both overarching installation narratives and information about individual objects has been an intensely debated topic. This audience may include individuals with limited prior knowledge of classical antiquity, some of whom may consider all white marble statues as vaguely Greek or Roman. Indeed, just as recent research on the multivalence of Roman art has emphasized that ancient viewers did not necessarily interpret monuments in the ways their patrons intended, so too the same principle applies to museum visitors, who may enjoy and even learn from their visit without taking away from it the themes or content intended by the curators and other museum staff. Numerous recent surveys have revealed that museum visitors on average spend very little time reading labels or supplementary materials such as didactic panels, maps, and timelines (see e.g., Fritsch 2011; Falk and Dierking 2013, 116–18). Even if an individual visitor reads some labels from start to finish, he or she is unlikely to read an entire gallery's worth, and there is little way for those writing the labels to know *which* will get read. As a result, recent label-writing guidelines (such as Trench 2011) emphasize the need for label copy that is accessible, engaging, and brief—often limited to no more than 100 words and sometimes to as little as half that length. In addition to written labels, a number of museums have experimented with providing interpretive material through such interactive means as cellphone tours, computer terminals (used with great success, for example, in the study gallery at the Metropolitan Museum of Art), and QR codes (which efficiently provide multilingual label copy in the recently reinstalled sculpture galleries of the Palazzo Massimo). It remains to be seen whether these new and constantly evolving technologies will prove more effective than traditional interpretive methods.

Putting Scholarship on Display

The challenge of communicating effectively with visitors through gallery installations bedevils a number of other issues that have recently been of interest both to academics and museum professionals working with Roman sculpture. Most difficult, and also most critical, in my opinion, is how to convey the complex relationship between Roman sculptures, particularly of mythological subjects (*Idealplastik*), and their Greek antecedents (see essay 3.3, Anguissola). Museum installations long reflected a scholarly value system that described—and sometimes dismissed—such works as copies of (lost) Greek masterpieces, with galleries of "Greek" art often populated with later, Roman marble statues essentially standing in for their presumed Greek prototypes. Some museums retain this practice: the central, vaulted gallery of Greek art at the Metropolitan Museum of Art is perhaps the most prominent example. In addition to downplaying their Roman connections, labeling statues as copies of Greek works can cause confusion for visitors, who may take the word "copy" to mean "not ancient."

Yet conveying the sophistication of Roman imitations and reinterpretations of Greek sculpture, as well as the new contexts and meanings given to traditional compositions by their Roman patrons (for bibliography see essay 3.3, Anguissola), is not easily achieved in a museum gallery. Several museums have relocated such statues to be shown with other Roman objects and use labels to evoke their Greek connections. In the Altes Museum in Berlin, in addition to a selection of Roman statues displayed in the ground-floor Greek galleries, one of the Roman galleries on the upper floor invites consideration of the relationship between Roman and Greek sculptures and addresses the related issue of stylistic retrospection (Scholl and Maischberger 2010). Most effective seem to be displays that present more than one replica of the same type, though this approach is possible only in museums whose collections have the depth to permit such comparisons. A case in the Fitzwilliam Museum, for example, invites visitors to compare two Hellenistic or early imperial statuettes of Aphrodite Anadyomene (Budde and Nicholls 1964, 53–4) and to observe both their remarkable similarity and the many subtle differences between them. Other new installations, including the Palazzo Massimo and the Ny Carlsberg Glyptotek, also show multiple replicas of the same subject—two crouching Aphrodites in Rome (Gasparri and Paris 2013, 215–17) and a group of Athenas in Copenhagen (figure 1.4.3; Moltesen 2002, 76–81). These installations convey both the popularity of such compositions among the Romans as well as the variations that distinguish one version from another.

At a more general level, the abundant recent research into the processes by which Roman sculptures were created (see Part II, Production and Distribution) corresponds well with museum visitors' frequently expressed curiosity about how statues and other

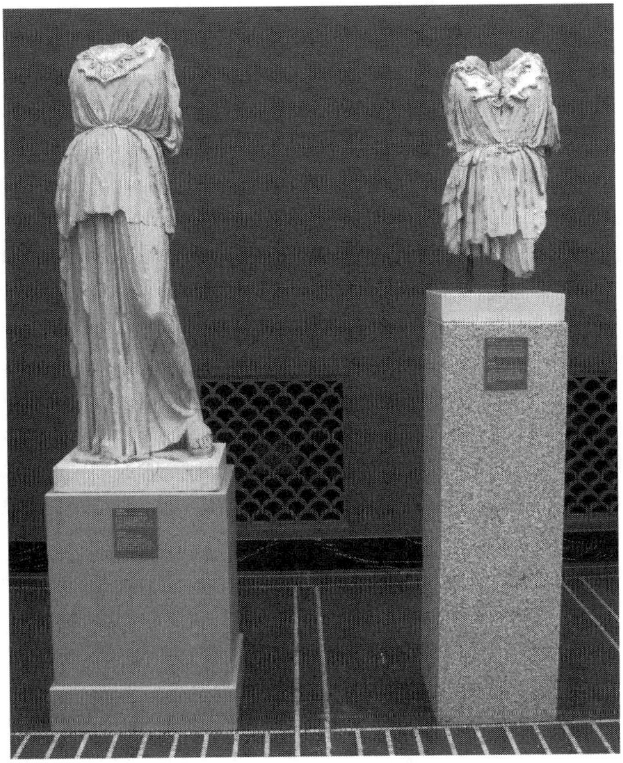

FIGURE 1.4.3 Two Roman torsos of Athena of the same type but with differing treatment of the drapery and the aegis in the Ny Carlsberg Glyptotek, Copenhagen.

objects were made in antiquity. Museums have much potential to explore these issues in their galleries, as some already do. Marble sculptures displayed in the round offer welcome opportunities to point out tool marks, joins, and other evidence for the working methods of ancient sculptors. The British Museum's gallery on life in Greece and Rome includes an informative case with examples of chisels and other stoneworking tools displayed next to marble fragments bearing different kinds of tool marks. Some museums, like the Museum of Fine Arts, Boston, also present didactic panels that discuss bronze working and the process of lost-wax casting. And a number of museums now display objects to emphasize the polychromy that once completed most ancient statues (see essay 2.6, Abbe). In the Ny Carlsberg Glyptotek, for example, colored casts placed next to some of the sculptures suggest how their polychrome surfaces could originally have appeared, while extended labels provide additional images and scientific evidence for pigments no longer visible to the naked eye.

Another technical issue of growing interest is the treatment of restorations added to ancient sculptures between the sixteenth and nineteenth centuries. Such restorations are largely a phenomenon of Roman sculptures from early excavations in Italy. The restorations themselves have become an object of study, and work on this topic has developed in tandem with the flourishing scholarship on Renaissance and later collections (see essays 1.1, Bartman; and 1.2, Podany). Because restored statues sometimes have extensive additions that substantially alter the ancient composition or include parts that did not belong to the same ancient work, some museums—most famously, the Munich Glyptothek—removed these misleading postantique interventions in the early and mid-twentieth century. Derestoration led to further problems, however: breaks were often so extensively recut to attach the restorations that the derestored cores conveyed little of the ancient work, and some were distractingly unattractive. In recent decades most museums with sculptures from old collections have become much more cautious in their approach to restorations. Several conservation projects, including those presented in a conference at the Getty Museum in 2001 (Grossman, Podany, and True 2003), exemplify this approach, with curators and conservators often leaving restorations in place or choosing to remove selectively only the most problematic elements. In many museums the restorations remain in place on statues in the galleries, but without any indication to the visitor of what parts of the statue are not ancient, while others have made this information available through publications (e.g., Schröder 2004; Fendt 2011). A few museums, including the Palazzo Altemps, the Metropolitan Museum of Art, and the San Antonio Museum of Art, have begun to add drawings to their labels indicating the presence of restorations. At the Getty Villa, color-coded labels accompanying several sculptures indicate successive phases of restoration and intervention.

The spread of Roman culture to far-flung provinces and the role of sculptures and other art forms as expressions of cultural identity have likewise received much recent scholarly attention (see Part V, Regions and Provinces). Museum installations that display objects in regional styles together with classicizing works can suggest the cultural variation that permeated the empire and the many ways in which sculptures record local responses to Roman rule and to classicizing Roman art. A number of recent installations include sections devoted to art and artifacts from Rome's provinces. And several have incorporated, for example, tomb reliefs from Palmyra or mummy portraits from Egypt alongside reliefs and sarcophagi from Italy to reflect the variety of funerary practices in different parts of the empire. The Louvre's new suite of galleries devoted to the eastern Mediterranean under the Roman Empire, which bring together material from several curatorial departments and include works from Egypt and sites throughout the Near East and Asia Minor, conveys well the rich cultural diversity of this region (Bel et al. 2012). In the newly reopened Neues Museum in Berlin, a gallery devoted to the Roman provinces leads to two that focus on material from "Rome's Northern Neighbors" and on the migration period and early medieval Europe. Collaboration between the museum's departments has resulted in an installation that reflects points of contact and continuity between Rome and Germany.

The issue of contexts and how to convey them has become particularly contested in recent years in light of intensified opposition to the collecting of undocumented antiquities and the return of antiquities by a number of American museums to Italy, Greece, and Turkey (for diverse perspectives, see Chippindale and Gill 2000; Brodie and Tubb 2002; Robson, Treadwell, and Gosden 2006; Watson and Todeschini 2006; Cuno 2008; 2009; Felch and Frammolino 2011). Understandably, few museums have chosen to address these complicated issues, which often have thorny legal ramifications, in their galleries. An increasing number of institutions have, however, made more provenance information about their collections publicly available, especially via searchable databases on their websites. Changes stemming from the restitutions and surrounding debate will have long-term effects: many American museums collecting in this field have adjusted their acquisition policies in accordance with the guidelines established by the Association of Art Museum Directors (2013). Museums that had seen their antiquities collections grow rapidly in the late twentieth century may find future growth slower and more focused on works from old collections. Instead, as a result of the returns and the memorandum of understanding between Italy and the United States signed in 2001 and renewed in 2006 and 2011 (http://eca.state.gov/files/bureau/it2011mouext.pdf), as well as special occasions like the celebration of 2013 as the Year of Italian Culture in the United States, more exhibitions and long-term loans are coming to the United States from Italian museums. Greece and the United States signed a similar memorandum of understanding in 2011 (http://eca.state.gov/files/bureau/gr2011mou.pdf), and it is to be hoped that in the future more such collaborations with countries holding extensive archaeological remains will become possible.

Many of the issues mentioned here have been explored in "special" exhibitions. Because of their temporary nature and the possibility of including works from multiple collections, exhibitions can develop more focused narratives elaborating on specific themes than is often possible in permanent collection galleries. Special exhibitions often address current topics and, through the accompanying catalogs and programs, provide a venue for presenting significant new research. *I, Claudia: Women in Ancient Rome*, for example, with its accompanying catalog (Kleiner and Matheson 1996) became a landmark in the study of women in the Roman world. The exhibitions *Bunte Götter* (Brinkmann and Wünsche 2003) and *The Color of Life* (Panzanelli 2008) presented important new research on polychromy, while *The Herculaneum Women* (Daehner 2008) and *From Caligula to Constantine* (Varner 2000) addressed respectively the replication and reuse of portraits. Other exhibitions have focused on the image, patronage, and milieu of specific individuals, including Nero (Tomei and Rea 2011), Hadrian (Adembri, Melucco Vaccaro, and Reggiani 2000; Opper 2008), and Constantine (Sena Chiesa 2012). *Ulisse: Il mito e la memoria* (Andreae and Parisi Presicce 1996) and *Aphrodite and the Gods of Love* (Kondoleon 2011) examined mythological subjects and the complex interplay between their representations in Greek and Roman art. Exhibitions such as *Versailles et l'Antique* (Maral and Milovanovic 2012) and *Hearst, the Collector* (Levkoff 2008) have addressed collectors and collecting in the centuries following the Renaissance. And exhibitions have also explored the modern reception of Roman sculpture, as in *Modern Antiquity* (Green and Daehner 2011) and a recent exhibition of Picasso's prints at the British Museum (Coppel 2012), both of which juxtaposed Roman statues with classically inspired works by celebrated twentieth-century artists.

A very positive trend in the last few years has been the number of exhibitions made up of loans from Italy and from other European museums to institutions that have less extensive antiquities collections, such as *Roman Art from the Louvre*, which toured several American museums in 2007 and 2008 (Giroire and Roger 2007). The nearly ubiquitous exhibitions on Pompeii (including D'Ambrosio, Guzzo, and Mastroroberto 2003; Mattusch 2008; Meller and Dickmann 2011; and Roberts 2013) as well as those focusing on the villas of Stabiae (Pesce 2005) have likewise brought to public view many works that would otherwise be in storage and thus inaccessible to the public. And two recent exhibitions on Roman portraiture at the Capitoline Museums brought together under a single roof some of the most famous sculptures from European museums, which could otherwise be compared only via photographs (La Rocca and Parisi Presicce 2011; 2012).

Conclusion

The end of the twentieth century and beginning of the twenty-first have been a period of rapid change for museums. The issues presented here have developed at the same time as museums have faced decreases in public funding and as their role in modern society has been debated. Recent installations of Roman art reflect new approaches by museum professionals both to displaying their collections and to engaging their visitors. Temporary exhibitions continue to provide not only opportunities to present new research, but also to explore innovative methods of exhibition design and interpretation. Museums provide a space in which visitors from all walks of life can encounter Roman sculptures in person—to marvel at the skill of ancient artisans, to enjoy the beauty of these works, and to learn about the past. Such experiences will undoubtedly continue to change—and, hopefully, will continue to become more rewarding—as museums evolve yet further in the coming decades.

Bibliography

Adembri, B., A. Melucco Vaccaro, and A. M. Reggiani. 2000. *Adriano: Architettura e progetto.* Milan: Electa.

Andreae, B., and C. Parisi Presicce. 1996. *Ulisse: il mito e la memoria.* Rome: Progetti Museali Editore.

Association of Art Museum Directors. 2013. "Guidelines on the Acquisition of Archaeological Material and Ancient Art." https://aamd.org/standards-and-practices.

Barbanera, M. 2008. "The Impossible Museum: Exhibitions of Archaeology as Reflections of Contemporary Ideologies." In *Archives, Ancestors, Practices: Archaeology in the Light of Its History*, edited by N. Schlanger and J. Nordbladh, 165–77. New York: Berghahn.

———. 2013. "I musei archeologici di Roma alla ricerca di una propria identità." In *Il museo impossibile: Storie di archeologia; Istituzioni, uomini, idee*, 43–85. Rome: Aracne.

Bartman, E. 2004. "The New Galleries of Ancient Art at the Walters Art Museum, Baltimore." *AJA* 108: 79–86.

Bartman, E., and H. Nagy. 2007. "Classical Art in Copenhagen." *AJA* 111: 787–94.

Bel, N., C. Giroire, M.-H. Rutschowscaya, and F. Gombert-Meurice. 2012. *L'Orient romain et byzantin au Louvre*. Arles: Actes Sud.

Bertoletti, M., M. Cima, and E. Talamo. 2007. *Centrale Montemartini: Musei Capitolini*. Rev. ed. Milan: Mondadori Electa.

Bilsel, C. 2012. *Antiquity on Display: Regimes of the Authentic in Berlin's Pergamon Museum.* Oxford: Oxford University Press.

Blythe, S. G., and B. Palley. 2011. "'Reading the Walls': A Study of Curatorial Expectation and Visitor Perception." In *Museum Gallery Interpretation and Material Culture*, edited by J. Fritsch, 221–33. London: Routledge.

Borbein, A. H. 2004. "Scultura antica: Retrospettiva e prospettiva su un campo dell'archeologia classica caduto in discredito." In *Storie dell'arte antica: Atti del Convegno "La storia dell'arte antica nell'ultima generazione; Tendenze e prospettive,"* edited by M. Barbanera, 33–8. Rome: Libreria dello Stato.

Borromeo, G. E., and C. C. Goulet, eds. 2001. *Rethinking the Romans: New Views of Ancient Sculpture*. Providence: Museum of Art, Rhode Island School of Design.

Brinkmann, V., and R. Wünsche, eds. 2003. *Bunte Götter: Die Farbigkeit antiken Skulptur.* Munich: Staatliche Antikensammlungen und Glyptothek.

Brodie, N., and K. W. Tubb, eds. 2002. *Illicit Antiquities: The Theft of Culture and the Extinction of Archaeology*. London: Routledge.

Budde, L., and R. Nicholls. 1964. *A Catalogue of the Greek and Roman Sculpture in the Fitzwilliam Museum, Cambridge*. Cambridge: Cambridge University Press.

Burn, L. 2012. "Introduction: Greece and Rome at the Fitzwilliam Museum." *Journal of the History of Collections* 24: 285–7.

Chippindale, C., and D. W. J. Gill. 2000. "Material Consequences of Contemporary Classical Collecting." *AJA* 104: 463–511.

Cohen, B. 2008. "Museum Reviews Editorial Statement." *AJA* 112: 531–2.

Coppel, S. 2012. *Picasso Prints: The Vollard Suite*. London: British Museum Press.

Cuno, J. 2008. *Who Owns Antiquity? Museums and the Battle over Our Ancient Heritage.* Princeton: Princeton University Press.

Cuno, J., ed. 2009. *Whose Culture? The Promise of Museums and the Debate over Antiquities.* Princeton: Princeton University Press.

D'Ambrosio, A., P. G. Guzzo, and M. Mastroroberto, eds. 2003. *Storie da un'eruzione: Pompei, Ercolano, Oplontis*. Milan: Mondadori Electa.

Daehner, J., ed. 2008. *The Herculaneum Women: History, Context, Identities*. Los Angeles: J. Paul Getty Museum.

De Angelis d'Ossat, M., and A. Capodiferro, eds. 2011. *Palazzo Altemps: Le collezioni*. Milan: Mondadori Electa.

Dyson, S. L. 1998. *Ancient Marbles to American Shores: Classical Archaeology in the United States*. Philadelphia: University of Pennsylvania Press.

Falk, J. H. 2009. *Identity and the Museum Visitor Experience*. Walnut Creek, CA: Left Coast.

Falk, J. H., and L. D. Dierking. 2013. *The Museum Experience Revisited*. Walnut Creek, CA: Left Coast.

Felch, J., and R. Frammolino. 2011. *Chasing Aphrodite: The Hunt for Looted Antiquities at the World's Richest Museum*. Boston: Houghton Mifflin Harcourt.

Fendt, A. 2011. *Archäologie und Restaurierung: Die Skulpturenergänzungen in der Berliner Antikensammlung des 19. Jahrhunderts*. 3 vols. Berlin: Walter de Gruyter.

Fentress, E. 2007. "Around the Temple: The New Galleries of the Capitoline Museum." *AJA* 111: 365–9.

Francis, D., S. Slack, and C. Edwards. 2011. "An Evaluation of Object-Centered Approaches to Interpretation at the British Museum." In *Museum Gallery Interpretation and Material Culture*, edited by J. Fritsch, 153–64. London: Routledge.

Fritsch, J., ed. 2011. *Museum Gallery Interpretation and Material Culture*. Routledge Research in Museum Studies 2. London: Routledge.

Gasparri, C., and R. Paris, eds. 2013. *Palazzo Massimo alle Terme: Le collezioni*. Milan: Mondadori Electa.

Giroire, C., and D. Roger. 2007. *Roman Art from the Louvre*. New York: Hudson Hills.

Giuliani, L. 2000. "Antiken-Museen: Vergangenheit und Perspektiven einer Institution." In *Klassische Archäologie: Eine Einführung*, edited by A. H. Borbein, P. Zanker, and T. Hölscher, 77–90. Berlin: Dietrich Reimer.

Green, C., and J. M. Daehner. 2011. *Modern Antiquity: Picasso, de Chirico, Léger, Picabia*. Los Angeles: J. Paul Getty Museum.

Grossman, J. B., J. Podany, and M. True, eds. 2003. *History of Restoration of Ancient Stone Sculptures*. Los Angeles: J. Paul Getty Museum.

James, N. 2010. "Ashmolean Museum Transformed." *Antiquity* 84: 556–7.

Kampen, N. B. 2003. "On Writing Histories of Roman Art." *ArtB* 85: 371–86.

Kleiner, D. E. E., and S. B. Matheson, eds. 1996. *I, Claudia: Women in Ancient Rome*. New Haven: Yale University Art Gallery.

Kondoleon, C., ed. 2011. *Aphrodite and the Gods of Love*. Boston: MFA Publications.

La Rocca, E., and C. Parisi Presicce, eds. 2011. *Ritratti: Le tante facce del potere*. Rome: Mondo Mostre.

———. 2012. *L'età dell'equilibrio: Traiano, Adriano, Antonino Pio, Marco Aurelio*. Loreto: Tecnostampa.

Levkoff, M. L. 2008. *Hearst, the Collector*. New York: Harry N. Abrams.

MacGregor, N. 2010. *A History of the World in 100 Objects*. New York: Viking.

Maral, A., and N. Milovanovic, eds. 2012. *Versailles et l'Antique*. Paris: Artlys.

Mattusch, C. C., ed. 2008. *Pompeii and the Roman Villa: Art and Culture around the Bay of Naples*. New York: Thames and Hudson.

Meller, H., and J.-A. Dickmann, eds. 2011. *Pompeji-Nola-Herculaneum: Katastrophen am Vesuv*. Munich: Hirmer.

Miniero, P. 2000. *Il Museo Archeologico dei Campi Flegrei nel Castello di Baia*. Naples: Electa Napoli.

Moltesen, M. 2002. *Imperial Rome II, Statues: Catalogue, Ny Carlsberg Glyptotek*. Copenhagen: Ny Carlsberg Glyptotek.

———. 2007. "The Reopened Getty Villa." *AJA* 111: 155–9.

Newhouse, V. 2005. *Art and the Power of Placement*. New York: Monacelli.

Opper, T. 2008. *Hadrian: Empire and Conflict*. Cambridge: Harvard University Press.

Panzanelli, R., ed. 2008. *The Color of Life: Polychromy in Sculpture from Antiquity to the Present*. Los Angeles: J. Paul Getty Museum.

Pesce, A., ed. 2005. *In Stabiano: Exploring the Ancient Seaside Villas of the Roman Elite*. Castellammare di Stabia: Nicola Longobardi Editore.

Picón, C. A. 2007. "A History of the Department of Greek and Roman Art." In *Art of the Classical World in the Metropolitan Museum of Art: Greece, Cyprus, Etruria, Rome*, by C. A. Picón, et al., 3–23. New York: Metropolitan Museum of Art.

Pitman, B., and E. Hirzy. 2010. *Ignite the Power of Art: Advancing Visitor Engagement in Museums*. Dallas: Dallas Museum of Art.

Powers, J. 2008. "The River City Celebrates a Classical Past." *Apollo* 167 (February): 50–55.

Powers, J., and J. Johnston, eds. 2012. *The San Antonio Museum of Art: Guide to the Collection*. San Antonio: San Antonio Museum of Art.

Roberts, P. 2013. *Life and Death in Pompeii and Herculaneum*. London: British Museum Press.

Robson, E., L. Treadwell, and C. Gosden, eds. 2006. *Who Owns Objects? The Ethics and Politics of Collecting Cultural Artefacts*. Oxford: Oxbow.

Rudolph, W. 2008. "Museum." *New Pauly, Classical*, 3: 689–97.

Scholl, A., and M. Maischberger. 2010. "Antike Welten: Griechen, Etrusker und Römer im Alten Museum; Die neue Dauerausstellung der Antikensammlung." *JPKB* 46: 203–216.

Schröder, S. F. 2004. *Katalog der antiken Skulpturen des Museo del Prado in Madrid*. Vol. 2, *Idealplastik*. Mainz: Philipp von Zabern.

Scott, S. 2006. "Art and the Archaeologist." *WorldArch* 38: 628–43.

Sena Chiesa, G., ed. 2012. *Costantino 313 d.C.: L'editto di Milano e il tempo della tolleranza*. Milan: Mondadori Electa.

Siapkas, J., and L. Sjögren. 2013. *Displaying the Ideals of Antiquity: The Petrified Gaze*. London: Routledge.

Swain, H. 2007. *An Introduction to Museum Archaeology*. Cambridge: Cambridge University Press.

Tomei, M. A., and R. Rea, eds. 2011. *Nerone*. Milan: Mondadori Electa.

Trench, L. 2011. "Gallery Text at the V&A: A Ten Point Guide." Victoria and Albert Museum. http://www.vam.ac.uk/content/articles/v/v-and-a-gallery-text-guidelines/.

Varner, E. R., ed. 2000. *From Caligula to Constantine: Tyranny and Transformation in Roman Portraiture*. Atlanta: Michael C. Carlos Museum.

Watson, P., and C. Todeschini. 2006. *The Medici Conspiracy: The Illicit Journey of Looted Antiquities, from Italy's Tomb Raiders to the World's Great Museums*. New York: Public Affairs.

Zanker, P. 2003. "I bei nuovi musei archeologici e la mancanza di visitatori." *BollMC* 17: 5–12.

CHAPTER 1.5

THREE-DIMENSIONAL SCANNING AND MODELING

BERNARD FRISCHER

Introduction: The Nature and Purpose of Three-Dimensional Digital Scanning and Modeling of Sculpture

This contribution presents the general issues of three-dimensional (3-D) data capture ("scanning"), modeling, restoration, and online publication of works of sculpture with special reference to projects involving Roman sculpture. We may best begin with the observation that the 3-D digital model (3DDM) of a statue is the twenty-first-century equivalent of the cast. The 3DDM inherited from the cast its principal art-historical and archaeological functions and added to them some new uses that are possible, or at least practical, only through the use of digital technology.

Borbein (2000) defined the primary advantage of the cast as accurate *representation* of the statue. As such, it is superior to other forms (such as a photograph or drawing) because, like the object it illustrates, the cast is three-dimensional, and its scale is 1:1. Secondary advantages include *reproducibility*—casts can easily be duplicated; *portability*—once the cast has been transported from the site of the original statue to a distant school or laboratory, it is generally placed on a base with wheels so that it can be moved easily as necessary (for example, to facilitate comparison with another statue or to be seen under different lighting conditions); and *experimentability*—hypotheses of restoration, such as adding a missing limb or painting vanished colors, can be attempted on a cast with a freedom that is generally not possible in the case of an original. The 3DDM offers the same ability to represent with submillimeter accuracy the features of a complex form such as a statue; like any digital file, it is copied or reproduced; it is easily transported—or transmitted—long distances and instantaneously as a digital file over the Internet; and it can provide an efficient and flexible medium for experimentation. Indeed, the 3DDM arguably potentially can do all these things with greater ease, speed, economy, and flexibility than can the cast. It is also safer. Whereas cast making requires the material constituting the mold to be applied to the object, 3-D data capture requires no contact and thus poses less of a risk to the original. And, as a digital asset, the 3DDM can also be integrated into larger contexts than can the cast, such as reconstructions of the original space in which the statue was erected or of now-vanished collections in which it was once housed. In brief, the 3DDM is a powerful aid to *visualization* (see, in general, Ware 2012) in art history and archaeology.

3-D data capture, which is the foundation of the 3DDM, grew out of the fields of survey and precision measurement. As the laser was developed in the 1950s and 1960s (Bertolotti 2004) and commercialized in the 1970s and 1980s, laser scanners made it possible to acquire from an object such as a building or a landscape thousands or even millions of points per second with great accuracy and high resolution. In sculptural studies, a statue was traditionally surveyed with calipers. Normally, in monographic publications of sculpture, the dimensions reported were limited to height and sometimes width, typically rounded off to the centimeter or half centimeter (5 mm), giving at best an error tolerance of approximately +/− 2 mm, the limit that human vision can detect (Bianchini 2007, 64). With the advent of 3-D scanners, it has become possible to survey rapidly not just one or two sets of points on a statue but millions or even hundreds of millions of points covering its entire surface. A modern scanner typically acquires as many as five million points per second at a resolution of 0.25 mm and with an accuracy of 0.015 mm. In comparison with traditional calipers, the modern 3-D data collector thus offers twenty times the resolution beyond the limits of human vision, over 133 times the accuracy, millions of times the detail in terms of points acquired, and an immeasurable increase in speed. The result is not just more accurate measurement of the work of art but something entirely new: a closely packed set of XYZ spatial coordinates for millions of points on the surface of the statue. These data can be seen as lists of numbers in ASCII text; but more interestingly, each set of XYZ coordinates for a single point on the statue's surface can also be rendered by a computer and displayed on a monitor as a point of light, sometimes (depending on the instrument used for data collection) containing RGB color information. If all the data acquired are so displayed, the result is a "point cloud" (or "cloud of points"), which, when viewed from a certain distance, resembles the statue scanned. When RGB information is included, the point cloud looks photorealistic. When we join the points to form polygons, a surface (or "mesh") is formed onto which we can then map digital photographs of the actual surface of the object, if we want to create a 3DDM of the current condition of the statue. Alternatively, we can map images of the original material (marble, bronze, etc.) onto the mesh. If we wish, we can digitally restore any damage to the surface or supplement any lost elements, such as noses, limbs, or paint. The result can give us a good idea of how the object looked when it was new.

Pioneering Projects

The earliest instruments manufactured that could be used for 3-D data collection of small objects such as sculpture started to be marketed in the late 1990s. For a while, the high expense of 3-D data collectors, the difficulty in using them, and the training required to process the data they generate were barriers to entry for art historians and archaeologists. Nevertheless, potential applications to the field of cultural heritage were quickly appreciated, at least by engineers and computer scientists. Thus, as early as 1992, Stanford computer scientist Marc Levoy had conceptualized the "3-D fax machine," and in 1996, he scanned a statuette of the Buddha. By 1998, he had initiated the Digital Michelangelo Project (Levoy et al. 2000), whose ambitious goal was to scan statues and buildings by Michelangelo (http://graphics.stanford.edu/projects/mich/). Among other achievements of the project has been the publication online of a highly detailed 3DDM of the David, with two billion polygons. Other early projects were initiated by computer scientists and electrical engineers (cf. Beraldin et al. 1997; Rushmeier, Taubin, and Guéziec 1997; Beraldin et al. 2000; Rocchini et al. 2001; Lingua and Rinaudo 2002; Stumpfel et al. 2003; Tsakiri, Ioannidis, and Carty 2003; Guidi, Beraldin, and Atzeni 2004). These projects all have in common that they entailed scanning and modeling the *current state* of sculpture such as Michelangelo's David, the Minerva of Arezzo, Ramses II, the Parthenon Frieze, and Donatello's Maddalena.

Inspired by this body of work, and collaborating with one of the pioneers, in 2004–5 we used the new technology in a way that might more readily occur to an archaeologist than an engineer: digital restoration and reconstruction of damaged or lost works of sculpture. The project to reconstruct the vanished original portrait statue of Epicurus entailed scanning the miniature bronze bust in the Museo Archeologico Nazionale di Napoli (inv. no. 5465), the torso in the Museo Archeologico Nazionale di Firenze (inv. no. 70990), and the author's own right arm for the missing limb. The resulting model of the head had to be scaled to fit the torso, and a series of issues had to be confronted about the orientation of the head, the gesture of the right arm, and the materials used in the original statue. The variant possible solutions for these issues were put into a table consisting of twelve cells. Each cell was illustrated by an appropriate 3DDM (see Frischer 2014). Another example of the utility of this application appeared in 2007 when Jansen and his team digitally restored the statue and niche of the Small Buddha in Bamiyan, which the Taliban had destroyed in 2001 (Jansen et al. 2008).

Terminology

As in any field, 3-D digital modeling has its own technical terminology. For 3DDMs, the semantic field is twofold: one set of vocabulary refers to the technology used to create the 3DDM, the other signifies the nature of the representation expressed by the 3DDM.

The technological process of creating a 3DDM begins with data capture. Typically a series of points with XYZ coordinates is collected, resulting in a point-cloud representation of the object. The points are then joined to form a mesh of polygons. The conversion from the point cloud to the mesh is done so that specialized software can organize, optimize, and manipulate the raw data. Thus we distinguish between 3DDMs that are point clouds and those that are mesh (or "polygonal") models. When the object of interest no longer exists or has suffered a great deal of damage, it must be recreated by a digital artist using whatever information happens to survive, for example fragments of the object, illustrations in other media, and literary descriptions. Such 3DDMs are called "hand models." A good overview of model types may be found in Vaughan (2012, 102–112).

With regard to the second dimension, we proposed in 2002 the following definition of terms regarding 3DDMs of sites, which has since proven to be helpful and is applicable as well to 3DDMs of statues: (1) original model; (2) state model; (3) restoration model; and (4) reconstruction model. The original model shows the surviving ancient material. The state model shows the object in its current condition, which may well include changes, modifications, and (in the cast of a cultural heritage artifact) modern restorations. The restoration model derives from the original model, which it brings back to an earlier state, typically (but not necessarily) its condition when new. We use the term "reconstruction model" when the surviving fragments are nonexistent or so exiguous as to require a great deal of hypothesizing to supplement all that is lacking (cf. Frischer and Stinson 2007, 51).

Reflecting on the pioneering works mentioned in the preceding section, we may say that the earliest work by the engineers and computer scientists were state models; our model of Epicurus and the Amazon Sciarra from Hadrian's Villa (figure 1.5.1, see color insert) are restoration models. As an example of a reconstruction model, our 3DDM of the statue of Marsyas in the Roman Forum (https://vimeo.com/15808133, time code 03:07–03:59) may be cited. As an example of an original model, we can cite our project on the Pan-Nymph statue group in the Staatliche Kunstsammlungen Dresden (figure 1.5.3).

Data Capture and Resolution

The methods and instruments used for 3-D data capture depend on the intended application of the 3DDM to be created. In monographic publications or documentation for conservation one will want to create a high-resolution representation of the statue. "High-resolution" here means from tens of millions to hundreds of millions or even billions of polygons in the mesh. In other words, the more polygons defining the surface features of the object being modeled, the greater the detail that results. Conservators might wish to examine tool marks, and studies show that these require resolution on the submillimeter level (see Levoy et al. 2000, 131). In more didactic applications for the Internet (e.g., in serious games), the model can be created in lower resolution (< 1 million polygons) given the limitations of game engines in supporting polygonal models. For high-resolution models, the appropriate instrument employed is a scanner (e.g., Phase Shift, Structured Light, and Coherent Frequency Modulated Continuous Wave Radar). For lower-resolution models, digital photographs are taken all around the object to be modeled. The photographs are then processed by software exploiting the principle of "structure from motion" (Szeliski 2010, 303–333).

Problems Typically Encountered in Data Collection

Regardless of the instrument used for data capture, it is important to consider how cooperative the material of the statue is to the process of 3-D data capture. Marbles that have a very crystalline surface experience subsurface scattering of light when scanned. This effect is worse when the surface is polished. When a surface is not cooperative, the resulting scattering of the laser's light results in noise, which is visually disturbing (on this issue see Levoy et al. 2000, 133; Godin et al. 2001, 2–3). In such cases, it may be preferable to scan a good plaster or resin cast, since those materials are highly cooperative to the scanning process (cf. now Pollini and Storage 2012, 32). A second issue concerns color: dark objects are less cooperative than light ones, because they absorb light. Once again, a cast may be preferable, or one can use a scanner that does not depend on the object's color. We encountered such a problem in scanning the dark bronze bust of Epicurus in the Museo Archeologico Nazionale di Napoli (inv. no. 5465). The solution was to use a scanner that worked on the principle of Coherent Frequency Modulated Continuous Wave Radar.

Validity and Utility of Using Casts Instead of Originals

The plaster and resin of casts may be materials that lend themselves to 3-D data capture more readily than bronze or many marbles, but is it methodologically sound to rely on even a well-made, first-generation cast instead of the original in collecting the 3-D data of a statue? Borbein traced the decline in prestige of the cast from the sixteenth to the twentieth centuries (Borbein 2000; also see essay 1.2, Mallampati Gleason). Many art historians and museum curators today, especially in Anglo-Saxon countries, are skeptical about the reliability of casts. In the last decades of the twentieth century, few cast collections survived intact in American universities and museums—the most glaring example of disrespect is the decision of the Metropolitan Museum of Art in New York in 2006 to dispose of its large cast collection (Vogel 2006; Mattusch 2012). This prejudice is not well grounded, at least if it rests on a claim that casts do not accurately reproduce the original. Elsewhere we show that the difference between a cast and an original is generally trivial in art-historical terms, that is within the already accepted margin of error reported above of +/– 2 mm used in typical catalogs and publications in the field (Frischer 2014).

Casts are also useful in another situation that can arise with statues, especially sculptural groups. A model will only contain those features that the data collector can reach. But some statues have occluded parts. A famous example from the repertoire of Roman art is the Laocoön, where we find a complex interplay of serpent coils, arms, and limbs. Levoy even made bold to state that it would be forever "unscannable" (Levoy 2002). In 2009–2010, we scanned the original in the Vatican as well as the cast made by Magi in 1957. The Magi cast consisted of the seven constituent parts of the original marble statue, which could be disassembled, thereby eliminating all the occlusions. The data that the scanner could not reach on the original were easily collected from the relevant parts of the cast (figure 1.5.2; www.digitalsculpture.org/laocoon/index.html).

Postprocessing

The Laocoön project raises the question of how one manipulates the raw scan data. For high-resolution models, dedicated software is used, such as the freeware Meshlab (http://meshlab.sourceforge.net/) or the proprietary solutions Geomagic (www.geomagic.com/en/), Polyworks (www.innovmetric.com/), and Rapidform (www.rapidform.com). The software is used to register the different scans (which can number in the dozens or even hundreds) that typically constitute a campaign of 3-D data collection on a statue as the scanning instrument is moved around, under, and over all parts of the object. Once all the data are entered and aligned, the software makes a point cloud, generates the mesh, and provides tools for fixing flaws, such as filling in holes where data are lacking. For low-resolution models, processing software such as 123D Catch (www.123dapp.com/catch), Recap (recap.autodesk.com), or PhotoScan (www.agisoft.ru/) is used. The digital photographs taken to document the statue are loaded in the software, which processes them and returns an initial model. The technician edits the initial model to prepare the final version.

Restoration

Thus far, the results of data capture and postprocessing should yield a state model of the statue. If a restoration model is needed, additional work must be done to edit, not the scan data and model, but the original object scanned. Of course, the process of "editing" referred to here is purely conceptual, not physical. If the statue (or a cast of one) is ancient, it may well be missing a limb or other extremity such as a nose or ear. Alternatively, it may be necessary to edit out a modern restoration that the scholar or conservator believes is mistaken and to install a digital replacement in its place. The surface of ancient sculpture is often scratched and/or dented, and such defects must be repaired. The original color will be at best faded, at worst completely lost. At this stage of the work, software such as Zbrush (www.pixologic.com/zbrush/) will be indispensable. Equally critical is consultation with various relevant experts so that, for example, modern restorations can be distinguished from ancient repairs, supplementation of parts for which evidence is missing can be based on relevant parallels, traces of surviving polychromy on the original statue can be detected, and a complete repainting of the statue that reflects ancient practice and style can be attempted.

Reconstruction

When the ancient original statue has been lost and no copies survive (even in fragmentary state), a reconstruction model must be created purely on the computer using software. As noted, we call this process "hand modeling." At most, if a 2-D image of the lost work survives, then the image can be digitized, vectorized, and used as part of the hand-modeling process. Many 3-D modeling software packages can be used for making a reconstruction model, including the open-source Blender (www.blender.org/) and the proprietary 3DS Max (http://usa.autodesk.com/3ds-max/).

Publication

Once finished, digital models can be rendered at print quality (typically TIFF format at 600 dpi) and used as illustrations for scholarly books and papers. It is easy to generate whatever views may be required such as frontal, rear, profile, three-quarters perspective, or others. Of course, 3DDMs can also remain in digital format. In this case, the model has many uses. It can be published online as a video through a web service such as YouTube. It can be inserted into a 3-D reconstruction of its original architectural context, which can be interactively explored using a game engine. It can be distributed through P3D (http://p3d.in) or Sketchfab (http://sketchfab.com), which are web services providing embed codes that support publication of an interactive version of the model on HTML pages. With a 3-D printer, it can even be used to create physical models at a variety of scales.

There are advantages and disadvantages to each form of digital publication. Videos can be produced in high definition (1080p) and made freely available through web services such as Vimeo and YouTube, but they offer only one, fixed lighting solution and point of view. The statue is typically shown slowly rotating 360° on a virtual turntable. Putting a 3DDM into a game engine has the advantage of architectural recontextualization and interactive viewing with six degrees of freedom, but it has the disadvantage that the 3DDM must typically be decimated to a small fraction of its total geometry to run in a game engine. The reduction in detail can be drastic: a full model of a statue may consist of tens or even hundreds of millions of polygons, but no object in a popular game engine such as Unity3D (http://unity3d.com/) may be larger than 65,000 polygons. The web services P3D and Sketchfab support medium-resolution models (up to several million polygons), which provides more geometric detail than do game engines. They do not at present support high-resolution models, and they have other limitations that, one may hope, will be overcome in due course. Three-dimensional prints can provide highly accurate physical expressions of the state or restoration model. Their main disadvantage is size: 1:1 reproductions of life-size sculpture are still prohibitively expensive. The common sizes of consumer-level 3-D prints (1 in. to 12 in.) may be too small to be of much practical use to art historians and archaeologists.

Paradata and the London Charter

In whatever medium or format the 3DDM is made public, it is important that it conform to the principles of the London Charter for the Computer-Based Visualization of Cultural Heritage (www.londoncharter.org/). Taking its point of departure from collaborative research led by the author (Frischer et al. 2002), the charter's goal is to propose best practices, so that "[D]igital heritage visualisation is, and is seen to be, at least as intellectually and technically rigorous as longer established cultural heritage research and communication methods." The key to achieving this aim is to promote transparency via paradata to allow others to evaluate the methods and choices made for each 3DDM visualization (Beacham, Denard, and Niccolucci 2006). The glossary of the charter defines this neologism as "information about human processes of understanding and interpretation of data objects" (www.londoncharter.org/glossary.html). Thus, when a 3DDM is published, there should always be associated with it a paradata report that lists sources of information and reveals and explains any hypothetically restored or reconstructed elements. Paradata might be compared to footnotes and bibliography in a work of print scholarship.

CASE STUDIES

For Roman art historians and archaeologists, the foregoing is mere background to what is truly of interest: actual examples of how 3-D digital technologies can help to promote discipline-specific instruction and research. Several case studies, therefore, will show how 3DDMs have been used thus far in creating state, restoration, and reconstruction models of Roman sculpture. We will also discuss which research issues are best addressed using 3DDMs, including experimental restorations of lost polychromy; re-experiencing sculpture in its ancient or postantique context; testing alignments between statues and celestial phenomena; and investigating volumetric issues such as recutting.

The Amazon Sciarra: The 3DDM as a New Kind of Cast

The Digital Hadrian's Villa Project (DHVP) of the Virtual World Heritage Laboratory (VWHL) has the aim of creating a 3-D digital model of the terrain, buildings, furnishings, fountains, gardens, and grounds of Hadrian's Villa, the World Heritage Site in Tivoli, Italy. Over 140 statues survive that have a known provenience from the villa (Raeder 1983, 29–122). The overwhelming majority of statues were either found out of context (e.g., in the Pantanello) or else their find spot was not precisely recorded. The DHVP therefore decided to concentrate on including in its model those statues that could be placed with some confidence inside the virtual villa.

A case in point is the Amazon of the Sciarra type that was found at the rounded, north end of the Canopus basin (Antiquarium, Hadrian's Villa, inv. no. 2266). This statue type has recently been the subject of studies to recover traces of color still detectable on three ancient versions in Copenhagen (Ny Carlsberg Glyptotek, inv. no. 1568), Berlin (Pergamon Museum, inv. no. Sk. 7), and Ecija (inv. nos. 8041–8197; see Østergaard 2010; Sargent and Therkildsen 2010). These studies showed some consistencies of polychromy among the three copies but also some variation. On some important general features the copies agreed: for example, the hair atop the head was painted yellow or reddish yellow. The skin on the face and body was painted in a realistic way and not left unpainted. Red and blue were the predominant colors of the clothing, though there were some differences in detail in how the colors were applied. The footwear (including the missing soles) was painted to suggest sandals, even though in the bronze original the Amazon probably wore riding boots (Østergaard 2010, 57). These results suggest that a copy such as that from Hadrian's Villa, on which no investigation of polychromy has yet been undertaken, can be restored in an experimental way to reflect the consensus of coloration that has emerged from studies of other versions. Where one copy has color preserved and the others not (e.g., for the wound on the Amazon's side, where red is preserved on the Copenhagen copy but not on the others; Østergaard 2010, 57), we have not taken absence of evidence as evidence of absence. Instead, we assume that a great deal of evidence is presently irrecoverable, given the condition of the statues and the limits of the techniques used by conservators to detect ancient pigment. Hence, where a trace of color survives on a detail from one or another copy, we have used that color in our digital restoration of the example from the Canopus (figure 1.5.1). This use of 3DDMs as a support for experiments of the restoration of polychromy reflects an earlier tradition of using casts and can be paralleled in the field of Roman archaeology by Zink and Piening's 3DDM of the colorized Temple of Palatine Apollo (2009), Borghini and Carlani's colorized 3DDM of the reliefs decorating the Ara Pacis (Liverani 2010; Rossini 2010), and the VWHL's own projects on the Augustus of Prima Porta (www.digitalsculpture.org/augustus/index.html) and the portrait of Caligula in the Virginia Museum of Fine Arts (www.digitalsculpture.org/caligula/index.html).

Laocoön: 3DDMs Illustrating a Statue's Current State and Past Use

In 2008, we scanned the Laocoön statue group in the Vatican Museums (inv. no. 10059, statue group; 1064, "Pollak" right arm of the father). In order to fill in any gaps caused by occlusions, we also digitized the seven pieces of the cast made by Magi in 1957 (inv. no. 57780). The resulting state model (figure 1.5.2) was posted along with related scholarly materials on the VWHL's Digital Sculpture website (www.digitalsculpture.org/laocoon/index.html).

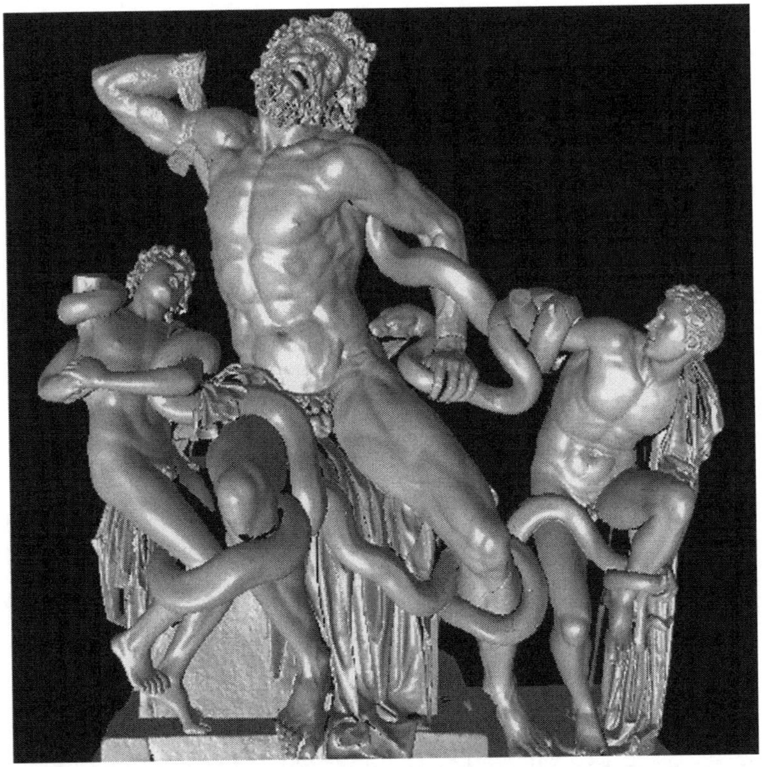

FIGURE 1.5.2 View of the 3DDM of the Laocoön. Data collected from the original and Magi cast in the Vatican Museums by B. Breuckmann, L. Wurmser, D. Koller, and C. Keller. 3-D model by B. Breuckmann. Sponsored by the Samuel H. Kress Foundation.

There are many potential uses of a digital model such as Laocoön. It can serve as a platform for experiments in the restoration of polychromy (Queyral 2003); now that we know its provenience (Volpe and Parisi 2009), we can recontextualize it in the Horti Maecenatis; we can use it to recreate lost modes of viewing. As an example of the latter, we used the 3DDM to simulate the experience of Grand Tourists in seeing the statue by torchlight at night (Mattos 2006).

Beyond Illustration: The 3DDM as a Heuristic Tool for Recovering Lost Meaning

The preceding examples may be considered uses of the 3DDM for purposes of illustration. They incorporate information we had prior to making the model but do not add to our stock of knowledge. But as I have pointed out elsewhere (Frischer 2008), visualizations can also support experimental research that takes its point of departure from knowledge and hypotheses existing prior to creation of the 3DDM and then uses the 3DDM to ask the question: "if this is true, then what follows?"

A case in point is our project to restore the fragments of the Pan-Nymph statue group in the Staatliche Kunstsammlungen Dresden (www.digitalsculpture.org/pan-nymph/index.html). In approximately 1890, Georg Treu disassembled the statue after recognizing that it was a Baroque pastiche combining elements of at least three unrelated ancient statues. Before we began the project, the twenty-three ancient and baroque fragments of the work survived on a pallet in storage. There was also a photograph with a frontal view of the statue group dating to c. 1890, taken just before the statue group was disassembled. While the photograph was a great aid in determining how the digitized fragments could be reintegrated, the fact that it was two-dimensional meant that a critical portion was not visible: the relationship of the left hand of the Pan figure to the right side of the Nymph's head. Once we had recovered the third dimension and restored this part of the statue, we learned that in fact Pan is shown doing something we did not have reason to suspect from the photograph: he is pulling on the ponytail of the Nymph (figure 1.5.3). This gesture explains the Nymph's expression: her face is shown with the startle reflex (Ekman and Friesen 1985).

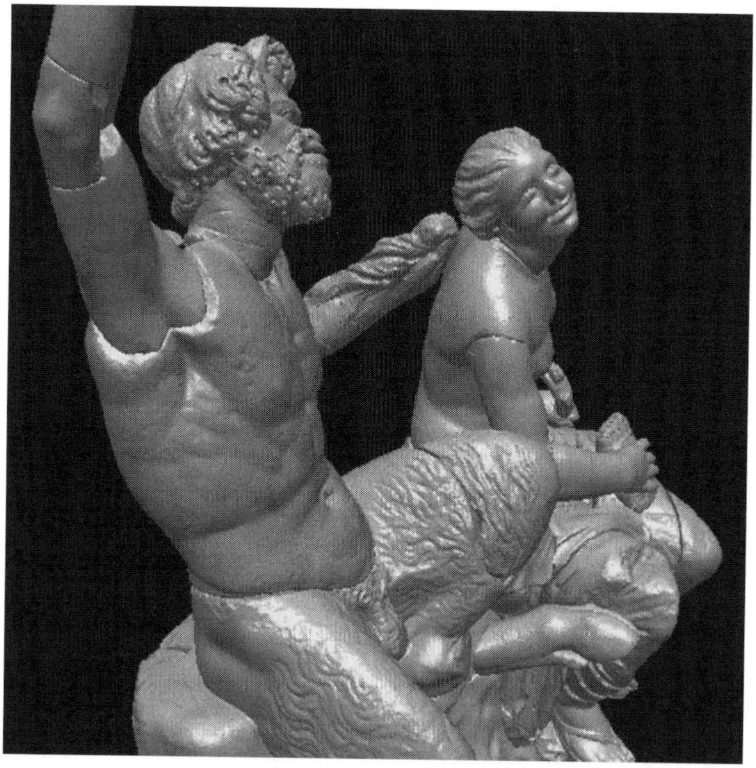

FIGURE 1.5.3 Detail of 3DDM of Pan-Nymph in the Dresden State Museums. Data collection by C. Keller, D. Koller, and B. Frischer. 3-D modeling by J. Page, Direct Dimensions. Sponsored by the Samuel H. Kress Foundation.

Beyond Illustration: The 3DDM as a Heuristic Tool for Recovering Lost Celestial Alignments

The Pan-Nymph project was a relatively straightforward example of heuristic use of a 3DDM. Another exploratory use of 3DDMs promises subtle and interesting contributions to our understanding of Hadrian's Villa at Tivoli and the role of its various sculptural installations. The VWHL has created a virtual world of Hadrian's Villa and has incorporated a solar tracker, allowing us to set the date and time of day for the year AD 130. While details are presented elsewhere (Frischer and Fillwalk 2013), here it suffices to note that we have already confirmed the thesis presented by Mangurian and Ray (2008) that at sunset on the summer solstice there was an alignment between the sun and the statue niche of the lower rotunda in the feature given the modern name Roccabruna (figure 1.5.4, see color insert). We restored the space as suggested by De Franceschini and Veneziano in their book on solstitial alignments in this part of the villa (2011), placing into the niche a 3DDM of one of the statues of Isis (Capitoline Museums, inv. no. MC 744) found in an unknown context at the villa. Thus, the building's architecture and its sculptural installations were designed to honor Isis, whose main festival took place on the summer solstice. This confirmation was not possible by autopsy, because the wobbling of the earth on its axis has changed the position of the sun in the sky on the summer solstice today.

Beyond Illustration: The 3DDM as a Heuristic Tool for Detection of Recutting

Another heuristic use of a 3DDM is the study by Pollini and Storage (2012) of a head of Augustus in the J. Paul Getty Museum (inv. no. 78.AA.261). Earlier scholarship had led to the conclusion that the head was originally a Caligula, recut after the emperor's assassination as an Augustus of Type V (Prima Porta: Pollini and Storage 2012, 34, 36). On the basis of a comparison of the 3DDM of the Getty head of Augustus and the 3DDM of another head in the Getty showing Caligula (inv. no. AA.155), Pollini and Storage demonstrated that when the Augustus head is aligned with that of Caligula, the face of Augustus protrudes c. 6 mm beyond Caligula's. But if the Augustus head had been recut from an original Caligula head, the opposite would be the case. On the basis of a comparison of the 3DDM of Augustus with the two-dimensional image of an Augustus in Stuttgart (inv. no. 65/12), it was concluded that the Getty Augustus was slightly reworked, not from a head of Caligula, but from that of an Augustus of a different type: a subtype of Type IV. This analysis uses the 3DDM as a resource for the kind of study of craniofacial landmarks that is used in the anthropometrical analysis of the human head for reconstructive and plastic surgery (Pollini and Storage 2012, 31n4). As Pollini and Storage (2010, 40) point out, many art-historical controversies regarding portraits that have been recut (or are suspected of having been recut) could be objectively resolved if this approach were applied.

Conclusion

3DDMs of ancient sculpture are still a relatively new form of scholarly expression and communication. Given their wide range of application and the ease with which they can be created, we can safely predict that in the near future there will be large, free, online libraries of 3DDMs of ancient sculpture available for use by students and scholars alike. In effect, the Internet will make it possible for anyone interested in ancient sculpture to have her own digital cast collection comparable in size and quality to the great physical cast collections, such as those in Rome, Basel, and Berlin. Let us hope that as more and more 3DDMs are made, they are collected, vetted, and made available through a reliable web-based archive (cf. Pollini and Storage 2012, 37, who call for the creation of "a database of three-dimensional models that would allow us to make comparisons" between different busts and statues). Terminological clarity must also be maintained, so that both the creator and user understand the nature and intent of the model. The best-practice guidelines of the London Charter should be observed so that the potential of 3DDMs to be as "reliable and robust" a form of scholarly expression is realized. Finally, the potential of 3DDMs for heuristics should be kept in mind. The true value of 3DDMs is probably less as illustrations than as tools for making experiments and recreating experiences that would otherwise be physically or practically impossible.

Bibliography

Beacham, R., H. Denard, and F. Niccolucci. 2006. "The London Charter: Introduction." London Charter for the Computer-Based Visualisation of Cultural Heritage. http://www.londoncharter.org/old-introduction.html.

Beraldin, J.-A., L. Cournoyer, M. Rioux, F. Blais, S. F. El-Hakim, and G. Godin. 1997. "Object Model Creation from Multiple Range Images: Acquisition, Calibration, Model Building, and Verification." In *International Conference on Recent Advances in 3-D Digital Imaging and Modeling: Proceedings, May* 12–15, 1997, *Ottawa, Ontario, Canada*, 326–33. Los Alamitos, CA: IEEE Computer Society Press.

Beraldin, J.-A., F. Blais, P. Boulanger, L. Cournoyer, J. Domey, S. F. El-Hakim, G. Godin, M. Rioux, and J. Taylor. 2000. "Real World Modeling through High Resolution Digital 3D Imaging of Objects and Statues." *ISPRS Journal of Photogrammetry and Remote Sensing* 55(4): 230–50.

Bertolotti, M. 2004. *The History of the Laser*. London: IOP.

Bianchini, M. 2007. *Manuale di rilievo e di documentazione digitale in archeologia*. Rome: ARACNE.

Borbein, A. H. 2000. "Zur Geschichte der Wertschätzung und Verwendung von Gisabgüssen antiker Skulpturen (insbesondere in Deutschland und in Berlin)." In *Les moulages de sculptures antiques et l'histoire de l'archéologie: Actes du colloque international Paris, 24 octobre* 1997, edited by H. Lavagne and F. Queyrel, 29–43. Geneva: Droz.

De Franceschini, M., and G. Veneziano. 2011. *Villa Adriana architettura celeste: I segreti dei solstizi.* Vol. 1, *Accademia Villa Adriana*. Rome: Giorgio Bretschneider.

Ekman, P., and W. V. Friesen. 1985. "Is the Startle Reaction an Emotion?" *Journal of Personality and Social Psychology* 49: 1416–26.

Frischer, B. 2008. "From Digital Illustration to Digital Heuristics." In *Beyond Illustration: 2D and 3D Digital Technologies as Tools for Discovery in Archaeology*, edited by B. Frischer and A. Dakouri-Hild, v–xxiv. BAR-IS 1805. Oxford: Archaeopress. www.frischerconsulting.com/frischer/pdf/Frischer_Heuristics.pdf.

———. 2014. "3D Data Capture, Restoration and Online Publication of Sculpture." In *3D Modeling in Archaeology and Cultural Heritage: Theory and Best Practices*, edited by F. Remondino and S. Campana, 137–44. BAR-IS 2598. Oxford: Archaeopress.

Frischer, B., and J. Fillwalk. 2013. "The Digital Hadrian's Villa Project: Using Virtual Worlds to Control Suspected Solar Alignments." In *Proceedings of 2012: 18th International Conference on Virtual Systems and Multimedia (VSMM 2012)*, edited by G. Guidi, 49–56. Piscataway, NJ: IEEE.

Frischer, B., F. Niccolucci, N. S. Ryan, and J. A. Barceló. 2002. "From CVR to CVRO: The Past, Present and Future of Cultural Virtual Reality." In *Virtual Archaeology: Proceedings of VAST 2000*, edited by F. Niccolucci, 7–18. BAR-IS 1075. Oxford: Archaeopress.

Frischer, B., and P. Stinson. 2007. "The Importance of Scientific Authentication and a Formal Visual Language in Virtual Models of Archeological Sites: The Case of the House of Augustus and the Villa of the Mysteries." In *Interpreting the Past: Heritage, New Technologies, and Local Development; Proceedings of the Conference on Authenticity, Intellectual Integrity and Sustainable Development of the Public Presentation of Archaeological and Historical Sites and Landscapes. Ghent, East-Flanders,* 11–13 *September 2002*, edited by N. A. Silberman and D. Callebaut, 49–83. Brussels: Flemish Heritage Institute. www.frischerconsulting.com/frischer/pdf/Frischer_Stinson.pdf.

Godin, G., M. Rioux, J.-A. Beraldin, M. Levoy, L. Cournoyer, and F. Blais. 2001. "An Assessment of Laser Range Measurement on Marble Surfaces." Paper presented at the 5th Conference on Optical 3D Measurement Techniques, Vienna, Austria, October 1–4, 2001. http://graphics.stanford.edu/papers/marble-assessment/marbre_gg_final2e_coul.pdf.

Guidi, G., J.-A. Beraldin, and C. Atzeni. 2004. "High-Accuracy 3-D Modeling of Cultural Heritage: The Digitizing of Donatello's 'Maddalena.'" *IEEE Trans Image Process* 13(3): 370–80.

Jansen, M., G. Toubekis, A. Walther, M. Döring-Williams, and I. Mayer. 2008. "Laser Scan Measurement of the Niche and Virtual 3D Representation of the Small Buddha in Bamiyan." In *Layers of Perception: Proceedings of the 35th International Conference on Computer Applications and Quantitative Methods in Archaeology (CAA), Berlin, Germany, April 2–6, 2007*, edited by A. Posluschny, K. Lambers, and I. Herzog, 83–90. Bonn: Dr. Rudolf Habelt.

Levoy, M. 2002. "Why is 3D Scanning Hard?" Invited address at 3D Processing, Visualization, Transmission, Padua, Italy, June 19, 2002. http://graphics.stanford.edu/talks/3Dscanning-3dpvt02/3Dscanning-3dpvt02_files/v3_document.htm.

Levoy, M., K. Pulli, B. Curless, S. Rusinkiewicz, D. Koller, L. Pereira, M. Ginzton, et al. 2000. "The Digital Michelangelo Project: 3D Scanning of Large Statues." In *SIGGRAPH '00: Proceedings of the 27th annual conference on Computer graphics and interactive techniques*, 131 44. New York: ACM Press. doi: 10.1145/344779.344849.

Lingua, A., and F. Rinaudo. 2002. "The Statue of Ramsete II—Integration of Digital Photogrammetry and Laser Scanning Technique for 3D Modeling." In *The CIPA*

International Archives for Documentation of Cultural Heritage. Vol. 18, 18–21 *Sept. 2001, Potsdam, Germany*, edited by J. Albertz, 206–211. Berlin: CIPA.

Liverani, P. 2010. "New Evidence on the Polychromy of Roman Sculpture." In *Circumlitio: The Polychromy of Antique and Mediaeval Sculpture*, edited by V. Brinkmann, O. Primavesi, and M. Hollein, 290–302. Munich: Hirmer.

Mangurian, R., and M. A. Ray. 2008. "Re-drawing Hadrian's Villa." *Perspecta: The Yale Architectural Journal* 41: 113–16.

Mattos, C. 2006. "The Torchlight Visit: Guiding the Eye through Late Eighteenth and Early Nineteenth Century Antique Sculpture Galleries." *RES: Anthropology and Aesthetics* 49–50: 139–50.

Mattusch, C. 2012. "Plaster Casts: Past, Present and Future." *JRA* 25: 985–8.

Østergaard, J. 2010. "The Sciarra Amazon Investigation: Some Archaeological Comments." *Tracking Colour: The Polychromy of Greek and Roman Sculpture in the Ny Carlsberg Glyptotek, Preliminary Report* 2: 50–60.

Pollini, J., and W. Storage. 2010. "Recutting Roman Portraits: Problems in Interpretation and the New Technology in Finding Possible Solutions." *MAAR* 55: 23–44.

———. 2012. "Computer Technology and Three-Dimensional Models in Determining the Recutting of Roman Portraits: The Getty Augustus." In *Interdisciplinary Studies on Ancient Stone. ASMOSIA 9*. Documenta 23, edited by A. Gutiérrez, P. Lapuente, and I. Rodà, 31–7. Tarragona: Institut Català d'Arqueologia Clàssica.

Queyrel, F. 2003. "Les couleurs du Laocoon." In "Le Laocoon: Histoire et réception," edited by E. Décultot, J. Le Rider, and F. Queyrel, special issue *Revue Germanique Internationale* 19: 57–70.

Raeder, J. 1983. *Die statuarische Ausstattung der Villa Hadriana bei Tivoli*. Frankfurt: Peter Lang.

Rocchini, C., P. Cignoni, C. Montani, P. Pingi, R. Scopigno, R. Fontana, M. Greco et al. 2001. "3D Scanning the Minerva of Arezzo." In *ICHIM 2001 Conference*, Vol. 2: 265–72.

Rossini, O. 2010. "I colori dell'Ara Pacis: Storia di un esperimento." *Archeomatica* 3: 20–25.

Rushmeier, H., G. Taubin, and A. Guéziec. 1997. "Applying Shape from Lighting Variation to Bump Map Capture." In *Rendering Techniques '97: Proceedings of the 8th Eurographics Rendering Workshop*, edited by J. Dorsey and P. Slusallek, 35–44. New York: Springer.

Sargent, M. L., and R. H. Therkildsen. 2010. "Research on Ancient Sculpture Polychromy with Focus on a 2nd Century CE Marble Amazon." In *Tracking Colour: The Polychromy of Greek and Roman Sculpture in the Ny Carlsberg Glyptotek, Preliminary Report*, edited by J. S. Østergaard, Vol. 2: 27–49. Copenhagen: Ny Carlsberg Glyptotek.

Stumpfel, J., C. Tchou, N. Yun, P. Martinez, T. Hawkins, A. Jones, B. Emerson, and P. Debevec. 2003. "Digital Reunification of the Parthenon and its Sculptures." In *VAST '03: Proceedings of the 4th International Symposium on Virtual Reality, Archaeology and Intelligent Cultural Heritage*, edited by D. Arnold, A. Chalmers, and F. Niccolucci, 41–50. Aire-la-Ville, Switzerland: Eurographics Association.

Szeliski, R. 2010. *Computer Vision: Algorithms and Applications*. London: Springer.

Tsakiri, M., C. Ioannidis, and A. Carty. 2003. "Laser Scanning Issues for the Geometric Recording of a Complex Statue." In *Proceedings of the 6th Conference on Optical 3-D Measurement Techniques, 22–25 September 2003, Zurich, Switzerland*, edited by A. Gruen and H. Kahmen, 214–22. Zurich: ETH Zurich.

Vaughan, W. 2012. *Digital Modeling*. Berkeley: New Riders.

Vogel, C. 2006. "Going to Auction: Pieces of History." *New York Times*, January 13.

Volpe, R., and A. Parisi. 2009 "'. . . In una vignia de uno gentile homo romano. . .' Il luogo di ritrovamento del Laocoonte." *BullCom* 110: 81–110.
Ware, C. 2012. *Information Visualization*. 3rd ed. Waltham, MA: Morgan Kaufmann.
Zink, S., and H. Piening. 2009. "*Haec aurea templa:* The Palatine Temple of Apollo and Its Polychromy." *JRA* 22: 109–121.

PART II

PRODUCTION AND DISTRIBUTION

CHAPTER 2.1

MARBLE QUARRIES

Ancient Imperial Administration and Modern Scientific Analyses

PATRIZIO PENSABENE AND
ELEONORA GASPARINI
TRANSLATED BY
MASSIMO CARLUCCI

Introduction

During the past fifty years, identifying ancient quarries and determining marble sources have become central to research related to multiple aspects of the Graeco-Roman world (Pensabene 2013). Understanding the history of quarry use and identifying the origins of marbles used in specific monuments provide indispensable ways to understand the historical and economic dynamics behind the prestige bestowed by the use of marbles and colored stones. Both the quantity and the quality of the marbles employed in architecture and in sculpture allowed local elites the opportunity to stand out on account of their riches and to represent their own power. Particularly famous are the stones quarried in the earliest times: granites, porphyries, and alabasters from Egypt; and from Greece, Pentelic marble from Athens as well as other marbles from the islands. As colored stones and marbles vary greatly in their hues, tones, patterns, inclusions, weathering, and characteristic breakage, visual inspection is usually sufficient for their identification; in contrast, for white marbles, visual observation alone is often misleading, because similar nuances of color and crystal-size can be found in different geographic regions. For example, the white marbles with a coarse grain from Proconnesos in Turkey and those from the quarries of Almadén de la Plata and of Mija in Baetica (Spain) cannot be distinguished by sight; the same applies to white marbles with small grain size of sculpture quality from Mount Pentelikon in Greece and Carrara in Italy. Archaeometric analyses are therefore indispensable.

But if, on the one hand, the archaeometric analyses offer a degree of certainty, on the other hand, we must not give up our own capacity to judge within historical and archaeological contexts, as this can often offer an important corrective to conclusions provided by the multiple results of scientific analyses. The importance of routinely determining the provenance of the marbles used both in architecture and in sculpture lies in the fact that the most prestigious stones were not only used in the regions where they were quarried, and sometimes settlements with plentiful supplies of local marble used imported stone as well (see essay 5.5, Ng). Stones were also frequently carried by sea on ships specially built for that purpose throughout the whole Mediterranean, the Black Sea, and also (to a lesser extent) along the Atlantic coastline from Gibraltar to Britain. Sometimes mainland cities far from the sea would import the most famous marbles for the prestige attached to them, even when good local stone was also available, spending huge amounts of money for overland transport, which costs much more than transport by river or sea (see essay 2.7, Russell). For these reasons, the first aim of research on marbles is to determine their provenance, which also assists in identifying stone-carving workshops, the patrons' intent, and more generally, the hierarchy of values attached to the use of different stones. This phenomenon accounts for the widespread occurrence more or less all over the Roman Empire of columns in *cipollino* marble from Euboea (Greece); in granite from Troade (Turkey); in *breccia corallina* from Bithynia (Turkey); and in Aswan granite: for example, the Aswan granite *tetrapyla* in Gerasa (in Jordan) and in Palmyra (in Syria) and the *propylaea* both in Aswan and Troad granites of the huge temple at Baalbek (in Lebanon).

After identifying the main marble districts of the Mediterranean, this essay will review the evidence for the history of use of white marble (and to a certain extent colored marbles) during the Roman period, including its early application in the late Republic, Caesar's recognition of the Luni quarries, Augustus's transformation of the city of Rome from brick to marble, and the imperial acquisition and control of marble quarries around the Mediterranean during the Augustan and subsequent periods. Though this handbook's main focus is sculpture, throughout our essay architectural uses will also be discussed, first because in many cases the same quarries supplied both architectural and sculptural marbles, but also because the urban aediculated facades of the Romans necessitated sculptural decor as well (see essay 4.1, Longfellow). The essay also highlights the distinction between marble production destined for civic use and that for private consumption. Finally, current developments in scientific analyses are reviewed.

Main Marble Districts of the Mediterranean

The quarries producing marbles for building and decorating were spread around the entire Mediterranean, and most towns had nearby quarries available, geology permitting (figure 2.1.1). Such quarries usually belonged to the nearest cities or to private people,

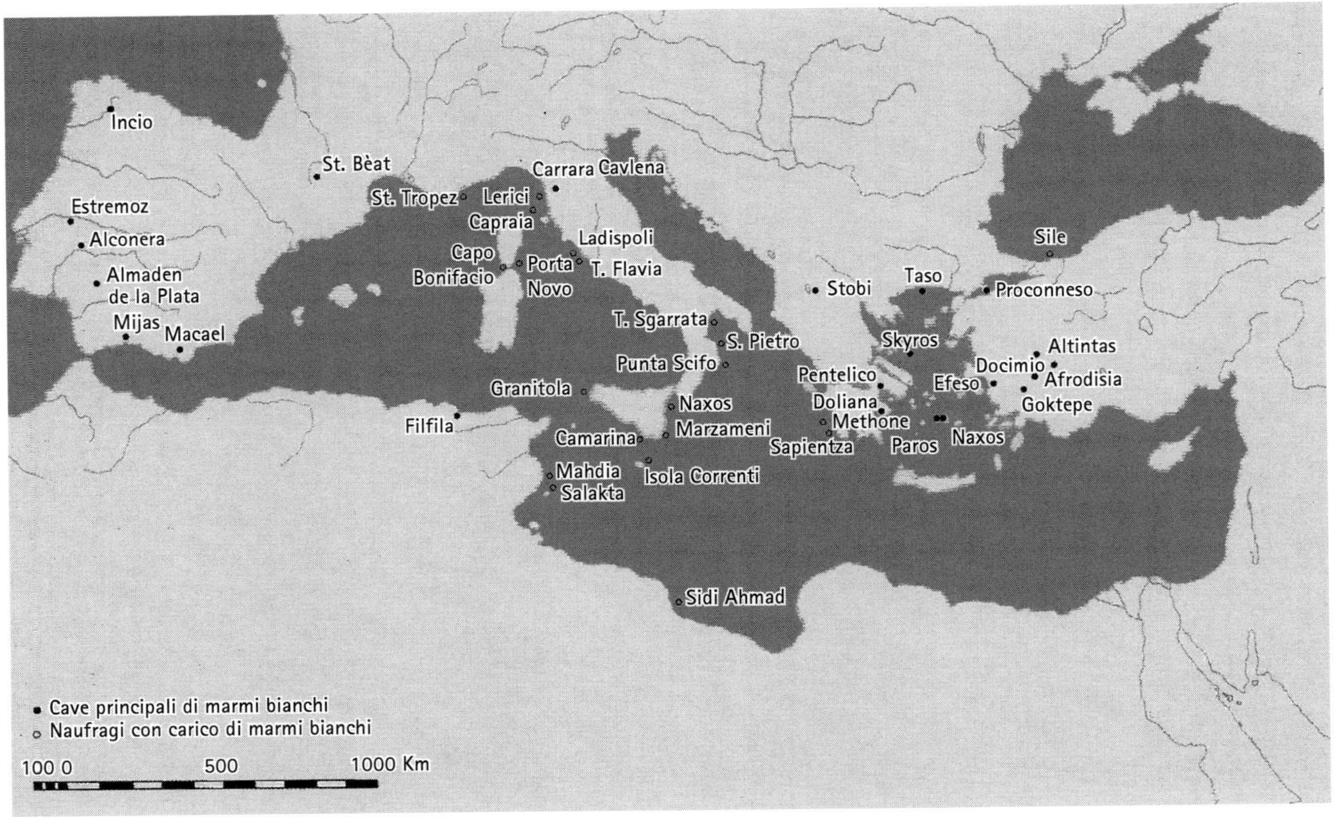

FIGURE 2.1.1 Map of the principal quarries of white marbles in the Roman Empire.

and their exploitation was granted to specialized companies on the basis of rent or contracts. Some marbles, like *pavonazzetto, africano, portasanta, cipollino, giallo antico*, and granite from Aswan and the Troad were exported all around the Mediterranean. What differentiated these marbles from the ones used only locally or in one province is the much higher transport cost compared to that of the local quarries and their visual contrast to the familiar local stone(s).

Within the Roman Empire, the imperial administration came to control three main quarrying zones of the most prestigious white marbles and colored stones. The first zone corresponds to mainland Greece and the Greek islands (see essay 5.4, Sturgeon) with their very ancient quarries of white marble: Mount Pentelikon, Paros, Naxos, and Thasos (figure 2.1.2); the quarries of colored marbles rarely used in pre-Roman times, but much exploited in the imperial age (Lazzarini 2007), such as those of *cipollino* and *fior di pesco* from Euboea; *rosso antico, nero antico*, and *serpentine* from the Peloponnesus; the Skyros *breccia* from the island of the same name in the Sporades; and eventually the *verde antico* from Thessaly. Only this very last quarry was opened in the imperial age (around the second century AD), while the others began to be intensively exploited at the end of the republican era.

The second zone is represented by the western section of Turkey and her surrounding islands (see essay 5.5, Ng) where the huge quarries of *portasanta* on the island of Chios, *africano* near Teos, *breccia corallina* in Bithynia, red *cipollino* or Iasos marble in Caria, granite in the Troad, and alabaster in Phrygia predated the Roman conquest.

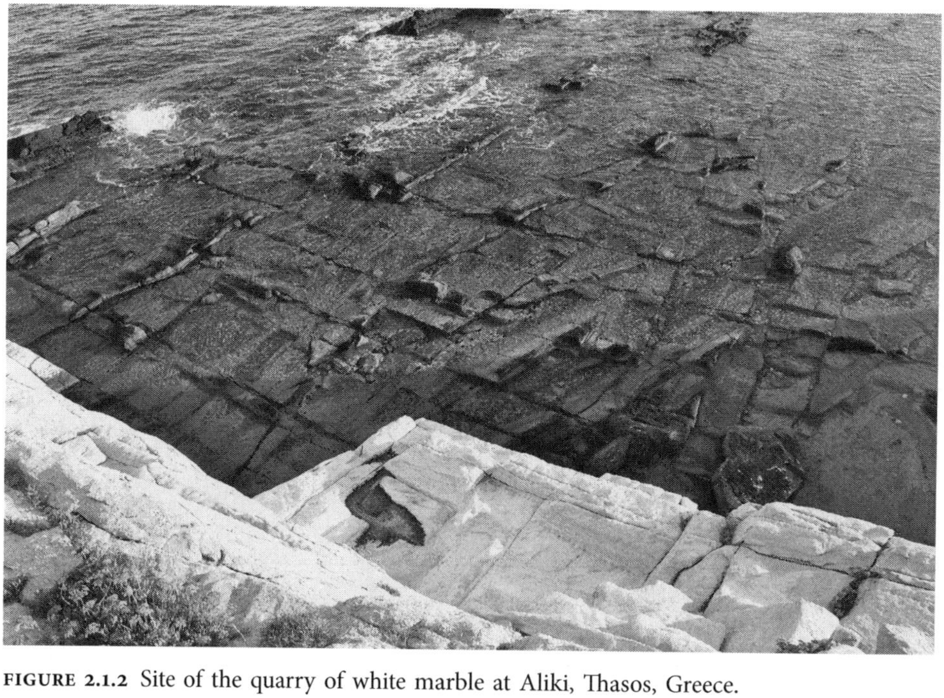

FIGURE 2.1.2 Site of the quarry of white marble at Aliki, Thasos, Greece.

The quarries of the small island of Proconnesos in the Sea of Marmara are to be noted, where white marble, much used for architecture, sarcophagi, and statuary of minor quality, was extracted. Also notable are the Dokimeion quarries in Phrygia from which was extracted *pavonazzetto*, one of the most valuable stones of antiquity, as well as a good-quality white marble used for sarcophagi and statuary.

The third zone, in the eastern desert of Egypt, had been first exploited in pharaonic times (see essays 3.7, Swetnam-Burland; and 5.6, Riggs). From there came porphyry, Marmor Claudianum (Forum granite), basanites, other types of porphyries and granites, among them the pink granite excavated in the Aswan quarries near the Nile and, along its course, quarries of alabaster.

Other large quarries stood out especially on account of the widespread distribution of their products that can best be described as interprovincial (used both locally and in nearby provinces, compared to that of other regional quarries whose stone was only used locally), but not empire-wide. Examples of interprovincial quarries include those of *giallo antico* near Simitthus in Numidia (Africa), white marble at Luni near Carrara (Italy), and *broccattello* in the Tarraconensis (Hispania; see essay 5.2, Jiménez and Rodà).

Augustus and the State's Acquisition of the Quarries

At the moment when the Romans conquered the eastern Mediterranean in the late Republic, they began to import and employ colored marble columns and slabs from the East and marble statues from Attica and other artistic Mediterranean centers, like Pergamon and Rhodes, in imitation of Hellenistic rulers and elites. This phenomenon should be connected, on the one hand, to the fact that at that time the quarries of Italian marble were not exploited and, on the other hand, to the political situation of Rome, which had just consolidated her power in the Mediterranean. Thus marble acquired ideological meanings in Rome, as a way to transmit the image of power and to celebrate the importance of the families from which the political rulers of the Senate came (Pensabene 2002, 4). At this time the sea transport of marbles accelerated.

It was Caesar who first thought of exploiting the white marble from Luni (Carrara) for his building projects in Rome (Dolci 1989, 11–54), as importing sufficient stone from the Pentelic quarries would be prohibitively expensive. Augustus inherited the project and carried it out on an even a larger scale. He transformed almost all the ancient buildings of the Forum Romanum and the Palatine and included marble in his new constructions as well. We can recall what Suetonius wrote: "Augustus found Rome a city built in brick and left it one of marble" (*Aug.* 28; figure 2.1.3). Echoing Rome, in the new provinces, an extensive urbanization of cities began to take place

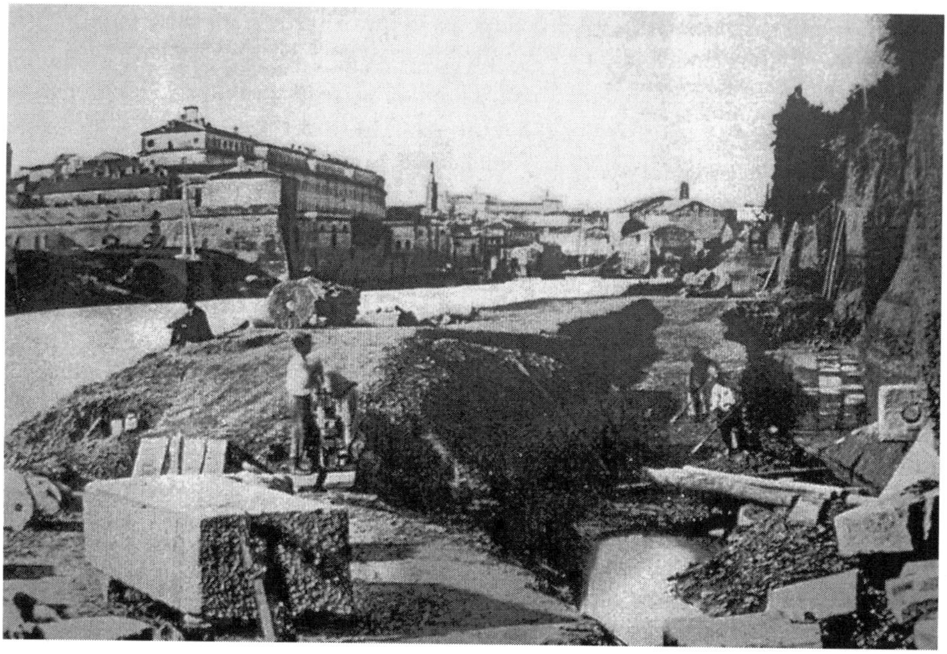

FIGURE 2.1.3 Excavations of the harbor along the Tiber in the nineteenth century, Rome.

during the Augustan period. As a result of this policy, the construction of monumental architecture such as theaters, temples, and baths with their statuary decoration was encouraged, thus making obligatory the use of marbles to imitate the grandeur of Rome.

The scale of Augustus's building projects resulted in an administrative practice aimed at the state's direct control of those quarries supplying the marbles for public architecture in Rome, for the statues decorating her monuments, and for the imperial residences (figure 2.1.4, see color insert). This situation led to a policy of acquisition by conquest (in the case of Egypt), confiscation, purchase, or inheritance of the quarries, until the three zones discussed in the previous section were firmly under the control of the imperial administration. Between the Augustan and the Claudian age the most important quarries of the Mediterranean came under imperial power. We have a lot of information about the system of administration of the quarries, because blocks that were meant for Rome were inscribed with the year of production by consular dates, the number of the block, and other abbreviations that vary depending on the quarry and the period.

On the other hand, quarries producing only for nearby cities or regions remained in the hands of private people or municipalities. At the same time precise laws established the rights of both the quarry owners and of the entrepreneurs renting extraction concessions. The practice common in earlier centuries of placing orders at local sculpture workshops or at prestigious workshops existing in famous artistic centers such as Athens continued. Statues, reliefs, and architectural furnishings like candelabra, *trapezophori* (table supports), *oscilla*, and basins could be purchased directly or through dealers (*mercatores*).

J. B. Ward-Perkins was the first to hypothesize a model for the system of distribution of marbles for architectural and statuary artifacts—semicrafted or semipolished—produced in view of the demand and which presuppose even for the quarries owned by the emperor a close collaboration with the distribution systems, whether dominated by the private market or directly controlled by the state (Ward-Perkins 1992).

Imperial Administration and Control: Concessions and Contracts

We should like to emphasize that by the end of the reign of Augustus, the emperor had established a near monopoly on the use of marbles in the public architecture and sculpture in the city of Rome that stretched all the way back to the quarries from which the stones were extracted. The expenses borne by the state administration concerned the organization of the extraction activity, the first squaring of the blocks in the quarries, the transport, and the crafting in the workshops. But soon the practice of quarry concessions given to entrepreneurs necessitated an administrative and bureaucratic organization to control the production, and a whole system of marks grafted on the blocks was created to distinguish those destined to Rome from the portion of the production that represented the earnings of the entrepreneurs (Fant 1993). In terms of the white marbles, the quarries directly controlled by the imperial administration presented two types of production, differing in their quality and destination:(1) marbles destined for architecture, more standard, often white-bluish, and with veins (even in the case of Pentelic marble and not only that of Luni and Proconnesos), though even the architectural marbles were to a great extent painted (see essay 2.6, Abbe); (2) marbles for statuary, with uniform color and possibly without slits or darker veins, which were also painted. The quarry blocks in Parian marble, a prestigious marble for statuary, found in the state warehouse of Porto (*statio marmorum*) were marked, as were the more prestigious colored marbles sent to Rome.

At the same time, marble commerce also thrived to satisfy the needs of private people and of the governments of individual municipalities. Trade was based on the "imperial" marbles too, which could be marketed for the profit of the contracting companies or sometimes also of the cities that still held the property of sections of the marble districts supplying Rome. New studies of the marks identifying the blocks transported from the quarries as well as the epigraphic documentation available in the quarries have led us to believe that their system of exploitation was based on a model analogous to that of the exploitation of other mines and of the production of bricks in the vicinity of Rome.

The juridical mechanism (Hirt 2010; Russell 2013) is called *locatio conductio rei* (the administration leases out the excavation rights to private contractors) or *locatio conductio operis* (the administration hires private contractors to assume specific sectors to quarry), but it is not always very easy to distinguish the different situations, both of which can be found in the same quarry, at different periods or in different sectors. The emperor, as the owner of the land, and his administration acted as *locator*, authorizing the *conductores* to extract a certain quantity of marble. State officials like the *procurators marmorum* controlled the situation, so that a substantial share of this production went directly to the imperial administration. Staff that supervised the mining districts at the same time depended on the *procurator* residing in the *statio marmorum* in Rome. Other important figures were the *rationarii*, generally imperial slaves or freedmen (recognized by the mark *ex ratio* followed by a name, inscribed on the blocks), who, during periods of particular demand for marble for the imperial constructions in Rome, rapidly organized the collection of blocks and shafts (Russell 2013). They did not operate in the quarries, but in the marble yards (like those of Rome and Portus, where the products of the quarries were stocked: Bruzza 1877, 39–46; Dubois 1908), or in deposits near the quarries, or also in the harbors from where ships sailed for Rome. The *conductores* and the *rationarii* made their profit from the available remains of the production, which consisted in a large part of the material coming from the extracting activities. That all means that marble from imperial quarries was not only destined for Rome and for the needs of the imperial house, but it ended up in a controlled market, which local elites could exploit for provincial building activity.

In order to better understand the quarry exploitation system organized by the Romans, we should make a distinction between the "imperial" marbles coming from quarries controlled directly by imperial administrators and the "local" marbles used for columns and decorations from quarries in private ownership. These latter materials can also be thought of as "substitution" or "imitation" marbles, because their use derives from the necessity for provincial cities to get marble for new monumental architecture in a quick and cheap way, looking for the nearest quarries. This need led to the employment of local stones similar to the more prestigious "imperial" marbles. The phenomenon is evidenced in Hispania by the white marble quarries at Estremoz (Portugal) and at Almadén de la Plata near Seville (Andalusia), and in Gaul at Saint-Béatin the Pyrenees (Nogales and Beltrán 2009; see essay 5.2, Jiménez and Rodà). In these cases the blocks were not carved with the marks of the Roman administration, because they were not of imperial ownership and were worked for private trade.

Marble Destined for Civic and Private Use

In the case of marbles acquired on the market we have been able to distinguish between those destined for public, civic monuments and those for private residences. As a matter of fact the workshops implied are different insofar as an order by private people could more easily make use of products available on the market and from small workshops. On the other hand, a public order, for instance for the building and the furnishing of a temple or a theater, seems more likely to refer to a large-size workshop able to satisfy the request: columns and trabeation elements of a large size were necessary for temples (see, for instance, the gigantism characterizing the architecture of the Hispanic and Gallic cities of the Julio-Claudian age, or of the cities in Asia Minor of the Flavian through the Severan eras). With regard to theaters, sculpted reliefs and statues for the stage building, columns of different colors to set on two or three superimposed orders, capitals, and elements of trabeation were necessary. The public edifices of large and medium-size cities would call for such a large number of architectural and statuary marbles, of lining slabs and so on, that they could have been satisfied only by an organization of workshops connected with the quarries and the marble distribution centers near the ports. However, we ought to make a distinction between cities placed near marble quarries able to satisfy their needs—for instance Ephesus and the Belevi quarries, and Italica and the Almadén de la Plata quarries—and cities located in areas without quarries in their vicinity. Such was the case for many cities in Cilicia, Lydia, Syria, Tripolitania, and Cyrenaica, or even in Sicily and southern Italy, where only quarries of limestone and other local stones existed. We ought to consider also the case of cities where intense building activity required such a large quantity of marble and number of workshops that the demands could not be satisfied by local resources. As an example, we must consider the city of Rome, which from the end of the first century needed to make use also of Proconnesian marble and of other eastern workshops as the supply of Luni marble was not sufficient.

When, on the other hand, artifacts were destined only for private individuals for their residences or funerary monuments, it is possible to speak more extensively of commercial dynamics linked to supply and availability. Less is known about market demand and the process of ordering sculptures. One can wonder whether it was worthwhile for a marble trader to keep stock in his warehouse ready to be finished to order or whether stock was put together only for already received commissions. But even in this case, the production of small statuary groups or of single statues used as *trapezophori* or to furnish niches and apses in gardens or fountains—examples of which were found in Greece and in the Dokimeion quarries—would demonstrate that some production of small objects already existed in workshops near the quarries in anticipation of orders. The small size of these statues called for only a small financial investment that could be easily borne by the workshops and the *negotiatores* who bought them. Further research is needed on this category of production destined for private people, in particular on the roles of customers and carvers and the ordering system. Moreover, regarding statues, it is necessary to distinguish between the presence of blocks bought by the workshops, more often on the basis of orders but also in view of demand, and sculptures acquired from a second-hand market (Russell 2013). This is the case with reused statues, which could easily be reworked: for example, honorific or funerary statues, which in the course of time had been removed from their original context (Russell 2013, 314; see essay 2.3, Varner). During the imperial age a process of production over time became popular. In fact, the bodies of the statues could be sculpted long before the portrait heads that were executed at the time of purchase by the client who wanted to represent either himself or a special person (see essays 2.3, Varner; and 3.4, Wood). The same happened to luxurious sarcophagi, such as those from Attica and Dokimeion, where the sarcophagi were completely sculpted, with the exception of the portrait heads, which could be finished off only at the moment of the delivery (see essay 4.4, Ewald).

In the last decades, on the basis of Ward-Perkins's studies, the importance of three main artistic centers has been emphasized: Athens, Aphrodisias, and Dokimeion (Ward-Perkins1992). We know that they were important centers of the production and export of sculpture: objects like table stands, vases, columns, and above all, sarcophagi, were indeed exported all over the empire from these cities, as we can determine from shipwrecks, like that at Punta Scifo near Crotone in Calabria (Italy). Inscriptions show that the objects were produced in workshops near the quarries and tightly connected to the extraction process (Pensabene 1998, 350–51). This is why we need to focus on the organization controlled by the state, but left to private hands, that was at the base of the whole marble trade.

Scientific Analyses

It is difficult, if not impossible, to distinguish the quarry provenance of white marbles simply by sight, yet much further analysis of marble artifacts depends upon ascertaining marble origins accurately. Prestige, cost, quality, and transport are just some of the factors at play. In recent decades, archaeometric approaches have been used to analyze the principal characteristics of white marbles, beginning with samples taken from ancient quarries that have been studied for their petrographic, isotopic, and geochemical properties. But so far, the numerous studies on marble provenance have led to only partial results from a scientific point of view, and an interdisciplinary approach has been recognized as indispensable for better understanding the properties and of the use of white marbles in antiquity (Lazzarini 2004, 113–25). Starting from known petrographic, isotopic, and geochemical properties of marble from specific ancient quarries, it has been possible to create databases and diagrams against which to compare samples taken from ancient artifacts of unknown marble to determine probabilities for their quarry origins. Several analytic techniques are in use, and the most authoritative studies combine the results from all these methods.

Geoscientific sampling techniques should respect as much as possible the aesthetic and historical contents and the physical integrity of the artifact, so as to minimize the impact on sculptures. Only one sample should be taken from any object, preferably from a hidden part of the artifact, consisting of a small chip of marble between 0.5 cm and 2.5 cm in diameter, from which must be obtained a thin section for microscopic analysis, as well as powder for mass-spectrometer (isotopic) analysis. With statues worked in the round, from which it is not possible to detach even the smallest splinter, one can use a drill with a 3 mm point to obtain a very small quantity of powder for mass-spectrometer analysis from an inconspicuous location.

The classic method, visual examination of the stone surface with the naked eye and consideration of which quarries are physically closest or considered most prestigious, cannot be completely rejected, because it is a "common sense" test against which to compare the plausibility of results obtained by more scientific methods.

The most authoritative results combine mineralogical-petrographic examination of thin sections with the determination of the carbon (C) and oxygen (O) stable isotopic ratios of the same sample. This approach takes advantage of the best existing database for the commonly used marbles in antiquity, whose parameters must be known in order to work through comparisons. The mineralogical-petrographic study uses polarizing microscopes and focuses on Maximum Grain Size (MGS) measurement and the study of crystal morphology from thin sections (Moens et al. 1988). X-ray diffraction (XRD), also conducted on thin sections, permits the study of the crystal structure of the materials and can establish the form and size of the elementary cells of the crystal and how the atoms are set inside the crystal itself.

Stable-isotope analysis measures the ratios of particular isotopes, δ18O and δ13C, within marble samples ground to a fine powder. Isotopic-ratio measurements of carbon and oxygen have led to the discrimination of some Greek marbles from Attica and the Cyclades (Craig and Craig 1972, 401–3) and of marbles from several quarries of Asia Minor (Manfra, Masi, and Turi 1975, 215–21; Cramer 2004). However, the data is sometimes ambiguous, and the overall picture is complex. Also promising, but more expensive, is strontium-isotope analysis (Pentia, Herz, and Turi 2002); although the high price of these studies makes it difficult to conduct, especially in the case of large-scale investigations on quarry and artifact samples.

Cathodoluminescence (CL) is based on the principle of luminescence induced by bombarding a sample of rock with electron beams produced by a cathode. It can be observed by a particular petrographical microscope equipped with a photography system with a void-and-cathode camera. This methodology adds information to the conventional petrographical analysis of the stones that would be difficult to obtain otherwise. Electron Paramagnetic Resonance (EPR) spectroscopy consists of a technique for the study of materials with unpaired electrons. It has been shown that the application to marble samples of CL and EPR spectroscopy together with the other methods discussed above can determine the quarry origins of an artifact's marble.

It has recently been possible to create data banks based on a catalog of "outer patterns," which allowed even nongeologists to apply systematic marble determination criteria. It was useful also to add digitized microphotographs of whole thin sections in order to obtain a qualitative and semiquantitative overview and distinction of essential fabric patterns. Therefore updated databanks of the analyses of the mineralogical-petrographical and geochemical characteristics have been put at scholars' disposal (Gorgoni et al. 2002). They concern the main quarries of white marbles active during antiquity, such as the ones at Paros, Naxos, Thasos, and Mount Pentelikon in Greece; Carrara in Italy;

and Aphrodisias, Afyon, and Marmara in Asia Minor (sources of Dokimeion and Proconnesian marble that were widely used in antiquity).

Today, the prevailing approach, which gives more reliable results for marble provenance research, consists of studying samples with at least two independent analytical methodologies and processing all the obtained information together. Even if petrographic patterns are of uppermost importance, a multivariate approach proves to be necessary, because of the overlapping of properties of marble quarries. In fact, researchers have ascertained that one or two geogenic characteristics alone are not sufficient for provenance determination.

Laboratories applying archaeometry to the study of marbles are rare both in Europe and in the United States. Prominent laboratories, research groups, and scholars frequently performing marble analysis include LAMA (Laboratorio di Analisi dei Materiali Antichi, Università IUAV) in Venice, the CNR (Consiglio Nazionale delle Richerche—Istituto di Struttura della Materia) in Rome, the ICAC (Istitut Català d'Arqueologia Clàssica) in Spain, the Laboratory of Archaeometry at the National Center for Scientific Research in Greece, and, in the US, Robert Tykot at the Laboratory for Archaeological Science at the University of South Florida and Scott Pike at Willamette University .

An important stimulus for scientific investigations in the archaeometric field over the last two decades has been provided by ASMOSIA (Association for the Study of Marbles and Other Stones in Antiquity; Gutiérrez, Lapuente, and Rodà 2012) and its members: new methods have been proposed and many new marbles and quarries, both major and minor, have been recognized.

Based on the results of scientific analyses, some famous sculptures once thought to be Roman copies have now been reclaimed as Greek originals or copies whose provenance can be specified as from Greece (Attic workshops) or from Phrygia (white Dokimeion). For example, the famous Dying Gaul and the group of the suicidal Gaul with his dead wife, carved from white Dokimeion marble, are now thought to be originals from the late Hellenistic period, when the kings of Pergamon controlled the Phrygian quarries in their dominion.

The recent discovery of the quarries of Göktepe, south of Aphrodisias (Turkey), has provided an important contribution to our understanding of the materials of Roman sculpture. These quarries produced statuary-grade white and black marbles: now, thanks to analytical and archaeometric tests (Attanasio, Bruno, and Yavuz 2010), we know that they were traded all over the Mediterranean, especially during the second century AD. Hadrian used these marbles in his villa at Tivoli, for instance, for the two famous Centaurs.

The importance of identification based on scientific data is obvious. For example, sculptures of uncertain attribution can be linked to a well-defined atelier or production area. Well-dated artworks can, in turn, help to establish the chronology of quarrying activity at particular sites. And the identification of shipwreck marbles permits us to reconstruct ancient trade routes (Russell 2013, 331–61). Moreover, when we recognize the original quarries of deteriorated marbles, we can obtain newly cut stone in order to make restorations, substitutions, or copies.

Conclusion

The central role of marble—both white and colored—in imperial-period civic and private realms has stimulated new research on the history of quarry use, the imperial administration of Mediterranean quarries, and scientific methods for determining quarry origins of marble artifacts and monuments. Historical, archaeological, and scientific data must be considered together to understand both the logistics (administrative and physical) and the meaning of marble in the Roman realm. Discoveries and studies of new quarries, as well as continued scientific determinations of marble provenance of specific artifacts or groups of artifacts, will yield further understanding of the economic, social, and political role of marble and marble quarries in the Roman world.

Bibliography

Attanasio D., M. Bruno, and A. B. Yavuz. 2010. "Villa Adriana e l'uso dei marmi Afrodisiensi dalle cave di Göktepe." In *Villa Adriana: Una storia mai finita*, edited by M. Sapelli Ragni, 81–90. Milan: Electa.

Bruzza, L. 1877. "Gli scavi dell'Emporio." In *Triplice Omaggio alla Santità di Papa Pio IX nel suo giubileo episcopio*, 39–46. Rome: Tipografia della Pace.

Craig, H., and V. Craig. 1972. "Greek Marble Determination of Provenance by Isotopic Analysis." *Science* 176: 401–403.

Cramer, T. 2004. "Multivariate Herkunftsanalyse von Marmor auf petrographischer und geochemischer Basis: Das Beispiel kleinasiatischer archaischer, hellenistischer und römischer Marmorobjekte der Berliner Antikensammlung und ihre Zuordnung zu mediterranen und anatolischen Marmorlagerstätten." PhD diss., Technische Universität Berlin.

Dolci, E. 1989. *Il Marmo nella civiltà romana*. Carrara: Internazionale marmi e macchine.

Dubois, C. 1908. *Etude sur l'administration et l'exploitation des carrières: Marbres, porphyre, granit, etc. dans le monde romain*. Paris: Fontemoing.

Fant, J. C. 1993. "Ideology, Gift and Trade: A Distribution Model for the Roman Imperial Marbles." In *The Inscribed Economy*, edited by W. V. Harris, 145–70. JRA Supplement 6. Ann Arbor: University of Michigan.

Gorgoni, C., L. Lazzarini, P. Pallante, and B. Turi. 2002. "An Updated and Detailed Mineropetrographic and C-O Stable Isotopic Reference Database for the Main Mediterranean Marbles Used in Antiquity." In *ASMOSIA 5, Boston, June 1998*, edited by J. J. Herrmann, Jr., N. Herz, and R. Newman, 115–31. London: Archetype.

Gutiérrez, A., P. Lapuente, and I. Rodà, eds. 2012. *Interdisciplinary Studies on Ancient Stone. ASMOSIA 9*. Documenta 23. Tarragona: Institut Català d'Arqueologia Clàssica.

Hirt, A. M. 2010. *Imperial Mines and Quarries in the Roman World: Organizational Aspects, 27 BC–AD 235*. Oxford: Oxford University Press.

Lazzarini, L. 2004. "Archaeometric Aspects of White and Coloured Marbles Used in Antiquity: The State of the Art." *Periodico di Mineralogia* 73: 113–25.

———. 2007. *"Poikiloi lithoi, versiculores maculae": I marmi colorati della Grecia antica; Storia, uso, diffusione, cave, geologia, caratterizzazione scientifica, archeometria, deterioramento*. Pisa: Fabrizio Serra.

Manfra, L., U. Masi, and B. Turi. 1975. "Carbon and Oxygen Isotope Ratios of Marbles from Some Ancient Quarries of Western Anatolia and Their Archaeological Significance." *Archaeometry* 17: 215–21.

Moens, L., P. Roos, J. De Rudder, P. De Paepe, J. van Hende, R. Marechal, and M. Waelkens. 1988. "A Multi-Method Approach to the Identification of White Marbles Used in Antique Artifacts." In *Classical Marble: Geochemistry, Technology, Trade*, edited by N. Herz and M. Waelkens, 243–50. NATO ASI Series E 153. Dordrecht: Kluwer Academic.

Nogales, T., and J. Beltrán, eds. 2009. *Marmora* Hispana: *Explotación y uso de los materiales pétreos en la Hispania Romana*. Rome: "L'Erma" di Bretschneider.

Pensabene, P. 1998. "Il fenomeno del marmo nella Roma tardo-repubblicana e imperiale." In *Marmi antichi.* Vol. 2, *Cave e tecnica di lavorazione, provenienze e distribuzione*, edited by P. Pensabene, 333–90. Studi Miscellanei 31. Rome: "L'Erma" di Bretschneider.

———. 2002. "Il fenomeno del marmo nel mondo romano." In *I marmi colorati della Roma imperiale*, edited by M. De Nuccio and L. Ungaro, 3–67. Venice: Marsilio.

———. 2013. *I marmi nella Roma antica*. Rome: Carocci.

Pentia, M., N. Herz, and B. Turi. 2002. "Provenance Determination of Classical Marbles: A Statistical Test Based on 87Sr/86Sr, 18°/16° and 13C/12C Isotopic Ratio." In *ASMOSIA VI, Venice, June 15–18, 2000*, edited by L. Lazzarini, 219–26. Padua: Bottega d'Erasmo Aldo Ausilio.

Russell, B. 2013. *The Economics of the Roman Stone Trade*. Oxford: Oxford University Press.

Ward-Perkins, J. B. 1992. *Marble in Antiquity: Collected Papers of J.B. Ward-Perkins*, edited by H. Dodge and B. Ward-Perkins. Archaeological Monographs of the British School at Rome 6. London: British School at Rome.

CHAPTER 2.2

MARBLE CARVING TECHNIQUES, WORKSHOPS, AND ARTISANS

AMANDA CLARIDGE

INTRODUCTION

THE quantity of marble sculpture that was produced in the Roman period, rising to an all-time peak during the first three centuries AD, has been thought to have required very different methods and modes of production from those that had prevailed earlier among the Greeks. To understand this profusion of production, twentieth-century scholars turned to modern sculptors and the sculptural industry that centers on the marble quarries at Carrara, Italy, and postulated a similar industrialized system of factory-sized workshops, practicing multiple divisions of labor, supplying finished works at long distance to a highly commercialized art market. In truth, Carrara's system developed as a by-product of the northern European industrial revolution of the mid-eighteenth century (Magenta 1866, 22–39; Bernieri 1983, 18–35), and it has no obvious relevance to the Roman world. Furthermore, as this paper will demonstrate, none of the technical evidence supports this idea. Roman production levels undoubtedly rose, but they could have been achieved simply by increasing the supply of the raw material (see essay 2.7, Russell) and by multiplying the numbers of skilled hands at work, with no fundamental change in the processes of sculpting, the size and locations of workshops, or the nature of sculpting as a profession.

This essay surveys the archaeological, literary, and epigraphic evidence for marble carving techniques, workshops, and artisans. Increased understanding of the artistic processes and those who undertook the creation of marble statuary sheds light on artistic traditions, aspects of the Roman economy, and a major industry whose products played a central role in late republican and imperial Roman world.

Marble Carving

Tools and Techniques

Toolmarks on sculpture, supplemented by depictions in funerary reliefs (Zimmer 1982, nos. 91–8) and finds from excavations indicate that Roman sculptors continued to use the same basic types of iron tools that had been developed among the Greeks of the sixth century BC (Bluemel 1969; Nolte 2006; for illustrations of tool types, see Rockwell 1993a), though the quality of the iron, forging, and tempering had improved. Depending on the size of the work and the amount of stone to be removed, the initial phases (called "roughing-out") were done with wooden-handled, iron-headed hand-picks with pointed tips and/or pointed chisels struck with an iron-headed hammer. As the shaping got closer to the eventual surface the pointed tools were exchanged for the finer, less powerful action of claw or toothed chisels, commonly with four or five slightly rounded teeth, which removed the furrows left by the points and prepared the way for the definitive carving to be done with edged chisels, whether curved (roundel) or square (flat). Roman flat chisels could be very robust (probably cross-cut), capable of replacing claw chisels in the transition from roughing-out to definitive form. Deep channels, hollows, and gaps were achieved with the aid of drills, which worked without shock. Drill bits were forged like chisels, with a rounded or flat bladed tip but a pyramid-shaped head, which fitted into a wooden stock with a handle at the top. The stock was turned back and forth either by the sculptor himself with a bow or by an assistant with straps. To make a deep channel, a series of vertical holes was drilled close together in a line and then the bridges knocked out, to be further shaped by chiseling, for which a special channeling tool (with an extra-thin shaft) was often employed. The "running drill," which has entered the literature as a means of making a channel in a single operation, is a phantom, based on a misunderstanding of the German "laufende Bohrer" (Pfanner 1988). Drillwork developed into a virtuoso skill in the later second century AD, used to great effect in the shaping of hair, beards, drapery, foliage, and fur. The definitive carving was then followed by other tools that did not involve shock: rasps, scrapers, and abrasives (emery, corundum, volcanic scoria, and quartz sand are variously attested). The main aim was to produce a stun-free and thus durable surface, to which paint and wax would then be applied.

Although the backs and occasionally the unfinished parts of otherwise finished sculpture can provide good evidence for tool types and sequences of tool use (Rockwell 1993a; 1993b), sculptural methods are best illustrated by genuinely unfinished sculpture. Over 200 examples exist, widely distributed around the empire; most are tiny statuettes, hardly representative, but even the statuettes show that not all sculptors approached their work in quite the same way or used quite the same toolkit. Sculptors in Athens, for instance, tended not to use claw chisels. They went directly from fairly cursory shaping with points to curved or flat chisels, handled in long parallel strokes. Other sculptors used progressively finer points to a much more advanced stage, then claws, then curved and flat chisels. One determining factor could be the type of marble being worked—some are harder or softer or more brittle to work than others (Claridge 1985). Some sculptors, depending on where they were trained, may have learned to work different kinds of marble with equal facility; others learned the customary local technique for one particular type.

Recent research has demonstrated that at all periods, from archaic Greece to late antiquity, the processes of creating marble sculpture did not stop at the marble surface (see essay 2.6, Abbe). Sculptures were painted, silvered, or gilded, including the flesh surfaces, even those treated to high polishes and virtuoso drilling. The incision of the pupil and iris of the eye, which became a regular practice around AD 130, did not replace a painted effect (as has been thought); rather, it emphasized and enhanced it.

Figure Types, Approaches to Form, and the Practice of Joining

Many of the figure types used in Roman statuary were very solid and straightforward to carve in marble, thanks to their upright frontal poses and the all-enveloping nature of their dress. Only the neck, wrists, and ankles were potential weak points, if exposed: a veil avoided the neck problem, the hands might be wrapped in folds, or positioned against the body; the ankles could be wearing boots. If arms and hands were to project far from the body, they could be carved in one piece with the rest of the figure, but usually remained anchored to it by one or more bridges of stone (a strut or *puntello*). Alternatively, they were carved out of separate pieces of stone and attached with the aid of an iron dowel set in the middle of the join that relieved the strain and was actually stronger than a strut (Claridge 1990). The join could be made invisible by making it coincide with a natural feature, such as an overfold of drapery or the end of a sleeve, and it allowed a better quality of stone to be used for the addition. Heads could be worked separately for the same reasons. The body itself could be made in two halves, joined horizontally, like the drums of a column. Positioned carefully, such joins could greatly reduce the size of block(s) required for the body and also the amount of stone that had to be removed in the roughing-out (Claridge 1988). Depending on where it was to be set up, the back of the figure could be left as solid stone (in the manner of a high relief); roughed out with the rest at the start, but not given further shape; or shaped with the rest, but not given a final finish (nor painted).

Other less well-draped subjects, the nudes and seminudes, and all those in more active poses, almost invariably required extensive drilling if they were to be achieved in a single block of stone and fully in the round, intrinsically demanding not only blocks of better quality but more skill and considerably more time on the part of the carver (drilling is never a shortcut; Pfanner 1988, 670). This, of course, might have been their appeal to patrons—their greater cost was manifest in the finished product to a public presumably well versed in such matters. Heads and arms were sometimes worked separately and joined in nude statuary, but the incidence of all such joins drops after the first century AD. Marble statuary in the second and early third centuries gets much larger and is more blatantly monolithic, favoring poses which entailed enormous gaps and massive bridging struts (Hollinshead 2002). Figures with outflung gestures are combined with huge lateral supports shaped into trees or other landscape accessories or in groups of two and three, providing mutual support. The art of joining continued to be of use for repairs and in cases of reuse, when the head on an existing statue was replaced or when it was given a new attribute (such as a wreath or a diadem). In the early third century sculptors combined marble and iron to make statues with an armature of iron rods inserted in the arms and legs, so that the figure did not even require a plinth.

Models, Measuring Points, and Mechanisms of Copying

A marble sculpture, unlike a bronze, does not require a model as part of the production process; the design can exist only in the sculptor's head, to be worked out directly in the stone. The larger, more ambitious, and complicated the concept, however, and the more the forms twist or turn in the block, the more likely the sculptor is to make a model, especially when the subject is unfamiliar or is to be made from life (since a living model cannot be expected to hold a pose long enough for the sculptor to capture the likeness directly in stone). Pliny tells of the sculptor Pasiteles visiting the docks to model a caged lion in clay from life (*HN* 36.40) and of other sculptors in Rome in the last century BC who were celebrated for their preparatory models of clay (*proplasmata; HN* 35.155–6). Models allow the marble sculptor to experiment in three dimensions, to convey ideas clearly to patrons, to estimate exactly the size of the block(s) required and possible approaches to it, to employ a whole team of assistants if necessary to help with the actual carving, and, if wished, to repeat exactly the same design again.

It is the reproductive function of Roman models that has attracted most attention, on the understanding that any Greek-looking figure could reproduce a lost bronze work of the classical or Hellenistic period (see essays 3.1, Fullerton; and 3.3, Anguissola). Small discrepancies in a given "copy series" are variously explained as the result of deficiencies in the models or the skills of "copyists;" larger errors are excused on the grounds that the translation of a bronze design into marble will have required adjustments (though why such translations should have been attempted at all is not easy to explain; Andreae 1992). Fragmentary plaster sculptures found at Baiae on the Bay of Naples in 1954 have been interpreted as models from a local marble sculptor's workshop, since some can be matched to familiar marble types known locally, albeit with some difference in volume, which suggests the molds used had been taken from bronzes (Landwehr 1985; Gasparri 1995; see essays 2.4, Mattusch; and 3.3, Anguissola). However, the Baiae "casts" show no signs of having been used as models, and plaster was a Roman sculptural medium in its own right (D'Alessandro and Persegati 1987; Barone 1994).

More reliable physical evidence of models exists in the form of measuring points—small bosses of stone left protruding from a carved surface, with or without a small hole in the top. They are found on all sorts of finished and unfinished work, both freestanding and in relief, and at all periods, from the early classical pediments at Olympia to the third century AD (Bluemel 1969, 48–56; Pfanner 1989, 236–51). There may be only one point, located on a salient feature or what is likely to have been the center of the block or the center of the design, as on the rear of the statue of Augustus from Prima Porta. Or there can be multiple such bosses—the largest number is twenty-seven, on an unfinished statue of a captive Dacian found in Rome (figure 2.2.1), where they appear all over the front and sides of the body, but not on the back (Pfanner 1989, 151f, figs. 14a–c). On heads, they are usually arranged in a triangle, with two on the hair over the brow and a third on the chin. On a training piece from Rome of Hadrianic date (figure 2.2.2; Lorenz 2009), the master sculptor has carved the head in relief on the right, leaving three points as he went (two on the cheek and one in the hair), and the apprentice has copied that model to the left, with three points in the same positions, in his case with small holes in them, where he has used a compass. This example, however, shows that such points cannot be taken as evidence of the existence of separate models, only that one existing work

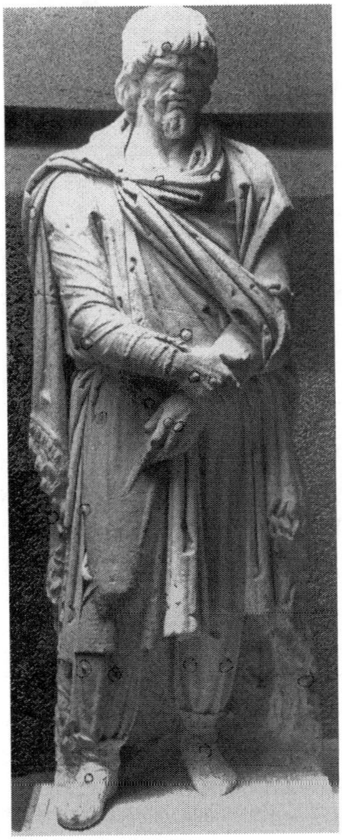

FIGURE 2.2.1 Unfinished statue of a Dacian prisoner, from the Campus Martius in Rome, c. AD 110. Vatican Museums, Museo Gregoriano Profano ex Lateranense inv. no. 10543.

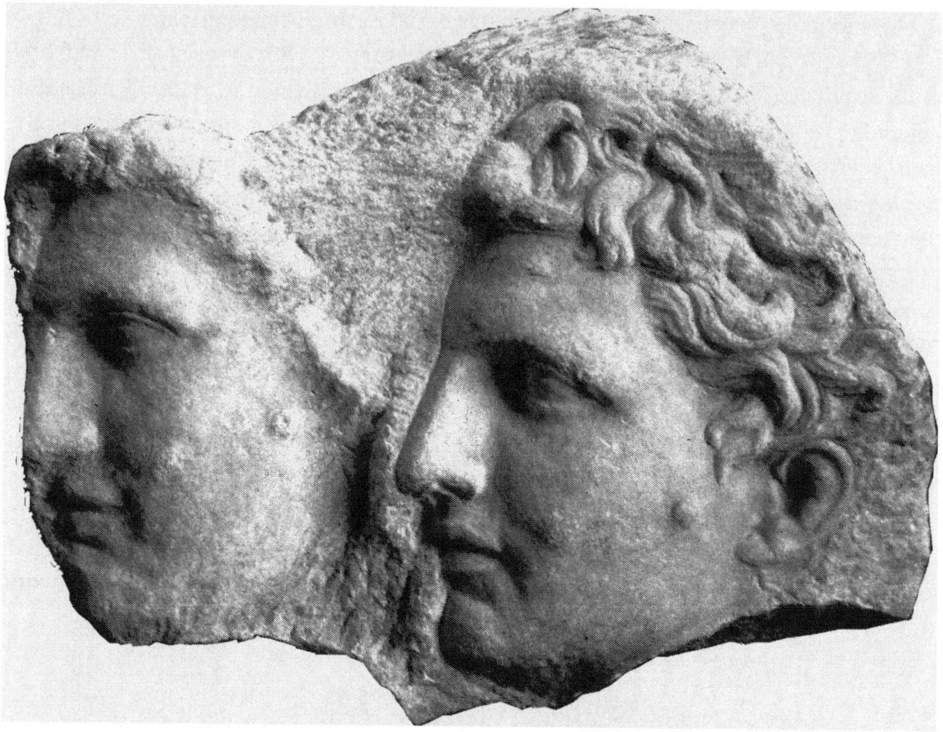

FIGURE 2.2.2 Apprentice training piece: head by master sculptor on right, by pupil on left. c. AD 120. Rome, Palazzo della Cancelleria, S. Lorenzo in Damaso excavation storerooms.

might serve as a model for another. The Dacian prisoner, therefore, could be the master model for a series of similar figures all produced by the same workshop, or the last in the series that turned out to be surplus.

These points cannot be equated with a modern system known as "pointing off," which operates with the aid of three fixed points and is capable of great precision, permitting the divisions of labor characteristic of Carrara's sculpture industry. This system was invented only around 1760, probably in Paris (Ayres 1985, 146–53), and always leaves additional evidence in the form of tiny drill holes (*punti*) peppering the surface of unfinished work, still detectable in finished work. No such *punti* are found on ancient Roman sculpture (unless the work is a modern forgery).

Workshops and the Location of Production

Roman marble-carvers, like their Greek predecessors and most modern counterparts, will have learned their trade on the job as part of a workshop, a term which can describe both a group of craftsmen and the place where they work. The Latin word *officina* had this same double sense, used by some sculptors when "signing" their work, but also inscribed on a quarry face, where it identified the sphere of operation of a given team of quarrymen. The individual block being extracted was called a *locus* (place or work-site). An extracted block could be transferred to sculptors while still in the quarry for more work to be done on it, lessening the weight before moving it any further, though the amount that could be done depended, again, on the size and shape of the finished product. Discards in Roman quarry debris consist mainly of architectural elements, especially Corinthian capitals in roughed-out state and blocks destined for sarcophagi. Finds of part-worked statuary are very rare, which probably means that Roman sculptors rarely worked in quarries, though could also mean that they were more successful in choosing their blocks (or adapting them to other purposes in the event of a flaw). To avoid the high risk of breakage in transit, the bulk of the carving, whether or not it was started in the quarry, would usually have been done after the block had been transported to its destination. There, too, the detailed processes of production would be conditioned by the size and shape of the work and where it was to be installed.

Many Roman work-sites were temporary and ephemeral, consisting only of the block set up in the open air, in or adjacent to the building where the work was to be installed, with perhaps an awning strung on poles to provide some cover, and leaving no trace in the archaeological record except a layer of marble chippings and dust. In Rome, for example, thick deposits from working and polishing marble have been recorded over a large area of the western Campus Martius (Maischberger 1997, 108–156), associated with a scatter of raw blocks and pieces of unfinished marble sculpture. The area apparently represents the site of a large marble yard with its own special quay on the river, serving the adjacent monumental building program on the Campus and in the imperial forums under Trajan and Hadrian. Sculptors making freestanding statues for the new projects set up shop there, working each statue to an advanced stage, able to use one as the model for the next, and then did the final finishing after the statue had been lifted into position. Figurative reliefs could also have been partly carved off-site, as long as the design occupied a single block, but they too will have been finished *in situ*, and continuous friezes were probably always carved entirely *in situ*, since the composition crossed over several blocks. Concentrations of marble-working debris like those in Rome, including unfinished sculpture, have been found in the harbor areas of Puteoli in Italy (Camodeca et al. 2001) and Delos in the Aegean (*BCH* 29, 1905, 16), and are attested epigraphically at Ephesus in Asia Minor (*IvE* 23; Bouras 2011).

The work both off- and on-site could be divided up and distributed among as many separate hands as could physically share the block (and scaffolding). A technical analysis of the frieze on Trajan's Column (an area of some 200 m^3 containing some 2,600 figures and masses of other detail in low relief) has suggested that its carving was done *in situ* by just eight or ten sculptors, apparently working in pairs, one usually doing the foreground figures, the second filling in the background (Rockwell 1989, 249–58). They carved freehand, laying out the design as they went, from the bottom to the top of the shaft. No doubt there was additional help in the form of apprentices, fetchers and carriers of tools, and a squad of blacksmiths to keep the tools sharp. Whether the carvers of Trajan's Column all belonged to a single large organization, led by one or two of their number or the division into pairs signifies four to five smaller workshops working in collaboration is difficult to tell: although individual sculptural "hands" can be distinguished by quirks of form and workmanship, the style and technique of their carving are so comparable that they probably had very similar training.

From the Augustan to the Severan period, there was an almost continuous program of building by the emperors in and around Rome and further afield, and a huge amount of building also by wealthy private individuals, representing opportunities for sculptors to perpetuate their workshops and establish new ones. Such "branch" workshops could have run into their thousands by the second century AD, spreading from Rome out into the rest of Italy and the western provinces, wherever there was a market for their work, and eventually spawning their own local offshoots. In Gaul, Spain, and North Africa, works of a strongly "metropolitan" character dominate local production in the first century AD, but by the second and third centuries there is a far greater variety of workmanship, with some distinctive regional peculiarities that suggest sculptors were being trained locally. In Greece and Asia Minor (modern Turkey), of course, many cities had good local sources of marble and much older traditions of marble sculpture than Rome. They could have supplied much of the expertise on which Rome's tradition was initially built and may have continued to be a source of skilled labor thereafter (for the training of sculptors at Aphrodisias-in-Caria, see Van Voorhis 1998). The literary and epigraphic record provides many eloquent examples.

Rome and many other cities offered a large enough market for marble workers to have been based there permanently, supplying a particular product to a particular clientele. Several depictions of sculptors at work survive from around the empire. A funerary altar from Rome of the early second century AD (D'Ambra 1998, 95, fig. 58) shows a sculptor in a knee-length workman's tunic seated on a stool with a cushion, putting the finishing touches to the pedestal of a portrait medallion of a girl, while a lady with an expensive hairstyle (either his wife or his patroness) looks on. He may have specialized in funerary portraiture, the carver of the portraits on his own epitaph. A loculus slab from Rome now in Urbino shows a Greek named Eutropos (*EAA* s.v. *marmorarius*, 671, fig. 1037; Durnan 2000, 33, fig.14), who stands to the left in the longer tunic of the later empire and is perhaps also the man shown at work, seated on a high stepped stool as he drills the lion's head on a strigillated vat-shaped sarcophagus with the help of one assistant (probably a slave, since he wears a shorter tunic). The lid for the sarcophagus, mounted on two supports to the right, bears Eutropos's name. A tomb monument at Bordeaux, France (figure 2.2.3), from about AD 170 shows a sculptor called M. Se(cundus) Amabilis, seated in a niche, which he is literally carving for himself; the Amandus F named below, who set the monument up, was probably his brother (*F*[*rater*]), and in the same business (Charles-Picard 1961). A scene carved in relief on the bottom edge of a sarcophagus found at Ephesus (Smith 2011, 67, fig. 4.7) shows two master-sculptors (in long tunics), one seated at work on a male portrait statue, the other carving a portrait bust. Between them a slave (in a loincloth) is polishing a marble table leg on a large wooden bench.

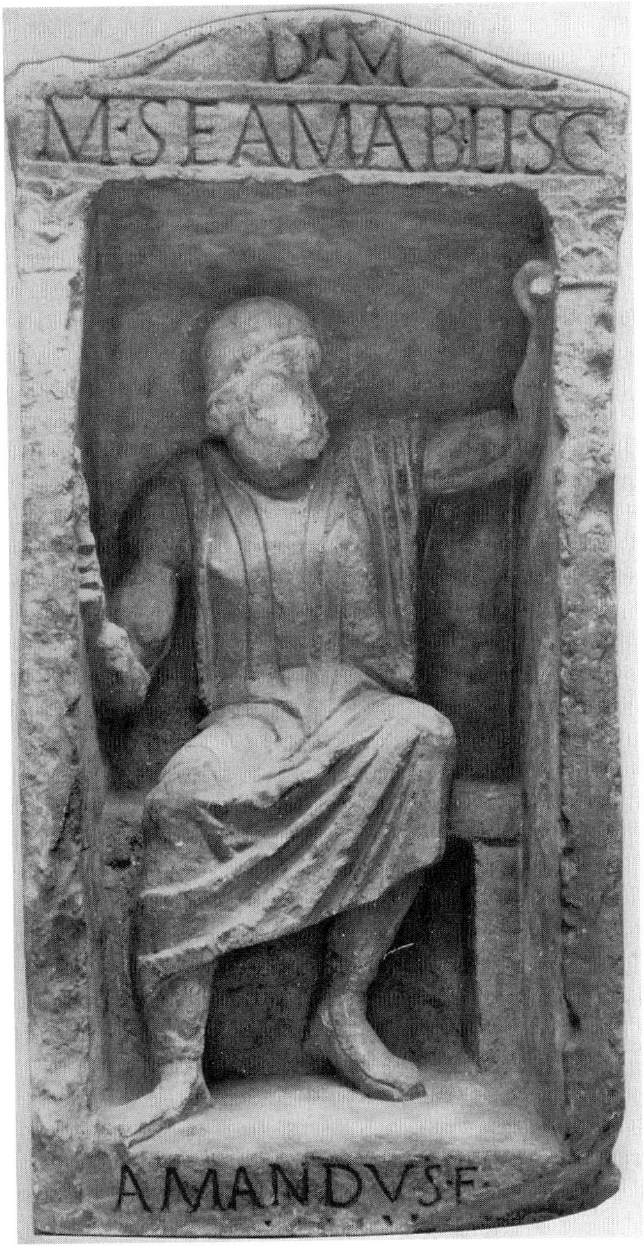

FIGURE 2.2.3 The sculptor Amabilis at work on his own funerary monument, c. AD 170. Bordeaux, Musée d'Aquitaine, inv. no. 60.1.82 (from cast in EUR, Museo della Civiltà Romana).

Two much smaller figures in shorter tunics are presumably young apprentices: that to the left is drawing on a board propped against a wall, the other is holding a drill (?) for the carver of the bust. The range of products, work-benches, and stools could signify built premises.

Private houses or rows of shop units (*tabernae*) in residential quarters at Delos (Marcadé 1969, 102–5; Nolte 2006, 281–9), Pompeii (Mustilli 1950), Sabratha (Barone 1994, 46–54), Thysdrus (Slim 1996, 40), and various other sites have yielded evidence of marble working. At most, two or three rooms were involved, and the occupation was fairly short-lived, suggesting that the sculptors were only temporary residents, like C. Avianius Evander, who occupied the *sacrarium* of the house of C. Memmius at Mytilene in 50 BC (Cic. *Fam.* 13.2). A "sculptor's studio" has been identified in the center of the city at Aphrodisias (Rockwell 1991; Van Voorhis 2012), but its activity dates from the fourth century AD, apparently using old statuary as raw material, not freshly quarried stone, and its location is unlikely to be typical of earlier periods, when the outskirts of the city would be more logical.

A large multi-aisled building of the second century AD adjacent to the quarries at Simitthus (Chemtou, Tunisia) was interpreted by its excavators in the 1970s as a "marble factory" but was in origin a military barracks (Rakob 1993, 121; Mackensen 2000), and the evidence for its use by marble workers dates from the fourth century AD, making dishes from quarry scrap for a local market (Rüger 1997). A factory-scale workshop has also been hypothesized (in part on stylistic grounds, in part extrapolating from Simitthus) in highland Phrygia, specializing in Asiatic columnar sarcophagi in Dokimeion marble for export (Waelkens 1982). The sarcophagi certainly reached a market well beyond the immediate region (mostly in the East, though a few went to Italy), and it is argued that sending a team of sculptors with a roughed-out block to complete on site would be too expensive (Wiegartz 1974). However, "economy" was probably never a concern; the sarcophagi were by far the largest and most luxurious to be had; the costs of bringing the marble and specialist craftsmen in from outside could have been their main appeal. Sculpture "factories" have also been envisaged in the case of the Neo-Attic products in Pentelic marble (reliefs, vases, candelabra, and sarcophagi), located in Athens or Piraeus so as to be convenient to their models on the one hand and sea transport on the other, but their existence is purely hypothetical.

Artisans: Origins, Status, and Signatures

It has been claimed (most influentially by Richter 1951a) that the status of sculptors and of sculpture as an art form was lower under the Roman Empire than it had been in Greece. Partly, this is an expectation born of modern rather than ancient value judgments as to the merits of Greek versus Roman sculpture, but it is also fuelled by the fact that we know relatively few Roman sculptors by name, while their individual "identities" as sculptors are obscured by conflation of their work with that of a lost Greek past. Actually, literary and epigraphic sources indicate the continued presence in the Roman world of skilled sculptors who enjoyed much the same kind of privileged relationship with their elite patrons as their Greek forerunners had and whose art was prized as much as it had ever been in the Greek world, perhaps more so.

The sculptors recorded in Rome in the last two centuries BC are mainly Greeks and very versatile, capable of making almost any material into any sculptural form their patrons desired. Families of sculptors from Athens, already accustomed to traveling widely to execute commissions in the East, were brought over or gravitated to Rome, where they worked in both bronze and marble (see essay 3.6, Touchette). Best known are the descendants of Polycles and his sons Polycles and Timarchides, this last probably one of many Greek artists brought back by the general Marcus Fulvius Nobilior to celebrate his triumph in 186 BC (Livy 39.22.1–2). Timarchides made a cult statue for the temple of Apollo in 179 BC and perhaps several others. His sons Polycles and Dionysios both became sculptors, carrying out various commissions in Rome for cult statues and other public dedications in the 150s and 140s BC. Dionysios later worked with his nephew, named Timarchides after his grandfather, on a statue set up in honor of an Italian businessman on the island of Delos around the 120s BC (Coarelli 1970). Active in Rome in the first half of the first century BC was Pasiteles, a south Italian Greek, whom we noted above as a modeler in clay. He worked also in ivory, metal, and marble (Donderer 1988), turning his hand to statues, reliefs, and tableware, and wrote a five-volume book on the "world's most celebrated works of art" (*nobilia opera in toto orbe*; Plin. *HN* 36.40; see essay 3.3, Anguissola). His pupil Stephanos signed a small statue of an athlete (Loewy 1885, no. 374; see essay 3.3, Anguissola), and Stephanos's pupil Menelaos (Loewy 1885, no. 375) took credit for a large statue group of Parian marble, both found in Rome. Arcesilaus (d. 42 BC), of unknown origin, was similarly multitalented, making major cult statues and fine wine vessels in metals, and was also an accomplished sculptor in marble. The Roman writer Varro (116–27 BC) owned Arcesilaus's Lioness teased by Cupids, some of whom were making it drink from a horn, others tying sandals to its feet, all carved out of a single block (Plin. *HN* 36.41), while Arcesilaus's group of Centaurs carrying Nymphs tops Pliny's list of marble works on display in the public library (Rome's first) built by C. Asinius Pollio in commemoration of a triumph he was awarded in 39 BC.

It is noticeable that several of these late republican sculptors called themselves "pupil of" rather than give their patronymic, which might mean they were slaves or that the professional acknowledgement was of greater import: not born into a sculpture family, they were newcomers to the trade, whose craftsman-base was expanding to meet Roman demand. One name Pliny mentions is not even Greek—a certain Coponius (the *nomen* of a Roman plebeian gens), who made the statues of the Nations for the porticus of the Theater of Pompey (*HN* 36.41). Then there is the name C. Vib(ius) Ruf(us -inus) cut into the upper surface of the plinth of one of the Caryatids from the Forum of Augustus (Ungaro and Del Moro 2007, 159, fig. 214), which is difficult to explain except as a maker's (less probably a supplier's) mark. He has the *tria nomina* of a Roman citizen, though he could have been a freedman. Part of a later imperial monument, the Extispicium relief in the Louvre, has the name M. Ul(pius) Orestes carved on the front hoof of the bull (Tortorella 1988). Orestes was surely an imperial freedman and more conventionally has a Greek cognomen. Whether he was really a Greek, any more than Vibius Rufus was a Roman, is anybody's guess. In both cases, the names will have been invisible from the ground; if their purpose was official, it was only temporary; otherwise they are most simply read as private statements of professional satisfaction.

Not just the emperors but other wealthy Romans will have regularly included sculptors among their slave *familia* to maintain their art collections and to make new works (Arcesilaus is described as *familiaris* of L. Lucullus, Plin. *HN* 35.155); there is also evidence of these patrons setting up their slaves in business to work for others. The C. Avianius Evander mentioned above working on Mytilene and known to Cicero was the Greek freedman of an Italian (probably Campanian) family that had migrated east in the late second century BC. His patron was M. Aemilius Avianianus, a friend of Cicero (D'Arms 1972, 211–2). Evander later went to Alexandria in the retinue of Mark Antony (probably in 39 BC), and after Actium to Rome, where he was employed by Octavian to replace the head of the cult statue of Diana (an antique by Timotheus) in the new Temple of Apollo and Diana on the Palatine, dedicated in 28 BC (Plin. *HN* 36.32).

The Cossutii, another family of businessmen from Campania, appear to have specialized in marble in the last two centuries BC, combining quarrying, shipping, and sculpting (Rawson 1975). A Marcus Cossutius Menelaos was named on a fragment of marble drapery in Rome (now lost) and a Marcus Cossutius Cerdo, a freedman of Marcus, was recorded on a pair of small statues of Pan (now in the British Museum) found in a villa at Lanuvium, south of Rome. On Paros (source of the finest white marble), a funerary altar was dedicated to a Marcus Cossutius, and a Marcus Cossutius Aphrodeisieus ("the Aphrodisian," i.e., from Aphrodisias-in-Caria) signed a statue base there in the Augustan period or shortly before.

Sculptors who were free citizens of Athens dominate the epigraphic record well into the first century AD, leaving their names in Greek on marble works both in their home city and abroad, in quantity at Olympia and Cyrene, also at Sparta, Butrint, on the Bay of Naples, and at Rome (Loewy 1885, nos. 313–46; Stewart 1979). Sculptors from other cities in Attica, from Paros, and from Asia Minor (Ephesus, Dokimeion, Nicomedia, Miletus, and Tralles) are also attested. A certain Carus of Puteoli caught the signature habit, perhaps having worked with an Athenian called Aphrodisios, since each made and signed (in Greek) a version of the same draped female figure type, both found at nearby Baiae (Zancani Montuoro 1933).

Traveling sculptors from Aphrodisias-in-Caria become more numerous as the Athenian signatures thin out (Squarciapino 1943). The city apparently had no previous tradition of marble sculpture and may have owed its expertise to Roman initiatives. The Aphrodisian M. Cossutius on Paros has already been mentioned; another Aphrodisian with a Roman *nomen*, Cornelius, signed a statue base at Olympia. Some took names with Latin endings, such as Koblanos, who signed as "his work" a statue of a youthful boxer in Pentelic marble at Surrentum (Bay of Naples) in the early first century AD. He or a near-contemporary namesake may have been the author of a portrait bust (his own?) found at Aphrodisias (Smith et al. 2006, 230, cat. no. 110, pls. 87–8). In the first

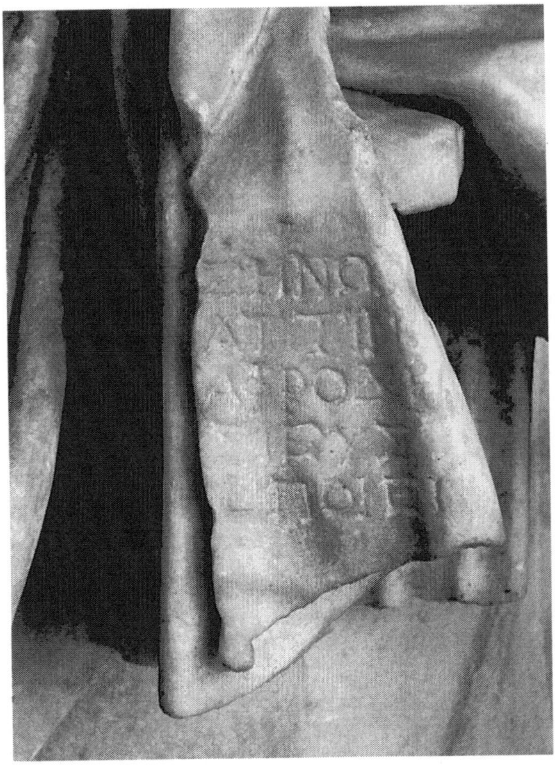

FIGURE 2.2.4 Signature of the sculptor Zenon, son of Attinas, of Aphrodisias, on a fold of drapery beside knee of a seated togate statue, c. AD 110. Rome, Palazzo Altemps, inv. no. 8641.

half of the second century AD a string of Aphrodisian sculptors called Zenas or Zenon and Alexandros signed works found at Lyttos on Crete, Syracuse, and Rome. In Rome, a Zenon, "having decorated many cities" built and decorated a tomb for his son with his own hands, while a Zenon, son of Attinas, signed a large statue of a seated philosopher (figure 2.2.4). The prestige of sculpture as an occupation at Aphrodisias in the Severan period is shown by an M. Aurelius Zenas, son of [. . .]nos, who made a statue of his sculptor father, on the occasion that he was honored by the Council and People for his "moral excellence" (Erim and Reynolds 1989, 533, no. 19, pl. 206). A youth called Aurelius Dionysos, with an equally long pedigree and said to be well-born, who had died before his time, was honored by the Council and People for his skill in the art of modeling (Erim and Reynolds 1989, 531, no. 18). A competition for statue makers (*agonaton agalmatopoioi*) held as part of public games around AD 190 was won by a sculptor whose name is lost, but his father's name is that of an important local family (Ritti 1971; Erim and Reynolds 1989, 530, no. 17). Three other Aphrodisian sculptors called Zenon, Chryseros, and Andronicus, who signed between them a group of at least twelve over-life-size statues found in fragments on the Esquiline Hill in Rome, were free citizens who all shared the imperial family name Flavius (Moltesen 2000). Zenon declares himself to be ἀρχιερεὺς καὶ διασημότατος (chief priest and *perfectissimus*), both titles indicating fairly high status, the latter an honor awarded for personal service to the emperor. It has been argued that this title must date from the fourth century AD (Roueché and Erim 1982), over a century later than the statues would normally be dated on stylistic and technical grounds, but this designation is not unknown in imperial circles in the second century AD.

That carving of marble sculpture was quite a respectable pursuit elsewhere in the Greek East in the second century AD is shown by *The Dream* or *Lucian's Career*. Lucian was born a citizen of Samosata in Syria in about AD 125. His grandfather had been a sculptor, two uncles were sculptors of some fame, and as a boy he had amazed his friends by his skill in modeling (like Dionysos at Aphrodisias). He tried his hand at marble, but broke a block and was punished by a beating, so he took up philosophy instead and a career of words.

Pride in authorship was probably the main motive behind the signatures discussed above. They had some precedents in the earlier Greek world, where the sculptors of a given work were named in small lettering on the front, side, or sometimes the back of its dedicatory base; from the first century BC onward these signatures move on to the work itself, to the front of the plinth, on the support, or on drapery at knee or ankle height. This struck Richter (1951b) as a negative development, but actually represents the normal eye level of a human spectator, making the signature more visible. Slaves, freedmen, and freeborn are all represented. The normal phrase used in the Greek signatures is "so-and-so made it," which might mean "had it made"; in Latin the verb is sometimes more explicit "carved it" or "by his hand." In Italy, Spain, and North Africa, the name in the genitive is quite often preceded by *ex officina* (from the workshop of), indicative of stronger team identity, though not necessarily a larger working unit (for examples and general discussion, Calabi Limentani 1958).

Bibliography

Andreae, B. 1992. "Die römischen Kopien in Marmor nach griechischen Meisterwerk in Bronze als Ausdruck der römischen Kultur." *StIt* 10: 21–30.

Ayres, J. 1985. *The Artist's Craft: A History of Tools, Techniques and Materials*. Oxford: Phaidon.

Barone, G. 1994. *Gessi del Museo di Sabratha*. Rome: "L'Erma" di Bretschneider.

Bernieri, A. 1983. *Storia di Carrara moderna (1815–1935)*. Pisa: Pacini.

Bluemel, C. 1969. *Greek Sculptors at Work*. Second edition, revised by B. Ross. London: Phaidon.

Bouras, C. 2011. "La circulation des pierres et le port d'Éphèse." In *Λευκός Λίθος: Marbres et autres pierres de la mediterraneé antique* (ASMOSIA 8), edited by P. Jockey, 495–508. Paris: Kathala.

Calabi Limentani, I. 1958. *Studi sulla società romana: Il lavoro artistico*. Milan: Istituto editoriale cisalpino.

Camodeca, G., F. Maniscalco, E. Ronchetti, and L. Russolillo. 2001. "Ricerche sul Vicus Lartidianus di Puteoli." In *Forma Maris*, edited by P. A. Gianfrotta and F. Maniscalco, 95–105. Naples: Massa.

Charles-Picard, G. 1961. "Sur une famille de sculpteurs d'Aquitaine, d'apres une stele funéraire du Musée de Bordeaux." *RA* 2: 96–100.

Claridge, A. 1985. "Sulla lavorazione dei marmi bianchi nella scultura di età romana." In *Marmi Antichi: Problemi d'impiego, di restauro e d'identificazione*, edited by P. Pensabene, 113–25. Rome: "L'Erma" di Bretschneider.

———. 1988. "Roman Statuary and the Supply of Statuary Marble." In *Ancient Marble Quarrying and Trade*, edited by J. Clayton Fant, 139–52. BAR-IS 453. Oxford: Archeopress.

———. 1990. "Ancient Techniques of Making Joins in Marble Statuary." In *Marble: Art Historical and Scientific Perspectives on Ancient Sculpture*, 135–62. Los Angeles: J. Paul Getty Museum.

Coarelli, F. 1970. "Polykles." *Studi miscellanei* 15: 81–9.

D'Alessandro, L., and F. Persegati. 1987. *Scultura e calchi in gesso*. Rome: "L'Erma" di Bretschneider.

D'Ambra, E. 1998. *Roman Art*. Cambridge: Cambridge University Press.

D'Arms, J. H. 1972. "CIL X.1792: A Municipal Notable of the Augustan Age." *HSCP* 76: 207–16.

Donderer, M. 1988. "Nicht Praxiteles, sondern Pasiteles: Eine signierte Statuenstütze in Verona." *ZPE* 73: 63–8.

Durnan, N. 2000. "Stone sculpture." In *Making Classical Art: Process and Practice*, edited by R. Ling, 18–36. Stroud: Tempus Publishing.

Erim, K. T., and J. M. Reynolds. 1989. "Sculptors of Aphrodisias in the Inscriptions of the City." In *Festschrift für Jale Inan*, edited by N. Başgelen **and** M. Lugal, 517–38. Istanbul: Arkeoloji ve Sanat Yayınları.

Gasparri, C. 1995. "L'officina dei calchi di Baia." *RM* 102: 173–87.

Hollinshead, M. B. 2002. "Extending the Reach of Marble: Struts in Greek and Roman Sculpture." In *The Ancient Art of Emulation*, edited by E. K. Gazda, 117–52. Ann Arbor: University of Michigan Press.

Landwehr, C. 1985. *Die antiken Gipsabgüsse aus Baiae: Griechische Bronzestatuen in Abgüssen römischer Zeit*. Berlin: Mann.

Loewy, E. 1885. *Inschriften griechischer Bildhauer mit Facsimiles*. Leipzig: B.G. Teubner.

Lorenz, T. 2009. "Rilievo con teste virili." In *L'antica Basilica di San Lorenzo in Damaso*. Vol. 2, *I materiali*, edited by C. L. Frommel and M. Pentiricci, 99–101. Rome: De Luca.

Mackensen, M. 2000. "Erster Bericht über neue archäologische Untersuchungen im sog. Arbeits- und Steinbruchlager von *Simitthus*/Chemtou (Nordwesttunisien)." *RM* 102: 487–503.

Magenta, C. 1866. *L'industria dei marmi di Carrara, Massa e Serravezza*. Florence: Tip Regno d'Italia G. Faziola.

Maischberger, M. 1997. *Marmor in Rom: Anlieferung, Lager- und Werkplätze in der Kaiserzeit*. Wiesbaden: Dr. Ludwig Reichert.

Marcadé, J. 1969. *Au Musée de Délos: Étude sur la sculpture hellénistique en ronde bosse découverte dans l'île*. BÉFAR 215. Paris: E. de Boccard.

Moltesen, M. 2000. "The Esquiline Group: Aphrodisian Statues in the Ny Carlsberg Glyptotek." *AntP* 27: 111–29.

Mustilli, D. 1950. "Botteghe di scultori, marmorari, bronzieri e caelatores in Pompeji." In *Pompeiana: Raccolta di studi per il secondo centenario degli scavi di Pompei*, edited by A. Maiuri, 206–29. Naples: Gaetano Macchiaroli.

Nolte, S. 2006. *Steinbruch-Werkstatt-Skulptur: Untersuchungen zu Aufbau und Organisation griechischer Bildhauerwwerkstätten*. Göttingen: Vandenhoeck and Ruprecht.

Pfanner, M. 1988. "Vom 'laufenden Bohrer' bis zum 'bohrlosen Stil': Überlegungen zur Bohrtechnik in der Antike." *AA* 1988: 667–76.

———. 1989. "Über das Herstellen von Porträts: Ein Beitrag zu Rationalisierungsmassnahmen und Produktionsmechanismen von Massenware im späten Hellenismus und in der römischen Kaiserzeit." *JdI* 104: 157–257.

Rakob, F. 1993. *Simitthus*. Vol. 1. *Die Steinbrücke und die antike Stadt*. Mainz: Philipp von Zabern.

Rawson, E. 1975. "Architecture and Sculpture: The Activities of the Cossutii." *PBSR* 43: 36–47.

Richter, G. M. A. 1951a. *Three Critical Periods in Greek Sculpture*. Oxford: Clarendon Press.

———. 1951b. "Who Made the Roman Portrait Statues—Greeks or Romans?" *PAPS* 95: 184–91.

Ritti, T. 1971. "Gare di scultura ad Afrodisia." *RendAccLinc* series 8, 26: 189–97.

Rockwell, P. 1989. *Lavorare la pietra: Manuale per l'archeologo, lo storico dell'arte e il restauratore*. Rome: Nuova Italia Scientifica.

———. 1991. "Unfinished Statuary Associated with a Sculptor's Studio." In *Aphrodisias Papers 2*, edited by R. R. R. Smith and K. T. Erim, 127–43. JRA Supplement 2. Ann Arbor: University of Michigan.

———. 1993a. *The Art of Stoneworking: A Reference Guide*. Cambridge: Cambridge University Press.

———. 1993b. "Tools in Ancient Marble Sculpture." In *Archeologia delle attività estrattive e metallurgiche*, edited by R. Frankovich, 177–94. Florence: All'insegna del Giglio.

Roueché, C., and K. Erim. 1982. "Sculptors from Aphrodisias: Some New Inscriptions." *PBSR* 50: 102–115.

Rüger, C. B. 1997. "Zu Marmorschalen in Chemtou." *RM* 104: 379–85.

Slim, H. 1996. *El Jem: Ancient Thysdrus*. Tunis: ALIF.

Smith, R. R. R. 2011. "Marble Workshops at Aphrodisias." In *Roman Sculpture in Asia Minor*, edited by F. D'Andria and I. Romeo, 63–76. JRA Supplement 80. Portsmouth, RI: Journal of Roman Archaeology.

Smith, R. R. R., S. Dillon, C. H. Hallett, J. Lenaghan, and J. Van Voorhis. 2006. "Production and Technique." *Roman portrait statuary from Aphrodisias*, 29–34. Aphrodisias 2. Mainz: Philipp von Zabern.

Squarciapino, M. F. 1943. *La Scuola di Afrodisia*. Studi e materiali del Museo dell'Impero Romano 3. Rome: Governatorato di Roma.

Stewart, A. F. 1979. *Attika: Studies in Athenian Sculpture of the Hellenistic Age*. Supplementary Paper 14. London: Society for the Promotion of Hellenic Studies.

Tortorella, S. 1988. "Il rilievo dell'extispicium del Museo del Louvre" *ScAnt* 2: 476–95.

Ungaro, L., and M. P. Del Moro. 2007. *Il museo dei fori imperiali*. Milan: Electa.

Van Voorhis, J. 1998. "Apprentices' Pieces and the Training of Sculptors at Aphrodisias." *JRA* 11: 175–92.

———. 2012. "The Working and Re-working of Marble Statuary at the Sculptor's Workshop at Aphrodisias." In *Ateliers and Artisans in Roman Art and Archaeology*, edited by T. M. Kristensen and B. Poulsen, 38–54. JRA Supplement 92. Portsmouth, RI: Journal of Roman Archaeology.

Waelkens, M. 1982. *Dokimeion: Die Werkstatt der repräsentativen kleinasiatischen Sarkophage: Chronologie und Typologie ihrer Produktion*. Berlin: Mann.

Wiegartz, H. 1974. "Marmorhandel, Sarkophagherstellung und die Lokalisierung der kleinasiatischen Säulensarkophage." In *Mansel'e Armağan = Mélanges Mansel I*, edited by E. Akurgal and U. B. Alkim, 345–83. Ankara: Türk Tarih Kurumu Basımevi.

Zancani Montuoro, P. 1933. "Repliche romane di una statua fidiaca." *BullCom* 61: 25–58.

Zimmer, G. 1982. *Römische Berufsdarstellungen*. Berlin: Mann.

CHAPTER 2.3

REUSE AND RECARVING

Technical Evidence

ERIC R. VARNER

INTRODUCTION

ROMAN history, across time and media, encompassed an entrenched culture of reuse. During the height of the Republic, sculptures were recontextualized in Rome on a vast scale. Victorious generals such as Lucius Mummius and Marcus Marcellus spoliated Corinth and Syracuse of their statues and transferred them to Rome for display (Rutledge 2012, 32–45). In the late first century BC, an entire group of pedimental sculpture, likely from the fifth-century Temple of Apollo at Eretria, was imported to Rome, where it adorned the newly renovated Temple of Apollo Medicus (figure 6.3.1, see essay 6.3, Shaya; La Rocca 1985, 76–8).

Nowhere is the Roman tendency to recycle more readily apparent than in portrait sculpture. In the imperial period, countless surviving Roman likenesses in marble reveal rich histories of multiple identities. A recent survey of the practice lists over 500 recarved images encompassing both private representations and imperial images and spanning the first through fifth centuries AD (Prusac 2011, 131–58). In all cases, the original iterations of the portraits are disclosed through legible technical traces of recutting. New identities never entirely obliterate the initial likeness through simple superimposition. The reconfiguration of a portrait, especially mass-produced images of emperors or other imperial family members, results in a cumulative composition whose hybrid elements act as semantic signs that can be likened to intertextual references in Roman literature (Galinsky 2008). In effect, the visual clues left in recut likenesses act like embedded quotations in literature that refer back to earlier compositions, although the degree of intentionality may not be as intense or self-conscious as in the texts.

The recarving of Roman sculpture was clearly recognized in the early twentieth century, especially in the Cancelleria reliefs (Magi 1945) and the recut portraits from the Trajanic, Hadrianic, and Aurelian reliefs reused on the arch of Constantine

(L'Orange and Von Gerkan 1939; Leander Touati 1987), as well as the erasures on the interior panels depicting the Severan family from the Arch of the Argentarii (Haynes and Hirst 1939) and the Aurelian panels of Triumph and Liberalitas where Commodus was excised (Ryberg 1967; Angelicoussis 1984). However, the issue of reuse in Roman sculpture did not begin to be fully explored until the publication of H. Blanck's groundbreaking monograph of 1969, *Wiederverwendung alter Statuen als Ehrendenkmäler bei Griechen und Römern*. Blanck's work exposed the widespread nature of sculptural reuse and opened new avenues for reinterpreting significant numbers of Roman sculptures. Within approximately a decade, three important treatments had appeared that focused on the recarved marble likenesses of Rome's "bad" emperors of the first century, Caligula, Nero, and Domitian, as a result of memory sanctions (*damnatio memoriae*) enacted against them (Bergmann and Zanker 1981; Jucker 1981; Pollini 1984). Beginning in the 1980s, most catalogs of Roman portrait sculpture have paid very close attention to technical analyses of recarving (see for example Fittschen and Zanker 1983; 1985; Boschung 1989; Johansen 1994–5; Alexandridis 2004; Fittschen, Zanker, and Cain 2010), as have more general handbooks (Kleiner 1992; Fejfer 2008; Bol 2010) and monographs such as those of C. Brian Rose (1997) and Dietrich Boschung (2002) on Julio-Claudian dynastic groups. Articles and monographs have explored further the technical aspects of recut portraits and refined their corpus (for example, Harrison 1990; Varner 2004; Prusac 2006; Ambrogi 2009–10; Prusac 2011; and articles from a symposium, "The Good, the Bad and the Altered," organized by Gregory Bucher at Creighton University in 2009: Bucher and Freeman 2010; De Puma 2010; Pollini and Storage 2010; Varner 2010; for some alternative perspectives, see also Fittschen 2012). This essay will focus on close technical analysis of surviving marble portraits, as well as gem portraits, to reveal the widespread nature of reuse that encompasses imperial and private likenesses ranging from the republican through the late Roman period. As will be shown, the large body of evidence also holds important aesthetic and historiographical implications for the production and reception of portrait images.

Techniques of Transformation

Like all reworked sculpture, altered portraits exhibit anomalies of form, proportion, and carving technique. In most cases, these sculptural redactions required substantial modifications to the physiognomy and coiffure to transform one likeness into another effectively. Certain aspects of the portrait, however, generally remained fixed, such as the position of the eyes, nose, mouth, and ears. Noses and ears in particular are especially difficult to recut, because they are projecting elements. In some instances, sculptors opted to replace these protruding elements entirely, as in the case of a portrait of Elagabalus remodeled as his younger cousin and successor, Severus Alexander, now on display in the Centrale Montemartini (inv. no. 2457, h. 0.255 m.: Fittschen and Zanker 1985, 121–2, no. 101, pl. 124). The contours of eyes could be slightly altered by redrilling the tear ducts and reshaping with flat and rounded chisels. Jawlines and chins could be reconfigured, most usually with flat and claw chisels. Point and claw chisels were also efficient tools for initially removing elements of the coiffure before retooling with the flat chisel or drill. In some cases, especially at the back of the head where details would be less visible, sculptors never went beyond the removal process with point and claw chisels. Recarved sculptures were usually refinished with the rasp in order to give the new image consistent surfaces, although discrepancies between old and new finishes can be discernible.

The emendations to marble sculptures often resulted in noticeable asymmetries of the eyes and mouth, as well as chins that recede from the frontal plane of the face. As supporting elements, the necks of recarved portraits are minimally modified and, as a result, can appear disproportionately thick in comparison with the reduced sculptural volumes of the face.

The delicate foliage of wreaths like the *corona civica*, with its serrated oak leaves, or the *corona triumphalis*, with laurel, are often substantially undercut or deeply drilled and almost impossible to refashion. In many recut portraits with wreaths, the headgear as well as the top of the head are left substantially intact, again resulting in visible disproportionalities between the upper and lower sections of the image. For example, a head of Caligula from the cycle of Julio-Claudian images at ancient Rusellae was reconfigured as Claudius (figure 2.3.1, Grosseto Museo Archeologico e d'Arte della Maremma, inv. no. 97765: Rose 1997, 116–18, cat. 44, esp. 118; Boschung 2002, 70, no. 20.9, pl. 60.1). Caligula's individual locks were removed with the punch and claw chisels, and the *corona civica* remains untouched. As a result, the crown and top of the head are considerably larger than the reduced proportions of the recarved facial features.

Precisely the same stonemasons who created sculpture *ex novo* were employed to recarve marbles and, as noted, they used the same basic tools of point chisel, flat chisel, claw chisel, and drill. Peter Rockwell's groundbreaking work on stone-carving techniques, together with Dietrich Boschung and Michael Pfanner's explorations of portrait production, have facilitated the physical analysis of reconfigured images in terms of techniques and tool marks, and further underscored that the recarving of portraits posed enormous technical challenges, because of the relatively fixed positions of the sensory organs as well as the limited sculptural volumes with which to work (Rockwell 1993; 1996; 1999; Boschung and Pfanner 1988; Pfanner 1989). New developments in three-dimensional imaging that model the new portrait within the envelope of the original likeness in particular should provide enormous amounts of useful new evidence (Pollini and Storage 2010; see essay 1.5, Frischer).

In fact, recutting a portrait was a far more difficult sculptural operation than starting from scratch. Although sometimes attributed primarily to economic motives, the choice to recarve sculpture can be much more ideologically and aesthetically driven, as attested by the large numbers of finely recarved imperial portraits of the first and early second centuries AD, reused during periods of acknowledged economic prosperity. Indeed, by the first century AD, sculptors, especially portrait specialists working in Rome and its environs, had acquired an admirable facility with the techniques of recutting preexisting

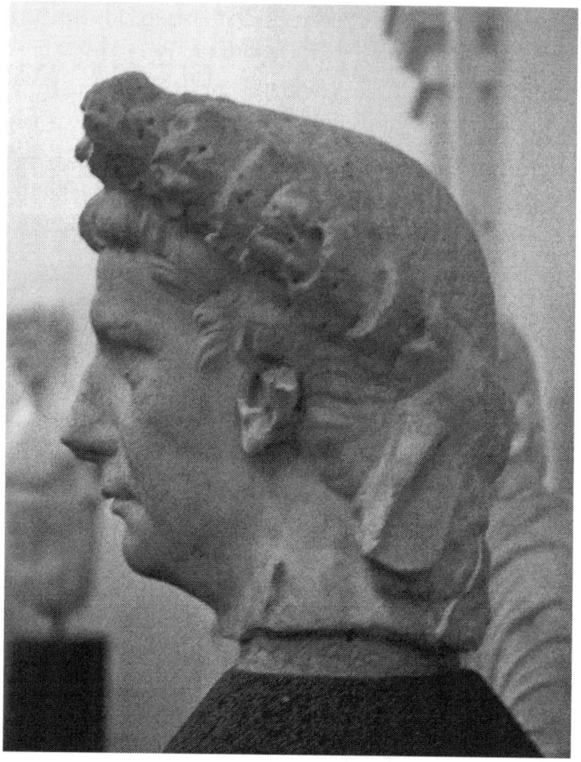

FIGURE 2.3.1 Caligula/Claudius. Grosseto, Museo Archeologico e d'Arte della Maremma, inv. no. 97765.

sculptures. Close examination of sculptural details and approaches to design on the column of Marcus Aurelius has revealed individual ateliers of sculptors at work on the monument (Beckmann 2011), and it seems likely that there may have been specific workshops at the capital that subspecialized in recarving portraits. While reconfigured imperial images are found most frequently in the environs of Rome, numerous examples from the provinces attest to a wide diffusion of the technical processes associated with reuse throughout the empire, as in a colossal head of Nero recut to Augustus from Athribis in Egypt (Alexandria, Graeco-Roman Museum, h. 0.79 m.: Bonacasa 1972). The sculptor's workshop at Aphrodisias also provides important evidence from the provinces for the practice of resculpting preexisting portraits. The transformation of a large third-century bust of a philosopher into a private portrait in the fourth century was never completed. The interruption of the work may have been caused by insurmountable technical difficulties relating to the size and placement of the original ears in relation to the substantially reduced proportions of the new face, or, intriguingly, the piece may have been used in training apprentice sculptors in the art of recarving (Van Voorhis 2012, 48, fig. 7).

Portraits of condemned emperors and other members of the imperial family were also redeployed negatively through disfigurement, as for instance a bronze bust of Caligula in a Swiss private collection (see figure 6.6.1, and essay 6.6, Kristensen). Often the sensory organs are attacked, with mutilations to the eyes, nose, mouth, and ears of the image. Defaced images, then, were repurposed as a negative testament to the condemned individual's posthumous reputation. Evidence in disfigured marble portraits for the same kinds of chisels and mallets used in stone carving suggest that sculptors themselves were active agents in mutilating likenesses, just as they recarved portraits into new representations. Sculpture was also reused through "reinscription," when the dedicatory inscriptions on statue bases were recarved (Højte 2005). Recarved or replacement portraits could accompany the newly inscribed or reinscribed bases. In many cases, however, the statues that accompanied the bases do not appear to have been modified. Reinscription encompassed both imperial and private portraits and was especially common in the eastern Mediterranean, where many earlier classical and Hellenistic statues were reused with amended inscriptions (Platt 2007; Shear 2007; Keesling 2010; Krumeich 2010). Dio Chrysostom famously decried the practice at Rhodes (*Or.* 31.8).

Transformative Histories

Already in the late Republic, the Roman cultural proclivity for reusing sculpture is plainly evident. For example, two seated statues of Greek poets were transformed with recut Roman portrait heads. The head of a seated statue of the new comedy poet Posidippus was recarved into an anonymous Roman (figure 2.3.2). Primarily the flat chisel was used to recut the facial features and hair entirely, but remnants of the original hair locks and the inscription on the base of the statue confirm its original identity (Musei Vaticani, Galleria delle Statue, inv. no. 735: Fittschen 1992; Zanker 1995, 137–45; Spinola 1999, 42–4, no. 51; Dillon 2006, 93–5). The statue body has been left intact with its Greek tunic and *himation*, but the shoes have also been refashioned tellingly into elite Roman footgear, the *calcei senatorii* or the *calcei patricii* (Fittschen 1992, 236–7). Apparently the Roman patron, sculptor, and viewers were not troubled by the combination of a veristic late republican portrait head with the inscribed statue body of a Greek poet, undoubtedly meant to communicate the intellectual accomplishments and refinements of the sitter. The recut Posidippus was discovered together with another seated statue of a poet, the Pseudo-Menander, at S. Lorenzo in Panisperna under the pontificate of Sixtus V, and it too had been remodeled with a veristic portrait head (Musei Vaticani, Galleria delle Statue, inv. no. 588: Fittschen 1992; Zanker 1995, 143; Spinola 1999, 41–2, no. 50).

In the later Republic, the phenomenon is by no means limited to Greek poets transformed into Roman citizens. A portrait of a woman in the Centrale Montemartini has had her initial melon hairstyle modified into the *nodus* coiffure made popular by Augustus's wife, Livia, and his sister, Octavia, c. 40–30 BC (figure 2.3.3; inv. no. 3356, h. 0.35 m.: Fittschen and Zanker 1983, 38, no. 40, pls. 50–51). The rolled plaits of the melon are still visible at the sides and back of the head, but were carved away over the temples where large rectangular mortises were chiseled into the old coiffure to anchor

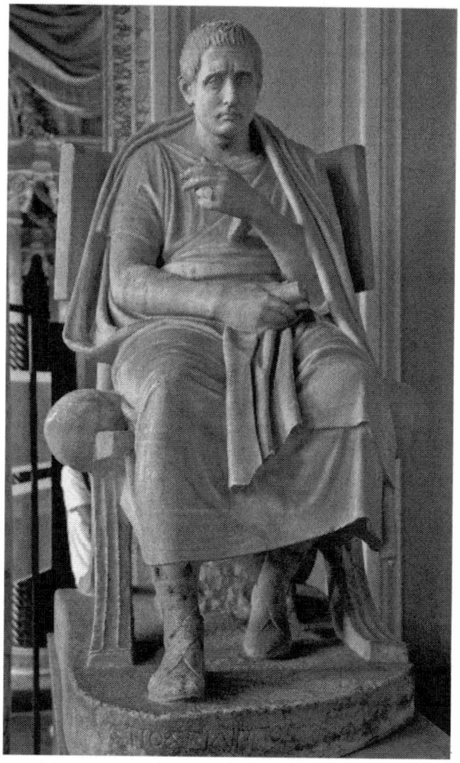

FIGURE 2.3.2 Posidippus/late republican portrait. Rome, Musei Vaticani, Galleria delle Statue, inv. no. 735.

separately worked marble pieces of the new coiffure, which likely would have resembled the waves of hair brushed back over braids along the sides of the face comparable to contemporary *nodus* portraits of Livia and Octavia. A flat section over the forehead was chiseled back for the addition of the *nodus* itself. The sitter's original *mellonenfrisur* would have been closely associated with Cleopatra VII, as seen for instance in a portrait likely carved in Rome during her sojourn there between 46 and 44 BC (Musei Vaticani, Museo Gregoriano Profano, inv. no. 38511, h. 0.39 m., from the Villa of the Quintilii: Ricci 1998, 95, no. 37, pl. 8; Walker and Higgs 2001, 218–19, no. 196). The change from the melon hairstyle associated with Cleopatra and her Ptolemaic ancestresses, like Arsinoe II, to the more emphatically Roman *nodus* championed by Livia and Octavia almost certainly reflects the shifting political allegiances of the sitter and her family in the years surrounding the Battle of Actium and the defeat of Antony and Cleopatra. The insertion of the portrait into the more honorific herm format furthermore indicates that the subject is of some importance.

By the early imperial period, it is the memory sanctions leveled against Rome's condemned emperors that provide the major impetus for sculptural transformations in portraiture. Marble images of Caligula, Nero, and Domitian that ranged from life-sized to colossal formats were recarved in vast numbers. These likenesses were

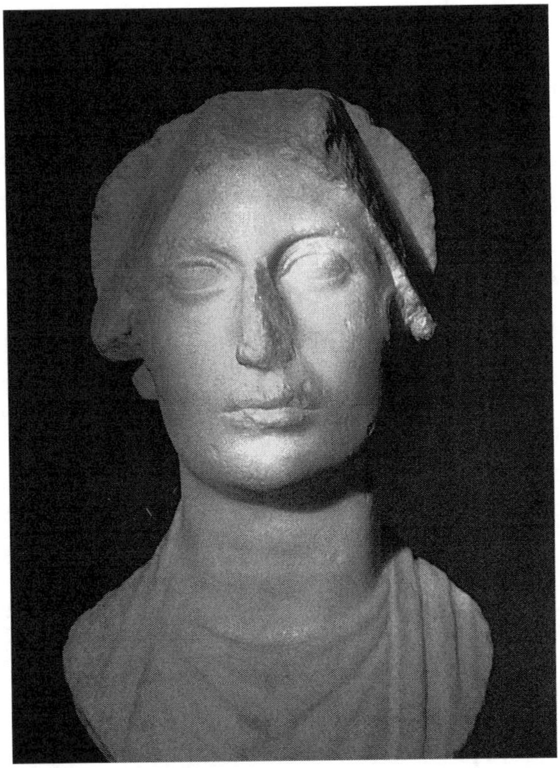

FIGURE 2.3.3 Late republican female portrait. Rome, Centrale Montemartini, inv. no. 3356.

usually reconfigured into representations of immediate successors, or revered predecessors, most often Augustus. For instance, at least fifteen portraits of Caligula have been recarved into depictions of Claudius, while at minimum twelve have been recut to Augustus (see Prusac 2011, 131–3, nos. 6–14, 16–18, 33–47). The political ramifications of these transfigurations are clear as the images of condemned emperors are coopted by the new regime.

Close technical analysis of many of these portraits, however, also holds important implications for methodological and historiographical developments in the discipline. An important bust of Claudius in Kassel exhibits clear traces of its reworking, including remnants of point and claw chisel marks over most of the back of the head where the original coiffure has been removed (Museumlandschaft Hessen Kassel Antikensammlung Schloss Wilhelmsöhe, inv. no. SK 116, h. 0.535 m.: Gercke and Zimmermann-Elseify 2007, 230–32, no. 73). Nevertheless, several locks of the original hairstyle—including the beginnings of the swallowtail part on the nape of the neck at the back of the head, a characteristic feature of Caligula's coiffures—are still visible. The flat chisel was used to smooth down the areas on the neck where Caligula's hair was removed. The hair on the top of the head, over the forehead, and around the ears was entirely rechiseled. The overall volume of the face was reduced and the chin recedes from the frontal plane, but the smoothly modeled and youthful appearance of the facial features was largely retained from the original Caligulan likeness. This head has been singled out as best representative of an entire type of Claudius's portraits, the "Kassel Type" (see Boschung 1993, 70), yet most of its salient features are the direct result of recarving, rather than any putative affinities with a prototype. A second variant of Claudius's Kassel type has also been reconfigured from a likeness of Caligula and at some later period combined with a Trajanic or Hadrianic statue body draped with a *paludamentum* to which the head did not originally belong (Aquileia, Museo, inv. no. 57, h. 2.01 m.: Mian 2009, 180–86, fig. 2), while a third example of the Kassel type in Athens also seems to have been recarved from Caligula (Athens, National Archaeological Museum, inv. no. 430, h. 0.42 m.: Kaltsas 2002, 318, no. 665). Indeed, several of the most important formal aspects of the entire type, including the youthful facial features and longer hair, have more in common with the representations of Caligula; at least three of the seven commonly identified replicas of the Kassel type were recut from earlier portraits.

Small-scale glyptic portraits on cameos could also be recarved. A portrait of Claudius in Vienna (Kunsthistorisches Museum 18, inv. no. IX A 23, h. 14.5 cm: Boschung 1989, 51–2, 90, 116, no. 36, sketch 29, pl. 30.4) was recut from Caligula, while a depiction of Titus in Florence originally portrayed Nero (Florence, Museo Archeologico, inv. no. 14546, 7.9 x 6.5 cm: Megow 1993). In the Vienna cameo, the veil that covered Caligula's head was cut away and a laurel crown carved out of it. In the Florence cameo, the remains of Nero's coiffure are clearly visible behind the laurel crown. In general, the recarved cameos exhibit the same sculptural anomalies as their marble counterparts, albeit in smaller scale. In one unique example, a rock crystal intaglio was recut, with a figure of Victory carved over a preexisting figure of Geta sacrificing together with Caracalla and Septimius Severus (Atlanta, Emory University, Michael C. Carlos Museum, inv. no. 2003.25.2: Varner 2004, 77, 172, 277–8, no. 7.9). The recarving of imperial gem portraits would continue well into late antiquity (Gagetti 2011).

Very rarely, imperial female portraits were subjected to reconfiguration. A statue of Agrippina from Herculaneum was refashioned from a portrait of Messalina, her predecessor as Claudius's wife (Museo Archeologico Nazionale di Napoli, inv. no. 6242, h. 1.81 m.: Wood 1999, 247, n. 114; Tomei and Rea 2011, 234, no. 13). As with the Posidippus and Pseudo-Menander from the late Republic, the statue body was left untouched, but the portrait head was resculpted and the coiffure completely modified. The chisel was used to transform Messalina's coiffure, which consisted of deeply drilled curls, into Agrippina's arrangement of modeled waves running along the side of the head from a central part. The waves framing the face are uncharacteristically punctuated with drilled holes, which are in fact the remains of the drilled voids at the center of the ringlets that would have been part of Messalina's original coiffure. The face has been only minimally redone and the resulting likeness is more generic and bland than many of Agrippina's portraits. The substantial reduction in the volume of the hair that occurred as a result of the recarving has made the coiffure somewhat flat in comparison to the majority of Agrippina's other images.

Male imperial portraits in marble continued to be modified into the early second century. Like Caligula and Nero before him, Domitian was subjected to memory sanctions after his assassination on 18 September AD 96. At least twenty-six of his images were physically recarved into representations of his successors, Nerva and Trajan, and occasionally his predecessor, Titus (Prusac 2011, 115–39, 91–2). Indeed, thirteen of Nerva's sixteen extant likenesses (approximately 80 percent) initially depicted Domitian, which underscores how entrenched the practice of sculptural recycling had become. After Domitian, however, the recarving of imperial portraits witnesses a virtual hiatus of over a century.

Private portraits were, however, recarved in the second and early third centuries, and Prusac catalogues ten male and twenty-four female portraits from this period (2011, 138–9, nos. 148–58; 140–41, nos. 173–97). The reconfiguration of female portraits often concentrated on the coiffure: hairstyles in many portraits were removed in their entirety and replaced with new marble wigs (Brilliant 1975; Hermann 1991). A portrait of a Hadrianic woman in the Museo Capitolino has had its original hair removed, likely with point and claw chisels, to add a new Severan nest coiffure carved from a separate piece of marble (figure 2.3.4; Rome, Museo Capitolino, Stanza degli Imperatori 35, inv. no. 488, h. 0.575 m.: Fittschen and Zanker 1983, 104–6, no. 155; Prusac 2011, no. 193, fig. 11a–b). The join of the new marble wig to the head is clearly visible and mimics the way in which

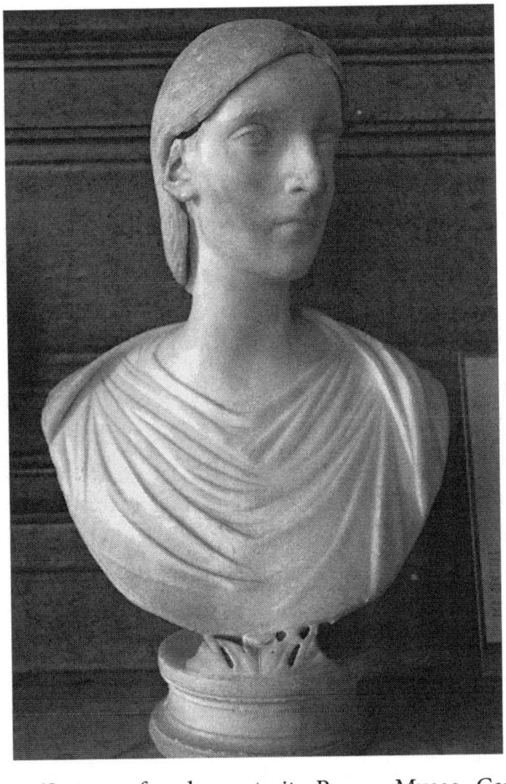

FIGURE 2.3.4 Hadrianic/Severan female portrait. Rome, Museo Capitolino, Stanza degli Imperatori 35, inv. no. 488.

real wigs made out of hair sit on top of the head. The facial features have also been substantially adapted and the ears completely rechiseled from the original mass of the portrait. The drilled indentation of the initial ear canal is still visible in front of the new ear, which sits in front of the marble wig. The eyes have also been recarved and the tear ducts redrilled. The substantial sculptural alterations of the portrait create disproportional relationships among the wig, head, neck, and bust.

Some of the reconfigured portraits from the second and early third centuries could cross gender boundaries, including a Severan woman in Copenhagen recarved from a representation of Antinous and a Severan girl recut from a Hadrianic togate male bust (Ny Carlsberg Glyptotek, inv. no. 3286, h. 0.32 m.: Johansen 1994–5, 3: 200–201, no. 88; Museo Capitolino, Vestibolo, inv. no. 2746, h. 0.425 m.: Fittschen and Zanker 1983, 103–4, no. 152, pl. 180; on male-to-female and female-to-male reconfigurations, see Prusac 2011, 112–13). Other remodeled portraits—like those carved from architectural elements—crossed entire boundaries of sculptural categories. Examples include a male portrait sculpted out of an anta capital (Princeton University, Art Museum, inv. no. 1953.25, h. 0.375 m.: Antonaccio 1992), a female portrait recut from an architectural fragment with *cymation* molding (Ny Carlsberg Glyptotek, inv. no. 1860, h. 0.38 m.: Johansen 1994–5, 3: 206, no. 91), a female portrait carved from a helmeted deity, perhaps Minerva or Mars (Princeton University, Art Museum, 1989.55, h. 0.305 m.: Prusac 2011, 140, no. 169), and a female portrait recrafted from a colossal toe, presumably from a statue of a deity (Stuttgart, Württembergisches Landesmuseum, inv. no. 1.13: Galinsky 2008, 12, fig. 15).

By the middle of the third century, imperial portraits begin to be recarved again in large numbers, although the reconfigurations are no longer occasioned by memory sanctions leveled against "bad" emperors. Several portraits of Gallienus, of his first and second types, were recut both from representations of revered Julio-Claudian predecessors and from images of Hadrian; recarved portraits of Gallienus include a portrait refashioned from Augustus in Copenhagen and another from Hadrian in Rome (Ny Carlsberg Glyptotek 768, inv. no. 832, h. 0.53 m.: Johansen 1994–5, 3: 128, no. 53; Museo Torlonia, inv. no. 603: Prusac 2006, 113, fig. 6; Prusac 2011, 142, no. 213, fig. 20a–b). Here, the sculptural recycling is positively motivated and designed to link the current emperor Gallienus with good emperors of the past. Similar sculptural reconfigurations may have been carried out in relief sculpture as well; evidence for recutting of the coiffure of Hadrian suggests that the reliefs from the Arco di Portogallo were updated, possibly with portraits of Gallienus substituted for Hadrian and of Gallienus's mother Mariniana for Sabina (La Rocca 1986, 29–30; Kleiner 1992, 134, 235, 445; Kinney 1997, 133–4; Prusac 2006, 115; 2011, 52; Tortorella 2011, 309). Modifications to imperial reliefs in Rome would continue in the later third and early fourth centuries with the recarving of the Claudian reliefs for the Arcus Novus reconfigured to celebrate the *decennalia* of Maximian and Diocletian in 293 (Laubscher 1976; Kinney 1997, 129–33, 145–6; for the recarved portraits, see in particular Cagiano de Azevedo 1951, 40, no. 11, pl. 5; 46–8, no. 21, pl. 19), and the Trajanic, Hadrianic, and Aurelian reliefs reworked for the Arch of Constantine. Indeed, the principate of Gallienus initiates a long period in the history of Roman imperial portraiture that is marked by a profound preference for recycled images. Two representations of Maxentius have been recarved from preexisting likenesses of Augustus and evoke similar ideological associations of the new emperor with Augustus as in the reworked portraits of Gallienus (Ostia, Museo, inv. no. 70: Blanck 1969, 54, no. A 31, pls. 22–3; Romeo 1999, 211, figs. 31–2; Prusac 2011, 143, no. 233; [formerly] Rome, private collection: Giuliano 1991, 7, figs. 5–8; Parisi Presicce 2012, 110). Constantine continues the practice, and the majority of his surviving type 2 portraits, introduced in 311 to mark his *quinquennalia*, are recarved from earlier images. Constantine's portraits are recycled from Augustan, Trajanic, and Hadrianic images, as well as from likenesses of his defeated rival Maxentius (Fittschen and Zanker 1985, 149–51; Knudsen 1988; Evers 1991, 799–800; Romeo 1999; Schäfer 1999; Hannestad 2007; La Rocca and Zanker 2007; Ambrogi 2009–2010, 342, n. 111; Parisi Presicce 2012, 112–13). A colossal head of one of Constantine's sons, either Constantius II or Constans, has also been reconfigured from an earlier portrait and confirms the continuation of sculptural repurposing in the later Constantinian period (figure 2.3.5; Palazzo dei Conservatori, Sala dei Fasti Moderni, inv. no. 2822, h. 0.96 m.: Fittschen and Zanker 1985, 156–7, no. 125, pl. 156). The coiffure at the back of the head has been worked away with point and claw chisels, and the facial

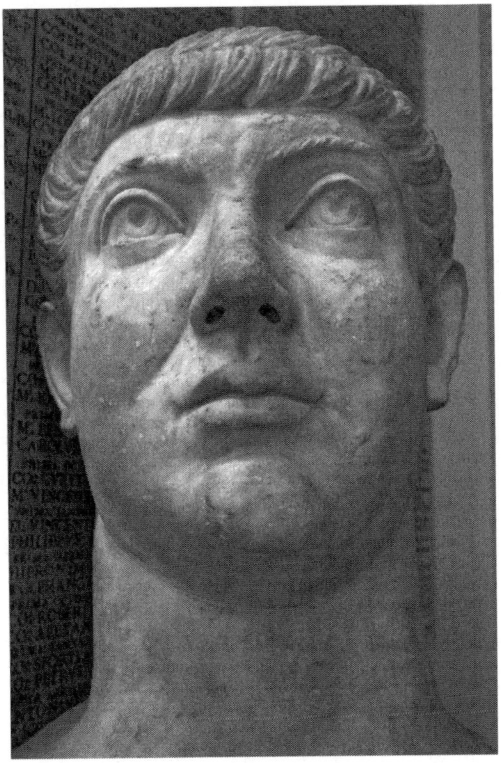

FIGURE 2.3.5 Constantius II or Constans (?), recarved from an earlier imperial portrait. Rome, Palazzo dei Conservatori, Sala dei Fasti Moderni, inv. no. 2822.

features and coiffure substantially reformulated with the flat chisel. The eyes have been enlarged and the tear ducts deeply drilled. The direction of the locks around the ears suggests that the original colossus may have been a replica of Trajan's first portrait type.

Conclusion: Aesthetics, Ideology, and Legibility

Awareness and examination of Roman sculptural praxis greatly inform the interpretation and meaning of Roman statuary. Technical as well as stylistic analysis is also of fundamental importance for deciphering early modern restoration and repair of Roman sculpture (Bianchi Bandinelli 1946; Grossman, Podany, and True 2003; see also essay 1.2, Podany). For ancient Romans, Peter Stewart has highlighted the cultural significance of statues as Rome's "other population," as well as their function as *simulacra* and *signa* (2003). The technical transformation of these images through recarving and reuse, as well as through mutilation, was not merely an opportunistic strategy for repurposing, but rather held important aesthetic and ideological implications for ancient audiences (Vout 2008). Changes effected by sculptors were not rote mechanical operations devoid of signification, but instead active modes of communication between image and viewer.

Ideological imperatives are readily discernible in works like the Cancelleria Reliefs, where the recarving of Domitian into Nerva facilitates a displacement of historical and political events. Nevertheless, repurposing of sculpture took part in a broader cultural aesthetic of reuse, which by the late Roman period was predominant. Massive amounts of sculpture became available in the later third century for often creative recontextualization as a direct result of the urban dislocations occasioned by the construction of the Aurelian Walls (Coates-Stephens 2001). Reuse of sculpture as spolia activated concepts of *renovatio memoriae* and *translatio memoriae* (Kinney 1997; Hansen 2003), where older monuments and their associated memories could be renovated, revived, or translated into new identities entirely. Repurposed sculptures were quite literally *rediviva saxa*, "renewed stones" (*Cod. Theod.* 15.1.19; Alchermes 1994, 167n2).

Although the Romans reused both figural and architectural marble sculpture across time and in vast quantities, portrait heads provide some of the most compelling evidence for recarving. The bodies of portrait statues themselves were seldom recut, but were reconfigured with substituted heads or altered inscriptions. The transformative process was mostly confined to one likeness reconfigured as another of similar scale, but singular instances of architectural or other types of sculpture recut as portraits, as well as striking discrepancies in scale between the original and altered image, underscore the pervasive and entrenched nature of the practice.

The reconfiguration of Roman sculpture, especially in portraits, was almost always legible and operative in individual as well as communal and cultural memory for several generations (Elsner 2003; Assmann 2006, 8–9). It is precisely the technical evidence preserved in transformed sculptures that gives meaning—both ideological and aesthetic—to the changes that have occurred and allows those changes to be legible. In addition, the substantial technical challenges entailed in the recutting of preexisting images confirm that recarving was not a rote or mechanical repurposing, but rather an intentional and deliberate choice on the part of sculptors and patrons with deeply embedded cultural, historical, and political significance.

Bibliography

Alchermes, J. 1994. "Spolia in Roman Cities of the Late Empire: Legislative Rationales and Architectural Reuse." *DOP* 48: 167–78.

Alexandridis, A. 2004. *Die Frauen der römischen Kaiserhauses: Eine Untersuchung ihrer bildlichen Darstellung von Livia bis Iulia Domna*. Mainz: Philipp von Zabern.

Ambrogi, A. 2009–2010. "Una statua togata dal 'Ginasio Romano' di Siracusa: Un caso di riempiego nella Sicilia tardoantica." *RendPontAcc* 82: 293–371.

Angelicoussis, E. 1984. "The Panel Reliefs of Marcus Aurelius." *RM* 91: 141–205.

Antonaccio, C. 1992. "Style, Reuse and Context in a Roman Portrait at Princeton." *AA* 1992: 441–52.

Assmann, J. 2006. *Religion and Cultural Memory: Ten Studies*. Translated by R. Livingston. Palo Alto: Stanford University Press.

Beckmann, M. 2011. *The Column of Marcus Aurelius: The Genesis and Meaning of a Roman Imperial Monument*. Chapel Hill: University of North Carolina Press.

Bergmann, M., and P. Zanker. 1981. "'Damnatio Memoriae' Umgearbeitete Nero- und Domitiansporträts: Zur Ikonographie der flavischen Kaiser und des Nerva." *JdI* 96: 317–412.

Bianchi Bandinelli, R. 1946. "An Antique Reworking of an Antique Head." *JWarb* 9: 1–9.

Blanck, H. 1969. *Wiederverwendung alter Statuen als Ehrendenkmäler bei Griechen und Römern*. Studia Archeologica 11. Rome: "L'Erma" di Bretschneider.

Bol, P. ed. 2010. *Die Geschichte der antiken Bildhauerkunst*. Vol. 4, *Plastik der römischen Kaiserzeit bis zum Tode Kaiser Hadrians*. Mainz: Philipp von Zabern.

Bonacasa, N. 1972. "Ritratto Colossale di Augusto del Museo Greco-Romano di Alessandria." *RM* 79: 221–34.

Boschung, D. 1989. *Die Bildnisse des Caligula*. Vol. 1.4 of *Das römische Herrscherbild*. Berlin: Mann.

———. 1993. "Die Bildnistypen der iulisch-claudischen Kaiserfamilie." *JRA* 6: 39–79.

———. 2002. *Gens Augusta: Untersuchungen zu Aufstellung, Wirkung und Bedeutung der Statuengruppen des julisch-claudischen Kaiserhauses*. Monumenta Artis Romanae 32. Mainz: Philipp Von Zabern.

Boschung, D., and M. Pfanner. 1988. "Antike Bildhauertechnik." *MüJb* 39: 7–28.

Brilliant, R. 1975. "One Head, Three Problems." *RM* 82: 135–63.

Bucher, G., and M. Freeman. 2010. "The 'Joslyn Augustus' and the 'Good, Bad and Altered' Symposium at Creighton University." *MAAR* 55: 3–13.

Cagiano de Azevedo, M. 1951. *Le antichità di Villa Medici*. Rome: La libreria dello stato.

Coates-Stephens, R. 2001. "Muri dei bassi secoli in Rome: Observations on the Re-use of Statuary in Walls Found on the Esquiline and Caelian after 1870." *JRA* 14: 217–38.

De Puma, R. 2010. "Is This Our Augustus?" *MAAR* 55: 15–21.

Dillon, S. 2006. *Ancient Greek Portrait Sculpture: Contexts, Subjects, and Styles*. Cambridge: Cambridge University Press.

Elsner, J. 2003. "Iconoclasm and the Preservation of Memory." In *Monuments and Memory, Made and Unmade*, edited by R. S. Nelson and M. Olin, 209–232. Chicago: University of Chicago Press.

Evers, C. 1991. "Remarques sur l'iconographie de Constantin: À propos du remploi de portraits des 'bons empereurs.'" *MÉFRA* 103(2): 785–806.

Fejfer, J. 2008. *Roman Portraits in Context*. Berlin: Walter De Gruyter.

Fittschen, K. 1992. "Zur Rekonstruktion griechischer Dichterstatuen 2 Teil: Die Statuen des Poseidippos und des Ps. Menander." *AM* 107: 229–71.

———. 2012. "Über das Umarbeitung römischen Porträts." *JRA* 25: 637–44.

Fittschen, K., and P. Zanker. 1983. *Katalog der römischen Porträts in den Capitolinischen Museen und den anderen kommunalen Sammlungen der Stadt Rom*. Vol. 3, *Kaiserinnen- und Prinzessinnenbildnisse Frauenporträts*. Mainz: Philipp von Zabern.

———. 1985. *Katalog der römischen Porträts in den Capitolinischen Museen und den anderen kommunalen Sammlungen der Stadt Rom*. Vol. 1, *Kaiser- und Prinzenbildnisse*. Mainz: Philipp von Zabern.

Fittschen, K., P. Zanker, and P. Cain. 2010. *Katalog der römischen Porträts in den Capitolinischen Museen und den anderen kommunalen Sammlungen der Stadt Rom*. Vol. 2, *Die männlichen Privatporträts*. Berlin: Walter de Gruyter.

Gagetti, E. 2011. "Three Degrees of Separation: Detail Reworking, Type Updating and Identity." In *Gems of Heaven: Recent Research on Engraved Gemstones in Late Antiquity*, edited by C. Entwistle and N. Adams, 135–48. London: British Museum.

Galinsky, K. 2008. "Recarved Imperial Portraits: Nuances and Wider Contexts." *MAAR* 53: 1–25.

Gercke, P., and N. Zimmermann-Elseify. 2007. *Antike Steinskulpturen und Neuzeitliche Nachbildungen in Kassel Bestandskatalog*. Mainz: Philipp Von Zabern.

Giuliano, A. 1991. "Augustus-Constantinus." *BdA* 68–9: 3–10.

Grossman, J. B., J. Podany, and M. True, eds. 2003. *History of Restoration of Ancient Stone Sculptures*. Los Angeles: J. Paul Getty Museum.

Hannestad, N. 2007. "Die Porträtskulpturen zur Zeit Konstantines des Grosse." In *Konstantin der Grosse = Imperator Caesar Flavius Constantinus: Ausstellungskatalog*, edited by A. Demandt and J. Engelmann, 96–116. Mainz: Philipp von Zabern.

Hansen, M. F. 2003. *The Eloquence of Appropriation: Prolegomena to an Understanding of Spolia in Early Christian Rome*. AnalRom Supplement 33. Rome: "L'Erma" di Bretschneider.

Harrison, E. B. 1990. "Repair, Reuse, and Reworking of Ancient Sculpture." In *Marble: Art Historical and Scientific Perspectives on Ancient Sculpture*, edited by M. True and J. Podany, 163–85. Malibu: J. Paul Getty Museum.

Haynes, D. E. L., and P. D. Hirst. 1939. *Porta Argentariorum*. London: Macmillan.

Hermann, J. J., Jr. 1991. "Re-arranged Hair: A Portrait of a Roman Woman in Boston and Some Recarved Portraits of Earlier Imperial Times." *JMFA* 3: 35–50.

Høtje, J. M. 2005. *Roman Imperial Statue Bases from Augustus to Commodus*. Aarhus: Aarhus University Press.

Johansen, F. 1994–5. *Roman Portraits*. 3 vols. Copenhagen: Ny Carlsberg Glyptotek.

Jucker, H. 1981. "Iulisch-claudische Kaiser- und Prinzenporträts als 'Palimpseste.'" *JdI* 96: 236–316.

Kaltsas, N. 2002. *Sculpture in the National Archaeological Museum, Athens*. Los Angeles: J. Paul Getty Museum.

Keesling, C. M. 2010. "The Hellenistic and Roman Afterlives of Dedications on the Akropolis." In Krumeich and Witschel 2010, 303–328.

Kinney, D. 1997. "*Spolia: Damnatio* and *Renovatio Memoraie*." *MAAR* 42: 117–48.

Kleiner, D. E. E. 1992. *Roman Sculpture*. New Haven: Yale University Press.

Knudsen, S. E. 1988. "The Portraits of Constantine the Great: Types and Chronology, A.D. 306–337." PhD diss., University of California, Santa Barbara.

Krumeich, R. 2010. "Vor klassischem Hintergrund: Zum Phänomen der Wiederwendung älterer Statuen auf der Athener Akropolis als Ehrenstatuen für Römer." In Krumeich and Witschel 2010, 329–98.

Krumeich, R., and C. Witschel, ed. 2010. *Die Akropolis von Athen im Hellenismus und in der römischen Kaiserzeit*. Wiesbaden: Reichert.

La Rocca, E. 1985. *Amazzonomachia: Le sculture frontonali del tempio di Apollo Sosiano*. Rome: De Luca.

———, ed. 1986. *Rilievi storici Capitolini: Il restauro dei pannelli di Adriano e di Marco Aurelio nel Palazzo dei Conservatori*. Rome: De Luca.

La Rocca, E., and P. Zanker. 2007. "Il ritratto colossale di Costantino del Foro di Traiano." In *Res bene gestae: Richerche di storia urbana su Roma Antica in onore di Eva Margherita Steinby*, edited by A. Leone, D. Palombi, and S. Walker, 145–68. LTUR Supplement 4. Rome: Quasar.

Laubscher, H. P. 1976. "Arcus Novus und Arcus Claudii: Zwei Triumphbögen an der Via Lata in Rom." *NAkG* 1976(3): 67–108.

Leander Touati, A.-M. 1987. *The Great Trajanic Frieze: The Study of a Monument and of the Mechanisms of Message Transmission in Roman Art*. ActaRom 4.45. Stockholm: Paul Åströms.

L'Orange, H. P., and A. Von Gerkan. 1939. *Der spätantike Bildschmuck des Konstantinsbogens*. Berlin: Walter de Gruyter.

Magi, F. 1945. *I Relievi Flavi del Palazzo della Cancelleria*. Rome: G. Bardi, presso la Pontificia Accademia di Archeologia.

Megow, W. R. 1993. "Zum Florentiner Tituskameo." *AA* 1993: 401–8.

Mian, G. 2009. "'Cicli' imperiali giulio-claudi ad Aquileia e lungo la costa adriatica orientale." In *Les ateliers de sculpture régionaux: Techniques, styles et iconographie; Actes de Xe Colloque International sur l'art provincial romain, Arles et Aix-en-Provence 21–23 mai 2007*, edited by V. Gaggadis-Robin, A. Hermary, M. Reddé, and C. Sintes, 179–88. Arles: Centre Camille Julian / Musée départemental Arles Antique.

Newby, Z., and R. Leader-Newby, eds. 2007. *Art and Inscriptions in the Ancient World*. Cambridge: Cambridge University Press.

Parisi Presicce, C. 2012. "Costantino e i suoi figli: Il nuovo volto dei potenti." In *Costantino 313 d.C.: L'editto di Milano e il tempo di tolleranza*, edited by G. S. Chiesa, 109–121. Milan: Mondadori Electa.

Pfanner, M. 1989. "Uber das Herstellen von Porträts: Ein Beitrag zu Rationalisierungsmaßnahmen und Produktionsmechanismen von Massenware im späten Hellenismus und in der römischen Kaiserzeit." *JdI* 104: 157–257.

Platt, V. 2007. "'Honour Takes Wing': Unstable Images and Anxious Orators in the Greek Tradition." In Newby and Leader-Newby 2007, 247–71.

Pollini, J. 1984. "*Damnatio Memoriae* in Stone: Two Portraits of Nero Recut to Vespasian in American Museums." *AJA* 88: 547–55.

Pollini, J., and W. Storage. 2010. "Recutting Roman Portraits. Problems in Interpretation and the New Technology in Finding Possible Solutions." *MAAR* 55: 23–44.

Prusac, M. 2006. "Re-carving Roman Portraits: Background and Methods." *ActaAArtHist* 20: 105–130.

Prusac, M. 2011. *From Face to Face: Recarving of Roman Portraits and the Late-Antique Portrait Arts*. Leiden: Brill.

Ricci, A., ed. 1998. *La Villa dei Quintili: Fonti scritte e fonti figurate*. Rome: Lithos.

Rockwell, P. 1993. *The Art of Stoneworking: A Reference Guide*. Cambridge: Cambridge University Press.

———. 1996. *Tecnologie della lavorazione dell pietra*. Padua: Centro di Formazione Maestranze Edili e Affini di Venezia e Provincia.

———. 1999. *Lavorare la pietra: Manuale per l'archeologo, lo storico dell'arte e il restauratore*. Rome: La Nuova Italia Scientifica.

Romeo, I. 1999. "Tra Massenzio e Costantino: Il ruolo delle officine urbane ed ostiensi nel creazione del ritratto costantiniano." *BullCom* 100: 197–228.

Rose, C. B. 1997. *Dynastic Commemoration and Imperial Portraiture in the Julio-Claudian Period*. Cambridge: Cambridge University Press.

Rutledge, S. H. 2012. *Ancient Rome as a Museum: Power, Identity, and the Culture of Collecting*. Oxford: Oxford University Press.

Ryberg, I. S. 1967. *Panel Reliefs of Marcus Aurelius*. Monographs on Archaeology and Fine Arts 14. New York: Archaeological Institute of America.

Schäfer, T. 1999. "*Felicior Augusto, Melior Trajano*: Das Bildnis von Konstantin in New York." In *Antike Porträts zum Gedachtnis von Helga von Heintze*, edited by H. Von Steuben, 295–302. Möhnesee: Bibliopolis.

Shear, J. 2007. "Reusing Statues, Rewriting Inscriptions and Bestowing Honors in Roman Athens." In Newby and Leader-Newby 2007, 221–46.

Spinola, G. 1999. *Guide Cataloghi Musei Vaticani*. Vol 4, *Il Museo Pio Clementino*. Rome: Musei Vaticani.

Stewart, P. 2003. *Statues in Roman Society: Representation and Response*. Oxford: Oxford University Press.

Tomei, M. A., and R. Rea, eds. 2011. *Nerone*. Milan: Mondadori Electa.

Tortorella, S. 2011. "Divi e dive del passato: L'apoteosi imperial." In *Ritratti: Le tante facce del potere*, edited by E. La Rocca, C. Parisi Pressice, and A. Lo Monaco, 303–313. Rome: Roma Capitale, Musei Capitolini, MondoMostro.

Van Voorhis, J. 2012. "The Working and Reworking of Marble Statuary at the Sculptor's Workshop in Aphrodisias." In *Ateliers and Artisans in Roman Art and Archaeology*, edited by T. M. Kristensen and B. Poulsen, 38–54. JRA Supplement 92. Portsmouth, RI: Journal of Roman Archaeology.

Varner, E. R. 2004. *Mutilation and Transformation: "Damnatio Memoriae" and Roman Imperial Portraiture*. Leiden: Brill.

———. 2010. "Reconfiguring Roman Portraits: Theories and Practices." *MAAR* 55: 46–56.

Vout, C. 2008. "The Art of 'Damnatio Memoriae.'" In *Un discours en images de la condamnation de mémoire*, edited by S. Benoist and A. Daguet-Gagey, 152–72. Metz: Centre Régional Universitaire Lorrain D'Histoire.

Walker, S., and P. Higgs, eds. 2001. *Cleopatra of Egypt: From History to Myth*. Princeton: Princeton University Press.

Wood, S. 1999. *Imperial Women: A Study in Public Images, 40 B.C.–A.D. 68*. Leiden: Brill.

Zanker, P. 1995. *The Mask of Socrates: The Image of the Intellectual in Antiquity*. Berkeley: University of California Press.

CHAPTER 2.4

BRONZES

CAROL C. MATTUSCH

Introduction

The study of classical bronze statuary was once primarily a philological and stylistic endeavor, in which scholars turned to Pliny the Elder's *Natural History* book 34 for answers to their questions about the identity and authorship of famous Greek bronze statues, and then tried to match statues discussed in the text with extant Roman marble sculptures in the classical style, which were identified as copies of particular Greek bronzes. But scholars now recognize that Romans produced their own statuary in the classical style (see essay 3.3, Anguissola) and that Romans generally preferred marble sculpture over bronze statuary, despite the additional costs involved in its production. At the same time, some Roman philhellenes were so committed to the idea of ancient Greece that they collected bronze statues, as if they were Greeks, as well as bronze busts and herm-portraits, both of which were distinctly Roman.

Today the investigation of classical bronzes has come to include attention to ancient production techniques and the application of modern technologies to bronzes, such as X-radiography, endoscopy, and chemical analysis. And yet Greek and Roman bronzes cannot be differentiated reliably, in part because of a lack of technical and scientific studies. To date, technical studies do not serve to differentiate alloys and methods of production from one period to the next or from one location to another. Perhaps a technical and analytical database for ancient bronzes, like that currently underway at the Louvre, might allow for the identification of such patterns (Descamps and Mille 2013).

Taking molds from Greek bronze statues and using them to produce copies—often marble—was common Roman practice, to judge from Lucian's remark about the Hermes of the Athenian Agora: "the one beside the Painted Stoa: he is covered with pitch from being molded upon every day by the statue-makers" (Lucian *Iupp. Trag.* 33). Making copies of important statues was a thriving industry (Ridgway 1984, 31–6). Theophrastus recommends plaster "for (taking) impressions, which seems to greatly surpass the other materials, and it is used for this especially in Greece, owing to its stickiness and smoothness" (Theophr. *On Stones* 67). Pliny the Elder also mentions the use of plaster models (Plin. *HN* 35.156). Despite the literary sources, there is little archaeological evidence for plaster models, with the exception of the finds from a Roman marble shop at Baiae on the Bay of Naples that yielded many fragmentary plaster casts intended to produce marble copies of Greek bronze statues, including the Athenian Tyrant-Slayers by Kritios and Nesiotes, three types of Amazons, and, most famous of all, the Doryphoros by Polykleitos (Landwehr 1985). The molds taken from famous bronze images in Greece, like the Tyrant-Slayers and the Hermes in the Agora, could also, however, be used to produce bronzes. One such survivor is the head from a life-size bronze statue of an Amazon, which may be Roman in date (Princeton 1997, 19).

Since relatively few ancient bronze statues have been found in modern times, scholars and collectors often ascribe greater importance to them than to ancient marbles, of which there are many examples, including numerous repetitions of a single image. The dearth of evidence was largely responsible for the growth of the modern notion that Greek bronzes were "originals" that the Romans copied endlessly in marble, a material judged to be of lesser value. Now that the number of bronze statues surviving in multiples is growing, scholars recognize that lost-wax casting is basically a reproductive technology. One need only think that when Marcus Scaurus was aedile in 58 BC, 3,000 bronze statues were installed on the stage of a temporary theater in Rome (Plin. *HN* 34.36; 36.113). Surely among these statues, as among those of the most famous and most productive Greek bronze artists, there were many repetitions or editions of particular statue-types. Nonetheless, the rarity of ancient bronzes ensures that their value on today's art market remains higher than that of ancient marbles and that this category of Roman sculpture is not as broadly studied or understood as others. After a brief introduction to the role of bronzes in public monuments and private collections and the Roman interest in Greek styles in bronze, this essay surveys the evidence (both literary and archaeological) for Roman bronze technology, discusses the role of modern metal analyses in our understanding of the production and use of bronzes in the Roman world, and explains the demise and disappearance of many of the classical bronzes that once populated the Roman sculptural landscape.

Public Monuments in Bronze: Literary *Testimonia*

Pliny the Elder's history of Roman bronze statuary begins with an image of Ceres that was erected in 485 BC. Then came portrait statues, leading to rivalry of various kinds. Greek nudes with spears and Roman *togati* competed with heroic statues wearing the cuirass, the cloak, and more personalized garb (Plin. *HN* 34.15–18). Statues of men were placed on columns as a sign of their importance (Plin. *HN* 34.27). Among the finest of all were the equestrian statues of men and of women (Plin. *HN* 34.28; Lahusen and

Formigli 2001). When Constantius visited Rome in AD 357, he was most impressed by the vast Forum of Trajan, and, not being able to construct anything so grand himself, he said he wished only to copy the (bronze) equestrian statue of the emperor standing in the forecourt. The Persian prince Ormisda is reported to have responded, "First, oh ruler, if you can, have a stable built like this one, so that the horse you plan to create can move around as freely as the one we see here" (Amm. Marc. 16.10.15–16).

Early bronze statues in the Roman Forum that honored Romans rather than gods were limited to three feet in height, but this rule was often disregarded: in the second century BC, a short poet erected a tall statue of himself (Plin. *HN* 34.24). In the same century, Cato objected to having statues of women set up in the provinces, but eliminating such honors in Rome was not his decision to make (Plin. *HN* 34.31). Chariot-groups honored women as well as men, and by Augustan times a bronze chariot-group might be drawn by as many as six horses or by elephants (Plin. *HN* 34.19, 34.28).

From the third century BC onwards, Roman generals brought back to Italy vast numbers of bronze statues as loot from the Greek world: Marcellus from Syracuse in 212, Aemilius Paullus from Macedonia in 168, Mummius from Corinth in 146, and Sulla from Athens in 86. Cicero noted that "in the public record you can find the number of statues, the size, shape, and attitude of each one of them" (*Verr.* 2.1.21.57). By the first century BC, art dealers in Greece were also selling antique sculptures to Roman collectors, such as Cicero in the 60s BC and, much later, Pliny the Younger, who also owned bronze statues of all the emperors (Plin. *Tra.* 10.8). Even so, in the first century AD, Pliny the Elder estimates that there were still about 12,000 bronze statues standing in Athens, Olympia, Delphi, and Rhodes (Plin. *HN* 34.36).

The literary evidence regarding the numbers of bronze statues erected in the city of Rome leaves no doubt that the production of bronze honorary statues was a thriving business, even though relatively few bronzes have survived, in contrast to the far greater number of extant marbles. These public statues were not carefully individualized portraits for the most part, but rather standardized images that celebrated the familiar. Anyone walking through Rome's public sector would have seen statues whose meaning was easily recognizable by the body, the gesture, and the attributes, as well as the inscription. There was undoubtedly a great deal of repetition among classical bronze statues representing statesmen and war heroes. According to the literary *testimonia*, the city of Rome became overly cluttered with honorific bronze statues on more than one occasion. A storm in 182 BC blew down many bronze statues installed on the Capitoline Hill and in the Circus Maximus (Livy 40.2.1–3). Building and renovation projects that were conducted in 179 by the censors Aemilius Lepidus and M. Fulvius Nobilior included the removal of statues from the colonnade surrounding the Temple of Capitoline Jupiter (Livy 40.51.2–6). Twenty years later, the censors had all statues of magistrates removed from around the Forum except for those dedications that had been voted by the people or the Senate (Plin. *HN* 34.30). These were not the bronzes that had been brought back as booty from Greece, Sicily, and the East, but statues that had been produced to honor Romans.

Private Collections and Bronzes: The Statues from the Villa of the Papyri

The Villa of the Papyri, a Roman seaside villa at Herculaneum on the Bay of Naples uncovered during the middle of the eighteenth century, yielded a vast collection of bronzes. The partial excavation of that villa might be described as the earliest scientific excavation of a classical site. A plan was drawn to scale, notes were kept, and findspots were recorded (Mattusch and Lie 2005). As a result, the Villa of the Papyri provides a unique view of the kinds of bronzes that were collected for decor in a Roman country house. Sixty-three large-scale bronzes were found, a number that has never been equaled at any other site. To date far fewer marbles have been found in the villa, indicating a predilection of these homeowners not just for Greek styles but also for the medium that had been preferred in Greece. These wealthy Roman villa-owners were eclectic in their taste, with a marked preference for Greek subjects and styles, ranging from archaizing to classicizing and Hellenistic with the addition of a few Roman republican and imperial portraits. There are statues, busts, herms, and garden ornaments, most with Greek subjects—athletes, intellectuals, generals, dynasts, and Athena—and statues of animals, rural deities, and naked children. All the works from the Villa of the Papyri are Roman, however, and they were evidently produced locally.

The sculpture collection was assembled over the duration of the villa's existence, perhaps nearly 200 years, until its destruction in AD 79. Thanks to the notes taken during the early excavations, it has been possible to reconstruct where particular statues and busts were installed. The collection and its installation did not follow a single overall program; rather, the statues were arranged as the owners desired at the time when they purchased a particular group of works, such as bronze busts of Greek rulers in the atrium (Mattusch and Lie 2005, 353–9), bronze statues in a large garden and its surrounding colonnade, and Pentelic marble herms of Greek intellectuals placed along the sides of a pool at the center of the garden.

Greek Styles in Roman Bronze Sculpture

Especially in the republican period but in imperial Rome as well, there was great demand for reproductions of famous antique Greek bronze statues, the finest perceived as being produced by Greek artisans, whether their works were ordered in marble or in bronze (Ridgway 1984; Landwehr 1985). For example, a bronze head of the famous classical Doryphoros (Spear-Bearer) by Polykleitos (figure 3.3.1), adapted for use as a herm in a private courtyard of the Villa of the Papyri, is inscribed on the front as having been made by the Athenian Apollonios, son of Archias (Museo Archeologico Nazionale di Napoli, inv. no. 4885), parentage that would have enhanced his own credentials (even though he evidently lived in Italy) and thus increased the marketability of the bronzes that he produced (Mattusch and Lie 2005, 276–82). The inscription is in Greek, and the producer and his father were Greeks. Its production in bronze by a Greek artisan signifies further admiration of what had been the preferred medium in Greece. The buyers for the Villa of the Papyri at Herculaneum also preferred works in the classical style, and most of their large works were bronze. In looking at the many marble examples of the Doryphoros and of other classical types of statues, one might wonder how many bronze examples—or editions—of the whole statue were produced during Roman times to satisfy hellenophiles who insisted on having bronzes in their collections, since most of these bronze versions are gone today.

Romans bought sculptures in all the old styles, such as the five ever-popular early classical young women known as the Herculaneum Dancers, bronze versions of which came from the colonnade surrounding the large garden of the Villa of the Papyri at Herculaneum (Mattusch and Lie 2005, 195–215; Dwyer 2012, 312–14). It may be that these classical types, alongside archaizing works, were especially popular during the 20s BC as part of Augustan promotion of reviving Rome's ancestral values and engendering nostalgia for the past (Hallett 2012, 100). One might wonder how many Roman buyers were discriminating enough to distinguish between classical and classicizing, archaic and archaizing works, and how often forgers passed off contemporary Roman works as ancient Greek ones.

In fact, modern scholars were initially misled by a bronze head of an Apollo or kouros-type (Museo Archeologico Nazionale di Napoli, inv. no. 5608) from the Villa of the Papyri, identifying it as an archaic Greek head that had been cut from a statue (figure 2.4.1), even though the many surviving statues from sixth-century Greece are marble. Stylistically, this bronze head appears to be archaic. The head is frontal, with corkscrew curls and a long braid wrapped around the head, the lips form an "archaic smile," eyebrows and lips are inlaid with copper, and the effect of the whole to a Roman audience would have been decidedly antique. There are prominent drip-marks on the back of the bust, such as one would expect to see on the interior of an indirect lost-wax casting, but definitely not on the exterior. The bust has irregular edges that appear to be broken, though they are not: they are finished edges that were cast to look as if they had been broken. Thus close examination has revealed that this head is a Roman archaizing bust with intentionally old-fashioned details, perhaps even an intentional forgery that misled the avid buyers from the Villa of the Papyri (Mattusch and Lie 2005, 236–42).

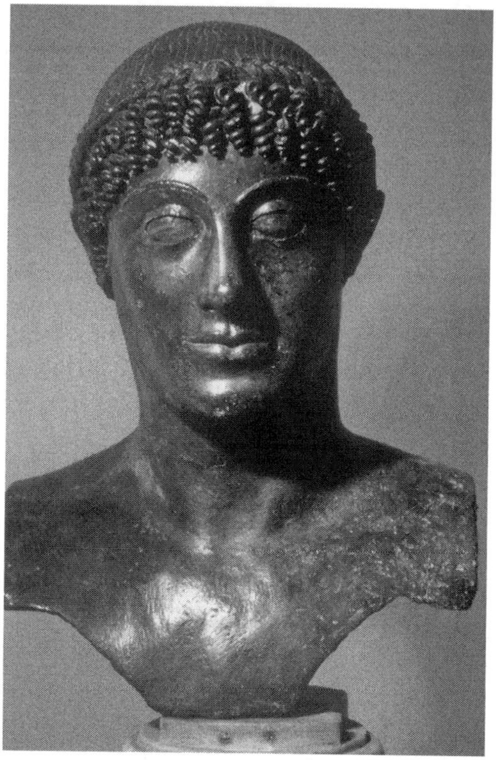

FIGURE 2.4.1 Archaizing Roman bronze bust of a youth with "archaic" ringlets and irregular lower edge of bust that was cast so as to appear broken. Museo Archeologico Nazionale di Napoli, inv. no. 5608.

Roman Bronze Technology

Literary *Testimonia*

Ancient bronze-casting technology was highly sophisticated, far more flexible in its application than scholars once thought, and capable of meeting the high demand for public monuments and private collections in bronze (Mattusch 1988, 22–30; 1996, 141–90). On the subjects of where the metals for Roman bronzes were mined and how they were refined and cast, there are few useful literary *testimonia*. Even Pliny the Elder provides very little information beyond saying that Cyprus is a source for copper and Spain for lead; he does not mention Etruria as being a source for lead. Different locales were known for specific types of bronzes and for different foundry practices yielding particular results (Plin. *HN* 34.94–6).

Regarding statuary, Pliny explains only roughly how to produce the correct alloy: first melt the lump (*massa*), then add a one-third portion of reused metal that has been bought up (*coempti*). He implies—but does not actually say—that the lump of metal should contain lead along with copper (Plin. *HN* 34.97–8). Beyond this, Pliny does not directly address the production of bronzes, except in a couple of cases to note something that impresses him.

Pliny once visited the workshop of the highly successful bronze artist Zenodorus, where a colossal statue of Nero as the sun god was being produced. He marveled "not only at the remarkable resemblance in the clay model, but also at the extremely small sticks [*surculi*] that are the first part of the work that are made" (Plin. *HN* 34.46). Pliny saw two works in progress: the clay model for the colossal statue of Nero and an armature over which another clay model was to be built, the first steps in the design of a statue. These two models would have occupied the studio area of the workshop, where visitors were brought to admire and place orders for the artist's designs. Visitors were not there to study the production of statues, and therefore literary sources do not describe many of the essential production steps or the spaces dedicated to them, such as the rooms devoted to clay, wax, pouring, and coldwork, and to tasks ranging from molding to finishing the waxes, to casting, joining, cleaning, and finishing the bronzes. Each phase of the process, taking the mold, making the wax, detailing the wax (if needed), pouring the bronze, cleaning, joining, and patinating, might be handled by different individuals. In an indirect reference to the division of labor, Horace describes a craftsman who can model fingernails and make wavy locks but who regrets that he cannot make the whole statue (Hor. *Ars P.* 32–5).

Material Evidence

In Pliny's opinion, Zenodorus was the only contemporary bronze artist who was any good. Otherwise, the art of working bronze had been forgotten (Plin. *HN* 34.47), and Pliny had nothing more to say about it. Modern scholars who are interested in the production of Roman bronze statues rely upon the physical evidence provided by surviving bronzes, ancient workshop debris, postantique processes, and, more recently, upon scientific analyses of ancient bronzes. As a result, we know that ancient sculptors in bronze mainly used the indirect lost-wax casting process, with variations from one foundry to another. The most telling evidence is provided by examination of the inside surfaces of ancient bronzes, which reveals brush marks, tool marks, drips, seams, and occasional fingerprints (Mattusch 2008). These marks reproduce the application of wax to the interior surfaces of master molds taken from a clay model and substitute for that model during its reproduction in bronze.

Lost-wax casting was and is essentially an indirect process, with innumerable variations, and it was used in antiquity for the production of multiples, editions, and unique works (figure 2.4.2). The process began with an artist's or designer's model, from which skilled artisans took clay or plaster piece molds. They poured and brushed wax into these master molds, creating a thin wax lining that could be removed from the molds and assembled to produce a hollow wax working model, nearly identical to the original clay model. This wax could be adjusted and refined before casting, or the working model

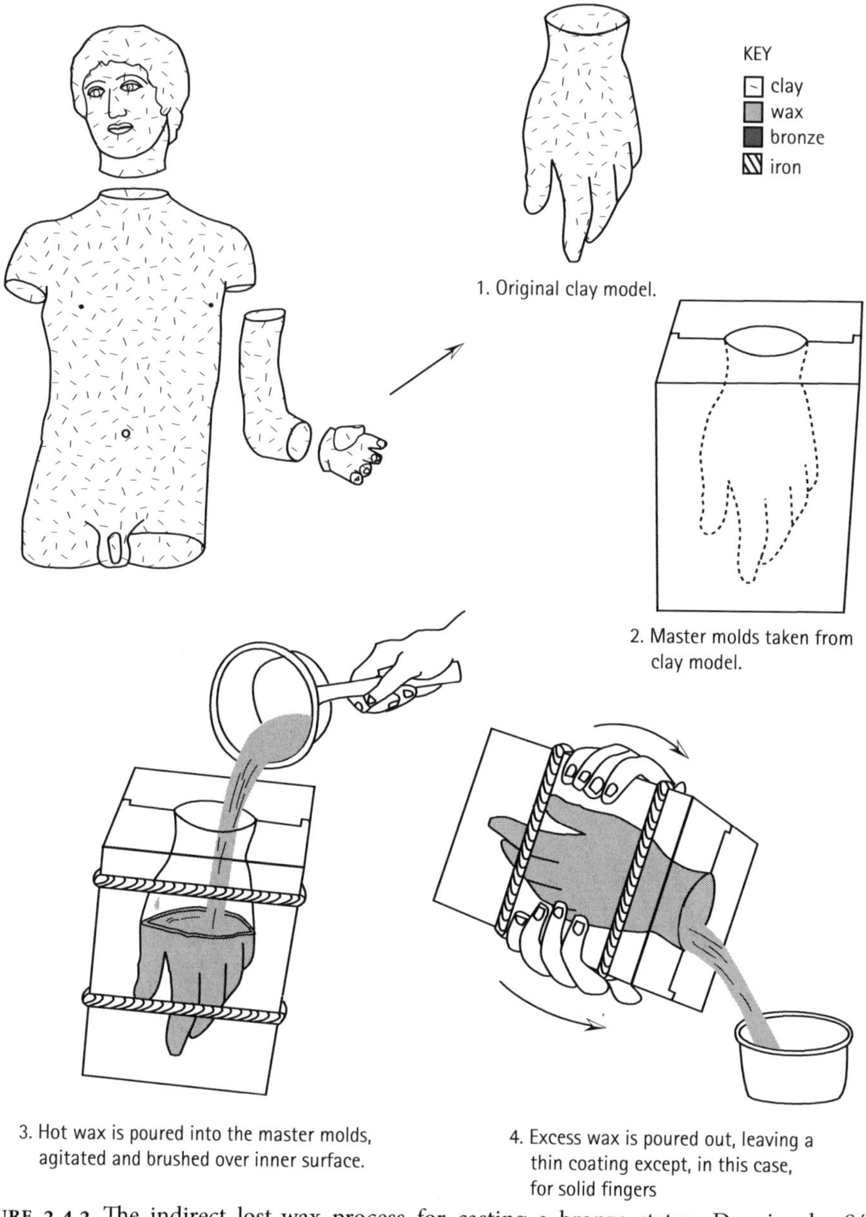

FIGURE 2.4.2 The indirect lost-wax process for casting a bronze statue. Drawing by Séan Hemingway.

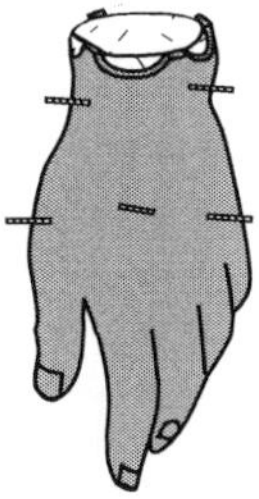

5. Finished wax working model with fingernails marked, clay core poured inside, and metal chaplets stuck through wax into core.

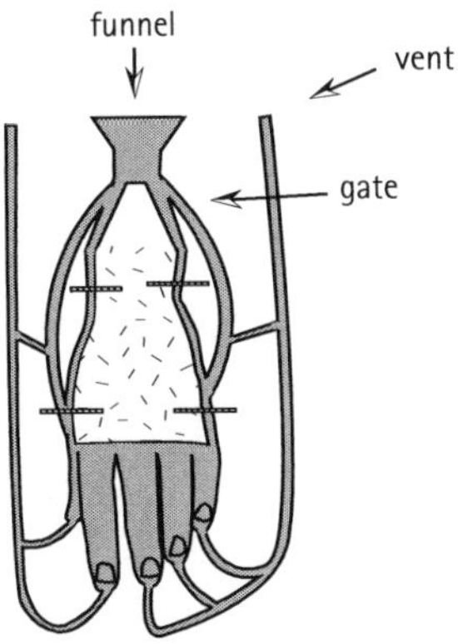

6. Cross section of wax working model with wax funnel, gates, and vents attached.

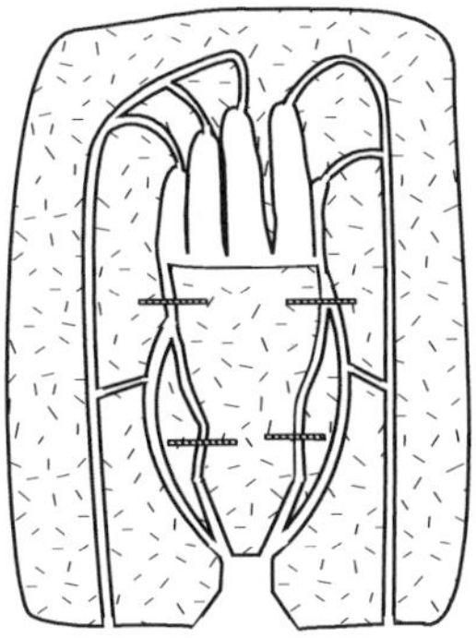

7. Cross section of investment mold inverted for baking, with hollow tubes where wax working model and gate system have been burned out.

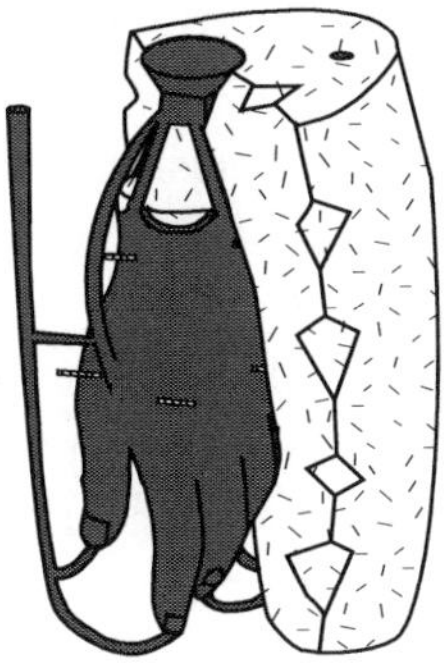

8. Bronze has been poured, investment mold partially broken away.

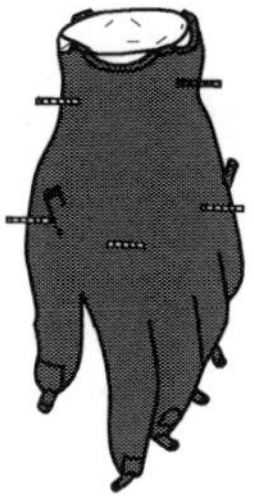

9. Cast bronze hand with core, chaplets and clipped gate system.

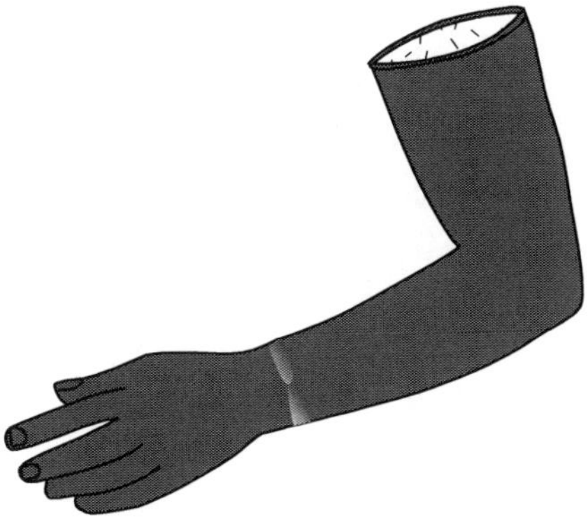

10. Hand joined to arm by flow weld.

FIGURE 2.4.2 (Continued)

could be cast in bronze, just as it came from the master molds. The master molds could be reused to produce more wax models from which could be cast as many bronzes as there were buyers for the work, either exact replicas or worked over in the wax to make slightly different versions or editions of the model.

An artist's input on the wax working model could be used to individualize two statues that were otherwise based on a standardized model for a general, a philosopher, a hero, or the like. A new edition might involve adjusting wax limbs or adding or embellishing particular features, such as ears, free-hanging locks of hair, or a beard, all in the wax. This method might be used for the separately cast head of a portrait statue, whose body was of a standard and oft-repeated type. The resulting bronze head has thick and uneven walls, whereas a statue's body normally has thin regular walls, indicating that minimal reworking of the wax working model was needed before the wax was invested with clay for the pour. But the wax added to the wax working model was not preserved after casting, and in the case of a miscasting, the individualization was lost. Thus, it is not unusual to find that a Roman portrait head has fairly thin and even wax walls, meaning that the face has been reproduced directly from a detailed original model or design, as would have been done for the widely disseminated portraits of members of the imperial family. In the case of a private individual, however, a relatively thin indirect casting strongly suggests that the portrait was molded directly from the face of the sitter. This practice can be traced back to the fourth-century BC bronze artisan Lysistratos, who Pliny the Elder claims was the first artisan to take a plaster mold from a person's face, pour wax into the mold, and then correct (*emendare*) the wax (Plin. *HN* 35.153). A life-mask process may well be reflected in an extraordinarily realistic portrait of an older man from the Villa of the Papyri (figure 2.4.3; Museo Archeologico Nazionale di Napoli, inv. no. 5634): the interior contours of the bronze generally follow the exterior; the thicker metal at the lips, the chin, and the outer rims of the ears reveals that these were features augmented in the wax before casting (Mattusch and Lie 2005, 270–72).

The finished wax working model was cut up into manageable parts, and each section was filled with a fine clay core anchored by means of iron or bronze pins (known as chaplets or core-pins) that reached from the core through the wax and finally into an outer clay investment mold. The cored and invested wax statue-parts were baked to dry the clay and burn out the wax, after which molten bronze was poured into clay funnels and channeled downward into the molds to cast the individual sections of the statue.

After the pour, the clay investment molds were broken away, the blackened bronze sections were cleaned, the surfaces polished, and the sections were joined mechanically or metallurgically. A draped statue might be produced in twenty to thirty separately cast sections, the notched and soldered joins concealed beneath the folds of tunic and toga. Nudes were sometimes cast in no more than six or eight major parts, their fabricators taking advantage of natural anatomical divisions like the line below the jaw and around the hairline on the back of the neck to conceal the metallurgical or welded joins (Mattusch and Lie 2005, 189–92). Flow welding involved pouring molten bronze into ovals cut along the join between two separately cast pieces; these may appear as a chain of pale oval shapes along the join. If fusion was not satisfactory, rows of small

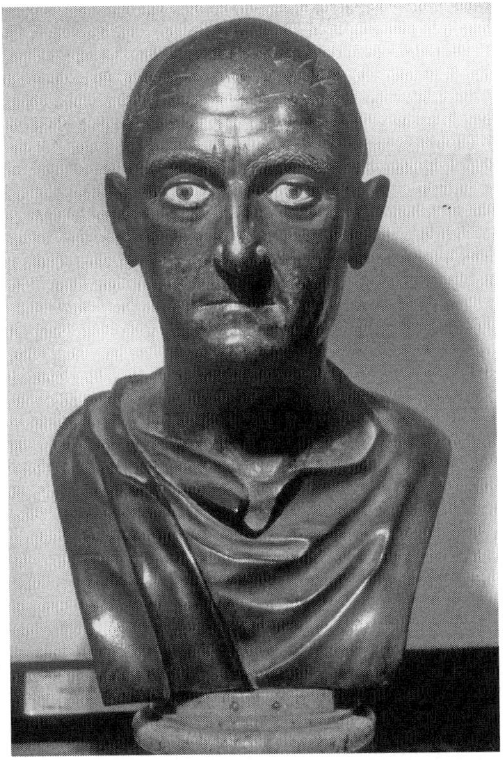

FIGURE 2.4.3 Roman bronze portrait of a man with a shaved head. The stippled head, lines and lump on the forehead, and eyebrows were detailed in the wax; the bone and stone eyes were inset after casting. Museo Archeologico Nazionale di Napoli, inv. no. 5634.

rectangular patches might be added to reinforce the welded joins. The bronze surface around casting flaws and the small square holes left behind by chaplets (core-pins) were cut out and squared, and surface patches were hammered into place. Some patches are less than 0.005 m square, whereas others may be much larger and may be polygonal rather than square or rectangular.

Color, Gilding, and Finishing

Today the use of mechanical methods for cleaning ancient metals has reduced the damage to the metal that was caused in the past by invasive chemical cleansing, thus revealing some further evidence for coloring and gilding Roman bronze statues. The preservation of ancient patinas and the increased visibility of color variations in the metal may lend credence to remarks by ancient authors that bronzes had different colors, though they tend to ascribe the color to alloy rather than to patination. Corinthian bronze was said to be whitish because of having some gold or silver in the alloy. Pliny advises that Delian bronze differs in color from Aeginetan bronze (Plin. *HN* 34.10), and an alloy that was preferred for portrait statues was "liver-colored" (Plin. *HN* 34.8). Furthermore, Plutarch (*Quaest. conv.* 5.1.2) mentions a statue whose face was a different color from the body.

Catullus (80.1) describes a certain individual as being paler than a gilded statue. The gilding of a statue was of course subject to the availability of funding and increased a statue's value significantly. Pliny the Elder tells an unusual story about a bronze statue of the young Alexander the Great by Lysippos, which Nero had gilded, thereby increasing its monetary value at the expense of its aesthetic value. When the gilding was removed, even though the slots for attachment were unsightly, the value of the plain bronze statue nonetheless increased (Plin. *HN* 34.63). The Roman practice of leaf-gilding, in which an adhesive such as mercury was used to apply leaf-thin sheets of gold to a non-tin-bronze, did not damage the surface of a statue and required far less gold. The equestrian statue of Marcus Aurelius on the Capitoline Hill in Rome was gilded in this manner, as were the Hercules in the Palazzo dei Conservatori in Rome and the Horses of San Marco in Venice.

Finishing touches might include insetting bone and stone or glass eyes encased in copper lashes, though occasionally the eyes were simply marked in the wax and reproduced in the bronze. Tin or silver teeth might be attached within an open mouth, and inlays could include copper lips and nipples, tin or silver fingernails, earrings, and a headband or drapery border. Wreaths and bracelets in copper, tin, and even gold or silver were sometimes added to statuettes kept securely in private homes (Mattusch and Lie 2005).

Metal Analysis

To date, not many Roman bronzes have been systematically analyzed, few by comparable methods, and only one group from a single context—those from the Villa of the Papyri. Although analyses cannot be used to determine the origins of the metal components or of an object, quantitative analyses have provided an important new dimension in the study of ancient bronze statuary. For example, chemical analyses have been made of the major, minor, and trace elements in bronzes from the Villa of the Papyri at Herculaneum using inductively coupled plasma mass spectrometry (ICP-MS) and electron probe microanalysis (EPMA). Both methods test a few of the same elements, thus providing a check for accuracy of results. Other evidence was provided by X-radiography and by examination of technical features, alongside more traditional studies of subjects, styles, sizes, and types of works, making it possible to recognize products from several local workshops (Mattusch and Lie 2005, 138–40, 333–4). Bronze workshops had specialties: works that were of one particular type, of a certain style, or that possessed some standardized features. A buyer might want a pair of sculptures—identical or mirror images—or variations on a theme. But workshops also had their own supplies of metals, and when the same batch of bronze was used to cast two or more bronzes at the same time, that fact can be revealed by the trace elements present in those bronzes.

Copper, tin, and lead are the principal intentional ingredients of ancient bronzes. Statuary bronzes tend to contain between 70 and 90 percent of copper and less than 10 percent of tin, but lead content ranges widely, from less than 1 percent to nearly 30 percent. Lead lowers the melting point of the alloy and increases the fluidity of molten bronze during casting, facilitating the casting of large pieces. A sufficient percentage of lead also promotes fusion during the joining of cast sections by flow welding.

Trace elements appear in an alloy because they were present in the ores from which the major elements were smelted. Unlike the principal elements, these traces can be used to identify objects cast from a single batch of metal and to confirm that bronzes matching in design, style, and subject matter were likely to have been made at one and the same time. For example, bronze busts of three Hellenistic dynasts from the atrium of the Villa of the Papyri are all of the same size, style, and type, and they also share the same trace elements, suggesting that they comprised a single commission and that they were cast as a group (Museo Archeologico Nazionale di Napoli, inv. nos. 5590, 5596, and 5600). Perhaps the buyer also had it in mind at the time of his order that he wanted to place these three large and impressive busts in his atrium (Mattusch and Lie 2005, 260–68).

Another example of trace element analyses contributing to our further understanding of the production and distribution of bronze statuary comes from a bronze in the sunken Mahdia ship. Between 100 and 70 BC, a Roman vessel on its way home from the eastern Mediterranean ran off course and sank off the coast of Tunisia. It was carrying a 300-ton cargo: some Greek pieces such as a few fourth-century BC Attic reliefs and inscriptions that may have been picked up or plundered in Greece along with a Hellenistic bronze statue of Eros, but mostly new items, including sixty to seventy marble columns, a few marble capitals, bronze candelabra, marble relief-kraters and figural tondi, four marble seated children intended for a fountain, and twenty-three bronze *klinai* with serially numbered legs (Hellenkemper Salies, von Prittwitz und Gaffron, and Bauchhenss 1994) along with a bronze herm and a bronze statue.

The bronze herm, representing Dionysos (Bardo National Museum, Tunis, inv. no. F 107) bore an inscription naming the second-century BC artist Boethos of Kalchedon as the maker. That herm has four extraordinarily close parallels that clearly chronicle the persistence of a popular image in both marble and bronze. One of the parallels is a bronze herm of the same size, uninscribed but missing an arm-boss that could have borne an inscription (J. Paul Getty Museum, inv. no. 79.AB.138). This herm, like the Mahdia herm, has a trace of cobalt in the alloy, meaning that the two were likely to have been cast at the same time from the same batch of metal (figure 2.4.4). The degradation of the surface of the Mahdia herm is the result of its having been damaged by marine organisms during its centuries in the sea, but the very close resemblance between the two bronzes is nonetheless undeniable (Mattusch 2014, 135–9).

(a) (b)

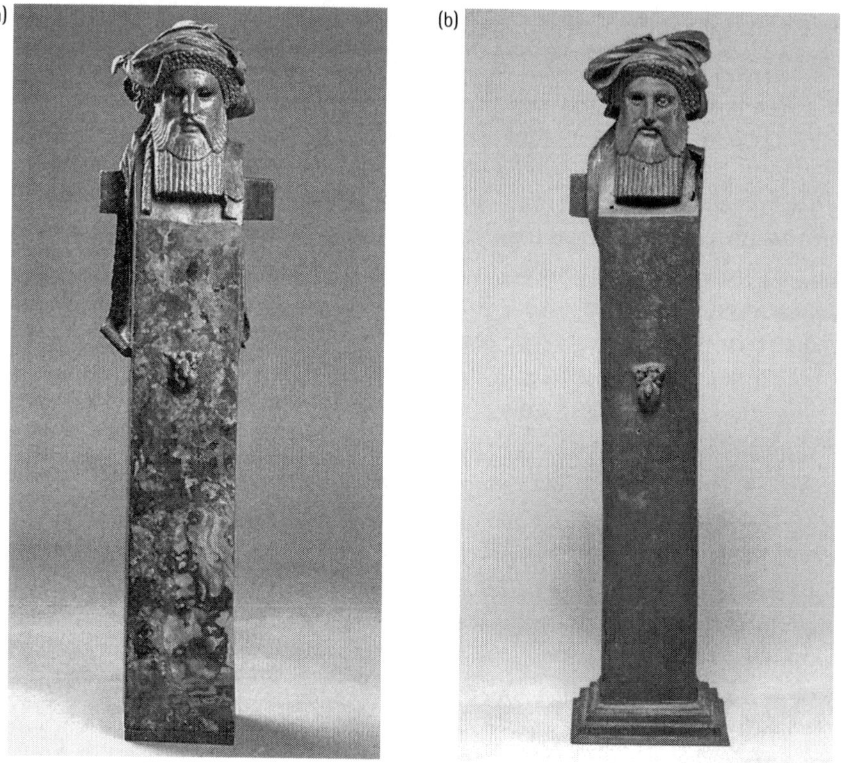

FIGURE 2.4.4 The Mahdia herm (left) and the Getty herm (right). Their dissimilar surface conditions result from their having been subjected to different conditions over the centuries, the former degraded from burial at sea, the latter, with sharper features, from an unknown context. Mahdia herm: Bardo National Museum, Tunis, inv. no. F 107; Getty herm: J. Paul Getty Museum, Malibu, inv. no. 79.AB.138.

Reuse and Removal of Bronze

As noted above, precious few ancient bronzes survive from antiquity, though we have literary (and some enticing archaeological) evidence for vast quantities of these once displayed throughout the public and private realms. What became of the scores of bronze sculptures from antiquity? Bronzes have always been vulnerable because of their value as scrap metal. A statue might be sent to market as scrap metal if the honoree had been forgotten, if the statue had fallen into disrepair, if it represented a politician who had fallen from favor, or if it represented a pagan in a Christian world. Pliny the Younger delighted at seeing the faces of Domitian's (emperor from AD 81 to 96) statues smashed by sword and ax, and he wished that blood and pain might follow every blow to a statue. He hoped that from the shattered (bronze) bodies and mutilated limbs that were being consumed by flames some good and useful works would be produced. (Plin. *Pan.* 52). In other words, *damnatio memoriae*, which included destroying the statues of an unpopular ruler (see essays 2.3, Varner; 3.8, Witschel; and 6.6, Kristensen), provided some relief to those who suffered under his rule, and Pliny seemed to condone the use of this particular scrap metal for the production of utilitarian day-to-day objects.

Once bronze statues no longer carried their original meanings or functions or had been irreparably damaged, they could be broken up, the pieces carted away to be sold as scrap for remelting and reuse in workshops that produced weapons, tools, and also new statues. Bronzes were shipped to Roman foundries from conquered cities and defeated armies. A dealer in scrap metal was and is always in the market for new stock, because (as noted above) scrap metal is regularly added to the mix for a bronze casting. Today the cost of scrap metal is less than half of 1 percent of the appraised value of a statue, but it is nonetheless a profitable market, if one considers the many uses for bronze. The Romans conquered the Etruscan city of Volsinii in 264 BC specifically for its 2,000 bronze statues (Plin. *HN* 34.34), which were presumably sent to workshops for their value as scrap metal, perhaps no more than 1 percent of the value of the statuary, but a sizeable haul for a scrap-metal dealer. Battle provided further resources. Spurius Carvilius cast a colossal statue of Jupiter on the Capitolium from the breastplates, greaves, and helmets of the Samnites, who had been defeated by Rome in 293 BC, and then, after the colossus was finished, Carvilius used the leftover filings to make a standing statue of himself that he placed at the feet of Jupiter (Plin. *HN* 34.43).

Close to Brindisi on the Italian coast, a ship went down in the sixth century AD with a cargo of scrap bronze, bits and pieces of as many as one hundred smashed statues that were apparently on their way to being sold as scrap metal (Marinazzo 2010). The bronze fragments have been dated between the fourth century BC and the late second or early third century AD. They included bits and pieces of public statuary, a powerful young ruler in a hipshot pose, an older man of letters with tousled hair and a long beard, an official wearing a toga, a few bare feet, hands with ringed fingers, and two colossal arms, one of them raised in a declamatory gesture with a pointing forefinger. There are also portraits of male and female members of Rome's Julio-Claudian dynasty. The early Christians had no use for the public statuary of the classical world, and so in the sixth century the statue-parts in this cargo were being sent off for recycling.

The one-hundred-foot-tall Colossus of Rhodes, representing Helios, set a record for its size and beauty, and it yielded 980 camel-loads of scrap metal when its fragments were carted off by the Saracens in AD 653 (Constantine Porphyrogennetos, *De administrando imperio* 20–21). Completed in 280 BC by Chares, a student of Lysippos, the statue was felled by an earthquake just fifty-six years later, in 224 BC (Strabo 14.2.5), yet it maintained its reputation as a world wonder during the 877 years that it lay on the ground in pieces. Pliny the Elder had no praise for contemporary Roman bronze-workers, with the exception of Zenodorus, whose Greek name brings to mind the outstanding reputations enjoyed by Greek artists and artisans employed by wealthy Roman patrons. Surely Zenodorus had in mind the universally admired world-wonder on Rhodes when he designed his own colossal bronze statue of the emperor Nero in the guise of Helios.

Conclusion

Traditional philological and stylistic approaches to the study of Roman bronzes are still valid, but careful visual examination of statuary—inside and out—and scientific analysis of the bronze itself have generated significant advances in our understanding of Roman bronzes. Production techniques and artistic practice are closely linked, and it is now clear that no single approach can yield all the answers or provide reliable guidelines for dating a sculpture. As scholars in a wide range of disciplines uncover new evidence and discover more avenues for investigation, our understanding of these rare survivors of a major ancient industry will continue to evolve.

Bibliography

Descamps, S., and B. Mille. 2013. "Recherches sur les techniques des bronzes grecs et romains: La base Héphaïstos." Musée du Louvre, Département des Antiquités grecques, étrusques et romaines. http://www.louvre.fr/en/recherches-sur-les-techniques-des-bronzes-grecs-et-romains-la-base-hephaistos.

Dwyer, E. 2012. "Collectible Singletons." *Arethusa* 45(3): 305–318.

Hallett, C. H. 2012. "The Archaic Style in Sculpture in the Eyes of Ancient and Modern Viewers." In *Making Sense of Greek Art*, edited by V. Coltman, 70–100. Exeter: University of Exeter Press.

Hellenkemper Salies, G., H.-H. von Prittwitz und Gaffron, and G. Bauchhenss, eds. 1994. *Das Wrack: Der antike Schiffsfund von Mahdia*. 2 vols. Cologne: Rheinland-Verlag.

Lahusen, G., and E. Formigli. 2001. *Römische Bildnisse aus Bronze: Kunst und Technik*. Munich: Hirmer.

Landwehr, C. 1985. *Die antiken Gipsabgüsse aus Baiae: Griechische Bronzestatuen in Abgüssen römischer Zeit*. Berlin: Mann.

Marinazzo, A. 2010. *I Bronzi di Punta del Serrone: Dal mare al Museo Provinciale di Brindisi*. Bari: Mario Adda.

Mattusch, C. C. 1988. *Greek Bronze Statuary: From the Beginnings through the Fifth Century B.C.* Ithaca: Cornell University Press.

———. 1996. *Classical Bronzes: The Art and Craft of Greek and Roman Statuary*. Ithaca: Cornell University Press.

———. 2008. "Metalworking and Tools." In *The Oxford Handbook of Engineering and Technology in the Classical World*, edited by J. P. Oleson, 569–95. Oxford: Oxford University Press.

———. 2014. *Enduring Bronze: Ancient Art, Modern Views*. Los Angeles: J. Paul Getty Museum.

Mattusch, C. C., and H. Lie. 2005. *The Villa dei Papiri at Herculaneum: Life and Afterlife of a Sculpture Collection*. Los Angeles: J. Paul Getty Museum.

Princeton Art Museum. 1997. *In Celebration: Works of Art from the Collections of Princeton Alumni and Friends of The Art Museum, Princeton University*. Princeton: Art Museum, Princeton University.

Ridgway, B. S. 1984. *Roman Copies of Greek Sculpture: The Problem of the Originals*. Ann Arbor: University of Michigan Press.

CHAPTER 2.5

TERRACOTTAS

ADI ERLICH

Introduction

"Terracottas" is the common term for objects made of clay other than pottery vessels, including statues, figurines, architectural elements, pipes, sarcophagi, stamps, lamps, and the like. Another common term, "coroplastic arts," recalls the type of Greek artisan who created them, the coroplast (κοροπλαστής). For this essay, I will refer only to coroplastic products that may be considered "sculpture," mainly figurines. In addition to small figurines there are also large-scale clay statues (see essay 3.6, Touchette), but those are rare due to their fragility and the difficulties in modeling them. Therefore, the majority of terracotta sculptures are small-scale, measuring 5–50 cm in height, with most approximately 30 cm tall.

Large-scale sculptures are often examined in regard to their display context and how they were perceived by the viewer. Terracotta figurines, however, are considered just like other small artifacts in terms of use: how they were held, moved around, dedicated, smashed, and deposited. Terracotta figurines differ from many other sculptures not only in their scale but also (and foremost) in their method of production. Unlike stone and large bronze sculptures that are made individually, terracotta figurines are normally mold-made and mass-produced. The production method, which did not change much throughout antiquity, had a strong impact on aspects of repetition (series and generations of production), distribution of types, and iconography. Hence, most terracottas fall between the categories of sculpture and pottery: they constitute small statues from the point of their form and iconography, and in a way also meaning, but they represent small clay products in terms of production, distribution, and usage.

With regard to quality and uniqueness, terracottas with stereotyped designs and rough details are usually inferior to bronze and stone sculpture (Burford 1972, 107). On the other hand, terracottas present many advantages for the study of Roman art and culture. They are numerous, varied, and reflect a range of aspects of daily life as well as religious iconography. Their frequency allows quantitative research that is impossible with large-scale sculpture. Terracottas represent all classes of society, especially under-represented groups. Lastly, unlike stone and bronze statues, terracottas are often found in archaeological context, and therefore their date and function are often more secure than those of large sculptures. Terracotta figurines and statuettes ideally mediate between art and craft, two categories that merged in antiquity.

Historiography: From Typology through Production to Context

Except for famous works like the Apollo of Veii, terracottas are often absent from general studies and textbooks of Roman art and in books on regional art in the empire. Other scholars have included terracottas in discussions of crafts but not of the arts, emphasizing their inferior quality compared to bronze and marble (Higgins 1976, 105). For example, a chapter dedicated to "Terracotta revetments, figurines and lamps" in Henig's *Handbook of Roman Art* (Bailey 1983, 191–204) represents terracottas as material culture rather than part of the medium of sculpture. Therefore, the refreshing and unprecedented choice to include terracottas in this handbook may provide us with new perspectives on Roman sculpture.

The history of research on terracotta figurines presents a shift both in interest and in methods. During the end of the nineteenth century and the first half of the twentieth century, scholars focused on typology, iconography, and identification of subjects portrayed in terracottas. Typology is still the best way to begin research on Roman terracottas and to establish a catalog of a given assemblage. However, it seems that typology is useful largely for scholars who study terracottas, since our typologies do not reflect faithfully the use of terracottas by the ancients, who did not produce them or use them sorted or classified into types.

From the 1950s to the 1990s, the focus shifted to production and producers. Nicholls's seminal paper (1952) on production methods of Greek terracottas served as a turning point. During these years many Roman workshops were excavated and published, especially those in the northwestern provinces but also examples in Egypt and elsewhere in the Roman Empire (Bémont, Jeanlin, and Lahanier 1993; Rodziewicz 2005). The focus on coroplasts and their craft brought to light aspects of series production and generations, workshops specializing in specific types, manufacture shared with other clay objects, diffusion of molds and types, and distribution of products (Uhlenbrock 1990). Experimental archaeology has also been helpful (Ramos Sáinz and Fuentes Ghislaín 1998). Furthermore, advanced methods for analyzing clay fabrics and their origins have been used in terracotta studies, such as petrographic analysis, portable X-ray fluorescence spectroscopy (pXRF), and neutron activation analysis (NAA) (Bémont, Jeanlin, and Lahanier 1993; Bouquillon, Hasselin Rous, and Laugier 2010).

Interest in context and its meaning has increased greatly over the past few decades. Thanks to controlled excavations that resulted in finds of large groups of figurines from secure contexts, scholars have turned their attention to the function and use of terracottas from the moment they left the workshops until the final contexts in which they were found. Another development goes beyond the terracottas themselves, examining what was dedicated, placed, and/or deposited with them, whether secular or sacred objects. Examples of this contextual approach are numerous in recent years, like the series on Italian deposits, *Corpus delle stipe votive in Italia* (for a review, see Ginge 1993).

Principles of Production

The manufacture technique of Greek and Roman terracottas was similar (Nicholls 1952; Higgins 1976; Uhlenbrock 1990, 15–21; Burn and Higgins 2001, 18–20). The stages of production included the preparation of a clay or plaster mold from an archetype or a ready-made figurine—sometimes separate molds for the front, the back, the head, or the arms, but more often only two molds for the front and back. The mold is retouched and fired, and then ready for mass production of figurines. Thin layers of clay are set in the molds and withdrawn gently. The different parts are then retouched, refined, and joined to create a hollow figurine. Handmade parts are added; sometimes a vent is cut in the back; and sometimes white coating is applied. In some cases only parts of these stages are carried out. Subsequently the figurine is fired in the kiln in low to medium temperature. After firing (although in some cases before) the figurine is coated with a lime wash and painted. Coroplastic production is often done in generations, i.e. derivative production of a cast from a mold, a mold from a figurine, and the next generation from the second mold, and so on. This method can be recognized in a decrease of the size of figurines due to the shrinkage of clay at each stage (Miller Ammerman 2002, 12–14).

In most workshops the coroplasts were anonymous and did not specialize in figurines only. However there are certain regions in the Roman Empire, especially in Asia Minor and Gaul, where coroplasts signed their figurines and other terracotta products (Kassab 1988; Bémont, Jeanlin, and Lahanier 1993, 96–123). The inscriptions on the figurines' bases or backs include signatures, monograms, signs, and letters, and allow us to identify certain workshops, to date figurines more precisely, and to follow the distribution of types made by those coroplasts.

Function and Meaning of Terracottas

The function and meaning of terracottas in the Roman world do not differ fundamentally from those of clay figurines in other ancient cultures in the Mediterranean.

Interpreting terracotta figurines is not easy, since obstacles and cultural bias make interpretation indecisive (for a methodological discussion, see Ucko 1968, 409–444; Voigt 1983, 186–95).

The interpretation of terracottas can be divided into three categories: general use, function, and meaning. For example, a terracotta figurine from a temple implies general religious and ritual use. But questions remain regarding the object's specific function. How was it purchased? From whom and by whom? Under what circumstances did it arrive at the temple (public ceremony, festival, private vow, etc.)? How was the object used (by its owner, by its dedicator, by religious officials), and how and why was it kept, deposited, and/or discarded? Meaning is the most difficult to address, because it deals with symbolism and the role that terracottas played in society. Given the limits of the evidence, this kind of interpretation becomes elusive.

There are three main ways to address the questions of the general use, function, and meaning of figurines. First is through typological and iconographic analyses; for example, clear divine iconography or types with religious connotation may apply to a religious meaning and probably also function. But as noted above, these approaches often fail to reveal the exact function and related questions of who used the figurine, where, and when. The second approach analyzes the archaeological context of the terracottas (for example, graves, sanctuaries, houses). The archaeological context is often insufficient for explaining the function of terracottas, however, because though findspot may tell us where terracottas were used, it does not explain how they functioned. Moreover, the archaeological context is often the last stop of the object, and does not necessarily tell us about the terracotta's whole life from the moment it left the kiln. For example, a certain terracotta figurine can be a possession of a child during his lifetime and also a funerary object buried with him after his death.

The third approach employs ethnographic studies that examine modern societies and project their habits back onto people in antiquity (Hamilton et al. 1996). There are limitations with this method as well. Ethnographic studies of figurines are usually conducted with tribal or illiterate societies, dissimilar to those of Roman times. While ethnographic studies generate a set of options, they generally do not provide a clear answer for specific cases. Nevertheless, the combination of these three methods, together with a close examination of a given repertoire and external sources (texts, visual depictions), may lead us to a better understanding of how terracottas functioned and what they stood for in Roman society.

Generally speaking, Roman figurines are related to three main spheres: religious use as votives in temples or sanctuaries; domestic use as objects of household cult, decoration, or toys; and funerary use as grave goods. The meaning and role of Roman terracottas are often interpreted in two directions: on the one hand positive—the guarantee of fertility, abundance, and good health, and on the other preventive—via apotropaic and protective roles.

Main Centers of Terracotta Production and Use in the Roman World

Italy

Italy is a good starting point, not only because it is the heart of the Roman world, but also because Italian terracottas are dated as early as Etruscan and republican Italy (see essay 3.2, de Grummond). Already in Etruscan times local artisans specialized in clay, available in many parts of Italy far more than any other material. Some remarkable terracotta pediments of the second through first centuries BC have survived, such as the relief from Via di San Gregorio with nearly life-size figures of a mythological sacrifice (Ferrea 2002; see essay 3.6, Touchette). Most of the coroplastic production in republican times however, consisted of smaller terracotta figurines. Architectural terracottas were not as common as in previous periods, especially in the late republican period (Rous 2009). Nevertheless, terracotta production reached its peak during the republican period, and decreased in the time of the empire. The coroplastic production of Italy in the fourth through first centuries BC can be divided into two groups representing different spheres of influence: the Etruscan-Roman tradition of central Italy (Etruria, Latium, and Campania) and the Hellenistic tradition of the rich cities of Magna Graecia (Campania, southern Italy, and Sicily; see Comella 1981).

In central Italy the local tradition was strong. Rural sanctuaries have yielded large quantities of votives. The technique and material were Etruscan (Söderlind 2000–2001, 241–73), the types and iconography had a mixture of Greek and Italic features, and the religious practice and beliefs were basically local Roman. The main types (votive heads, standing figures, women, swaddled babies, animals, fruits, and anatomical models) are all considered to be related to fertility and healing cults.

A typical genre of Italian votive offerings are the anatomical models (figure 2.5.1), including masks, limbs and other external or internal body parts (Fenelli 1975; Comella 1981; Potter 1985). Such models were common in Etruria, Latium, and Campania from the fourth century BC until the late Republic. They reflect belief in the power of different gods to cure (eyes, ears, limbs, or internal organs) and reproduce (uteri, male organs, and swaddled babies). It should be noted, though, that anatomical models are not restricted or exclusive to healing shrines, and often they are integral to other cults. In Glinister's words, "they represent the generic power of deities over the major aspects of human life" (2006, 13).

Another characteristic type of Italian offerings are the votive heads or half-heads, which are made in Etruscan, Hellenistic, and Roman styles (Nagy 1988, 14–19; Söderlind 2002, 369–75). The heads, which have no specific attributes, are not considered portraits. It has been suggested that heads and other anatomical parts that are often found

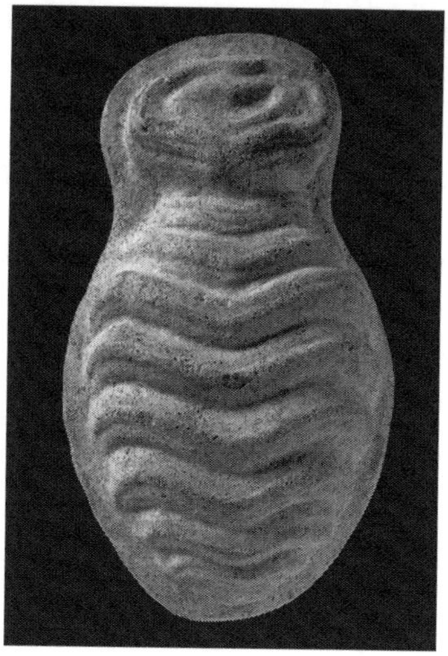

FIGURE 2.5.1 Terracotta model of uterus from Italy. Fourth to second centuries BC. London, British Museum.

together belong to the same category: the heads represent cure from headache, and both were dedicated to deities of cure and fertility (Nagy 1988, 28). Otherwise, the heads might be votives representing the dedicators.

Depictions of women with children appear in Italian terracottas in large quantities and reflect childbirth and the tending of children. The swaddled babies may stand for thanksgiving for a successful delivery. Depictions of women and children became increasingly widespread all over the Mediterranean during the fourth century BC.

A better understanding of the votives can be achieved if we look more closely at their contexts and associated finds. Some sanctuaries contain different kinds of models, while others seem to specialize in certain organs (Macintosh Turfa 1994, 20). At Gravisca in Etruria, votives were found *in situ* in rooms of a sanctuary, enabling us to identify the deities according to inscriptions and concentration of types (Comella 1978). As no male organs were discovered, but many female ones were, the site was easily identified as a women's shrine. In another case, at Satricum in Latium, an attempt was made to study all the votives deposited there, whether terracottas or not. From this holistic analysis, Bouma argued that the cult was a local votive tradition with some conscious external influences (1996).

In addition to their religious significance in healing and fertility cults, the anatomical models and heads have also been examined from sociomedical and sociopolitical perspectives. Although many of the terracotta organs are life-size and bear no deformities, they testify to specialized medical practices in republican Italy (Potter 1985; Macintosh Turfa 1994). It is generally believed that the anatomical models found outside of Rome in Italy and beyond spread from Rome, and some argue that the spread of such models reflects Roman colonization (Comella 1981; Söderlind 2000–2001). However, it is more likely that these anatomical models represent a wider *koine* that goes beyond the power of Rome (Glinister 2006).

Indeed, cheap terracottas served as mediators between individuals or groups and supernatural powers, and not between political powers and the masses. Therefore they should be examined not only in light of political history, but also in cultural and anthropological contexts. An innovative approach to the anatomical models might analyze the construction of body image in Italian society. The deconstruction of the body into organs, the nonindividualistic character of the organ dedicated, and the very act of dedicating part of oneself to the deity, even in the form of a model, await detailed study.

The second major group of terracottas from Italy comes from the rich cities of southern Italy and Sicily, where a classical and Hellenistic tradition of terracottas lasted until the end of the third century BC, when the Romans arrived and sacked these cities (Bell 1990). The prosperous cities of Campania from the second century BC to the first century AD also yielded terracottas in Hellenistic style, often found in temples (Miller Ammerman 2002) or houses, where they were stored in cupboards and served in domestic cults or as decorations (D'Ambrosio and Borriello 1990, 13). Most were the Hellenistic *Tanagra* type (figures of draped, standing females). Other types include divinities such as Aphrodite and Eros, Bacchus and his circle, and Minerva, among others. Also present are busts, theatrical and sports motifs, realistic figures, animals, and types based on imperial statuary, such as portrait busts of males and boys (Besques 1986). The types and style are Hellenistic. Unlike their Greek counterparts, however, the figurines are frontal with heavily set, disproportionate forms, and with somber expressions.

The Northwestern Provinces, Africa Proconsularis, and Spain

When we shift from Italy to the northwestern provinces, we move forward chronologically to the first three centuries AD, and, in terms of findspot, we shift from votive deposits to two main production areas along river valleys, which correlate in technique, types, and style.

Many terracotta workshops operated in central Gaul during the first through third centuries AD. The main centers were at Allier (Vichy) and its vicinity (Bémont, Jeanlin, and Lahanier 1993, fig. 2). They produced terracottas for the Gaulish region and exported them to Switzerland, Belgium, Holland, Austria, Britain, and Spain (Bémont, Jeanlin and Lahanier 1993, 218–52).

The coroplasts of central Gaul and the technique they employed are well known, thanks to excavated workshops and signatures that sometimes appear on molds and figurines (Van Boekel 1983, 203–230; Bémont, Jeanlin, and Lahanier 1993, 96–123). The coroplasts of central Gaul often used white, pure fabric with high kaolin and low chalk and iron content, plastic enough to be molded. It was fired in reducing circumstances, resulting in white clay, a perfect ground for coloring. In many cases the coroplasts manufactured other products of clay such as terra sigillata pottery, with the figurines as secondary products of those kilns. Indeed, the frontality of the figurines and the fact they were produced in a few molds only (front, back, head) imply a shared pottery production and not a specialized coroplastic craft. Many molds have been discovered, as well as some archetypes. Production in generations was common.

The Gaulish repertoire is varied, with themes conveying a mixture of Graeco-Roman and Gaulish iconography (Rouvier-Jeanlin 1972, 28–34; Van Boekel 1983, 231–6; Bémont, Jeanlin, and Lahanier 1993, 130–34). It includes Roman and local deities of whom Venus is first and foremost. The goddess of love is usually depicted nude or semidraped, following Hellenistic types, but her frontal pose and rigid style, wide hips, and elaborate hairdos reflect local tastes. Modern scholars consider a common plaque figurine type of a nude female surrounded by apotropaic motifs to be a local variant of Venus in a shrine. Other popular Gallo-Roman deities appearing as figurines include Minerva, Fortuna, Eros and Psyche in a symmetric pose, Celtic Epona, and Celtic and Roman Mercury.

The popular motif of motherhood is represented by two main types: a plaque-like figurine depicting a woman with children on her sides or in front of her, with concentric circles around the figures; and a woman seated on a wicker chair with one baby or twins suckling in a symmetrical pose. Frequently found in domestic contexts and in tombs, both types either represent motherhood and fertility in general or may depict a local mother-goddess and thus suggest private religious beliefs (Rouvier-Jeanlin 1972, 32). Other types are riders on horses, gladiators, copies of the Hellenistic motif of the thorn puller, and animals. Another common type depicts busts of women or busts of smiling bald toddlers. The main iconographical themes are of women and children, not of men. It seems that most of the types—symbols of love, fecundity, maternity, and prosperity—are related to female gender roles and connotations in Gallo-Roman society.

As for style, the Gaulish figurines are rough, massive, and hardly retouched. Despite the different repertoire of types, the style resembles Gaulish bronze, stone, and wood sculpture (Bémont, Jeanlin, and Lahanier 1993, 104–9). The terracottas are dated according to their context, style, and the female figurines' hairstyles (Rouvier-Jeanlin 1972, 26–7; Bémont, Jeanlin, and Lahanier 1993, 131). Through the centuries the figurines became more simplified, more frontal, and more stereotyped.

Besides at workshops, the Gaulish figurines are discovered in three main contexts: domestic, funerary, and religious (Rouvier-Jeanlin 1972, 27–9; Van Boekel 1983, 238). At dwellings the types are religious, with mostly female divinities, above all the so-called mother-goddess. Figurines with protective qualities are often found in *lararia*. In graves, animal figurines and especially wild beasts predominate, perhaps due to the funerary role of lions, bulls, and so on. Terracottas portraying animals and fruits are favored in children's tombs, perhaps serving as substitute offerings. A specific type seems to predominate in each sanctuary (Bémont, Jeanlin, and Lahanier 1993, 139–42).

Another region with production centers is further to the north, along the rivers of the Rhine-Mosel, with the main workshops of Cologne and Trier. These operated for slightly longer than the Gaulish centers (first through fourth centuries AD), and their products are found in Germania Inferior, the northern part of Germania Superior, and the north of Gallia Belgica (Van Boekel 1983, 207–216). The Rhine-Mosel terracottas were often made in plaster molds, resulting in bulges on their surfaces, and they are characterized by the inferior quality of the finishing and assembly of the two halves (Van Boekel 1983, 224–7; Bémont, Jeanlin, and Lahanier 1993, 228). Other technical differences from central Gaulish workshops include the lack of vents and the modeling of the plinths and the busts' backs. Variations in typology are minor. Masks, rare at Gaulish centers, appear in shrines and houses, probably serving apotropaic, Bacchic, and decorative functions (Van Boekel 1983, 231–8; 1986, 276–86; Rose 2006).

Both the Gaulish and Rhine-Mosel productions were distributed throughout northwestern Europe (Van Boekel 1983; 1986; De Beenhouwer 1991; Bémont, Jeanlin, and Lahanier 1993, 218–52; Von Gonzenbach [1986] 1995). In Britain, for example, 90 percent of Roman terracottas were of central Gaulish manufacture (Bémont, Jeanlin, and Lahanier 1993, 240–52). Venus (or some local deity assimilated with her) and a woman seated in wicker chairs with two babies are the most popular types (figure 2.5.2; Jenkins 1957; 1958).

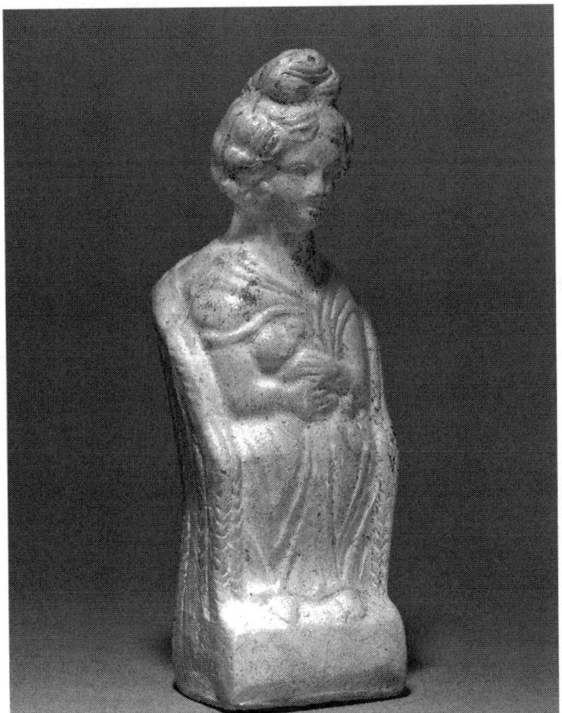

FIGURE 2.5.2 Terracotta of a woman seated in a wicker chair and holding a baby, from a Roman cemetery at Welwyn Grange, Hertfordshire. Second century AD. London, British Museum.

To sum up, northwestern terracottas are distinctive in the information they provide about production, distribution, and use. They were produced together with other clay products and, among other functions, served as votives. They seem to exist alongside other sculptural types in stone, wood, and bronze, rather than merge with them. The predominance of female motifs is noticeable and may hint at the users' identity, as well as at the concerns the figurines present—mainly fertility and maternity.

The southern Mediterranean also yielded terracottas, especially Africa Proconsularis and Spain. The old Punic traditions were not strong, and most of the production shows an ordinary assortment of Roman types: Greek deities, musicians, actors and gladiators, busts, and animals (Du Coudray La Blanchère and Gauckler 1897, 131–45, pls. 29–33; Deneauve 1987; Bonifay 2004, 431–5). Terracottas are found mostly in tombs, such as the cemetery of Hammamet (Pupput) in Tunisia (Bonifay 2004, 431–5) and at Granada (Ruiz Fernández and Molina Fajardo 1982).

Greece and Asia Minor

Greece and Asia Minor were the home of terracotta figurines in earlier periods, from the archaic through Hellenistic times, yet during the Roman period the production and use of terracottas decreased or ceased. At the Athenian Agora, after a gap of some 200 years, production of late Roman terracottas (third through fourth centuries AD) reappeared, with notably lesser quality (Grandjouan 1961). Terracottas were manufactured together with other pottery products and signed by the same artisans. Figurines were produced in two molds only (both clay and plaster), rather than in a modular system of separate molds for torsos, limbs, and heads, as was customary in the Hellenistic period. The Roman repertoire included canonical Greek and Roman deities with some foreign apotropaic divinities; enthroned women with children or other attributes, similar to the Gaulish type; motifs related to the theater and to a lesser extent the games—actors, masks, mimes and pantomimes, trained animals, gladiators and wrestlers; phallic objects; a selection of children's toys—puppets, dolls, toys on wheels, and rattles; busts of children and adults; and representations of daily life and fashion.

In a few centers of Asia Minor, especially at Myrina, Smyrna, and Tarsus, production increased in the early Roman era. Late Hellenistic types and religious traditions continued, as did the practice of copying well-known sculptural types (Bartman 1992, 20–22).

About 2000 figurines have been excavated from tombs dated between the third century BC and the first century AD at the relatively insignificant city of Myrina, situated between Smyrna and Pergamon (Burr 1934; Mollard-Besques 1963; Burn and Higgins 2001, 113–14). The Myrinian terracottas were closely related to Pergamene workshops (Töpperwein 1976, 171–2, 193–8). The figurines of the first century BC to the first century AD lost their freshness and became more metallic and ornate, showing less careful workmanship. Between 60 BC and AD 30 artisans often signed their figurines (Burr 1934, 7–25; Mollard-Besques 1963, pls. 13–25; Kassab 1988). The most productive and well-attested signatures are of Diphilos and Menophilos. Diphilos worked from AD

20 to 70 and made terracottas in sculptural style, including draped women, Aphrodite, Erotes, and groups. His work is considered to be great in quantity but poor in quality, with unfinished surfaces and dull style. Menophilos (figure 2.5.3) worked in the same era, producing terracottas of better quality (Burford 1972, 107).

Smyrna produced terracotta figurines from Hellenistic times until it was damaged in an earthquake in AD 178. Most of the terracottas, made from a distinctive clay, have no secure provenance (Besques 1972, 153–6; Burn and Higgins 2001, 127–8; Hasselin Rous, Laugier, and Martinez 2009). The repertoire of Smyrna is mostly characterized by the large quantity of figurines portraying distorted figures, pathological conduct, disabled people, and comic actors (Besques 1972, pls. 221–47, 306–323, 324–31). The meaning of these types is debatable, and possibilities range from apotropaic or cultic objects to theater souvenirs (Garland 1995, 105–122; Burn and Higgins 2001, 128).

At Tarsus, terracottas were produced from the Hellenistic period until the second century AD (Goldman 1950, 298–306). The figurines were manufactured in multiple plaster molds. Roman figurines of gods follow the Hellenistic sculptural tradition with new types starting from the late first century AD. Figurines wearing wreaths with ivy leaves and a ribbon or diadems are hallmarks for the early imperial local industry. Other Roman types are theatrical masks, horsemen, realistic figures, and grotesques.

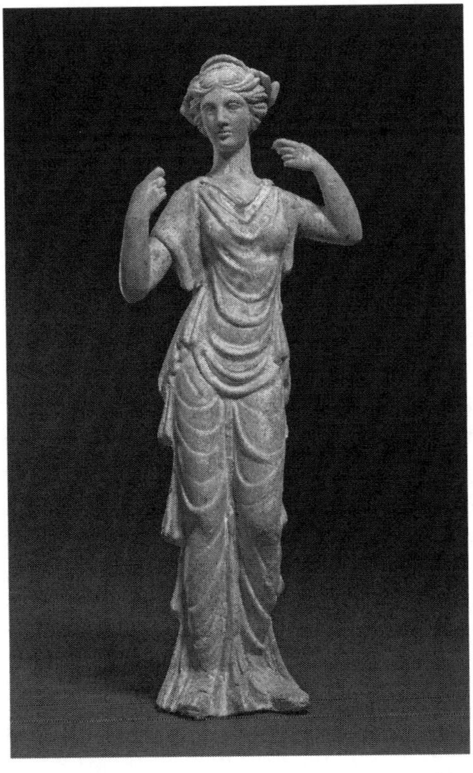

FIGURE 2.5.3 Terracotta from Myrina depicting Aphrodite, signed by Menophilos. First century AD. London, British Museum.

The Levant

During Roman times terracotta production in the Levant also decreased significantly. In Syria, figurines and plaques were found only at Dura Europos and Palmyra (Seyrig 1985, 301–315; Downey 2003). Other centers were far beyond the river Euphrates and the empire's borders in Parthia. Most of the Dura Europos figurines are handmade, such as the most popular horseman type. Surprisingly, hardly any nude female figurines, which constitute a prominent part of Mesopotamian assemblages, occur at the site. Moreover, Aphrodite and Heracles are common at Dura in sculpture and painting, but are absent from the terracottas. Therefore Downey (2003, 11–12) suggests that terracottas were used largely by the less Hellenized segment of the population. Again, as we saw in the northwestern provinces and Italy, terracottas and large sculptures often diverge in subject and function.

In Roman Syria-Palestine and Arabia, terracotta figurines are found in the same three contexts they are discovered elsewhere: shrines, tombs, and dwellings. Two centers are worthy of note. One is the workshop of figurines and lamps found at Gerasa (Jerash), dated to around AD 100 (Iliffe 1944), with a repertoire similar to that of Tarsus (Aphrodite and other Greek deities, masks, riders, animals). Similar figurines were found in temples or shrines in the region (unpublished). Another workshop, at Beit Nattif in Palestine, dates to the third through fifth centuries AD (Baramki 1936). It also produced figurines together with lamps but exhibits a change in technique: both lamps and figurines were produced in stone molds, in what seems to be a new practice in Byzantine Palestine (Sussman 1980; Erlich and Foerster 2012). Two main types of the Beit Nattif workshop depict horsemen and nude women in a shrine (figure 2.5.4).

Egypt

Unlike the Levant, terracotta production in Egypt did not decrease in Roman times but increased and advanced. Roman terracottas developed directly from the Hellenistic-Ptolemaic tradition, with a mixture of Greek and Egyptian motifs executed in a distinct local style. The production peaked in the mid-second through mid-third centuries, declined in the mid-third century, and ceased in the fourth century AD (Fjeldhagen 1995, 14). Terracottas are found both in production centers and in their destination contexts, especially domestic settings. Unfortunately most of the terracottas that have been published come from museums and collections and have no good provenance (e.g., Dunand 1990; Fischer 1994; Fjeldhagen 1995; Török 1995; Bailey 2008).

Terracottas were produced in the cities of the Delta (Naucratis, Alexandria, and Canopus) and up the Nile (Coptus, Edfu), but especially in the *chora* of the Fayum. The coroplasts used coarse clay made of Nile mud, which turns brown after firing, and cast the figurines in plaster or clay molds, with the back often plain and convex (Fjeldhagen 1995, 10–13; Rodziewicz 2005, 39). The workmanship is generally mediocre, and workshops also manufactured other products (Rodziewicz 2005).

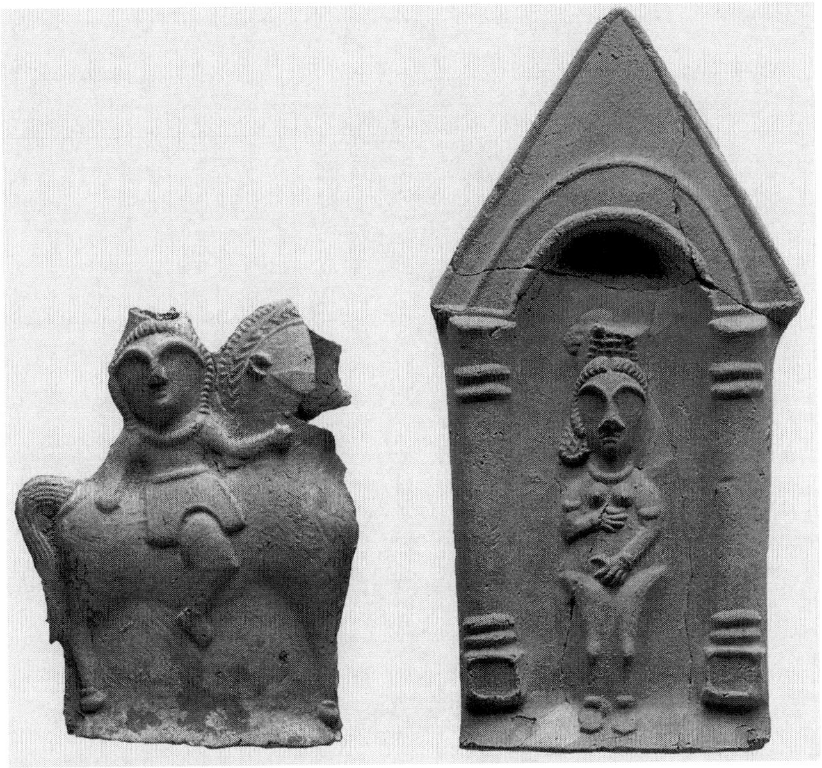

FIGURE 2.5.4 Two terracottas of the Beit Nattif workshop in Israel: horse rider and a nude woman in a shrine. Third to fourth centuries AD. Jerusalem, Israel Antiquities Authority.

Besides in workshops, Egyptian terracottas are discovered mostly in dwellings and to a lesser degree in tombs and shrines (Nachtergael 1995; Bailey 2008, 1–2). The terracottas were placed in domestic shrines, frescoed *aediculae*, or niches. These figurines represent private religious practices, with people praying to them, suspending them, or placing them on altars. Their main function was to protect from supernatural powers and to aid the fertility of humans, animals, and the fields. This domestic cult should not be viewed as polarized from the formal cult in the temples, as both were complementary (Frankfurter 1998, 131–42; Dunand and Zivie-Coche 2004, 302–3). The predominant use of these figurines in domestic cult rather than official cult is demonstrated by the popular types: Harpocrates predominates in terracottas, whereas cult places dedicated to him are few; Bes did not have cult sites; while Isis is the only one who enjoys both cult sites and many figurines. The evidence represents an Egyptian *koine* of mostly religious types, of which Harpocrates (figure 2.5.5) predominates (Nachtergael 1995, 235–8; Fischer 1995). Fischer (1994; 1995) has tried to establish a chronology of types, but it is uncertain, as many of the figurines have no reliable provenance and their context is not well established.

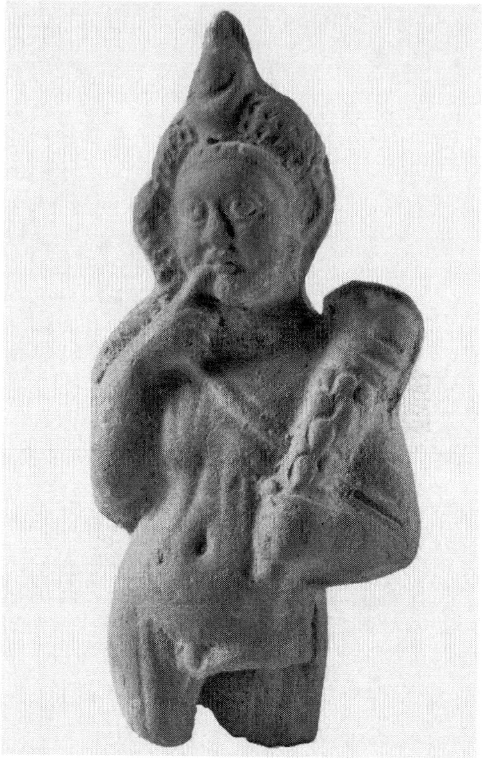

FIGURE 2.5.5 Terracotta of Harpocrates from Egypt. First to second centuries AD. Haifa, National Maritime Museum.

The types may be instructive for the study of ethnicity, as often the local Egyptian types co-occur with non-Greek (Demotic) papyri in relatively poor houses and therefore may point to a local population (Nachtergael 1995, 235–8). The main types show Egyptian deities and demons (Harpocrates, Isis and Isiac figures, Sarapis, Bes); local figures related to fertility (naked women, *orans*-like females with huge coiffures, "baubo," and phallic figures); participants in cult (priests and priestesses, dancers, and musicians); Greek deities; aspects of daily life (human figures, home scenes, outdoor scenes, slaves, army, actors, and grotesques); and animals that can be considered as toys or emblems of deities (Fischer 1995; Bailey 2008).

To sum up, Egypt is unique among Roman centers of terracotta production. It is the only region in which a local Egyptian goddess, Isis, rules, rather than Aphrodite/Venus. It is also the only region where the iconography of an infant god (Harpocrates) prevails over his mother or any other adult deity. Furthermore, it is the only area in which terracottas are so extensively related to private cult and popular beliefs and found mostly in domestic contexts (or funerary, again private). The uniqueness of Egyptian terracottas relates to the lengthy and strong Pharaonic tradition.

Conclusion

Roman terracottas draw a complex picture. Italy was home to a rich coroplastic tradition, but only until the dawn of the empire, when production there decreased greatly. The first century AD witnessed the decline of old centers of coroplastic production in Greece, Asia Minor, and Cyprus, and the flourishing of other centers with local styles in Gaul and Egypt. The decline of Roman terracottas in the third through fourth centuries preceded the end of the Roman Empire.

While workshops specializing in coroplastic production were common in the Hellenistic period, by the Roman period most workshops also manufactured other pottery products. Does that make those terracotta figurines pottery, not sculpture? In support of this interpretation, the technical process was simplified, and the style became more rough and dull.

As for types, they are indeed varied, but seem to be related to two main fields: the cycle of love, fertility, and children's welfare, and the apotropaic and protective sphere. Terracottas served as private—not public—sculpture and were often the possession of marginalized groups in society—women, children, and poor people. Save for representations of a few standard Graeco-Roman deities, the choice of types shows a strong preference for popular themes (such as Venus and maternity) in most regions. It seems that terracottas, cheap and mass-produced, served largely as reflections of the feeling, beliefs, and aspirations of the lower classes in Roman society.

Bibliography

Bailey, D. M. 1983. "Terracotta Revetments, Figurines, and Lamps." In *A Handbook of Roman Art: A Survey of the Visual Arts of the Roman World*, edited by M. Henig, 191–204. Oxford: Phaidon.

———. 2008. *Catalogue of Terracottas in the British Museum*. Vol. 4, *Ptolemaic and Roman Terracottas from Egypt*. London: British Museum Press.

Baramki, D. C. 1936. "Two Roman Cisterns at Beit Nattif." *QDAP* 5: 3–10.

Bartman, E. 1992. *Ancient Sculptural Copies in Miniature*. Columbia Studies in the Classical Tradition 19. Leiden: Brill.

Bell, M. 1990. "Hellenistic Terracottas of Southern Italy and Sicily." In *The Coroplast's Art: Greek Terracottas of the Hellenistic World*, edited by J. P. Uhlenbrock, 64–70. New Rochelle, NY: A. D. Caratzas.

Bémont, C., M. Jeanlin, and C. Lahanier, eds. 1993. *Les figurines en terre cuite gallo-romaines*. DAF 38. Paris: Éditions de la Maison des sciences de l'homme.

Besques, S. 1972. *Catalogue raisonné des figurines et reliefs en terre cuite grecs, étrusques et romains*. Vol. 3, *Époques hellénistique et romaine, Grèce et Asie Mineure*. Paris: Éditions des musées nationaux.

Besques, S. 1986. *Musée national du Louvre: Catalogue raisonné des figurines et reliefs en terre cuite grecs, étrusques et romains*. Vol. 4, *Époques hellénistique et romaine*. Part 1, *Italie méridionale—Sicilie—Sardaigne*. Paris: Éditions des musées nationaux.

Bonifay, M. 2004. *Etudes sur la céramique romaine tardive d'Afrique*. BAR-IS 1301. Oxford: Archaeopress.

Bouma, J. W. 1996. "*Religio Votiva*: The Archaeology of Latial Votive Religion: The 5th–3rd c. BC Votive Deposit South West of the Main Temple at 'Satricum' Borgo Le Ferriere." PhD diss., University of Groningen.

Bouquillon, A., I. Hasselin Rous, and L. Laugier 2010. "Smyrne et ses productions artistiques: Bilan des analyses scientifiques menées sur les figurines en terre cuite et les marbres smyrniotes du musée du Louvre." *Anatolia Antiqua* 18: 321–8.

Burford, A. 1972. *Craftsmen in Greek and Roman Society*. London: Thames and Hudson.

Burn, L., and R. A. Higgins. 2001. *Catalogue of Greek Terracottas in the British Museum*. Vol. 3. London: British Museum Press.

Burr, D. 1934. *Terra-cottas from Myrina in the Museum of Fine Arts, Boston*. Vienna: Adolf Nachfolder.

Comella, A. 1978. *Il materiale votivo tardo di Gravisca*. Archaeologica 6. Rome: Giorgio Bretschneider.

———. 1981. "Tipologia e diffusion dei complessi votivi in Italia in epoca medio- e tardo-republicana." *MÉFRA* 93(2): 717–803.

D'Ambrosio, A., and M. R. Borriello. 1990. *Le terrecotte figurate di Pompei*. Rome: "L'Erma" di Bretschneider.

De Beenhouwer, J. 1991. "Roman Terracotta Statuettes from a Closed Find at Tongeren and their Relation to the Köln, Trier and Central-Rhine Production Centres." *ActaArchLov* 30: 61–93.

Deneauve, J. 1987. "Figurines et lampes africaines." *AntAfr* 23: 197–251.

Downey, S. B. 2003. *Terracotta Figurines and Plaques from Dura-Europos*. Ann Arbor: University of Michigan Press.

Du Coudray La Blanchère, F., and P. Gauckler. 1897. *Catalogue du Musée Alaoui*. Paris: Ernest Leroux.

Dunand, F. 1990. *Catalogue des terres cuites gréco-romaines d'Égypte*. Paris: Réunion des musées nationaux.

Dunand, F., and C. Zivie-Coche. 2004. *Gods and Men in Egypt: 3000 BCE to 395 CE*. Translated by D. Lorton. Ithaca: Cornell University Press.

Erlich, A., and G. Foerster. 2012. "Zoomorphic Vases of the Fourth–Sixth Centuries from the North of Palestine." In *Christ is Here! Studies in Biblical and Christian Archaeology in Memory of Michele Piccirillo, ofm*. Studium Biblicum Franciscanum, Collectio Maior 52, edited by L. D. Chrupcała, 1–10. Milan: Terra Santa.

Fenelli, M. 1975. "Contributo per lo studio del votivo anatomico: I votivi anatomici di Lavinio." *ArchCl* 27: 206–52.

Ferrea, L. 2002. *Gli dei di terracotta: La ricomposizione del frontone da via di San Gregorio*. Milan: Electa.

Fischer, J. 1994. *Griechische-römische Terrakotten aus Ägypten: Die Sammlungen Sieglin und Schrieber*. Tübingen: E. Wasmuth.

———. 1995. "The Change of Religious Subjects in Graeco-Roman Coroplastic Art." In *Alessandria e il mondo ellenistico-romano: Studi in onore di Achille Adriani*, edited by N. Bonacasa and A. Di Vita, 308–313. Rome: "L'Erma" di Bretschneider.

Fjeldhagen, M. 1995. *Catalogue of the Graeco Roman Terracottas from Egypt*. Copenhagen: Ny Carlsberg Glyptotek.

Frankfurter, D. 1998. *Religion in Roman Egypt: Assimilation and Resistance*. Princeton: Princeton University Press.

Garland, R. 1995. *The Eye of the Beholder: Deformity and Disability in the Graeco-Roman World*. Ithaca: Cornell University Press.

Ginge, B. 1993. "Votive Deposits in Italy: New Perspectives on Old Finds." *JRA* 6: 285–8.

Glinister, F. 2006. "Reconsidering 'Religious Romanization.'" In *Religion in Republican Italy*, edited by C. E. Schultz and P. B. Harvey, 10–33. Cambridge: Cambridge University Press.

Goldman, H. 1950. *Excavations at Gözlü Kule, Tarsus*. Vol. 1, *The Hellenistic and Roman Periods*. Princeton: Princeton University Press.

Grandjouan, C. 1961. *Terracottas and Plastic Lamps of the Roman Period*. Agora 6. Princeton: American School of Classical Studies at Athens.

Hamilton, N., J. Marcus, D. W. Bailey, G. Haaland, R. Haaland, and P. J. Ucko. 1996. "Viewpoint: Can We Interpret Figurines?" *CAJ* 6(2): 281–307.

Hasselin Rous, I., L. Laugier, and J.-L. Martinez. 2009. *D'Izmir à Smyrne: Découverte d'une cité antique*. Paris: Musée du Louvre éditions.

Higgins, R. A. 1976. "Terracottas." In *Roman Crafts*, edited by D. E. Strong and D. Brown, 105–9. London: Duckworth.

Iliffe, J. H. 1944. "Imperial Art in Trans-Jordan: Figurines and Lamps from a Potter Store at Jerash." *QDAP* 11: 1–26.

Jenkins, F. 1957. "The Cult of *Dea Nutrix* in Kent." *Archaeologia Cantiana* 71: 38–46.

———. 1958. "The Cult of the 'Pseudo-Venus' in Kent." *Archaeologia Cantiana* 72: 60–76.

Kassab, T. D. 1988. *Statuettes en terre cuite de Myrina: Corpus des signatures, monogrammes, lettres et signes*. Istanbul: Institut français d'études anatoliennes d'Istanbul.

Macintosh Turfa, J. 1994. "Anatomical Votives and Italian Medical Traditions." In *Murlo and the Etruscans: Art and Society in Ancient Etruria*, edited by R. D. De Puma and J. P. Small, 224–40. Madison: University of Wisconsin Press.

Miller Ammerman, R. 2002. *The Sanctuary of Santa Venera at Paestum II: The Votive Terracottas*. Ann Arbor: University of Michigan Press.

Mollard-Besques, S. 1963. *Catalogue raisonné des figurines et reliefs en terre cuite grecs et romains*. Vol. 2, *Myrina*. Paris: Éditions des musées nationaux.

Nachtergael, G. 1995. "Chronique: Terres cuites de l'Égypte gréco-romaine; À propos de quatre Catalogues récents." *Chronique d'Égypte* 70: 254–94.

Nagy, H. 1988. *Votive Terracottas from the "Vignaccia", Cerveteri, in the Lowie Museum of Anthropology*. Archaeologica 75. Rome: Giorgio Bretschneider.

Nicholls, R. V. 1952. "Type, Group and Series: A Reconsideration of Some Coroplastic Fundamentals." *BSA* 47: 217–26.

Potter, T. W. 1985. "A Republican Healing-Sanctuary at Ponte di Nona near Rome and the Classical Tradition of Votive Medicine." *Journal of the British Archaeological Association* 138: 23–47.

Ramos Sáinz, M. L., and L. Fuentes Ghislaín. 1998. *Arqueología experimental: La manufactura de terracotas en época romana*. BAR-IS 736. Oxford: Archaeopress.

Rodziewicz, M. D. 2005. *Early Roman Industries on Elephantine*. Elephantine 27. Archäologische Veröffentlichungen 107. Mainz: Philipp Von Zabern.

Rous, B. 2009. "An Age without Images: Architectural Decoration in the Late Republican Period." In *Deliciae Fictiles IV: Architectural Terracottas in Ancient Italy; Images of Gods, Monsters and Heroes*, edited by P. Lulof and C. Rescigno, 84–94. Oxford: Oxbow.

Rose, H. 2006. *Die römischen Terrakottamasken in den Nordwestprovinzen: Herkunft, Herstellung, Verbreitung, Funktion*. Monumenta Artis Romanae 37. Wiesbaden: Reichert.

Rouvier-Jeanlin, M. 1972. *Les figurines gallo-romaines en terre cuite au Musée des antiquités nationales*. Supplément à Gallia 24. Paris: Éditions du Centre national de la recherche scientifique.

Ruiz Fernández, A., and F. Molina Fajardo. 1982. "El conjunto de terracotas de una tumba romana en Almuñecar (Granada)." *MM* 23: 318–46.

Seyrig, H. 1985. *Scripta Varia: Mélanges d'archéologie et d'histoire*. Paris: Librairie orientaliste Paul Geuthner.

Söderlind, M. 2000–2001. "Romanization and the Use of Votive Offerings in the Eastern *Ager Vulcentis*." *OpRom* 25–6: 89–102.

———. 2002. *Late Etruscan Votive Heads from Tessennano: Production, Distribution, Sociohistorical Context*. Rome: "L'Erma" di Bretschneider.

Sussman, V. 1980. "Molds for Lamps and Figurines from a Caesarea Workshop." *'Atiqot* 14: 76–9.

Töpperwein, E. 1976. *Terrakotten von Pergamon*. Berlin: Walter de Gruyter.

Török, L. 1995. *Hellenistic and Roman Terracottas from Egypt*. Rome: "L'Erma" di Bretschneider.

Ucko, P. J. 1968. *Anthropomorphic Figurines of Predynastic Egypt and Neolithic Crete with Comparative Material from the Prehistoric Near East and Mainland Greece*. London: Andrew Szmilda.

Uhlenbrock, J. P., ed. 1990. *The Coroplast's Art: Greek Terracottas of the Hellenistic World*. New Rochelle, NY: A. D. Caratzas.

Van Boekel, G. M. E. C. 1983. "Roman Terracotta Figurines and Masks from the Netherlands: Introduction and catalogue I (Apollo-Fortuna)." *Berichten van de Rijksdienst voor het Oudheidkundig Bodemonderzoek* 33: 197–359.

———. 1986. "Roman Terracotta Figurines and Masks from the Netherlands: Catalogue III and Conclusions." *Berichten van de Rijksdienst voor het Oudheidkundig Bodemonderzoek* 36: 25–404.

Voigt, M. M. 1983. *Hajji Firuz Tepe, Iran: The Neolithic Settlement*. University Museum Monograph 50. Philadelphia: University Museum, University of Pennsylvania.

Von Gonzenbach, V. (1986) 1995. *Die römischen Terracotten in der Schweiz: Untersuchungen zu Zeitstellung, Typologie und Ursprung der mittelgallischen Tonstatuetten*. Bern: Francke.

CHAPTER 2.6

POLYCHROMY

MARK B. ABBE

INTRODUCTION

ALTHOUGH the phrase "ancient Roman sculpture" may conjure up, for many, a rather limited palette of pristine white marbles and corroded green bronzes, in antiquity Roman statuary was richly embellished with various forms of painting, gilding, silvering, and inlay. This polychromy was fundamental not only to the striking immediacy of such works, but also to their individual definition and to their complex and nuanced meanings. The media of large-scale Roman statuary—ivory, metal, stone, terracotta, plaster, and wood—all belonged to the broader ancient Mediterranean tradition of polychrome sculpture and received various forms of applied coloration, from opaque applications that effectively obscured the sculpture's substrate, such as thick painting and metal leaf, to thin translucent forms of painting, glazing, and waxing that enhanced the material qualities of the sculptural substrate's medium. The polychromy of Roman sculpture varied widely, from vividly mimetic, presenting a "real-looking" virtual likeness, to emphatically stylized, artful and symbolic, elevated and removed from everyday life. Such polychrome styles were, of course, not mutually exclusive and were often combined in a rich visual language of associations and connotations.

Although the modern term polychromy (deriving from the Greek word *polychrómatos*, "multicolored": *poly* "many" plus *chroma* "color") is often used to mean painting, it properly encompasses the full range of color media applied to sculpture and related aesthetic phenomena (Marincola 2004). Studies of artistic materials and techniques form the foundation for fundamentally broader considerations of the complex visual appearances and aesthetics of images, such as the conditions of their original display and viewing, and their materiality, that is the distinctly cultural and historical use of materials, often precious and exotic, with highly symbolic and evocative qualities (Clerbois and Droth 2011).

In the early twenty-first century the polychromy of Greek and Roman sculpture has become a subject of increasing interest and research (Brinkmann and Wünsche

2003; Rouveret, Duvel, and Naas 2006; Brinkmann and Wünsche 2007; Panzanelli, Schmidt, and Lapatin 2008; Brinkmann, Primavesi, and Hollein 2010). Recent studies build upon a long history of scholarship and often reinvestigate questions raised in the nineteenth century (Reutersward 1960, 1–34). Patrik Reutersward's monograph on the coloration of Greek and Roman sculpture (1960), though dated, remains a standard point of reference in many discussions of color on Roman statuary. Excellent recent overviews of various aspects of Roman sculptural polychromy, both marble (Liverani 2008; Østergaard 2008; Liverani 2009; 2010) and bronze (Descamps-Lequime 2006; Formigli 2013), are available. The intuitive character of most earlier research has increasingly given way to a variety of new interdisciplinary approaches that combine archaeological and historical study with detailed methods of examination and scientific characterization of the extant vestiges of coloration (Bourgeois and Jockey 2003; Brinkmann 2007; Verri 2009; Abbe, Borromeo, and Pike 2012). Such research has the potential to reveal, often quite dramatically (Bourgeois and Jockey 2005; Verri, Opper, and Deviese 2010), both the extent and the complexity of polychromy preserved at the brink of invisibility in what constitutes a new micro-stratigraphic surface archaeology of ancient sculpture. This research is increasingly documented with microscopic images, cross-sections, and scientific materials analysis. Presenting these results in a more accessible form remains challenging: color reconstructions of what statuary "actually looked like" are difficult and inevitably subjective, because the remains of polychromy are incomplete and often have altered over time; their original hue, brightness, and surface appearance can rarely be precisely reconstructed with certainty (Brinkmann et al. 2007; Wünsche 2007; Brinkmann, Koch-Brinkmann, and Piening 2010, 68–85; Zimmer 2012).

Roman sculpture preserves a more extensive and richly varied corpus of polychromy than any other period of classical antiquity. Despite growing interest in Roman sculpture during the last half-century, the systematic study of such coloration is in its infancy compared to that of the adjacent Greek and Medieval periods. The essential historical resource remains Reutersward's 1960 groundbreaking monograph on the polychromy of Greek and Roman statuary, which, though invaluable, is increasingly dated, intuitive in many of its conclusions, and largely devoid of illustrations. The striking disconnect between the wealth of evidence and the nascent state of its investigation offers extensive opportunities for new research that can add unprecedented levels to our understanding of Roman sculpture.

A wealth of secondary evidence for sculptural polychromy survives from the Roman period: representations of colored statuary in Roman mural painting, mosaics, and illustrated manuscripts (Moormann 1988; 2008; and essay 6.4, Moormann) and an abundance of literary and epigraphic sources describing the color and materiality of statuary, both real and fictional, from a wide range of historical and cultural perspectives (Primavesi 2007; Bradley 2009b; Mandel 2010; Barry 2011). Much of this evidence remains only summarily investigated, and future studies of polychromy will profit through increased interdisciplinary study combining all types of evidence.

This essay provides a brief introduction to the decorative techniques used on the principal extant media of Roman sculpture—white marble, colored stone, and bronze—from c. 100 BC to AD 300, when the vast majority of extant Roman sculpture was produced. As our knowledge and understanding of the range and historical definition of Roman sculptural polychromy remain limited, several caveats are appropriate. First, given the geographical extent, chronological span, and diverse cultures contained within the Roman Empire, a single, uniform tradition of sculptural polychromy should not be assumed. Even within a specific location and historical period, polychromy varied widely according to display, genre, context, and purpose: the often-noted stylistic plurality of Roman sculpture extended to its coloration and one should think in terms of *polychromies* rather than a single, uniform *polychromy*, though we remain only at the beginning of defining the changes to the language of color in Roman sculpture. Second, regarding terminology, it is also worth noting that the modern orthodox juxtaposition of monochromy and polychromy in many discussions of sculpture remains unattested in antiquity. This modern and fundamentally rhetorical language has no ancient pedigree and is probably unproductive, if not obstructive, to the proper material and historical evaluation of many interesting and nuanced forms of polychromy in which the coloration *on* and materiality *of* the substrates were inseparable. Paint, for example, enriched and enhanced the prized translucency of marble on many celebrated works, such as Praxiteles's Aphrodite of Knidos (Ps.-Lucian *Amor* 15; Mandel 2010, 309), in a sophisticated relationship between polychrome application and substrate material.

Finally, it should be emphasized that the polychrome effects of Roman statuary should be understood within the broader hierarchy of materials and broad aesthetics of Graeco-Roman statuary. In antiquity the most esteemed sculpture was made of sumptuous precious materials. For example, the splendor of chryselephantine (gold and ivory) sculptures contributed to their mimetic simulacra of divine radiance and a materially embodied lustrous, radiant epiphany associated with the divine to the degree that these materials were thought to have added something to religion (Quint. *Inst.* 12.10.9). Gold, silver, and ivory spoke immediately to the prestige of the commission and were generally restricted to images of the gods and sculptural honors of exceptional status. The more limited use of these materials, especially gold, on the flesh, hair, or drapery embodied significant symbolic and ideological concepts. Bronze and marble, though less precious, were prized sculptural materials that technique and artisanship could significantly elevate. A true-to-life polychrome "realism," so prized in modern scholarship, was not the sole overriding aim of mimetic sculpture. Ancient notions of mimesis often were materially mediated, and materials added definition and symbolic meaning to the identity, function, and status of the work. Although less celebrated materials such as terracotta, plaster, and wood could obtain highly naturalistic effects with the aid of excellent craftsmanship, their materials were less esteemed and generally emulated the aesthetics of more celebrated sculptural media.

Artistic Practice

Little is recorded about the artisans who created the polychrome finish on sculpture in Roman antiquity. The raw materials and techniques employed on statuary were not specific to the artistic genre, and most artists were known for their specialized craft skill with materials (e.g., encaustic painter) rather than the product or artistic medium to which it was applied (e.g., panel painting versus sculpture). Collaborations between specialist craftsmen must have been common in creating the polychrome effects on statuary. Plutarch suggestively likened the interconnected work of encaustic painters, gilders, and tempera painters in defining sculpture to the complementary roles that actors play in the production of a drama (*De glor. Ath.* 348 E 11). Pliny's famous anecdote (*HN* 35.133) that the celebrated classical Greek sculptor Praxiteles's favorite sculptures from his workshop were those painted by the contemporary painter Nicias no doubt spoke to similar relationships between marble sculptors and painters in his own day (Primavesi 2007, 203–4). Large metropolitan centers supported highly specialized craftsmen who excelled in specific aspects of sculptural polychromy: funerary epitaphs from Rome record more than one *oculararius faber*, that is the "maker of eyes" inlaid into high quality statuary (Lahusen and Formigli 2001, 463). A highly unusual epitaph of an Aphrodisian sculptor suggestively identifies him as *agalmatopoios enkaustes*—that is, as both a statue-maker (of images of the gods) and an encaustic-painter, the most distinguished medium of painting (Löwy 1885, 376, no. 551).

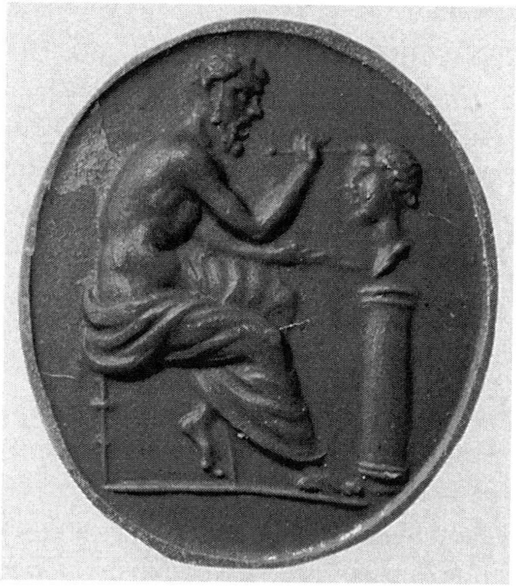

FIGURE 2.6.1 Impression of intaglio ring stone with seated Greek artisan painting a portrait of a Roman woman with a fashionable *nodus* hairstyle. Carnelian, from Italy, c. 20 BC. H. 1.3 cm. New York, Metropolitan Museum of Art.

A rare, if not singular, image of an artist creating the polychrome finish on sculpture from the Roman period is preserved on a personal carnelian ring stone (figure 2.6.1) from Italy dating to last decades of the late first century BC (Richter 1956, 437, no. 434). A seated Greek painter, with a full beard and himation and holding a flat mollusk-shell-like palette, gently applies a brush-like instrument to the hair of a female portrait bust with a distinctively Roman female *nodus*-coiffure that was fashionable in the Augustan period. The painting technique (presumably tempera) is secondary to the definition of the social status of this painter of sculpture, who is represented far removed from the banausic labor of the marble yard (compare Lucian *Somn.* 9) in an era when Greek painters increasingly migrated to Roman patrons in Italy to create portraits in the ever more widespread medium of white marble.

White Marble

Marmor (transliterated from the Greek *mármaron*, meaning "gleaming stone") was a celebrated sculptural material in Roman culture, as the vast corpus of extant marble sculpture amply attests. An imported luxury material in Rome and southern-central Italy, marble was a focus of competitive display by the Roman aristocracy during the republican period and became increasingly available in Italy after the opening of the local Luna quarries in the late first century BC and across the empire with the development of both a private and imperial administration (*ratio marmorum*) of marble production (Hirt 2010; see also essay 2.1, Pensabene and Gasparini). Painted white marble significantly diversified the polychrome language of Roman sculpture by adding a richer, more expressive and complex range of painterly effects than bronze or painted terracotta, including sophisticated modes of painted "naturalism" that appear to have appealed to Roman aesthetic sensibilities in both their portraiture and art. The polychromy of Roman sculpture continued the nuanced coloration of marble sculpture in the Hellenistic Greek world (Blume 2010; Bourgeois and Jockey 2010). The archaeological record displays a general expansion in the Roman market for marble sculpture in the first century AD when Pliny famously described marble sculpture as a thriving art in his own day, unlike the dying arts (*ars moriens*) of bronze statuary and painting (Isager 1991, 174–8, 209–211). During the peak of production in the second half of the second and early third centuries AD, marble effectively supplanted bronze as a leading medium of sculpture for portraits and other forms of sculpture. Many statues are distinguished by exquisitely refined techniques, including deeply drilled hairstyles, engraved irises and drilled pupils, and highly polished flesh areas, the overall aim of which was to create heightened realistic and dramatic effects akin to contemporary modes of self-stylization. Details previously rendered in paint—such as eyes, eyebrows, hair, and beards—were now increasingly rendered in the marble itself, suggesting the increased intimacy between painting and sculptural definition. Contrary to views of this period as an era of alleged sculptural monochromy (Reuterswärd 1960, 218–27), even the high polishes on the best metropolitan portraits were subtly colored (Skovmøller and Therkildsen 2012).

Painting was probably the most delicate and refined form of ancient sculptural polychromy. From the ancient sources two binding media appear to have been most common: tempera (using a water-soluble binding agent such as egg) and encaustic (defined by its wax medium and the *enkaustikos* ["burning in" process] by which colors were bonded to the substrate). The numerous and often contradictory descriptions of these painting methods attest to the flexibility of ancient practice (Berger 1904; Büll 1963; Koch 2000). Artists were, of course, well aware that the binding medium used with a pigment affects the color, translucency, and optical qualities of a painted surface, and presumably employed multiple methods to obtain differing results on a single work.

The process of painting marble sculpture frequently began with localized underpainting—usually in red, yellow, or black—that defined features otherwise unrepresented in the sculptured form, often with masterful precision, such as details of the hair, eyes, eyebrows, and eyelashes that survive on many sculptures (e.g., the Copenhagen portrait head of Caligula: Østergaard 2007). Such underpainting, which defined the sculpted white canvas (similar to "underdrawing" on painting) and provided a base color for the definition of the desired color hue and value, often appears to have been a distinct phase of the multistage painting process; often it is the only painting that remains on sculpture due to the more-common loss of the subsequent painting for reasons that remain poorly understood.

On flesh areas, subsequent painting often survives only in protected locations, such as in the mouth, nostrils, ears, and corners of the eyes. More extensive coloration is preserved to an exceptional degree on the Treu Head, a mid-second-century AD head of a goddess discovered in Rome in 1884 (figure 2.6.2, see color insert). This sculpture is a powerful demonstration of the sophisticated technique, artful dexterity, and subtle employment of color that defined much polychromy of Roman marble statuary. The color of the flesh, for example, is composed of a combination of no fewer than six finely mixed pigments (calcite, a pink organic lake, carbon black, red hematite, yellow goethite, and Egyptian blue). It was thinly applied across the flesh area (preserved to a thickness of c. 70 microns) and appears to have exploited the natural translucency of the Parian marble substrate (Verri, Opper, and Deviese 2010). Translucent highlights on the cheeks and neck were rendered with thin layers of finely ground calcite, and more opaque shadows were defined in the corners of the mouth and around the eyes to enhance the sculpted form. The refined painting is strikingly akin in process and materials to the best painting preserved on wooden panels from Roman Egypt.

Flesh tones on marble sculpture challenge common modern assumptions about classical marble statuary, as do the highly detailed, brightly colored costumes that, in antiquity, presumably made statues both legible and conspicuous, and indeed could have differentiated otherwise similar types. Many examples display a complex range and nuanced patterning of pigments, such as the Prima Porta Augustus, whose expensive and highly localized painted coloration on the cuirassed costume drew attention to its specific mythological scenes and elevated characterization (Liverani 2003; 2004). The extensive coloration preserved on the drapery of a statue of Venus from a private house in Pompeii (figure 2.6.3, see color insert) originally created a sharp narrative contrast: the bright yellow, blue, and pink palette on the drapery of the living goddess was effectively juxtaposed with a more subdued and seemingly older palette of yellow, green, and black on the archaistic statue support (Carrella et al. 2008, 24–5).

Gilding and other precious-metal leafs were a common form of embellishment on the hair, garments, and attributes of marble sculpture. Gold leaf could be applied directly to the sculptural substrate or on top of pigmented, bole-like preparation layers. Generally yellow or red in color, these underlayers imparted visual warmth to the metal leaf and allowed the leaf to be smoothed or burnished to a pristine, reflective surface. Large areas of gilding were often additionally prepared with a thick, white preparatory ground before the bole layer to assist in creating a uniform gilded surface. The overall gilding of marble statuary to create, in effect, a brilliant golden image appears to have been a common—and increasingly recognized—practice (Bourgeois and Jockey 2005, 257–9; Abbe 2010, 280–84). The high-quality marble replica of the Diadoumenos (Fillet-Binder) by Polykleitos from Delos—the first securely dated precise marble replica of an earlier work of Greek sculpture, commissioned by a Roman patron—was entirely covered in gilding, including the palm tree support (Bourgeois, Jockey, and Karydas 2009). Such golden surfaces (on marble and other sculpture media) often received additional definition, including areas of contrasting matte and polishes and painted glazing to define detail and shadows of the sculptured form (Abbe 2011).

After sculptures in marble and other materials were carefully finished and polished they were routinely covered with wax and glazing. The most common word for these surface and aesthetic treatments is the Latin word *ganosis* (Vitr. *De arch.* 7.9.3), transliterated from the Greek *ganou* ("to polish" or "to glaze"), the suggestive metaphorical meaning of which is "to delight." Ancient authors assumed that the precious and delicate polychromy of sculpture required both protection and maintenance (Plut. *Quaest. Rom.* 98; *Mor.* 74D) and many sculptures were repainted and regilded over their long histories due to wear, redeployment, and changes in fashion, meaning, and the aesthetics of the large display context and environment (Liverani 2003, 132–3; Abbe 2010, 181–4).

While the complete nuanced language of sculptural polychromy in different genres, contexts, and historical periods awaits further investigation, recent research is adding new levels of meaning to our understanding of Roman sculpture. Modern scholarship on Roman sculpture has often viewed formal replication (or "copying") to be an overwhelming, if not defining, aspect of Roman statuary (see essay 3.3, Anguissola). The apparent sameness of Roman sculpture is increasingly recognized to be fundamentally deceptive: while replication does reflect the manufacture of sculpture and was an important aid to its legibility, where modern viewers perceive an apparent uniformity (e.g., on the precisely replicated marble "copies" of lost Greek bronzes), there existed in antiquity a diversity of polychrome definition (Sargent and Therkildsen 2010; Østergaard 2010, 50–60; see essay 1.5, Frischer). While the polychromy of such works presumably was loosely prescribed by lost pattern books and texts (some illustrated) like Pasiteles's *Opera nobilia* (*or Mirabilia*) and Varro's *De imaginibus* (Plin. *HN* 35.11, 36.39), the coloration of each individual work was undoubtedly largely defined in its immediate context according to its subject matter, function, intended site-specific reading, and other nearby artworks. Moreover, close scrutiny of Roman sculpture reveals not uniformity, but rather a remarkable variety of carving techniques, styles, surface textures, finishes, and polishes. Often historically defined, such marble techniques (like the alloys of Roman bronzes) are increasingly understood in relation to—and as preparations for—different types of polychrome applications and highly refined visual effects (Abbe 2011; Skovmøller and Therkildsen 2012). Such research has begun to explain Roman marble sculptural technique and to define interrelationships between the craft traditions of sculptural media—ivory, marble, bronze, and so on—often studied in isolation. The evidence for the original polychromy of Roman sculpture thus exists not only in the vestiges of extant coloration, but also in the refined techniques of creating sculpture.

Colored Stones and Porphyry

Interest in the color and materials of sculpture in the Roman period is strikingly manifest in the unprecedented range of high-quality statuary carved in colored stones from the reign of Augustus onward. This spectrum of rare geological materials was quarried from distant areas of the empire, often by the imperial administration or *ratio marmorum* (De Nuccio and Ungaro 2002; Hirt 2010). These stones were viewed as wondrous natural materials and were prized for their color, texture, hardness, and exotic origins (Plin. *HN* 36.44–63; Bradley 2009a, 89–93). Although large-scale statuary in colored stones was always rare compared to both white marble and bronze statuary and the more widespread use of these same colored materials in architecture, such sculptures tended to be of exceptional quality, and a high proportion were imperial commissions, concentrated in and around Rome, or imperial benefactions in the broader empire. Small-scale sculpture in a limited range of colored stones constituted a broader, emulative phenomenon (Gregarek 1999).

The natural color of these stones was, of course, integral to the polychrome effect of colored-stone statuary. Virtuoso carving and high polishes conspicuously displayed the stone's color and surface patterning to highlight the sculpture's exceptional materiality. Sculptors masterfully carved the often extremely hard stones to create dynamic relationships between the color, material, and subject matter of these figured images in what constitutes a uniquely polychrome sculptural art of the Roman imperial period.

The largest number of sculptures carved in colored stones are created in various dark black and green stones (basalt, *nero antico, bigio morato*), often but not exclusively from Egypt. A small number of imperial portraits continued a Ptolemaic tradition of portraiture in hard dark Egyptian stones. Most dark stones were used in top-quality decorative statuary, often of Egyptian gods such as Isis or Serapis or for the realistic depiction of the dark skin of Africans (Baratte 2001). Crisply carved in a distinctively "metallic" style and highly polished, these hard stones deceptively evoked the color and surface appearance of old dark-patinated, "antique" Greek bronzes in a more expensive, durable, and technically challenging material (Belli Pasqua 1995).

Colored stones were often named after their geographical origin and thus acquired regional and cultural associations. The distinctive mottled white and violet *pavonazzetto* marble from Dokimeion in Asia Minor known as *marmor phrygium* was used in state victory monuments during the Augustan period to represent subjugated "eastern" Parthian barbarians (Schneider 1986; see essay 2.7, Russell). The variegated, veined marble evoked the colorful oriental costumes of the defeated and materially embodied the imperial subjection of these far-flung domains. However, the majority of sculptures carved from *pavonazzetto* and other colored stone were primarily decorative and carry little explicit imperial symbolism. *Marmor phrygium* was used in mythological statuary with subjects associated with its origins in Asia Minor: Ganymede, Attis, and Marsyas, or the East more generally (Stat. *Silv.* 1.5.37–8, 2.2.87; Gregarek 1999). The mottled purple, red, and white color of the stone was masterfully used in the illusionistic representation of the bruised and flayed body of the Hanging Marsyas (Weis 1992, 20–21, 57; Gregarek 1999, 23; see essay 3.3, Anguissola). Various wine-red stones (*rosso antico*) often had associations with Dionysos and evoked the tawny skin of his retinue. Translucent yellow, green, and banded alabasters from the eastern Mediterranean were used to evoke the colored drapery of the gods, usually eastern gods, with their extremities added in white marble (Gregarek 1999, 170, 182, 190–91).

Additional types of polychromy were essential to the illusionism of colored stone sculpture. Inset eyes, metal additions, and in some cases stone intarsia and glass inlay were incorporated into these works. This rich variety of materials was complemented with painting and other more fugitive forms of polychromy on the garments, hair, eyes, and lips, akin to the more limited polychrome conventions on decorative white marble sculpture (Gregarek 1999, 45–7; Baratte 2001).

The purple color of porphyry, an extremely hard rock found in the remote Eastern Desert of Egypt, was selectively used in imperial commissions for the drapery of the Olympian gods and the *toga purpurea* of the emperor (Delbrueck 1932; Del Bufalo 2012). The head and limbs of such images were usually added in white marble, as in other colored stone statuary. Porphyry became a larger focus of imperial portrait statuary in the Tetrarchy when its royal color (like the purple cloth) acquired highly symbolic and formalized associations with imperial validity, authority, strength, and power. Imperial porphyry workshops produced centrally distributed portrait statuary with a new emphatic and formalized image for the explicitly monarchic system (Bergmann 1977, 163–79; Del Bufalo 2012; Last Statues of Antiquity [LSA] database, http://laststatues.classics.ox.ac.uk). These imperial portraits were monolithic—that is carved entirely of porphyry—so at least symbolically the royal purple color imbued the whole of the imperial image. The original polychrome effect of these porphyry statues is difficult to reconstruct: the eyes received inlay, indirect details of the carving and finishing indicate the hair, beards, and elements of the imperial costume were painted and/or gilded, but it remains unclear whether the flesh areas were painted (Delbrueck 1932, 6; Laubscher

1999, 242–4; Von Bülow and Wulf-Rheidt 2009, 17). Porphyry remained the most distinguished material for imperial portraits into late antiquity.

Bronze

Pliny and other Roman writers praised bronze statuary's bright, eye-catching appearance (it literally gleamed with prestige and distinction) and its ability to capture portraits in minute fidelity to nature (Lahusen and Formigli 2001, 13–16). Frequently kept polished and free of corrosion, the metal's sheen was a particularly prized effect for civic honorific statuary and favored for votive sculpture. Although bronze permitted a more circumscribed range of polychromy than painted marble, a remarkably broad and flexible range of coloration was created in the Roman period through the manipulation of its metallic composition, colorful inlaid materials, artificial patination, and extensive gilding and silvering (see essay 2.4, Mattusch).

Alloys of bronzes—composed of copper, tin, lead, and less commonly small amounts of zinc, silver, and gold—were manipulated to produce specific colors. Although ancient authors briefly describe "named" Greek alloys of specific origin (e.g., from Delos, Aegina, Corinth), prized for their chromatic values, these remain largely elusive in the extant archaeological record or, in the case of the Corinthian bronzes (*Corinthium aes*), are the subject of ongoing debate (Giumlia-Mair and Craddock 1993; Jacobson and Weitzman 1995; Descamps-Lequime 2006, 86–9). The colors of bronze varied in hue from reddish pink to golden brown and in value from pale white to dark gray. Representations of bronze sculpture in Roman wall painting suggest something of their standard range of actual appearances from yellow (the alloy itself or gilded), to red, dark brown, and green (Moormann 1988; 2008; and essay 6.4, Moormann).

Bronze undergoes dramatic color changes during working and finishing, and the artist's manipulation of the color values of the alloy and its final metallic sheen were prized and protected, if not enhanced, with translucent bitumen (*asphaltos*, Plin. *HN* 34.15) and other translucent materials applied to the surface, vestiges of which have begun to be discerned (Formigli 2013). Extensive maintenance, of course, was required to maintain bronze's radiance and prevent disfiguring corrosion (as described by Plutarch at Delphi: *De Pyth. or.* 395.2–4; Schröder 1990, 81–4, 114–30).

Naturalistic inlay and localized precious-metal leaf—gold and copper eyebrows, copper lips and nipples, silver teeth and nails, and so on—heightened the individual forms of sculpture to add greater lifelike realism. Inlaid eyes imparted a striking, radiant gaze and an immediate mental presence, with irises and pupils (rendered in colored glass, obsidian, or colored stone) framed by the bright "whites" of the eyes (stone, bone, or ivory) and bronze eyelashes. Even realistic red paste is preserved in the tear ducts (caruncles) of the eyes of the portrait of Augustus from Meroë (Lahusen and Formigli 2001, 58–60). Other nonfigural elements—garments, diadems, wreaths, jewelry, shoes, and attributes—were frequently embellished with polychrome metal inlay. Purple, red, yellow, and white metal alloys, as well as gold and silver, evoked the colorful patterns of luxury textiles, from the simple purple *clavus* of a Roman tunic to elaborate silvered and gilded decorative patterns on the borders of garments. Such polychromy is abundant not only on small bronzes (Franken 2010), but also on scattered finds of top quality large-scale statuary, such as the large drapery fragment of a *paludamentum* from an imperial statue group adorning a triumphal arch of Caracalla in Volubilis, Mauretania (Boube-Piccot 1969, 87–103). The extensively inlaid and patinated bronze was defined by a rich combination of purple, black, red, yellow, and white inlay (composed of at least six alloys of copper, silver, and tin) complemented with gilding and silvering. Large registers, separated by minute decorative patterning, represent barbarian captives flanking a *trophaeum*, captive weapons and arms, and sea creatures. Such inlay represented the elaborate ceremonial textiles in the high and later empire that remained largely the reserve of imperial decorum, like the *toga picta* and long *chlamys* (Gehn 2012, 22–5, 226).

Bronze statuary was frequently further embellished with gold leaf to add still greater distinction. Gilding is attested from at least the second century BC and became widespread in the imperial period, especially in honorific statuary of both the imperial family and local elite of the empire (Lahusen and Formigli 2001, 505–521). Bronze statues were gilded by diffusion bonding or applying gold leaf using an adhesive or heat and an amalgam of mercury and gold, so-called “fire gilding” (La Niece and Craddock 1993). Although gilded statuary may have required less day-to-day maintenance than regular bronze, regilding was often required and extant bronze sculptures preserve multiple sequential applications of gold leaf (e.g., the head of Minerva from Bath with six layers of gold leaf: Oddy et al. 1990, 120).

Recent studies have revealed broad historical changes in the alloys of Roman bronze during the imperial period and their relationship to sculptural practices. Pliny’s often dismissed comments on the decline of bronze working in his time (*HN* 34.46–7) appear, in fact, to align with increased lead content, simplification of techniques, and increased gilding of statuary (Hallett 2004; Lahusen and Formigli 2001, 501–4). Replacing the Greek tradition of copper-tin alloys, an increased use of lead to inexpensively bulk the bronze and aid its flow during casting also sacrificed its surface luster and coloration. This change in alloy was part of a broader economizing trend in bronze sculpture, in which the naturalistic coloration of inlaid eyes, lips, and details were reduced as the flexible, nuanced polychrome language of the increasingly refined production of marble sculpture eclipsed bronze sculpture in the second century AD. This reduction of the naturalistic polychromy of bronze demonstrates the growing symbolic coloration of honorific sculpture in the later Roman world.

The extent to which large-scale Roman bronze sculpture was deliberately artificially patinated and perhaps even painted is disputed and difficult to determine (La Niece and Craddock 1993; Descamps-Lequime 2006). While much of the evidence for such delicate and subtle surface coloration on classical bronzes may be lost due to corrosion and historic cleaning practices, research has made solid gains by focusing on the distinctive lustrous black sulfide-rich layers found on large-scale bronzes. Ambiguities often remain, as what some identify as a product of deliberate patination others interpret as a natural corrosion product of the anaerobic aqueous burial environments in which most well-preserved ancient bronzes are found (Mello, Parrini, and Formigli 1984; Mello 2003). Some cases are, however, increasingly clear: the rich black surface (chalcocite) on a statue of a child Dionysos from the Fayum in Egypt (figure 2.6.4, see color insert) is demonstrably preburial and fortuitously preserved in its dry deposition context (Mattusch 1996, 237–42). The shiny black surface of this bronze was deliberately contrasted with silver foil on the eyes and teeth to create a strong bichrome effect, akin to a visual effect evident in dark black and green colored stone sculptures with inlaid white eyes and teeth, and to evoke the prized dark surfaces of old "antiques" from ancient Greece (Gregarek 1999, 147–8; Baratte 2001).

Conclusion

The study of polychromy significantly enriches our understanding of Roman statuary by bringing us closer to the original visual appearance and definition of these sculptures. It thereby adds new levels of understanding to the complex and often nuanced aesthetics, meanings, and historical and cultural reception of these images in antiquity. Our understanding of the rich, complex, and diverse traditions of sculptural polychromy in the Roman world remains in its infancy, and much work is needed in both the re-examination of known objects in collections and the investigation of newly discovered archaeological material. Significant progress will come from applying and developing the current interdisciplinary methodologies to the study of works of exceptional preservation whose ancient display contexts can be defined in detail and, ideally, modeled in their environmental, cultural, and historical richness. Despite the ravages of time, proper study and consideration of the extant remains of ancient polychromy of Roman sculpture remains indispensable for a proper historical and cultural understanding of the remarkable tradition of superbly crafted statuary from Roman antiquity. The investigation of such polychromy promises to be a particularly rich and rewarding field of research in the twenty-first century.

Bibliography

Abbe, M. B. 2010. "Recent Research on the Painting and Gilding of Roman Marble Statuary at Aphrodisias." In Brinkmann, Primavesi, and Hollein 2010, 277–89.

———. 2011. "A Roman Replica of the 'South Slope Head': Polychromy and Identification." *Source: Notes in the History of Art* 30: 18–24.

Abbe, M. B., G. E. Borromeo, and S. Pike. 2012. "A Hellenistic Greek Marble Statue with Ancient Polychromy Reported to be from Knidos." In *Interdisciplinary Studies on Ancient Stone. ASMOSIA 9*. Documenta 23, edited by A. Gutiérrez, P. Lapuente, and I. Rodà, 763–71. Tarragona: Institut Català d'Arqueologia Clàssica.

Baratte, F. 2001. "Exotisme et décor à Aphrodisias: La statue de jeune noir de l'ancienne collection Gaudin." *MonPiot* 80: 57–80.

Barry, F. 2011. "A Whiter Shade of Pale: Relative and Absolute White in Roman Sculpture and Architecture." In Clerbois and Droth 2011, 31–62.

Belli Pasqua, R. 1995. *Sculture di età romana in "basalto."* Rome: "L'Erma" di Bretschneider.

Berger, E. 1904. *Die Maltechnik des Altertums*. Munich: Georg D. W. Callwey.

Bergmann, M. 1977. *Studien zum römischen Porträt des 3. Jahrhunderts n. Chr.* Bonn: Rudolf Habelt.

Blume, C. 2010. "When Colour Tells a Story: The Polychromy of Hellenistic Sculpture and Terracotta." In Brinkmann, Primavesi, and Hollein 2010, 220–57.

Boube-Piccot, C. 1969. *Les bronzes antiques du Maroc*. Vol. 1, *La statuaire*. Études et travaux d'archéologie marocaine 4. Paris: Éditions Recherche sur les Civilisations.

Bourgeois, B., and P. Jockey. 2003. "Le geste et la couleur: Stratégies de mise en couleurs de la sculpture hellénistique de Délos." *BAC* 30: 65–77.

———. 2005. "La dorure des marbres grecs: Nouvelle enquête sur la sculpture hellénistique de Délos." *JSav* 2: 253–316.

———. 2010. "The Polychromy of Hellenistic Marble Sculpture in Delos." In Brinkmann, Primavesi, and Hollein 2010, 224–39.

Bourgeois, B., P. Jockey, and A. Karydas. 2009. "New Researches on Polychrome Hellenistic Sculptures in Delos, III: The Gilding Processes; Observations and Meanings." In *Leukos lithos: Marbres et autres roches de la Méditerranée antique, ASMOSIA 8*, edited by P. Jockey, 645–61. Paris: Karthala.

Bradley, M. 2009a. *Colour and Meaning in Ancient Rome*. Cambridge: Cambridge University Press.

———. 2009b. "The Importance of Colour on Ancient Marble Sculpture." *Art History* 32: 427–57.

Brinkmann, V. 2007. "Research in the Polychromy of Ancient Sculpture." In Brinkmann and Wünsche 2007, 20–27.

Brinkmann, V., S. Kellner, U. Koch-Brinkmann, and J. S. Østergaard. 2007. "The Coloration of the Caligula Portrait." In Brinkmann and Wünsche 2007, 186–91.

Brinkmann, V., U. Koch-Brinkmann, and H. Piening. 2010. "Alte Gewänder in Neuem Look, Beobachtungen zu den Farben der pompejanischen Artemis." In *Die Artemis von Pompeji und die Entdeckung der Farbigkeit griechischer Plastik*, edited by V. Brinkmann and M. Kunze, 69–86. Ruhpolding: Franz Philipp Rutzen.

Brinkmann, V., O. Primavesi, and M. Hollein, eds. 2010. *Circumlitio: The Polychromy of Antique and Mediaeval Sculpture*. Munich: Hirmer.

Brinkmann, V., and R. Wünsche, eds. 2003. *Bunte Götter: Die Farbigkeit antiker Skulptur*. Munich: Staatliche Antikensammlungen und Glyptothek.

———, eds. 2007. *Gods in Color: Painted Sculpture in Classical Antiquity*. Munich: Staatliche Antikensammlungen und Glyptothek and Stiftung Archäologie.

Büll, R. 1963. *Wachsmalerei: Enkaustik und Temperatechnik unter besonderer Berücksichtigung antiker Wachsmalverfahren*. Frankfurt: Farbwerke Hoechst.

Carrella, A., L. A. D'Acunto, N. Inserra, and C. Serpe, eds. 2008. *Marmora pompeiana nel Museo archeologico nazionale di Napoli: Gli arredi scultorei delle case pompeiane*. Rome: "L'Erma" di Bretschneider.

Clerbois, S., and M. Droth, eds. 2011. *Revival and Invention: Sculpture through Its Material Histories*. Oxford: Peter Lang.

Del Bufalo, D. 2012. *Porphyry: Red Imperial Porphyry; Power and Religion*. Turin: Umberto Allemandi.

Delbrueck, R. 1932. *Antike Porphyrwerke: Studien zur spätantiken Kunstgeschichte*. Berlin: Walter de Gruyter.

De Nuccio, M., and L. Ungaro, eds. 2002. *I marmi colorati della Roma imperiale*. Venice: Marsilio.

Descamps-Lequime, S. 2006. "La polychromie des bronzes grecs et romains." In Rouveret, Dubel, and Naas 2006, 79–92.

Formigli, E., ed. 2013. *Colore e luce nella statuaria antica in bronzo: Indagini archeometriche e sperimentali*. Rome: "L'Erma" di Bretschneider.

Franken, N. 2010. "Bunte Bronzen." In *Bunte Götter: Die Farbigkeit antiker Skulptur*, edited by V. Brinkmann and A. Scholl, 162–9. Berlin and Munich: Staatliche Museen zu Berlin and Hirmer.

Gehn, U. 2012. *Ehrenstatuen in der Spätantike: Chlamydati und Togati*. Wiesbaden: Reichert.

Giumlia-Mair, A. R., and P. T. Craddock. 1993. *Corinthium aes: Das schwarze Gold der Alchimisten*. Mainz: Philipp von Zabern.

Gregarek, H. 1999. "Untersuchungen zur kaiserzeitlichen Idealplastik aus Buntmarmor." *KölnJb* 32: 33–284.

Hallett, C. H. 2004. "Technological Advance and Artistic Decline? A History of Bronze-Working in the Roman Period." *JRA* 15: 487–501.

Hirt, A. M. 2010. *Imperial Mines and Quarries in the Roman World: Organizational Aspects, 27 BC–AD 235*. Oxford: Oxford University Press.

Isager, J. 1991. *Pliny on Art and Society: The Elder Pliny's Chapters on the History of Art*. London: Routledge.

Jacobson, D. M., and M. P. Weitzman. 1995. "Black Bronze and the 'Corinthian Alloy.'" *CQ* 45: 580–3.

Koch, N. J. 2000. *Techne und Erfindung in der klassischen Malerei: Eine terminologische Untersuchung*. Munich: Biering und Brinkmann.

Lahusen, G., and E. Formigli. 2001. *Römische Bildnisse aus Bronze: Kunst und Technik*. Munich: Hirmer.

La Niece, S., and P. Craddock, eds. 1993. *Metal Plating and Patination: Cultural, Technical, and Historical Developments*. London: Butterworth-Heinemann.

Laubscher, H. P. 1999. "Beobachtungen zu tetrarchischen Kaiserbildnissen aus Porphyr." *JdI* 114: 207–52.

Liverani, P. 2003. "Die Polychromie des Augustus von Prima Porta, vorläufiger Bericht." In *Neue Forschungen zur hellenistischen Plastik: Kolloquium zum 70. Geburtstag von Georg Daltrop*, edited by G. Zimmer, 121–40. Eichstätt-Ingolstadt: Katholische Universität Eichstätt-Ingolstadt.

———. 2004. "L'Augusto di Prima Porta." In *I colori del bianco: Policromia nella scultura antica*, edited by H. Bankel and P. Liverani, 235–42. Rome: De Luca.

———. 2008. "La policromia delle statue antiche." In *Escultura romana en Hispania: Actes de la V renunión internacional celebrada en Murcía del 9 al 11 de noviembre de 2005*, edited by J. M. N. Celdrán and E. C. Guerri, 65–86. Murcia: Tabularium.

———. 2009. "Observazioni sulla policromia e la doratura della scultura in età tardoantica." In *Il colore nel Medioevo: Arte, simbolo, tecnica; Pietra e colore; Conoscenza, conservazione e restauro della policromia; Atti delle giornate di studi, Lucca 22–23–24 novembre 2007*, edited by P. A. Andreuccetti and I. L. Cervelli, 9–22. Lucca: Istituto storico lucchese.

———. 2010. "New Evidence on the Polychromy of Roman Sculpture." In Brinkmann, Primavesi, and Hollein 2010, 290–302.

Löwy, E. 1885. *Inschriften griechischer Bildhauer*. Leipzig: B. G. Teubner.

Mandel, U. 2010. "On the Qualities of the 'Colour' White in Antiquity." In Brinkmann, Primavesi, and Hollein 2010, 303–23.

Marincola, M. 2004. "Polychromy." In *The Encyclopedia of Sculpture*, edited by A. Bostöm, 1318–22. New York: Fitzroy Dearborn.

Mattusch, C. C., ed. 1996. *The Fire of Hephaistos: Large Classical Bronzes from North American Collections*. Cambridge, MA: Harvard University Art Museums.

Mello, E. 2003. "Studio metallografico, analitico, microanalitico e mediante tecniche spettroscopiche di analisi delle superfici di due campioni prelevati dalle statue di Riace." *In I bronzi di Riace: Restauro come conoscenza*, edited by A. M. Vaccaro and G. de Palma, 1: 185–202. Rome: Artemide.

Mello, E., P. Parrini, and E. Formigli. 1984. "Alterazioni superficiali dei bronzi di Riace: Le aree con patina nera della statua A." In *Due bronzi da Riace*, edited by G. Triches, 1: 147–56. BdA Serie Speciale. Rome: Instituto Poligrafico e Zecca dello Stato.

Moormann, E. M. 1988. *La pittura parietale romana come fonte di conoscenza per la scultura antica*. Assen: Van Gorcum.

———. 2008. "Statues on the Wall: The Representation of Statuary in Roman Wall Painting." In *The Sculptural Environment of the Roman Near East: Reflections on Culture, Ideology, and Power*, edited by Y. Z. Eliav, E. A. Friedland, and S. Herbert, 197–224. Leuven: Peeters.

Oddy, W. A., M. R. Cowell, P. T. Craddock, and D. R. Hook. 1990. "The Gilding of Bronze Sculpture in the Classical World." In *Small Bronze Sculpture from the Ancient World: Papers Delivered at a Symposium Organized by the Departments of Antiquities and Antiquities Conservation and Held at the J. Paul Getty Museum, March 16–19, 1989*, 103–24. Los Angeles: J. Paul Getty Museum.

Østergaard, J. S. 2007. "Caligula in the Ny Carlsberg Glyptotek, Copenhagen: Reconstructing the Polychromy of a oman Portrait." In Brinkmann and Wünsche 2007, 178–83.

———. 2008. "Emerging Colors: Roman Sculptural Polychromy Revived." In Panzanelli, Schmidt, and Lapatin 2008, 40–61.

———, ed. 2010. *Tracking Colour: The Polychromy of Greek and Roman Sculpture in the Ny Carlsberg Glyptotek; Preliminary Report 2*. Copenhagen: Ny Carlsberg Glyptotek.

Panzanelli, R., E. D. Schmidt, and K. Lapatin, eds. 2008. *The Color of Life: Polychromy in Sculpture from Antiquity to the Present*. Los Angeles: J. Paul Getty Museum.

Primavesi, O. 2007. "Colorful Sculptures in Ancient Literature? The Textual Evidence Revisited." In Brinkmann and Wünsche 2007, 192–209.

Reutersward, P. 1960. *Studien zur Polychromie der Plastik, Griechenland und Rom: Untersuchungen über die Farbwirkung der Marmor- und Bronzeskulpturen*. Stockholm: Svenska Bokförlaget.

Richter, G. M. A. 1956. *Catalogue of Engraved Gems: Greek, Etruscan and Roman*. Rome: "L'Erma" di Bretschneider.

Rouveret, A., S. Dubel, and V. Naas, eds. 2006. *Couleurs et matières dans l'antiquité: Textes, techniques et pratiques*. Paris: Éditions rue d'Ulm.

Sargent, M. L., and R. H. Therkildsen. 2010. "Research on Ancient Sculptural Polychromy with Focus on the 2nd Century CE Marble Amazon." In Østergaard 2010, 27–49.

Schneider, R. M. 1986. *Bunte Barbaren: Orientalenstatuen aus farbigem Marmor in der römischen Repräsentationskunst*. Worms: Wernersche Verlagsgesellschaft.

Schröder, S. 1990. *Plutarchs Schrift De Pythiae oraculis*. Stuttgart: Teubner.

Skovmøller, A., and R. H. Therkildsen. 2012. "On the High Gloss Polish of Roman Sculpture." In *Tracking Colour: The Polychromy of Greek and Roman Sculpture in the Ny Carlsberg Glyptotek: Preliminary Report* 3, edited by J. S. Østergaard, 35–46. Copenhagen: Ny Carlsberg Glyptotek.

Verri, G. 2009. "The Spatially Resolved Characterisation of Egyptian Blue, Han Blue and Han Purple by Photo-Induced Luminescence Digital Imaging." *Analytical and Bioanalytical Chemistry* 394(4): 1011–21.

Verri, G., T. Opper, and T. Deviese. 2010. "The 'Treu Head': A Case Study in Roman Sculptural Polychromy." *British Museum Technical Research Bulletin* 4: 39–53.

Von Bülow, G., and U. Wulf-Rheidt. 2009. *Felix Romuliana: Der Palast des Kaisers Galerius und sein Umfeld; Eine serbisch-deutsche Kooperation*. Berlin: Deutsches Archäologisches Institut.

Weis, A. 1992. *The Hanging Marsyas and Its Copies: Roman Innovations in a Hellenistic Sculptural Tradition*. Rome: Giorgio Bretschneider.

Wünsche, R. 2007. "On the Coloring of the Munich Bronze Head with a Victor's Fillet." In Brinkmann and Wünsche 2007, 118–31.

Zimmer, G. 2012. "Die Farbe des Metalls: Möglichkeiten der Farbgestaltung bei Grossbronzen." In *"Bronzes grecs et romains, recherches récentes": Hommage à Claude Rolley, L'Institut National d'Histoire de l'Art, Actes des colloques*, edited by M. Denoyelle, S. Descamps-Lequime, B. Mille, and S. Verger. Paris: INHA. http://inha.revues.org/3986.

CHAPTER 2.7

TRANSPORT AND DISTRIBUTION

BEN RUSSELL

INTRODUCTION

STONE and bronze, favored by Roman artists for their durability, are heavy materials that are both difficult and expensive to transport. A life-size figure in marble, with an approximate volume of 1 m^3, weighs about 2700 kg (2.7 metric tons); most limestones weigh marginally less, granites slightly more. A marble sarcophagus chest of average proportions would weigh at least 3–5 metric tons—roughly the same as an average-size car. Bronze, by comparison, is around 7–9 metric tons per m^3, meaning that a hollow life-size bronze statue can weigh 400–500 kg. Moving large pieces of either stone or bronze was not only logistically challenging, therefore, but also labor-intensive, in many cases requiring specialist lifting equipment. As a result, throughout history, most sculptors, like builders, have tended to use raw materials from the most easily accessed sources.

All of this makes the long-distance trade in both artists' materials and actual works of art that developed in the Roman period even more remarkable. This trade was driven by demand for high-quality materials, the sources of which were irregularly distributed across the Roman world, coupled with demand for works of art from the best-known artistic centers. These grew dramatically from the second century BC onward, reaching their zenith, in terms of both intensity and extent, in the second century AD. While this phenomenon was not solely Roman, the scale of demand for both raw materials and finished works of art outstripped anything that had come before.

The interregional aspect of the Roman art market, especially in the first three centuries AD, is revealed by a number of different datasets that this essay will explore. Literary and epigraphic sources highlight the mobile nature of craftsmen in this period and provide insight into the ordering of works of art; finds from quarrying sites and shipwrecks reveal the condition in which this material was supplied and transported;

distribution patterns show that sculptors obtaining supplies as well as customers seeking high-quality products cast their nets increasingly wide.

Mobile Craftsmen

Sculptors certainly moved around in the Roman period to be as close as possible to the main markets for their products. As early as the sixth century BC, the Etruscan sculptor Vulca traveled to Rome to undertake several commissions for Tarquinius Priscus (Plin. *HN* 35.157; Plut. *Vit. Publicola* 13; see essay 3.2, de Grummond). The literary sources also refer to many Greek sculptors who came to Rome from the second century BC onward (Plin. *HN* 35.154–7, 36.35–44; Pollitt 1986, 162–3; Coarelli 1996, 67–84). While some simply passed through the city for the completion of specific commissions, others settled permanently. Major names, like Timarchides and later Arkesilaos and Pasiteles, lived and worked in Rome, and in turn influenced new generations of craftsmen (Toynbee 1951, 18–26; see essays 2.4, Mattusch; 3.3, Anguissola; and 3.6, Touchette).

Analogous literary testimony in the imperial period is rare and in its place we rely on often ambiguous epigraphic evidence. Inscribed signatures on finished works are a case in point. These record the name of either the carver or workshop owner, but occasionally they also give their hometown. Sculptors from well-known artistic centers—Athens in Greece or Dokimeion (modern Iscehisar) and Aphrodisias in Turkey—were especially keen to let their civic affiliations be known (Squarciapino 1943, 12–17; Toynbee 1951, 23–6). It is usually assumed that sculptors did so when working overseas, and thus this practice is used as evidence for the kind of mobility recorded in the written sources. But at Aphrodisias a third-century AD sculptor called Polyneikes records that he is an Aphrodisian even when signing a statue erected in that very city's theater (Roueché and Erim 1982, 102–3). While these inscriptions do sometimes note where the creators were from, then, they do not tell us where the objects in question were actually carved.

Other epigraphic evidence for the mobility of sculptors is more clear-cut. An association of carvers from Nicomedia in northwestern Turkey is attested at Nicopolis-ad-Istrum in northern Bulgaria (*IGBulg.* 2.674). It can be assumed that only permanent residents, or at least those settled in the city for some time, would have formed themselves into such a corporate body. Dokimeian carvers, who presumably maintained close contact with suppliers in the famous white and polychrome marble quarries of their hometown, also moved around. A pair of brothers, who define themselves as sculptors from Dokimeion, dedicated an altar at Iconium (modern Konya, Turkey) in the first or second century AD (McLean 2002, no. 45). An Alexandrian sculptor named on two statue bases at Gerasa in Jordan also seems to have been genuinely active in that city, since one of these objects is in local limestone and must have been carved at Gerasa (Friedland 2013, 107–8). Across the empire, at Bath in Britain, we find Priscus son of Toutus, who describes himself as a *lapidarius cives Carnutenus*—a stone-worker from the area around Chartres in northern France (*RIB* 1.149).

At Rome, there is a high concentration of sculptors' signatures and other epigraphic evidence for immigrant craftsmen and their suppliers, including the Aphrodisian sculptor Zenon, who recorded on a herm of Hadrianic date, now in the Vatican Museums, that he had settled in Rome after working in numerous other cities (*CIG* 3.6233; Strong and Claridge 1976, 195). On another famous epitaph the sculptor Novius Blesamus states that he "decorated the city and the whole world with statues" (*CIL* 6.23083: *hic olim statuis urbem decoravit et orbem*). To judge from his name, Novius may have been a northern Italian of Celtic origin. The raw materials that these sculptors relied on had to be imported; specialist stone suppliers are also attested, such as Marcus Aurelius Xenonianus Aquila from Bithynia in northwestern Turkey, who operated in the capital in the third century AD (*SEG* 4.106).

Transporting Raw Materials

Many of these mobile sculptors traveled to areas lacking sources of high-quality materials, especially marble, and consequently had to import them. The movement of craftsmen and the long-distance supply of their raw materials were therefore closely related. Even sculptors operating in resource-rich areas, however, took advantage of established commercial networks, especially maritime ones, to import the best-quality materials from elsewhere.

Most stone intended for sculpture would have been quarried and transported either as unshaped or roughly squared blocks. Unshaped blocks had the advantage of offering the carver as much stone as possible to work with, and it seems likely that the series of amorphous Parian blocks found in and around the Fossa Traiana at Portus, near Rome, were intended for statue production (Pensabene 1994, 121–2, nos. 54–60). Recently, similar blocks, irregular in form, have been discovered at the Göktepe quarries in Turkey, where fine-grained white and black marble, widely used for statuary, was extracted (Attanasio, Bruno, and Yavuz 2009, 323–4). Blocks could also have been imported roughly squared, a multipurpose format that allowed them to be used for a range of projects. At Cyrene in eastern Libya, most statues were carved in white Parian and Pentelic marble from Greece and apparently from blocks of relatively standard sizes that were subdivided as required (Kane and Carrier 1988, 204).

The materials for bronze sculpture production were also moved around in a raw form. Bronze is an alloy of copper, tin, and sometimes lead, the key sources of which were Cyprus, Spain, and later Britain. The Capo Bellavista A and Lavezzi A shipwrecks off Sardinia and the Port-Vendres B wreck off southern France all contain copper ingots and are datable to the late first century BC or first century AD, though to what use these materials were to be put is uncertain (Parker 1992, 112, 239, 331). Most major urban centers probably had bronze foundries capable of handling these materials, though Pliny the Elder tells us that the best bronze came from Greece, especially Corinth, Delos, and Aegina (Plin. *HN* 34.6–11; see essay 2.4, Mattusch). Although there is little physical evidence for it, we should not rule out the possibility that sculptors might have imported preprepared alloys from these well-known centers.

Transporting Partly Finished Statues

While it made sense to ship stone blocks before they were carved into fragile forms, a significant volume of this material would end up being discarded during the carving process. For this reason, stone sculptures were routinely roughed out before transport, their overall forms defined to reduce their weight but with any potentially fragile details left unworked. This process made particular sense when the sculptor was based at the quarry or wanted to select and test material immediately after its extraction.

A good example of a roughed-out statue in transit is the colossal cuirassed male, over 4.50 m tall, from the shipwreck near Şile in northwestern Turkey (figure 2.7.1; Asgari 1990, 125–6; Russell 2013b, 231–4, fig. 8.4). Probably representing an early fourth-century AD emperor (though sometimes dated to the second century AD), it was found alongside a

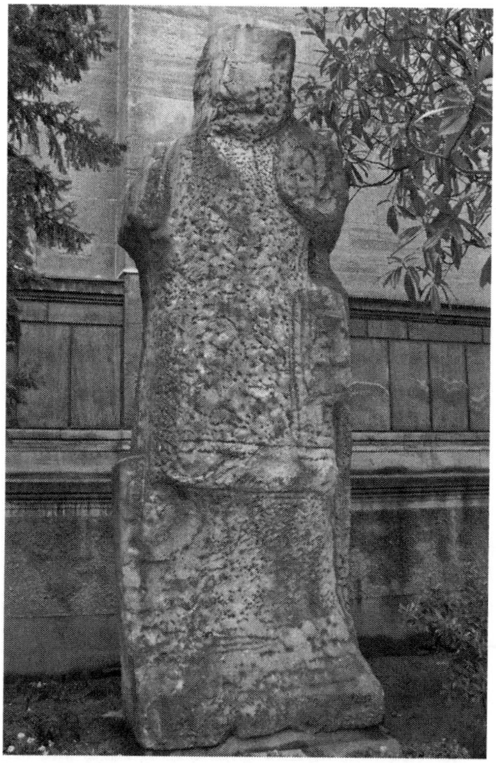

FIGURE 2.7.1 Colossal marble statue from the Şile shipwreck on display outside the Istanbul Archaeological Museum.

similarly roughed-out but life-size female bust. Part of a mixed cargo of various marble objects, both of these statues were carved in white Prokonnesian marble, roughly point chiseled with only the basic lines of their forms defined. These statues could have been in transit between two teams of carvers, one responsible for roughing-out at the quarry, the other for finishing on site, but it is equally possible that one team of carvers was undertaking all of this work, accompanying the roughed-out objects en route. An alternative possibility is that the whole cargo is a later, perhaps Byzantine, collection of older material being transported to somewhere in northern Asia Minor, but without further analysis of the small finds from the site, the exact date of the wreck will remain in doubt.

Remains from quarrying sites show that the Şile statues are not anomalies. A statue of a togate male carved to an identical state was recently found in the Vila Viçosa white marble quarries near Estremoz in Portugal, and a handful of other examples have been recorded in white marble quarries on Thasos and on Paros in the Aegean (Koželj 1988, 10, pl. 12, ill. 18; Waelkens, De Paepe, and Moens 1988, 20; Mañas and Fusco 2008, 493–5, fig. 4). At Dokimeion in Turkey, roughed-out statues have been found in both the white marble and the purple-streaked so-called *pavonazzetto* marble also quarried at this site (Bruno 2002, 186–8). This practice of roughing out sculpture was not limited to marble quarries. Four life-size statues in the limestone quarries at Xylophagou on Cyprus were all finished to the same degree as the Şile statues (Karageorghis 1969, 494–7, figs. 130–33). Particularly remarkable is the pair of roughed-out equestrian statues, usually interpreted as third-century AD emperors, from the sandstone quarries near Breitfurt in Germany (Röder 1960). These weigh roughly 5000 kg each and are the largest Roman statues found north of the Alps.

Transporting Finished Works

Despite the risks associated with transporting finished sculptures, nearly or fully finished statues are more common finds in Roman shipwrecks than roughed-out ones. Two near-finished white marble statues have been found off southern Italy: a second-century AD nude male from the sea off Marsala in Sicily and an early third-century AD group representing Eros and Psyche, from the Punta Scifo A wreck off Calabria (Pensabene 2002, 37–8, fig. 15; Arata 2005, no. 44). Arata's catalogue (2005) of similar finds includes numerous fully finished statues. Among these are five white marble statues with holes for the insertion of heads found off Cephalonia in western Greece that are dated to the Roman imperial period; a porphyry statue of a seated emperor from off Ascalon on the western coast of Israel; a white marble female statue from the Golfo di Baratti in Tuscany; and from Spain, a white marble statue of Diana from Benalmadena near Málaga and another of a male from near Cadiz (Arata 2005, nos. 6, 8, 10, 14, 47). Recently, a third-century AD shipwreck has been discovered off Porticcio in southern Corsica that contained at least two white marble busts of the emperor Philip the Arab and his wife, Otacilia Severa, two life-size statues of the same subjects, as well as several smaller statuettes, a cargo of amphorae, and 230 kg of window glass (the Porticcio A wreck: Massy 2013, 110–14).

Some of these finds might have been personal possessions being moved around by their owners, but most appear to have been new products, produced in a finished state even though they were destined for onward transport. A pair of life-size imperial statues from the Prokonnesian white marble quarries in Turkey, probably fourth century AD in date, show that carving was sometimes taken to an advanced stage at the quarry (Asgari 1990, 126, fig. 29; Attanasio 2003, pl. 28.1). They are finished apart from their heads, which were left for final carving on arrival or by other craftsmen. A finished *pavonazzetto* marble statue of a Dacian was also found in the Çakırsaz quarry near Dokimeion in Turkey (Waelkens 1985). The risk of damage during transport was evidently deemed worth taking if it meant having this piece completed by sculptors at the quarries.

Good evidence for a sizeable trade in old or second-hand sculpture alongside these new products confirms much of what the literary sources tell us about the art market. One of the most important collections of fully finished material in transit comes from the site of the Mahdia shipwreck off eastern Tunisia (figure 2.7.2; see essay 2.4, Mattusch). This vessel sank in the early first century BC carrying roughly 300 metric

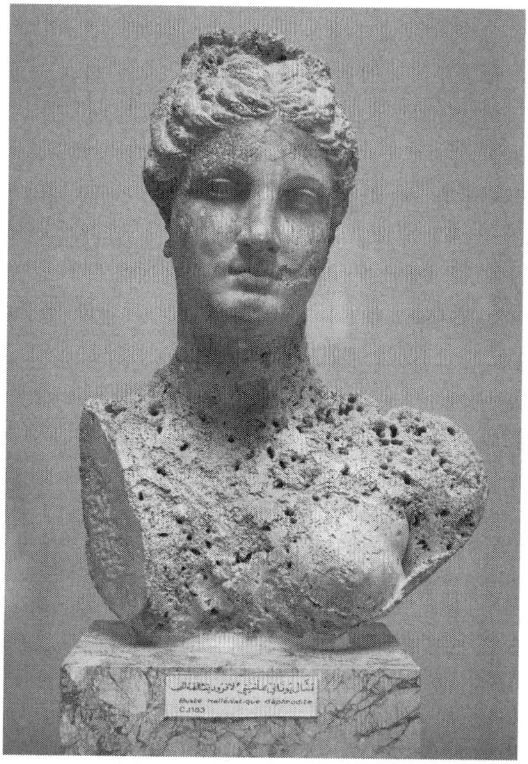

FIGURE 2.7.2 Marble bust of Aphrodite from the Mahdia shipwreck, now in the Musée National du Bardo, Tunis.

tons of architectural elements, furniture, and marble and bronze statues, all apparently loaded at Athens. Some of these objects were new, Neo-Attic products designed for the Italian market, but others were clearly old: a bronze herm signed by a certain Boethos (figure 2.4.4a) and another depicting a winged boy, both datable to the mid- to late second century BC (Mattusch 1994, 435–7; Söldner 1994); a series of five Greek inscriptions from various contexts; and four Attic grave reliefs of the fourth century BC (Bauchhenss 1994; Petzl 1994).

Another shipwreck, found off Antikythera, datable to the second quarter of the first century BC, contains a similar mix of new and old. Among the new are probably the forty or so marble statues, most very fragmentary, depicting deities and heroes. Among the clearly old are bronzes of a young male, perhaps Perseus, and a bust of a philosopher (figure 2.7.3), respectively fourth- and third-century BC originals (Vlachogianni 2012). Some of this material might have been booty, but there was also considerable demand for antique statues that could have been bought through more conventional channels. Indeed, enormous quantities of old statues continued to be shipped through the entire Roman period, this activity perhaps reaching a peak with the adornment of Constantinople in the fourth century AD (Bassett 2004, 37–49).

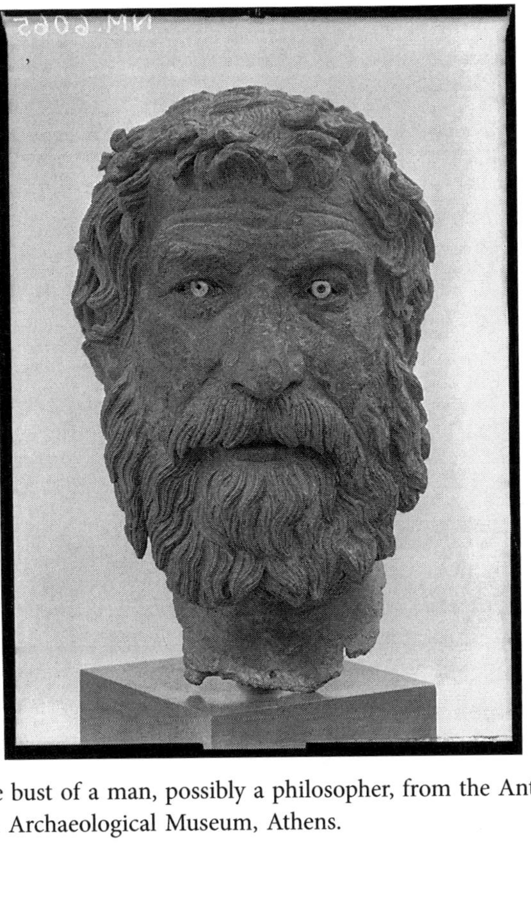

FIGURE 2.7.3 Bronze bust of a man, possibly a philosopher, from the Antikythera shipwreck, now in the National Archaeological Museum, Athens.

At least some of the large-scale classical or Hellenistic bronzes found elsewhere in the Mediterranean probably also come from Roman shipwrecks, among them the statues of Zeus or Poseidon and the boy rider from off Cape Artemision in northern Euboea, Greece, as well as the Riace bronzes from off Calabria, southern Italy (Mattusch 1996, 31–5). Moreover, the fragmentary life-size bronze of a mounted Augustus dredged up between Lemnos and Euboea in the Aegean seems to show that the transport of finished bronze artifacts was not limited to antiques (Arata 2005, no. 28).

Unlike the roughed-out statues found at certain shipwrecks and a number of quarrying sites, these statues were finished works, ready for display. Most of them probably already had secured buyers eagerly awaiting their arrival. Cicero's letters to Atticus famously provide testimony to the long-distance ordering of sculpture of the kind that the Mahdia and Antikythera ships were delivering (Cic. *Att.* 1.8.2, 1.9.2, 1.10.3; see essay 6.1, Squire). Through this close friend and part-time art dealer based in Athens, Cicero purchased a range of statues of athletic and intellectual subjects suitable for various rooms in his villa, arranging for their transport to Italy.

Later literary evidence also supports the archaeological evidence for the movement of finished statues. In a well-known passage of his *Periplus Maris Euxini*, often quoted in this context, Arrian asks the emperor Hadrian to send him three statues, depicting the emperor and two divinities, for the refurbishment of a temple in Trapezus on the Black Sea coast of Turkey (Arr. *Peripl. M. Eux.* 1.4–2.1). Furthermore, in his life of the philosopher Apollonios of Tyana, Philostratos recounts a tale in which his protagonist rebukes a merchant setting sail from the Piraeus near Athens with a speculative cargo of votive statues in gold, marble, and ivory for sale on the open market (Philostr. *V A* 5.20). Apollonios contrasts this trade in finished work with what he regards as the more traditional system that saw carvers travel with their raw materials to undertake commissions. However, the evidence summarized above—for the movement of raw materials as well as for roughed-out, nearly, and fully finished statues and for mobile sculptors—shows there was no single system in any one period and certainly no shift over time. The method selected depended very much on the choices of the individual sculptors and their clients.

Overland Transport

Not all sculpture was moved by sea. Overland transport and its challenges also need to be considered. Land vehicles could not have carried the loads that ships managed, and finished sculpture would have been vulnerable to damage during transport over uneven roads. Even so, statues were clearly moved around by land, often over long distances. Few quarries were located directly on the coast, so landlocked production centers, like the workshops surrounding the Dokimeian quarries, had little choice but to move their commodities by land, roughed-out or perhaps even finished (Waelkens 1982, 124–7).

Identifying sculpture in transit on land is often impossible, but scattered documentary evidence refers to overland transport of works of art. A papyrus from the Dakhleh

Oasis in Egypt, for instance, refers to the transport of statues (Worp 1995, 83–5, no. 29). This document, from Kellis, consists of a receipt for the transportation of statues to Alexandria in AD 330. Whether they were bronze, faience, or terracotta, these were apparently finished items and, since transport amounted to a total cost of 9 talents of silver, they were obviously being moved a long way. An interesting inscription from Mactar in Tunisia also provides evidence for the movement of a finished bronze statue both overland and by sea (Picard 1968). In this text, Sextus Iulius Possessor, a procurator originally from the city, records his gift of a "bronze statue conveyed from overseas" (*statuam aheneam transmare advectam*). Since Mactar is far inland, this same statue must also have been brought by wagon from the coast. A statue being transported upright in a wagon is shown on a wall painting from the Villa di San Marco at Stabiae in Italy depicting a construction scene (Adam and Varène 1980, 216–17, fig. 2). Over long distances, however, finished statues must have been carefully stowed, probably lying down, in crates or surrounded with packing material.

Distribution Patterns

Archaeological and documentary evidence reveals the variety of forms in which sculpture and the raw materials for its production were transported. Assessing accurately where certain materials ended up being used, however, has always been complicated by the fact that distinguishing between white marbles by eye is notoriously unreliable. The development of reliable archaeometric techniques for identifying the provenance of stone, since the 1980s, has changed this (see essay 2.1, Pensabene and Gasparini). By revealing exactly which materials were used where and for what, these data provide an important insight into the distributive mechanisms underlying this traffic. Archaeometric data are also useful for highlighting differences between media—between stone used for building and sculpture, for instance, or for sarcophagus production.

Data from the Levant, where particular attention has been paid to this question, are especially revealing in this regard. By the mid-second century AD the large-scale import of white marble was well established in the coastal centers of this region, which lacked its own marble resources. In architectural contexts the import of choice, alongside polychrome stones from a variety of sources, was white Prokonnesian marble (Fischer 1998, 257). Analysis of statuary, at both coastal centers and far inland, however, provides different results, with statues having been identified in white marble from the Pentelic, Parian, and dolomitic Thasian quarries in Greece, the Prokonnesian and Dokimeian quarries in Turkey, and possibly even marble from other quarries in Turkey, like those around Aphrodisias and Ephesos (Wielgosz et al. 2002; Wielgosz 2008; Wielgosz and Degryse 2008, 69–73; Friedland 2013). This pattern is not limited to the Levant. At Ostia, in Italy, statues in Luna marble from Carrara in northern Italy have been identified alongside others in Pentelic, Parian, Thasian, Prokonnesian, Aphrodisian, and

Dokimeian marble (Lazzarini et al. 2007); two recent campaigns of analysis at Hadrian's Villa near Tivoli in Italy, meanwhile, found sculpture in all of these materials as well as the fine-grained marble from Göktepe in Turkey (Lapuente et al. 2012; Pensabene et al. 2012). Even at these well-connected sites a much smaller range of white marbles are found in architectural contexts.

Why this discrepancy? On the one hand, it could be argued that sculptors based at these centers increasingly drew on a wider range of raw materials as they became available, much more so than their colleagues in the building industry. Although stone carving is a generally conservative craft and it is often assumed that sculptors worked in only one or perhaps two materials, this tendency should not be overstated (Rockwell 1993, 2–5). In their various studies on sculpture in Thasian dolomitic marble, Herrmann and Newman argued that such was the stylistic range of these objects that there was no way they could all be attributed to Thasian sculptors. In other words, local sculptors all across the Roman world imported Thasian marble as a raw material favored for its durability and whiteness (Herrmann and Newman 1995, 75–8). In choosing what material to use, a stone carver will assess the suitability of the different options for the job at hand, their workability, and cost, which will be heavily determined by how easy they are to get hold of. While building materials would be needed in bulk, which might limit the quarries that could feasibly supply them, sculptors required only single blocks and could be more flexible in their selection.

On the other hand, the archaeological and documentary evidence discussed above shows that sculpture was also often purchased and transported quite differently from architectural material. Stone components for buildings were usually shipped en masse, in roughed-out or unworked form (Russell 2011a, 147–8). Statues, in contrast, were often shipped individually, alongside other stone elements or different cargoes altogether; they were routinely bought and sold as single items, often fully finished products rather than raw materials. The range of materials used for statuary at sites all around the Mediterranean shows that individual customers engaged with a wide range of sculptors and suppliers in what was a highly dynamic marketplace. Customers evidently sought out products from prestigious artistic centers or even individual sculptors. Athenian, Dokimeian, Aphrodisian, and Nicomedian sculptors were especially in demand. These sculptors were presumably known for the quality of their work but perhaps also for their particular specialties. In the case of sarcophagi it is possible to distinguish between particular producers based on the style of their products, such was the level of specialization: Attic sarcophagi, for instance, are always carved in Pentelic marble and consistently share enough stylistic characteristics to identify them as the products of a limited body of craftsmen (Russell 2011b, 127–31). Whether this specialization ever existed in the case of statue production is open for debate. Several inscriptions from Asia Minor refer to "Aphrodisian" carvings, but these might just have been works done by Aphrodisians (Chaisemartin 1999, 264). No convincing evidence links any single statue type to a single producer. Statues of the Large Herculaneum Woman type, to give one example, are carved in a wide range of materials and vary considerably in finish, as a recent catalogue of them shows (Trimble 2011, 64–74). Clearly no single maker oversaw their production, and the same holds true for other canonical statue types.

Individual sculptors appear to have drawn on a wide repertoire of forms and motifs and it was their skill in executing these rather than the originality of their composition that customers valued. How these designs themselves were transmitted is another question altogether. Traveling sculptors would certainly have helped to spread popular styles, and imported statues must have had a similar effect, acting as models for local craftsmen. Designs for particular statues could also have been circulated in the form of sketches, models (in plaster or terracotta), and perhaps even marble or bronze prototypes, but how controlled this process was in the case of imperial portraits, for example, remains uncertain (Pfanner 1989; Smith 1996).

The Sarcophagus Trade

The discussion above has concentrated on statuary, partly because archaeometric analysis has had a major impact in this area. In terms of sheer clarity of patterns of supply and demand, though, the sarcophagus trade warrants special attention. Sarcophagi are more easily categorized and their place of origin more readily identified macroscopically than other forms of sculpture. Indeed partly finished sarcophagi at the quarries, alongside finds from shipwrecks and sites all across the Roman world, allow the routes taken by these objects and the stages of production that they passed through to be closely followed.

Roughed-out sarcophagi are known from numerous white marble quarries, but particular concentrations have been identified on Prokonnesos and Thasos. Usually this work was limited to hollowing-out and basic squaring, but sometimes more detailed roughing-out was undertaken at the quarry. A series of round-ended (so-called *lēnos*) sarcophagi in various states of finish have been found in the dolomitic marble quarries at Saliara and Cape Vathy on Thasos, for example (Wurch-Koželj and Koželj 1995). Some were also left with projecting protomes along one of their sides for the carving of lions' heads, a decorative motif popular at Rome. Both the Prokonnesian and Thasian quarries were well positioned to supply overseas markets, and the sarcophagi produced at them were effectively raw materials for carvers based elsewhere. The rectangular chests roughed out on Prokonnesos, for instance, were shipped to the Black Sea, the western and southern coasts of Turkey, the Levant, Alexandria, and the Adriatic (Ward-Perkins 1992, 82, fig. 58; Koch 2011, 15–21). In all of these areas local producers added the final level of decoration to these objects, adapting them to regional tastes.

The largest market for sarcophagi between the second and fourth centuries AD, however, was Rome. Numerous sarcophagus producers emerged here to take advantage of this demand (Koch and Sichtermann 1982, 267–72). Archaeometric analysis has shown that these producers imported roughed-out chests from a wide range of quarries, among them the Prokonnesian, Thasian, Luna, Pentelic, and Ephesian ones (Van Keuren et al. 2011). These producers must have communicated closely with the quarries, sending specifications as required, and indeed the *lēnos* sarcophagi found on Thasos were clearly intended for this market.

Two shipwrecks off southern Italy, both of which were carrying sarcophagi in Thasian marble probably destined for Rome, provide remarkable evidence for the form in which these roughed-out sarcophagi were shipped. The first, off San Pietro in Bevagna in Puglia, contains a cargo of roughed-out *lēnos* sarcophagi, dated to the third century AD. Of the twenty-three sarcophagi comprising this cargo, ten are round-ended *lēnos* sarcophagi (seven with projecting protomes), nine are simple rectangular chests, while four are rectangular chests with round-ended interior cavities; all are carved in white Thasian dolomitic marble (Ward-Perkins and Throckmorton 1965; Petriaggi and Davidde 2010). A similar cargo has been identified at the nearby Torre Sgarrata wreck (figure 2.7.4). The vessel that sank here, again probably in the late second or early third century AD, carried eighteen rectangular sarcophagus chests in two varieties of Thasian marble, calcitic and dolomitic (Throckmorton 1969; Calia et al. 2009). Both the Torre Sgarrata and San Pietro cargoes were relatively large, around the 150–60 metric ton mark, and each of these sarcophagi weighs 3–5 metric tons (on other stone cargoes: Russell 2011a; 2013a). To purchase all of the chests and contract a ship to carry them would have required substantial capital outlay, presumably from either a major workshop in the capital, a specialist supplier, or possibly multiple carvers clubbing together (Russell 2011b, 137).

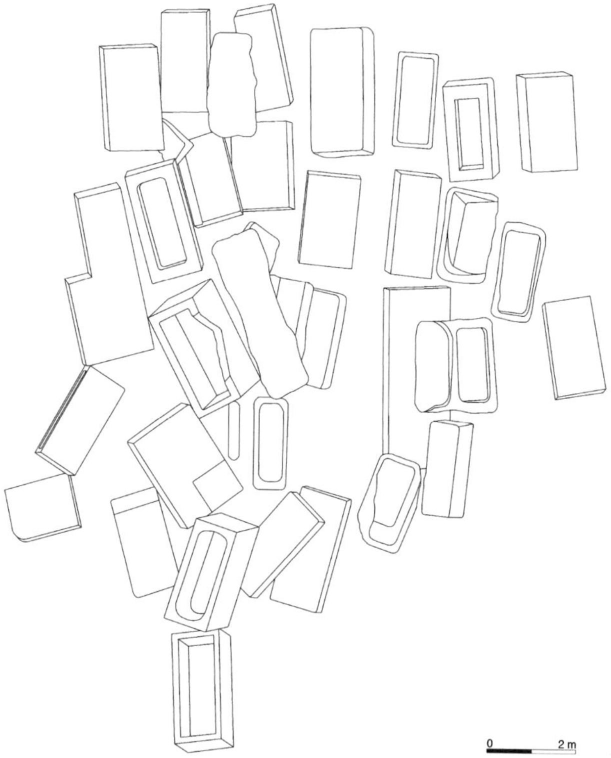

FIGURE 2.7.4 Plan of the cargo of the Torre Sgarrata shipwreck off Puglia (based on Throckmorton 1972, 13).

Not all sarcophagus producers, however, relied on roughed-out forms from distant quarries. The well-known Attic and Dokimeian producers made use of their local materials and carved them to a finished or at least near-finished state before transport (Russell 2011b, 123–31). Attic sarcophagi, produced in and around Athens and carved in Pentelic marble, were widely distributed along the Mediterranean coast, while sarcophagi in Dokimeian marble, especially the famous columnar, so-called Asiatic sarcophagi, are found throughout Turkey as well as in Italy and the Levant (Waelkens 1982, 9, pl. 31). These expensive, ornately carved products were created by a limited body of sculptors trained in a shared tradition, probably all from Athens and Dokimeion respectively. Whether they were dispatched from these sites fully finished or roughed out and accompanied by a team of sculptors to finish them has been widely debated (Ward-Perkins 1956; Wiegartz 1974, 348–50). At the moment, little evidence supports the hypothesis that they were transported roughed out. The only two Attic sarcophagi to have been recovered from the seabed, perhaps from shipwrecks, are indeed fully finished (Arata 2005, 166, 197).

Sarcophagi, even when fully carved, were heavy objects, so it is not surprising that it was predominately customers in coastal centers who bought them. Nevertheless, these were prestigious items, one-time purchases which were also often made to contain whole families. For this reason, sarcophagi were occasionally imported far inland, even to areas where imported building materials are scarce (Ward-Perkins 1992, 83, fig. 59).

Conclusion

The long-distance trade in sculpture and the raw materials for its production developed in response to increasing demand for high-quality works of art in marble and bronze across the Roman world. While this demand had its roots at Rome in the third and second centuries BC, it soon spread to other areas of the Roman world, with marble and bronze becoming the preferred materials for high-end, elite artistic production. In areas that had no indigenous traditions of working in these media, where there were no marble resources or the necessary metals to make bronze, customers were reliant on imports. Such was the demand for high-quality materials of any type, however, that even fine limestone or sandstones were highly sought-after and transported significant distances. While most stone objects were probably transported either as raw blocks or partially roughed out, statues and sarcophagi were certainly also traded in a finished form, despite their fragility. The raw materials for bronze statuary production must also have been widely distributed, though tracing them is difficult, and there is clear evidence for a trade in finished bronzes. The sculptors who worked these materials were also mobile, traveling with single commissions or moving overseas on a longer-term basis to be closer to their customer base. The routes traveled by these objects and individuals are revealing not simply of economic but also cultural and artistic connectivity, as well as the relationship between sculptors, their customers, and the various other individuals (such as quarrymen and shippers) involved in the production and distribution of sculpture.

Bibliography

Adam, J.-P., and P. Varène. 1980. "Une peinture romaine représentant une scène de chantier." *RA* 1980(2): 213–38.

Arata, F. P. 2005. *Opere d'arte dal mare: Testimonianze archeologiche subacquee del trasporto e del commercio marittimo di prodotti artistici*. Rome: Libreria dello Stato.

Asgari, N. 1990. "Objets de marbre finis, semi-finis et inachevés du Proconnèse." In *Pierre Éternelle du Nil au Rhin: Carrières et prefabrication*, edited by M. Waelkens, 106–126. Brussels: Crédit Communal.

Attanasio, D. 2003. *Ancient White Marbles: Analysis and Identification by Paramagnetic Resonance Spectroscopy*. Studia Archaeologica 122. Rome: "L'Erma" di Bretschneider.

Attanasio, D., M. Bruno, and A. B. Yavuz. 2009. "Quarries in the Region of Aphrodisias: The Black and White Marbles of Göktepe (Muğla)." *JRA* 22.1: 312–48.

Bassett, S. 2004. *The Urban Images of Late Antique Constantinople*. Cambridge: Cambridge University Press.

Bauchhenss, G. 1994. "Die klassichen Reliefs." In Hellenkemper Salies, von Prittwitz und Gaffron, and Bauchhenss 1994, 375–80.

Bruno, M. 2002. "Considerazioni sulle cave, sui metodi di estrazione, di lavorazione e sui trasporti." In De Nuccio and Ungaro 2002, 179–94.

Calia, A., M. T. Giannotta, L. Lazzarini, and G. Quarta. 2009. "The Torre Sgarrata Wreck: Characterization and Provenance of White Marble Artefacts in the Cargo." In *ASMOSIA 7*, edited by Y. Maniatis, *BCH* Supplement 51: 333–42.

Chaisemartin, N. de. 1999. "Technical Aspects of the Sculptural Decoration at Aphrodisias in Caria." In *Archéomatériaux: Marbres et autres roches; ASMOSIA 4*, edited by M. Schvoerer, 261–8. Bordeaux: Presses Universitaires de Bordeaux.

Coarelli, F. 1996. *Revixit ars: Arte e ideologia a Roma; Dai modelli ellenistici alla tradizione repubblicana*. Rome: Edizioni Quasar.

De Nuccio, M., and L. Ungaro, eds. 2002. *I marmi colorati della Roma imperiale*. Venice: Marsilio.

Elsner, J., and J. Huskinson, eds. 2011. *Life, Death and Representation: Some New Work on Roman Sarcophagi*. Millennium Studies 29. Berlin: Walter de Gruyter.

Fischer, M. L. 1998. *Marble Studies: Roman Palestine and the Marble Trade*. Konstanz: Universitätsverlag Konstanz.

Friedland, E. A. 2013. "The Carving of Classical Sculpture in the Roman Near East." In *Ateliers and Artisans in Roman Art and Archaeology*, edited by T. M. Kristensen and B. Poulsen. JRA Supplement 92: 101–118.

Gutiérrez, A., P. Lapuente, and I. Rodà, eds. 2012. *Interdisciplinary Studies on Ancient Stone. ASMOSIA 9*. Documenta 23. Tarragona: Institut Català d'Arqueologia Clàssica.

Hellenkemper Salies, G., H.-H. von Prittwitz und Gaffron, and G. Bauchhenss, eds. 1994. *Das Wrack: Der antike Schiffsfund von Mahdia*. Vol. 1. Cologne: Rheinland-Verlag.

Herrmann, J. J., Jr., and R. Newman. 1995. "The Exportation of Dolomitic Marble from Thasos: Evidence from Mediterranean and Other Collections." In Maniatis, Herz, and Basiakos 1995, 73–86.

Herz, N. and M. Waelkens, eds. 1988. *Classical Marble: Geochemistry, Technology and Trade.* NATO ASI series E: Applied Sciences 153. Dordrecht: Kluwer Academic.

Kane, S., and S. Carrier. 1988. "Relationships between Style and Size of Statuary and the Availability of Marble at Cyrene." In Herz and Waelkens 1988, 197–206.

Karageorghis, V. 1969. "Chronique des fouilles à Chypre en 1968." *BCH* 93: 431–569.

Koch, G. 2011. "Sarcofagi di età imperiale romana in Asia Minore: Una sintesi." In *Roman Sculpture in Asia Minor*, edited by F. D'Andria and I. Romeo, 9–29. JRA Supplement 80. Portsmouth, RI: Journal of Roman Archaeology.

Koch, G., and H. Sichtermann. 1982. *Römische Sarkophage*. Munich: C. H. Beck.

Koželj, T. 1988. "Les carrières des époques grecque, romaine et byzantine." In *Ancient Marble Quarrying and Trade*, edited by J. C. Fant, 3–79. BAR-IS 453. Oxford: Archeopress.

Lapuente, P., P. León, T. Nogales, H. Royo, M. Preite-Martinez, and P. Blanc. 2012. "White Sculptural Materials from Villa Adriana: Study of Provenance." In Gutiérrez, Lapuente, and Rodà 2012, 364–75.

Lazzarini, L., P. Pensabene, M. Preite-Martinez, and B. Turi. 2007. "La determinazione della provenienza dei marmi usati nella statuaria e nei rilievi." In *Ostiensum marmorum decus et decor: Studi architettonici, decorativi e archeometrici*, edited by P. Pensabene, 619–27. Studi Miscellanei 33. Rome: "L'Erma" di Bretschneider.

Mañas, I., and A. Fusco. 2008. "Canteras de *Lusitania*: Un anális arqueológico." In *Marmora Hispania: Explotación y uso de los materiales pétreos en la Hispania romana*, edited by T. Nogales and J. Beltrán, 481–522. Hispania Antigua, Serie Arqueológica 2. Rome: "L'Erma" di Bretschneider.

Maniatis, Y., N. Herz, and Y. Basiakos, eds. 1995. *The Study of Marble and Other Stones Used in Antiquity; ASMOSIA* 3. London: Archetype.

Massy, J.-L. 2013. *Archéologie sous-marine en Corse antique*. CahArchSubaq 20. Fréjus: Cahiers d'archéologie subaquatique.

Mattusch, C. C. 1994. "Bronze Herm of Dionysos." In Hellenkemper Salies, von Prittwitz und Gaffron, and Bauchhenss 1994, 431–50.

———. 1996. "The Preferred Medium: The Many Lives of Classical Bronzes." In *The Fire of Hephaistos: Large Classical Bronzes from North American Collections*, edited by C. C. Mattusch, 15–43. Cambridge, MA: Harvard University Art Museums.

McLean, B. H. 2002. *Greek and Latin Inscriptions in the Konya Archaeological Museum*. Regional Epigraphic Catalogues of Asia Minor 4. London: British Institute of Archaeology at Ankara.

Parker, A. J. 1992. *Ancient Shipwrecks of the Mediterranean and Roman Provinces*. BAR-IS 580. Oxford: Archaeopress.

Pensabene, P. 1994. *Le vie del marmo: I blocchi di cava di Roma e di Ostia; Il fenomeno del marmo nella Roma antica*. Rome: Ministero per i Beni Culturali e Ambientali.

———. 2002. "Il fenomeno del marmo nel mondo romano." In De Nuccio and Ungaro 2002, 3–67.

Pensabene, P., F. Antonelli, L. Lazzarini, and S. Cancelliere. 2012. "Archaeometric Analyses of White Marbles from Hadrian's Villa (Tivoli, Italy) and the Use of Pentelic and Dokymaean Marbles in the Statuary of the So-Called Canopus." In Gutiérrez, Lapuente, and Rodà 2012, 104–8.

Petriaggi, R., and B. Davidde. 2010. "The Sarcophagi from the Wreck of San Pietro in Bevagna (Taranto): The Subject of New Works by the Istituto Superiore per la Conservazione ed il restauro." *Archaeologia Maritima Mediterranea* 7: 131–7.

Petzl, G. 1994. "Die Inschriften." In Hellenkemper Salies, von Prittwitz und Gaffron, and Bauchhenss 1994, 381–98.

Pfanner, M. 1989. "Über das Herstellen von Porträts: Ein Beitrag zu Rationalisierungsmassnahmen und Produktionsmechanismen von Massenware im späten Hellenismus und in der römischen Kaiserzeit." *JdI* 104: 157–257.

Picard, G.-C. 1968. "Un témoinage sur le commerce des objets d'art dans l'empire romain: La statue de bronze de 'l'Apollon' de Mactar, offerte par S. Julius Possessor." *RA* 1968(2): 297–314.

Pollitt, J. J. 1986. *Art in the Hellenistic Age*. Cambridge: Cambridge University Press.

Rockwell, P. 1993. *The Art of Stoneworking: A Reference Guide*. Cambridge: Cambridge University Press.

Röder, J. 1960. "Die Reiter von Breitfurt: Technische Betrachtungen." *Mitteilungen des historischen Vereins der Pfalz* 58: 96–109.

Roueché, C., and K. Erim. 1982. "Sculptors from Aphrodisias: Some New Inscriptions." *PBSR* 50: 102–115.

Russell, B. 2011a. "*Lapis transmarinus*: Stone-Carrying Ships and the Maritime Distribution of Stone in the Roman Empire." In *Maritime Archaeology and Ancient Trade in the Mediterranean*, edited by D. J. Robinson and A. I. Wilson, 139–56. OCMA Monographs 7. Oxford: School of Archaeology.

———. 2011b. "The Roman Sarcophagus 'Industry': A Reconsideration." In Elsner and Huskinson 2011, 119–47.

———. 2013a. "Roman and Late-Antique Shipwrecks with Stone Cargoes: A New Inventory." *JRA* 26: 331–61.

———. 2013b. *The Economics of the Roman Stone Trade*. Oxford Studies on the Roman Economy. Oxford: Oxford University Press.

Smith, R. R. R. 1996. "Typology and Diversity in the Portraits of Augustus." *JRA* 9: 30–47.

Söldner, M. 1994. "Der sogenannte Agon." In Hellenkemper Salies, von Prittwitz und Gaffron, and Bauchhenss 1994, 399–430.

Squarciapino, M. F. 1943. *La Scuola di Afrodisia*. Studi e materiali del Museo dell'Impero Romano 3. Rome: Governatorato di Roma.

Strong, D., and A. Claridge. 1976. "Marble Sculpture." In *Roman Crafts*, edited by D. Strong and D. Brown, 195–207. London: Duckworth.

Throckmorton, P. 1969. "Ancient Shipwreck Yields New Facts—and a Strange Cargo." *National Geographic* 135: 282–300.

———. 1972. "Romans on the Sea." In *A History of Seafaring Based on Underwater Archaeology*, edited by G. Bass, 65–86. London: Thames and Hudson.

Toynbee, J. M. C. 1951. *Some Notes on Artists in the Roman World*. Collection Latomus 6. Brussels: Latomus.

Trimble, J. 2011. *Women and Visual Replication in Roman Imperial Art and Culture*. Cambridge: Cambridge University Press.

Van Keuren, F., D. Attanasio, J. J. Herrmann Jr., N. Herz, and L. P. Gromet. 2011. "Multimethod Analyses of Roman Sarcophagi at the Museo Nazionale Romano, Rome." In Elsner and Huskinson 2011, 149–88.

Vlachogianni, E. 2012. "Sculpture." In *The Antikythera Shipwreck: The Ship, the Treasures, the Mechanism*, edited by N. E. Kaltsas, E. Vlachogianni, and P. Bouyia, 62–115. Athens: National Archaeological Museum.

Waelkens, M. 1982. *Dokimeion: Die Werkstatt der repräsentativen kleinasiatischen Sarkophage: Chronologie und Typologie ihrer Produktion*. Archäologische Forschungen 11. Berlin: Mann.

———. 1985. "From a Phrygian Quarry: The Provenance of the Statues of the Dacian Prisoners in Trajan's Forum at Rome." *AJA* 89: 641–53.

Waelkens, M., P. De Paepe, and L. Moens. 1988. "Quarries and the Marble Trade." In Herz and Waelkens 1988, 11–28.

Ward-Perkins, J. B. 1956. "The Hippolytus Sarcophagus from Trinquetaille." *JRS* 46: 10–16.

———. 1992. *Marble in Antiquity: Collected Papers of J. B. Ward-Perkins*. Edited by H. Dodge and B. Ward-Perkins. Archaeological Monographs of the British School at Rome 6. London: British School at Rome.

Ward-Perkins, J. B., and P. Throckmorton. 1965. "The San Pietro Wreck." *Archaeology* 18(3): 201–9.

Wiegartz, H. 1974. "Marmorhandel, Sarkophagherstellung und die Lokalisierung der kleinasiatischen Säulensarkophage." In *Mansel'e Armağan = Mélanges Mansel*, edited by E. Akurgal and U. B. Alkim, 1: 345–83. Ankara: Türk Tarih Kurumu Basımevi.

Wielgosz, D. 2008. "Marble Sculptures from the Archaeological Museum of Bosra." *Marmora* 4: 57–64.

Wielgosz, D., and P. Degryse. 2008. "Provenance of the Imperial Marble Group from Philippopolis (Shahba, Syria): Archaeometric Evidence." *Marmora* 4: 65–74.

Wielgosz, D., L. Lazzarini, B. Turi, and F. Antonelli. 2002. "The Origin of the Marble Sculptures from Palmyra." In *Interdisciplinary Studies on Ancient Stone: ASMOSIA 6*, edited by L. Lazzarini, 389–402. Padua: Bottega d'Erasmo.

Worp, K. A., ed. 1995. *Greek Papyri from Kellis: I (P.Kell.Gr.), Nos. 1–90*. Dakhleh Oasis Project: Monograph No. 3. Oxford: Oxbow.

Wurch-Koželj, M., and T. Koželj. 1995. "Roman Quarries of Apse-Sarcophagi in Thasos of the second and third Centuries." In Maniatis, Herz, and Basiakos 1995, 39–50.

PART III

STYLES AND GENRES

CHAPTER 3.1

STYLE

Applications and Limitations

MARK D. FULLERTON

Introduction: The Problems of Style in Roman Sculpture

For as long as scholars have arranged ancient works according to stylistic criteria, they have worked from an assumption that style should develop according to an organic model of growth, perfection, and decline. As "natural" as it seems to us today, this model is by no means the rule among early cultures; there is little trace of it in the exquisitely crafted artistic outputs of ancient Egypt, Mesopotamia, and the Aegean Bronze Age, nor does it play much of a role in our understanding of art across the Mediterranean in the first millennium AD. The model was developed, embraced, and even reinforced already in antiquity. It is implicit in the brief accounts of sculpture and painting found in the works of Cicero, Quintilian, and Pliny, who themselves drew on much earlier sources (Pollitt 1974, 73–84). In modern times, of course, the primary source of the model is Winckelmann ([1764] 2006, 227–44; Brendel [1953] 1979, 18–24). Although his terms for the sequential stylistic eras differ from those used today, the chronological periods themselves and even his stylistic assessments live on. Significantly for the study of Roman art, he termed the entire period after the era of Lysippos and Alexander as an "age of imitators"—a characterization that has had enormous impact on approaches to both Hellenistic and Roman art ever since.

Rather than focus on the dismissive tone of Winckelmann's assessment of Hellenistic and Roman art (Fullerton 2003), we might instead embrace the ways in which his observation is correct. A great deal of Roman art, especially monumental, official, and elite art, reflects a desire to own and display objects that resemble the products of other cultures, primarily Greek. Yet, there are distinct challenges in analyzing the artistic works of "imitative" cultures, because the very concepts of imitation and influence are neither obvious nor neutral but are themselves interpretive and evaluative. Modern scholarship seeks to nuance such terms by investigating the dynamics of cultural interaction, attempting to identify just what features are shared or borrowed, on what kinds of objects, through what mechanisms of exchange, and, especially, by which segments of society (Gazda 2002; Perry 2005).

Two basic models offer themselves, depending on the circumstances of the cultural interaction. In the first, the contact is ongoing, and the works of the recipient culture repeat the developments of the "donor" culture as each new stage is revealed; implicitly, the imitative works are later than and, ostensibly, qualitatively inferior to their models. This diachronic diffusion model results in works often termed "provincial"; the most obvious examples in our period are provided by many treatments of Greek colonial or Etruscan art (most conspicuously, Boardman 1994). A contrasting model entails a relationship between two different cultures that is dramatically altered when one conquers and endeavors to rule the other. This model has been applied to "imperial" forces in the ancient world, for example, Akkadians, Assyrians, Persians, Mycenaeans, Macedonians, and, of course, Romans. In this synchronic appropriation model, the ruling culture assimilates the subject culture's art, including the entire history of its artistic accomplishment, all at once (Pollitt 1978; Gruen 1992, 84–182). Therefore, rules or patterns for which styles are used and how they are used develop in order for art to accomplish its communicative mission, and different styles are often combined to form "eclectic" works.

These models, however imperfect and approximate, are useful for thinking about processes and especially valuable for understanding the Roman situation, which is subject to both the diachronic and synchronic models. The Romans, like the Etruscans, were involved in significant intercultural exchange with the Greek *poleis* during the first centuries after the city's foundation. Thus, their art during the eighth through fourth centuries BC followed a very similar development, one that reflects in general terms the sequence observable in Greece. However, as Rome extended its contacts through conquest of the western Greek and Punic worlds, its historical and cultural trajectories diverged sharply from those of Etruria. With the astonishingly rapid extension of Roman hegemony over the Hellenistic eastern Mediterranean in the second century BC, the situation of artistic production, acquisition, and employment in Rome and its serial colonial acquisitions was utterly transformed. It was at this time that the Romans developed their own visual language of empire, characterized by a complex system of styles drawn from the artistic traditions of both conqueror and conquered (Beard and Henderson 2001). Moreover, the cultures they encountered and appropriated at that time were decidedly different from that of Greece in the classical period. The Hellenistic monarchs, mostly Macedonian in origin, had themselves developed successful means to express power and exercise control, means that fully employed the possibilities of public sculpture and included a visual language that was already a mix of traditional and innovative figures and styles. The Romans quickly adopted their strategies.

The story of Roman stylistic development is therefore a stratigraphic phenomenon, with layers of "influence" that must be peeled away, and each understood in its own context, in order to reveal sources and speculate on signification. Like a real, rather than ideal, stratigraphy, the layers are not always equal in depth, easily separated, or evenly documented. For example, when we see a Roman imperial work in classical style, can we tell whether it references the classical era, a Hellenistic classicizing work, or even an early Etrusco-Roman work of the classical period (Elsner 2006; Hölscher 2006)? Would the motives for that stylistic choice be different according to which source was in play? What is obvious here, as was already obvious to Brendel a half century ago ([1953] 1979, 9), is that the interpretation of style in Roman sculpture is not the same matter as in the study of Greek sculpture and that the organizational structure that works for the latter is insufficient for the former.

Structuring Phenomena

Periodization of Style and the Teleology of Abstraction

Many models for a stylistic assessment of Roman sculpture can be found in the two centuries of scholarship on the topic, but most work simultaneously from two parallel conceptual frameworks. Both of these were operative at the end of the nineteenth and early twentieth centuries, when the first modern histories of Roman art were written in a series of attempts to rescue it from the marginalization it had suffered in Winckelmann's account (Brendel [1953] 1979, 28–68). One is the a priori assumption, as hinted above, that Roman art can be organized into a sequence of definable stylistic periods, as had been done for Greek art before Alexander. However, since the Roman material does not adhere to the organic model of development used for the Greek, the result was a sequence of styles that do not always flow logically or coherently from one period to the next. Nor did all scholars apply the same stylistic criteria. In the case of Greek art, one tends to explain style in terms of the governing values and principles of the society, which are similarly detectible in contemporaneous literature, philosophy, and religion. As these values and principles change, so do their various cultural manifestations. For Roman art, however, explanations were sought in the distinct historical periods defined by the persons of power within the society—from the patrician aspirants of the later Republic to the succeeding sequence of imperial dynasties. Eventually this model came to characterize stylistic phases in the personalities and/or policies of the emperors themselves, giving us, for example, an "Augustan," "Flavian" or "Hadrianic" artistic style (e.g., Toynbee 1934; Zanker 1988; Henderson 2003; see essay 4.7, Petersen).

It is possible in this way to organize Roman style into a system that makes accessible a comprehension of the whole process, as for Greek art. Yet, both the phases themselves and their sequence are qualitatively different from their Greek counterparts, lacking the internal rationality, stylistic exclusivity, and strict unidirectionality of the organic model. Thus the defining characteristics of a given era can, even must, repeat: we hear of both Augustan and Hadrianic "classicism" or Flavian and Severan "baroque." This system retains from histories of Greek art the presumed inseparability of prevailing values and artistic styles, but, as appropriate to a distinctly Roman historical situation, it differs in the assumptions that it makes about how values change and who effects each transformation. Change in Greek art, to put it simply, is a natural outgrowth of the highly agonistic nature of classical Greek society and institutions. Whatever the reason that Greek art developed the *way* it did, it did so *because* artists desired or needed to improve their product either from their own sense of technical *aretē* or because of the equally competitive orientation of their patrons. Roman art, understood as a reflection of a sequence of dynastic forces, must then change (or not change) in accordance with each ruler's efforts to emphasize continuity or discontinuity with his predecessor(s).

The second organizational framework is more empirical than the historicist account, and actually preceded it as a basis for structuring a development of Roman art (Brendel [1953] 1979, 25–47). It is based on an obvious truth concerning Roman sculptural style: the distinct formal differences between the styles that prevail in official state sculpture of the early empire and those from three centuries later. This too has an analogue in Greek art, in which the stylistic system seeks to illustrate and explicate a similar formal change, but in reverse. In Greece the change is from a style that is linear, flat, and conceptual (geometric) to one that is rounded, three-dimensional, and perceptually convincing (late classical); in Roman art the change is from the "naturalism" of late republican and Augustan Hellenism to the "abstraction" of tetrarchic art. Moreover, not only the directions but also the defining qualities of the Greek and Roman stylistic changes were entirely different, the latter, unlike the former, being neither organic nor exclusive, neither linear nor unidirectional. Since the Roman process is entirely different, to a viewer conditioned to understand stylistic change in terms of the Greek model, it was counterintuitive and thus more demanding of explanation. Although most fourth-century AD art looks different from first-century art, the nature of the change and the intermediate steps in the process do not make very useful chronological markers.

The main goals, then, of most histories of Roman sculptural styles are to identify the prevailing style or styles of each time period, seek an explanation for the use of those styles in the backgrounds, tastes, and intentions of those wielding power, explain the transitions between succeeding dynasties in ways that also explain stylistic change (or continuity), and finally elicit a coherent, compelling, and congruent account of how and why abstraction came to prevail. For the how, one seeks out aspects of Roman art in which the basic features of abstraction—for example strong contrasts of light and shadow and simplified forms—might be detected from an early stage. Proposed formal models range from the chiaroscural sculpture of Hellenistic and imperial Asia Minor, to the oriental formalism of sculpture in the Roman Near East, to the "provincial" simplicity of sculptural styles in the northern European provinces. For the why, still assuming a top-down process in the determination of fashion, scholars seek explanation in the origins or affiliations of later emperors, which come to represent a full range of ethnic origins and social classes. All such views contextualize these formal changes within a third century AD characterized by a growing spirituality and dissatisfaction with classical humanism, as well as the rigid, even formalistic socioeconomic and political structures of the Tetrarchy itself (L'Orange 1965; Elsner 1998).

Dualistic Models

These systems of periodization provide useful structures for organizing information about Roman sculpture, specifically the phenomena of style, and suggest ways of thinking about the relationships among history, style, and development. Indeed, many Roman art texts to this day apply them at the very least as an organizational scheme, and thus they tend to frame, explicitly or implicitly, the account itself (Kampen 2003, 379–80). Yet period-based schemes can result in only a partial understanding; while able to accommodate one category of variation, the geographic, they tend to underevaluate others. First, a focus on the "official" art of imperial portraiture and commemorative relief can marginalize works made for even the prosperous members of the nonruling classes (see essay 4.7, Petersen). Second, even within the realm of "official" art, the quest to define phases often obscures the significant variation in the styles actually used. Such plurality, if recognized, is often marginalized as an unexamined eclecticism, mistaking that descriptive term for an interpretive one. Like the organic developmental model from which it is born, a totalizing, historicist system of stylistic phases cannot easily abide pluralism of style.

One step in this direction can be seen in histories of Roman art that sought to address this conflict through hypothesizing dualistic economic, political, and social structures in Rome and the empire. Such an account equates Italic versus Greek styles with "popular" versus "great" art and postulates that the strongly Hellenizing and idealizing forms of Roman imperial art are a direct continuation of a similarly graecophilic orientation among the republican patrician and equestrian elite from which the *imperatores* and earlier emperors emerged. The less privileged preferred more abstract forms and more realistic effects, but this stylistic schism was not simply a product of the polarizing social consequences of the Mediterranean conquest, when the Roman aristocracy embraced the Hellenistic art of Rome's defeated adversaries. A similar dichotomy can be detected in Etrusco-Italic art, starting when Greeks first came in numbers to the Italian peninsula. Villanovans and early Etruscans maintained their own ceramic traditions in unpainted, and often handmade, impasto and bucchero at the same time that they eagerly purchased (and imitated) wheel-made Greek geometric, orientalizing, archaic, and classical vases (Brendel [1978] 1995).

The contributions of this structure were not limited to uncovering the origins of pluralism in the style of Roman art or its proposed model for understanding the social signification of Roman sculptural style. In its eventual Marxist form it also offers a possible explanation for the eventual prevalence of abstraction in the late empire. During the third century, men of unprecedentedly modest means often occupied the imperial title, not simply common citizens and offspring of freedmen but even sons of peasants whose career began as foot soldiers. It might be inferred that the styles preferred in their reigns might reflect this background by drawing on formal traditions familiar to them. This view has many weaknesses as a single explanation (Kampen 2010), but the emergence of abstraction resulted from a variety of forces, and surely the socioeconomic element was one of them.

Pluralistic Models: Semantics and Semiotics

Just as the socially determined dualistic model of stylistic diversity arises from Marxist critical theory of the earlier twentieth century, so too a semiotic model arises from contemporaneous structuralist linguistic theory. While the former explains pluralism within the prevailing periodic stylistic system, the semiotic model essentially inverts the process by centering on stylistic diversity itself, not historical interpretation and its implied system of change. Yet, neither historical explanation nor identification of meaning need be abandoned; it is simply that style, and more specifically the interaction of similar and different stylistic features and figural types, is seen as the key to eliciting meaning from images. In other words, one works from stylistic system to meaning to context rather than from context to meaning to style.

While this approach to Roman art, as a consciously pursued method, is relatively recent, its roots are quite deep. In the mid-nineteenth century it was recognized that of the many Roman sculptures of divine subjects rendered in one or another of the Greek sculptural styles, some were probably copies of lost Greek works, while others were Roman creations employing Greek stylistic features without following any single model (Ridgway 1984; Gazda 2002; Hallett 2005; see essay 3.3, Anguissola). The term "Neo-Attic," originally coined for Greek sculptors of both copies and original creations in earlier styles, soon came to be used more widely for the latter phenomenon, especially in relief sculpture (Fullerton 2003; Gazda 2002). The scholarship on these stylistic phenomena enjoyed a revival from the 1960s onward, driven both by scholars of Greek sculpture, increasingly uneasy with their dependency on Roman works as a means to construct their corpus, and by Romanists wishing to evaluate these sculptures as the Roman works that they obviously were (e.g., Hölscher [1987] 2004, 3; Zanker 1974; Kousser 2008).

The semiotic system emerged from a convergence of interests shared by all parties invested in the study of such "imitative" material. First, one who sought to explain *why* a Roman sculptor would make a work in one or another of these pre-existing styles needed to determine what such choices would bring to the meaning of the work. The coexistence of all these styles strongly suggests that meaning lies in both similarity and difference—whether compared to the universe of possible stylistic referents or to other styles and figures present in the same or adjacent works. That linguistics already had terms for these relationships—paradigmatic and syntagmatic, respectively—suggested the usefulness of a semiotic model. Second, since the forms of Neo-Attic work repeat over a long period of time, and most examples have no find context, the inherent advantages of an ahistoricist reading were obvious.

Tonio Hölscher's "semantic" system remains the most influential model of this type ([1987] 2004; Elsner 2004). His work also is rooted in the traditions of thinking about idealized sculptures (58–76), but perhaps his most valuable contribution is his detection of the system in the more purely "Roman" realms of portraiture and commemorative relief (38–58, 77–82). Central to his treatment is the explicit distinction between "figure," which is the core element of a signifying system that remains consistent throughout Roman art, and "style," which follows a different, "temporal" process (16–18). The former has to do with established figural types and compositional schemes; the latter deals with largely technical qualities such as the depth of relief sculpture and the degree of sharpness in the rendering of details like drapery folds and anatomical divisions. Style, as it is understood in the present essay, has, rather, to do with the actual forms of those features (and others, like pose) and their association with characteristics of a particular stage in the Greek development. It therefore encompasses elements from both "figure" and "style" as distinguished by Hölscher, while classifying much of what he would call "style" as "technique." As it seems to conflate three separate qualities, therefore, Hölscher's demarcation between figure and style is not always easy to draw, especially since, as he himself observes, styles can be as classicizing as figural types (16).

Hölscher's temporal stylistic system creates an area of compromise with the desire for an historical stylistic development, whether unitary or dualist. He describes a pattern that moves from planar figures and sharply defined forms in the Augustan era to an increasingly soft and volumetric carving of details in Flavian work. Should the development be pushed beyond this, which Hölscher does not, it would be seen to lead to the greater chiaroscuro in sculptures of the Antonine and Severan eras. Additionally, Hölscher emphasizes that one result of his semantic system is an increasing abstraction of content resulting from the standardization of forms (88–92), causing a stock figure within a sculptured scene to serve not as a physical participant but as a sign for an abstract concept. One might, although Hölscher does not, argue that this abstraction of content, combined with increased chiaroscuro, contributes to the abstraction of form and, inseparably, style that characterizes the third and following centuries AD. In this respect, then, an association between date and form can be constructed, but the pluralistic nature of the Roman development makes any such system both partial and provisional.

A distinction must also be drawn between Hölscher's semantic system, which primarily focuses on the association between figure and meaning, and a semiotic process, which situates a figural type or stylistic feature in a world of diverse visual imagery. The latter approach seeks to identify possible referents, to determine which referents are potentially relevant, and to consider how this interplay of image and referential universe was operative in the minds of designer and viewer alike, through analogy with literary intertext (Fullerton 1997). By focusing on the construction of meaning by both participants, formal diversity is further complicated by experiential diversity. There are obvious advantages to this last approach. As this inverted view of artistic style is more broadly based than the more strictly historicist accounts, it is more culturally based and less situationally determined, which better accommodates "timeless" categories of Roman sculpture such as idealized statuary and relief. Moreover, for monuments that *are* datable without recourse to the evidence of style, this more nuanced form of reading can reveal an exceptionally rich process of interplay among image, viewer, and context, as is demonstrated below.

Applications and Limitations

To summarize, the situation of style and interpretation in the study of Roman sculpture is one that offers both challenges and opportunities, both of which result from a stratigraphic process of stylistic development conditioned by a series of stimuli, largely non-native, that follow both the "provincial" and the "eclectic" models of cultural interaction. What one finds, when organizing or interpreting Roman sculpture in terms of style, is a diversity of forms, sources, and mechanisms of influence for which one must attempt to account. The resulting styles, each with its own component processes, can be sorted into three general categories.

The so-called native Italic or Etrusco-Roman styles (see essay 3.2, de Grummond) can be traced back to the beginnings of art in Iron Age Italy, when they continued to develop parallel with Greek and Syro-Phoenician imports and their imitations. Since the last are taken, from their emulation of expensive goods, to have functioned as markers of elite status, the less obviously imitative works tend to be associated with both "native" and "middle class" strata. In fact there were multiple motivations for their usage, and they were employed, in Etruscan and Roman art alike, by the wealthiest patrons. A prime example is the use of a realistic or "direct" form of representation, rather than one that is more generic or idealistic (and thus Hellenizing) in portraiture. Its roots can be traced through Hellenistic and classical funerary sculptures back to canopic urns of the seventh century BC. Yet many or most of these sculpted monuments contain the remains of the very wealthy, and the "veristic" style of later republican portraits (like the wax *imagines* that provided its probable prototype) was the very marker of the most privileged classes. Here the point seems to have been the antiquity and autochthony of the *gens*, which are manifested in what seems a specifically Roman form of characterization, although the Hellenistic world also reveals significant experimentation in strikingly honest modes of representation of the non-Greek and nonideal. Indeed, some scholars attribute "Roman" verism to Hellenistic Greek sculptors (Smith 1981; Tanner 2000). More clearly Italic, perhaps, is the use, especially in relief sculpture, of simplified linear forms, squat "unclassical" figural proportions, and planar paratactic compositions. These features exist in Etruscan art (e.g., Brendel [1978] 1995, fig. 246) literally side-by-side with more purely Hellenizing subjects and forms, a juxtaposition that provides an important basis for dualistic structures of stylistic assessment, but in contexts suggesting that the difference is not to be found in social standing alone.

A second group of styles, the Hellenizing (see essays 3.3, Anguissola; and 3.6, Touchette), is the logical result of the first, since the native styles are identified primarily by their differences from these imitative styles. The processes of influence are complex, consisting both of emulations of contemporary Greek forms and referencing of very ancient models, and further nuanced by the archaizing tendencies that occur within each stage of Greek art and culminate under the Macedonian dynasties of the Hellenistic era. It might well be said that the most characteristic qualities and applications of Roman visual Hellenism were taken over by Rome from these Hellenistic monarchs together with their realms.

During the empire, a third group of stylistic developments arises that derives specifically from mutual interaction between Rome and her subject cultures (see Part V, Regions and Provinces). Initially consisting of provincial versions of Roman forms, they come increasingly in the high empire to include the influence of the native and hybrid forms on the products of the capital itself. The latter phenomenon must have been at least one of the forces that led to the rise of abstraction in late antiquity.

A universe of sculptural style that admits such diversity inevitably limits the use we can make of style in assigning dates to specific works. A sculpture that employs a style evocative of that of the Parthenon, for example, might reasonably be postulated to be Augustan, because some much-studied works set up under the first emperor prominently display such features. Yet style alone is not conclusive, because many other eras used classicizing styles. The inverse problem is that of the stylistic period. The lack of uniformity and exclusivity in the connection of sculptural styles with historical epoch eliminates the likelihood of convincingly using those styles to explore a comprehensive artistic *Zeitgeist* for a particular reign or dynasty. Whereas one can argue that the style of the pedimental sculptures from the Sanctuary of Zeus at Olympia reflects the confidence and humanism resulting from the victory over Persia, or that the cool idealism of the Parthenon frieze captures the quasi-heroic status awarded itself by the demos of Periclean Athens, one can only say that the classicism of an Augustan or Flavian sculpture simply manifests one possible set of prevailing principles and values.

Therefore embracing rather than suppressing the complexity of Roman sculptural style is necessary in order to interpret it, but such an approach brings its own limitations. The objective is to assess a work of sculpture in terms of the style or styles it employs against what we may or may not know about the context of its creation and display. But even if this context can be reasonably fixed, the traditions or influences operative on the decision as to how the sculpture should look are not always obvious. Archaistic sculptures might be thought to imitate the archaic, but very few of them look at all like actual archaic work, and most derive from an archaistic tradition that originates in high classical Athens and develops its own diverse array of variants throughout the Hellenistic world (Fullerton 1990, 2–12). Similarly, the classicism of an Augustan work might have nothing to do with classical Greece but instead be a continuation of a well-documented strain of classicism in Hellenistic art.

The process is obviously additive, so the situation becomes more complex with time. Hadrianic classicism, for example, might reasonably allude to the golden age of Pericles or to the classicism of Hellenistic Pergamon, given the emergence of Asia at that time as a seat of considerable economic power and influence, or it might situate Hadrian in the tradition of Augustus, the model for all future *Augusti*. A consideration of the circumstances of Hadrianic classicism suggests yet another possibility—an association with the classical and classicizing traditions that were still living among the aristocrats of the imperial East and are evident in the philosophical, religious, and rhetorical developments we term the Second Sophistic. The emphasis on visual referentiality, therefore, has its own risks, primary among which is a continual deferral of the signifying process that in the best of circumstances might lead to a "richer" reading of signification, but if taken to its nihilistic extreme, can also allow style to consume iconography, thus making meaning irretrievable.

The Gemma Augustea: Style, Content, Context

Stylistic analysis is a comparative process, a truism nowhere more applicable than in the study of Roman sculpture. Given the genesis, evolution, and interactions of styles and influences, it is essential to embrace that comparative nature and consider how all the diverse available stylistic possibilities define both themselves and one another in a reciprocal process. As noted above, these frames of reference can be present in the same work (syntagmatic) or absent but implicated by their immanent possibility as an alternate stylistic choice (paradigmatic). Thus, of all the systems of stylistic interpretation that have been outlined here, the semiotic method, which employs this linguistic model, stands the best chance of offering a useful approach, despite its own limitations. Hölscher's system, for example, focuses primarily on the paradigmatic; he identifies the conventional associations of type with meaning and demonstrates how those meanings operate in a context historically situated by considerations external to stylistic analysis itself. The syntagmatic relationships among those figures (and, more importantly, styles, which are necessarily part of the same system) remain a byproduct of the inherently eclectic nature of his system. They are not, in the examples he offers, used as a means to *determine* meaning, let alone historical context. In other words, the traditional analytical divide between iconography/iconology and style remains unbridged. But need that be the case?

By way of illustration, I would like to look briefly at one very famous work of Roman sculpture—the Gemma Augustea (figure 3.1.1). This exceptionally large and exquisitely sculptured cameo is of unknown provenience, having been in Vienna for over four centuries; there is nothing by which to date it outside the cameo itself. Although it brings together an array of mostly familiar and identifiable figures, its broader meaning, and thus historical context, has been a point of much speculation. Most analyses focus on the specific identities and possible meanings of the separate figures and combine them to form a summative assessment (e.g., Pollini 1993). Although the interaction of figures within the separate groupings that constitute the overall composition is often noted, less attention is paid to the relationships among those groupings, not simply iconographic but also stylistic. Yet just such a consideration, which surely provides a means to explore *how* this monument signifies, also provides a clue as to *what* it specifically references.

It is common now in the study of representational programs to distinguish three separate realms of iconographic operation—the divine/heroic, the allegorical, and the

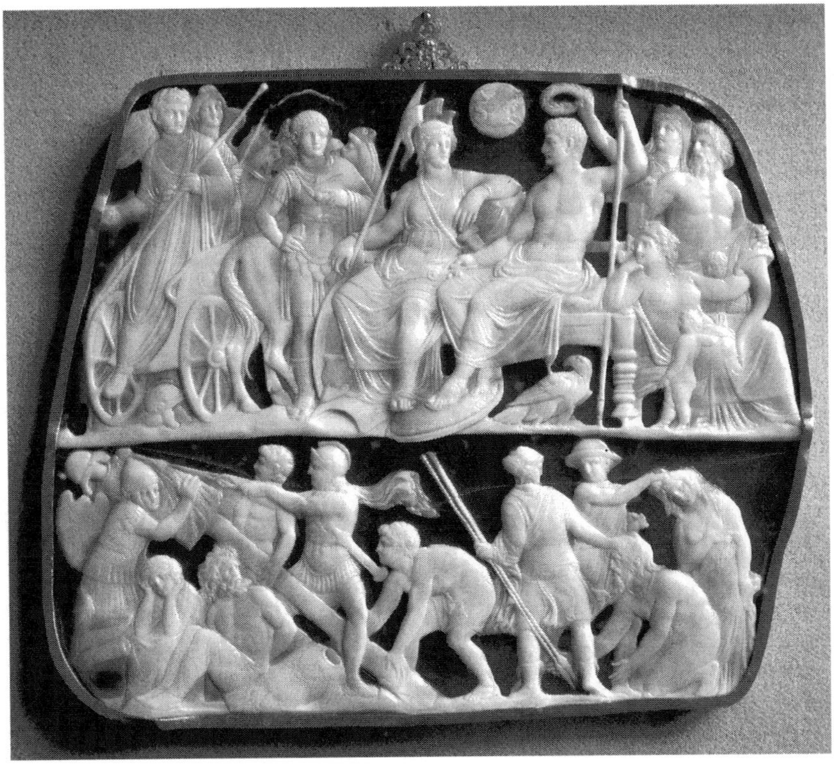

FIGURE 3.1.1 Gemma Augustea. First century BC. Sardonyx. Vienna, Kunsthistorisches Museum.

historical (e.g., Stewart 1985). The borders among them are not impermeable, but the distinction remains a useful one and is certainly applicable here. The divine realm on the Gemma Augustea occurs in the group indicated as the monument's focal point through both composition and scale—the seated images of Augustus and the goddess Roma. Many are troubled by the idea that Augustus is shown as a god before his apotheosis, but it is difficult to escape the conclusion that he is shown as such. The attributes of Jupiter—eagle and scepter—surely suggest this, as does colocation on a throne (a common Roman device that suggests shared equal authority) with the goddess herself. Style, too, is used to set these figures apart. Their forms—drapery, physiognomy, facial features—are strongly classicizing, and possible specific referents come quickly to mind. The seated Augustus is often compared to the Capitoline Jupiter, as it is known from coins (Pollini 1993, 260–66), but his pose is far more relaxed; even more languid is the figure of Roma, whose left arm is thrown back over the seat back and whose right hand rests limply on its arm. Neither of these figurations is typical for its subject, but together they clearly capture the mood and style of the Zeus and Hera from the east frieze of the Parthenon. Roma and Augustus do not actually become Jupiter and Juno here, but they are rendered in a manner—a style—that suggests a comparable power and parallel relationship. They seem then to serve here not simply as allegorical figures but specifically as the god and goddess worshipped in provincial temples to Roma and Augustus throughout and after the Augustan epoch, a point to which we shall return.

To the right of this group is an allegory: an earth goddess reclines in front of personifications of the ocean (Okeanos) and the inhabited world (Oikoumene), who holds a crown above the *princeps*'s head. Reprising themes and imagery of the Ara Pacis and Primaporta Augustus, these figures stand both for the ubiquity of the prosperity brought about by the ascendance of Augustus and the active endorsement of rule by the ruled herself. Yet these figures are separated from the central group by their stylistic forms, which derive from the late classical or Hellenistic prototypes; these not only are *decor*—appropriate—to personification and allegory (Perry 2005, 28–77) but also clearly contrast with the high classical associations of the enthroned deities.

Similarly separated by both scale and style are the figures at left, which are shown, by the relative realism of their portrait faces and official Roman garb, to be historical figures portrayed as *triumphator* and *imperator*. One could extend this analysis to the lower register, where allegory and history mix freely, as do sculptural forms. The point here is the subjugation of the provinces by means of a Roman army composed in large part of provincials, with the elision of stylistic and ethnic realms reflecting (as does the Oikoumene figure above) an open acceptance by the conquered of the benefits of embracing *romanitas*. Style here is also used to mark off the not yet acquiescent, in the form of the bound captive at left, rendered in a Hellenistic "baroque" style, and thereby creates yet another triad, distinguishing among the Roman, the Romanized, and the yet to be tamed non-Roman.

On this gem, therefore, style and the process by which styles mutually define one another complement the scene's signification through iconography and attributes. It serves as an equal force in the monument's construction of meaning, perhaps even more persuasively for being effectively subliminal. The styles of the subsidiary figures are applied as appropriate to the subject matter and emphasize by contrast the patent classicism—and divine referents—of Roma and Augustus. Therefore, owing to style as much as sign, scale, and composition, the viewer is brought back to the centrality and divinity of the enthroned pair. We must conclude that these two figures and their status as the recipients of cult activity are the focus of this cameo.

Yet the most common interpretation of the gem is that it has to do with succession (Pollini 1993, 267–9). The togate figure at left is taken to be Tiberius, who celebrated (and refused) triumphs earned in the time of Augustus; his younger comrade in arms is then his nephew, and enforced heir, Germanicus, who also campaigned in the northern provinces in later Augustan times. They would then represent two stages of succession provided for by Augustus in the form of his son and grandson by adoption, both of whom are worthy of imperial rank owing to their experience pacifying and thus nurturing forces in the empire. But this reading is at pains to explain the patent prominence and stylistic distinction of Roma and Augustus; indeed most studies struggle to explain, or explain away, Augustus's figuration as a god without dating the monument after his death.

A proper appreciation for the signifying force of style supports here an alternative reading that the cameo commemorates the inauguration of the Roma/Augustus cult in

12 BC by Tiberius and his brother Drusus at Lugdunum in Gaul and in 9 BC by Drusus alone at Oppidum Ubiorum in Germany, renamed Ara Ubiorum at that time (Fishwick 2002, 5–40). The gem likely references both. If it shows Tiberius not with Germanicus but with Germanicus's father, the gem could thus date a generation earlier than is commonly maintained (Fullerton 2009; for a similar date and specifically Gallic reading: de Grummond 2012). The establishment of the cult in the western provinces was a major component in Augustus's use of religion to pacify and control a region that was unaccustomed, unlike the eastern Mediterranean, to ruler worship of any kind. Moreover, the cult itself, especially at Ara Ubiorum on the Rhine, maintained its connections with the imperial family, including not just Drusus, who founded it, but his sons Germanicus and Claudius, as well as his granddaughter Agrippina II, in whose name it was made a colony in AD 50 (*Colonia Claudia Ara Agrippiensium*, modern Cologne). Such a reading of the gem explains the strong focus on the cultic pair, surrounded and highlighted by figures of conquest and acquiescence, of barbarian and ally, using myriad styles and stylistic associations to emphasize a diverse realm unified by the transcendent immanence of Roma and Augustus in divine, classical form.

Conclusion

The organic nature of Greek sculptural development, and the even more highly constructed schemes we use to comprehend it, have long caused scholars to see style in Roman sculpture, which adheres to no such pattern, as a "problem" either to be solved or wished away. It is equally possible, however, that the problem is one of our own creation. We tend to understand meaning in Greek styles as the inevitable product of the cultural conditions and values of a particular place and time. The interplay of stylistic tradition and artistic choice that characterizes Roman sculpture liberates the interpretive process from any such determinism. Style is therefore no longer a "problem" in the study of Roman sculpture, because it stands at the very core of the signifying process, and the *application* of stylistic analysis as a means to elicit meaning (and thereby, sometimes, even date) surely outweighs its *limitation* in fulfilling roles that Hellenocentric modes of thinking can unwittingly assign.

Bibliography

Boardman, J. 1994. *The Diffusion of Classical Art in Antiquity*. Princeton: Princeton University Press.

Beard, M., and J. Henderson. 2001. *Classical Art: From Greece to Rome*. Oxford: Oxford University Press.

Brendel, O. J. (1953) 1979. *Prolegomena to the Study of Roman Art*. New Haven: Yale University Press. Reprinted essay, originally published 1953, with additional essay covering the intervening decades.

———. (1978) 1995. *Etruscan Art*. 2nd edition with additional bibliography. New Haven: Yale University Press.

de Grummond, N. 2012. "The Gemma Augustea: Not Made for Rome." *Archaeological Institute of America 113 Annual Meeting: Abstracts v.35*, 28. Boston: Archaeological Institute of America.

Elsner, J. 1998. *Imperial Rome and Christian Triumph: The Art of the Roman Empire, AD 100–450*. Oxford: Oxford University Press.

———. 2004. "Foreword." In Hölscher (1987) 2004, xv–xxxi.

———. 2006. "Classicism in Roman Art." In Porter 2006, 270–97.

Fishwick, D. 2002. *The Imperial Cult in the Latin West: Studies in the Ruler Cult of the Western Provinces of the Roman Empire*. Vol. 3, *Provincial Cult*. Pt. 1, *Institution and Evolution*. Leiden: Brill.

Fullerton, M. D. 1990. *The Archaistic Style in Roman Statuary*. Mnemosyne Supplement 110. Leiden: Brill.

———. 1997. "Imitation and Intertextuality in Roman Art." *JRA* 10: 427–40.

———. 2003. "*Der Stil der Nachahmer*: A Brief Historiography of Stylistic Retrospection." In *Ancient Art and its Historiography*, edited by A. A. Donohue and M. D. Fullerton, 92–117. Cambridge: Cambridge University Press.

———. 2009. "Roma and Augustus on the Gemma Augustea." *Abstracts 2009*, 151. New York: College Art Association.

Gazda, E. K. 2002. "Introduction: Beyond Copying: Artistic Originality and Tradition." In *The Ancient Art of Emulation: Studies in Artistic Originality and Tradition from the Present to Classical Antiquity*, edited by E. K. Gazda, 1–24. Ann Arbor: University of Michigan Press.

Gruen, E. S. 1992. *Culture and National Identity in Republican Rome*. Ithaca: Cornell University Press.

Hallett, C. H. 2005. "Emulation versus Replication: Redefining Roman Copying." *JRA* 18: 419–35.

Henderson, J. 2003. "*Par Operi Sedes:* Mrs. Arthur Strong and Flavian Style, the Arch of Titus and the Cancelleria Reliefs." In *Flavian Rome: Culture, Image, Text*, edited by A. J. Boyle and W. H. Dominik, 229–54. Leiden: Brill.

Hölscher, T. (1987) 2004. *The Language of Images in Roman Art*. Translated by A. Snodgrass and A. Künzl-Snodgrass. Cambridge: Cambridge University Press. Originally published as *Römische Bildsprache als semantisches System*.

———. 2006. "Greek Styles and Greek Art in Augustan Rome: Issues of the Present versus Records of the Past." In Porter 2006, 237–69.

Kampen, N. B. 2003. "On Writing Histories of Roman Art." *ArtB* 85(2): 371–86.

———. 2010. "Plebeian Art, Roman." In *The Oxford Encyclopedia of Ancient Greece and Rome*, ed. by M. Gagarin, 5: 316–18. Oxford: Oxford University Press.

Kousser, R. M. 2008. *Hellenistic and Roman Ideal Sculpture: The Allure of the Classical*. Cambridge: Cambridge University Press.

L'Orange, H. P. 1965. *Art Forms and Civic Life in the Late Roman Empire*. Translated by Dr. and Mrs. Knut Berg. Princeton: Princeton University Press.

Perry, E. 2005. *The Aesthetics of Emulation in the Visual Arts of Ancient Rome*. Cambridge: Cambridge University Press.

Pollini, J. 1993. "The Gemma Augustea: Ideology, Rhetorical Imagery, and the Creation of a Dynastic Narrative." In *Narrative and Event in Ancient Art*, edited by P. Holliday, 258–98. Cambridge: Cambridge University Press.

Pollitt, J. J. 1974. *The Ancient View of Greek Art: Criticism, History, and Terminology.* New Haven: Yale University Press.
———. 1978. "The Impact of Greek Art on Rome." *TAPA* 108: 155–74.
Porter, J. I., ed. 2006. *Classical Pasts: The Classical Traditions of Greece and Rome.* Princeton: Princeton University Press.
Ridgway, B. S. 1984. *Roman Copies of Greek Sculpture: The Problem of the Originals.* Ann Arbor: University of Michigan Press.
Smith, R. R. R. 1981. "Greeks, Foreigners, and Roman Republican Portraits." *JRS* 71: 24–38.
Stewart, A. F. 1985. "History, Myth, and Allegory in the Program of the Temple of Athena Nike at Athens." In *Pictorial Narrative in Antiquity and the Middle Ages*, edited by H. L. Kessler and M. S. Simpson, 53–73. Studies in the History of Art 16. Washington, DC: National Gallery of Art.
Tanner, J. 2000. "Portraits, Power, and Patronage in the Late Roman Republic." *JRS* 90: 18–50.
Toynbee, J. C. M. 1934. *The Hadrianic School: A Chapter in the History of Greek Art.* Cambridge: Cambridge University Press.
Winckelmann, J. J. (1764) 2006. *History of the Art of Antiquity.* Translated by H. Mallgrave. Los Angeles: J. Paul Getty Museum. Originally published as *Geschichte der Künst des Ältertums.*
Zanker, P. 1974. *Klassizistische Statuen: Studien zur Veränderung des Kunstgeschmacks in der römischen Kaiserzeit.* Mainz: Philipp von Zabern.
———. 1988. *The Power of Images in the Age of Augustus.* Translated by A. Shapiro. Ann Arbor: University of Michigan Press.

CHAPTER 3.2

ETRUSCAN CONNECTIONS

NANCY T. DE GRUMMOND

Introduction

Etruscans inhabited the opposite side of the Tiber River from the Romans and from prehistoric times shared a culture with them. Written sources and archaeological evidence reveal extensive interactions between the two ethnicities. Veii, one of the *duodecim populi* ("Twelve Peoples"; Livy 7.21.1) of the Etruscans, was the closest to Rome, only 17 km distant; today it can even be reached by city bus from Rome. From Veii came to Rome the most famous of Etruscan artists, Vulca, who created important sculptures for the temple of Capitoline Jupiter in the sixth century BC (Plin. *HN* 35.157). Not much further away were two other *populi*, at Caere (modern Cerveteri), where the Vestal Virgins took refuge when the Gauls attacked Rome in 390 BC (Livy 5.40), and at Tarquinii, from which the Tarquin dynasty came to Rome in the seventh century BC, destined to build the Capitoline temple and remake the urban fabric of the city (Livy 1.34; Dion. Hal. *Ant. Rom.* 3.67–9).

These city-states lay close to that part of the Mediterranean the Greeks called the Tyrrhenian (i.e., "Etruscan") Sea, and farther up the coastline to the north were other major *populi* at Vulci and Vetulonia, both of which had significant relations with Rome. Servius Tullius, the second of the Etruscan kings of Rome (sixth century BC) had close ties with Vulci, where he was known as Macstrna, and Vetulonia is said to have provided Rome with insignia of power such as the ivory *sella curulis*, the *fasces*, and the curved musical instrument called the *lituus* (Sil. *Pun.* 8.484–9; cf. Livy 1.8; Diod. Sic. 5.40.1). Dramatic confirmation of the literary evidence came from the discovery of a bundle of iron rods and a double axe in a seventh-century BC tomb at Vetulonia (Camporeale 1967). Tombs at other Etruscan sites have yielded examples of the ivory folding stool and representations in archaic Etruscan art that show a magistrate sitting on such a chair; further, a bronze musical *lituus* has been found with a bronze axe head of the seventh century BC at Tarquinii (Bonghi Jovino 2010, 168–70).

At a greater distance from Rome, but closely connected through the artery of the Tiber, lay Volsinii (modern Orvieto) and Clusium (Chiusi). The notorious sack of Volsinii in 264 BC resulted in the capture and transport to Rome of 2000 bronze statues (Plin. *HN* 34.34). Further, a statue and cult of the principal god of the Etruscans, called Vertumnus by the Romans, came from Volsinii to reside in the area in Rome known as the Vicus Tuscus (the "Etruscan Quarter"; cf. Prop. 4.2). As for Clusium, the great king called Lars Porsenna by the Romans made his well-known attack on the city in the late sixth or fifth century BC, and may even have ruled Rome for a time (Tac. *Hist.* 3.72).

Also relevant, but at a later date, are the cities of northern Etruria, in particular Arretium (Arezzo) and Volaterrae (modern Volterra), which were among seven Etruscan cities that supplied goods to the fleet of Scipio for his invasion of Hannibal's Africa in 205 BC. Arretium donated a staggering amount of bronze armory and other supplies, while Volaterrae gave grain and fittings for ships (Livy 28.45). Arretium had come under Roman dominance as early as 301 BC when nobles of the Cilnii family summoned Roman forces to help them subdue an uprising of the lower classes. Later Volaterrae was besieged for two years by the armies of Sulla (82–80 BC) and subsequently was colonized, while Arretium, which had also sided with Marius against Sulla, likewise received a colony. Leading citizens of these famed old Etruscan towns developed ties with Romans of similar status, so that there are reports of Cicero defending in court a woman from Arretium and his good friend from Volaterrae, Aulus Caecina (*pro Caecina*, 69 BC). Perhaps the most famous Etruscan integrated into Roman culture was the Aretine Maecenas, of the Cilnii, who became a minister and patron for the arts as well as a political advisor under Augustus. The lustrous red-gloss pottery produced at Arretium, especially during the period of Augustus, featured signatures with both Etruscan and Roman names, as well as names from the Hellenistic East.

These few examples of the numerous interactions between Romans and Etruscans demonstrate sustained contact over many centuries (for a concise review of Etruscan-Roman history, see Richardson 1964, 63–87; for a lengthy analysis, Harris 1971). They reveal a complicated relationship between Rome and a number of different Etruscan cities, each with its own history, special characteristics, conflicts, and subjugations, with Etruscans ruling Romans and alternately Romans dominating Etruscan cities. Against this backdrop of fluid political and military power occurred the exchange of wealth, of artistic tendencies and artifacts, of social practice, of religious and ritual customs and beliefs. The point of these observations for the present essay is that they indicate how difficult it is to speak of influence flowing in only one direction, as might be suitable if the topic at hand were limited to Etruscan influence on Roman art. Instead the emphasis here will be placed on a shared, evolving cultural matrix, out of which emerged a specifically defined Roman art toward the end of the Republic and the beginning of the empire, coinciding with the time when the Etruscans disappeared from history as a recognizable entity.

There are further complications. The Etruscans intermingled similarly and in varying degrees with other cities in Latium, such as Praeneste, Satricum, Tusculum ("Little Etruscan Town"), and numerous other sites in pre-imperial central Italy. The culture of the city of Rome itself has been traced by tradition and through archaeology to the early

Latin sites of Gabii and Alba Longa. Entangled with these strands are the cultural currents flowing from Greece, the Near East, and the Hellenistic East into Rome, sometimes mediated by the Etruscans or Praeneste. The boundaries between the various centers were permeable, and it may be best not to attempt to separate them artificially but to think in terms of a common culture in central Italy.

With all of these aspects of context in mind, we shall address the most significant areas of artistic connection between Etruscans and Romans, the depiction of the human figure and the beginnings of early monumental sculpture, through various questions of iconography (the toga), subject matter (the procession), and genre (portraiture).

The Human Figure

The study of these connections in sculpture begins with an examination of the approach to representing the human figure in central Italy, which relates to ritual needs more than to aesthetic factors as in Greek sculpture. A vivid example of this concept lies in the tradition of canopic urns from Clusium (figure 3.2.1), in which the ash urn for cremated

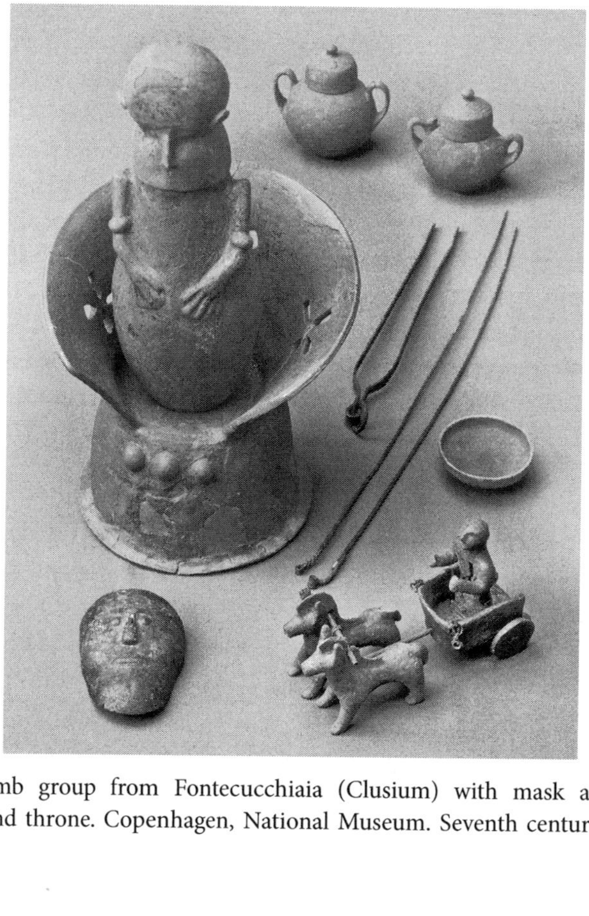

FIGURE 3.2.1 Tomb group from Fontecucchiaia (Clusium) with mask and canopic urn including head and throne. Copenhagen, National Museum. Seventh century BC.

remains was given human attributes, so that the vessel might preserve some of the individuality of the deceased; it was often placed upon a chair so that the ancestor could attend a banquet in his or her honor.

A tomb group dating to the seventh century BC, from Fontecucciaia in the territory of Clusium (Gempeler [1973?], 22, 159–60, no. 7; Torelli 2000, 31, 585–6), shows the typical features, with the urn proper endowed with braceleted arms, the lid turned into a rudimentary head with ears and nose, and the newly reconstituted person set upon a chair of honor. A bronze face-mask found in the same grave may have been attached to a second—bronze—ash urn; it is one example from a small group of masks made of bronze and terracotta that have been found in Etruscan tombs. Sometimes they show holes that would have been used to attach the mask to an urn by wire or string (Cristofani 2000, 289, no. 110). There probably were cloth masks as well, attached to the urns by sewing, since some canopic heads have holes in the face that would have served to attach cloth. These may be considered forerunners of Roman ancestral masks (the well-known *imagines*; see essay 3.4, Wood). The impulse to hold onto the most characteristic part of the individual, the face, at the time he or she passes away, is present in both cultures. The canopic heads of Clusium showed increasing realism through the sixth and fifth centuries; with these examples one may speak of portraiture in only the most generic terms, but at an advanced stage Etruscan faces in funerary art became quite realistic—one might even say veristic. During the second and first centuries BC, Etruscans and Romans alike created numerous portraits that basically served the purpose of making the individual appear alive. In both cultures there was a deep-seated tradition of ancestor worship that provided the conceptual framework for various rituals directed toward that end (Colonna and Von Hase 1986; Damgaard Andersen 1993; Flower 1996, 339–51).

The Fontecucchiaia tomb group also shows the use of the sculpted figurine to serve religious purposes. Here a diminutive, modeled terracotta human is driving a two-horse chariot, no doubt to make the journey to the afterlife in a symbolic way. Similar ritual figures have been found in tombs of Latium and Etruria, as early as the ninth century and continuing into the seventh century BC. In particular they have been found in the Alban Hills above Rome, in connection with ash urns in the shape of a hut of a type shared by Latium and Etruria (Bartoloni et al. 1987). This "House of the Dead" sometimes had with it a miniature baked clay image best identified as the deceased inhabiting the place. An example from Rocca di Papa shows the roughly modeled figure standing and extending his right arm forward to hold a drinking cup (h. 16 cm; Colonna 1976, 83).

Early Monumental Sculpture

There are various instances of sculpture on a larger scale employed to represent Etruscan ancestors. Of particular interest is the Tomba delle Statue from the site of Ceri in the territory of Caere, featuring two seated male figures holding scepters, probably insignia of office, carved out of the tufa bedrock and dated to the early seventh century BC (h.

of the figures, 103 and 105 cm; Colonna and Von Hase 1986). The different medium and setting create quite a distinct effect from that observed in the figurines, but in addition, there is a different meaning to the figures, which are not images of the deceased but rather may be interpreted as ancestors who welcome the new arrivals to their company. Other monumental sculptures from Etruscan tombs present yet other interpretations. Nearly life-size statues made of a local calcareous stone from a necropolis at Cecina near Volaterrae, showing figures stripped to the waist, may be representations of mourners (eighth century BC). Monumental mourning figures made of local stones have been identified also at Vetulonia and Clusium (c. 600 BC).

Literary Evidence

Monumental sculpture makes its first appearance in Rome during the legendary period of the Etruscan kings, traditionally dated from 616 to 509 BC. Literary sources connect it especially with the Capitoline temple to Jupiter, Juno, and Minerva, begun by Tarquinius Priscus, who is said to have summoned the artist Vulca from nearby Veii to make a cult image of Jupiter, according to Varro, quoted by Pliny the Elder (*HN* 35.157). Pliny describes the statue as made of terracotta and colored red (presumably on the face and skin) according to custom. He further notes that Vulca created terracotta *quadrigae* for the temple *in fastigio* (on the gable) and a statue of Hercules, called *fictilis* in his time. Livy (1.55–6) and Plutarch (*Poplicola* 14) attributed the construction of the temple instead to Tarquinius Superbus, grandson or son of Priscus, who ruled traditionally from 534 to 509 BC, suggesting that the time frame for Vulca was considerably later. The later dating works well with evidence from archaeology and is preferred by most scholars. The *quadrigae* of Vulca were doubtless part of a system for decorating the superstructure of the temple with terracotta sculpture, leading scholars to connect the name and workshop of Vulca with an impressive series of acroteria discovered at the Portonaccio temple at Veii, dating to the last quarter of the sixth century BC. Life-size terracotta statues of Apulu and Hercle stood on bases in a shape that would have fit well over the main ridge pole of the temple. The style is distinctive, utilizing conventions with pronounced ridges and grooves for drapery and musculature, imparting a fierce and intense character to the figures.

The Capitoline Wolf

Until recently the striking life-size hollow-cast bronze of a she-wolf that was placed on the Capitoline Hill in the fifteenth century AD and that is universally regarded as a great symbol of the ancient city of Rome was thought to be an Etruscan relic of archaic times. The highly stylized mane and severe outline, along with the rigidity and intensity of the limbs and face of the Wolf, were used to support comparisons with the style of the molded terracottas from Veii attributed to Vulca. A date of c. 500–475 BC has often been recommended for the Wolf, setting it in a chronological framework inviting comparison with another famed sculpture of a crouching animal, the Chimaera from Arezzo, a hollow-cast bronze inscribed in Etruscan, dated to the late fifth or early fourth century BC (Cianferoni 2012, 25). The Chimaera shows a similar patterning and stylization of the hair, but a greater naturalism in the muscles and sinews as the creature recoils and strikes a defensive pose that is more convincing than that of the Wolf. The connection with the Etruscans was strengthened by the existence of Etruscan cultic traditions associated with wolves, including a fourth-century BC sandstone grave stele from Bologna that depicts a female wolf suckling a single child, easily explained as showing a story similar to the myth of Romulus and Remus nursed by the she-wolf on the banks of the Tiber (Briguet 1986, fig. IV.31).

Recent research on the sculpture, however, including examination of the bronze-casting technique, studied during restoration of the piece (Carruba 2006), has led to a dramatic challenge to the dating of the Wolf itself. (The naturalistically rendered twins beneath the teats of the Capitoline Wolf were set there in the fifteenth century and have long been recognized as not ancient.) In general bronzes from ancient Italy are quite rare, and generalizations may be dangerous, but recent studies argue that the Capitoline Wolf was cast in one piece, a technique practiced in the Middle Ages in Italy, whereas ancient bronzes were normally cast in parts (as was the Chimaera). Other details of workmanship and style help to link the piece with medieval art (Giumlia-Mair 2012, 177), and carbon dates from organic material extracted from the interior of the bronze sculpture have consistently given dates in the thirteenth century AD (Bartoloni 2010, 10). The considerable uproar over the possibility that the famous and iconic statue may be medieval has focused attention on a number of topics that have bearing on the relationship between Etruscan and Roman sculpture and created a climate of excited re-evaluation of technology, technique, metallurgy, style, and iconography.

Roof Decoration

Archaeological evidence for the first monumental temples in Rome comes from the sixth century BC. The temples of the archaic period are generally agreed to compare closely with Etruscan examples in ground plan and elevation and, like many Etruscan temples, they were adorned on the roof with elaborate polychrome terracottas, as early as the first half of the sixth century. These roofing systems were used not only for temples, as in Greece, but also for public structures and houses. Relief revetment plaques of a kind used in Etruria have been excavated in the Roman Forum, associated with the Regia and the Curia Hostilia and dated to c. 590–580 BC, showing motifs of an advancing armed rider and of a bull-headed man wearing a short tunic, walking between parading felines (Cristofani 1990, 61; Winter 2009, 178–80). In the second half of the sixth century, a great variety of revetment plaques appear at a number of sites in Rome, including the Palatine, the Capitoline, and the Forum. Especially popular are the plaques with chariot processions, good examples of which are provided by reliefs dated c. 530 BC from the sacred area at the foot of the Capitoline Hill in the Forum Boarium, found underneath the church of

Sant'Omobono (Winter 2009, 316–17). They show *bigae* and *trigae*, with couples (male and female) riding in the chariots and male attendants striding alongside as well as in front of and behind the chariots. The horses are sometimes winged, suggesting that the procession relates to the divine. The close connection with Etruria and also with Latium is demonstrated by the fact that the molds for these revetment plaques were also used at Veii and at Velletri, south of Rome. What is regularly referred to as the Veii-Rome-Velletri system of roof decoration shows many instances of this kind of transfer of materials. For example, plaques of identical type featuring chariot races with *bigae* and *trigae* occur on the Palatine and the Capitoline, as well as at Veii and Velletri. The dynamics of the workshops will probably never be completely clear, especially as to whether the terracotta workers were sedentary or traveling (Winter 2009, 538), but a credible hypothesis is that an artist like Vulca might carry his molds with him when he traveled to serve patrons outside his home city.

Also during this later archaic phase, handmade clay statues, nearly life-size, were created for the sacred area of Sant'Omobono. A pair of figures—a male in a lion skin and a female wearing a helmet—are thought to have been set up together as acroteria for a temple of Mater Matuta, dated c. 530 BC (figure 3.2.2; Winter 2009, 379–80). Two groups with similar iconography of the same date have been found at Veii in the Portonaccio sanctuary, perhaps also once used as acroteria (Colonna 2001, 67–8; Winter 2009, 377–9). Further, scraps of similar statues occur at Latin Satricum, Velletri, and possibly Caprifico (Lulof 2000). These figures are routinely referred to as Herakles and Athena, an identification that is generally correct, except that in Etruria the pair would have been called Hercle and Menrva and in Rome and elsewhere, Hercules and Minerva. The statues from Sant'Omobono have frequently been interpreted as making a political statement, implying that Tarquinius was supported by a goddess, presumably Mater Matuta, just as Hercules was supported by Minerva. Ritual considerations may be of significance as well, for the cult of Hercules, one of the earliest in Rome, had its center in the Forum Boarium. Hercules is sometimes said to have established there the Ara Maxima for his own cult at the time of the first king on the site of Rome, Evander, an action prophesied by the ruler's goddess mother Carmenta (Livy 1.7). The cult was rich in details, for there was also in the Forum Boarium a statue of Hercules in bronze supposedly dedicated by Evander, which was traditionally decked out in ritual dress during triumphal processions (Plin. *HN* 34.33).

The references to Evander seem to allude to a pre-Etruscan stratum of religious activity in the Forum Boarium, but a number of the bits of information about activity there resonate with the Etruscan connection. The large-scale terracotta sculptures are dated to the time period when most scholars argue the Capitoline temple was under construction by Tarquinius Superbus and Vulca was invited from Veii to Rome. Vulca's Hercules Fictilis could easily have resembled the clay acroterion of the hero from Sant'Omobono, although one may argue convincingly that the Apulu of Veii is actually quite different in style from the Hercules. The bronze statue of Hercules in triumphal costume, a rather unusual garb, may also connect with Etruscan ritual, since the Roman triumph was profoundly influenced by Etruscan practices. Among the changes brought by the Etruscans were the use of a chariot by the *triumphator*, instead of his going on foot or by horse; the dress of the *triumphator* in ornate tunic and toga and the practice of painting the face

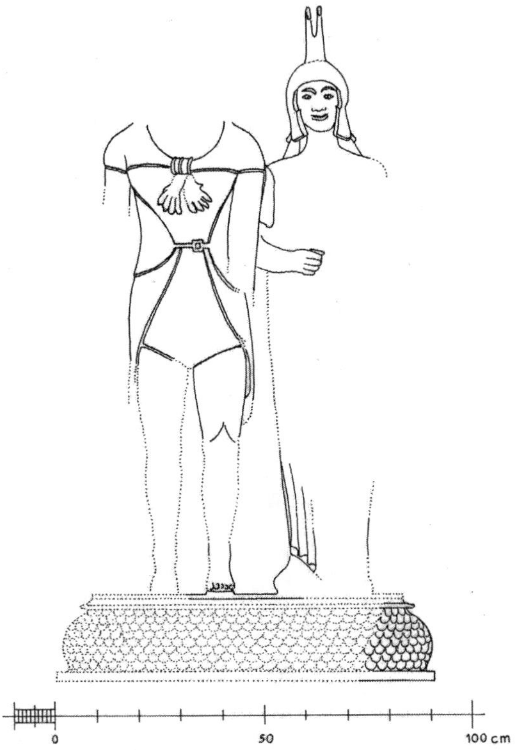

FIGURE 3.2.2 Hercules and Minerva, acroteria from the sacred area of Sant'Omobono, Rome. Late sixth century BC. (Winter 2009, fig. 6.16.2).

red, both based on the appearance of the terracotta Jupiter of Vulca; and the goal of the triumph as the Tarquin Temple of Capitoline Jupiter (Bonfante Warren 1970, 57; Versnel 1970; *contra* Beard 2007, 231–3, with unwarranted objections).

The Toga

The crescent-shaped mantle known to the Romans as the toga is referenced in literary sources as being used in Rome at the time of Tarquinius Priscus, and was recognized universally as having Etruscan connections (Dion. Hal. *Ant. Rom.* 3.16; Stone 1994, 13). The garment appears in Etruscan art around the middle of the sixth century BC (Bonfante 2003, 48). A series of Etruscan bronzes of the late archaic period give quite a good idea of what the mantle was like in this early phase (Richardson 1953, 115–21). It was frequently worn without a tunic underneath, draped over the left arm, and leaving the right arm and shoulder bare. When worn ritually by a *triumphator*, the toga was decorated with embroidery (*toga picta*); underneath it would be a *tunica palmata*, a flowered tunic, also known as the *tunica Jovis*, because the garment belonged to Capitoline

Jupiter (Juv. 10.38). Further decoration was sometimes created on the border of the toga, which was set off by a broad stripe of purple in the *toga praetexta*.

A good early Etruscan example of the ornate toga and tunic is provided by a small bronze of unknown provenance in Heidelberg, showing a bearded male clutching a large thunderbolt, identified as Tinia, the Etruscan counterpart of Jupiter (figure 3.2.3). The toga is incised with numerous small circles, probably meant to represent embroidery, framed by lines presumably intended to indicate folds, and the border is offset by the way it is folded across the

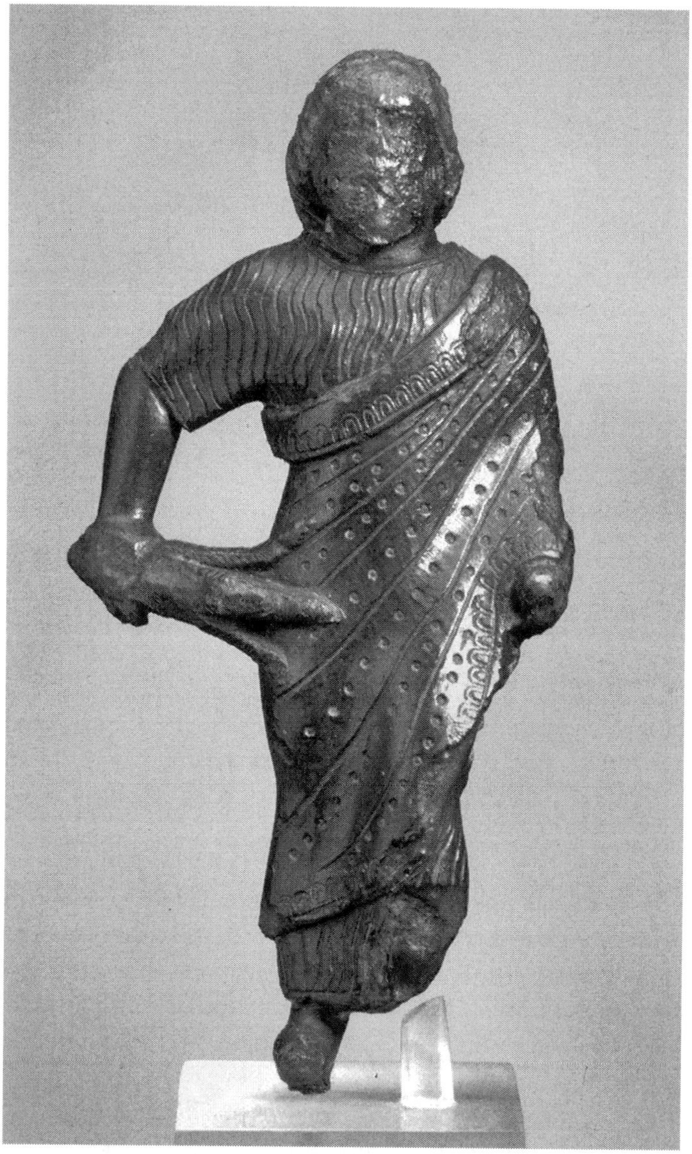

FIGURE 3.2.3 Tinia, bronze statuette of unknown provenance. Fifth century BC. Heidelberg University, Antikenmuseum.

chest and by a decoration with an ovolo pattern. A similar decoration is seen on the hem at the bottom. The wavy lines of the tunic seem to indicate the crinkly texture of the cloth (presumably linen) rather than decoration, but in general add to the rich impression of the dress of the dignified god. All in all, the image may give some idea of the clothing of Capitoline Jupiter and the nature of ritual triumphal dress in Rome in this early period.

The dress scheme in the Heidelberg statuette of a god is not very different from what may be seen in the much later bronze life-size honorific and votive statue of an actual person, an Etruscan orator, found near Lake Trasimeno (figure 3.2.4; Cristofani

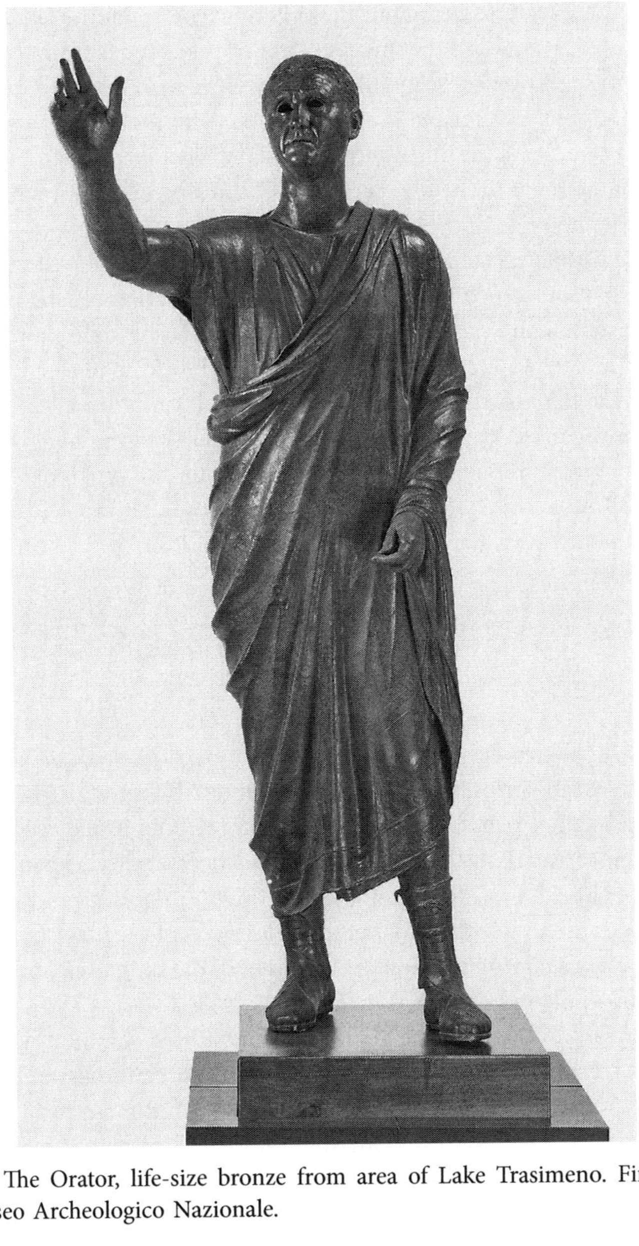

FIGURE 3.2.4 The Orator, life-size bronze from area of Lake Trasimeno. First century BC. Florence, Museo Archeologico Nazionale.

2000, 300). He wears a toga of a very similar length, with a roll of cloth across the chest replacing the articulated border in the Tinia figure and with a stripe at the bottom offset by tubular piping and ornamented by an inscription in Etruscan, telling the name of the man, Aule Meteli. The tunic is also familiar, though here the fabric is more likely wool, and the sleeves are a little shorter. In addition, the tunic features a stripe on the proper right side of the orator, the only part where the garment is visible. (Certainly there would have been a symmetrical stripe on the left side.) Reddish copper inlay made clear the difference in color of the stripes and the tunic. The term *toga exigua*, "skimpy toga," is often applied to the togas displayed in statuary in the first century BC, and the phrase does serve to bring out the difference between the late Etruscan / late republican representations and the images of voluminous togas from the period of the empire. This phrase, however, originally used by Horace to describe the toga of Cato (Hor. *Epist.* 1.19.12–14), was meant as a kind of joke, and modern usage is thus off the mark. Togas of the archaic period are in fact often even shorter than the one worn by Tinia and any of the togas of the first century BC, limiting even more the usefulness of the term *toga exigua*.

The hair of Aule Meteli is cut in the close-cropped style of the first century BC, known from Roman depictions on coins and statuary, and the highly realistic portrayal of the face is also consistent with Roman art of the late Republic. The high-strapped shoes have been compared in turn to Etruscan archaic boots and to Roman senatorial boots that likely evolved from the Etruscan fashion. Without the inscription in Etruscan the work might have been regarded by modern scholarship as a key monument in the history of Roman art. The point to remember is that the long history of syncretism and evolution of Etruscan and Roman dress, social and religious customs, and artistic traditions make it impossible to identify this statue as purely Etruscan or Roman.

The Procession

The importance of the triumph and the popularity of chariot parades and races at Rome in the archaic Etruscan period have already been noted. In both Etruria and Rome, the rituals associated with processions became ever more complicated and enriched with details, and the purposes of the processions became more diverse, expanding especially into funerary practice. From Etruscan tomb paintings, sarcophagi, and ash urns comes an abundance of evidence for the ritual of the procession of the magistrate, which must have been intended as a recapitulation of the career of the individual, framed as a journey of glory or triumph to the afterlife.

Several significant examples appear in Etruscan painted tombs at Tarquinii in the fourth and third centuries BC (Pieraccini 2015). These paintings are rich in detail, showing various motifs that are well known from later Roman examples in sculpture: magistrates with attendants carrying rods or axes, throngs in togas, family groups including children, one looking like nothing so much as the procession of Augustus and his family on the Ara Pacis (Conlin 1997, 23–4; Pieraccini 2015; see essay 3.5, Sobocinski and Wolfram Thill).

The magistrate's procession also appears sculpted on stone sarcophagi from Caere, Tarquinii, Tuscania, Vulci, and Volaterrae of the third through second centuries BC and on alabaster ash urns from Volaterrae dating to the second and first centuries BC (Holliday 1990; 2002; Bruni 2004, 28–31; Van der Meer 2004). The schemes on these reliefs are convincingly viewed as forerunners of Roman triumphal scenes, such as the procession of Titus on the Arch of Titus (fig. 3.5.1, essay 3.5, Sobocinski and Wolfram Thill) or the depiction of Septimius Severus on his arch at Leptis Magna. As Ryberg notes, the Etruscan symbolic procession features laurel wreaths, lictors, musicians, sacrificial implements, and even the placards and platters for carrying effigies and trophies that are part of representations of the Roman triumph (1955, 16).

A tufa sarcophagus from Tuscania provides a good example (figure 3.2.5). The chest is carved with a procession moving from right to left, in which the deceased appears driving a *biga* led forward by a naked winged youth and followed by three attendants with bundles of rods and a musician. The inscription above the scene gives his name, Vel Atna, and reveals that he was *zilath* (*praetor*) and also connected with a *maruchva*, a word that may refer to a college of priests. The magistrate wears a toga that leaves his right arm free to hold the reins (now missing). The attendants also wear togas, as is clear from the curved hemline, but with a variant draping in which the right arm is actually wrapped and the left arm is brought forward to hold the rods. The togas in the painted processions mentioned above frequently show a similar wrapping of the right arm, suggesting that this manner of draping was related to ritual. Cicero seems to describe such a custom when he refers to wearing the toga *ad cohibendum brachium* (*Cael.* 5.11), though the passage does not relate to a funeral but rather to a program of discipline for young men and perhaps specifically in relation to learning rhetorical gesturing (Richardson and Richardson 1966). More to the point here, the wrapping of the right arm is very common in Roman funerary reliefs dating to the first century BC of full-length figures, such as the togate man and wife from the Via Statilia, or various half-length figures in freedman art of the same period and later (Kleiner 1992, 41, 79). Thus there is an Etruscan

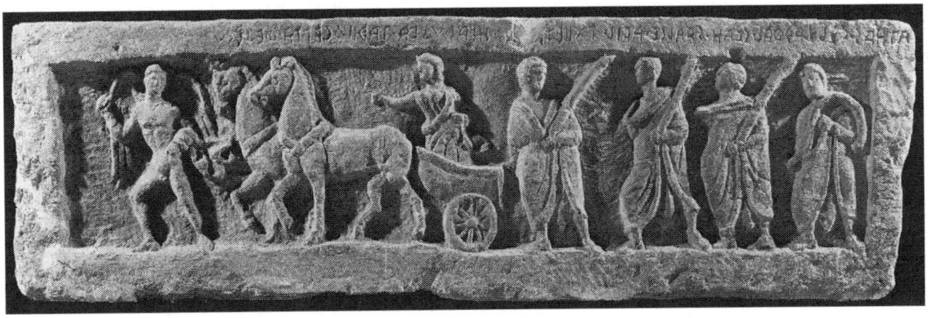

FIGURE 3.2.5 Procession to the afterlife, stone sarcophagus from the Tomba Campanari, Tuscania. London, British Museum. Third century BC.

connection for this type of ritual funerary dress, though in Rome it becomes associated with a class different from the grand noble families of the Etruscans. According to Kleiner, freedmen sometimes used heroic nudity for the depiction of the deceased as a way of showing elevated status, and it may be that the fashion *ad cohibendum brachium* had a similar motive.

The scenes in paintings and on sarcophagi and ash urns surely are based on real rituals that took place at Etruscan funerals. The winged demons and spirits that appear are often spoken of as evidence that the depictions were imaginary, but that need not be the case at all. It is entirely possible that individuals dressed up to play roles as members of the family who accompanied the deceased on the journey to the afterlife, and it would not require a great effort for others to don costumes to play the role of underworld demon escorts. The extensive corpus of evidence of Etruscan processions to the afterlife has a direct parallel in the Roman ritual of wearing wax ancestor masks (*imagines*) described by Polybius in the second century BC (6.53–4; Flower 1996, chap. 4). Also resonating with the Etruscan monuments is the description of the funeral of Sulla in 78 BC (App. *B Civ.* 1.105–6), detailing the procession through Italy with the statesman's body on a litter, attended by horsemen and trumpeters, bearers of the *fasces* and standards, priests and priestesses in proper costume, and senators and other magistrates.

The Portrait

The background described above creates a framework for studying a final area of artistic connection between Etruscans and Romans: the portrait (see essay 3.4, Wood). Looking at syncretized rituals and traditions in central Italy from the Iron Age to the late Republic, we recognize a complex of shared ideas and physical manifestations of those ideas rooted in a desire to prolong the memory—and thus the life—of prominent members of society. The development of ancestor worship is at the core of practices celebrating the careers of magistrates by means of chariot parades, triumphs, and dramatized funeral processions. Ritual dress and attributes were used in real life and were represented in art as essential ingredients in these events. It is not surprising that attempts to imitate the appearance of the individuals led to a focus on the head and face even as much as dress in defining the individual. The use of masks in a funerary context is one manifestation, while an increasing tendency toward realism is another.

The Etruscan statue of the orator Aule Meteli from the first century BC (figure 3.2.4) shows the latter tendency fully developed. The facial features are quite individualized, characterizing a man perhaps forty to fifty years old, with furrowed brow, wrinkles at the bridge of the nose and at the corners of the eyes, asymmetrical lips, and a slight malocclusion of the jaw. His haircut also follows a particular fashion of his time rather than a convention for representing hair. It has long been recognized that the orator belongs in a group of portraits found in Italy made of bronze or terracotta dating from the middle to late Republic or the late Etruscan period (c. 300 BC to first century BC).

These include: (1) a clay votive head from the Manganello sanctuary at Caere with asymmetrical framing lines around the mouth and a nose so bent out of shape that it has been conjectured that it was broken; the man's very close-cropped hair places him in the first century BC (Torelli 2000, cat. 304); (2) the bronze head traditionally called Brutus, with its strong aquiline nose, wide, thin asymmetrical mouth, piercing gaze, and a short beard and longish hair that should place it earlier in the sequence (300–250 BC; Cristofani 2000, 297–9, no. 124); and (3) a bronze head of a young man from Fiesole (ancient Faesulae) with heavy jaw and slack lips, as well as furrows in the brow (300 BC; Cristofani 2000, 297, no. 123). The heads are always facing front, rather than turning in space, and have been characterized as factual and objective, showing a style native to Italy as opposed to the dramatic, emotional, and free-moving portrait heads in the style of the Hellenistic kingdoms.

A parallel trend has been recognized in carved stone portraits of the same period (Gazda 1973). Characterized as "vernacular" portraiture, and similarly showing a lack of Hellenistic conventions, these images are found especially in freedmen reliefs, showing a frontal and vertical head presented in an objective way (see essay 4.7, Petersen). Features are indicated with lines and angles more than with volumes. The gaze is steady and the mouth firmly set. When the body is indicated, the artist shows a lack of interest in anatomical correctness, as in the Via Statilia couple (Kleiner 1992, 40–41), where the shoulders are narrow and the connection of parts of the bodies is unclear. Similar tendencies in head and body are seen in numerous Etruscan images beginning as early as the canopics of the archaic period and abounding in the third to first centuries BC. Examples include images of the deceased on stone sarcophagi from Tarquinii (Herbig 1952), terracotta sarcophagi from Tuscania (Gentili 1994), and alabaster ash urns from Volaterrae (Maggiani 1985, esp. 74–95).

Finally, it has also been argued that even the technique used in cutting the stone of Roman sculptures is Italian vernacular rather than Greek. This theory applies to subjects in portraiture and also in relief that were carved out of such locally available stones as tufa and travertine, which were never supplanted by marble in Etruscan sculpture, though the Carrara quarries were known as early as the sixth century BC and marble was used occasionally. In cutting the brittle, porous stone, the sculptors would have utilized especially the chisel, whether flat or rounded, as opposed to the drill or abrasives achieving an effect of high polish. This vernacular practice gave a rough-hewn, tooled surface to some Etruscan and republican Roman stone carving, in contrast to the smooth effects on Greek marble statuary (Conlin 1997, 63–4).

Conclusion

As the literary, archaeological, and artistic evidence demonstrate, a range of connections between the Etruscans and Romans manifest themselves in works of sculpture created in Rome and Etruria from the Iron Age down to the time of the founding of the empire. Geographical proximity allowed easy and natural transference of artistic, religious, and cultural practices. Public rituals of the funeral and of political life seem to have been especially important for creating the milieu within which cultural sharing occurred, affecting matters of iconography, style, and technique. Connections can be seen in sculptures in terracotta, bronze, and marble, whether in relief or in sculpture in the round, exemplified by figures small and large. This essay has placed emphasis on the time when Etruscan civilization still retained some of its identity—even as power was relinquished by Etruria to Rome—and the customs described above were living ones in both cultures. The story continued in the empire, when many aspects of characteristic Etruscan activities, such as the parade of the magistrate, realistic portraiture, and the use of the human figure as a vehicle for religious and ritual rather than aesthetic values, remained embedded in Roman artistic traditions.

Bibliography

Bartoloni, G., ed. 2010. *Lupa Capitolina: Nuove prospettive di studio*. Supplementi e Monografie della rivista Archeologia Classica 5, n.s. 2. Rome: "L'Erma" di Bretschneider.

Bartoloni, G., F. Buranelli, V. D'Atri, and A. De Santis. 1987. *Le urne a capanna rinvenute in Italia*. Rome: Giorgio Bretschneider.

Beard, M. 2007. *The Roman Triumph*. Cambridge, MA: Belknap.

Bonfante, L. 2003. *Etruscan Dress*. Updated edition. Baltimore: Johns Hopkins University Press.

Bonfante Warren, L. 1970. "Roman Triumphs and Etruscan Kings: The Changing Face of the Triumph." *JRS* 60: 49–66.

Bonghi Jovino, M. 2010. "The Tarquinia Project: A Summary of 25 Years of Excavation." *AJA* 114: 161–80.

Briguet, M.-F. 1986. "Art." In *Etruscan Life and Afterlife*, edited by L. Bonfante, 92–173. Detroit: Wayne State University Press.

Bruni, S. 2004. "Le processioni in Etruria." In *Thesaurus cultus et rituum antiquorum* (*ThesCRA*), 1: 21–32. Los Angeles: J. Paul Getty Museum.

Camporeale, G. 1967. *La Tomba del Duce*. Florence: Leo S. Olschki.

Carruba, A. M. 2006. *La Lupa Capitolina: Un bronzo medievale*. Rome: De Luca.

Cianferoni, G. C. 2012. "La Chimera." In Iozzo, Cianferoni, and Setari 2012, 15–25.

Colonna, G., ed. 1976. *Civiltà del Lazio primitivo*. Rome: Multigrafica Editrice.

———. 2001. "I.F.5. Gruppo di Ercole e di Minerva." In *Veio, Cerveteri, Vulci: Città d'Etruria a confronto*, edited by A. M. M. Sgubini, 67–8. Rome: "L'Erma" di Bretschneider.

Colonna, G., and F. W. Von Hase. 1986. "Alle origini della statuaria etrusca: La Tomba delle Statue presso Ceri." *StEtr* 52: 13–59.

Conlin, D. 1997. *The Artists of the Ara Pacis*. Chapel Hill: University of North Carolina Press.

Cristofani, M., ed. 1990 *La grande Roma dei Tarquini*. Rome: "L'Erma" di Bretschneider.

———. 2000. *I bronzi degli etruschi*. Novara: Istituto Geografico De Agostini.

Damgaard Andersen, H. 1993. "The Etruscan Ancestor Cult: Its Origin and Development and the Importance of Anthropomorphization." *AnalRom* 21: 7–66.

Flower, H. 1996. *Ancestor Masks and Aristocratic Power in Roman Culture*. Oxford: Clarendon Press.

Gazda, E. K. 1973. "Etruscan Influence in the Funerary Reliefs of Late Republican Rome: A Study of Roman Vernacular Portraiture." *ANRW* 1.4: 855–70.

Gempeler, R. [1973?]. *Die Etruskischen Kanopen: Herstellung, Typologie, Entwicklungsgeschicte*. Einsiedeln: Benziger.

Gentili, M. D. 1994. *I sarcophagi etruschi in terracotta di età recente*. Rome: Giorgio Bretschneider.

Giumlia-Mair, A. 2012. "The Technology of Bronze Statuary." In Iozzo, Cianferoni, and Setari 2012, 167–84.

Harris, W. V. 1971. *Rome in Etruria and Umbria*. Oxford: Clarendon Press.

Herbig, R. 1952. *Die jüngeretruskischen Steinsarkophage*. ASR 7. Berlin: Mann.

Holliday, P. J. 1990. "Processional Imagery in Late Etruscan Funerary Art." *AJA* 94: 73–93.

———. 2002. *The Origins of Roman Historical Commemoration in the Visual Arts*. Cambridge: Cambridge University Press.

Iozzo, M., G. C. Cianferoni, and E. Setari, eds. 2012. *Myth, Allegory, Emblem: The Many Lives of the Chimaera of Arezzo*. Rome: ARACNE.

Kleiner, D. E. E. 1992. *Roman Sculpture*. New Haven: Yale University Press.

Lulof, P. 2000. "Archaic Terracotta Acroteria representing Athena and Heracles: Manifestations of Power in Central Italy." *JRA* 13: 207–219.

Maggiani, A., ed. 1985. *Artigianato artistico: L'Etruria settentrionale in età ellenistica*. Milan: Electa.

Pieraccini, L. 2015. "Etruscan Wall Painting: Insights, Innovations, and Legacy" In *A Companion to the Etruscans*, edited by A. Carpino and S. Bell. Chichester/Malden, MA: Wiley-Blackwell.

Richardson, E. H. 1953. "The Etruscan Origins of Early Roman Sculpture." *MAAR* 21: 75–124.

———. 1964. *The Etruscans: Their Art and Civilization*. Chicago: University of Chicago Press.

Richardson, E. H., and L. Richardson, Jr. 1966. "*Ad cohibendum brachium toga*: An Archaeological Examination of Cicero, *Pro Caelio* 5.11." *YCS* 19: 251–68.

Ryberg, I. S. 1955. *Rites of the State Religion in Roman Art*. MAAR 22. Rome: American Academy in Rome.

Stone, S. 1994. "The Toga: From National to Ceremonial Costume." In *The World of Roman Costume*, edited by L. Bonfante and J. L. Sebesta, 13–45. Madison: University of Wisconsin Press.

Torelli, M. 2000. *Gli etruschi*. Monza: Bompiani.

Van der Meer, L. B. 2004. *Myths and More on Etruscan Stone Sarcophagi (c. 350–c. 200 B.C.)*. Louvain: Peeters.

Versnel, H. S. 1970. *Triumphus: An Inquiry into the Origin, Development and Meaning of the Roman Triumph*. Leiden: Brill.

Winter, N. 2009. *Symbols of Wealth and Power: Architectural Terracotta Decoration in Etruria and Central Italy, 640–510 B.C.* MAAR Supplement 9. Ann Arbor: University of Michigan Press.

CHAPTER 3.3

"IDEALPLASTIK" AND THE RELATIONSHIP BETWEEN GREEK AND ROMAN SCULPTURE

ANNA ANGUISSOLA

Introduction

The Villa of the Papyri at Herculaneum is one of the best preserved displays of sculptures in a Roman house: the vast selection of marbles and bronzes that adorned the villa's hallways and courtyard is now on display in the Museo Archeologico Nazionale di Napoli (see essays 2.4, Mattusch; 4.3, Gazda; and 6.1, Squire). One particularly famous piece is the bronze bust of a youth, remarkable for its elegant workmanship and the accurate treatment of face and hair (figure 3.3.1). This bust dates to the age of Augustus and has been recognized as a copy of the head of one of the most celebrated bronze masterpieces of the Greek world: the Spear-Bearer or Doryphoros made by Polykleitos in the mid-fifth century BC. Significantly, the Herculaneum bust was signed by an artist named Apollonios, son of Archias and native of Athens. The name is written in tidy Greek characters in a prominent position on the front side of the bust (Mattusch 2005, 276–7, 279–82).

The works of Polykleitos—especially his famous athletes, the Doryphoros (Spear-Bearer) and the Diadoumenos (Fillet-Binder)—epitomize the relationship between Greek and Roman sculpture (cf. Marvin 1997; 2008, 151–64). Latin literature used both the Doryphoros and Diadoumenos as evocative rhetorical tropes (Neumeister 1990; Settis 1992). Like Myron with his Diskobolos (the Discus-Thrower) and Lysippos with his Apoxyomenos (the Scraper), Polykleitos was the author of images whose gesture had become synonymous with the statue itself. The Greek title and the gesture concurred to create both a visual and a conceptual unity that indelibly fixed those statues in the minds of Roman viewers. Seneca (*Ep.* 65.5–7), for instance, refers

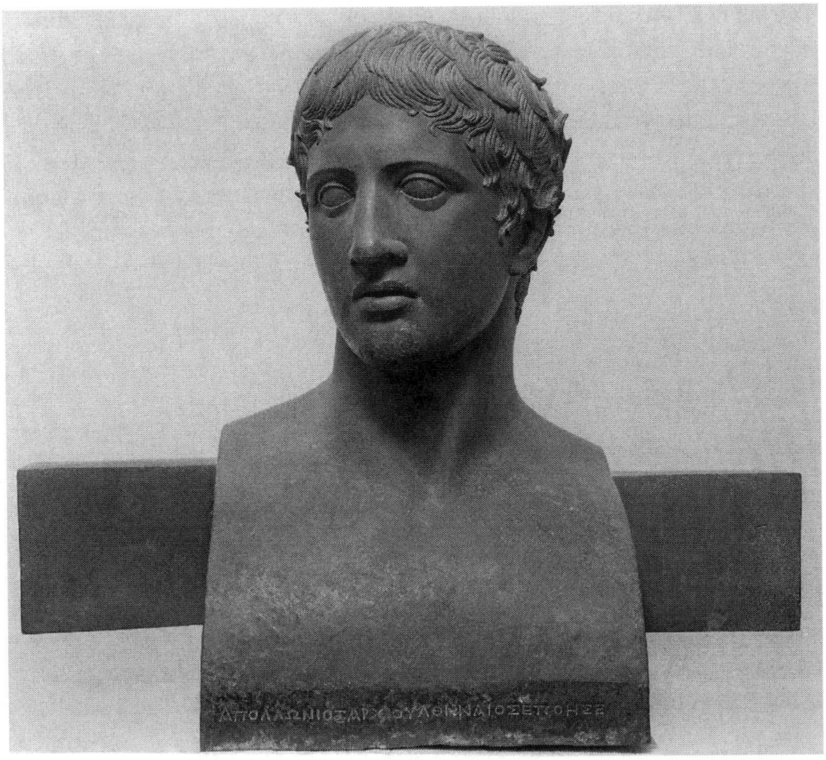

FIGURE 3.3.1 A Roman bronze bust (Augustan period) from the Villa of the Papyri at Herculaneum. The head is a copy of that of the Doryphoros by Polykleitos. Museo Archeologico Nazionale di Napoli, inv. 4885.

to Polykleitos's Doryphoros and Diadoumenos when summarizing Aristotle's theory on causes: after mentioning the first two "causes" of a statue, material and the artist, he illustrates the concept of "form" (*forma*) by referring to Polykleitos's statues as notable examples of how form not only provided titles to images, but also became their content. Pliny the Elder describes the Spear-Bearer and the Fillet-Binder as a *viriliter puer* and a *molliter iuvenis* respectively—a "manly looking boy" and a "soft-looking youth," definitions that embody the whole spectrum of athletic youth (*HN* 34.55; Rackham 1961, 169). The fame of the model, mentioned by several Greek and Latin authors and widely copied in antiquity, was such that Apollonios's replica must have been easily recognizable for the Herculaneum villa's cultivated owner and his guests, although only the head was represented (and the characteristic posture omitted). That the copyist signed this work indicates that skill in reproduction was valued in and of itself. The person who purchased and displayed the bronze head of the Doryphoros may have appreciated at once its intrinsic artistic quality, the fame of its prototype, and the provenance from a given workshop guaranteed by the signature.

Inside the villa, this piece belonged to a larger collection that included a number of marble and bronze heads generically resembling the style of Polykleitos (Warden 1991; Warden and Romano 1994; Mattusch 2005). Works like the head signed by Apollonios that either replicate or loosely imitate older Greek prototypes form a substantial group in the corpus of Roman sculpture. In the public spaces of any major city of the Roman Empire, as well as inside most high-profile homes, visitors encountered a landscape crowded with statues of gods and heroes. First and foremost thanks to their format and style, these divine and mythological figures were based on Greek models familiar to a vast majority of viewers (Zanker 1979, 284–99). The questions that this material raises and that the present essay aims to address revolve around the thorny issue of originality in Roman visual culture and relate to intertwined cultural, functional, and technological factors.

The Modern Construction of Roman Copies

That Roman art, and sculpture in particular, depended heavily upon Greek antecedents in matters of subject, style, and iconography has been common opinion for centuries (Marvin 2008, 16–167). In the early eighteenth century, learned travelers such as Joseph Addison and Jonathan Richardson Jr. first conjectured that most ancient statues known in their time were actually Roman copies after lost Greek prototypes (Barbanera 2006, 9–13; 2008, 41–4; 2011; Anguissola 2012, 25–6). This idea—together with the general assumption that Roman art had principally a retrospective character—was occasionally explored in Johann Joachim Winckelmann's foundational account of classical art (Potts 1980; see essays 1.2, Podany; and 3.1, Fullerton).

By the mid-nineteenth century, tracing lost Greek works of art through their alleged Roman replicas had become a compelling task for scholars. Relying on plaster casts and, after 1850, on the new medium of photography, experts on ancient art developed a methodology known as *Kopienkritik* (copy criticism) to catalog and understand Graeco-Roman sculpture (Anguissola 2012, 31–8). The book published in 1893 by the German archaeologist Adolf Furtwängler, *Meisterwerke der griechischen Plastik*, is the most remarkable and influential example of this method (Fullerton 2003, 102–5; Perry 2005, 81–4; Marvin 2008, 144–50). Furtwängler's project combined both *Meisterforschung* (research on the masters) and *Kopienkritik*. The former refers to the analysis of ancient literary sources in order to collect available information on particular artists and their works (see essay 2.4, Mattusch). Sifting through the massive quantity of Roman statues in classical style, Furtwängler isolated a number of marble figures or fragments that apparently derived from a set of common types. He assumed that these widely replicated types corresponded to masterpieces of the Greek classical era, particularly those very bronzes created by the artists mentioned by Pliny the Elder and the other ancient literary sources. In order to reconstruct the lost originals, Furtwängler employed a comparative analysis of the copies, inspired by the work of philologists engaged in the reconstruction of original texts through multiple later manuscript copies (Gazda 1995, 124–9; 2002, 4–8; Marvin 2008, 142–4).

This approach presumes that copies were crafted to meet a demand for replicas of Greek masterpieces; that copies needed therefore to be as faithful as possible; and that the fame of an image could be inferred from (i.e., was directly proportional to) the number of copies made. Obviously, looking through the works of the Roman period in search of their models fosters a simplistic view of the relationship between Greek and Roman art, with the consequence of drastically marginalizing the latter (see essay 3.1, Fullerton). Nevertheless, the identification of many celebrated masterpieces mentioned by Greek and Latin authors revealed a corpus of vanished "masterpieces of Greek sculpture" foundational for our knowledge of Greek art and its stylistic evolution. A paradigmatic example of this method was the identification of Polykleitos's Doryphoros, which Karl Friedrichs "rediscovered" in 1863 by combining the literary sources and the extant replicas of a statue whose format and balance corresponded to those described by the ancient authors (Anguissola 2012, 34).

During the late twentieth century, a parallel evolution of Greek and Roman archaeology led, on the one hand, to de-emphasizing the role of copies for the history of Greek art and, on the other hand, to their rediscovery in the sphere of Roman civilization. Historians of Roman art have underlined the importance of viewing images created according to Greek styles and iconographies as genuine expressions of Roman taste, culture, interests, and values (see essay 6.2, Trimble). This shift was grounded in the idea that the problem depended mostly on inappropriate modern assumptions and terminology. According to this view, advocated in particular by Brunilde Ridgway, Raimund Wünsche, and Paul Zanker during the 1970s (Ridgway 1970; Wünsche 1972; Zanker 1974; Ridgway 1977), many Roman sculptures derived from Greek prototypes should rather be considered as creations in the visual arts, akin to the achievements of Latin literature, in which powerful engagement with Greek models produced entirely new works by Roman authors (cf. Anguissola 2012, 38–42).

German scholars, in particular, engaged in the task of establishing a functional terminology to describe the relationship between Greek models and derived Roman works, acknowledging a wider range of possibilities. Behind this effort stood the awareness that the definitions one employs in order to deal with the phenomena of archaism, classicism, and copying will inevitably affect the conclusions about origin, development, and meaning. These taxonomic attempts resulted in the idea that the intentional and faithful copy (*Kopie*) or replica (*Replik, Wiederholung, Nachbildung*) of a model (*Vorbild*) should be distinguished from several other categories of works that display more or less consistent variations on the prototype. Prototype images could undergo transformation (*Umbildung*) and stylistic changes (*Umstilisierung*), could be combined with other types (*Kontamination*), or be used (*Benutzung, Verwendung*) to manufacture entirely inventive creations. New figures inspired by Greek antecedents (*Neuschöpfungen*) could in their turn become models for further artworks. At the same time, these concepts were tentatively connected to terms drawn from the Latin language of rhetoric and literary practice. Following this line of comparison, faithful copying was equated to the Latin *interpretatio* or literal translation. Free rendering (*Umbildung*) was thought to correspond to the exercise of *imitatio*, while the creation of inventive works of art (*Neuschöpfung*) came to be translated as *aemulatio* (Anguissola 2012, 39, 42).

Within this framework, the term "ideal sculpture" (in German *Idealplastik*) was coined to refer to Greek-style images of gods and mythological figures in Roman art, without prejudging their degree of indebtedness to particular classical models (a concept that has been recently investigated in the light of current research trends by Kousser 2008). The underlying assumption behind the use of this new hermeneutical category was that Roman spectators had a more open and flexible approach toward imitation than modern scholars. Therefore, when confronted with copies or other "imitations," Roman viewers would have considered a broader range of questions that did not necessarily focus (only) on the artwork's precise degree of fidelity to its model, but rather concerned the appropriateness of images, styles, and genres to their context and the message they were meant to broadcast.

These basic ideas, more precisely defined and reformulated, have gradually picked up a large and influential following among experts on Roman art (as discussed in Hallett 2005a). Today, one of the first notions that a student of archaeology learns is that quotations of Greek sculptural styles, masters, and masterpieces played a central role within Roman culture, essentially because they provided the visual vocabulary for artistic expression of "new Roman" values and qualities, also referred to as a "semantic system." The heavy Roman reliance on Greek art, as is especially evident in the sphere of sculpture, should be understood in terms of a creative approach to working within the conservative tradition of a culture where the *antiqui*, the "old masters," occupied an exceptionally exalted position (Gazda 2002, 1–24; Perry 2005). Behind the choice of artworks and styles that should be emulated was the pervasive principle of appropriateness (*decor*/*decorum*; in Greek πρέπον), which guided the selection of images according to function and context (cf. M. Fuchs 1999, 75–9; Perry 2002, 156–7; 2005, 28–64).

From Multiples to the Art of Multiplying

In terms of production, copying older images is by no means a Roman invention (Strocka 1979; Ridgway 1984; 1989). In classical Greece, for instance, the display of identical (or nearly identical) pendant statues may be required by the context (e.g., the Korai from the Erechtheion in Athens), and the production of multiple funerary or votive reliefs may depend on commercial or religious purposes (as attested by the double Telemachos relief from the Athenian Asklepieion). In addition, seriality was inherent in the process developed for bronze statuary, the classical medium of sculpture *par excellence*. The method of lost-wax casting (also known as *cire perdue*) allowed the production of a number of identical finished works derived from the same clay model (Mattusch 1999, 75–82; see also essay 2.4, Mattusch).

It is clear that the existence—centuries before the rise of Rome—of well-established practices and technologies for creating multiples and replicas requires that we frame our knowledge about Roman copies within a broader perspective. If the serial production of art was in itself not a technical innovation of the Romans, where does the distinctive nature of Roman copies lay?

The spread of copies after classical masterworks is attested for the first time during the Hellenistic period and has been recognized as inherent in court practice at Pergamon around the mid-second century BC (Niemeier 1985, 108–110, 128–9, 145–6, 154–7). This characteristic interest in classical art, both sculpture and painting, eventually led to the production of imitative artworks (Anguissola 2012, 75; 2013, 6–7).

At about the same time, a significant turn in the use and display of art took place in Rome. "Original" Greek art from the conquered cities in Magna Graecia, Sicily, and the eastern Mediterranean reached Rome during the second century BC as war booty dedicated by generals to serve as *ornamenta* in public spaces (Cirucci 2005; Bravi 2012). Items that did not find a place in temples or other public buildings could be purchased by private citizens: the inauguration of a trade in artistic goods from Sicily, Greece, and Asia Minor seems to have been well under way after Mummius's sack of Corinth in 146 BC (Miles 2008, 156).

From the late second and especially in the first century BC, sculptors' workshops in Greece and Asia Minor increasingly catered to Roman and Italian customers, producing copies after classical Greek masterpieces and inventive "retrospective" artworks based on the same tradition (Cain 1998, 1234–5). The materials from the shipwrecks of Mahdia (off the coast of Tunisia, cf. W. Fuchs 1963; Hellenkemper Salies, von Prittwitz und Gaffron, and Bauchhenss 1994; see essays 2.4, Mattusch; and 2.7, Russell) and Antikythera (an island between Crete and the Peloponnese, cf. Bol 1972; see essay 2.7, Russell) provide critical evidence for the production and trade of art at the turn of the second to first centuries BC. The first cargo vessel probably set sail from Athens, the second from Delos, both aiming at Rome and its environs: their holds were packed with sculptures produced according to the styles and models of late classical and Hellenistic art.

By the mid-first century BC, workshops founded and led by Greek sculptors may have been numerous in Rome, too (M. Fuchs 1999). Significantly, the late Hellenistic through the early imperial period of Rome mark the age of transition from art collections as holy dedications and commemorations of triumphs to collecting as a social and intellectual phenomenon, connected to established practices of connoisseurship, private art patronage, and the art market (Bounia 2004; see essays 4.6, Kellum; and 6.3, Shaya).

Among the foremost artists who worked in Rome in the first century BC, the sculptor Pasiteles, said by Pliny the Elder to have been of Greek ancestry, is particularly relevant (see essay 3.6, Touchette). Pasiteles hailed from a *polis* of Magna Graecia and thus was later awarded Roman citizenship through the *Lex Plautia Papiria* of 89 BC.

According to the account handed down by the sculptor's contemporary, Varro, later quoted by Pliny, Pasiteles executed a series of high-profile commissions in Rome during the late Republic and was also acclaimed for his theoretical writings (*HN* 36.39). Unlike most other known theoretical works by ancient artists, which seem to have concentrated on technology and composition, the five-book treatise written by Pasiteles offered a historical overview of Greek art based on a succession of masterpieces (the no-longer extant *quinque volumina nobilium operum in toto orbe*, "five volumes about the famous masterpieces of all the world"). This collection of *mirabilia* (marvels) may have offered substantial insight into the dynamics of reception and the role of the old Greek masters at a key moment for the history of Roman sculpture (Anguissola 2012, 20–21, 32, 82–5, 90, 114, 174). Together with other sources, Pasiteles's books provided Pliny the Elder with essential information to articulate his canon of Greek sculptors and works. It is likely that Pliny may have derived from the account written by Pasiteles his sequence of styles and authors that omits the early Hellenistic period and postulates the death of art in the early third century BC (*cessavit ars*) and its rebirth in the mid-second century BC (*rursus revixit*), contemporary with the emergence of Neo-Atticism (for this discussion Rouveret 1989, 458–9; Pucci 2003, 24–7; see essays 3.6, Touchette; and 6.1, Squire).

The school of Pasiteles, which is known to us through a number of extant works, developed a language based on the creative imitation of classical prototypes and the repetition of a standardized repertoire (Simon 1987; M. Fuchs 1999, 81–3). To judge from the best-known product of his school, the so-called Stephanos Athlete (or Albani Athlete; figure 3.3.2), Pasiteles's interest in the history of Greek sculpture also deeply affected the production of his students, who created profoundly classicizing sculptures. This under-life-size statue of an athlete is identified by a Greek inscription as the work of Stephanos, pupil (*μαθητής*) of Pasiteles (Kousser 2008, 146–9). The artist took inspiration from the severe style of the early classical era (480–450 BC) for his overall concept and elements such as the flat-footed *contrapposto* and the tightly braided cap of hair. At the same time, he adopted the slender proportions typical of late classical sculpture, as known for instance from the works of Lysippos (fourth century BC). The youth that Stephanos created by drawing on a variety of prototypes, combining the format of early classical athletes with a softly modeled body, seems to have enjoyed remarkable popularity in the Roman period, as the eighteen preserved replicas and imitations suggest (Zanker 1974, 49–54).

This evolution from functional multiplication to purposeful retrospection resulted in a situation where copied art from much earlier periods and a different culture not only seems to dominate Roman production, but also to be a fundamental instrument of communication. Within the visual code developed by the Romans, signifier (images and styles of the Greek tradition) and signified (concepts pertaining to individual and civic qualities) were closely related.

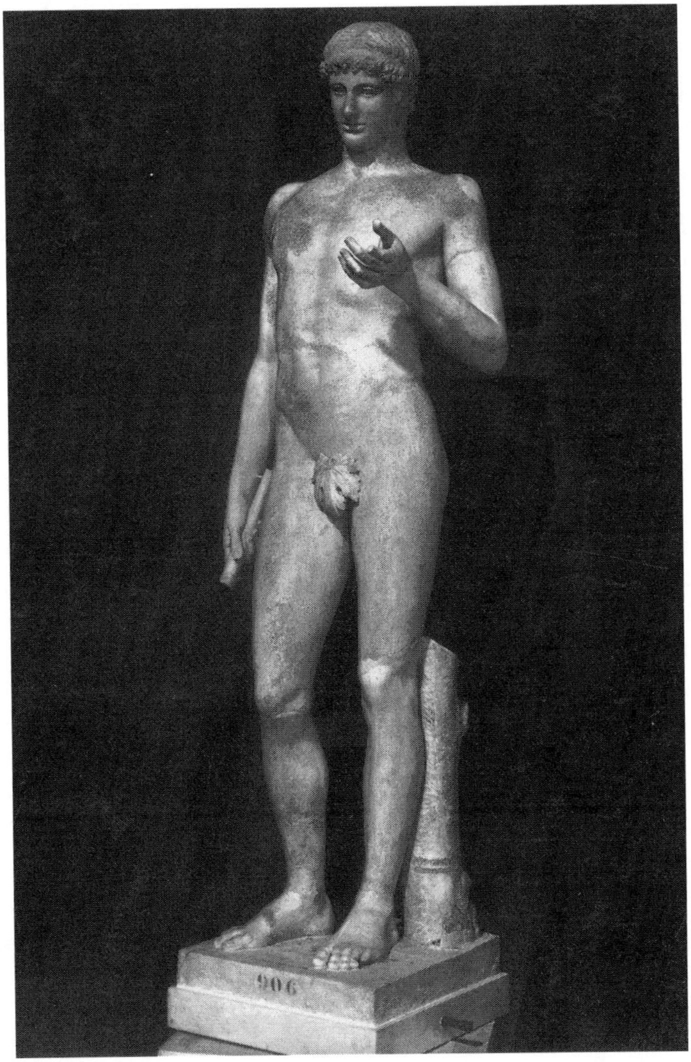

FIGURE 3.3.2 Marble statue of the so-called Stephanos Athlete (mid-first century BC). The sculptor Stephanos signed his work and presented himself as a pupil of Pasiteles. Rome, Museo di Villa Albani, inv. 906.

A Serial Art

The sculptural types that gave rise, in the Roman period, to large replica series cover the entire range of possible relationships between Roman creations and their Greek antecedents: intentional copies from classical Greek masterworks (as seen in the evidence for the Doryphoros and Diadoumenos by Polykleitos or the Diskobolos by Myron); popular classical images whose origins are unknown (e.g., the so-called Fréjus Aphrodite); and generic Greek-looking creations which loosely imitate the style of a given artist (e.g., the "Polykleitan" athletes or the "Praxitelean" boys) or combine the traditions of disparate chronological periods (like the Stephanos Athlete). Although images in a classical style—from the severe to the late classical—seem to prevail, some Hellenistic-style types are likewise preserved in a large number of replicas, such as the "red" and "white" versions of the Hanging Marsyas (see essay 1.5, Frischer), erotic groups (*symplegmata*) like the Dresden Hermaphrodite and Satyr, or the numerous figures of Venus inspired by Praxiteles's Aphrodite of Knidos.

Throughout any one given replica series, material, dimensions, and stylistic features of the items could either remain constant or undergo radical modifications. Even the identity of each member of the series could vary according to the choice of attributes attached to the standard body type. For example, one familiar classical type of a youth, known as the Westmacott Ephebe from the conventional name given to the eponymous statue in London, could provide the standard iconographic framework for individualized figures of human or divine boys—such as winged Icarus or Bacchus crowned with grapes and clothed in animal skin (Zanker 1974, 23–5; Bartman 2002, 254–5). A striking case of "individualized repetition" is known from the sculpture collection displayed in the Villa of Hadrian at Tivoli. The set of statues placed around the Canopus seems to have been selected with an eye for repetition and symmetrical pendants. On the west side of the pool, the colonnade was interrupted by four copies of the Korai from the Erechtheion in Athens (the Caryatids), which replaced as many columns. The short curved northern side was adorned, in the spaces of the intercolumniations, with two slightly different Amazons of the so-called Sciarra and Mattei types, facing each other on the opposite sides of the pool. Two almost identical male figures occupied a symmetrical position at this end of the stretch of water. Because their format and style derive from the same fifth-century BC prototype, they can be identified with the gods Mercury and Mars only thanks to details such as, respectively, winged sandals and weapons (Raeder 1983, 87–8, nos. 84–5).

The extent of available options within the constraint of a consistent series is evident when considering, for instance, the group of statues derived from one of the best-known athletes of the classical era: the Discus-Thrower or Diskobolos by Myron. The image of this lost statue, cast in bronze in the mid-fifth century BC, was recovered in 1781 by Giovanni Battista Visconti, the successor of Winckelmann as curator of Papal antiquities, thanks to the discovery of a full-size replica on the Esquiline (figure 3.3.3). The Diskobolos is known today from a large replica series, copied in several media and in many sizes (Anguissola 2005). Among the more traditional replicas there are many differences in detail: sometimes the pose portrays extreme tension, but sometimes the musculature is more relaxed; the turn and inclination of the torso vary widely; the figure relies on more or less visible supports. One bronze statuette now in the Munich Antikensammlungen stretches the limits of the type. The proportions of the torso are altered, the body twist is emphasized, and the head looks nothing like a classical athlete, sporting long and thick locks framing a florid face with round cheeks and large eyes (cf.

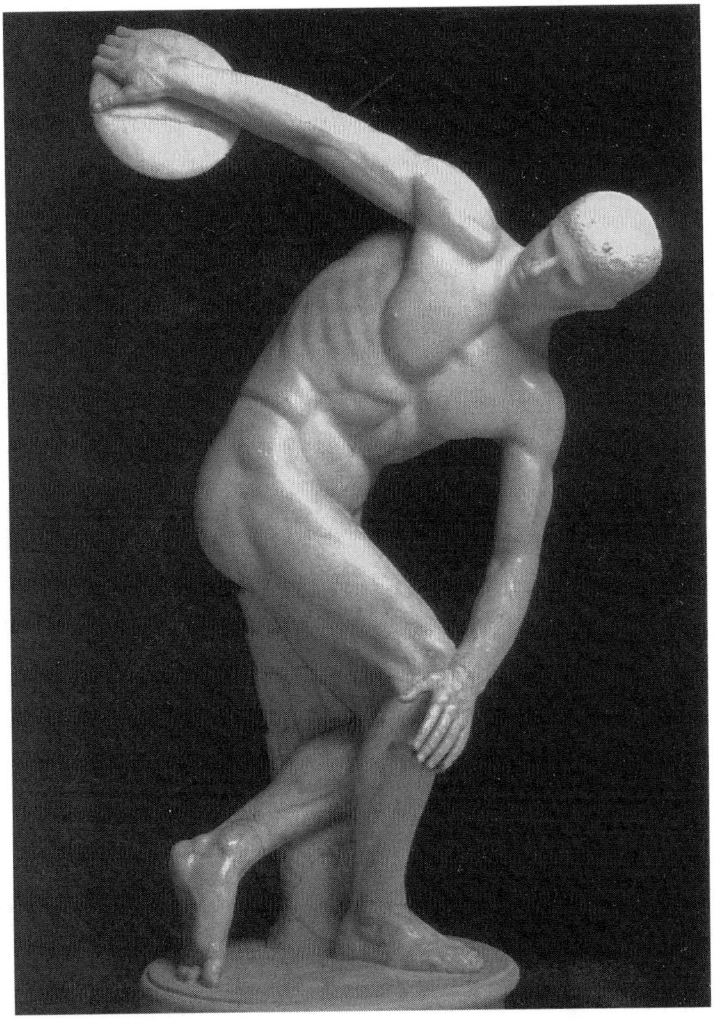

FIGURE 3.3.3 Marble copy (early Antonine period) of the Diskobolos by Myron, found in 1781 on the Esquiline. Rome, Museo Nazionale Romano, inv. 126371.

Anguissola 2005, 329–31, no. 26). As demonstrated by Elizabeth Bartman (1992), miniatures of famous masterpieces can hardly be discounted as merely secondary evidence for the history of copying and the reception of Greek art in Rome. Miniatures offered the possibility, on the one hand, to use either cheaper or extremely costly materials and, on the other hand, to modify the prototypes easily. The wider range of choices allowed by the format provides exceptional insight into the tastes and visual literacy of a wider public and reveals how deeply the memory, knowledge, and manipulation of Greek art impacted the everyday life of the Romans.

Extreme modifications of a given type include combination with a portrait head. This widespread—and typically Roman—practice also relies on the pervasive logic of appropriateness (*decor*): iconographies and styles from the Greek past could be associated with certain concepts and therefore be more or less appropriate for a given subject (e.g., on the one hand, the *dignitas, pondus, maiestas, auctoritas, gravitas, sanctitas* expressed by the creations of the classical masters, on the other hand, the characteristic *amoenitas* and *voluptas* of late classical and Hellenistic art). Not only certain styles but also particular artists were considered expressions of a tight rhetoric of concepts and ideals (Hölscher [1987] 2004): the Romans, for instance, saw Pheidias as the master of majesty (*maiestas*) appropriate for divinities; Polykleitos as the matchless creator of heroes and their ideal grace (*decor supra verum*); and Lysippos as the greatest portraitist for his "truth" (*veritas*) to the human subject—a quality shared by Praxiteles, too (as described by Quint. *Inst.* 12.9.8–9; see essay 6.1, Squire).

Since the Roman art of portraiture called for an attributive description of the person's social standing, role, history, and qualities, a set of stock bodies derived from well-known Greek prototypes, whose ideal meaning was understood by the whole community of viewers, provided an efficient visual code to Roman patrons (cf. Hallett 2005b). The Roman penchant for interchangeable parts, each of which could have independent origins, was matched by an equal inclination toward stylistic diversity (see essay 3.6, Touchette).

A number of examples are known for this technique of combination. The famous marble portrait of a Julio-Claudian prince discovered on the Esquiline in Rome and now at the Louvre Museum in Paris provides a perfect case in point to observe how such ancient pastiches functioned. The figure combines a portrait head and the replica of a classical Greek body: a type of Hermes, known to art historians as the Hermes Ludovisi, originally created in the mid-fifth century BC (Hallett 2005b, 175–6). Similarly, Roman women could be portrayed with sculptural types emphasizing their respectable social identity (e.g., the Large Herculaneum Woman, as discussed by Trimble 2011) or their beauty, implicit in the choice of being represented in the guise of Venus (see essay 4.8, D'Ambra and Tronchin). To modern eyes, the combination of the individual head of a middle-aged woman and the seductive body of the Capitoline Venus makes a sharp contrast, as in the example of a portrait statue from a villa near Lake Albano and today in Copenhagen, dating to the age of Trajan. A comparable effect is achieved by a late Antonine female portrait found in the environs of Santa Croce in Gerusalemme in Rome and now in the Belvedere Court of the Vatican Museums, which combines a portrait head with the figure type of the Knidian Aprodite (Hallett 2005b, 201, pls. 121–2).

Portrait statues constructed with various stock body types often show remarkable differences between the treatment of the head and the rest of the figure, suggesting that carvers with different specializations (portraitists and copyists) collaborated within a single workshop. Sometimes, however, the same artist could be commissioned to create both portraits of notable citizens and copies of ideal sculpture (e.g., a female portrait and a copy of the so-called Tiber Apollo from the seaport town of Cherchel in Algeria, both dating to the Antonine period; cf. Landwehr 2010, 45).

Nowhere else have full-scale copies been found in such impressive quantity as in Rome and Campania. Nonetheless, recent regional studies about the distribution of copies after Greek masterpieces show that they also enjoyed considerable popularity outside the "core area" of Rome and central Italy. The study of replica series within a given geographical context provides information on the role that famous masterpieces played in staging prestige and collective identities (exemplary in this respect is Trimble 2011, with regard to the replicas of the so-called Large Herculaneum Woman). Thorough analysis of the copies from classical and late classical models found in the cities of the province Gallia Narbonensis, for instance, has demonstrated that these statues, probably imported from other regions of the empire, played a fundamental role in the efforts of monumentalization and self-presentation of the local elites (Slavazzi 1996). Recent publications of understudied regions—Spain, North Africa, the ancient Near East—suggest that similar patterns could apply here, too (see part V, Regions and Provinces). Along the *limes*, the situation must have been different due to reduced access to high-quality materials, accomplished artists, and luxury trade. Nonetheless, the use of established sculptural types seems to have been similarly widespread and to have constituted a long-lasting phenomenon over the centuries of Roman occupation.

Most sculptural types reached their apogee in the Hadrianic and Antonine period, during the second century AD. At this time of the empire's greatest wealth, increased exploitation of marble mines throughout the Mediterranean contributed to a period of prolific artistic production. In particular, colored marbles allow clear identification of quarry origins and chronology, as well as of particular associations between subject and material (Gasparri 1994, 269–70, 278). Basalt (green schist), for instance, seems to have been employed between the age of Augustus and that of Hadrian, first for copies after fifth-century BC classical models and from the Flavian age for figures of Hellenistic origin, too (cf. also Belli Pasqua 1995). Toward the end of this period, dark marbles (*bigio antico*) also came into use, often for works depending on the Hellenistic sculptural tradition of Rhodes and Asia Minor. Red marble (*rosso antico*) is comparatively rare and was used in a limited number of workshops, such as the one that produced the Red Faun in the Capitoline Museums. From the Augustan age onward, Phrygian marble or *pavonazzetto* enjoyed particular appreciation for subjects connected to eastern stories or environments, such as the Sperlonga Ganymedes, images of barbarian captives (Schneider 1986), and the "red" Marsyas (e.g., Weis 1992, cat. nos. 15, 19, 39).

The Technologies of Imitation

Clearly, a visual culture that relied so heavily on the replication of familiar types required efficient means for mass production of copies and stock bodies. Already in the late nineteenth century, scholars postulated that ancient Roman copyists worked with the aid of mechanical methods similar to those known in later times. Plaster or clay models (Duthoy 2012, 102–5), derived from casts of the originals, were available to Roman copyists, who could translate shape and proportions on the new block of marble thanks to pointing and triangulation (Pfanner 1989; Touchette 2000; Anguissola 2012, 34–5, 60n38).

Models, however, were expensive tools. Experimental archaeology has demonstrated that, since elastic materials such as silicon for molds were unknown in antiquity, making a cast of a full-sized statue must have been a long and challenging process (Landwehr 2010, 37). The artisan responsible for the production of these casts, the *gypsarius*, was entrusted with the delicate task of creating reliable and sturdy models without damaging their prototype. The first step toward a reliable plaster model was the creation of the so-called negative cast (Landwehr 1982, 16–18). All attached attributes of the bronze statue (e.g., crowns, jewelry, etc.) had to be removed, while details such as tinplate eyelashes were covered with protective wax. The same procedure had to be followed for elaborate hairstyles: protruding or spiral-shaped locks had to be either wrapped or removed. Afterward, plaster casts of small zones of the surface could be made one by one. These smaller casts were later pieced together and secured by using fresh plaster and an inner frame made of bone, wood, or cane. At the end, a mixture of oil and wax could be spread on the figure in order to strengthen the plaster surface.

Our knowledge of ancient plaster casts depends largely on one exceptional discovery, made in 1954 in the Campanian town of Baiae, a Roman seaside resort on the Bay of Naples, a short distance from the dynamic port of Puteoli (see essay 2.4, Mattusch). There, discarded in an underground space beneath the so-called Baths of Sosandra, archaeologists found around 400 fragments of plaster casts, once owned by a Roman sculptors' workshop active in the first two centuries AD (Landwehr 1982; 1985). These fragments seem to have belonged to plaster figures used for replicas after Greek models of the fifth and fourth centuries BC (figure 3.3.4), as well as for eclectic variations of unknown classical prototypes.

The number and quality of the casts corroborate previously posited theories of a high-end workshop. Traces of defensive measures, such as the removal of attached details and the protection of delicate parts with wax or pitch, confirm that at least some of the casts owned by the Baiae sculptors had been taken directly from the bronze originals. The spread at Baiae itself and in the Phlegraean area of marble copies after the prototypes included in the hoard of plaster casts attests to the activity of this workshop. According to Carlo Gasparri, who based his conjectures on the corpus of replicas ascribed to these sculptors, the workshop began its activity around the age of Augustus, thanks to Greek artists who had probably emigrated from Athens; later on, local sculptors may have taken on the business (Gasparri 1994, 274; 1995, 184–7). The latter continued to carve marble statues into the first century AD that privileged the Attic repertoire from the second half of the fifth (the era of the Parthenon) and the early fourth centuries BC. The activity of this workshop seems to have continued well into the second century AD, and in the Hadrianic period the Baiae sculptors traded their creations on a larger scale and reached the city of Rome. Coincidental with the development of new commercial routes was a substantial renewal of their repertoire, which came to include prototypes from the late severe style such as the so-called Aphrodite Sosandra, the Omphalos Apollo, the Giustiniani Hestia, and the Ludovisi Peplophoros (Gasparri 1995; cf. also Gasparri 1989).

Faithful copying was as tricky and time consuming as the task of carving fully "new" statues. In view of the difficulties and costs of the casting process, as well as of the expenses

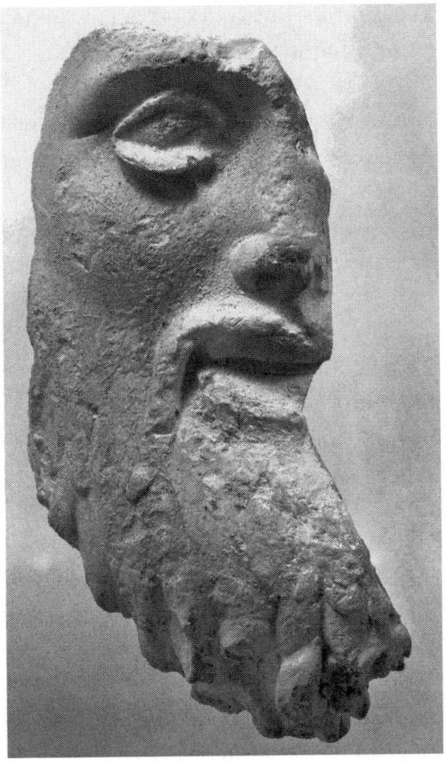

FIGURE 3.3.4 Fragment of a plaster cast used to produce copies of the statue of Aristogeiton, one of the two figures from the group of the Tyrant-Slayers. Baiae, Museo Archeologico dei Campi Flegrei, inv. 174.479.

for shipping the finished plaster models, we may argue that copies, often dismissed by modern art historians as inferior products of mechanical replication, must have had a different value in the eyes of sophisticated Roman connoisseurs, depending on their artistic quality. Besides, the "mechanical" pointing technique could not guarantee perfectly truthful results without the creative intervention of the copyist, who could count on a grid of references which indicated only a set of crucial points (see Pfanner 1989, 236–51, for a list of statues that preserve traces of the points). General proportions and overall shape could be translated onto the new block of marble directly from the model, but the rendering of details, especially hairstyle and drapery, mirrors the individual sensibility of the copyists—and therefore often the specific taste and stylistic idiosyncrasies of their epoch.

Conclusion

In light of these remarks, it is difficult to escape a radical challenge to our ideas about the relative value of copies, and therefore about their place in the visual imagery of the

Romans. Certainly, the concept of "Roman copies after Greek originals," as posed by nineteenth and early twentieth century art historians, fails to account for the pervasive retrospection that permeated Roman art at a deep level. It has been widely recognized that, for the most part, known Roman statues are inventive creations loosely indebted to some Greek prototypes rather than intentional copies. Nevertheless, the conceptual framework within which we consider the relationship between Greek and Roman sculpture should not neglect to account for the spread and success of true copies intended, manufactured, and displayed to establish a clear relationship to a given Greek masterpiece (or, as it is the case with the Stephanos Athlete and its replica series, to an inventive "classicizing" Roman creation).

With all of the emphasis that Roman culture seems to have put on the artists' ability to play with tradition, two literary sources on painting and engraving reveal that the taste for creative emulation coexisted with a radically different attitude that may well have extended to the sphere of sculpture. Lucian, who wrote in the second century AD a long ekphrasis on a famous classical Greek painting, the Centaurs by Zeuxis, confidently resorts to a replica in order to present this artwork (*Zeuxis* 3; cf. Perry 2005, 91–4; Anguissola 2012, 73–5). The original had been lost long before, when it was shipped to Italy in the aftermath of Sulla's seizure of Athens. However, Lucian, who lived six centuries after the Greek painter and over two centuries after the original painting had sunk off of Cape Maleas (in the southeast of the Peloponnese), takes it for granted that a copy he had seen in Athens provides the means to judge not only the original's subject and iconography, but also the precision of Zeuxis's line, his mastery of the palette, the quality of his brushwork, and his management of shadows! The copy—implicitly—functions as substitute for the original of indisputable status. Similarly, one of the most famous accomplishments of Zenodorus, a fashionable sculptor of Pliny the Elder's time and the creator of the sun colossus for Nero, was the successful emulation of two silver cups chased in the fourth century BC by the Greek engraver Kalamis (Hallett 2005a, 432–3; Marvin 2008, 224). The similarity of their metalwork was such that, according to Pliny (*HN* 34.47), the two artists deserved to be held as equal in terms of artistic achievements (*ars*).

If the capacity to create variations of a given repertoire was a much-esteemed quality for rhetoricians, poets, and artists alike, who used Greek art as a source of inspiration for "originally Roman" creations, these sources suggest that the skill to reproduce an illustrious prototype with exactitude—and therefore the cultural value of copies—was by no means marginal in theory and everyday practice—even in the eyes of skilled viewers.

On the one hand, the Roman artists used complicated and expensive techniques to make full-scale copies of Greek and even Roman "classicizing" masterpieces. On the other hand, they worked according to methods that resulted in their work bearing the stamp of their own era. This process conferred on these statues a paradoxical double nature that may have been crucial in determining their appreciation in the eyes of the Romans. Copies and other retrospective statues could be valued as sophisticated works of art, both recognizable and authoritative, which explicitly acknowledged their place within a revered tradition (Geominy 1999).

The potential of copies as instruments for communication may explain in part the reasons for their exceptional spread in the homes and cities of the Romans, according to a taste that finds no parallel in other periods of Western art history. Undoubtedly, repeated images and standardized bodies were often chosen because they belonged to a widespread language of clichés, to fill the architectural spaces as conventional commonplaces, or provide a reliable language on which individual references could be built (Zanker 1992). Nonetheless, their potential for the manipulation of collective memory constitutes one fundamental aspect in the Roman ethos of visual repetition. For the Romans, references to the chronologically distant "ancient" Greek *opera nobilia* were layered over hints to the "modern" Roman artifacts or places closer in time to the contemporary viewers, as well as to a rhetoric of styles that had become commonplace (Hölscher [1987] 2004). From this perspective, the exactitude of copies relative to one another is of little historical value without the consideration of other factors. What matters is neither (only) faithfulness nor (only) the ideal content associated with the styles of one or another Greek artist; instead, the importance lies in the narratives that certain relationships recalled (to which faithfulness could be instrumental).

The idea of multiple references and levels to which the concept of "copy" applies can be tested on one of the rare instances where both original and copies have reached our times: the Caryatids from the Athenian Erechtheion and their Roman replicas (Schmidt 1973; Lauter 1976; Varner 2006, 282). In the case of both the Caryatids on the attic story of the portico in the Forum of Augustus and of those embellishing the Canopus at Hadrian's Villa in Tivoli, no doubts exist about their dependence upon the Athenian prototypes. However, it remains impossible to determine exactly which was the cultural and chronological landscape that these images intended to recall. Was the quotation really meant to recall the great Athens of the fifth century BC or did it refer, rather, to the contemporary cultural capital of Greece? It is just as likely, indeed, that the Caryatids were expected to create a link to Athens, as it was during the years, respectively, of Augustus and Hadrian, when well-maintained ancient classical monuments were integrated within the new Roman landscape (cf. Alcock 2002, 51–73). This conjecture becomes all the more intriguing when we think, on the one hand, about the role that a classicizing visual code played under Augustus or, on the other hand, about the urban flourishing that Athens underwent during the years of Hadrian, the hellenophile. This chain of considerations expands when considering a third series of Caryatids, from the Forum of the Spanish town of Mérida (*Augusta Emerita*). Along the attic of the portico, built in Claudian-Neronian times, relief Caryatids alternated with shields (De La Barrera 2000, 105–110, nos. 371–96, 161–2). Although their general shape indirectly depends upon the Erechtheion's maidens, it is clear that their presence has little to do here with the religious and political geography of the Athenian Acropolis—but imitates the lavish setting of the Forum of Augustus, to reflect the prestige of Rome in the little provincial town.

As part of a landscape—both physical and mental—sculptures, paintings, and buildings are involved in the complex interplay between experience and memory, whence the semantics and meaning of places take their origin. The evident difficulty in placing real copies and creative imitations along a quantitative scale of "faithfulness" and relative value challenges us to conceive of a broader and more inclusive narrative of Roman art—and in particular of Roman sculpture—that accommodates both formally innovative creations and self-consciously retrospective works.

Bibliography

Alcock, S. 2002. *Archaeologies of the Greek Past: Landscape, Monuments, and Memories*. Cambridge: Cambridge University Press.

Anguissola, A. 2005. "Roman Copies of Myron's Discobolus." *JRA* 18: 317–35.

———. 2012. *"Difficillima imitatio": Immagine e lessico delle copie tra Grecia e Roma*. Rome: "L'Erma" di Bretschneider.

———. 2013. "Die Kunst der Nachahmung: Reflexe einer technischen Sprache in den Griechischen und Römischen Quellen." *Indo-European Linguistics and Classical Philology* 17: 3–15.

Barbanera, M. 2006. *Original und Kopie: Bedeutungs- und Wertewandel eines intellektuellen Begriffspaares seit dem 18. Jahrhundert in der Klassischen Archäologie*. Stendal: Winckelmann-Gesellschaft.

———. 2008. "Original und Kopie: Aufstieg und Niedergand eines intellektuellen Begriffspaares seit dem 18. Jahrhundert in der Klassischen Archäologie." In *Original und Kopie: Formen und Konzepte der Nachahmung in der antiken Kunst*, edited by K. Junker and A. Stähli, 35–61. Wiesbaden: Reichert.

———. 2011. *Originale e copia nell'arte antica*. Mantua: Tre Lune.

Bartman, E. 1992. *Ancient Sculptural Copies in Miniature*. Columbia Studies in the Classical Tradition 19. Leiden: Brill.

———. 2002. "Eros's Flame. Images of Sexy Boys in Roman Ideal Sculpture." In Gazda 2002, 249–71.

Belli Pasqua, R. 1995. *Sculture di età romana in "basalto."* Rome: "L'Erma" di Bretschneider.

Bol, P. C. 1972. *Die Skulpturen des Schiffsfundes von Antikythera*. Berlin: Mann.

Bounia, A. 2004. *The Nature of Classical Collecting: Collectors and Collections, 100 BCE–100 CE*. Aldershot: Ashgate.

Bravi, A. 2012. *"Ornamenta urbis": Opere d'arte greche negli spazi romani*. Bari: Edipuglia.

Cain, H.-U. 1998. "Copie dai *mirabilia* greci." In *I Greci oltre la Grecia*, edited by S. Settis, 1221–44. I Greci: Storia cultura arte società 3. Turin: Einaudi.

Cirucci, G. 2005. "Sculture greche di VI–IV secolo a.C. reimpiegate nella Roma antica: Una proposta di sintesi." *RivIstArch* 28: 9–57.

De La Barrera, J. L. 2000. *La decoración arquitectónica de los foros de Augusta Emerita*. Rome: "L'Erma" di Bretschneider.

Duthoy, F. 2012. *Sculpteurs et commanditaires au IIe siècle après J.-C. Rome et Tivoli*. Rome: École Française de Rome.

Fuchs, M. 1999. *"In hoc etiam genere Graeciae nihil cedamus": Studien zur Romanisierung der späthellenistischen Kunst im 1. Jh. v. Chr.* Mainz: Philipp von Zabern.

Fuchs, W. 1963. *Der Schiffsfund von Mahdia*. Tübingen: Wasmuth.

Fullerton, M. D. 2003. "*Der Stil der Nachahmer*: A Brief Historiography of Stylistic Retrospection." In *Ancient Art and its Historiography*, edited by A. A. Donohue and M. D. Fullerton, 92–117. Cambridge: Cambridge University Press.

Furtwängler, A. 1893. *Meisterwerke der griechischen Plastik: Kunstgeschichtliche Untersuchungen*. Leipzig: Giesecke and Devrient.

Gasparri, C. 1989. "Una officina di copisti in età medio-imperiale." In *The Greek Renaissance in the Roman Empire*, edited by S. Walker and A. Cameron, 96–101. London: Institute of Classical Studies.
———. 1994. "Copie e copisti." *EAA* Supplement 2: 267–80.
———. 1995. "L'officina dei calchi di Baia." *RM* 102: 173–87.
Gazda, E. K. 1995. "Roman Sculpture and the Ethos of Emulation: Reconsidering Repetition." *HSCP* 97: 121–156.
———, ed. 2002. *The Ancient Art of Emulation: Studies in Artistic Originality and Tradition from the Present to Classical Antiquity*. Ann Arbor: University of Michigan Press.
Geominy, W. 1999. "Zwischen Kennerschaft und Cliché: Römische Kopien und die Geschichte ihrer Bewertung." In *Rezeption und Identität: Die kulturelle Auseinandersetzung Roms mit Griechenland als europäisches Paradigma*, edited by G. Vogt-Spira and B. Rommel, 38–58. Stuttgart: Steiner.
Hallett, C. H. 2005a. "Emulation versus Replication: Redefining Roman Copying." *JRA* 18: 419–35.
———. 2005b. *The Roman Nude: Heroic Portrait Statuary, 200 BC–AD 300*. Oxford: Oxford University Press.
Hellenkemper Salies, G., H.-H. von Prittwitz und Gaffron, and G. Bauchhenss, eds. 1994. *Das Wrack: Der antike Schiffsfund von Mahdia*. Vol. 1. Cologne: Rheinland-Verlag.
Hölscher, T. (1987) 2004. *The Language of Images in Roman Art*. Translated by A. Snodgrass and A. M. Künzl-Snodgrass. Cambridge: Cambridge University Press. Originally published as *Römische Bildsprache als semantisches System*.
Kousser, R. M. 2008. *Hellenistic and Roman Ideal Sculpture: The Allure of the Classical*. Cambridge: Cambridge University Press.
Landwehr, C. 1982. *Griechische Meisterwerke in römischen Abgüssen: Der Fund von Baia; Zur Technik antiker Kopisten*. Frankfurt am Main: Liebieghaus.
———. 1985. *Die antiken Gipsabgüsse aus Baiae: Griechische Bronzestatuen in Abgüssen römischer Zeit*. Berlin: Mann.
———. 2010. "The Baiae Casts and the Uniqueness of Roman Copies." In *Plaster Casts: Making, Collecting and Displaying from Classical Antiquity to the Present*, edited by R. Fredriksen and E. Marchand, 35–46. Berlin: Walter de Gruyter.
Lauter, H. 1976. *Die Koren des Erechtheion*. AntP 16. Berlin: Mann.
Marvin, M. 1997. "Roman Sculptural Copies or Polykleitos: The Sequel." In *Sculpture and Its Reproductions*, edited by A. Hughes and E. Ranfft, 7–28. London: Reaktion.
———. 2008. *The Language of the Muses: The Dialogue between Roman and Greek Sculpture*. Los Angeles: J. Paul Getty Museum.
Mattusch, C. C. 1999. "Lost-Wax Casting and the Question of Originals and Copies." In *I grandi bronzi antichi*, edited by E. Formigli, 75–82. Siena: Nuova Immagine Editrice.
———. 2005. *The Villa dei Papiri: Life and Afterlife of a Sculptural Collection*. Los Angeles: J. Paul Getty Museum.
Miles, M. M. 2008. *Art as Plunder: The Ancient Origins of Debate about Cultural Property*. Cambridge: Cambridge University Press.
Neumeister, C. 1990. "Polyklet in der römischen Literatur." In *Polyklet: Der Bildhauer der griechischen Klassik*, edited by H. Beck, P. C. Bol, and M. Bückling, 428–49. Mainz: Philipp von Zabern.
Niemeier, J.-P. 1985. *Kopien und Nachahmungen im Hellenismus: Ein Beitrag zum Klassizismus des 2. und frühen 1. Jhs. v. Chr.* Bonn: Habelt.
Perry, E. 2002. "Rhetoric, Literary Criticism, and the Roman Aesthetics of Artistic Imitation." In Gazda 2002, 153–71.

Perry, E. 2005. *The Aesthetics of Emulation in the Visual Arts of Ancient Rome*. Cambridge: Cambridge University Press.

Pfanner, M. 1989. "Über das Herstellen von Porträts: Ein Beitrag zu Rationalisierungsmassnahmen und Produktionsmechanismen von Massenware im späten Hellenismus und in der römischen Kaiserzeit." *JdI* 104: 157–257.

Potts, A. 1980. "Greek Sculpture and Roman Copies I: Anton Raphael Mengs and the Eighteenth Century." *JWarb* 43: 150–73.

Pucci, G. 2003. "L'antichità greca e romana." In *Estetica della scultura*, edited by L. Russo, 9–46. Palermo: Aesthetica.

Rackham, H., trans. 1961. *Pliny, Natural History*. Vol. 9, *Books XXXIII–XXXV*. Loeb Classical Library. Cambridge, MA: Harvard University Press.

Raeder, J. 1983. *Die statuarische Ausstattung der Villa Hadriana bei Tivoli*. Frankfurt: Peter Lang.

Ridgway, B. S. 1970. *The Severe Style in Greek Sculpture*. Princeton: Princeton University Press.

———. 1977. *Archaic Styles in Greek Sculpture*. Princeton: Princeton University Press.

———. 1984. *Roman Copies of Greek Sculpture: The Problem of the Originals*. Ann Arbor: University of Michigan Press.

———. 1989. "Defining the Issue: The Greek Period." In *Retaining the Original: Multiple Originals, Copies, and Reproductions*, edited by K. Preciado, 13–26. Washington, DC: National Gallery of Art.

Rouveret, A. 1989. *Histoire et imaginaire de la peinture anciennne (Ve siècle av. J.-C.–Ier siècle ap. J.-C.)*. Rome: École Française de Rome.

Schmidt, E. E. 1973. *Die Kopien der Erechtheionkoren*. AntP 13. Berlin: Mann.

Schneider, R. M. 1986. *Bunte Barbaren: Orientalenstatuen aus farbigem Marmor in der römischen Repräsentationskunst*. Worms: Wernersche Verlagsgesellschaft.

Settis, S. 1992. "Fortuna del Diadumeno: I testi." *NumAntCl* 21: 51–68.

Simon, E. 1987. "Kriterien zur Deutung Pasitelischer Gruppen." *JdI* 102: 291–304.

Slavazzi, F. 1996. *"Italia verius quam provincia": Diffusione e funzione delle copie di sculture greche nella Gallia Narbonensis*. Naples: Edizioni Scientifiche Italiane.

Strocka, V. M. 1979. "Variante, Wiederholung und Serie in der griechischen Bildhauerei." *JdI* 94: 143–73.

Touchette, L.-A. 2000. "The Mechanics of Roman Copy Production?" In *Periplous: Papers on Classical Art and Archaeology Presented to Sir John Boardman*, edited by G. R. Tsetskhladze, J. Prag, and A. Snodgrass, 344–352. London: Thames and Hudson.

Trimble, J. 2011. *Women and Visual Replication in Roman Imperial Art and Culture*. Cambridge: Cambridge University Press.

Varner, E. R. 2006. "Reading Replications: Roman Rhetoric and Greek Quotations." In "Art and Replication: Greece, Rome and Beyond," edited by J. Trimble and J. Elsner, special issue *Art History* 29(2): 280–303.

Warden, P. G. 1991. "The Sculptural Program of the Villa of the Papyri." *JRA* 4: 257–61.

Warden, P. G., and D. G. Romano 1994. "The Course of Glory: Greek Art in a Roman Context at the Villa of the Papyri at Herculaneum." *Art History* 17: 228–54.

Weis, A. 1992. *The Hanging Marsyas and Its Copies. Roman Innovations in a Hellenistic Sculptural Tradition*. Rome: Giorgio Bretschneider.

Wünsche, R. 1972. "Der Jüngling vom Magdalensberg: Studie zur römischen Idealplastik." In *Festschrift Luitpold Dussler*, edited by J. A. Schmoll, M. Restle, and H. Weiermann, 45–80. Munich: Deutsche Kunstverlag.

Zanker, P. 1974. *Klassizistische Statuen: Studien zur Veränderung des Kunstgeschmacks in der römischen Zeit*. Mainz: Philipp von Zabern.

———. 1979. "Zur Funktion und Bedeutung griechischer Skulptur in der Römerzeit." In *Le classicisme à Rome aux Iers. siècles avant et après J.C.*, edited by T. Gelzer, H. Flashar, and O. Reverdin, 283–314. Geneva: Fondation Hardt.

———. 1992. "Nachahmen als kulturelles Schicksal." In *Probleme der Kopie von der Antike bis zum 19. Jahrhundert*, edited by C. Lenz, 9–24. Munich: Bayerische Staatsgemäldesammlungen.

CHAPTER 3.4

PORTRAITURE

SUSAN WOOD

Introduction: Function and Context

Portraits, which we shall define here as recognizable likenesses of individuals, were ubiquitous in the ancient Roman world. People of the empire did not merely observe these images, but interacted with them in politics, religious ritual, and even the most banal of everyday activities. An exchange of money, for example, always involved at least a passing glance at the faces on the obverses of coins, and from the late Republic onward, those obverses frequently bore portrait profiles. The identity of that person, and the authority that his image conveyed, were instantly recognizable throughout the empire (Matt. 22:20–21). Sculptural portraits were media for another sort of exchange: a display of gratitude or loyalty toward the honoree by his city, by his clients, or by the Roman Senate and People. Statues of prominent citizens decorated public spaces, sometimes in deliberately obstructive positions that made the honoree impossible to ignore or forget (Stewart 2003, 133–6). Annual rituals or distributions of food or money to the public might take place at those statues to ensure that the statue's meaning would remain fresh in people's minds (Fejfer 2008, 66–70, 223–4; see essay 4.6, Kellum).

Architectural niches in public buildings usually held sculpture, including portrait statues of imperial figures and of prominent local citizens (see essay 4.1, Longfellow). The former would demonstrate the loyalty of the community to Rome, their acceptance of the emperor's legitimate authority and that of his chosen heirs (Pollini 1987; Rose 1997). The latter would usually honor the patron whose euergetism had paid for the building's construction. Portrait images also appeared in relief, on public monuments like the Ara Pacis, and on private sarcophagi. Both types of work could show the portrait figure interacting either with human or with divine and mythological figures.

The home of an elite family might boast several types of portraits. During the time of the Republic, these so-called *imagines* could include wax masks of the family's prominent men (Pollini 2012, 29–39). These were functional objects, through which actors would reanimate these ancestors by literally impersonating them—assuming their *personae* (masks)—during the funerals of family members. At other times, the shrines that contained those masks would advertise the family's aristocratic lineage to visitors. Later, during the empire, marble or bronze herms and busts replaced the fragile masks in the atrium (figure 3.4.1). These more durable objects did not need protective containers, thus allowing the clients of an elite citizen to admire his illustrious ancestors every time they entered the atrium of his house (Fejfer 2008, 90–91). Portraits of historical figures such as philosophers, poets, and intellectuals might also decorate an aristocratic residence like the Villa of the Papyri at Herculaneum (see essays 2.4, Mattusch; 3.3, Anguissola; 4.3, Gazda; and 6.1, Squire). These too could have functional as well as decorative value. An elite man's activities would entail public speaking. Meaningful objects in familiar settings, such as these images of literati, could serve as mnemonics for composing and memorizing orations (Quint. *Inst.* 11.2. 17–21). Another venue for portraits was the tombs that lined roadsides outside city gates. These monuments often sought to perpetuate the memory of loved ones by capturing the attention of passersby. A traveler might pause to admire a beautifully or innovatively designed tomb, perhaps to rest on a convenient bench in a shady garden provided for his benefit, to contemplate the images of the deceased and to read their names (Petron. *Sat.* 71; Davies 2000; Petersen 2003; Fejfer 2008, 105–110). Within the tombs, portrait likenesses in statuary or on sarcophagi

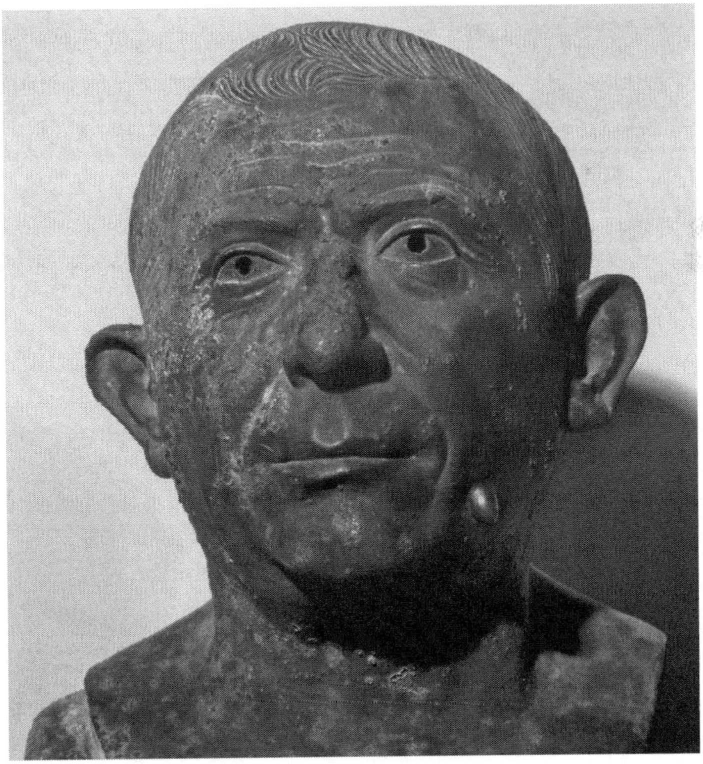

FIGURE 3.4.1 Portrait herm of Lucius Caecilius Iucundus, from the atrium of his house in Pompeii. Museo Archeologico Nazionale di Napoli.

served a more intimate audience, the living relatives who paid their respects to the dead on holidays like the *Rosalia* and *Parentalia*. Privately owned luxury objects such as cameos decorated with individual or group portraits might serve the dual purpose of ostentation and declaration of political loyalty or personal attachment.

The concept of the individualized portrait was not unique to any one ancient culture, but clearly it found enthusiastic reception in the culture of Rome. A society that attached great significance to veneration of ancestors would welcome a way to preserve the likeness of a parent or grandparent, along with his name and the record of his accomplishments. Meanwhile, a candidate for public office had to perform an *ambitio*, or "making of the rounds," during which this literally *ambitious* man made his face and name familiar to voters. A man lucky enough to be honored with a public statue, or to have an ancestor thus honored, possessed a great advantage in achieving recognition (Stewart 2003, 129–30). And as the territories of Rome expanded, the empire's subjects in far-flung provinces needed some way to display their respect to powerful figures, even when those men were not physically present. A portrait statue in these circumstances could make an acceptable substitute for the man himself (Tanner 2000, 31–6). In later years, the statue of the absent emperor conferred legitimacy on governmental proceedings by embodying his authority.

Problems and Issues

For obvious reasons, then, Roman portrait images have been a focus of interest for centuries for collectors, historians, antiquarians, archaeologists, and art historians. But there are numerous issues surrounding their study. Most surviving portraits are fragmentary and bereft of context; information that would have been immediately apparent to an ancient observer often requires laborious detective work to understand. Coins typically preserve not only a face but also an inscription that provide the individual's name. However, numismatic portraits are tiny and show only a profile view. Sculptures, which typically break at narrow points, seldom survive with portrait head and body in one piece, and indeed were frequently not made that way in the first place. Portrait specialists routinely carved acrolithic heads for insertion into separate torsos. Complicating the issue still further, a portrait might change identities in antiquity through recutting or the simple substitution of one portrait head for another (see essay 2.3, Varner). Images of emperors who came to bad ends, such as Nero and Domitian, frequently underwent such a fate (Varner 2004; see essays 2.3, Varner; and 6.6, Kristensen). Sometimes, the identity of the original subject is relatively easy to determine. In other cases, signs of reworking may be obvious, but the earlier form more difficult to reconstruct. Pollini and Storage (2012) have recently employed digital scanning and computer modeling to test some hypotheses about recutting (see essay 1.5, Frischer).

During the later third and fourth centuries, economic breakdown and lack of readily available stone encouraged the reuse of earlier sculpture (see essay 3.8, Witschel).

Recutting, indeed, drove many stylistic changes during that period (Prusac 2011, 47–78). Sometimes, the secondary sculptor might simply remove the hair or beard, replacing it with linear chisel strokes that indicated short stubble. Other portraits reveal more extensive alteration (e.g., figure 2.3.4, Museo Capitolino inv. no. 488: Fittschen and Zanker 1983–2010, 3: 104–6, no. 155, pl. 182–3). The traits that give many third-century and later portraits their compelling power are precisely those likely to result from recutting: large, deeply set eyes with highly arched upper lids, elongated faces with strongly undulating contours, deep furrows that tear through masses of stone, or, conversely, short and compact faces with geometrically simplified features (figure 3.4.2). Many such characteristics, initially imposed by technical restrictions, eventually became codified in Byzantine icon painting (L'Orange 1973, 32–42; Sande 1993).

Alterations to portraits continued long after antiquity. Collectors and dealers did and sometimes still do restore headless statues with alien portraits, creating new and deceptive contexts for both components. And if it is rare for a statue to survive with its original head, the survival of a statue with its original inscribed base is even rarer (see essay 4.5, Tuck). Not even the archaeological provenance of many surviving objects can be ascertained. How, then, are we to understand these objects in their rich nexus of social functions and connections?

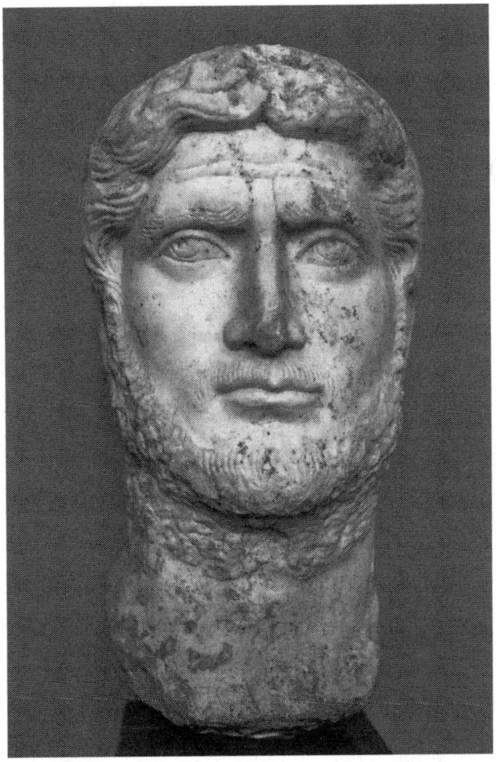

FIGURE 3.4.2 Colossal portrait head of Gallienus, probably recut from a portrait of Hadrian. Copenhagen, Ny Carlsberg Glyptotek.

Iconography and Typology

The first question that any surviving portrait presents is tedious but necessary: whom does this work represent? When the subject is a private person, the answer can seldom be more than generic: "a Roman citizen," "a freedman," "a priestess of Isis," "a military officer." If the portrait represents an emperor or a member the imperial family, however, we can often attach both a name and a biography to the face. Coins bear both identifying inscriptions and portraits that allow us to match the (admittedly tiny) profiles and hairstyles of the individual with works in other media. Hair, indeed, is likely to be replicated with more precision than facial features, since a linear pattern is easier to copy accurately than the subtle nuances of physiognomy. Even if coin portraits are not available, we can sometimes deduce identity from archaeological context. If a portrait survives together with other identifiable sculptures, for example, we can occasionally infer kinship between the subjects of the portraits. Wealthy and prolific philanthropists like Herodes Atticus sponsored building projects with accompanying portrait statue groups that enable us to identify the patron himself, members of his family, and close associates.

Another scholarly concern is typology: identifying replicas that recognizably follow a common original. Roman artists had the means to duplicate sculptures with considerable fidelity. Bronzes could be cast in multiple copies from molds (see essays 2.4, Mattusch; and 3.3, Anguissola), while marble carvers could use measuring devices to triangulate key points in three dimensions, allowing accurate reproduction of volumes (Pfanner 1989; see essay 3.3, Anguissola). Every replica, however, would reflect the distinctive techniques of its workshop, and would differ subtly from others. Determining which works follow a common original despite their individual variations and which do not, despite a general similarity to the type, is a necessary task. Such types can frequently be recognized even when we cannot name the person they represent: for example, prominent men of the Roman Republic who merited numerous public statues, but did not appear on coinage (Megow 2005). Most museum catalogs and other such standard reference works on portrait sculpture necessarily devote their primary attention to these issues of identification, both of the subject and of his or her portrait type (e.g., Poulsen 1962–74; Kersauson 1986–96; Kleiner 1992; Johansen 1994–5; and the series *Das römische Herrscherbild*).

Complicating the issue of typology is the fact that a public figure might have more than one official portrait type (Carandini 1969; Fittschen 1982; Flory 1993; Winkes 1995; Bartman 1998). A new portrait generally commemorated some important event, but a change in the style of a portrait could also signal a shift in the focus of political rhetoric. Portraits of Rome's first emperor, Augustus, for example, display consistently recognizable features and proportions throughout his life, but demonstrate marked stylistic changes. Octavian Caesar's early portraits from the time of the civil wars are dramatically expressive, with thick, wind-blown hair, an intense expression, a strong turn of the neck, and—frequently—an upturned gaze. These likenesses emphasize his precocious charisma by inviting comparison with Alexander the Great. Some of his statues, furthermore, appear to have represented him in complete or partial nudity, like a Hellenistic king or legendary hero. After he became emperor and acquired the title Augustus in 27 BC, his likenesses take on serene expressions and quieter poses, suitable to the founder of the Pax Augusta (figure 3.4.3). The statues in heroic costume give way to presentations of the first citizen in his strictly mortal and constitutional capacities, wearing the toga or military armor (Hallett 2005, 160–69). Having consolidated his power, Augustus needed to convince the Roman Senate that he did not have regal ambitions and intended to exercise only the authority that they granted to him.

Once an emperor had disseminated these prototypes to copyists, however, he effectively lost control over them. Members of the imperial family rarely dedicated their own statues. Such an honor had to be conferred on one by others, and the recipient was expected to act with due modesty about accepting (Stewart 2008, 103–5). The tastes and aesthetic goals of the patron, then, undoubtedly affected the interpretation of the type. Furthermore, the process of copying inevitably introduced variations that were then perpetuated, as those replicas in turn provided models for later portraits (Albertson 2004). Regional tastes in the provinces would assert themselves in these replica series along with the official style of Rome. At Aphrodisias, for example, the Sebasteion reliefs

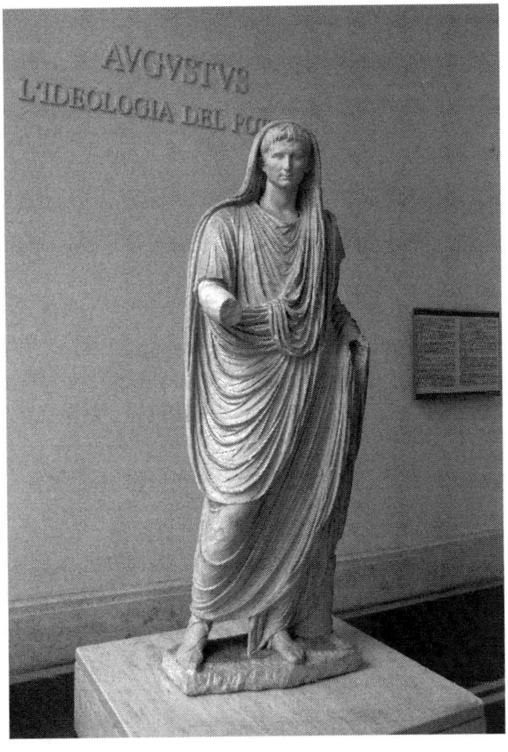

FIGURE 3.4.3 Portrait statue of Augustus wearing the toga and preparing to sacrifice, from the Via Labicana. Rome, Museo Nazionale Romano, Palazzo Massimo.

represented the Julio-Claudians in recognizable, if sometimes rather simplified, copies of their official types (Smith 2006, 47; see essay 4.6, Kellum). But the local sculptors placed these figures into narrative compositions that had no precedents in art from the capital (Smith 1987, 99–101, 116–17). At Perge, the city gate of Plancia Magna displayed portrait statues of imperial women that ignored official prototypes altogether, following the older Hellenistic tradition of purely idealized representations on which inscriptions conferred identity by fiat. The local patron, Plancia Magna, whose statue was found just outside this gate and evidently stood on a display wall along the roadside, likewise appeared in an ideal, classical format. Neither she nor the imperial women wore contemporary coiffures (Inan and Rosenbaum 1966, 72–3, no. 36, 78, no. 47; Inan and Alföldi-Rosenbaum 1979, 248, no. 225, pls. 158.1–3, 159, 160.2, 271.4; Alexandridis 2004, 239, 2.2.12, no. 14; Dillon 2010, 156–9). Emperors might place some restrictions on how they were to be represented: Domitian, for example, required that in the sacred space of the Capitoline, no images of him were to be set up except in precious metals and of a minimum weight (Suet. *Dom.* 13.2). This order may have reflected Domitian's megalomania, as later historians assume, or perhaps a desire to ensure that any votive offerings to Jupiter in his image were worthy of their surroundings. In any case, these statues also illustrate another way in which Domitian lost control over his likenesses: after his assassination, all of them were melted down (Plin. *Pan.* 52, 1–5).

Portrait iconography and typology, then, have always been dominant concerns of scholars, prompting some to wonder when we will ever be able to proceed beyond them. The answer to that question, unfortunately, is never, or at least not as long as new material continues to emerge. Identification should never be an end in itself, but we must always be prepared for the discovery that will demolish elegant theories. One example can suffice for all: the excavations of the Antonine period theater at Sessa Aurunca in Italy yielded a magnificent polychrome marble statue that must have stood in the most prestigious location of the *scaenae frons*, directly above the central door of the stage (Sessa Aurunca Castello Ducale inv. no. 297048; Cascella 2002, 67, no. 6, 71–3, figs. 36–9; Reggiani 2004a, 128–33; 2004b, 12–14, fig. 2). The woman whom the statue represents does not appear on any extant imperial coins. Inscriptions, however, establish that the patron who rebuilt the theater after an earthquake was Mindia Matidia, the great-niece of the emperor Trajan, sister-in-law of Hadrian, and aunt by adoption of Antoninus. The statue in the place of honor, therefore, almost certainly represented Matidia—and its identification in turn allows us to attach that name to five extant replicas of the same portrait type (Fittschen 1996, 46–7).

The discoveries at Sessa Aurunca not only provide us with a name for these six portraits, but also require us to discard earlier proposals for their identification. We must now reject a once-plausible effort by Hausmann (1959, 200–202) to recognize Matidia in the magnificent Busta Fonseca, one of the most justly famous extant Roman portrait sculptures (Rome, Museo Capitolino, inv. no. 434; Fittschen and Zanker 1983–2010, 3: 53–4, no. 69, pl. 86–7). The temptation to attach a distinguished name to such a distinguished work is intense, but the lady's facial structure and proportions differ too much from those of the Sessa Aurunca type to support the identification. She must therefore be sadly relegated once again to the status of "Private citizen, name unknown." In other respects, however, the Busta Fonseca does not need a name to be understood in a broader context. The sheer virtuosity both of the marble carving and of the flamboyant coiffure that it reproduces tells us volumes about the wealth, ostentation, and competition to display status among the Roman elite (Fejfer 2008, 351–7). The coiffure would have demanded the skilled labors of at least two and perhaps more hairdressers and probably an hour or more of patience on the part of the lady herself (Stephens 2008, 125–31, figs. 20, 21; 2012).

Formal Analysis

Roman patrons and sculptors had access to a variety of styles, which they could use contemporaneously, and often even within the same monument, depending on what they deemed appropriate for the setting. Stylistic analysis, then, is rarely useful for determining dates of Roman sculpture (see essay 3.1, Fullerton). On the other hand, stylistic analysis of a portrait does yield information about the ethos that the patron wished to convey. Imperial portraits, by definition, reflect the political rhetoric and agenda of the current *princeps*, who might present himself as a warrior, philosopher, demigod, or unpretentious mortal, depending on circumstances. Portrait sculptors attempting to convey these personae might choose from idealized or veristic, ornate or austere, serene or emotional styles, to name a few of their options.

Imperial tastes would inspire emulation by private citizens, but adoption of the official style was never universal. At Pompeii, where the disaster of AD 79 preserved many works in datable contexts, portraits of private citizens continued to follow the harshly realistic style of the Republic well into the period of the empire (figure 3.4.1), although the Augustan and Julio-Claudian preference for youthful, idealized images (figure 3.4.3) dominated imperial sculpture (Welch 2007, 566–73). Within the atria of private homes, where a family displayed its social status and lineage, many patrons preferred an emphasis on maturity and experience. The prosperous freedmen of Pompeii, like newly rich people everywhere, enthusiastically embraced this traditional style of the older elite.

Body Types and Meaning

Clothing, jewelry, and similar attributes instantly communicated information to the Roman viewer that is often lost to us (Sensi 1980–81; Wrede 1981; Mikocki 1995; Sebesta and Bonfante 2001). We do know, however, many of the standard formulae for the bodies of statues, some but not all drawn from Greek prototypes: the cuirassed statue for a general or emperor, the togate figure for a male citizen, with the drapery drawn over his head if he is shown performing a sacrifice, a variety of draped figures for women (figure 3.4.4), and nude figures that assimilate the subject to a hero or deity. The great demand for portrait statues would have made the creation of original compositions for every statue utterly impractical. The technical demands of quarrying and transportation likewise favored the use of a few standard formats (Trimble 2011, 64–103). The bodies, unlike the heads, were rarely personal likenesses. Nude statues of women with realistically aged faces but the bodies of youthful, ideal Venus often amuse modern observers. They would not have made the same impression on an ancient viewer, who understood the voluptuous torso as a signifier of personal qualities rather than a literal representation (Stewart 2003, 51–4; Hallett 2005, 219–22; Fejfer 2008, 124–8). This sort of a statue, then, conveyed that the deceased had been a loving and beloved wife. Likewise, no one would have believed that the elderly Claudius or the portly Nero had the muscular bodies of Polykleitan athletes. Everyone, nonetheless, could understand the assimilation of the head of state to Jupiter, Sol, or Achilles. These bodies, often described as costumes, might find a better analogy in uniforms that signify group rather than personal identity. Judicial robes, clerical vestments, academic regalia, and white medical coats obscure rather than reveal individual form, but instantly convey authority, membership in an elite group, and—theoretically, at least—adherence to high moral and ethical standards.

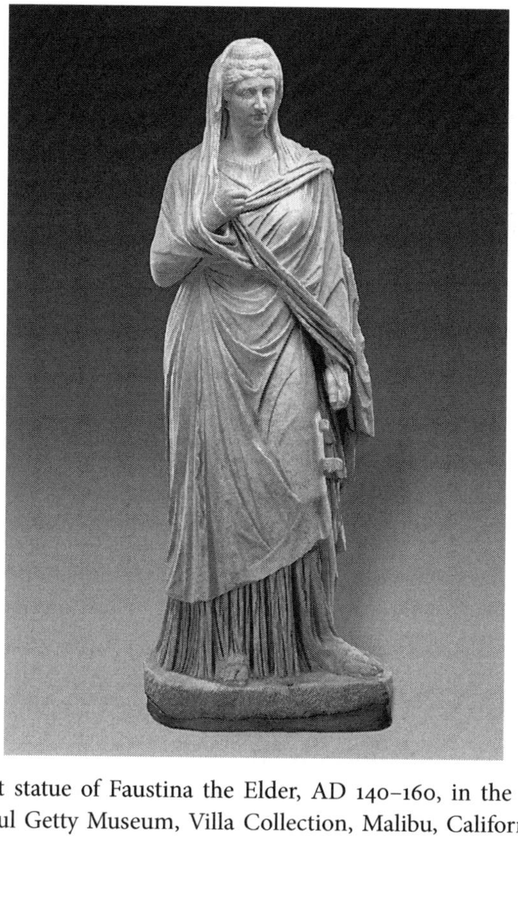

FIGURE 3.4.4 Portrait statue of Faustina the Elder, AD 140–160, in the Large Herculaneum Woman format. J. Paul Getty Museum, Villa Collection, Malibu, California.

Despite, or perhaps precisely because of, its repetitiveness, a widely used statuary format like the Large Herculaneum Woman (figure 3.4.4) communicated important information about the subject's wealth (the opulent layers of drapery), beauty, modesty, and social graces (Vorster 2007, 120–21; Dillon 2010, 60–102; Trimble 2011, 244–59). Furthermore, the formats could accommodate subtle variations, such as attributes in the hands and the presence or absence of a veil. Color could also have individualized the replicas. At least two statues of the Small Herculaneum type preserve traces of their original paint, and the two works clearly did not use the same color schemes (Wood 2008, 306–7; see essay 2.6, Abbe).

Cuirassed statues of generals likewise look monotonously, but deceptively, similar. These statues were probably roughed out at marble quarries into formulaic poses; at least one such unfinished statue has survived in the cargo of a shipwrecked vessel (Trimble 2011, 81–5, fig. 2.2; see essay 2.7, Russell). Buyers at the point of delivery could then have the statues completed according to their own specifications. Elements such as gorgoneia, griffins, victories, tritons, candelabrae, and floral ornaments appear again and again, yet these elements offer a surprisingly broad range of permutations (Stemmer 1978, 152–62). They could allude to victories by land or by sea, ongoing conflicts or successfully concluded campaigns, and could glorify a living emperor or a deified predecessor. Whether or not the emperor actually wore such a cuirass is as irrelevant as whether or not the torso accurately represents his physical proportions. These are ideological—as opposed to physical—representations of individuals.

Occasionally, however, an honorific statue might break surprisingly with tradition, adopting a body type that was unorthodox for portraiture. Mindia Matidia's image at Sessa Aurunca, for example, did not assume one of the standard formats for elite women. Instead, she appeared as an Aura, or breeze, in a running pose with filmy drapery that billowed around her in ornamental scrolls. The unorthodox choice may have made a punning reference to the name "Aurunca," transforming Matidia into a *genius loci* for the city, with its breezy hillside setting. It also required an impressive expenditure: this figure, unlike the popular draped types, did not have a compact or self-contained composition that made economic use of the stone. It was not cut from a single block but assembled from at least three of Aphrodisian marble and *bigio morato*, both of which were costly imports (Cascella 2012, 75). Such a unique and site-specific commission paid special honor to the patron by flaunting its expense.

Display Contexts

The original placement of a statue inevitably affected how viewers interacted with it. Scientifically excavated sites that allow us to reconstruct these settings are immensely valuable. The sculptural finds from the shrine of the Augustales at Misenum cast light on the cult of the imperial family, and of how that college of priests adapted to changing regimes (see essays 4.5, Tuck; and 4.6, Kellum). The building of Eumachia at Pompeii, the nymphaeum of Annia Regilla at Olympia (Pomeroy 2007, 84–103), and the city gate of Plancia Magna at Perge demonstrate how a local patron might appear in relation to imperial statues (see essays 4.5, Tuck; and 4.6, Kellum). The living donor and his or her living relatives might appear in the same structure or façade, but at a different level from the imperial statues, or the donor's statue might appear near, but not within, the structure where the imperial statues stood. The city gate of Plancia Magna at Perge illustrates this latter approach: a statue of Plancia Magna and another base that once supported a bronze statue of the same lady came to light near, but significantly not within, the horseshoe-shaped enclosure of the gate where the imperial statues appeared. The marble statue of Plancia Magna, however, also demonstrates that a statue might have had more than one context in antiquity. A handsome display wall on the exterior of the public baths just outside the city gate flanked the courtyard that led to Plancia Magna's city gate. The marble portrait statue of Plancia Magna stood in a niche of that wall—which postdated her lifetime by more than half a century. The Severan-era wall may have replaced an earlier one at the same location, but perhaps the statue originally stood elsewhere (Fejfer 2008, 363–5, fig. 302 E; Trimble 2011, 166–9, fig. 4.6).

At some sites, excavators can reconstruct the positions of the statues in an architectural setting, because statues have remained more or less where they fell when the building collapsed. Archaeological context, however, is not always the same thing as original setting. Sculptures could be moved from their original locations and sometimes repurposed; a statue might have more than one context in antiquity as well as in later periods (Stewart 2003, 129–30; Plin. *HN* 34.30). Even when works do not survive in their original placements, however, or do not survive at all, it is sometimes possible to reconstruct the composition of public statuary groups from inscriptions and other such evidence (Rose 1997; Boschung 2002; Ruck 2007; see essay 4.5, Tuck).

Regional Styles

In an empire as large and culturally diverse as Rome's, distinctive regional responses to portraiture, as to any other art form, inevitably develop (see essays in part V, Regions and Provinces). Some cities of Greece and Asia Minor already had strongly established sculptural traditions of their own that continued to thrive after the Roman conquest. Other regions, like Britain, had virtually no traditions of statuary, and have yielded hardly any portrait sculpture from the Roman period (Stewart 2003, 174–9; see essay 5.1, Cassibry). But in some provinces and regions, we find a cross-fertilization of Graeco-Roman traditions with very different local aesthetics.

The sculpture of Roman Egypt demonstrates this sort of hybridization (see essay 5.6, Riggs). In the antechamber of the well-preserved Kom el-Shoqafa catacomb at Alexandria stood two portrait statues, a male and a female. The man's face is furrowed with age, his frowning expression conveying Roman *gravitas*. He wears a full mass of curly hair that reveals slight balding at the temples and crown. The woman's face is more youthful, and she wears her hair in the same fashion as Caligula's sisters. From the necks downward, however, both these statues are entirely Pharaonic in their stances, proportions, and drapery: the man wears a traditional kilt, the woman a tight linen sheath-dress (Venit 2002, 129–34, figs. 108–111). Other Egyptian statuary from the Roman period melds the two traditions more completely: seated figures wear Graeco-Roman costume and hold Roman funerary garlands. They sit, however, in rigidly frontal poses, hands resting on their knees, their bodies rendered in the blocky form of Pharaonic art (Albertson 2002–3).

At the Syrian frontier city of Palmyra, we see a comparable phenomenon. Palmyrene tombs, like those of Italy, featured individualized portrait busts of deceased family members. Most of the Palmyrenes whom these reliefs represent wore Greek garments draped in well-established patterns. Men would loop the himation around the shoulders, forming a sling under the right arm, while matrons would demurely adjust their veils, a gesture of modesty equally familiar in Greek and Roman art. The sharp-edged carving of the features, however, and the decoratively linear hair and drapery have roots in Parthian art. Some attributes and items of clothing are likewise local, such as the ornate turbans of the women, while certain mannered and formulaic gestures repeat themselves frequently (Skupińska-Løvset 1999; Heyn 2010). The unique fusion of Parthian and classical elements formed a style that is instantly recognizable even in objects that have long since left their place of origin (Fejfer 2008, 163–6, pl. 17).

Conclusion: Reconstructing Contexts

In recent decades, scholars have achieved remarkable recontextualizations of ancient sculpture through archival research, and have sometimes reunited ancient works in ways that illuminate their meaning. The excavation records of the Horti Lamiani in Rome, for example, cast surprising new light on the original display of the well-known bust of Commodus as Hercules. The bust had been discovered between torsos of tritons that had probably flanked and supported the portrait within a circular frame (Cima and LaRocca 1986, 88–94, 173–6). This composition is familiar from sarcophagi, in which sea creatures carry an *imago clipeata* of the deceased. That funerary imagery, in turn, identifies this sculpture as a posthumous image of Commodus, after Septimius Severus had rehabilitated and deified him. A sculpture formerly interpreted to reflect the absurd megalomania of a bad emperor, then, takes on a new meaning. The rhetoric of Commodus's Hercules portrait is not egomaniacal but elegiac. It presents an eloquent, albeit thoroughly false, representation of a good ruler who has died young but whose noble deeds have won him immortality.

Conventional drawings, three-dimensional models, and plaster casts have always been valuable tools, but computer modeling has opened up a dramatic range of possibilities for studying ancient portraiture and for reconstructing its architectural settings (see essay 1.5, Frischer). While several digitally-based research projects are discussed elsewhere in this volume, here it seems useful to highlight one that involves a very famous Roman imperial portrait, its history of display, and the stewardship of cultural heritage. Digital image files were used to replicate the equestrian statue of Marcus Aurelius, when the fragile condition of the original bronze required its removal to an indoor display. During the process, nothing touched the delicate ancient surface except a laser beam that recorded measurements, from which numerically controlled machining then produced a three dimensional replica. Conservators then took molds not from the original but from this replica to produce the bronze copy that now stands on the Campidoglio. The twentieth-century bronze replica preserves the focus of Michaelangelo's magnificent architectural design, as well as one of the statue's historical contexts, while the original now stands inside the Palazzo dei Conservatori.

Finally, the most indispensable and yet frustratingly elusive context in which we must attempt to understand portraits is that of the societies that produced them: the economic forces that drove patronage and production; the values that the works of art reflected; the religious beliefs for which they sometimes served a ritual function; and the social hierarchies that they demonstrated and affirmed. When context or inscriptions allow us to recognize a portrait relief as a family of freedmen, for example, the ways in which the subjects present themselves can tell us much both about their actual status in society and their aspirations (Kockel 1993, 49–55). Imperial images, as noted above, necessarily carry political meaning. However, in this area our reconstructions of ancient art depend on the most fragile of evidence, the most subjective interpretations, and the methods most susceptible to personal bias.

The study of Roman art and archaeology is inextricable from the study of portrait likenesses and vice versa. Scholars of the last thirty years have rightly focused on understanding these works in their contexts: physical, historical, political, social, and ritualistic. Any effort to reconstruct context, however, must begin with careful examination of the object, its current condition, apparent original form, and, if possible, place of discovery. Reconstruction of contexts demands collaboration among art historians, field archaeologists, numismatists, epigraphers, philologists, geologists, mineralogists, and computer engineers. Collaborations between academics, collectors, and museums have produced significant results, particularly in the plan and realization of exhibitions. The Horti Lamiani exhibition, mentioned above, is an impressive example of such recontextualized ancient objects. Another is the loan of the Large and Small Herculaneum Women from the Dresden Albertinum to the J. Paul Getty Museum, which produced an informative exhibition and much valuable new scholarship by both German and American archaeologists (Daehner 2007). And all of us share a mutual responsibility to protect the integrity of archaeological sites and to discourage clandestine excavation, which destroys or damages huge volumes of irreplaceable information. Archaeological sites of the Roman Empire will continue to yield likenesses of individuals as long as sites remain to be excavated. The identities of those portrait subjects and the settings and functions of their images will continue to enlarge, enrich, and sometimes unexpectedly change our understanding of life, death, religion, and politics in the Roman Empire.

Bibliography

Albertson, F. C. 2002–3. "Two Limestone Statues from Roman Egypt." *Cantor Arts Center Journal* 3: 6–15.

———. 2004. "The Creation and Dissemination of Roman Imperial Portrait Types: The Case of Marcus Aurelius Type IV." *JdI* 119: 259–306.

Alexandridis, A. 2004. *Die Frauen des römischen Kaiserhauses: Eine Untersuchung ihrer bildlichen Darstellung von Livia bis Iulia Domna*. Mainz: Philipp von Zabern.

Bartman, E. 1998. *Portraits of Livia: Imaging the Imperial Woman in Augustan Rome*. Cambridge: Cambridge University Press.

Boschung, D. 2002. *Gens Augusta: Untersuchungen zu Aufstellung, Wirkung und Bedeutung der Statuengruppen des julisch-claudischen Kaiserhauses*. Monumenta Artis Romanae 32. Mainz: Philipp von Zabern.

Carandini, A. 1969. *Vibia Sabina*. Florence: Leo S. Olschki.

Cascella, S. 2002. *Il Teatro Romano di Sessa Aurunca*. Marina di Minturno: Caramanica Editore.

———. 2012. "Uso e riuso dell'antico a Sessa Aurunca (DE): Il caso dei marmi del teatro Romano." *Diagnosis for the Conservation and Valorization of Cultural Heritage: Atti del Terzo Convegno Internationale*, edited by L. Campanella and C. Piccioli, 62–84. Naples: Diagnosis of Cultural Heritage. http://www.diagnosisculturalheritage.com/index.php/book/book-2012.

Cima, M., and E. La Rocca, eds. 1986. *Le Tranquille dimore degli dei: La residenza imperiale degli Horti Lamiani*. Venice: Marsilio.

Daehner, J., ed. 2007. *The Herculaneum Women: History, Context, Identities*. Los Angeles: J. Paul Getty Museum.

Davies, P. J. E. 2000. *Death and the Emperor: Roman Imperial Funerary Monuments from Augustus to Marcus Aurelius*. Cambridge: Cambridge University Press.

Deutsches Archäologisches Institut. 1939–. *Das römisches Herrscherbild*. 14 vols. Berlin: Mann.

Dillon, S. 2010. *The Female Portrait Statue in the Greek World*. Cambridge: Cambridge University Press.

Fejfer, J. 2008. *Roman Portraits in Context*. Berlin: Walter de Gruyter.

Fittschen, K. 1982. *Die Bildnistypen der Faustina Minor und die Fecunditas Augusta*. AbhGött 126 ser. 3. Göttingen: Vandernhoeck and Ruprecht.

———. 1996. "Courtly Portraits of Women in the Era of the Adoptive Emperors (98–180) and their Reception in Roman Society." In *I Claudia: Women in Ancient Rome*, edited by D. E. E. Kleiner and S. B. Matheson, 42–52. Austin: University of Texas Press.

Fittschen, K., and P. Zanker. 1983–2010. *Katalog der römischen Porträts in den Capitolinischen Museen und den anderen kommunalen Sammlungen der Stadt Rom*. 3 vols. Berlin: Philipp von Zabern.

Flory, M. 1993. "Livia and the History of Public Honorific Statues for Women in Rome." *TAPA* 123: 287–308.

Hallett, C. H. 2005. *The Roman Nude: Heroic Portrait Statuary, 200 BC–AD 300*. Oxford: Oxford University Press.

Hausmann, U. 1959. "Bildnisse zweier junger Römerinnen in Fiesole." *JdI* 74: 164–202.

Heyn, M. K. 2010. "Gesture and Identity in the Funerary Art of Palmyra." *AJA* 114(4): 631–61.

Inan, J., and E. Alföldi-Rosenbaum. 1979. *Römische und frühbyzantinische Porträtplastik aus der Türkei: Neue Funde*. Mainz: Philipp von Zabern.

Inan, J., and E. Rosenbaum. 1966. *Roman and Early Byzantine Portrait Sculpture in Asia Minor*. London: Oxford University Press.

Johansen, F. 1994–5. *Roman Portraits*. 3 vols. Copenhagen: Ny Carlsberg Glyptotek.

Kersauson, K. de. 1986–96. *Catalogue des portraits romains*. Vol. 1, *Portraits de la République et d'époque Julio-Claudienne*. Vol. 2, *De l'année de la guerre civile (68–69 après J.-C.) à la fin de l'Empire*. Paris: Editions de la Réunion des musées nationaux.

Kleiner, D. E. E. 1992. *Roman Sculpture*. New Haven: Yale University Press.

Kockel, V. 1993. *Porträtreliefs stadtrömischer Grabbauten: Ein Beitrag zur Geschichte und zum Verständnis des spätrepublikanisch-frühkaiserzeitlichen Privatporträts*. Mainz: Philipp von Zabern.

L'Orange, H. P. 1973. *Likeness and Icon*. Odense: Odense University Press.

Megow, W.-R. 2005. *Republikanische Bildnis-Typen*. Frankfurt: Peter Lang.

Mikocki, T. 1995. *Sub specie deae: Les impératrices et princesses romaines assimilées à des déesses: Etude iconologique*. RdA Supplement 14. Rome: "L'Erma" di Bretschneider.

Petersen, L. H. 2003. "The Baker, His Tomb, His Wife, and Her Breadbasket." *ArtB* 85(2): 230–57.

Pfanner, M. 1989. "Über das Herstellen von Porträts: Ein Beitrag zu Rationalisierungsmaßnahmen und Produktionsmechanismen von Massenware im späten Hellenismus und in der römischen Kaiserzeit." *JdI* 104: 157–257.

Pollini, J. 1987. *The Portraiture of Gaius and Lucius Caesar*. New York: Fordham University Press.

———. 2012. *From Republic to Empire: Rhetoric, Religion, and Power in the Visual Culture of Ancient Rome*. Norman: University of Oklahoma Press.

Pollini, J., and W. Storage. 2012. "Computer Technology and Three-Dimensional Models in Determining the Recutting of Roman Portraits: The Getty Augustus." In *Interdisciplinary Studies on Ancient Stone. ASMOSIA 9*. Documenta 23, edited by A. Gutiérrez, P. Lapuente, and I. Rodà, 31–7. Tarragona: Institut Català d'Arqueologia Clàssica.

Pomeroy, S. 2007. *The Murder of Regilla: A Case of Domestic Violence in Antiquity*. Cambridge, MA: Harvard University Press.

Poulsen, V. 1962–74. *Les portraits Romains*. 2 vols. Copenhagen: Munksgaard.

Prusac, M. 2011. *From Face to Face: Recarving of Roman Portraits and the Late-Antique Portrait Arts*. Leiden: Brill.

Reggiani, A. M., ed. 2004a. *Adriano: Le Memorie al Femminile*. Milan: Electa.

Reggiani, A. M. 2004b. "Un Ritratto di Matidia Minore da Tivoli e la galleria celebrativa della Domus Augusta." In *Lazio e Sabina* 2, edited by J. R. Brandt, X. Dupré i Raventós and G. Ghini, 11–22. Rome: De Luca.

Rose, C. B. 1997. *Dynastic Commemoration and Imperial Portraiture in the Julio-Claudian Period*. Cambridge: Cambridge University Press.

Ruck, B. 2007. *Die Grossen dieser Welt: Kolossalporträts im antiken Rom*. Archäologie und Geschichte 11. Heidelberg: Verlag Archäologie und Geschichte.

Sande, S. 1993. "The Icon and its Origin in Graeco-Roman Portraiture." In *Aspects of Late Antiquity and Early Byzantium*, edited by L. Rydén and J. O. Rosenqvist, 75–84. Stockholm: Svenska forskningsinstitutet i Istanbul.

Sebesta, J. L., and L. Bonfante, eds. 2001. *The World of Roman Costume*. Madison: University of Wisconsin Press.

Sensi, L. 1980–81. "Ornatus e status sociale delle donne romane." *AnnPerugia* 18: 55–102.

Skupińska-Løvset, I. 1999. *Portraiture in Roman Syria: A Study in Social and Regional Differentiation within the Art of Portraiture*. Łódź: Wydawnictwo Uniwersytetu Łódzkiego.

Smith, R. R. R. 1987. "The Imperial Reliefs from the Sebasteion at Aphrodisias." *JRS* 77: 88–138.
———. 2006. *Roman Portrait Statuary from Aphrodisias*. Mainz: Philipp von Zabern.
Stemmer, K. 1978. *Untersuchungen zur Typologie, Chronologie und Ikonographie der Panzerstatuen*. Berlin: Mann.
Stephens, J. 2008. "Ancient Roman Hairdressing: On (Hair)pins and Needles." *JRA* 21: 110–32.
———. 2012. "Flavian-Trajanic Hairstyle: Orbis Comarum." YouTube.com, October 1. http://www.youtube.com/watch?v=Vs9fLwm-9-k.
Stewart, P. 2003. *Statues in Roman Society: Representation and Response*. Oxford: Oxford University Press.
———. 2008. *The Social History of Roman Art*. Cambridge: Cambridge University Press.
Tanner, J. J. 2000. "Portraits, Power, and Patronage in the Late Roman Republic." *JRS* 90: 18–50.
Trimble, J. 2011. *Women and Visual Replication in Roman Imperial Art and Culture*. Cambridge: Cambridge University Press.
Varner, E. 2004. *Mutilation and Transformation: "Damnatio Memoriae" and Roman Imperial Portraiture*. Leiden: Brill.
Venit, M. S. 2002. *Monumental Tombs of Ancient Alexandria: The Theatre of the Dead*. Cambridge: Cambridge University Press.
Vorster, C. 2007. "Greek Origins: The Herculaneum Women in the Pre-Roman World." In Daehner 2007, 113–39.
Welch, K. 2007. "Pompeian Men and Women in Portrait Sculpture." In *The World of Pompeii*, edited by P. Foss and J. Dobbins, 550–84. New York: Routledge.
Winkes, R. 1995. *Livia, Octavia, Julia*. Louvain-la-Neuve: Art and Archaeology Publications.
Wood, S. 2008. Review of Daehner 2007. *New England Classical Journal* 35(4): 304–7.
Wrede, H. 1981. *Consecratio in Formam Deorum: Vergöttlichte Privatpersonen in der römischen Kaiserzeit*. Mainz: Philipp von Zabern.

CHAPTER 3.5

MONUMENTAL RELIEFS

MELANIE GRUNOW SOBOCINSKI AND
ELIZABETH WOLFRAM THILL

Introduction

Since the formal study of Roman art began, monumental reliefs have featured prominently in the academic literature, including textbooks (D. E. E. Kleiner 1992) and historiographic studies (Brendel [1953] 1979; Kampen 2003; Elsner 2004). During early efforts to distinguish Roman from Greek art, monumental reliefs held center-stage as among the most indisputably "Roman" sculptures of the corpus. Scholars comparing Roman monumental reliefs to classical Greek architectural reliefs, which almost exclusively featured widely spaced mythological figures against an unsculpted background, argued that the handling of space and historicized narrative in the Roman works constituted the definitive stylistic features of a distinctive "Roman" art. Otto Brendel pointed out, however, that the eclectic yet synchronous styles and wide geographic spread of art under the Roman Empire made the hunt for definitive unifying features a futile exercise ([1953] 1979, with earlier bibliography).

Reliefs also played an important role in early analyses of eclecticism in Roman art. Ranuccio Bianchi Bandinelli's work on "Hellenistic" and "plebeian" styles in Roman art (1970), for example, depends heavily on monumental reliefs, from the so-called Altar of Domitius Ahenobarbus to the Column Base of Antoninus Pius. Indeed, many discussions of the artistic transition to late antiquity draw upon stylistic comparisons between the Column of Trajan and that of Marcus Aurelius or among the pastiche of reliefs on the Arch of Constantine (for a critical assessment, see Elsner 2000; for current approaches, see essay 3.8, Witschel).

Monumental reliefs also garnered attention due to their supposed connection to historic events. Beyond being interpreted as illustrations of events, those panels that seemed to be aligned with historical moments or periods (from the evidence of inscriptions and portrait heads) became linchpins in a methodology that employed stylistic analysis to determine chronology for otherwise undatable reliefs. Gerhard Koeppel's series of *Bonner Jahrbücher* articles (1983–92) represent one extreme in the spectrum of historical-stylistic analysis, attempting to put all known "historical" reliefs from the city of Rome into chronological order. He associated each relief with a historical monument or event if possible and, when not possible, with dates determined by fine-grained sequences of artistic styles. Although some of his chronological proposals are open to debate, Koeppel's articles remain an essential survey of the best-known reliefs and their bibliographies.

More recently, scholars have also analyzed monumental reliefs within their iconographic and physical contexts. Such studies often include other media, such as coins, gems, and privately commissioned sculpture, and the placement of reliefs within monuments and urban programs. Seminal works include Inez Scott Ryberg's study of the depiction of sacrifice (*Rites of the State Religion in Roman Art*, 1955) and Paul Zanker's assessment of the Augustan period (republished in translation as *The Power of Images in the Age of Augustus*, 1988). These two groundbreaking works demonstrate how the study of major monuments that preserve relief decoration can be integrated within broader studies of Roman society. Monumental reliefs have been also used as evidence to reconstruct the content or appearance of now-lost triumphal paintings (Lusnia 2006), pedimental groupings (Fishwick [2003] 2007), funerary practices and topographic sightlines (Davies 2000), and military commentaries and campaigns (Lepper and Frere 1988).

Nomenclature

Although the corpus of often large-scale public reliefs produced mainly under the Principate in Rome are among the best-known and most studied of Roman sculptures, questions of definition, function, and nomenclature for these reliefs have become unusually complicated and intertwined. The popular English nomenclatures "historical relief" and "state relief" both carry methodological baggage.

The term "historical relief" originated in the belief that a defining characteristic of this genre was the illustration of actual historical events (Strong 1907; Torelli 1982). This hypothesis concentrated interest on establishing a date for each piece, identifying which particular events were depicted, and integrating the interpreted images into the history of the relevant emperor's rule. Many scholars, however, have pointed out limitations in this approach. First, closer inspection reveals frequent difficulties in identifying individual historical events securely and evidence that reliefs often record idealized rather than "real" events. For example, scholars struggle to identify an appropriate historical procession for the reliefs of the Ara Pacis Augustae, since the individuals depicted were never all together in Rome around the time of the altar's establishment or dedication (in 13 and 9 BC, respectively; see Rose 1990; Billows 1993; Rehak 2001, 124–33). Clearly, the reliefs cannot be read in the same light as a journalistic photograph.

Second, such reliefs often include allegorical figures. To draw again from the Ara Pacis, the supposedly historical reliefs of the processions are only one part of the monument, which also included four smaller relief panels showing allegorical personifications and mythohistorical scenes (see essay 4.8, D'Ambra and Tronchin). The term "historical relief" is of limited value to describe a seated Roma, and referring to the altar as a "historical relief" monument privileges the procession reliefs in our modern understanding of the monument (Holliday 1990; Galinsky 1992). Furthermore, allegorical figures are often found within depictions of historical scenes, such as the Victory joining Titus in his triumphal chariot on the Arch of Titus (figure 3.5.1). Such inclusions belie the assumption that the primary intention of these reliefs was documentary.

A third, related problem with the term "historical relief" is that it tends to unduly emphasize the narrative elements of complex monuments. For instance, the majority of the Ara Pacis is covered by nonnarrative motifs, specifically simulacra of a traditional rustic shrine on the interior and vegetal designs on the exterior. Even the tiny animals found within the curving acanthus vines convey ideas of fertility and rebirth brought about in the new Augustan Golden Age (Kellum 1994). The nonnarrative relief elements are thus essential components of the overall theme of the monument, but are poorly served by the term "historical relief."

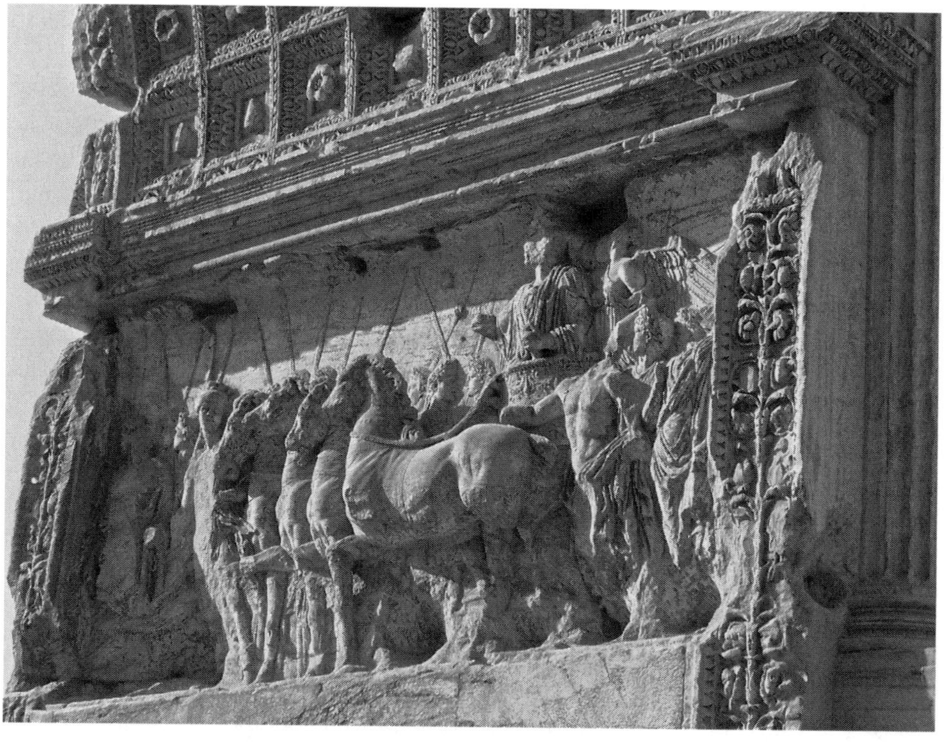

FIGURE 3.5.1 Chariot Relief, Arch of Titus, Rome.

The term "state relief" that has also been used to describe such relief sculptures (Hamberg 1945; Ryberg 1955) assumes a different unifying characteristic: their commission through official channels of the Roman state. As a result, "state relief" may be taken to imply a coordinated propagandistic effort on the part of state actors, along the lines of modern nation-states. This nomenclature privileges the questions of patronage and function and implies answers to those questions that the evidence does not necessarily support. Moreover, it favors the study of relief monuments from Rome itself and contributes to the neglect of provincial examples. The Roman governance, patronage, and honorary systems are all so different from those familiar today that such misleading language should be avoided if possible (Ewald and Noreña 2010).

In particular, despite the inscribed proclamations that relief monuments were dedicated by the Senate and people of Rome, the term "state relief" supports the traditional assumption that the emperor directed or at least approved the reliefs' designs. Recently, some scholars have tended toward more literal interpretations of the few dedicatory inscriptions that survive *in situ* with associated reliefs (e.g., the Arches of Septimius Severus and Constantine in Rome; see essays 4.5, Tuck; and 4.6, Kellum). They consider how the reliefs might have functioned within a complex dialogue between Senate and emperor, specifically as a means of expressing the Senate's expectations for proper imperial behavior (see the papers in Ewald and Noreña 2010, especially Mayer 2010). Such scholarship emphasizes that the Roman "state" was hardly a stable, uniform entity, and that the precise role of anyone vis-à-vis design and iconography is near impossible to determine even with epigraphic or literary evidence of patronage.

The challenge of interpreting preserved dedicatory inscriptions calls attention to another problem, namely that such inscriptions are rare exceptions, not the rule. For the majority of the reliefs in question, the use of the finest marbles, high-quality workmanship, large scale, and imperial iconographic themes (battle, *adlocutio, adventus*, triumph, sacrifice, apotheosis, etc.) generally imply installation on public structures, and thus the patron(s) must have expended extraordinary amounts, whether individually or as a group. Nevertheless, basing the nomenclature of an entire sculptural category on an assumption regarding patronage and imperial involvement, however likely, can be seen as problematic, especially given our limited evidence for the mechanisms of patronage.

The phrases "monumental relief," "commemorative relief," and the unadorned term "relief" are more neutral and therefore useful for scholars. We have titled this essay "monumental reliefs" because we wish to emphasize the importance of form and context for future innovative study of this material. The phrase "monumental reliefs" evokes, first of all, the scale and quality of the reliefs, as well as their architectural setting. While the original contexts of most reliefs have been lost, their original settings—whether arch, altar, temple, forum, or other public structure—contributed to the essential messages and visual effects of the reliefs and should not be neglected. Indeed, some Roman building types were optimized for the display of extensive relief programs (Hölscher 2009). The word "monumental" also evokes its etymological root, *monumentum*, a Latin word whose full meaning is not perfectly understood but which surely denoted something that commemorated a person, family, or event (Meadows and Williams 2001; see essay 4.4, Ewald).

Chronology and Distribution

The earliest surviving monumental reliefs from the Roman world date to the late republican period. While the prominence of relief ornamentation on so many different types of public buildings as seen in the Roman Empire was unprecedented, Etruscan (see essay 3.2, de Grummond) and Hellenistic antecedents (e.g., the Telephos Frieze of Pergamum; Dreyfus and Schraudolph 1996) need to be considered as part of this genre's development.

Though no precisely equivalent Greek reliefs survive, the earliest extant Roman reliefs have strong Hellenistic connections. The Monument of Aemilius Paullus in Delphi (168–167 BC) features a battle frieze against a flat background. The preserved dedicatory inscription records that the monument was taken by L. Aemilius Paullus from a defeated Macedonian king, leading to speculation as to whether the frieze was added or altered by its new Roman patron, and whether its imagery can be tied to historic events and the emergent medium of monumental reliefs (Kähler 1965; Boschung 2001). The so-called Altar of Domitius Ahenobarbus, recovered from the Campus Martius and also dated to the second century BC, combines a (possibly spoliated) frieze depicting a marine wedding procession with a scene depicting a census and a sacrifice overseen by Mars himself (Kuttner 1993; Stilp 2001). The relief from the Piazza della Consolazione, of uncertain date and significance, displays a series of military trophies without narrative context (Hölscher 1980; 1988, 384–6).

Republican monumental reliefs as preserved are thus an eclectic mixture that both differs from and anticipates later reliefs. The extent to which the competitive building projects in the late Republic included relief sculptures is uncertain, but by the Augustan period, high-quality reliefs often illustrating quasi-historical events regularly adorned public structures. The production of monumental reliefs would continue unabated in Rome until the third century AD, when civil wars brought about an abrupt halt. After a brief revival under the Tetrarchs and Constantine, monumental reliefs effectively ceased to be erected in Rome for centuries, although similar monuments were erected elsewhere (e.g., the Arch of Galerius in Thessaloniki: D. E. E. Kleiner 1992, 418–25; the Column of Theodosius in Istanbul: Becatti 1960).

Another interesting facet of monumental reliefs is their geographical distribution. The vast majority of monumental reliefs have been recovered in Rome itself. The few notable exceptions to this rule mostly seem to be connected to particular efforts to assert connections to Rome (see essays in part V, Regions and Provinces). Some of these reliefs, such as the so-called Tellus or Pax Relief from Carthage (now in the Louvre), seem to be close, if not exact, copies of monuments in the capital, in this case one panel of the Ara Pacis (Zanker 1988, 172–9, 313–15). Provincial monumental reliefs, however, often differ in key ways from their presumed models. The quality of production, the style, and the iconography vary more than in the capital. For example, compare the stylized figures in the processional frieze of the Augustan Arch in Susa (Fogliato 1992; Letta 2006–7; Moede 2007a) with the classicizing frieze of the Ara Pacis, or the abstract duels of Trajan's Tropaeum at Adamklissi (Florescu 1965; Coulston 2003) with the naturalistic battles of the Column of Trajan. The Sebasteion at Aphrodisias (Smith 2013) combines the general subject (praise of the imperial family) and style of monumental reliefs in Rome with (to our knowledge) unprecedented quantity, setting (190 panels in a monumental portico), and imagery (e.g., Claudius's Rape of Britannia). Apparent instances of monumental reliefs in the capital that influenced other media in the provinces are rare but not unknown: for example, the Monument of Philopappus borrows triumphal imagery from monuments such as the Arch of Titus (figure 3.5.1) and repurposes it for a funerary relief in Athens (figure 3.5.2; D. E. E. Kleiner 1992, 233–5).

It is nearly impossible to assess to what extent the reliefs that survive reflect what was actually produced. It is probably significant that so many reliefs have been recovered from Rome itself, although additional excavation and documentation throughout the empire will almost certainly bring forth previously unknown reliefs, such as the relief fragments from Nikopolis celebrating Augustus's victory at Actium (Greece; see essay 5.4, Sturgeon). At the same time, major monuments such as the Column of Theodosius have vanished within recorded memory (Becatti 1960). Some smaller-scale pieces, in stone and other media, have been interpreted as reproducing elements of long-lost monumental reliefs in Rome. For example, the silver cups from Boscoreale (buried by the eruption of Vesuvius in AD 79) feature high-relief elements that find parallels in much

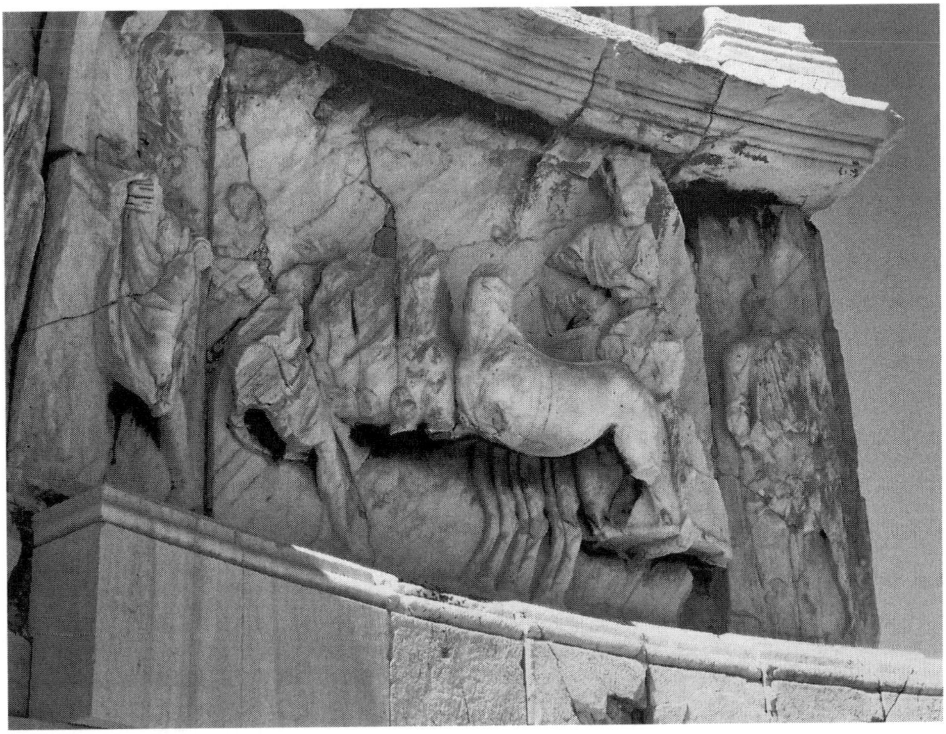

FIGURE 3.5.2 Detail of the relief from the Monument of Philopappus, Athens.

later monumental reliefs, leading to a hypothesized common model in Rome (Kuttner 1995). Such cautionary tales warn against taking the preserved corpus of monumental reliefs as an unambiguous sample of ancient production.

Methodology

The process of studying reliefs encompasses the techniques discussed elsewhere in this volume (attention to material, workmanship, polychromy, iconography, chronology, setting, function, reception, etc.), yet other considerations are particular to the genre. Since reliefs were inevitably embedded in larger monuments (such as columns, arches, altars, temples, tombs, etc.), the interpretation of a relief cannot be disentangled from its context. In relief, the individual units of iconographic analysis, including portraits and personifications, body types and clothing, equipment and attributes, animals and vegetation, representations of architecture and landscape features, are part of a larger composition, and much of the meaning is drawn from the interaction of elements. Tonio Hölscher's exploration of Roman art from a semiotic perspective ([1987] 2004) relies heavily upon reliefs to illustrate key points. Hölscher emphasizes that choices regarding iconography, composition, and style communicate ideological messages in addition to their literal content (see also Bal and Bryson 1991; Huet 1996; Elsner 2000).

Monuments frequently encompass many reliefs of different sizes. For instance, the Arch of Trajan at Beneventum includes twelve large panels on the main façades, a narrow, small-scale triumph frieze running around all four sides, two massive horizontal panels in the passageway, and a small square panel in the passageway vault (Rotili 1972). We caution that when working with a set of relief panels such as the two surviving Cancelleria reliefs, their original dimensions and the total quantity of relief on the monument for which they were carved are truly unknowable. For fragmentary reliefs, the unknowns multiply even further.

The large format of monumental reliefs has allowed some research on detecting the work of individual sculptors as well as the processes by which the reliefs were carved (Rockwell 1985; Leander Touati 1987; Conlin 1997; Beckmann 2011). Many reliefs have damaged, abraded, or recarved surfaces (La Rocca 1986), so monuments suitable for such studies are exceptions. In addition, for these studies, direct access to the monuments (often involving scaffolding) is necessary. Extensive postclassical restorations, alterations, and reinstallation on later structures make determining the original appearance of some reliefs very difficult indeed. For example, upon installation several stories high on the façade of the Villa Medici in Rome, panels of the so-called Ara Pietatis (see below) were subdivided and surrounded by additional stucco figures and new backgrounds to create novel pastiches; as a result, photographs of casts of these reliefs are usually reproduced instead, often without noting that fact (e.g., D. E. E. Kleiner 1992, figs. 119–20).

In fact, access to reliefs is a continual problem. A surprising percentage of monumental reliefs remain poorly photographed and minimally published to this day. Photographs tend to feature shots of full "scenes" and neglect details, except for those of interest to a particular study (i.e., close-ups of drapery folds support chronological arguments and faces support portrait identifications). New studies thus are often best served by direct examination of the reliefs themselves. For reliefs that are typically inaccessible, such as the heights of the Column of Trajan, casts can allow up-close examination and measurement (Wolfram Thill 2010), sometimes preserve details that have been lost, especially to pollution (Coulston 1988, 6–10, 79–80), and can facilitate the reunion of fragments now in different museums (e.g., the so-called Dono Hartwig Monument split between the Kelsey Museum in Ann Arbor and the Palazzo Massimo in Rome: Gazda and Haeckl 1996).

Context

One of the two most glaring methodological challenges in the study of monumental reliefs is the absence of archaeological context. Reliefs surviving *in situ* demonstrate clearly that topographic location, architectural setting, and panel arrangement were critical to their effect and therefore their interpretation. To give an oft-repeated example, the large passageway relief panels in the Arch of Titus (D. E. E. Kleiner 1992, 183–90) that represent a triumphal procession are augmented by their position inside the arch, so that the viewer walking through the arch joined the procession (figure 3.5.1). The arch depicted in the spoils panel (figure 3.5.3) raises further questions of possible topographic connections between reliefs and (now lost) buildings.

The modern barriers that currently block off the arch's passageway, and thus inhibit the visitor's ability to experience the reliefs as an ancient viewer would have, also serve as an example of how differences from the ancient context can affect modern viewers' perceptions of the reliefs. In certain situations this disparity can be nearly impossible to appreciate fully: the Column of Trajan, to give another much-discussed example, now stands in the open, but was originally surrounded closely by a dense grid of buildings that would have greatly hindered the ancient viewer's ability to see the monument itself, let alone the details of the reliefs (Dillon 2006, 259; Wolfram Thill 2011, 285). Immersive 3-D digital reconstructions of entire monuments within the cityscape could potentially address some of these issues.

Even within a monument, the arrangement of the reliefs could drastically affect their interpretation. The relief panels on the sides of the Arch of Trajan at Beneventum are still *in situ* and arranged so that scenes more directly relevant to the capital are on the side facing Rome, and scenes relevant to the provinces are on the side facing away from the city. In contrast, eight of a suite of Antonine arch panels were reused in the Arch of Constantine, and three are immured in the Capitoline Museum (Ryberg 1967; Angelicoussis 1984; La Rocca 1986). We wonder whether the Antonine panels, which also present a mixture of scenes inside and outside the capital, were originally arranged

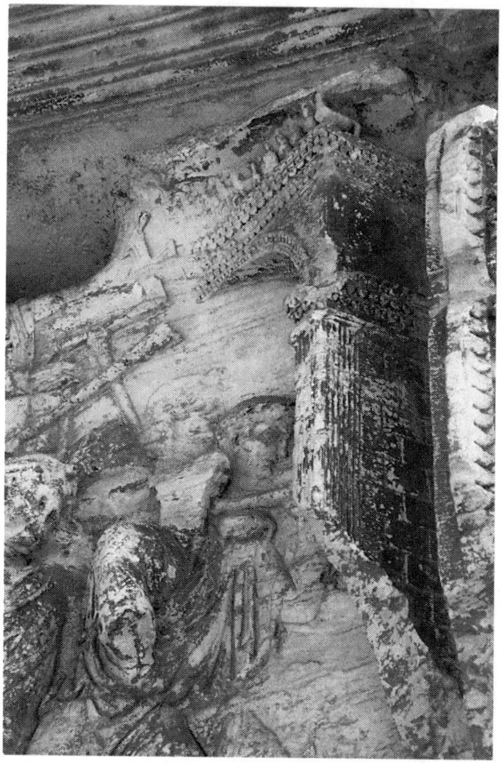

FIGURE 3.5.3 Detail of the arch from the Spoils Relief, Arch of Titus, Rome.

in a topographic pattern similar to that on the Beneventum Arch. Or were they arranged in chronological order to produce a narrative effect similar to the Column of Trajan (Ryberg 1967)? To what extent were they also organized thematically to emphasize the emperor's virtues (Angelicoussis 1984)? Even more fundamentally, did the panels belong to one arch or two? How many panels are missing from the series? Different answers to these questions change the significance of the reliefs.

The secondary life of monumental reliefs poses a significant problem for scholars. The Arch of Constantine, decorated almost entirely with spoliated sculpture from earlier periods, is the most famous example of the reuse of major pieces of sculpture within the ancient world; still, no consensus regarding the origins of the reliefs, how or why they came to be reused, or how they were interpreted by the contemporary viewer has yet emerged (F. S. Kleiner 2003; Marlowe 2004). The existence of marble dumps and the removal, transport, and reuse of reliefs haunts scholars who attempt to find significance in some recorded find spots. The Anaglypha, for example, depict the buildings around the Forum Romanum where they were excavated (Hammond 1953; Torelli 1982, 89–118). While scholars have seen much significance in this coincidence, the reliefs were set on postantique bases and immured in a medieval structure (Giuliani and Verduchi 1987, 1: 79–83), meaning they could have been brought from anywhere in the city at any time, either because of or independent of the buildings they show.

Date

In an ideal situation, a dedicatory inscription including a clear date is paired with an *in situ* relief. Only a few such examples exist, however, and even these rare examples can be afflicted by arguments regarding potential discrepancies between the monument's dedication date and the execution and completion of the associated sculpture (Richmond 1969, 229–38; Claridge 1993). An emperor's portrait, another dating method, provides only a terminus post quem, and many imperial portraits have been replaced or reworked. The imperial portraits of the Cancelleria reliefs, currently those of Nerva and Vespasian, were reworked from portraits of Domitian (Pfanner 1981; Hölscher 1992). Scholars often cannot agree about which heads represent imperial family members (Ara Pacis: Rose 1990; Holliday 1990; Koeppel 1992; Beneventum Arch: Richmond 1969, 229–38; Gauer 1974; D. E. E. Kleiner 1992, 228).

When lacking epigraphy or portraiture, scholars use style to date monumental reliefs. Such subjective judgments often fail to provide a convincing chronological argument. The Anaglypha have been dated to both the Trajanic (Hölscher 2002, 141–2; Tortorella 2012, 57–8) and Hadrianic periods (D. E. E. Kleiner 1992, 248–50; Kuttner 1995, 44–51) based on style and content. Similarly, a famous collection of relief fragments, alternatively known as the Valle-Medici reliefs (after the owners of the largest number of surviving fragments) or as the so-called Ara Pietatis (a once widely accepted identification by Bloch 1939; convincingly rejected by Koeppel 1982), for several decades functioned as a chronological linchpin defining Claudian style, but a firm date for them has proved elusive; since 1982 they have been variously dated to the reign of almost every Julio-Claudian emperor (Tiberius: Rehak 1990; Claudius: La Rocca 1994; Nero: Fuchs 2011).

The lure of identifying a historical event and naming a monument tempts scholars with the promise of a new fixed point for the chronology of styles and with the enticing possibility of an elaborate interpretation of the relief itself. We argue that broad distinctions can be offered in cases like the Valle-Medici reliefs (Julio-Claudian) or the Anaglypha (early second century AD), but further refinement of our chronological schemes on stylistic grounds alone is more often than not impossible (see essays 3.1, Fullerton; and 3.4, Wood). Dating a relief to the Trajanic period while excluding a Hadrianic date based on diagnostic criteria such as drapery folds will always be a speculative enterprise. We can offer here only a note of caution, rather than a solution to this problem. Methodologically, ambiguity should be accepted and a wider date range promulgated for some monuments, as D. E. E. Kleiner has modeled for the Anaglypha (1992, 248–50), until further evidence (if any) helps define the chronology more closely.

Because well-dated monuments—such as the Ara Pacis and the Column of Trajan—admit such close readings of the evidence, scholars become frustrated when similarly complex monuments cannot be convincingly linked to a date and historic event (for instance, the various proposals regarding the so-called Altar of Domitius Ahenobarbus from the republican era, better labeled the Paris-Munich reliefs). Interpretations resulting from "what if" readings of monuments based on speculative identifications, however, cannot support further analysis, and sometimes get (inappropriately) entrenched into introductory textbooks. On the other hand, precisely because some reliefs cannot be given a conclusive interpretation, like the stunning but relatively neglected Vatican-Terme processional relief fragments (Liljenstolpe 1996), they are often avoided in favor of objects with more certain significance.

Even with a precise date, the problems of artistry and patronage, of who determined which aspects of a given relief and why, remain almost unknowable. Few Roman texts mention architects or sculptors, and only one relevant sculptor's signature has been discovered (on the Extispicium relief in the Louvre: Laugier 2007; see also essay 2.2, Claridge). To our knowledge, no mention of monumental reliefs per se has been identified in Roman literature. How the layout or even content of a relief was determined or interpreted is therefore a realm of speculation.

Conclusion: Opportunities for Future Study

Despite over 200 years of scholarship and numerous intellectual challenges, the study of monumental reliefs remains an exciting field, open to advances both archaeological and methodological. For example, the forthcoming Manfred Lautenschläger Forschungsprojekt on "Politik und Monument im griechischen und römischen Altertum," which intends to pair an extensive computer database with traditional publications, including a two-volume overview of Roman monumental reliefs by Tonio Hölscher, may open numerous doors for future scholarship.

The potential of 3-D scanning and illustration is tantalizing as well, especially for exploring otherwise inaccessible reliefs (see essay 1.5, Frischer). A 3-D detailed scan of the Column of Marcus Aurelius could allow for full exploration of compositional and iconographic relationships within and between scenes, horizontally, vertically, and rotationally. Although reliefs are sometimes treated as if two-dimensional (an unfortunate repercussion of reliance upon frontal photographs of complete panels), three-dimensional interplay between elements can shift readings of scenes in critical ways (Huet 1996; Beard 2000; Elsner 2000).

Also intriguing are the links between reliefs and other media, both public and private. Coins and medallions are obvious comparanda (Ryberg 1955; Sobocinski 2009; Wolfram Thill 2014). Although sarcophagi and private funerary reliefs often share motifs and techniques with their monumental cousins (Beckmann 2011; see essay 4.4, Ewald), not much comparative work has been done, except when they share iconographies. The same is true for reliefs on religious themes (Moede 2007b; see also essays 4.2, McCarty; and 4.7, Petersen). Carved gems like the Gemma Augustea, relief incorporated into free-standing sculptures such as the carved cuirass on the Augustus Primaporta, mosaics, and wall paintings all offer further points of connection and comparison. Continuing research on polychromy (see essay 2.6, Abbe) is beginning to allow analysis of reliefs in terms of coloration and potentially in direct comparison with wall painting as well (Ara Pacis: Liverani 2010; Arch of Titus: Piening 2013; Column of Trajan: Del Monte, Ausset, and Lefevre 1998).

Of increasing interest is the small detail within larger compositions. Studies of representations of architecture have been popular lately (Quante-Schöttler 2002; Sobocinski 2009; 2014; Wolfram Thill 2010; 2011), and monumental reliefs provide evidence for otherwise vanished sculptures (Madigan 2013) and sculptural groups such as the quadrigae surmounting the arch depicted on the Arch of Titus (figure 3.5.3). While these representations are interpretive rather than documentary, they provide key evidence regarding the reception of sculpture in various contexts (Sobocinski 2009; 2014; see essays 4.1, Longfellow; and 6.4, Moormann).

Explorations of weaponry (Coulston 1989) and other assorted "marginalia" have taken overlooked elements of the reliefs and set them in a new context. Scholars are also moving beyond the emperor to study the roles of women (Zanker 2000; Dillon 2006), children (Uzzi 2005), and barbarians (Rose 1990; Hölscher 1999; Coulston 2003; Heitz 2009) in monumental reliefs. Scholars increasingly recognize, furthermore, that not all elements in reliefs need be independently significant (Wolfram Thill 2010; 2011; Sobocinski 2014). Not every depicted temple is the Temple of Jupiter Optimus Maximus, and not every woman in a monumental relief is a captured foreign queen. The inclusion of generic elements, and the implications of this practice for the interpretation of monumental relief, warrants further exploration.

As interpretations of monumental reliefs have shifted from historical illustrations to complex, ideologically driven compositions, scholars continue to derive novel insights from these well-studied pieces. While identifying and documenting reliefs and relief fragments is still a time-consuming process, subject to the vagrancies of chance and access, new methodologies can be explored within an extensive corpus. Crucial issues still need further analysis. The concentration of monumental reliefs in the imperial capital, for example, has yet to be fully appreciated; better comparative data for provincial monuments is needed. A rich history of scholarship provides a solid foundation for future research, as well as a field for historiographical investigation. Although rooted in the earliest days of interest in Roman sculpture, the study of monumental reliefs looks forward to a promising future.

Bibliography

Angelicoussis, E. 1984. "The Panel Reliefs of Marcus Aurelius." *RM* 91: 141–205.

Bal, M., and N. Bryson. 1991. "Semiotics and Art History." *ArtB* 73: 174–208.

Beard, M. 2000. "The Spectator and the Column: Reading and Writing the Language of Gesture." In Scheid and Huet 2000, 265–79.

Becatti, G. 1960. *La colonna coclide istoriata: Problemi storici, iconografici, stilistici.* Rome: "L'Erma" di Bretschneider.

Beckmann, M. 2011. *The Column of Marcus Aurelius: The Genesis and Meaning of a Roman Imperial Monument.* Chapel Hill: University of North Carolina Press.

Bianchi Bandinelli, R. 1970. *Rome: The Center of Power, 500 B.C. to A.D. 200*. Translated by P. Green. New York: George Braziller.

Billows, R. 1993. "The Religious Procession of the Ara Pacis Augustae: Augustus' *Supplicatio* in 13 B.C." *JRA* 6: 80–92.

Bloch, P. 1939. "L'Ara Pietatis Augustae." *MÉFRA* 56: 81–120.

Boschung, D. 2001. "Überlegungen zum Denkmal des L. Aemilius Paullus in Delphi." In *Rome et ses provinces: Genèse et diffusion d'une image du pouvoir*, edited by C. Evers and A. Tsingarida, 59–72. Brussels: Timperman.

Brendel, O. J. (1953) 1979. *Prolegomena to the Study of Roman Art*. New Haven: Yale University Press.

Claridge, A. 1993. "Hadrian's Column of Trajan?" *JRA* 6: 5–22.

Conlin, D. A. 1997. *The Artists of the Ara Pacis: The Process of Hellenization in Roman Relief Sculpture*. Chapel Hill: University of North Carolina Press.

Coulston, J. C. N. 1988. "Trajan's Column: The Sculpting and Relief Content of a Roman Propaganda Monument." PhD diss., Newcastle University.

———. 1989. "The Value of Trajan's Column as a Source for Military Equipment." In *Roman Military Equipment: The Sources of Evidence*, edited by C. van Dreiel-Murray, 31–44. BAR-IS 476. Oxford: British Archaeological Reports.

———. 2003. "Overcoming the Barbarian: Depictions of Rome's Enemies in Trajanic Monumental Art." In *The Representation and Perception of Roman Imperial Power*, edited by L. de Blois, 389–424. Amsterdam: Gieben.

Davies, P. J. E. 2000. *Death and the Emperor: Roman Imperial Funerary Monuments from Augustus to Marcus Aurelius*. Cambridge: Cambridge University Press.

Del Monte, M., P. Ausset, and R. A. Lefevre. 1998. "Traces of Ancient Colours on Trajan's Column." *Archaeometry* 40(2): 403–412.

Dillon, S. 2006. "Women on the Columns of Trajan and Marcus Aurelius and the Visual Language of Roman Victory." In Dillon and Welch 2006, 244–71.

Dillon, S., and K. Welch, eds. 2006. *Representations of War in Ancient Rome*. Cambridge: Cambridge University Press.

Dreyfus, R., and E. Schraudolph, eds. 1996. *Pergamon: The Telephos Frieze from the Great Altar*. 2 vols. San Francisco: Fine Arts Museums of San Francisco.

Elsner, J. 2000. "From the Culture of *Spolia* to the Cult of Relics: The Arch of Constantine and the Genesis of Late Antique Forms." *PBSR* 68: 149–84.

———. 2004. "Foreword." In Hölscher (1987) 2004, xv–xxxi.

Ewald, B. C., and C. F. Noreña, eds. 2010. *The Emperor and Rome: Space, Representation, and Ritual*. Cambridge: Cambridge University Press.

Fishwick, D. (2003) 2007. "Iconography and Ideology: The Statue Group in the Temple of Mars Ultor." *AJAH* 2(1): 63–94.

Florescu, F. B. 1965. *Das Siegesdenkmal von Adamklissi Tropaeum Traiani*. Bonn: Habelt.

Fogliato, D. 1992. *L'arco di Augusto a Susa*. Collegno: Gruppo Archeologico "Ad Quintum."

Fuchs, M. 2011. "Der gerettete Staat: Die Krise des Jahres 59 n.Chr. und die Tempelreliefs Valle-Medici." In *Kunst und Politik, Religion und Gedächtniskultur: Von der späten Republik bis zu den Flaviern*, edited by H. Meyer, 139–55. Munich: Biering und Brinkmann.

Galinsky, K. 1992. "Venus, Polysemy, and the Ara Pacis Augustae." *AJA* 96: 457–75.

Gauer, W. 1974. "Zum Bildprogramm des Trajansbogens von Benevent." *JdI* 89: 308–335.

Gazda, E., and A. Haeckl. 1996. *Images of Empire: Flavian Fragments in Rome and Ann Arbor Rejoined*. Ann Arbor: Kelsey Museum of Archaeology.

Giuliani, C. F., and P. Verduchi. 1987. *L'area centrale del Foro Romano*. 2 vols. Florence: Leo S. Olschki.
Hamberg, P. G. 1945. *Studies in Roman Imperial Art, with Special Reference to the State Reliefs of the Second Century*. Copenhagen: Ejnar Munksgaard.
Hammond, M. 1953. "A Statue of Trajan Represented on the 'Anaglypha Traiani.'" *MAAR* 21: 125, 127–83.
Heitz, C. 2009. *Die Guten, die Bösen und die Hässlichen: Nördliche "Barbaren" in der römischen Bildkunst*. Hamburg: Kovač.
Holliday, P. 1990. "Time, History, and Ritual on the Ara Pacis Augustae." *ArtB* 72: 542–57.
Hölscher, T. 1980. "Die Geschichtsauffassung in der römischen Reprasentationskunst." *JdI* 95: 265–321.
———. (1987) 2004. *The Language of Images in Roman Art*. Translated by A. Snodgrass and A. Künzl-Snodgrass. Cambridge: Cambridge University Press. Originally published as *Römische Bildsprache als semantisches System*.
———. 1988. "Historische Reliefs." In *Kaiser Augustus und die verlorene Republik*, edited by M. R. Hofter, 351–400. Mainz: Philipp von Zabern.
———. 1992. "Monumenti politici di Domiziano: Stabilità e sviluppo dell'iconografia politica romana." In *La storia, la letteratura e l'arte a Roma da Tiberio a Domiziano*, 293–309. Mantua: Accademia nazionale Virgiliana.
———. 1999. "Alle Welt für Traian: Beobachtungen zur Darstellung von Fremdvölkern an traianischen Staatsdenkmälern." In *Imago antiquitatis: Religions et iconographie du monde romain*, edited by N. Blanc and A. Buisson, 281–9. Paris: De Boccard.
———. 2002. "Bilder der Macht und Herrschaft." In *Traian: Ein Kaiser der Superlative am Beginn einer Umbruchzeit?*, edited by A. Nünnerich-Asmus, 127–44. Mainz: Philipp von Zabern.
———. 2009. "Architectural Sculpture: Messages? Programs? Towards Rehabilitating the Notion of 'Decoration.'" In *Structure, Image, Ornament: Architectural Sculpture in the Greek World*, edited by P. Schultz and R. von den Hoff, 54–67. Oxford: Oxbow.
Huet, V. 1996. "Stories One Might Tell of Roman Art: Reading Trajan's Column and the Tiberius Cup." In *Art and Text in Roman Culture*, edited by J. Elsner, 9–31. Cambridge: Cambridge University Press.
Kähler, H. 1965. *Der Fries vom Reiterdenkmal des Aemilius Paullus in Delphi*. Berlin: Mann.
Kampen, N. B. 2003. "On Writing Histories of Roman Art." *ArtB* 85(2): 371–86.
Kellum, B. A. 1994. "What We See and What We Don't See: Narrative Structure and the Ara Pacis Augustae." *Art History* 17: 26–45.
Kleiner, D. E. E. 1992. *Roman Sculpture*. New Haven: Yale University Press.
Kleiner, F. S. 2003. "The Arch of Constantine: Roman Art in Microcosm." In *Hommages à Carl Deroux*. Vol. 4, *Archéologie et histoire de l'art, religion*, edited by P. Defosse, 174–9. Collection Latomus 277. Brussels: Latomus.
Koeppel, G. 1982. "Die 'Ara Pietatis Augustae:' Ein Geisterbau." *RM* 89: 453–5.
———. 1983–92. "Die historischen Reliefs der römischen Kaiserzeit." Pts. 1–9. *BJb* 183: 61–144; 184: 1–65; 185: 143–213; 186: 1–90; 187: 101–157; 189: 17–71; 190: 1–64; 191: 135–98; 192: 61–122.
Kuttner, A. 1993. "Some New Grounds for Narrative: Marcus Antonius's Base (the Ara Domitii Ahenobarbi) and Republican Biographies." In *Narrative and Event in Ancient Art*, edited by P. Holliday, 198–229. Cambridge: Cambridge University Press.
———. 1995. *Dynasty and Empire in the Age of Augustus: The Case of the Boscoreale Cups*. Berkeley: University of California Press.

La Rocca, E., ed. 1986. *Rilievi storici Capitolini: Il restauro dei pannelli di Adriano e di Marco Aurelio nel Palazzo dei Conservatori*. Rome: De Luca.

———. 1994. "Arcus et Arae Claudii." In *Die Regierungszeit des Kaisers Claudius (41–54 n.Chr.): Umbruch oder Episode?*, edited by V. M. Strocka, 267–93. Mainz: Philipp von Zabern.

Laugier, L. 2007. "Relief Showing the Reading of Auguries and Declaration of Sacred Vows." In *Roman Art from the Louvre*, edited by C. Giroire and D. Roger, 232–3. Manchester, VT: Hudson Hills.

Leander Touati, A.-M. 1987. *The Great Trajanic Frieze: The Study of a Monument and of the Mechanisms of Message Transmission in Roman Art*. ActaRom 4.45. Stockholm: Paul Åströms.

Lepper, F., and S. Frere. 1988. *Trajan's Column: A New Edition of the Cichorius Plates; Introduction, Commentary, and Notes*. Gloucester: Alan Sutton.

Letta, C. 2006–7. "Per una rilettura storica del fregio dell'arco di Susa." *RendPontAcc* 79: 343–64.

Liljenstolpe, P. 1996. "The Vatican Procession Relief in Rome: Trajan Re-dedicating the Temple of Quirinus?" *AA* 1996: 527–38.

Liverani, P. 2010. "New Evidence on the Polychromy of Roman Sculpture." In *Circumlitio: The Polychromy of Antique and Mediaeval Sculpture*, edited by V. Brinkmann, O. Primavesi, and M. Hollein, 290–302. Munich: Hirmer.

Lusnia, S. S. 2006. "Battle Imagery and Politics on the Severan Arch on the Roman Forum." In Dillon and Welch 2006, 272–99.

Madigan, B. 2013. *The Ceremonial Sculptures of the Roman Gods*. Monumenta Graeca et Romana 20. Leiden: Brill.

Marlowe, E. 2004. "'That Customary Magnificence which is Your Due': Constantine and the Symbolic Capital of Rome." PhD diss., Columbia University.

Mayer, E. 2010. "Propaganda, Staged Applause, or Local Politics? Public Monuments from Augustus to Septimius Severus." In Ewald and Noreña 2010, 111–34.

Meadows, A., and J. Williams. 2001. "*Moneta* and the Monuments: Coinage and Politics in Republican Rome." *JRS* 91: 27–49.

Moede, K. 2007a. "Der Augustusbogen von Susa: Römische Rituale ausserhalb Roms." In *Römische Bilderwelten: Von der Wirklichkeit zum Bild und zurück*, edited by F. Hölscher and T. Hölscher, 133–44. Heidelberg: Verlag Archäologie und Geschichte.

———. 2007b. "Reliefs, Public and Private." In *A Companion to Roman Religion*, edited by J. Rupke, 164–75. Malden, MA: Blackwell.

Pfanner, M. 1981. "Technische Beobachtungen an den Cancelleria-Reliefs." *AA* 1981: 514–18.

Piening, H. 2013. "Examination Report: The Polychromy of the Arch of Titus Menorah Relief." *Images* 6: 26–9. doi: 10.1163/18718000-12340002.

Quante-Schöttler, D. 2002. *Ante aedes: Darstellung von Architektur in römischen Reliefs*. Hamburg: Dr. Kovač.

Rehak, P. 1990. "The Ionic Temple Relief in the Capitoline: The Temple of Victory on the Palatine?" *JRA* 3: 172–86.

———. 2001. "The Fourth 'Flamen' of the Ara Pacis Augustae." *JRA* 14: 284–8.

Richmond, I. 1969. *Roman Archaeology and Art: Essays and Studies*. London: Faber.

Rockwell, P. 1985. "Preliminary Study of the Carving Techniques on the Column of Trajan." In *Marmi antichi: Problemi d'impiego, di restauro e d'identificazione*, edited by P. Pensabene, 101–5. Rome: "L'Erma" di Bretschneider.

Rotili, M. 1972. *L'arco di Traiano a Benevento*. Rome: Istituto Poligrafico dello Stato.

Rose, C. B. 1990. "'Princes' and Barbarians on the Ara Pacis." *AJA* 94: 453–67.

Ryberg, I. S. 1955. *Rites of the State Religion in Roman Art*. MAAR 22. Rome: American Academy in Rome.
———. 1967. *Panel Reliefs of Marcus Aurelius*. Monographs on Archaeology and Fine Arts 14. New York: Archaeological Institute of America.
Scheid, J., and V. Huet, eds. 2000. *La colonne Aurélienne: Autour de la colonne Aurélienne; Geste et image sur la colonne de Marc Aurèle à Rome*. Turnhout: Brepols.
Smith, R. R. R. 2013. *The Marble Reliefs from the Julio-Claudian Sebasteion*. Aphrodisias 6. Darmstadt: Philipp von Zabern.
Sobocinski, M. G. 2009. "Porta Triumphalis and Fortuna Redux: Reconsidering the Evidence." *MAAR* 54: 135–64.
———. 2014. "Visualizing Architecture Then and Now: Mimesis and the Capitoline Temple of Jupiter Optimus Maximus." In *A Companion to Roman Architecture*, edited by R. Ulrich and C. Quenemoen, 446–61. Chichester and Malden, MA: Wiley-Blackwell.
Stilp, F. 2001. *Mariage et Suovetaurilia: Etude sur le Soi-disant "Autel Ahenobarbus"*. Rome: Giorgio Bretschneider.
Strong, E. 1907. *Roman Sculpture from Augustus to Constantine*. New York: C. Scribner's Sons.
Torelli, M. 1982. *Typology and Structure of Roman Historical Reliefs*. Ann Arbor: University of Michigan Press.
Tortorella, S. 2012. "Monumenti statali fra Traiano e Marco Aurelio: Esibizione del potere e provvidenze imperiali." In *L'età dell'equilibrio, 98–180 d.C.: Traiano, Adriano, Antonino Pio, Marco Aurelio*, edited by E. La Rocca, C. Parisi Presicce, and A. Lo Monaco, 52–9. Rome: MondoMostre.
Uzzi, J. D. 2005. *Children in the Visual Arts of Imperial Rome*. Cambridge: Cambridge University Press.
Wolfram Thill, E. 2010. "Civilization Under Construction: Depictions of Architecture on the Column of Trajan." *AJA* 114: 27–43.
———. 2011. "Depicting Barbarism on Fire: Architectural Destruction on the Columns of Trajan and Marcus Aurelius." *JRA* 24: 283–312.
———. 2014. "The Emperor in Action: Group Scenes in Trajanic Coinage and Monumental Reliefs". *AJN* Second Series 26: 87–140.
Zanker, P. 1988. *The Power of Images in the Age of Augustus*. Translated by A. Shapiro. Ann Arbor: University of Michigan Press.
———. 2000. "Die Frauen und Kinder der Barbaren auf der Markussäule." In Scheid and Huet 2000, 163–74.

CHAPTER 3.6

ARCHAISM AND ECLECTICISM

LORI-ANN TOUCHETTE

INTRODUCTION

THOUGH Pliny (*HN* 34.52) represents art as dead, only to be reborn in the mid-second century BC, the evidence from Rome demonstrates a continuum of art production from the seventh through the second centuries BC (i.e., the archaic through classical and later Hellenistic periods). Perhaps Coarelli (1996, 15–84) is correct in seeing the declaration as an attempt to reclaim art from the perceived decadence of the Hellenistic period through a return to classicism—and here I would add archaism—promoted through the so-called Neo-Attic workshops. In fact, archaism and eclecticism, although often marginalized in scholarship, are central to an understanding of Roman sculpture of the republican and early imperial periods.

Any consideration of archaism and eclecticism requires a definition of terms, especially since the categories are modern rather than ancient. "Archaistic" is used here to refer to all Roman (or more inclusively, post-480 BC) sculpture that contains archaic traits in pose, drapery, hairstyle, and facial features. Although Ridgway (2002, 142–53) retained the traditional use of "archaizing" to refer to works predominantly archaic in style and "archaistic" for works that combine archaic features with the style of their period, Fullerton (1990) and Zagdoun (1989) argue persuasively that this distinction is too subjective. Here, I also extend the term to refer to the use of retrospective sculptural materials such as terracotta. "Eclecticism" can be applied to everything from sculptural style, whether predominantly archaistic, classicizing, or Hellenistic, to the use of varied styles within a single sculpture or a collection of works, or even a period. The most complete treatment of eclecticism is presented by Perry, who defines eclecticism in Roman art with reference to "a work of art [that] depends for its inspiration on two or more models, subject types or period styles" (Perry 2005, 111).

From the second century BC on, Roman sculptural production in a broad range of materials took as its starting point Greek originals or Greek style. These new Roman works stood side-by-side with statues created by Greek artists living and working in Rome and with Greek originals from a variety of dates that had been taken as booty from Magna Graecia, Greece, and elsewhere in the Hellenistic East and set up in Rome. Eclecticism was a direct result of this influx of masses of looted and purchased Greek sculpture in multiple styles, which influenced Greek artists heavily in their formulation of a new language of images for their Roman patrons.

Terracotta sculpture serves as a link between these two points of departure due to its use first as a necessity in marble-poor archaic and republican Rome and then as a conscious archaism in the late republican and early Augustan periods (see essay 2.5, Erlich). The late republican and early Augustan periods have been linked to an "archaic revival" (Hallett 2012). Moreover, La Rocca (2010), Strazzulla (2010), and others have argued that a "renaissance" in terracotta sculpture in the late republican and early imperial periods can be linked to archaism and eclecticism. I posit that the production of the workshops of the famous Neo-Attic sculptors Pasiteles and Arcesilaos can be associated with the (re)birth of a truly Roman art through the creation of sculpture in terracotta, a material that evoked the Roman archaic past. These terracotta works, in an eclectic mix of archaic, classical, and Hellenistic style, stood beside works by the same masters in stone and metal that proclaimed their connections to Greek cultural traditions.

Although archaism and eclecticism can be demonstrated in art of the republican through late antique periods, this essay will focus on the late republican and early imperial periods and on the city of Rome itself, where excavations allow us to reconstruct a continuum of Greek-style art in the Roman period. After a discussion of the relative rarity, origins, and meaning of archaistic style, I will use a group of archaistic herms to introduce a discussion of what archaism and eclecticism can tell us about the relationship between Greek and Roman art. To reinforce my thesis of the connection between Neo-Attic sculptors and the creation of a truly Roman art, the final section will focus on the schools of Polycles and Pasiteles, relating them to a survey of terracotta sculpture in Rome and its environs from the archaic through late republican periods, ending at the Augustan Temple of Apollo on the Palatine.

Archaism: Rarity, Origins, and Meaning

Archaistic sculpture is relatively rare in the corpus of statuary preserved from the Roman period. One need only compare the 119 statues treated in Fullerton's catalog of archaistic freestanding sculpture (1990) to the more than one hundred copies after the Capitoline Venus, 115 copies of Praxiteles's Leaning Satyr, or more than eighty copies of the Dancing Maenad reliefs. Therefore, archaistic works have tended to be marginalized in favor of the more copious sculptural production in Hellenistic and classical style.

Two monographs, by Zagdoun (1989) and Fullerton (1990), present opposed interpretations of the origins of archaistic style. Can the establishment of all major archaistic figure types be traced to the fourth century BC and thus be identified as Greek (*pace* Zagdoun) or should we accept Fullerton's argument that links them to Hellenistic and Roman production of the second century BC and later? Their conclusions are central to the current debate on Roman copies, with some scholars continuing to utilize *Kopienkritik* for the interpretation of Roman replicas, whereas others would like us to see the vast majority of Roman copies reinterpreted as Roman creations (see essay 3.3, Anguissola). If Fullerton and others have noted that the archaistic style is necessarily eclectic and retrospective, so too are the majority of sculptures (after Greek models) that filled the theaters, fora, and domestic spaces of the Roman world.

Whatever one's interpretation of the prototype for individual archaistic sculptures, all would agree that archaic style was already utilized in fifth-century Greece to endow certain images with greater sanctity. Archaism had lost its novelty long before its appropriation in the Roman world, and in both Greek and Roman contexts it was not associated with a particular chronological period. Instead, its significance was religious, conferring greater venerability on images of the gods and their followers. In fact, the vast majority of archaistic images represent the gods of the Greek and Roman pantheon. The few exceptions are personifications, such as Spes, whose cult, tellingly, was newly introduced by Augustus and for whose image the Princeps chose to use archaistic style.

In addition, archaistic style may have been used to recall lost original cult statues. Examples of replication and its sacred ramifications have been collected by Anguissola (2007). The late sixth-century BC archaic head of Athena Promachos from the Palatine is an intriguing case. Some scholars have associated it with the archaic sculptors Bupalos and Athenis (Plin. *HN* 36.13), whereas others identify it as the Palladium Palatinum, brought by Aeneas from burning Troy. According to Dionysius of Halicarnassus (*Ant. Rom.* 1.93.3, 2.66.5), the image stolen by Diomedes and Odysseus was an exact copy of the original, set up as a decoy. The original was thereby preserved, so it (and its power) could be transferred by Aeneas to Italy and finally to Augustus's Temple of Vesta Palatina. In another example of the phenomenon, La Rocca (2010, 260–62, cat. I.19) interprets the archaistic Dioscuroi of the second century BC from the Lacus Juturna as examples of "cultural archaism," citing their imitation of the archaic originals of the Temple of the Dioscuri.

Four female marble herms from the Horti Maecenatiani (figures 3.6.1–2) serve as exemplars of two trends in archaistic style of the Roman period distinguished by Fullerton (1990, 191): direct imitation of archaic prototypes and increased eclecticism. Standard archaic elements such as stylized hair, swallowtail drapery, and archaic smiles recall the *korai* of the archaic Acropolis. The closest parallel for their heads is an archaistic Athena (Fullerton 1990, 81, fig. 23), but the plait around the head is characteristic of male athletes (see "Orestes and Pylades," below). Although the format of the herm is late archaic, their clothing (at odds with true archaic works) is characterized by a *peplos*

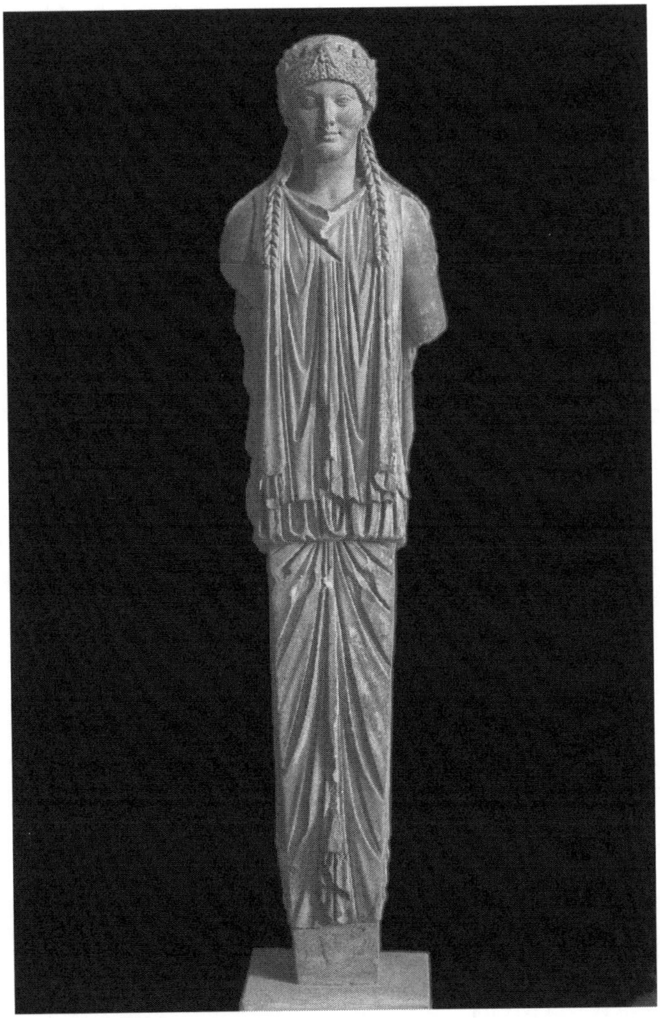

FIGURE 3.6.1 Archaistic female herm from the Horti Maecenatiani. Rome, Musei Capitolini, inv. no. 1095.

with various over-folds. The herms represent both close replication within each pair and more pronounced variation between the two sets, articulated through different treatment of their clothing, both the length of the overfold and the presence or absence of an under-chiton.

Might these herms have had a religious significance? Whereas the finds of archaistic *korai* in Greece have been tied to sanctuaries, the villa contexts of Roman *korai* (or Maenads) have stripped them of their votive significance, and they have been interpreted as merely decorative. Indeed, Fullerton emphasizes the decorative character of archaistic works (1990, 198), extending the term to Neo-Attic reliefs. Pollitt (1986, 178) uses the same term to define Neo-Attic reliefs, but makes a distinction between the reliefs and archaistic freestanding sculpture. Perhaps Pollitt and Fullerton are

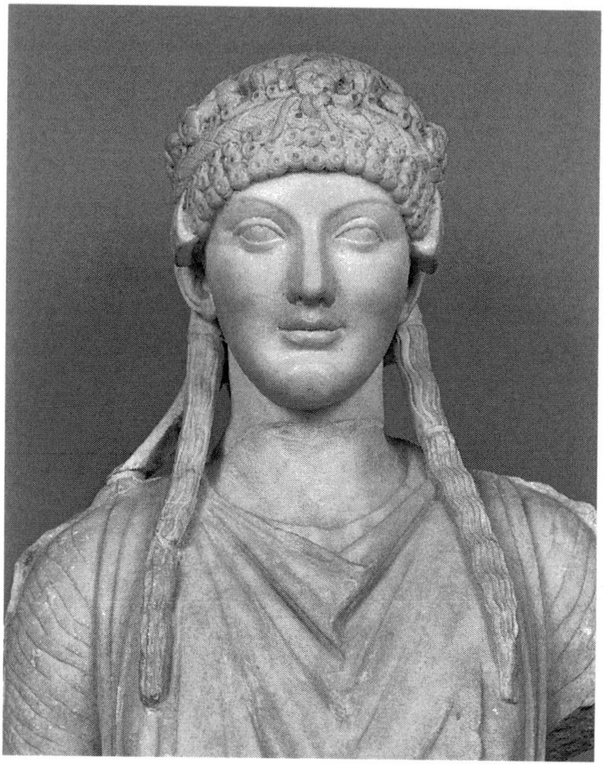

FIGURE 3.6.2 Archaistic female herm from the Horti Maecenatiani. Rome, Musei Capitolini, inv. no. 1100.

misled by those very qualities of grace and other-worldliness that rendered archaistic art attractive to the Romans (Hallett 2012). Rather than divesting the works of their religious character, archaistic style reinforced their sacrality by rendering them timeless. Elsewhere, I have argued that Neo-Attic reliefs retained their sacred power (Touchette 1995) and by extension the moral charge of archaistic statuary should not be denied.

As part of the sculpture collection of the Horti Maecenatiani, these herms also reveal the eclectic nature of Roman collecting and display in the late republican and early imperial period, since these pieces come from a collection of over 300 pieces, varied in style, subject, and material (Häuber 1991). The four archaizing herms were displayed alongside Greek originals, such as the Villa Albani relief and an early classical grave stele, and Roman-period copies mostly in classicizing and Hellenistic style. The similarly eclectic collection of Asinius Pollius combined works of the Neo-Attic artists Arcesilaos, Cleomenes, and Stephanos with statues by the fourth-century BC Greek masters Praxiteles (or perhaps we should read Pasiteles?), Cephisodotus, and Scopas (Plin. *HN* 36.23–4, 36.33–4).

Archaism, Eclecticism, and the Relationship between Greek and Roman Sculpture

Artists' signatures have been little integrated into the study of Roman copies, except as a means of identifying artists and linking their names to literary references in Pliny and others (see essay 2.2, Claridge). This area of research, however, has much to teach us about Roman perception and reception of copies after Greek originals and works in Greek style. Collectors and authors of the Roman period relied on signatures for the attribution of statuary to specific sculptors. Pausanias's description of Greece is replete with examples where he notes that the inscription states the name of the sculptor. So strong is his reliance on inscriptional evidence that Pausanias records even the names of obscure sculptors about whom nothing else is known (5.24.1). In the absence of inscriptions, Pliny and his contemporaries were lost; many famous statues were unattributed or attributed to more than one sculptor.

Epigraphic and Literary Evidence for the Identity of Sculptors

The standard term for Greek-style sculpture made for the Roman market, Neo-Attic, coined more than half a century ago and implying Athenian identity of the sculptors, seems less accurate in the face of the evidence of sculptors' signatures (Cain and Dräger 1994, 825). Indeed, artists' signatures reveal a range of ethnics: certainly Athenians, but also Rhodians, Ephesians, Aphrodisians, and others (see essays 2.2, Claridge; 2.6, Abbe; 2.7, Russell; 3.8, Witschel; and 5.4, Sturgeon). The placement of the signatures on the statue itself instead of on the base reinforces the argument that these signed pieces were made for the export market, as does the citation of the ethnic (rather than deme) of the artists. The choice of Greek for the signatures emphasizes the "Greekness" of the works. As Hallett (2005b, 428–35) points out, the Romans wanted works that through their reference to the Greek past conferred a greater value on the Roman present. In fact, Greek signatures appear on a range of works: copies after famous Greek masterpieces, ideal sculpture, and Neo-Attic reliefs (as they are still called). Typical of artist signatures of the Roman period is the name of the artist and his ethnic followed by ΕΠΟΕΙ "made (it)." Sometimes the patronymic is included.

Not all artists' signatures were in Greek. Signatures in Latin are attested from the fourth century BC in Italy. On a series of late third century BC architectural terracottas, the name of the Greek artist and the term *epoi* are transliterated into Latin (Susini 1965). By the late republican period, the signatures are in Latin, signed by the artist in a *tabula ansata* at the top of the relief. Arretine ware is signed in Latin script; Greek names are simply transliterated into Latin (e.g., La Rocca et al. 2013, 278–79, cat. VII.9). In general, art forms that were viewed as Roman, such as terracotta architectural reliefs and lamps, are signed in Latin, even by Greek artists; art forms that were viewed as Greek are signed in Greek. The language of the signature is determined by Roman perception of the work, not the nationality, ethnicity, or native language of the artist.

In his treatment of *artifices* of the Roman period, Pliny simply lists the Greek names of the artists working in bronze and marble. According to De Angelis (2008), what makes art Roman for Pliny is its topographical position in Rome (or Italy) and, sometimes, Roman patronage. The sole exception is when Pliny turns to terracotta sculpture, where he draws a clear distinction between Greek and Italic artistry. Pliny's list of *plastae laudatissimi* ("the most esteemed clay-modelers," *HN* 35.154–6) opens with Damophilus and Gorgasus, who signed their work for the Temple of Ceres in Rome in a Greek verse inscription. In the closing chapter, immediately after referring to Pasiteles's use of clay models, Pliny returns to the question of Greek versus Italic, attributing to Varro the statement that this art was elaborated most successfully by Italy and by Etruria in particular (*HN* 35.156).

Three Influential Workshops: The Schools of Polycles, Arcesilaos, and Pasiteles

I would like to explore the relationship posited between Italic art and terracotta by looking at three schools of Greek sculptors who worked in Rome from the second to first centuries BC. La Rocca (2013, 185) considers the first-century BC workshops of Pasiteles and Arcesilaos to be the *locus* of the amalgamation of the classicizing trend (represented by the second-century BC sculptor Polycles and his school) with archaic, severe, and early Hellenistic elements, thereby creating a new visual language. I would like to suggest that Arcesilaos and Pasiteles and the artists of his school emphasized the universal quality of their works by suppressing their ethnicity. Instead, they relied on the material of their works (bronze and marble or terracotta) to communicate the pieces' Greek or Roman nature.

Pliny's list of artists associated with the rebirth of art in the 156th Olympiad (156–153 BC) includes the Athenian sculptor Polycles (Stewart 2012). Scholars have reconstructed the *oeuvre* of Polycles and his family through a combination of literary sources and signatures. In Greece, these artists sign with their deme (Thorikos), whereas their works on Delos and at Rome use the ethnic (Athenian). On Delos, the portrait statue of C. Ofellius Ferus is signed by Dionysios and Timarchides (Stewart 1990, 305, T 160, fig. 839; Hallett 2005a, 103–4, pl. 51), and the inscription includes their ethnic and patronymics. Interestingly, Preisshofen and Zanker (1970–71) cite this work as the earliest surviving eclectic sculpture, as it combined a retrospective body with a now-missing, but presumably veristic Roman portrait, in the manner of other Roman portraits from Delos. In

Rome, the workshop of Polycles and his family seems to have specialized in cult statues, with an emphasis on copies after famous works (Plin. *HN* 36.35).

The home and parentage of Arcesilaos are unknown. His most famous work in Rome was the cult statue of Venus, likely made of terracotta, in the Temple of Venus Genetrix (Plin. *HN* 35.155–6). Pliny (*HN* 35.155), quoting Varro, reveals that the clay models (*proplasmata*) of Arcesilaos sold for more among artists than the finished works of others. The same artist was paid a talent for the archetype of a krater, which most likely was a workshop model rather than a cast of a Greek original. Pliny also notes works by Arcesilaos in marble (a group of Nymphs and Centaurs owned by Asinius Pollius; a lioness with Cupids worked out of single block; Plin. *HN* 36.41).

The name of the first-century BC artist Pasiteles has become synonymous with eclecticism in Roman sculpture. A sculptor skilled in both bronze casting and marble sculpture, he was a Greek from Magna Graecia who became a Roman citizen (Plin. *HN* 36.39), thereby mediating between these two worlds. Even in the Roman period, it seems that his reputation exceeded his identifiable works (Plin. *HN* 36.39–40). His encyclopedic interests are demonstrated by his five-volume treatment of *nobilia opera* of the entire world (see essays 2.6, Abbe; and 3.3, Anguissola). In addition to attributing to him the ivory statue of Jupiter in his temple in the Portico of Metellus, Pliny lists Pasiteles among the best sculptors working in silver (*HN* 33.156; seconded by Cic. *Div.* 1.36.79) and elsewhere adds: "Varro also praised Pasiteles, who called modeling the mother of sculpture in metal and stone, and who, although he was pre-eminent in these arts, never made anything before he had made a clay model" (*HN* 35.156; Stewart 1990, 306, T 164). Although no signed works associated with him have survived, a signed marble strut reads ΠΑΣΙΤΕΛΗ[Σ] ΕΠΟΕΙ ("Pasiteles made [it]"). The absence of both ethnic and patronymic is noteworthy (Donderer 1988).

Pasiteles's style has been reconstructed through the works of Stephanos (who signed marble statues as "pupil of Pasiteles") and Menelaos ("pupil of Stephanos," also known from signatures). The severe-style head of the Stephanos Youth in the Villa Albani (Koortbojian 2002, 182, pl. 8.9) is combined with a high classical body; the proportions reflect the fourth-century BC Lysippan canon (figure 3.3.2). This under-life-size work served in turn as a model for several sculpture groups on the same scale. The Orestes and Pylades in the Louvre repeats the Stephanos Youth type in combination with a Praxitelean male with a severe-style head that recalls the Omphalos Apollo (La Rocca et al. 2013, 206–7, cats. III.8.1–2; cf. Stewart 1990, figs. 285–6). In the Naples Orestes and Electra, the Stephanos Youth type reappears with a female figure whose head (a close match for the male head of Pylades) is feminized through the addition of a low chignon. Wincklemann identified another group in Rome as Orestes and Electra (figure 3.6.3), this time signed by Menelaos, the pupil of Stephanos (ΜΕΝΕ /ΛΑΟΣ / ΣΤΕΦΑ / ΝΟΥ / ΜΑΘΗ / ΤΗΣ / ΕΠΟΙ / ΕΙ), possibly identical with the Marcus Cossoutios Menelaos known from a now-lost signature on a drapery fragment (Rawson 1975, 39). He might have been related to the freedman Marcus Cossoutios Cerdo, son of Marcus, who signed two sculptures of Pan now in the British Museum in Greek, transliterating his Roman name (Fuchs 1999, pls. 54–9; the spelling indicates a first-century BC date, Rawson 1975, 39). All signatures

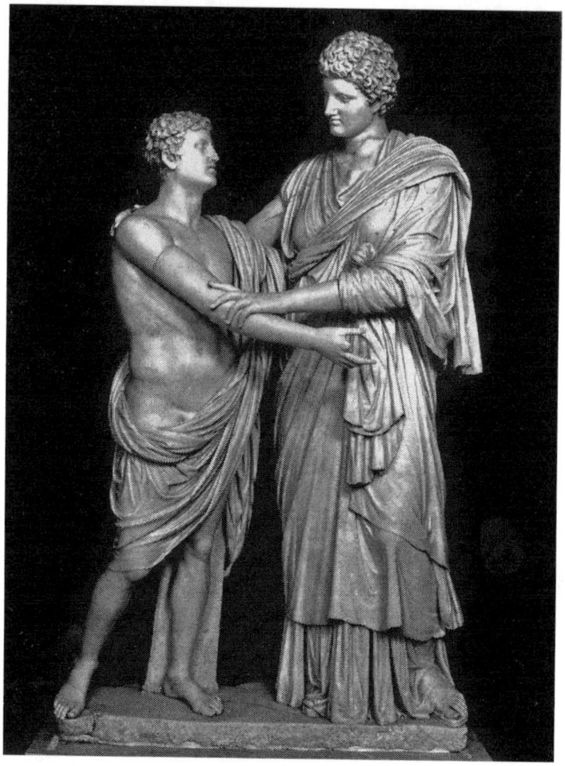

FIGURE 3.6.3 Marble statue group of Orestes and Electra signed in Greek by Menelaos, the pupil of Stephanos. Rome, Museo Nazionale Romano, inv. no. 8604.

attributed to Pasiteles's school of sculptors are in Greek; it is unusual that they consistently sign without their ethnic.

Eclecticism in the school of Pasiteles could be stylistic, uniting figures modeled on prototypes of different periods. In the San Ildefonso Group (see essay 6.1, Squire, figure 6.1.2), the Praxitelean body of one twin is beefed up to match the musculature of his Polykleitan brother, modeled on the Westmacott Athlete. The latter's head reproduces lock for lock the hair of the bronze Doryphorus herm from the Villa of the Papyri (see essay 3.3, Anguissola, figure 3.3.1; Stewart 1990, figs. 380–81). A small-scale archaistic *kore* is called into service as a strut. The Electra in Naples represents the fusion of male and female models in a single figure, whereas Menelaos's Orestes and Electra combines figures in two different scales. Electra is over life-size, whereas Orestes's dimensions match those of the two-thirds-life-size Stephanos Youth.

In terms of ancient responses to eclecticism, a passage from the early first-century BC *Rhetorica ad Herennium* (4.6.9) admonishes artists to avoid combining body parts modeled after different masters. Perry (2005, 116–17) suggested that this passage was to be read as a warning to pupils, rather than a reflection on the working process of masters. Most importantly, Perry proposes a counter argument to the disparaging view of eclectic works that focuses on the artist's ability to fuse several models into a new and harmonious whole, expanding the argument of Preisshofen and Zanker (1970–71). Thus, eclecticism permitted the artist to transform the visual tradition in response to contemporary needs.

The question is whether we can relate these texts to the reality of sculptural production in the workshop of Pasiteles and others. Read in a different fashion, the passage seems almost a recipe for eclectic sculpture. Perhaps it is a response to contemporary sculpture production associated with Pasiteles. Although Perry (2002, 161) argues that "the principle of eclecticism dictates, quite rightly, that surpassing any single model is actually easier than reproducing it," her interpretation seems at odds with ancient workshop practice and the eclectic Pasitelean works discussed above.

Can we also connect Pasiteles and his school with the production of statuary in terracotta, a material and process congruent with his eclectic style? Excavations on the Palatine in the early 1980s yielded approximately fifty fragments of a series of almost life-size terracotta statues. Similar terracotta works discovered in the 1860s excavations on the Palatine are now lost. Several heads and some drapery fragments have been reconstructed. Fuchs (1999, 70, pls. 64.1–4) compares the face of the best preserved male head (figure 3.6.4) to the archaizing bronze head of a kouros from the Villa of the Papyri (Fuchs 1999, pl. 26; see essay 2.4, Mattusch, figure 2.4.1). The empty sockets for

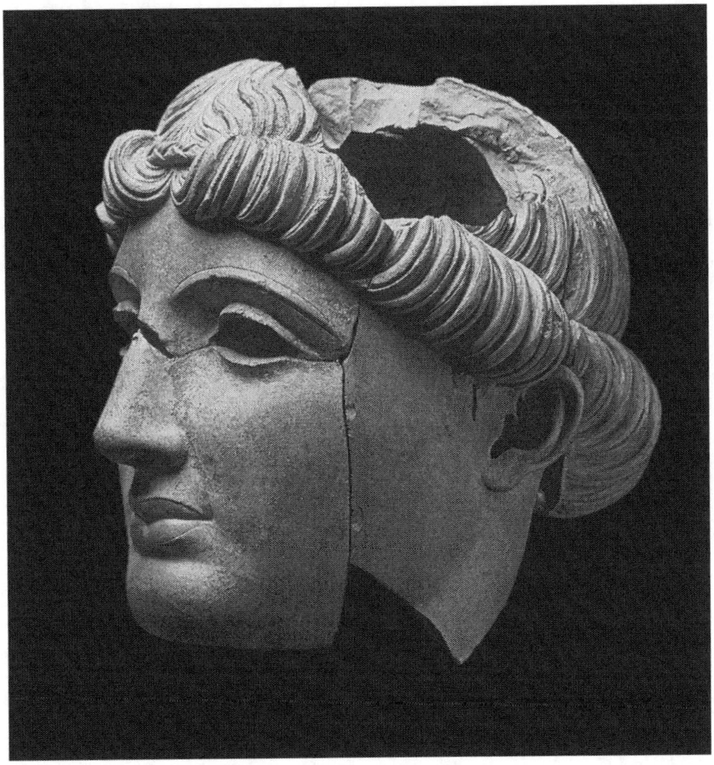

FIGURE 3.6.4 Head of a male, life-size terracotta sculpture from the Domus Tiberiana, Palatine Hill, Rome. Rome, Museo Nazionale Romano, inv. no. 375847.

the insertion of inlaid eyes and the incision outlining the contours of the mouth recall bronze production. The closest parallel for the rolled hairstyle is the Pylades head (see above). The hairstyle of another fragmentary male head matches the head of the Capitoline Charioteer lock for lock (Fuchs 1999, pl. 65.1–3, cf. La Rocca and Parisi Presicce 2010, 311, cat. III.22), itself modeled on the Omphalos Apollo (Stewart 1990, figs. 285–6). Thus, the terracottas on the Palatine share critical iconographic and stylistic details with works known epigraphically as belonging to the school of Pasiteles.

Fuchs (1999, 69, 85–8) is no doubt correct in interpreting the terracottas from the Palatine not as *proplasmata* (*pace* Tomei 1992), which are more likely to have been plaster casts or unfired clay working models, but as works of art in their own right, worthy of display beside similar works in marble and bronze. The high quality of the clay and the exquisite execution mimicking the best of bronze working confirm this reading. Yet, their very eclecticism is a reflection of workshop practice. Their scale seems to have been determined by plaster casts of Greek originals or Roman retrospective works (Landwehr 1985). In comparison, note the regularity in scale of the various versions of the Stephanos Youth, sometimes to odd effect, as in the case of the Orestes and Electra in Rome, where the discrepancy in scale between the two figures may be explained by different-sized models. Other groups, such as the Orestes and Pylades in Paris and the Orestes and Electra in Naples, demonstrate the workshop's reliance on piece molds. The same head is utilized for both Pylades and Electra (with minor changes to create a female hairstyle). Therefore I agree with Tomei (1992), who attributed the Palatine terracottas to a workshop in the tradition of Pasiteles.

Archaism, Eclecticism, Terracotta, and Roman Sculpture

Earlier, I noted that Pliny distinguishes between Greek and Italic artists only in his treatment of terracotta works. Lysistratos, the brother of Lysippos, was said to be the first to "mold a likeness in plaster from the face itself." Lysistratos is credited not only with the invention of the technique of making corrections on the wax casting but also that of taking casts from statues, "and this method advanced to such an extent that no figures or statues were made without a clay model." (Plin. *HN* 35.153; Stewart 1990, 293, T 133). Pliny continues by noting that this demonstrates that modeling in clay preceded bronze casting chronologically. Interestingly, the next passages (Plin. *HN* 35.154–7) introduce modelers in clay in Rome, starting with Damophilus and Gorgasus and progressing through Arcesilaos to end with Pasiteles.

How did terracotta sculpture come to be associated with a specifically Roman form of art that transcended style? As Coarelli notes (1996, 15), "the formation of an Italic-Roman culture is inseparable from its very origins with Greek models." Nowhere is this more demonstrable than in Rome, where the fusion of Greek, Roman, and Etruscan culture was the norm from the time of the legendary kings. One need only think of Tarquinius Priscus, the Etruscan king of Rome, whose father was the Corinthian Demaratus (Livy 1.34.2). Moreover, Pliny (*HN* 35.152) ascribes to Demaratus the introduction of the art of modeling in clay to Italy, since the modelers Euchir, Diopus, and Eugrammus accompanied him in his flight from Corinth (the traditional birthplace of ceramics).

The early sixth-century BC temple from the Sanctuary of Sant'Omobono in Rome, perhaps dedicated by the Etrusco-Corinthian Tarquinius Priscus, has been linked iconographically to contemporary temples in Corfu (Greece) and Syracuse (Magna Graecia), all built by members of the exiled Bacchiads of Corinth (Winter 2005). The pediments of those Greek temples are adorned with a central Gorgon with heraldic felines, and the early sixth-century BC Sant'Omobono temple in Rome featured a terracotta Gorgon with terracotta flanking felines in the pediment. La Rocca (2010, 100) notes the dependence of Etruscan-Italic sculpture of the sixth and fifth centuries BC on Greek models as also reflected in the terracotta statues of Apollo, Herakles, and Latona on the contemporary Temple of Apollo at Portonaccio (see essay 3.2, de Grummond). Both these and the smaller terracotta acroteria from the Portonaccio temple (Winter 2005, 248, fig. 3) have been linked to the workshop of the terracotta quadriga of Rome's Capitoline temple.

The archaic Temple of Jupiter Optimus Maximus is a prime example of the long tradition of eclecticism and the use of terracotta in Roman sculpture. Its sixth-century BC terracotta architectural sculpture and the terracotta cult statue of the god, attributed to the Etruscan artist Vulca and commissioned by Tarquinius Superbus (Plin. *HN* 35.157) were combined over the centuries with a truly eclectic mix of works in different styles (see essay 3.2, de Grummond). A bronze quadriga replaced the terracotta one destroyed by lightning in the late third century BC. Golden shields were added by M. Aemilius Lepidus and Aemilius Paullus a century later.

An early fifth-century BC fragmentary Amazon in terracotta has also been linked to the presence of Greek artists in Rome (Lulof 2007, 27, fig. 23). Its technique finds closest parallels in terracottas from Greece and Magna Grecia, where similar figures served as temple acroteria. It is tempting to associate the piece with the first of the coroplasts mentioned by Pliny (35.154), the Greek artists, Damophilus and Gorgasus, who decorated the Temple of Ceres in Rome (496–493 BC). Indeed, an essentially continuous tradition of large-scale terracotta sculpture production can be documented in Rome and its environs through the fourth, third, and second centuries BC, including eclectic works based on fifth-century BC models (La Rocca and Parisi Presicce 2010).

Cato the Elder's lament concerning the ridiculing of the traditional terracotta gods of the past in the face of the influx of bronze and marble statuary into the city as booty after the sack of Syracuse in 211 BC (Livy 34.4.3–4) suggests an important shift in the material used for sculpture production in Rome. But Rome remained a world full of terracotta gods. Pliny reports that many cult images and temple pediments in terracotta were visible in his day, "admirable for their technical and artistic merit, and for their intrinsic durability; more venerable than gold, and certainly more innocent." (*HN* 35.158; trans.

Hallett 2012, 226n54). The choice of terracotta for new works in this latter age must have signaled traditionalism and sanctity.

In Rome, the mid-second-century BC terracotta temple pediment from Via San Gregorio (La Rocca and Parisi Presicce 2010, 247–9, cat. I.2) contains a mix of divinities clearly based on fourth-century and Hellenistic Greek models. The mid-first-century BC seated goddess from Ostia demonstrates the continuity in the terracotta tradition of cult statues (La Rocca and Parisi Presicce 2010, 273, cat. I.32). The monumental body is modeled on fourth-century BC Greek sculpture; her strongly classicizing face was molded then gilded. If the style of the sculpture is eclectic, its material—terracotta—is undoubtedly archaistic.

A very fragmentary first-century BC architectural sculpture group in terracotta from the via Latina includes both eclectic and archaizing elements: a bearded male who may represent Jupiter (a fragment of a hand holds a thunderbolt; Fuchs 1999, pl. 66.3); a youthful archaistic head (Fuchs 1999, pl. 66.6); another male head (with the full cheeks of the severe style) that corresponds closely to one of the Palatine cache heads (Fuchs 1999, pl. 66.4, cf. 66.2); and a female head after a fourth-century BC prototype (Fuchs 1999, pl. 66.5). The high quality of the clay and the technique in which the eyes were inlaid in another material, reminiscent of bronze working, also ties these works with the school of Pasiteles, whose founding sculptor, as we have seen, worked in terracotta as well as in marble, bronze, and ivory.

Finally, our survey takes us back to the Palatine. Terracotta architectural reliefs adorned the complex that included the Sanctuary of Apollo and the house of Augustus (La Rocca et al. 2013, 226–7, cat. V.2). The reliefs are eclectic and archaizing not only in their style but also in their material. They recall the multitude of painted terracottas that symbolized continuity with the Italic past of the city and in particular those of the original Temple of Jupiter Optimus Maximus (burned in 83 BC), the archetypal Tuscan temple that the Temple of Apollo (Vitr. *De arch.* 3.3.4–5) imitated in marble. Augustus may have commissioned the Palatine terracotta gods for the same sanctuary on the Palatine, presenting himself as the restorer of the Republic and paralleling his restoration of traditional cults and temples associated with the origins of Rome. These eclectic works in clay paid homage to the traditional material of archaic Rome while taking their inspiration from retrospective models of the Greek world.

Conclusion

Archaism and eclecticism are by nature retrospective styles, and their use in Roman art is inextricably related to the historical relationship of Rome to Greece, visible in the second-century BC phenomena of the transfer to Rome of original Greek sculpture and the creation of new works by Greek artists living and working in Rome. Though these styles appear in a range of materials, the extensive use of terracotta, the traditional material of the Italic past, marked these works, whose styles certainly evoked Greek cultural traditions, as specifically Roman. Because of the link between these styles and the early development of Roman art, archaism and eclecticism are central to the study of Roman sculpture.

Bibliography

Anguissola, A. 2007. "Retaining the Function: Sacred copies in Greek and Roman Art." *RES: Anthropology and Aesthetics* 51: 98–107.

Cain, H.-U., and O. Dräger 1994. "Die sogenannten neuattischen Werkstätten." In *Das Wrack: Der antike Schiffsfund von Mahdia*, vol. 2, edited by G. Hellenkemper Salies, H.-H. von Prittwitz und Gaffron, and G. Bauchhenss, 809–829. Cologne: Rheinland-Verlag.

Coarelli, F. 1996. *Revixit ars: Arte e ideologia a Roma; Dai modelli ellenistici alla tradizione repubblicana*. Rome: Edizioni Quasar.

De Angelis, F. 2008. "Pliny the Elder and the Identity of Roman Art." *RES: Anthropology and Aesthetics* 53–4: 79–92.

Donderer, M. 1988. "Nicht Praxiteles, sondern Pasiteles: Eine signierte Statuenstütze in Verona." *ZPE* 73: 63–8.

Fuchs, M. 1999. *"In hoc etiam genere Graeciae nihil cedamus": Studien zur Romanisierung der späthellenistischen Kunst im 1. Jh. v. Chr.* Mainz: Philipp von Zabern.

Fullerton, M. D. 1990. *The Archaistic Style in Roman Statuary*. Mnemosyne Supplement 110. Leiden: Brill.

Gazda, E. K., ed. 2002. *The Ancient Art of Emulation: Studies in Artistic Originality and Tradition from the Present to Classical Antiquity*. Ann Arbor: University of Michigan Press.

Hallett, C. H. 2005a. *The Roman Nude: Heroic Portrait Statuary, 200 BC–AD 300*. Oxford: Oxford University Press.

———. 2005b. "Emulation versus Replication: Redefining Roman Copying." *JRA* 18: 419–35.

———. 2012. "The Archaic Style in Sculpture in the Eyes of Ancient and Modern Viewers." In *Making Sense of Greek Art*, edited by V. Coltman, 70–100. Exeter: University of Exeter Press.

Häuber, R. C. 1991. *Horti Romani: Die Horti Maecenatis und die Horti Lamiani auf dem Esquilin; Geschichte, Topographie, Statuenfunde*. Cologne: Häuber.

Koortbojian, M. 2002. "Forms of Attention: Four Notes on Replication and Variation." In Gazda 2002, 173–204.

La Rocca, E. 2010. "La maestà degli dèi come apparizione teatrale." In La Rocca and Parisi Presicce 2010, 95–114.

———. 2013. "La costruzione di una nuova classicità." In La Rocca et al. 2013, 184–201.

La Rocca, E., and C. Parisi Presicce, eds. 2010. *I giorni di Roma: L'età della conquista*. Rome: Skira.

La Rocca, E., C. Parisi Presicce, A. Lo Monaco, C. Giroire, and D. Roger, eds. 2013. *Augusto*. Milan: Mondadori Electa.

Landwehr, C. 1985. *Die antiken Gipsabgüsse aus Baiae: Griechische Bronzestatuen in Abgüssen römischer Zeit*. Berlin: Mann.

Lulof, P. S. 2007. "L'Amazzone del Esquilino: Una nuova ricostruzione." *BullCom* 108: 1–31.

Perry, E. 2002. "Rhetoric, Literary Criticism, and the Roman Aesthetics of Artistic Imitation." In Gazda 2002, 153–71.

———. 2005. *The Aesthetics of Emulation in the Visual Arts of Ancient Rome*. Cambridge: Cambridge University Press.

Pollitt, J. J. 1986. *Art in the Hellenistic Age*. Cambridge: Cambridge University Press.
Preisshofen, F., and P. Zanker 1970–71. "Reflex einer eklektischen Kunstanschauung beim Auctor *Ad Herrenium*." *DialArch* 4–5: 100–119.
Rawson, E. 1975. "Architecture and Sculpture: The Activities of the Cossutii." *PBSR* 43: 36–47.
Ridgway, B. S. 2002. *Hellenistic Sculpture III: The Styles of ca. 100–31 BC*. Madison: University of Wisconsin Press.
Stewart, A. F. 1990. *Greek Sculpture: An Exploration*. New Haven: Yale University Press.
———. 2012. "Hellenistic Freestanding Sculpture from the Athenian Agora, Part 2: Demeter, Kore, and the Polykles Family." *Hesperia* 81: 655–89.
Strazzulla, M. J. 2010. "L'architettura religiosa di Roma tra tradizione e innovazione." In La Rocca and Parisi Presicce 2010, 83–94.
Susini, G. 1965. "Il coroplasta Dionisio di Colofone." *ArchCl* 17: 302–5.
Tomei, M. A. 1992. "Statue di Terracotta del Palatino." *RM* 99: 171–228.
Touchette, L.-A. 1995. *The Dancing Maenad Reliefs: Continuity and Change in Roman Copies*. BICS Supplement 62. London: Institute of Classical Studies.
Winter, N. 2005. "Gods Walking on the Roof." *JRA* 18: 241–51.
Zagdoun, M.-A. 1989. *La sculpture archaïsante dans l'art hellénistique et dans l'art romain du haut-empire*. BÉFAR 269. Paris: Boccard.

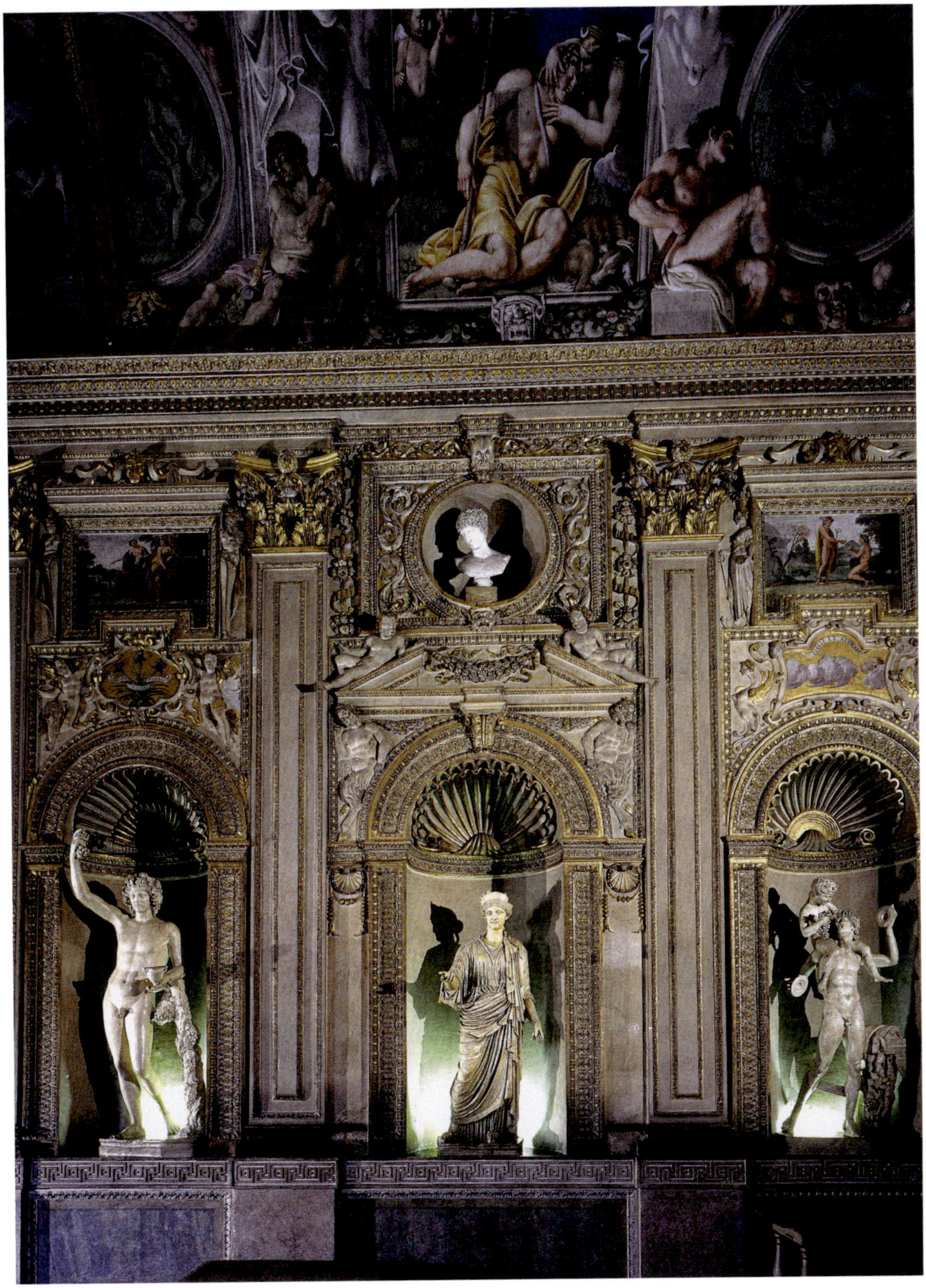

FIGURE 1.1.3 Vault with frescos of gods and cupids, woodwork, and niches with classical sculptures, Carracci Gallery, Palazzo Farnese, Rome, Italy. 1601.

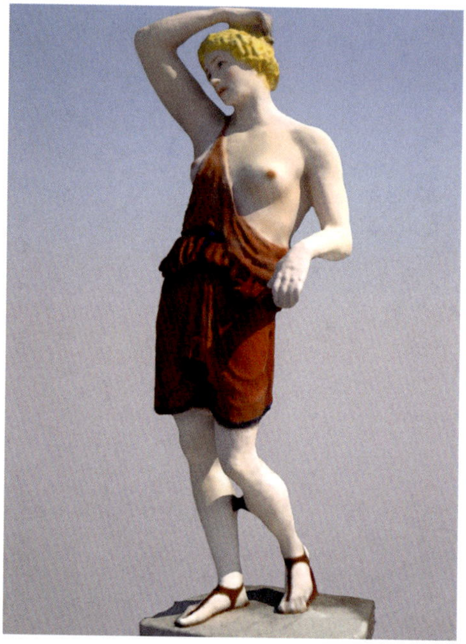

FIGURE 1.5.1 3DDM of the Amazon Sciarra from the Canopus of Hadrian's Villa with color restored. 3-D data collected by B. Frischer from the cast in the Skulpturhalle, Basel. 3-D modeling and restoration by M. Brennan. Sponsored by NSF grant # 1018512.

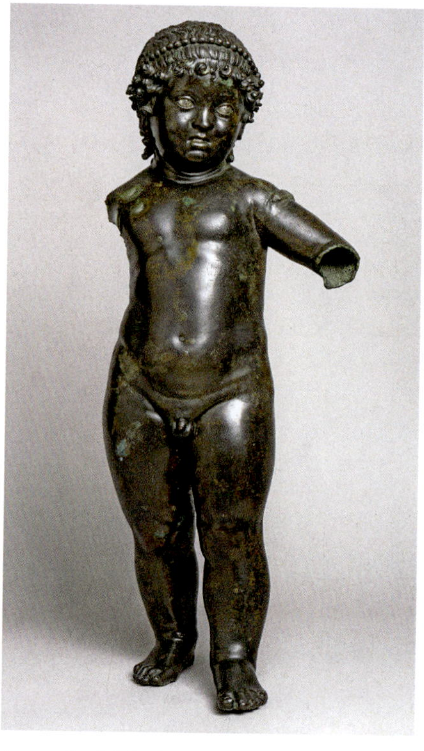

FIGURE 2.6.4 Bronze statue of child Dionysos with sulfide-rich black patination and silvered eyes and teeth. From Fayum, Egypt. Mid-first century BC to mid-first century AD. H. 62.9 cm. St. Louis, Saint Louis Art Museum.

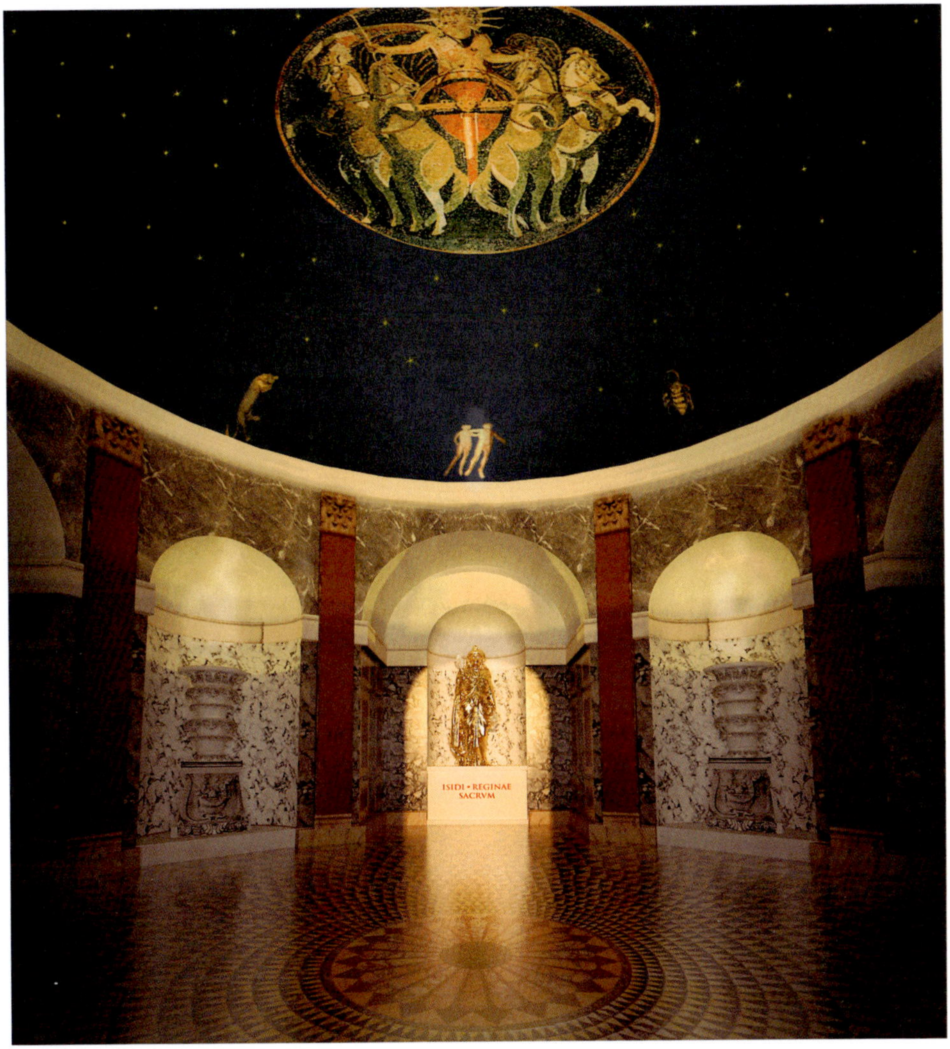

FIGURE 1.5.4 3DDM of the lower rotunda of Roccabruna, Hadrian's Villa. 3-D hand modeling by M. Brennan. Sponsored by NSF grant # 1018512.

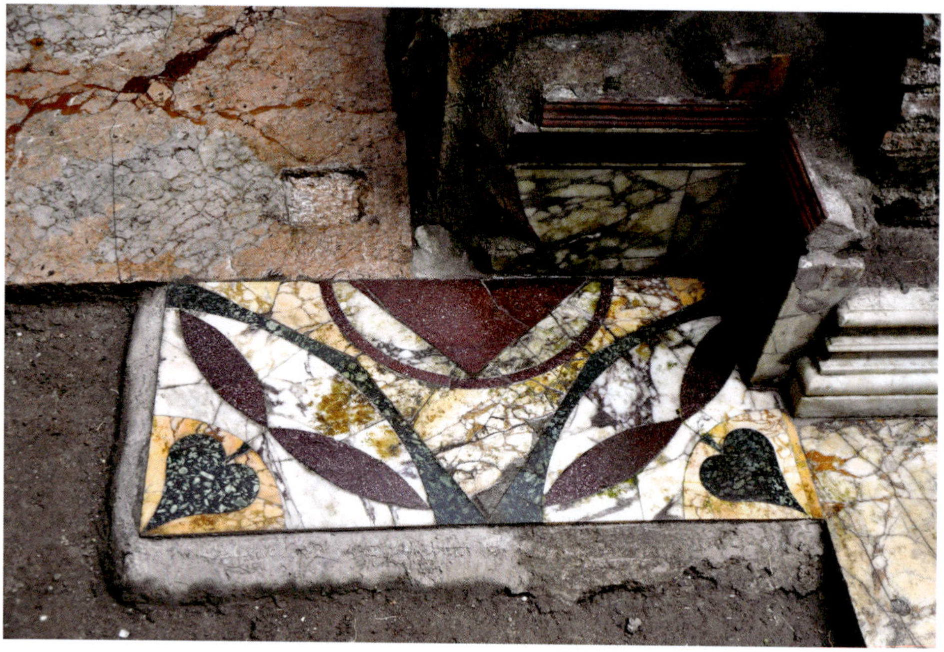

FIGURE 2.1.4 So-called Bagni di Livia, a part of Nero's imperial palace, Rome.

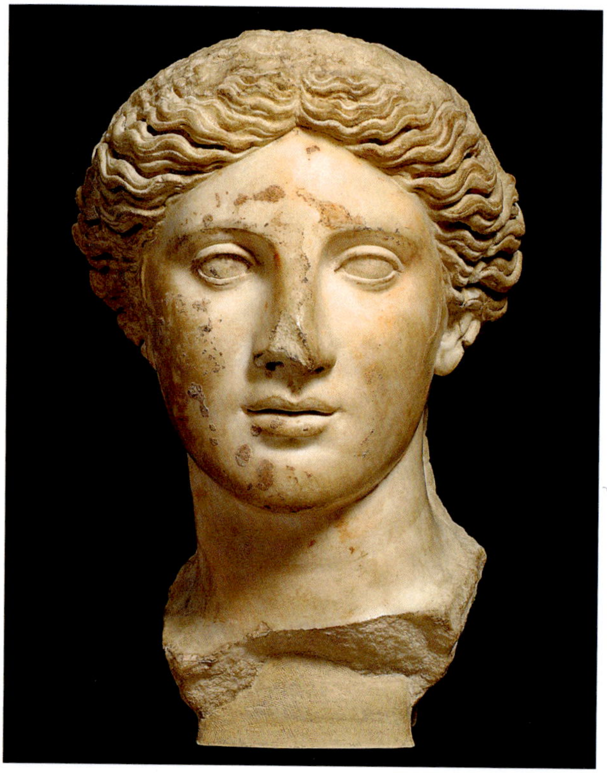

FIGURE 2.6.2 Head of a goddess, the so-called Treu Head. Parian marble with extensive vestiges of painting on hair, eyes, and flesh areas. From Rome, Esquiline Hill, c. AD 140. H. 38.1 cm. London, British Museum.

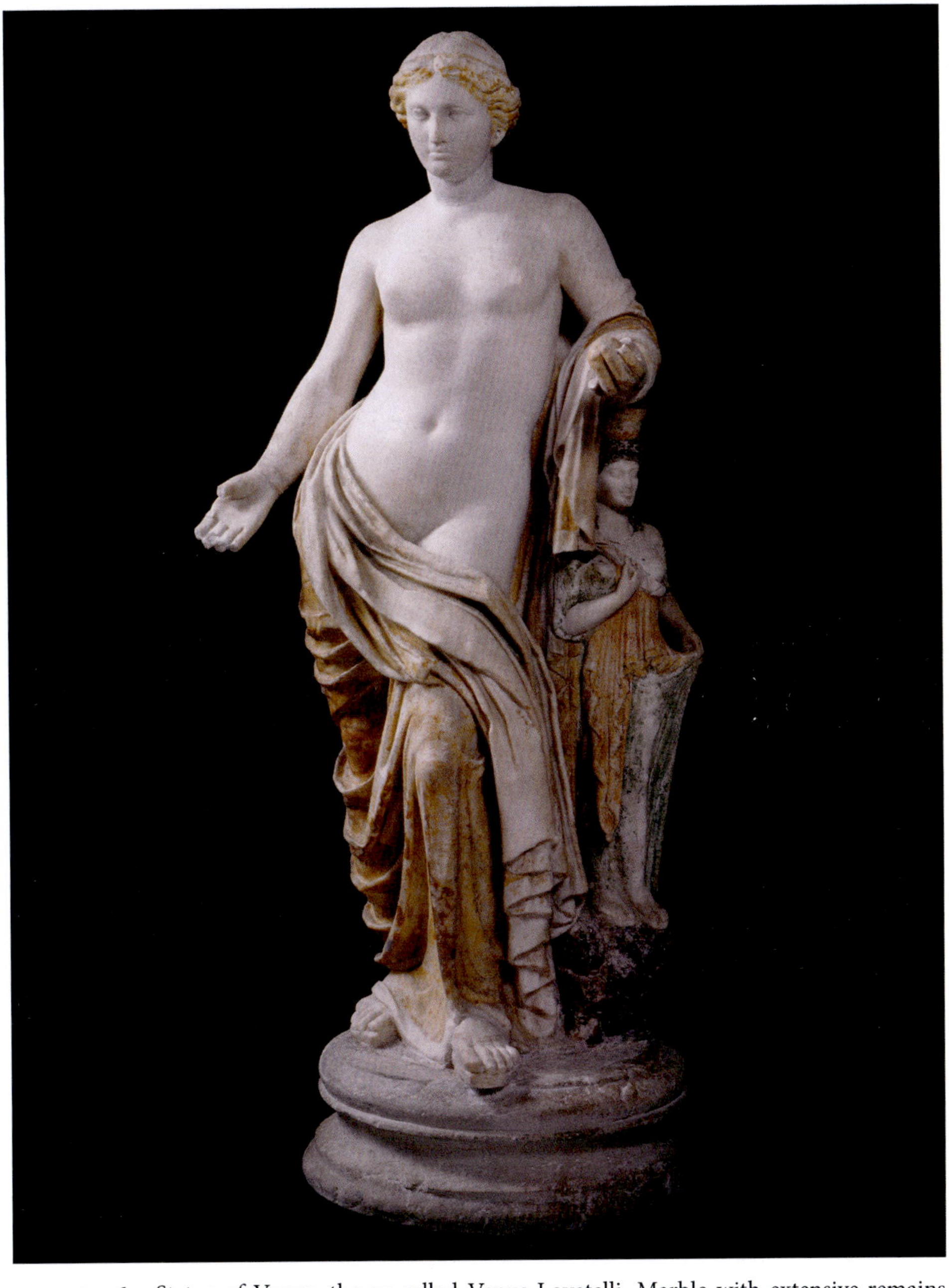

FIGURE 2.6.3 Statue of Venus, the so-called Venus Lovatelli. Marble with extensive remains of painting. From Pompeii, c. first century BC. H. 104 cm. Museo Archeologico Nazionale di Napoli.

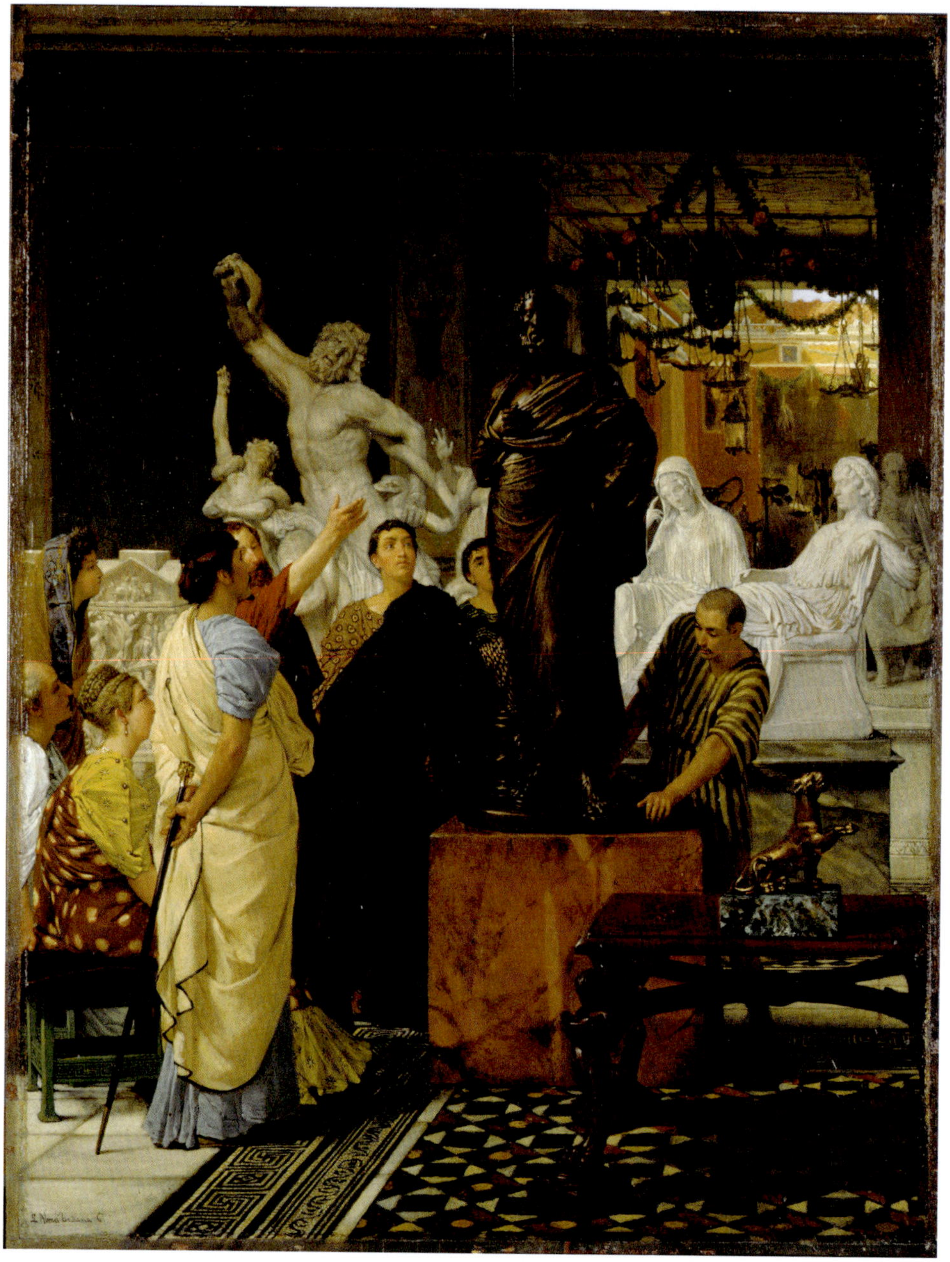

FIGURE 6.1.1 Lawrence Alma-Tadema, *A Dealer in Statues, or, A Sculpture Gallery in Rome at the Time of Augustus* (Opus XLIX), 1867, oil on panel, 61.5 × 46.9 cm. Montreal Museum of Fine Arts, purchased by the Horsley and Annie Townsend Bequest (inv. no. 1980.2).

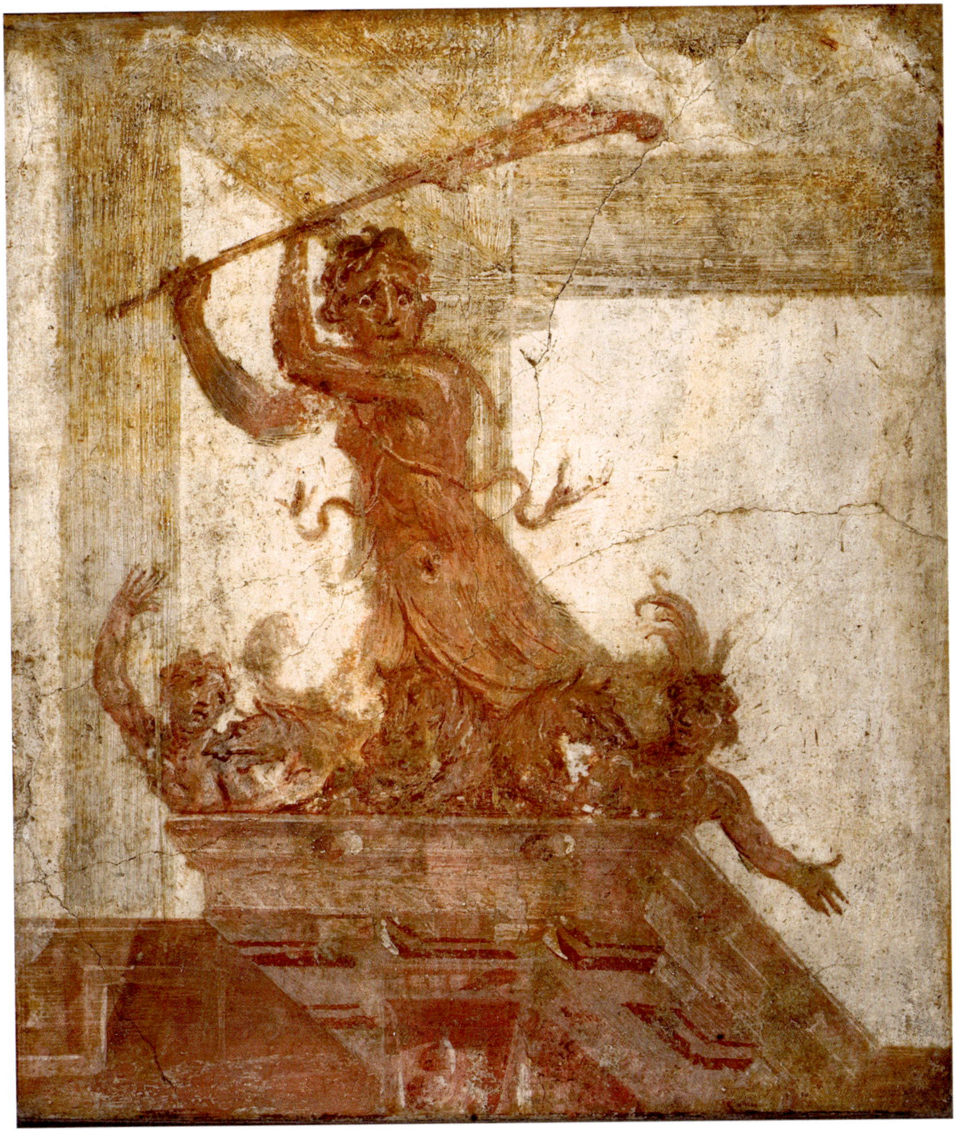

FIGURE 6.4.1 Fourth-Style wall painting showing a Triton as an acroterium, from the Villa of Ariadne in Castellammare di Stabia. Museo Archeologico Nazionale di Napoli, inv. no. 8860.

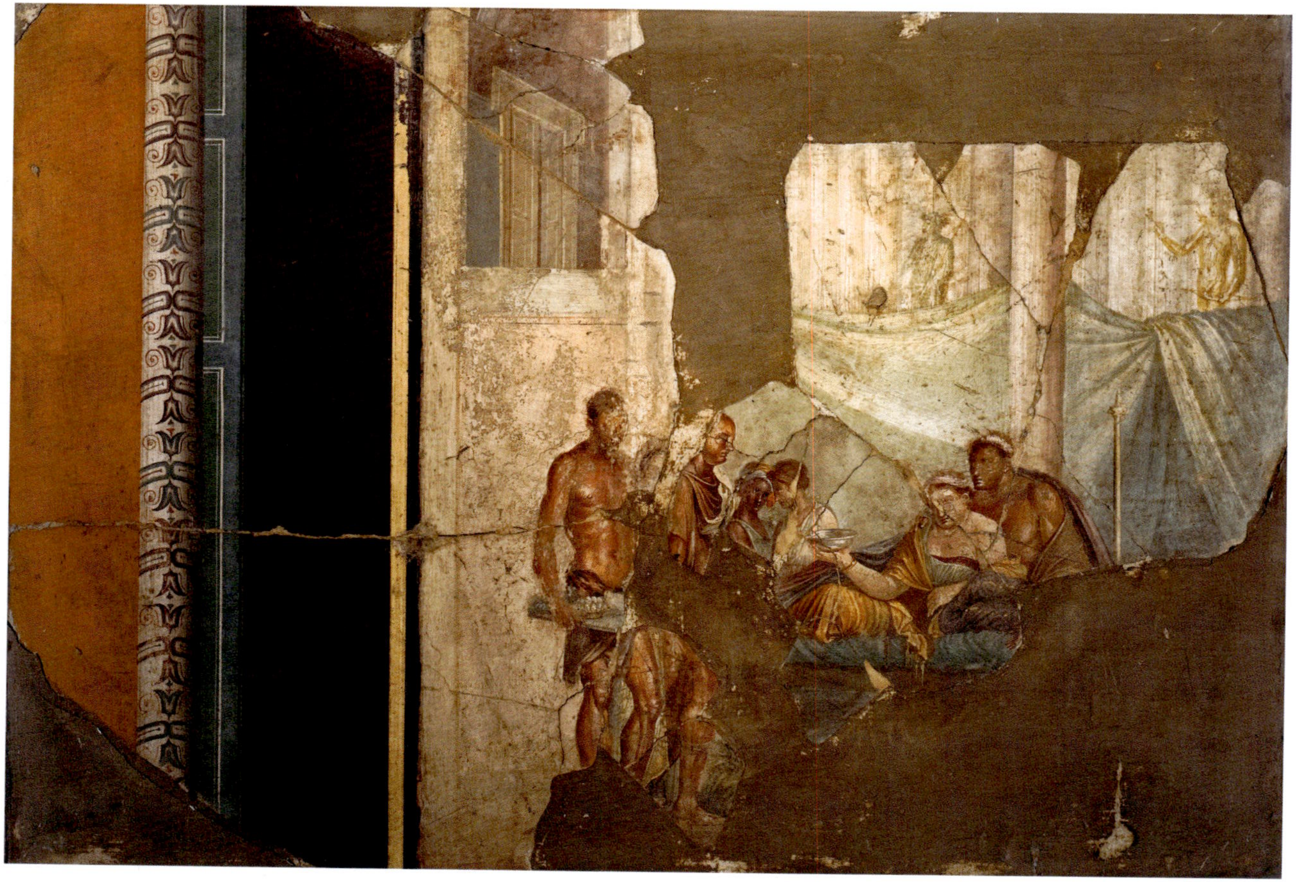

FIGURE 6.4.2 Third-Style wall painting known as "Sophonisba and Massinissa", showing a banqueting scene with statues of Apollo and Dionysus as embellishments of the interior, from the House of Joseph II in Pompeii. Museo Archeologico Nazionale di Napoli, inv. no. 8968.

CHAPTER 3.7

EGYPTIAN-STYLE MONUMENTS

MOLLY SWETNAM-BURLAND

INTRODUCTION

IN this essay, I discuss Roman-period sculptures fashioned in Egyptian styles and their relationship with imported Egyptian antiquities. I treat exclusively artworks found outside of the province of Aegyptus and focus on the period following Rome's annexation of the territory as a province in 30 BC (for sculpture within Roman-controlled Egypt, see essay 5.6, Riggs). Egyptian-looking works of art from Roman Italy and the provinces are sometimes referred to as aegyptiaca, Egyptiana, pharaonica, or exotica—all modern terms that stress their unique external appearance and indicate that these monuments were not of Egyptian provenance or manufacture, but made in Italy in what was perceived to be an Egyptian style. Such terms create a conceptual divide between artworks created in foreign or antique styles and other artworks produced in Rome. As a result, sculptures in the Egyptian mode are not often included in general surveys of Roman art; they are presumed to be of interest only to specialists in the Italian cults to the Egyptian gods or taken as emblematic of an imperial fad, an Egyptomania of the classical period. In the last decade, however, a number of scholars have questioned the value of categories and boundaries that have segregated aegyptiaca from other Roman material culture (Versluys 2002; 2010; Vout 2003; Elsner 2006; Swetnam-Burland 2007; 2015; Petersen 2012, 328–32). It is undeniable that as Egypt came within Rome's imperial dominion and the flow of goods from Egypt to Rome grew, so too did an awareness of the place, its culture, and its religion, and so too did appreciation for Egyptian-looking artworks. But this phenomenon was no short-lived craze; rather it was a broad, deep, and enduring trend that spanned centuries—dependent upon patterns of trade and shifts in population that affected the empire as a whole.

Roman sculptures in Egyptian styles range from reliefs and statues worked in the round, to monumental columns with sculpted decoration, to obelisks with sunken-relief carving. Some reproduce imported Egyptian "originals" one-to-one; others affect an Egyptian-looking style; still others depict Egyptian subjects, but according to prevailing Italian artistic conventions. Because the study of these materials has grown, in some senses, into a subdiscipline, interested students and scholars should consult both older, pathbreaking scholarship on Egyptian and Egyptianizing materials and the cult of Isis (Malaise 1972; Roullet 1972; Dunand 1973) and more recent exhibition catalogs and compendia (Arslan et al. 1997; Walker and Higgs 2001; Beck, Bol, and Bückling 2005; De Caro 2006) to become acquainted with the corpora. Though I focus here on the plastic arts, it is important to be aware that many media drew upon Egyptian motifs, including frescoes (De Vos 1980), mosaics, precious-metal plate, seals, gems (Sfameni 2003; Veymiers 2009), and cameo glass. In addition, representations of the land and residents of Egypt, both in the form of personifications and peopled landscapes, were popular in sculpture and in two-dimensional media like painting and mosaics. Though these often do not have a foreign visual style, they are nevertheless germane to discussions that press beyond connoisseurship, seeking to understand the wider appeal of Egyptian culture in the Roman context (Versluys 2002; Swetnam-Burland 2009).

It is clear that aegyptiaca of all sorts appealed to Roman audiences on the basis of their distinctiveness. These artworks were exotic in that they advertised a connection with a place geographically distant, renowned for its powerful gods, fertile lands, and long history. Greek and Roman authors knew the land of the Nile as a place with "upside-down" customs relative to Greek and Roman norms, animal worship chief among them (for literary discourse on Egypt, see Smelik and Hemelrijk 1984; Vasunia 2001; Moyer 2011; Parker 2011; Manolaraki 2012). At the same time, Aegyptus was a real place, crucial to the economic stability of the empire. Visitors from all around the Mediterranean admired the land for its antiquity; they were particularly drawn to the pyramids or monuments like the Colossi of Memnon. Many travelers were there first in administrative or commercial capacities and were tourists second (Foertmeyer 1989). Egypt's agricultural products were vital to daily life throughout the empire; its granites adorned public monuments; its gems and mineral resources (not to mention the spices, textiles, and perfumes that moved westward through Alexandria) enabled many forms of elite conspicuous consumption. Throughout this essay, I adopt the view that, despite this foreign façade, we can best understand Egyptian and Egyptian-looking sculptures in Italy if we treat them just as we do other kinds of Roman material culture, fronting questions about context and thinking carefully about manufacture. First, I examine the phenomenon of the importation of Egyptian antiquities. Next, I turn to their influence on sculptures of Roman production, particularly in contexts intended to evoke or honor the Egyptian gods.

Egyptian Sculptures Imported to Italy

Contact between Egypt and Italy predated Roman annexation of Aegyptus by centuries. Egyptian artifacts and materials, including ivory, lapis lazuli, and faience, appear in funerary contexts in Etruria, Campania, and Magna Graecia during the orientalizing period (c. 720–525 BC), a feature of the extensive pan-Mediterranean trade in portable luxuries. Contact and commerce between Egypt and Italy continued throughout the Republic, based on trade, diplomacy, and military intervention. Yet, by and large, trade was sporadic, especially relative to the later imperial networks that moved grain in bulk directly from Alexandria to Rome. Rome's dependence on Egyptian staple commodities was an imperial phenomenon and enabled commerce in all manner of other goods, including many smaller luxury products like refined papyrus, perfumes, spices, precious metals, and both Egyptian antiquities and newly quarried colored granites, marbles, and basalts. Though there are monuments from the Republic that reflect an interest in Egypt, including the well-known Nile mosaic from Palestrina, the greatest taste for aegyptiaca followed conquest. In broadest strokes, imported materials became more common, available, and affordable to a wider range of patrons following annexation. In turn, imports inspired the creation of new works in Egyptian mode.

Egyptian sculptures brought to Italy range widely in size, material, and subject matter. Though the corpus is diverse, a few patterns suggest that Romans, above all, valued pieces that looked Egyptian to them. Romans preferred sculptures inscribed with the hieroglyphic script or that represented kings and queens, sphinxes, or exotic animals (for a concise summary in list form, see Roullet 1972, appendix III; Lollio Barberi, Parola, and Totti 1995). Efforts to find a common thread among these works confound what may seem obvious assumptions on the part of students or scholars first confronted with the material, whether Romanists or Egyptologists. Almost all Egyptian antiquities brought to Rome were antiques in the sense that they were already centuries old at the time of their removal to Italy, yet few come from those periods of history most studied today. The majority belong to the late period (664–525 BC) or Ptolemaic period (323–30 BC). The reasons for these preferences are many. Egyptian art of the late period is known for its archaism, a deliberate return to the visual styles of earlier periods, part of a comprehensive effort by the Egyptian kings to hail a return to a golden age. Monuments of the period are known for the high quality of their carving and exhibit those traits most often thought to define Egyptian visual style (a stable canon of proportions, combined perspective, symbolic use of color). Most Ptolemaic works imported to Rome also adhere to Egyptian visual conventions. Material from both the late and Ptolemaic periods would also have been plentiful in Roman Egypt, particularly in the region of the Delta, close to the port city of Alexandria. Thus, the selected materials were both readily available and pleasing to the eye in their "Egyptian-ness." The abundance of later Egyptian artifacts in the Italian corpus makes sense for both aesthetic and practical reasons.

Yet the fact that Romans in Italy prized Egyptian sculptures that exhibited an antique style raises what seems a fundamental question: how did Romans outside Egypt understand this material, featuring exotic iconography and inscribed with foreign text? Some might put the question differently, asking whether Romans used or valued these artworks as residents of Aegyptus did, or as or Egyptians of the distant past had done. There are no easy answers. Only a select minority of people living outside Egypt, for instance, would have been able to read the hieroglyphic script, though many would have recognized hieroglyphs as a form of Egyptian writing (Iversen 1971; for a "translated" monument, Lambrecht 2001). And, as pictorial symbols, hieroglyphs also served a decorative function Romans could appreciate. Pliny the Elder, for example, described the writing on obelisks as *scalpturae* and *effigies*, "carved engravings" and "representations," and knew that they conveyed information, though he was not himself able to read them (Plin. *HN* 36.64). Other evidence suggests that hieroglyphs could be read allegorically or even taken literally, as representations of men, women, animals, and so on. They were therefore meaningful—not according to their former linguistic values but on a visual, symbolic level. The Roman reuse of Egyptian imported sculptures severed these objects' connections with the contexts from which their original, culture-specific meanings derived. Furthermore, in most instances Romans did not use or display imported materials according to Egyptian precedent. It can be useful, then, to think of these materials as having Egyptian lives and Roman afterlives. Whatever new symbolism these monuments acquired stemmed, without doubt, from the fact that they were recognizable as Egyptian. But this was Egypt as it was understood by others. Elusive though the Roman meanings attached to aegyptiaca may be, what answers there are come from studying them within their Italian contexts (Swetnam-Burland 2007; 2015).

Egyptian materials have been found in a wide range of contexts, from the humble and private to the imperial and public. By far the richest collections of Egyptian antiquities are associated with cult centers of the Egyptian gods in Italy, including the Iseum and Serapeum Campense (Lembke 1994a) and other shrines in Rome, and the temples of Beneventum (Müller 1969), Pompeii (Tran Tam Tinh 1964; De Caro 1992), Cumae (Caputo 2010), and many others. In these settings, imported material helped set an "Egyptian" tone and sometimes was treated as sacred. Even in these instances, however, we often lack evidence for the manner of display of specific pieces. Many came to light during the early modern reurbanization of Rome or were found in postclassical deposits, reused as building material or found in middens. For example, an impressive Ptolemaic granite bull was found on the Esquiline Hill in several fragments in the gardens of the Palazzo Brancaccio (figure 3.7.1). Since its discovery, the sculpture has been associated with a possible cult site in the region, and other Egyptian-looking works found in the area, including heads of Isis and Serapis, certainly lend credence to the theory (Roullet 1972, cat. 267; Kater-Sibbes and Vermaseren 1975, cat. 28; and for possible reconstruction, Haüber and Schütz 2010). Recent scholarship, however, problematizes the assumption that all Egyptian and Egyptian-looking artworks were religious in nature—the byproduct of a scholarly tradition that, though of high quality, was guided chiefly by interest in the history of the Egyptian cults in the Mediterranean. The mere presence of Egyptian and Egyptian-looking sculptures in any given context need not indicate that the site served as a place of veneration; nor did all representations of Egyptian deities serve cultic functions (Versluys 2002, 15–17). Certainly, many imported works belonged in sanctuaries, and they can be used in the study of ancient religion. Nevertheless, it is essential to press our explanations beyond superficial generalizations by taking into account context, condition, manufacture, and local votive and commemorative practice.

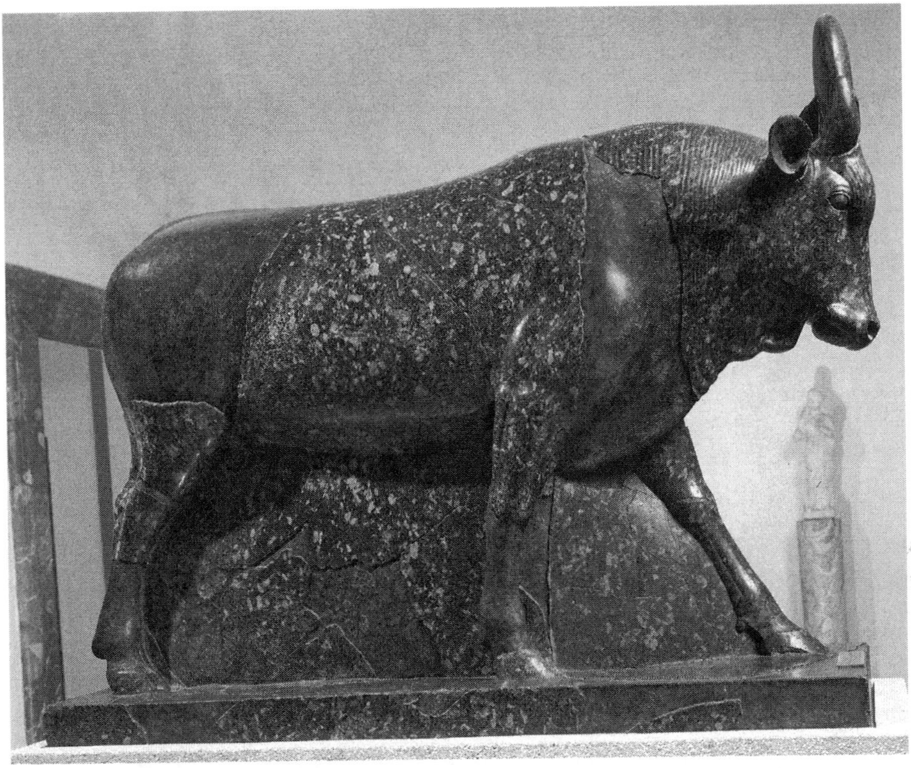

FIGURE 3.7.1 Apis bull, c. second century BC, discovered on the Esquiline Hill in 1886.

Consider the example of a shrine to the Egyptian gods located near the church of San Martino ai Monti on the Esquiline hill, so well preserved at the time of its discovery that it stood intact, complete with its sculptures (Ensoli Vittozi 1993). The brick construction shows that it was constructed in the imperial period, perhaps at that time functioning as a public shrine. But by the fourth century AD, it had been incorporated into an elite residence. Whoever owned the shrine in its final phases venerated the Egyptian gods. A life-size Isis-Fortuna of the second century AD, with traces of gilding still evident, stood in the central niche; the lateral walls had shelves for displaying the shrine's other contents (figure 3.7.2). The finds included ritual paraphernalia, such as small portable altars and lamps, numerous sculptures (including busts and figurines of Serapis, Harpocrates, Venus, Hercules, Diana, and Mars), and an imported Egyptian artifact—a steatite stela of Ptolemaic date bearing an image of Horus standing on a crocodile, surrounded by hieroglyphic texts (Lollio Barberi, Parola, and Totti 1995, no. 26; Arslan et al. 1997, VI.50). Similar objects in their original Egyptian contexts were magical. The image of Horus in this guise proclaimed his ability to control the forces of chaos, and the texts included efficacious formulae (Ritner 1989; Gasse 2004). Though we do not know if Roman audiences understood them in this way, similar imported stelae have been associated with sanctuary sites, including the Iseum and Serapeum Campense (Lembke 1994a, cat. 27; Arslan et al. 1997, V.3). Nevertheless, the precise ritual function

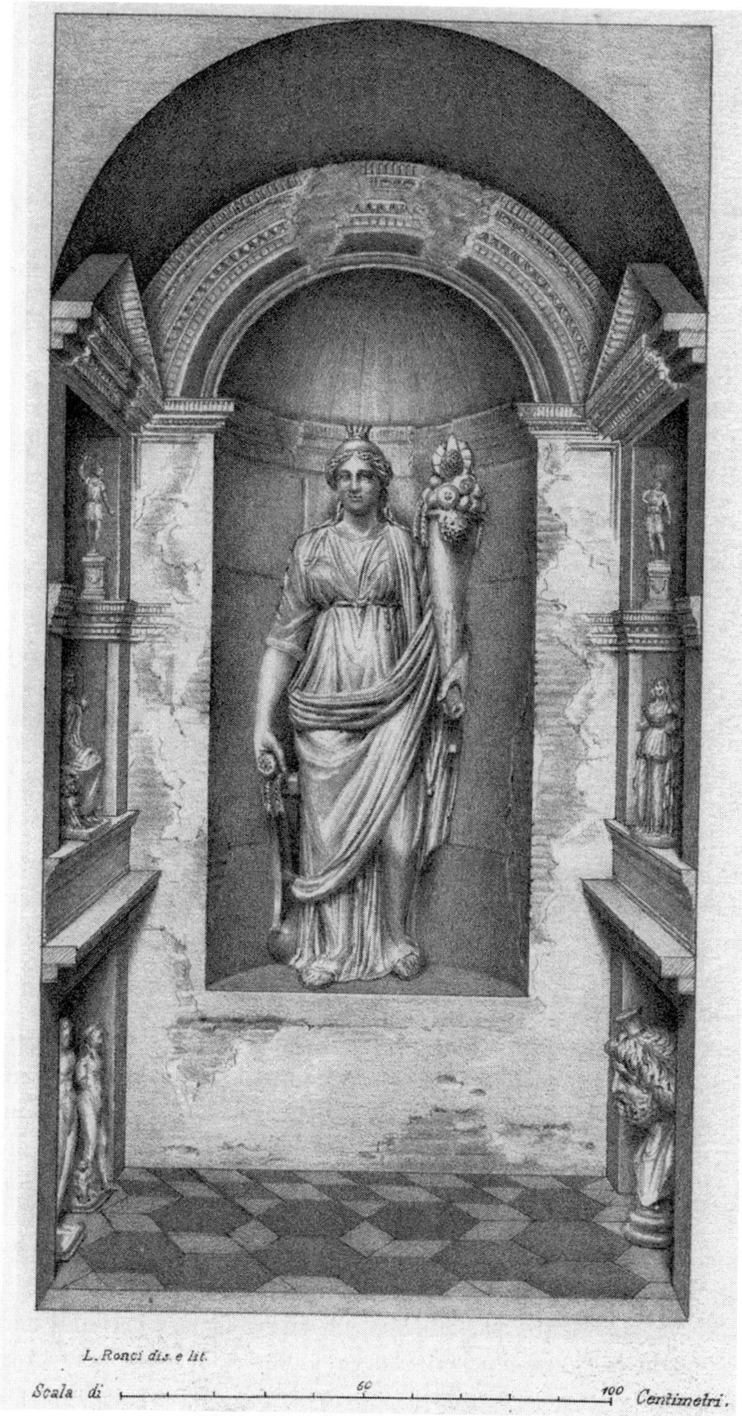

FIGURE 3.7.2 Drawing of *aediculum* on the Esquiline with Isis and assemblage, c. AD 300 (after Visconti 1885, Tav. IV).

of this unusual object—which would have been nearly 600 years old at the time of deposition—is elusive.

If we shift our perspective, placing as much emphasis on the object's place in the assemblage as upon its Egyptian origin, the piece makes greater sense. Particularly curious is that the stela exhibits significant surface damage, possibly caused by burning (Visconti 1885, 33). Most of the other sculptures in this collection were also antiques, second or third century AD in date, and seemingly gathered from diverse contexts, including perhaps imperial *horti*. Others also showed signs of having been repurposed. Two herms, for example, seem to have been architectural spolia (Ensoli Vitozzi 1993, nos. 2–3). Many sculptures were in fragmentary condition, lacking heads, hands, or noses. One female divinity, otherwise unidentifiable, also showed signs of burning (Ensoli Vitozzi 1993, no. 10). In sum, the collection assembled in the shrine's late antique phase brought together a number of artworks, most of them reused, and as a result weathered to greater and lesser degrees. Sacred meaning was newly invested in these sculptures, which eclipsed or enhanced the purposes for which they had been made centuries before. What was once a votive dedication or architectural adornment now became an emblem of the divine. Even the statue of Isis, though it may have served as a cult statue in an earlier phase of its existence, must be understood thus: the gilding evident on the piece is consistent with late antique maintenance (Abbe 2010; see essay 2.6, Abbe). The meaning, in other words, is not inherent to the artwork, but derives from the viewer's existing knowledge and first-hand experience, which may involve touching, dressing, painting, or engaging with the sculpture in other physical ways (see essay 6.5, Perry). Indeed, the damage to the stela may have resulted from such an intervention in an earlier phase of its Roman life, for there are examples of imported materials that were ritually broken (e.g., the imported ushabty from the temple of Isis in Pompeii, found broken and interred, Swetnam-Burland 2007). What some may find surprising is that, despite its foreign manufacture, the imported Ptolemaic sculpture was treated more *like* other materials from the same collection than *unlike* them.

Imported Egyptian sculptures stand at a disciplinary crossroads. They testify to two different times and places—reflecting the history and culture of the Egyptian craftsman and patrons who created and commissioned them, and the history and culture of the Romans who imported, modified, and redisplayed them. The Roman taste for Egyptian sculptures was not connoisseurship, in that it did not rest on authoritative knowledge of their former uses and symbolisms. Rather, Romans chose materials based on their availability and in accordance with their own worship of Isis, Serapis, and many other deities. These artworks were valuable in many senses. They were recommodified by trade, moved across the Mediterranean at great expense, and eventually sold to new owners. Their granite and marble material, too, was luxurious and prestigious, used also for Roman sculptures including both those in Egyptian styles and those in traditional Graeco-Roman visual vernacular (on colored marmora, De Nuccio and Ungaro 2002; see essay 2.6, Abbe). Symbolic meaning, however, was audience- and context-dependent.

Roman Sculptures in "Egyptian" Style

Though it can be useful to distinguish between imported and Italian-made artworks on the basis of manufacture (that is, treating the former as Egyptian and the latter as Roman), both spoke to the same tastes and in many cases were commissioned and dedicated by the same patrons. Often, they were displayed together, integrated into diverse collections. A number of Egyptian-looking sculptures, to take a well-known example, were discovered at Hadrian's Villa at Tivoli (Raeder 1983; Calandra 2000; Pensabene 2010). Some were found in an area that is now thought to be the remains of a temple built for the Egyptian gods or in honor of the deified Antinous (Adembri and Mari 2006; Mari and Sgalambro 2007). Others, however, were found throughout the villa, and—though antiquarian interest and early undocumented excavations make determining their findspots difficult—were clearly part of extraordinary, eclectic groups. Egyptian-looking sculptures and frescoes have been associated with the Palaestra (Ensoli 1999; Newby 2002; De Vos 2004) and the so-called Canopus or Scenic Canal (Grenier 1989). It is possible that the sculptures belonged to shrines within these structures, but both were also areas known for their lavish displays, suggesting a broader audience. Isolating the Egyptian-looking material from other artworks found in proximity risks limiting the scope of interpretation. The sculptures from the canal, for example, in addition to the collection of Egyptian-looking works thought to indicate the presence of a Serapaeum, incorporated iterations of popular types, including the Nile and Tiber, Sciarra, Mattei, and Sciarpa Amazons, reproductions of the karyatids from the Erechtheion and the Forum of Augustus, and many others. Furthermore, Egyptian-inspired artworks played to eclectic tastes even in those contexts where an exotic decor would seem most essential to the establishment of sacred space. The temple of Isis in Pompeii, so well preserved, is a good example. The sanctuary owned some imported Egyptian objects. But the sculptures dedicated by initiates also included representations of Venus and Bacchus as well as portraits. In other words, just as with Roman sculptures that relate to Greek originals, we must consider the appropriation of Egyptian style as integral to the Romans' own aesthetic.

Considering the relationship between works of Egyptian and Italian manufacture, however, can help us understand how artists learned of and came to emulate Egyptian styles. Some Italian-made works reproduce imported sculptures closely or feature texts copied from imports. In some cases, the new sculpture was intended to complement the one on which it was based, and they were displayed together (e.g., two sphinxes, Swetnam-Burland 2007; two queens from the Horti Sallustiani, Hartswick 2004, 130–38). In other cases, imports served as templates that Italian artists drew upon to imbue new creations with seemingly authentic Egyptian features. Looking in more depth at Egyptian obelisks brought to Rome at imperial behest and those made in Italy and carved by local sculptors illustrates this process in action.

Obelisks taken from Egypt were marvels of engineering, symbols of Rome's control of a vast empire. As noted above, hieroglyphs and carved decoration were fundamental to their appeal, intriguing because they appeared to contain secret wisdom and to tell of ancient Egyptian kings (D'Onofrio 1967; Iversen 1968; Parker 2003; 2007; Schneider 2004; 2005; Curran et al. 2009; Swetnam-Burland 2010). Though less famous, a number of obelisks in Italy were quarried or carved during the Roman period both in Egypt and Italy. Some—including Domitian's obelisk, today in the Piazza Navona, and that dedicated to Antinous, standing on the Pincian Hill—were imperial monuments, with custom texts intended to enhance their inclusion in specific settings. Because both were moved after antiquity, however, the nature of these settings is unknown. There is considerable debate about the latter, which some believe was created for a memorial in Rome or at Hadrian's Villa, but which others think was created for display in Antinoopolis and only subsequently brought to Rome (Renberg 2010, appendix). Because it makes specific references to Rome and current events, however, Domitian's obelisk appears to have been carved in Italy, for inclusion in the Iseum and Serapaeum Campense (Parker 2007; for translation, Bricault 2005, 501/0124). There are also a few obelisks commissioned at private initiative, most small in scale and serving as dedications in sanctuaries. All were made of imported stone and carved in Italy, and a few have legible hieroglyphic inscriptions, which reference their Roman dedicators. These monuments attest to the involvement of priests or others trained in hieroglyphic script to compose the texts. But these individuals were rare practitioners of a highly specialized skill (Swetnam-Burland 2011), and they should not be equated with the artisans who carved the monuments. Study of Egyptianizing sculptures that employ sunken relief, in both granite and marble, suggests that their artisans were locals (Parlasca 2003). Furthermore, some obelisks feature fanciful writing or reproduce real texts taken out of context. Perhaps the most telling case is that of the Trinità dei Monti obelisk, originally from the Horti Sallustiani, whose text is a character-for-character duplicate of the obelisk today in the Piazza del Popolo (Hartswick 2004, 52–8; Swetnam-Burland 2010). To carve the new obelisk required resizing the characters and labor-intensive onsite carving. Because few could read them in the literal sense, that the new obelisks bear hieroglyphs served to authenticate them, making them bearers of Egyptian-ness despite their Italian production. These obelisks, therefore, are at once Egyptian *and* Roman. They functioned on many levels as symbols of Egypt, its religions, and its culture, but were worked by local craftsmen using the same methods employed to reproduce artworks of other appearances—including those inspired by Greek masters.

Still other Roman-made works were free compositions or iterations of recurring types (e.g., Eingartner 1991 on Isis-types). There is no consistent Egyptian style evident in Roman-made works, which drew on modes of representation from different periods of Egyptian history and which also vary in iconography. Much art deemed Egyptianizing, furthermore, is not foreign in style, but *does* present Egyptian subjects. Representations of exotic animals and deities were particularly popular, though not all of this material was religious. The cult of Isis required initiation and created tight-knit, hierarchical cultic communities. Yet much knowledge about the Egyptian gods was not rarified. The myths of Isis were in wide enough currency that Roman authors drew on them in poetry and prose, on the assumption that their readers already had some familiarity with the stories (for an introduction to the primary sources with excellent bibliography, Bricault 2005; 2013). Thus, many artworks in Egyptian styles would have had a religious resonance perceptible to the uninitiated, evoking the homeland of these deities in ways that had positive associations. Conversely, it is not possible to infer a solely religious purpose for an artwork based on its depiction of Isis or its style.

A late first- or early second-century relief panel of Luna marble from Arriccia (figure 3.7.3) depicts a performance within a sanctuary, with both performers and their audience clapping in time (Lembke 1994b). The scene represents an Egyptian ritual, perhaps the *navigium Isidis*, celebrating Isis as protector of seafaring. That the scene relates to the Egyptian cults is clear from the setting. A large telamon wearing a kilt stands to the far right, supporting a colonnade filled with Egyptian statues, including an Apis bull, baboons, and a throned goddess, possibly Isis herself. This work was not, however, found in a sanctuary, where such a ceremony might take place, but was reused as the covering for a simple burial. The grave was humble, a simple pit lined with marble slabs, many of them worked in a way that suggested they once served as architectural ornamentation. The relief, along with a tile, served as a cover for the burial. It is possible that the tomb belonged to an initiate in the cult of Isis (Lembke 1994b). But, though it is most likely that the relief was first intended for a monumental, public setting, it need not have been religious. We may take the piece as some evidence for Egyptian religion, in the depiction of the dance, without leaping to the conclusion that the piece instantiates ritual or belonged to a shrine. What is clear, above all, is the artistic value of the piece. Throughout, the sculptor created an experience of movement and rhythm, by juxtaposing the dancers, shown in a combination of profile, rear, and three-quarters view, with the repetition of static forms, the colonnade above and the birds below. Its style—that is, the rendering of three-dimensional space and the proportions of the figures—is not

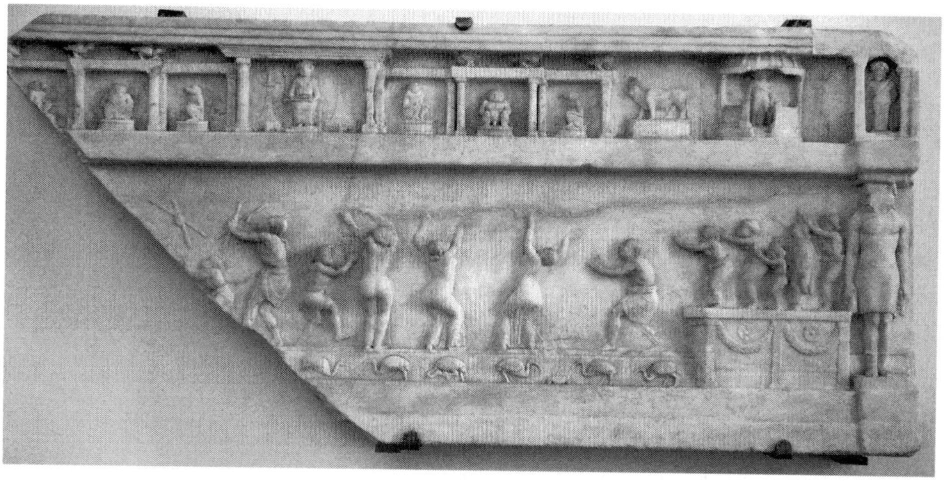

FIGURE 3.7.3 Relief of an Isiac ceremony, imperial period, found in a burial in Arriccia.

particularly Egyptian, despite the exotic subject matter. The relief represents the pinnacle of craftsmanship, attesting to the technical skill of Italian artists, the availability of fine marble, and the value of sculptural handicraft as spolia long after it had served its original purpose.

Throughout, I have suggested that we benefit from treating Egyptian-looking sculptures as we would other Roman material culture. This holds true even for those striking examples in which Egyptian visual conventions were deliberately borrowed. Portraits of Antinous as pharaoh are a case in point. The most often illustrated example is a full-body composition (figure 3.7.4), associated alternately with the Poikile at Hadrian's Villa or with the so-called Canopus (Raeder 1983, 1.136; cf. Grenier 2008, 61). The portrait adopts Egyptian dress and posture. Antinous stands with left foot forward, shoulders squared,

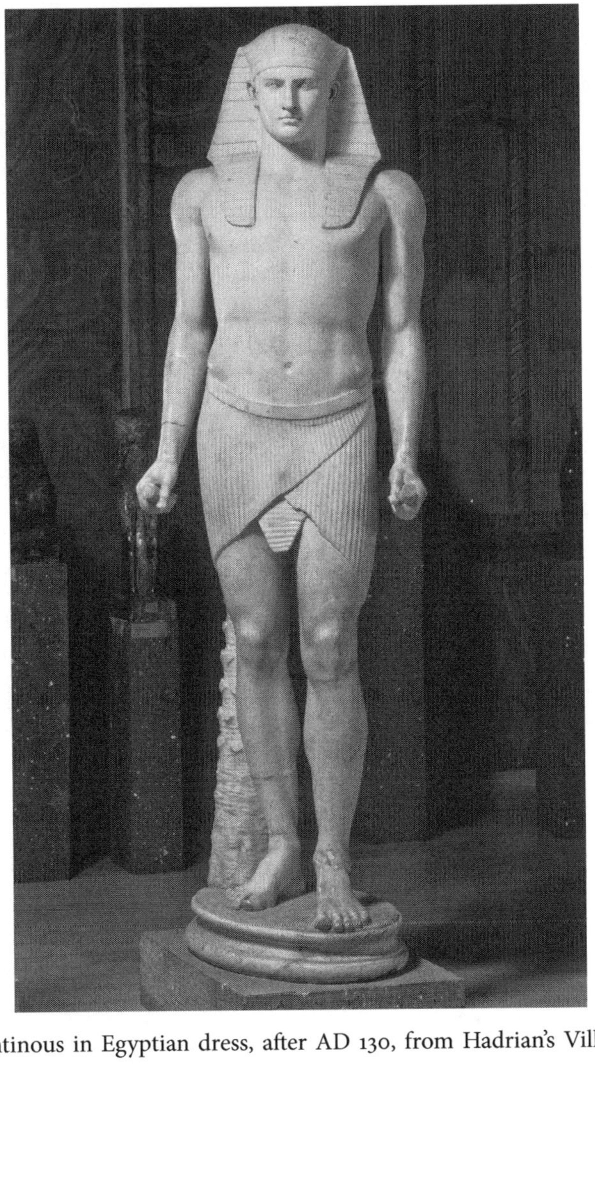

FIGURE 3.7.4 Antinous in Egyptian dress, after AD 130, from Hadrian's Villa.

and arms tensed. In some regards, the Roman artists got certain conventions "wrong" by Egyptian standards. In each hand, Antinous holds a short dowel, a nod to the Egyptian practice of representing the negative space between the palms. The Roman artists, however, have interpreted this feature as if it were a physical object. The work is also not Egyptian in its approach to the human form. It conforms to contemporary practices for treating the body as a whole—in so doing revealing how difficult it would be to hold the posture in real space. The rear view (Meyer 1991, Tafel 107) shows how deeply Antinous's back arches to tip his pelvis forward, allowing the hips to appear level from the front. Throughout, the sculptors have lavished attention on anatomy, even acknowledging the position of the body underneath the thick fabric of the kilt.

The adoption of a foreign mode of representation is purposeful here, but also fictive. That is to say, the "Egyptian" aspects of the sculpture are not part of a visual *koine* that developed organically and was legible to members of the cultural group that produced it. In Egyptian convention, for example, the body was depicted in two-dimensional media so as to show each part from the ideal vantage, according to a canon of proportions. Sculptures were also made according to the canon, to ensure a sense of harmony relative to other artworks (Davis 1990; Robins 1994). Here, however, the "Egyptian" features serve a different purpose: to enhance the sculpture as a suitable memorial for Antinous by stressing his divinity after death. There are a number of similar works in this mode, sometimes referred to as the Egyptian Antinous or Antinous-Osiris (Meyer 1991, IA5; Grenier 2008, 61–2). This fact gives us useful purchase on the Vatican Antinous's appeal. Just as other posthumous portrait statues presented him in the guise of Silvanus, Bacchus, or Apollo by drawing on well-known sculptural types, the Egyptian-style portraits relied on their viewers' immediate ability to recognize the work's relationship with typical depictions of gods or heroes. This common device in imperial portraiture, which juxtaposed the ideal body and individualized features to create a visual metaphor, revealed something of the internal character of the person depicted. The sculptures of Antinous as pharaoh were effective, in other words, *because* many viewers could recognize them as "Egyptian" and as "regal" without further explanation. And, indeed, this realization may lead us back to reconsidering these portraits as truly unique. Michael John Versluys (2012) and Caroline Vout (2005) have both argued for new ways to approach representations of Antinous. Vout argues that the identification of Antinous portraits presumes that sculptures fall within rigid systems of classification, leading scholars to overlook some examples and to accept canonical identifications for others too readily. The scientistic approach overlooks idiosyncrasy. Not all portraits of youthful men in Egyptian dress need be Antinous (examples from Hadrian's Villa and from the estate of Herodes Atticus in Brexiza: Vout 2005, 90n44; 92n55). And not all representations of Antinous in Egyptian dress need be taken as reflecting a cultic association with Osiris. As with so many examples of aegyptiaca, they are effective as artworks not because they express some literal truth, but because they draw on generalized associations of Egypt as an ancient land of kings and deeply felt religious conviction. They simultaneously evoke Egypt as a place of the past and as a real part of the Roman world.

Conclusion

As the foregoing has shown, there is no single category of Roman-produced sculptures evoking Egypt. Rather, there are many, loosely related by subject, theme, and material, but with as many differences as commonalities. The study of these sculptures benefits from consideration equivalent to that accorded any other Roman artwork, including the full range of approaches discussed in this volume: formal and iconographic study; three-dimensional reconstruction; marble analysis; distribution and dissemination of type; awareness of the value of handicraft as spolia, and so on. Furthermore, that Italian-made sculptures adopt a foreign style offers fruitful opportunity for considering Roman aesthetics more broadly. Artists working in Italy not only reproduced originals more or less one-to-one, but created works in a number of styles, materials, and genres from sculpture in the round, to painting, to the minor arts. In this regard, Egyptian-looking artworks provide a useful counterpoint to the Roman taste for artworks of Greek inspiration.

Despite their unusual appearance, Egyptian-looking artworks are central to the study of Roman sculpture, writ large. They illustrate how one conquered territory exerted a lasting and powerful influence on the arts of the capital city of Rome. They reflect the virtuosity of the craftsmen of Roman Italy, possessed of the ability to work with visual vocabularies beyond their own vernacular and even to mix them in hybrid works drawing on multiple conventions and styles. Many of the social engines that shaped elite tastes—including formal education and travel—also contributed to the emulation of Egyptian styles. And, because so many Egyptian-inspired works used costly decorative stones, these sculptures speak directly to the place of the plastic arts in luxury culture.

Bibliography

Abbe, M. B. 2010. "Recent Research on the Painting and Gilding of Roman Marble Statuary at Aphrodisias." In *Circumlitio: The Polychromy of Antique and Mediaeval Sculpture*, edited by V. Brinkmann, O. Primavesi, and M. Hollein, 277–89. Munich: Hirmer.

Adembri, B., and Z. Mari. 2006. *Suggestioni egizie a Villa Adriana*. Milan: Electa.

Arslan, E., F. Tiraditti, M. Abbiati Brida, and A. Magni, eds. 1997. *Iside: Il mito, il mistero, la magia*. Milan: Electa.

Beck, H., P. C. Bol, and M. Bückling, eds. 2005. *Ägypten, Griechenland, Rom: Abwehr und Berührung*. Tübingen: Ernst Wasmuth.

Bricault, L. 2005. *Recueil des inscriptions concernant les cultes isiaques*. Mémoires de l'Académie des Inscriptions et Belles-Lettres 31. Paris: De Boccard.

———. 2013. *Les cultes isiaques dans le monde gréco-romain: Documents réunis, traduits, et commentés*. Paris: Les belles lettres.

Bricault, L., and M. J. Versluys, eds. 2003. *Isis en Occident: Actes du IIème Colloque international sur les études isiaques, Lyon III 16–17 mai 2002*. Leiden: Brill.

Bricault, L., M. J. Versluys, and P. G. P. Meyboom, eds. 2007. *Nile into Tiber: Egypt in the Roman World, Proceedings of the 3rd International Conference of Isis Studies, Faculty of Archaeology, Leiden University, May 11–14, 2005*. Religions of the Graeco-Roman World 159. Leiden: Brill.

Calandra, E. 2000. "Il programma figurativo del Canopo." In *Adriano: Architettura e progetto*, edited by B. Adembri, A. Melucco Vaccaro, and A. Maria Reggiani, 68–72. Milan: Electa.

Caputo, P. 2010. "Aegyptiaca from Cumae: New Evidence for Isis Cult in Campania; Site and Materials." In *Mystic Cults in Magna Graecia*, edited by G. Casadio and P. Johnston, 235–50. Austin: University of Texas Press.

Curran, B., A. Grafton, P. Long, and B. Weiss. 2009. *Obelisk: A History*. Boston: MIT Press.

Davis, W. 1990. *The Canonical Tradition in Egyptian Art*. Cambridge: Cambridge University Press.

De Caro, S., ed. 1992. *Alla ricerca di Iside: Analisi, studi e restauri dell'Iseo pompeiano nel Museo di Napoli*. Rome: ARTI.

———, ed. 2006. *Egittomania: Iside e il mistero*. Milan: Electa.

De Nuccio, M., and L. Ungaro, eds. 2002. *I marmi colorati della Roma imperiale*. Venice: Marsilio.

De Vos, M. 1980. *L'egittomania in pitture e mosaici romano-campani della prima età imperiale*. ÉPRO 84. Leiden: Brill.

———. 2004. "Una ricontestualizzazione degli aegyptiaca nella cosiddetta Palestra di Villa Adriana." In *Atti del Convegno Symposium Ägyptische Einflüsse in Griechenland und Rom, Frankfurt am Main 28–11/30–11 2002*, edited by P. Bol, 207–213. Frankfurt: Liebighaus.

D'Onofrio, C. 1967. *Gli obelischi di Roma*. Rome: Bulzoni.

Dunand, F. 1973. *Le culte d'Isis dans le bassin oriental de la Méditerranée*. ÉPRO 26. Leiden: Brill.

Eingartner, J. 1991. *Isis und ihre Dienerinnen in der Kunst der römischen Kaiserzeit*. Mnemosyne Supplement 115. Leiden: Brill.

Elsner, J. 2006. "Classicism in Roman Art." In *Classical Pasts: The Classical Traditions of Greece and Rome*, edited by J. I. Porter, 270–97. Princeton: Princeton University Press.

Ensoli, S. 1999. "Prêtres d'Isis en marble rouge antique: Antinuös dans le 'Palestre' de la Villa Adriana." In *Hadrien: Trésors d'une villa imperial*, edited by J. Charles-Gaffiot and H. Lavagne, 79–83. Milan: Electa.

Ensoli Vittozi, S. 1993. "Le sculture del 'larario' di S. Martino ai Monti: Un contest recuperato." *BullCom* 95: 221–43.

Foertmeyer, V. 1989. "Tourism in Graeco-Roman Egypt." PhD diss., Princeton.

Gasse, A. 2004. *Les stèles d'Horus sur les crocodiles*. Paris: Réunion des musées nationaux.

Grenier, J.-C. 1989. "La décoration statuaire du 'Serapeum' du 'Canope' de la Villa Adriana: Essai de reconstitution et d'interprétation." *MEFRA* 101(2): 925–1019.

———. 2008. *L'Osiris Antinoos*. CENIM 1. Montpelier: Université Paul Valéry.

Hartswick, K. 2004. *The Gardens of Sallust: A Changing Landscape*. Austin: University of Texas Press.

Haüber, C., and F. Shütz. 2010. "The Sanctuary Isis et Serapis in Regio III in Rome: Preliminary Reconstruction and Visualization of the ancient Landscape using 3/4D–GIS Technology." In "Congresso di Archeologia A.I.A.C. 2008," special issue *Bollettino di Archeologia On Line*, 0: paper D/session3/article 7, 82–94. http://www.bollettinodiarcheologiaonline.beniculturali.it/documenti/generale/7_SCHUTZ_HAUBER.pdf.

Iversen, E. 1968. *Obelisks in Exile*. 2 vols. Copenhagen: Gad.

———. 1971. "The Hieroglyphic Tradition." In *The Legacy of Egypt*, edited by J. R. Harris, 171–93. Oxford: Clarendon Press.

Kater-Sibbes, G. J. F., and M. J. Vermaseren. 1975. *Apis II: Monuments from outside Egypt*. ÉPRO 48. Leiden: Brill.

Lambrecht, B. 2001. "L'Obélisque d'Hermapion." *Le Muséon: Revue d'études orientales* 114: 51–95.

Lembke, K. 1994a. *Das Iseum Campense in Rom: Studie uber den Isiskult unter Domitian*. Archäologie und Geschichte 3. Heidelberg: Verlag Archäologie und Geschichte.

———. 1994b. "Ein Relief aus Arriccia und seine Geschichte." *RM* 101: 97–102.

Lollio Barberi, O., G. Parola, and M. P. Totti. 1995. *Le antichità egiziane di Roma imperiale*. Rome: Istituto Poligraphico e Zecca dello Stato, Libreria dello Stato.

Malaise, M. 1972. *Les conditions de pénétration et de diffusion des cultes égyptiens en Italie*. 2 vols. ÉPRO 21–2. Leiden: Brill.

Manolaraki, E. 2012. *Noscendi Nilum Cupido: Imagining Egypt from Lucan to Philostratus*. Trends in Classics 18. Berlin: Walter de Gruyter.

Mari, Z., and S. Sgalambro. 2007. "The Antinoeion of Hadrian's Villa: Interpretation and Architectural Reconstruction." *AJA* 111: 83–104.

Meyer, H. 1991. *Antinoos: Die archäologischen Denkmäler unter Einbeziehung des numismatischen und epigraphischen Materials sowie der literarischen Nachrichten: Ein Beitrag zur Kunst- und Kulturgeschichte der hadrianisch-frühantoninischen Zeit*. Munich: Wilhelm Fink.

Moyer, I. 2011. *Egypt and the Limits of Hellenism*. Cambridge: Cambridge University Press.

Müller, H. 1969. *Der Isiskult im antiken Benevent und Katalog der Skulpturen aus den Ägyptishcen Heligtümen del Sannio zu Benevent*. Müncher Ägyptologische Studien 16. Berlin: B. Hessling.

Newby, Z. 2002. "Sculptural Display in the So-Called Palaestra of Hadrian's Villa." *RM* 109: 59–82.

Parker, G. 2003. "Narrating Monumentality: The Piazza Navona Obelisk." *JMA* 16 (2): 193–215.

———. 2007. "Obelisks Still in Exile: Monuments Made to Measure." In Bricault, Versluys, and Meyboom 2007, 209–222.

———. 2011. "India, Egypt and Parthia in Augustan Verse: The Post-Orientalist Turn." *Dictynna* 8. http://dictynna.revues.org/691.

Parlasca, K. 2003. "Ägyptisierende Tempelreliefs und Architecturelemente aus Rom." In Bricault and Versluys 2003, 405–420.

Pensabene, P. 2010. "Arredo statuario del Canopo di Villa Adriana." *Lazio e Sabina* 7: 17–32.

Petersen, L. 2012. "Collecting Gods in Roman Houses: The House of the Gilded Cupids (VI.16.7, 38) at Pompeii." *Arethusa* 45(3): 319–32.

Raeder, J. 1983. *Die statuarische Ausstattung der Villa Hadriana bei Tivoli*. Reihe 38, Archäologie Bd. 4. Frankfurt: Peter Lang.

Renberg, G. 2010. "Hadrian and the Oracles of Antinous." *MAAR* 55: 160–98.

Ritner, R. 1989. "Horus on the Crocodiles: A Juncture of Religion and Magic." In *Religion and Philosophy in Ancient Egypt*, 103–116. Yale Egyptological Studies 3. New Haven: Yale Egyptological Seminar.

Robins, G. 1994. *Proportion and Style in Egyptian Art*. Austin: University of Texas Press.

Roullet, A. 1972. *The Egyptian and Egyptianizing Monuments of Imperial Rome*. ÉPRO 25. Leiden: Brill.

Schneider, R. M. 2004. "Nicht mehr Ägypten, sondern Rom: Der neue Lebensraum der Obelisken." *Städel Jahrbuch*, Neue Folge 19: 155–79.

———. 2005. "Römische Bildern äegyptischer Obelisken." In Beck, Bol, and Bückling 2005, 416–26.

Sfameni, C. 2003. "Fra religione e magia: Temi isiaci nelle gemme di età imperiale." In Bricault and Versluys 2003, 377–404.

Smelik, K. A. D., and E. A. Hemelrijk. 1984. "'Who Knows Not What Monsters Demented Egypt Worships?' Opinions on Egyptian Animal Worship in Antiquity as Part of the Ancient Conception of Egypt." *ANRW* 2.17.4: 1852–2000, 2337–57.

Swetnam-Burland, M. 2007. "Egyptian Objects, Roman Contexts: A Taste for *aegyptiaca* in Italy." In Bricault, Versluys, and Meyboom 2007, 113–36.

———. 2009. "Egypt Embodied: The Vatican Nile." *AJA* 113(3): 439–57.

———. 2010. "*Aegyptus Redacta*: The Egyptian Obelisk in the Augustan Campus Martius." *ArtB* 72: 135–53.

———. 2011. "'Egyptian' Priests in Roman Italy." In *Cultural Identity and the Peoples of the Mediterranean*, edited by E. Gruen, 336–53. Los Angeles: Getty Research Institute.

———. 2015. *Egypt in Italy: Visions of Egypt in Roman Imperial Culture*. Cambridge: Cambridge University Press.

Tran Tam Tinh, V. 1964. *Essai sur le culte d'Isis à Pompéi*. Paris: De Boccard.

Vasunia, P. 2001. *The Gift of the Nile: Hellenizing Egypt from Aeschylus to Alexander*. Berkeley: University of California Press.

Versluys, M. J. 2002. *Aegyptiaca Romana: Nilotic Scenes and the Roman Views of Egypt*. Religions in the Graeco-Roman World 144. Leiden: Brill.

———. 2010. "Understanding Egypt in Egypt and Beyond." In *Isis on the Nile: Egyptian Gods in Hellenistic and Roman Egypt; Proceedings of the IVth International Conference of Isis Studies; Michael Malaise in honorem*, edited by L. Bricault and M. J. Versluys, 7–36. Leiden: Brill.

———. 2012. "Making Meaning with Egypt: Hadrian, Antinous and Rome's Cultural Renaissance." In *Egyptian Gods in the Hellenistic and Roman Mediterranean: Image and Reality between Local and Global*, edited by M. Versluys and L. Bricault, 25–40. Mythos: Revista di storia delle religioni, Supplement 3. Caltanissetta: Salvatore Sciascia.

Veymiers, R. 2009. *Hileōs tō phorunti: Sérapis sur les gemmes et les bijoux antiques*. Brussels: Académie Royale de Belgique.

Visconti, C. 1885. "Del larario e del mitrèo scoperti nell'Esquilino presso la chiesa di S. Martino ai Monti." *BullCom* 13: 27–36.

Vout, C. 2003. "Embracing Egypt." In *Rome the Cosmopolis*, edited by C. Edwards and G. Woolf, 177–202. Cambridge: Cambridge University Press.

———. 2005. "Antinoos, Archaeology, and History." *JRS* 95: 80–96.

Walker, S., and P. Higgs, eds. 2001. *Cleopatra of Egypt: From History to Myth*. Princeton: Princeton University Press.

CHAPTER 3.8

LATE ANTIQUE SCULPTURE

CHRISTIAN WITSCHEL

Introduction

This essay deals with the production and the use of sculpture during the period of late antiquity, that is from the middle of the third to the late sixth century AD. Late antique sculptures have been found in most parts of the Mediterranean, but there is a marked predominance of finds from the eastern half of the Roman Empire. In these regions we can also locate some of the most important production centers, especially in the city of Aphrodisias in Asia Minor (see essay 5.5, Ng). This essay will concentrate on sculpture in the round and especially on honorific portraits and mythological statues that were to be seen both in the public places of late antique cities and in domestic settings (see essays 3.3, Anguissola; 3.4, Wood; 4.1, Longfellow; and 4.3, Gazda). These genres were an important component of society and culture in the Roman Empire and can thus serve as a test case for changing attitudes and mentalities during the last phase of antiquity. Other types of sculpture like sarcophagi or decorated table stands were also of some importance during this period, but as they were characterized by different spheres of use and perception they will not be considered here.

Defining the subject one could also refer more broadly to "sculpture in late antiquity" in order to focus on the specific situation during this period, when the strict separation between old and new with regard to sculpture became blurred: many statues were no longer freshly carved, but consisted of older pieces that were reused, repaired, reworked, put together by using different elements, relocated, or arranged in a new setting. Also important is how people during this period dealt with the innumerable works of sculpture they had inherited from earlier times, as these statues still formed an important part of life in late antiquity (Smith 2007, 204–6; Aurenhammer and Sokolicek 2011).

The traditional approaches to studying Roman sculpture, especially the art-historical method that uses stylistic criteria and tries to arrange individual objects in a sequence in order to date them, have also been applied to late antique sculpture, mainly by German and Scandinavian scholars (L'Orange 1933; Severin 1972; Özgan and Stutzinger 1985;

Kiilerich 1993b; Meischner 2001). But this approach does not account for the peculiar conditions of production and workshop organization that prevailed during this period. A linear and unbroken development of stylistic trends—the precondition for any stylistic dating—is not readily discerned when looking at late antique sculpture. Quite the contrary, in certain phases, such as during the early fourth century AD, a kind of "stylistic chaos" seems to have been dominant, as different modes of expression and carving techniques were used simultaneously (Bergmann 1990; 1999, 67; and essay 3.1, Fullerton), leading to difficulties in assigning dates to specific objects that are central for the understanding of late antique art. For this reason, it seems better to concentrate on other ways of approaching the subject. I prefer an analysis that takes into account the sculptures' spatial setting and their function within late antique society. Such an approach should focus on the practices and perceptions that people in late antiquity applied to statues. After a brief history of the study of late antique sculpture, this essay will therefore consider the production and use of sculpture in this period, some of the main genres involved, and finally the treatment of statues produced in earlier times.

Historiography

Late antique sculpture was long neglected in classical studies—as were other aspects of late antique archaeology outside the Christian sphere. If the topic was explored at all, it was often approached with negative assumptions, such as a presumed decline both in aesthetic principles and in artistic skills. The point of comparison for this evolutionary model was the preceding imperial age (from the first to the early third century AD) when many high quality sculptures and portraits were produced. Only in the last several decades has a more intensive and less prejudiced treatment of late antique sculpture emerged (see the papers in Bauer and Witschel 2007; Eliav, Friedland, and Herbert 2008; Dally and Ratté 2011; D'Andria and Romeo 2011; Kristensen and Poulsen 2012), initiated by Peter Brown's 1971 rehabilitation of late antiquity as a period of cultural vitality rather than of "late Roman decadence." Now scholars caution that care must be taken in applying value judgments influenced by modern prejudices and that it might be unwise to regard the situation in Hellenistic and early imperial times as the only valid parameters from which to approach the situation in late antiquity.

Other dominant concepts of earlier scholarship have also been called into question, such as the presumed turn of late antique art production toward forms of higher abstraction and the concomitant loss of individuality—especially in the portraits of this age—combined with a reduction in the naturalism that has long been regarded as a hallmark of classical art. In that mode of thought, late antiquity was seen as an "age of spirituality" transformed by the triumphant power of the Christian church into a sort of protomedieval society (Kitzinger 1977; Weitzmann 1979; see below). Such constructs produce a biased and rather teleological narrative that has been rightly criticized in recent scholarship (Smith 1997; 1999; 2011).

Current scholarship instead stresses many forms of continuity that connected the imperial age with late antiquity, and sees the latter period as basically still dominated by "antique" structures. On the other hand, the effects of significant change in many realms of life after the middle of the third century should not be underestimated. It therefore seems best to view late antiquity as an epoch in its own right that was characterized by a number of divergent trends, which also affected the production and treatment of sculpture during this period.

Changes and Continuities in the Production and Use of Sculpture in Late Antiquity

In terms of quantities, there can be no doubt that the production of new statuary declined markedly in the whole empire from the middle of the third century AD onward. This decrease affected all genres of sculpture in the round and was in itself part of a wider change in the forms of social communication and representation, as can be seen by the parallel abatement in the "epigraphic habit." On the other hand, this drastic reduction in the number of newly carved statues in late antiquity does not mean that the sculptural medium had lost its meaning in the lives of contemporary people. There were still numerous statues to be seen in the cities of the empire, many of them inherited from previous periods and now reused, recarved, and/or rearranged in a new setting. Literary and pictorial sources make it clear that statues still held an important place in the cultural discourses of late antiquity (Bauer and Witschel 2007, 1–24). Furthermore, there were major differences in the speed and extent of the changes in production among the different regions of the empire: whereas in some parts of the West like Spain or Gaul the practice of making new statues for public presentation had already died out more or less completely by the early fourth century AD, other regions showed more continuity. In some places like Aphrodisias statues were still freshly carved until the early sixth century AD. But even here the numbers were much reduced in comparison to those of the imperial period (Smith 1999, 173; Smith et al. 2006, 9–13, 74). While the "statue habit" thus had a longer life in the East, lingering on into the sixth century AD, even in the metropolis of Constantinople the widespread production and use of statuary seems to have come to an end in the late sixth or early seventh century (Stichel 1982, 21–35; Bauer 2003).

When we ask what might have caused this marked decline in quantities, we must be careful to avoid seemingly easy answers. For example, it has been argued that the main reason for the reduction in the production of new sculpture was the depressed economic situation in late antiquity—people simply did not have enough money to spend on such objects as statues. The change in sculptural demand, however, also occurred in economically stable regions and is therefore likely due to choice: rich members of the elite now chose to invest their money in areas other than statuary (see Borg and Witschel 2001, 78–90).

It has also been claimed that a general decline in artistic skills might have led to the downward turn in sculptural production during late antiquity. But this explanation does not satisfy, either. At places like Aphrodisias sculptural workshops were still carving high-quality pieces. In fashionable sectors of late antique artistic production, like mosaics and silverware, no decline of craftsmanship can be detected—quite the contrary seems true. A more convincing scenario than a general "decline" of the arts posits first a lack of demand for many previously popular products. In many cities of the empire people now invested their money in other forms of social representation and no longer commissioned extensive sculptural programs. Fewer orders made sculpting a less attractive career option, and this development in turn led to the disappearance of many specialized workshops that had supplied the much higher demand of the imperial age. The remaining late antique workshops, coping with fewer commissions (and less money) for sculptural products, developed some interesting strategies to handle this situation. In particular, the recycling of older statues now became a dominant trend (Prusac 2011; see essay 2.3, Varner) that could take different forms—from a slight recarving of a portrait head in order to adapt it to contemporary fashions of hairstyle to a complete remodeling of a whole sculptural monument by reusing pieces (including statue bases) of different origins and putting them together in a new composition. Pastiches of the latter kind were quite common in late antiquity (examples from Aizanoi and Aphrodisias: Von Mosch 1995; Smith 2001). They look rather awkward to modern eyes more familiar with the products of classical art, but late antique preferences for recycling earlier pieces seem to have led to new forms of aesthetics and changes in the perception of sculptural monuments (figure 3.8.1; see essay 3.1, Fullerton).

A third interpretive model links the decline in the production of sculpture to the rise of Christianity during the fourth century AD. Early Christian authors did indeed sometimes exhibit a hostile attitude toward statues in the public realm, especially those of gods and of "idols" in general. However, even when the Christian church had become the dominant force in religious and (to some degree) in social life at the end of the fourth century AD, it did not try to conquer the public spaces of Roman cities by annihilating the existing sculptural decoration or replacing it with statues that had a Christian meaning (Kiilerich 1993a; Bauer and Witschel 2007, 13–15). It is remarkable that we know of almost no statue set up in a public place depicting either a figure of Christian mythology or a member of the church hierarchy. On the other hand, Christian violence against statues in the public sphere, even against those with a clear pagan connotation, was rarer than one might expect. We do know of some spectacular cases in which a Christian mob, often led by the local bishop, destroyed pagan temples and smashed statues identified as *idola* (Stewart 1999; Trombley 2008; see essay 6.6, Kristensen). But that does not seem to have been the regular way of dealing with the huge numbers of statues that populated the squares and streets of Roman cities. More often a less destructive method of religious "purification" was felt to be sufficient and made it possible to keep the statues,

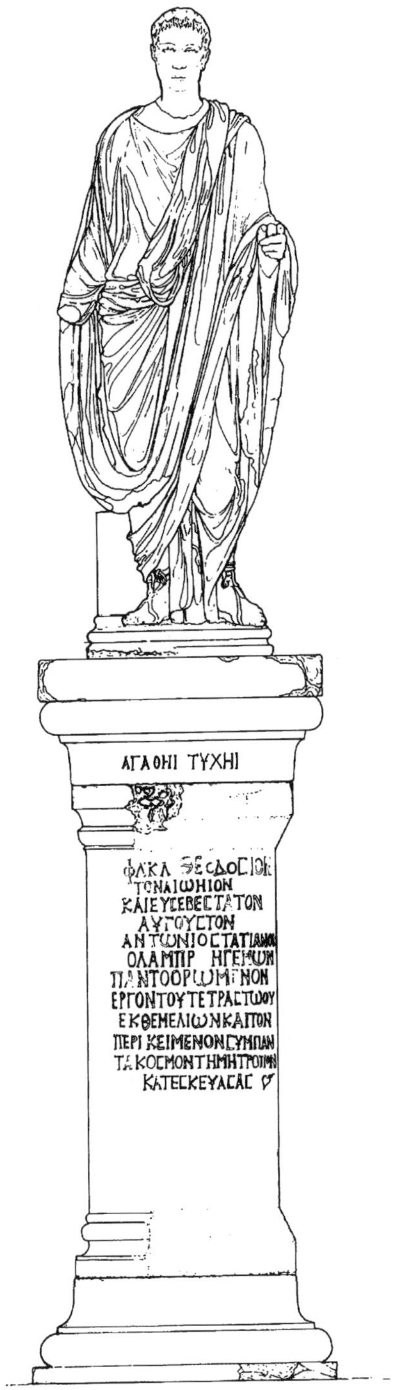

FIGURE 3.8.1 Restored elevation of the monument of Theodosius (I or II) from Aphrodisias, assembled from different reused elements (Smith 2001, fig. 34).

even those of pagan gods, in place where they were often still to be seen in the fifth and sixth centuries.

Moreover, there was a strong desire, also expressed in the law codes of late antiquity, to preserve as much of the cultural heritage of earlier times as possible, which explicitly included sculptural works that now were to be regarded as *ornamenta* of the cities (Witschel 2007, 116–17, 123). This attitude was shared by many Christians, who saw no problem in viewing sculptures in the public sphere as works of art as long as no cultic practice was connected to them (Prudent. *c. Symm.* 1.502–5). We even sometimes encounter Christians actively engaged in the preservation of sculptures with a pagan content (examples from Aquileia and Rhodes: Zaccaria 2000; Deligiannakis 2008). The public sphere of the cities, which was the traditional stage for social communication and commemoration, thus became a sort of neutral zone where traditional civic values and the common identity of a town could be cultivated by all inhabitants regardless of their religious affiliation. In this context sculptures still played an important role, and in most cases clergy made no effort to change this situation. The Christianization of state and society thus had at best only a very indirect effect on the development of sculptural production in late antiquity.

A final observation can be added: it is quite obvious that in specific contexts of late antique life sculpture in the round had lost its previous importance as a medium of exhibiting social and cultural values and was replaced with other forms of artistic expression. This turn away from sculpture is especially true for two settings of great importance in late antiquity, namely the interior of church buildings and the grandiose villas of the elite. In both contexts sculpture played only a minor role (though it was still present in some of the larger villas). Now the dominant artistic media were colorful floor-mosaics and sumptuous wall paintings. Muth (2007) has argued that these media allowed for a higher degree of narrativity and thus more direct engagement with the beholder than sculpture, and therefore were preferred. But again this (useful) observation cannot serve as the sole explanation for the changing attitudes toward sculpture in late antiquity, as the inverse trend can also be documented. The possession of a rich array of sculptural monuments was still regarded as a hallmark of *urbanitas*. Indeed, after Constantine established Constantinople as the new metropolis of the East, it had to be equipped with a collection of statues worthy of its increased prominence (Basset 2004). In order to achieve this goal, huge numbers of statues from all the provinces of the East were brought in successive phases to Constantinople where they adorned the public places and buildings of the city.

Genres

We now take a closer look at three of the most important genres of sculpture in the round: portraits of emperors and other members of the *domus Augusta*; honorific sculptural monuments for elite men and women; and statues or statuettes depicting gods or other mythological figures, so-called ideal sculpture.

With regard to late antique imperial portraits in sculpture (Delbrueck 1933; Stichel 1982; Smith 1997; Hannestad 2001a; Schade 2003, 72–94; see essay 3.4, Wood) we are again confronted with a steep decline in numbers that became ever more marked after the end of the fourth century (Smith 1985, 215–21). This decrease is at first surprising, because the literary sources (collected in Kruse 1934) show that in the same period an increasing importance was attached to the veneration of the imperial likeness. From the middle of the third century onward every new emperor would send his image to all towns of the empire, where it was received in a carefully staged ceremony (Bruun 1976). However, the dominant medium for the imperial image changed: most of the *imagines* distributed by late antique emperors seem to have been painted images of a small size rather than freshly carved sculpted portraits. The centrally organized distribution of imperial images was a novel feature of late antiquity; and despite the change in medium, it shows that the imperial portrait was still extremely important at a political level both for the emperor himself and for his subjects.

In late antiquity very few sculpted imperial portraits depended upon centrally designed prototypes (Schade 2003, 77–8). Whereas the use of fixed types had been a hallmark of the imperial portraiture of the Principate, most portraits in this period were individual creations by local sculptors in which the physiognomy of an emperor could vary quite considerably from one image to another (Smith 1997, 176–8). Instead of easily recognized facial likenesses in which the emperor always looked more or less the same, from the early fourth century onward distinctive symbols of power made it possible for everyone to identify images of the ruler. The most important of these new attributes was the diadem. In addition, the size of the statues and the material now also mattered more than ever, as some late antique imperial statues were of colossal format (like the famous statue in Barletta: Stichel 1982, 61–3) or made of porphyry (figure 3.8.2; Laubscher 1999).

Other ways of communicating the distinctive qualities of the ruler included an increasing expressivity of the central features of the face (such as enlarged eyes) and a nonindividual, always youthful, and hieratic appearance of the imperial image. Such traits can be seen as an indication of the omnipresence and strength of an emperor who would watch everything taking place in his realm. These stylistic phenomena have often been interpreted as belonging to a growing tendency of late antique art toward abstraction or even spirituality, but it is much more convincing to regard them as deliberate choices to enhance the absolute power of the late antique monarch (Smith 1997, 194–201). This change was a decisive break with earlier forms of imperial representation: whereas the portraits of emperors in the first and second centuries had emphasized the fact that rulers were (at least in theory) not different from the rest of the population by avoiding distinctive royal symbols, in late antiquity the dividing line between the superhuman ruler and the normal mortals was clearly expressed through visual language. Consequently, another characteristic feature of the portraiture of the Principate, namely the fashioning of private portraits after the model of the emperor, now came to an end (Bergmann 2005).

Similar changes can be observed with regard to honorific statues of nonimperial persons. These private portraits had been numerous in the late Hellenistic and early

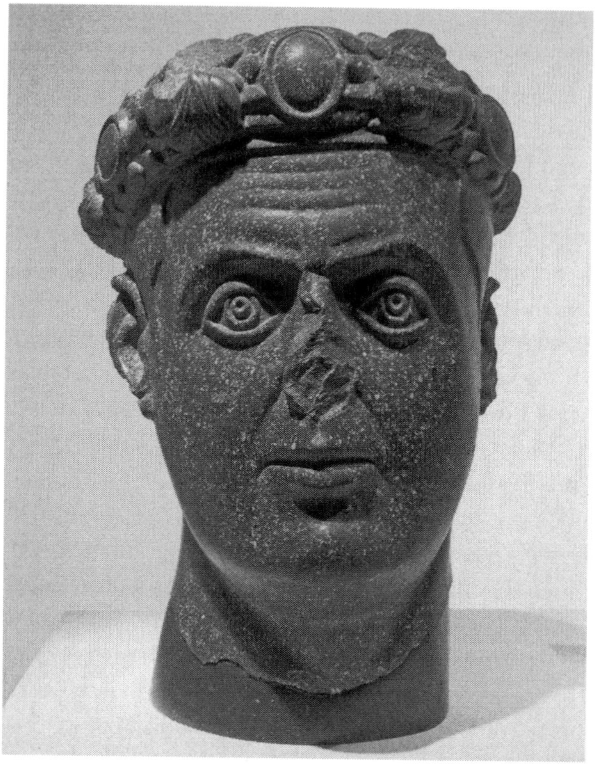

FIGURE 3.8.2 Portrait of a Tetrarch (Galerius?) in porphyry from Gamzigrad/Romuliana. Zaječar, National Museum, inv. no. 1477.416.

imperial periods up to the earlier third century AD, when the main public places of towns all around the Mediterranean had been filled with hundreds of such monuments. In the competitive social structures of that age the dedication of a portrait statue had been one of the most important means to honor persons of outstanding social prestige who had distinguished themselves either by service for the community or by lavish gifts (see essay 4.5, Tuck). In late antiquity this habit continued to a certain extent, but the number of monuments and the range of individuals who would receive such an honor was now much more restricted. Members of the purely local elite, who had been granted a considerable share of honorific statues during the Principate, dropped out more or less completely. Their absence was certainly connected to wider changes in the social hierarchy at the municipal level during late antiquity, but it seems rash to interpret this development as a sign of the collapse of the traditional ways of civic life.

The individuals who continued to be honored with statues in late antiquity were nearly all members of the imperial elite, particularly senators, very often acting as governors or in some other official post (Smith 2002). For the depiction of this cosmopolitan elite in the East, new visual codes modeled upon the prevailing fashions in Constantinople and the other imperial capitals were devised. One easily recognizable feature of these statues was their dress (Smith 1999, 176–82; Gehn 2012): most of them were either equipped with a *chlamys* (the official dress of late antique magistrates, with strong military connotations, only now also depicted in statues) or a new-style toga (used especially for the more traditional senatorial magistracies), whereas the old civic dress of the local elite of the East, the *himation*, was used only rarely. The new situation can be seen most clearly in some of the provincial capitals of late antiquity like Corinth, Ephesos, and Aphrodisias (Foss 1990; Smith 1999; A. R. Brown 2012), where governors and other high-ranking officials were granted statues wearing these costumes (figure 3.8.3).

The stylistic treatment of these honorific portraits shows some tendencies similar to those noted in the images of emperors: especially in those monuments which were presented in public, an intensification of expression was achieved through a heightening and even exaggeration of certain facial features, like enlarged eyes. This move away from a more naturalistic rendering of physiognomies is again not to be interpreted as an indication of an increasing movement toward a late antique "spirituality" or a loss of artistic skill, but as a strategy to show the main qualities of a good governor, alluded to in the inscriptions on the statue base but now also given a striking visual expression (Smith 1999, 182–8).

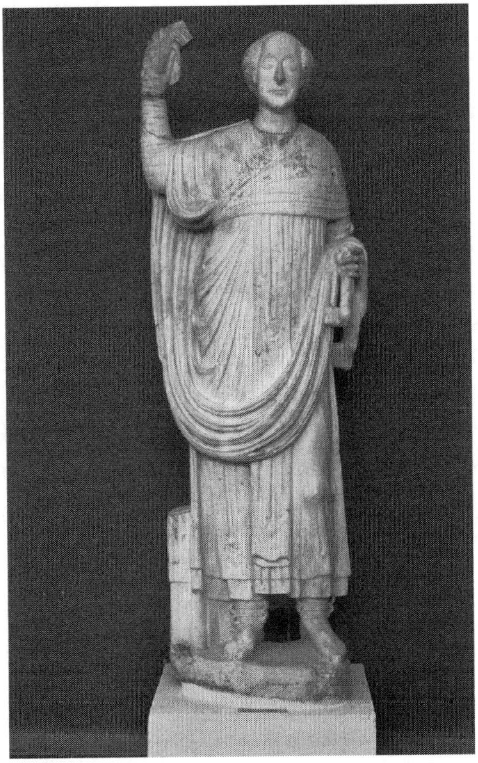

FIGURE 3.8.3 Statue of a high-ranking late antique magistrate (Stephanos?) wearing a toga, from Ephesos. Efes Müzesi Selçuk, inv. no. 1402.

Many of these honorific statues were created out of preexisting sculptures through recarving and/or pastiche. The same tendencies can be seen when we examine the bases of sculptural monuments, many of which were also reused. Again we notice a change both in technique and in aesthetics. The new texts often look irregular, as though engraved by inexpert stonemasons. It would certainly be wrong, however, to conclude from this observation that honorific inscriptions no longer had a value for social prestige. To the contrary, we can note that their messages had become more elaborate: instead of the rather short and crisp prose texts which had been the rule in earlier periods, in late antiquity the verse epigram became standard in the East (Robert 1948; Smith 1999, 174–5). It praised the individual honored in an artificial and archaizing language, and a high degree of education was required to understand the often rather obscure allusions in these inscriptions.

A number of these texts point out that the function of the sculptural monument was not only to present the image of the person honored to contemporary spectators but also to preserve his *memoria* for the future. Of course this idea was not new, but it was stressed more explicitly here than in earlier inscriptions (Witschel 2007, 117–8). This phenomenon is interesting, because it can be questioned whether honorific statues and inscriptions were really still the main medium for expressing social status. We have seen above that many local elites in the Roman Empire had discontinued the "statue habit" already at the beginning of the late antique period. But this development does not mean that these people had simultaneously disappeared from the municipal scene. Literary sources show that they were still actively engaged in civic affairs and in acts of munificence. But they no longer expected an honorific statue as a reward; instead, they wanted elaborate acclamations, which were carefully staged and shouted by the whole populace. Such performative acts seem to have become more important for other fields of representation as well (Borg and Witschel 2001).

In the mid-third century AD the copying of familiar statue types of gods, heroes, and other mythological figures from the classical and Hellenistic periods, which had been a dominant feature of sculptural production in the Roman Empire (see essay 3.3, Anguissola), came nearly to an end (Willers 1996). Yet, we can observe that there were still some workshops in late antiquity that were able to produce ideal sculpture (especially miniature pieces but probably also some life-size statues) of a high quality, and these production centers might have been active until the early fifth century AD. Accordingly, there must still have been a demand for these pieces, especially in the sumptuous *domus* and villas of the aristocrats. The latter—whether pagan or Christian—were eager to show off their *paideia*, and statues or statuettes of the mythological genre still appealed for this purpose. In southern Gaul, some late antique villas exhibited a collection of often small-scale statuary (Stirling 2005). Many of these pieces were heirlooms from earlier periods, sometimes apparently acquired through a sort of art market, but in quite a few places there were also some freshly carved sculptures (figure 3.8.4). Most impressively, the owner of the famous villa of Chiragan ordered a whole new set of sculptures in the mid-fourth century AD (Bergmann 1999, 26–43). Although the demand was certainly not nearly as high as in the previous epoch, it was still sufficient to sustain a small number of specialized workshops that could produce sculpture with a strong retrospective tendency.

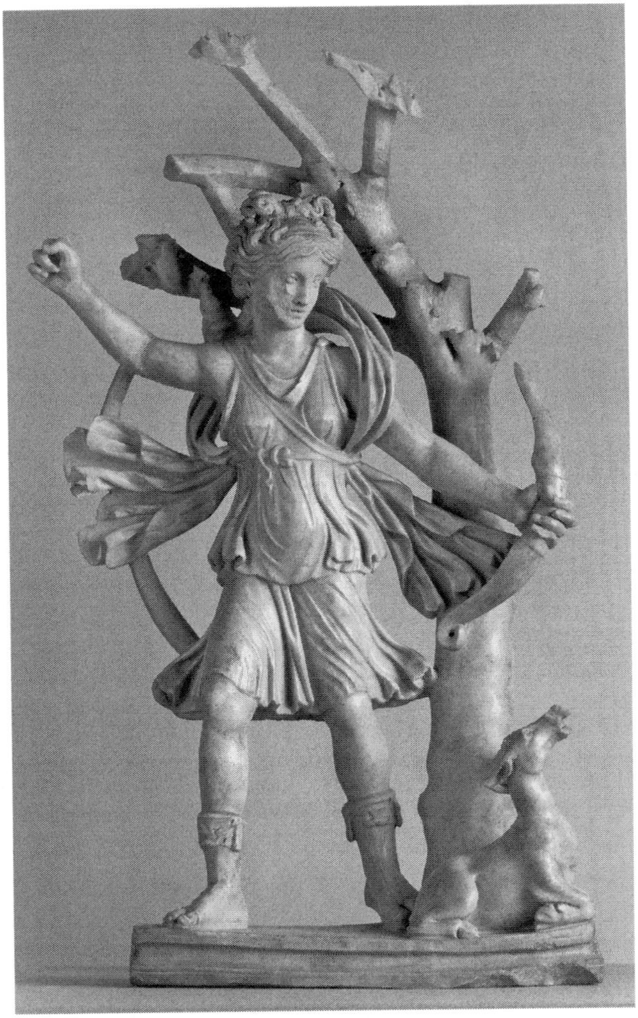

FIGURE 3.8.4 Statuette of Diana from the villa of Saint Georges de Montagne. Bordeaux, Musée d'Aquitaine, inv. no. 71.16.1.

The last statement, however, needs some qualification, as it is connected to an ongoing debate about the date of some key pieces of (presumably) late antique sculpture. A good example is a group of five mythological statues from the Esquiline in Rome, now in Copenhagen (Moltesen 2000). The group was signed by a man from Aphrodisias named Flavius Zenon whose role as producer might be inferred from the verb in the inscription, *epoiei* (literally, "he made it"). By using prosopographical criteria, this man can be dated to the Constantinian period (Erim and Roueché 1982), which would date the Esquiline group to the same age, although stylistically it would fit much better into the late second century. This contrast between epigraphic information and stylistic dating would mean that in the earlier fourth century Aphrodisian sculptors could still fabricate statues that looked like those of the second century. As other sculptures with similar features can be added to this group (Kiilerich and Torp 1994; Bergmann 1999; Hannestad 2012), we are confronted with a broader phenomenon, which in turn could shatter our established notions about a linear stylistic development from the imperial period to late antiquity (see essay 3.1, Fullerton). While there are good reasons to think that the whole model of continuous stylistic evolution might be misguided, in this case one needs to be careful: it is not absolutely certain that the word *epoiei* indicates that Zenon (or rather the stonemasons in the workshop he seems to have owned) fabricated a completely new set of sculptures. Instead, the phrase could mean that Zenon had rearranged and restored earlier pieces (see Smith 2007, 214–5; Bauer and Witschel 2007, 8–11)—a practice quite common in late antiquity, as we have already seen. If the latter hypothesis were true, there would be no need to date all these sculptures to the fourth century AD after all. Indeed, the late dating of these pieces has also been criticized on stylistic grounds (Breitner 2008); and in many cases no consensus has been reached yet. For example, a statue of a youthful *togatus* from Aphrodisias is dated by some scholars to the early second century (Smith et al. 2006, 108–111, no. 3) and by others to the mid-fifth century (Hannestad 2012, 83–6).

The Treatment of Pre-Existing Sculpture in Late Antiquity

With regard to late antiquity it is certainly not enough to concentrate on newly produced sculpture, as there was no strict separation between old and new in this period. We therefore must examine briefly the different ways in which sculptures made in earlier times were treated in late antiquity. By the beginning of the period a huge mass of sculpture had accumulated all around the Mediterranean, and people therefore had to develop different strategies for dealing with this multitude of statues. We have already seen that from the middle of the third century AD onward there was a massive increase in the reuse and reworking of older sculpture, especially for honorific monuments (Prusac 2011). A good example of the different working processes that were simultaneously executed in a single context (new production, restoration, storing of older pieces in a marble yard, etc.) is a sculptor's workshop at Aphrodisias, which seems to have been active until the early fifth century AD (Rockwell 2008; Smith 2011, 68–9; Van Voorhis 2012). The restoration of older sculptures in order to preserve them was a remarkable feature of late antique craftsmanship, and it is interesting to see how much effort and technical skill was sometimes invested in the upkeep of earlier monuments (cf. Hannestad 1994, although many of his propositions remain controversial). A similar attitude can be observed in those cases in which older statues were relocated from "ugly places" to a new setting in which they were often rearranged to give them a new meaning (Lepelley 1994; Roueché 2002; Witschel 2007, 122–4). Such relocation and reuse demonstrates again that statues still played an important role in the shaping of a civic identity. Large numbers of statues, however, fared much less well during late antiquity. They could be taken from their original location to be reused as building material, as in the town-wall of Aphrodisias (Smith et al. 2006, 10–11) or in the many "statue walls" that have been detected in Rome (Coates-Stephens 2001). In the latter case smashed statues from earlier times served as the foundation walls for large aristocratic *domus*, which themselves were sometimes adorned with statuary of a similar kind. It is difficult to know why in a specific context one statue inherited from previous times was left in place or even renovated, while a neighboring sculpture was condemned as building material. It is unlikely that these choices were random, but unfortunately we have no sources that elucidate the decision-making process.

Finally, a word about Christian attitudes toward older sculpture as observed in practice (which was often quite different from the ideas of Christian authors): as we have seen, the violent destruction of pagan sculpture by Christians was apparently rather the exception than the rule. In most cases Christians used strategies in dealing with the huge amount of existing sculpture in the public sphere that allowed them to purify these objects from their demonic aspects while at the same time keeping them in place (Hannestad 1999). We have quite a lot of evidence for this cleansing or Christianization of statues: a cross could be incised into the forehead of an imperial portrait (figure 3.8.5) or the genitals of a naked mythological figure could be chiseled away (Hannestad 2001b; examples from Ephesos and Miletos: Auinger and Rathmayer 2007, 248–52, 254–7; Dally

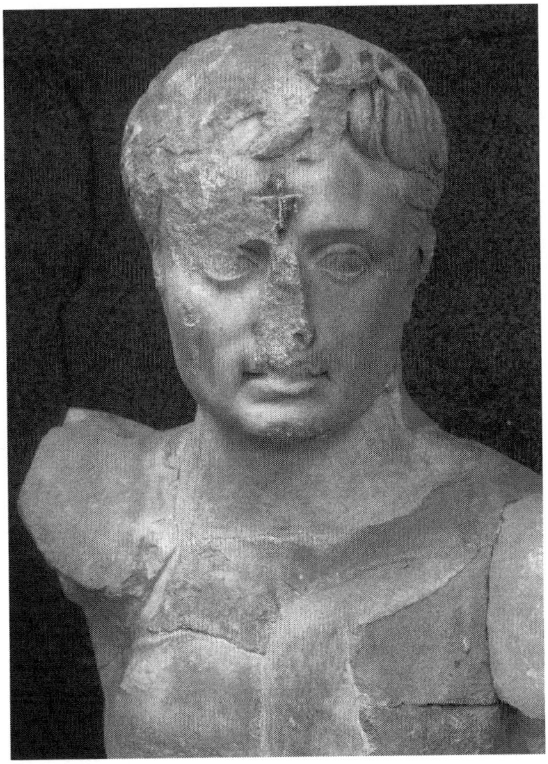

FIGURE 3.8.5 Portrait of Augustus with an incised cross on the forehead from Ephesos. Efes Müzesi Selçuk, inv. no. 1957.

et al. 2011, 92–8). Sculpture was thus embedded in the different processes of change that affected late antique society.

Conclusion

It is necessary to approach the phenomenon of late antique sculpture with several interpretive models in mind, as widely divergent trends were at work that affected both the production of new pieces and the treatment of older ones. While we have seen quite massive changes like the clear reduction in quantities, we could also observe some rather striking cases of continuity, for example in the ongoing fabrication of high-quality sculpture. It is therefore not easy to formulate a final verdict: on the one hand, we have seen that sculptures had lost a good deal of their former importance and function to the point that they could even end up as building material; but on the other hand, we have encountered a number of situations in which statues were still indispensable and a great deal of energy was invested in them. The "ancient" way of dealing with statues only seems to have come to an end in the later sixth century AD. The final extinction of a tradition that had lasted for centuries can be seen as one of the decisive turning points in the transition from antiquity to the Middle Ages.

Bibliography

Auinger, J., and E. Rathmayer. 2007. "Zur spätantiken Statuenausstattung der Thermen und Nymphäen in Ephesos." In Bauer and Witschel 2007, 237–69.

Aurenhammer, M., and A. Sokolicek. 2011. "The Remains of Centuries: Sculptures and Statue Bases in Late Antique Ephesus; The Evidence of the Upper Agora." In Dally and Ratté 2011, 43–66.

Bassett, S. 2004. *The Urban Image of Late Antique Constantinople*. Cambridge: Cambridge University Press.

Bauer, F. A. 2003. "Statuen hoher Würdenträger im Stadtbild Konstantinopels." *ByzZeit* 96: 493–513.

Bauer, F. A., and C. Witschel, eds. 2007. *Statuen in der Spätantike*. Wiesbaden: Reichert.

Bergmann, M. 1990. "Nr. 254: Kaiserporträt der Jahre 293–313 n.Chr." In *Antike Kunstwerke aus der Sammlung Ludwig*. Vol. 3, *Skulpturen*, edited by E. Berger, 383–401. Mainz: Philipp von Zabern.

———. 1999. *Chiragan, Aphrodisias, Konstantinopel: Zur mythologischen Skulptur der Spätantike*. Wiesbaden: Reichert.

———. 2005. "La ritrattistica privata di età costantiniana: L'abbandono del prototipo imperiale." In *Costantino il Grande: La civiltà antica al bivio tra Occidente e Oriente*, edited by A. Donati and G. Gentili, 156–65. Milan: Silvana.

Borg, B., and C. Witschel. 2001. "Veränderungen im Repräsentationsverhalten der römischen Eliten während des 3. Jhs. n.Chr." In *Inschriftliche Denkmäler als Medien der Selbstdarstellung in der römischen Welt*, edited by G. Alföldy and S. Panciera, 47–120. Stuttgart: Steiner.

Breitner, G. 2008. "*Simulacra artis pretio metienda*: Studien zur Erforschung spätantiker mythologischer Rundplastik." PhD diss., University of Mainz.

Brown, A. R. 2012. "Last Men Standing: *Chlamydatus* Portraits and Public Life in Late Antique Corinth." *Hesperia* 81: 141–76.

Brown, P. 1971. *The World of Late Antiquity from Marcus Aurelius to Muhammad*. London: Thames and Hudson.

Bruun, P. 1976. "Notes on the Transmission of Imperial Images in Late Antiquity." In *Studia Romana in honorem Petri Krarup septuagenarii*, edited by K. Ascani, 122–31. [Odense]: Odense University Press.

Coates-Stephens, R. 2001. "*Muri dei bassi secoli* in Rome: Observations on the Re-Use of Statuary in Walls Found on the Esquiline and Caelian after 1870." *JRA* 14: 217–38.

Dally, O., and C. Ratté, eds. 2011. *Archaeology and the Cities of Asia Minor in Late Antiquity*. Ann Arbor: Kelsey Museum of Archaeology.

Dally, O., M. Maischberger, P. I. Schneider, and A. Scholl. 2011. "The Town Center of Miletus from Roman Imperial Times to Late Antiquity." In Dally and Ratté 2011, 81–101.

D'Andria, F., and I. Romeo, eds. 2011. *Roman Sculpture in Asia Minor*. JRA Supplement 80. Portsmouth, RI: Journal of Roman Archaeology.

Delbrueck, R. 1933. *Spätantike Kaiserporträts von Constantinus Magnus bis zum Ende des Westreichs*. Berlin: Walter de Gruyter.

Deligiannakis, G. 2008. "Christian Attitudes towards Pagan Statuary: The Case of Anastasios of Rhodes." *Byzantion* 78: 142–58.

Eliav, Y. Z., E. A. Friedland, and S. Herbert, eds. 2008. *The Sculptural Environment of the Roman Near East: Reflections on Culture, Ideology, and Power*. Leuven: Peters.

Erim, K. T., and C. Roueché. 1982. "Sculptors from Aphrodisias: Some New Inscriptions." *PBSR* 50: 102–115.

Foss, C. 1990. "Stephanus, Proconsul of Asia, and Related Statues." In *History and Archaeology of Byzantine Asia Minor*, chap. 3. Aldershot, Hampshire: Variorum.

Gehn, U. 2012. *Ehrenstatuen in der Spätantike: Chlamydati und Togati*. Wiesbaden: Reichert.

Hannestad, N. 1994. *Tradition in Late Antique Sculpture: Conservation—Modernization—Production*. Aarhus: Aarhus University Press.

———. 1999. "How Did Rising Christianity Cope with Pagan Sculpture?" In *East and West: Modes of Communication; Proceedings of the First Plenary Conference at Mérida*, edited by E. Chrysos and I. Wood, 173–203. Leiden: Brill.

———. 2001a. "The Ruler Image of the Fourth Century: Innovation or Tradition." *ActaAArtHist* 15: 93–107.

———. 2001b. "Castration in the Baths." In *Macellum: Culinaria Archaeologica Robert Fleischer zum 60. Geburtstag von Kollegen, Freunden und Schülern*, edited by N. Birkle, 67–77. Mainz: N. Birkle.

———. 2012. "Mythological Marble Sculpture of Late Antiquity and the Question of Workshops." In Kristensen and Poulsen 2012, 75–112.

Kiilerich, B. 1993a. "Sculpture in the Round in the Early Byzantine Period: Constantinople and the East." In *Aspects of Late Antiquity and Early Byzantium*, edited by L. Rydén and J. O. Rosenqvist, 85–97. Uppsala: Almqvist and Wiksell.

———. 1993b. *Late Fourth Century Classicism in the Plastic Arts: Studies in the So-Called Theodosian Renaissance*. Odense: Odense University Press.

Kiilerich, B., and H. Torp. 1994. "Mythological Sculpture in the Fourth Century A.D.: The Esquiline Group and the Silahtarağa Statues." *IstMitt* 44: 307–316.

Kitzinger, E. 1977. *Byzantine Art in the Making: Main Lines of Stylistic Development in Mediterranean Art, 3rd–7th Century*. London: Faber and Faber.

Kristensen, T. M., and B. Poulsen, eds. 2012. *Ateliers and Artisans in Roman Art and Archaeology*. JRA Supplement 92. Portsmouth, RI: Journal of Roman Archaeology.

Kruse, H. 1934. *Studien zur offiziellen Geltung des Kaiserbildes im römischen Reiche*. Paderborn: Schöningh.

Laubscher, H. P. 1999. "Beobachtungen zu tetrarchischen Kaiserbildnissen aus Porphyr." *JdI* 114: 207–252.

Lepelley, C. 1994. "Le musée des statues divines: La volonté de sauvegarder le patrimoine artistique païen à l'époque théodosienne." *CahArch* 42: 5–15.

L'Orange, H. P. 1933. *Studien zur Geschichte des spätantiken Porträts*. Oslo: Aschehoug.

Meischner, J. 2001. *Bildnisse der Spätantike, 193–500: Problemfelder; die Privatportraits*. Berlin: Edition BNB.

Moltesen, M. 2000. "The Esquiline Group: Aphrodisian Statues in the Ny Carlsberg Glyptotek." *AntP* 27: 111–29.

Muth, S. 2007. "Das Manko der Statuen? Zum Wettstreit der bildlichen Ausstattung im spätantiken Wohnraum." In Bauer and Witschel 2007, 341–55.

Özgan, R., and D. Stutzinger. 1985. "Untersuchungen zur Porträtplastik des 5. Jhs. n. Chr. anhand zweier neugefundener Porträts aus Stratonikeia." *IstMitt* 35: 237–74.

Prusac, M. 2011. *From Face to Face: Recarving of Roman Portraits and the Late-Antique Portrait Arts*. Leiden: Brill.

Robert, L. 1948. "Épigrammes relatives à des gouverneurs." *Hellenika* 4: 35–114.

Rockwell, P. 2008. "The Sculptor's Studio at Aphrodisias: The Working Methods and Varieties of Sculpture Produced." In Eliav, Friedland, and Herbert 2008, 91–115.

Roueché, C. 2002. "The Image of Victory: New Evidence from Ephesus." In *Mélanges Gilbert Dagron*, edited by V. Déroche, 527–46. TravMém 14. Paris: Association des amis du Centre d'histore et civilisation de Byzance.

Schade, K. 2003. *Frauen in der Spätantike—Status und Repräsentation: Eine Untersuchung zur römischen und frühbyzantinischen Bildniskunst*. Mainz: Philipp von Zabern.

Severin, H.-G. 1972. *Zur Portraitplastik des 5. Jahrhunderts n. Chr*. Munich: Institut für Byzantinistik u. Neugriech. Philologie.

Smith, R. R. R. 1985. "Roman Portraits: Honours, Empresses, and Late Emperors." *JRS* 75: 209–221.

———. 1997. "The Public Image of Licinius I: Portrait Sculpture and Imperial Ideology in the Fourth Century." *JRS* 87: 170–202.

———. 1999. "Late Antique Portraits in a Public Context: Honorific Statuary at Aphrodisias in Caria, A.D. 300–600." *JRS* 89: 155–89.

———. 2001. "A Portrait Monument for Julian and Theodosius at Aphrodisias." In *Griechenland in der Kaiserzeit: Neue Funde und Forschungen zu Skulptur, Architektur und Topographie*, edited by C. Reusser, 125–36. Zürich: Institut für Klassische Archäologie der Universität Bern.

———. 2002. "The Statue Monument of Oecumenius: A New Portrait of a Late Antique Governor from Aphrodisias." *JRS* 92: 134–56.

———. 2007. "Statue Life in the Hadrianic Baths at Aphrodisias, AD 100–600: Local Context and Historical Meaning." In Bauer and Witschel 2007, 203–235.

———. 2011. "Marble Workshops at Aphrodisias." In D'Andria and Romeo 2011, 63–76.

Smith, R. R. R., with S. Dillon, C. H. Hallett, J. Lenaghan, and J. Van Voorhis. 2006. *Aphrodisias II: Roman Portrait Statuary from Aphrodisias*. Mainz: Philipp von Zabern.

Stewart, P. 1999. "The Destruction of Statues in Late Antiquity." In *Constructing Identities in Late Antiquity*, edited by R. Miles, 159–89. London: Routledge.

Stichel, R. H. W. 1982. *Die römische Kaiserstatue am Ausgang der Antike: Untersuchungen zum plastischen Kaiserporträt seit Valentinian I (364–375 n. Chr.)*. Rome: Giorgio Bretschneider.

Stirling, L. M. 2005. *The Learned Collector: Mythological Statuettes and Classical Taste in Late Antique Gaul*. Ann Arbor: University of Michigan Press.

Trombley, F. R. 2008. "The Destruction of Pagan Statuary and Christianization (Fourth–Sixth Century C.E.)." In Eliav, Friedland, and Herbert 2008, 143–64.

Van Voorhis, J. A. 2012. "The Working and Re-Working of Marble Statuary at the Sculptor's Workshop in Aphrodisias." In Kristensen and Poulsen 2012, 39–54.

Von Mosch, H.-C. 1995. "Eine neue Replik des Satyrs mit der Querflöte und ihre Aufstellung in spätantikem Kontext." *AA* 1995: 741–53.

Weitzmann, K., ed. 1979. *Age of Spirituality: Late Antique and Early Christian Art, Third to Seventh Century*. New York: Princeton University Press.

Willers, D. 1996. "Das Ende der antiken Idealstatue." *MusHelv* 53: 170–86.

Witschel, C. 2007. "Statuen auf spätantiken Platzanlagen in Italien und Africa." In Bauer and Witschel 2007, 113–69.

Zaccaria, C. 2000. "Permanenza dell'ideale civico romano in epoca tardoantica: Nuove evidenze da Aquileia." In *Aquileia romana e cristiana fra II e V secolo*, edited by G. Bandelli and C. Zaccaria, 91–113. Antichità altoadriatiche 47. Trieste: Editreg.

PART IV

SPATIAL AND SOCIAL CONTEXTS

CHAPTER 4.1

ARCHITECTURAL SETTINGS

BRENDA LONGFELLOW

Introduction

In sixth-century AD Rome, statues were so numerous and ubiquitous that Cassiodorus (*Var.* 7.15) proclaimed their population to rival that of men. This urban populace, which crowded public fora and major arteries, civic edifices and sacred complexes, communal gardens and monumental fountains, had accumulated over the centuries, so that second-century BC archaizing statues of the heroes Castor and Pollux shared the Lacus Iuturnae in the Forum Romanum with an honorific statue of the emperor Constantine. Because the production of statuary had decreased dramatically over the late third, fourth, and fifth centuries AD, most of the free-standing statues visible to Cassiodorus were centuries older than the administrator writing about them (see essay 3.8, Witschel).

The vibrancy of the urban congregation of statues alluded to by Cassiodorus is a characteristic feature of Roman cities throughout the empire; from Spain to Syria, people encountered urban landscapes filled not only with free-standing statues but also with architectural monuments designed to be densely occupied by statuary. The overall effect of such congregations is represented in the Via Sacra relief from the Tomb of the Haterii in Rome (figure 4.1.1). Here, statues of emperors, deities, heroes, horses, and eagles stand on and are framed by arches, occupy the upper stories of the exterior façade of the Flavian amphitheater, and peer out from the interior of a temple to Jupiter (see essay 6.4, Moormann). This relief reflects the number and types of statues found in civic centers and on urban monuments across the Roman Empire. The elaboration of architectural monuments like arches and amphitheaters with statues probably seemed natural to someone walking along the Via Sacra in the Trajanic period, in large part because civic amenities had been embellished with similar statues for centuries. This essay will discuss when and how three-dimensional statues came to be associated with an increasing variety of contexts in republican Rome and then consider the physical and social display contexts of statues associated with civic monuments throughout the Roman Empire. The focus is on freestanding sculpture outside of funerary contexts, leaving aside the

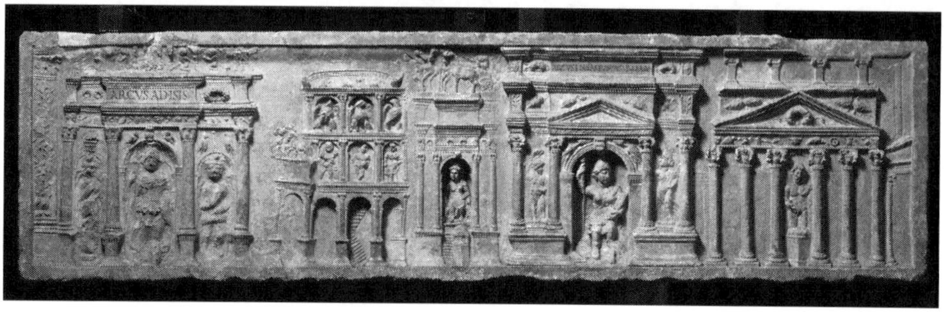

FIGURE 4.1.1 Relief from the Tomb of the Haterii on the Via Labicana, Rome. Late first/early second century AD. Marble. W: 1.58 m. Vatican Museums, Lateran Coll. 9997.

interrelated categories of art, like relief sculpture and paintings, though they shared physical and contextual space with the three-dimensional statues. To begin, I provide a brief overview of the recent scholarly trends in the study of sculpture associated with architectural edifices.

Historiography

Although portraits and ideal statues stood side by side in antiquity, and although conventional scholarship for both has primarily focused on issues of connoisseurship, typology, and chronology, they have often been discussed separately in modern scholarship. This separatist approach was particularly evident through the 1970s, when sculptural finds from particular cities or civic monuments were often categorized by type rather than findspot, with the result that the portraits and ideal statues that had shared a single architectural edifice in antiquity were discussed independently from one another. For example, Jale Inan planned to publish the sculptural finds from the city of Side in Pamphylia in three volumes organized by sculptural type: portraits, ideal sculpture, and funerary finds (Inan 1975, viii). The volume on ideal sculpture contains 457 fragments of approximately one hundred statues. The focus of the catalog is twofold: to use *Kopienkritik*, or the analysis of copies, to decide how closely each work reflected the reputed original statue as well as to determine what may be regarded as additions made by the copyist; and to use the stylistic similarities observed among the Roman statues to define local and regional workshop characteristics. The catalog is organized by the date of the presumed original as well as by the size and completeness of the statue from Side. Thus, the catalog begins with fragments of large-scale statues referencing Greek sculptures, like the Discobolos of Myron, before discussing statuettes recalling Roman creations, like Jupiter Capitolinus. The catalog concludes with limbs and other miscellaneous fragments of figures and animals. This organization not only emphasizes the then-prevailing interest in using the existing statues found at Side to augment the reconstruction of statuary prototypes, but also reinforces the assumption of J. J. Winckelmann and his followers that Greek art was fundamentally superior to Roman.

Over the last few decades, more and more studies of ideal statues have shifted the primary focus away from *Kopienkritik*, which often results in the dismissal of extant statues as perfunctory replicas, and toward a consideration of the Roman contexts of statuary (Ridgway 1984; Bartman 1988; Marvin 1993; Gazda 1995; Kousser 2008; Marvin 2008; see essay 3.3, Anguissola). Vitruvius alludes to how such statues expressed the function of the civic edifice within which they were set, and this understanding of the primary purpose of Roman ideal statuary fundamentally changed the course of scholarship on statues. By the 1980s, scholars became increasingly interested in categorizing and contextualizing the types of ideal statues associated with particular architectural settings. These studies have resulted in a more precise understanding of the types of statues commonly used in certain kinds of urban amenities, including theaters (Bejor 1979; Fuchs 1987; Sturgeon 2004), fountains (Bol 1984; Ghedini 1985; Schmidt-Colinet 1985; Rathmayr 2011), and baths (Manderscheid 1981; Marvin 1983; Özren 1996). Mary Sturgeon (2004, 22) noted that the architecture of the Hadrianic theater at Corinth was conceived with the sculptural program in mind: the conspicuous variety in the heights, widths, and embellishments of sculptural niches built into the edifice suggests that these niches were constructed in order to accommodate statues of certain sizes and distinction. Such perceptible coordination between architecture and sculptural ensemble indicates that individual statues were matched with their intended settings from the beginning of the architectural process. This synchronization is also noticeable when considering the formal qualities of the ideal statues themselves. Orientation, size, and the extent to which a statue was finished in the round depends in large part on its intended placement at ground level or higher up in the architectural framework, as well as its planned destination in a niche, between columns in a portico or doorway, or on a statue base meant to be circumambulated.

Innumerable portraits were also created for architectural contexts (see essay 3.4, Wood), and the planned interdependency of architecture and decorative program shaped the appearance and presentation of these statues as well. Thus, portrait statues understood apart from their architectural contexts are missing key explicatory elements, but such contextual studies are a relatively recent development in the field. The traditional focus has been on using *Kopienkritik* to identify and date portrait head types. Given that few statues can still be associated with inscribed statue bases, this typological model remains an essential component of portraiture studies, but there is a growing interest in balancing discussions of portrait heads with analyses of body types, costumes, gestures, intended settings, and social contexts. Increasingly, scholars combine a close reading of statues with their associated texts and settings, addressing how portraits functioned within and contributed to specific cultural, architectural, and geographical contexts (Tanner 1990; Gazda and Haeckl 1993; Smith 1998; Hallett 2005; Smith et al. 2006; Fejfer 2008; Trimble 2011). Furthermore, ideal statues and portraits that once shared the same edifice or cityscape are now often treated as symbiotic components of a larger picture. As the interdependency of portraits and ideal statues, art and architecture has become more central to scholarship, interest has rotated between reconstructing statuary ensembles within architectural contexts and contextualizing such creations. Of recent interest are the potential intentions of the patron responsible for such creations and the various ways prospective audiences might perceive these ornamented spaces (Boatwright 1993; Zanker 2000; Stewart 2003; Bravi 2011; Longfellow 2011). The rest of this essay provides a general overview of the social context for urban sculptural ensembles, first by considering how portraits and ideal statues came to be the most common sculptural types in republican Rome, and then by addressing the relationship of portraits and ideal statues to architectural amenities created in the imperial period, concentrating on the common expectations for the sculptural groupings and their function within urban edifices.

Honorific and Ideal Statues in Republican Rome

The statue types most frequently mentioned in republican Rome by contemporary and later historical sources can be divided into two categories, portraits (see essay 3.4, Wood) and ideal statues (see essay 3.3, Anguissola), and these are generally associated with fora and sacred locales. In a Roman community, one of the highest honors available to an individual was an honorific statue set up in the forum or in another highly trafficked area of the city. Such portrait statues were awarded not only by the senate and people in Rome but also by a variety of governmental bodies in other cities, as well as by religious organizations, craftsmen's guilds, and individuals. Closely related to and probably derived from the Hellenistic practice of dedicating statues of benefactors and members of the royal family, these statues monumentalized the mutually beneficial relationship between patron and community and preserved the benefactor's reputation in perpetuity. The earliest known archaeological evidence for statues honoring Roman citizens comes from the Greek East. Inscribed bases in the city of Phanotea in Phocis and on the island of Cos demonstrate that these communities honored T. Quinctius Flamininus with statues around the time he declared the freedom of the Greeks in 196 BC. Although little epigraphic or sculptural evidence exists for honorific portrait statues in Rome before the first century BC, later literary sources suggest that honorific statues may have stood in the sanctuaries and open spaces of Rome as early as the fourth century BC (Sehlmeyer 1999, 48). Livy (8.13.9) records that the Senate set up equestrian statues in the Forum Romanum for the consuls C. Maenius and L. Furius Camillus after their victory over the Latins in 338 BC. Pliny the Elder (*HN* 34.30) cites L. Piso when he states that the censors of 158 BC removed all the statues in the Forum Romanum that had not been approved by the Roman senate or people, an action that suggests there may have been a glut of statues set up by individuals and professional groups (Lahusen 1983). By the death of Caesar, honorific and other types of portrait statues had become so common that Rome's civic centers and sanctuaries were probably once again crowded with statues honoring generals, administrators, dignitaries, and other elites. Each statue expressed information about the person represented through the portrait head, accompanying inscription, body position, and costume. The most common body types in republican Rome were equestrian statues for those being honored for their military service and togate statues for those honored as magistrates and priests. Cuirassed and nude body types, which were used for honorific statues of Romans in the eastern Mediterranean by the early first century BC, had joined the sculptural repertoire in Rome by the Caesarian and Augustan periods, respectively (Hallett 2005, 97–8; Fejfer 2008).

Like portrait statues, the incorporation of ideal statues into the cityscape of Rome can be associated with Roman interactions with the Greek world, and particularly with the wars of expansion that resulted in the conquest of Greek cities in Sicily and the East. With the conquest of Syracuse by M. Claudius Marcellus in 211 BC, massive quantities of ideal statues were paraded through the streets of Rome as part of the subsequent triumphal processions and less prestigious *ovationes* (Pollitt 1978). Conquest was closely tied to religious piety, and literary and archaeological evidence indicate that most of the manubial statues in republican Rome that were not melted down were displayed in sanctuary contexts. From the Etruscan cult statue of Juno that willingly relocated to a new shrine on the Aventine after the sacking of Veii in 396 BC to the colossal Greek statue of Hercules by Lysippos that came to the Capitoline "in chains" after Tarentum fell in 209 BC, the plundered statues mentioned by literary sources are invariably associated with the venerable sanctuaries and triumphal temples of Rome (Livy 5.22.3–8; 5.12.4–7; 27.16.7; Strabo 6.3.1; see essay 6.3, Shaya). The most commonly mentioned display areas for such statues are sacred locales located in areas along the triumphal route, including those of the Circus Flaminius, the Forum Boarium, the Forum Romanum, and the Capitoline Hill. Archaeological evidence for manubial statues along the triumphal route may include the statue bases recovered from the Area Sacra di Sant'Omobono and associated with the twin temples in the Forum Boarium (McDonnell 2006, 73). These bases held a total of thirty bronze statuettes, each two to three feet tall. One of the statue bases is inscribed with the name of M. Fulvius Flaccus, who celebrated a victory over the Volsinii in 264 BC. The size and number of statuettes associated with these bases suggest they may be associated with Flaccus's triumphant return to Rome, which Pliny (*HN* 34.34) states was accompanied by 2000 small Etruscan statues. By placing manubial statues like these along the triumphal route, generals visually reminded the Roman public of their respective victories while simultaneously comparing their success to those of their predecessors and providing exemplars for future generations.

The strong link between sacred space and manubial display continued as more architecturally complex sacred precincts were introduced in Rome during the second and first centuries BC. These included sanctuaries demarcated by porticos, which provided bounded spaces for crowds of people and sculpture. After defeating the Macedonians in 148 BC, Q. Caecilius Metellus built the earliest known example of a sacred portico adjacent to the Circus Flaminius, which served as the traditional staging ground for Roman triumphs. A square enclosure surrounded by a double colonnade, the portico enfolded the marble temple that Metellus built for Jupiter Stator as well as a preexisting temple for Juno Regina. It also served as a permanent display arena for statues that Metellus had taken as plunder from Macedonia, including the equestrian statues by Lysippos that had formed the Granikos Monument at Dion. This monument had been commissioned by Alexander the Great in honor of his comrades who had died during the pivotal battle at the Granikos River (Vell. Pat. 1.11.2–5). When Metellus moved these famous statues to Rome and placed them in the sacred portico amid other spoils of war, he found a powerful way to bind his victory visually with those of the greatest conqueror known to the Romans, Alexander the Great.

The second and first centuries BC were a transformative period for sculptural displays in Rome. Not only does the number of statues known in the archaeological record increase dramatically, but also the range of edifices with which statues are associated multiplies. Alongside the increasingly elaborate sacred contexts for exhibiting triumphal booty, generals used other types of display monuments, like temporary theaters and arches, the latter of which were called *fornices* in the republican period (Wallace-Hadrill 1990). The genesis for combining statues with civic amenities located outside of sacred precincts may again be traceable to the late third and second centuries BC, when the Roman cityscape was inundated with manubial statues, and generals competed to showcase their spoils of war in innovative ways. The earliest triumphal *fornices* mentioned in later historical sources are those erected by L. Stertinius in 196 BC to celebrate his victories in Spain. Livy (33.27.4) references three arches, all of which supported gilded statues, presumably of gods, family members, or Stertinius himself. The second option may be most probable, given that Livy (37.3.7) reports that P. Scipio constructed an arch on the Capitoline Hill that supported seven gilded statues of his family members only six years after Stertinius had built his *fornices*. Two of the three arches constructed by Stertinius were located in the Forum Boarium in front of the twin temples and thus may have been part of the sanctuary complex, perhaps serving as entrances. The third was located in the Circus Maximus, where not only horse races but also gladiatorial combats and animal fights took place throughout the republican period. From its earliest beginnings, the Circus Maximus was sacred to gods like Murcia and Sol, but the placement of the arch in this entertainment venue rather than a forum or purely sacred space is notable.

By 186 BC, a statue of the Roman goddess Pollentia also stood in the Circus Maximus, probably on the spina running down the middle of the racetrack (Livy 39.7.8–9). Livy's multiple references to statues in the Circus Maximus during the first quarter of the second century BC suggest that he considered the circus to be an expected place for sculptural display at that time. Indeed, games, festivals, and other dramatic spectacles provided a ready audience for conspicuous sculptural displays, making entertainment buildings a particularly rich arena for the expansion of the sculptural population in Rome. Outside of Rome, Livy (45.33.5) mentions that L. Aemilius Paullus awed the crowd gathered for his victory games at Amphipolis in 167 BC by displaying the loot of Macedonia. Contemporaries of Aemilius Paullus built temporary theaters in Rome for their votive games (*ludi scaenici*); such edifices also provided a place to display plundered statues and other types of booty after the triumphal parade and before they were either melted down or transitioned to their permanent locales, primarily temples and domestic spaces. By massing the loot in a single locale before its dispersal, victorious generals dazzled the Roman populace with the enormous influx of treasures that were arriving in Rome as a direct result of their leadership and military prowess. The display potential of victory performances and games may well have influenced the architectural development of the multistoried *scaenae frons*, the back wall of the stage building in a Roman theater (Klar 2006). In 58 BC, the aedile M. Aemilius Scaurus built a temporary theater in Rome so elaborate that it featured a three-story *scaenae frons* containing, by Pliny the Elder's count, 360 columns and 3000 bronze statues (Plin. *HN* 34.36; 36.5, 50, 114–15; Cic. *Sest.* 116). Rome's first and largest permanent theater was dedicated by Pompey the Great in 55 BC with gymnastic and musical competitions, horse races, and wild animal fights (Cic. *Fam.* 7.1.2–4; Plut. *Vit. Pomp.* 52; Cass. Dio 39.38.1). Although there is some uncertainty over whether it had a wooden or stone *scaenae frons*, Pompey's entertainment venue featured a large number of statues, including a statue of Victory that Cassius Dio (50.8.3) reports as falling from the *scaenae frons* in 32 BC. In addition to the *scaenae frons*, this immense complex had countless places for statues to be displayed. For instance, freestanding statues could have stood in the orchestra, in the portico above the *cavea* that provided access to the temple of Venus Victrix, and in the enormous quadriporticus behind the stage building, which provided shade, greenery, and leisure space for the people of Rome. The statues adorning this victory complex came from any number of places. Some statues associated with the complex were war booty from Pompey's campaigns, others were obtained by Atticus on behalf of Cicero, and still others were commissioned for the new venue (Plin. *HN* 7.34; 36.41; Cic. *Att.* 4.9.1; Cass Dio. 50.8.3). The most famous of the last group were the statues by Coponius of the fourteen nations conquered by Pompey, which have been variously associated with the quadriporticus and the portico above the *cavea* (Plin. *HN* 36.41; Suet., *Ner.* 46).

As will be typical of later sculptural displays associated with theaters, the known statues from the theater complex of Pompey combined references to Pompey's victories with deities associated with music and drama, particularly Apollo and the muses. In addition to the statue of Victory mentioned by Cassius Dio, other statues associated with the *scaenae frons* include an Apollo, Thalia, and another Muse now in the Villa Borghese, as well as an Euterpe in the Louvre (Fuchs 1987, 6–7). Muses are also firmly associated with the theater at Aphrodisias in Asia Minor, which is one of two theaters that provide early archaeological evidence for permanent two-story *scaenae frons* (the other example is at Iguvium [modern Gubbio] in Italy, which has a head more tentatively identified as a Muse associated with its *scaenae frons*). Dedicated by G. Julius Zoilos in the 20s BC, the theatrical backdrop to the stage at Aphrodisias featured a group of Apollo being crowned by two Muses, each of which holds a tragic mask. Located in the central niche of the upper story of the *scaenae frons*, this group mirrors the basic use of the theater for theatrical performances and musical competitions. This simple correlation between the function of the theater and the ideal sculptures is one that is expected for all types of Roman buildings.

Statues in Architectural Contexts across the Roman Empire

In the imperial period, fountains, baths, and other types of architectural monuments developed elaborate marble walls faced with columnar screens and superimposed *aediculae* for statues. These animated walls are commonly positioned where large groups of people might congregate, whether near a fountain at an urban crossroads or in the *frigidarium*, the cold plunge pool of a bathing complex. One of the last monument types to adopt such display architecture was the monumental fountain. The earliest known fountain with a multistory aediculated façade is the Hydrekdocheion of C. Laecanius Bassus in Ephesus, dedicated in AD 78–79. It features a large, open air basin framed on three sides by a multistoried façade wall. Like most aedicular façade walls created in the second half of the first century AD, this theatrical backdrop displayed a mixture of portraits and ideal statuary, the latter of which included multiple Aphrodites, tritons, and river gods (Fossel and Langmann 1983). Such statues relate thematically to the function of the building as a fountain.

According to Vitruvius, the purpose of an ideal statue is to explicate its architectural context. He makes this point while telling how Licymnius, a mathematician from Tralles, used the solecism of the citizens of Alabanda in Asia Minor to convince his fellow citizens to change the *scaenae frons* of their theater into something more acceptable. "[I]n their gymnasia all the statues are of lawyers pleading cases, whereas in the forum there are discus throwers, runners, and ballplayers. Thus the inappropriate placement of the statues with regard to their site has won the city the reputation for poor judgment. Now let us see to it that this scene building does not transform us, too, into Alabandeans. . ." (*De arch.* 7.5.6; translated by Rowland and Howe 1999). With this story, Vitruvius emphasizes how the disregard of the basic Roman rules of *decorum* adversely affected others' opinions of the city.

As more statues are studied within their architectural contexts, however, it becomes increasingly apparent that sculptural ensembles do not strictly adhere to Vitruvius's ideal. Indeed, most partially preserved sculptural groups include ideal statues that do not obviously relate to the basic function of the monument. Some seemingly errant statues may have referred not to the basic function of the architectural type but to earlier phases, later renovations, or even a range of anticipated functions. Other statues make reference to the patron, like the victory statue in the theater complex of Pompey, while still others make reference to the shared history of communities using the space.

Even with the apparent uniformity of subject matter, limited statue types, and prevailing conventions of *decorum*, there was ample opportunity for benefactors and local populations to display their sense of self through sculptural ensembles, and they used both portraits and ideal statues to do so. Such allusions seem to be an expected part of the display, as many ideal statues erected in urban amenities are best understood as references to communal or individual expressions of identity. In Ephesus, for instance, the Hydrekdocheion of Laecenius Bassus was soon joined by a second massive fountain. Known as the Hydrekdocheion of Trajan (dedicated AD 102–114), this edifice had a pi-shaped aedicular façade that contained statues of Androkles, the legendary founder of Ephesus, and Dionysus, a primary deity in the Ephesian pantheon. The façade also held a statue of Aphrodite, a deity associated with water as well as fertility, and thus appropriate for a fountain. But the Ephesians worshipped Aphrodite in several locales and guises, and thus the statues of Aphrodite in both the Hydrekdocheion of Laecenius Bassus and that of Trajan could be understood not only as referencing the basic function of the monument type but also as emphasizing an aspect of local religious identity.

Still other ideal statues are not as easily explained, and thus serve as important reminders not only of the many lacunae in our knowledge about societal expectations for such displays but also of the likelihood that the basic assumptions Romans held about appropriate sculptural displays may have fluctuated over time and across geographical regions. In bath complexes, for instance, statues associated with water and health, like Neptune, Venus, Asclepius, and Hygeia, are intermixed with imperial and elite portraits, as well as ideal statues of heroes and athletes like the Doryphoros and Hercules. More often than not, however, other ideal statues are also found in bath complexes, and sometimes the statues of expected deities or heroes are so different from their normal portrayal that they defy ready explanation. The range of ideal statues found in the Baths of Antoninus Pius in Carthage suggests that more than local identity and *decorum* was on display in this complex. Beyond the expected sea god and several Venuses (up to three), the assemblage includes multiple statues of Bacchus, Apollo, and Minerva, as well as one each of Mercury, Mars, and Juno.

Like the sculptural arrangement in theaters and other complexes, baths accommodated sculptures both in niches and on bases placed on floors. The *frigidarium* was typically one of the largest and most centrally located rooms in a bathing complex; its size and prominent location meant that it frequently contained more statues in niches and on the floor than most other rooms in the same bathing complex. Statues also tended to congregate around the *natatio*, or swimming pool; in *palaestrae*, or exercise courts surrounded by porticoes; and in *tepidaria*, or warm bathing rooms (Manderscheid 1981). At the massive Baths of Caracalla in Rome (dedicated AD 216), over one hundred freestanding statues are known from the central bathing block alone, and many of these come from the *frigidarium* (Marvin 1983; De Laine 1997, 266–7).

The statues associated with this room include the renowned Farnese Hercules (figure 4.1.2), which faced into the *frigidarium* from the columned entryway separating the cold bathing room from a neighboring space known as room 14E. As Paul Zanker (2010, 66) has pointed out, the flawless nudity of ideal statues set within the context of bathing complexes provides unattainable models for bathers concerned with the realities of their own bodies. Hercules is a heroic figure commonly incorporated into bathing complexes, but the tension between the Farnese Hercules's abject weariness and brawny strength permits the statue to engage with and possibly enhance a bather's state of mind before and after exercise in a way that few other ideal statue types can. Moreover, the utter exhaustion of the Farnese Hercules

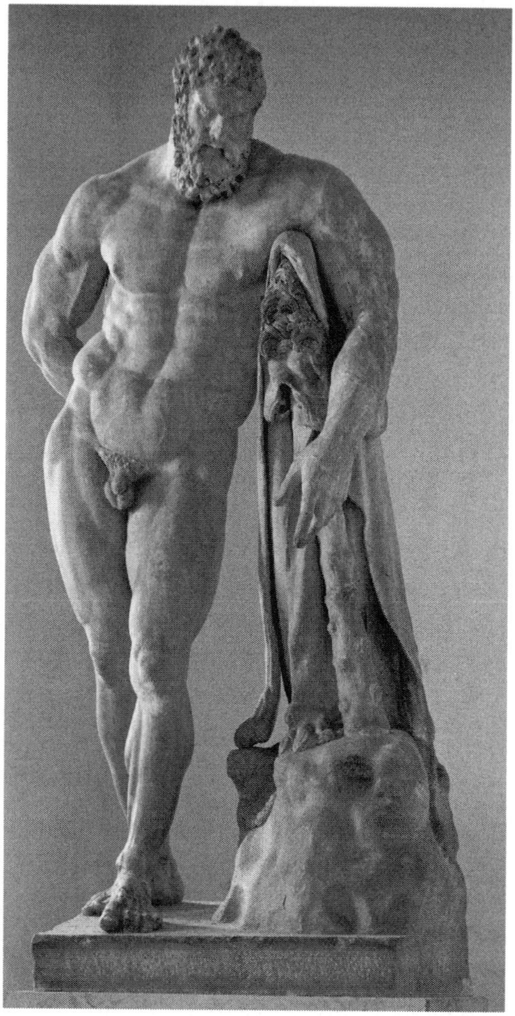

FIGURE 4.1.2 Hercules from the Baths of Caracalla, Rome, signed by Glykon of Athens, c. AD 220. Marble. Museo Archeologico Nazionale di Napoli.

adds a narrative aspect to the space that is best understood by someone who has walked behind the statue and seen the apples of Hesperides held loosely in the hand behind his back; with these apples, Hercules has completed his twelve labors. It is rare for statues of the weary champion to include the apples, and this modification to the type perhaps drew enough attention to this statue that it adds more than simply ambiance to the architectural space. Indeed, the impact of the statue probably was magnified by its placement in the southern intercolumniation between the *frigidarium* and room 14E, where it formed a pendant pair with the equally large and burly Hercules that occupied the northern intercolumniation. Labeled dismissively as the "Latin" Hercules because of unfavorable comparisons with the Farnese

Hercules, which is signed by the Athenian sculptor Glykon, the second Hercules statue is approximately the same size as the Farnese Hercules and presents a variation of the same type but lacks the apples held behind the back. Displayed together as pendants, these two colossal statues dwarfed the bathers passing between them.

The few other extant statues thought to have shared floor space with the Farnese Hercules indicate that the architecture of the *frigidarium* framed not only the activities of the bathers but also the spectacles created by the statues, both individually and combined. A statue of Achilles provides a striking formal parallel to the Farnese Hercules. Like the Farnese Hercules, this statue requires someone to walk around the sculptural group in order to appreciate the scene. Achilles steps forward confidently, with someone's leg casually slung over his left shoulder. From the back, one can see Troilus hanging upside down over Achilles's back; the dead boy's entrails are seeping out of his fatal wound. Although this sculptural group features the quintessential Homeric hero, the scene it narrates at best tangentially alludes to the function of the bathing complex as a place of exercise. Rather, the group seems staged to evoke a visceral reaction, and this unexpected drama in turn probably affected the bather's experience of the architectural space.

Vitriuvius presents *decorum* as it was understood during the early Augustan period, and the potential differences between the predictable displays alluded to by Vitruvius and the varied reality in the first through third centuries AD perhaps also can be seen in the discrepancy between eastern and western cities in the display of ideal athletes and athletic portrait statues (Fejfer 2008, 37–9). In the western empire, baths, gymnasia, and other places of exercise commonly featured ideal statues of athletes and heroes both in niches and on statue bases. For instance, one Doryphoros now in the Museo Archeologico Nazionale di Napoli was found in the Samnite Palaestra in Pompeii. In the eastern empire, however, ideal statues of athletes and heroes often shared the exercise spaces with honorific statues of prize-winning athletes holding ties to the community. In the second and third centuries AD, these statues were also found in other areas of the city. In Aphrodisias, for instance, statues of victorious athletes were also set up in the theater and near the city gate. Thus, the basic expectations about appropriate statuary display were not completely homogeneous across time or geography.

Ideal statues referencing the function of the monument in which they stood and the shared mytho-history of the community and benefactor were commonly intermixed with portrait statues of the emperor, imperial family members, local elites, and benefactors. These sculptural displays served as permanent reminders of individual and communal connections to local and imperial interests, and thus provided another way for communities and elites to emphasize their status in local, regional, and imperial circles and contexts. Organization of such displays within the multistoried aedicular façade was often hierarchical: gods or imperial family members occupy the larger lower story; local elites, heroes, and lesser divinities occupy the smaller upper stories. In Hadrianic Perge, for instance, Plancia Magna monumentalized the existing Hellenistic city gate by adding an interior court framed by a two-story aedicular façade. The niches in the lower story contained statues of gods, while the upper story held statues of her family and of Perge's mythical founders (Boatwright 1993).

In early Antonine Aphrodisias, the Agora gate featured a two-story aedicular façade containing colossal statues of members of the imperial family in the lower story and smaller statues of local elites and honorands above (Smith et al. 2006, 48). Such multi-storied sculptural programs could be understood in any number of ways: as individual statues, in vertical or horizontal segments, or as a single collective ensemble (Newby 2003, 200). Each reading draws any number of connections between the deities and individuals represented, and blurs the lines between human and divine realms as well as local and imperial identities. Coordinated with their architectural setting, such multivalent sculptural ensembles evoke more than ideal and portrait statues could do alone and often build up an image of the community that connects local social, political, and religious histories with a contemporary Roman context (see essay 4.6, Kellum).

Over 5000 portraits of Roman emperors and their families are extant, suggesting that hundreds of thousands of imperial portraits once intermingled with portraits of private elites and ideal statues in architectural monuments, sanctuaries, and civic centers across the Roman Empire (Fittschen 2010, 221). Often these imperial images received honors and became objects of religious devotion, simultaneously imparting legitimacy to the administrative and sacred events that happened beneath their gaze. In Apamea-on-the-Orontes, for instance, statues of Antoninus Pius, Marcus Aurelius, and Lucius Verus stood on ledges located halfway up three column shafts of the colonnade lining the main street. These statues bore witness to the ephemeral spectacles taking place on the street

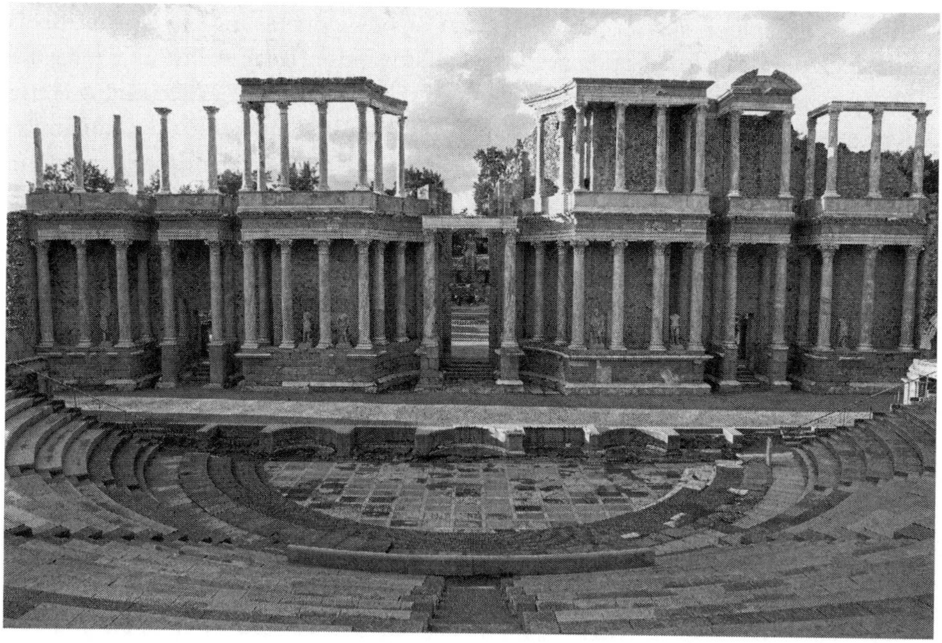

FIGURE 4.1.3 Roman theater in Colonia Augusta Emerita (Mérida, Spain). Constructed 16/15 BC by M. Vipsanius Agrippa. The current configuration of the *scaenae frons* may date to the time of Trajan or Hadrian.

below, ceremonies that included processions of portable effigies of the same emperors. In the theater at Colonia Emerita Augusta (modern Mérida), statues of Julio-Claudian family members occupied the *scaenae frons* and the *sacellum* in the adjacent portico (figure 4.1.3); in the theater of Dionysos in Athens, at least four and possibly twelve honorific statues of Hadrian stood in the *cavea*. While the imperial statues at Emerita faced the audience, those at Athens faced the stage, turning their backs on the audience and blocking the view. Under the multiple gazes of the emperor, the ceremonies, performances, and other spectacles taking place in the theater were reflected back on the participants and spectators as imperially sanctioned events. In both theaters, the interaction of the imperial portraits with architectural setting and ephemeral event revealed and enhanced the unique relationship between city and the ruling power.

Conclusion

Writing in the first century AD, Severianus explained the ubiquity of imperial images: "Since the emperor cannot be present everywhere, it is necessary to set up a portrait of the emperor at tribunals, in marketplaces, at meetings, and in theaters. In fact, a portrait must be present in every place in which a magistrate acts, so that he might sanction whatever transpires" (*In Cosmogoniam* 6.5, translated by Ando 2000, 233). This basic function of imperial statues may explain why they stood not only in nodal spaces but also in transitional locales, like a bridge in Mauretania Caesariensis and the city gate at Timgad/Thamugadi (both in Algeria). It also may explain why such statues are fairly rare in bath complexes: in Manderscheid's study of the sculptural decoration of sixty-six bath complexes (1981), portraits of the emperor comprise only about 3 percent of the sample. More appropriate for baths, apparently, were ideal statues and statues of donors, whether local elite or imperial. Moreover, the numbers of portraits of emperors fluctuate according to geography. Until the second century, the provinces along the Danube and the Black Sea as well as western North Africa, northern Asia Minor, and Syria do not have evidence for imperial statues (Højte 2005, 102). Once imperial statues appear in these regions, however, they are juxtaposed with ideal statues and images of local elites in architectural amenities (like baths, amphitheaters, and basilicas) that can often be taken as markers of Roman social ideas. In each edifice, local and imperial traditions contextualized and nuanced the sculpture display.

Bibliography

Ando, C. 2000. *Imperial Ideology and Provincial Loyalty in the Roman Empire*. Berkeley: University of California Press.

Bartman, E. 1988. "*Decor et Duplicatio*: Pendants in Roman Sculptural Display." *AJA* 92(2): 211–25.

Bejor, G. 1979. "La decorazione scultorea dei teatri romani nelle province africane." *Prospettiva* 17: 37–46.

Boatwright, M. T. 1993. "The City Gate of Plancia Magna in Perge." In *Roman Art in Context: An Anthology*, edited by E. D'Ambra, 189–207. Englewood Cliffs: Prentice Hall.

Bol, R. 1984. *Das Statuenprogramm des Herodes-Atticus-Nymphäums*. OlForsch 15. Berlin: Walter de Gruyter.

Bravi, A. 2011. "Le immagini negli spazi pubblici di Perge in epoca Adriana." In D'Andria and Romeo 2011, 302–18.

D'Andria, F., and I. Romeo, eds. 2011. *Roman Sculpture in Asia Minor*. JRA Supplement 80. Portsmouth, RI: Journal of Roman Archaeology.

De Laine, J. 1997. *The Baths of Caracalla: A Study in the Design, Construction, and Economics of Large-scale Building Projects in Imperial Rome*. JRA Supplement 25. Portsmouth, RI: Journal of Roman Archaeology.

Fejfer, J. 2008. *Roman Portraits in Context*. Berlin: Walter de Gruyter.

Fittschen, K. 2010. "The Portraits of Roman Emperors and Their Families: Controversial Positions and Unsolved Problems." In *The Emperor and Rome: Space, Representation, and Ritual*, edited by B. Ewald and C. Noreña, 221–46. Cambridge: Cambridge University Press.

Fossel, E., and G. Langmann. 1983. "Das Nymphaeum des C. Laecanius Bassus in Ephesos." *AntW* 14: 53–5.

Fuchs, M. 1987. *Untersuchungen zur Ausstattung römischer Theater in Italien und den Westprovinzen des Imperium Romanum*. Mainz: Philipp von Zabern.

Gazda, E. K. 1995. "Roman Sculpture and the Ethos of Emulation: Reconsidering Repetition." *HSCP* 97: 121–56.

Gazda, E. K., and A. F. Haeckl. 1993. "Roman Portraiture: Reflections on the Question of Context." *JRA* 6: 289–302.

Ghedini, F. 1985. "Sculture dal ninfeo e dal pretorio di Gortina." *ASAtene* 63: 63–248.

Hallett, C. H. 2005. *The Roman Nude: Heroic Portrait Statuary, 200 BC–AD 300*. Oxford: Oxford University Press.

Højte, J. M. 2005. *Roman Imperial Statue Bases: From Augustus to Commodus*. Aarhus: Aarhus University Press.

Inan, J. 1975. *Roman Sculpture in Side*. Ankara: Türk Tarih Kurumu Basımevi.

Klar, L. S. 2006. "The Origins of the Roman *Scaenae Frons* and the Architecture of Triumphal Games in the Second Century B.C." In *Representations of War in Ancient Rome*, edited by S. Dillon and K. Welch, 162–83. Cambridge: Cambridge University Press.

Kousser, R. M. 2008. *Hellenistic and Roman Ideal Sculpture: The Allure of the Classical*. Cambridge: Cambridge University Press.

Lahusen, G. 1983. *Untersuchungen zur Ehrenstatue in Rom*. Rome: Giorgio Bretschneider.

Longfellow, B. 2011. *Roman Imperialism and Civic Patronage: Form, Meaning and Ideology in Monumental Fountain Complexes*. Cambridge: Cambridge University Press.

Manderscheid, H. 1981. *Die Skulpturenausstattung der kaiserzeitlichen Termenanlagen*. Monumenta Artis Romanae 15. Berlin: Mann.

Marvin, M. 1983. "Freestanding Sculptures from the Baths of Caracalla." *AJA* 87: 347–84.

———. 1993 "Copying in Roman Sculpture: The Replica Series." In *Roman Art in Context: An Anthology*, edited by E. D'Ambra, 161–88. Englewood Cliffs: Prentice Hall.

———. 2008. *The Language of the Muses: The Dialogue between Greek and Roman Sculpture*. Los Angeles: J. Paul Getty Museum.

McDonnell, M. 2006. "Roman Aesthetics and the Spoils of Syracuse." In *Representations of War in Ancient Rome*, edited by S. Dillon and K. Welch, 68–90. Cambridge: Cambridge University Press.

Newby, Z. 2003. "Art and Identity in Asia Minor." In *Roman Imperialism and Provincial Art*, edited by S. Scott and J. Webster, 192–213. Cambridge: Cambridge University Press.

Özren, A. 1996. "Die Skulpturenausstattung kaiserzeitlicher Theater in der Provinz Asia, am Beispiel der Theater in Aphrodisias, Ephesos und Hierapolis." *Thetis* 3: 122–8.

Pollitt, J. J. 1978. "The Impact of Greek Art on Rome." *TAPA* 108: 155–74.

Rathmayr, E. 2011. "Die Skulpturenausstattung des C. Laecanius Bassus Nymphaeum in Ephesos." In D'Andria and Romeo 2011, 130–49.

Ridgway, B. S. 1984. *Roman Copies of Greek Sculpture: The Problem of the Originals*. Ann Arbor: University of Michigan Press.

Rowland, I. D., and T. N. Howe. 1999. *Vitruvius: Ten Books on Architecture*. Cambridge: Cambridge University Press.

Schmidt-Colinet, A. 1985. "Skulpturen aus dem Nymphäum von Apamea/Syria." *AA* 1985: 119–33.

Sehlmeyer, M. 1999. *Stadtrömische Ehrenstatuen der republikanischen Zeit: Historizität und Kontext von Symbolen nobilitären Standesbewusstseins*. Stuttgart: Franz Steiner.

Smith, R. R. R. 1998. "Cultural Choice and Political Identity in Honorific Portrait Statues in the Greek East in the Second Century A.D." *JRS* 88: 56–93.

Smith, R. R. R., with S. Dillon, C. H. Hallett, J. Lenaghan, and J. Van Voorhis. 2006. *Aphrodisias II: Roman Portrait Statuary from Aphrodisias*. Mainz: Philipp von Zabern.

Stewart, P. 2003. *Statues in Roman Society: Representation and Response*. Oxford: Oxford University Press.

Sturgeon, M. 2004. *Sculpture: The Assemblage from the Theater*. Corinth 9.3. Princeton: American School of Classical Studies at Athens.

Tanner, J. 1990. "Portraits, Power, and Patronage in the Late Roman Republic." *JRS* 90: 18–50.

Trimble, J. 2011. *Women and Visual Replication in Roman Imperial Art and Culture*. Cambridge: Cambridge University Press.

Wallace-Hadrill, A. 1990. "Roman Arches and Greek Honours: The Language of Power at Rome." *PCPS* 36: 143–81.

Zanker, P. 2000. "Bildräume und Betrachter im kaiserzeitlichen Rom: Fragen und Anregungen für Interpreten." In *Klassische Archäologie: Eine Einführung*, edited by A. Borbein, T. Hölscher, and P. Zanker, 205–226. Berlin: Dietrich Reimer.

———. 2010. "By the Emperor, For the People: 'Popular' Architecture in Rome." In *The Emperor and Rome: Space, Representation, and Ritual*, edited by B. Ewald and C. Noreña, 45–88. Cambridge: Cambridge University Press.

CHAPTER 4.2

RELIGIOUS DEDICATIONS

MATTHEW M. MCCARTY

Introduction

If geographically and culturally remote from Rome itself, a temple in Uley (Gloucestershire, Britain) offers an instructive view of the range of ways figurative sculpture might be deployed in a sacred environment in the Roman Empire (Woodward and Leach 1993). At the back of a portico, set atop a podium, towered a finely carved, over-life-size, limestone statue of the god Mercury flanked by a goat and a cockerel, a visual focus of the space (figure 4.2.1). Smaller stone statues stood elsewhere in the sanctuary, as did a series of small altars carved with images of the god, reproducing the schema of the larger statue (figure 4.2.2). A relief of imported white marble—an expensive and exotic commodity in Britain—stood out from these other dedications. Bronze statuettes of deities, and a variety of other objects ranging from coins to personal adornments were also dedicated within the precinct. Visitors seeking restitution inscribed pleas for divine justice on lead sheets. Every autumn, hundreds of goats were slaughtered for the god and feasted upon by worshippers from across the region.

The sculptural assemblage from Uley raises a number of questions pertinent to the study of religious dedications throughout the Roman world. To what extent are such dedications commensurate with sculptures from other contexts? What were the purposes and functions of dedicating objects—and figurative sculpture in particular? Are dedicated sculptures fundamentally different than the range of other dedications made in sanctuaries? To what extent were such dedications indices, or commemorations, of something else, and of what: the god, the god's actions, the dedicant, the dedicatory act? How and why did the objects and rituals of dedication change over time?

Like Uley, many sanctuaries across the Roman world were replete with sculpted representations. Yet of the four types of places elaborated with sculpture across the Roman world—public spaces, tombs, houses, and sanctuaries—studies of the sanctuary sphere remain relatively underdeveloped theoretically and methodologically. My focus here will rest primarily upon the roles of sanctuary sculpture in relation to civic statuary and

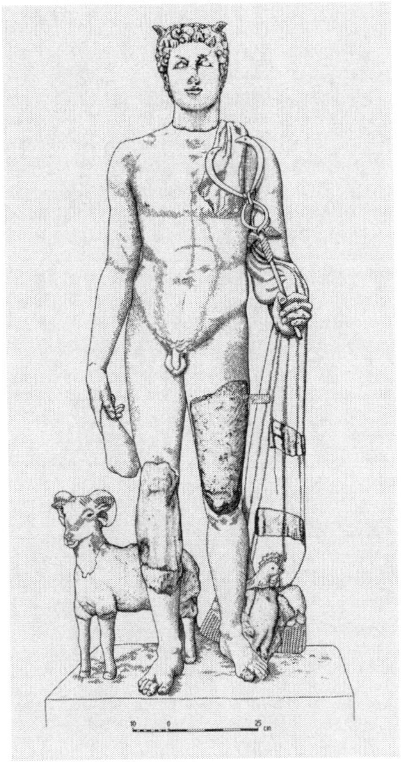

FIGURE 4.2.1 Statue of Mercury (proposed reconstruction), from the Sanctuary of Mercury, West Hill, Uley, Gloucestershire. Late second century AD.

other types of sanctuary dedications, as well as upon the ways in which sanctuary sculpture engages with ritual, not just as an object of ritual dedication or as a locus of practices. There are, of course, a number of other ways in which temple sculpture might be interrogated. Did sanctuary visitors approach the sculptures with a particular mode of "religious viewing" as Elsner (1996) suggests? The conceptual stakes of figuring gods, and representing them in particular ways, are also unsettled. While statues of the gods might serve to make a god present and visible, perhaps luxuriating in the tensions raised by the practice of figuration (Platt 2011), Cliff Ando (2010) has suggested that such interpretations are the legacy of Christian polemic and that Roman images of the gods do not sit on a scale of iconicity: Roman gods were never invisible or immaterial to begin with. The problems of figuration and the choices of particular schemata for gods become more fraught in parts of the empire where such practices are rare or nonexistent prior to the imperial period or Roman conquest. There, any changes in the practices and technologies surrounding sculpted gods must have taken into account a range of social pressures, changing power hierarchies, and novel ways of creating knowledge about the gods.

If there is a dearth of general accounts of votive sculpture in the imperial-period Roman world, the topic has been more fully explored for the Greek world (Van Straten

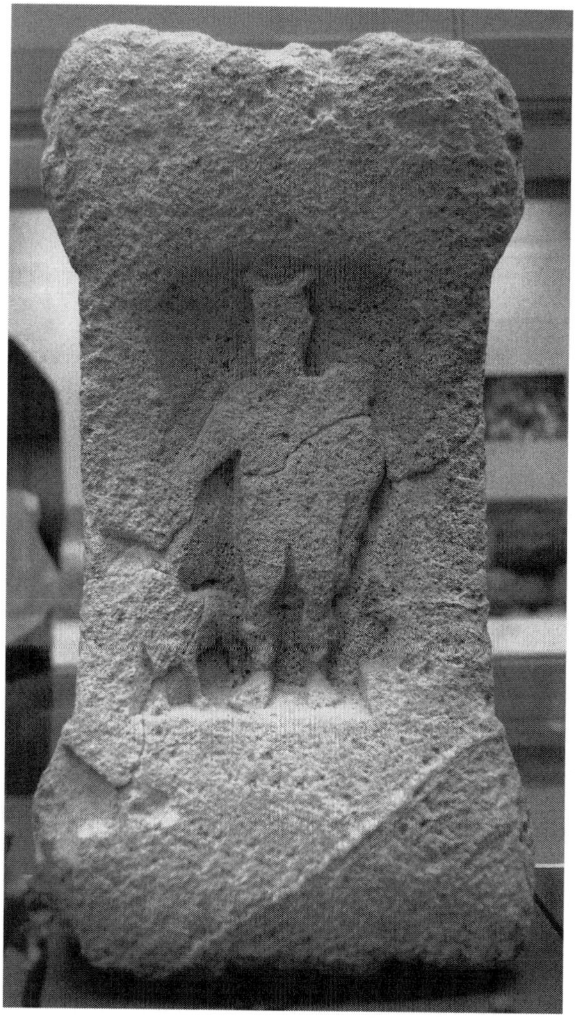

FIGURE 4.2.2 Altar with Mercury, from the Sanctuary of Mercury, West Hill, Uley. Limestone, late second or third century AD. London, British Museum.

1995), and for Italy up through the late Republic. The lack of synthetic works on Roman imperial-period sanctuary dedications may partly be a product of the problematic assumption that a relatively universal, unchanging logic of gift-exchange with the gods offers a mostly complete explanation of all sanctuary dedications (Rüpke 2007, 154–65; Osborne 2004). Of course, the other reason for few synthetic works, save occasional region-based studies (Schörner 2003; McCarty 2010a), lies in the sheer diversity of sculpted offerings and their functions within particular sanctuaries and cult communities. Even if there are families of resemblance and a few common themes in sculptural dedications and the practices surrounding them, religion in the Roman world was a fundamentally local affair.

In what follows, I suggest that religious dedications demand different approaches and questions than those used for other genres of sculpture, especially honorific statuary. Sculpted dedications can, of course, provide insight regarding social structures, yet focusing only on dedicants' self-representation limits investigation to a minor aspect of the objects. Parsing the many interfaces between such sculpture and religious practices and their variations across time and space remains the most promising avenue of research both into Roman sculpture and religion. A few words are necessary about the problems inherent in understanding "religion" and its sculptural corollaries in the ancient world before turning to four of the ways sculpted dedications were enmeshed with religion: as objects of ritual dedication, as objects akin to ritual, as recipients of ritual, and as subjects capable of shaping the significance of ritual for participants.

Religion and Votives in the Roman World

"Religion" is a notoriously amorphous term, and modern definitions, worked out primarily from nineteenth-century Protestant ideals (Masuzawa 2005; Nongbri 2013), rarely translate well into the ancient world. Most recent accounts of religion in the Roman world have emphasized correct ritual practice—orthopraxy, as opposed to the Christian notion of orthodoxy (correct belief)—as its central component and sacrifice as the paradigmatic ritual act (Scheid 2005). Epigraphic evidence suggests—at first glance—that this ritual system is primarily transactional. Every year, the Arval Brethren, a club of elite Romans, would selectively inscribe their religious activities, including a formal declaration: if the gods had kept the emperor safe during that year, then the Arvals would return the next year and offer the gods specific sacrifices and, in some cases, statues. The ubiquity of variations on the epigraphic formula *votum solvit libens merito* ("he deservedly fulfilled the vow") on the altars, reliefs, and statuary dedicated in sanctuaries across the Latin world has been taken to confirm that this type of formal exchange not only sat at the heart of Roman religion, but also serves as a full and satisfying explanation for the bulk of sanctuary sculpture and practices. The sculptural assemblages dedicated in sanctuaries, though, suggest that such a model is only partially valid.

At the same time, religious life was not a neatly bounded phenomenon, but one interlaced with a variety of other discourses and social structures. These connections might exist at the political level, creating the "civic religion" of the myriad towns across the empire, but might also be tied to a range of other social frameworks created by a community of visitors to particular sanctuaries (McCarty 2010a). Since most societies across the Roman world, especially on the civic level, had certain common characteristics and structures that developed under Roman rule, it is unsurprising to find similarities in religious life and dedicatory practice (Rives 2007, although it overemphasizes a normative picture). Yet the level of diversity across the Roman world in ritual practices, whether stemming from pre-Roman rites or as newly created traditions, cannot be overestimated. To that end, each assemblage of sculpture must be understood on its own terms, in its local and network contexts, before building outward to look at wider patterns in the Roman world.

"Religion" also did not exist in and of itself: everything we might term "religion" was mediated in a variety of forms, from dinnertime conversations about the gods, to dramatic spectacles of public sacrifice, to responses a viewer might have to an image, to the aggregate of offerings made by individuals. In a world without formal religious education, and where sacred texts were rare, knowledge about the gods and how to relate to them depended especially on the rituals and visual environments of sanctuaries. As such, the objects dedicated in sanctuaries played an important role in the construction and perpetuation of ideas about the gods, relations with them, and the functioning and ordering of human society. Given the range of meanings and explanations which participants could place upon the same sequence of ritual actions or objects, seeking significance within the gestures and things themselves is nearly impossible; but when connected to the full visual and phenomenological environment of a sanctuary, the complete assemblage of actions and images could work to produce its own system of signification. Articulating how such systems worked and how they varied across time and space within the Roman Empire remain the key challenges for understanding religious sculpture in the Roman world.

If "religion" cannot be disentangled from a host of other discourses, bracketing "religious sculpture" or sculpted dedications is itself arbitrary. Around Rome, sculpted altars and bases for tripods were erected within garden-shrines, establishing scenic, personal, "sacro-idyllic landscapes" like those seen in Pompeian wall painting (Dräger 1994). In fora, city council houses, and other public spaces, inscriptions on some bases proclaim that their statues were not simply products of the euergetic exchange that created Roman cityscapes, but also dedicated to particular deities: often those linked explicitly to civic life (Zimmer and Wesch-Klein 1989). Carved altars and gravestones set up in necropoleis across the Roman world were explicitly dedicated to the Dis Manes (see essay 4.4, Ewald), and at Rome itself, matters of burial were overseen by the priestly college of pontifices and thus might be considered part of—or at least contiguous with—"religion." All of these contexts of sculpture dedication might count as religious, but here, I will focus on sculptural assemblages from sanctuaries.

Sculpted dedications from sanctuaries do not necessarily reflect the same concerns and social dynamics as civic-honorific sculpture, although many recent studies of sculptured dedications borrow heavily from paradigms used in the civic realm of sculpture, seeing sanctuary assemblages as indicative of competition for prestige among local elites (McGowen 2010). Such accounts build from the dichotomy that underpinned Jacob Burckhardt's 1884 essay on Greek votives: a fundamental difference between "simple, pious, private" offerings—terracottas, coins, the seemingly anonymous dedications at sanctuaries—and large-scale, public sculpture, which was "secular" and meant to communicate something about the dedicant. Not only are the public/private and sacred/secular distinctions problematic, but the types of social claims made by sculptures dedicated in sanctuaries are rarely competitive, as will be shown below. The question of how sculpted offerings differ from other types of sculpture and from other types of dedications must be revisited.

Location and the level of traffic from visitor-viewers is a crucial factor in determining the types of offerings and the social claims that they might make. The inscriptions associated with dedications to the gods in central civic-spaces, for example, are loquacious compared to those found in contemporary sanctuaries: the former often include details about the dedicant's career and the circumstances of dedication, whether promised as part of a campaign for election, or given as a bequest. Such details and precision are almost entirely absent from sanctuary dedications in the West. The different types of location and inscription frame the associated sculpture within markedly different social discourses. By contrast, the large and heavily visited Panhellenic sanctuaries of the East—including Olympia, Delphi, Epidauros (Schörner 2003)—as well as the urban temple-porticoes of cities like Rome, were filled with honorific portrait statues and long inscriptions detailing their subjects' careers, along with similar portrait statues and inscriptions explicitly dedicated to gods.

Also, the level of visibility of sculpture in sanctuaries—unlike in fora—is itself uncertain: how often cella doors were open to reveal the treasures and sculptures inside is unclear, and probably varied by temple and region. Most sculptural dedications, though, seem to have sat in the precincts around the temple buildings, or in porticoes; in many sanctuaries, they were periodically cleared and buried or placed in storage areas. Sanctuaries that sat outside of urban centers were destinations in themselves, requiring a fixed intention of visiting—even if only for a stroll through the portico.

Ample evidence for viewers' responses to sanctuary sculpture implies at least occasional visibility and direct engagement with the images: at Uley, for example, the reduplication of the large statue's schema in the smaller altars implies that the statue was seen and known by other dedicators (see essay 6.4, Moormann). Most sanctuaries, save large healing centers or important civic temples, were not prime social advertising space. Unlike civic sculpture, sanctuary dedications more often work in a manner akin to ritual practices themselves: to emphasize repetition, and to create a range of conceptual and visual ties to sanctuary-specific practices and concerns. Indeed, if discourses of "religion" in the Roman world revolve around practices, then understanding religious sculpture requires teasing apart the ties between rituals and sculpted objects.

Objects of Dedication

All dedications, including sculpted ones, were inextricably linked to ritual actions, including their dedication. Peter Stewart (2010) has argued that the adoption and contours of "sculpture habits" in various parts of the empire can broadly be linked to specific communities of users, market forces, geography, and geology; ritual practices must emphatically be added to this list. Sculptured dedications were the outcome of certain rituals, including vows to the gods, and were always in dialogue with these practices.

In Gaul, Germany, and Britain, patterns of stone sculpture dedication broadly follow patterns of civic/honorific and tomb sculpture erection (McGowen 2010; see essay 5.1, Cassibry), though there are also clear distinctions: the Cotswold region (Britain), for example, lacks much civic statuary, but sanctuary sculpture is abundant. No "sculpture habit" spread across all realms; such general practices as sculpture carving may play a role—it is easier to procure carved monuments for a sanctuary when there is a sculpture workshop nearby—but they are not the only impetus for dedicating sculpture in temples.

Similarly, in North Africa, the sculpture-dedicating habit spread as part of a particular rite (McCarty 2010b), even if the numbers of dedications can be linked to the adoption of more general stoneworking practices (see essay 5.3, Baratte and Chaisemartin). The majority of thousands of votive stelae dedicated to Saturn over the imperial period come from generally wealthy communities who produced a range of carved-stone monuments; for example, the military and veteran communities of Thamagudi and Lambaesis (Algeria), the source of over half of the votive stelae in the province of Numidia, also erected nearly 20 percent of inscriptions in the entire province. Yet a number of other communities who did not adopt broad inscriptional and sculpture habits also erected the votive stelae, suggesting that the pattern of general stone-monument use does not map neatly onto religious dedications. Instead, the African stelae are tied to a particular ritual: they were commissioned and dedicated in conjunction with a holocaust sacrifice, usually of either infants or ovicaprines, whose remains were placed in an urn and buried. By their placement above or immediately adjacent to the urns with sacrificial remains, the stelae were closely linked to the sacrifice, though not every sacrifice included the dedication of a stela: even if incorporated as an element of a specific chain of ritualized actions, sculpture dedication was always exceptional, rather than the norm.

Over 150 "confession stelae" of Asia Minor were set up in village temples of Lydia and Phrygia, most between the mid-second and mid-third centuries AD; many are sculpted with reliefs related to their divine recipients or other themes (e.g., figure 4.2.3; Petzl 1994). These stelae all outline a series of particular events in their inscriptions: the dedicant committed an offense against the god, the god punished him or her (sometimes many years later), the dedicant became aware of and expiated the crime, then dedicated the stela. If this general sequence of misfortune and expiation—minus stela dedication—was practiced in a similar manner prior to the first century AD, it has left no trace. Whether a new (and perhaps exceptional) addition to preexisting practices, or an entirely new practice, the confession stelae must be seen as the products of a specific regional ritual.

In North Africa and Asia Minor, even if sculptural dedication was always an exceptional feature of ritual, it predated the Roman imperial period. In the northwest, by contrast, the wide spread of figurative offerings is a new feature of the imperial period, whether in wood (the shrines at Chamelières and the Source de la Seine, both of which seem to be active primarily from the first century AD: Romeuf 1986), terracotta, stone, or bronze.

One facet of explanation for the rise of sculpture as sanctuary offerings, set alongside the general adoption of sculpture habits, is the wider participation in new rites, and in particular, the *votum*: the dedicant makes a vow to dedicate something to the god if the god provides a service; the favor is granted; the dedicant makes the offering, which could be sculptural. Two types of archaeological evidence serve as indices of the spread of this rite in the northwest: the omnipresent epigraphic formulae (*votum solvit*) and the appearance of clay seals, which might have sealed tablets containing *vota* (Derks 1995). In addition, changes in the interface between religion and social ordering expedited by Roman conquest made access to the gods, via these new types of rites, more widespread, and no longer the preserve of the elite: offerings of all kinds proliferate from the first century AD (Bradley 1990). At least some of the sculpture found in sanctuaries of the northwest provinces was the product of this new—and more widely available—ritual practice (Van Andringa 2002, 122–3).

Sculptural dedication in sanctuaries was always part of a chain of rites. In one sense sculpture was commensurate with other types of offerings (animal sacrifices, coins, miniature vessels). As an unusual offering, however, it could also serve different or complementary purposes. Not every *votum* promised a sculpture; not every holocaust sacrifice in North Africa received a stela; not every expiation in Lydia and Phrygia resulted in dedication of a confession stela.

Objects Like Ritual: Repetition and Seriation

Most sculptural dedications resulted from specific types of ritualized practices for dealing with the gods, and the sculptures often functioned analogously to ritual itself by creating a visibly stable and repeated model of divine-human relations.

It may well be that the immediate personal intent of one dedicant was commensurate with that of another. Although very rarely reconstructable on the basis of surviving evidence, there seem to be three general types of occasion for dedication: an external stress (sickness, bad harvest, natural disaster); an anxiety that might be regular or one-time (preserving health, hoping for a good harvest, undertaking a dangerous voyage); or some great blessing that demanded acclamation and thanksgiving to the god. These occasions sometimes determined the form of a given offering: sculptures of votaries that emphasize physical pathologies, as at the first-to-third-century AD healing sanctuary of the goddess Sequana at the Source de la Seine (France), record the types of ailments for which people made sculptured offerings (Aldhouse-Green 1999).

More usually, though (especially outside healing shrines), we can only guess at the particular occasion that prompted the dedication of sculpture and other objects in a sanctuary; such reasons are rarely indicated iconographically or epigraphically. Their absence is telling. If the Arval Acts suggests a concern in ritual practice with publicly proclaiming the terms of a transaction with the gods in specific and legalistic terms, such specificity is usually eschewed in sculpted offerings. At Uley, the inscription displayed on one of the small altars records the name of the dedicant and that he fulfilled his vow, but not why that vow was made. The image shows only the god. Commemorating the specifics of the occasion or reproducing the level of specificity that might have occurred in the original vow is not the goal of the sculpture. This generality also stands in sharp contrast to the specificity of the curse-tablets from the site, where the crime suffered is clearly defined: the theft of an animal, a bridle, a cloth. Explicitly commemorating and communicating details about a particular event or set of circumstances was not a central concern of most sanctuary sculpture, unlike these other technologies for relating to the gods.

Where relatively complete assemblages of sculpted offerings survive, a minority bear inscriptions, suggesting again that their role is not primarily as commemorations of a particular individual or action (in contrast to civic or tomb sculpture). Only about a third of the nearly 2000 stelae dedicated in North Africa from the first century AD onward have any inscription. Even though the stelae were dedicated at particular moments and linked to the denouement of a single holocaust sacrifice, their iconography was largely standardized. If each stela could be seen as the index of a single act by a specific individual, particularizing the occasion or naming the person was not a main concern of the sculpture. Similarly, at the healing sanctuary of Hercules Salutaris at Deneuvre (Moitrieux 1992), of the forty figured stelae and altars that survive nearly complete, only three include the name of the dedicant and a votive formula. The images of Hercules on these stelae and altars differed, but all repeated one of two main figure-types: Hercules leaning on his club or raising it. The majority of sculpture did not offer specific information about the occasion of dedication or the dedicant.

The point of particular visual formulations in dedicated sculpture was rarely to commemorate, reproduce, or communicate the specific circumstances of dedication or dedicant, but to sit within wider patterns of offerings and iconographies: to be part of a series. Terracotta offerings, made in series in molds, are particularly apt for this role (see essay 2.5, Erlich). Throughout Gaul, even if the practices of dedicating terracotta statuettes in sanctuaries differed widely by site and microregion, terracotta assemblages from sanctuaries show less variation in iconography than those from funerary contexts (Bémont, Jeanlin, and Lahanier 1993): there were expectations as to what types of terracottas were suitable for dedication, even if the statuettes themselves may not have been visibly displayed. Repetition was a central concern.

Even when inscriptions occur in connection with dedications, their silence on specific circumstances, their refusal to provide a unique narrative in favor of formulae like *votum solvit libens merito* serves a deliberate purpose: reiteration of a normative relationship and series of events rather than particulars. As in ritual practices themselves, the claim to repetition—perhaps with minor variation—is central.

A focus on repetition makes apparent exceptions especially interesting. The confession stelae of Asia Minor provide a wealth of details often absent from other sculptural dedications and use such details to give an illusion of accuracy and completeness: the date (by the local calendar), the crime, and sometimes further circumstances. The images—and not every confession stela includes them—also vary widely: at least two show the crime taking place; several, the body parts afflicted with the god's punishment; ten, worshippers acclaiming the god; and the rest, the gods or their attributes. One stela, dedicated by Severus, describes how he was punished for not allowing temple servants to cut branches for festive wreaths from his orchard (figure 4.2.3). The accompanying image shows Severus shooing a man with a pruning knife away from a tree. Such features guaranteed the "uniqueness" of the event while confirming that no crime, however petty or however long ago, escaped the god's notice. Yet the texts seem to follow a master script, and Richard Gordon (2008) has argued that the variations were selected by their patrons in response to specific social pressures: the need for the guilty party to explain his or her misfortune by providing an authoritative account of the crime, for example.

Yet the degree of variation is more pronounced when the confession stelae from different sites are gathered together. Although the stelae lack contexts, the images chosen within a particular sanctuary seem generally to repeat one another; three stelae probably from the same sanctuary of Zeus of the Twin Oaks at Mons Toma (Turkey), for example, all show two figures standing side-by-side above the inscriptions. Within a

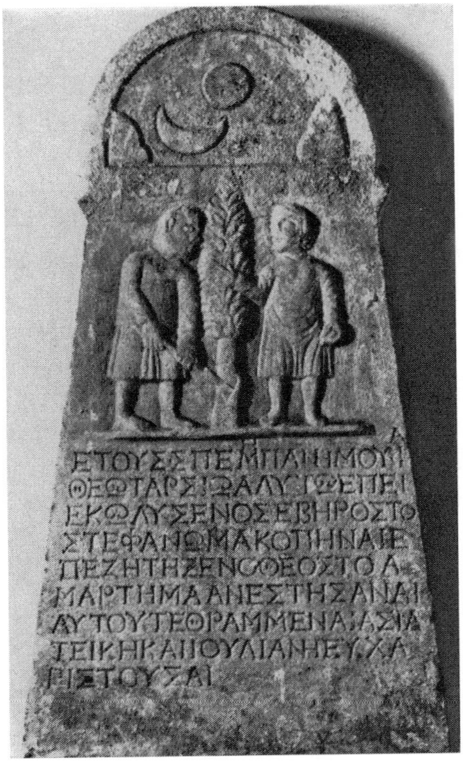

FIGURE 4.2.3 Severus's confession stela, probably from northeast Lydia. Limestone, AD 200/201. Private collection.

single sanctuary, the prevailing visual pattern serves, as with the repeated formulae and invocations in the inscriptions, to demonstrate an overarching regularity, even if the narrative details might differ.

The other main exception to this rule of seriation lies in healing sanctuaries. There, too, individual narratives about illness, personal engagement with the god, and miraculous cures were emphasized: at the Asklepeion of Pergamon, for example, plaques showing afflicted body parts were routinely dedicated and included details about the votary. Alongside such sculpted offerings, a range of other objects are hinted at by inscriptions that include inventories of personal offerings: bracelets, clothing, adornments. All of these personal narratives and indices of individual pilgrims healed at the shrine—whether commemorated in sculpture or figured plaques, in inscribed altars, or personal objects—build on a master script to establish a set pattern of the god's engagement with visitors' bodies (Petsalis-Diomidis 2010).

The stability of human and divine relations was in the interest of a sanctuary's staff, a group whose role in dedications is often overlooked. Despite the recent emphasis on the agency of individual dedicants, sculptural dedications must have required at least some approval from those in charge of the sanctuary; erecting offerings was not a free-for-all. Hellenistic lists of rules for conduct in sanctuaries demonstrate such concerns over personal dedications in the East (e.g., Sokolowski 1969, no. 43); elsewhere, when found *in situ*, the arrangement of dedications in sanctuaries, such as the neat rows of stelae in North African temples, hints at such controls. As much as general social expectations and the dedicant's choice might affect the selection of particular types of offering, the role of temple authorities should not be forgotten in this equation: if nothing else, they determined what could be dedicated and displayed—and where—within the sanctuary. Gordon (2008) sees evidence in the confession stelae inscriptions for a negotiation between temple authorities and dedicants in crafting an appropriate narrative; that process of negotiation may have included monument type and iconography.

The use of a sanctuary's services and spaces as a means to establish an exchange with the gods was generally on an *ad hoc* basis, with the exception of calendar-based events like the autumn goat sacrifices at Uley. The display of offerings, especially those explicitly marked by inscriptions proclaiming that they fulfilled a vow (demonstrating that the god had met his part of the bargain) or manifesting successful healing, proved the efficacy of the god and sanctuary apparatus. In communities with multiple sanctuaries, and for sanctuary centers that aimed to draw pilgrims, the display of sculpted offerings and high levels of investment provided a competitive advantage: evidence that the sanctuary and its staff were worth the price of its service.

Recipients of Ritual

In addition to being objects of dedicatory practices or analogous to ritual in their seriation, religious dedications also served as loci for subsequent ritual actions (Gladigow

1994). Much ink has been spilled on the status of divine statues dedicated in sanctuaries and on the applicability of the modern category of "cult statue" for certain dedications in temples. There is no discrete lexical category in Greek or Latin for such special dedications (Stewart 2003, 19–35, 184–95). But not all dedications in a sanctuary occupied the same visual, ritual, and conceptual status.

From a Roman legal perspective, Macrobius (*Sat.* 3.11.6, not dealing directly with sculpture) suggests that two key distinctions mattered in determining the status of an object in a temple: when it was dedicated—things consecrated together with the temple were inalienable *sacra*—and the use to which the object was put—things essential to sacrifice were also inalienable. As the perceived participant in and recipient of such sacrifices (Vitr. *De arch.* 4.5), a statue dedicated in the heart of a temple would fulfill both criteria. Spatial hierarchies in temples could also be "practical" determinants of a dedication's perceived status: at the imperial cult shrine at Misenum, for example, statues of the primary recipients of cult—deified emperors—were placed inside the shrine, while living emperors were placed outside, alongside honorific statues of priests and deities who were "guests" in the sanctuary (Estienne 2010).

In practice, sculptural dedications centrally placed in a temple's cella and often dedicated with the building (or at its renovation) became centers of cult and visual foci to which subsequent "peripheral" dedications responded. Rarely did carved stone dedications beyond the largest, most centrally placed (and often in the most expensive material) statue serve as recipient of offerings, or direct participants in cult; smaller statues in precious metal or wood dedicated in a temple might, however, be carried in processions. At Ammaedara (Tunisia), an open-air sanctuary to Saturn began in the first century AD as a shrine filled with lines of stelae that showed Saturn in a number of guises and schemata; by analogy with other stela-sanctuaries, each of these monuments may have been a site for later offerings as well. Later, a new temple to Saturn was built, an over-life-size marble statue of the god enthroned was set in the cella, and a large sacrificial altar built in front. From that moment on, smaller sculpted limestone dedications in the sanctuary portico depicted Saturn with the same enthroned type (figure 4.2.4), demonstrating the visual importance and centrality of the new marble image. In other words, the building of the temple and installation of a high-status image converted a sanctuary that had been polycentric in its cult practices and visual choices into one where a single statue served as a new, and only, visual and sacrificial center (McCarty 2011b). A similar phenomenon can be seen at Uley: although the relative chronology of the statue and altars is unclear, it is probable that the votive altars responded to the new and central image of the god.

If the category of "cult statue" is a redescriptive one, it is still useful to denote the way certain sculptural dedications in the Roman world received material, spatial, visual, and ritual priority in their sanctuaries. Yet even when not themselves loci of cult, figured dedications could also work in other ways to establish and reinforce the connections between ritual and image.

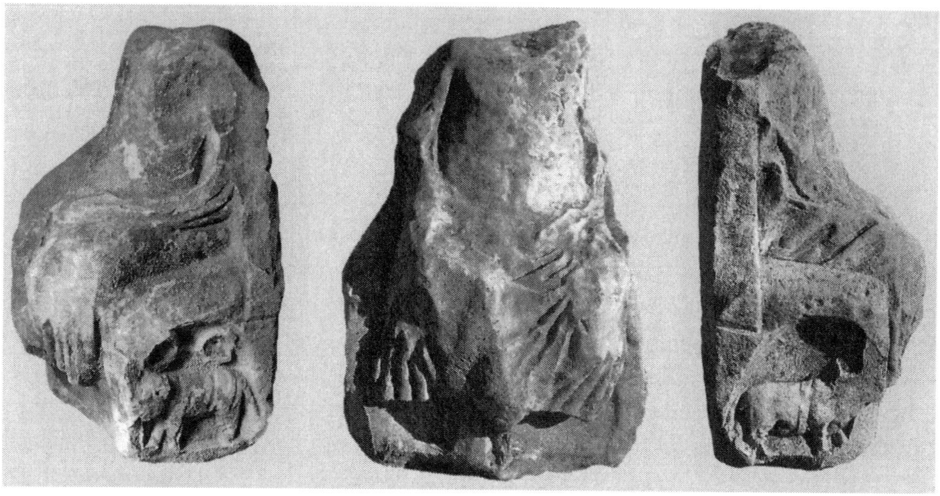

FIGURE 4.2.4 Statuette of Saturn, from Sanctuary of Saturn, Haïdra. Limestone, late second or third century AD.

Sculpture and Other Offerings: Ritual Engagement and Creating Contexts

Sculpted dedications could also be tied to ritual more explicitly. At Uley, two animals flanked the statue of Mercury: a goat to his right and a cock to his left. At least two votive altars reproduce this schema. The Uley dedications closely connect with practices at the site. Male goats were the most common sacrificial offering, while cocks appeared as significant offerings at Uley only in the period when the temple was built and the statue dedicated; although goats are common in the late Iron Age/first-century AD deposits, chickens appear only later. Establishing a causal relationship or even chronological priority between the images and the incorporation of a new type of animal offering is impossible; nevertheless, the iconography associated with the god not only worked to identify and particularize the god himself, but to tie him to a particular set of rites and offerings made at this sanctuary.

Similarly, other features of the Uley altars make reference to a range of practices. In their forms, they hint at the act of sacrifice. An inscribed—but fragmentary—altar from Uley includes below the image of the deity a series of carved leaves that resemble the thin, precious-metal leaves dedicated as offerings there. Even the money purse held by Mercury could draw to mind the frequent coin offerings in the sanctuary.

In other words, the iconography of these altars connected a wide range of rites and types of dedications found in the sanctuary. Set alongside practices, the altars established a relatively closed and predominantly self-referential system of signification.

Meanwhile, an image-type of Mercury popular across the empire could be particularized through its association with the rites that took place there.

Uley is one of many sanctuaries where sculptural dedications engage with, link, and perhaps even serve to explain the range of ritual practices enacted, even if the exact nature of these ties varies by site. At Hadrumetum (Tunisia), changes in the iconography of stelae map onto and reinforce changes in ritual practice in a number of ways; for example, as individual burned sacrifices disappear from the site in the second century AD, images of animal victims on the stelae serve both as substitutes and to maintain a visible and physical link with the older traditions (McCarty 2011a). Likewise, at Ammaedara, one of the limestone statuettes of Saturn adds sacrificial animals on each side (figure 4.2.4; McCarty 2011b). If the main statue offered a "canonical" image of the deity, a center to which other offerings in the sanctuary might respond, the smaller offering draws an explicit link between the god and the sacrificial rites practiced at the site. Further east, in a written account of the rites to Hercules at Sikyon (Greece), Pausanias describes how an image of the god serves to make theological claims about the hero-god by uniting two different types of sacrifice (Elsner 1996). Finally, Peter Stewart (2003, 195–207) has suggested that even lamps with representations of the gods on them—whether in the central tondo of clay examples or atop more elaborate bronze lamps—create a "virtual" sacrificial relationship between the lamp-user and the deity, as the lamp's flame imitates a burning altar.

In all of these cases—and others from across the Roman world—images are enmeshed with practices. These bonds might be highlighted figuratively by showing, creating ties to, and offering commentaries on particular rites (or, as at Uley, perhaps even encouraging particular kinds of sacrifices), or by simulating ritual engagements with the god. If the lamps did this in a very general way, the other examples reflect the sanctuary-specific nature of the rites and concerns. Nevertheless, sanctuary sculpture cannot be fully understood without reference to the wider sets of ritual practices that took place either through the sculpture or side-by-side with it.

Jas Elsner (1995, 190–245) has suggested that one of the major transformations from "pagan" to Christian art was due to a reconfiguration of the bond between practice and image: Roman religious art sought to reproduce ritual actions (see essay 3.5, Sobocinski and Wolfram Thill), while in the case of the art of "mystery cults" (including Mithraism and Christianity), ritual practices developed out of, or as exegeses of, representations in sanctuaries. If nothing else, the sculpted dedications described above suggest that such relationships are hardly so neat: that sculpture from all periods and types of cult might engage with, shape, and respond to ritual on a number of levels.

Conclusion

The dedication of religious sculpture in sanctuaries of the Roman world was always linked to particular local or regional rites. In some sanctuaries, such as the Pergamene Asklepeion, sculptural dedications might generally function analogously to other types of offerings, such as articles of clothing, given under similar circumstances. In other sanctuaries, such as Uley, sculpted offerings could play slightly different roles and even draw imagined connections among the ways visitors to the sanctuary might relate to the gods. Reducing such dedications to a universal notion of votivity obscures these site-specific practices and ways of engaging with sculpture. Even when a product of more widespread ritual technologies like the *votum* or when reproducing schemata popular across the empire, sanctuary sculpture could respond to (or shape) the rites of its particular temple, as at Uley. In the repetition of particular images and the frequent downplaying of particular circumstances, such offerings could present a stable vision of divine-human interaction in a given temple; at the same time, such repetition works to create a local and reflexive system of signification. It is essential, when interrogating such dedications, to see them in their numerous ritual contexts, as part and parcel of ancient religion—not just as instruments of social structuring or prestige competition or as simple commemorations of a single moment.

Bibliography

Aldhouse-Green, M. J. 1999. *Pilgrims in Stone: Stone Images from the Gallo-Roman Sanctuary of Fontes Sequanae*. BAR-IS 754. Oxford: Archeopress.

Ando, C. 2010. "Praesentia Numinis I: The Visibility of Roman Gods." *Asdiwal* 5: 45–73.

Bémont, C., M. Jeanlin, and C. Lahanier, eds. 1993. *Les figurines en terre cuite gallo-romaines*. Paris: Éditions de la Maison des sciences de l'homme.

Bradley, R. 1990. *The Passage of Arms: An Archaeological Analysis of Prehistoric Hoards and Votive Deposits*. Cambridge: Cambridge University Press.

Burckhardt, J. (1884) 1919. "Die Weihgeschenke der Alten." In *Jacob Burckhardt: Vörtrage, 1844–1887*, edited by E. Dürr, 173–82. Basel: Schwabe.

Derks, T. 1995. "The Ritual of the Vow in Gallo-Roman Religion." In *Integration in the Early Roman West: The Role of Culture and Ideology*, edited by J. Metzler, 111–27. Luxembourg: Musée national d'histoire et d'art.

Dräger, O. 1994. *Religionem significare: Studien zu reich verzierten römischen Altären und Basen aus Marmor*. RM-EH 33. Mainz: Philipp von Zabern.

Elsner, J. 1995. *Art and the Roman Viewer: The Transformation of Art from the Pagan World to Christianity*. Cambridge: Cambridge University Press.

———. 1996. "Image and Ritual: Reflections on the Religious Appreciation of Classical Art." *CQ* 46: 515–31.

Estienne, S. 2010. "The Status of Divine Images in the Temples of Rome." In *Divine Images and Human Imaginations in Ancient Greece and Rome*, edited by J. Mylonopoulos, 257–71. Leiden: Brill.

Gladigow, B. 1994. "Zur Ikonographie und Pragmatik römischer Kultbilder." In *Iconologia Sacra: Mythos, Bildkunst und Dichtung in der Religions- und Sozialgeschichte Alteuropas*, edited by H. Keller and N. Staubach, 9–24. Berlin: Walter de Gruyter.

Gordon, R. 2008. "Raising a Sceptre: Confession-Narratives from Lydia and Phrygia." *JRA* 17: 177–96.

Masuzawa, T. 2005. *The Invention of World Religions*. Chicago: University of Chicago Press.

McCarty, M. M. 2010a. "Votive Stelae, Religion, and Cultural Change in Africa Proconsularis and Numidia." DPhil diss., Oxford University.

———. 2010b. "Soldiers and Stelae: Votive Cult and the Roman Army in North Africa." In "Congresso di Archeologia A.I.A.C. 2008," special issue *Bollettino di Archeologia On Line*, 0: paper B/session 10/article 4, 34–43. http://www.bollettinodiarcheologiaonline.beniculturali.it/documenti/generale/4_McCARTY.pdf.

———. 2011a. "Representation and the 'Meaning' of Ritual Change." In *Ritual Dynamics in the Ancient Mediterranean*, edited by A. Chaniotis, 203–234. Stuttgart: Steiner.

———. 2011b. "Beyond Models and Diffusion, Centres and Peripheries." In *Roma y las provincias: Modelo y diffusion*, edited by T. Nogales and I. Rodà, 439–49. Rome: "L'Erma" di Bretschneider.

McGowen, S. L. 2010. *Sacred and Civic Stone Monuments of the Northwest Roman Provinces*. BAR-IS 2109. Oxford: Archaeopress.

Moitrieux, G. 1992. *Hercules Salutaris: Hercule au sanctuaire de Deneuvre (Meurthe-et-Moselle)*. Nancy: Presses universitaires de Nancy.

Nongbri, B. 2013. *Before Religion: A History of a Modern Concept*. New Haven: Yale University Press.

Osborne, R., ed. 2004. *The Object of Dedication*. World Archaeology 36.1. Abingdon: Routledge.

Petsalis-Diomidis, A. 2010. *Truly Beyond Wonders: Aelius Aristides and the Cult of Asklepios*. Oxford: Oxford University Press.

Petzl, G. 1994. "Die Biechtinschriften Westkleinasiens." *EpigAnat* 22: 1–175.

Platt, V. J. 2011. *Facing the Gods: Epiphany and Representation in Graeco-Roman Art, Literature and Religion*. Cambridge: Cambridge University Press.

Rives, J. B. 2007. *Religion in the Roman Empire*. Malden, MA: Blackwell.

Romeuf, A. M. 1986. "Ex-voto en bois de Chamalières (Puy-de-Dôme) et des Sources de la Seine." *Gallia* 44: 65–89.

Rüpke, J. 2007. *Religion of the Romans*. Translated by R. Gordon. Cambridge: Polity.

Scheid, J. 2005. *Quand faire, c'est croire: Les rites sacrificiels des Romains*. Paris: Aubier.

Schörner, G. 2003. *Votive im römischen Griechenland: Untersuchungen zur späthellenistischen und kaiserzeitlichen Kunst- und Religionsgeschichte*. Stuttgart: Steiner.

Simon, E. 1992. "Mercurius." *LIMC* 6: 500–554.

Sokolowski, F. 1969. *Lois sacrées des cités grecques*. Paris: De Boccard.

Stewart, P. 2003. *Statues in Roman Society: Representation and Response*. Oxford: Oxford University Press.

———. 2010. "Geographies of Provincialism in Roman Sculpture." *RIHA Journal* 5. http://www.riha-journal.org/articles/2010/stewart-geographies-of-provincialism.

Van Andringa, W. 2002. *La religion en Gaule romaine: Piété et politique (Ier–IIIe siècle apr. J.-C)*. Paris: Errance.

Van Straten, F. 1995. *Hiera Kala: Images of Animal Sacrifice in Archaic and Classical Greece*. Leiden: Brill.

Woodward, A., and P. Leach. 1993. *The Uley Shrines: Excavation of a Ritual Complex on West Hill, Uley, Gloucestershire*. London: English Heritage.

Zimmer, G., and G. Wesch-Klein. 1989. *Locus datus decreto decurionum: Zur Statuenaufstellung zweier Forumsanlagen im römischen Afrika*. Munich: Beck.

CHAPTER 4.3

DOMESTIC DISPLAYS

ELAINE K. GAZDA

Introduction

Sculptures adorned the domestic spaces in which elites as well as non-elites performed a variety of social and religious rituals. Whether in a town house, a villa, or a palace, displays of sculpture worked in concert with the architecture, gardens, wall paintings, floor mosaics, furnishings, and many other elements of the physical environment. Displays were calculated to present the owner and his or her household in the best possible light for a wide range of visitors who viewed these installations under a diverse set of social circumstances. This essay begins with an overview of domestic sculptural types and media and the household contexts in which they are typically found. Following a brief historiography of the study of displays of sculpture in domestic settings, discussion centers on the nature of the evidence along with the problems it presents for reconstructing sculptural arrangements, and then outlines the different traditions and principles of display that coalesced in the Roman domestic environment. A few key examples from archaeological sites in Campania and the Roman provinces highlight approaches to interpreting the sculptures in relation to their larger visual and social settings and suggest how sculptural displays themselves encouraged the active participation of the viewer in constructing meaning (see essay 6.2, Trimble). The essay concludes with commentary on future directions in the study of Roman domestic display and notes the potential benefits of current visualization technologies for reconstructing sculptural displays within their domestic contexts.

Types of Sculptures and Typical Display Contexts

Sculpture in many forms adorned all elite and many non-elite residences—palaces, villas, and townhouses alike. The display of sculpture was largely confined to those areas of the house that were accessible to the general public and invited guests. Although each household's sculpture represents an individual's preferences, several domestic spaces were ordinarily used for its display. As the symbolic and functional seat of the father's and family's power, the traditional atrium would have housed ancestor portraits and often a shrine of the household gods, though *lararia* were often placed in gardens or near service areas (e.g., Oplontis, Villa A). The center of the space marked by the *impluvium* provided a prime location for a statue or a decorated wellhead or table that was clearly visible from the entrance (Dwyer 2012). The garden (*hortus*), often enclosed by a peristyle, was also a common place for displaying sculpture: along paths marking planting beds, in fountains, or in shrines. Dining rooms contained portable sculptures, some used as lamp stands, others as tabletop decorations. Cubicula might also be sites of sculptural display, especially for small pieces that rewarded close looking.

The types of sculpture on display were many and varied. Apart from freestanding statues in various sizes that populated the spaces just mentioned, reliefs were set into the walls of porticoes; masks, *oscilla*, and *peltae* hung between peristyle columns; and *pinakes* were elevated on pedestals amid formally arranged greenery. Decorative terracotta antefixes capped roof tiles along the eaves, ornate capitals crowned columns, and both vegetal and figural relief sculptures ran the length of entablature friezes. On the interior, frescoed walls of the rooms were trimmed with stucco moldings, and stucco reliefs decorated ceilings (Ling 1999). Household furnishings, too, were adorned with attachments of statuettes and appliqué reliefs. Among these might be ornaments on couches, carved marble table supports, ivory-clad thrones and folding stools, bronze cupboard door pulls, and locking mechanisms on strongboxes. Not only furniture but many other types of household objects sported sculptural decorations; even items of personal identity and adornment—seal stones, jewelry, hairpins, combs, mirrors, cosmetic boxes, and the like. A variety of media, some very costly, were employed: bronze, silver, gold, ivory, marble, porphyry, onyx, alabaster, glass, and bone are among them. Together these many forms of sculpture made up a substantial part of the setting of self-display in which patrons and their families routinely presented their status, wealth, and personal tastes.

This essay, however, cannot do justice to the full range of sculptural displays. Rather, my goals here are: (1) to outline the available evidence and the issues that have concerned scholars of domestic displays of sculpture over time; (2) to call attention to some principles of design favored by Romans for the display of sculpture using a few key examples of well-preserved sculptural assemblages in Italy and the Roman provinces from the late Republic to the late empire that show both continuity and change; and (3) to indicate some directions that the study of sculptural displays in residential settings is beginning to take.

Historiography

Sculptural display in the domestic realm, along with the closely related topic of collecting, has interested scholars since the Italian Renaissance—a time when ancient texts constituted the principal sources of information about the proper way to adorn an upper-class Roman residence. Until the advent of systematic archaeological excavations, the original display contexts of sculptures remained of little interest and largely unknown (see essays 1.1, Bartman; and 6.1, Squire).

With discoveries like the Villa of the Papyri (see essays 2.4, Mattusch; 3.3, Anguissola; 3.6, Touchette; and 6.1, Squire) in the middle of the eighteenth century, this situation began to change. With an abundance of material evidence, which steadily increased over time with further excavation at Campanian sites and elsewhere in the Roman world, scholars could compare the archaeological evidence to what Roman and Greek authors had said about the proper ornamentation of a house belonging to a Roman grandee.

Yet, as discoveries continued throughout the nineteenth and into the twentieth century, most studies of sculpture found in domestic spaces took the form of typologies and catalogs that isolated the sculptures from their display contexts. The dominant tendency was to treat sculptures as well as other objects taxonomically, as members of larger categories such as portraiture, replicas of Greek originals, mythological reliefs, *oscilla*, fountain heads, furniture, altars, votive statuettes, and the like. Often objects were segregated by medium as well. Although by the later nineteenth century, photography was assisting excavators in documenting the locations of finds, in many excavated houses that were opened to the public, sculptures were set up in atria and gardens to enhance tourists' experience of reconstructed domestic environments but without much regard for the sculptures' original locations; other sculptures were removed to museums for safe-keeping.

In the twentieth century, both the architecture and the contents of Campanian houses and villas became major topics of scholarly investigation from archaeological, art historical, and sociohistorical perspectives. At the same time a number of important discoveries of sculptural assemblages were made. In the 1950s and 1960s, excavations at Stabiae unearthed several villas, and remarkable discoveries were made at the villa of Tiberius at Sperlonga, at Punta Epitaffio near Baiae, and at the Blue Grotto on Capri. In addition, in the 1960s and 1970s excavations at Oplontis revealed an extensive collection of marble sculptures, many found *in situ*.

In 1968, Cornelius Vermeule published two articles and in 1977 a book that addressed the display contexts of statues, especially those made in mirror image. Eugene Dwyer's archival and onsite research on several excavated Pompeian houses and their contents marked a new direction of inquiry, one that saw the reintegration of the architecture of houses and the objects and other materials that had been discovered in them. Dwyer's dissertation of 1974 on the sculpture and other contents of five Pompeian houses, followed by his book of 1982 on the same topic, made clear the value of studying all the material evidence for reconstructing the domestic sculptural environment. In an article of 1979, Dwyer summarized the Pompeian evidence for sculptural display, discussing sculptures in relation to their typical display locations and pointing the way to more comprehensive study of sculptural display. Meanwhile Wilhelmina Jashemski had begun to do systematic research on the gardens of Pompeii and the surrounding region, which contributed important insights into the display of sculptures in relation to planting arrangements and other features of the surrounding space, including paintings, fountains, shrines, and the like. Others followed suit (Jashemski 1979–93; Hill 1981).

The 1980s and 1990s saw a dramatic increase in interest in the domestic sphere in general and a concomitant concern for the social and spatial contexts of artworks found in houses and villas around the empire from the Republic to late antiquity. John D'Arms' book *Romans on the Bay of Naples* (1970) had stimulated scholars to investigate the social importance of Roman villas and houses and their decor in light of the social requirements of the Roman elite. Paul Zanker's 1979 article on villas as models for townhouses also proved highly influential as did Andrew Wallace-Hadrill's 1988 article on the social structure of the Roman house. For the study of domestic displays of sculpture, Richard Neudecker's thorough compendium of sculptures from Roman villas in Italy (1988) provided a basic research tool. John Clarke's *Houses of Roman Italy* (1991) and my own edited volume, *Roman Art in the Private Sphere* (1991), added momentum to this growing trend.

Concurrently, detailed documentation and reexamination of individual houses in Pompeii and Herculaneum provided more reliable information on which to base reconstructions of sculptural displays. That work continues today, including the ongoing German series *Häuser in Pompeji*, the British project at the House of the Menander (I.10.4), the Anglo-American project at the insula of the House of the Vestals (VI.i.7), the Swedish project at the insula of the House of Caecilius Iucundus (V.1.26), and the large-scale conservation and documentation project at Herculaneum. With more complete archaeological knowledge of domestic environments, scholars have been able to consider the visual and iconographic interplays between sculptural displays and the other elements of visual decor and to attempt to reconstruct the viewer's experience of entire environments (Clarke 1991; B. Bergmann 2002; Powers 2006).

While the townhouses and villas of Campania have long provided scholars with the bulk of material evidence for the study of Roman domestic environments (and they continue to do so, if current scholarship is any indication), the city of Rome has yielded important sculptural finds for centuries, many purportedly from elite houses, palaces, and *horti*. Most of these sites, however, were greatly disturbed by later construction and poorly documented in early excavations, with the result that display contexts are very difficult—if not impossible—to reconstruct. One of the exceptions is the domus found in the Via Cavour, which has yielded valuable insights into sculptural display (Bartman 1988; 1991). Excavations of cities, especially in the Greek East and North Africa, and increasingly in the western, northwestern, and northern provinces of the empire have expanded the range of evidence for studying domestic sculptural displays.

Many studies have taken a programmatic approach, which focuses on seeking thematic coherence among the sculptures and finding the authoritative original meaning of a given assemblage. Though such studies yield many insights into Roman notions of aesthetics and meaning and the functions of Roman art (see essay 6.1, Squire), it has become clear that no one interpretation of any assemblage of sculpture can suffice—the same collection can be interpreted convincingly in different ways (Bartman 1991; Warden 1991). Rather, scholars began to embrace the concept of eclecticism as an underlying principle of Roman collecting and display (see essay 3.6, Touchette). Scholarly thinking about eclecticism was once dominated by judgments of quality based on modern rather than Roman criteria. Now, however, it is recognized as a defining characteristic of cultivated Roman taste (Perry 2005; Tronchin 2012a and b). In addition, postmodern approaches embrace the multivalency of images, and studies of sculptural display increasingly acknowledge the mutability of meaning, rooted in individual viewers and their knowledge and life experience, and the activities performed in relation to the sculptural display (see part VI, Viewing and Reception). Studies of wall painting have also suggested how sculpture would have contributed to a multimedia environment and, in turn, how this wider semantic field enriches our understanding of sculpture's role in the daily life of Romans (Bergmann 2002).

Persistent Problems of Reconstruction

In order to visualize the displays themselves, and as a prerequisite to exploring variability in meaning, one needs to deal with the Roman source material, whether textual or artifactual, and the archival records from excavations. Yet problems of reconstruction abound. As noted above, early excavators often rearranged sculptures to enhance sites for visiting tourists without much regard for actual findspots. Even recorded findspots, however, may not reflect the arrangement that the Roman owners preferred when the houses were habitable. This problem is best illustrated in the Vesuvian region, where damage from the series of earthquakes that occurred in AD 62 and the years immediately following prompted many homeowners to remove valued sculptures to safer locations while their houses and villas underwent repair. Moreover, the eruption of AD 79 happened before many of those repairs were completed and the sculptures could be returned to their original locations.

Other problems further complicate the situation. Although from the late nineteenth century onward better documented excavations at sites in Campania and elsewhere in the Roman world have yielded ever more reliable evidence for sculptural displays in domestic contexts, scholars must take into account the fact that sculptures, unlike wall paintings and floor mosaics, were portable and *could be moved at will*. In addition, since many collections of sculpture were built up over time, with each addition the owner could rearrange the display; and successive owners would have reshaped the contexts of viewing as well. Conversely, as the many building phases on the Palatine hill in Rome attest, expansion or reworking of structures also prompted the updating of sculptural programs. We must recognize that sculpture arrangements as revealed by excavation represent only the last phase of their use (see essay 6.6, Kristensen).

The intrinsic value of the materials from which sculptures were made poses another problem. Many sculptures were removed from their display contexts and either reused or destroyed. Thousands of bronze sculptures were melted down in late antiquity, sometimes to create currency, and even more marble statues were burnt in lime kilns for building material—a fate shared by sculptures in public settings. Thus, ideal situations for analyzing displays of sculpture in their ancient domestic contexts are few and far between.

Traditions of Sculptural Display

Romans were certainly not the first to display sculpture in their homes, but their displays constituted a unique blend of republican and foreign traditions. Republican aristocratic traditions included the display of ancestor portraits (*imagines*—restricted to the aristocracy; see essay 3.4, Wood), statuettes and painted images associated with religious rites celebrated in the house, and displays of spoils of war (Welch 2006). Literary sources suggest that these forms of display were largely centered in the atrium but that spoils consisting of the armor of defeated enemies were often displayed outside. As Rome expanded into the eastern Mediterranean, many works of art and other treasures were brought to the city as spoils of war to be dedicated in sanctuaries or put on public view (see essays 3.6, Touchette; and 6.3, Shaya). The display of foreign, mainly eastern, luxuries in private homes in Rome gave rise to conflicting values. In luxury villas in Campania and elsewhere, art collections and their display occasioned severe criticism on the part of conservative Romans who equated them with a decline in moral values (see essays 3.6, Touchette; and 6.1, Squire).

Perhaps partly in response to the danger of exposing oneself to this kind of criticism, Romans became concerned about the appropriateness of their sculptural displays whether in the public or the private sphere (Perry 2005). Cicero's letters to Atticus reveal his concern that sculptures he collected would be appropriate in subject for the spaces in which he intended to display them (Marvin 1989; see essays 2.7, Russell; and 6.1, Squire). Archaeological finds tell us more about what was considered appropriate for display in a garden. Subjects related to nature and fertility were common. The relationship between nature and art could be expressed in surprising ways. Cicero (*QFr.* 3.1.5; Littlewood 1987, 12) tells us of a gardener who had planted so much ivy that the sculptures in the garden appeared to be gardeners themselves, offering their ivy for sale!

Bartman (1991) cites a passage of Lucian's "Teller of Lies" that implies another modern criterion—that of authenticity—was of little concern to Romans. Referring to Myron's Diskobolos as one of the sculptures in his (apparently private) collection, Lucian's narrator does not distinguish between the version of this famous work that Myron's own workshop had produced in the first half of the fifth century BC and what must have been a replica of this work that Lucian's Roman collector displayed in his house. From this same passage in Lucian we can glean that the criterion of appropriateness that had preoccupied Cicero was at work here, too. The athlete and the general both found an appropriate place in a courtyard setting where such conversations about artworks took place—much as in a Hellenistic gymnasium. Educated Romans knew that works of sculpture were not (or at least should not) be randomly placed within the domestic setting. The art market and industry responded to Roman concerns by producing a limited repertoire of sculptures of suitable subjects.

Some Common Principles of Display

Evidence of the sculptures themselves, along with remains of bases and various types of pedestals for statues and herms found onsite, and architectural forms (such as niches, shrines, and fountains) with remains of attachments for statues, all provide concrete evidence for how sculptures were displayed in domestic contexts. From this evidence certain common principles can be gleaned. First and foremost, sculptures were displayed in the most accessible spaces of a residence and in formal relation to architectural elements. They complemented the plan of a room or garden. Single statues of high value might be shown in a central position in the atrium or in a statue niche in the peristyle placed so as to be clearly visible from a distance (Dwyer 2012). Sculptures of the same type might be shown as pendants (Bartman 1988; 1991) or in mirror reversal. Statues lined garden paths or acted as focal points at the end of a pool. Principles of display also resonated with rhetorical principles such as *similitudo, vicinitas*, and *contrarium* (Brilliant 1984). Applied to sculpture, images that were similar, near, or antithetical could stimulate certain kinds of reflection on the part of the viewer. Such general rules were frequently bent to suit such nonbuilt settings as natural grottoes, where sculptures might be arranged within lightly modified irregular spaces to produce a scenographic effect.

Because similar display principles applied to wall paintings and mosaics, the various media often created a coordinated, dynamic visual interplay. Add the movement of people who viewed these multimedia domestic environments as they participated in daily activities, formal ritual occasions, and social events, and we can begin to imagine the overall calculated visual effects that encouraged a variety of readings of such displays.

Domestic Displays from the Late Republic to Late Antiquity

In the following survey of selected examples of domestic displays of sculpture, I intend both to highlight patterns of sculptural display and to point to continuities and modifications that occurred in response to different forms of domestic architecture and social situations. I focus on the Bay of Naples, where the evidence for the late Republic and early empire is most abundant then briefly sketch the general contours of the evidence for Rome and other sites in Italy and Rome's provinces.

The Bay of Naples in the Late Republic and Early Empire

The single most important (and arguably the earliest) discovery of a sculptural display, the Villa of the Papyri, was documented by Swiss engineer Karl Weber, whose detailed plan of the villa, which indicates the purported findspots of the sculptures, has been employed by numerous scholars who have attempted to interpret the meaning of the display (see essays 2.4 Mattusch; 3.3, Anguissola; 3.6, Touchette; and 6.1, Squire). But the accuracy of this plan of the still largely buried villa has been questioned, leaving scholars to debate its value for reconstructing the sculptural arrangement (Warden 1991, 258); and we lack access to other elements of the villa's decor to examine visual and semantic interplays among media. Therefore, I focus here on the better documented and far more accessible Villa A, the so-called Villa of Poppaea at Oplontis.

Located in the middle of modern Torre Annunziata, some five kilometers west of Pompeii, a large portion of Villa A began to be excavated in the 1960s and is now accessible to the public. The sculpture from the villa, the second largest collection known from this region, has received far less attention than that of the Villa of the Papyri, but it is of paramount importance for our consideration of questions of domestic display. The excavators carefully documented the sculptures' findspots, and though a number of them had been moved, probably during renovations that were necessitated by earthquake damage in the 60s AD, others were still *in situ*, close to their original bases (De Caro 1976; 1987). In addition, large portions of the gardens and of the restored building are visible, as are numerous important wall paintings of the second, third, and fourth Pompeian styles with corresponding pavements. A nuanced study by Bettina Bergmann (2002) on art and nature at Oplontis clearly demonstrated the benefits of taking this larger semantic field into account. Her contextual analysis of the visual and intellectual interplays among the villa's landscape, gardens, wall paintings, architecture, and sculptures provides a model for viewing sculptural displays as components of dynamic multimedia, multisensory environments.

The sculptural displays at Villa A (figure 4.3.1) illustrate a number of common devices that worked to elicit responses from viewers. Along a path in the north garden, herm portraits of a Julio-Claudian woman and a young boy alternated with herms of Venus and a young Bacchus (since stolen)—juxtapositions likely intended to allude to the divine status of the two Julio-Claudian subjects. Two male and two female centaurs may have been displayed as pendants in a fountain in the north garden, though they were found under the west portico of the villa's north façade, perhaps moved there for safekeeping (De Caro 1976; 1987). Similar juxtapositions and pendants occur in the sculptural display in the east garden where life-size marble statues and herms were arrayed along the east and south sides of the enormous swimming pool. On the east were two victories alighting, one flanked on the south by a statue of a youth and the other by Artemis or an Amazon on the north. A herm of Hercules bracketed each end of the surviving display. The implicit themes of valor and victory were amusingly echoed in the erotic group of a satyr and hermaphrodite wrestling at the south end of the pool. This group, along with a large

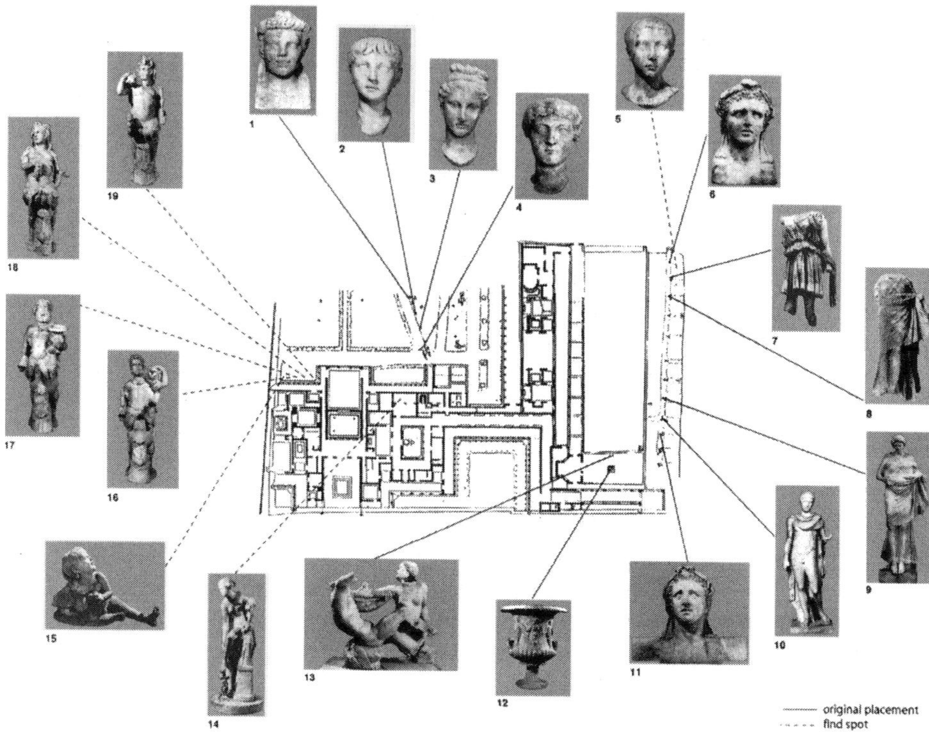

Marble sculpture found at the villa at Oplontis:*

1. Crowned head of the child Bacchus (originally on pillar of African marble) (h. 93 cm).
2. Portrait of boy (on herm of African marble), Julio-Claudian (h. 28 cm).
3. Head of Venus (on cipollino marble pillar) (h. 36 cm).
4. Portrait of woman (on grey-blue marble pillar), Julio-Claudian (h. 32 cm).
5. Portrait of boy, Julio-Claudian (h. 27 cm).
6. Hercules bust (on white marble herm) (h. 44 cm).
7. Amazon type (on plinth of Sarno limestone) (as is, 1.15 m).
8. Nike (h. with base 1.76 m, includes lost head).
9. Nike (pendant to no. 8) (h. with base 1.76 m).
10. Ephebe (pendant to no. 7) (h. 1.54 m; with base, 1.60 m).
11. Hercules bust (on white marble herm) (pendant to no. 6) (h. 42 cm).
12. Neo-Attic bell crater fountain, Pentelic marble in square marble pool (h. 109.5 cm, base 48 x 48 x 6.2 cm).
13. Satyr and Hermaphrodite (h. 1 m) (on rectangular marble plinth) (91 x 58 cm).
14. Venus untying her sandal, Parian or Dokimian marble (h. 52.5 cm).
15. Boy with duck fountain (h. 46 cm).
16. Centaur with boar, blue-veined white marble (h. 90 cm).
17. Centaur with a crater, blue-veined white marble (h. 90 cm).
18. Centauress with a lyre, blue-veined white marble (h. 90 cm).
19. Centauress with a fawn, blue-veined white marble (h. 90 cm).

* All date to the late 1st c. B.C. and early 1st c. A.D. Several more marble fragments, including pieces of figural sculpture and architectural reliefs, were in the process of restoration and found stored in various rooms throughout the complex, along with a few terracottas. See De Caro 1976, 184-225; id. 1987, 88-126.

FIGURE 4.3.1 The sculptural displays at Villa A, Oplontis.

crater with relief decoration of dancing warriors, punctuated the axial view to the sea. The sculptures along the east side of the pool illustrate another of the common principles of design—architectural alignment. Each statue stood in front of a tree as if to echo the position of a corresponding column of the portico on the opposite side of the pool.

The splendid sculptural tableaux at Baiae, Sperlonga, and the Blue Grotto on Capri illustrate still other forms of display. As home to famous thermal mineral baths, the resort town of Baiae had attracted the vacationing senatorial elite at least as early as the late second century BC (D'Arms 1970), and from the time of Augustus onward emperors favored this area as a retreat as well. At Punta Epitaffio, adjacent to Baiae, underwater excavations in the 1960s recovered the architectural remains of an elaborate dining hall along with much of its sculptural ornamentation. At the far end of the hall a marble group representing the Blinding of Polyphemus was set into an apse symbolic of the cave in which the action took place (figure 4.3.2). Symmetrically arranged niches along the walls leading to the apse contained single statues. Two represent the youthful Bacchus and a portrait of a young girl who is thought to portray Octavia Claudia, daughter of the emperor Claudius and Messalina. The butterfly she held likely alluded to Psyche, the lover of Eros, the son of Venus, who appears in the ensemble as a small child standing on the arm of Antonia Minor, Claudius's mother, herself crowned and wearing the garment of Venus Genetrix, the mythical mother of the Julian line. A fragmentary draped male torso that may have represented Augustus, Tiberius, or Claudius himself stood alongside (Andreae 1983, 53). What is preserved of the statuary ensemble strongly suggests a dynastic theme, replete with allusions to divinity and to the heroic exploits of Odysseus on his voyage home from the Trojan War, a voyage that took him along this very coast of Italy. The water channel that surrounds the dining couches and the central pool perhaps alluded to his voyage. The placement of sculptures in symmetrical niches that lead the eye toward the central apse offers another instance of a display dictated by architectural design. Yet the formality of the arrangement would have been animated by daylight or torchlight reflecting from the water and playing on both the diners and the statues.

Such theatricality is even more evident in natural grottoes, such as the one at the Villa of Tiberius at Sperlonga (see essay 6.1, Squire). Here, too, the placement of sculptures was guided by the natural features or "architecture" of the cave. As at Punta Epitaffio, a tableau of the Blinding of Polyphemus occupied the furthest recess, but the main focal point was the group representing Scylla's attack on Odysseus's ships at the center of the circular pool. The Roman architect regularized the circle with a concrete embankment that

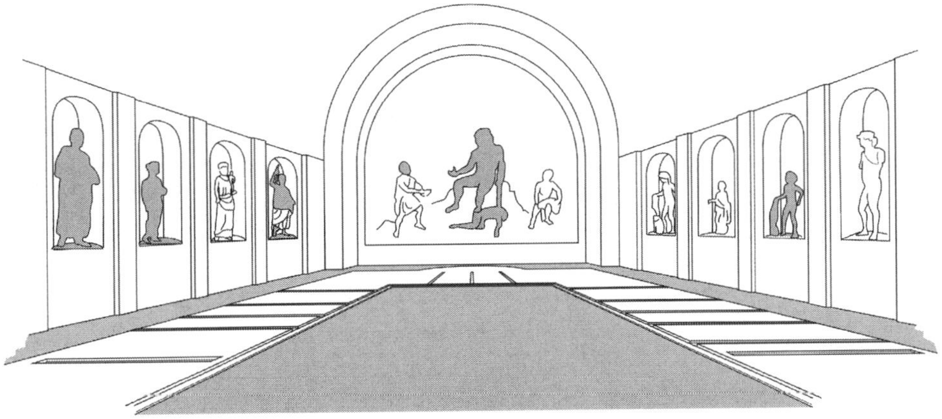

FIGURE 4.3.2 Reconstruction of the sculptural display at Punta Epitaffio, Baiae. Preserved sculptures (left to right): Antonia Minor, male lower torso, Odysseus, wineskin bearer, Bacchus with panther, Octavia Claudia, and Dionysus. Shaded parts are hypothetical.

allowed one to walk around the edge of the pool and peer into the recesses of the grotto. Just outside the cave, a dining platform served as the principal viewpoint for guests, who could gaze at the sculptural spectacle from their couches. Torchlight within the grotto must have provided dramatic illumination, again reflected from the pool, and it is not hard to imagine animated performances taking place amid the sculptures. Guests may even have taken boat rides around the pool, experiencing the sculptural display from ever-changing angles. Such interactive viewing of sculpture was not uncommon in the Roman world (Stewart 2003, 263–4). At Capri's Blue Grotto, boat rides must have been the main means of viewing the sculptural displays arrayed around the central cave and along inner passageways that served as a nymphaeum for the Roman villa on the cliffs above. In 1964, Italian divers retrieved two badly deteriorated marble sculptures of marine creatures, at least one of them identifiable as a triton blowing a conch. The other may represent Neptune. Another triton emerged in 1974, along with a headless peplophoros, an altar, two bases, and other fragments (Federico and Miranda 1998, 215–16, 260–63). The assemblage suggests an elaborate display that would reward comprehensive study.

Displays in Campanian Town Houses

While villas offer the most spectacular examples of domestic display, a number of townhouses in Herculaneum and Pompeii incorporated similar arrangements, albeit on a much smaller scale. Long regarded as inferior imitations of their more splendid presumed paradigms, they have been described disparagingly as "a marionette theater," "kitsch," and "Disneyland." Recent scholarship, however, has reassessed the displays in Pompeian houses, finding that they reflect visually sophisticated and culturally aware planning on a par with that encountered in villa displays. Studies of the House of the Gilded Cupids have suggested site-specific meanings and possible neighborhood-specific relationships (Powers 2006; Petersen 2012), while the sculpture collection of the House of Octavius Quartio has been reassembled with the goal of assessing its eclectic aesthetic and thematic heterogeneity (Tronchin 2011). Such studies demonstrate that the principles of display exemplified by villas at Oplontis and elsewhere were shared by smaller-scale domestic sculptural displays.

Italy in the Mid- to Late Empire

Among the many sculpture collections known from Rome and environs during the imperial period, frustratingly few display contexts are known (Neudecker 1988). The sculptural display associated with the Villa of Hadrian at Tivoli (see essays 1.5, Frischer; 3.3, Anguissola; and 3.7, Swetnam-Burland) thus serves as the principal example, even though many of its sculptures were removed from the site long ago and without careful documentation. The area of the villa known as the Serapeum, however, preserves symmetrical sculpture niches in the walls of the half-vaulted dining

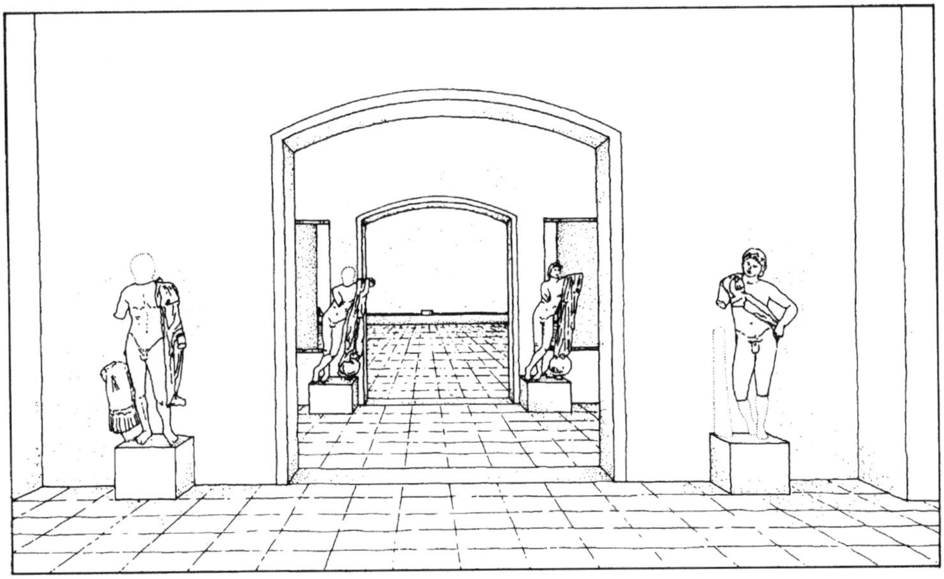

FIGURE 4.3.3 Pendants from *domus*, Via Cavour, Rome.

hall and a centrally located base that may once have held a Scylla group reminiscent of the one at Sperlonga (Adembri 2012). The adjacent canal of the canopus, with its restored line of nearly identical Erechtheion caryatids and Sileni along one side and symmetrically placed statues of gods at one end of the long pool, also suggests that principles of display observed in Campanian villas and houses remained operative in the second century. In Rome a rare find of a *domus* in the Via Cavour yielded evidence of sculptural pendants (figure 4.3.3)—a display strategy that may have had more to do with aesthetics and connoisseurship than with subject matter (Bartman 1988; 1991). Another example of wringing insights from partially preserved display contexts is Linda Roccos's 2002 study of statues of Apollo Citharoedus from four villas near Rome, in which she demonstrates how the meaning of this statue type changed according to the ensemble to which it belonged.

Villas and Town Houses in the Roman Provinces up to Late Antiquity

The display of sculptures in domestic contexts continued throughout the empire into late antiquity (Stirling 2005, 165–227; see part V, Regions and Provinces). Here just a few examples must suffice. In the Greek East, the assemblage of statuettes from a shrine in the Panayia Domus at Corinth shows the continued importance of household shrines as contexts of display (Stirling 2008). Likewise in Ephesus, *lararia* continued to be important. Portraits of Livia and Tiberius associated with the imperial cult were found in a such a shrine in Terrace House 2 at Ephesus, and numerous other sculptures were on view in this complex well into the third century (Rathmayr 2006). At Aphrodisias, shield portraits from a late-antique mansion (Smith 1996, 70–71) stand out as examples of both continuity and novelty in the fifth century. Late-antique villas in Spain and Gaul have yielded numerous mythological and other sculptures (see essay 5.2, Jiménez and Rodà), but few of the sculptures can be related to their display contexts (Stirling 2007). The range of subjects, however, suggests that the traditional concern for appropriateness persisted. The villa at Chiragan in Gaul preserved an astonishing array of sculptures that has fueled debate over their date and place of production, a debate complicated by the collection's growth over time and its deliberate destruction and burial in the early fifth century (M. Bergmann 1999). North Africa has also provided evidence of domestic sculptural display in the late antique era (see essay 5.3, Baratte and Chaisemartin). At Carthage, excavations at the House of the Greek Charioteers uncovered a small marble statuette group of Ganymede and the Eagle, which may have been displayed in a niche in the dining room or in the peristyle, possibly paired with a group of Leda and the Swan, another of Jupiter's conquests that were so derided by the Church Fathers of this period (Gazda 1981). In Egypt, Alexandria's Kom el-Dikka district yielded a fair amount of fragmentary sculpture of traditional types, some of them found in domestic contexts of the late-antique period but with little evidence of their original display locations (Rodziewicz 1984). Even from houses in small provincial towns like those at Karanis in the Fayum (Gazda et al. 1978) there is evidence of sculptural display, most likely in household shrines (figure 4.3.4).

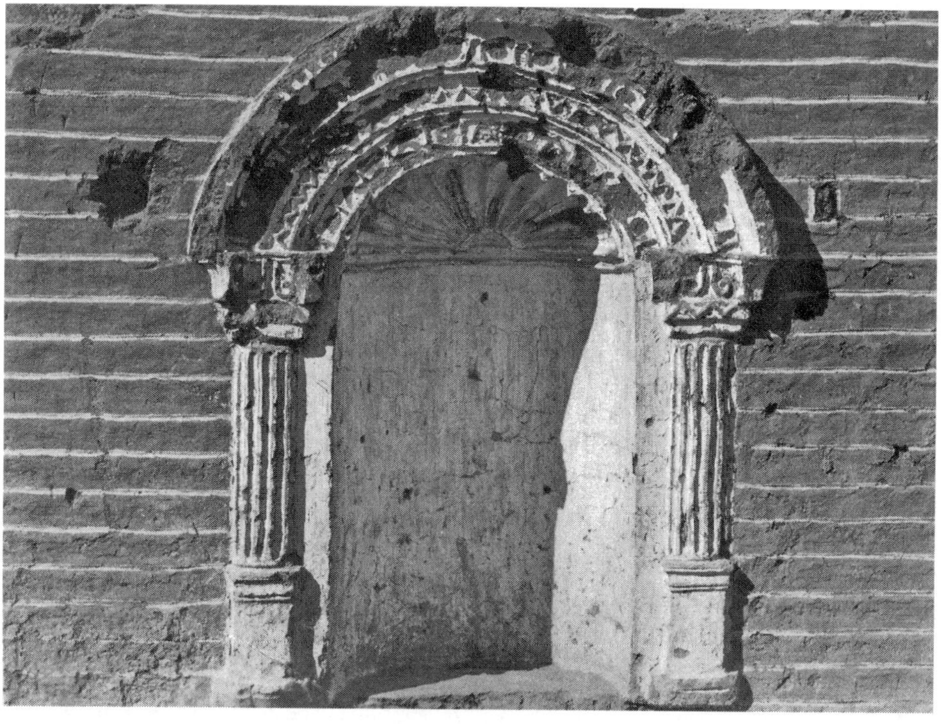

FIGURE 4.3.4 Sculpture niche in house C119, Karanis, Egypt. Kelsey Museum of Archaeology, University of Michigan.

Conclusion

While the groundwork of documenting archaeological contexts, analyzing forms and media, and identifying subjects of individual sculptures or groups of sculptures remain fundamental first steps in the interpretive process, scholars are increasingly concerned with the dynamic interplay among all elements of the visual environment and how viewers of different educational and social backgrounds interacted with and understood the visual elements of that environment as they participated in the social rituals that it framed. It is no longer enough to isolate one medium from the rest. For understanding how the design of the display itself worked to elicit varying responses, simulating the visual environments of domestic display is essential. Bergmann's introduction of physical models, such as the one of Villa A at Oplontis, to aid in studying spatial relations, lines of sight, and a multitude of viewing possibilities established the utility of this approach. Now 3-D navigable models, such as the one produced by the current Oplontis Project in collaboration with the King's Visualization Lab in London, are proving to be an even more flexible tool, making it possible to follow various paths through the domestic spaces and to see more concretely how sculptures interacted with visual images in other media and with views into the neighborhood and the landscape beyond. As immersive technologies continue to develop (see essay 1.5, Frischer), the incorporation of other sensory effects will add yet another dimension to the viewing experience. Indeed, the future study of domestic display is not only exciting, but is "virtually" without limit.

Bibliography

Adembri, B. 2012. "Villa Adriana e l'Egitto." In *Antinoo: Il fascino della bellezza*, edited by M. Sapelli Ragni, 93–107. Milan: Mondadori Electa.

Andreae, B. 1983. "Le Sculture." In *Baia: Il ninfeo imperial sommerso di Punta Epitaffio*, 49–66. Naples: Edizione Banca Sannitica.

Bartman, E. 1988. "*Decor et Duplicatio*: Pendants in Roman Sculptural Display." *AJA* 92(2): 211–25.

———. 1991. "Sculptural Collecting and Display in the Private Realm." In Gazda 1991, 71–88.

Bergmann, B. 2002. "Art and Nature in the Villa at Oplontis." In *Pompeian Brothels, Pompeii's Ancient History, Mirrors and Mysteries, Art and Nature at Oplontis, and the Herculaneum "Basilica"*, by T. McGinn, P. Carafa, N. de Grummond, B. Bergmann, and T. Najbjerg, 87–120. JRA Supplement 47. Portsmouth, RI: Journal of Roman Archaeology.

Bergmann, M. 1999. *Chiragan, Aphrodisias, Konstantinopel: Zur mythologischen Skulptur der Spätantike*. Wiesbaden: Reichert.

Brilliant, R. 1984. *Visual Narratives: Storytelling in Etruscan and Roman Art*. Ithaca: Cornell University Press.

Clarke, J. R. 1991. *The Houses of Roman Italy, 100 B.C.–A.D. 250: Ritual, Space and Decoration*. Berkeley: University of California Press.

D'Arms, J. H. 1970. *Romans on the Bay of Naples: A Social and Cultural Study of the Villas and Their Owners from 150 B.C. to A.D. 400*. Cambridge, MA: Harvard University Press.

De Caro, S. 1976. "Sculture dalla 'Villa di Poppea' in Oplontis." *CronPomp* 2: 184–225.

———. 1987. "The Sculptures of the Villa Poppaea at Oplontis: A Preliminary Report." In MacDougall 1987, 77–133.

Dwyer, E. J. 1974. "Pompeian Sculpture in its Domestic Context: A Study of Five Pompeian Houses and their Contents." PhD diss., New York University.

———. 1979. "Sculpture and Its Display in Private Houses of Pompeii." *Pompeii and the Vesuvian Landscape*, 59–77. Washington, DC: Archaeological Institute of America.

———. 1982. *Pompeian Domestic Sculpture: A Study of Five Pompeian Houses and Their Contents*. Rome: Giorgio Bretschneider.

———. 2012. "Collectible Singletons." *Arethusa* 45(3): 305–318.

Federico, E., and E. Miranda, eds. 1998. *Capri Antica: Dalla preistoria all fine dell'età romana*. Capri: Edizioni La Conchiglia.

Gazda, E. K. 1981. "A Marble Group of Ganymede and the Eagle from the Age of Augustine." In *Excavations at Carthage, 1977, Conducted by the University of Michigan*. Vol. 6, edited by J. H. Humphrey, 125–78. Ann Arbor: Kelsey Museum.

———, ed. 1991. *Roman Art in the Private Sphere: New Perspectives on the Architecture and Decor of the Domus, Villa, and Insula*. Ann Arbor: University of Michigan Press.

Gazda, E. K., with C. Hessenbruch, M. Allen, and V. Hutchinson. 1978. *Guardians of the Nile: Sculptures from Karanis in the Fayoum, c. 250 B.C.–A.D. 450*. Ann Arbor: Kelsey Museum of Archaeology.

Hill, D. K. 1981. "Some Sculpture from Roman Domestic Gardens." In *Ancient Roman Gardens*, edited by E. B. MacDougall and W. F. Jashemski, 81–94. Dumbarton Oaks Colloquium Series in the History of Landscape Architecture 7. Cambridge, MA: Harvard University Press.

Jashemski, W. F. 1979–93. *The Gardens of Pompeii, Herculaneum and the Villas Destroyed by Vesuvius*. 2 vols. New Rochelle: Caratzas Brothers.

Ling, R. 1999. *Stuccowork and Painting in Roman Italy*. Aldershot: Ashgate.

Littlewood, A. R. 1987. "Ancient Literary Evidence for the Pleasure Gardens of Roman Country Villas." In MacDougall 1987, 7–30.

MacDougall, E. B., ed. 1987. *Ancient Roman Villa Gardens*. Dumbarton Oaks Colloquium Series in the History of Landscape Architecture 10. Washington, DC: Dumbarton Oaks.

Marvin, M. 1989. "Copying in Roman Sculpture: The Replica Series." In *Retaining the Original: Multiple Originals, Copies, and Reproductions*, edited by K. Preciado, 29–45. Studies in the History of Art 20. Washington: National Gallery of Art.

Neudecker, R. 1988. *Die Skulpturenausstattung römischer Villen in Italien*. Mainz: Philipp von Zabern.

Perry, E. 2005. *The Aesthetics of Emulation in the Visual Arts of Ancient Rome*. Cambridge: Cambridge University Press.

Petersen, L. H. 2012. "Collecting Gods in Roman Houses: The House of the Gilded Cupids (VI.16.7, 38) at Pompeii." *Arethusa* 45(3): 319–32.

Powers, J. D. 2006. "Patrons, Houses, and Viewers in Pompeii: Reconsidering the House of the Gilded Cupids." PhD diss., University of Michigan.

Raeder, J. 1983. *Die statuarische Ausstattung der Villa Hadriana bei Tivoli*. Frankfurt: Peter Lang.

Rathmayr, E. 2006. "Götter-und Kaiserkult im privaten Wohnbereich anhand von Skulpturen aus dem Hanghaus 2 in Ephesos." In *Römische historiche Mitteilungen* 48: 103–134.

Roccos, L. J. 2002. "The Citharode Apollo in Villa Contexts: A Roman Theme with Variations." In *The Ancient Art of Emulation: Studies in Artistic Originality and Tradition from the Present to Classical Antiquity*, edited by E. K. Gazda, 273–93. Ann Arbor: University of Michigan Press.

Rodziewicz, M. 1984. *Alexandrie III: Les habitations romaines tardives d'Alexandrie.* Warsaw: Editions scientifiques de Pologne.

Smith, R. R. R. 1996. "Archaeological Research at Aphrodisias, 1986–1992." In *Aphrodisias Papers 3*, edited by C. Rouché and R. R. R. Smith, 10–72. JRA Supplement 20. Ann Arbor: Journal of Roman Archaeology.

Stewart, P. 2003. *Statues in Roman Society: Representation and Response.* Oxford: Oxford University Press.

Stirling, L. M. 2005. *The Learned Collector: Mythological Statuettes and Classical Taste in Late Antique Gaul.* Ann Arbor: University of Michigan Press.

———. 2007. "Statuary Collecting and Display in the Late Antique Villas of Gaul and Spain: A Comparative Study. In *Statuen in der Spätantike*, edited by F. A. Bauer and C. Witschel, 304–321. Wiesbaden: Reichert.

———. 2008. "Pagan Statuettes in Late Antique Corinth: Sculpture from the Panayia Domus." *Hesperia* 77: 89–161.

Tronchin, F. 2011. "The Sculpture of the Casa di Octavius Quartio at Pompei." In *Art, Industry and Infrastructure in Roman Pompeii*, edited by E. Poehler, M. Flohr, and K. Cole, 33–49. Oxford: Oxbow.

———. 2012a. "Introduction: Collecting the Eclectic in Roman Houses." *Arethusa* 45(3): 261–82.

———. 2012b. "Roman Collecting, Decorating, and Eclectic Practice in the Textual Sources." *Arethusa* 45(3): 333–45.

Vermeule, C. C. 1968. "Graeco-Roman Statues: Purpose and Setting." Pts. 1 and 2. *Burlington Magazine* 110 (787): 545–58; (788): 607–613.

———. 1977. *Greek Sculpture and Roman Taste: The Purpose and Setting of Graeco-Roman Art in Italy and the Greek Imperial East.* Ann Arbor: University of Michigan Press.

Wallace-Hadrill, A. 1988. "The Social Structure of the Roman House." *PBSR* 56: 43–97.

Warden, P. G. 1991. "The Sculptural Program of the Villa of the Papyri." *JRA* 4: 257–61.

Welch, K. E. 2006. "*Domi Militiaeque*: Roman Domestic Aesthetics and War Booty in the Republic." In *Representations of War in Ancient Rome*, edited by S. Dillon and K. E. Welch, 91–161. Cambridge: Cambridge University Press.

Zanker, P. 1979. "Die Villa als Vorbild des späten pompeijanischen Wohngeschmacks." *JdI* 94: 460–523.

CHAPTER 4.4

FUNERARY MONUMENTS

BJÖRN C. EWALD

INTRODUCTION

In the city of Rome itself, it has been estimated that there would have been somewhere between 10.5 and 14 million burials from the time of Augustus to that of Constantine (Bodel 2008, 179). The several thousand funerary monuments that are preserved from the same period—though only a small fraction of the original number, and even though produced by patrons from a wide social spectrum—clearly signaled status. So a systematic survey of Roman funerary monuments from the entire Roman Empire or just Rome itself remains a rather daunting task. Too great are the variations across time and space, the social and gender differences, and the discrepancies observable in the funerary habits and contexts from one city to the next, with exceptions to almost every rule. In fact, Roman funerary monuments, tomb contexts (Dresken-Weiland 2003; Borg 2013), and inscriptions offer a near unlimited potential for writing microhistories of Roman lives and deaths.

The topic of Roman funerary art encompasses multiple genres of sculpture (freestanding and relief: Wrede 1981; Fejfer 2008); funerary rituals and practices at every social rank (Toynbee 1971; Prieur 1986; De Filippis Cappai 1997; Corbeill 2004, 67–106; Carroll 2006; Brink and Green 2008; Andreu, Espinosa, and Pastor 2011); and the reception, historiography, and afterlife of funerary monuments and the role they played in the formation of the discipline of art history (Elsner 2010; Erasmo 2012; Zanker and Ewald 2012, 1–21). Setting aside the extraordinary thematic complex of imperial funerals and apotheosis (Arce 1988; Beard and Henderson 1998; Davies 2000; Arce 2010; see essay 4.6, Kellum), this essay surveys private funerary monuments with sculptural decoration from the city of Rome of the later first century BC to the third century AD: reliefs, altars, urns, *kline* monuments, and sarcophagi.

The Latin *monumentum* (from *monere*, to remind, admonish, advise), often used in funerary inscriptions, is not coextensive with our modern use of the term "monument" (see essay 3.5, Sobocinski and Wolfram Thill). Its semantic spectrum comprised not only the burial marker—the monument in a modern sense—but larger structures, such as a tomb building or funerary precinct surrounding a funerary altar (Boschung 1987, 12–13). Likewise, the terminology for the classes of funerary monuments was often fluid. The term *ara*, for example, indicated both funerary urns and altars in Latin funerary inscriptions (Boschung 1987; Sinn 1987). While I adhere to established archaeological terminologies and typological classifications in this essay, they do not always reflect ancient naming and perceptions of such monuments. Commonly used ancient terms for various classes of funerary monuments include *memoria*, *mnema*, and *mnemeion*. These terms applied to inscriptions, to any type of stele or funerary marker, to entire tombs, and even to literary works (Häusle 1980, 29–40; cf. Boschung 1987, 12–13; Walker 1985). *Memoria* was utterly material: in a society without coherent eschatology, without common trust in rebirth or postmortal existence, and with vastly diverging belief systems, the monument itself guaranteed the memory of the deceased. The principal function shared by funerary monuments was the preservation of an individual's memory and the fight against oblivion. Funerary monuments were placed under legal and magical protection, because they were the only reliable form of long-term, postmortal presence among the living (Häusle 1980, 64–131).

This function involved a perception of the ontological status of monuments and images slightly different from our own: funerary monuments and effigies of the deceased could function as "doubles" of and substitutes for the deceased (Arce 2010; Bettini 2011), who was believed to be somehow present in them, and they were sometimes attributed qualities and agency we would associate with the actual person (Bettini 1999, 187–212; 2011, 225–37; Arce 2010). For this substitutive function, it was irrelevant whether effigies or monuments were produced during or after the life of the honorand, or whether the images had been commissioned by the deceased himself, by his relatives, or others. The emphatically substitutive function of the image could even pose a threat to the living individual whose social persona the monument continued post mortem, as expressed by fears of encountering one's *Doppelgänger* while still alive (Bettini 1999, 228–36; 2011, 171–91). It is quite possible that the phenomenon of unfinished portrait heads on Roman sarcophagi (Andreae 1984; Huskinson 1998; Smith 2012) has something to do with such (occasional) feelings of unease vis-à-vis one's image. When the dead and the living are united, as in the reliefs of Roman *liberti* (Kockel 1993), the addition of a *viv(-it)* to the name in inscriptions can make explicit who was alive and who was not at the time the monument or image was erected; often, however, this distinction was not made.

In what follows, I survey the most common classes of funerary monuments with sculptural decoration, commenting on current interpretations of them. To conclude, I consider the sociology and patronage of these funerary monuments and how their evolution from the first and third centuries AD possibly reflects a broader change in mentality and a shift toward increasing concern with death and its finality.

Classes of Roman Funerary Monuments with Sculptural Decoration

Roman Funerary Reliefs of *Liberti*

Funerary reliefs come into fashion among Roman freedmen and -women (*liberti*) in the early first century BC (Zanker 1975; Kleiner 1977; Kockel 1993; Pflug 1997; Zanker and Ewald 2012, 176–8). Almost 300 examples are currently known (Kockel 1993). The bulk of the material dates to the years 40–10 BC, and most are carved from Luni marble (Kockel 1993, 57–8). Numbers decline sharply in the first century AD, although production continued into the second century AD.

Most reliefs depict half portraits of the upper body, including the hands, which gesture to communicate virtues of the individuals or relationships between figures (figure 4.4.1). Fewer show portrait busts or entire figures. Framing is usually simple, but can include vegetation, architectural elements, or attributes reflecting professions. German scholars have nicknamed the boxed-in half-length figures *Fenstergucker*, or window-peekers (Zanker 1975). The meaning of the format is unclear; the few reliefs documented *in situ* decorated the façades of house-type and altar-type tombs, among others (Kockel 1993, 7–9). These reliefs were thus intended to confront passersby directly, inviting them to contemplate the likenesses and read out loud the inscriptions carved into the lower margin of the reliefs or the wall of the tomb itself. Nevertheless, such reliefs occasionally appear in the interior of tombs, such as *columbaria*, where one late example was found.

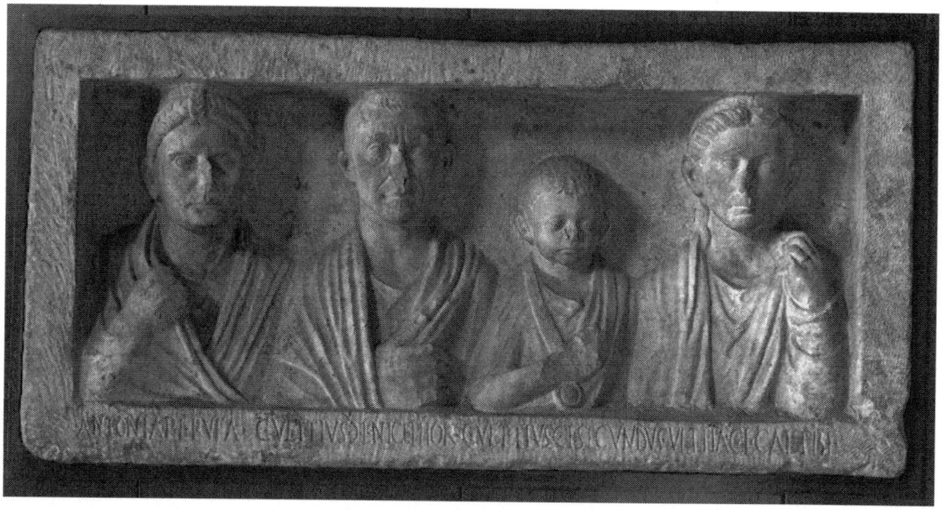

FIGURE 4.4.1 Funerary relief of the Vettii (Kockel 1993, 145, no. H 13). Vettius Nicephor (second from the left) and Vettia Calybe (right) were still alive when the relief was made, as is indicated by the *v(ivit)* above their names. Vettius's wife, Antonia Rufa (left), as well as his son, Vettius Secundus (with *bulla*), had apparently already died. All of the adults were *liberti*. Late first century BC. Rome, Via Po.

The most compelling interpretation of the half- and full-body relief portraits suggests that they imitated in an abbreviated form the statues that decorated elaborate multi-story tombs (Kockel 1993, 7–14, 77–81), the statue galleries on display in public spaces, or even the aristocratic portraits that adorned public buildings (Pflug 1997, 501). They probably did not imitate the cupboards (*armaria*) in which aristocratic Romans kept the images of their ancestors (*imagines maiorum*; Kockel 1993, 12–14). In most of these reliefs, the artists focused on the face (*vultus, facies*) and gestures as bearers of meaning and as a vehicle for identifying the tomb occupants and their relations to one another (Corbeill 2004; Bettini 2011, 131–68). The depiction of similar facial characteristics was often employed to produce a "family look" (Kockel 1993, 67–70). In this respect, portrait reliefs are related to the aristocratic *imagines maiorum*, which likewise amounted to "a sort of iconographic archive of the family's physical features" (Bettini 2011, 158).

The social status of the patrons explains the overwhelming popularity of the toga, the Roman national costume, as the most common mode of representation for men (Kockel 1993, 15–24). The toga not only announces achieved social status, but also distinguishes between generations. Old men wear a particularly old-fashioned, tightly draped toga. Young men can be shown in the toga or in a heroizing scheme, with naked upper body and sword (but without other common heroic formulae, such as turned head or opened mouth), which harks back to aggrandizing Hellenistic statue types and, in this specific context, likely refers to an office as military tribune (*tribunus militum*: Kockel 1993, 24–5). The rights to marry and have legitimate offspring were the most important benefits of *liberti* status (Zanker 1975); therefore the women are shown in a common *pudicitia* scheme, which celebrates female qualities of modesty and chastity, often clasp hands with their husbands (*dextrarum iunctio*) as a sign of their marital status (Kockel 1993, 25–31, 35–53), and have veiled heads to emphasize their virtues. The children often wear the *bulla* (figure 4.4.1), the amulet of the freeborn male child, and are prominently positioned (Zanker 1975, 289–91; Kockel 1993, 53–4). As the first in the family to have the full rights of freeborn Roman citizens, the hopes of the family—sometimes shattered prematurely—rested upon them.

Roman Funerary Altars

The typology and decoration of Roman funerary altars was entirely in line with their cultic function (Boschung 1987); except for the inscription they are almost indistinguishable from altars for the gods. In fact, altars for deities could even be rededicated to the *manes* of Roman individuals, and vice versa (Boschung 1987, 12). Garlands, sacrificial instruments, candelabra, tripods, and other iconographic elements expressed the idea that pious duties toward the deceased had been fulfilled and also defined the funerary precinct as a *locus religiosus*. Gorgoneia and other apotropaic symbols provided magical protection against violation and reuse, a concern voiced by many funerary inscriptions.

Funerary altars become popular in Rome during the reign of Tiberius, perhaps under the influence of the altars of the *Lares* that had been erected in Rome's 265 neighborhoods (*vici*) (Boschung 1993). The chronological distribution of Roman funerary altars centers on the late first and the early second centuries AD. Over the course of the second century

AD, numbers declined sharply, and only a few examples were produced in the third and fourth centuries AD (Boschung 1987, 53). The idea of honoring the dead with a public display of *pietas* was already present in the monumental altar tombs of the first century BC (Boschung 1987, 53); in a development typical for the art of the early imperial period, the funerary altars are sharply reduced in terms of size, but more refined and precious in terms of decoration and material, which is usually marble. The direct successors of the altars are the second-century AD garland sarcophagi; they take up many motifs found on garlanded funerary altars, including mythological vignettes (Boschung 1993, 40–41).

The early altars show mainly garlands and emulate altars for deities, while the Neronian and Flavian altars offer a richer repertoire of forms, including architectural framings; in the early second century AD, designs become simpler again. Figural representations become more popular after the Flavian period, including reclining figures, togate figures, Dionysiac figures, sea creatures, and mythological scenes such as the abduction of Proserpina or the death of Archemoros. There was also room for portraits of the deceased and their relatives, in the form of small-scale or miniature busts (figure 4.4.2), portraits in shells, or the couple itself, often in *dextrarum iunctio* (Boschung 1987, 50–52; Kleiner 1987). The imagery of Roman funerary altars usually communicates

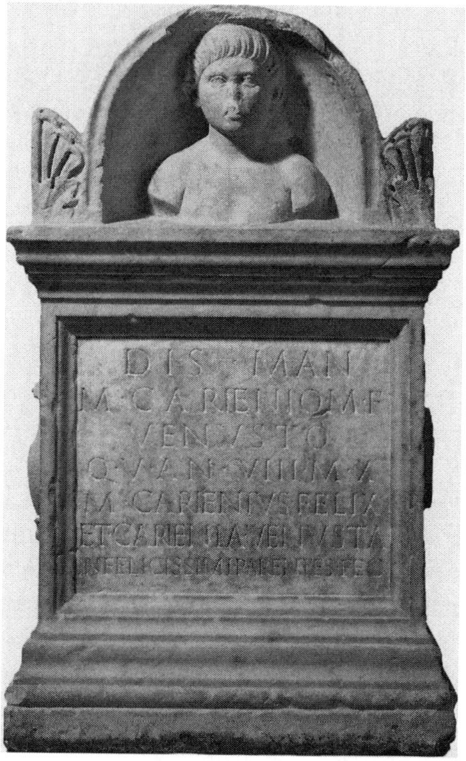

FIGURE 4.4.2 Funerary altar of eight-year-old Carienius Venustus (Boschung 1987, 88, no. 349). Second century AD. Toronto, Royal Ontario Museum (formerly London, Lansdowne House).

fulfillment of pious duties toward the deceased; commemoration and praise of individuals and couples in an elevating, aggrandizing, and poetic fashion; celebration of marital concord; and it begins to make use of mythological themes, as either metaphorical laments of the human condition or evocations of the pleasures of being.

Roman Marble Urns

With over 700 examples known, mostly from Rome and Ostia, marble urns are comparable to altars in number (Sinn 1982; 1987). They served as containers for the cremated remains of the deceased (the ashes and bones that had been gathered, sprinkled with wine, and wrapped in a cloth) and various grave goods, such as coins, *unguentaria* filled with perfume oils, or even jewelry (Sinn 1987, 13). Chronologically, the urns spread from the Augustan period into the third century, with the bulk of the material dating from the Neronian to the Trajanic period (figure 4.4.3). Their popularity thus parallels that of the altars, to which they are closely related. Marble urns were a more

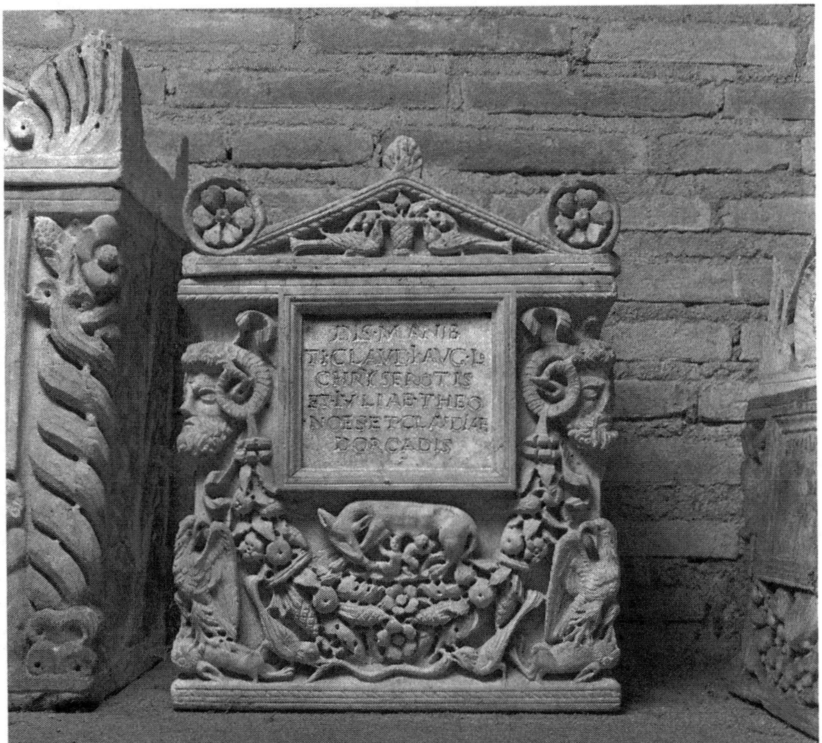

FIGURE 4.4.3 Funerary urn of Claudius Chryseros, Iulia Theonoe, and Claudia Dorcas, with *Lupa romana* under the tabula (Sinn 1987, 143, no. 204). Chryseros was a *libertus* of either Claudius or Nero. Early Flavian. Rome, Museo Nazionale Romano, inv. no. 297191. From Rome, Via Appia, Vigna Codini, Tomb III.

expensive and exclusive option than terracotta urns (*ollae*): among the 460 loculi (containing two *ollae* each) in the Columbarium I in Vigna Codini in Rome, for example, only twelve were marble (Sinn 1987, 14n30). Marble urns were usually intended for single burials, but some urns have as many as three consecutive inscriptions, indicating use for three burials. Some were conceptualized as double urns from the beginning, with two or more *tabulae* next to one another. These multiple urns are similar to sarcophagi in shape. Libation holes for the pouring of wine onto the remains allowed continued interaction with the dead (a second hole could provide drainage). Such urns resemble similarly equipped funerary altars.

In accordance with a general shift toward more "inward-looking" forms of representation that begins in the late first century BC (Hesberg and Zanker 1987; Hesberg 1992; Feraudi-Gruénais 2001; 2003), marble urns were intended to decorate the tomb interior, not the exterior (like the reliefs of the *liberti*), or a funerary precinct (in the case of the altars). The urns stood in grave chambers of various sizes, from the large columbaria of the early imperial period to small family tombs (Sinn 1987, 12–14). They were placed in niches, on pedestals in front of a wall, simply on the ground, or even buried. Unbound to the cultic format of the altar, the typology and decoration of the urns illustrates how the sculptors attempted to come to terms with and interpret the new function of the urns as permanent receptacles for the remains. The artists and their patrons mostly opted for hybrid designs that draw on various aspects of the tomb, as both a house of the dead (Wallace-Hadrill 2008) and as a place at which the survivors fulfilled their religious duties toward the deceased (Sinn 1987, 63–5). The most common form is that of a rectangular box with a roof-shaped lid and gable, which defines the urn as a house or a miniature shrine for the dead—though the urn itself was placed within the larger structure of the tomb, which was also conceptualized as a *domus aeterna*. Isodomic blockwork in relief, pilasters, and prominent doors (a feature that will recur on the sarcophagi) also allude to the *domus aeterna*. Sometimes couples take leave at the opened doors (Sinn 1987, 63), or victories open the doors. Whether doors signify the entrance to the *domus aeterna* or that of the underworld, they clearly emphasize the liminality of death as a moment of separation and passage into another realm. The corners of the roof-shaped lids can be crowned by acroteria, while the pediments are decorated with idyllic motifs (such as birds or sea creatures), or somewhat more authoritative attributes such as eagles or honorific wreaths. Often, the lids end in *pulvini* reminiscent of altars, making explicit the religious dimension of the tomb (figure 4.4.3). Other urns resemble chests (Sinn 1987, 23) or imitate the shape of wicker baskets in order to illustrate their function as containers, like the famous example that probably comes from the tomb of the baker Eurysaces. It is not clear if associations with a bread basket or with a Dionysiac *cista mystica* (depicted on other urns) were intended. The particular aesthetic interest in this shape seems to be the imitation of wicker in marble, a mannered and self-conscious illusionism that renders an inexpensive, ephemeral material in a more precious, permanent medium.

The most common decoration is vegetation (Sinn 1987, 56–62): garlands, trees and branches, even scrollwork, reminiscent of that found on the Ara Pacis, and also inhabited by a rich fauna of birds and insects. Such decoration defines the urn as a symbolic place of bliss (*locus amoenus*) for the dead, by evoking the same positive ideas of peaceful repose that were also associated with lush funerary gardens (*cepotaphia*; Toynbee 1971, 94–100; Sinn 1987, 56–62). The omnipresence of laurel trees and wreaths shows how heavily the artists borrowed from the *aurea aetas* iconography of Augustan art. These references, however, remain playful and largely stripped of their political connotations. Even an emphatically Roman motif such as the *lupa Romana* with the twins becomes a positive symbol of nurturing piety (figure 4.4.3); in one case it alludes, as the inscription suggests, to fraternal love—without (we must assume) any sinister secondary meanings (Sinn 1987, 71). The deceased themselves (and sometimes living relatives) can be evoked in the form of miniature busts in shells or are carried by figures (such as Erotes) that were meant to reflect positively on the deceased's physical qualities. Scenes of *dextrarum iunctio* reflect on the significance of marriage for the *liberti* who dominated this class of monuments. Largely absent, however, are themes such as the profession of the deceased or his office. From the second century, the thematic development of the urns corresponds to that of the sarcophagi (as did that of the funerary altars), with a range of mythological themes such as the abduction of Proserpina (often used on urns for males as a symbol for the love of the couple), Meleager, Venus and Adonis, Hippolytus and Phaedra.

Kline Monuments

Kline monuments, that is depictions of the deceased reclining on a couch, were used from the Augustan period into the third century and are relatively rare. Most date from the Flavian to the early Antonine periods (Wrede 1971; 1981; Koch and Sichtermann 1982, 58–61; Zanker and Ewald 2012, 185–90), thus they preceded and perhaps influenced the mass production of sarcophagi. The motif of reclining figures had a long history, including Greek and Etruscan precedents. *Kline* monuments could be used in a variety of ways. Since cremation was still dominant when they came in fashion, they sometimes accommodated the ashes of the deceased. They could also be prepared to receive the offering of libations. In this respect they are related to the urns and altars on which similar symposium imagery can sometimes be found. In the case of a *kline* monument in Copenhagen, the cup held by the reclining male functioned as a libation hole, allowing the commemorators to fulfill their religious duties while literally "dining with the dead." But *kline* monuments could also cover a burial in a *forma* or a simple sarcophagus; in these cases their function was practically that of the later sarcophagus lids, which similarly depict reclining figures. *Kline* monuments were also placed on bases, on the floor of a grave chamber or funerary precinct, or in a niche, and could thus serve as funerary monuments in their own right (Koch and Sichtermann 1982, 59). The famous crane relief from the tomb of the Haterii depicts the female deceased in the guise of just such a monument, which we have to imagine as having been part of the funerary shrine below (Wrede 1971).

The substitutive function of *kline* monuments is made particularly obvious by the three-dimensional rendering of a body on a *kline*, often understood as a portrayal of the deceased in a happy beyond. Often the honorand is shown sleeping, with flower garland in hand, as if she had gently nodded away at a symposium (figure 4.4.4). Sleep is here used as a rather transparent and consoling euphemism for death. But beyond that, more concrete associations with the body lying in state or even with the wax effigies placed on biers or couches for funerals *in effigie* would have been inevitable. The combination of an actual body, hidden from view in a container or sarcophagus (*theke*), with an openly displayed effigy on a *kline* above the body is attested for the funerals of both Augustus and Pertinax (Cass. Dio 75.4.2–5; Erasmo 2008; Arce 2010). Other *kline* monuments use a more upright, wakeful pose (Roller 2006). Similar funerary iconographies had been used since the Hellenistic period, illustrating the patron's opulent lifestyle and *savoir vivre*. On one (now lost) example, the *kline* monument of a certain Saturneinos, the inscription identifies the deceased with Dionysos (Wrede 1981, 261, no. 174). Males and females can be equipped further with various gendered attributes of domestic luxury, such as thick pillows, garlands, drinking cups, erotes, or dogs. The rendering of the body can also vary considerably, and sometimes depicts both men and women as partially

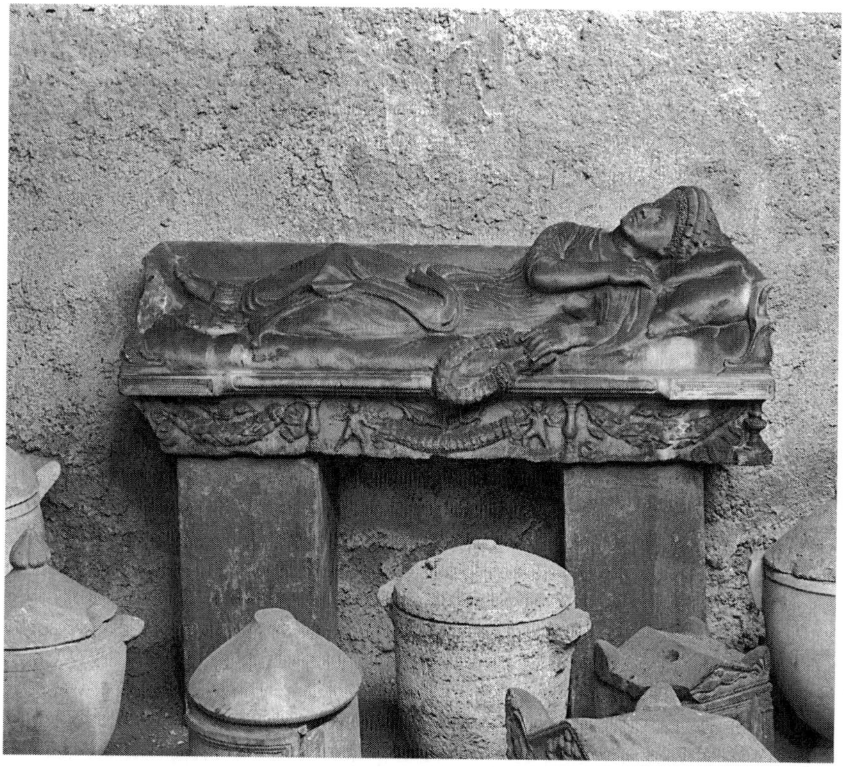

FIGURE 4.4.4 *Kline* monument depicting a woman holding a garland. Early second century AD. Rome, Museo Nazionale Romano, inv. no. 72879.

nude. The attention drawn to the body anticipates the corporeal aesthetic of Roman mythological sarcophagi, on which half- (or even entirely) naked mythological figures can also be used for comparison and identification. In the later second century, the dominant ideal of the couple appears on the *kline* monuments; around the same time, reclining couples also begin to be featured on the *kline* lids of both Roman and eastern sarcophagi.

Sarcophagi

Relief decorated marble sarcophagi come into fashion in various parts of the Roman Empire during the second century AD (figure 4.4.5). The general function of sarcophagi was the containment, preservation, and concealment of one or several bodies, as is shown by the slight elevation for the head usually found inside on the right; still, some sarcophagi were used for cremation burials. The decomposing body was literally concealed by the marble facade of the sarcophagus front which often displayed the immaculate marble bodies of gods and heroes, as a substitute and "redemption" for death and decay (Ewald 2011). The emergence of sarcophagi is thus related to the gradual transition from cremation to inhumation during the second century (Nock 1932), although it has often—and rightly—been noted that the popularity of elaborate, relief decorated sarcophagi is not an inevitable consequence of this change in burial customs. Rather, what contributed to the wide diffusion of relief decorated sarcophagi must have been the possibilities offered by the new format itself: for increased self-presentation (albeit in a private venue), for sprawling mythological storytelling, and for an intensified visual discourse about life, love, death, corporeality, emotions, virtues, and family relations. At Rome the thematic range found on relief sarcophagi is firmly situated within these thematic coordinates, which moreover corresponded to the rather private character of the tomb as a memorial space for the family unit; the latter could include slaves, freedmen, and friends who could also be buried in such family tombs (Feraudi-Gruénais 2001; 2003). However, the actual contexts and circumstances of viewing and display of sarcophagi varied greatly across the Roman Empire. Though most often displayed in tombs, sarcophagi could also occasionally be buried in the floor of tomb chambers, so that their relief decoration was no longer visible; at the other extreme, they could be raised by funerary platforms and high bases in the open so that they could be seen from afar, as is the case in the necropolis of Tyre in Lebanon (Linant de Bellefonds 1985; De Jong 2010).

In terms of quantity, sarcophagi are the most numerously preserved body of funerary art. A rather conservative estimate puts the number of extant pieces (and fragments thereof) found across the Roman Empire at between 12,000 and 15,000 (Koch 1993, 1), suggesting that sarcophagi must have originally numbered in the hundreds of thousands, depending on the ratio between lost and extant pieces one uses in such calculations (e.g., Smith 2012). Thus, in most places, this type of burial must have been somewhat affordable. The greatest number of sarcophagi (about 6000, according to Koch 1993, 94), as well as the greatest variety of sarcophagus shapes and themes, is found

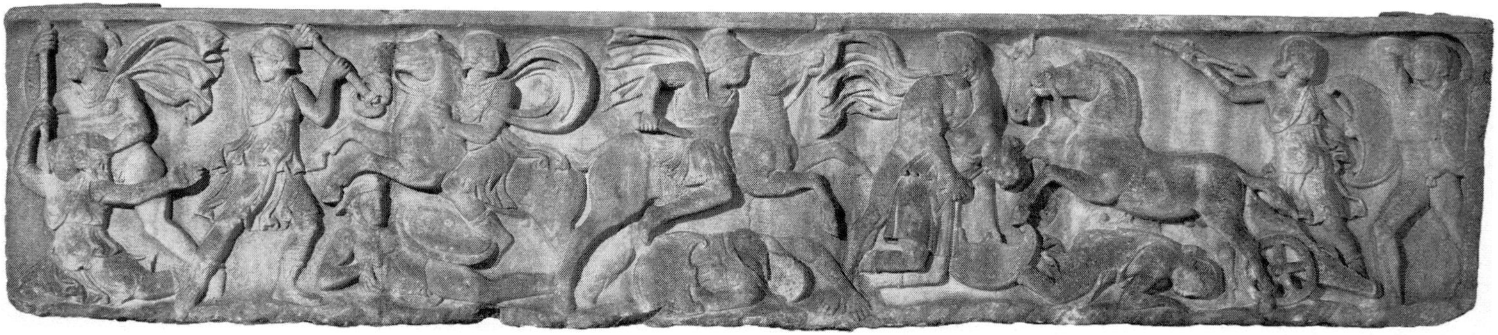

FIGURE 4.4.5 Roman sarcophagus with Amazonomachy. Mid-second century AD. Toronto, Royal Ontario Museum.

in the city of Rome itself (Koch 1993, 2). Other types of Roman funerary sculpture, such as the few urns, altars, and funerary reliefs of *liberti* produced in the second century, began to use decorative motifs pioneered on sarcophagi. Apart from Rome and Ostia, important workshops (or "centers of production": Koch and Sichtermann 1982; Koch 1993) were located in Athens and Asia Minor (Ephesos, Aphrodisias, Dokimeion). Upon closer inspection, however, the picture becomes complicated: raw materials (often marble from a variety of quarries, in particular Prokonnesos in the Sea of Marmara) and sarcophagi in various stages of completion were traded along the lines of a complex and only superficially researched network of trade relations (Walker 1985; Koch 1993, 3–17; Russell 2011). In addition, many local workshops throughout the empire carved sarcophagi from either locally available or imported materials (limestone or marble), often imitating the design of costly imports.

Sarcophagi come in a great variety of shapes and types (Koch 1993, 17–32). Sarcophagi at Rome usually emphasize the sarcophagus front, while the sides can be summarily carved and the back is often left undecorated. Sarcophagi from Athens and Asia Minor, however, tend to be carved on all four sides, giving them the character of an independent *heroon*. Many of them were (perhaps recursively or self-referentially) displayed in tombs that were also understood as *heroa* (Cormack 2004). As has been observed in the case of the marble urns, the different types of sarcophagi provide clues as to how the new format could be conceptualized (Elsner 2012; Platt 2012). Vat-shaped sarcophagi are often decorated with Dionysiac scenes, thus conceptualizing the tomb as a positive space of abundance and bliss. Columnar sarcophagi evoke the impression of an elaborate *heroon* or a decorative facade in which statues of mythological figures or the sarcophagus patrons are displayed. Strigillated sarcophagi, particularly popular in Rome during the third century, provide visual interest while at the same time simplifying figural decoration; they illustrate the gradual emergence of a new late antique aesthetic and the turn away from the abundant mythological storytelling of the late second and early third centuries.

In terms of interpretation, mythological sarcophagi are one of the most contested bodies of material in Roman art history, because of the complexity of the reliefs, which lend themselves to a variety of hermeneutic approaches (Nock 1946; Koch and Sichtermann 1982, 583–623; Elsner and Huskinson 2011; Elsner and Wu 2012; Zanker and Ewald 2012). Older symbolic interpretations anachronistically projected concern about the afterlife and used textual references to recognize in sarcophagi a kind of eschatology in images that turned pagan Romans into mere proto-Christians. Recent approaches, however, emphasize the autonomy and primacy of the visual tradition over (and even against) presumed literary references, and read the sarcophagus imagery as a system of signification that was based primarily on visual analogies and cross-connections rather than textual references (Koortbojian 1995; Zanker and Ewald 2012). A particular concern of scholarship over the past few decades has been the question of how the mostly Greek myths depicted on sarcophagi were tailored and appropriated for their Roman purposes (Giuliani 1989; Müller 1994; Koortbojian 1995; Bielfeldt 2005; Elsner and Huskinson 2011; Zanker and Ewald 2012). Recent scholarship also examines the possible meanings of the complex formal and thematic shifts observable on Roman sarcophagi from the second to fourth centuries (Ewald 2012; Zanker and Ewald 2012). Other topics of interest are the contexts and viewing conditions of sarcophagi (D'Ambra 1988; Bielfeldt 2003; Dresken-Weiland 2003; Borg 2013; Meinecke 2014), portraiture (Newby 2011; Birk 2013), polychromy (Liverani 2010), the selection and creation of specific iconographies for certain social or age groups (Huskinson 1996; Wrede 2001; Ewald 2003; Reinsberg 2006), the sarcophagus trade (Russell 2011; see essay 2.7, Russell), and cross-cultural comparisons with China (Elsner and Wu 2012).

Sociology and Patrons

Who was able to afford a funerary monument with sculptural decoration during the imperial period? In the most general terms, it is certainly correct to connect the wealth of monuments to the existence of a large, monument-producing "middle class" (Mayer 2012), whose economic potency, desire for representation, and resulting visibility in the archaeological record did not necessarily correspond to their legal status or political relevance. But the link between the social class of patrons and the iconography of a funerary monument is rarely as straightforward as in the case of the funerary reliefs of Roman *liberti*, whose analysis by P. Zanker (1975) has become something of a model case for the sociohistorical interpretation of Roman funerary art. Conclusive evidence can come only from inscriptions, which teach us that some classes of monuments were preferred by customers from certain social groups, while others were used by a wider range of clients; they demonstrate that preferences shifted over time, and that the size and context of a funerary monument mattered. An examination of inscriptions from Roman imperial period tombs with painted and stucco decoration demonstrated that nearly all were owned by members of the lower orders of society (Feraudi-Gruénais 2001; 2003). Examination of the over 500 inscriptions on Roman marble relief urns yielded similar results: the patrons were mainly slaves and freedmen who had worked either in private households or in the imperial administration; the latter were important agents and multipliers of new funeral fashions and imperial iconographies in the private realm (Sinn 1987, 84–7). From the later second century on, however, when inhumation had become the new fashion, soldiers and military veterans play a more important role as patrons of marble urns; they apparently continued to practice cremation, perhaps because they often died abroad and were cremated in the field. In single cases, marble urns were even used for equestrians and senators (Sinn 1987, 86n745). Funerary altars are found across the entire social spectrum, though the ones used by the aristocracy were larger (over 1 m in height) than those used by patrons from lower classes (Eck 1998). Altars were mostly commissioned by imperial freedmen and slaves as well as "craftsmen, money changers,. . . musicians and actors" (Boschung 1987, 55), but we also have a good number of altars for equestrians, senators, and even members of the imperial court, such as the son-in-law of the emperor Claudius (Boschung 1987, 55; 1993, 37). Inscriptions on Roman funerary altars occasionally mention the actual prices of such monuments: 10,000 sesterces in the case of one altar; 50,000 sesterces in the case of an ensemble of two altars, or about one-sixth the annual salary of an imperial procurator of high rank (Boschung 1987, 39).

The clientele of marble sarcophagi appears to have been just as varied. The cost of an elaborate mythological sarcophagus has been estimated to be about a year's salary for an equestrian military officer of high rank (Fittschen 1975) but the great numbers of extant sarcophagi and fragments demonstrate that they were clearly in reach of many. The inscriptions, which have never been studied comprehensively (cf. Dresken-Weiland 2003), reveal a remarkable range of clients, as well as considerable regional variation. We encounter patrons from all walks of life, from freedmen to consuls, from a musician turned pimp or slave trader to high military officers, from craftsmen to star rhetoricians. In Aphrodisias in Caria, for example, marble was so readily available that many ex-slaves were able to commission garland sarcophagi with inscriptions (Smith 2008). In Roman Tyre (modern Lebanon), on the other hand, rich purple-producers and dyers imported immensely expensive (Attic) sarcophagi with heroic scenes from Athens, which were proudly displayed on funerary platforms in the open (Chéhab 1984; Linant de Bellefonds 1985; De Jong 2010). As far as the city of Rome is concerned, we again find slaves and freedmen at the lower end of the spectrum, for example in the case of the sarcophagi from the mausoleum of the Marcii (Mausoleum Phi) on the Via Cornelia in Rome, or the sarcophagi from the tomb of the Octavii on the Via Triumphalis (Feraudi-Gruénais 2001, 59–60, 63–5). At the top end, senators and equestrians probably commissioned the lavish, large-scale third-century sarcophagi with singular iconographies (Wrede 2001; Ewald 2003; Reinsberg 2006; Zanker and Ewald 2012, 182–4). To what extent they inspired the development of new themes and iconographies is controversial (Wrede 2001; Ewald 2003); it appears that thematic shifts observable on Roman sarcophagi from the mid-second to the late third centuries AD may indicate profound changes of attitudes toward life and death and not just sociohistorical transformations. In the greater scheme of things, the development of Roman funerary art cannot be separated from the emergence of new forms of subjectivity that had ultimately been engendered by the advent of the imperial system (Bartsch 2006; Alston and Spentzou 2011). These processes of individuation encompassed an intensified reflection on and concern with death and its finality, combined with an increasing reluctance to accept this finality, by setting something more permanent—a funerary monument or image—against it (Wrede 1971; Ewald 2012).

Bibliography

Alston, R., and E. Spentzou. 2011. *Reflections of Romanity: Discourses of Subjectivity in Imperial Rome*. Columbus: Ohio State University Press.

Andreae, B. 1984. "Bossierte Porträts auf römischen Sarkophagen: Ein ungelöstes Problem." *MarbWPr* 1984: 109–128.

Andreu, J., D. Espinosa, and S. Pastor, eds. 2011. *Mors omnibus instat: Aspectos arqueológicos, epigráficos y rituales de la muerte en el Occidente Romano*. Madrid: Liceus Ediciones.

Arce, J. 1988. *Funus Imperatorum: Los funerales de los emperadores romanos*. Madrid: Alianza Editorial.

———. 2010. "Roman Imperial Funerals *in effigie*." In Ewald and Noreña 2010, 309–324.

Bartsch, S. 2006. *The Mirror of the Self: Sexuality, Self-Knowledge, and the Gaze in the Early Roman Empire*. Chicago: University of Chicago Press.

Beard, M., and J. Henderson. 1998. "The Emperor's new Body: Ascent from Rome." In *Parchments of Gender*, edited by M. Wyke, 191–220. Oxford: Oxford University Press.

Bettini, M. 1999. *The Portrait of the Lover*. Berkeley: University of California Press.

———. 2011. *The Ears of Hermes: Communication, Images, and Identity in the Classical World*. Columbus: Ohio State University Press.

Bielfeldt, R. 2003. "Orest im Medusengrab: Ein Versuch zum Betrachter." *RM* 110: 117–50.

———. 2005. *Orestes auf römischen Sarkophagen*. Berlin: Reichert.

Birk, S. 2013. *Depicting the Dead: Self-Representation and Commemoration on Roman Sarcophagi with Portraits*. Aarhus: Aarhus University Press.

Bodel, J. 2008. "From Columbaria to Catacombs: Collective Burial in Pagan and Christian Rome." In Brink and Green 2008, 177–242.

Borg, B. 2013. *Crisis and Ambition: Tombs and Burial Customs in 3rd Century CE Rome*. Oxford: Oxford University Press.

Boschung, D. 1987. *Antike Grabaltäre aus den Nekropolen Roms*. Bern: Stämpfli.

———. 1993. "Grabaltäre mit Girlanden und frühe Girlandensarkophage: Zur Genese der kaiserzeitlichen Sepulkralkunst." In *Grabeskunst der römischen Kaiserzeit*, edited by G. Koch, 37–42. Mainz: Philipp von Zabern.

Brink, L., and D. Green, eds. 2008. *Commemorating the Dead: Texts and Artifacts in Context; Studies of Roman, Jewish, and Christian Burials*. Berlin: Walter de Gruyter.

Carroll, M. 2006. *Spirits of the Dead: Roman Funerary Commemoration in Western Europe*. Oxford: Oxford University Press.

Chéhab, M. 1984. "Fouilles de Tyr: La nécropole, 2. Description des fouilles." *BMusBeyr* 34: 1–482.

Corbeill, A. 2004. *Nature Embodied: Gesture in Ancient Rome*. Princeton: Princeton University Press.

Cormack, S. 2004. *The Space of Death in Roman Asia Minor*. Vienna: Phoibos.

D'Ambra, E. 1988. "A Myth for a Smith: A Meleager Sarcophagus from a Tomb in Ostia." *AJA* 92: 85–99, 311.

Davies, P. J. E. 2000. *Death and the Emperor: Roman Imperial Funerary Monuments from Augustus to Marcus Aurelius*. Cambridge: Cambridge University Press.

De Filippis Cappai, C. 1997. *Imago mortis: L'uomo romano e la morte*. Naples: Loffredo.

De Jong, L. 2010. "Performing Death in Tyre." *AJA* 114: 597–630.

Dresken-Weiland, J. 2003. *Sarkophagbestattungen im Westen des römischen Reiches*. Freiburg: Herder.

Eck, W. 1998. "Grabmonumente und sozialer Status in Rom und Umgebung." In *Bestattungssitte und kulturelle Identität*, edited by P. Fasold, T. Fischer, and H. Von Hesberg, 29–40. Cologne: Rheinland.

Elsner, J. 2010. "Alois Riegl and Roman Classical Archaeology." In *Alois Riegl Revisited: Beiträge zu Werk und Rezeption*, edited by P. Noever, A. Rosenauer, and G. Vasold, 45–57. Vienna: Austrian Academy of Sciences.
———. 2012. "Decorative Imperatives between Concealment and Display: The Form of Sarcophagi." *RES: Anthropology and Aesthetics* 61–2: 178–95.
Elsner, J., and J. Huskinson, eds. 2011. *Life, Death and Representation: Some New Work on Roman Sarcophagi*. Millennium Studies 29. Berlin: Walter de Gruyter.
Elsner, J., and H. Wu. 2012. "Editorial." *RES: Anthropology and Aesthetics* 61–2: 5–21.
Erasmo, M. 2008. *Reading Death in Ancient Rome*. Columbus: Ohio State University Press.
———. 2012. *Death: Antiquity and its Legacy*. London: Tauris.
Ewald, B. C. 2003. "The Social History of Roman Funerary Art and its Limits." *JRA* 16: 561–70.
———. 2011. "Myth and Visual Narrative in the "Second Sophistic" – a Comparative Approach: Notes on an Attic Hippolytos Sarcophagus in Agrigento." In Elsner and Huskinson 2011, 261–307.
———. 2012. "Paradigms of Personhood and Regimes of Representation: Some Notes on the Transformation of Roman Sarcophagi." *RES: Anthropology and Aesthetics* 61–2: 41–64.
Ewald, B. C., and C. F. Noreña, eds. 2010. *The Emperor and Rome: Space, Representation, and Ritual*. Cambridge: Cambridge University Press.
Fejfer, J. 2008. *Roman Portraits in Context*. Berlin: Walter de Gruyter.
Feraudi-Gruénais, F. 2001. *Ubi diutius nobis habitandum est: Die Innendekoration der kaiserzeitlichen Gräber Roms*. Wiesbaden: Ludwig Reichert.
———. 2003. *Inschriften und "Selbstdarstellung" in stadtrömischen Grabbauten*. Rome: Edizioni Quasar.
Fittschen, K. 1975. *Der Meleager-Sarkophag*. Frankfurt: Liebieghaus.
Giuliani, L. 1989. "Achill-Sarkophage in Ost und West." *JBerlMus* 31: 369–93.
Häusle, H. 1980. *Das Denkmal als Garant des Nachruhms: Beiträge zur Geschichte und Thematik eines Motivs in lateinischen Inschriften*. Munich: Beck.
Hesberg, H. 1992. *Stadtrömische Grabbauten*. Darmstadt: Wissenschaftliche Buchgesellschaft.
Hesberg, H., and P. Zanker, eds. 1987. *Römische Gräberstraßen: Selbstdarstellung, Status, Standard*. Munich: Bayerischen Akademie der Wissenschaften.
Huskinson, J. 1996. *Roman Children's Sarcophagi*. Oxford: Oxford University Press.
———. 1998. "Unfinished Portrait Heads on Later Roman Sarcophagi." *PBSR* 66: 129–58.
Kleiner, D. E. E. 1977. *Roman Group Portraiture: The Funerary Reliefs of the Late Republic and Early Empire*. New York: Garland.
———. 1987. *Roman Imperial Funerary Altars with Portraits*. Rome: Giorgio Bretschneider.
Koch, G. 1993. *Sarkophage der römischen Kaiserzeit*. Darmstadt: Wissenschaftliche Buchgesellschaft.
Koch, G., and H. Sichtermann. 1982. *Römische Sarkophage*. Munich: Beck.
Kockel, V. 1993. *Porträtreliefs stadtrömischer Grabbauten: Ein Beitrag zur Geschichte und zum Verständnis des spätrepublikanisch-frühkaiserzeitlichen Privatporträts*. Mainz: Philipp von Zabern.
Koortbojian, M. 1995. *Myth, Meaning and Memory on Roman Sarcophagi*. Berkeley: University of California Press.
Linant de Bellefonds, P. 1985. *Sarcophages attiques de la nécropole de Tyr: Une étude iconographique*. Paris: Editions Recherche sur les Civilisations.

Liverani, P. 2010. “New Evidence on the Polychromy of Roman Sculpture.” In *Circumlitio: The Polychromy of Antique and Medieval Sculpture*, edited by V. Brinkmann, O. Primavesi, and M. Hollein, 290–302. Munich: Hirmer.

Mayer, E. 2012. *The Ancient Middle Classes: Urban Life and Aesthetics in the Roman Empire, 100 BCE–250 CE*. Cambridge, MA: Harvard University Press.

Meinecke, K. 2014. *Sarcophagum posuit: Römische Steinsarkophage im Kontext*. Sarkophag-Studien 7. Wiesbaden: Harassowitz.

Müller, F. 1994. *The So-Called Peleus and Thetis Sarcophagus in the Villa Albani*. Leiden: Brill.

Newby, Z. 2011. “In the Guise of Gods and Heroes: Portrait Heads on Roman Mythological Sarcophagi.” In Elsner and Huskinson 2011, 189–227.

Nock, A. D. 1932. “Cremation and Burial in the Roman Empire.” *HTR* 25(4): 321–59.

———. 1946. “Sarcophagi and Symbolism.” *AJA* 50: 140–60.

Pflug, H. 1997. Review of Kockel 1993. *BJb* 197: 497–505.

Platt, V. 2012. “Framing the Dead on Roman Sarcophagi.” *RES: Anthropology and Aesthetics* 61–2: 213–27.

Prieur, J. 1986. *La mort dans l'antiquité romaine*. Rennes: Ouest France.

Reinsberg, C. 2006. *Vita Romana*. Part 3 of *Die Sarkophage mit Darstellungen aus dem Menschenleben*. ASR 1.3. Berlin: Mann.

Roller, M. 2006. *Dining Posture in Ancient Rome: Bodies, Values and Status*. Princeton: Princeton University Press.

Russell, B. 2011. “The Roman Sarcophagus ‘Industry’: A Reconsideration.” In Elsner and Huskinson 2011, 119–47.

Sinn, F. 1982. “Urnen.” In Koch and Sichtermann 1982, 41–58.

———. 1987. *Stadtrömische Marmorurnen*. Mainz: Philipp von Zabern.

Smith, R. R. R. 2008. “Sarcophagi and Roman citizenship.” In *Aphrodisias Papers 4: New Research on the City and its Monuments*, edited by C. Ratté and R. R. R. Smith, 347–94. JRA Supplement 70. Providence, RI: Journal of Roman Archaeology.

———. 2012. “Monuments for new citizens in Rome and Aphrodisias.” In *Kunst von Unten? Stil und Gesellschaft in der antiken Welt von der “arte plebea” bis heute*, edited by J.-A. Dickmann, R. von den Hoff, and F. Pirson, 171–84. Wiesbaden: Reichert.

Toynbee, J. M. C. 1971. *Death and Burial in the Roman World*. Ithaca, NY: Cornell University Press.

Walker, S. 1985. *Memorials to the Roman Dead*. London: British Museum.

Wallace-Hadrill, A. 2008. “Housing the Dead: The Tomb as House in Roman Italy.” In Brink and Green 2008, 39–78.

Wrede, H. 1971. “Das Mausoleum der Claudia Semne und die bürgerliche Plastik der Kaiserzeit.” *RM* 78: 125–66.

———. 1981. *Consecratio in Formam Deorum: Vergöttlichte Privatpersonen in der römischen Kaiserzeit*. Mainz: Philipp von Zabern.

———. 2001. *Senatorische Sarkophage Roms: Der Beitrag des Senatorenstandes zur römischen Kunst der hohen und späten Kaiserzeit*. Mainz: Philipp von Zabern.

Zanker, P. 1975. “Grabreliefs römischer Freigelassener.” *JdI* 90: 267–315.

Zanker, P., and B. C. Ewald. 2012. *Living with Myths: The Imagery of Roman Sarcophagi*. Translated by J. Slater. Oxford: Oxford University Press.

CHAPTER 4.5

EPIGRAPHY AND PATRONAGE

STEVEN L. TUCK

INTRODUCTION

THIS essay examines the context in which sculptures (largely portraits) were vowed and dedicated through the analysis of inscriptions on statue bases, the majority of whose statues are no longer extant. Detailed study of these inscriptions provides us with critical evidence for the habits of erecting statues across the Roman world (Forbis 1996; Højte 2005; Fejfer 2008). They typically reveal the identity of the statue, the honoree, the name and titles of the dedicator(s), and the date of dedication. On some occasions inscriptions can also reveal original display location, cost, artist, materials, and form. From these basic facts conclusions about the patterns of sculptural dedications can be drawn and some basic statistical studies performed (Duncan-Jones 1982; Højte 2005). More importantly, perhaps, this information, both individually and in aggregate, reveals the social, religious, and political world of which sculpture is a product. For example, one of the most important facts concerning sculptural dedication (often misunderstood by scholars) is that neither the emperors themselves nor their administrations ever dedicated statues of emperors; imperial portraits are always third-party dedications (Højte 2005, 167). As such, study of the inscriptions found on statue bases is actually a study of the dynamics of power, public display, and the context for the creation of sculpture in the Roman world. Such important issues can only be studied with the inscriptions as they reveal the layers of dialogue and competing and complementary values of different levels of Roman society.

The study of epigraphic evidence informs the study of sculpture in critical ways. The epigraphy on statue bases and dedications can allow the study of no longer extant sculptures, helping to mitigate the loss of statues, particularly the disappearance of virtually all metal sculpture from the Roman world due to recycling (see essay 2.4, Mattusch). Inscribed statue bases are particularly important because they are often reused very nearly *in situ*, whereas the statues they once held, both the primary and secondary dedications, are almost always missing. The bases, therefore, can provide a history of sculptural display in a space, as well as evidence of individual dedication. Not only scholars find this material notable: the existence of so much epigraphic material associated with sculpture suggests its importance in antiquity. That Romans paid close attention to at least some inscriptions is demonstrated by references in literary sources (Højte 2005, 42) and honorary decrees (Rose 1997, 73) to the texts of inscriptions on statues; in fact, one of these ancient sources (Plin. *HN* 3.136–7) even mentions an inscription that is still extant. More commonly the central role of these inscriptions in Roman society is demonstrated by the multiple examples of posthumous erasure of the names of condemned former emperors, a phenomenon known generally as *damnatio memoriae* (Flower 2006; see essay 2.3, Varner). Testimony for the awareness of and attention to the inscriptions of statues is vividly provided by the provision in the *Senatus Consultum de Cn. Pisone Patre* (Potter and Damon 1999, ll. 82–4) in which the Senate decrees that the name of Piso be eliminated from the statue of Germanicus: *utiq(ue) nomen Cn. Pisonis / patris tolleretur/ ex titulo statuae Germanici Caesaris, quam ei sodales / Augustales in campo ad / aram Providentiae posuissent.* This form of *damnatio memoriae* differs from the wiping out of the names and images of honorees and extends this common treatment to the dedicator of public sculpture indicating the significance of the identities of both individuals.

After a brief review of the nature and formulae of the inscriptions associated with the dedication of statuary, this essay will demonstrate how epigraphic material can shed light on patronage and specific historical events, the dialogue that occurred through sculptural dedication, and the use of statuary to connect individuals, local communities, and groups with each other and the imperial family.

Tituli, Their Formulae, and the Nature of Epigraphic Evidence Associated with Statues

The *tituli* (titles, labels, or captions) from statues are formulaic with a certain amount of expected regional and temporal variation (Salomies 1994). The basic formula (Højte 2005, 19–21) consists of the name of the honoree and the name of the dedicator, generally in that order, followed by (from most to least common) the date, circumstances or motivation for the dedication, cost, and name of the artist. The consistency of these elements and their order combined with the regular abbreviation of every common name, title, and verb of giving allows even the most fragmentary inscriptions to be restored, so that we can confidently add additional examples to the corpus of sculptural displays and study fragmentary inscriptions to great benefit. Formulaic imperial titles allow the assignment of many sculptural dedications to very narrow date ranges based on our historical knowledge of the emperors' reigns. For example, an inscription of seven whole and six partial letters, *Aurel] io[/]Germ[anico] / Sar]matio[/ principi i]vven[tutis*, can be restored as a statue dedicated to Commodus erected at Puteoli between 7 July AD 175, and 27 November AD 176, the date on which this final Antonine ruler dropped the title *princeps iuventutis* (Tuck 2005, 11). The sculpture itself and the name(s) of dedicator(s) are lost, but its existence, subject, and possible placement (at the findspot?) are preserved. In addition to recording individual examples such as this, much work has been done in recent years creating databases of inscriptions. Essentially the inheritors of the *Corpus Inscriptionum Latinarum* (*CIL*) and other earlier print collections, digital databases are fully searchable by name, term, string, or even portion of a word, often illustrated with photographs, and easily amended and augmented. The fragmentary *titulus* above can be studied with tens of thousands of others to determine patterns of commemoration and the distribution and range of formulae as well as to answer a host of questions about sculptural patronage for which the data were previously unavailable or extremely difficult to collect.

Another thirteen-letter inscription reveals even more about patronage, specific historical events, and the movement of sculpture in the Roman world. A statue base in the sanctuary of Apollo at Pompeii bears the inscription: L MVMMIS L KVSVL (retrograde), referring to Lucius Mummius, the Roman general who sacked Corinth in 146 BC. Here the inscription is in Oscan, demonstrating that it was written just for this community, since it is the only Oscan inscription out of seventeen extant examples recording benefactions from Mummius (Yarrow 2006, appendix 1). A number of ancient sources relate that Mummius distributed a portion of the spoils from Corinth to allied communities, and this inscription must mark one such gift (Yarrow 2006). We do not know for certain the iconography of the sculpture that this base once supported, but the cuttings atop the statue base indicate that it was bronze. It has been suggested that the Apollo or Artemis statues found in the sanctuary were spoils from Corinth (De Caro 1994, 110) and originally belonged on this and another base with an almost identical profile found in the same portico (Descœudres 2007, 11). Pausanias (5.24.4) also credits Mummius with being the first Roman ever to make a dedication at a Greek sanctuary. This base, therefore, provides evidence for a number of statements in literary sources and may also offer possible origins for the bronze statues of Apollo and Artemis. It also demonstrates the usefulness of inscriptions in dating sculptural dedications. Since Mummius is referred to only as consul, the dedication must be after 146 BC but prior to 142 BC when he was elected censor. So, these distributions seem to have occurred relatively rapidly in the year of or that following his triumph in Rome. Finally, the inscription is notably in the nominative, which gives the *titulus* the appearance of a label, but actually is used to identify the dedicator of a sculpture (Harrison 1993, 205–211; Højte 2005, 180). Even the briefest of *tituli* allow us to restore the date, form, context, and significance of sculptures and the dialogue that took place in sculptural dedication in the Roman world.

Individual Patronage and Municipal Reciprocity

The examples discussed above could be considered unidirectional dedications, in which an individual or group dedicated a statue of a particular subject in a public space. While these examples add to our knowledge of patronage and sculpture in the Roman world, other sets of inscriptions reveal more about the complex interactions that occurred around sculptural patronage and the dynamics of public beneficence. Here, I offer two examples.

The first involves two inscriptions on sculptural dedications from Pompeii associated with a certain Cuspius and made in the aftermath of the AD 62 earthquake; a large statue niche in the north passageway into the arena of the amphitheater of Pompeii has this inscription carved on the block below it (figure 4.5.1):

> C(aius) Cuspius C(ai) f(ilius) Pansa pater d(uum)v(ir) i(ure) d(icundo) / IIII quinq(uennalis) praef(ectus) i(ure) d(icundo) ex d(ecreto) d(ecurionum) lege Petron(ia) (*CIL* 10.858 = *ILS* 6359)

The inscription is typically misunderstood as labeling the subject of the sculpture in the niche as an honorific statue of Cuspius. The existence of a paired statue niche with his son's name below it (*CIL* 10.859 = *ILS* 6359a) has led to a further misinterpretation of this passageway as "the shrine to the family" (Franklin 2004, 172). The use of the nominative, however, denotes Cuspius as the dedicator, not the subject. In fact, the subject of the sculpture is not known. The remains of a metal grill anchored into the stone that protected the statue, however, suggests that it was a nearly life-size precious-metal statue, probably of a deity or emperor (Cooley and Cooley 2004, 47). Poppaea Sabina, whose birthplace was Pompeii, married Nero in AD 62. Perhaps valuable metal statues of the imperial couple faced each other across this passageway. Because of its location, the audience for the sculpture was restricted to participants in the *pompa* that initiated a set of games. It seems most likely that the dedication was placed deliberately to be viewed by those members of the local magistracies and priesthoods who entered here with the *pompa* and were seated in the *ima cavea* also accessible through this passageway. The inscription and indirect evidence of material of the sculpture suggest a dedication designed by a member of the local elite to speak to a limited audience of other elites, certainly drawn from across the region (Benefiel 2004; Tuck 2008). The occasion of the dedication is thought to have been the restoration of the amphitheater following the earthquake of AD 62 when Cuspius was appointed prefect. Additional support for that as the occasion as well as a clear statement of the community's response to his work is provided by another inscription. It was found in the forum of Pompeii on a statue base decorated with gladiatorial motifs and supporting a statue of Cuspius:

> C(aio) Cuspio C(ai) f(ilio) Pansae / IIvir(o) i(ure) d(icundo) quart(um) quinq(uennali) / ex d(ecreto) d(ecurionum) pec(unia) pub(lica)

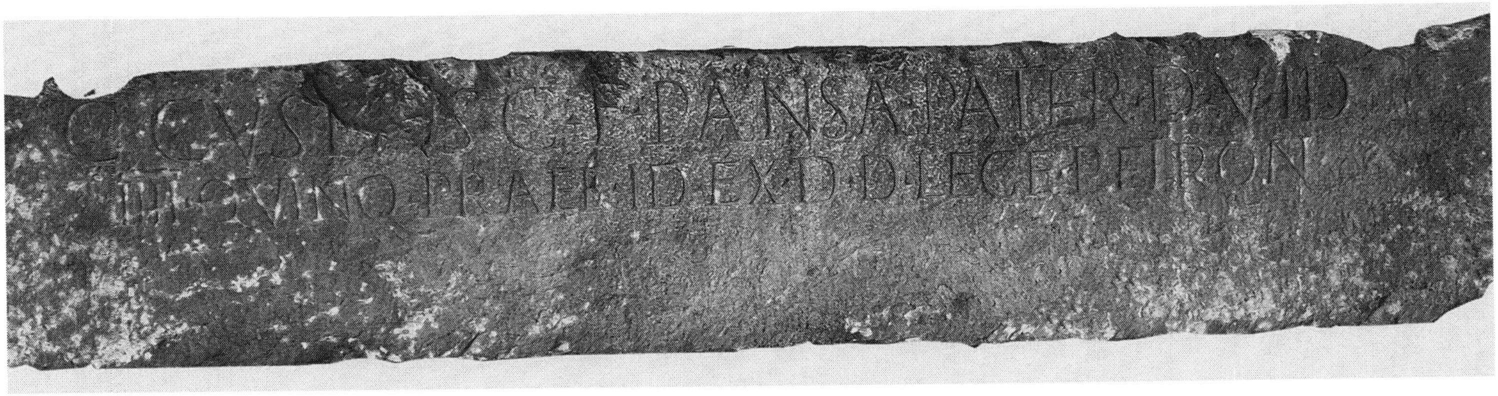

FIGURE 4.5.1 Dedicatory inscription below niche in the north passageway of the amphitheater of Pompeii, c. AD 62.

Cuspius's name as the leading element here does not mean that he is the dedicator as in the *titulus* above. Instead, the use of the dative names him as the subject of the statue and the honoree. Together the two inscriptions provide an example of the dialogue that occurred in sculpture across the Roman world as public benefactors were commemorated in turn by local communities with publicly funded dedications of honorific statues. In this instance the original dedication may have also served to highlight a connection between the imperial family and the local community.

Another example of a complex interaction revealed by epigraphy comes from the city of Perge in the province of Lycia and Pamphylia, where a woman named Plancia Magna was responsible for many public sculptures incorporated into the well-preserved rebuilt city gate (Boatwright 1991; 1993; see essays 3.4, Wood; 4.1, Longfellow; 4.6, Kellum; and 5.5, Ng). Not only do these dedications provide a more extensive display of beneficence and response, they also demonstrate how *tituli* can be useful in preserving dedications by patrons who are not otherwise attested in the literary record. At Perge, Plancia Magna's sculptural display (dating to AD 121) was arranged within twenty-eight statue niches, half on either side of the gate and arrayed on two stories of a wall that defined the interior courtyard of the gate. A monumental triple passage arch was also erected, set between the gate and the city and adorned with additional sculpture. The sculptures in the courtyard niches fall into two categories: deities in the lower niches and city founders, both distant and more recent, in the upper. The deities included Apollo, Aphrodite, the Dioscuri, Heracles, Hermes, and Pan. Statue bases from the upper niches record dedications to Kalchas the Argive, Labos the Delphian, Leonthus the Lapith, Machaeon the Thessalian, Minyas the Orchomenian, Mopsos the Delphian, Rixos the Athenian, M. Plancius Varus (father of Plancia Magna), and C. Plancius Varus (brother of Plancia Magna), all labeled as city founders. The dedicatory inscriptions of the display equate Plancia's immediate family with the heroic city founders who are themselves placed in proximity to the deities, probably selected from those with sanctuaries in Perge. Missing is the city's most important deity, Artemis Pergaia, for whose statue a viewer only needed to turn toward the triple passage arch that spanned the road into the city.

The inscriptions on the arch indicate a different and more privileged sculptural display. Unlike the Greek inscriptions on the courtyard bases, all the arch inscriptions are in both Latin and Greek. Dedicatory inscriptions on both faces name Plancia Magna as the patron of the arch. The bases associated with the arch record dedications to Artemis Pergaia and the Tyche (or Genius) of Perge along with living and divine members of the imperial family, including Divus Augustus, Divus Nerva, Divus Traianus, Diva Marciana, Diva Matidia, Hadrian, Plotina Augusta, and Sabina Augusta. The titles on Hadrian's base are datable to AD 121, chronologically anchoring the entire lavish display. Creating a dynastic imperial monument, even one that incorporated deities, was a form of beneficence that first came about under Augustus and spread under the Julio-Claudians (Rose 1997, 32–50). Programmatic displays arranged in a *scaenae frons* format such as Plancia Magna's are known from many examples across the Roman East in the second and third centuries (Bol 1984; Burrell 2006; Longfellow 2011; see essay 4.1, Longfellow). A message of the entire display is the insertion of the imperial family among those deities most directly responsible for the success of Perge along with the ancestors and relatives of Plancia who defined the city.

The aggrandizement of Perge and the emperors extended as well to Plancia Magna, whose prominent name was clear to all literate viewers. In addition, reciprocity in the form familiar from the example of Cuspius may be seen in two slightly later inscribed statue bases dedicated to Plancia by Perge's city council and assembly and by its council of elders (Boatwright 1993, 200) that named her as priestess of Artemis Pergaia and priestess of the Mother of the Gods. The example of Plancia, her image, and her name were prominent in a nearby display just outside the gate, in a wall at least 10 m in length with three statue niches. The center statue was of an unknown male while the two flanking niches held statues of Plancia: one dedicated by M. Plancius Pius to his patroness, and the other dedicated by M. Plancius Alexandros naming Plancia as priestess of the imperial cult. The inscriptions from Perge demonstrate reciprocity of Plancia's benefaction through the dedication of additional public sculpture. In fact, inscriptions preserve the names of hundreds of women who dedicated sculptures across the Roman world, although these actions are nearly invisible in the literary records. Clearly, women established public personas through sculpture; Plancia's programmatic displays also characterized her community's public identity.

Sculptural Displays and Imperial Dynasty

While Plancia's extensive benefaction represents a synchronic dedication, inscriptions on other works illustrate the agglutinative nature of imperial sculptural displays assembled over long periods by both individuals and groups. More than 2300 dedications to the imperial family have been documented across the Roman world (Højte 2005, 217). They generally commemorate either an event that occurred in the life of the dedicator (the vast majority), or an event in the life of the honoree (*pace*: Højte 2005, 179). Events in the life of the dedicator include manumission, retirement, election to public office, and the like. An inscribed base for a statue of Trajan (*CIL* 6.40489) illustrates the dedicator's priorities. Of the nine lines in the inscription, seven detail the career of the dedicator, while only two give the name and titles of the emperor. Inscriptions clearly document statuary erected in response to imperial deaths and accessions. Even though scholars have claimed that imperial statues also commemorated imperial triumphs, visits, anniversaries, and other events, little or no evidence supports such assertions. While isolated statues of a single emperor are known, in other cases statue groups were set up either all at once or in phases, on a single base or on separately inscribed bases.

Extensive evidence for some of the earliest sculptural dedications to the imperial family can be found at Ephesus, where multiple monuments to Julius Caesar, Augustus, and Livia were erected (Price 1984, 254–7). Among the sculptural groups to Augustus, one

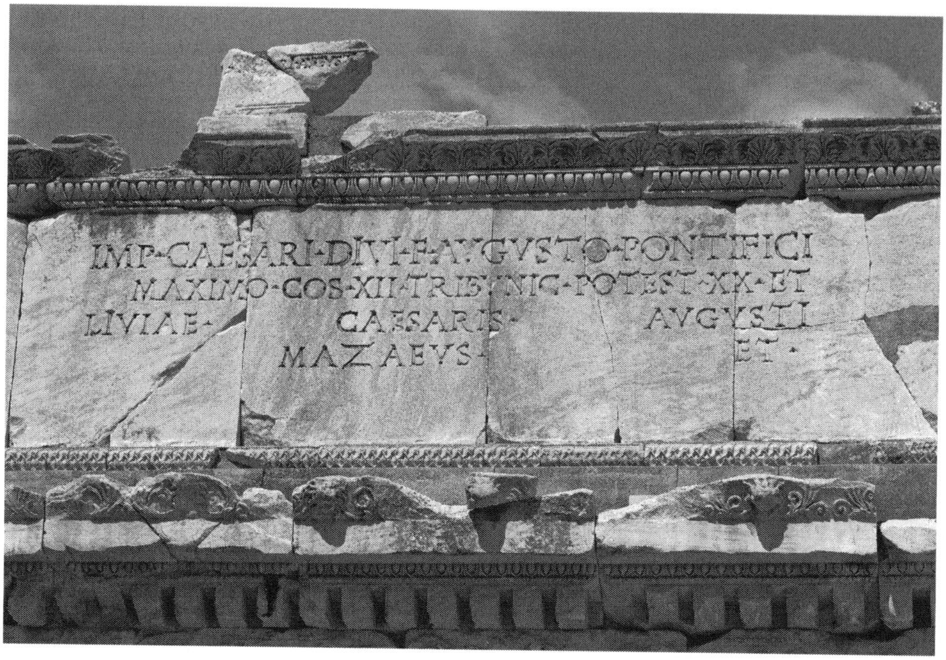

FIGURE 4.5.2 Dedication of Mazaeus from market gate at Ephesus (Mithridates section not shown); note the statue base to Lucius Caesar placed on the top of the gateway, 4/3 BC.

topped a triple passage arch that served as an entrance to the agora of Ephesus, dedicated in 4/3 BC as the letter channels for the missing bronze dedicatory inscription reveal (*AE* 1904, 98; Rose 1997, no. 112; Højte 2005, Augustus 166) (figure 4.5.2):

> Imp(eratori) Caesari Divi f(ilio) Augusto pontifici / maximo co(n)s(uli) XII tribunic(ia) potest(ate) XX et / Liviae Caesaris Augusti // M(arco) Agrippae L(uci) f(ilio) co(n)s(uli) tert(ium) imb(eratori)(!) tribunic(ia) / potest(ate) VI et / Iuliae Caesaris Augusti fil(iae) // Mazaeus et Mithridates patronis

Cuttings on the top of the gate prove that the arch served as a monumental statue base for an imperial dynastic group, restorable from the inscription as originally consisting of statues of Augustus and Livia paired on a common base above the left passage and statues of Agrippa and Julia paired on a single base above the right. The motivation for the dedication seems to have been a desire by the two freedmen to recognize their patrons and patrons' wives. The occasion is less certain. It may have been planned during Agrippa's and Julia's travels in the area from 16 to 13 BC or, more probably, in 12 BC on the death of Agrippa. In either event Augustus's titles date from the year 4/3 BC when Julia was married to Tiberius, a fact that is ignored in the nomenclature and pairing of statues, none of which survive.

A separate, freestanding base for a statue of Lucius Caesar was also found during excavations. It could not have been part of the original statue group on the top of the gate, since his name is not included in the dedicatory inscription. A base for his brother

Gaius was not found, suggesting that this was not set up on the occasion of their adoption by Augustus, but more likely in AD 2 on the death of Lucius. Whether Gaius was similarly commemorated upon his death in AD 4 is unknown, but the nomenclature referring to Lucius as a son of Augustus, which he was by adoption, rather than Agrippa, his birth father, leads to the conclusion that the statue was set up next to Augustus (Rose 1997, 174). The inscriptions represent two separate reactions to changing dynastic realities in the imperial family. One event, the marriage of Tiberius and Julia, is ignored, while a subsequent event, the death of Lucius, seems to have led to the augmentation of the display. This *titulus* reveals the desire to commemorate a direct connection between individuals and the imperial family. It also allows the significant observation that the formulae of *tituli* do not necessarily follow those found in more official dedications. The variations illustrate the needs and desires of the dedicators and possibly the context for the dedication.

A different solution to the problems of dynastic commemoration is found in a set of inscriptions from Rome associated with a shrine to the imperial cult dedicated by the *aenatores*, a group of musicians who play bronze instruments. Because this dynastic commemoration was dedicated by a group rather than an individual and its main monument eventually took the form of a single updated statue group rather than one with auxiliary additions as at Ephesus, these dedications provide unique examples of multigenerational corporate dedicators, illustrating the continuity of sculptural display and its role as a medium for public benefactions by an organization. They also demonstrate the use of inscriptions to write the history, sometimes very complex, of a dynastic monument. At the shrine, discovered in 1992 between the Arch of Constantine and the northeast corner of the Palatine, excavators found a fragmentary bronze sheet from the front of a base for a single statue (*CIL* 6.40334) and a long, rectangular marble base designed to accommodate five or six statues with several inscriptions along the sides (*CIL* 6.40307). Such a bronze sheet, originally anchored to the front of a base for a bronze statue, is a rarely found form of inscription, as these sheets generally suffer the same fate as the bronze statues themselves (Højte 2005, 182). Its inscription reads:

> Ti(berio) Cla[ud]io Ti(beri) f(ilio) / [Ne]roni / pon[t(ifici) co(n)s(uli) II i]mp(eratori) II / [ae]n(e)ator[e]s tubicines / l[iti]cines co[r]nicines / Romani

Tiberius's nomenclature and titles give a date between 8 BC and 4 BC (Morizio 1996; Boschung 2002). Since he went into voluntary exile on Rhodes in 6 BC, the period from 8 BC to 7 BC seems far more likely for such an expensive dedication (on the cost of imperial statues, see Højte 2005, 52–6). The musicians who dedicated the statue included the *tubicines*, who played a straight horn; *liticines*, players of the curved trumpet; and *cornicines*, players of the large bronze instrument that wrapped around the player's body. All of these were originally military instruments, but were also used at Rome for sacred ceremonies, processions, and in the games at the Colosseum, and these players were all joined into a single organization of *aenatores* (Vincent 2013). The proximity of this shrine to the Colosseum may be significant here or it may be coincidental, as it is also adjacent to the triumphal procession route, another venue for these players. The

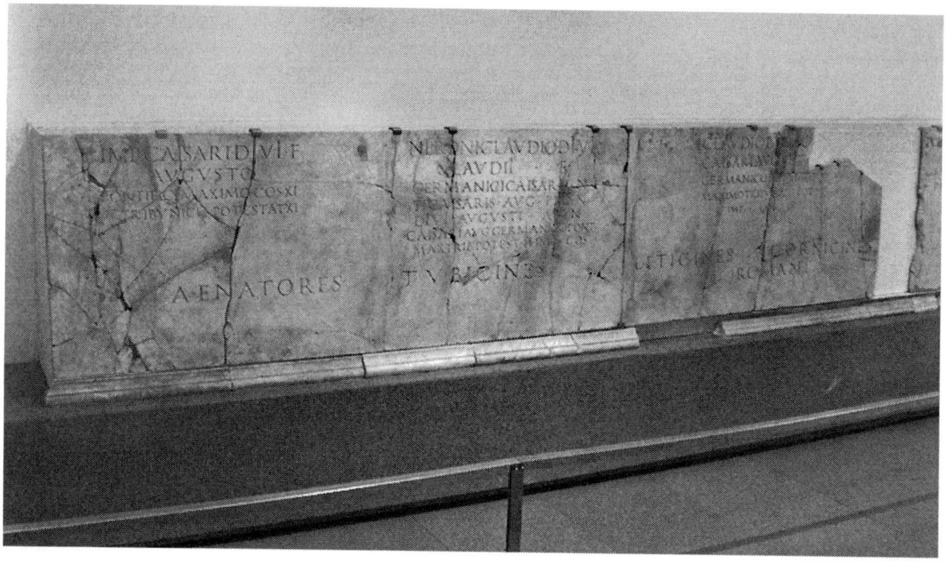

FIGURE 4.5.3 Three of the four *tituli* on the large base dedicated by the *aenatores* at Rome, c. AD 56.

inscriptions on the large marble base have a more complicated history than the bronze sheet, but also provide us with an extraordinary multigenerational series of dedications to the imperial family by the same body of dedicators (figure 4.5.3):

> Imp(eratori) Ca<e=I>sari divi f(ilio) / Augusto / pontifici maximo co(n)s(uli) XI / tribunicia potestat(e) XI // Neroni Claudio divi / Claudii f(ilio) / Germanici Ca<e=I>saris n(epoti) / Ti(beri) Ca<e=I>saris Aug(usti) pron(epoti) / divi Augusti abn(epoti) / Ca<e=I>sari Aug(usto) Germanico pont(ifici) / max(imo) trib(unicia) potest(ate) II imp(eratori) co(n)s(uli) // Ti(berio) Claudio Drusi f(ilio) / Ca<e=I>sari Augusto / Germanico pontifici / maximo tribunicia pot(estate) / imp(eratori) co(n)s(uli) II // Iuliae Au[gustae] / Agri[ppinae] / Germanic[i Caesaris f(iliae)] / divi Cla[udi uxori] // Aen(e)atores tubicines liticines cornicines Romani / {Romani}

The facing from this large base survives in three sections. It preserves *tituli* of four missing bronze statues that were once set above each inscription spaced the length of the base. The names of the dedicators run across the bottom of all the slabs with the word *Romani*, the only portion of the dedicators' name on the final slab under the fourth inscription, also repeated under the third inscription. In order from the left, the inscriptions name four members of the imperial family from the first century. On the far left is Augustus, his nomenclature and titles datable to between 6 March 12 BC and 11 June 11 BC. To his right was a statue of Nero dedicated sometime from late AD 55 to 56. Third in line was a statue of Claudius with titular formulae datable to 1–25 of January AD 42. Finally, a statue of Agrippina was on the far right, probably contemporary with the statue of Nero in AD 55–6. The dates and names allow us to reconstruct the history of display here at the shrine and demonstrate that the musicians made dedications here over a period of seventy years.

The statues of Augustus and Claudius were, like that of Tiberius, probably set up on individual bases in 11 BC and AD 42. In AD 55, shortly after Nero came to power, the large dedication was created to make a visual link between Nero, his mother, and the deified members of the dynasty. At that time the large base was created and the *tituli* of Augustus and Claudius were copied onto it without being updated, preserving the evidence of prior dedications by the *aenatores*. Shortly after her death in AD 59, Agrippina's statue was removed along with the slab that carried her *titulus* as well as the last word of the dedication, *Romani*. The word *Romani* was then inscribed on the Claudius slab below the names *liticines* and *cornicines*. Study of the inscriptions reveals the history of the dedications that were made or altered in 11 BC, 7 BC, AD 42, AD 55, and AD 59, all in the names of the *aenatores*, who seem to have maintained their connection to this cult site until it was destroyed in the great fire of AD 64. These dedications are credited only to the organization; none of the members are named. These *tituli* illustrate the attempts of a professional organization whose work relied on public events to navigate the changing world of the Julio-Claudian dynasty, demonstrating their support of and loyalty to the imperial family while adjusting the display to remove dedications to dead and dishonored members. It charts a form of flexible sculptural patronage designed to promote the interests of a specific group.

In other instances, such as the Caserma dei Vigili at Ostia, the dedications range from completely anonymous to those credited to an organization or those dedicated by an individual on behalf of an organization. The headquarters (Caserma) of the firefighters (Italian, *vigili*; Latin, *vigiles*) at Ostia was originally constructed under Domitian. As rebuilt during the reign of Hadrian, a two story structure surrounded an open rectangular courtyard; the main entrance on one short end faced a temple-like shrine for the worship of the emperors on the other end of the courtyard. This type of space is known from military camps, the Villa of Hadrian, and civic sites around the Roman Empire. Within the shrine are dedications to members of the imperial family, including at least two inscribed marble altars and four marble statue bases, some of which carried life-size or larger precious-metal statues like the ones dedicated by Cuspius at Pompeii. The inscriptions record dedications to Lucius Aelius Verus Caesar, adoptive son of Hadrian (AD 137), Antoninus Pius (AD 138), Marcus Aurelius (a base from AD 140–44 and an altar from AD 162), Lucius Verus (AD 162), and Septimius Severus (an altar from AD 194–5). The dedication to Septimius Severus is inscribed over an erased text, probably originally a dedication to Commodus. In the courtyard are several other bases. Dedications to Septimius Severus, his sons Geta and Caracalla, and his wife Julia Domna (all from AD 207) were set against the columns and brick piers across the front of the shrine. The text to Geta was erased after he had been murdered in AD 211. To the left are dedications to Caracalla (AD 211), Gordianus III (AD 239), and his wife, Furia Sabinia Tranquillina (AD 241–4). In a nearby room a statue base with a dedication to Diadumenianus (AD 218) was found.

The *tituli*, although ranging over a century in date, are consistently inscribed with monumental lettering with very few abbreviations on very high-quality marble bases.

They display one notable development and that is in the pattern of attributing patronage. The oldest inscriptions carry only the name and titles of the emperor whose statue they labeled. The early Marcus Aurelius inscription, for example, reads:

> M(arco) Aurelio Caesari / Imp(eratoris) Caesaris T(ito) Aeli Hadriani / Antonini Augusti Pii filio / Divi Hadriani Nepoti Divi Traiani / pronepoti Divi Nervae abnep(oti) co(n)s(uli) / Optimo ac Piissimo (*CIL* 14.4366)

However, beginning with the AD 162 altar of Marcus Aurelius and base of Lucius Verus, the *cohortes vigilum* are credited with the dedications, but in the simplest terms, with the number of the *cohors* added to the inscription as a final line:

> Imp(eratori) Caesari / Divi Antonini Filio Divi Ha / driani Nep(oti) Divi Traiani Par / thici Pronep(oti) Divi Nervae Abn(epoti) / L(uci) Avrelio Vero Aug(usto) Trib(unicia) Pot(estate) II / Co(n)s(uli) II / Cohortes VII Vig(ilum) (*CIL* 14.4376)

The next development is seen in the third-century inscriptions which are dedicated in the name of the *praefectus*, and, sometimes, the *subpraefectus*, and eventually the *praepositus* of the *vigiles*:

> Iuliae / Aug(ustae) / Matri Augusti / Et Kastrorum / Sub Cn(aeo) M(arco) Rustio Rufino / Pr(aefecto) Vig(ilum) E(gregio) V(iro) / Curantibvs / C(aio) Laecanio Novatilliano / Subpr(aefecto) Et / M(arco) Fl(avio) Raesiano Trib(uno) Coh(ortis) II Vig(ilum) / Praeposito Vexillationis (*CIL* 14.4386)

The pattern seems clear. The initial dedications were inscribed exclusively with the name of the honoree. About thirty years later the expectation became one of acknowledging the *vigiles* whose responsibility for the dedications had previously been understood. Then, beginning about thirty years after that, the desire for personal recognition and aggrandizement led to the listing of the names of the officers in charge of the 320 men stationed here. The final dedication in the series, to Furia Sabinia Tranquillina (AD 241–4), is a fourteen-line inscription of which only five lines list the names and titles of Furia, while nine are given over to the names and titles of the dedicators. None of these dedications give an indication of the circumstances under which they were erected. Some may have been dedicated to celebrate events in the lives of the dedicators, such as their commencement of term of office. Judging by the dates, however, it seems that sculptural dedications were a customary response to the accession of a new emperor, as many of these dedications were made in the year following a new emperor's taking office or undergoing a major change in status (Fishwick 1987, 482, 501). The renewal of service oaths at the start of the new year might be the occasion for these dedications. The shift to include recognition of the officers of the *cohortes* reflects the primary audience of the shrine: present and subsequent members of the same organization. The display reinforces the loyalty of the organization as a whole as well, as the *pietas* of the officers, perhaps self-consciously designed as models for their successors. In contrast to the consistent anonymity of the first-century musicians of the previous example, here the *tituli* reveal changes during the second and third centuries in the recognition of the dedicators. The names and titles of

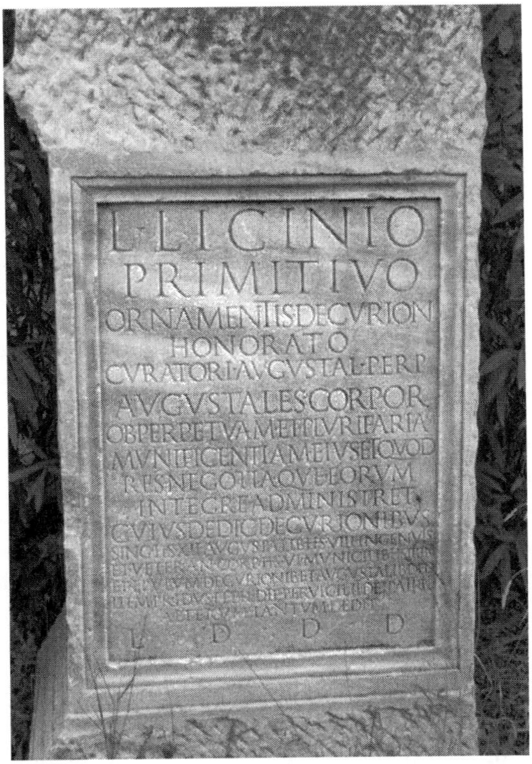

FIGURE 4.5.4 Statue base for L. Licinius Primitivus from the Sacellum of the Augustales, Misenum, AD 169.

the officers gradually take on a greater role perhaps celebrating their individual *pietas* or perhaps reflecting the increasing uncertainty of the third century and the need to more explicitly declare support for the rapidly changing imperial family.

Similar issues of personal aggrandizement, corporate identity, and benefaction are found in a shrine to the imperial cult at Misenum. Here, however, a more extensive dialogue is revealed as a freedman is honored for his beneficence and that honor is extended by his widow to solidify his reputation and her rise in status in this religious group and community. The *sacellum* of the Augustales of Misenum, a shrine and headquarters of a group of freedmen priests to the cult of the emperors (Fishwick 1987, 609–619; see essay 4.6, Kellum), featured ten statue bases found in the courtyard in front of the *sacellum* and under the surrounding portico (figure 4.5.4). Among them the base of the now-missing bronze statue of Q. Cominius Abascantus erected by his wife, Nymphidia Monime, carries inscriptions on three sides, which chart a series of events whose sequence can be reconstructed (D'Arms 2000, 143; Zevi 2000). The sequence began with Cominius's dedication of two statues in the forum and associated grants of money to members of the town by AD 147. Shortly following this series of benefactions, the Augustales responded by awarding him *ornamenta decurionalia* and other honors, all recorded in the first inscription on the front of the base. After his death, his widow dedicated his statue and made a further grant of money, as the first inscription (on the front of the base) describes. A second inscription added later in AD 148 by the executor of Cominius's estate documents bequests and legacies to the Augustales (on the right side of the base). Early in AD 149, Monime was adlected in the college of the Augustales as recorded in their decree, the third inscription added to the base (on the left side). A single statue proves the imperial cult as a vehicle for advancement, but the dialogue of patronage and beneficence occurs only between local members of the community.

Conclusion

Epigraphy offers some major contributions to the study of Roman sculpture and its patronage. The basic details and conditions of sculptural dedication including date, physical location, cost, form, context, and dedicators of a sculpture or sculptural group are preserved by their *tituli*. More importantly, this information can be analyzed for social, religious, military, and personal structures and patterns across the Roman world. By study of the epigraphy sculpture is discovered to have been used by local elites, such as Plancia Magna at Perge, to establish or assert their place in the community. It is used, as at Ephesus under Augustus, by other locals—arguably subelite—to announce personal relationships with the highest levels of Roman society. Assemblages of sculptures, notably to the emperors and imperial family, show a dialogue of patronage and commemoration that reveals the social, religious, and political world of which sculpture is a product.

It is clear that worship of the imperial cult or even celebration of the imperial family is a remarkably important medium for municipal advancement across the Roman world. Our evidence for the reciprocal exchanges that occur at the local level comes almost exclusively from epigraphy with well-understood examples from Ostia, Misenum, and Rome. Many others could be added of course. The practical result of these dedications is the social and political establishment and advancement of individuals, families, and groups whose public beneficence included sculptural displays.

The work of collecting inscriptions and applying basic analysis to them to understand patterns, whether spatial, chronological, or social, is well established by now. Coupled with an understanding of the patterns of imperial epithets and projected qualities, the dialogue between dedicator and honoree seems prescriptive and based on terms established by the imperial family. Future study of these materials is likely to challenge that. As the Ephesus dedication exemplified variation from the contemporary arrangement of the imperial family based on the freedom of choice by the patrons, an understudied area for the same type of variation is epithets. Dedicators certainly selected epithets not found in official images and documents and therefore not reflecting official versions of the imperial image. For example, groups of sculptural dedications (*CIL* 6.1066, 6.31338a, vel sim.) cite the *indulgentia* of Caracalla, not one of his officially celebrated virtues (Noreña 2001; 2011). Use of the inscriptions now available through searchable online databases will likely allow us to reconstruct a dialogue in sculpture and epigraphy whose form was as much the creation of the dedicators as the imperial honorees.

Online Databases of Inscriptions

Epigraphic Database Heidelberg: http://edh-www.adw.uni-heidelberg.de/

Electronic Archive of Greek and Latin Epigraphy: http://www.edr-edr.it/

Epigraphik-Datenbank Clauss-Slaby: http://www.manfredclauss.de/

Corpus Inscriptionum Latinarum: http://cil.bbaw.de/

Arachne, the central object database of the German Archaeological Institute (DAI) and the Archaeological Institute of the University of Cologne includes scans of *CIL*: http://arachne.uni-koeln.de/drupal/

Bibliography

Benefiel, R. 2004. "Pompeii, Puteoli, and the Status of a *Colonia* in the Mid-First Century AD." In *Pompei, Capri e la Penisola Sorrentina*, edited by F. Senatore, 349–68. Rome: Bardi.

Boatwright, M. T. 1991. "Plancia Magna of Perge: Women's Roles and Status in Asia Minor." In *Women's History and Ancient History*, edited by S. Pomeroy, 249–72. Chapel Hill: University of North Carolina Press.

———. 1993. "The City Gate of Plancia Magna in Perge." In *Roman Art in Context: An Anthology*, edited by E. D'Ambra, 189–207. Englewood Cliffs: Prentice Hall.

Bol, R. 1984. *Das Statuenprogramm des Herodes-Atticus-Nymphäums*. OlForsch 15. Berlin: Walter de Gruyter.

Boschung, D. 2002. *Gens Augusta: Untersuchungen zur Aufstellung, Wirkung und Bedeutung der Statuengruppen des julisch-claudischen Kaiserhauses*. Monumenta Artis Romanae 32. Mainz: Philipp von Zabern.

Burrell, B. 2006. "Separating the Aedicular Facade from the Imperial Cult in Roman Asia Minor." *AJA* 110(3): 437–69.

Cooley, A. E., and M. G. L. Cooley. 2004. *Pompeii: A Sourcebook*. London: Routledge.

D'Arms, J. H. 2000. "Memory, Money, and Status at Misenum: Three New Inscriptions from the Collegium of the Augustales." *JRS* 90: 126–44.

De Caro, S. 1994. *Il Museo Archeologico Nazionale di Napoli*. Naples: Electa.

Descœudres, J. P. 2007. "History and Historical Sources." In *The World of Pompeii*, edited by J. J. Dobbins and P. W. Foss, 9–27. London: Routledge.

Duncan-Jones, R. 1982. *The Economy of the Roman Empire: Quantitative Studies*. Cambridge: Cambridge University Press.

Fejfer, J. 2008. *Roman Portraits in Context*. Berlin: Walter de Gruyter.

Fishwick, D. 1987. *The Imperial Cult in the Latin West: Studies in the Ruler Cult of the Western Provinces of the Roman Empire*. Vol. 2, pt. 1. Leiden: Brill.

Flower, H. I. 2006. *The Art of Forgetting: Disgrace and Oblivion in Roman Political Culture*. Chapel Hill: University of North Carolina Press.

Forbis, E. 1996. *Municipal Virtues in the Roman Empire: The Evidence of Italian Honorary Inscriptions.* Stuttgart: Teubner.

Franklin, J. L., Jr. 2004. *"Pompeis Difficile Est": Studies in the Political Life of Imperial Pompeii.* Ann Arbor: University of Michigan Press.

Harrison, G. M. W. 1993. *The Romans and Crete.* Amsterdam: Adolf M. Hakkert.

Højte, J. M. 2005. *Roman Imperial Statue Bases: From Augustus to Commodus.* Aarhus: Aarhus University Press.

Longfellow, B. 2011. *Roman Imperialism and Civic Patronage: Form, Meaning and Ideology in Monumental Fountain Complexes.* Cambridge: Cambridge University Press.

Morizio, V. 1996. "La base in bronzo con dedica a Tiberio." In *Meta Sudans I: Un'area sacra in Palatio e la valle del Colosseo prima e dopo Nerone*, edited by C. Panella, 115–31. Rome: Istituto poligrafico e Zecca dello Stato.

Noreña, C. F. 2001. "The Communication of the Emperor's Virtues." *JRS* 91: 146–68.

———. 2011. *Imperial Ideals in the Roman West: Representation, Circulation, Power.* Cambridge: Cambridge University Press.

Potter, D. S., and C. Damon. 1999. "The *Senatus Consultum De Cn. Pisone Patre.*" *AJP* 120(1): 13–41.

Price, S. R. F. 1984. *Rituals and Power: The Roman Imperial Cult in Asia Minor.* Cambridge: Cambridge University Press.

Rose, C. B. 1997. *Dynastic Commemoration and Imperial Portraiture in the Julio-Claudian Period.* Cambridge: Cambridge University Press.

Salomies, O. 1994. "Observations on the Development of the Style of Latin Honorific Inscriptions during the Empire." *Arctos* 28: 63–106.

Tuck, S. L. 2005. *Latin Inscriptions in the Kelsey Museum: The Dennison and De Criscio Collections.* Ann Arbor: University of Michigan Press.

———. 2008. "Scheduling Spectacle: Factors contributing to the Dates of Pompeian *Munera*." *RStPomp* 19: 25–34.

Vincent, A. 2013. "Les *aenatores*: Une catégorie de musiciens au service de la cité." In *Le statut du musicien dans l'Antiquité: Egypte, Mésopotamie, Grèce, Rome*, edited by S. Emerit, 239–58. Bibliothèque d'étude 159. Le Caire: Presses de l'IFAO.

Yarrow, L. 2006. "Lucius Mummius and the Spoils of Corinth." *Scripta Classica Israelica* 25: 57–70.

Zevi, F. 2000. "The Epigraphic Evidence." In *Il Sacello degli Augustali di Miseno: Museo archeologico dei Campi Flegrei nel Castello di Baia*, edited by P. Miniero, 47–62. Naples: Electa.

CHAPTER 4.6

IMPERIAL MESSAGES

BARBARA KELLUM

Introduction

In AD 148, Cornelius Fronto, writing to the imperial heir apparent Marcus Aurelius, declared: "You know how in all the banks and stands and storefronts and shops and arcades and entryways and windows, everywhere and every moment, images of you all are displayed to the public—they are badly painted, sure, and most of them are shaped or carved under the inspiration of a thick, or should I say a mud-caked Muse, but when your image, no matter how unlike you, catches my eye on my way, this never happens without jolting from my mouth the gape and the dream of a kiss" (*ad Marc. Caes.* 4.12.6 [van den Hout]; trans. Richlin 2007, 144). Though the profoundly emotional response of Fronto, the emperor's tutor, to this viewing experience may be what most immediately catches readers' imaginations (Richlin 2007, 143–7), two other aspects of this passage are of interest for our exploration of sculptural delivery of imperial messages: first, the sheer ubiquity of images of the imperial family to which the text attests, and second the authorship of those likenesses across a wide social spectrum and for a variety of purposes.

More than twenty-five years ago, Paul Zanker, in his now-classic *The Power of Images in the Age of Augustus*, insisted that there was no "propaganda machine" at work in the imperial messages of Augustan Rome; rather a new visual language of peace and prosperity with the emperor at its center was gradually internalized in acts of patronage at every social level, empire-wide (Zanker 1988, 3, 291, 335–6). Zanker's work is important for many reasons, but for our purposes here, it highlights the visual dialogue initiated by a range of patrons (imperial and non-imperial) that occurred empire-wide through sculptural representations of the emperor and imperial family, often depicted along with members of the local elite. As this essay will outline, imperial messages were communicated through large quantities of statuary that fulfilled many functions and came in a range of formats. Most importantly, this essay will demonstrate that these imperial messages were often initiated by the emperor himself, the imperial family, or imperial agents, but that patronage of sculpture which broadcast imperial messages was also undertaken by local elite and other nonimperial individuals. I suggest that the sculptural evidence demonstrates that Romans were cognizant of and actively participated in this visual, sculptural dialogue and employed it not only to further imperial ideals but also to establish their own identities within a political and social milieu dominated by the emperor.

Quantity, Function, and Format

The omnipresence of images of the emperor is in itself difficult to overestimate. Michael Pfanner has calculated that during the era of Augustus alone, between 25,000 and 50,000 imperial statues were produced, and of course the numbers grew exponentially reign by reign thereafter (Pfanner 1989, 178–9). These imperial likenesses served many roles. Statues functioned as major punctuators of urban space and constituted an entire population in themselves, both at Rome and across the empire (Ando 2000, 233–45; Stewart 2003; Noreña 2011, 200–218). Interactions with statues of the emperor could be intense. In most courtrooms around the Roman world a statue of the emperor served as his proxy, and what was done or said in front of the statue was tantamount to doing or saying it before the emperor himself (Apul. *Apol.* 85, in Sabratha, Tripolitania). Statues of the emperor could serve as places of asylum for citizens and slaves alike (Philostr. *V A* 1.15; Plin. *Ep.* 10.74), but under tyrannical rulers they could prove deadly as well: under Tiberius, carrying a coin or a ring stamped with an image of the emperor into either a privy or a brothel was also potentially a capital offence (Suet. *Tib.* 58, cf. Sen. *Ben.* 3.26); during the reign of Caracalla, men were supposedly condemned to die for urinating too close to imperial statues (SHA *M. Ant.* 5.7). Equal and opposite, images of the emperor could become sites for popular intervention. For example, after Nero had murdered his mother, Agrippina, a sack was hung around the neck of a statue of Nero with a note saying he "deserved the sack," the punishment of the parricide: to be sewn into a sack with a dog, a cock, a snake, and a monkey, and thrown into the sea (Suet. *Ner.* 45.2, cf. *Aug.* 31.1). And of course the pulling down of the statues of condemned emperors was fundamentally important to the censure of them in the public memory, even if in practice these images were often refashioned into portraits of their successors (Suet. *Dom.* 23; Varner 2004; Fejfer 2008, 377–80).

In terms of format, portraits of the emperor came in all shapes and sizes, from colossal statues to miniature busts, although statuary types were conventionally few: the togate statue, the statue in military cuirass, the heroic nude or seminude statue, and the theomorphic (colossal: Pekáry 1985, 84–7; miniature: Dahmen 2001; types: Niemeyer 1968; Fejfer 2008, 395–404). Of course, imperial likenesses also appeared in the monumental relief sculpture that covered public buildings (see essay 3.5, Sobocinski and Wolfram Thill). Since the emperor's portrait also appeared on the obverse of coins, he was present in everyday financial transactions large and small.

The careful study of coin hoards and the central mint has yielded in-depth information about patterns of circulation and the ideological effectiveness of imperial ideals—peace, concord, and the virtues of the emperor—which the reverse types of the coins communicated (Wallace-Hadrill 1986; Noreña 2011). Although there is no doubt that prototypes of portrait statues of the emperor and his family were created in Rome, the pattern of their empire-wide distribution remains hypothetical (Rose 1997, 57–9; Fejfer 2008, 407–425; Mayer 2010, 112–14). Over the past twenty years, however, close scrutiny of imperial portrait statue groups across the Roman world has revealed a great deal, establishing secure correspondences between portrait and inscription and arriving at a whole new level of understanding of the politics of imperial portrait display (Rose 1990, 463–7; 1997).

Patronage: Imperial

In terms of patronage at Rome, imperial family monuments were decreed by the Senate, as were major monuments such as the still-extant Ara Pacis (*RG* 12; Torelli 1982, 27–61) or the arch in the Circus Flaminius populated with statues of Germanicus and members of his extended family. However, the Senate was not the only player in the game of constructing imperial messages. The emperor played a role as well. For example, beginning in 7 BC Augustus established—or revived—the cults of Rome's neighborhoods by gifting each with a pair of statuettes of the Lares Augusti. The Belvedere altar actually shows the emperor, his toga reverently pulled over his head just as on the Ara Pacis, handing the statuettes to the local *magistri vici*. On a grander scale, imperial- or Senate-sponsored monuments at Rome included the better-known monuments such as arches, imperial fora, and the treasure-packed porticoed complexes that became the hallmark of Rome in the early imperial period (see essays 4.1, Longfellow; and 6.3, Shaya).

These porticoed complexes structured the fabric of the city itself (Strabo 5.3.8) and put on display a staggering array of works of art garnered as booty in the conquest of the Greek East. These were works from all stylistic periods—the archaic to the Hellenistic—and provided the basis for what Tonio Hölscher has identified as the "semantic system" of Roman art, emulating Greek styles in Roman genres such as portraiture and historical relief (Hölscher [1987] 2004). Others have characterized these spaces as veritable museums for the display of Greek plunder which served both as markers of cultural sophistication and as the ultimate indicators of Rome's imperial power (Rutledge 2012, 31, 123–57, 221–62; see essay 6.3, Shaya). The emphasis here is on these objects as Greek cultural property utilized to create a narrative about the divine and heroic heritage of the *princeps*. For example, the many statues of Aphrodite in the Augustan Porticus of Octavia were to be associated with the descent of the Julian line from the goddess's Roman equivalent Venus, while the spectacular Battle of Granikos group in the same porticus—featuring life-size bronze statues of Alexander the Great and his twenty-five young lieutenants by the fourth-century sculptor Lysippos—was, like the Alexander memorabilia in many Augustan buildings, intended to link the emperor with the famed Macedonian world conqueror (Rutledge 2012, 261–2).

Still, it is worth bearing in mind that many of these Augustan complexes freely juxtaposed Greek masterpieces with objects of natural wonder. In the Saepta Julia, which Agrippa adorned with paintings and the marble statues of Olympus and Pan and of Chiron and Achilles by Praxiteles or Scopas—works considered "so valuable that their keepers must answer for their safety with their lives" (Plin. *HN* 36.29, trans. Eichholz 1971)—a one-hundred-foot larchwood beam from the wide-span roof of the adjacent Diribitorium (voting hall in the Campus Martius) was also proudly on display and much acclaimed as a miracle of cutting-edge technology (Cass. Dio 53.23; Plin. *HN* 16.201, 36.102). In Augustan Rome, larchwood beams as well as Greek works of art and new statues were a part of imperial message making and all elements were metamorphosed to serve contemporary purposes.

Thus the very ancient ivory image of the warrior goddess Athena Alea from Tegea by the sixth-century BC sculptor Endoeus that stood at the entry of the Forum of Augustus carried with it a very modern message about the emperor's transporting it to Rome after the defeat of Mark Antony and his allies, among whom were the Tegeans (Paus. 8.46.1–5). Another treasure-house, the *Aedes Concordiae Augustae*—dedicated by the heir apparent Tiberius in AD 10 on 16 January, the day Augustus had assumed his cognomen—was filled with Greek artwork, but these statues were artfully arranged to bespeak the contemporary message of *pax deorum*, the very essence of Concordia Augusta, mirroring the balance struck between members of the imperial family and between social orders within the state, and ultimately reflecting the order of the cosmos itself (Kellum 1990). Although carefully structured, this program was not systematic or intended to be read detail for detail. Rather everywhere one looked—from the bronze sculptures by the Hellenistic sculptor Baton depicting Apollo and Juno (respectively the divine mainstay and arch-nemesis of Aeneas during most of the *Aeneid*), here reconciled (Plin. *HN* 34.73), to the teamwork of the paired rams, which leapt from the corners of the acanthus foliage of the temple's interior order—there were multiple embodiments of Concordia Augusta made manifest.

This phenomenon of instantiation through representation characterizes all the treasure-filled building complexes of Augustan Rome and gave tangible form to imperial concepts. In establishing his new dynasty, Vespasian made sure that his magnificent Templum Pacis had a panoply of Greek art by Lysippos, Pheidias, Praxiteles, and Cephisodotus among others on display as well as the famed captured spoils from the temple in Jerusalem (Rutledge 2012, 272–84). As Josephus observed "To be sure, into that temple were collected and contained everything which men previously travelled all over the world to see" (*BJ* 7.162, trans. Thackeray 1976), but as Carlos Noreña has articulated so well, it is the personification to which the complex is dedicated, *Pax* in her military aspect: "*Pax* was a core ideal in the official construction of Vespasian's public image and one of the central claims on which the legitimacy of his principate was based" (Noreña 2003, 29). The complex was a public celebration of empire touted in both the dedication of the building in AD 75 and in an all-time spike in the depiction of *Pax* on denarii produced in the same year. This coordination of two systems of imperial communication is good indication of a well-oiled imperial message-making machine (Noreña 2003, 31–41).

One of the most boldly innovative as well as the most controversial triumphal monuments in the city of Rome is the Column of Trajan in his Forum (see essay 3.5, Sobocinski and Wolfram Thill). The 155 scenes of Trajan's Dacian campaigns spiraling up the column have long been the passion of military historians, who relish its minutely detailed representations of the Roman army (Lepper and Frere 1988). *In situ*, however, it is a different story. The column height—35 m atop its massive base—and its placement in close proximity to the libraries and the Basilica Ulpia—make the continuous narrative on the column impossible to follow as the helical bands of sculpture rise relentlessly upward toward the sky. Some have suggested that viewing the column from the second story of the libraries and the basilica might have made some portions more legible, and Penelope Davies has argued that the repeated circumambulation required to see the monument may have ritual significance as the column functioned as Trajan's tomb (Davies 1997). Both Salvatore Settis and Richard Brilliant have also analyzed the vertical correspondences between scenes and other visual devices including the use of paint that would have highlighted the figure of the emperor and underscored the main message of his omnipresence in this epic drama (Brilliant 1984, 90–108; Settis 1988). Although I think the Column of Trajan may have yet more to reveal about our own text-bound assumptions regarding how to "read" a monument and about what makes Rome's visual culture a distinctive one (Veyne 1988), it was in the second century at least clearly considered a good mode via which to broadcast imperial messages, since it served as the model for the Column of Marcus Aurelius, and the relationship between the two is capably assessed by Martin Beckmann in his recent monograph on the later column (Beckmann 2011).

Although Trajan's Forum with its column was the last of the imperial fora built in Rome, other traditional forms of imperial commemoration persisted, one of which was the triumphal arch. The new Severan dynasty was honored by a massive arch erected in AD 203, voted on by the Senate, built adjacent to the Curia in the Forum Romanum, and dedicated to Septimius and his sons Caracalla and Geta in honor of Septimius's Parthian victories. The large relief panels detailing the victories are adaptations of the helical bands of the Columns of Trajan and Marcus Aurelius, with the figure of the emperor depicted frontally to emphasize him the more (Brilliant 1967; Newby 2007, 201–6; Mayer 2010, 127–8).

One late example of urban orchestration of sculpture (and architecture) on a massive scale to broadcast imperial messages comes from the Arch of Constantine, erected just after this once-tetrarch became emperor in AD 312. As Elizabeth Marlowe has demonstrated, the placement of the Arch of Constantine, built to commemorate his victory over Maxentius at the Milvian Bridge, was aligned so that the central passageway of the arch framed the colossal bronze statue of the sun god Sol, which was first erected by Nero at the entry to his Golden House (Marlowe 2006). Vespasian had rededicated the statue to Sol, and although it had undergone various alterations over time, including an attempt to identify it with Maxentius's deceased son Divus Romulus (the fragments of the enormous inscription which accomplished this transformation found in the attic of the Arch of Constantine itself), the 38 m statue was reclaimed by Constantine for Sol in all his divine majesty. The brilliant interplay between the colossal statue of Sol and the arch would have begun as soon as a viewer caught sight of them along the Via Triumphalis and continued as s/he approached, with the relationship affirmed by several representations of Sol on the arch itself. This savvy placement of the arch also reframed the whole of the Colosseum Valley to which it gave entry, drawing together Hadrian's Temple of Venus and Rome, the Flavian amphitheater, and the Meta Sudans fountain in a new configuration that underscored Constantine's own supposed dynastic link with the Flavians and with the monuments of great emperors of the past, also demonstrated in the various spoliated relief sculptures from earlier imperial monuments incorporated into the arch.

Patronage: Local

For the present, however, in terms of patronage, it is both the breadth of the social net that was being cast and the loose connection to what has sometimes been termed "the imperial cult" that I would like to emphasize (Fishwick 1987–2005, 3:3.273–82; Beard, North, and Price 1998, 1: 348–63). Practices varied across time and space, but often the empire-wide distribution of imperial portraits and the broadcasting of imperial messages are intimately related to local officials or elite who are in one way or another associated with the emperor. In Italy and the West, members of the Augustales usually took the lead. Once thought to be simply municipal priests of the imperial cult, increasingly the Augustales have come to be regarded as an organized *ordo* of wealthy municipal freedmen next in social status to the *decuriones* (members of the town council; Ostrow 1985; D'Arms 2000). The remains of the *sacellum* of the Augustales at Misenum vividly illustrates the melding of these roles. The shrine featured two over-life-size marble statues of the heroically nude emperors Vespasian and Titus, and a bronze equestrian statue that started off life as a portrait of Domitian but was transformed into his successor Nerva after Domitian's *damnatio memoriae* (Muscettola 2000, 29–38). Ten additional statue bases in the precinct once carried statues of other emperors and divinities and at least two statues commemorating individual members of the Augustales. The base for the statue of Q. Cominius Abascantus, *curator perpetuus* of the Augustales, erected by his wife, Nymphidia Monime, in AD 148, bears three inscriptions that document the arrangements for the perpetuation of his memory in painstaking detail. The Augustales were provided a legacy in Cominius's will, intended to guarantee that every year at the Parentalia the statues of the Protectress of the Fleet and the Genius of the Town, which Cominius had erected in the Forum, be cleaned, oiled, and decorated with roses and violets and that every year on his birthday, December 17, there be an athletic performance, with ten pairs of wrestlers and a banquet for select municipal officials at his garden tomb. Perfumed nard was to be poured over his remains and honeyed wine provided for the populace, as well as a cash donation distributed according to status: 20 sesterces to decurions, 12 to each member of the Augustales, and lesser amounts to those lower on the social hierarchy (D'Arms 2000, 127–35). The public and performative aspects of these annual events and the intermingling of the memory of the individual Augustalis with the image of the emperor stamped on each of those sesterces speaks to the multiple ways in which imperial messages became integral to everyday lives.

Given the bounty of Cominius's bequest, it is perhaps not surprising that the third inscription on the statue base records the fact that the Augustales adlected his widow and heir Nymphidia into their corporation. This is the first evidence of women in the Augustales, but at Misenum at least it was not the last: in the 160s AD the *pronaos* of the *sacellum*—also termed the *Templum Augusti*—was refurbished by the priestess Cassia Victoria in her name and that of her deceased husband, the Augustalis L. Laecanius Primitivus. It is *their* portraits that appear in the *clipeus* at the center of the pediment surrounded by the oak-leaf *corona civica* held aloft by winged Victories (Muscettola 2000, 38–42; Fejfer 2008, 81–2). The couple's hair and beard styles are those popularized by the Antonine court, but the portrait features especially of Cassia Victoria are very individualized. This confluence of the imperial and the local pertains in every detail, for the *corona civica* had first been fastened above the doorway of Augustus's house on the Palatine (*RG* 34), but was soon adapted in municipal contexts as a sign of the Augustales, while the winged Victories, the quintessential symbol of imperial success, served simultaneously as an *image parlante* of the dedicator's name, Cassia Victoria.

A similar combination of the local and the imperial appears at the city gate complex at Perge in Lycia et Pamphylia (modern Turkey) where Plancia Magna, a major civic benefactress, refurbished the Hellenistic city gate during the Hadrianic period and was honored with a marble portrait statue at the front of the complex dedicated by her freedman Marcus Plancius Pius and honoring her as "priestess of the mother of the gods for life" and "high priestess of the emperors" (trans. Trimble 2011, 185). The body chosen for Plancia Magna's statue was the so-called Large Herculaneum Woman, a type that was popular for the civic portraiture of local and regional elites in the second century, but not often employed in empresses' portraits (Trimble 2011, 178–9). It seems significant, therefore, that when portraits of the empresses Sabina and Faustina Minor were added to the gate complex, it was Plancia Magna's statue type of the Large Herculaneum Woman which was utilized for the two empresses (Trimble 2011, 231). The same body type also likely unified imperial and nonimperial women at the giant Nymphaeum of Herodes Atticus and his wife, Regilla, at Olympia, which the wealthy Athenian sophist and exconsul built to honor his family and their close links to the imperial family (Trimble 2011, 237–44).

Imperial Messages: Reception and Response

But if these were the messages being broadcast, do we have any traces of how—or whether—they were received? I believe there is material evidence that Romans both comprehended how objects bespoke imperial ideals and made use of that understanding to themselves participate in imperial message-making and at the same time establish their own identities. For instance, sometime toward the end of Augustus's reign, Numerius Lucius Hermeros Aequitas, freedman of Numerius, one of Rome's neighborhood magistrates (*vicomagistri*) serving for the third time, dedicated a statue base (Lott 2004, 161–5, 209–210). The base to Venus Augusta has on it an image of doves drinking from a basin, certainly a free interpretation of a motif from the celebrated mosaic composition of the Pergamene artist Sosus as described by Pliny (*HN* 36.184). When the inscription was first published in 1980, Silvio Panciera pointed out this source and duly noted that doves were birds of Venus (Panciera 1980, 203–4). True enough, but I will urge that there is more here to be gleaned about the relationship between monument and dedicator. This was one of three statuary dedications by Numerius Lucius Hermeros Aequitas as one of the *vicomagistri* for the Forum Boarium, and in each instance, arguably, the monument is as much about himself as it is about the Augustan deities honored. His is the first name of three listed on the inaugural board of *vicomagistri*, which dedicated a statue to the August Mercury (Lott 2004, 184). At this point, he had only his former slave name—Hermeros—as cognomen, but Mercury (Hermes) was half his namesake. For his next dedication in AD 4/5, however, when Numerius Lucius was *magister iterum*, he pulled out all the stops and helped dedicate not only a statue of Hercules—a popular deity in the area of the Cattle Market—but also sets of gold and silver scales, which gained him the added cognomen Aequitas (Lott 2004, 201). This honorary cognomen was no mean achievement, since it laid claim to what was in time to become one of the emperor's own virtues (Wallace-Hadrill 1981; Noreña 2001, 157–8), and weights and measures were of active interest to everyone involved in commerce.

In making his final dedication to Venus Augusta, as *magister vici* for the third time, Mr. Equitable may well have emulated one of the several statues of Venus that stood in imperial buildings of Augustan Rome. As a terracotta votive with the same dove-decorated statue base suggests, it may well have been a variant on the Aphrodite Anadyomene type, a nearby example of which by the first-century BC artist Polycharmes stood in the Temple of Jupiter Stator within the Porticus of Octavia, built by the sister of the *princeps* (Plin. *HN* 36.35–6). The compliment to the first emperor was multifaceted, since Apelles's famous painting of the same subject, Venus's birth from the sea, was the centerpiece of Augustus's Temple of Divus Julius, and Venus herself was the progenitor of the Julian line (Plin. *HN* 35.91). Simultaneously, however, she belonged equally to someone half of whose original slave name (Hermeros) was that of the goddess's own son Eros. I would even suggest that Venus's doves on Hermeros Aequitas's statue base—both on the water basin at the front and happily feeding on the side panel—amusingly allude to his own repeated duties, for, as *magister vici*, he would have been responsible for administrating the water and grain supplies for the neighborhood (Lott 2004, 161–5, 236n189). No merely sycophantic gift to an all-powerful emperor was this; it was an artful balance of appearing to honor an imperial deity, while at the same time defining the self in a local context.

Indeed across the empire, at scales great and small, civic patrons followed suit in custom-tailoring imperial imagery to their own circumstances. At Aphrodisias in Caria, a city in Roman Asia Minor, two local families constructed a monumental Sebasteion. One family—two brothers, Menander and Eusebes, with Eusebes's wife, Apphias—dedicated the propylon and north portico, which was then restored by Apphias with her daughter and two grandsons after an earthquake. The south portico and temple were the project of two more brothers, Diogenes and Attalus as well as Attalus's wife, Attalis Apphion, and these buildings were then restored by Diogenes's son, Tiberius Claudius Diogenes. Tiberius Claudius Diogenes received Roman citizenship under the emperor Claudius, and the building and restoration period as a whole extends from the reign of Tiberius to the early reign of Nero (Smith 1987, 90). A portion of the southern portico has been reconstructed and begins to suggest just how awe-inspiring this long pathway to the temple must have been, with its tall three-storied porticoes decorated with large relief panels on the upper two stories. Seventy complete or fragmentary relief panels survive from the southern portico and freely juxtapose scenes from Greek mythology with representations of the imperial family and its conquests. Since the temple was for the city-goddess Aphrodite as well as the imperial family, it is not surprising that Venus and her son Aeneas—the origins of the Julian line—play a major role here with the Birth of Eros, Aeneas departing Troy (en route to Rome), and the Three Graces clearly recognizable in the reconstructed portion of the south portico. Images of the emperor and other gods appear in the upper story, such as an image of Claudius conquering Britannia, where the emperor's portrait features have been painstakingly rendered for recognizability on a head that somewhat outsizes his heroically nude body. This scene of conquest that took place literally a world away was also labeled to help in its identification (Smith 1987, 97, 115–17; 2013). It was displayed next to a panel with a winged Victory and, on the other side of the Victory, a similar grouping of Nero overcoming Armenia. The two emperors with the swooning female figures before them resonated not only with one another but also with the relief of Achilles and the fallen Amazon queen Penthesilea from this ensemble. Altogether there were 180 relief panels in the complex. For Aphrodisias, which owed its own recent rise to prominence to Rome and the Julian line, the Sebasteion and its reliefs unabashedly revel in Rome's imperial power, while simultaneously celebrating their city's own connection to it through their namesake local goddess, Aphrodite.

This trend of private elaboration on imperial messages continues in the second and third centuries AD, both in Rome itself and in the provinces, as can be demonstrated with two examples that honor the Severan dynasty. In AD 204 Rome's bankers (*argentarii*) built a diminutive arch in the capital city's Forum Boarium featuring frontal images of the imperial family making sacrifice, and strategically balancing a large-scale image of Septimius Severus and Julia Domna sprinkling incense atop a smaller vignette of the culmination of the ritual, the slaughter of the bull, surely a neighborhood favorite in this, the Cattle Market (Forum Boarium). Outside Rome at Leptis Magna, in gratitude to Septimius Severus, who had lavished attention on their city, his birthplace, by restructuring the harbor and building a magnificent main road and a gigantic forum and basilica complex, the citizens commissioned a dramatic tetrapylon. It was, however, not only the emperor's martial prowess and his *pietas* that were on display in the reliefs that covered this arch, but so too his god-like appeal, cast in city-of-Rome terms, since Septimius Severus was depicted as Jupiter Optimus Maximus and Julia Domna as Juno (Newby 2007, 206–211; Wilson 2007, 295–307; Mayer 2010, 128–30).

Conclusion

Even after the late third century AD, when there was no longer an emperor in the city of Rome, Roman imperial messages had something of an afterlife. At the Sebasteion in Aphrodisias, for example, although much of the northern portico collapsed before the mid-fourth century and the temple too was mostly dismantled, the southern portico served as a retail and crafts center in the fourth through fifth centuries and, as the graffiti confirm, served a populace of Christians and Jews. Of the eighty reliefs on the south portico, only nine were carefully defaced and those seem to have been selected because of their strong association with the worship of the local goddess Aphrodite or of what were perceived to be powerful pagan *daimones* which might do harm. Other mythological scenes, deities like healthful Hygieia, and Victories were left intact, and so too were images of the emperor, even though the genitals of nude figures were tidied up so as not to disturb Christian shoppers (Smith 2012; see essays 3.8, Witschel; and 6.6, Kristensen). Indeed in the commercial arena imperial images continued for several centuries: Byzantine emperors were standard on coinage, and in the marketplace, at least until the seventh century, crossbeam weights (often termed steelyard weights) for measuring bulk goods took the form of busts of the emperor, or more often empress, still the gold standard, as it were, by which all things were measured (McClanan 2002, 29–64). Mr. Equitable (Numerius Lucius Hermeros Aequitas), the neighborhood magistrate from the first-century Forum Boarium, would have felt right at home.

Across time and empire-wide, imperial messages were broadcast by everyone from emperors to members of municipal elites to wealthy freedpersons, each for their own distinctive purposes. Tracing the dynamics of this proliferation highlights how diverse these monuments were and yet also underscores some commonalities. All were in their own ways emperor-centric and shared what might be termed a system of knowledge that was characteristically imperial, with its emphasis on order and on use of hierarchy. The very precise annual rank-based cash donation in memory of Cominius the Augustalis from Misenum in the Antonine period comes to mind—20 sesterces to each

Decurion, 12 to each member of the Augustales, and so on—but again it was generated on a local level and for individual purpose. Imperial message makers were everywhere, and often, in context, the seductiveness of their visual statements about emperor and empire must have proved downright irresistible. Still, capturing hearts and minds empire-wide could prove a challenge, and as visually oriented as this culture was, there seem to have been attempts to engage the other senses as well, as two final objects from far-flung corners of the empire suggest. These are two molds for the cakes distributed to the populace at sacrifices (Varro *Rust.* 2.8.1), one found at Sirmium in Pannonia and the other at Silchester in Britain. The example from Sirmium takes the form of a Genius of an emperor making sacrifice, and the one from Silchester shows Septimius Severus making sacrifice before military standards (Boon 1958, 184–5; Thomas 1980). Here was an opportunity to consume—literally—the image of the emperor as a treat! This and other such ephemeral activities may well have worked their magic, as much as the monuments discussed here, in fully assimilating the emperor and imperial messages into the lives of everyday Romans.

Bibliography

Ando, C. 2000. *Imperial Ideology and Provincial Loyalty in the Roman Empire.* Berkeley: University of California Press.

Beard, M., J. North, and S. R. F. Price. 1998. *Religions of Rome.* 2 vols. Cambridge: Cambridge University Press.

Beckmann, M. 2011. *The Column of Marcus Aurelius: The Genesis and Meaning of a Roman Monument.* Chapel Hill: University of North Carolina Press.

Boon, G. C. 1958. "A Roman Pastry-Cook's Mould from Silchester" *AntJ* 38: 237–40.

Brilliant, R. 1967. *The Arch of Septimius Severus in the Roman Forum.* MAAR 29. Rome: American Academy in Rome.

———. 1984. *Visual Narratives: Storytelling in Etruscan and Roman Art.* Ithaca: Cornell University Press.

Dahmen, K. 2001. *Untersuchungen zu Form und Funktion kleinformatiger Porträts der römischen Kaiserzeit.* Münster: Scriptorium.

D'Arms, J. H. 2000. "Memory, Money, and Status at Misenum: Three New Inscriptions from the *Collegium* of the Augustales." *JRS* 90: 126–44.

Davies, P. J. E. 1997. "The Politics of Perpetuation: Trajan's Column and the Art of Commemoration." *AJA* 101: 41–65.

Eichholz, D. E., trans. 1971. *Natural History of Pliny, vol. 10: Books 36–37.* Loeb Classical Library. Cambridge, MA: Harvard University Press.

Ewald, B. C., and C. F. Noreña, eds. 2010. *The Emperor and Rome: Space, Representation, and Ritual.* Cambridge: Cambridge University Press.

Fejfer, J. 2008. *Roman Portraits in Context.* Berlin: Walter de Gruyter.

Fishwick, D. 1987–2005. *The Imperial Cult in the Latin West: Studies in the Ruler Cult of the Western Provinces of the Roman Empire.* 3 vols. Leiden: Brill.

Hölscher, T. (1987) 2004. *The Language of Images in Roman Art.* Translated by A. Snodgrass and A. Künzl-Snodgrass. Cambridge: Cambridge University Press. Originally published as *Römische Bildsprache als semantisches System.*

Kellum, B. A. 1990. "The City Adorned: Programmatic Display at the *Aedes Concordiae Augustae*." In *Between Republic and Empire: Interpretations of Augustus and His Principate*, edited by K. A. Raaflaub and M. Toher, 276–307. Berkeley: University of California Press.

Lepper, F., and S. Frere. 1988. *Trajan's Column: A New Edition of the Cichorius Plates; Introduction, Commentary, and Notes*. Gloucester: Alan Sutton.

Lott, J. B. 2004. *The Neighborhoods of Augustan Rome*. Cambridge: Cambridge University Press.

Marlowe, E. 2006. "Framing the Sun: The Arch of Constantine and the Roman Cityscape." *ArtB* 88: 223–42.

Mayer, E. 2010. "Propaganda, Staged Applause, or Local Politics? Public Monuments from Augustus to Septimius Severus." In Ewald and Noreña 2010, 111–34.

McClanan, A. 2002. *Representations of Early Byzantine Empresses*. New York: Palgrave Macmillan.

Muscettola, S. A. 2000. "The Sculptural Evidence." In *The Sacellum of the Augustales at Miseno*, edited by P. Miniero and translated by C. Fordham, 29–45. Naples: Electa.

Newby, Z. 2007. "Art at the crossroads? Themes and styles in Severan art." In Swain, Harrison, and Elsner 2007, 201–249.

Niemeyer, H. G. 1968. *Studien zur statuarischen Darstellung der römischen Kaiser*. Berlin: Mann.

Noreña, C. F. 2001. "The Communication of the Emperor's Virtues." *JRS* 91: 146–68.

———. 2003. "Medium and Message in Vespasian's Templum Pacis." *MAAR* 48: 25–43.

———. 2011. *Imperial Ideals in the Roman West: Representation, Circulation, Power*. Cambridge: Cambridge University Press.

Ostrow, S. E. 1985. "'Augustales' along the Bay of Naples: A Case for Their Early Growth." *Historia* 34(1): 64–101.

Panciera, S. 1980. "Nuovi luoghi di culto a Roma dalla testimonianze epigrafiche." In *Archeologia Laziale III: Terzo incontro di studio del Comitato per l'archeologia laziale*, 202–213. Rome: Consiglia nazionale delle ricerche.

Pekáry, T. 1985. *Das römische Herrscherbild*. Vol. 3, pt. 5, *Das römische Kaiserbildnis in Staat, Kult und Gesellschaft, dargestellt anhand der Schriftquellen*. Berlin: Mann.

Pfanner, M. 1989. "Über das Herstellen von Porträts: Ein Beitrag zu Rationalisierungsmaßnahmen und Produktionsmechanismen von Massenware im späten Hellenismus und in der römischen Kaiserzeit." *JdI* 104: 157–257.

Richlin, A. 2007. *Marcus Aurelius in Love: The Letters of Marcus and Fronto*. Chicago: University of Chicago Press.

Rose, C. B. 1990. "'Princes' and Barbarians on the Ara Pacis." *AJA* 94: 453–67.

———. 1997. *Dynastic Commemoration and Imperial Portraiture in the Julio-Claudian Period*. Cambridge: Cambridge University Press.

Rutledge, S. H. 2012. *Ancient Rome as a Museum: Power, Identity, and the Culture of Collecting*. Oxford: Oxford University Press.

Settis, S., ed. 1988. *La Colonna Traiana*. Torino: G. Einaudi.

Smith, R. R. R. 1987. "The Imperial Reliefs from the Sebasteion at Aphrodisias." *JRS* 77: 88–138.

———. 2012. "Defacing the Gods at Aphrodisias." In *Historical and Religious Memory in the Ancient World*, edited by B. Dignas and R. R. R. Smith, 283–326. Oxford: Oxford University Press.

———. 2013. *The Marble Reliefs from the Julio-Claudian Sebasteion*. Aphrodisias 6. Darmstadt: Philipp von Zabern.

Stewart, P. 2003. *Statues in Roman Society: Representation and Response*. Oxford: Oxford University Press.
Swain, S., S. Harrison, and J. Elsner, eds. 2007. *Severan Culture*. Cambridge: Cambridge University Press.
Thackeray, H. St. J., trans. 1976. *Josephus*. Loeb Classical Library. Cambridge, MA: Harvard University Press.
Thomas, E. B. 1980. "Religion." In *The Archaeology of Roman Pannonia*, edited by A. Lengyel and G. T. B. Radan, 177–206. Lexington: University of Kentucky Press.
Torelli, M. 1982. *Typology and Structure of Roman Historical Reliefs*. Ann Arbor: University of Michigan Press.
Trimble, J. 2011. *Women and Visual Replication in Roman Imperial Art and Culture*. Cambridge: Cambridge University Press.
Varner, E. R. 2004. *Mutilation and Transformation: "Damnatio memoriae" and Roman Imperial Portraiture*. Boston: Brill.
Veyne, P. 1988. "Conduct without Belief and Works of Art without Viewers." Translated by J. Ferguson. *Diogenes* 36(1): 1–22.
Wallace-Hadrill, A. 1981. "Galba's Aequitas." *NC* 141: 20–39.
———. 1986. "Image and Authority in the Coinage of Augustus." *JRS* 76: 66–87.
Wilson, A. 2007. "Urban Development in the Severan Empire." In Swain, Harrison, and Elsner 2007, 290–326.
Zanker, P. 1988. *The Power of Images in the Age of Augustus*. Translated by A. Shapiro. Ann Arbor: University of Michigan Press.

CHAPTER 4.7

NON-ELITE PATRONAGE

LAUREN HACKWORTH PETERSEN

Introduction

In 1862, the excavation of a small Pompeian house that connects to a cloth-treatment workshop (VII.12.17/21) led to the discovery of several bronze serving pieces, glass vessels, and a bronze statue of the god Bacchus (Dwyer 1982, 53–6). The bronze Bacchus is especially noteworthy: it measures 0.63 m tall, making it rather large and suggesting that it was a display piece rather than an object of veneration within a small domestic shrine; its pose derives from late classical models, with the S-curve of the torso being a hallmark of the fourth-century BC sculptors Praxiteles and Lysippos; and because it was found in the cloth-treatment workshop it is assumed to have come from the collapsed upper floor belonging to the connecting house (figure 4.7.1). Due to the location of the statue and elegant tableware—in a house/workshop—one scholar made the following observation: "In a neighborhood of taverns and brothels, such a rich collection of bronzes appears anomalous. It is known only that the owner was the proprietor of a fullonica [or cloth-treatment workshop], and thus a member of a prosperous but not socially exalted class" (Dwyer 1982, 53). At the time, the reasoning behind this statement was typical of much scholarship concerning the character of non-elites and their artistic patronage in the Roman world: non-elites owned and/or labored in shops and workshops (instead of earning an income from the land and properties as the elites did) and therefore did not have the means or the leisure to indulge in the collecting of expensive sculpture. In the last few decades much has changed, as scholars have sought to write a more dynamic and inclusive history of Roman art by challenging some of the discipline's biases and exploring the meanings of artistic patronage by non-elite individuals in a variety of contexts (Clarke 2003; Stewart 2008; Mayer 2012).

This essay explores how scholars have come to categorize some sculptures as non-elite and what this category has meant for the study of Roman sculpture (and, by implication, Roman art more generally). Specifically, this essay addresses the social history of Roman sculpture. It confronts some of the elite-centered paradigms that shape how we have

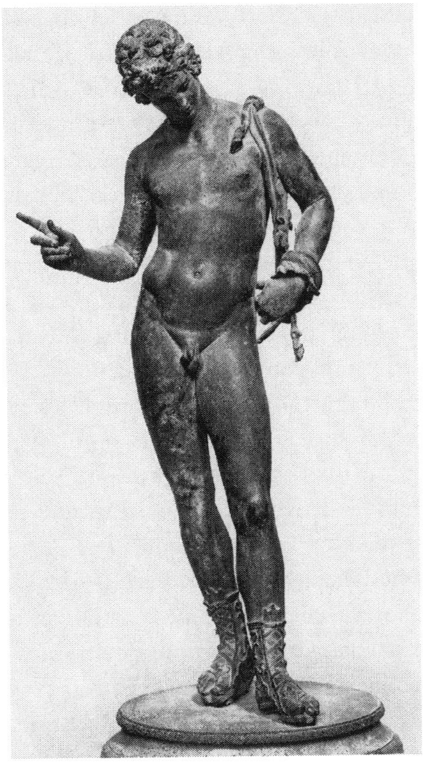

FIGURE 4.7.1 Statue of Bacchus, from workshop VII.12.17/21, Pompeii. Museo Archeologico Nazionale di Napoli.

seen and described non-elite Roman sculpture, namely in direct comparison to its elite counterparts. This elite/non-elite dichotomy, I suggest, is both reductive and essentializing: it limits how scholars have interpreted the artistic legacy of the diverse individuals who fell outside elite circles. Instead, more nuanced approaches may help us to re-see—on their own terms—the individuals of financial means who engaged in artistic patronage to communicate their messages.

To begin, it is useful to think about the concept of the patron as it pertains to Roman sculpture. The definition seems straightforward enough: it is the person who commissioned a work of art. Most visible (and the grandest) were the monuments and portraits of the emperor and his family. Indeed, the emperors were the most powerful individuals among Rome's citizens and had the means to commission sculpture on an unprecedented scale. The issue, however, is thornier than it first appears. Although the epigraphic evidence can often point to the patron of monuments, we tend to identify imperial monuments by the dedicatee (see essay 4.5, Tuck). Perhaps more often than we would like to admit, there is some ambiguity over who actually controlled and/or approved the message and the process, even if the result is emphatically connected with an emperor (e.g., the inscription on the Arch of Septimius Severus that identifies the Senate and People of Rome [*SPQR*] as the patrons, not the dedicatees; see essays 3.5,

Sobocinski and Wolfram Thill; 4.5, Tuck; and 4.6, Kellum). Due to the high profile of the emperors and their families, it is relatively easy to assign dates to the large number of sculptures honoring them. Hence the history of Roman art, and the organizing principle of surveys of Roman art and sculpture, has traditionally been one based on the chronological succession of emperors, after an initial chapter or chapters on Etruscan precedents and the art of the Republic (e.g., D. E. E. Kleiner 1992; Ramage and Ramage 2008; F. S. Kleiner 2010 intersperses thematic chapters with imperially focused ones). When dynasties were fragile, such as during the civil wars of the first and third centuries, imperially driven chapter titles succumb to more historically descriptive ones, but the material is still examined through the lens of the ruling elite. In other words, the emperors and their presumed sculptural commissions and portraits have been and continue to be the primary apparatus for narrating the history of Roman art (Stewart 2004, 3–4).

It is important to bear in mind that there is nothing particularly "natural" or self-evident about this organizing principle. Roman art, eclectic in terms of style and largely produced by anonymous artists or artisans, does not lend itself to traditional art historical narratives (see essays 3.1, Fullerton; and 3.6, Touchette). Art historians have thus turned to the known and most visible patrons (and dedicatees) of art—the emperors and their retinue—as a means of developing a narrative and, perhaps more significantly, of discussing stylistic changes and continuities in Roman sculpture. Clearly this paradigm has meant a primacy given to imperial patronage and subjects, not only in narrating the history of Roman art, but also in terms of scholarly priorities.

Defining "Non-Elite"

When it comes to studying the non-elite patronage of Roman art, we face a staggering array of objects that are not so easily categorized. The term "non-elite" covers a broad swath of society from successful businesspeople to the working poor and slaves. Non-elite art is usually identified in genres such as funerary portraits of freedmen (ex-slaves) from Rome and Pompeii (Zanker 1975; D. E. E. Kleiner 1977; see essays 4.4, Ewald; and 6.2, Trimble), reliefs and frescoes depicting people working or with tools of a trade from throughout the empire (Kampen 1981; D'Ambra 1988; Clarke 2003, 78–81, 85–7, 95–129; see essay 4.8, D'Ambra and Tronchin), and neighborhood altars (Lott 2004; see essay 4.2, McCarty), in addition to decorative ensembles in modest-sized houses (Zanker [1979] 1998; Clarke 1991; 2003). Most apparent are the artistic commissions of former slaves, especially those who identify themselves by name and status with an L for *libertus* or *liberta* in funerary reliefs in the early imperial period (Zanker 1975; D. E. E. Kleiner 1977; see essay 6.2, Trimble, and figure 6.2.4). In fact, early work on the artistic commissions of former slaves led to the scholarly category "freedman art," which inadvertently became a ready-made way to describe art commissioned by those outside of elite circles, even without epigraphic evidence. While we can talk about sculpture of former slaves when inscriptions explicitly identify them as such, in the absence of status indicators we should exercise caution and not make assumptions about the precise status of artistic patrons and hence the presumed motives of such patrons (Petersen 2006).

Compared to imperial monuments, only a small number of the surviving sculptures commissioned by non-elites are addressed in synthetic narratives of Roman art (Clarke 2003 begins to fill this lacuna). The aforementioned bronze statue of Bacchus is a case in point: it and its owner rarely make an appearance except in highly specialized studies. We know nothing about the owner or occupants except that the house was connected to a cloth-treatment workshop, a setting defined by historians as categorically non-elite. Perhaps the very anonymity of such patrons contributes to the problem: we know little about the patrons themselves beyond their presumed non-elite status, and so their sculptural commissions tend to be relegated to the margins of Roman art history (akin to anonymous works of art from the Renaissance period onward). In contrast, those about whom we know something (usually through epigraphy) are made more visible, such as freed slaves, as their patronage finds a parallel with elite commissions.

Nonetheless, in the last few decades, scholars started to bring much-needed attention to non-elite sculpture. This trend basically began with the work of Ranuccio Bianchi Bandinelli (*arte plebea* / plebeian art) followed by the scholarship of Natalie Kampen (Roman working women), John Clarke (ordinary Romans), Peter Stewart (Roman art and social history), Eve D'Ambra and Guy Métraux (citizens, soldiers, and freedmen), and now Emanuel Mayer (the Roman middle-classes), to name just a few. These scholars have been instrumental in releasing the grip that the emperors have held on the history of Roman sculpture (see also Knapp 2011, on non-elites more generally, and essays in Bell and Ramsby 2012). Moreover, Kampen's call to write histories (plural) of Roman art instead of *the* history of Roman art invites us to embrace the diversity of Roman art—from large-scale sculptures to small-scale pieces, from sumptuous materials to the relatively inexpensive, and from Rome to the provinces.

Despite this much-needed, excellent scholarship, one methodological issue still finds its way into most studies of non-elite sculpture: a dependency (perhaps unconscious) on elite models in assessing the quality or effectiveness of sculpture. For example, we tend to see the front panel of the Altar of the Vicus Aesculeti, which comes from Rome and dates to the Augustan era, by what it does not do, rather than by what it does do: what it communicates and how (figures 4.7.2 and 4.7.3; Clarke 2003, 81–5; Lott 2004, 142–4, 186). From the altar's inscriptions and imagery, we know that it was commissioned by four administrators of one of the city's *vici* (the *vicomagistri*). These minor local officials oversaw the infrastructure of their ward, including fire and crime prevention as well as traffic control (Lott 2004, 81–127). This altar was set up within the Vicus Aesculeti to commemorate the *vicomagistri* publicly and to provide a space for ritual and sacrifice when honoring the neighborhood Lares of the crossroads (*Lares compitales*) and the Genius of the emperor. Indeed, on each of the two side panels a figure of a Lar standing on a projecting pedestal is carved in high relief. On the best-preserved panel (figure 4.7.3), the Lar has one hand raised and holds a large laurel branch in the other, while he looks down in quiet solemnity. With one leg slightly forward, his

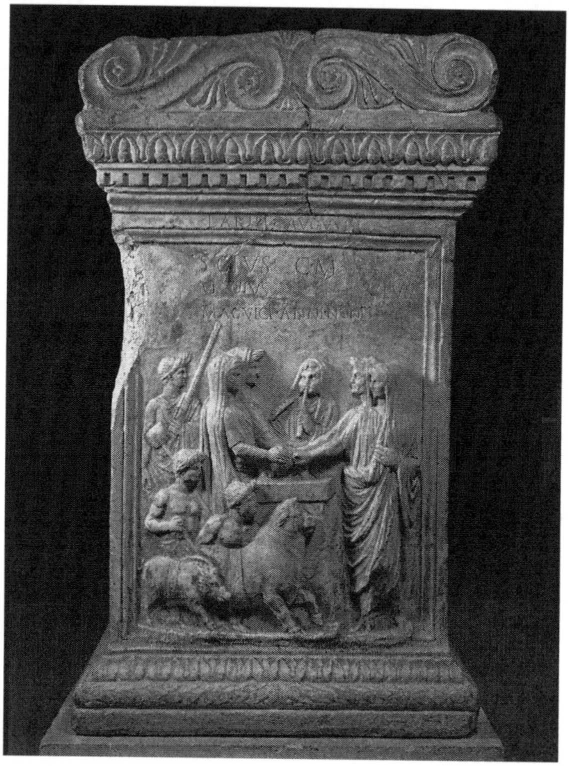

FIGURE 4.7.2 Altar of the Vicus Aesculeti, front side, showing the *vicomagistri* sacrificing at an altar. Augustan period, Rome.

drapery appears to be fluttering. In many respects, the deity is depicted in the classical style that characterizes much of Augustan art (Zanker 1970–71; 1990, 239–63). The back of the altar depicted a *corona civica* (oak crown), now only partially legible (Lott 2004, 143). The front, the side that has garnered the most scholarly attention, depicts the four *vicomagistri* performing a sacrifice at an altar. Each is dressed in a toga with the edge covering his head, as required for sacrifices. Also present are the various customary attendants: two *victimarii* (the bare-chested men who slaughter the animals) behind a pig and a bull to be sacrificed, a *tibia* player, and a lictor. The toga worn by all four *vicomagistri* signals their status as Roman citizens, but does not reveal whether they were freeborn or freed. Overall, the iconography of the sacrifice scene is familiar (akin to images of an emperor sacrificing) and would have been as recognizable to viewers in antiquity as it is to scholars today (Lott 2004).

It appears that the name of each of the four *vicomagistri* was inscribed on the altar, providing us with a window into its patronage. Fragments of a name survive above each Lar: P. Clodius P. L. (on the right side) and [...] S. L. L. Salvius (on the left side). With the L in each name standing for *libertus*, we know that at least two of the *vicomagistri* dedicating this altar were former slaves; the other two names are poorly preserved, so it must

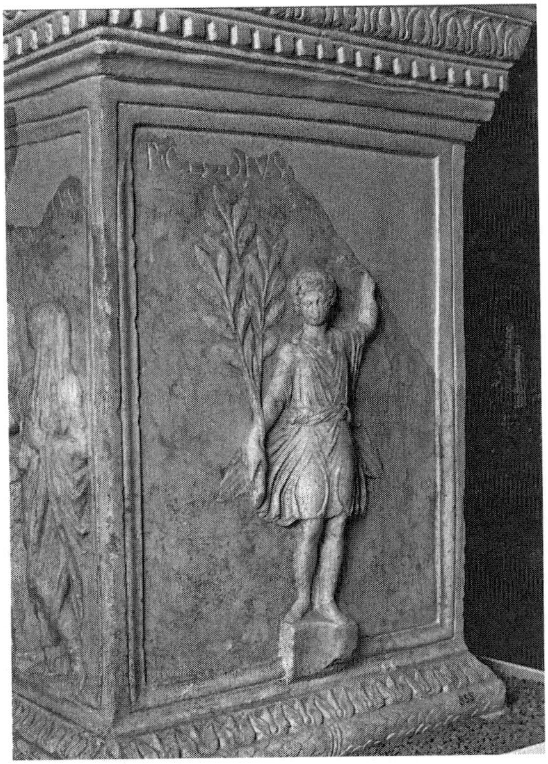

FIGURE 4.7.3 Altar of the Vicus Aesculeti, Lar figure on the right side of the altar. Augustan period, Rome.

remain conjecture as to whether these individuals were former slaves as well (Panciera 1987; Clarke 2003, 292n27). Based on two of the inscriptions, in combination with the subject matter of the front relief—four individuals making a sacrifice, as opposed to one—scholars confidently put this altar in the scholarly category of non-elite art, as at least two of its patrons were former slaves and the *vicomagistri* were minor local officials. And this is precisely the point at which interpretations of the altar's imagery become problematic.

More than a simple category, the term non-elite carries much baggage. Non-elite Roman sculpture is typically viewed as imitating sculpture commissioned by the elite, which is to say that the elite set the standards and the non-elite—everyone else—emulated that style, most times naively so. This model, also known as "trickle-down aesthetics," has in the past driven discussions of non-elite Roman art (Zanker 1975; D. E. E. Kleiner 1977; Zanker [1979] 1998, 135–203; for critiques of this model, see Petersen 2006; Mayer 2012, 100–212). Art history, however, seems to have some backing in the words of the ancients themselves. In fact, art historians typically turn to Petronius's vivid literary depiction of Trimalchio, the *nouveau riche* former slave who apes his social betters in the oft-cited *cena Trimalchionis* of *The Satyrica*. What makes the character of

Trimalchio so humorous, if not downright comical, is that he seems to try, with all of his wealth, to affect the culture of the elite, but in the end it is all pretension that falls short, and these shortcomings tend to be the most memorable moments of the story. In this regard, Trimalchio's missteps and bungles have become a way of seeing and interpreting the artistic patronage and choices not only of wealthy freed slaves, but also of non-elites more broadly, who are presented as financially successful social climbers who lack noble birth and whose artistic commissions are viewed as vapid imitation of elite ones (a tendency I have elsewhere called "Trimalchio Vision," as it relates to artistic commissions thought to be by former slaves; Petersen 2006).

One recent discussion of the Altar of the Vicus Aesculeti illustrates just how this literary tradition and the dichotomy of elite/non-elite patronage may limit our assessments. Although Clarke's bold work on art and ordinary Romans has thrown open the door to visual material that had been long neglected by scholars, it unwittingly reveals how conditioned we tend to be by discourses that privilege elite artistic forms (and he is surely not alone in this regard). For example, upon identifying two of the patrons of the altar—freedmen and hence non-elite residents of Rome—Clarke's discussion continues with a description of the relief presenting the figures standing around the altar and concludes with some remarks about the lictor holding the *fasces* (bound rods). A brief comparison of the iconography is then made with the lictors that appear on the Ara Pacis of Augustus, at which point Clarke offers the following observation: "Clearly this modest relief [of the Altar of the Vicus Aesculeti] crows a bit in imitation of important state religious ceremony, considering that the duties of the *vicomagistri* were local and discrete" (Clarke 2003, 83). The implication is that even though Augustus granted the *vicomagistri* the privilege of two lictors to accompany them, and that their responsibilities included sacrifices to the Genius of Augustus and the *Lares compitales*, to portray publicly that privilege and those responsibilities by using recognizable iconography drawn from imperial sources must have somehow transgressed an unstated social boundary. Indeed, the concluding sentence of the analysis invokes the usual trope of trickle-down aesthetics: "If the altar of the *magistri* of the Vicus Aesculeti, despite its modest execution, seemed familiar to the ancient viewer, it is because it imitated elite monuments of the state religion" (85).

These statements point to the crux of the problem, namely the use of elite monuments as a standard against which other monuments are assessed. In the case of the Altar of the Vicus Aesculeti, we can readily point to several imperial commissions that contain similar scenes of sacrifice, albeit typically with the lone or isolated figure of the emperor sacrificing rather than four local magistrates gathered around an altar. Because two of this relief's patrons are known to be freedmen/non-elite, the similarity is classified as purely derivative (and even "crowing in imitation"). Yet one could argue that in order for the scene to be comprehended, the patrons and artist turned to a familiar composition and stock imagery. Everything about the iconography of the front panel matches literary descriptions of the roles and perquisites of these officials, and the size of the altar (1.05 m tall) is itself relatively modest. The issue is perhaps not one of naive imitation but instead of legibility and standard visual vocabulary. This last notion is particularly evident with respect to the scale of the two *victimarii* and sacrificial animals at left. Depicted in smaller proportions than the four *vicomagistri* and two attendants, these figures make a symbolic appearance; they are props to the action performed by the protagonists (*contra* Zanker 1990, 131, who characterizes the animals as "absurdly small"). Such a visual device (or hierarchy of size) occurs in Roman sculpture produced throughout the empire. By way of comparison, the frieze from the Arch of Augustus at Susa (northern Italy), contemporary with the Altar of the Vicus Aesculeti, depicts sacrificial victims in an unnaturally large scale, with a gigantic pig being especially noteworthy. Bianchi Bandinelli has suggested this play of scale was symbolic so as to underline "the importance of the solemnly accomplished religious act which sanctioned the political treaty" signed between the king of Susa and Rome (1970, 57). In other words, this manipulation of scale helps to convey the message of the elite monument. The same could be said of the Altar of the Vicus Aesculeti, emphasizing as it does the four *vicomagistri*. In this regard, there is nothing particularly "non-elite" with respect to the visual conventions of the altar, except that our knowledge of its patrons seems to affect how we see the monument—as derivative—and how we do not see it, namely as a monument that utilizes a traditional visual language.

In the absence of inscriptional evidence that links a piece of sculpture with its patron, the tendency is to connect it with a type of owner based on any available criteria. One is location, where the object was found, as was the case with the bronze statue of Bacchus from Pompeii. Because it seems to have fallen from an upstairs floor of the house connected to a cloth-treatment workshop, the presumption has been that its owner was a prosperous but non-elite individual. Let us interrogate the assumptions behind this interpretation. It used to be that Pompeian studies viewed the devastating earthquake of AD 62 as the event that ushered in a decline in both the social and urban fabric of the city. With the city in disrepair, many of the well-to-do inhabitants, so it was argued, left the city, while non-elites, namely freedman, infiltrated the city and began to make their mark, most visibly with the commercial shops and workshops associated with houses (Maiuri 1942). This narrative has since been substantially revised from both political and archaeological perspectives (Wallace-Hadrill 1994, 118–42; Mouritsen 1996; Mayer 2012; Ball and Dobbins 2013). What emerges is a picture in which commercial activities cannot be attached so firmly or exclusively to non-elites. A city's elite citizens are now imagined to have had substantial interests in commercial activities—from renting out workshops connected to domestic units to engaging dependents in business affairs. Moreover, the economically and socially mobile middle classes complicate the stark dichotomy usually drawn between the elites and non-elites (Mayer 2012). In other words, while the owner(s)/occupant(s) of the house / cloth-treatment workshop with the statue of Bacchus may not have been elite in the strict sense of the term (that is, not belonging to the senatorial nobility), they may have been among the thousands of individuals whose economic activities and opportunities afforded the ability to purchase and display finely sculpted objects and to participate in Roman conventions of decorating one's house to the extent that financial resources allowed.

Based on the sculpture's material and execution, there is nothing particularly "non-elite" or derivative about the bronze Bacchus, except that its style looks to late classical models for inspiration—and this is an important and related point. The pose and style of the deity, as noted, loosely imitate those of sculptures by Praxiteles and Lysippos. In fact, much Roman sculpture takes its cues from the Greek world, a situation that had once relegated Roman art to being the stepsister to Greek art (see essay 3.3, Anguissola). More recently, art historians have vigorously challenged this notion, so that Roman art now stands on its own—sometimes looking to the Greek world to convey specific messages and other times engaging indigenous forms that seem better suited to the subject matter (see essays 3.2, de Grummond; 3.6, Touchette; 3.7, Swetnam-Burland; and the essays in part V, Regions and Provinces). With respect to the former, the works of Tonio Hölscher, Elaine Gazda, Ellen Perry, Miranda Marvin, Peter Stewart, Christopher Hallett, and Elizabeth Bartman, to name only a few, have been instrumental in thinking about Roman sculpture in context to tease out the meanings of its use of Greek models.

Hölscher's essay on the language of Roman art, for instance, argues that Roman image-making embraced Greek forms to express Roman ideals. The basic premise of Hölscher's argument is that in Roman art formal choices were dictated by social and political content; form and content are inextricably linked in Roman art, producing a visual language with its own syntax. In regard to depicting gods, the classical style of Polykleitos or the late classical styles of Praxiteles or Lysippos were considered by the Romans to convey the ideals of truthfulness and beauty appropriate for the gods (Hölscher [1987] 2004, 86–102). Specifically, Roman images of Bacchus, on account of the god's youth and sensuous appearance, looked to the aforementioned late-classical sculptors to convey his attributes. What Hölscher's argument means is that the Pompeian owner of the bronze statue of Bacchus found in the house/workshop engaged in Roman traditions of sculpture collecting, albeit on a relatively limited scale in comparison with villa owners. While the anonymity of the owner of the sculpture of Bacchus in combination with its findspot have led to categorization of this statue as "anomalous" and by implication as non-elite, we should be suspicious of this type of categorization, for it does little to reveal the practices of patronage among well-to-do business people, individuals who may have had a significant impact on the art market in Roman cities, as Mayer's recent study on the middle-classes has aptly demonstrated.

Two other criteria that have also been deployed in characterizing sculpture as non-elite focus on subject matter and style. As we saw with Hölscher's study of the language of Roman art in reference to the use of Greek styles, subject and style tend to go hand-in-hand, especially in regard to elite patronage. Yet certain subjects, namely images of work, and a non-Hellenic-looking style have been identified simply and self-evidently as belonging in the sphere of non-elite sculptural commissions, because they look different than sculptures commissioned by elite citizens. What if non-elite sculpture were similarly read, with nuance and depth, as fully participating in this complex semantic system of image making?

Rethinking "Non-Elite"

The work of Bianchi Bandinelli was among the earliest in challenging vigorously the elite-centric story of Roman art. Despite some limitations, his ideas are still useful as a starting point. Writing nearly fifty years ago, Bianchi Bandinelli sought to explain how the visual characteristics of Roman art were tied explicitly to class concerns, especially in the media of relief sculpture and portraiture. Specifically, he identifies two traditions in Roman art—the patrician and the plebeian traditions (Bianchi Bandinelli 1967; 1970, 51–105; 1971, esp. 23–38). The patrician tradition (*arte aulica*) is tied to the elites in the capital, Rome, and is indebted to Hellenic artistic traditions, whereas the plebeian tradition—*arte plebea*—emerges in municipalities throughout Italy and is characterized by nonnaturalistic or symbolic proportions, frontal views of figures, an overall lack of pictorial perspective, and expressive qualities. The plebeian trend, he proposes, reflects the artistic patronage of lower-level office holders, soldiers, freedmen, and colonists, and belongs to the realm of historical narratives and relief (Bianchi Bandinelli 1967, 17). This trend, according to Bianchi Bandinelli, forms the basis of late antique art, with the style that characterizes *arte plebea* becoming the hallmark of imperial commissions of late antiquity. Of course, part of his theory stems from his own Marxist agenda. But as an historian of Roman art and archaeology, he also turns to the freedman character Trimalchio, who has come to represent the classic up-from-under figure, and finds in him a largely positive model. Moreover, Bianchi Bandinelli adheres to the belief that one style is not necessarily of higher aesthetic value than the other; rather, each is determined primarily by class interests.

Despite his efforts to explain plebeian art in positive terms, dualisms prevail in Bianchi Bandinelli's theory—classical/unclassical and patrician/plebeian—although he does explore overlappings, cross-pollination, and borrowings in the early imperial period (Bianchi Bandinelli 1970, 64). For example, in his discussion of early imperial funerary monuments of local magistrates, he comments on "the frequency with which Hellenistic rules of naturalism were jettisoned in order to emphasize action, and enhance the figure of the donor," while allowing for "borrowings from the tradition of official [i.e., elite] art" (58). With the Altar of the Vicus Aesculeti, we can see borrowings from official art, including the more or less Hellenic rendering of the togate figures and Lares, combined with a clear use of hierarchy of size as a means to emphasize the action and the donors themselves. This mode of representation becomes common in later imperial art commissions, as with the scenes of sacrifice on the Column of Trajan, where Trajan and his retinue are depicted in a Hellenic manner, except that the figure of the emperor stands isolated from and taller than the others. The Altar of the Vicus Aesculeti, I would think, therefore speaks not to an artistic patronage that naively imitates the elite, but rather to one in which economically and socially mobile consumers and patrons of sculpture effectively articulate their place in society, and with it values that transcend elite/non-elite categories among Rome's citizens.

More difficult to discuss in these terms, however, are reliefs showing Romans busy at work or with the tools of their trade. They abound in the corpus of Roman sculpture—from those depicting various activities of a large bakery running along the top of the Monument of Eurysaces in Rome, to the small-scale terracotta reliefs of a midwife and a smith, among others, adorning the exterior of tombs at the Isola Sacra necropolis outside Ostia Antica. Within the frieze from the Monument of Eurysaces, for example, the busyness of the bakery is shown by the vigorous movements of the workers in contrast to the togate officials who stand to oversee various aspects of the bread-making process, one of whom may be Eurysaces himself, although we cannot be certain (figure 4.7.4). The location, scale, materials, and expense of the monument suggest that Eurysaces' baking enterprise was quite successful. Even so, the scholarly tendency has been to categorize this monument as non-elite because of its unabashed celebration of work, alongside the unclassically rendered (i.e., non-Greek-inspired) images of labor. Here a single relief plane defines the space, the figures stand out in isolation from each other, and varying proportions work together to project the image of this bakery. One scholar viewed the frieze as done in "a lively but unselfconscious narrative style," and this type of characterization is common (D. E. E. Kleiner 1992, 109). But one wonders, with the frieze high above viewers standing on the street, if the choice was more self-conscious than we have allowed it to be, with the compositional features enhancing the legibility of the protagonists and their symbolic import.

In fact, we still have much to learn from the language we use to describe sculptures of and for non-elites. As art historians, making visual comparisons and articulating what we see are the mainstays of our profession. The acts of seeing and verbalizing are rarely neutral exercises, however. The language brought to bear in a description usually contains some sort of comparison, whether explicit or not, and thus a set of value judgments, whether or not the writer is aware of them. And the act of seeing—what we

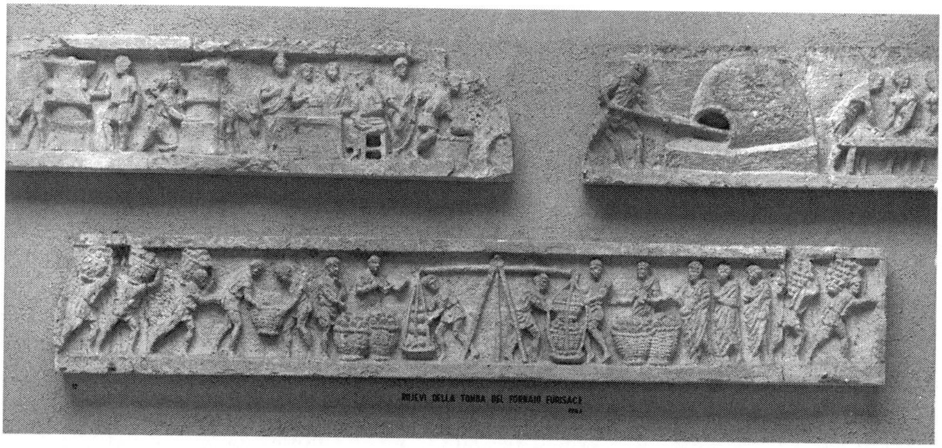

FIGURE 4.7.4 Cast of reliefs showing a bread-making enterprise, from the Monument of Eurysaces. Augustan period. Museo della Civiltà Romana, Rome.

choose to see, and what we do not see—is also culturally constructed (Donohue 2005; cf. Ackerman 1962 on style more generally; and Webster 2008, 140, albeit in a different Roman context). Analyses of style extrapolate relationships among works of art, as they are derived from drawing comparisons and contrasts based on visual characteristics. Stylistic categories can be immensely useful to organize bodies of artistic material and generate historical narratives (Ackerman 1962). However, much is at stake in defining categories of style, as the traditional focus of Roman art history has been on imperial art, that is elite art (actually ultra-elite, rising above any local elite) that took its cues early on from the Greek world and that has become the standard against which all else is compared.

Two interpretations of a funerary stele of a shoemaker illustrate what is at stake in discussions of non-elite sculpture (figure 4.7.5). This monument comes from Rome and contains an inscription below a portrait-bust of the deceased that reads, "Gaius Julius Helius, shoemaker at the Porta Fontinalis, built this monument, while living, for himself, Julia Flaccilla, daughter, Gaius Julius Onesimus, freedman, and his freed slaves and theirs" (*CIL* 6.33914: *C(aius) Iulius Helius sutor a / Porta Fontinale fecit sibi et / Iuliae Flaccillae fil(iae) et C(aio) Iulio / Onesimo liberto libertabusque / posterisque eorum v(ivo) f(ecit)*). Although not explicitly stated in the inscription, the assumption has been that

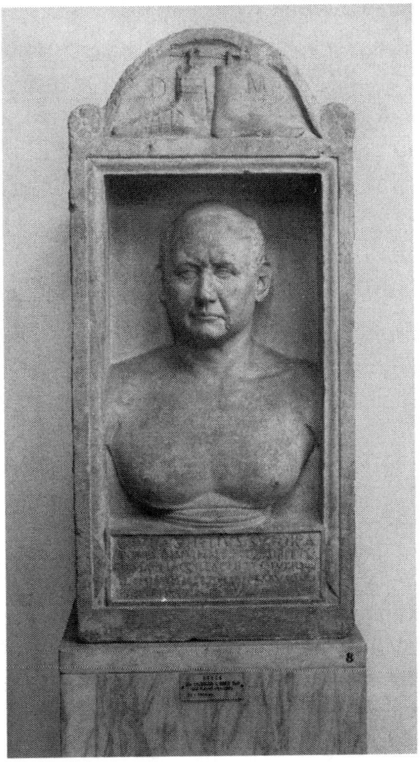

FIGURE 4.7.5 Funerary stele of a shoemaker. Second century, Rome.

C. Iulius Helius was a former slave, with a daughter, Flaccilla, who was born after he was freed (D'Ambra 1998, 39); however, we cannot be certain based on the nomenclature. What we can say for certain, based on the inscription and the sculpted relief of two shoe lasts, one outfitted with a sandal, is that the monument announces the deceased's profession as a shoemaker. Dated to the early second century AD, the portrait recalls those of the Republic, in which the vigorous, youthful bodies of leaders could be combined with aged facial features to connote experience and long service to the state (on this topic more generally, see Hallett 2005b). If one compares this portrait with those of Rome's powerful elite, this monument seems to aim high but fall short due to the fact that it belongs to a shoemaker, who was of markedly lower standing than a senator or a general. In specific reference to the aged portrait type, a type that was subsequently commissioned among former slaves, one scholar comments: "It was as if the freedmen achieved respectability simply by manipulating the external signs of status" (D'Ambra 1998, 46). And of this monument in particular: "The nudity of this bust aspires to a different ideal of a heroic, divinely inspired power—but the allusion seems gross for the commemoration of a shoemaker" (48).

Examining the stele for what it discloses—rather than contrasting it with elite counterparts and values—Mayer's recent reassessment offers new ways of seeing middle-class artistic commissions. With respect to the funerary stele of the shoemaker, he suggests, for example, that the aged portrait might signal his "prolonged business success" (Mayer 2012, 117). While such a statement may seem a bit trite, substituting business for political activities, his analysis goes further. Taking a cue from Kampen's work, Mayer notes that the shoemaker also provides the location of his business enterprise (at or near the Porta Fontinalis on the Campus Martius), a location that was prominent and much sought after, suggesting not only the shoemaker's success in general, but more pointedly his success in a keenly competitive environment. This achievement was worth commemorating in its own right, in a way that was generally consistent with Roman memory-making practices (120). The monument was thus effective in conveying a message that would have been legible to its audiences, because it "spoke" a language familiar to a range of individuals but was specific to this particular patron (see essay 6.2, Trimble).

Conclusion

The stele of the shoemaker is rather typical of funerary monuments discovered within Italy and throughout the empire. Museums and their storage areas are filled with such objects, but proportionately few find their way into the histories of Roman art or sculpture. Moreover, sculptures of all types (portraits, reliefs, freestanding, altars, stelai, and so forth) belonging to non-elite Romans, though perhaps not as conspicuous or grand as the imperial art forms in Rome, were everywhere: in houses, bars, tombs, temples, sanctuaries, and city streets. We would still benefit, I suggest, from a greater awareness of the biases that infiltrate our assessments of sculpture, biases that derive from preconceived notions concerning the findspot, subject matter, style, or patronage, if known. There is, in fact, a real opportunity to re-see and rewrite the histories of Roman sculpture: to interrogate the priorities that drive the elite/non-elite dualism, namely an unqualified valuation of Hellenic-looking art; to ask new questions of non-elite art rather than putting it in a seemingly self-evident container; and to embrace pluralities that are not so easily reduced to stylistic categories. Doing so invites us to rethink the long-held assumptions that lie behind stylistic designations based on dualisms, in which one side of the dichotomy is viewed positively (classical/elite) and the other side is viewed negatively, seen for what it is not (un-classical/non-elite). We need to be forthright in acknowledging the limitations of such a paradigm just as we need to open up new ways of seeing, describing, and narrating the histories of Roman sculpture. Until we do so, we will continue to construct a history of Roman sculpture that places on the margins material that was arguably omnipresent and has much to tell us about the Romans.

Bibliography

Ackerman, J. 1962. "A Theory of Style." *Journal of Aesthetics and Art Criticism* 20(3): 227–37.

Ball, L., and J. Dobbins. 2013. "Pompeii Forum Project: Current Thinking on the Pompeii Forum." *AJA* 117(3): 461–92.

Bartman, E. 1991. "Sculptural Collecting and Display in the Private Realm." In *Roman Art in the Private Sphere: New Perspectives on the Architecture and Decor of the Domus, Villa, and Insula*, edited by E. K. Gazda, 71–88. Ann Arbor: University of Michigan Press.

Bell, S., and T. Ramsby, eds. 2012. *Free at Last! The Impact of Freed Slaves on the Roman Empire*. London: Bristol Classical Press.

Bianchi Bandinelli, R. 1967. "Arte plebea." *DialArch* 1(1): 7–19.

———. 1970. *Rome: The Center of Power, 500 B.C. to A.D. 200*. Translated by P. Green. New York: George Braziller.

———. 1971. *Rome, The Late Empire: Roman Art, A.D. 200–400*. Translated by P. Green. New York: George Braziller.

Clarke, J. R. 1991. *The Houses of Roman Italy, 100 B.C.–A.D. 250: Ritual, Space, and Decoration*. Berkeley: University of California Press.

———. 2003. *Art in the Lives of Ordinary Romans: Visual Representation and Non-Elite Viewers in Italy, 100 B.C.–A.D. 315*. Berkeley: University of California Press.

D'Ambra, E. 1988. "A Myth for a Smith: A Meleager Sarcophagus from a Tomb in Ostia." *AJA* 92: 85–99, 311.

———. 1998. *Roman Art*. New York: Cambridge University Press.

D'Ambra, E., and G. Métraux, eds. 2006. *The Art of Citizens, Soldiers, and Freedmen in the Roman World*. BAR-IS 1526. Oxford: Archeopress.

Donohue, A. 2005. *Greek Sculpture and the Problem of Description*. Cambridge: Cambridge University Press.

Dwyer, E. J. 1982. *Pompeian Domestic Sculpture: A Study of Five Pompeian Houses and Their Contents*. Rome: Giorgio Bretschneider.

Gazda, E. K., ed. 2002. *The Ancient Art of Emulation: Studies in Artistic Originality and Tradition from the Present to Classical Antiquity*. Ann Arbor: University of Michigan Press.

Hallett, C. H. 2005a. "Emulation versus Replication: Redefining Roman Copying." *JRA* 18: 419–35.

Hallett, C. H. 2005b. *The Roman Nude: Heroic Portrait Statuary, 200 BC–AD 300*. Oxford: Oxford University Press.

Hölscher, T. (1987) 2004. *The Language of Images in Roman Art*. Translated by A. Snodgrass and A. Künzl-Snodgrass. Cambridge: Cambridge University Press. Originally published as *Römische Bildsprache als semantisches System*.

Kampen, N. B. 1981. *Image and Status: Roman Working Women in Ostia*. Berlin: Mann.

———. 1995. "On Not Writing the History of Roman Art." *ArtB* 77(3): 375–78.

———. 2003. "On Writing Histories of Roman Art." *ArtB* 85(2): 371–86.

Kleiner, D. E. E. 1977. *Roman Group Portraiture: The Funerary Reliefs of the Late Republic and Early Empire*. New York: Garland.

———. 1992. *Roman Sculpture*. New Haven: Yale University Press.

Kleiner, F. S. 2010. *A History of Roman Art*. Boston: Wadsworth.

Knapp, R. 2011. *Invisible Romans: Prostitutes, Outlaws, Slaves, Gladiators, Ordinary Men and Women... the Romans that History Forgot*. London: Profile.

Lott, J. B. 2004. *The Neighborhoods of Augustan Rome*. Cambridge: Cambridge University Press.

Maiuri, A. 1942. *L'ultima fase edilizia di Pompei*. Rome: Istituto di studi romani.

Marvin, M. 2008. *The Language of the Muses: The Dialogue between Roman and Greek Sculpture*. Los Angeles: J. Paul Getty Museum.

Mayer, E. 2012. *The Ancient Middle Classes: Urban Life and Aesthetics in the Roman Empire, 100 BCE–250 CE*. Cambridge, MA: Harvard University Press.

Mouritsen, H. 1996. "Order and Disorder in Late Pompeian Politics." In *Les Élites municipales de l'Italie péninsulaire des Gracques à Néron*, edited by M. Cébeillac-Gervasoni, 139–44. Naples and Rome: Centre Jean Bérard, Ècole Française de Rome.

Panciera, S. 1987. "Ancora tra epigrafia e topografia." In *L'Urbs: Espace urbain et histoire (1er siècle avant J.-C.–IIIe siècle après J.-C.)*, 61–86. Rome: École Française de Rome.

Perry, E. 2005. *The Aesthetics of Emulation in the Visual Arts of Ancient Rome*. Cambridge: Cambridge University Press.

Petersen, L. H. 2006. *The Freedman in Roman Art and Art History*. Cambridge: Cambridge University Press.

Ramage, N., and A. Ramage. 2008. *Roman Art*. 5th ed. Upper Saddle River, NJ: Prentice Hall.

Stewart, P. 2003. *Statues in Roman Society: Representation and Response*. Oxford: Oxford University Press.

———. 2004. *Roman Art*. Oxford: Oxford University Press.

———. 2008. *The Social History of Roman Art*. Cambridge: Cambridge University Press.

Wallace-Hadrill, A. 1994. *Houses and Society in Pompeii and Herculaneum*. Princeton: Princeton University Press.

Webster, J. 2008. "Slavery, Archaeology and the Politics of Analogy." *Archaeological Dialogues* 15(2): 139–49.

Zanker, P. 1970–71. "Über die Werkstätten augusteischer Larenaltäre und damit zusammenhängende Probleme der Interpretation." *BullCom* 82: 147–55.

———. 1975. "Grabreliefs römischer Freigelassener." *JdI* 90: 267–315.

———. (1979) 1998. *Pompeii: Public and Private Life*. Translated by D. L. Schneider. Cambridge, MA: Harvard University Press.

———. 1990. *The Power of Images in the Age of Augustus*. Translated by A. Shapiro. Ann Arbor: University of Michigan Press.

CHAPTER 4.8

GENDER

EVE D'AMBRA AND FRANCESCA TRONCHIN

INTRODUCTION

IN the late 1960s, scholars questioned the canon of works that constituted the field of Roman sculpture. In particular, they sought out art and artifacts that documented the lives of Roman citizens unattested in the ancient historical sources (Bianchi Bandinelli 1967). In the study of classical art and archaeology, the question of gender arrived at the same moment as the new social history that aimed to redefine history from below. Workers' struggles, rather than court intrigues, took center stage. Classicists asked where the silent women of Rome were and found tales of stoic mothers and courageous daughters in the ancient written sources (Pomeroy 1975). Livy's account of the founding of Rome and Plutarch's exemplary lives, however, focus on elites, and the occasional mention of womenfolk concerns the privileged, political classes. In the wake of the social upheavals of the late sixties, art historians and archaeologists turned their attention to the monuments commissioned by the lower echelons of Roman society. Some scholars sought to include ignored works of art in the corpus; others aimed to demonstrate the dominant influence of imperial art, for instance, the immense appeal of Augustan classicism, or, conversely, the gulf between court art and that of humble citizens (see essay 4.7, Petersen). The question of gender was first posed at this juncture—when Roman art was viewed in terms of its full range of patrons, from senators to ex-slaves, from metropolitan Rome to remote provinces.

Gender refers to the construction of sexual identities, usually articulated in terms of anatomical and sociocultural differences (Montserrat 2000, 154). In the classical world male and female were polarized into a binary system in which the male was aligned with strength, wisdom, virtue, initiative, and integrity, while the female was identified with weakness, ignorance, vice, indolence, and deceit (Kampen 1996b, 16). Heteronormativity, in which the sexual norm is presumed to be heterosexuality, also shaped depictions of gender. Thus the female was inherently secondary and, therefore, powerless, in the patriarchal society of Rome. Yet, women's biological role as mothers rendered them crucial to the empire and its well-being, and the good wife and mother were enshrined in the household (Treggiari 1991; Dixon 1992). In reality, boundaries were somewhat blurred in the social hierarchy that endowed elite women with honor and respect, as well as some influence (J. P. Hallett 1984). In the following, we begin with the moment at which representations of women became significant in the study of Roman sculpture and then turn to issues of gender in reliefs, portraits, and mythological sculpture. If our inquiry into gender favors the female, it is because images of women in ancient Rome demonstrated difference in a male-dominated culture.

Gender and Status

The book that changed the field was Natalie Boymel Kampen's *Image and Status: Roman Working Women in Ostia* (1981). This groundbreaking volume considered the iconography of female vocation across a variety of activities (from retail trade to artisanal production and professional services), and pointed out gendered differences in the imagery: male-dominated production of tools or equipment in comparison with the prominence of female social relationships and caregiving (Kampen 1981). Other than minimal antiquarian interest in crafts and trades, until this study there had been little interest in art depicting the lives of anonymous Romans. That labor—and women's work specifically—was depicted at all in Roman art had not previously been thought worthy of investigation (Brown 2000).

Women's work involved service to customers, represented in scenes of women selling goods in market stalls or shops, or the care of infants and children, as seen in the sarcophagi depicting biographical narratives of male subjects from birth to the attainment of high office (Kampen 1981; 1982, 65). Nurses in the latter appear as subsidiary figures in scenes of the protagonist's attainment of political and military power, also evoked with female figures personifying virtues or abstract ideas underlying the social order. Kampen's study of the second- and third-century reliefs from Ostia traced the contours of a culture coexistent with that of the court of Rome and senatorial aristocracies.

The literal, nonsymbolic style of funerary reliefs (although some may have served as shop signs as well) represent simplified figures and generic scenes of street life (Kampen 1981). They do not reference the ideal forms of Hellenic statuary, and mythological allusions are usually absent. For example, one relief represents a produce saleswoman who stands in a market stall made from trestle tables (figure 4.8.1). She is framed by her goods, which are rendered with sufficient linear detail to identify garlic, cauliflower, and zucchini. The half-figure behind the table shows the simplified and rough forms of a rounded face with hair pulled back and a body clothed in a loose tunic and mantle. Lacking the individualized facial features of a portrait, the figure instead appeals with a gesture that signals speech with the two little fingers in a closed position while the others are extended on the oversized hand. The grocer is shown pointing to her goods and addressing a potential customer in the characteristic tactic of the "hard sell,"

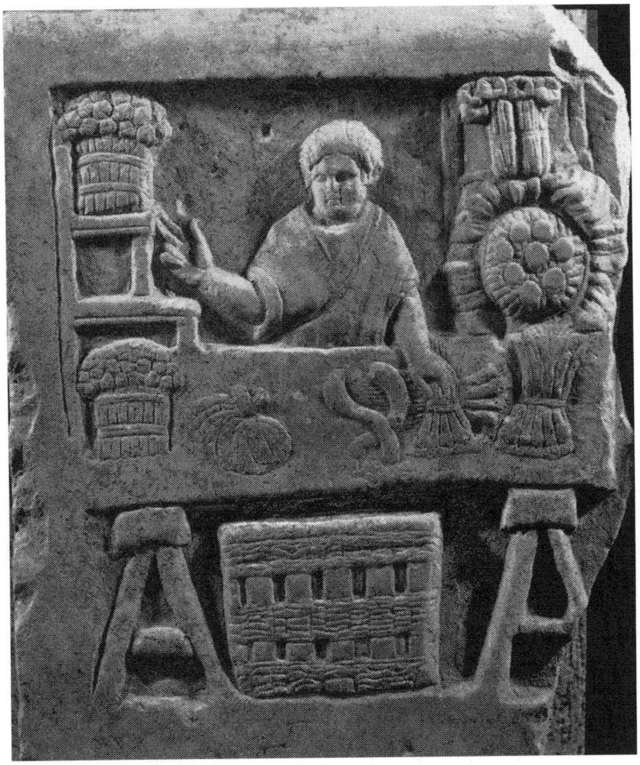

FIGURE 4.8.1 Greengrocer's Relief, late second or early third century AD. Ostia, Museo Ostiense.

demonstrating her mettle at attracting customers in a crowded market (D'Ambra 2007, 139). The saleswoman appeals directly to the viewer, who stands in for the passersby at the marketplace. The reliefs commissioned by working-class patrons tend to depict figures placed frontally who are dominated, if not subsumed, by objects, the goods they sell or produce. The scenes and settings typically appear to be containers for the inventory of items, arranged in rows or stacks in a shallow space. Often more closely observed and finely detailed than the figures, the trade goods come into sharp focus as the means of making a living.

This relief and many others like it commemorate saleswomen in scenes that characterize the teeming, competitive atmosphere of the marketplace. The corpus of Latin inscriptions includes epitaphs of a female dealer in grains, a mosaic worker, and perfumer, among many others. The reliefs depict the most public aspects of their jobs: the greengrocer hawking her wares, a poultry seller carrying out a transaction at her stall, and so on; women are the focus of attention and activity. This aspect of their labor made the women appear disreputable and degraded to elite men, who characterized them as aggressive, shameless, and surely willing to sell their bodies as easily as they would a head of garlic (D'Ambra 2007, 140). Notably, the reliefs celebrate the qualities that ensured the women's success and also demonstrated their marked difference from the modest and demure matrons of means. The reliefs and inscriptions indicate that women worked alongside their husbands or supported themselves in a variety of occupations or professions, yet they remain largely invisible in the texts of poets and historians who provided the standard accounts of Roman life.

Natalie Kampen's contribution lies in her focus on the status and public roles of women in one community within a circumscribed period. Her analysis of the rather style-less style of the reliefs from Ostia, with their shallow spatial setting, the clutter of sharply-contoured objects, and the simplified figure style with no individualization, also applies to reliefs in the provinces. Working people across the empire conveyed their identity in art through their occupations. Rather than reflecting regional differences, reliefs commemorated artisans and merchants in a remarkably similar style, as seen in the blacksmiths' reliefs from the Isola Sacra Necropolis in Ostia and Aquileia in northern Italy, as well as in monuments to service staff, such as the wet nurse Severina in Cologne (Kampen 1976, 164–6, 178–9, fig. 61).

In subsequent essays, Kampen extended her interest in gender to the state reliefs of the Augustan period with mythological or allegorical subjects (see essay 3.5, Sobocinski and Wolfram Thill). The themes from the founding of Rome conveyed a sense of the social order and the ideal roles of men and women, rulers and their subjects, Romans and barbarians. Patriarchy maintained a strict hierarchy of values that privileged the dominant male citizen at the expense of the female, characterized by scholars in the eighties as "the other," that is a lower being, chaotic, unruly, and closer to nature. In the ancient accounts of the early city, female sexuality was seen to undermine the institutions of family and the state if not kept in check. In particular, unmarried women served as intermediaries for outsiders to gain access to Rome, as in Livy's accounts of the Sabine women and Tarpeia (Kampen 1988, 15–19). Indeed, a public building in the center of the Roman Forum, the Basilica Aemilia, featured a sculptural frieze representing scenes from the legendary founding of Rome, with the Rape of the Sabine Women and the Punishment of Tarpeia among the extant panels (figure 4.8.2). The fragmentary reliefs depict

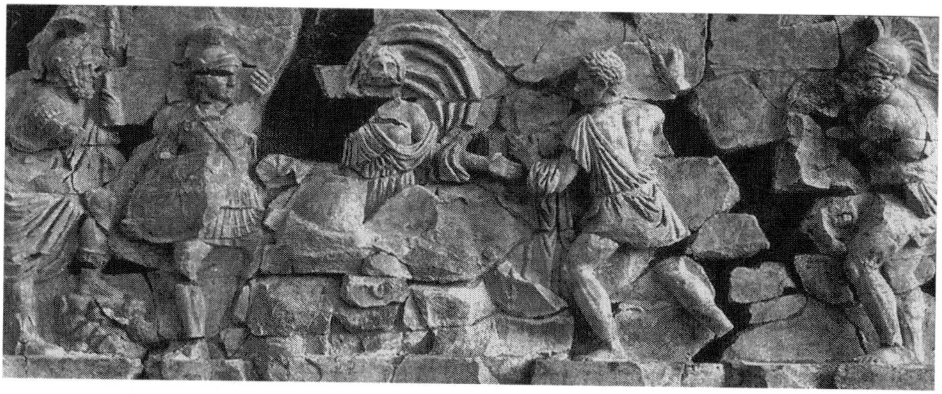

FIGURE 4.8.2 Relief from the Basilica Aemilia, Punishment of Tarpeia. Augustan period. Rome, Antiquarium of the Roman Forum.

the Sabine women under assault with their arms flung out and streaming locks of hair. The Sabine women, however, become Roman wives and are thus transformed from outsiders to insiders: their identity and allegiances change. The Roman Tarpeia, on the other hand, has allowed the enemy to enter the city, and for this she is punished by the foreigners she has helped: the relief depicts the Sabines crushing her with their shields. Even those who profited from her treachery scorned her actions. The themes celebrated women who assumed Roman values as their own as exemplary citizens. Furthermore, Kampen observed that the classicizing style of the reliefs, recalling Hellenic art of the fifth to fourth centuries BC, underlined the theme's implications of the overriding triumphalism and destiny of Rome (Kampen 1988, 19).

Another monument from Augustan Rome, the Ara Pacis Augustae, was decorated with relief sculpture that commemorated the dedication of the altar and set the historical event in the heroic context of early Rome. One panel depicts a resplendent full-figured female with two babies on her lap. The theme of regeneration of the Roman populace and the natural world is writ large in the relief that represents the health and well-being of Rome: the human figures take center stage with the enthroned earth mother flanked by the personification of breezes, as indicated by their billowing drapery, while the stalks of grain refer to the thriving fields and the diminutive animals to the resilience of the herds. While the identification of the female figure as Tellus is somewhat controversial (she has also been called Italia and Pax, among others), the iconography of fertility is very apparent in her voluptuous body and attendant figures. It is characteristic that the fecund female body is equated with the land, now blooming forth without interruption due to the Augustan peace. In this example of state art, motherhood is idealized as Tellus, the figure with the handsome facial features of a goddess and whose cleavage and midriff are revealed through clinging and nearly transparent garments, an outfit that would bring scandal to a Roman matron. Clearly Tellus is a figure from the realm of art and, as such, would have been distinguished from a Roman matron by viewers; yet, the pure and rarefied version of femininity in this scene, with its visual linking of babies and breasts as well as the motherly lap cradling fruits of the field, plays into traditional ideals of womanhood. The political and patriotic aspects of Augustan themes appealed to many citizens throughout the empire who commissioned works of art and architecture in emulation of the famed Roman monuments for their own cities. For example, a relief from Carthage in North Africa seems to be a close copy of this panel (Zanker 1988, 313–14). A showy edifice in Pompeii featured the vine scroll ornament of the Ara Pacis, which, no doubt, enhanced its elegance and demonstrated the worldliness of the woman, Eumachia, who built it for her fellow citizens (D'Ambra 2012, 400–413).

Natalie Kampen also turned to imperial monuments of later periods to analyze representations of women under imperial rule. The categories of gender and status proved effective in the analysis of female figures, whether Dacian women forced into exile as seen on the Column of Trajan or Julia Domna depicted on the Quadrifrons Arch in Leptis Magna (Kampen 2009, 38–63, 82–103). As mothers of the next generation, women maintained the social order by transmitting values and norms. Imperial women like Julia Domna were often assimilated to personifications that enlarged their presence and endowed them with authority, if in name only. The authority of imperial women, however, lacked any basis in public office, so remained informal and intermittent as they occasionally stepped in as surrogates. In propaganda the emperors' wives or daughters were confined to the domestic and dynastic spheres, with imagery bearing the high gloss of Hellenic art. On the other hand, those who felt the rough hand of imperial might, such as the vanquished Dacian women, were represented with sufficient ethnographic detail to identify them as barbarians indigenous to specific contested regions (for costume, see Sebesta and Bonfante 1994). Despite the curiosity their representations probably aroused in Roman spectators, the Dacian women gained a degree of dignity as they were portrayed struggling to keep their families together. In the pioneering studies of Natalie Kampen, gender became a trenchant analytical tool, particularly when inflected with the variables of social status. Rather than conceptualizing woman as other, this fulcrum allowed scholars to observe how the category of woman was represented within a highly differentiated social structure.

Statue Types

Representations of women in Rome were common in both the public and private spheres (see essay 3.4, Wood). Unfortunately, today, many are unidentifiable, though they were once labeled by inscriptions on their bases (now lost) and may also have been recognizable via portrait heads (often also now detached from preserved pieces). Statues erected in fora honored outstanding women of the leading families. Since the only public office women could hold were priesthoods, they were notably disadvantaged in the Roman competition for honors, titles, and other marks of public acclaim (Nicols 1989, 117–42). Only about 10 percent of honorific statues represented women (Trimble 2011, 216). We might expect that these statues offered realistic depictions of elite women in comparison to the simplified figures of saleswomen identified by their stock in trade. Female portrait statues, however, appear formulaic and standardized with heavily draped bodies in the manner of goddesses. Women were portrayed in a limited number of statue types (the Pudicitia, Ceres, the Kore Albani, Hera Borghese, and the Small and Large Herculaneum Woman types) derived from Hellenic tradition (Fejfer 2008, 335; see essay 3.4, Wood). Whether these statue types were specifically identified with the various goddesses by Roman patrons likely did not matter; more important was the presence of the statues amidst displays of male honorific figures in the most prestigious quarters of cities. The statues endowed honor upon women deemed worthy and gave them visibility. The latter, however, was tempered by their representation in the form of familiar female figures from the repertory of classical culture and the state religion. That the statue types had not changed for hundreds of years enhanced their venerability and linked the women with tradition and the cultural legacy of Hellenism under Rome (Trimble 2011, 198, on the type of the Large Herculaneum Woman as "a generic form of classicism").

The female honorific statue embodies a deep contradiction in Roman society: in order to be ennobled in the form of a statue, the women assumed the form of goddesses or personified virtues. This guise elevated them above their peers but effectively masked their identity with conventional poses, drapery suited to divinity, and often idealized faces. In other words, the images of women of substance all looked somewhat alike, as the conventional statue types allowed for limited modification or individualization. Male honorific statues also can be classified into standard types, but these were rooted in the experience of their political participation celebrated in active, heroic forms. Men were commemorated in statues as orators, warriors, and priests, roles in which they participated in civic life and through which they made careers, whereas women were distinguished by sculptural forms that transformed them into divinities or abstractions, figures larger than life but without reference to their conditions of existence.

In the past scholars have made much of the minor differences among the various female statue types in order to identify and classify them. Although grounded in closely observed details, the literature, paradoxically, has demonstrated the rigid replication of types to create appearances of uniformity (e.g., variations are found in the positions of arms and patterns of drapery folds with bundles at the shoulders or hips). The monotony of draped female figures reflects Roman attitudes that, in contrast to public, political men, wives and mothers should recede from sight and exert moral influence, if at all, within the religious and domestic spheres.

Portraits and Likeness

The popularity of standardized statue types to create the effect of uniformity produced immediately recognizable, monumental images for esteemed women (Trimble 2011, 200–205). If the sculptural bodies were not realistic representations of their subjects, then were the heads also borrowed from the classical repertory? Or were the heads portraits with individualized likenesses in order to modify or customize the statues? Social protocols of gender affected the development of portraits, and to understand the differences in development and function of both female and male portraits, it is necessary to turn to their model, the imperial portrait.

The emperor's portrait forms the *Zeitgesicht* (the period face), the features and style of which were emulated in the portraits of citizens. Yet, the male private portraits (that is, portraits from outside the imperial family) are not identical with the imperial models (Fejfer 2008, 270–85), but were individualized for recognition. The emperor's portrait clearly leads the way, while the other images follow. The portraiture of imperial women, however, has been more difficult to distinguish from the private female portraits, and, in fact, the heads of unidentified women often bear elaborate adornment in the form of coiffures (331–69). It appears that the emperors' female relatives were not always in the vanguard. First of all, imperial women of the high empire are less visible in the ancient sources, both written texts and artifacts. They tend to be represented by fewer sculptural portrait types. In addition, the marble heads of busts or full-length statues were usually found without inscribed bases to identify them by name.

The study of coins has established the basis for identifying representations of imperial personages, including imperial women (Wood 1999, 63–70, 88–92, 289–95). Yet coins' miniature portraits in profile, their shallow relief, and the lack of noses on many sculpted heads in the round, limit the value of comparisons between these two portrait types (Fejfer 2008, 411). Furthermore, on coins imperial women's images on obverses tend to be paired with personifications of virtues on reverses, such as *Concordia, Fecunditas*, and *Castitas* (Alexandridis 2010, 201–4). The personified virtues are abstract in concept and depicted as veiled and draped female figures with attributes. They are virtually interchangeable as stock types. The canon of female virtues ornamented coins to support the moral and ethical foundations of society and the empire. The imagery distances viewers from the imperial women, who appear simply as fixtures to round out the political agenda of the imperial court.

Imperial female portraiture has long been characterized as realistic heads with fashion hairstyles (Bartman 2001, 1–25). While modern scholarship has submitted the female heads to intense analysis in order to delineate features of individual likenesses, minimal descriptive detail means that many female portraits cannot stand up to this level of scrutiny. In fact, homogeneity tends to be a marked characteristic of female heads, and faces of women in the imperial household may not have been at all easily recognized even when their husbands or fathers ruled Rome. The number of female heads, their limited number of portrait types, and their relationship to the coin profiles are rather different than those of the emperor (Alexandridis 2010, 219–24).

The interpretive problem lies in the production of portraits, attitudes about making women visible, and the tradition of representation. Although we know very little about the production of portraits, we must question how many women of any rank modeled for sculptors, given ideals of modesty and, in the case of imperial women, the chasm in social status between the artisans and the women of the imperial court. Propriety demanded modesty and self-restraint from women, who receded from public view in most instances. By adopting portraits with generic or classicizing features, sculptors endowed women with ennobled presences and greater stature. Portraits were produced after other portraits, and when depicting women, sculptors often made use of the venerable tradition of representing them as beautiful, ageless goddesses. Instead of being surprised by uniformity among female portraits, perhaps we should be startled by the extent to which their conventional sets of features were individualized (Dillon 2010, 131–4). There are, however, periods in which female portrait faces assumed a greater degree of individualization.

Abstraction and Adornment

Adornment appeared in period styles that featured showy or striking coiffures (Stephens 2008, 110–32). *Cultus* (i.e., adornment and dress) entailed the regimens of labor, care, and control over the body and its outward appearance that resulted in refinement and sophistication (Olson 2008, 9). The style of the Flavian and Trajanic periods is often described as realistic, with harsh or aging physiognomies sharing broad features under elaborate or architectonic coiffures. Although the scholarship attributes hairstyles to tastes of the imperial women, the enduring appeal of the so-called Flavian coiffure suggests that other phenomena were at work beyond that of copying the styles of imperial women (D'Ambra 2013). The hairstyle marked the women beneath it as members of a group of matrons whose inherent dignity was demonstrated by their impeccable grooming and comportment. As the coiffure spread across the empire and endured, it very well may have expressed a cosmopolitan style projecting high culture and status.

Status has been thought to have been the primary factor in representation that trumped gender: elite female patrons preferred the classicizing forms that embodied ideals of beauty, while women of the lower social orders were portrayed in a vernacular style characterized by reductive, inorganic forms. This generalization does not hold true in portraits and funerary statues in which anonymous (many lower-status, occasionally freedwomen) women donned elaborate coiffures or adopted the resplendent body of Venus in styles that overtook those of the imperial women's imagery (D'Ambra 1996). It is peculiar in a starkly hierarchical society that the women of the imperial house did not dominate nor even stand out from the women below them in rank in their imagery (Fejfer 2008, 344–5). Since the emperor's wife held no political office and performed a loose array of traditionally female duties involving cult and patronage, neither dedicated costumes nor attributes defined her iconography. The suppression of explicit individualized features has confounded scholars, who have retreated to the complexity of the highly wrought coiffures instead. Yet, the reserved faces with limited descriptive detail were capable of representing a broad swath of womanhood with a sense of the appropriate characteristics of dignity and integrity. The definition of the portrait requires some latitude to include these highly standardized and formulaic heads. But again, we must remember that inscribed plaques, usually engraved on bases separate from their statues (and now lost), completed the function of commemorative statues by identifying their subjects specifically (Trimble 2011, 181–96) and often named titles and honors achieved by women (see essays 3.4, Wood; and 4.5, Tuck).

Action Figures

Proto-Barbies

The best testimony of the wide influence and appeal of the female sculptural portrait lies in its use for girls' dolls. More commonly made of rags, dolls were also carved of ivory and a few of these from the second century AD are finely produced with high levels of workmanship. One in particular evokes the idealized female portraits of the Antonine women through its pristine facial features and tower coiffure (figure 4.8.3). Its adult figure also appears ready to be dressed in the high-belted tunics favored by the popular statue types. The doll was found with its seventeen-year-old female owner, Crepereia Tryphaena, in her sarcophagus in the city of Rome (Sommella Mura 1983, 10–16). Although Crepereia Tryphaena was nearing maturity, she apparently had not cast off the doll that accompanied her to the grave. The doll, with its looks of a sculpture in miniature, took part in the girl's life, rather than being erected as a monument to it.

The ivory doll bears some resemblance to female portrait sculpture of the mid-second century AD due to the finesse of its workmanship (down to the fingernails) and the

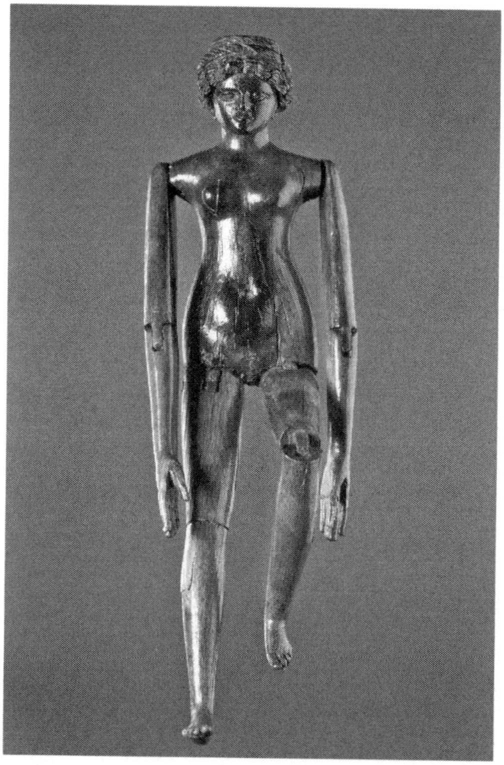

FIGURE 4.8.3 Doll of Crepereia Tryphaena, mid-second century AD. Rome, Musei Capitolini, Centrale Montemartini.

period style of the coiffure. The facial features, however attractive, have been simplified to the point of caricature with overly large almond-shaped eyes and small, pursed lips. It does not portray an individual but, rather, projects to the doll's owner an image of a lovely, fair maiden. That the doll possessed a grooming kit with a mirror (also interred with the girl and her doll) suggests that the games played included studying the face in the mirror and applying the techniques of beautification (D'Ambra 2007, 61–2). Small ivory combs and jewelry also belonged to the doll, who wore a ring to which a tiny key was attached—the key opened the box of grooming accessories.

Precious possessions under lock and key point to the imaginary world inhabited by Crepereia Tryphaena and her doll. The fine contours of the doll's face and figure demonstrate how ideals of sculptural form serve to introduce girls to the requirements of a refined and sophisticated appearance. As artifacts deriving from artistic traditions, such dolls functioned as hand-held sculpture. Hands were intended to move the doll's limbs, supplied with joints at the shoulders, elbows, hips, and knees. Tasks such as changing the doll's clothes probably kept Crepereia Tryphaena busy with her toy, though in other games the doll's movements brought her into the girls' world with a semblance of life. In imaginative play, the doll as a sculpture in miniature engaged with Crepereia Tryphaena in very different ways than statues, which only seemed to step off their pedestals in myth or poetry (see essay 6.5, Perry). Given that the female body and its beautification was considered in poetic terms as a work of art, it is fitting that some Roman girls played with dolls that resembled honorific statues (D'Ambra 2013).

Heroes and Leaders

Toy figures found in boys' tombs consisted of action figures, such as soldiers or gladiators. A preference for action figures also marks the monumental statuary of the emperor and elite males. Sculpture distinguishes the emperor and the senatorial leadership in their various roles as statesmen and orators, generals, or priests of the state religion (Fejfer 2008, 181–212). Marble or bronze figures feature the heads of state mounted on spirited steeds, declaiming with scrolls in hand, or in the act of offering to the gods with heads veiled. As much as these figures evoke aspects of military command, public service, or ceremonial duties, they are statuary types with conventions of their own.

Clothing characterizes the role of the figure in male sculpture, and the same subject was depicted in different costumes that befit his various offices and appointments. As the female honorific sculpture adapted Hellenic models that featured idealization, male statue types typically represented youthful bodies at their peak of development and among these, the nude portrait statue raises provocative issues. Nudity is frequently considered a hallmark of classical visual culture, and contrary to many modern Western conventions, there was a rather firm division between nudity and eroticism in antiquity—naked figures were not necessarily sexual. Nakedness had originally been viewed as a shameful state for outsiders and other non-elites like slaves and prisoners, but later came to signify positive agonistic, heroic, or divine associations for a male portrait sitter when viewed through a Hellenic lens (Bonfante 1989; C. H. Hallett 2005, chap. 3). As with many things Greek, nudity in portraiture was initially avoided in the visual crafting of Roman male identity, but private patrons had adopted the costume of "heroic nudity" as early as the first century BC, as seen in the Tivoli General (figure 6.2.1) and the Pseudo-Athlete from Delos. Indeed it is not until Greek visual culture effectively usurped the native Etruscan over the course of the late Republic that the transition from clothed gods (Etruscan) to nude ones (Greek) took place. The acceptance of nudity in the Roman visual language came first to images of gods before being deemed appropriate for mortal men (C. H. Hallett 2005, 89–92). The type of nudity eventually chosen for Roman male portraits was aspirational, asserting the virility and athleticism of the sitter through an idealized and muscular physique; this state of undress evoked the perfection and vigor of great gods and heroes.

Nude male portraits frequently employed weapons as attributes, likely to clarify this undressed state as heroic rather than vulnerable, yet male nudity need not be motivated by a specific mythological narrative. The exposure of the female body, however, required justification by the mythological vignette of Venus bathing, which evoked the Roman matron's beautification regime and the female stylization of the self (D'Ambra 1996, 219–32; 2000, 101–114). Both male and female nude portraits employed the attributes of divinities, not to suggest apotheosis, but that the sitter possessed the superior characteristics of the emulated god (C. H. Hallett 2005, 225–9). The poses of the nude male figures also communicated physical strength through posture and gesture: well-balanced *contrapposto*, a raised arm, face squarely regarding the viewer. Often the wrinkled faces of the portrait heads seem to clash with their powerfully formed physiques, as in the portrait statue of Claudius in the guise of Jupiter. The divine body replaces the emperor's own figure, known for various physical defects or deficiencies, as accounted in the ancient written sources (Suet. *Claud.* 2–4).

Hermaphrodites and Hermaphroditus

Hermaphrodites present a special case in Roman constructions of sexual and gender identity in their endowment with both male sex organs and female breasts; in Roman eyes they violated natural laws of anatomy and defied the categories of the social order. While the myths of Hermaphroditus inspired depiction of hermaphrodites in sculpture and domestic wall-painting (Diod. Sic. 4.6.5; Ov. *Met.* 4.285–388), actual intersex people were mostly reviled by the Romans and seen as ill portents (Livy 31.12). The fourth-century AD author Ausonius described hermaphrodites as either sexually apathetic or prone to excessive passion. Hermaphroditus more emphatically contravenes expected Roman gender norms than, say Omphale, yet images of the double-sexed figure are more popular, according to the surviving archaeological evidence (Ajootian 1990; Kampen 1996a). No doubt, the popularity of the hermaphrodite reflected fascination with the doubling of sexual attributes and the abundance of vitality this implied. The most familiar sculptural type of Hermaphroditus, the Sleeping Hermaphrodite

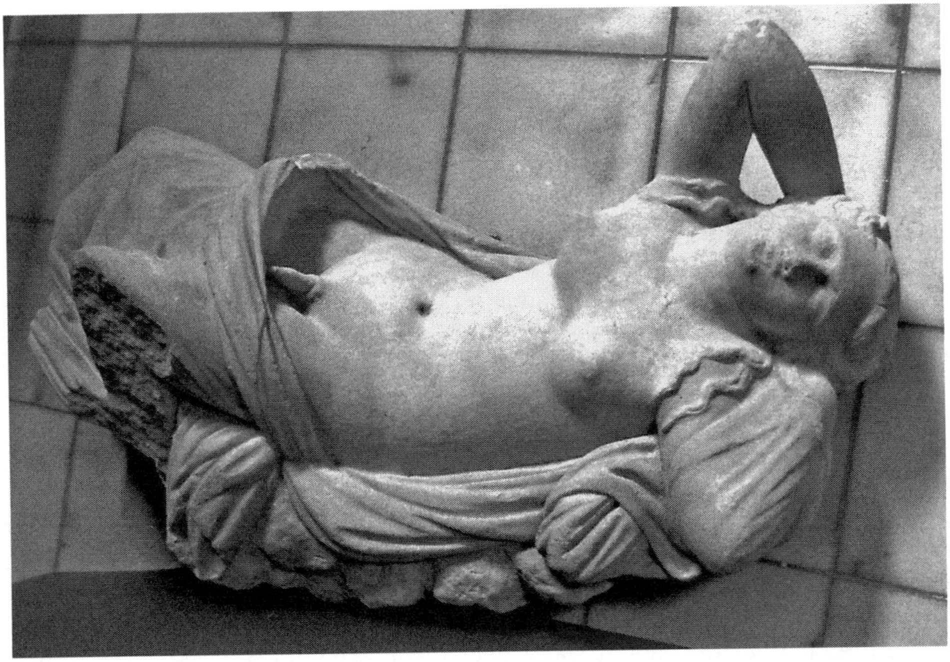

FIGURE 4.8.4 Sleeping Hermaphrodite, first century AD. Pompeii, Ufficio Scavi.

who twists his/her body to present male and female sex organs to viewers on opposite sides of the sculpture, offering the opportunity for a titillating surprise, has excessively colored modern interpretations of this subject. Yet a number of other depictions of Hermaphroditus offer the viewer direct access to both male genitalia and female breasts in one glance (figure 4.8.4). The *anasyromenos* type wears a garment that reveals the female breasts and lifts the hem of the dress to reveal male genitals (Ajootian 2000, 220–23). The lifting of the garment is an essential element of this type of hermaphrodite image: as women's garments concealed their pubic region even if the breasts were clearly rendered under the cloth, Hermaphroditus must raise his/her skirt to distinguish him/herself as not simply female. The aggressive gesture of exposure suggests that statues of hermaphrodites may have served to avert the evil eye, in the manner of Priapic imagery in Roman domestic gardens (Ajootian 2000, 230; Clarke 2007, 180).

Sexuality and Sexual Behavior in Roman Sculpture

As has been noted above, much of the iconography of female figures in Roman sculpture emphasized their fertility and sexual attractiveness to men, yet these images were not explicitly sexual. Statues of goddesses, as in the Venus types, appropriately exploited the divinity's appealing fleshiness in nude representations. The opportunity to eroticize male figures did not go unmissed by Roman sculptors; a class of *Idealplastik* representations of vaguely mythological young men has been singled out as a genre of "sexy boys" because of the subjects' youthful, lithe, nude forms and poses that draw attention to their genitalia (Bartman 2002). This category of eroticized young men in sculpture can be viewed as an exception to the rule of heteronormativity in Roman visual culture, as these figures were likely commissioned by men.

Sexuality or eroticism in Roman sculpture can be difficult to interpret, and it should be noted that overtly sexual scenes are effectively absent, being more the purview of Roman painting (as in scenes from the Suburban Baths at Pompeii; Clarke 1998, 212–40). *Symplegmata*, however, are indeed scenes of intercourse yet are exclusively mythological in nature as the couplings include at least one nonhuman, like the group of a satyr and a hermaphrodite from Villa A at Oplontis or Pan and a goat from the Villa of the Papyri at Herculaneum (Stähli 1999). Other examples of explicit sexual scenes are found in the so-called minor arts, and the best-known and most controversial example of such a scene is the silver Warren Cup, with its depiction of homosexual activity on a rather luxurious object (figure 4.8.5; Clarke 1993; 1998, 61–78). The figured relief scene displays the style and technique found in monumental relief sculpture, and its subject matter

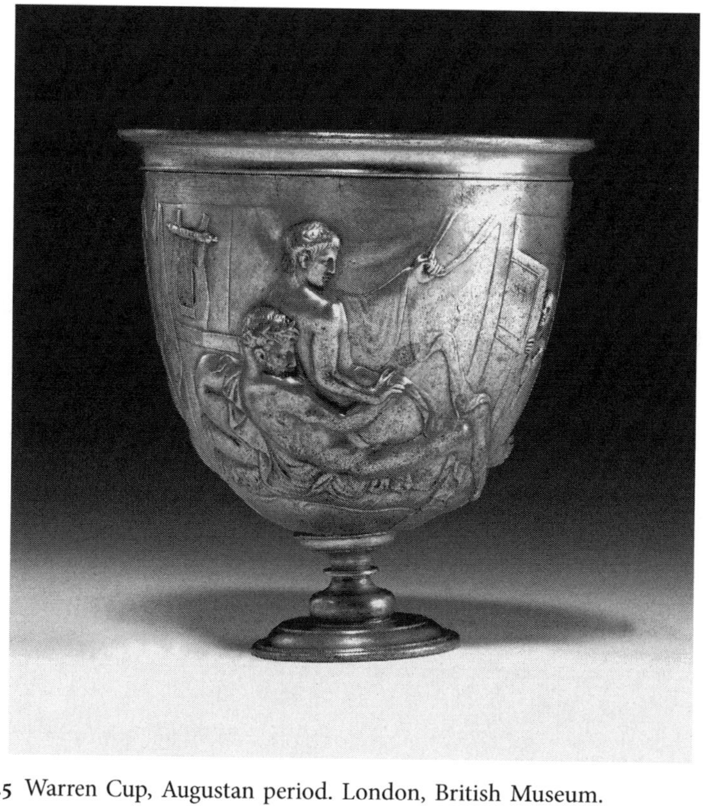

FIGURE 4.8.5 Warren Cup, Augustan period. London, British Museum.

appealed to a rarefied group of connoisseurs or collectors. With its Augustan date, the Warren Cup forms the antithesis to the Tellus panel of the Ara Pacis. The panel on the state altar and the silver goblet both display the elegance of high classical style, with graceful symmetry, masterful balancing of relief layers, fine details, full-bodied figures with chiseled profiles, and recondite allusions to myth and *paideia*. Yet the Ara Pacis represents the female body as nature, the fruits of which sustained the empire, while the couplings on the silver vessel contravened state-sanctioned morality. The bombastic appeal of the former with its complex symbolic repertory may have gone over the heads of some Romans, although its linking of the female form with fields in harvest was easy to grasp. The frank sexuality of the Warren Cup may have evoked an intellectual nostalgia for the Greek symposium from those who had never experienced it, so to attribute it to those who flouted the Augustan moral campaign would be overreaching. An erotic charge takes effect at different intensities in the two works.

Conclusion

Scholarship on Roman sculpture now deploys a more expansive identification of "the Romans," including patrons and viewers of sculpture from the lower social orders and the edges of the empire. Ranuccio Bianchi Bandinelli first brought attention to the problem of "the other" in imperial society within and without the city of Rome (see essay 4.7, Petersen). Gender is implicit in this configuration of the other, defined by difference and represented as the opposite of the elite male citizen of metropolitan Rome. In Bianchi Bandinelli's groundbreaking studies, those outside of the empire or barely enfranchised within it assumed its forms of representation through appropriation or adaptation. Natalie Boymel Kampen's early scholarship explored gender within the lower social orders of the freed and freeborn working classes, a realm in which the classicizing forms of Hellenic art had no purchase. Although social status was a determinative of the reliefs' style, gendered differences are apparent in the emphasis on gestures and human contact in the working women's commemorations. The classically draped figures of elite women erected in public, initially dismissed because they all looked alike, turn out to be portraits of individuals despite their highly conventional types and features. As the human body dominated the sculptural repertory, gender figured prominently to make visible both social norms and transgressive states.

Bibliography

Ajootian, A. 1990. "Hermaphroditos." *LIMC* 5(1): 268–85.

———. 2000. "The Only Happy Couple: Hermaphrodites and Gender." In Koloski-Ostrow and Lyons 2000, 220–42.

Alexandridis, A. 2010. "The Other Side of the Coin: The Women of the Flavian Imperial Family." In *Tradition und Erneuerung: Mediale Strategien in der Zeit der Flavier*, edited by N. Kramer and C. Reitz, 191–237. Berlin: Walter de Gruyter.

Bartman, E. 2001. "Hair and the Artifice of Roman Female Adornment." *AJA* 105(1): 1–25.
———. 2002. "Eros's Flame: Images of Sexy Boys in Roman Ideal Sculpture." In *The Ancient Art of Emulation: Studies in Artistic Originality and Tradition from the Present to Classical Antiquity*, edited by E. K. Gazda, 249–71. Ann Arbor: University of Michigan Press.
Bianchi Bandinelli, R. 1967. "Arte plebea." *DialArch* 1(1): 7–19.
Bonfante, L. 1989. "Nudity as a Costume in Classical Art." *AJA* 93(4): 543–70.
Brown, S. 2000. "'Ways of Seeing' Women in Antiquity: An Introduction to Feminism in Classical Archaeology and Ancient Art History." In Koloski-Ostrow and Lyons 2000, 12–42.
Clarke, J. R. 1993. "The Warren Cup and the Contexts for Representations of Male-to-Male Lovemaking in Augustan and Early Julio-Claudian Art." *ArtB* 75(2): 275–94.
———. 1998. *Looking at Lovemaking: Constructions of Sexuality in Roman Art*. Berkeley: University of California Press.
———. 2007. *Looking at Laughing: Humor, Power, and Transgression in Roman Visual Culture, 100 B.C.–A.D. 250*. Berkeley: University of California Press.
D'Ambra, E. 1996. "The Calculus of Venus: Nude Portraits of Roman Matrons." In Kampen, ed. 1996, 219–32.
———. 2000. "Nudity and Adornment in Female Portrait Sculpture of the 2nd Century AD." In Kleiner and Matheson 2000, 101–4.
———. 2007. *Roman Women*. Cambridge: Cambridge University Press.
———. 2012. "Women on the Bay of Naples." In *A Companion to Women in the Ancient World*, edited by S. L. James and S. Dillon, 400–413. Oxford: Blackwell.
———. 2013. "Mode and Model in the Flavian Female Portrait," *AJA* 117: 511–25.
Dillon, S. 2010. *The Female Portrait Statue in the Greek World*. Cambridge: Cambridge University Press.
Dixon, S. 1992. *The Roman Family*. Baltimore: Johns Hopkins University.
Fejfer, J. 2008. *Roman Portraits in Context*. Berlin: Walter de Gruyter.
Hallett, C. H. 2005. *The Roman Nude: Heroic Portrait Statuary, 200 BC–AD 300*. Oxford: Oxford University Press.
Hallett, J. P. 1984. *Fathers and Daughters in Roman Society: Women and the Elite Family*. Princeton: Princeton University Press.
Kampen, N. B. 1976. "Images and Status of Roman Working Women: Second and Third Century Reliefs from Ostia." PhD diss., Brown University.
———. 1981. *Image and Status: Roman Working Women in Ostia*. Berlin: Mann.
———. 1982. "Social Status and Gender in Roman Art: The Case of the Saleswoman." In *Feminism and Art History*, edited by N. Broude and M. D. Garrard, 63–78. New York: Harper and Row.
———. 1988. "The Muted Other." *ArtJ* 47: 15–19.
———. 1996a. "Omphale and the Instability of Gender." In Kampen, ed. 1996, 233–46.
———. 1996b. "Gender Theory in Roman Art." In Kleiner and Matheson 1996, 14–25.
———, ed. 1996. *Sexuality in Ancient Art*. Cambridge: Cambridge University Press.
———. 2009. *Family Fictions in Roman Art: Essays on the Representation of Powerful People*. Cambridge: Cambridge University Press.
Kleiner, D. E. E., and S. B. Matheson, eds. 1996. *I, Claudia: Women in Ancient Rome*. New Haven: Yale University Art Gallery.
Koloski-Ostrow, A. O., and C. Lyons, eds. 2000. *Naked Truths: Women, Sexuality, and Gender in Classical Art and Archaeology*. London: Routledge.

Montserrat, D. 2000. "Reading Gender in the Roman World." In *Experiencing Rome: Culture, Identity, and Power in the Roman Empire*, edited by J. Huskinson, 153–81. London: Routledge.
Nicols, J. 1989. "*Patrona Civitatis*: Gender and Civic Patronage." In *Studies in Latin Literature and Roman History V*, edited by C. Deroux, 117–42. Brussels: Latomus.
Olson, K. 2008. *Dress and the Roman Woman: Self-Presentation and Society*. London: Routledge.
Pomeroy, S. 1975. *Goddesses, Whores, Wives, and Slaves: Women in Classical Antiquity*. New York: Schocken.
Sebesta, J. L., and L. Bonfante, eds. 1994. *The World of Roman Costume*. Madison: University of Wisconsin Press.
Sommella Mura, A. 1983. *Crepereia Tryphaena: Un tesoro nascosto di 2000 anni fa*. Torino: Fabbri.
Stähli, Adrian. 1999. *Die Verweigerung der Lüst: Erotische Gruppen in der antiken Plastik*. Berlin: Dietrich Reimer.
Stephens, J. 2008. "Ancient Roman Hairdressing: On (Hair)pins and Needles." *JRA* 21: 110–32.
Treggiari, S. 1991. *Roman Marriage*. Oxford: Oxford University Press.
Trimble, J. 2011. *Women and Visual Replication in Roman Imperial Art and Culture*. Cambridge: Cambridge University Press.
Wood, S. 1999. *Imperial Women: A Study in Public Images, 40 B.C.–A.D. 68*. Leiden: Brill.
Zanker, Paul. 1988. *The Power of Images in the Age of Augustus*. Translated by A. Shapiro. Ann Arbor: University of Michigan Press.

PART V

REGIONS AND PROVINCES

CHAPTER 5.1

NORTHERN GAUL, GERMANY, AND BRITAIN

KIMBERLY CASSIBRY

Introduction

Supernatural Cernunnos, sculpted with antlers bearing Celtic torques, still draws attention to the earliest major monument in Paris, the Pillar of the Sailors (figure 5.1.1). Such sculptures seldom appear in surveys of Roman art, yet they have been central to debates about provincial art, religion, and identity because of an unusual historical circumstance. The region's patrons, unlike residents of the empire's Mediterranean territories, did not commission stone monuments with dedicatory inscriptions prior to conquest. Roman sculptural and commemorative practices offered a new way to perpetuate cultural heritage and express personal perspectives on empire. Cernunnos, for instance, counts among many Celtic deities named for the first time on the Pillar of the Sailors, itself the first of many monuments set up by prosperous indigenous navigators. The pillar and other dedications concerned with cultural memory feature below in the sections "Religious Sculpture and Imperial Syncretism" and "Funerary Sculpture and the Mobility of Provincial Patrons." The essay begins, though, with an overview of the region's thematically diverse sculptures, their study, and their evolving role in the field's debates about Roman imperialism.

Boundaries, Evidence, and Approaches

This essay's geographic scope heeds recent calls to look across provincial boundaries in order to challenge both scholarly parochialism and the traditional center-to-periphery paradigm of cultural influence (Walter 2000; Stewart 2009; Kampen 2014). No fewer than six provinces—Gallia Aquitania, Gallia Lugdunensis, Gallia Belgica, Germania

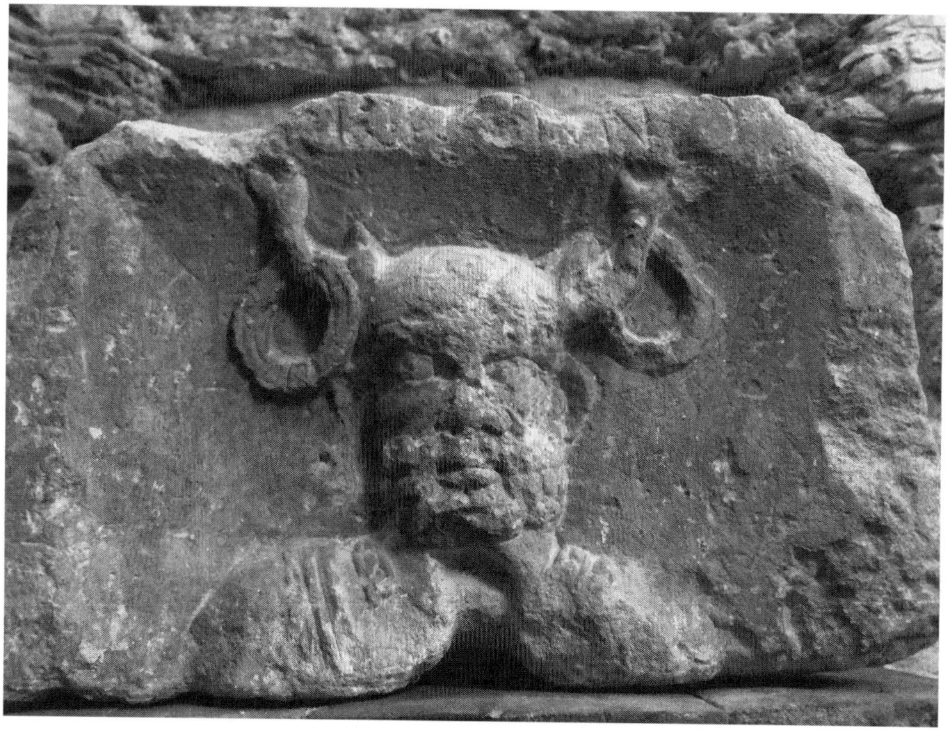

FIGURE 5.1.1 Detail of Cernunnos, Pillar of the Sailors, AD 14–37, Paris, France. Paris, Musée National du Moyen Age—Musée de Cluny.

Superior, Germania Inferior, and Britannia—fall within the region. Nine modern nations—France, the Netherlands, Luxembourg, Belgium, Germany, Switzerland, England, Wales, and Scotland—now claim this same territory and foster independent research programs. Yet there are good reasons to consider the lands together: circulation studies suggest that the area formed an interactive zone under Roman rule, while southern Gaul (Gallia Narbonensis; see essay 5.2, Jiménez and Rodà) was oriented toward Italy (Rothe 2012, 247).

The genres, themes, and historiography of the region's sculptural corpus also distinguish these northern provinces from southern Gaul and Italy. Craftsmen here produced a substantial body of relief sculptures. Those visualizing deities have inspired postcolonial critiques of syncretism, the integration of religious realms. Reliefs on funerary monuments have drawn the attention of scholars reconstructing the identities of the provinces' residents. Cult statues of Celtic and Graeco-Roman gods and portrait statues of emperors and citizens survive in smaller numbers and have elicited fewer discussions. Historical and state reliefs are extremely rare (see essay 3.5, Sobocinski and Wolfram Thill); figurines in terracotta (see essay 2.5, Erlich), stone, and metal are quite abundant.

More than forty catalog volumes have not yet fully recorded the region's extensive sculptural corpus. Émile Espérandieu's catalogs for Roman Gaul and Roman Germany revolutionized study in the early twentieth century (1907–1938; 1931). With supplements (Espérandieu, Lantier, and Duval 1947–1981), new editions (*Nouvel Espérandieu*, Lavagne 2003–), and an online database (http://nesp.mmsh.univ-aix.fr/index.htm), the series remains the touchstone for Roman Gaul. Catalogs addressing either Roman Germany or Britain now appear in the empire-wide series *Corpus Signorum Imperii Romani*, published under the direction of national institutes and organized by site and subject. As excavations continue in every province, the catalogs will require attentive updating.

Because stone sculptures became prominent only after conquest, they might seem to offer evidence of successful Romanization, a process loosely and traditionally defined as Rome's transformation of provincial culture through coercive incentives. Yet patrons often commissioned sculptures to commemorate indigenous gods and enduring tribal affiliations and in doing so transformed the parameters of Roman art. Frustrated by the "Romanization" paradigm's intransigence in the face of contradictory evidence, many scholars now seek to recover diverse provincial identities, despite the risk of merely turning the rejected model on its head by pursuing difference instead of uniformity (Hingley 2005; Mattingly 2014). Martin Pitts (2007) has rightly warned that "identity" is a slippery modern concept to apply to the past, especially when archaeological evidence is considered in isolation, rather than as the result of dynamic social practice. This essay approaches cultural change as a multilateral negotiation at the local level, wherein aspects of Rome's own hybrid culture were adopted and diversified according to the traditions of communities and priorities of patrons. In considering how patrons and their craftsmen constructed identities in text and image, this essay focuses on relief sculptures grounded in religious and funerary acts of commemoration.

Even a brief survey of the sculptures' patrons reveals a broad cross-section of society. Affluent businessmen like *nautae* (shippers) commissioned both funerary and religious monuments, including the sculpture of Cernunnos mentioned above (figure 5.1.1). Local politicians, especially *decuriones* (city councilmen), funded major monuments like Jupiter Columns in Roman Germany (figure 5.1.2). Troops stationed at the British and Rhineland frontiers commissioned a substantial number of sculpted votive plaques and tombstones, not only for themselves but also for their spouses and former slaves (figures 5.1.3–4). Such soldiers, from Italy and increasingly from the provinces, played a crucial role in transmitting sculptural practices not only within the military but to civilian groups, too.

Less is known about the region's sculptors. They rarely if ever signed their work and seem to have set up few monuments asserting their own identities. Scholars assume that most were indigenous (Webster 1997, 172; Green 2003b, 47), while a few immigrants may have accompanied mobile military units (Kampen 2006, 130–32). Because anyone with artistic aptitude could be trained to sculpt in a certain technique, attempts to read a craftsman's geographic origins in his carving remain risky.

Assessing the quality of the sculptures these craftsmen produced has sharply divided specialists, who often lament the lack of naturalism (lifelike proportions and volumes in coherently integrated figures) and recognizable Graeco-Roman styles (like neoclassicism or verism). The damaged and fragmentary Cernunnos relief, for example, reveals

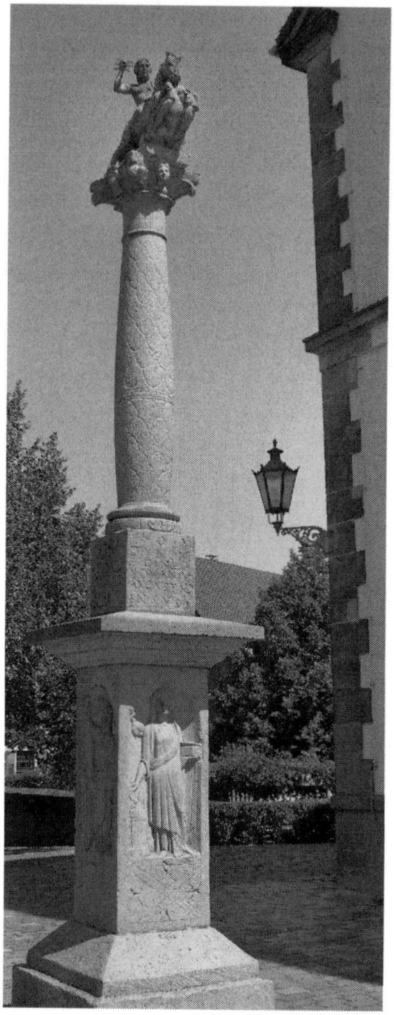

FIGURE 5.1.2 Cast of a Jupiter Column, second to third centuries AD, Ladenburg, Germany. Ladenburg, Lobdengau-Museum Ladenburg.

a typically mixed approach, with no clear stylistic affiliation: the facial features possess lifelike proportions, but the eyes seem asymmetrical, the ears barely attached to the head, and the neck impossibly short (figure 5.1.1). Earlier generations studied reliefs like the Cernunnos head despite their perceived aesthetic deficiencies. More recently, some have wondered if such appearances might be intentional. Natalie Kampen, for instance, has suggested that the "generic" styles found on construction commemoration plaques (called "legionary distance slabs") from the Antonine Wall in Scotland "forged a sense of commonality" among international soldiers accustomed to diverse non-elite traditions (Kampen 2006, 132). Miranda Green has gone further and connected naturalism to Romanness and argued that sculptures entirely lacking it reject Rome (2003b).

In wholly unnaturalistic sculptures, Catherine Johns sees instead a "naïve" lack of artistic skill and training (2003a). She has also drawn attention to materials: the region's stones did not hold fine details (Johns 2003b; also Stewart 2010). Ultimately, the act of commemoration (Kampen 2006, 132) and the subject matter (Stewart 2009, 269) seem to have mattered most to patrons. Sculptures structuring religious, funerary, and civic exchanges did not necessarily require flawlessly executed naturalism or recognizable Graeco-Roman styles to function effectively.

Historical Background: Conquest, Tribes, and Artistic Precedents

In interpreting the region's sculpture, outdated notions of first contact between Romans and residents must be set aside: goods and peoples circulated for centuries prior to the slow advance of the empire's border (Woolf 1997, 2011). Southern Gaul having been annexed by Rome around 120 BC, northern Gaul subsequently fell to Caesar in the 50s. His heir Augustus divided the northern territory into the provinces Gallia Aquitania, Lugdunensis, and Belgica in 27 BC (Wightman 1985; Woolf 1998; Le Bohec 2008; Ferdière 2011). Britannia formed in AD 43, principally in England then spreading west into Wales and north into southern Scotland (Breeze 2006; De la Bédoyère 2006; Mattingly 2007; Hobbs and Jackson 2010). Germania Superior and Inferior officially took shape around AD 85, after more than a century of occupation and combat (King 1990; Wamser, Flügel, and Ziegaus 2000; Carroll 2001; Bechert 2007). By the fifth century AD, the Roman Empire had begun to abandon the northern provinces, many of which had been reorganized and renamed in the intervening years.

Resident tribes possessed distinct names (such as Parisii, Remi, Treveri, etc.), which persisted into the Roman era and are often still employed by their continuously occupied cities (Paris, Reims, Trier, etc.). Greek and Roman authors have caused enduring confusion by inconsistently ascribing these tribes to larger ethnic groups, such as Britons, Celts, Gauls, Belgae, and Germans (Woolf 2011). For rhetorical purposes, they often overemphasized differences, especially in the mixed Rhineland zone (C. Wells 1995; Krebs 2011). Many scholars, responding to perceived commonalities in language and/or material culture, now use "Celtic" as an overarching term of convenience for Iron Age tribes throughout Europe and the British Isles (Koch 2007, 1), yet doing so is highly controversial (James 1999; Collis 2003).

No written treatise of any kind survives from the era of tribal independence, although nascent literacy seems to have preceded Roman rule (Lambert 2003, 71–89; Lacroix 2011). Caesar, writing in the 50s BC, relates that the Gauls used the Greek alphabet for most matters, though the druids insisted on the oral transmission of their own knowledge (*BG* 6.14). Long before conquest, however, the region's tribes had shared a preliterate mindset and saw the world in ways literate societies (then and now) struggle to comprehend (P. Wells 2012). The subsequent spread of dedicatory inscriptions reveals a significant shift in mentality, while also capturing, for the first time, the words residents adopted to describe themselves.

Statues were relatively rare prior to Roman rule, as were full representations of the human form. Tribal craftsmen excelled instead at portable metalwork decorated in the abstract La Tène style, which often emphasized the metamorphosis and disarticulation of plants, animals, and humans (Harding 2007; Garrow, Gosden, and Hill 2008; Müller 2009; Garrow and Gosden 2012). Only isolated groups of stone sculpture have been found (none with dedicatory inscriptions). In the fifth and fourth centuries BC, sculptors working primarily east of the Rhine created a few statues and relief sculptures, notably the Hirschlanden and Glauberg warriors, the Pfalzfeld pillar, and the Heidelberg head (Frey 1998; Armit and Grant 2008). In the fifth to second centuries, the warrior elite of southernmost Gaul set up stone statues of seated soldiers holding human heads, notably at Entremont and Roquepertuse (Py 2011, 83–182; Armit 2012, 127–95). A later group, from the late second and first centuries BC, occurs at Paule (northwestern France), where statuettes less than a meter tall portray human figures, perhaps ancestors, with stocky proportions and blunt features (Ménez et al. 1999). Wooden statues of humans and animals, often unnaturally proportioned, have been excavated in greater numbers from sacred springs and sanctuary enclosures (Webster 1995b), where rare anaerobic conditions may have arrested an intended transformation of a spiritually charged medium (Green 2004, 98–102). Dendrochronological dates typically range from the late second century BC to the first century AD in France and Germany; an earlier series exists in Britain (Green 1998, 20–21). As with written words, experimentation with figural sculpture preceded conquest, but developed in radically new directions thereafter.

Religious Sculpture and Imperial Syncretism

Sculptural dedications from the Roman era reveal that the region's residents supplicated deities from every corner of the empire. Mithras, a supposedly Persian god popular with the army, received iconographically complex altarpieces throughout the Rhineland and even as far away as London (Londinium, Britannia; Turcan 1993). Egyptian Isis had a temple at Mainz (Mogontiacum, Germania Superior) full of votive gifts (Witteyer 2004). Greek and Roman deities appeared in every major city, and, unusually, even took precedence over historical subjects on the region's few commemorative arches, including those at Besançon (Vesontio Sequanorum, Germania Superior), Reims (Durocortorum Remorum, Gallia Belgica), Mainz, and London (Walter 1985; Fornasier 2003; Cassibry 2008; McGowen 2010). I focus here, however, on sculptures of the region's own gods, because they have inspired a substantial debate about syncretism.

Indigenous gods and goddesses are known principally through sculptures and inscriptions of the Roman era (Hatt 1989; Nerzic 1989, 47–68; Green 1995, 465–88; Deyts 1998). For prior centuries, we know neither how residents conceived of the divine realm nor whether they represented aspects of it figurally. Caesar's *Gallic War* offers insight into the situation in the 50s BC, a period of crisis not necessarily indicative of earlier times. He claims that the Gauls recognized deities comparable to Mercury, Apollo, Mars, Jupiter, and Minerva, and that they frequently represented the one like Mercury; he gives no Gallic names, only classical equivalents (*BG* 6.17). The Germans, he contends, considered forces like the sun, fire, and moon divine (*BG* 6.21). Though evidence is scant, most scholars assume that the regionally distinct gods later attested in Roman sculptures did exist—at least conceptually—before conquest. They then consider whether such divine beings were empowered or disempowered by being named, represented figurally, and connected to Graeco-Roman partners (Webster 1995a).

Relief sculptures visualize independent, coalesced, and cooperative deities; Latin dedicatory inscriptions preserve valuable information about names. The popular Epona (an equestrian goddess), for instance, appears only with horses on votive altars, plaques, and figurines (Green 2003a, 102–6; Webster 2003, 46–50). Paired deities of the same gender could merge, as in the gilt bronze cult statue of Sulis-Minerva from Bath (Aquae Sulis, Britannia). Gods and goddesses might also be juxtaposed as "married" couples, as on many Mercury and Rosmerta plaques, or in larger groups, as on the Cernunnos, Apollo, and Mercury altar from Reims (both considered below). Three concerns have animated the most promising discussions of this varied corpus: gender precedence, hierarchies of image and text, and the appropriation of Roman sculptural traditions for pre-Roman cult practices.

Gendered power relations have been read in divine "marriages," which almost always match indigenous goddesses with Graeco-Roman gods. Representations of regional conquest as potential rape—as when the emperor Claudius threatens the female personification of Britannia in the Sebasteion relief from Aphrodisias, Turkey—suggest one interpretive paradigm wherein the male figure, and by extension Rome, dominates (Ferris 2000, 55–60; Rodgers 2003). Jane Webster (1997), however, notes the more prominent political and social roles attributed to Celtic women by classical authors and accepts the hypothesis of a strong "feminine principle in Celtic divinity" (175–6). Analyzing widespread sculptural dedications to Rosmerta and Mercury (primarily in central and eastern Gaul, but also in Germany and Britain), she suggests that their marriage "shows the subversion of a Roman deity to the power of an important local goddess" and that the "Romanized medium of stone imagery" enhances the subversiveness (177). Likewise, Green sees *Gallitas* (Gallicness) expressed by the female partner and *Romanitas* (Romanness) by the male, and asserts that the female, "with her consistent imagery of fertility, abundance, and regeneration, may be the dominant partner" (2003a, 97).

Visual analysis of juxtaposed deities reveals mostly egalitarian representations. Divine couples like Rosmerta and Mercury appear as figures of similar height standing side by side: neither in pose, nor in scale, nor in composition does one dominate (Green

2003a, 109–110). In contrast, some dedications visually emphasize a native deity. On the Cernunnos altar from Reims, now lacking an inscription, the god appears as an antlered man seated in a cross-legged pose (Pray Bober 1951, 50; Deyts 1998, 120; Altjohann 2003, 69). Central to the composition, he would tower over the flanking Apollo and Mercury if he stood.

Cernunnos can be identified on the Reims altar and elsewhere because his image is labeled on the Pillar of the Sailors (*Pilier des Nautes*; figure 5.1.1). The pillar's Latin dedication honors Jupiter Optimus Maximus alone, but the program of relief sculptures preserves an unprecedented array of regional and Graeco-Roman deities and heroes, all with names inscribed above them (Adam 1984; Lejeune 1988). Scholars alternately prioritize the hierarchical inscription or the visually egalitarian reliefs in their interpretations. William von Andringa (2009) has argued that this pillar and comparable dedications enact a subordination of indigenous gods to the Roman pantheon's leader. Henri Lavagne (1984) persuasively reads a moment of possibility, when the coexistence of the patrons' preferred deities from both pantheons seemed feasible. The patrons' perspective merits further consideration. In the dedicatory inscription, they call themselves the *Nautae Parisiaci*, a corporation of shippers from the Parisii tribe. With a monument originally rising nearly five meters, they made their mark on the Roman cityscape just beginning to emerge in Paris (Lutetia Parisiorum, Gallia Lugdunensis).

The Pillar of the Sailors has been cited, controversially, as an archetype for the German provinces' most distinctive and pervasive type of monument, the Jupiter Columns (Hatt 1952). The cult that produced them was regionally circumscribed and may have perpetuated indigenous practices and beliefs. Bauchhenss and Noelke (1981) have cataloged fragments from well over 500 examples in the German region, and at least ten each from Belgium and Britain; the columns also appear in northeastern Gaul (Walter 1970), but practically nowhere else in the empire. Dedications peaked around AD 200, and their enduring value is attested in secondary inscriptions recording restorations (Kousser 2010).

The emphatically polytheistic, highly customized Jupiter Columns could rise to 15 m or more (figure 5.1.2). Dedicatory inscriptions honor Jupiter Optimus Maximus, as do crowning statue groups showing the god either enthroned, often alongside his consort Juno, or on horseback riding down a snake-tailed monster. The latter iconography is inspired by Greek Gigantomachies (battles of gods and giants), though neither Jupiter nor his Greek counterpart Zeus were traditionally equestrian gods. The four-sided bases typically bear relief sculptures of other Graeco-Roman deities. Mercury, Minerva, Juno, and Hercules recur most often, though patrons varied their selections considerably. Above the base, a "Wochengötterstein" ("gods of the week stone") could also increase the number of gods represented. The column shafts themselves preserve scale patterns and, occasionally, vines and small-scale gods. Corinthian column capitals hold female personifications of seasons.

The monuments' significance divides scholars, who locate their perceived efficacy either in the Roman era or the prehistoric past. Green (1986) has hypothesized that the columns reimagine rituals in sacred woods; for her, scale patterns conjure bark on skeuomorphs of trees. She argues further that the wheel emblems occasionally borne by Jupiter equate him with indigenous sky gods. Woolf (2001), however, insists that patrons would not have remembered pre-Roman practices so long after conquest. His evocative phrase, "Jupiter Columns rivaled each other like skyscrapers over Manhattan" (127), points to another aspect of their appeal. Jupiter Columns became a prestige monument in Roman Germany and northeastern Gaul, where the eye-catching form found favor with local elites, including city councilmen (*decuriones*) and their families, as well as soldiers (Woolf 2001, 121–2; Cassibry 2008). Potent divine intercedents, the columns drew mundane attention to those who could afford lavishly effective votive offerings.

Funerary Sculpture and the Mobility of Provincial Patrons

Sculpted funerary monuments with inscribed dedications likewise appeared in the region only after conquest (McGowen 2010, 89–97). Towering pillar tombs with extensive iconographic programs, like those at Bartringen and Igel (both Gallia Belgica), deserve wider renown (Scheid 2003; Kremer 2009). Here, however, I focus on the more modest tombstones, which have illuminated the identities of itinerant Roman soldiers, indigenous merchants, and their spouses. The social and geographic mobility attested in their words and images merits greater consideration in future studies of imperial circulation.

Roman soldiers acknowledged mortality by making provisions for personal monuments (Hope 2001; 2003). A cavalry tombstone, set up around AD 100 and excavated at Lancaster (Britannia) in 2005, offers new evidence for the degree of customization permitted by the genre's flexible schema (figure 5.1.3; Schleiermacher 1984; Bull 2007; Iles and Shotter 2009, 68–87). After invoking the Roman gods of the underworld (*Dis Manibus*), the inscription names the deceased "Insus, son of Vodullus, member of the Treveri tribe" (from Trier, Augusta Treverorum, Gallia Belgica) and connects him to the "Ala Augusta," one of many cavalry units for auxiliary soldiers (who became eligible for Roman citizenship upon retirement, if they lived that long). The relief sculpture follows convention by visualizing Insus in Roman armor, astride a horse, and trampling an enemy; the foe's decapitation, however, is unique among known cavalry stones. Both rider and horse are carved competently, vigorously, and legibly, rather than with finely nuanced transitions. The composition cleverly collapses the space between viewer and viewed: Insus's snarling steed leaps beyond the architectural frame. Cavalryman, Treveran, Roman, noncitizen, itinerant—these are just a few aspects of Insus's identity captured in this monument, which once towered 2 m tall on the road leading into Lancaster's fort.

Although such military tombstones played a crucial role in spreading general awareness of funerary commemoration, not all civilian communities adopted the habit. Hope

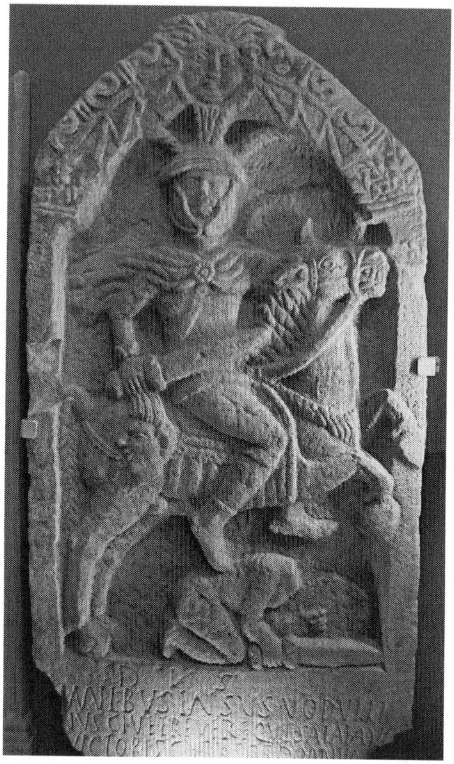

FIGURE 5.1.3 Tombstone of Insus the Treveran, c. AD 100, Lancaster, Britain. Lancaster, Lancaster City Museum.

argues that in Britannia, tombstones "were of particular relevance to immigrants and outsiders who used the medium to assert their identity in a strange land" (1997, 246). The more plentiful civilian tombstones of northern Gaul and Germany, in contrast, offer insight into the professional pride of indigenous men.

The stele of Blussus from Mainz, for instance, addresses his work as a *nauta* (shipper), the same occupation claimed by the patrons of Paris's Pillar of the Sailors. A Latin inscription, unusually repeated on both sides, asserts that Blussus lived seventy-five years, that his wife Menimane initiated the monument during her lifetime, that a house slave lay in the same spot, and that a son called Primus ultimately set up the stele (Selzer 1988, 95–8, 168–9). Primus ("First") is an unimaginative Latin name contrasting with his parents' mellifluous indigenous ones; the inscription omits mention of the tribal affiliations their names lead us to expect. The three sculpted figures convey affluence: a bejeweled woman and a man holding a bulging bag of coins sit side by side; a boy (either Primus or the house slave) stands behind and between them. On the back of the tombstone, a small but accurately carved ship further glosses the source of Blussus' prosperity. In his business, he may have profited from ancestral expertise in navigating the regions' extensive river networks, which were never fully supplanted by Roman roads (De Izarra 1993). Many other *nautae* are attested epigraphically, especially at Lyon

(Lugdunum, capital of Gallia Lugdunensis), which stood at the confluence of the Rhône and Saône rivers.

Funerary portraits like those of Blussus and Menimane indirectly preserve evidence for changes in regional dress, as clothes themselves rarely survive (Wild 1985, 366). Blussus, for example, wears the sleeved Gallic tunic falling to mid-calf and the hooded Gallic cape, an indigenous garment that remained popular in the Rhineland and northern Gaul during the Roman era. Menimane is clad in the eponymous Menimane's ensemble, which included a long-sleeved inner bodice (visible at her wrists), a sleeveless tunic draped from three brooches, and an outer cloak with elaborate folds (Wild 1985, 394–5). To judge from brooch finds and reliefs on other tombstones, her mode of dress was popular in the former territory of the Treveri tribe (originally spanning from Trier to the Rhine river), but fell from fashion by the end of the first century AD, not long after Menimane modeled it on her mid-century tombstone (Rothe 2012, 237–9). Subsequently, women in the area joined those across Germany, northern Gaul, and Britain in favoring the Gallic ensemble, a new mode of dress that reimagined and lengthened the long-sleeved Gallic tunic still worn by men. Ursula Rothe (2012) describes the sartorial invention as a "Third Way" that neither perpetuated prior female dress nor adapted Rome's own belted fashions for women. Significantly, she sees greater regional integration as the catalyst. For Rothe, the garment "symbolized membership in a cultural sphere that stretched beyond the local community, but not as far as Rome" (244). Innovation could bypass Rome altogether without signifying dissent.

Such regional networks intersected with wider imperial circuits connecting one periphery to another. A tombstone from Arbeia (South Shields, Britannia), the easternmost fort along Hadrian's Wall, commemorates a freed slave in a way that links this northern frontier to the island's southern end as well as to a leading city of the eastern Mediterranean (figure 5.1.4; Toynbee 1962, 160). Dated around AD 200, the monument also preserves longstanding tribal and city affiliations. The formulaic Latin inscription honors a thirty-year-old woman named Regina, described both as a member of the Catuvellauni tribe (based in southeast England) and as the freed slave and wife of Barates from Palmyra (Syria). Beneath the Latin, the bereaved husband (whose own tombstone may survive at the Corbridge fort nearby) had a phrase of mourning added in the Palmyrene dialect of Aramaic. Above the text, Regina sits on a wicker chair in a baroque niche of a kind common in the architecture around the eastern Mediterranean but rare in Britain. She gestures to a box and holds what seem to be sewing implements related to the basket of wool on her left. Significantly, she wears the long-sleeved Gallic garment popular in the second century AD. Though damaged, the tombstone still conveys in text, image, and form many aspects of Regina's identity: emancipated, married, Gallic, Catuvellaunian, Roman, wife of a Palmyrene.

Other inscribed provincial sculptures also help reconstruct empire-wide networks. In Arbeia's site museum, Regina's stele stands beside another one controversially attributed to the same Syrian artist (figure 5.1.4; Stewart 2009, 267–9). An inscription gives the deceased's name (Victor) and identifies him as a freed slave of the Maurish people (North Africa). His master (and perhaps lover) Numerianus of the *Ala I Asturum*, an auxiliary

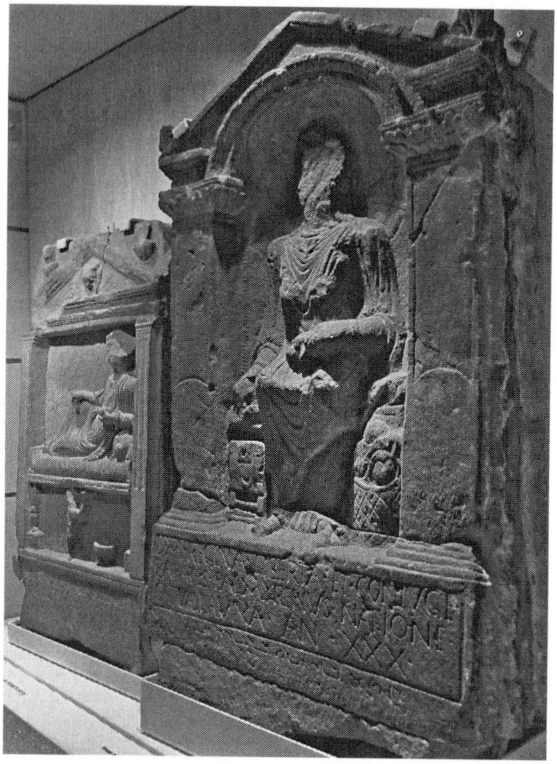

FIGURE 5.1.4 Tombstones of Victor and Regina, second to third centuries AD, South Shields, Britain. South Shields, Arbeia Roman Fort and Museum.

unit originally recruited from Spain, had him depicted in a banquet scene (*Totenmahl*), a tombstone motif popular with both soldiers and civilians. Although Victor and his master, along with Regina and hers, typically appear in studies of Roman Britain, their tombstones establish connections to opposite corners of the Mediterranean and illuminate the personal experience of long-distance cultural exchange. They show one way provincial sculptures could supplement commodities, portable art, and inscriptions in the study of the empire's dynamic circulation.

Conclusion: Rethinking the Canon(s)

Scholars disagree vehemently about the current state of Roman art's canon and even more about its reformulation (Kampen 2003). Even so, the debate merits mention here because so few sculptures from northern Gaul, Germany, and Britain have appeared in general overviews, especially in the English language. This *Handbook*'s incorporation of an essay on the topic promises a more inclusive future, as do other essays in the volume. What remains to be seen is whether specialists concerned with regional canons will increasingly pursue connections among them and whether they will find an effective way to integrate more provincial material into a truly empire-wide Roman art history.

Bibliography

Adam, J.-P. 1984. "Le Pilier des Nautes, Essai de Restitution." In Musée Carnavalet 1984, 299–306.
Altjohann, M. 2003. "Cernunnos-Darstellungen in den gallischen und germanischen Provinzen." In Noelke 2003, 67–80.
Armit, I. 2012. *Headhunting and the Body in Iron Age Europe.* Cambridge: Cambridge University Press.
Armit, I., and P. Grant. 2008. "Gesture Politics and the Art of Ambiguity: The Iron Age Statue from Hirschlanden." *Antiquity* 82: 409–422.
Bauchhenss, G., and P. Noelke. 1981. *Die Iupitersäulen in den germanischen Provinzen.* Cologne: Rheinland.
Bechert, T. 2007. *Germania Inferior: Eine Provinz an der Nordgrenze des Römischen Reiches.* Mainz: Philipp von Zabern.
Breeze, D. J. 2006. *Roman Scotland.* London: Batsford.
Bull, S. 2007. *Triumphant Rider: The Lancaster Roman Cavalry Tombstone.* Lancaster: Lancaster Museums.
Carroll, M. 2001. *Romans, Celts and Germans: The German Provinces of Rome.* Stroud: Tempus.
Cassibry, K. 2008. "Provincial Patrons and Commemorative Rivalries: Rethinking the Roman Arch Monument." *Mouseion* 8(3): 417–50.
Collis, J. 2003. *The Celts: Origins, Myths, and Inventions.* Stroud: Tempus.
De Izarra, F. 1993. *Hommes et Fleuves en Gaule Romaine.* Paris: Éditions Errance.
De la Bédoyère, G. 2006. *Roman Britain: A New History.* London: Thames and Hudson.
Deyts, S., ed. 1998. *À la Rencontre des Dieux Gaulois: Un défi à César.* Paris: Réunion des Musées Nationaux.
Espérandieu, E. 1907–38. *Recueil général des bas-reliefs, statues et bustes de la Gaule romaine.* 11 vols. Paris: Imprimerie Nationale.
Espérandieu, E. 1931. *Recueil général des bas-reliefs, statues et bustes de la Germanie romaine.* Paris: G. van Oest.
Espérandieu, E., R. Lantier, and P.-M. Duval. 1947–1981. *Recueil général des bas-reliefs, statues et bustes de la Gaule romaine. Suppléments.* 5 vols. Paris: Presses Universitaires de France.
Ferdière, A. 2011. *La Gaule Lyonnaise.* Paris: Picard.
Ferris, I. 2000. *Enemies of Rome: Barbarians through Roman Eyes.* Stroud: Sutton.
Fornasier, B. 2003. *Les Fragments architectureaux des arcs triomphaux en Gaule Romaine.* Paris: Les Belles Lettres, Presses Universitaires Francs-Comtoises.
Frey, O.-H. 1998. "The Stone Knight, the Sphinx, and the Hare." *PPS* 64: 1–14.
Garrow, D., and C. Gosden. 2012. *Technologies of Enchantment? Exploring Celtic Art: 400 BC to AD 100.* Oxford: Oxford University Press.
Garrow, D., C. Gosden, and J. D. Hill, eds. 2008. *Rethinking Celtic Art.* Oxford: Oxbow.
Green, M. 1986. "Jupiter, Taranis and the Solar Wheel." In *Pagan Gods and Shrines of the Roman Empire*, edited by M. Henig and A. King, 65–76. Oxford: Oxford University Committee for Archaeology.
———. ed. 1995. *The Celtic World.* New York: Routledge.

Green, M. 1998. "God in Man's Image: Thoughts on the Genesis and Affiliations of Some Romano-British Cult Imagery." *Britannia* 29: 17–30.
———. 2003a. "Poles Apart? Perceptions of Gender in Gallo-British Cult-Iconography." In Scott and Webster 2003, 95–118.
———. 2003b. "Alternative Iconographies: Metaphors of Resistance in Romano-British Cult-Imagery." In Noelke 2003, 39–48.
———. 2004. *An Archaeology of Images: Iconology and Cosmology in Iron Age and Roman Europe*. London: Routledge.
Harding, D. W. 2007. *The Archaeology of Celtic Art*. London: Routledge.
Hatt, J.-J. 1952. "Les monuments gallo-romains de Paris, et les origines de la sculpture votive en Gaule romaine. I. Du pilier des nautes de Paris à la colonne de Mayence." *RA* Sixth Series 39: 68–83.
———. 1989. *Mythes et Dieux de la Gaule*. Paris: Picard.
Hingley, R. 2005. *Globalizing Roman Culture: Unity, Diversity and Empire*. London: Routledge.
Hobbs, R., and R. Jackson. 2010. *Roman Britain: Life at the Edge of Empire*. London: British Museum Press.
Hope, V. 1997. "Words and Pictures: The Interpretation of Romano-British Tombstones." *Britannia* 28: 245–58.
———. 2001. *Constructing Identity: The Funerary Monuments of Aquileia, Mainz, and Nîmes*. BAR-IS 960. Oxford: Archaeopress.
———. 2003. "Trophies and Tombstones: Commemorating the Roman Soldier." *WorldArch* 35(1): 79–97.
Iles, P., and D. Shotter, eds. 2009. *Lancaster's Roman Cemeteries*. Lancaster: Lancaster University Centre for Northwest Regional Studies.
James, S. 1999. *The Atlantic Celts: Ancient People or Modern Invention?* Madison: University of Wisconsin Press.
Johns, C. 2003a. "Art, Romanisation, and Competence." In Scott and Webster 2003, 9–23.
———. 2003b. "Romano-British Sculpture: Intention and Execution." In Noelke 2003, 27–38.
Kampen, N. B. 2003. "On Writing Histories of Roman Art." *ArtB* 85(2): 371–86.
———. 2006. "The Art of Soldiers on a Roman Frontier: Style and the Antonine Wall." In *The Art of Citizens, Soldiers, and Freedmen in the Roman World*, edited by E. D'Ambra and G. Métraux, 125–34. BAR-IS 1526. Oxford: Archaeopress.
———. 2014. "Roman Art and Architecture in the Provinces and Beyond the Roman World." In *The Oxford Handbook of Greek and Roman Art*, edited by C. Marconi, 395–413. New York: Oxford University Press.
King, A. 1990. *Roman Gaul and Germany*. Berkeley: University of California Press.
Koch, J. 2007. *An Atlas for Celtic Studies: Archaeology and Names in Ancient Europe and Early Medieval Ireland, Britain, and Brittany*. Oxford: Oxbow.
Kousser, R. 2010. "A Sacred Landscape: The Creation, Maintenance, and Destruction of Religious Space in Roman Germany." *RES: Anthropology and Aesthetics* 57–8: 120–39.
Krebs, C. 2011. "Borealism: Caesar, Seneca, Tacitus, and the Roman Discourse about the Germanic North." In *Cultural Identity in the Ancient Mediterranean*, edited by E. Gruen, 202–221. Los Angeles: Getty Research Institute.
Kremer, G. 2009. *Das frühkaiserzeitliche Mausoleum von Bartringen (Luxembourg)*. Luxembourg: Musée National d'Histoire et d'Art.
Lacroix, J. 2011. "Un Peuple sans Écriture?" In *Qui étaient les gaulois?*, edited by F. Malrain and M. Poux, 144–55. Paris: Universcience Éditions/Éditions de la Martinière.

Lambert, P.-Y. 2003. *La langue gauloise*. Paris: Éditions Errance.
Lavagne, H. 1984. "Le Pilier des Nautes." In Musée Carnavalet 1984, 275–98.
———., ed. 2003–. *Nouvel Espérandieu: Recueil général des sculptures sur pierre de la Gaule*. 4 vols. Paris: Académie des Inscriptions et Belles-Lettres.
Le Bohec, Y. 2008. *La province romaine de Gaule Lyonnaise: Du Lyonnais au Finistère*. Dijon: Faton.
Lejeune, M. 1988. "Parisii, Paris, L14." In *Recueil des Inscriptions Gauloises (R.I.G.)*, Vol. 2.1, edited by P.-M. Duval, 157–76. Paris: Éditions du Centre National de la Recherche Scientifique.
Mattingly, D. J. 2007. *An Imperial Possession: Britain in the Roman Empire, 54 BC–AD 409*. New York: Penguin.
———. 2014. "Identities in the Roman World: Discrepancy, Heterogeneity, Hybridity and Plurality." In *Roman in the Provinces: Art on the Periphery of Empire*, edited by L. Brody and G. Hoffman, 35–59. Chestnut Hill, MA: McMullen Museum of Art, Boston College.
McGowen, S. L. 2010. *Sacred and Civic Stone Monuments of the Northwest Roman Provinces*. BAR-IS 2109. Oxford: Archaeopress.
Ménez, Y., P. R. Giot, M. F. Laubenheimer, E. Le Goff, and C. Vendries. 1999. "Les Sculptures Gauloises de Paule (Côtes d'Armor)." *Gallia* 56: 357–414.
Müller, F., ed. 2009. *Art of the Celts: 700 BC to AD 700*. Berne: Historisches Museum.
Musée Carnavalet. 1984. *Lutèce: Paris de César à Clovis*. Paris: Société des Amis du Musée Carnavalet.
Nerzic, C. 1989. *La Sculpture en Gaule Romaine*. Paris: Éditions Errance.
Noelke, P., ed. 2003. *Romanisation und Resistenz in Plastik, Architektur und Inschriften der Provinzen des Imperium Romanum: Neue Funde und Forschungen*. Mainz: Philipp von Zabern.
Pitts, M. 2007. "The Emperor's New Clothes? The Utility of Identity in Roman Archaeology." *AJA* 111(4): 693–713.
Pray Bober, P. 1951. "Cernunnos: Origins and Transformations of a Celtic Divinity." *AJA* 55: 13–51.
Py, M. 2011. *La Sculpture Gauloise Méridionale*. Paris: Éditions Errance.
Rodgers, R. 2003. "Female Representation in Roman Art: Feminising the Provincial 'Other.'" In Scott and Webster 2003, 69–93.
Rothe, U. 2012. "Treveran Women's Dress and the 'Gallic Ensemble.'" *AJA* 116: 235–52.
Scheid, J. 2003. "Les Reliefs du mausolée d'Igel dans le cadre des représentations romaines de l'au-delà." *AntCl* 72: 113–40.
Schleiermacher, M. 1984. *Römische Reitergrabsteine: Die kaiserzeitlichen Reliefs des triumphierenden Reiters*. Bonn: Bouvier Verlag Herbert Grundmann.
Scott, S., and J. Webster, eds. 2003. *Roman Imperialism and Provincial Art*. Cambridge: Cambridge University Press.
Selzer, W., ed. 1988. *Römische Steindenkmäler: Mainz in Römischer Zeit*. Mainz: Philipp von Zabern.
Stewart, P. 2009. "Totenmahl Reliefs in the Northern Provinces" *JRA* 22: 253–74.
———. 2010. "Geographies of Provincialism in Roman Sculpture." *RIHA Journal* 5. http://www.riha-journal.org/articles/2010/stewart-geographies-of-provincialism.
Toynbee, J. 1962. *Art in Roman Britain*. London: Phaidon.
Turcan, R. 1993. *Mithra et le mithraicisme*. Paris: Les Belles Lettres.

Von Andringa, W. 2009. *La religion en Gaule Romaine: Piété et Politique, Ier–IIIe siècle apr. J.-C.* Paris: Éditions Errance.

Walter, H. 1970. *La Colonne Ciselée dans la Gaule Romaine.* Annales Littéraires de l'Université de Besançon 119. Paris: Les Belles Lettres.

———. 1985. *La Porte Noire: Contribution à l'étude de l'art triomphal des Gaules.* Centre de Recherches d'Histoire Ancienne 65. Annales Littéraires de l'Université de Besançon 321. Paris: Les Belles Lettres.

———, ed. 2000. *La sculpture d'époque romaine dans le nord, dans l'est des Gaules et dans les régions avoisinantes: Acquis et problématiques actuelles.* Besançon: Presses Universitaires Franc-Comtoises.

Wamser, L., C. Flügel, and B. Ziegaus, eds. 2000. *Die Römer zwischen Alpen und Nordmeer: Zivilisatorisches Erbe einer europäischen Militärmacht.* Mainz: Philipp von Zabern.

Webster, J. 1995a. "'Interpretatio': Roman Word Power and the Celtic Gods." *Britannia* 26: 153–61.

———. 1995b. "Sanctuaries and Sacred Places." In Green 1995, 445–64.

———. 1997. "A Negotiated Syncretism: Readings on the Development of Romano-Celtic Religion." In *Dialogues in Roman Imperialism: Power, Discourse, and Discrepant Experience in the Roman Empire*, edited by D. J. Mattingly, 165–84. JRA Supplement 23. Portsmouth, RI: Journal of Roman Archaeology.

———. 2003. "Art as Resistance and Negotiation." In Scott and Webster 2003, 24–51.

Wells, C. 1995. "Celts and Germans in the Rhineland." In Green 1995, 603–619.

Wells, P. 2012. *How Ancient Europeans Saw the World.* Princeton: Princeton University Press.

Wightman, E. M. 1985. *Gallia Belgica.* Berkeley: University of California Press.

Wild, J. P. 1985. "The Clothing of Britannia, Gallia Belgica, and Germania Inferior." *ANRW* 2.12.3: 362–423.

Witteyer, M. 2004. *Das Heiligtum für Isis und Mater Magna: Texte und Bilder.* Mainz: Philipp von Zabern.

Woolf, G. 1997. "Beyond Romans and Natives." *WorldArch* 28(3): 339–50.

———. 1998. *Becoming Roman: The Origins of Provincial Civilization in Gaul.* Cambridge: Cambridge University Press.

———. 2001. "Representation as Cult: The Case of the Jupiter Columns." In *Religion in den germanischen Provinzen Roms*, edited by W. Spickermann, 117–234. Tübingen: Mohr Siebeck.

———. 2011. *Tales of the Barbarians: Ethnography and Empire in the Roman West.* Malden, MA: Wiley-Blackwell.

CHAPTER 5.2

HISPANIAE AND NARBONENSIS

ALICIA JIMÉNEZ AND ISABEL RODÀ

INTRODUCTION

ROME's first territorial bases on the Iberian peninsula were the military encampments established during the republican period as a result of the Second Punic War (218–201BC) at Emporiae in northeasternmost Spain (modern Empúries) and Tarraco (modern Tarragona). The completion of the conquest of the Iberian peninsula, which did not occur until two centuries later (19 BC), made it possible to carry out a further major restructuring program, particularly in the northern third of the peninsula. Inscriptions document the various attempts by which the three Hispaniae (Citerior or Tarraconensis, Baetica, and Lusitania) were formed (Alföldy 2000). A similar process took place in southern Gaul, where Rome got involved as a consequence of the Second Punic War. However, the establishment of Roman power in the *provincia* Gallia Transalpina, an important overland route to the Iberian peninsula, took place in 121 BC, that is, at a later date than in the Hispaniae. Gallia Transalpina of the republican period became known as Gallia Narbonensis in the Augustan period. Its capital, *Colonia Narbo Martius*, is modern Narbonne (France).

Ancient authors such as Pliny the Elder (*HN* 3.4) and Pomponius Mela (2.5, 3.2; Woolf 1998, 50–51) grouped Narbonensis with its neighboring Mediterranean provinces, and not with the rest of Gaul. In this essay, we aim to establish connections and contrasts between the sculptural production of the Hispaniae and Narbonensis. This essay focuses on the four centuries from the beginning of the Roman conquest to end of the second century AD. It asks whether there was a characteristically provincial way of producing and consuming sculpture in the Roman Empire and how the sculptures produced in the Hispaniae and Gallia Narbonensis were distinctive. We also aim to investigate to what extent it is possible to perceive in sculpture the tensions among local elements, the alleged models from Rome, and influences from other provinces.

In general, we can say that the areas most exposed to Mediterranean contact (the eastern coastal regions of Iberia, the Baetis/Guadalquivir Valley, and Narbonensis) were those in which the sculpture presents the greatest formal similarities to that of the Italian peninsula, while in the western, central, and northern regions of the Iberian peninsula, the differences are greater. Sculptures from these provinces varied in appearance, genre, function, material, and display context, but all were linked by the common denominator of Roman colonization.

The persistence of pre-Roman traditions in the Indo-European area of the Iberian peninsula was especially important (Rodríguez Colmenero 2012). Changes in sculpture production of the Hispaniae intensified during the second half of the first century BC in connection with the foundation of *coloniae* during the Caesarean-Augustan period, the increase in immigration from the Italian peninsula, and new settlements of a military nature. The blurry boundary between Iberian and Roman sculpture (Rodà 1998) will be the starting point from which we will be able to explain many of the regional variations in the sculpture of the Hispaniae and Narbonensis during the imperial period. In the official, public sculpture from the Hispaniae and Narbonensis, the dissemination of the same models gives the appearance of uniformity of production. On the other hand, in the private sphere, it is possible to detect particularities of each area that are closely linked to autochthonous traditions and materials.

The bibliography on Roman sculpture in the Hispaniae has increased considerably in the last two decades thanks to the publication of the *Corpus Signorum Imperii Romani España* (*CSIR España*), of which six volumes were published between 2002 and 2012, as well as the volume dedicated to Portugal in 1990. Rodrigues Gonzalves has also published a monograph on Roman sculpture in Portugal (2007). The proceedings of seven conferences on Roman sculpture in Hispania have now been published (*Actas, Reunión sobre escultura romana en Hispania* [*RERH*]: I, Mérida 1992; II, Tarragona 1995; III, Córdoba 1997; IV, Lisbon-Cascais 2002; V, Murcia 2005; VI, *Segobriga* 2008; VII, Santiago de Compostela-Lugo 2011). For Narbonensis, two volumes of the series *Nouvel Espérandieu*, edited by Henri Lavagne, cataloging Roman stone sculpture in Gaul (I, Vienne 2003; IV, Fréjus 2013), are fundamental. Nogales and Rodà (2011) includes papers on all the provinces discussed in this essay.

The Sculpture of Cultural Contact: The Republican Period (Third to First Centuries BC)

Sculpture existed in some of these regions before the conquest. Certain local workshops in southern Spain (e.g., Osuna, Estepa, and Torreparedones) and in the southeast (e.g., Cerro de los Santos), continued to be active during the republican period. It is precisely from these preexisting, local workshops that we have the largest number of sculptures that can be dated to this period (J. Beltrán 2009, 20), rather than from the first Roman settlements on the Iberian peninsula (i.e., Tarraco, Valentia, Corduba, Italica, and Carteia). The sculptures produced between the fourth and second centuries BC in settlements with Greek traditions, such as Emporion (Emporiae under the Romans), had little influence on the towns in their immediate surroundings. Indeed, with the exception of certain imports, such as the Pentelic and Parian marble Asclepius-Serapis statue (second century BC), the Pentelic marble altar (perhaps late third century BC), and the fragment of a lion from the settlement of Mas Castellar (modern Pontós, dated to the fifth century BC or slightly later), these local communities do not seem to have produced sculptures in this period (Sanmartí 2007, 248, 253; Noguera and Rodríguez Oliva 2008).

One example of an early work that seems related to local traditions is a relief of Minerva, preserved in the walls of Tarraco (figure 5.2.1). It may be one of the first carvings made by Roman artisans outside Italy. Despite its Italian connections, the image differs from Roman sculptures in that the umbo of the shield displays the head of a wolf, instead of Medusa (Grünhagen 1976–7). The relief was embedded in the earliest section of Tarraco's walls, the construction of which began at the end of the third century BC, and was found in connection with a graffito in archaic Latin, "M. Vibio(s) Men(e)rva" (Manius Vibius [dedicated this to] Minerva), that is considered one of the oldest Latin inscriptions of Hispania (Alföldy 1981).

As with this relief, it is often difficult to establish who could have been the patrons for some of the works from this period. Are the features that resemble Roman sculptures a reflection of the introduction of new artistic trends to provincial productions or a consequence of commissions to local artisans by Roman colonists? Particular attention should be paid to the fact that, the origins of the sculptors and their clients notwithstanding, the context in which the statues and stelae of the northeast are found in this period, mainly

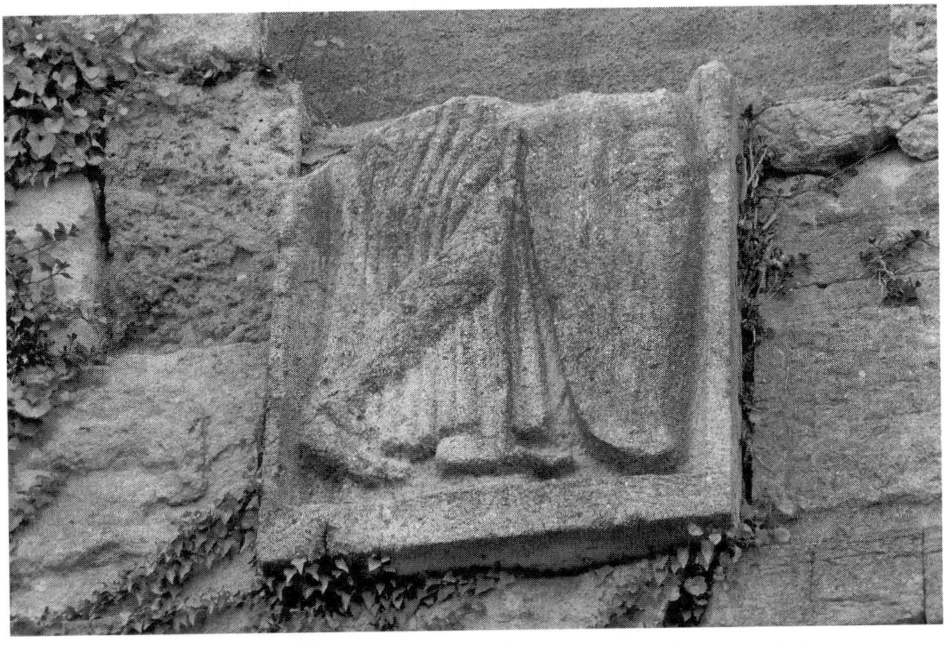

FIGURE 5.2.1 Minerva, republican city walls, Tarragona. Late third century BC.

suburban necropolises and shrines, can best be understood as a continuation of local practices. This pre-Roman habit contrasts with the placement of sculptures both inside and outside the towns in public and private spaces during the first years of the empire.

Necropolises in the Hispaniae were the first to be decorated with Italic-type monuments, as can be seen, for example, in the remains of funerary altars found in Córdoba (Vaquerizo and Murillo 2010, 481–2). These were initially placed not in the vicinity of settlements, as was usually the case for sculptures during the Iron Age, but along the roads entering the towns, particularly from the second half of the first century BC. Some regions, especially in the south (at archaeological sites such as Castulo, Gadir, and Carissa Aurelia), maintained the pre-Roman custom of placing animal sculptures on some tombs, often depictions of lions (Chapa 1985; Pérez 1999, 16; Rodríguez Oliva 2003; Beltrán and Loza 2005). Other reliefs that may have been part of funerary monuments, such as those found in Osuna (Seville province), appear to reflect traditional local rituals, including libations, music, and offerings and possibly funerary games involving combats. The presence of archaistic elements in the dress (e.g., the belt buckle of a flautist, reflecting fourth-century BC prototypes) or the armament (as can be seen in the representation of a *falcata*, the characteristic Iberian curved sword, figure 5.2.2), reinforce the traditional nature of the images. In other reliefs found at the same archaeological site, soldiers are

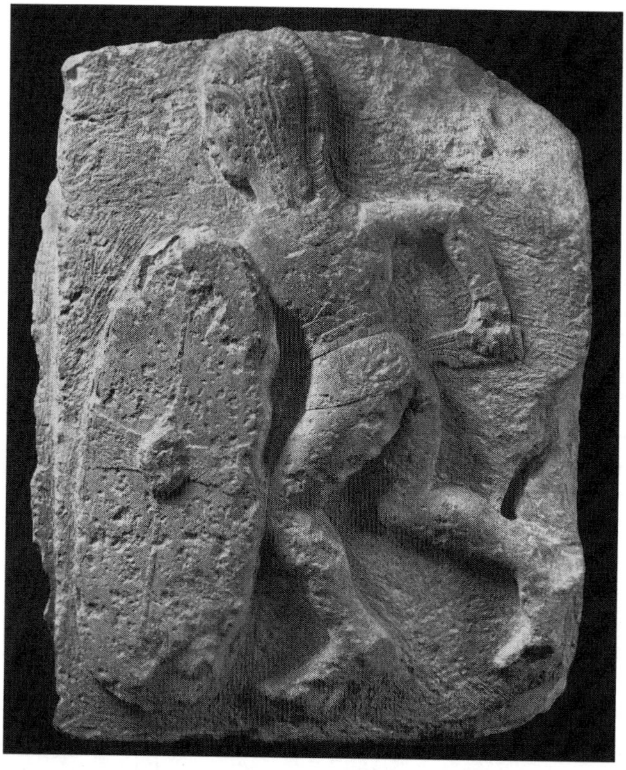

FIGURE 5.2.2 Warrior from Osuna. Third to second centuries BC. Museo Arqueológico Nacional, Madrid, inv. no. 38424.

depicted wearing parts of the Roman uniform (*lorica, ocreae*, and *caligae*). The combination of local and Roman elements takes on greater importance because in other locations Roman legionaries are depicted, such as those found in Estepa (León 1998, 97–106; Beltrán and Salas 2002, 246–8; Bendala 2007, 32–4).

At a time when the large-scale trade in marble had yet to begin, another typical example of the use of local stone to reflect iconographies linked directly to the Italic repertoire is the funerary monument of Malla (Barcelona province: Rodà 1993; 1998). One of its blocks depicts Ionic columns on the sides and the procession of a magistrate; another has Herculean iconography (Hercules, Nessus, and Deianira on one face and Hercules on Mount Olympus on the other).

A similar process can be seen in some pre-Roman sanctuaries not abandoned after the conquest, where the materials from the Roman period share a characteristic hybrid language. Some of these pre-Roman sanctuaries, such as Cerro de los Santos (modern Montealegre del Castillo, Albacete), La Encarnación (modern Caravaca de la Cruz, Murcia), and La Luz (modern Verdolay, Murcia), began to be monumentalized and decorated with Ionic or Tuscan capitals and architectural terracottas during the second century BC. At Cerro de los Santos depictions of females reminiscent of local sculptures from the fourth and third centuries BC, both for their posture (seated upright with an offering in their hands) and their elaborate clothing, shared the sacred area of the shrine with male ex-votos that were beginning to include standing figures with elements that in Rome symbolized citizenship—togae, *bullae*, and *calcei* (Ramallo 1993; Noguera 1994; Ramallo 2004, 126–9; Jiménez 2011).

The sculpting techniques and the materials used (different types of limestone and sandstone, stuccoed and painted) and the size of the sculptures (larger than the terracotta ex-votos typically found in late republican shrines on the Italian peninsula; see essay 2.5, Erlich) perpetuated local forms of representation to which were added not only elements of Roman dress, but sometimes also inscriptions in the Iberian or Latin scripts with the names of the dedicators or of their communities.

PROVINCIAL SCULPTURE UNDER THE ROMAN EMPIRE

First Century AD

Major changes in the amount and role of statuary came only following the conclusion of the conquest of the Iberian peninsula in 19 BC. Two factors influenced the spread of sculpture at this time. First, the dissemination of official models and dynastic propaganda of Augustus and the imperial family that filled public places with images encouraged the trend of self-representation among the elite and all those who had sufficient financial resources to pay for statues, either free-standing or in relief (Garriguet 2001; León 2001; Rosso 2005; 2006; Nogales and Gonçalves 2008; León 2009, 204–227). The second factor was the trade in raw materials that led to the circulation throughout the Mediterranean of all types of stone, including marble, porphyry, granite, limestone, and alabaster. Old quarries increased production and new quarries opened in various parts of the Iberian peninsula, extracting the Baetican marbles of Almadén de la Plata (Seville province) and Mijas (Málaga province), Lusitanian marble from the Borba-Estremoz area, the limestone of Santa Tecla in Tarragona, Buixcarró in Xàtiva, and the so-called *broccatello* from Tortosa (Àlvarez et al. 2009). Although the origins of the stone of most sculptures in Narbonensis still need to be determined, the use of pink limestone from la Couronne (Martigues, Bouches-du-Rhône) and yellowish shelly limestone from Beaumont-du-Ventoux seems to indicate the presence of local workshops in the time of Augustus (Delestre 2009, 28). It should be noted that in Hispania no remains of wooden sculpture have been found, and significant examples in terracotta are few and far between, as are bronze pieces. Neither do we have *signa aurea* (statues made of gold) or *argentea* (silver) in the Hispaniae, although they are referred to in some epigraphic sources; in Narbonensis the first and most important surviving piece is the silver-plated portrait of a private man found at Vasio Vocontiorum (modern Vaison-la-Romaine; figure 5.2.3; Braemer 1968; Bezin 2001).

We should also mention the near complete loss of bronze sculptures from the first two centuries of the era, although a few superb pieces from the first century have been

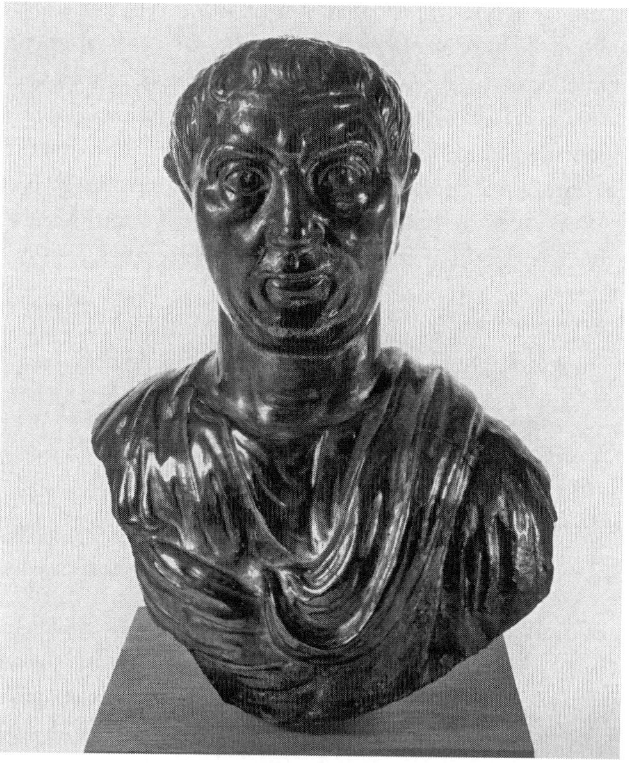

FIGURE 5.2.3 Silver male portrait from Vaison. First half of the third century AD. Musée archéologique Théo Desplans. Vaison-la-Romaine, inv. no. 990.03 009.

preserved, such as the portrait of Tiberius found at Mago (Maó), the Hypnos from Jumilla (a type subsequently followed by the example from Almedinilla), and the Flavian lady from Emporiae (García y Bellido 1949, n58; Arce and Caballero 1990; Vaquerizo and Noguera 1997, 150–59; Tugores 2005, 65; Claveria and Koppel 2007; Carreras 2012, 108–9).

Examples of extraordinary sculptural decoration are also found inland, despite their distance from maritime or river transport routes habitually used for marble transport. For example, *Segobriga* (Cuenca province), thanks to the quarrying of *lapis specularis*, was endowed with splendid iconographic programs in its forum and theater (Noguera 2012). Another important recent discovery comes from the forum of an inland town in Baetica, Torreparedones (possibly *Colonia Ituci Virtus Iulia*), which, during the period of Tiberius, was monumentalized with an epigraph of major proportions (*litterae aureae* 0.265 m high and a maximum length of 13 m) inserted into the paving slabs of the square. It also had marble buildings and marble sculptures in the portico, including a Prima Porta–type portrait of Augustus from a local workshop and a portrait of the emperor Claudius reworked from one of Caligula, with a series of attachment points in which to fit a crown (Márquez 2012; Márquez, Ventura, and Morena 2013).

The dissemination and display of official models was particularly intensive in the fora of the provincial capitals, where parts of the sculptural program of the Forum of Augustus were reproduced at different times during the century. Caryatids and the group of Aeneas, Anchises, and Ascanius have been identified in Emerita (figure 5.2.4) and a possible sculpture of Romulus in Córdoba (De la Barrera and Trillmich 1996; Trillmich 1996a; 1996b; see essays 2.2, Claridge; 3.3, Anguissola; 6.1, Squire; 6.3, Shaya; 6.4, Moormann). In fact, the sculptural remains from capitals of the Hispaniae have allowed us to restore groups that we know were displayed in the Forum of Augustus but are no longer extant. Rome made its presence felt through partial copies that link the provinces to the center of power by depicting Roman ancestors that erase all traces of a local past from the official discourse (Dupré 2004; Nogales and Álvarez 2006; Nogales 2008; Jiménez 2010). We even find partial representations of this imagery (a caryatid) in a rural sanctuary not far away from Emerita, São Miguel da Mota (Évora, Portugal: Schattner, Fabiao, and Guerra 2008).

At the same time there was a huge rise in the popularity of the private portrait that, in many cases, followed the official models so closely that it is difficult to distinguish them from the effigies of members of the imperial family. Many Julio-Claudian "princes," "Livias," and "Agrippinas" are now being reattributed. For example, a couple from Azaila, now correctly identified as Quintus Iunius Hispanus and a female protector figure that could be a Nike or Juno herself, were previously thought to have been Augustus and Livia (Beltrán Lloris 2000, 49–53).

However, the most notable increase in the opulence of domestic decoration came about at the beginning of the Flavian era. During this period there was an increase in ornamental sculpture in villas, generally in the form of under-life-size sculptures and decorative items such as *oscilla*, round disks that were hung from trees or between

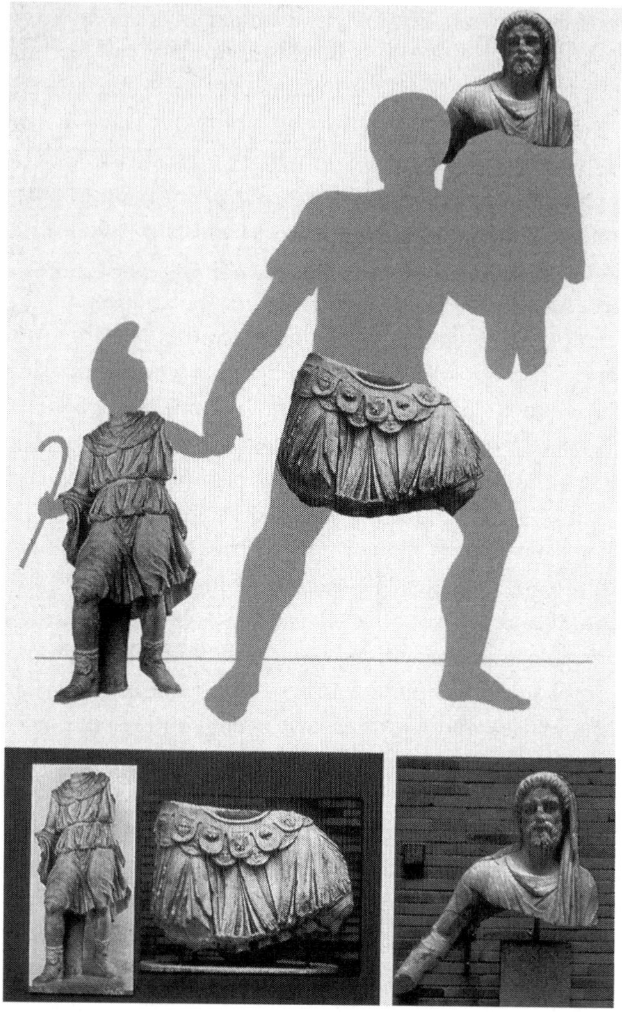

FIGURE 5.2.4 Aeneas group from Mérida. Julio-Claudian. Museo Nacional de Arte Romano, Mérida, inv. nos. 33676, 33675, and 34432.

columns (Koppel 1986–8), and herms in the form of busts of characters from the cortege of Bacchus (Peña 2009, 323–31).

Throughout the first century AD, Italic models were widely disseminated in the western Mediterranean, having a particular impact on Narbonensis, certain areas of Baetica, and the Levante coast of the Iberian peninsula. Funerary monuments incorporating Doric friezes (Joulia 1988) are widespread, but other motifs are more restricted geographically. For instance, in Barcino, monumental altars finished with *gorgoneia* were extraordinarily popular (Claveria 2008), as they were in the Alto Guadalquivir region of Baetica, but not in the capitals of the three provinces, as there is little evidence of the type in Narbonne, Tarragona, or Córdoba (Beltrán 2004; Baena and Beltrán 2002). Monolithic *cupae* are prevalent in Barcino and Emerita especially in the second and third centuries, while they are nonexistent in Narbonne and only four examples have been found in Tarragona (Andreu 2012). On the other hand, in Narbonne we find funerary monuments decorated with military trophies or scenes of daily life in relief, subjects not found in the north of Hispania (Rodà 2000).

The explanation for this phenomenon could lie not only in the law of supply and demand, but also in pre-Roman regional traditions and the different avenues of dissemination of the models that, in the case of Tarraconensis for example, could either have come directly from Italy or via Narbo, whose port was a true hub for redistribution of merchandise.

In both cases a primary role would have been played by the senatorial families from Italy who expanded their businesses both in Narbonensis and Tarraconensis through their respective networks of freedmen (Carreras and Guitart 2009; Carreras, Mullor, and Guitart 2013). In both Narbonensis and the coastal towns of northern Hispania former slaves played a fundamental role (Gayraud 1981, 411–76). In the first half of the first century AD the funerary monuments of Narbo and Barcino were quite similar in appearance, made from comparable local sandstones with grayish hues, using the same sculptural techniques, such as the deep perforation of the eyes and a deep groove to silhouette the figures. The similarities in the images of Priapus, Attis, and Atlas and reliefs with *fasces* and *lictores* on tombs of *seviri augustales* (priests of the imperial cult) in both regions are an emblematic example of this phenomenon (Rodà 2000; Carrier 2008). Later funerary monuments from Nemausus (modern Nîmes) also share these characteristics. In the case of Narbo, there appears to be a more obvious direct route from Italy for both freestanding or relief sculptures and architectural sculpture, as indicated by the sculptures of Augustus and Venus (Carrier 2005–6).

Despite obvious similarities between the regions, the diversity of sculpture in Hispaniae and Narbonensis is equally remarkable. On the Mediterranean coast, towns such as Emporiae, Barcino, Tarraco, and Carthago Nova (Koppel 1985; Noguera 1991; Rodà 1998; Koppel 2012; 2013) all have rich series of sculptures from the Julio-Claudian period. They are carved in Carrara marble that was brought in huge amounts to the different port towns, thanks to the fluidity of sea transport. This imported marble was also used in various ornamental elements, as we can see in the Corinthian capitals of the Carthago Nova theater (Ramallo and Ruiz 1998, 84–93; Gutiérrez and Rodà 2012) and even in the construction of the so-called provincial forum in Tarraco, for which rough Carrara marble was imported to be worked *in situ* (Mar et al. 2012, 352–9).

On the other hand, in the north of Lusitania and the Galician zone of Tarraconensis, sculptures are mainly found in private contexts in much smaller numbers, usually carved out of local hard granite with pre-Roman iconography (mostly boars and warriors). Thus, even when Italic-type models were used, such as in the stela of Adai (Lugo; figure 5.2.5), the result was adapted to the local aesthetic. In fact, the basic type came to be made up of stelae with representations of the deceased and a profusion of astral signs that, in many cases, demonstrates the survival of pre-Roman antecedents adapted to the tastes of a specific clientele, but with forms of representation common in the Roman Empire (Acuña and Casal 2010; Rodríguez Colmenero 2012; 2013).

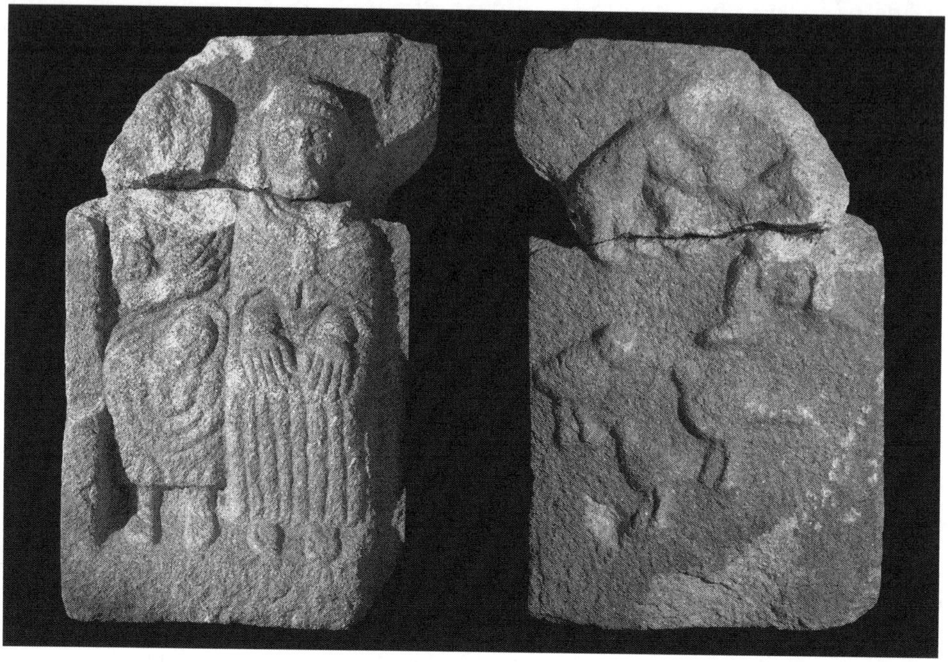

FIGURE 5.2.5 Stela from Adai, sides A and B. First century AD. Museo Provincial de Lugo.

In contrast, for those zones that had earlier permanent contact with Rome, it can be difficult to trace local elements due to longer familiarity with Hellenistic and Roman culture. It is therefore fundamental that we study the sculpture workshops (*officinae*), which are not always easy to identify (Nogales 2002; Gaggadis-Robin et al. 2009; Nogales and Rodà, 2014), and their clientele.

When we have an item carved out of local stone, there can be little doubt that it was made within a limited radius. However, in this group we can include pieces of extraordinary quality, such as most of the togate figures from Augusta Emerita carved out of good Lusitanian marble from Borba-Estremoz by the skillful hands of artisans from a workshop known particularly for the ornamentation of that town's forum. At the other extreme, we have the crude heads of Galicia, iconic images or portraits carved in Tarragona's lumaquela (clam sandstone) and the sandstone from the Montjuïc mountain in Barcelona, the quality of which is far from exceptional, although we should take into account that today we see them without their final layer of stucco that would have made them look more like marble (Koppel 1985, 87–9; 2009; Rodà 2009). When we are dealing with imported stone, such as Carrara marble, only series that show evidence of a workshop's peculiar habit or the existence of production waste can definitely confirm local manufacture (Rodà 1980).

The complex issues surrounding the patronage of these works are exemplified by the stelae of Lara de los Infantes that for so long have been considered crude representations of summarily "Romanized" personages from the Spanish Meseta (Abásolo

1974). Scholars have long questioned whether their Celtic undertones are local or not. However, most recently, these manifestations have been linked to sections of the army posted from other areas of Celtic influence, specifically northern Italy.

Second Century AD

This century was inaugurated with the reigns of two emperors from Hispania, Trajan and Hadrian, who were born in Baetican Italica. In the case of Trajan this fact had no palpable repercussion in the field of sculpture. Under Hadrian, however, the town of Italica was endowed with imported sculptural ornamentation that included some of the best pieces found on the Iberian peninsula, such as the Mercury, Venus, and Diana, all made of Parian marble and close to Greek originals, that decorated the upper part of the theater in the *vetus Urbs* (Rodríguez Oliva 2009, 82–9). A fountain from a foreign workshop depicting the Wolf and Twins in expensive *rosso antico* can also be dated to the time of Hadrian (Beltrán 2009, 301).

Likewise, to honor the memory of his predecessor and adoptive father, Hadrian funded a sumptuous temple complex, the so-called Traianeum, with a plan similar to that of Hadrian's Library in Athens and extensive use of imported marbles. The monument included a colossal statue of which only the toe of one foot in Parian marble remains. Most of the statues ended up in the numerous lime kilns that riddled the site (León 1988).

In Tarragona, a workshop has been detected that was active in the second (and possibly as early as the first) century, in which the marble used to make imperial portraits was worked. In this way it appears certain that the portraits of Marcus Aurelius and Lucius Verus found near the forum were manufactured in Tarraconensis (Koppel 1985, 33–5). The portrait of Drusus Minor found in Caesar Augusta (Zaragoza) probably also came from a workshop in Tarragona (Koppel and Rodà 2007, 113–15). Also from Tarragona is the very complete decoration of the *schola* of the *collegium fabrum*, presided over by the goddess Minerva, in which Hadrianic-period trends can be clearly seen (Koppel 1988).

The second century saw marked changes in certain areas. In Augusta Emerita, for example, private funerary portraits in the round were replaced by another fashion in sepulchral art: stelae bearing the image of the deceased (Nogales 1997; Edmondson, Nogales, and Trillmich 2001). Also during the reign of Hadrian, carved sarcophagi become more numerous (Claveria 2002). Dating from the time of Marcus Aurelius are some sculptures from Narbonne inspired by others from the Hellenistic period and similar to pieces produced in artistic centers of Italy and Asia Minor (Queyrel 2009) as well as a few of the highest-quality portraits found in Hispania, including the couples in the Palencia Museum and the Barcelona History Museum (Rodà 1992; Del Amo and Pérez 2006, 89–93) that reflect contemporary hairstyles; the two female faces are exact clones of that of Faustina Minor as are others from Hispania.

Villas continued to increase their sculptural programs (Koppel 1995; Koppel and Rodà 2008). We find particularly outstanding cases in the villas of El Ruedo in Almedinilla (Córdoba province; Vaquerizo and Noguera 1997) and Els Munts in Altafulla (Tarragona province; Koppel 2000). The latter is a splendid residence near the provincial capital with unique sculptures, given that in some cases they were larger than life-size, rare in villa finds. It has also provided us with such clearly Hadrianic figures as the statue of Antinous (Koppel 2000).

Conclusion

It is important to question how Roman imperialism was reflected in the art of the Hispaniae and Narbonensis four centuries after the beginning of the conquest. The works of the late republican period often perpetuated local carving techniques, materials, and traditional iconography in funerary and religious contexts that very probably continued pre-Roman practices in terms of their functions, locations, and arrangement of sculpture displays. Although some shrines were monumentalized at the end of the second century BC, the true moment of transformation came about, as it did in many other areas of material culture, in the second half of the first century BC and especially in the Augustan period. Marble imported from outside the Iberian peninsula demonstrates how the empire intensified the connectivity between the different regions of the Mediterranean. At the same time, local marble quarries were exploited wherever possible.

The sculptures that reflect a more intensive relationship with Rome come from towns that became provincial capitals following Augustus's reforms and thus hosted local versions of the Forum of Augustus in Rome. The models of imperial family statues from forums and basilicas were modified for a second time when they were adapted to the private sphere.

The fact that "provincialization" led not to unification but to territorial restructuring in the interests of Rome can be sensed from the major differences observed in the art from the same province, as in the case of the north and south of Lusitania or the coastal area and interior of Tarraconensis.

This model changed again during the Severan period. At that time there was a drastic reduction in the number of freestanding sculptures erected in Hispania and Narbonensis. This fact cannot be attributed only to the vicissitudes of the preservation (or not) of pieces, but also to a reduction in the desire for self-representation in statuary among the elites (see essay 3.8, Witschel), who had been the principal agents of the dissemination of sculpture during the first centuries of the empire.

Bibliography

Abad, L., and J. A. Soler, eds. 2007. *Arte Ibérico en la España mediterránea*. Alicante: Diputación Provincial.

Abásolo, J. A. 1974. *Epigrafía romana de la región de Lara de los Infantes*. Burgos: Diputación Provincial de Burgos.

Acuña, F., and R. Casal. 2010. "Revisitando la plástica galaico-romana." In *RERH* VI, edited by J. M. Abascal and R. Cebrián, 385–401. Murcia: Tabularium.

Acuña, F., R. Casal, and S. González. eds. 2013. *Actas de la VII Reunión de Escultura romana en Hispania*. Santiago de Compostela: Andavira.

Alföldy, G. 1981. "Die älteste römische Inschrift der iberischen Halbinsel." *ZPE* 43: 1–12.

———. 2000. "Das neue Edikt des Augustus aus El Bierzo in Hispanien." *ZPE* 131: 177–205.

Àlvarez A., A. Domènech, P. Lapuente, and À. Pitarch. 2009. *Marbles and Stones of Hispania*. Tarragona: Institut Català d'Arqueologia Clàssica.

Andreu, J., ed. 2012. *Las cupae hispanas: Origen, difusión, uso, tipología*. Zaragoza: UNED-Tudela.

Arce, J., and L. Caballero. 1990. *Los bronces romanos en España*. Madrid: Ministerio de Cultura.

Baena, L., and J. Beltrán. 2002. *Las esculturas romanas de la provincia de Jaén*. CSIR España 1.2. Murcia: Tabularium.

Beltrán Lloris, F. 2000. "La vida en la frontera." In *Roma en la Cuenca Media del Ebro*, edited by F. Beltrán Lloris, M. Martín-Bueno, and F. Pina Polo, 45–62. Zaragoza: Caja de Ahorros de la Inmaculada de Aragón.

Beltrán, J. 2004. "Monumenta sepulcrales en forma de altar con pulvinos de los territorios hispanorromanos: Revisión de materiales y estado de la cuestión." *ArchEspArq* 77: 101–141.

———. 2009. "Precedentes" and "El relieve." In León 2009, 17–39 and 277–319.

Beltrán, J., and M. L. Loza. 2005. "El 'Oso de Porcuna': Una escultura funeraria excepcional de la Hispania Romana." *Romula* 4: 163–76.

Beltrán, J., and J. Salas. 2002. "Los relieves de Osuna." In *Urso: A la búsqueda de su pasado*, edited by F. Chaves, 235–72. Osuna: Fundación de Cultura García Blanco.

Bendala, M. 2007. "El arte ibérico en el ámbito andaluz: Notas sobre la escultura." In Abad and Soler 2007, 21–38.

Bezin, C. 2001. "Bust masculí." In *Tarraco: Porta de Roma*, edited by I. Rodà, 141, no. 150. Barcelona: Fundació "la Caixa".

Braemer, F. 1968. "Sculptures en métal battu et repoussé de la Gaule Romaine et des Régions limitrophes." *RA* 2: 327–54.

Carreras, C., and J. Guitart. 2009. *Barcino I: Marques i terrisseries d'àmfores al Pla de Barcelona*. Corpus International des Timbres Amphoriques 15. Barcelona: Institut d'Estudis Catalans, Institut Català d'Arqueologia Clàssica.

Carreras, C., A. López Mullor, and J. Guitart. 2013. *Barcino II: Marques i terrisseries d'àmfores al Baix Llobregat*. Corpus International des Timbres Amphoriques 18. Barcelona: Institut d'Estudis Catalans, Institut Català d'Arqueologia Clàssica.

Carreras, T., ed. 2012. *Històries de tocador: Cosmètica i bellesa a l'Antiguitat*. Barcelona: Museu d'Arqueologia de Catalunya.

Carrier, C. 2005–6. "Sculptures augustéennes du théâtre d'Arles." *RANarb* 38–9: 365–96.

———. 2008. "Les sculptures trouvées dans la nécropole de la route de Beaucaire à Nîmes." *RANarb* 41: 153–68.

Chapa, T. 1985. *La escultura ibérica zoomorfa*. Madrid: Ministerio de Cultura.

Claveria, M. 2002. *Los sarcófagos romanos de Cataluña*. CSIR España 1.1. Murcia: Tabularium.

Claveria, M. 2008. "Los altares monumentales con *pulvini* del nordeste peninsular." In *RERH* V, edited by J. M. Noguera and E. Conde, 345–96. Murcia: Tabularium.

Claveria, M., and E. M. Koppel. 2007. "La gran escultura en bronce." In *Metalistería de la Hispania Romana*, edited by C. Fernández, 267–8. Sautuola 13. Santander: Consejería de Cultura y Deporte del Gobierno de Cantabria.

Del Amo, M., and F. J. Pérez. 2006. *Guía del Museo de Palencia*. Palencia: Junta de Castilla y León.

De la Barrera, J. L., and W. Trillmich. 1996. "Eine Wiederholung der Aeneas-Gruppe vom Forum Augustum samt ihrer Inschrift in Mérida (Spanien)." *RM* 103: 119–38.

Delestre, X. 2009. "Gaule Narbonnaise, provinces alpestres." In Gaggadis-Robin et al. 2009, 25–32.

Dupré, X., ed. 2004. *Las capitales provinciales de Hispania*. Vol. 1, *Córdoba: Colonia Patricia Corduba*. Vol. 2, *Mérida: Colonia Augusta Emerita*. Vol. 3, *Tarragona: Colonia Iulia Urbs Triumphalis Tarraco*. Rome: "L'Erma" di Bretschneider.

Edmondson, J., T. Nogales, and W. Trillmich. 2001. *Imagen y memoria: Monumentos funerarios con retratos en la Colonia Augusta Emerita*. Madrid: Real Academia de la Historia.

Gaggadis-Robin, V., A. Hermary, M. Reddé, and C. Sintes, eds. 2009. *Les ateliers de sculpture régionaux: Techniques, styles et iconographie*. Aix-en-Provence: Centre Camille Jullien; Arles: Musée départemental d'Arles antique.

García y Bellido, A. 1949. *Esculturas romanas de España y Portugal*. Madrid: CSIC.

Garriguet, J. A. 2001. *La imagen del poder imperial en Hispania: Tipos estatuarios*. CSIR España 2.1. Murcia: Tabularium.

Gayraud, M. 1981. *Narbonne antique des origines à la fin du IIIe siècle*. Paris: De Boccard.

Grünhagen, W. 1976–7. "Notas sobre el relieve de Minerva de la muralla de Tarragona." *Boletín Arqueológico* 4(133–40): 75–94.

Gutiérrez, A., and I. Rodà. 2012. "El mármol de Luni-Carrara en la fachada mediterránea de Hispania." In *Rome, Portus and the Mediterranean*, edited by S. J. Keay, 293–312. London: British School at Rome.

Jiménez, A. 2010. "Reproducing Difference: Mimesis and Colonialism in Roman Hispania." In *Material Connections: Mobility, Materiality and Mediterranean Identities*, edited by B. Knapp and P. van Dommelen, 38–63. London: Routledge.

———. 2011. "Pure Hybridism: Late Iron Age Sculpture in Southern Iberia." *WorldArch* 43(1): 102–123.

Joulia, J.-Cl. 1988. *Les frises doriques de Narbonne*. Collection Latomus 202. Brussels: Latomus.

Koppel, E. M. 1985. *Die römischen Skulpturen von Tarraco*. MF 15. Berlin: Deutsches Archäologisches Institut.

———. 1986–8. "Los relieves decorativos en Cataluña." *Empúries* 48–50(2): 8–20.

———. 1988. *La schola del collegium fabrum de Tarraco y su decoración escultórica*. Barcelona: Universitat Autònoma de Barcelona.

———. 1995. "La decoración escultórica de las *villae* en *Hispania*." In *Poblamiento rural romano en el sureste de Hispania*, edited by J. M. Noguera, 27–48. Murcia: Tabularium.

———. 2000. "Informe preliminar sobre la decoración escultórica de la villa romana de 'Els Munts.'" *MM* 41: 380–94.

———. 2009. "Los retratos funerarios en piedra de los talleres locales en Tarraco." In Gaggadis-Robin et al. 2009, 505–511.

———. 2012. "La escultura." In *Empúries: Municipium Emporiae*, edited by X. Aquilué, 117–26. Ciudades romanas de Hispania 6. Rome: "L'Erma" di Bretschneider.

———. 2013. "La decoración escultórica en el ámbito privado de la ciudad de Empúries." In Acuña, Casal, and González 2013, 149–79.

Koppel, E. M., and I. Rodà. 2007. "La escultura." In *Zaragoza: Colonia Caesar Augusta*, edited by F. Beltrán, 109–122. Ciudades romanas de Hispania 4. Roma: "L'Erma" di Bretschneider.

———. 2008. "La escultura de las *villae* de la zona noreste hispánico: Los ejemplos de Tarragona y Tossa de Mar." In *Las villae tardorromanas en el occidente del Imperio: Arquitectura y función*, edited by C. Fernández Ochoa, F. Gil Sendino and V. García-Entero, 108–114. Gijón: Ediciones Trea.

Lavagne, H., ed. 2003–. *Nouvel Espérandieu: Recueil général des sculptures sur pierre de la Gaule*. 4 vols. Paris: Académie des Inscriptions et Belles-Lettres.

León, P. 1988. *Traianeum de Italica*. Seville: Monte de Piedad y Caja de Ahorros de Sevilla.

———. 1998. *La sculpture des ibères*. Paris: L'Harmattan.

———. 2001. *Retratos romanos de la Bética*. Seville: Fundación El Monte.

———, ed. 2009. *Arte romano de la Bética: Escultura*. Seville: Fundación Focus-Abengoa.

Mar, R., J. Ruiz de Arbulo, D. Vivó, and J. A. Beltrán-Caballero. 2012. *Tarraco: Arquitectura y urbanismo de una capital provincial romana*. Vol. 1, *De la Tarragona ibérica a la construcción del templo de Augusto*. Tarragona: Universitat Rovira i Virgili, Institut Català d'Arqueologia Clàssica.

Márquez, C. 2012. "Dos nuevos retratos de Augusto en la provincia de Córdoba." *Romula* 11: 205–211.

Márquez. C., A. Ventura, and J. A. Morena. 2013. "El ciclo escultórico de Torreparedones (Baena, Córdoba)." In Acuña, Casal, and González 2013, 325–46.

Nogales, T. 1997. *El retrato privado en Augusta Emerita*. Badajoz: Diputación Provincial.

———, ed. 2002. *Materiales y técnicas escultóricas de Augusta Emerita y otras ciudades de Hispania*. Mérida: Museo Nacional de Arte Romano.

———. 2008. "Rómulo en el Augusteum del foro colonial emeritense." In *Le due patrie acquisite: Studi di archeologia dedicati a Walter Trillmich*, edited by E. La Rocca, P. León, and C. Parisi Presicce, 301–312. Rome: "L'Erma" di Bretschneider.

Nogales, T., and J. M. Álvarez. 2006. "Fora Augustae Emeritae: La 'interpretatio' provincial de los patrones metropolitanos." In *El concepto de lo provincial en el mundo antiguo*, edited by D. Vaquerizo and J. F. Murillo, 419–50. Córdoba: Universidad de Córdoba.

Nogales, T., and L. Gonçalves. 2008. "Programas decorativos públicos de Lusitania: Augusta Emérita como paradigma en algunos ejemplos provinciales." In *RERH* V, edited by J. M. Noguera and E. Conde, 655–99. Murcia: Tabularium.

Nogales, T., and I. Rodà. ed. 2011. *Roma y las provincias: Modelo y difusión; Actas XI Coloquio Internacional de Arte Romano Provincial*. Rome: "L'Erma" di Bretschneider.

———. 2014. "Talleres escultóricos/Sculpture workshops." In *Artifices Idóneos: Talleres, artesanos y manufacturas en Hispania*, edited by M. Bustamante and D. Bernal, 75–103. Anejos de ArchEspArq 72. Mérida: CSIC.

Noguera, J. M. 1991. *La ciudad romana de Carthago Nova: La escultura*. Murcia: Universidad de Murcia.

———. 1994. *La escultura romana de la provincia de Albacete (Hispania Citerior, Conventus Carthaginensis)*. Albacete: Instituto de Estudios Albacetenses.

———. 2012. *Segobriga: Provincia de Cuenca, Hispania Citerior*. CSIR España 1.4. Tarragona: Institut Català d'Arqueologia Clàssica.

Noguera, J. M., and P. Rodríguez Oliva. 2008. "Scultura ispànica in epoca repubblicana: Note su generi, iconografia, usi e cronologia." In *Iberia e Italia: Modelos romanos de integración territorial*, edited by J. Uroz, J. M. Noguera, and F. Coarelli, 379–453. Murcia: Tabularium.

Peña, A. 2009. "La escultura decorativa." In León 2009, 321–63.

Pérez, I. 1999. *Leones romanos en Hispania*. Madrid: Fundación Focus Abengoa.

Queyrel, F. 2009. "Un atelier de sculptures trouvées à Narbonne." In Gaggadis-Robin et al. 2009, 117–23.

Ramallo, S. F. 1993. "Terracotas arquitectónicas del santuario de La Encarnación (Caravaca, Murcia)." *ArchEspArq* 64: 71–98.

———, ed. 2004. *La decoración arquitectónica en las ciudades romanas de Occidente (Cartagena 2003)*. Murcia: Universidad de Murcia.

Ramallo, S. F., and E. Ruiz. 1998. *El teatro romano de Cartagena*. Murcia: Editorial KR.

Rodà, I. 1980. "Un retrat inèdit de Barcino i el taller escultòric local." *RStLig* 46: 41–52.

———. 1992. *Retrats romans: Les colleccions del Museu d'Història de la Ciutat*. Barcelona: Museu d'Història de la Ciutat.

———. 1993. "Escultura republicana en la Tarraconense: El monumento funerario de Malla." In *RERH* I, edited by T. Nogales, 207–219. Mérida-Madrid: Ministerio de Cultura.

———. 1998. "La difícil frontera entre escultura ibérica y escultura romana." In *Congreso Internacional Los iberos, príncipes de Occidente*, 265–73. Barcelona: Fundació "la Caixa."

———. 2000. "La escultura del sur de la Narbonense y el norte de Hispania citerior: Paralelos y contactos." In *RERH* III, edited by P. León and T. Nogales, 173–96. Madrid: Ministerio de Educación, Cultura y Deporte, Dirección General de Bellas Artes, Subdirección General de Museos Estatales.

———. 2009. "Los talleres de la ciudad de Barcino (Barcelona)." In Gaggadis-Robin et al. 2009, 513–29.

Rodríguez Colmenero, A. 2012. "Roma." In *Gallaecia petrea*, 206–317. Santiago de Compostela: Xunta de Galicia.

———. 2013. "Guerreros galaicos con inscripciones latinas: ¿indigenismo o romanización?" In Acuña, Casal, and González 2013, 285–309.

Rodrigues Gonzalves, L. J. 2007. *Escultura romana em Portugal*. Mérida: Museo Nacional de Arte Romano.

Rodríguez Oliva, P. 2003. "Esculturas zoomorfas de época romano-republicana de la provincia de Málaga." *Mainake* 25: 321–57.

———. 2009. "La escultura ideal." In León 2009, 41–151.

Rosso, E. 2005. "Elites et *imitatio*: La reprise par les élites des types statuaires impériaux." In *L'autocélébration des élites dans le monde romain: Contextes, images, textes*, edited by M. Cébeillac-Gervasoni, L. Lamoine, and F. Trément, 33–57. Clermont-Ferrand: Presses Universitaires Blaise Pascal.

———. 2006. *L'image de l'empereur en Gaule romaine: Portraits et inscriptions*. Paris: CTHS.

Sanmartí, J. 2007. "El arte en la Iberia septentrional." In Abad and Soler 2007, 239–64.

Schattner, T., C. Fabiao, and A. Guerra. 2008. "La cariátide de Sao Miguel da Mota y su relación con las cariátides de Mérida." In *RERH* V, edited by J.M. Noguera and E. Conde, 697–729. Murcia: Tabularium.

Trillmich, W. 1996a. "Los tres foros de Augusta Emerita y el caso de Corduba." In *Colonia Patricia Corduba: Una reflexión arqueológica*, edited by P. León, 173–95. Córdoba: Junta de Andalucía.

———. 1996b. "Reflejos del programa estatuario del *Forum Augustum* en Mérida." In *RERH* II, edited by J. Massó and P. Sada, 95–108. Tarragona: Museu Nacional Arqueològic de Tarragona.

Tugores, F., ed. 2005. *El món romà a les illes Balears*. Barcelona: Fundació "la Caixa."

Vaquerizo, D., and J. F. Murillo. 2010. "Ciudad y *suburbia* en *Corduba*: Una visión diacrónica (siglos II a.C.–VII d.C.)." In *Las áreas suburbanas en la ciudad histórica: Topografía, usos, funciones*, edited by D. Vaquerizo, 455–522. Córdoba: Universidad de Córdoba.

Vaquerizo, D., and J. M. Noguera 1997. *La villa de El Ruedo, Almedinilla (Córdoba): Decoración escultórica e interpretación*. Murcia: Servicio de Publicaciones Universidad de Córdoba, Universidad de Murcia.

Woolf, G. 1998. *Becoming Roman: The Origins of Provincial Civilization in Gaul*. Cambridge: Cambridge University Press.

CHAPTER 5.3

NORTH AFRICA

FRANÇOIS BARATTE AND
NATHALIE DE CHAISEMARTIN

Introduction

This essay addresses sculpture from the Roman provinces of North Africa—Mauretania, Africa Proconsularis, and Tripolitania—in the imperial period. Large collections of sculpture from this region are housed in museums of the major cities in the modern states of Morocco, Algeria, Tunisia, and Libya, including at Leptis Magna, Tripoli, and Sabratha (in Libya); Sousse and Tunis (in Tunisia); and Constantine, Sétif, Hippo, Algiers, and Cherchell (in Algeria). Few discoveries of sculptures have been made since G. C. Picard's treatment of this material in 1982. Further typological and thematic syntheses are warranted, such as that of M. Le Glay (1961; 1966) on African Saturn and that of N. Benseddik (2010) on Aesculapius. Studies are needed to augment work on issues of materials, techniques, and workshops, such as those focused on architectural sculpture by P. Pensabene (2003; 2006) and N. Ferchiou (1989). No survey of bronze sculptures from North Africa exists apart from the study of C. Boube-Piccot (1969) on bronzes of Morocco.

An important marker of the influence of the Roman way of life particularly from the second to the middle of the third centuries AD, sculpture plays an important role in the Romanized urban context of North Africa as well as in rural sanctuaries (see essay 4.2, McCarty) and cemeteries. The adoption, development, and influence of Roman sculpture in North Africa can be compared, at least for official sculpture, to that of Spain, though the western sector of Mauretania Tingitana has produced less evidence than Tripolitania and Africa Proconsularis.

As shown by the Mahdia shipwreck, the coast of North Africa lies along the trade routes for the transport to Italy of marble and works of art from Greece, Asia Minor, and Egypt. Though Roman rule in North Africa began in the middle of the second century BC, the earliest sculptures date to the Augustan era; until the reign of Trajan, sculpture is rare and mostly confined to coastal sites. It should be noted, however, that some earlier examples of architectural relief on mausolea, modeled on Hellenistic monumental decoration, such as those at Dougga (Rakob 1979, 156–8), Kbor Klib (129–32), and Chemtou (120–29), survive from Africa Proconsularis and the Numidian kingdoms.

The collections of Juba II and of his son Ptolemy in their capitals of Cherchell and Volubilis constitute a special case. Both had spent much time in Rome and were well traveled, especially in the eastern Mediterranean. The works of stone and bronze found in their capitals show a taste for works of Greek classicism, though some statues carved in Greek marbles appear to be Roman-period creations either imported or carved locally by traveling sculptors from the Aegean: portraits of family members, deities, and geographical allegories such as the head of Africa crowned with an elephant skin (Sintès and Rebahi 2003, n. 22).

One of the main issues for this region concerns the import of marble statuary—and the related technology—as well as the dissemination of models and works from the Graeco-Roman tradition common on the coast and in major cities to the interior cities, villages, and the fringe of the African *limes*. For example, an inscription of Sextus Iulius Possessor (*CIL* 2.1180 = *ILS* 1403) records that he sent a bronze statue from Alexandria to Maktar, located in the interior of Tunisia 140 km southwest of Tunis and also dedicated two statues of marble, perhaps carved on site (see essay 2.7, Russell). The contact between the art of the Graeco-Roman *koine* and the Libyo-Phoenician substrate of the region, linked to a different mode of social and religious expression, prompted changes in local sculptural traditions.

The study of this material, however, cannot be limited to dependency on Roman models (*stadtrömisch*) or the presence of prominent workshops and works coming from the Aegean or even from the often ill-defined "East." Instead, studies of groups of works, thematic or stylistic, historical or geographic, will allow us to understand the sculptural landscape of North Africa, through its contrasts and varying degrees of acculturation. This essay identifies the areas in which we feel most progress can be made.

Materials, Workshops, and Production

North Africa is rich in limestones but lacks sculptural marbles. From Tunisia come Kedel stone; Chemtou green stone; Thala gray limestone; colored marmoreal limestone (faux onyx), a poor but genuine marble; and yellow and purple Chemtou marble exported throughout the Roman world. From Algeria, the marble of Cap de Garde (*greco scritto*) was of little interest for statuary. And from Morocco a white marble from a quarry near Sala (Chellah, near Rabat) was only sporadically exploited for sculpture in antiquity.

Even today, white marble is an expensive import commodity in North Africa, and in the second century AD, Proconnesian marble sent directly from the quarries of Marmara by ship arrived in North Africa in the form of roughed-out forms and thick slabs for sawing into revetment. Sometimes the revetment slabs were used instead for rather thin statues to be displayed in front of a wall, such as the Ceres-Tyche of Gightis (Yacoub 1970, 101, no. C1030), a funerary statue of Borj el Amri (Slim and Fauqué 2001, 213), and a late togatus from Knaïs (Zeta) near Sousse (Chaisemartin 1987, 126, no. 182), all in Tunisia. Very few sculptures unearthed in North Africa were carved from the marbles of Asia Minor (Chaisemartin 2007), but those rare works are finished, high-quality products destined mostly for the domestic setting and clearly ordered by connoisseurs in the major coastal cities. The works of sculpture decorating public buildings are mostly from the workshops of Rome or Attica. They also reached the ports of North Africa as finished products, like the remains of the great acrolithic Jupiters from the Capitolia of Thuburbo Majus and Dougga (C. Poinssot 1983, 35), or in cargoes of unfinished statues accompanied by teams of sculptors who completed and sold them on demand (see essay 2.7, Russell). The "neck strut," an area of marble left at the back of the neck to reinforce the head during transport, is common. Often, sculptures are made of several parts, with the arms, parts of the head, or the attributes cut in separate pieces and joined at the destination.

Signatures of sculptors and dedications bearing their names or mention of the work done are rare: only the sculptors Saturninus in Oea (modern Tripoli: Apuleius, *De magia*, 61–3), Aristius Antiochus at Leptis Magna (Caputo 1949), and Asklepiades, a Bithynian sculptor from Nicomedia (Reynolds and Ward-Perkins [1952] 2009, no. 264), are known. Major projects, such as the Augustan forum at Byrsa near Carthage (Deneauve 1990), theaters throughout the region, the large baths of Hadrian in Leptis Magna (Finocchi 2012) and of Antoninus at Carthage (Lézine 1969), and the complex of Septimius Severus at Leptis Magna (Ward-Perkins 1993), hired sculpture workshops to carve of all the architectural and sculptural decoration of the building. These *officina* can come from distant art centers: M. F. Squarciapino (1974) proposed that the Severan forum at Leptis Magna was the work of an Aphrodisian workshop, while P. Pensabene (2006) attributed it to Bithynian workshops. Foreign sculptors certainly trained local apprentices in their techniques and styles as well as some sculptural types.

The major cities of North Africa have not produced archaeological evidence of sculpture workshops, except for the fragmentary plaster models of statues discovered in El Jem (Tunisia) (Slim and Fauqué 2001, 211–12). Thus it remains difficult to distinguish provincial statues from imported copies based on association with attested workshops in the region. Technical details show that the Capitoline Jupiter from the Odeon of Carthage (Yacoub 1970, 49, no. C. 921) is of local manufacture (Baratte 2012, 73, fig. 67). The nude Mars Gradivus from the same Odeon has been identified alternately as a "provincial" representation of Hadrian or as a statue of a contemporary African officer imitating a characteristic image of the emperor (Yacoub 1970, 46, no. C932). G. Caputo and G. Traversari (1976, 6–8) have posited a "grand atelier" at Leptis Magna, and it is likely that Iol Caesarea (Cherchell) and Carthage were production centers as well.

Foreign influence on local sculptural formats, materials, motifs, and styles is most obvious in the funerary realm. In Africa Proconsularis, where the use of stucco exteriors to adorn the walls of monuments exposed to the elements is characteristic, some burial coffers imitate the decor of imported Roman sarcophagi (including the funerary Eros, garlands, pastoral scenes, and offerings; Chaisemartin 1987, 93–8). Similar stuccoed exteriors and Roman influences are found on monumental Antonine tomb-cippi like that in Carthage representing the inauguration of a legate (Baratte 2012, 66–7) or that of the Flavio-Trajanic woman from La Malga (Slim and Fauqué 2001, 216). Egyptian mummy busts in plaster and stucco influenced the third-century AD images of the dead molded in this material at Thysdrus (El Jem: Slim and Fauqué 2001, 207–8) and Hadrumetum (Sousse: Chaisemartin 1987, 87–8, no. 131). A cippus with a plaster niche in Hadrumentum presents the young deceased between Dea Roma and a Muse (Chaisemartin 1987, 91–3, no. 134). Finally, at Sala in Tingitane, plaster is used for models of grotesque figures (Boube 1986).

Graeco-Roman Sculpture

In North Africa, Graeco-Roman statuary comes from monumental urban infrastructure, some mausolea, a few upper-class homes (e.g., Maison de la Cachette and Maison de la Volière in Carthage), and suburban sanctuaries. Inscriptions show that dedications of statues in the Roman fashion are concentrated almost entirely between AD 138 and 235, at the same time that Roman-style municipal life reached its peak in North Africa. Colossal representations modeled after works in Rome like the Livia-Tyche of Leptis Magna (Bianchi-Bandinelli et al. 1963, 44), the statues of the Temple of Apollo in Bulla Regia (Attya-Ouertani 1977), and the aforementioned Capitoline Jupiters impressed a public unevenly acculturated. Reproductions of works of the Greek tradition (*opera nobilia*, portraits of intellectual and historical figures) are very rare except in Tripolitania, which has more influence from the Neo-Attic tradition. Even cities located far from large coastal centers seem to have imported works of high-quality marble, like the Hercules of Thuburbo Majus (Yacoub 1970, 151, fig. 35) and the cuirassed statues of Ammaedara (Haïdra, Tunisia: Stemmer 1978, 38–9).

Four major categories of "Graeco-Roman" statuary are notable and will be surveyed here: (1) the cult statues and images offered in the temples and shrines of the gods of the Graeco-Roman pantheon or of Libyo-Phoenician, Egyptian, or Oriental origins, assimilated through Romanization; (2) mythological imagery decorating public buildings, such as the *scaenae frontes* of theaters, fountains, and baths, but also private houses; (3) monumental reliefs; and (4) portrait representations related to the imperial government and local civic institutions: living or deified emperors and their families and honorary statues of local authorities and supporters of the cities erected in the fora, basilicas, circuses, and amphitheaters.

Religious Sculptures

Among the cult or votive statues, examples clearly based on classical types (draped Jupiters, Aesculapius, Apollo Citharode of Hadrumetum and Bulla Regia, the huntress

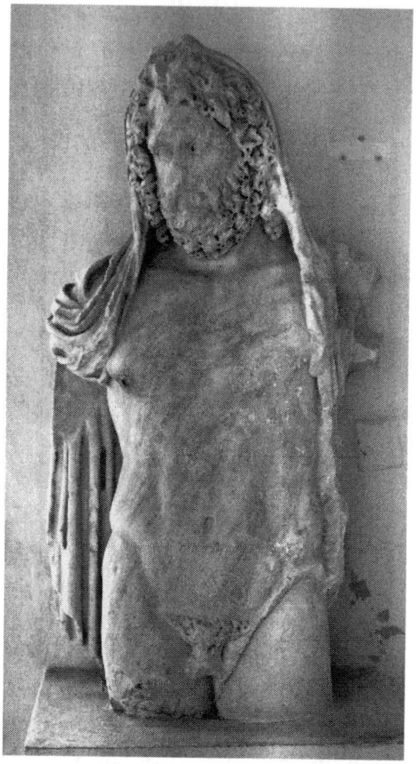

FIGURE 5.3.1 Saturn/Caelus from Hadrumetum, standing figure imitating Jupiter with his right arm encased in a vertical housing. Musée de Sousse, Tunisia.

Artemis, and Venus) appeared alongside original interpretations that seem to have been fashioned with very specific requirements in mind. For example, the standing Caelus/Saturn with veiled head and draped body discovered at Hadrumetum (figure 5.3.1), has a removable right arm in order to change the attribute to suit the needs of the cult calendar (Chaisemartin 1987, 18–20, no. 7). The two statues of Saturn Frugifer (Attya-Ouertani 1977, fig. 129; Baratte 2012, 74, fig. 69) and Athena Panthea of the Temple of Apollo at Bulla Regia reflect the syncretic religious orientation characteristic of North Africa. Heir to African Baal, Saturn appears seated on local stelae with his left hand near the face as in the Roman model, while some statues in the round (e.g., at Bulla Regia and Sousse) favor assimilation to standing Jupiter or Aesculapius. The head with "dreadlocks" in the Louvre from Cherchell—and until recently considered the portrait of Juba I—instead depicts a local deity with Numidian tendencies (Landwehr 2001). As in Gaul, Mercury is often depicted as a purveyor of wealth and trade, and statues of Aesculapius are also widespread. Heads of male deities carved in North Africa often carry heavy jeweled vegetal crowns like portraits of deified emperors, demonstrating permeability between them. Some alterations seem irreverent: for example, the Trajanic Lycian Apollo from the Baths of Leptis Magna was transformed into Antinous-Dionysus by sawing the head vertically and replacing the face (Bianchi-Bandinelli et al. 1963, fig. 11; Polidori et al. 1998, 96).

Female deities are mostly associated with prosperity: the Cereres (local variants of Demeter and Persephone), Venus, and Tyche/Fortuna. A headless Venus from Thysdrus (El Jem: Chaisemartin 2007, 221–9) in Aphrodisian marble carrying an Eros on her left shoulder with a cuirass for support was probably a Venus Genetrix. Some female figures, like the seated Tyche accompanied by a child from above the *cavea* of the theater of Leptis Magna (Caputo and Traversari 1976, no. 68, 76–9), remain unidentifiable although proposals include a mother goddess, one of the empresses of the late second century AD, or a personification of the city of Leptis accompanied by Septimius Severus as a child. The colossal statue of Livia from the sanctuary *in summa cavea* of the theater at Leptis (Caputo and Traversari 1976, no. 58, 76–9) demonstrates the same tendency towards syncretism as the statues from the Temple of Apollo at Bulla Regia: is Livia assimilated to Ceres, Cybele, or Tyche, or all three at once?

Mythological Sculptures

Many mythological sculptures adorned the nymphaea, theaters, and wealthy *domus* of North African cities. This imagery overlaps with contemporary mosaics in terms of the predominance of aquatic themes (marine thiasos, Eros and Nereids fishing or riding dolphins) and Dionysian figures (Satyrs, Sileni, Bacchants). Often smaller than life-size, these sculptures are, as in Gaul, serial productions of types, often imported from workshops of Asia Minor: for example, Dokimeion (Ganymede and eagle, Carthage: Gazda 1981; Orpheus, Sabratha: Ward 1970, cat. no. 25); Aphrodisias (torso possibly belonging to the judgment of Marsyas, El Jem: Chaisemartin 2007, 212–16); *bigio morato* ("dancer," El Jem: Chaisemartin 2007, 216–21; herms with "exotic" heads supporting a basin, Uthina: Association 1982, 119, no. 168–9); and Proconnesian statuettes produced by Bithynian workshops.

Monumental Reliefs

Several important examples of monumental relief survive from Romanized North Africa, beginning in the Augustan era and continuing to the third century AD. For example, the altar in Pentelic marble dedicated to the Gens Augusta in Carthage (L. Poinssot 1929), representing the flight of Aeneas, Apollo, Roma, and a scene of sacrifice led by the emperor Augustus is an import from Neo-Attic workshops in Rome, but may have inspired scenes of sacrifice on late stelae from the *tophet* in Sousse or the funerary monuments at Mactar. An Augustan relief from Carthage (Algiers Museum; Zanker 1987, 199–200, fig. 151) reproduces precisely the triad of the Temple of Mars Ultor in Rome. At the Bardo, a fragment coming from Utica and depicting a life-size pig wearing a sacrificial strip (*dorsuale*) shows a scene of *suovetaurilia* (Yacoub 1970, 31, no. C. 1173).

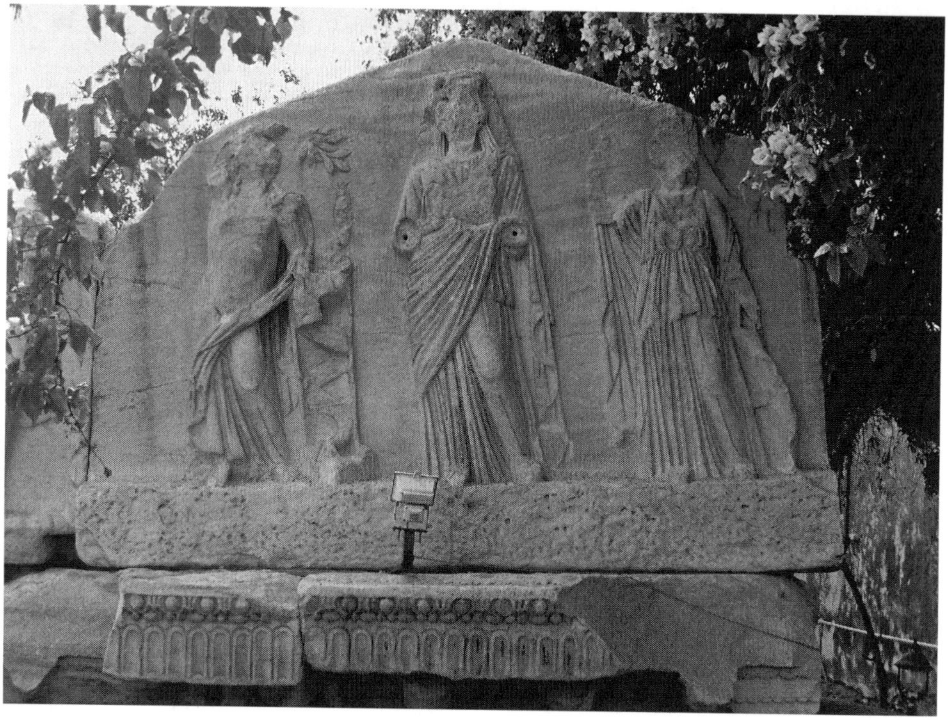

FIGURE 5.3.2 Central part of the pediment of the Temple of Genius Civitatis of Oea (modern Tripoli) depicting turreted Fortune between Apollo and Minerva. Tripoli, Libya.

At Hadrumetum a relief carved in Proconnesian marble presents a scene of imperial triumph with a northern captive datable to the second century AD (Chaisemartin 1987, 49–51, no. 43). Like the pillars of the eastern Barbarians from Meninx (Baratte and Ouertani 2004), the large Victories of Carthage probably refer to the Antonine imperial victories in the East (Lavagne 2012, 75–83; Baratte 2012, 41). The marble pediment of the Temple of *Genius coloniae* at Oea (modern Tripoli), dated AD 183 (figure 5.3.2), presents in classicizing style the paratactical figures of Tyche Polias, framed by Apollo and Minerva (the city's patron deities), and the Dioscuri (Polidori et al. 1998, 9). A re-examination of the nearby relief-decorated arch of Marcus Aurelius and Lucius Verus indicates that it honored the *virtus* of deified Antoninus Pius, with a secondary dedication to his successors (Arato 1996), and may be the work of North African sculptors imitating models from Rome. A Roman tomb covered with stucco from the cemetery of the *officiales* in Carthage, featuring the induction ceremony of a Roman legate of the Antonine period (mentioned above), resembles scenes of imperial *adventus*. On the other hand, the Severan reliefs of the *pulpitum* of Sabratha (Polidori et al. 1998, 173–81) and of the Arch of Septimius Severus at Leptis Magna (Bianchi-Bandinelli et al. 1963, 67–70), famous for its elaborate compositions, anticipate the conventions of late antique sculpture. Overall, however, Romanized North Africa preserves relatively few monumental relief panels (Baratte 2006) and the triumphal arches of Numidia and Africa Proconsularis do not carry figurative decoration.

Portraits

Sculpted representations of imperial families are a statistically significant category in Roman sculpture from North Africa due to the early construction of temples to the imperial cult and imperial groups included in the *fora* and *scaenae frontes* of theaters.

The series of portraits of the Mauretanian ruling family (Fittschen 1974) were certainly made by artists coming from Rome to Cherchell with copies at Sala (statue of Ptolemy; Boube 1990) and Volubilis (Boube-Piccot 1969, n. 1). At the other end of Roman North Africa have been unearthed three cycles of portraits of the Julio-Claudian family: one Tiberian displayed in the Temple of Rome and Augustus at Leptis Magna (Aurigemma 1940); a second one in the Old Forum of the same city, erected under Claudius; and a third that adorned the forum of the modest city of Zitha (modern Zian) on the southern coast of Africa Proconsularis (Queyrel 1993). The few Julio-Claudian portrait heads include the Augustus of Thysdrus (Boschung 1993, 191, Kat. 201) and of Hippo Regius (Baratte 2005, 156), the Livia of Carthage (Yacoub 1970, 47, no. C. 934), the colossal Octavia of El Jem (Chaisemartin 1983), and the Caligula of Musti (in Tunisia; Boschung 1989, 110, Kat. 14). The cuirassed statue of Cherchell copies an Augustan model but dates to the Claudian era, according to Landwehr (1993–2008, 4: 102–114). Three cuirassed statues of the first century come from the Forum of Hadrumetum (Chaisemartin 1987, 39–41, no. 31–3). In contrast for the Flavian period, we can mention only two heads of Vespasian from Bulla Regia (Slim and Fauqué 2001, 146) and Hippo (Baratte 2005, 154), and a head of Titus from Constantine (De La Blanchère 1890–1928, 2: no. 3, 93, pl. VI), as well as some cuirassed statues: Vespasian and Titus from Sabratha (Stemmer 1978, 62–3, no. V.10–11, 19, no. I.20, 26, no. II.7), torsos of Haïdra (Stemmer 1978, 38–9, no. III.15) and Carthage (Stemmer 1978, 40–41, no. III.20).

From the time of Trajan—represented by a colossal head from Hadrumetum assimilated to the *genius coloniae* of the city (Chaisemartin 1987, 32–4, no. 25) and a life-size head from Thuburbo Majus (Yacoub 1970, 73, inv. 3157)—the second-century portraits of the emperors (often colossal) multiply: in addition to cuirassed statues, very popular in North Africa (Stemmer 1978), Roman rulers are often depicted heroically nude or draped like Jupiter with a heavy wreath of laurel or oak with medallions: for example, Hadrian of Thysdrus in the Algiers Museum (Evers 1994, 82, cat. 5); Lucius Verus from the theater at Dougga, now in the Bardo Museum (Baratte 2012, 80, fig. 76); and a pair of seated statues of Marcus Aurelius and Lucius Verus from the theater at Bulla Regia (Zanker 1983, 32, pls. 19–20). The dynastic group from the Forum of Markouna (Algeria; Baratte 1983) from a local workshop features simplified treatment of hair and schematic faces.

A series of ten portraits of the empress Sabina wearing a diadem of serpentine curls gives an idea of how a formal model coming from Rome to Carthage was repeatedly copied (Carandini 1969, 138–43, nos. 4–14). Draped statues of empresses in North Africa are often represented as Ceres or as initiates into the Eleusinian mysteries (Carandini 1969, 141–2).

Septimius Severus, born in Leptis Magna, left two portraits there, one from the exedra of the Old Forum (Bonacasa-Carra 1980, 110, fig. 9) and another found to the north of the theater (Caputo and Traversari 1976, nos. 77, 98–100), and Julia Domna is represented as a Muse at Carthage (Yacoub 1970, 46, no. C.22). Colossal heads of cult statues of the couple were found in the temple to the *gens* Septimia at Cuicul (Jemila: McCann 1968, 153, no. 45; Sintès and Rebahi 2003, 66), while a head of Caracalla comes from Thuburbo Majus (Slim and Fauqué 2001, 146). The only third-century imperial portrait in North Africa is of Gordian I (figure 5.3.3) from Carthage (Bergmann 1977, 33–4).

Meanwhile, numerous honorary statues of notables, dedicated mainly between AD 138 and 235, testify to municipal life. The influence of Roman style is seen in the evolution of the drapery of the toga for men, hairstyles imitating those of the imperial family for both sexes, and the adoption of aspects of imperial physiognomy. On the other hand, a peculiarity of these provinces is the lack of attention to details of the musculature and of the forms of the body, and sometimes a tendency to an excessively poignant or expressive rendering of faces.

Women, whether priestesses or benefactors like Minia Procula at Bulla Regia (Attya-Ouertani 1977, 131), or the dead, like Crepereia Innula from Ammaedara (Haïdra: Fejfer 2008, 282–3), are enveloped in traditional drapery of Greek origin. North African examples of well-known types have been found, including the large and small Herculaneum women, Eumachia or Fundilia, *pudicitia*, or *palliata*. Models derived

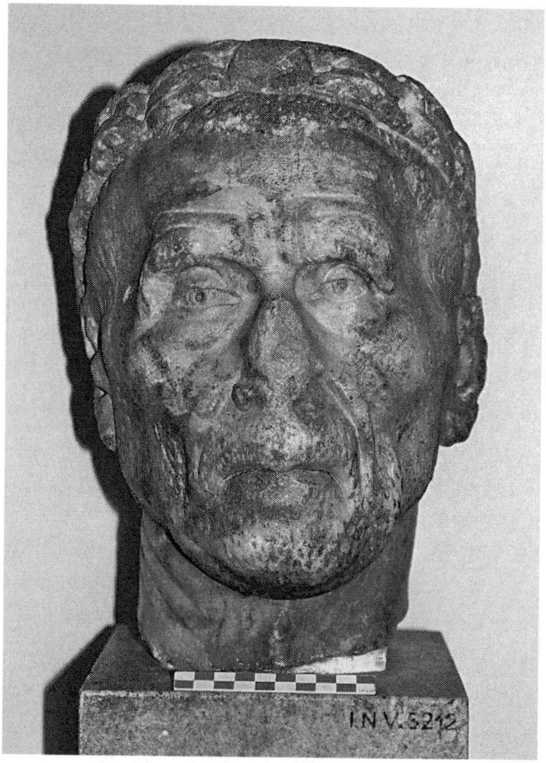

FIGURE 5.3.3 Portrait of Gordian I of Carthage wearing a wreath. Tunis, Musée du Bardo.

from images of Ceres, holding the ritual bunch of poppies and ears of wheat, were particularly popular. Such types include Kore, Phidian Demeter, and the so-called initiate (in vogue during the reign of Trajan) gathering her drape over the thigh.

Some original works depict local notables whose Libyan-Berber ethnicity is emphasized: Iddibal Caphada Aemilius from Leptis Magna (Equini-Schneider 1995), the African at Sabratha (Bonacasa-Carra 1980), and Lusius Quietus of Sousse (Chaisemartin 1989). The deceased represented as Hercules at Borj el Amri resembles third-century heads of Roman soldiers (Association 1982, 123–4, no. 174). The *togatus* with the turreted crown from the temple of Saturn at Dougga (Association 1982, 122, no. 173) seems assimilated to the *Genius* of the city, and his tense face dates to the third quarter of the third century.

A class of funerary statues apparently unique to North Africa depicts participants in circus and amphitheater games with their characteristic costumes and attributes: the charioteer or *sparsor* holding a small amphora from Carthage (Veyne, Beschaouch, and Ennabli 1995, 34–54); the fragmentary charioteer with the head of his horse from Sousse (Chaisemartin 1987, 42–3, no. 35); the statue of the *venator* wearing a mantle richly decorated with the ornate emblems of his association from Sidi Ghrib (figure 5.3.4; Baratte 1998; 2012, 46); and two fragmentary statues of hunters attacked in the amphitheater by a panther from El Jem and Haïdra (Baratte and Abdallah 2000, 50–79).

Sarcophagi

Though votive and funerary stelae are plentiful, sarcophagi are scarce and unevenly distributed from one end of North Africa to the other: absent in Mauretania Tingitana and Tripolitania, they are rare in Algeria except at Tipasa, and more numerous in Africa Proconsularis. While they constitute an excellent medium for images, secular, pagan, or Christian, and also contributed to memorializing the rank of the deceased in society, the complexity of their execution and their prices may explain their limited diffusion, except for late sarcophagi in locally quarried kedel limestone.

As in other genres of sculpture, both imported copies and locally made examples may be identified, some carved by skilled craftsmen who may have been trained in the major centers of production, others by other less experienced artisans occasionally demonstrating originality in the choice of decoration. Some unfinished sarcophagi at Carthage reflect different stages of completion (Fournet-Pilipenko 1961, cat. 103).

The majority of imported sarcophagi were from Rome, like the example discovered at Port Gueydon (Algeria) representing the myth of Bellerophon (Aymard 1935). North African productions are distinguished either by their workmanship or by significant changes in their decoration: an oval child's sarcophagus with a *clipeus*, discovered near Téboursouk (Tunisia), is more monumental (Baratte 2013); one from a hypogeum at Sousse depicts the young deceased three times (Museum of Algiers; Chaisemartin 1987, 84–5, no. 128); and a sarcophagus from central Tunisia depicts the four seasons in

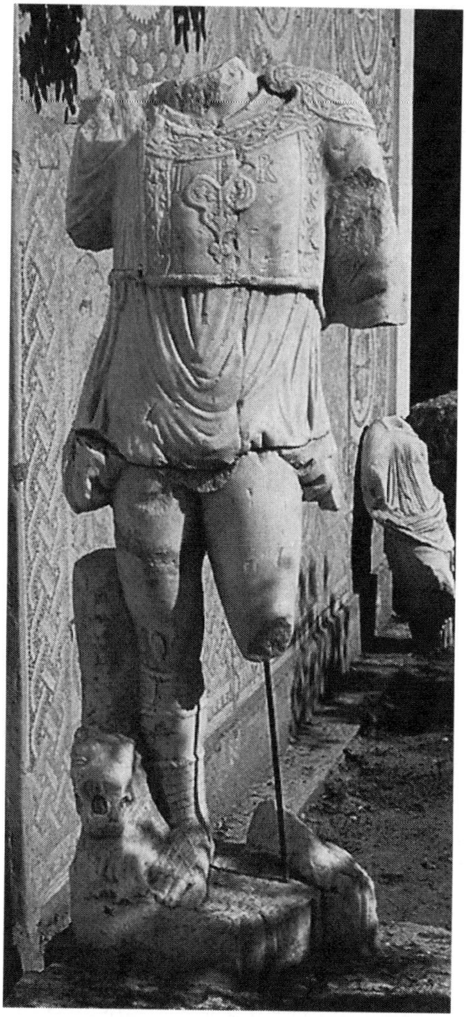

FIGURE 5.3.4 Portrait of a hunter from Sidi Ghrib (modern Tunisia) wearing a protective cloak decorated with the emblems of his professional association. Carthage, Musée de Carthage.

a distinctly non-Graeco-Roman, original iconography (Fournet-Pilipenko 1961, cat. 4). At Rusicade (modern Skikda, Algeria), a sarcophagus represents pastoral and hunting scenes in very low relief and is certainly a local product (Baratte 2007, 246–7). At Timgad (Algeria) and at Cincari (Tunisia), very original, grand vegetal scrolls decorate the front of sarcophagi (Fournet-Pilipenko 1961, cat. 129), unparalleled in the production of Rome. At Ucubi (El Gousset, Tunisia), the artisan, unfamiliar with carving this sort of sculpture, treated the relief as if it were a block of architecture, representing the deceased lying very awkwardly (perhaps inspired by images of Endymion; Fournet-Pilipenko 1961, cat. 163).

In addition to numerous strigillated examples, a few sarcophagi illustrate the career of the deceased, for example the sarcophagus of C. Statius Celsus from

Carthage (Himmelmann 1973, 311). Mythological themes are few (though examples of Bellerophon, Pelops, the Amazons, and the Muses survive), and the scarcity of Bacchic themes is surprising. On the other hand, representations of the seasons are common until the end of antiquity (e.g., Fournet-Pilipenko 1961, cat. 22). No sarcophagus relief illustrates circus games.

Christian sarcophagi are more unusual (Christern-Briesenick 2003). Apart from a few examples imported from Rome or Gaul (for example a sarcophagus with columns, now in the Museum of Algiers), one encounters sarcophagi of North African production, which are based on Roman models (like that from Chullu, Algeria) or develop a more original iconography, sometimes of high quality, such as that discovered at Lamta (Tunisia), which surprisingly blends hunting scenes and the *Traditio Legis* (Bejaoui 2002). There are also some high-quality works on which the figures are only etched or in very shallow relief. Some pieces eschew any classification.

In the fourth and fifth centuries, the production of kedel sarcophagi, carved from limestone quarried at the foot of Cap Bon in Tunisia, developed at Carthage. Often of good quality, these locally successful sarcophagi usually feature strigils complemented by floral motifs or Christian figures (such as the Good Shepherd). These limestone sarcophagi were also traded, most notably to Tarragona (Spain).

Local Votive and Funerary Reliefs

In Roman North Africa, the genre of local votive and funerary sculpture is widely represented by numerous relief stelae, especially in Africa Proconsularis, Numidia, and Mauretania Caesariensis (see essay 4.2, McCarty). Carved from local stones by workshops of sometimes modest locales and for sanctuaries of indigenous traditions, these reliefs usually represent dedicants or the dead sacrificing to deities. Saturn/Baal is the most common of these deities, who are often depicted in the upper register of the stela. More rarely the commemorated deceased appear in scenes of daily life or associated with their occupations: a priestess, couples embracing, soldiers (Ammaedara: Association 1982, cat. 150; Cherchell: Sintès and Rebahi 2003, cat. 35–8), an oil merchant (Sintès and Rebahi 2003, n. 57), and scenes of agricultural life (Association 1982, cat. 159).

One is struck by the great diversity of form, composition, and manufacture from one end of North Africa to the other, but also sometimes within the same site. Reliefs vary in depth from engraving to high relief, and along the continuum from abstraction to Roman-style realism. On some reliefs from Numidia, for example, clothing is treated in purely ornamental fashion. These differences reflect the uneven skills of artisans (as on the stela dedicated to Mercury at the Musée de Sétif; Sintès and Rebahi 2003, n.77), but also correspond to a greater or lesser familiarity with Roman culture. The narrow, pointed shape of the stela (figure 5.3.5) recalls Punic stelae reminiscent of obelisks. In some border regions (such as central Tunisia and Numidia), we encounter motifs borrowed from pre-Roman religious contexts, such as the symbol of Tanit, the presence

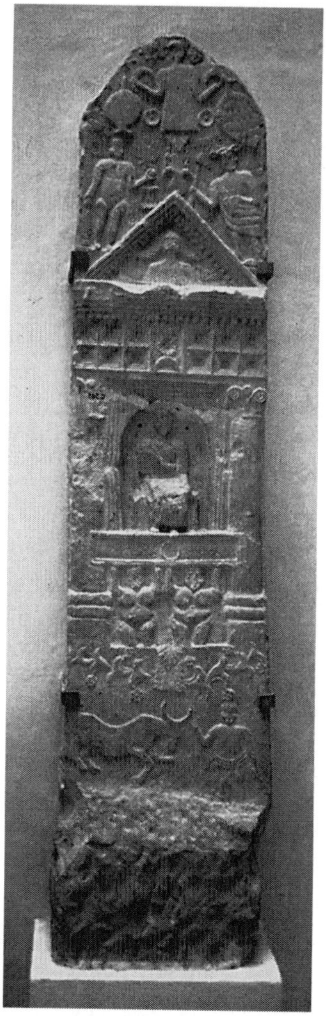

FIGURE 5.3.5 Stela of Maghrawa (called Ghorfa) depicting the sacrificial bull and victim below, the dedicant sitting in an *aedicula* carried by two Atlantes, whose front displays a bust of Saturn (?), and finally, at top, the gods Mercury and Venus and a schematic figure carrying a pomegranate and a pine cone. Tunis, Musée du Bardo.

of chthonic figures, offerings like gamma shaped votive cakes brought by the faithful, North African priestly costume, and stylized plants framing the dedicant (Berthier and Charlier 1955; Sintès and Rebahi 2003, 145–6).

Many headstones, especially those dedicated to Saturn, have a hierarchical organization. The registers of the composition, from the image of the sacrificial victim at the bottom to the god in the pediment, reflect the transition from the earthly world to the realm of the gods. The group of stelae from Maghrawa (formerly La Ghorfa) demonstrates the regional attachment to indigenous designs (M'Charek 1988; Moore 2000): the complex architectural framework supports a multitude of patterns and divine figures or symbols whose Roman appearance (Dioscuri) encompasses a different meaning.

Other scenes are taken from the repertoire of Roman religion: the sacrifice of a bull on the stela dedicated to Saturn from the sanctuary at Bou Kornein on the eastern shore of the Bay of Tunis (Association 1982, cat. 158) and a small group of stelae from Sousse depicting sacrifice in the manner of Julio-Claudian reliefs (Chaisemartin 1987, 61–75, nos. 70–75). Representations of indigenous deities are exceptional (Association 1982, cat. 161), and some reveal a partial adaptation of certain Roman motifs (Sintès and Rebahi 2003, n.76).

As dedicant, the deceased is represented mostly standing, except in rare groups of funerary stelae from coastal sites like Ulisippira (Henchir Zembra, Tunisia: Chaisemartin 1987, 101–4, no. 157–61) with busts in an architectural framework. In the central highlands, tables furnished with receptacles for food offerings are often decorated with a figured relief sunk into the vertical face of the stone (Deonna 1934, 12–21).

Numerous mausolea were erected in North Africa, but they rarely carry figurative architectural decoration. In southern Tunisia mythological representations appear in the first century on the mausoleum of El-Amrouni (Ferchiou 1989), while at Tataouine (Tunisia) and in southern Libya at Ghirza the motifs evoke the daily life of less-Romanized indigenous people (Brogan and Smith 1984).

Conclusion

In the fourth century AD, the role of sculpture in North Africa remained significant. Few statues have actually been found, but inscriptions attest to their presence. The latest stela dedicated to Saturn is dated precisely November 323 (Association 1982, cat. 160) and craftsmen still continued to represent the pagan deities, as the letter of St. Augustine sent in 389 to notables of Sufès (*Ep.* 50) about a statue of Hercules attests. Imperial effigies—such as the portrait of Constantius II from Carthage (Association 1982, cat. 175)—and portraits of elite members of society, like the statue of a child from Madaure (Mdaourouch, Algeria; Sintès and Rebahi 2003, n. 110), are still present in the cities, although in smaller numbers, as shown by inscriptions. Decorative statuary is still appreciated, as shown by the statuette of Ganymede discovered in the "House of the Greek Charioteers" in Carthage (Gazda 1981). Several sarcophagi and reliefs (like the marble table from Sbeitla with biblical scenes; Association 1982, 183, cat. 237) confirm the continuation of imports from Rome and Asia Minor.

However, around AD 400, the taste for three-dimensional sculpture seems to disappear in North Africa, as evidenced by the decline in statue dedications. Political difficulties and the weakening of municipal elites (especially after the Vandal invasion), the growing influence of the Church (distrustful of statuary), and a slow change in attitudes (more sensitive now to drawing and color than to volume), all no doubt explain the profound change that becomes more noticeable in the sixth and seventh centuries, when the Byzantines became masters of North Africa. Yet the sovereign Vandals themselves were fond of sculpture, as a mark of prestige associated with Roman culture. Thus in AD 455, according to Procopius (*Vand.* 3.5.5), King Genseric loaded ships with statues from the sack of Rome to take to North Africa.

At the same time in several regions of Africa Proconsularis and Numidia, local sculpture workshops were producing architectural elements with figurative decoration for churches (Christern 1976). After the Byzantine conquest, architectural sculpture for churches was frequently imported from Constantinople and Asia Minor. Thus, by the fifth and sixth centuries AD, the role of sculpture in North Africa had shifted dramatically.

Bibliography

Arata, F. P. 1996. "L'arco di Marco Aurelio a Tripoli (Oea): Una nuova ipotesi esegetica." In *Scritti di antichità in memoria di S. Stucchi*, edited by L. Bachielli and M. Bonnano Aravantinos, 9–30. Rome: "L'Erma" di Bretschneider.

Association Française d'Action Artistique. 1982. *De Carthage à Kairouan: 2000 ans d'art et d'histoire en Tunisie.* Paris: Association Française d'Action Artistique.

Attya-Ouertani N. 1977. "Les antiquités de Bulla Regia au Musée du Bardo." In *Les ruines de Bulla Regia*, by A. Beschaouch, R. Hanoune, and Y. Thebert, 123–32. CÉFR 28. Rome: École française de Rome.

Aurigemma, S. 1940. "Sculture del Foro Vecchio di Leptis Magna raffiguranti la dea Roma e principi della casa dei Giulio-Claudi." *AfrIt* 8: 1–74.

Aymard J. 1935. "La légende de Bellérophon sur un sarcophage du musée d'Alger." *MÉFRA* 52: 143–84.

Baratte, F. 1983. "Les portraits impériaux de Markouna et la sculpture officielle dans l'Afrique romaine." *MÉFRA* 95: 785–815.

———. 1998. "Un témoignage sur les *venatores* en Afrique: La statue de Sidi Ghrib (Tunisie)." *AntAfr* 34: 215–25.

———. 2005. "La Sculpture." In *Hippone*, edited by X. Delestre, 154–64. Aix-en Provence: Edisud.

———. 2006. "L'image impériale sur les reliefs de l'Afrique romaine." In *La transmission de l'idéologie impériale dans l'Occident Romain*, edited by M. N. Caballero and J.-M. Roddaz, 273–96. Bordeaux: Ausonius.

———. 2007. "A propos des sarcophages dans l'Afrique romaine: Thèmes et ateliers." In *Akten des Symposiums des Sarkophag-Corpus 2001*, edited by G. Koch, 241–50. Sarkophag-Studien 3. Mainz: Philipp von Zabern.

———. 2012. *Die Römer in Tunesien und Libyen: Nordafrika in römischer Zeit.* Darmstadt: Philipp von Zabern.

———. 2013. "Les sarcophages dans l'Afrique antique: Images romaines et provinciales." In *Iconographie funéraire romaine et société: Corpus antique, approches nouvelles?*, edited by F. Baratte and M. Galinier, 173–91. Perpignan: Presses universitaires de Perpignan.

Baratte, F., and Z. B. B. Abdallah. 2000. "Le sanctuaire de Saturne à *Ammaedara* (Haïdra, Tunisie): Documents inédits." *RA* 2000(1): 51–79.

Baratte, F., and N. Ouertani. 2004. "Un curieux ensemble sculpté de l'Afrique romaine: Les piliers de Méninx." In *Studi di archeologia in onore di Gustavo Traversari*, edited by M. Fano Santi, 47–62. Rome: Bretschneider.

Bejaoui, F. 2002. "Le sarcophage de Lemta." In *Akten des Symposiums "Frühchristliche Sarkophage," Marburg 1999*, edited by K. Kirchhainer and G. Koch, 13–18. Sarkophag-Studien 2. Mainz: Philipp von Zabern.

Benseddik, N. 2010. *Esculape et Hygie en Afrique*. Paris: Académie des Inscriptions et Belles-lettres.

Bergmann, M. 1977. *Studien zum römischen Porträt des 3. Jahrhunderts n. Chr.* Bonn: Rudolf Habelt.

Berthier A., and R. Charlier. 1955. *Le sanctuaire punique d'El Hofra à Constantine*. Paris: Arts et métiers graphiques.

Bianchi-Bandinelli R., E. Vergara Caffarelli, G. Caputo, and F. Clerici. 1963. *Leptis Magna*. Rome: Impresa Astaldi.

Bonacasa-Carra, R. M. 1980. "Ritratto di un dignitario libio nel Museo di Sabratha." *QAL* 11: 100–112.

Boschung, D. 1989. *Die Bildnisse des Caligula*. Berlin: Mann.

———. 1993. *Die Bildnisse des Augustus*. Berlin: Mann.

Boube, J. 1986. "Modèles antiques en plâtre près de Sala (Maroc)." *RA* 1986(2): 301–326.

———. 1990. "Une statue portrait de Ptolémée de Maurétanie à Sala (Maroc)." *RA* 1990(2): 331–60.

Boube-Piccot, C. 1969. *Les bronzes antiques du Maroc*. Vol. 1, *La statuaire*. Etudes et travaux d'archéologie marocaine 4. Rabat: Royaume du Maroc.

Brogan, O., and D. J. Smith. 1984. *Ghirza: A Libyan settlement in the Roman period*. Tripoli: Department of Antiquities.

Caputo, G. 1949. "Statua di Mitra e firma di Aristius Antiochus in Leptis Magna." *ArchCl* 1(2): 205–7.

Caputo, G., and G. Traversari. 1976. *Le sculture del teatro di Leptis Magna*. Rome: Bretschneider.

Carandini, A. 1969. *Vibia Sabina*. Florence: Leo S. Olschki.

Chaisemartin, N. de. 1983. "Note sur l'iconographie d'Octavie d'après un portrait provenant d'El Jem et conservé au Musée de Sousse." *AntAfr* 19: 35–61.

———. 1987. *Les sculptures romaines de Sousse et des sites environnants*. CSIR Tunisie Proconsulaire 2. CÉFR 102. Rome: École Française de Rome.

———. 1989. "Portraits d'un Africain." In *Festschrift für Jale Inan*, edited by N. Besgelen and M. Lugal, 449–59. Istanbul: Arkeoloji ve Sanat Tarihi Yayinlari.

———. 2007. "Le commerce des sculptures dans l'empire romain: Témoignages sur les échanges artistiques des ateliers d'Aphrodisias avec l'Afrique." In *Actes du colloque La Méditerranée d'une rive à l'autre*, edited by A. Laronde and J. Leclant, 201–229. Cahiers de la villa Kérylos 18. Paris: De Boccard.

Christern, J. 1976. *Das Frühchristliche Pilgerheiligtum von Tebessa: Architektur und Ornamentik einer spätantiken Bauhütte in Nordafrika*. Wiesbaden: Steiner.

Christern-Briesenick, B. 2003. *Repertorium der christlich-antiken Sarkophage*. Vol. 3, *Frankreich, Algerien, Tunesien*. Mainz: Philipp von Zabern.

De La Blanchère, R., ed. 1890–1928. *Description de l'Afrique du Nord, Musées et collections archéologiques de l'Algérie et de la Tunisie*. 22 vols. Paris: Leroux.

Deneauve, J. 1990. "Le centre monumental de Carthage: Un ensemble cultuel sur la colline de Byrsa." In *Histoire et archéologie de l'Afrique du Nord, 1. Carthage et son territoire dans l'antiquité*, 143–56. Paris: CTHS.

Deonna, W. 1934. "Mobilier Délien, I: Tables antiques d'offrandes avec écuelles et table d'autel chrétien." *BCH* 58: 1–90.

Equini-Schneider, E. 1995. "Problemi di ritrattistica leptitana: Ancora sulla statua di Iddibal Caphada Aemilius." *AfrRom* 11: 1085–9.

Evers, C. 1994. *Les portraits d'Hadrien*. Brussels: Académie royale de Belgique.

Fejfer, J. 2008. *Roman Portraits in Context*. Berlin: Walter de Gruyter.

Ferchiou, N. 1989. "Le mausolée de Q. Apuleus Maxssimus à El Amrouni." *PBSR* 57: 47–76.

Finocchi, P. 2012. *Le sculture delle terme adrianee di Leptis Magna*. Rome: Espera.

Fittschen, K. 1974. "Die Bildnisse der mauretanischen Könige und ihre stadtrömischen Vorbilder." *MM* 15: 156–73.

Fournet-Pilipenko, H. 1961. "Sarcophages romains de Tunisie." *Karthago* 11: 77–168.

Gazda, E. K. 1981. "A Marble Group of Ganymede and the Eagle from the Age of Augustine." In *Excavations at Carthage, 1977, Conducted by the University of Michigan*. Vol. 6, edited by J. H. Humphrey, 125–78. Ann Arbor: Kelsey Museum.

Himmelmann, N. 1973. *Typologische Untersuchungen an römischen Sarkophagreliefs des 3. und 4. Jahrhunderts n. Ch.* Mainz: Philipp von Zabern.

Landwehr, C., ed. 1993–2008. *Die römischen Skulpturen von Caesarea Mauretaniae*. 4 vols. Mainz: Philipp von Zabern.

Landwehr, C. 2001. "König Juba I oder Deus Maurus?" *JdI* 116: 277–97.

Lavagne, H. 2012. "Un relief de l'arc de triomphe du forum de Carthage conservé près d'Aix-en-Provence." *Monuments Piot* 91: 59–89.

Le Glay, M. 1961. *Saturne Africain: Monuments*. Vol. 1, *Afrique proconsulaire*. Paris: Arts et Métiers Graphiques.

———. 1966. *Saturne Africain: Monuments*. Vol. 2, *Numidie, Maurétanies*. Paris: Éditions du Centre national de la recherche scientifique.

Lézine, A. 1969. *Les thermes d'Antonin à Carthage*. Tunis: Société Tunisienne de Diffusion.

McCann, A. M. 1968. *The Portraits of Septimius Severus*. MAAR 30. Rome.

M'Charek, A. 1988. "Maghrawa, lieu de provenance des stèles punico-numides dites de la Ghorfa." *MÉFRA* 100(2): 731–60.

Moore. J. 2000. "Cultural identity in Roman Africa: The 'La Ghorfa' Stelae." PhD diss., McMaster University. https://macsphere.mcmaster.ca/handle/11375/6359.

Pensabene, P. 2003. "La Porta Oea e l'arco di Marco Aurelio a Leptis Magna: Contributo alla definizione dei marmi e del loro costo, delle officine e delle commitenze." *Quaderni di archeologia della Libya* 18: 341–67.

———. 2006. "Le scuole di Nicomedia e Afrodisia e i pilastri della basilica severiana di Leptis Magna." *Marmora* 2: 41–58.

Picard, G. Ch. 1982. "La sculpture dans l'Afrique romaine." In "150-Jahr-Feier Deutsches Archäologisches Institut Rom." *RM-EH* 25: 180–95.

Poinssot, C. 1983. *Les ruines de Dougga*. Tunis: Institut national d'archéologie et arts.

Poinssot, L. 1929. *L'autel de la Gens Augusta à Carthage*. Tunis: Tournier.

Polidori, R., A. Di Vita, G. Di Vita-Evrard, and L. Bachielli. 1998. *La Libye antique: Cités perdues de l'Empire romain*. Paris: Mengès.

Queyrel, F. 1993. "De Paris à Ziane: Identification d'un groupe julio-claudien." *AntAfr* 29: 71–119.

Rakob F. 1979. "Numidische Königarchitektur in Nordafrika." In *Die Numider, Reiter und könige nördlich des Sahara*, edited by H. G. Horn and Ch. B. Rüger, 119–71. Bonn: Rheinisches Landesmuseum.

Reynolds, J. M., and J. B. Ward-Perkins. (1952) 2009. *Inscriptions of Roman Tripolitania*. Enhanced electronic reissue edited by G. Bodard and C. Roueché. http://inslib.kcl.ac.uk/irt2009/index.html.

Sintès, C., and Y. Rebahi. 2003. *Algérie antique*. Arles: Éditions du Musée de l'Arles et de la Provence antiques.

Slim, H., and N. Fauqué. 2001. *La Tunisie antique: De Hannibal à Saint Augustin*. Paris: Mengès.

Squarciapino, M. F. 1974. *Sculture del Foro Severiano di Leptis Magna*. Rome: Bretschneider.

Stemmer, K. 1978. *Untersuchungen zur Typologie, Chronologie und Ikonographie der Panzerstatuen*. Berlin: Mann.

Veyne, P., A. Beschaouch, and A. Ennabli. 1995. "Statue d'aurige romain trouvée à Carthage." *RA* 1995(1): 39–54.

Ward, P. 1970. *Sabratha: A Guide to Visitors*. Cambridge: Oleander.

Ward-Perkins, J. B. 1993. *The Severan Buildings of Lepcis Magna: An Architectural Survey*. London: Society for Libyan Studies.

Yacoub M. 1970. *Le musée du Bardo: Musée Antique*. Tunis: Ministère des affaires culturelles.

Zanker, P. 1983. *Provinzielle Kaiserporträts*. Munich: Beck.

———. 1987. *Augustus und die Macht der Bilder*. Munich: Beck.

CHAPTER 5.4

GREECE

MARY C. STURGEON

INTRODUCTION

GREECE is extremely rich in marble sculpture of the Roman period, despite Rome's systematic destruction of Greek cities in the late third and second centuries BC and the reduction of the region to the status of a province. New finds are continually reported, new museum catalogs produced, and conference publications regularly bring Roman sculpture from Greece to our attention. This material is abundant and varied and the quality of some pieces is exceptional.

Ideal statues depicting deities, mythological figures, and personifications occupy a dominant position, along with imperial and private portraits, and architectural, funerary and votive reliefs. Copies, variations, and new creations inspired by archaic, classical, and Hellenistic Greek types were commissioned for public and private contexts. With such retrospective styles artists recall earlier works of art as characteristic of cultural knowledge and antiquarianism as well as cultural memory (Pollitt 1986, 164–84; Hölscher 2006; Kousser 2008; see essay 3.6, Touchette). The workshops that produced sculptures in retrospective styles, often referred to as Neo-Attic, achieved significant popularity in the second and first centuries BC.

In terms of literary evidence, of the ancient authors, Pausanias (mid-second century AD) provides the most information about sculpture in Greece. Visiting the important sites of his day, he recorded much of what he saw in the order he encountered it, paying special attention to Greek architecture, sculpture, and artists. In Messene he lists a number of statues of deities, which agrees with the order in which the statue bases were found (4.31.10; Habicht 1985, 44). Pausanias does the same on the Athenian Akropolis, where, walking east along the north side of the Parthenon, he mentions first the statue of the goddess Earth (Ge) and then of Timotheus, the son, and of Conon his father (1.24.3). Pausanias, however, was not always complete: he sometimes described sculptures made of costly materials but neglected the marble statues that stood beside them; he carefully examined centuries-old sculptures and often ignored works made during his own time.

Roman sculpture in Greece began to receive significant attention in the second half of the twentieth century. A steady development of interest is demonstrated by studies of portraits (Harrison 1953; Rüsch 1969; de Grazia 1973; Datsouli-Stavridi 1985). The 1997 installation of Roman sculpture in the National Archaeological Museum in Athens first made accessible to the public the full range of Roman sculptural types produced in Greece (Rhomiopoulou 1997). Scholars have also turned attention to finds from recent excavations, sculptures from known archaeological contexts, and technical features. Publications address questions of chronology, relationships to possible models and to contemporary works, workshop affiliations, techniques of carving, and marble type. Roman Greece remained a major center for the production of marble sculpture, actively responding to commissions from patrons at home, in Italy, and to the east through the late antique period (Kokkorou-Alevra 2001; Fittschen 2008).

This essay begins with a brief discussion of the special status of Greece vis-à-vis the impact of various Roman provinces on the artistic traditions of Rome followed by an overview of recent finds and evidence for sculptural production in Roman Greece. Then, I provide surveys of the sculptural evidence and trends notable in portraiture, ideal sculpture, architectural sculpture, and funerary statuary of Roman Greece. A final section on the late Roman period highlights this stylistically important period in which Greece plays a significant role.

Interest in the Past

Greece was unique among Roman provinces in the artistic allure it had on Rome. In addition to the enormous impact of Greek art on Rome evident during the late Republic (see essays 3.3, Anguissola; and 3.6, Touchette), during the imperial period several emperors, notably Augustus and Hadrian, cultivated an interest in classical art, which had a strong effect on the appearance and subjects of sculpture produced in Greece as well as that made for metropolitan contexts (Toynbee 1934; Zanker 1988; Spawforth 2012). The Augustan period preferred retrospective styles to express political ideals (Hölscher 2006), and the Augustan reliefs at Nikopolis include both archaic and classical forms.

Renewed interest in classical forms in the Hadrianic to early Antonine periods is exemplified by a set of reliefs found in Peiraieus. These large panels contain two-figured scenes adapted from the Amazonomachy on the shield of Athena Parthenos (Stephanidou-Tiveriou 1979). They were probably commissioned for a villa where they would have demonstrated the erudition of the wealthy patron. Private collections of contemporary and earlier sculptures have been discovered at such villas. Herodes Atticus's villa at Loukou has revealed a large group of sculptures of both Greek and Roman date (Spyropoulos 2001; Spyropoulos and Spyropoulos 2003). In a late Roman villa in the Panayia area at Corinth, nine statuettes—of Artemis (twice), Asklepios (twice), Dionysos, Herakles, Europa/Sosandra, Pan, and Roma—were found, probably from a domestic shrine. The subjects (except for Roma) and figure types are primarily traditional (Stirling 2008). Long-established Greek subjects are also used in figural table supports, especially popular in northern Greece, which continue through the fourth century (Despinis, Stephanidou-Tiveriou, and Boutiras 1997, 131–40, nos. 100–110; Ajootian 2000).

Recent Finds

Recent excavations have yielded many new sculptures. Excavations for the new Metro in Athens produced evidence for workshop activity in the National Gardens. A bronze male statuette and a foot from a large statue were found in the "Zappeion shaft" in a first-century BC context (Zachariadou 2001, 144–7, cat. nos. 126, 127). By the Makrygianni building south of the Akropolis, the area of the New Akropolis Museum, notable finds include large statuettes of foreign divinities, such as the Ephesian Artemis, Heliopolitan Zeus, and Egyptian deities (Trianti 2008). Messene has produced a large number of sculptures, including a Doryphoros and a Diomedes (Themelis 2000).

At Nikopolis the excavations at Octavian's victory monument commemorating the Battle of Actium have uncovered an altar with an extensive series of reliefs. The procession restored in the upper frieze is thought to represent Octavian's triple triumph of 29 BC (Zachos 2003; 2007). It is truly remarkable that this monument, likely the major precursor of the Ara Pacis in Rome, was erected in Roman Greece.

Artists, Materials, and Techniques

In the later third and second centuries BC, sculptors from Greece went to other places for work, especially Pergamon and Rome (see essays 3.3, Anguissola; and 3.6, Touchette). Perhaps this "brain drain" meant that few local sculptors were still practicing in Greece in the mid-first century BC, explaining why at that time statue bodies were reused, rededicated to different subjects by reinscribing their bases (Palagia 1997, 81; Varner 2004; see essay 2.3, Varner). The custom of artists seeking commissions abroad could be said to form part of an artistic exchange, for the Roman architect Cossutius went to Athens in the mid-second century BC to work on the temple of Olympian Zeus (Vitr. *De arch.* 7.17). Just decades after Sulla had sacked Athens in 86 BC, the Roman sculptor Quintus Pompeius was brought to Eleusis to work on the Lesser Propylaia, vowed by the Roman consul Appius Claudius Pulcher in 54 BC (Plin. *HN* 34.13, 36.38; Cass. Dio 53.27.2; Vitr. *De arch.* 1.1.5). At Messene a group of life-size sculptors' models is associated with the workshop of two Alexandrian sculptors who worked there in the Augustan period (Themelis 2012).

Despite references to artists by literary sources and the survival of some signatures, nothing is known about the artists as individuals. We can say, however, that signing practices had changed since the fifth century BC. At Olympia, for example, a signature is carved on the knee of the Large Herculaneum Woman figure from the pronaos of the Heraion, while the subject's name and the dedication are carved on the statue base (Trimble 2011, 122; see essay 2.2, Claridge). At Corinth the signature of an artist or workshop owner has been recognized on a marble revetment plaque from the theater (Sturgeon 2004, 49).

The majority of surviving sculptures are made of white marble. Marble from Mt. Pentele is widely used, but Thasian is prevalent in the north and occurs to some degree in central and southern Greece, as does Parian. Some non-Greek marbles are imported, as from Aphrodisias, Dokimeion, and Prokonnesos in Anatolia and Carrara in Italy, apparently in lesser amounts, but scientific analysis is necessary to confirm quarry origins. Some local stones are employed for sculpture, such as that from the Doliana quarries in Arkadia. Colored stones, such as alabaster and basalt, received only occasional use. Statue bases indicate that a substantial number of bronze statues once existed, but few survive. The bronze equestrian figure identified as Augustus found in the sea east of Euboea and the bronze woman from Sparta (Kaltsas 2002, 318, no. 664; 356, no. 756) are noteworthy.

Piecing, as in earlier periods, occurs especially with large-scale works (see essay 2.2, Claridge). The acrolithic technique was employed rarely (Despinis 2012). Contrary to typical practice, the stone segments are used not only for heads, arms, hands, and feet, but also for nude chests. The technique is employed for colossal statues of deities, such as the second-century Athena in Thessaloniki, and also for cuirassed statues. Technical features of these pieced sculptures, such as swallowtail cuttings, nonlevel attachment surfaces and lack of anathyrosis, are derived from wooden construction rather than marble.

Until c. 100 BC, the usual process of carving involved gradually working around the figure on all sides. In the Roman period, however, the practice shifted to working a piece evenly from front to back (Palagia 2006, 244–5). For example, an unfluted column drum partly converted into a funerary relief of a victorious athlete crowning himself is finished only in front (Kaltsas 2002, 352, no. 743).

A few sculptor's workshops have been excavated in Roman Greece. One is identified in the Library of Pantainos in Athens, where many marble chips, emery polishing basins, and unfinished sculptures were discovered, dating from the second to third centuries AD. Workshop activity also occurred along the Street of the Marble Workers, southwest of the Agora (Lawton 2006, 17–23). At Corinth unfinished marble feet, made for attachment but unused, were discovered in the Gymnasium-Bath complex, near a bronze foundry (Sturgeon 2003, 362–3). Such traces of workshop activity are tantalizing.

Freestanding Sculpture

Portraits

Imperial portraits are found throughout Greece, likely set up by cities and local elites to curry favor with the ruling powers. They occur in over-life-size and colossal scale, in heroic nudity and in cuirass, in civic centers and religious sanctuaries. Some dedications feature an imperial family group, such as those from the Metroon and the Nymphaeum of Herodes Atticus at Olympia. In Athens many statues of Hadrian were set up in the Olympieion and in the Theater of Dionysos. An impressive cuirassed statue sporting a relief of Dirce and the Bull was found on Naxos in 1986. At first thought to depict Antony, it has been reinterpreted as Caligula or Nero due to signs of intentional damage (Queyrel 2012).

Private portraits, also numerous, come from domestic, civic, and religious contexts. In the Athenian Agora, a head wearing a bust crown (unusual in Greece) possibly depicts a member of the Panhellenion, the federation of Greek cities established by Hadrian (Riccardi 2007). Other private portraits represent older men who were probably civic officials or *agonothetes* (officials in the athletic games) and young athletic victors. Portraits of Herodes Atticus, the patron and sophist from the mid-second century AD, are numerous, reflecting his many public benefactions.

Hero cults provided a different occasion for commissioning private portraits. In AD 130, for example, following the death of Hadrian's favorite, Antinous, hero cults were established in his honor and portraits created to perpetuate his memory (Meyer 1991; Vout 2007). Similarly, Herodes Atticus commissioned commemorative portraits of his pupil Polydeukion after his early death (Kaltsas 2002, 346–7, nos. 735, 736).

In second- and third-century Athens, which remained an important center of education, a large group of portraits on hermaic stelai represent the *kosmetes* (teachers) of the *ephebes* (youths). These monuments (dating from the Trajanic period through the mid-third century AD) display a remarkable range of styles and types; some resemble older portraits of Greek philosophers (Kaltsas 2002, 325–34, nos. 683–707).

Ideal Statuary

Ideal statuary, produced in all periods, demonstrates continued interest in classical forms and subject matter. Attic workshops active on Delos in the late second to mid-first century BC worked largely for Italian businessmen on the island (Stewart 1979). These workshops created copies of fifth-century BC athletic types, such as the Diadoumenos, and portraits, like the Pseudo-Athlete (now in Athens; Kaltsas 2002, 312, no. 654) in which a portrait head is combined with a Greek-inspired, nude athletic body type and a hand-on-hip gesture that recalls the Hellenistic Ruler (Pollitt 1986, 72–3, fig. 74). Although strange to modern eyes, the Pseudo-Athlete illustrates the way Roman art may draw from multiple sources to create a new, forceful image, the subject positioning himself in the tradition of Greeks who received their civic and athletic education in the gymnasium (Hallett 2005, 1–2, 106; Dillon 2006; see essay 3.6, Touchette). The ideal and the real are combined with the emblematic to create a new mode of self-representation.

Patrons continued to commission sculptures of traditional subjects, especially deities. Thus, abundant examples of Aphrodite, Artemis, and Athena are found (Karanastassis 1986–7), as well as Apollo, Dionysos, and Hermes. This range of subjects is exemplified in many centers, such as at Gortyn on Crete (Romeo and Portale 1998). Asklepios and Hygieia are important, and the Egyptian deities Isis and Serapis as well as their worshippers are prominent in the second century AD (Milleker 1985; Walters 1988). The fifth-century BC Amazon, Doryphoros, and Diomedes types are widespread as well.

Devotion to Hekate, the Mother of the Gods, Kybele, Nike, Poseidon, and Zeus are strong in many areas. In funerary contexts, portraits showing the deceased in the guise of a deity are often employed. A relative newcomer, Tyche/Fortuna, appears in many cities, as seen in the colossal heads from Sparta and Sikyon (Palagia 1994; 2010). At Corinth a colossal image of Tyche was set up in a small temple at the west end of the Forum, while a second head with a turreted crown, from a different statuary type, stood in the west pediment of Temple E. Personifications associated with rivers and springs, such as the Peirene spring at Corinth, evoke local elements in the landscape (Robinson 2011).

The Aphrodite from Epidauros exemplifies the high-quality work created in Greece and the kinds of issues raised by ideal statuary (figure 5.4.1; Katakis 2002). Made in c. AD

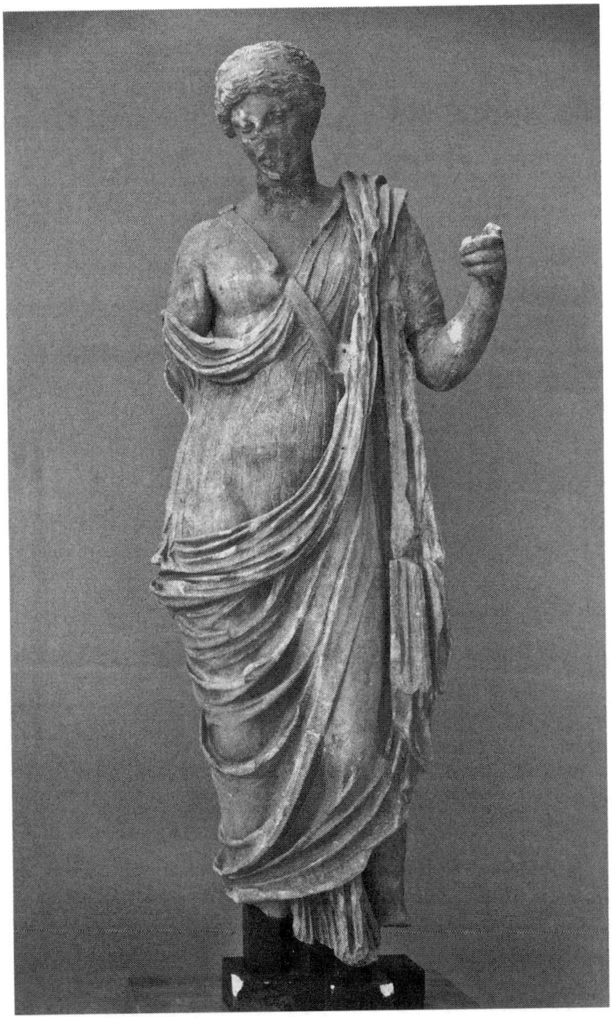

FIGURE 5.4.1 The Epidauros Aphrodite. Athens, National Museum 262.

40 of Parian marble, the Epidauros Aphrodite was found in the Sanctuary of Asklepios and is fairly well preserved. It conveys a classical image, but the identity of a possible prototype is unknown (Katakis 2002, 54–6, 145–7, 238–40, 300–302). The figure's stance follows the mid-fifth century tradition of Polykleitos of Argos, with the raised left shoulder counterbalanced by the raised right hip in a chiastic pose, the left foot pulled back. The figure exhibits a specific drapery style with ribbon folds in the chiton, which derive from c. 420 BC (Ridgway 1981, 111, 223). The strong diagonals established by the sword strap slung crosswise from the right shoulder, set in opposition to the line of the chiton edge passing beneath the right breast and paralleled by the bunched himation crossing to the right hip, derive from the early fourth century BC as does the emphasis on the nude body, almost completely revealed through the two garments.

Primary attributes of the Epidauros figure are the nude breast, the transparent garment, and the sword belt. The sword hilt was attached separately, and she may have carried a spear or sword in her left hand. These features establish the figure as an Armed Aphrodite, a type distinct from the one mentioned by Pausanias on Acrocorinth (2.5.1; Kousser 2008, 18–28). Three other examples of the type come from Italy, but in those figures the type has been adapted for other subjects by introducing a different feature such as an animal skin (Häuser 1902; Katakis 2002, 147).

As with other classical-type statuary, the Epidauros figure type would have been chosen because of its clear classical forms, whose associations would have been considered appropriate for the subject (Ridgway 1984, 6–14, 31–4, 81–6; Perry 2005). Typically, classical statuary types are employed for deities or new types are created with a similar aesthetic, as such forms give the subject the *dignitas* and *auctoritas* desired for the Roman audience (Elsner 2006).

Some portraits of elite Roman women present their subjects in the guise of Greek deities (Wrede 1981; Maderna 1988), but others use well-known Greek statue types, such as the Large and Small Herculaneum Women (Daehner 2007; Trimble 2011). For such portraits, replicating the work of a famous artist was unimportant in contrast to using forms that would evoke the classical past and convey a particular sentiment, such as modesty.

Architectural Sculpture

During the Roman period, the strong tradition of architectural sculpture in Greece continued on religious and civic buildings in the major centers. In Athens, the façade of the Theater of Dionysos incorporated three colossal statues and five pairs of architectural silenoi during its Hadrianic phase (Papastamati-von Moock 2012). The reliefs now on the stage front, the Bema of Phaedrus, probably belonged to an altar. Four other sets of reliefs belonging to second-century AD altars are known from Athens, including those from the Hadrianic Bouleuterion north of the Stoa of Attalos (Despinis 2003). In the Agora, giants and tritons embellish the Antonine phase of the façade of the Odeion of Agrippa.

In Corinth, the Hadrianic theater was a showpiece for architectural decoration. The *scaenae frons* displayed a colossal portrait of the emperor, three sets of Greek mythological reliefs on and between the column podia, local deities as high relief busts in the pediments, and a relief with confronting griffins above the *porta regia* (Sturgeon 2004). The inner walls of the Arch over the Lechaion Road supported Trajanic reliefs of captives and a sacrifice (Edwards 1994). The Captives' Façade, with male and female captives, stood in the second story of the southern façade of the Basilica on the Lechaion Road (Strocka 2010). Temple E, on the western hill overlooking the Forum, was also richly decorated, with over-life-size figures in the pediments and acroteria on the roof (Freeman 1941). Temple F at Eleusis also exhibited pedimental sculpture, modeled on figures in the Parthenon west pediment (Lindner 1982).

In Sparta, pilasters with hip-herms of Herakles formed part of the decoration of the theater in the Severan period (Palagia 1989). Muses enhanced the Odeum in Thessaloniki (Despinis, Stephanidou-Tiveriou, and Boutiras 1997, 123–5, nos. 93–6). The Actium monument at Nikopolis (see above) featured a richly decorated altar, and nymphaea at Argos and in the Athenian Agora supported marble statues (Longfellow 2011, 112–20, 122–30).

In Thessaloniki the large Arch of Galerius (see below), is abundantly covered with reliefs (Laubscher 1975), while the portraits on the small Arch of Galerius (now in the Archaeological Museum of Thessaloniki) are better preserved (Despinis, Stephanidou-Tiveriou, and Boutiras 1997, 184–9). Relief figures of deities and maenads on piers decorated the second story of the Stoa of the Idols ("The Incantadas"; Grammenos 2003, 154–5, 211, figs. 27, 28).

Funerary Sculpture

In Athens, some funerary reliefs continue the Hellenistic tall, narrow form of stelai. Main figures on such stelai often have elongated proportions; secondary figures are smaller. Philopappos, of the royal family of Commagene, boldly set his tall funerary monument atop a high hill (AD 114–116), claiming visibility for centuries (Kleiner 1992, 233–5; Von Moock 1998, 16). In northern Greece, funerary reliefs depicting a hunter on horseback are especially popular, as are reliefs with multiple heads (Despinis, Stephanidou-Tiveriou, and Boutiras 1997, 155–6, no. 125; 145–53, 159–61, nos. 114–23, 128–9).

Sarcophagi became one of the leading products of Athens, one of the three leading centers (with Rome and Dokimeion) for marble coffins. The production of decorated Attic sarcophagi occurs from c. AD 130 to AD 260, with demand increasing significantly after AD 200. A substantial number of Attic sarcophagi (over 65 percent) were intended for export (see essay 2.7, Russell). Attic sarcophagi are found as far afield as Britannia, Germania, Dacia, and Lusitania, and across coastal North Africa and the Levant. These monuments are common in Rome as well as in the coastal cities of Anatolia, Syria, and

Palestine (Koch and Sichtermann 1982, 366–475; Koch 2012). In the reliefs the carving of heads, garments, and ornament is sufficiently distinctive to facilitate attribution to Attic workshops. Reliefs generally occur on all four sides of Attic sarcophagi, so they are easily distinguished from rectangular Italian sarcophagi (characterized instead by primary relief decoration on the front, shallower reliefs on the sides, and a flat lid decorated by a narrow relief on one long side).

A sarcophagus from near Patras depicting Meleager and the Calydonian Boar Hunt provides an excellent example of Attic work of c. AD 160 (figure 5.4.2). Made of Pentelic marble, it employs the format typical of Attic sarcophagi from the second century: a rectangular box with a pitched roof, resembling a house of the dead (Koch 1975, 76, 138; Kaltsas 2002, 350).

Two hundred examples of the Calydonian Boar Hunt are known on Roman sarcophagi. The stock figure types used on the Patras sarcophagus occur in many representations of this subject, though the composition may vary. This subject probably suggested the *virtus*, or physical prowess and manhood, of the deceased as well as the tragedy of his death. In this context the Boar Hunt may also imply that the deceased, like Meleager, will live on in people's memory like great heroes of the past, victorious in the hunt as in war. Some scholars believe that the use of Meleager's hunt on sarcophagi establishes an unmistakable confrontation with death (Ewald and Zanker 2004, 56, 68, 70, 72).

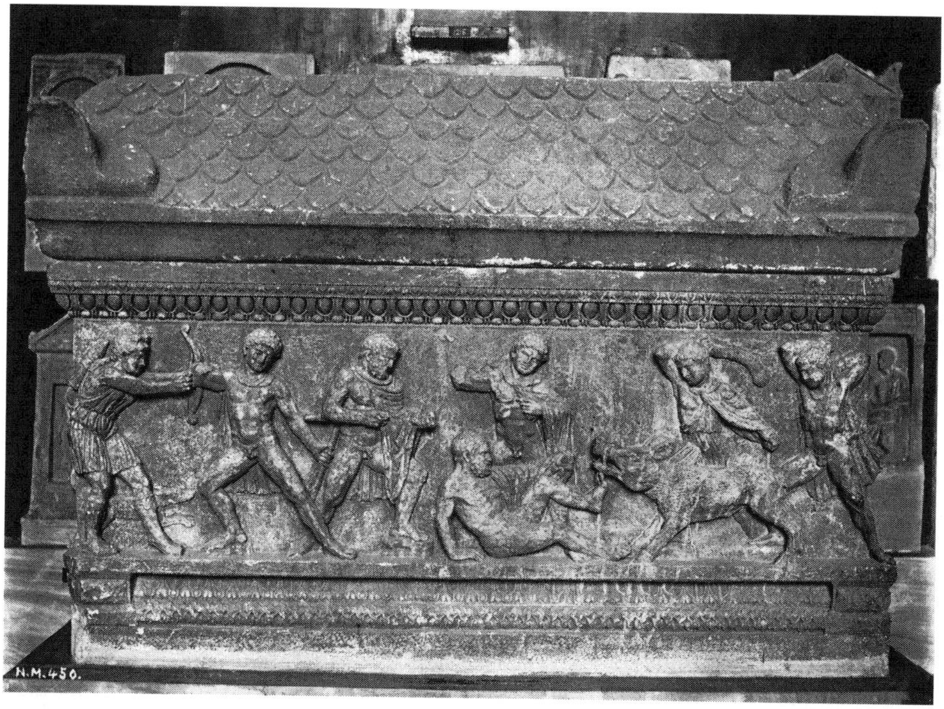

FIGURE 5.4.2 Attic Sarcophagus with Calydonian Boar Hunt from Patras. Athens, National Museum 1186.

This monument also raises issues of replication. Figure types on the Patras sarcophagus occur on two other monuments in Greece. One is the base of the cult statue in the Temple of Poseidon on the Isthmus of Corinth (Sturgeon 1987, 96–109, pls. 45–8). The Isthmia Atalanta and the chlamys-wearer behind her follow the same format as two figures on the Patras sarcophagus, but the placement—and thus the viewing—of them differs. On the sarcophagus Atalanta stands at the left end of the long side, while the figure behind her appears around the corner on the short side. On the Isthmian reliefs, however, these figures occur beside each other on the same flat panel.

Secondly, the format of one hunter on the Patras sarcophagus is replicated alone on a funerary stele where the figure is a set into the context of a personal hunt, not a mythological one (Kaltsas 2002, 353, no. 747). The deceased, Artemidoros from Bessa, is shown against a rocky landscape, which extends to the upper border of the scene, and contains goats, his dog, and his prey, which is, of course, a boar. This stele celebrates Artemidoros's life by emphasizing his *virtus* and commemorating him as a great hunter.

The Late Roman Period

During the Tetrarchy, Galerius as Augustus (AD 293–305) resided in his capital city, Thessaloniki. The massive Arch of Galerius, erected c. AD 300 to commemorate his military achievements and the Tetrarchy itself, is truly monumental (Kleiner 1992, 418–25). Originally shaped as an octopylon with a quadrifons arch in the center, it once functioned as the intersection of a major street and the gateway into Galerius's mausoleum complex. Two of the piers still standing retain reliefs, now quite worn, laid out in horizontal frameworks analogous to the decorative fields on sarcophagi, and badly damaged imperial portraits. Although the scenes seem designed to be read from top to bottom, the most important were placed at eye level. The small Arch of Galerius has well-preserved imperial portraits (Despinis, Stephanidou-Tiveriou, and Boutiras 1997, 184–9, no. 141).

Carving of three-dimensional figures in the late Roman period is reduced in quantity, but includes some outstanding examples. Primary among these are the portrait busts of a prominent couple from c. AD 410 (figures 5.4.3 and 5.4.4; L'Orange 1973, 54–71; Kiilerich 1993, 113, 120, 210). Exceptional work in Pentelic marble, these sculptures are among the best produced anywhere in this period. Scholars believe that they come from Thessaloniki, but the location of their discovery and their original place of display are unknown (Despinis, Stephanidou-Tiveriou, and Boutiras 2011, 192–200, nos. 522, 523).

The portraits display the clothing and hairstyles of the late antique period. The man's costume, two tunics, and a chlamys fastened by a button at the right shoulder, denotes his high-ranking position. Under each primary garment is a second garment. These garments are commonly seen in full-length statues of men from the fourth to sixth centuries especially in the East, but few busts in this garb are well preserved.

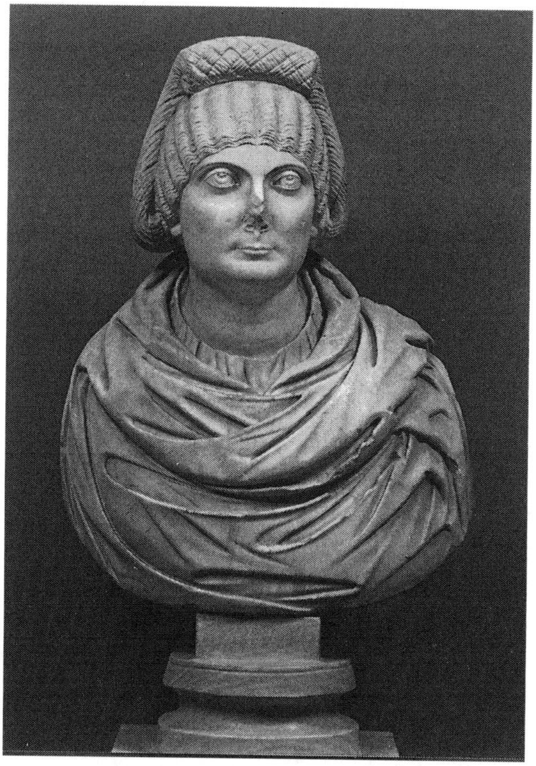

FIGURE 5.4.3 Late antique portrait of prominent woman. Archaeological Museum of Thessaloniki, inv. no. 1060.

The woman is shown dressed in a chiton and a himation that is draped around her shoulders and covers most of her chest except for the narrow edge of the chiton at the neck. This bust type is used for elite women from the period of Faustina the Elder through late antiquity. The woman's face is wide with prominent high cheekbones and square jaw. Above the low forehead an elaborate coiffure consists of a melon configuration in front, enhanced by an intricate arrangement of intersecting braids in back that are brought up over the crown. The intricate coiffure, which would have required a maid or two to fix, the mantle that encloses both arms, which implies that she had many servants and never had to use her hands, and the high quality of the portrait characterize the subject as a member of the wealthy upper class.

As with many private portraits, the individuals' names are unknown, but it is evident that they depict mature individuals of education and refinement. The man was probably an important magistrate or another kind of civic official. He and his wife may each have benefited the city by supporting important building projects and/or religious or athletic festivities. Their portraits, like those of other donors, may have been prominently displayed in the structure that they funded. The use of busts rather than full-length statues likely reflects the wishes of the patron rather than lack of funds, as the high quality of the

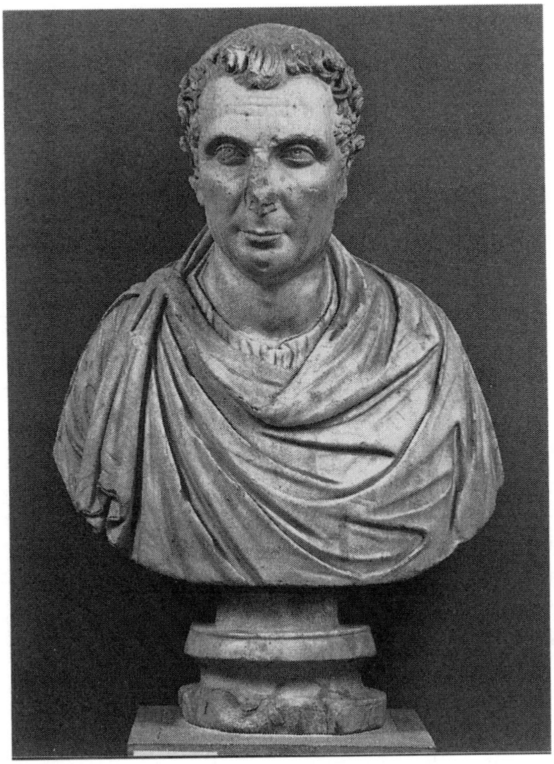

FIGURE 5.4.4 Late antique portrait of prominent man. Archaeological Museum of Thessaloniki, inv. no. 1061.

busts indicates that they would have been very costly. The bust form may have been preferred for display in an interior location, which is also indicated by their good condition.

The Thessaloniki male portrait resembles a head found in Corinth to the extent that they are said to depict the same personage (Vanderpool 2003, 379–80). If this assumption is correct, it suggests that the man occupied an important senior position in the administration of the Roman provincial governments of Greece. This personage may also have been a wealthy merchant whose interests were represented in both cities. The early fifth-century AD portrait busts from Thessaloniki show that wealthy patrons existed in late Roman times and that they were able to locate artists to fill their commissions (see also essay 3.8, Witschel).

Conclusion

Sculptures from Roman Greece illustrate the continuation of a strong tradition of marble carving that began in the mid-seventh century BC and extended at least to the fifth century AD. Production encompasses many statuary types and includes civic, personal, and religious objects such as funerary stelai and sarcophagi. Portraits exist in large numbers and exhibit a range of quality, as do images of divine and mythological subjects. The quality of Roman sculptures from Greece varied considerably, as it did elsewhere, but the sculptures reviewed here provide evidence of the high level of artistic skill and the significant ongoing patronage that supported the best carving traditions.

Bibliography

Ajootian, A. 2000. "A Roman Table Support at Ancient Corinth." *Hesperia* 69: 487–507.

Daehner, J., ed. 2007. *The Herculaneum Women: History, Context, Identities.* Los Angeles: J. Paul Getty Museum.

Datsouli-Stavridi, A. 1985. *Ρωμαϊκά πορτραίτα στὸ Ἐθνικό Ἀρχαιολογικό Μουσείο τῆς Ἀθήνας.* Athens: Michalas.

de Grazia, C. E. 1973. "Excavations of the American School of Classical Studies at Corinth: The Roman Portrait Sculpture." PhD diss., Columbia University.

Despinis, G. I. 2003. *Hochrelieffriese des 2. Jahrhunderts n. Chr. aus Athen.* Munich: Hirmer.

———. 2012. "Ακρόλιθα αγάλματα των ρωμαϊκών χρόνων." In Stephanidou-Tiveriou, Karanastasi, and Damaskos 2012, 19–34.

Despinis, G., T. Stephanidou-Tiveriou, and E. Boutiras. 1997. *Catalogue of Sculpture in the Archaeological Museum of Thessaloniki.* Vol. 1. Thessaloniki: National Bank Cultural Foundation.

———. 2011. *Catalogue of Sculpture in the Archaeological Museum of Thessaloniki.* Vol. 3. Thessaloniki: National Bank Cultural Foundation.

Dillon, S. 2006. *Ancient Greek Portrait Sculpture: Contexts, Subjects, and Styles.* Cambridge: Cambridge University Press.

Edwards, C. M. 1994. "The Arch over the Lechaion Road at Corinth and Its Sculpture." *Hesperia* 63: 263–308.

Elsner, J. 2006. "Classicism in Roman Art." In Porter 2006, 270–97.

Ewald, B. C., and P. Zanker. 2004. *Mit Mythen leben: Die Bilderwelt der römischen Sarkophage.* Munich: Hirmer.

Fittschen, K. 2008. "Über den Beitrag der Bildhauer in Athen zur Kunstproduktion im römischen Reich." In *Athens during the Roman Period: Recent Discoveries, New Evidence,* edited by S. Vlizos, 325–36. Athens: Benaki Museum.

Freeman, S. E. 1941. "Temple E." In *Corinth.* Vol. 1.2, *Architecture,* by R. Stillwell, R. L. Scranton, and S.E. Freeman, 166–236. Cambridge, MA: Harvard University Press.

Grammenos, D. V. 2003. *Roman Thessaloniki.* Thessaloniki: Thessaloniki Archaeological Museum.

Habicht, C. 1985. *Pausanias' Guide to Ancient Greece.* Berkeley: University of California Press.

Hallett, C. H. 2005. *The Roman Nude: Heroic Portrait Statuary, 200 BC–AD 300.* Oxford: Oxford University Press.

Harrison, E. B. 1953. *The Portrait Sculpture.* Agora 1. Princeton: American School of Classical Studies at Athens.

Häuser, F. 1902. "Die Aphrodite von Epidauros." *RM* 17: 232–54.

Hölscher, T. 2006. "Greek Styles and Greek Art in Augustan Rome: Issues of the Present versus Records of the Past." In Porter 2006, 237–69.

Kaltsas, N. 2002. *Sculpture in the National Archaeological Museum, Athens.* Los Angeles: J. Paul Getty Museum.

Karanastassis, P. 1986–7. "Untersuchungen zur kaiserzeitlichen Plastik in Griechenland." *AM* 101: 207–279; 102: 323–428.

Katakis, S. 2002. *Επίδαυρος: Τα γλυπτά τῶν ρωμαικὼν χρόνων ἀπὸ το ιερό του Απόλλωνος Μαλεάτα και του Ασκληπιού.* Athens: Archaeological Society in Athens.

Kiilerich, B. 1993. *Late Fourth Century Classicism in the Plastic Arts: Studies in the So-Called Theodosian Renaissance.* Odense: Odense University Press.

Kleiner, D. E. E. 1992. *Roman Sculpture.* New Haven: Yale University Press.

Koch, G. 1975. *Die mythologischen Sarkophage: Meleager.* ASR 12.6. Berlin: Mann.

———. 2012. "Οι αττικές σαρκοφάγοι και η σημασία τους για την τέχνη της αυτοκρατορικής εποχής." In Stephanidou-Tiveriou, Karanastasi, and Damaskos 2012, 35–56.

Koch, G., and H. Sichtermann. 1982. *Römische Sarkophage.* Munich: C. H. Beck.

Kokkorou-Alevra, G. 2001. "Δραστηριότητες των αττικών εργαστηρίων γλυπτικής την εποχή της ρωμαιοκρατίας." In *Καλλίστευμα Μελέτες προς τιμήν Όλγας Τζάχου-Αλεξανδρή*, edited by O. Tzachou-Alexandri and I. Levendi, 319–48. Athens: Kulturministerium.

Kousser, R. M. 2008. *Hellenistic and Roman Ideal Sculpture: The Allure of the Classical.* Cambridge: Cambridge University Press.

Laubscher, H. P. 1975. *Der Reliefschmuck des Galeriusbogens in Thessaloniki.* Berlin: Mann.

Lawton, C. 2006. *Marbleworkers in the Athenian Agora.* Princeton: American School of Classical Studies at Athens.

Lindner, R. 1982. "Die Giebelgruppe von Eleusis mit dem Raub der Persephone." *JdI* 97: 303–400.

Longfellow, B. 2011. *Roman Imperialism and Civic Patronage: Form, Meaning, and Ideology in Monumental Fountain Complexes.* Cambridge: Cambridge University Press.

L'Orange, H. P. 1973. *Likeness and Icon.* Odense: Odense University Press.

Maderna, C. 1988. *Iuppiter Diomedes und Merkur als Vorbilder für römische Bildnisstatuen: Untersuchungen zum römischen statuarischen Idealporträt.* Heidelberg: Verlag Archäologie und Geschichte.

Meyer, H. 1991. *Antinoos: Die archäologischen Denkmäler unter Einbeziehung des numismatischen und epigraphischen Materials sowie der literarischen Nachrichten: Ein Beitrag zur Kunst- und Kulturgeschichte der hadrianisch-frühantoninischen Zeit.* Munich: Wilhelm Fink.

Milleker, E. J. 1985. "Three Heads of Sarapis from Corinth." *Hesperia* 54: 121–35.

Palagia, O. 1989. "Seven Pilasters of Herakles from Sparta." In *The Greek Renaissance in the Roman Empire*, edited by S. Walker and A. Cameron, 122–9. BICS Supplement 55. London: University of London.

———. 1994. "Tyche at Sparta." In *An Obsession with Fortune: Tyche in Greek and Roman Art, YaleBull* 1994: 64–75.

———. 1997. "Classical Encounters: Attic Sculpture after Sulla." In *The Romanization of Athens*, edited by M. C. Hoff and S. I. Rotroff, 81–95. Oxford: Oxbow.

———. 2006. "Marble Carving Techniques." In *Greek Sculpture: Function, Materials and Techniques in the Archaic and Classical Periods*, edited by O. Palagia, 243–79. Cambridge: Cambridge University Press.

———. 2010. "Sculptures from the Peloponnese in the Roman Imperial Period." In *Roman Peloponnese III: Society, Economy and Culture under the Roman Empire; Continuity and Innovation*, edited by A. D. Rizakis and C. E. Lepenioti, 431–45. Meletemata 63. Athens: National Hellenic Research Foundation.

Papastamati-von Moock, C. 2012. "Θέατρο του Διονύσου Ελευθερέως: Τα γλυπτά της ρωμαϊκής σκηνής; χρονολογικά, καλλιτεχνικά και ερμηνευτικά ζητήματα." In Stephanidou-Tiveriou, Karanastasi, and Damaskos 2012, 129–50.

Perry, E. 2005. *The Aesthetics of Emulation in the Visual Arts of Ancient Rome.* Cambridge: Cambridge University Press.

Pollitt, J. J. 1986. *Art in the Hellenistic Age.* Cambridge: Cambridge University Press.

Porter, J. I., ed. 2006. *Classical Pasts: The Classical Traditions of Greece and Rome.* Princeton: Princeton University Press.

Queyrel, F. 2012. "Modes de représentation des Julio-Claudiens dans les Cyclades: Traditions régionales et reprises de schémas iconographiques." In Stephanidou-Tiveriou, Karanastasi, and Damaskos 2012, 417–31.

Rhomiopoulou, K. 1997. *Ἑλληνορωμαϊκά γλυπτά τοῦ Ἐθνικοῦ Ἀρχαιολογικοῦ Μουσείου.* Athens: Archaeological Receipts Fund.

Riccardi, L. A. 2007. "The Bust-Crown, the Panhellenion, and Eleusis: A New Portrait from the Athenian Agora." *Hesperia* 76: 365–90.

Ridgway, B. S. 1981. *Fifth Century Styles in Greek Sculpture.* Princeton: Princeton University Press.

———. 1984. *Roman Copies of Greek Sculpture: The Problem of the Originals.* Ann Arbor: University of Michigan Press.

Robinson, B. 2011. *Histories of Peirene: A Corinthian Fountain in Three Millennia.* Princeton: American School of Classical Studies at Athens.

Romeo, I., and E. C. Portale. 1998. *Gortina.* Vol. 3, *Le sculture.* Padua: Bottega d'Erasmo.

Rüsch, A. 1969. "Das kaiserzeitliche Porträt in Macedonien." *JdI* 84: 68–196.

Spawforth, A. J. S. 2012. *Greece and the Augustan Cultural Revolution.* Cambridge: Cambridge University Press.

Spyropoulos G. 2001. *Drei Meisterwerke der griechischen Plastik aus der Villa des Herodes Atticus zu Eva/Loukou.* Frankfurt: Peter Lang.

Spyropoulos, G., and T. Spyropoulos. 2003. "Prächtige Villa, Refugium und Musenstätte: Die Villa des Herodes Atticus im arkadischen Eua." *AntW* 34: 463–70.

Stephanidou-Tiveriou, T. 1979. *Νεοαττικά: Οἱ ἀναγλύφοι πίνακες ἀπὸ τὸ λιμάνι τοῦ Πειραιᾶ.* Athens: Archaeological Society in Athens.

Stephanidou-Tiveriou, T., P. Karanastasi, and D. Damaskos, eds. 2012. *Κλασική παράδοση και νεωτερικά στοιχεία στην πλαστική της ρωμαϊκής Ελλάδας.* Thessaloniki: University Studio Press.

Stewart, A. F. 1979. *Attika: Studies in Athenian Sculpture of the Hellenistic Age.* Supplementary Paper 14. London: Society for the Promotion of Hellenic Studies.

Stirling, L. M. 2008. "Pagan Statuettes in Late Antique Corinth: Sculpture from the Panayia Domus." *Hesperia* 77: 89–161.

Strocka, V. M. 2010. *Die Gefangenenfassade an der Agora von Korinth: Ihr Ort in der römischen Kunstgeschichte.* Regensburg: Schnell and Steiner.

Sturgeon, M. C. 1987. *Sculpture I: 1952–67.* Isthmia 4. Princeton: American School of Classical Studies at Athens.

———. 2003. "Sculpture of the Classical Style at Corinth: 1896–1996." In Williams and Bookidis 2003, 351–68.

———. 2004. *Sculpture: The Assemblage from the Theater.* Corinth 9.3. Princeton: American School of Classical Studies at Athens.

Themelis, P. 2000. *Ήρωες και ηρώα στη Μεσσήνη*. Athens: Archaeological Society in Athens.

———. 2012. "Έργα επωνύμων γλυπτών και εργαστήριο γλυπτικής πρώιμων ρωμαϊκών χρόνων στη Μεσσήνη." In Stephanidou-Tiveriou, Karanastasi, and Damaskos 2012, 177–91.

Toynbee, J. M. C. 1934. *The Hadrianic School: A Chapter in the History of Greek Art.* Cambridge: Cambridge University Press.

Trianti, I. 2008. "Eastern Deities from the Makrygianni Lot." In *Athens during the Roman Period: Recent Discoveries, New Evidence,* edited by S. Vlizos, 391–409. Athens: Benaki Museum.

Trimble, J. 2011. *Women and Visual Replication in Roman Imperial Art and Culture.* Cambridge: Cambridge University Press.

Vanderpool, C. d. G. 2003. "Roman Portraiture: The Many Faces of Corinth." In Williams and Bookidis 2003, 369–84.

Varner, E. R. 2004. *Mutilation and Transformation: "Damnatio Memoriae" and Roman Imperial Portraiture.* Leiden: Brill.

Von Moock, D. W. 1998. *Die figürlichen Grabstelen Attikas in der Kaiserzeit.* Mainz: Philipp von Zabern.

Vout, C. 2007. *Power and Eroticism in Imperial Rome.* Cambridge: Cambridge University Press.

Walters, E. J. 1988. *Attic Grave Reliefs that Represent Women in the Dress of Isis.* Hesperia Supplement 22. Princeton: American School of Classical Studies at Athens.

Williams, C. K., and N. Bookidis. 2003. *Corinth: The Centenary, 1896–1996.* Corinth 20. Princeton: American School of Classical Studies at Athens.

Wrede, H. 1981. *Consecratio in Formam Deorum: Vergöttliche Privatpersonen in der römischen Kaiserzeit.* Mainz: Philipp von Zabern.

Zachariadou, O. 2001. "Zappeion Shaft." In *Athens: the City Beneath the City; Antiquities from the Metropolitan Railway Excavations,* edited by L. Parlama and N. Stampolides, 132–41. Athens: Goulandris Museum.

Zachos, K. L. 2003. "The Tropaeum of the Sea-Battle of Actium at Nikopolis: Interim Report." *JRA* 16: 65–92.

———. 2007. "Τα γλυπτά του βωμού στο Μνημείο του Οκταβιανού Αυγούστου στη Νικόπολη: Μία πρώτη προσέγγιση." In *Nikopolis II: Proceedings of the Second International Symposium on Nikopolis, 11–15 September 2002,* edited by K. L. Zachos, 411–34. Preveza: Idryma Aktia Nikopolis.

Zanker, P. 1988. *The Power of Images in the Age of Augustus.* Ann Arbor: University of Michigan Press.

CHAPTER 5.5

ASIA MINOR

DIANA Y. NG

Chronology

Asia Minor had already developed a vibrant urban culture before the arrival and eventual rule of the Romans. Leading cities such as Ephesos and Smyrna were well established by the archaic period but others were founded or grew and prospered throughout the Hellenistic period, and had many of the architectural amenities—theaters, temples, agoras—typical of a Greek city. These structures were complemented by sculpture executed in regional styles, the most famous of which is associated with Pergamon. The Roman province of Asia was formed from Attalos III's bequest of Pergamon's vast territories in Asia Minor to the Senate in 133 BC. The province was consolidated throughout the first century BC, only to be partitioned into smaller provincial units in subsequent periods. As a result of this addition to the Roman domain and of other Roman involvements in Greece during the second century BC, Hellenistic sculptural style spread to Italy, appearing on such monuments as the so-called Altar of Domitius Ahenobarbus (see essay 3.5, Sobocinski and Wolfram Thill) and in examples of republican portraiture that were influenced by the ruler portraits that had flourished in the East (Rose 1997, 4–10).

The Julio-Claudian period saw the creation of important examples of what one might consider Roman sculpture in Asia Minor. The metropolitan influence that can be detected in objects from this period—ranging from imperial statues and dynastic groups to personal portraiture and public reliefs—relates directly to the contemporaneous construction of *neokoros* (or official imperial cult) temples in the region and to the accompanying promulgation of the imperial image (Rose 1997). Not only were Roman ideas and forms introduced to the region, but patterns for the hybridization of local and imperial styles and complex visual articulations of personal identity and political loyalty were also forged at this time. The art history corresponds to historical evidence for regional efforts to appeal to the imperial family via games and offerings and to the importance of the *neokoros* in establishing the hierarchy of prestige among the leading cities of Asia Minor (Ritti 1985; Burrell 2004). It must be noted, however, that Hellenistic qualities—in design, style, execution, and iconography—would always remain vital components in the sculpture of Asia Minor, to be used solely or in combination with Roman elements.

Sculptural production in Roman Asia Minor peaked during the second and third centuries AD, a time of stability and prosperity in the region and in the empire as a whole. In general, the development of the urban landscape continued on a grand scale with the patronage of imperial officials and local elites. Colonnaded streets, fountains, and baths were constructed, and gates and theaters were renovated or rebuilt as cities competed in beauty and prestige; all were decorated with elaborate marble façades. In these settings, large numbers of relief and freestanding portrait and mythological sculptures were placed (see essay 4.1, Longfellow). In addition, public spaces were populated with the portraits of civic benefactors, adding to the overall urban ornamentation while reaffirming communal social relationships.

The visual culture of late antiquity has long been part of the archaeological exploration of Asia Minor. The era's stylistic changes—increasing abstraction in imperial portraiture, representation of office and power rather than physiognomy, and the popularization of the court dress of Constantinople in private portraiture—are also visible in Asia Minor (Bauer and Witschel 2007, 1–17; see essay 3.8, Witschel). While the overall number of sculptures declined significantly, some portrait statues were still being produced in Asia Minor—and in high quality at Aphrodisias. The display contexts for statuary in cities like Ephesos and Aphrodisias changed, however, with sculpture being moved from public and political venues like the temple, agora, or the *bouleuterion* to what Smith terms "neutral" sites like bath complexes (2007, 207).

Important Sites for Roman Sculpture in Asia Minor

Roman Asia Minor boasts vast and widely distributed amounts of sculpture. Indeed, rich sculptural finds, such as those from Sagalassos in Pisidia, still await full publication (Mägele 2011). Nevertheless, certain sites are preeminent in sculptural studies for the quantity, quality, and variety of their preserved sculpture, as well as for related data on the sculptures' commission, display, and manufacture. In addition, these sites highlight different aspects of the sculptural tendencies of Asia Minor. Whereas Aphrodisias and Ephesos exhibit strong ties to the Roman imperial center, Hierapolis has a pronounced local focus in its sculptural material. Regional and city-specific styles can also be detected at many other sites, including Pergamon, Perge, and Side.

A large portion of the Roman sculpture from Aphrodisias in Caria has been recovered in very fine condition with a corpus that stretches from the republican period into the seventh century AD (Erim 1986). It is possible to see at Aphrodisias examples of the importance of Roman metropolitan influence on the region's artists as well as the emergence of local production systems that would become influential in their own right.

Aphrodisian sculpture is typified by its high quality of execution, especially in drill-work, textural contrasts and finish, expressiveness, and stylistic eclecticism. The majority of the statuary from the site is carved from the soft white marble available locally from the surrounding region (Rockwell 1996, 81–6; Long 2012, 81–7). The preservation of late republican and early imperial architectural sculpture from Aphrodisias such as that from the Zoilos monument and the Sebasteion has resulted in a great deal of scholarly attention to the site. These two buildings are notable, not only because of their preservation (due to seismic activity and subsequent rebuilding throughout Asia Minor, there is rather less material preserved from the early imperial period than from the second and third centuries), but also because they both exhibit a combination of the classical and Hellenistic sculptural traditions with the influence of the imperial iconography developed in Italy (Smith 1993). The Zoilos monument (a tomb or heroon to C. Julius Zoilos, a freedman of Octavian/Augustus) self-consciously uses the compositional schemes, deep carving, and personifications familiar from other Hellenistic elite and civic monuments in combination with Roman themes and iconography in order to articulate the exalted standing of this important intermediary between Aphrodisias and the Augustan regime (Smith 1993, 61–7). The Sebasteion, a precinct of the imperial cult and Aphrodite in the city, presented Aphrodisias as both Rome's subject and partner. Mythological panels, bearing Hellenistic influences, are paired with heroic depictions of Julio-Claudian emperors conquering geographical personifications while ethnic personifications stand watch (Smith 1987; 1988; 1990b; 2013). According to the excavators, personifications representing places and peoples in the hinterlands of the empire depend upon models from Rome (Smith 1988, 71–7). In contrast, the reliefs depicting Augustus and Julio-Claudian emperors betray the region's longstanding representational traditions of ruler veneration (Smith 1987, 134–8; Rose 1997, 164–9).

The role of powerful elites in facilitating the incorporation of Roman artistic styles at Aphrodisias can be seen again at the theater, which not only was decorated with architectural decoration that echoed the lush garlands and bucrania of Augustan art, but also was filled with freestanding statuary of deities and mythological figures, what is often referred to as "ideal sculpture" (Erim and Smith 1991; see essay 3.3, Anguissola). Representations of the Muses and Apollo (Erim and Smith 1991, 71–2) were obviously relevant to the function of the theater as a place of musical performance, but they were also linked to the Nike imagery that was propagated by Augustus in his own visual programs (74–9).

Ephesos, as the metropolis of the province of Asia, figured prominently in regional artistic trends. As at other prosperous cities in Asia Minor during the second and third centuries AD, Ephesos was endowed with numerous pieces of richly decorated architecture. Gifts from Roman imperial officials and local notables, these monuments—including but not limited to bath-gymnasia and fountains—featured high-quality reliefs and freestanding statuary that depicted the deities, heroes, and benefactors of the community. Sculptures of Androklos, the foundation hero of Ephesos, have been recovered from fountains and bath buildings standing alongside portrait statues of emperors and donors, such as that of Vedius Antoninus from the marble hall or so-called *kaisersaal* at the Baths of Vedius (Thür 1995; Dillon 1996). Such assemblages strongly suggest that these particular aediculated spaces accommodated both imperial worship and civic rituals (Yegül 1982; Burrell 2006).

The tradition of imperial portraiture at Ephesos has a long history, from the colossal portraits of Augustus and Livia recovered from the early imperial basilica to the relief portraits of Antonine emperors on the frieze of the remarkable Parthian Monument, erected in honor of Lucius Verus and Marcus Aurelius in AD 169. As a site of concentrated wealth and political prominence, Ephesos was able to draw upon the best sculptural workshops in the region, including those of Aphrodisias and Dokimeion. Locally quarried and imported stone were both used at this site to sate the tremendous demand for sculpture (Long 2012, 185–205). The ideal sculpture from the Austrian excavations at the site has been catalogued (Aurenhammer 1990; 2004) and highlights of the portraiture have appeared in print (Aurenhammer 2011); a full catalog of the portraiture is eagerly awaited. Studies of Ephesian architecture have shed light on the physical and historical contexts of the decorative sculptural programs. Indeed, the fortunate preservation of the architecture, coupled with careful excavation and publication, has made Ephesos one of the most studied sites for Roman sculpture not only in terms of typology but also in social history.

Other sites in Asia Minor also command attention. Cities such as Hierapolis in Phrygia reflect a strong preoccupation with local mythology and cult in their sculpture. The sculpture and epigraphy of this site have been published extensively over the years (D'Andria and Ritti 1985; Ritti 1985; D'Andria 2003; De Bernardi Ferrero, Ciotta, and Pensabene 2007). Though much of its early imperial art and architecture are lost to earthquake damage and subsequent rebuilding, Hierapolis does feature a significant Julio-Claudian monument, the so-called Tomba Bella. This monumental tomb showcases not only the classicizing style typical of the Julio-Claudian period, with its reliance on personifications, but also reveals the artistic flow of information across Asia Minor in this crucial period (Romeo 2011, 199–207). The structure bears, in the iconography and composition of its figural frieze, a striking resemblance to the Zoilos monument at Aphrodisias, suggesting that the tastes of Rome were quickly adopted—partially as indicators of appreciation for the Roman emperors—by the elites of the provinces.

The sculptural floruit of Hierapolis was in the second and early third centuries AD. Sculpture has been recovered throughout the city, including the areas of the agora and the intramural sanctuary of Apollo, as well as from the Roman-period urban theater (Bejor 1991). During the early Severan renovation of the theater's stage building, extensive biographical relief cycles of Apollo and Artemis—the patron god of the city and his twin—were added to the podium of the *scaenae frons* (D'Andria and Ritti 1985). These reliefs were complemented by statues of local notables, philosophers, and mythological beings installed in and around the stage building. While Bejor had identified the podium reliefs as the work of Dokimeian sculptors from the same region of Phrygia, and physical and epigraphic finds from Hierapolis indicate that the city's elite were eager customers of the neighboring Dokimeion and Thiounta quarries (1991, 90), subsequent analysis of the marble from the theater stage building shows that Thiounta and Aphrodisian stones were used for the majority of the stage building and reliefs and that only a portion of the architectural members were carved from Dokimeian marble (Attanasio and Pensabene 2002; Pensabene 2007, 294–6). Bejor conjectured that artists working in connection with Dokimeion and Thiounta marble quarries spread their style throughout the region, traveling to local workshops (Bejor 1991, 94), such as the ones that existed at Hierapolis, to produce works for the local market. Hierapolis also had large, highly decorated fountains. The Nymphaeum of the Amazons, which is in the preliminary stages of publication, featured reliefs of local gods and of the Amazons, who are very much part of the mythological history of Asia Minor (D'Andria 2011, 168–70). In this respect the iconography of the nymphaeum correlates with that of the theater reliefs of Apollo and Artemis, which depicted scenes from locally occurring myths, such as the flaying of Marsyas and the slaughter of the Niobids (D'Andria and Ritti 1985, 76, 183, 186).

Other sites that should be noted in a consideration of sculpture in Roman Asia Minor include Pergamon, Perge, and Side. Though Pergamon's Hellenistic sculpture has received much more attention than its Roman-period products, as an early capital of the province of Asia and the seat of the first *neokoros* it is a source of high-quality Roman portraiture (Inan and Rosenbaum 1966, 20–22). In addition, the second-century AD Red Hall also has important examples of Hadrianic Egyptianizing sculpture (Koester 1998). Excavations at Perge and Side have uncovered a rich variety of portrait and ideal sculptures along with well-decorated public architecture, much of which has yet to be published fully (Pehlivaner 1996). Perge may have hosted a local sculptural school that perhaps produced the statuary filling the city's monumental city gate, fountains, and bath complex (Mansel 1956; 1975; Newby 2003; Slavazzi 2007, 124–7). The high-quality finds from Side (Mansel 1963; Inan 1975) are similar, coming from monumental nymphaea and other buildings, including the enigmatic "Building M," a public building whose function has not been determined. Portraiture, mythological sculpture, and archaistic sculptural types were combined in this structure, perhaps to highlight local cult and to tap into classicizing tastes established in imperial circles in Rome (Slavazzi 2007, 131–6).

Topics and Themes in Roman Sculpture of Asia Minor

Prevalent topics, themes, and trends in the interpretation and study of Roman sculpture in Asia Minor in recent years include the physical contexts for sculpture; the social and cultural significance of sculpture, including portraiture; and the analysis of funerary sculpture, including sarcophagi.

Contextualization and Programmatic Sculpture

While the publication of Roman sculpture in catalogs based on genre or period is standard practice, in the past two decades there has a been an emphasis on reintegrating the sculpture recovered from various sites in Asia Minor into original physical contexts (Newby 2003; Slavazzi 2007; Longfellow 2011). The consideration of how sculpture and architecture together form a unified monument goes hand in hand with the physical reconstruction work taking place at various sites. Long and well-documented excavation histories at many sites make it possible to reconstruct many statuary programs in their original architectural settings.

Certain public spaces in the Roman cities of Asia Minor served as important loci for sculpture. These spaces were areas of high traffic or regular attendance, such as fountains, theaters, agoras, and the ornate colonnaded streets that connected these points. That statues, and in particular honorific portraits, should be placed to ensure maximum visibility to the community comes as no surprise (Stewart 2003; Smith et al. 2006, 9–19). However, much of the relevant textual data comes from Italy or the western parts of the empire, so the archaeological confirmation of this information in Asia Minor is important in establishing a standardized approach to the display of sculpture across the Roman Mediterranean. Indeed, the scholarly focus on recovering physical contexts is important precisely because: (1) it allows for better understanding of the statuary habits of Asia Minor in comparison to the rest of the Roman Empire; (2) it provides a surer grasp of the costs of complete monuments for their patrons; and (3) it lays the foundation for further interpretive work on sculptural displays, which integrates sculptural style, type, and technique but is not limited to these traditional topics.

A challenge in investigating the settings of sculpture—one that is not unique to Asia Minor—occurs when sculptures are excavated in obviously secondary contexts without any means to determine their original location or function. The late-antique inhabitants of these cities themselves moved statuary around, and many of these sites are close to modern towns that took advantage of readily available stone, architectural or sculptural, in constructing houses and other buildings. Nevertheless, current thinking gives much more credence to the idea of choice and curation in spolia, and less attention to presumed economic motivations. Scholars have detected a strong late-antique tendency to gather sculpture from throughout the city to create new displays that emphasized the appreciation of classical art, the prevalence of *ornamenta* as a mark of civic prestige, and the continued vitality of classical culture (Smith 2007; Stewart 2007). In the instance of Constantine's collection of famous classical and Hellenistic period works from throughout the empire in his new capital city, Bassett sees the promotion of ties both to the legacy of Rome and to Greek cultural heritage in order to articulate the new capital's standing as equal to western Roman imperial traditions (2004). Though style and typology are commonly used to date Roman sculpture, this practice can be problematic, as a sculpture's appearance can often reflect antiquarian or regional tastes that do not conform to periodization. In late-antique secondary contexts, however, stylistic and typological analyses are profitably used, not to pinpoint a sculpture's origin, but to clarify curatorial motivations for subsequent reuse as part of new "collections" or as evidence of new display habits developing in the period. That is, style and typology are considered as cultural and historical signifiers meaningful in certain ways to the viewer.

The scholarship on the social context of sculpture in Roman Asia Minor has been progressing on two (sometimes convergent) tracks: the interpretation of public sculptural programs and the study of honorific portraits as embodiments of elite identity and social relationships. The sites mentioned above figure prominently in this area of study, especially during the peak of the Roman Empire. Precisely because the physical contexts for statues of gods, heroes, emperors, and notables had been established with some degree of certainty, art historians then have been able to consider what was being articulated in unified sculptural programs. In general, common factors link the interpretations of these programs. The peak of architectural and public sculptural production coincides with the rhetorical—and arguably cultural—movement of the Second Sophistic. This movement had major proponents in Asia Minor and centered on fluency in Hellenic linguistic and educational traditions, especially on the part of the elites. This translated into a new valorization of Hellenic—that is, from the Greek mainland—roots and origins by Anatolian communities and a tendency for notables to demonstrate their personal *paideia* or "learnedness."

The Second Sophistic has become a standard framework for interpreting sculptural programs in Asia Minor, because representations of legendary founders from Greece are often prominently featured. In Ephesos, as mentioned earlier, the Athenian prince and founder Androklos was represented at multiple displays throughout the city. Perge's South City Gate, renovated and decorated in the Hadrianic period, held in its niches statues (now known only by their bases) of at least seven founders from different parts of Greece, including Delphi and Argos (Mansel 1956; Boatwright 1993; Newby 2003, 201; Slavazzi 2007, 124–7; see essays 3.4, Wood; 4.1, Longfellow; 4.5, Tuck; and 4.6, Kellum). In such cases, the sculpture decorating the large public fountains and gates served to project a civic identity that was not Anatolian but Hellenic, in keeping with the rhetoric of Greekness that dominated Sophistic culture. At the same time, the reach of the Second Sophistic is seen to extend also to depictions of regionally or locally specific elements, such as the representation of the rape and return of Persephone on the early Severan theater podium reliefs at Nysa (Lindner 1994) or the previously noted Hierapolitan theater reliefs. At Nysa, the incorporation of Roman soldiers and Papposilenus actors into the frieze suggests strongly that the story of Persephone's abduction on the plains of Nysa was recreated for the consumption of a Roman imperial audience (Lindner 1994, 145, no. 45; Newby 2003, 209). The connection between these theater friezes and, more broadly, among all the public sculptural programs that focused on the mythical past is that of an active cultural memory of local history and origins (Yildirim 2004). As the concept of cultural memory has taken a central place in the scholarship of the Second Sophistic, its application in the analysis of public sculpture is similarly important (Cordovana and Galli 2007). Moreover, the heuristic framework of the Second Sophistic can be used to investigate the motivations of the local notables who paid for the erection and decoration of the fountains, gates, and baths in Asia Minor. As elite identity is so closely connected to *paideia* in the Second Sophistic, programmatic sculpture that positioned elite portraits alongside the representations of legendary founders and local deities can be understood as the artistic expression of Greek cultural fluency—that these men (and some women) were aware of and prized the Hellenic traditions of their communities.

Portraiture

The Hellenic identity of the elites was often integral to their personal depictions beyond programmatic statuary. Asia Minor presents us with a large corpus of portrait statues, of which some were from sculptural programs in monuments, while others constituted honorific monuments in their own right. Catalogs of Roman portraits from Aphrodisias and Ephesos have either been published (Smith et al. 2006) or are in preparation, and Jale Inan and Elisabeth Alföldi-Rosenbaum's catalogs (1966; 1979) of Roman portraits from Asia Minor have been available for decades. Studies of portraiture in recent years have examined this important genre across the Roman Empire (see essay 3.4, Wood), and have focused more on the social functions of portraits than their formal characteristics (Stewart 2003; Fejfer 2008). The public portraiture from Asia Minor occupies an important place in these studies. While much of the textual and epigraphic sources that document Roman attitudes toward portraits are Italian and come from a distinctly Roman tradition, the evidence from Asia Minor, a deeply Hellenized province with a long portrait tradition, presents its own cultural and historical nuances.

For example, citizens at Aphrodisias were represented in various guises, both Greek and Roman (Smith et al. 2006, 9–19). The study of Roman-period portraiture in Asia Minor is heavily influenced by Smith's analysis (1998) of these honorific portraits—pioneering a thematic approach to the study of this corpus—which argued convincingly that the conscious selection of specific Greek or Roman costumes and coiffures such as the toga or the full beard for these statues articulated the personal and cultural identities of their elite subjects, who were culturally Greek but participated enthusiastically in the Roman imperial project. Indeed, one cannot fully consider the public honorific statue, so prominent in both the material record and the literary discourse of imperial Asia Minor, without knowledge of this argument for multivalent self-presentation.

Scholars also frequently cite Dio Chrysostom's orations, particularly his *Rhodian Oration* (for example, *Or.* 31.9, 31.28), and the *Corinthian Oration* attributed to Favorinus (*Or.* 37.8, 37.28) for their discussions of the recycling of portrait statuary. Peter Stewart and Jane Fejfer's geographically comprehensive volumes on Roman statuary and portraits both rely on these speeches for information on the recycling of statue bases (Stewart 2003; Fejfer 2008). In addition, Verity Platt's essay (2007) focuses on Dio

Chrysostom's objections to the reinscription of statue bases, observing that the communicative power of the honorific portrait monument is thereby disrupted. Of course, the reuse and removal of public portrait statuary is by no means restricted to Asia Minor; however, the centrality of the region's textual evidence for this practice cannot be denied. These studies and sources should be read alongside works such as the recent catalog from Aphrodisias, which provides the epigraphy from statue bases for the identities of and honors received by the statue subjects. Together, the archaeology and art history create a more complete social context for portrait statuary than has been available in the past. It is also necessary, when considering the public honorific statue in Roman Asia Minor, to remember its development from earlier practice (Wallace-Hadrill 1990, 150–54). The public portrait had been prominent in the urban life and elite identities of Asia Minor since the Hellenistic period, and the relationships between elites and their demanding local constituents embodied by these sculptures also in large part continued from the politics of that era.

As for the portraits from Asia Minor themselves, the quality ranges from competent to extremely fine. They correspond generally to known types commonly used across the empire, and sometimes combine metropolitan influence with Hellenistic softness and vigor (Inan and Rosenbaum 1966). Portraits of emperors follow styles established in Italy, such as the Prima Porta type for Augustus, though the more emphatic twists of the head point to eastern style (Inan and Rosenbaum 1966, 12–15). In addition, female relatives of emperors were often represented using Demeter types (Rose 1997, 53). The finish of the portraits also reveals local differences: Side's portraits feature a softer finish and smoother transitions between parts of the head, while Perge's are harder with more deeply carved lines in the face and hair (Inan and Rosenbaum 1966, 34–5). Ephesos, not surprisingly, boasts a large number of portraits, with examples dating from the Republic through late antiquity. While Aphrodisias produced high-quality portraits in all periods, its late antique portraits are especially outstanding (Inan and Alföldi-Rosenbaum 1979, 24–34). These Aphrodisian portraits retain the singular liveliness and expressiveness of their high imperial counterparts and their classical fluidity longer than late antique sculpture found elsewhere in the empire (Smith 1999, 184–5, 187). A series of shield portraits from a late antique house, depicting primarily Greek philosophers, including at least one master and one student, are fine examples of the work of sculptors at Aphrodisias and show that, even when drawing from classical prototypes in this late period, local artists introduced elements into the portraiture that highlighted the intellectual intensity and "dynamism" of their subjects, using techniques such as fine drill work that had long been a part of the local repertoire (Smith 1990a, 133–4 and passim; 1991, 163, 167).

Overall, there are typological commonalities and basic conventions that underlie the use of public portraits in the different parts of the empire, despite the Hellenistic influence over the practice in Asia Minor; in contrast, the themes and styles of public programmatic sculpture are generally seen to reflect very localized concerns and to be deeply tied to the cultural and political environment of Asia Minor.

Marble Studies and Sarcophagi

The study of marble quarries and workshops is also shedding new light on Asia Minor's sculptural industry. While for a long time, stylistic and palaeographical analysis and the attribution of works to specific "schools" have been part of the scholarship of Roman sculpture from Asia Minor (Squarciapino 1943; 1991), studies done at various sites in the region, including those noted above, have begun to reveal a general consensus that many of them had an active but limited sculptural industry, producing for the consumption of the local populace. Marble studies, using a combination of archaeological data and the analysis of physical properties, have helped to establish the sources of sculpture-grade stone used by these workshops. While the top-quality marbles from the Prokonnesos and Dokimeion certainly supported the beautification of the entire empire, other smaller Anatolian quarries, such as those near Ephesos, also exported some of their materials to other provinces (Fischer 1998, 255; Prochaska and Grillo 2012). Meanwhile, Long's new research (2012) shows that marble from numerous Anatolian quarries was exploited primarily, though not exclusively, to serve local and regional markets for marble buildings and sculpture. The additional importation of fine white stones into cities with a good supply of building-grade material, such as Hierapolis and Ephesos, not only indicates great demand for statuary marble, but also could signal desire for prestige and novelty (Pensabene 2007; Prochaska and Grillo 2012, 590; Scardozzi 2012, 575). Marble sourcing data combined with analysis of local workshop characteristics paint a complex picture of the sculpture industry in Asia Minor. Sculptors obviously were able to work locally quarried marble, but those from cities without local access to sculpture-grade stone, like Perge, nevertheless developed proficiency with regional imports. At the same time, quarry-based sculptors, along with their traveling or satellite colleagues, helped to make the most of material exported from home (Long 2012, 251). Evidence also suggests that some quarry-based prefabrication of sculpture occurred (Pensabene 2002; see essay 2.7, Russell). Marble sourcing studies therefore have the potential to provide insight on the economy of Asia Minor, the trade of materials across the province and empire, and the valuation of raw and finished materials, which would then enhance the understanding of sculptural commissions in Roman Asia Minor.

The study of Asiatic sarcophagi has benefited from these workshop and marble studies. This genre of Roman sculpture merits attention, especially because the Asiatic sarcophagi are closely connected with the industry in Rome (see essay 4.3, Ewald). Roman sarcophagi studies have a long publication history in German (for Asia Minor, important early works include Koch and Sichtermann 1982; Wiegartz 1965). Though Marc Waelkens had argued for the dominant importance of Dokimeion in Asia Minor's sarcophagus industry, due to what he saw as its influence via locally made exports on style in the region, and even on Italian production (1982, 106–110, 121–8), there are actually variations in style and motifs across Asia Minor. Several cities—including Ephesos, Perge, Laodicea, Aphrodisias, Prokonnesos—can be considered major regional production centers for sarcophagi in the Roman period (Koch and Sichtermann 1982; Işık

2007). Sarcophagi exports from Asia Minor were roughly fabricated at the quarries, and then finished at their ultimate destinations (Koch and Sichtermann 1982, 507–9; see essay 2.7, Russell). The question as to the origins of the popular compositions and iconographies—including garlands and columnar frames—found on Asiatic sarcophagi has been revisited recently, with evidence suggesting that these motifs originated in Rome and then were popularized in Asia Minor (Işık 2000, 113–17). These adapted motifs were subsequently reimported into Rome via the semi-finished products from eastern quarries and workshops, which were finally completed by Anatolian artists in satellite workshops. This two-way movement of artistic influence and craftsmanship between provinces and the imperial capital has been supported by examinations of both the stone and carving techniques of sarcophagi found in Rome (Koch 1982, 170–73; Işık 2000, 121–2). The formal interplays between sarcophagi from Asia Minor and those from Rome have allowed for very interesting work, notably Thomas's recent essay (2010) on the meaning of the aediculated, arcaded, and otherwise columnar designs of predominantly Asiatic—and, especially in the mid-second to mid-third centuries AD, Dokimeian—sarcophagi. Thomas argues that the adoption of these "microarchitectural" sarcophagi was a statement of cultural identity, *paideia*, and loyalty to the Roman Empire. His essay also ties the columnar displays on sarcophagi to the large-scale aediculated architecture of the Roman East and to the concurrent vogue for the display of both portrait and ideal sculptures in these elaborate façades.

Conclusion

Asia Minor, like other Roman provinces, produced sculpture that at once reflected both local traditions and Roman identity. The priorities of the Second Sophistic contributed to a heightened visual habit of cultural negotiation and expression of elite identity. The proliferation of sculpture in Roman Asia Minor was funded by the wealth of its leading cities and citizens and supported by the numerous marble quarries and workshops throughout the region, growing largely from an existing expectation for civic adornment. The study of this marble culture intersects with broader developments in the scholarship of Roman sculpture, while presenting valuable insights into various aspects of local style and practice.

Bibliography

Attanasio, D., and P. Pensabene. 2002. "I marmi del teatro di Hierapolis." In *Hierapolis: Scavi e ricerche IV; Saggi in onore di Paolo Verzone*, edited by D. De Bernardi Ferrero, 69–85. Rome: Giorgio Bretschneider.

Aurenhammer, M. 1990. *Die Skulpturen von Ephesos, Idealplastik I.* Vienna: Österreichischen Akademie der Wissenschaften.

———. 2004. "Sculptures of Gods and Heroes from Ephesos." In *Ephesos, Metropolis of Asia*, edited by H. Koester, 251–80. Cambridge, MA: Harvard Theological Studies.

———. 2011. "Late Hellenistic and Early Roman Imperial Portraits from Ephesos." In D'Andria and Romeo 2011, 101–116.

Bassett, S. 2004. *The Urban Image of Late Antique Constantinople*. Cambridge: Cambridge University Press.

Bauer, F. A., and C. Witschel, eds. 2007. *Statuen in der Spatäntike*. Wiesbaden: Reichert.

Bejor, G. 1991. *Hierapolis: Scavi e richerche III: Le statue*. Rome: Giorgio Bretschneider.

Boatwright, M. T. 1993. "The City Gate of Plancia Magna in Perge." In *Roman Art in Context: An Anthology*, edited by E. D'Ambra, 189–207. Englewood Cliffs: Prentice Hall.

Burrell, B. 2004. *Neokoroi: Greek cities and Roman emperors*. Leiden: Brill.

———. 2006. "False Fronts: Separating the Aedicular Facade from the Imperial Cult in Roman Asia Minor." *AJA* 110 (3): 437–69.

Cordovana, O., and M. Galli, eds. 2007. *Arte e memoria culturale nell'eta della Seconda Sofistica*. Catania: Prisma.

D'Andria, F. 2003. *Hierapolis of Phrygia (Pammukale): An Archaeological Guide*. Translated by P. Arthur. Istanbul: Ege yayınları.

———. 2011. "Gods and Amazons in the Nymphaea of Hierapolis." In D'Andria and Romeo 2011, 150–72.

D'Andria, F., and T. Ritti. 1985. *Hierapolis: scavi e richerche II: Le sculture del teatro*. Rome: Giorgio Bretschneider.

D'Andria, F., and I. Romeo, eds. 2011. *Roman Sculpture in Asia Minor*. JRA Supplement 80. Portsmouth, RI: Journal of Roman Archaeology.

De Bernardi Ferrero, D., G. Ciotta, and P. Pensabene, eds. 2007. *Hierapolis di Frigia II: Il teatro di Hierapolis di Frigia; Restauro, architettura ed epigrafia*. Genova: De Ferrari.

Dillon, S. 1996. "The Portraits of a Civic Benefactor of 2nd-c. Ephesos." *JRA* 9: 261–74.

Erim, K. 1986. *Aphrodisias: City of Venus-Aphrodite*. London: Muller, Blond and White.

Erim, K., and R. R. R. Smith. 1991. "Sculpture from the Theatre: A Preliminary Report." In Smith and Erim 1991, 67–98.

Fejfer, J. 2008. *Roman Portraits in Context*. Berlin: Walter de Gruyter.

Fischer, M. L. 1998. *Marble Studies: Roman Palestine and the Marble Trade*. Konstanz: Universtätverlag Konstanz.

Gutiérrez, A., P. Lapuente, and I. Rodà, eds. 2012. *Interdisciplinary Studies on Ancient Stone. ASMOSIA 9*. Documenta 23. Tarragona: Institut Català d'Arqueologia Clàssica.

Inan, J. 1975. *Roman Sculpture in Side*. Ankara: Türk Tarih Kurumu Basımevi.

Inan, J., and E. Alföldi-Rosenbaum. 1979. *Römische und frühbyzantinische Porträtplastik aus der Türkei: Neue Funde*. Mainz: Philipp von Zabern.

Inan, J., and E. Rosenbaum. 1966. *Roman and Early Byzantine Portrait Sculpture in Asia Minor*. London: Oxford University Press.

Işık, F. 2000. "Stadtrömisch oder kleinasiatisch? Zur Werkstattfrage der Girlandensarkophage der Hauptgruppe aus Rome." In *Munus: Festschrift für Hans Wiegartz*, edited by T. Mattern, 113–23. Münster: Scriptorium.

———. 2007. "Lokalisierung der Werkstätten der Girlandensarkophage der kleinasiatischen Hauptgruppe." In Koch, Fittschen, and Dally 2007, 279–89.

Koch, G. 1982. "Östliche Sarkophage in Rom." *BJb* 182: 167–208.

Koch, G., K. Fittschen, and O. Dally, eds. 2007. *Akten des Symposiums des Sarkophag-Corpus 2001, Marburg, 2–7 Juli 2001*. Mainz: Philipp von Zabern.

Koch, G., and H. Sichtermann. 1982. *Römische Sarkophage*. Munich: C. H. Beck.

Koester, H. 1998. "The Cult of the Egyptian Deities in Asia Minor." In *Pergamon, Citadel of the Gods: Archaeological Record, Literary Description, and Religious Development*, edited by Helmut Koester, 111–35. Cambridge, MA: Harvard Theological Studies.

Lindner, R. 1994. *Mythos und Identität: Studien zur Selbstdarstellung kleinasiatischer Städte in der römischen Kaiserzeit*. Stuttgart: F. Steiner.

Long, L. 2012. "Urbanism, Art, and Economy: The Marble Quarrying Industries of Aphrodisias and Roman Asia Minor." PhD diss., University of Michigan, Ann Arbor.

Longfellow, B. 2011. *Roman Imperialism and Civic Patronage: Form, Meaning, and Ideology in Monumental Fountain Complexes*. Cambridge: Cambridge University Press.

Mägele, S. 2011. "The Sculptural Evidence of Sagalassos in its Urban Context." In D'Andria and Romeo 2011, 319–35.

Mansel, A. 1956. "Bericht über Ausgrabungen und Untersuchungen in Pamphylien in den Jahren 1946–1955." *AA* 71: 34–120.

———. 1963. *Die Ruinen von Side*. Berlin: Walter de Gruyter.

———. 1975. "Die Nymphaeen von Perge." *IstMitt* 25: 367–72.

Newby, Z. 2003. "Art and Identity in Asia Minor." In *Roman Imperialism and Provincial Art*, edited by S. Scott and J. Webster, 192–213. Cambridge: Cambridge University Press.

Newby, Z., and R. Leader-Newby, eds. 2007. *Art and Inscriptions in the Ancient World*. Cambridge: Cambridge University Press.

Pehlivaner, M., ed. 1996. *Sculptures of the Museum in Antalya I*. Ankara: Dönmez.

Pensabene, P. 2002. "Le principali cave di marmo bianco." In *I marmi colorati della Roma imperiale*, edited by M. De Nuccio and L. Ungaro, 203–222. Venice: Marsilio.

———. 2007. "Gli elementi marmorei della scena: Classificazione tipologica e inquadramento nella storia della decorazione architettonica in Asia Minor." In De Bernardi Ferrero, Ciotta, and Pensabene 2007, 229–333.

Platt, V. 2007. "'Honour Takes Wing': Unstable Images and Anxious Orators in the Greek Tradition." In Newby and Leader-Newby 2007, 247–71.

Prochaska, W., and S. M. Grillo. 2012. "The Marble Quarries of the Metropolis of Ephesos and Some Examples of the Use for Marbles in Ephesian Architecture and Sculpturing." In Gutiérrez, Lapuente, and Rodà 2012, 584–91.

Ritti, T. 1985. *Hierapolis: Scavi e richerche I; Fonti letterarie ed epigrafiche*. Rome: Giorgio Bretschneider.

Rockwell, P. 1996. "The Marble Quarries: A Preliminary Survey." In *Aphrodisias Papers 3: The Setting and Quarries, Mythological and Other Sculptural Decoration, Architectural Development, Portico of Tiberius, and Tetrapylon*, edited by C. Roueché and R. R. R. Smith, 81–103. JRA Supplement 20. Portsmouth, RI: Journal of Roman Archaeology.

Romeo, I. 2011. "The 'Beautiful Tomb' and Civic Identity in Julio-Claudian Hierapolis." In D'Andria and Romeo 2011, 193–210.

Rose, C. B. 1997. *Dynastic Commemoration and Imperial Portraiture in the Julio-Claudian Period*. Cambridge: Cambridge University Press.

Roueché, C., and K. T. Erim, eds. 1990. *Aphrodisias Papers*. JRA Supplement 1. Ann Arbor: Journal of Roman Archaeology.

Scardozzi, G. 2012. "Ancient Marble and Alabaster Quarries near Hierapolis in Phyrgia (Turkey): New Data from Archaeological Surveys." In Gutiérrez, Lapuente, and Rodà 2012, 573–83.

Slavazzi, F. 2007. "Uso dei modelli e recupero del passato nei programmi scultorei ufficiali di età antonina in Asia Minore." In Cordovana and Galli 2007, 123–36.

Smith, R. R. R. 1987. "The Imperial Reliefs from the Sebasteion at Aphrodisias." *JRS* 77: 88–138.

———. 1988. "*Simulacra Gentium*: The *Ethne* from the Sebasteion at Aphrodisias." *JRS* 78: 50–77.

———. 1990a. "Late Roman Philosopher Portraits from Aphrodisias." *JRS* 90: 127–55.

———. 1990b. "Myth and Allegory in the Sebasteion." In Roueché and Erim 1990, 89–100.

———. 1991. "A New Portrait of Pythagoras." In Smith and Erim 1991, 159–67.

———. 1993. *Aphrodisias I: The Monument of C. Julius Zoilos*. Mainz: Philipp von Zabern.

———. 1998. "Cultural Choice and Political Identity in Honorific Portrait Statues in the Greek East in the Second Century AD." *JRS* 98: 56–93.

———. 1999. "Late Antique Portraits in a Public Context: Honorific Statuary at Aphrodisias in Caria, AD 300–600." *JRS* 99: 155–89.

———. 2007. "Statue Life in the Hadrianic Baths at Aphrodisias, AD 100–600: Local Context and Historical Meaning." In Bauer and Witschel 2007, 203–236.

———. 2013. *The Marble Reliefs from the Julio-Claudian Sebasteion*. Aphrodisias 6. Darmstadt: Philipp von Zabern.

Smith, R. R. R., with S. Dillon, C. H. Hallett, J. Lenaghan, and J. Van Voorhis. 2006. *Aphrodisias II: Roman Portrait Statuary from Aphrodisias*. Mainz: Philipp von Zabern.

Smith, R. R. R., and K. T. Erim, eds. 1991. *Aphrodisias Papers 2: The Theatre, a Sculptor's Workshop, Philosophers, and Coin Types*. JRA Supplement 2. Ann Arbor: Journal of Roman Archaeology.

Squarciapino, M. F. 1943. *La Scuola di Afrodisia*. Studi e materiali del Museo dell'Impero Romano 3. Rome: Governatorato di Roma.

———. 1991. "La scuola di Aphrodisias (dopo 40 anni)." In Smith and Erim 1991, 123–6.

Stewart, P. 2003. *Statues in Roman Society: Representation and Response*. Oxford: Oxford University Press.

———. 2007. "Continuity and Tradition in Late Antique Perceptions of Portrait Statuary." In Bauer and Witschel 2007, 27–42.

Thomas, E. 2010. " 'Houses of the Dead'? Columnar Sarcophagi as 'Micro-Architecture.'" In *Life, Death and Representation*, edited by J. Elsner and J. Huskinson, 387–435. New York: Walter de Gruyter.

Thür, H. 1995. "Der ephesische Ktistes Androklos und (s)ein Heroon am Embolos." *ÖJh* 64: 63–104.

Waelkens, M. 1982. *Dokimeion: Die Werkstatt der repräsentativen kleinasiatischen Sarkophage: Chronologie und Typologie ihrer Produktion*. Berlin: Mann.

Wallace-Hadrill, A. 1990. "Roman Arches and Greek Honours: The Language of Power at Rome." *PCPS* 36: 143–81.

Wiegartz, H. 1965. *Kleinasiatische Säulensarkophage: Untersuchungen zun Sarkophagtypus und zu den figürlich Darstellungen*. IstForsch 26.

Yegül, F. K. 1982. "A Study in Architectural Iconography: Kaisersaal and the Imperial Cult." *Art Bulletin* 64(1): 7–31.

Yildirim, B. 2004. "Identities and Empire: Local Mythology and the Self-Representation of Aphrodisias." In *Paideia, the World of the Second Sophistic*, edited by B. Borg, 23–52. Berlin: Walter de Gruyter.

CHAPTER 5.6

EGYPT

CHRISTINA RIGGS

INTRODUCTION

IN 2012, analysis of a Roman-period limestone statue of an enthroned god found in Egypt, now in the British Museum, revealed traces of rich pigment on its surface: red on the high-backed throne, two shades of green on the draperies, and yellow on the deity's arms as well as on his feathered face (figure 5.6.1; Beck, Bol, and Bückling 2005, 617, no. 196; see essay 2.6, Abbe). This statue was no Roman Jupiter or Mars or even the Graeco-Egyptian deity Sarapis, but Horus, the triumphant falcon-king and sky deity of Egyptian myths that were some three millennia old by the time Augustus brought Egypt under Roman sway. The overlapping feathers of the god's throat repeat on the surface of his mail armor shirt. A cloak fastened at the proper right shoulder gives way, around the lower body, to a himation that is richly draped but arranged with some uncertainty, as if the sculptor were unsure how the garment should be wrapped. Perhaps the sculptor worked from a two-dimensional representation rather than a three-dimensional model—sometimes a sign of forgery.

But the drapery of the Horus statue cannot cast doubt on its authenticity, for on the armor shirt and details of the feathered face, the pigment analysis identified Egyptian blue, a synthetic calcium-copper-silicate compound prized for its saturated hue and traded throughout the Mediterranean in ancient times. As its common name suggests, Egyptian blue was formulated and used in Egypt from the third millennium BC onward, one of a range of materials that mimicked the color of semiprecious stones like lapis and turquoise. The Horus statue bears some paint common during the Roman period as well: the paler green of the cloak derives from green earth, a pigment widely used throughout the empire but not attested in pharaonic Egypt (Dyer 2012). On this statue, which the British Museum purchased from Luxor antiquities dealer Mohammed Mohassib in 1912, the conjunction of these two pigments—one typically Egyptian, the other typically Roman—mirrors the conjunction of the Egyptian god and his Roman imperial form and, more broadly, the multifaceted nature of Roman Egyptian society. If

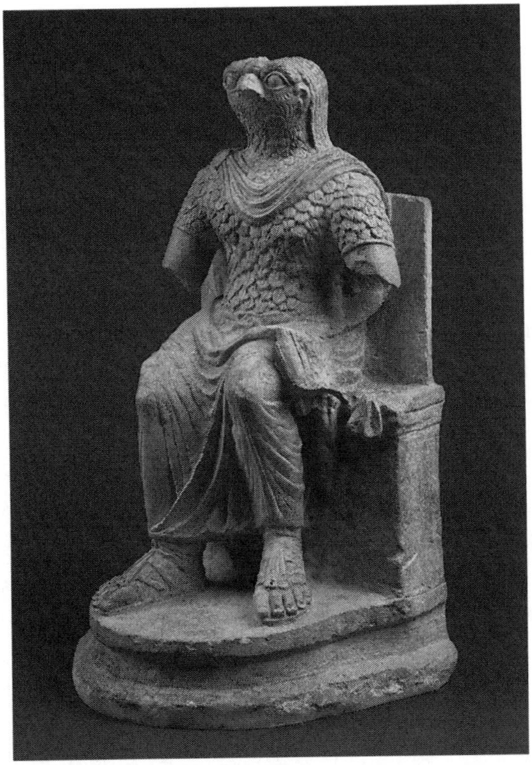

FIGURE 5.6.1 Statue of the Egyptian god Horus in Roman imperial dress with feather-patterned armor. Acquired in Egypt in 1912; probably from the vicinity of Luxor. Limestone, H 54.5 cm. London, British Museum, EA 51100.

the awkward draping of the lower body, the rough simplicity of the Egyptian limestone, and the brashness of the color scheme strike us today as provincial, dubious, or lacking in technique (and taste), we miss the mindset of the ancient viewer: in both Roman and Egyptian religious practice, statues like this manifested power, divine and otherwise. Imagine the statue set in a niche in some small shrine in southern Egypt, lit by flickering oil-lamps and veiled in a haze of incense, and this image of Horus becomes less ungainly, more otherworldly, which was surely its intended effect.

The Horus figure, with its combination of materials, hybrid form, and mixed subject matter (military and divine, human and animal, Egyptian and Roman) raises several themes that offer key insights about sculpture in Roman Egypt, a subject that tends to fall between the disciplinary cracks of classical archaeology and Egyptology, not to mention papyrology and epigraphy. Instead of documenting "types" or classifications of sculpture in Roman Egypt, this essay suggests directions that further research on such sculpture might take. I include a range of materials and media and examine the wide roles that sculpted images played in the visual experience and cultural life of Roman Egyptian society. The standard marble statue executed in the round, though certainly present in Roman Egypt, was only one aspect of sculptural production. After a brief look at the history of scholarship on sculpture in Roman Egypt, I consider the functions and contexts of statuary; the ways in which various materials made sculpture accessible to many; and sculptural evidence for long-distance connections between Egypt and the rest of the empire.

Studying Sculpture in Roman Egypt

Classical-looking objects of Roman date found on Egyptian sites have proven stubbornly difficult for scholars to categorize to their satisfaction, whether on the pages of publications or in the galleries of museums. In his 1903 volume of the Cairo Museum's *Catalogue générale*, entitled *Greek Sculpture*, C. C. Edgar defended his selections: "Many things in the list. . . are partly Greek and partly Egyptian, and a few are even more Egyptian than Greek. In dealing with antiquities of the Ptolemaic and Roman ages it is a constantly recurring difficulty where to draw the line" (Edgar 1903, i). Edgar's "Greek" category ranged from archaic *kouros*-type statuettes to Hellenistic stelae to "odds and ends" (xv) of Roman-era plaster figures and architectural sculpture. His interest lay in identifying the influence of classical forms on "native" Egyptian work, and vice versa, culminating in the "decline" (xvi) of sculpture in late antiquity. Edgar also explained the difficulties of accessing works in the museum, which at that point was in the process of transferring its collections to a new, purpose-built home in Ismailiya (now Tahrir) Square. New material kept arriving from excavations as well, and objects deemed to have a strong "Greek" character were often transferred to the Graeco-Roman Museum in Alexandria, founded in the 1890s (Botti 1900).

In the 1920s and 1930s, a series of publications from the Alexandria museum helped bring that collection to greater international attention (Breccia 1924; 1932; 1933; Adriani 1933–7), although a *Catalogue générale* modeled on that of the Cairo museum did not progress beyond a volume of Greek and Latin inscriptions and a report on the Shatby necropolis (Breccia 1911; 1912). The collections in Alexandria and Cairo formed the core of Paul Graindor's 1937 *Bustes et statues-portraits d'Égypte romaine*, to date the only monograph devoted to sculpture, of any kind, from Roman Egypt. Graindor also included a handful of works in European and American collections and documented pieces he had accessed through antiquities dealers in Cairo, limiting himself as much as possible to material he had seen in person. The book would, he hoped, be followed by others, though his death soon after publication meant that his plans were never realized. What Graindor produced was an initial offering meant to provide a representative selection of portrait busts and statues, which he arranged by categories rather than chronologically: imperial portraits, images of well-known individuals (such as Alexander the Great and Socrates), and anonymous portraits, first male, then female. Graindor devoted a final section to "works called Egyptianizing (*égyptisante*)," which were, he wrote, unjustly neglected (6). This group included representations of Roman emperors as pharaohs, wearing the *nemes*-head dress and standing upright in the left-leg-forward posture that was a long-established convention of Egyptian sculpture (see essay 3.7, Swetnam-Burland). Graindor also included in his "Egyptianizing" section examples of basalt statues from the village of Soknopaiou Nesos (Dime) on the far edge of Lake Moeris in the Fayum, whose seated and standing forms likewise conformed to Egyptian conventions (figure 5.6.2).

Fast forward several decades, and both of these groups—Roman emperors and the Dime statues—were the subject of quite different studies, enabled by a 1980s shift toward interdisciplinarity in the humanities, as well as an increasing openness to evaluating "provincial" forms of cultural production on their own terms. The Polish archaeologist Zsolt Kiss published studies of Roman imperial portraiture in Egypt, with an emphasis on identifying specific emperors in both classical and Egyptian-style sculpture (Kiss 1975; 1984). Stanwick (2002, 88–9) has revisited this topic in relation to representations of the Ptolemaic kings, whose Hellenized portraits, in combination with Egyptian features, created a successful model for Roman emperors in Egypt, though only a dozen or so such sculptures survive (Stanwick's Group G, 127–30, nos. G1 to G14). Where Edgar had spoken of decline, scholars like Stanwick now speak of transformation and acknowledge

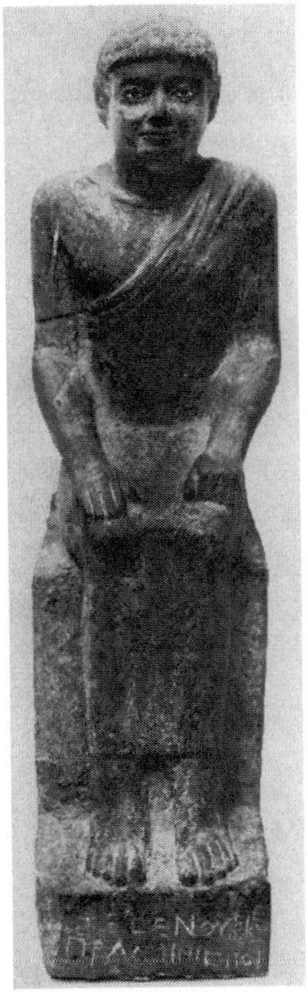

FIGURE 5.6.2 Seated statue of a man named Tesenuphis, a priest at Soknopaiou Nesos (Dime) in the Fayum, early first century AD. Basalt, H 50.0 cm. Cairo, Egyptian Museum, CG 1190.

the choices that artists and patrons made in adapting visual forms to specific contexts. More information about context can be gleaned from studies that draw together linguistic, archaeological, and artistic evidence, as Lembke (1998a; 1998b) has done for the Dime statues, demonstrating through the prosopography of their Egyptian and Greek inscriptions that the statues date to the late Ptolemaic and early Roman periods and commemorate priests who served in the local crocodile cult. The statues appear to have lined the causeway to the temple that dominated this agricultural village (Davoli 2012), a position considered unusual in Egyptian practice, where statues of private individuals were traditionally located within the restricted precinct of the temple itself. At the same time, the dark stone, inlaid eyes, and poses of the Dime statues represent one of the last attestations of this indigenous form, perhaps creating an intentionally "old-fashioned" effect for these representations of local worthies.

The Dime statues and Egyptian-form statues of emperors like Caracalla stand out as exceptions, however, since most sculpture in Roman Egypt was executed in the visual idiom of classical art, with statue forms similar to those of the Greek East in particular. Sculpture in the Egyptian style belonged to limited spheres, whether bold schemes like the Main Tomb at Kom el-Shugafa with its mirror-image second-century statues topped by portrait heads (Venit 2002, 124–45) or Egyptian temples extended or decorated under the empire (Minas-Nerpel 2012). Exploring the differences between classical and Egyptian art—and the presence or absence of interaction between the two—can be an important tool for studying certain objects and monuments, but should not be an end in itself. Trying to categorize sculpture along stylistic lines (as Edgar's efforts attest) can be more hindrance than help, and advances in the study of sculpture in Roman Egypt will depend on a more holistic approach, making full use of textual and archaeological evidence as well as the classical sculpture itself. The latter has yet to be collected and considered in the kind of corpus that Graindor seems to have envisioned, although Adriani's *Repertorio d'arte dell'egitto greco-romano* Series A, on "Scultura," made another attempt to do so, including Hellenistic works alongside Roman (Adriani 1961). The practicalities of academic specialization mean that both artistic and philological evidence tends to be divided between scholars trained in Classics on the one hand and Egyptology on the other; corpuses of material may facilitate more focused, thematic analyses (as, for instance, Parlasca's *Ritratti di mumie* [1969–80; Parlasca and Frenz 2003], published in the *Repertorio* as Series B, has done for mummy portraits), and both represent important future directions for study.

Settings and Subjects

The relationship between statues and the architecture around them adds to the complexity of characterizing statues as classical, Egyptian, or hybrid in form, since a "pure" statue in one form may have been erected in a setting that strongly evoked the other: for instance a Roman-style statue erected inside or in front of an Egyptian temple or an

Egyptian-form statue, like the Apis bull from the Serapeum at Alexandria, inscribed in Greek with the name of Hadrian, set up in a complex whose architectural language was entirely classical (Savvopoulos and Bianchi 2012, 56–9, cat. 13; McKenzie, Gibson, and Reyes 2004). Other sculpture adorned public buildings in the classical style, such as marble (according to the excavator) or more likely limestone statues perhaps representing the Muses, which were documented at the sizeable theater of Oxyrhynchus in the early 1920s together with red granite columns and limestone pilaster capitals, the latter now in the British Museum (Petrie 1925, 14–15, pls. xxxvi–xxxvii). Much more sculpture of this kind will have been incorporated into buildings that are now lost, given subsequent quarrying of ruins for construction materials and the widespread burning of limestone for lime.

Even where the material itself does not survive, the rich but understudied papyrological and epigraphic record in Roman Egypt might detail the mechanisms by which individuals and corporate bodies, like urban magistrates, commissioned and dedicated statues. Egyptian cities and *metropoleis* (the regional capitals) did not have town councils until the reign of Caracalla, but the system of magistracies enabled both the *poleis* (Alexandria, Naukratis, Ptolemais, and Antinoopolis) and the regional capitals, like Oxyrhynchus, to function in similar ways to cities in the Greek East, which would include the ability to grant honorific statue rights (Bowman and Rathbone 1992). From this administrative set-up and from surviving material, we can begin to gauge the experience and expectations of the magistrates and wider populace in such urban spaces, since some viewers were accustomed to high-caliber workmanship equal to anything erected in Rome or Aphrodisias. Such a familiarity was demonstrable not only in Alexandria, but in the regional capitals as well: a few miles away from Dime in the Fayum's main town, Arsinoe, superb marble busts of Augustus (the Prima Porta type), Livia, and Tiberius, now in Copenhagen, are said to have graced the amphitheater, and presumably helped mark the adoption of Tiberius in AD 5 (Johansen 1994–5, 1: 90–91, no. 33; 96–7, no. 36; 114–15, no. 45). Although these busts may be imports from Rome, their audience was local. Indeed, by the mid-first century AD, families from Arsinoe had begun to incorporate Roman-style encaustic painted portraits, with imperial hairstyles, in the wrapped mummies of the dead (Borg 2012). The marble busts and the painted panels and shrouds represent tiers of artistic execution relying upon the same aesthetic.

Throughout Egypt, people used sculpture, and images inspired by sculpture, in ways which scholars generally distinguish as funerary (or commemorative), honorific, and cultic (or divine). Without a firm provenance or inscriptional evidence, however, the difference between funerary and honorific works is not always clear in the Egyptian corpus and may have been fluid from an ancient perspective as well. Placing statues of living individuals (other than the pharaoh) on public, unrestricted view had not been part of indigenous Egyptian practice, but changes to both social organization and urban space over the course of the Hellenistic era may well have expanded this practice and introduced classical-style honorific statues, for instance in civic buildings and marketplaces. By the Roman period, the practice was well attested. For instance, at Oxyrhynchus, an over-life-size marble statue of a woman, dating to the second century AD, was found next to its columnar base in an open space, perhaps an agora near the town center (Alexandria, Graeco-Roman Museum 24008: Borg 2012, 615–16, fig. 37.1). Either findspot or sculptural form may point to honorific use, such as a statue of the Small Herculaneum woman type found at Tel Muqdam (Leontopolis) in the central Delta, whose oft-repeated form suggests its honorific function (Cairo, Egyptian Museum CG 27477: Edgar 1903, 22, pl. xii; compare Trimble 2000). Another example, also for a woman, is a statue found at Asyut (Lykopolis) and with a stance and draping similar to the *kore* types used as honorific statues in sanctuaries in the Greek East; the lost right arm most likely held out an offering *patera* (figure 5.6.3; Graindor 1937, 122–4, pl. lv). The Asyut statue is also of interest for the signature inscribed over the right knee, naming Ammonios son of Apollophanos as the sculptor.

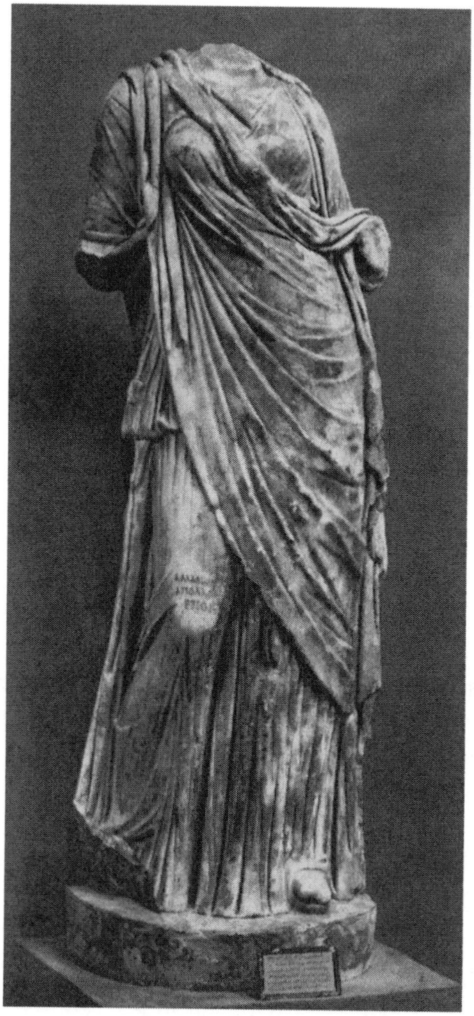

FIGURE 5.6.3 Statue of a woman found at Asyut (Lykopolis) in 1895. The Greek signature of the sculptor, Ammonios, son of Apollophanes, is carved above the right knee. Marble with traces of paint, H 145.0 cm. Alexandria, Graeco-Roman Museum, 3882.

Most of the largest concentration of honorific statues, from Alexandria and its environs, represent men and date to the second and third centuries AD (e.g., Graindor 1937, 103–7, pls. xli–xlii; Savvopoulos and Bianchi 2012, 74–5, no. 20; 76–7, no. 21; 138–9, no. 43; and 142–3, no. 45). The attributes of papyrus scrolls and cases (*capsae*) on several of these may point to erudition and decorum in general or specifically to holders of office and rank; two of the known statues depict toga wearers (Alexandria, Graeco-Roman Museum 3907: Graindor 1937, 106–7, no. 50, pl. xliib; Alexandria, Graeco-Roman Museum 27066: Savvopoulos and Bianchi 2012, 142–3, no. 45). Although these attributes and sculptural forms suggest an honorific function for the statues, findspots on the western and eastern edges of Alexandria, where the city's main cemeteries were located, suggest that they were part of funerary monuments instead (compare Savvopoulos and Bianchi 2012, on nos. 43 and 45). A cemetery used by the *legio II Germanica* at Sidi Gaber, to the east of the city, has yielded a number of commemorative reliefs (Schmidt 2003) and statues, including a reclining portrait of an older, bearded man holding a floral wreath (Alexandria, Graeco-Roman Museum 3897: Graindor 1937, 97–100, pl. xxxix; Borg 2012, 617, fig. 37.2). Another eastern suburb of Alexandria, Hagar el-Nawatieh, is the findspot of a mythologizing, under-life-size statue of a male figure wearing only a cloak, with a frontal, Egyptian image of the god Osiris carved on the support (Alexandria, Graeco-Roman Museum 20931: Graindor 1937, 96–7, pl. xxxviii; Savvopoulos and Bianchi 2012, 124–5, no. 37). Here, as elsewhere in Egypt, placing a classical figure in close proximity to an Egyptian deity created a visual "hybrid" particularly well suited to the funerary sphere.

Images of gods in Roman Egypt were as multiple as the gods themselves, and even where actual statues do not survive, representations like those on coinage or molded terracotta figures hint at the range of sculptural forms that existed. Statues of Sarapis were numerous, with several marble versions found at Alexandria (Kater-Sibbes 1973, 1–54; Schmidt 2005) and an impressive wooden head and torso at Theadelphia in the Fayum (Alexandria GRM 23352: Kater-Sibbes 1973, 15, no. 75; Empereur 1995, 5–6, fig. 4), giving an indication of how sculpture in other materials provided an important alternative to works in imported stone. As the Horus statue discussed at the start of this essay demonstrates, the visual language of classical art was the predominant form in which images of the gods were created, regardless of whether the deities had an earlier, Egyptian iconography. In addition to deities with an Egyptian origin, cults related to conventional Greek and Roman gods or to "new" cults from the East also thrived. For example, the Egyptian Museum in Cairo displays a damaged but no less impressive Mithras relief from Hermopolis Magna (JE 85747, illustrated in Bagnall and Rathbone 2004, color fig. 3.2.1), and a set of finely finished, marble statues discovered in Alexandria in 1973 includes an exquisite Aphrodite and Eros (Alexandria, Graeco-Roman Museum 29456: see Savvopoulos and Bianchi 2012, 156–9, no. 47h, with further literature at p. 148).

Two shrines found with some sculpture *in situ*—one at Luxor, the other at Ras el-Soda, near Alexandria—demonstrate how well classical sculpture served the widespread cult of Isis and Sarapis in particular. At Luxor, the "little Serapeum" is a brick-built, peripteral chapel set along the dromos of the Eighteenth-Dynasty (c. 1400 BC) Amun temple

(Golvin et al. 1981). An inscription records its dedication on Hadrian's birthday in AD 126 by an ex-*decurion*. The brick walls of the chapel were plastered and painted in imitation of marble, while its Egyptian-style doorway, with torus molding and sun disk, is carved sandstone. Inside the chapel, a low ledge or bench provided support for several statues, with an external niche on each of the side and back walls intended for more. When the chapel was discovered in 1951, excavators found fragments of an Osiris-*in-hydria* figure, the lower part of a draped male (perhaps Sarapis), two bulls (one limestone, one granite), and a near-life-size, headless statue of Isis, which has been re-erected on site. Both the structure of the chapel, with its low ledge and external niches, and the program of statues it contained, correspond to other shrines associated with the Isis and Sarapis cult, in Egypt as well as Italy. Statues of Isis, Harpocrates, and two large (meter-high) Osiris-*in-hydria*, together with a statue usually identified as Hermanubis, were found inside a late second-century shrine at Ras el-Soda, just east of Alexandria (Adriani 1940; Naerebout 2007; Savvopoulos and Bianchi 2012, cat. 48). Since relocated within the city, this limestone structure with marble prostyle Ionic columns was discovered in 1936. The fine statues were all remarkably intact, including an over-life-size statue of Isis in her typical Roman-era appearance, with knotted mantle, *situla* pail, and corkscrew curls. The Ras el-Soda shrine also included a marble altar, a pair of small, granite sphinxes, and a votive foot sculpted on a plinth, dedicated by one Isidoros to thank the gods for healing him after a carriage accident (Naerebout 2007, 507 n. 4). The array of sculpture found at Ras el-Soda points to the way in which such objects brought the worlds of gods and humans together, from the acts of commission and manufacture to devotion and commemoration. It embodied, in a quite literal sense, the social and political structures of society, through the creation and installation of statues representing emperors and members of the civic elite. Statues in every form peopled the cityscapes, cemeteries, and religious spaces of Roman Egypt, and this constant, near-ubiquitous presence gave sculpture an impact and influence exceeding the specific function of individual statues or groups. As with sculpture elsewhere in the Roman Empire, sculpture in Egypt informed an entire cultural mode of representation and visuality.

Sculpture in Society

The sculptural form signified an ideal, whether human or divine. Statues were often encountered as if they were living beings, imbued with agency—thus the strength of the reaction against them by early Christian fathers, like the abbot Shenute, and in earlier destructive practices as well (Stewart 2003, 261–99; Frankfurter 2008; see essays 4.2, McCarty; 6.5, Perry; 6.6, Kristensen). One of the best-known examples of *damnatio memoriae* in art, a painted wooden tondo of Septimius Severus, Julia Domna, Geta, and Caracalla, comes from Egypt; acquired through the art market and now in Berlin, the tondo may have been cut down from a larger format, and is usually assigned a provenance in the Fayum (Stewart 2003, 282, fig. 47; Rondot 2013, 33). Although its defacement of Geta is through the rubbing out of paint, rather than the chiseling away of relief or damage to a statue, the tondo and other images are what Stewart refers to as "statuesque," in that they ultimately refer to the abstract concept of a portrait statue, here specifically to busts (Stewart 2003, 92–117). In various media, including painting and relief, a statue-like appearance lent honor, *gravitas*, and prestige to portrait images where a full statue would have been unwieldy or unattainable.

The unattainability of portrait sculpture was a factor in Roman Egypt for a number of reasons, from the financial reach of patrons among the sub-elites of the regional towns and villages to the availability of materials and skilled artisans outside the major metropolitan areas. Decorum and suitability probably also helped determine who used which kind of image, with funerary art offering a wider scope for self-presentation. All these elements will have influenced the use of "statuesque" imagery in tomb paintings, grave reliefs, and mummy decoration. The well-known "mummy portraits," which were painted on wooden panels or linen shrouds and used on mummified bodies, make reference to portrait sculpture, whether as heads, busts, or full-length, statue-like figures, which sometimes include the base or plinth (e.g., Louvre N3076: Riggs 2006, 168–73, 278, no. 73, color pl. 9). Carved wooden coffins from Abusir el-Meleq, near the mouth of the Fayum, stood upright inside outer coffins in the form of Egyptian shrines; these coffins use the "arm-sling" statue posture replicated so often in statues and reliefs throughout the Greek East, here carved assiduously in soft wood that would have been plastered, painted, and gilded to heighten the effect (Riggs 2006, 148–55). Also from a funerary context, reliefs of men, women, and children set in niches were used in tombs at Oxyrhynchus, some recovered by Petrie in the same season he cleared the town's theater (Petrie 1925, 16–17, pls. xlv.10, xlvi.17) but others extracted after World War II and sold on the art market, often sawn out of their original niches (Severin 1995; Thomas 2000; Schmidt 2003, 149–55; Riggs 2012b). Carved in the soft, nummulitic limestone local to the area, these reliefs refer to sculptural forms in the stance and draping of the figures, many of whom gesture in offering to an altar on their right side. When finished with plaster and paint, the reliefs served the purpose for which they were designed, to no doubt dazzling effect—but contrast them with the full-scale, marble statue of a woman found near its pedestal in the same city's agora, and the difference in quality between these works, and presumably the social status of their subjects, becomes clear.

The prevalence of sculpture as a material and visual medium in the Roman world, including Roman Egypt, is thus attested well beyond the evidence of surviving statues themselves. Statues and the "statuesque" open a window onto works in other media, and in Egypt that applies especially to the sizeable corpus of lamps and terracotta figures attested both from excavated sites and the antiquities trade (Sandri 2012). Terracottas were miniaturized sculptures, made in multiples and therefore more affordable to, and readily acquired by, a wider cross-section of society (see essay 2.5, Erlich). Some resembled common statue types, such as enthroned figures of Sarapis and Isis. These deities were most frequently replicated in terracotta forms, along with Harpocrates and other child gods classed by this name. Other terracottas give a statuesque appearance to human figures like cult devotees, priests, or the pregnant "Baubo." Some terracottas use elevated form and visual language, but others (for instance, grotesque or priapic versions) inject a note of humor or satire into the sculptured world, letting us glimpse a tenor of discourse otherwise inaccessible.

Images reproduced on lamps and the use of lamps themselves provide another example of how statue imagery and devotional practice permeated visual culture and hence social strata. As Stewart (2003, 195–207) has argued, lamps could serve religious functions in several intersecting ways: as devotions themselves; as sources of light placed before a cult figure in a shrine or home altar; and through their iconography. Even more than terracotta figures or coins (another locus for "statuesque" imagery), lamps depict statues that refer to, if they do not actually replicate, cult images such as might be housed in temples. Like coins, the lamps themselves may depict temple façades that frame the statue or part of the statue inside (e.g., Stewart 2003, 201, fig. 33; see essay 6.4, Moormann) in much the same way that cult images were made visible through portable shrines or in the architecture of temples like the Luxor Serapeum and the Ras el-Soda chapel, both of which have a wider central intercolumniation to frame a view into the cella. Scholarship increasingly recognizes that the idea of the replicated "type"—based on a single cult image at a major temple—is a problematic and needlessly restrictive conception of ancient practice. Instead, statues embodied the gods, and a wide range of objects appropriately represented the gods *as* statues in form and function. By speaking the language of statues, such imagery heightened the experience of interaction with the divine, much as statue forms raised the potency and prestige of images incorporated in funerary art. The production and circulation of replicas (in the broadest sense) of divinities and cult participants extended both the time and space of religious encounter, allowing it to reach from the focused action and setting of a temple or festival to the more repetitive and quotidian spheres of domestic life and mortuary commemoration. The world of sculpture was not a world only of marble and metal, but of limestone, wood, and fired clay.

Materials and Material Culture

The stone most closely associated with Roman Egypt is the luxurious porphyry quarried in the eastern deserts, where military encampments at Mons Claudianus and Mons Porphyrites oversaw the logistics of the quarry operations and stone transport (Peacock and Maxfield 2007; Gates-Foster 2012). As an imperial monopoly, porphyry was primarily for export. Scarcely any Roman sculpture in porphyry has been found in Egypt, the primary exception being a spectacular enthroned emperor of the late third or early fourth century AD, which was found in Alexandria in the late nineteenth century and stands some 2.66 m high, even without its head (Alexandria, Graeco-Roman Museum 5954: Kiss 1984, 109; Savvopoulos and Bianchi 2012, 92–3, cat. 25). Other colored stones with long histories in the Egyptian artistic repertoire were used for high-status, even imperial statues in the Roman period, an example of hybrid sculptural practices combining materials and forms. Red granite, quarried at Aswan in the far south of Egypt, is attested for architectural elements as well as portrait and divine sculpture, such as a colossal head of

Caracalla (University of Pennsylvania E976: Graindor 1937, 145–6; Stanwick 2002, 130, no. G14, with further bibliography) and a statue of Harpocrates (or a child commemorated as the god, now in Lyon; Gabolde and Galliano 2000, 104–5, no. 76), both from the important town of Coptos at the Nile end of the Eastern Desert routes.

Large-scale bronze statues complemented the use of stone for public statues, such as the sculptures that topped honorific columns either singly (like "Pompey's pillar" at Alexandria) or in tetrastyle arrangements at the crossroads that defined urban space in Roman-period cities and towns of every size (Bailey 2012). The British Museum's well-known colossal head of Augustus, found buried under temple steps at Meroë in Sudan, was quite likely seized by Meroitic forces from one of the many sites that honored the first emperor in the wake of his annexation of Egypt (British Museum GR 1911.9–1.1: Walker and Higgs 2001, 272–3, no. 323; see essay 6.6, Kristensen). Another finely worked, over-life-size bronze head, said to have been found in or around Coptos, has often been published as an image of Hadrian, an unsupportable attribution. The head is no less interesting, however, for instead of an imperial portrait, it must be an honorific image of another high-status individual, perhaps one of the equestrian prefects who governed Egypt (figure 5.6.4; Alexandria, Graeco-Roman Museum: Graindor

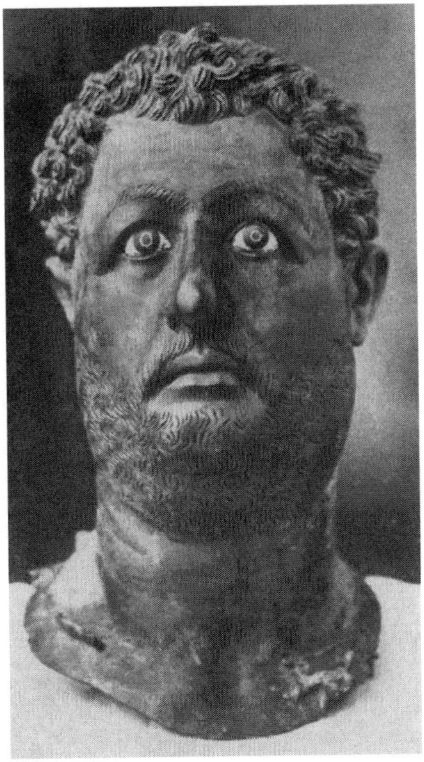

FIGURE 5.6.4 Bronze head with glass inlaid eyes, said to have been discovered at Qena together with fragments of the statue's drapery. Alexandria, Graeco-Roman Museum. H 37.0 cm.

1937, 50–52, pl. x; Empereur 1995, 24–5, fig. 37); fragments of drapery from the same statue are also recorded in the museum's collection. In addition to such spectacular pieces, bronze was the medium for smaller-scale sculpture, which, where it has survived, tends to be catalogued and discussed separately from stone sculpture. Bronze casting had a long history in pharaonic and Hellenistic Egypt, and in the Roman period it continued to serve a range of functions, especially for devotional images and figural lamps. Workshops and sources of raw materials within Egypt would have been capable of producing a range of works, although the possibility that imperial commissions, like the head of Augustus, were imported cannot be ruled out; metallurgical analysis might help clarify this.

Egypt lacked the marble quarries of Italy, Greece, and Turkey, the last two of which supplied material for statues and architectural sculpture in Egypt and the Near East (although there are marble quarries exploited in Egypt today, especially along the Red Sea). In the pharaonic era, a mineralized limestone with a creamy yellow, crystalline structure—variously termed indurated limestone, alabaster, or travertine—was quarried in Middle Egypt and used for high-quality sculpture, but by the Ptolemaic period, the stone was very rare. All the marble sculpture found in Hellenistic and Roman Egypt was thus imported to Egypt, either in a finished state or as blocks; sarcophagi and architectural relief lent themselves to being roughed out at source and finished once they had reached their destination. In publications of sculpture from Egypt, some scholars provide descriptions of the color or quality of the marble and may even hazard a guess as to its provenance. For example, Savvopoulos and Bianchi (2012, 148) suggest that the "greyish-white" color of the marble used for several sculptures discovered in Alexandria in 1973, including the Aphrodite and Eros mentioned above and a reclining Nile, indicates that the stone comes from the Marmara Sea. Such attribution via examination with the naked eye is not accurate, however (see essay 2.1, Pensabene and Gasparini), and any number of quarries around the Mediterranean are potential sources for marble imported to Egypt. Marble sourcing of pieces discovered in Roman Egypt would thus be a fruitful avenue of study, complementing work done on importation of marble in the Levant (see essays 2.1, Pensabene and Gasparini; 2.7, Russell; 5.7, Weber).

Although the bulk of marble statuary has been found in and around Alexandria, marble sculpture has been discovered in the towns and villages of the Delta and the Nile Valley as well, as indicated by the few examples discussed above, as well as others in catalogues like Graindor's and Edgar's. As the country's main port, Alexandria will have been the entry point for much of the marble and easily supported a number of thriving sculptors' workshops. The extent to which other cities and the regional capitals could also sustain specialist marble workshops is uncertain, although a building boom in the second century, with Hadrian's founding of Antinoopolis, provided ample employment. In smaller towns, sculptors may have worked a range of stones, especially the more plentiful Egyptian limestone. Itinerant sculptors are another possibility, perhaps following commissions in coordination with the supply of adequate marble. At present, the size and organization of any artist's workshop in Roman Egypt is poorly understood, but documentary evidence and sources like the price edict issued by Diocletian in AD 301 suggest avenues for research in this area (Cannata 2012).

In addition to its availability and relative ease of carving, one of the appeals of limestone for sculpture may have been its creamy white and yellow hues, which compared favorably with the color of most marble. Plaster too offered a certain similarity to the color of more prestigious marble and was molded into smaller-scale sculptures as well as mummy masks and covers, especially in Middle Egyptian cemeteries such as Tuna el-Gebel (Aubert and Cortopassi 2004; Borg 2012, 620–22). Both limestone and plaster relied on paint and gilding for their effect as well, with a richness that the chemical analysis of the British Museum's Horus statue has demonstrated. In certain contexts and aesthetic frameworks, painted limestone or plaster may have been more desirable than costly marble. The requirements and expectations of the intended audience were key in such artistic transactions, which makes it all the more important for scholarship to work across materials and consider where those materials may have had complementary, or oppositional, functions and values in ancient practice. The polyvalent significance of different materials, from stone to metal to the more humble media of wood and clay, embeds them in a web of cultural meanings related to the visual and material culture of statues.

Conclusion

In this overview of sculpture in Roman Egypt, I have suggested ways in which a range of objects, from marble statues to terracotta lamps, are connected through the form and function of statuary. The objects themselves have often been divided along disciplinary lines (Classics versus Egyptology, archaeology versus art history), whether in catalogues or in museums, and no published corpus yet brings together the imperial and private portrait statues, in any medium, in a way that would aid deeper analysis and allow connections to be made both within material from Egypt and between Egypt and other parts of the Roman Empire. What emerges, however, is a sense of the breadth and depth of the images themselves, in terms of their role in Roman Egyptian society. From the finest (and largest) marble and bronze statues to the replication and circulation of terracottas, sculpture shaped visual experience in Roman Egypt, enabling interaction with the gods and embodying and enacting the changes in social structure that were set in place by Roman reforms. The marble head of an empress and the plaster head of a mummy mask may occupy different museum galleries today and represent very different social strata, but they were part of one society and its multiple engagements with the sculpted image.

Bibliography

Adriani, A. 1933–7. *Sculture del Museo Greco-Romano di Alessandria.* 2 vols. Alexandria: Graeco-Roman Museum.

———. 1940. "Sanctuaire de l'époque romaine à Ras el Soda." *Annuaire du Musée Gréco-Romaine 1935–9*: 136–48.

———. 1961. *Scultura.* 2 vols. Repertorio d'Arte dell'Egitto Greco-Romano A.1–2. Palermo: Banco di Sicilia.

Aubert, M.-F., and R. Cortopassi. 2004. *Portraits funéraires de l'Égypte romaine.* Vol. 1, *Masques en stuc.* Paris: Réunion des Musées Nationaux.

Bagnall, R., and D. Rathbone, eds. 2004. *Egypt: From Alexander to the Early Christians. An Archaeological and Historical Guide.* London: British Museum.

Bailey, D. M. 2012. "Classical Architecture." In Riggs 2012a, 189–204.

Beck, H., P. C. Bol, and M. Bückling, eds. 2005. *Ägypten, Griechenland, Rom: Abwehr und Berührung.* Tübingen: Ernst Wasmuth.

Borg, B. 2012. "Portraits." In Riggs 2012a, 613–29.

Botti, G. 1900. *Catalogue des monuments exposés au Musée Gréco-Romain d'Alexandrie.* Alexandria: Graeco-Roman Museum.

Bowman, A., and D. Rathbone. 1992. "Cities and Administration in Roman Egypt." *JRS* 82: 107–127.

Breccia, E. 1911. *Iscrizioni greche e latine.* Catalogue genéral des antiquités égyptiennes du Musée d'Alexandrie. Cairo: Institut Français d'Archéologie Orientale.

———. 1912. *La necropoli di Sciatbi.* Catalogue genéral des antiquités égyptiennes du Musée d'Alexandrie. Cairo: Institut Français d'Archéologie Orientale.

———. 1924. *Le Musée Gréco-Romaine au cours de l'année 1922–23.* Alexandria: Pompeo.

———. 1932. *Le Musée Gréco-Romaine 1925–31.* Bergamo: Istituto Italiano d'Arti Grafiche.

———. 1933. *Le Musée Gréco-Romaine, II, 1931–1932.* Bergamo: Istituto Italiano d'Arti Grafiche.

Cannata, M. 2012. "Funerary Artists: The Textual Evidence." In Riggs 2012a, 597–612.

Davoli, P. 2012. "The Archaeology of the Fayum." In Riggs 2012a, 152–70.

Dyer, J. 2012. "The Art (and Science) of a Colourful, Cross-Culturally Dressing Statue." *British Museum (blog)*, November 2, 2012. http://blog.britishmuseum.org/2012/11/02/the-art-and-science-of-a-colourful-cross-culturally-dressing-statue/.

Edgar, C. C. 1903. *Greek Sculpture.* Catalogue général du Musée de Caire. Cairo: Institut Français d'Archéologie Orientale.

Empereur, J.-Y. 1995. *A Short Guide to the Graeco-Roman Museum, Alexandria.* Alexandria: Sarapis.

Frankfurter, D. 2008. "The Vitality of Egyptian Images in Late Antiquity: Christian Memory and Response." In *The Sculptural Environment of the Roman Near East: Reflections on Culture, Ideology, and Power*, edited by Y. Z. Eliav, E. A. Friedland, and S. Herbert, 659–78. Leuven: Peeters.

Gabolde, M., and G. Galliano. 2000. *Coptos: L'Égypte antique aux portes du desert (Lyon, Musee des Beaux-Arts, 3 Fevrier–7 Mai 2000).* Paris: Réunion des Musées Nationaux.

Gates-Foster, J. 2012. "The Eastern Desert and the Red Sea Ports." In Riggs 2012a, 736–48.

Golvin, J.-C., S. Abd el-Hamid, G. Wagner, and F. Dunand. 1981. "Le petit Sarapieion romain de Louqsor." *BIFAO* 81: 115–48.

Graindor, P. 1937. *Bustes et statues-portraits d'Égypte romaine.* Cairo: P. Barbey.

Johansen, F. 1994–5. *Roman Portraits.* 3 vols. Copenhagen: Ny Carlsberg Glyptotek.

Kater-Sibbes, G. J. F. 1973. *Preliminary Catalogue of Sarapis Monuments*. Leiden: Brill.

Kiss, Z. 1975. "Notes sur le portrait impérial romain en Égypte." *MDIK* 31: 293–302.

———. 1984. *Études sur le portrait impérial romain en Égypte*. Warsaw: Editions scientifiques de Polognes.

Lembke, K. 1998a. "Dimeh: Römische Repräsentationskunst im Fayyum." *JdI* 113: 109–137.

———. 1998b. "Private Representation in Roman Times: The Statues from Dimeh/Fayum." In *L'egitto in Italia dall'Antichità al Medioevo: Atti del III Congresso Internazionale Italo-Egiziano, Roma, CNR-Pompei, 13–19 Novembre 1995*, edited by N. Bonacasa, M. C. Naro, E. C. Portale, and A. Tullio, 289–95. Rome: Consiglio nazionale delle ricerche.

McKenzie, J., S. Gibson, and A. T. Reyes. 2004. "Reconstructing the Serapeum in Alexandria from the Archaeological Evidence." *JRS* 94: 73–114.

Minas-Nerpel, M. 2012. "Egyptian Temples." In Riggs 2012a, 362–82.

Naerebout, F. G. 2007. "The Temple at Ras el-Soda. Is It an Isis Temple? Is It Greek, Roman, Egyptian, or Neither? And So What?" In *Nile into Tiber: Egypt in the Roman World*, edited by L. Bricault, M. J. Versluys, and P. G. P. Meyboom, 506–554. Leiden: Brill.

Parlasca, K. 1969–80. *Ritratti di mumie*. Vols. 1–3. Repertorio d'arte dell'Egitto greco-romano B.1–3. Rome: Bretschneider.

Parlasca, K., and H. G. Frenz. 2003. *Ritratti di mumie*. Vol. 4. Repertorio d'arte dell'Egitto greco-romano B.4. Rome: Bretschneider.

Peacock, D., and V. Maxfield. 2007. *The Roman Imperial Quarries: Survey and Excavation at Mons Porphyrites 1994–1998*. Vol. 2, *The Excavations*. London: Egypt Exploration Society.

Petrie, W. M. F. 1925. *Tombs of the Courtiers and Oxyrhynchus*. London: British School of Archaeology in Egypt.

Riggs, C. 2006. *The Beautiful Burial in Roman Egypt: Art, Identity, and Funerary Religion*. Oxford: Oxford University Press.

———, ed. 2012a. *The Oxford Handbook of Roman Egypt*. Oxford: Oxford University Press.

———. 2012b. "Portraits, Prestige, and Piety: Images of Women in Roman Egypt." In *A Companion to Women in the Ancient World*, edited by S. L. James and S. Dillon, 423–36. Oxford: Wiley-Blackwell.

Rondot, V. 2013. *Derniers visages des dieux d'Égypte*. Paris: Louvre.

Sandri, S. 2012. "Terracottas." In Riggs 2012a, 630–47.

Savvopoulos, K., and R. S. Bianchi. 2012. *Alexandrian Sculpture in the Graeco-Roman Museum*. Alexandria: Bibliotheca Alexandrina.

Schmidt, S. 2003. *Grabreliefs im Griechisch-Römischen Museum von Alexandria*. Berlin: Achet Verlag.

———. 2005. "Serapis—ein neuer Gott für die Griechen in Ägypten." In Beck, Bol, and Bückling 2005, 291–304.

Severin, H.-G. 1995. "Pseudoprotokoptika." In *Divitiae Aegypti: Koptologische und Verwandte Studien zu Ehren von Martin Krause*, edited by C. Fluck, L. Langener, S. Richter, S. Schaten, and G. Wurst, 289–99. Wiesbaden: Dr. Ludwig Reichert.

Stanwick, P. E. 2002. *Portraits of the Ptolemies: Greek Kings as Egyptian Pharaohs*. Austin: University of Texas Press.

Stewart, P. 2003. *Statues in Roman Society: Representation and Response*. Oxford: Oxford University Press.

Thomas, T. K. 2000. *Late Antique Egyptian Funerary Sculptures*. Princeton: Princeton University Press.

Trimble, J. 2000. "Replicating the Body Politic: The Herculaneum Women Statue Types in Early Imperial Italy." *JRA* 13: 41–68.

Venit, M. S. 2002. *Monumental Tombs of Ancient Alexandria: The Theatre of the Dead.* Cambridge: Cambridge University Press.

Walker, S., and P. Higgs, eds. 2001. *Cleopatra of Egypt: From History to Myth.* London: British Museum Press.

CHAPTER 5.7

NEAR EAST

THOMAS M. WEBER-KARYOTAKIS

INTRODUCTION

THIS essay examines the history of sculpture in the provinces of Syria, Arabia, and Palaestina, comprising the modern states of Syria, Lebanon, Israel, Palestine, Jordan, Saudi Arabia, and Yemen, and—to a limited extent—southeastern Turkey and western Iraq. The most common term for this region in scholarship today is the ancient Near East. Because these areas had a variety of ethnic groups and cultures, whose boundaries shifted repeatedly over time, and yet there are general consistencies in the artistic traditions of these areas, they have been referred to as "Oriental" cultures, still occasionally used in this field as a technical term, though it is ultimately adopted from ancient Greek (i.e., outsider) perspectives on the area.

Recent excavations at Göbelki Tepe (upper Mesopotamia) uncovered stone stelae depicting animals or men dated to the pre-pottery Neolithic (tenth to ninth millennia BC). Later, around 7500 BC, life-size anthropomorphic figures, modeled out of mud over scaffolds of cane, were dumped in dwellings at 'Ain Ghazal, Jordan. It is not yet possible, however, to trace an uninterrupted evolution of sculptural production in the ancient Near East. The sculptures of the Babylonian and Assyrian empires through the Aramaic kingdoms down to the Hellenistic era have been only partially explored. On the other hand, the architecture, sculpture, and decoration of North Syria profoundly influenced and transformed Greek art during the eighth century BC, the period known as orientalizing. The artistic heritage of the eastern civilizations survives as a substratum from prehistory to present days: compositional and stylistic idioms such as hieratic frontality, abstraction, arabesque linearism, and cubic workmanship characterize the region's artistic production throughout the ages. It still existed, more or less apparent, when dominating Graeco-Roman powers arrived with their own visual language with its own parameters of interpretation.

This region is also known for a conflicted attitude toward figural art. The positions ranged from the devoted adoration of idols to strict prohibition of the graven image.

The latter stimulated extremist movements of iconoclasm, not only Jewish, but also Christian and Muslim (see essay 6.6, Kristensen). The discourse pro and contra imagery is a constant in the region's cultural history.

The Macedonian conquest of the Persian empire (331 BC) was not the first occasion upon which peoples of the Near East were confronted with Hellenic imagery. The first Greek statues arrived at the Levantine littoral and the Achaemenid palaces as trophies looted during the Persian Wars. The Phoenician nobility of the fifth century BC commissioned hybrid anthropomorphic sarcophagi, mainly carved out of white Aegean island marble (a rock geologically unavailable in the Levant), with lid portraits in the Greek severe style and Egyptian-style mummy coffins. Later, Phoenician officials in service of their Persian lords preferred mainstream Greek-style works of art such as the so-called Alexander sarcophagus, the Mourning Women sarcophagus, and the Satrap sarcophagus found in the cemeteries of Sidon. The general impact on figural art within the Levantine coastal towns and their Syrian hinterlands was limited, as imported marble was extremely expensive. Little is known about the public and private statuary displayed in the Hellenistic towns of the Syro-Seleucid empire. Only a few Greek masterpieces, such as the Tyche of Antioch by Eutychides and the Apollo of Daphne by Bryaxis come from the Syrian domains.

With the collapse of the Hellenistic kingdoms of the Near East and the rise of Roman supremacy during the first century BC, former court artists and their ateliers sought out local regional sovereigns, the Roman client kings in Syria (Commagene, Emesa, Idumaea), Palaestina (Hashmoneans and Herods), and northwestern Arabia (Nabateans), as well as the Aramaean Sheikhs in the southern Syrian basalt zone (Hauran and Decapolis) and in the Mesopotamian desert (Palmyra). Local sculptural styles developed an amalgam of Hellenistic and Oriental elements enriched by Roman components. The Graeco-Roman pantheon underwent an Oriental interpretation, including the introduction of the imperial cult after the establishment of the Principate (29 BC), an important political tool. The integration of this entire area into the *Imperium Romanum* was concluded by the establishment of the provinces of Syria (64/63 BC), Arabia (AD 105/6), and Palaestina (AD 135).

The material culture of the Near East during the Graeco-Roman period is often discussed in modern scholarship using the terms Hellenization or Romanization, which attempt to describe rather complex processes of cultural integration and also segregation. The acceptance or refusal of figural imagery depended upon a variety of factors beyond the scope of this article. Representations of gods and mortals, however, could be read by local audiences in various ways. It has been widely accepted that old Semitic divinities survived in a sometimes hybrid guise, assimilated with the divine Greek pantheon: Baal, Shamash, or Bel with the shape of Zeus, Allat with Athena, al-'Uzza or Astarte with Aphrodite, and so on. Pre-Islamic Arabs reacted to these representations with some ambivalence and often returned to a figurative syntax strongly influenced by their indigenous stone cults. The sometimes controversial but predominantly harmonious interaction commonly labeled "West versus East" was manifested in religion and tradition, in rhetoric, in politics, and (to some extent) in the monuments themselves.

This essay will survey the evidence for both native sculptural production and the import of statuary in Graeco-Roman styles and materials, noting instances, impetus, and importance of the influence of classical models on local works.

The sculptural material from the Roman Near East, apart from material from Palaestina and the Decapolis as well as local groups of the Palmyrene oasis and the Hauran mountain range, is still largely unexplored. Important surveys by A. Sabeh (1950) and H. Mussche (1957) remained unpublished (see also Will 1965; Balty 2004). One volume of the series *Sculptures from Roman Syria* (Weber and al-Muhammed 2006), an international joint venture run by specialists, organized by the Johannes Gutenberg-University at Mainz, Germany, and funded by the German Research Association (DFG), has been published and two more are in preparation: *Marble Statuary in the Bilad ash-Sham* (cited here as SRS 2) and *Metal Statuary in the Oriental Provinces* (cited here as SRS 3). Moshe Fischer's *Marble Studies* provides an important overview of the marble corpus from Roman Palestine (1998). A catalog of statues in all materials known from Jordan at the time of publication can be found in the author's *Gadara Decapolitana* (Weber 2002). Relevant monuments can today been seen in museums and private collections of the region, and much relevant sculpture is also currently in European and North American collections, such as the Louvre, the Ny Carlsberg Glyptotek, the National Gallery in Oslo, the Museum of Art History in Vienna, the Worcester Art Museum, the Princeton University Art Museum, the Cincinnati Art Museum, the Kelsey Museum of Archaeology, the Harvard Art Museums, and the University of Pennsylvania Museum.

The large-size sculptural monuments, carved in the round, may be divided into three main categories according to their material of fabrication: metal; marble and other imported stones; and indigenous rocks such as basalt, limestone, and, to certain extent, alabaster. There are, of course, other possible criteria to organize a brief overview, such as genres, provenance, or chronological periods of fabrication. The aspect of working materials, however, seems to the present author most appropriate to characterize one of the main phenomena of the region, the co-existence and interplay between imported and indigenous sculptural production. These genres comprise, of course, not only three-dimensional works, but also a large number of architectural reliefs, stelae, sarcophagi, and furniture such as table stands.

Metal Sculptures

The most precious statuary was made from noble metals and copper alloys, the latter commonly called bronze. Metal statues could be enhanced with other materials such as ivory, ebony, glass, and precious or semiprecious stones—not only to increase their value but also for aesthetic reasons of polychromy (see essay 2.6, Abbe). Due to their initial expense and due to recycling by melting, few metal statues survive (see essay 2.4, Mattusch). An inscription from the Arabian provincial capital of Bosra, for instance, reports a temple with a pure silver cult image of the Egyptian-based military god Zeus-Ammon, however, no physical evidence for the piece exists. The corpus of extant pieces or fragments of metal sculptures include, for example: a smaller-than-life-size Apollo from Seriana/Ezriye in the Palmyrenian desert (Gogräfe 2001; SRS 3, fig. 14), a gilded portrait of Empress Julia Domna from Salaminas/Selemiye (in Cambridge, Massachusetts; Skupińska-Løvset 1999, 103–4; SRS 3, fig. 3), a bronze weary Heracles leaning on his club from Seleucia-on-the Tigris (Bernard 1990; SRS 3, fig. 13), an unpublished arm fragment from Larissa-on-the-Orontes/Sheizar (Hama Archaeological Museum; SRS 3, fig. 15), and a composite cuirassed statue of Emperor Hadrian from Tel Shalem near Scythopolis / Beth Shean, Israel (Gergel 1991; SRS 3, fig. 8). The *Periplous Maris Erythraei* (Casson 1989, 28) mentions metal sculptures imported from Roman Egypt to Arabia Felix, and two large-scale bronzes of late third or early fourth century AD Arabian kings from Nakhlat al-Hamra (modern Yemen), created by the Greek artist Phokas and fitted by a local Himyarite metal worker named Lahay amm bear the distinctive artistic impact of the eastern Mediterranean realm (Weidemann 1983). A number of high quality bronzes in Graeco-Roman and Egyptian style from Djebel al-'Awd in Yemen (Fleischer 2012) and Qaryat al-Faw in Saudi Arabia (Al-Ghabban, André-Salvini, and Demargne 2010, 331–6, nos. 151–8) illustrate the rich imports to the Arabian peninsula during the Roman period. Workshops producing metal sculptures and instruments using the *cire perdue* casting technique (see essay 2.4, Mattusch) have been located, for instance, in Decapolitan Gerasa (modern Jerash, Jordan), Berytus (modern Beirut, Lebanon), and at Nabataean Petra (Khalil, Seigne, and Weber 2013; SRS 3).

Tantalizing evidence for a possible colossal gold and ivory statue in the region comes from literary evidence, which describes Herod I's homage to Augustus via the installation of a colossal statue of the emperor in a temple at the newly founded harbor of Caesarea Maritima. According to Josephus, this cult image resembled the famous Pheidian gold-ivory statue of enthroned Zeus at Olympia, considered one of the world wonders of antiquity (*BJ* 1.414). Livia, as Dea Roma, was represented in the manner of the enthroned Hera of Argos by (the older) Polykleitos. A colossal marble foot from Caesarea Maritima dating to the late first century BC may be a remnant of the enthroned emperor from this cult image group (Weber 2008, 253–8, esp. 237, figs. 3–5). The colossal size of these early imperial cult statue fragments led to the conclusion that they were constructed out of separately worked parts in the acrolithic technique, for which shiny white marble was used for flesh. In fact, parts of colossal human figures are preserved in the sanctuaries on Djebel Khalid on the middle Euphrates, at Caesarea Maritima, on the citadel of Amman/Philadelphia, and at Petra.

Imperial Marble Statuary

There were no local marble sources in the Levant (Pensabene 1997), however, so marble had to be imported from quarries in Italy, in Greece and its archipelago islands, or in Asia Minor. This trade had a profound effect upon the material culture of Near Eastern cities. Citizens acquired prefabricated elements for buildings, or, if they could not afford these, they might be able to have competent copies made in local materials. Public and private spaces could be adorned with sculpture, either mass-produced or specially commissioned. Rich individuals bought mythological statues and portraits produced by craftsmen skilled in classical styles, and they could be buried in imported marble sarcophagi. These marble imports stood in stark contrast to the statues produced in local styles and stones, such as the anthropomorphic funerary busts carved in limestone and employed by the Semitic inhabitants of the Hellenized Decapolitan cities, the Palmyrenian oasis, and upper Mesopotamia (Parlasca 1982; Skupińska-Løvset 1983; Parlasca 1985; Weber 2002, 227–31; Romano and Fischer 2009), which display a peculiar resistance to Roman veristic portraiture.

The uniformity and widespread nature of marble culture adopted in the region points to a deeply rooted desire for connection to Roman imperial social and political spheres. It should be noted, however, that this desire was mainly that of the social elites who could afford to finance such expensive objects, and who had the most to gain by aligning themselves with the international overlay of Roman imperial culture (Butcher 2003, 23). Recent archaeometric research to determine the provenances of imported marbles has added much to our understanding of trade routes, the connections of the Roman Near East to other imperial provinces, and patterns of sculptural import and dedication (Fischer 1998; Wielgosz 2008; Fischer 2009; Friedland and Tykot 2010; see essay 2.7, Russell), but the location of quarries is of little help in the longstanding debate about how to distinguish imported marble sculpture from locally fabricated works (Friedland 2012a).

A map showing the findspots of marble sculpture in the Near East (figure 5.7.1) demonstrates the routes used for the distribution of marble. Discernable are four major regions importing marble statuary: (A) The Syro-Phoenician-Levantine coastal line, including the area eastbound onto the rift extending from the Cilician Gates to the western Syrian Alawite mountains to the Lebanese Beqaa down to the valley of river Jordan and the Red Sea; (B) the inland cities east of the rift from Berrhoea/Aleppo in the north, down to Petra and Aila/Aqaba in the south; (C) the Syrian desert area; and (D) the Roman frontier cities along the Euphrates valley and beyond. The captions provide a preliminary statistic, based on the catalog entries in SRS 2 regarding the amount of marble statuary discovered in each area, though it must be noted that these numbers refer to better and more fully preserved items only and neglect very small fragments and pieces; in fact, we cannot always be sure whether individual fragments belong to separate pieces or whether they belong to a single statue, complicating the question of how many statues were present in each area. Nevertheless, the comparative totals presented in table 5.7.1 provide—to an extent—a representative picture and allow some fascinating observations.

Even though such statistical features are diminished by several external factors—as, for instance finds of larger caches (as at Antioch, Byblos, Berytus, Sidon, Caesarea Maritima, Scythopolis / Beth Shean, and Paneas / Caesarea Philippi), state of exploration of a site, destruction by lime burning, and so on—the picture is nonetheless significant: far more than two-thirds of the marbles come from the Mediterranean littoral and its immediate coastal hinterlands. The major part of the remaining third are finds from the interior cities, well connected to the harbors by the ancient road system and natural transport lines such as the Orontes River. About sixty pieces of the entire corpus found their way on tracks into the desert or along the empire's natural boundary following the Euphrates line and beyond.

The motivation to bring Greek masterpieces in the shape of copies to the Near East must be explained by a sociocultural interaction comparable to the modern Western lifestyle in many Middle Eastern cities. Certainly, some Greek and Roman foreigners more or less permanently settled in Syro-Phoenicia, Palaestina, and Arabia. On the other hand, indigenous families of upper social rank, educated in the academies of Greece and Italy, had a number of expatriates in the central Mediterranean. In their Phoenician, Syrian, Palestinian, or Arab households, Greek was for them the lingua franca, beside the quotidian Aramaic. The knowledge or even veneration of Greek religion and myths was fostered in such ambiences. Marble replicas of Greek deities and mythological figures such as Athena, Artemis, Zeus, Heracles, and others referring to famous archetypes of the Pheidian, Polykleitan, Lysippian, and Praxitelian schools were widely distributed in public and private spaces of those communities that proclaimed themselves as *poleis Hellenides*.

Impressive documents of such an environment are marble busts of Greek intellectuals found in various cities of Palaestina (Gersht 1996, 445–6) and the statue of flying

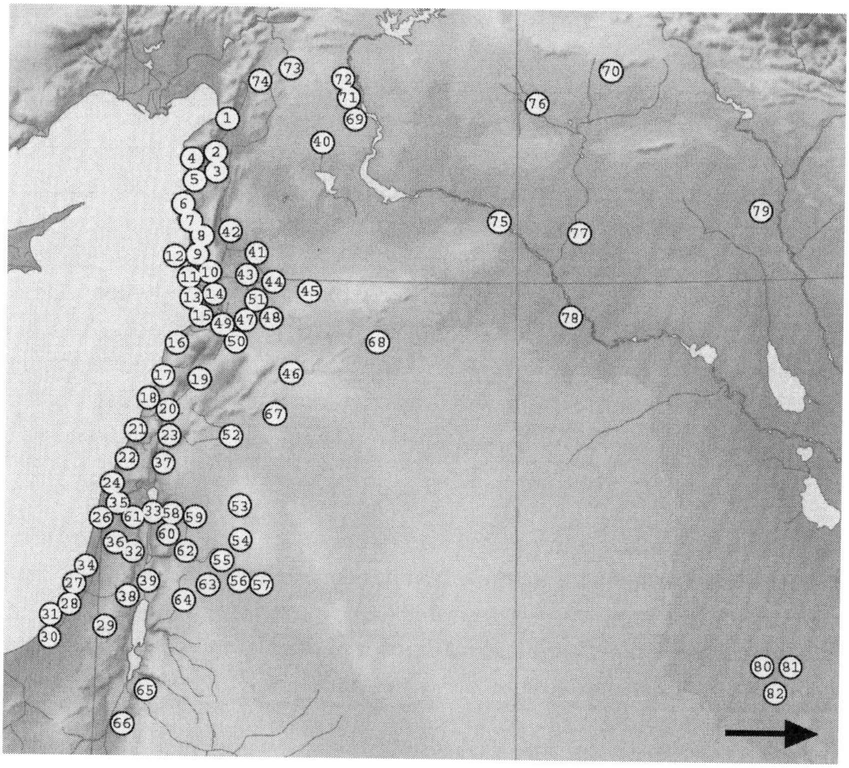

FIGURE 5.7.1 Map locating finds of Graeco-Roman marble sculpture in the Near East.

Table 5.7.1 Key to figure 5.7.1: Distribution of finds of Graeco-Roman marble sculpture.

Map #	Ancient name / modern name	Estimated # of statues
	(A) Syro-Phoenician-Levantine coastal line	
1	Alexandria ad Issum / Iskenderun	2
2	Antiocheia ad Orontem / Antakya	82
3	Daphne / Harbiye	52
4	Seleukeia ad Pieriam / Samadag	22
5	Bytyllion Hometerion / al-Mina	5
6	Laodikeia ad Marem / Ladhakiya	22
7	Gabala / Djebleh	9
8	Balaneia ad Chrysorrhoam / Banyas	5
9	Antarados / Tartus	6
10	Khirbet Lubnah	1
11	Enydra / Tell Ghamkha	1
12	Arados / Arwad	3
13	Marathos / Amrit	6
14	Iammoura / Yakhmour	1
15	'Azar	1
16	Tripolis / Trablus	3
17	Byblos / Jbeil	36
18	Berytus / Beirut	42
19	Heliopolis / Baalbek	49
20	Balmarcodes / Bait Mery	3
21	Sidon / Saida	156
22	Tyros / Sur	13
23	Bait Mare	1
24	Ptolemais / Akkon	4
26	Caesarea Maritima	?
27	Shuni-Maioumas	1
28	Ascalon	8
29	Diokletianopolis	1
30	Gaza	3
31	Anthedon	2
32	Neapolis / Nablus	1
33	Philoteria	1
34	Yavneh	1
35	Sepphoris / Zippori	?

(*Continued*)

Table 5.7.1 Continued

36	Samaria-Sebaste	9
37	Paneas-Caesarea Philippi / Banias	32
38	Aelia Capitolina / Jerusalem	10
39	Jericho / Khirbet al-Mafjar	1
	(B) The inland cities	
40	Batna	1
40bis	Kyrrhos	9
41	Qamkhana	1
42	Apameia ad Orontem / Qala'a Mudiq	24
43	Larissa ad Orontem / Sheiza	1
44	Epiphaneia / Hama	7
45	Salaminas / Selemiye	1
46	Nazala / Qaryateen	1
47	Emesa / Homs	24
48	Qatna	2
49	Tell Biseh	1
50	Laodikeia ad Libanum / Nebi Mend	1
51	Arethusa ad Orontem / Rastan	14
52	Damascus	2
53	Philippopolis / Shahba	4
54	Bosra	13
55	Umm id-Djimal	1
56	Qasr al-Hallabat	2
57	Hamman as-Sarah	5
58	Gadara / Umm Qais	28
59	Abila / Quelbeh	2
60	Pella / Tabaqat Fahil	2
61	Scythopolis / Beth Shean	19
62	Gerasa / Jerash	22
63	Philadelphia / Amman	15
64	Esbus / Husban	3
65	Khirbet ed-Dharih	1
66	Petra	**
	(C) Syrian desert	
67	Khirbet Ramadan	1
68	Palmyra / Tadmor	27
	(D) Euphrates frontier line and beyond	
69	Djebel Khalid	5

(*Continued*)

Table 5.7.1 Continued

70	Nisibis	1
71	Karkemish	1
72	Zeugma	3
73	Doliche	1
74	Islahiye	1
75	Zenobia / Halabiye	2
76	Resaina	1
77	Tell Sheikh Hammad	2
78	Dura Europos / Salhiye	5
79	Hatra	4
80	Susa	2
81	Persepolis	1
82	Tahtr-i-Zohak	1

Daidalos (Hannestad 2001; SRS 2, Phila-6) found at one of the slopes of the Amman citadel (figure 5.7.2). It represents the entirely Greek myth of the escape of this early hero of Greek art with his son Icaros from the dungeon on Crete, where king Minos kept him. Apart from requiring of the viewer a detailed knowledge of the myth, the figure and its mounting on a high façade above a pool of water provided a special challenge for the artist. Daidalos was certainly shown in the moment when his son, approaching the sun, dramatically crashed down into the sea. Modern art historians claim this extraordinary sculptural group originates in a late Roman atelier at Aphrodisias in Asia Minor. It is likely that a wealthy Decapolitan art connoisseur with a Greek intellectual background commissioned this group for the embellishment of his Arab hometown.

This part of the empire seems to have developed a certain antipathy toward naturalistic portraiture in the Graeco-Roman sense (for portraiture in Syria, see Skupińska-Løvset 1999; 2003). Only a few portraits of Hellenistic rulers are known today. Though nothing secure is known about the appearance of the Herodian and Nabataean client kings, as no heads of their portraits survive in the marble bodies associated with them, it seems that the kings adapted Hellenistic prototypes, for instance, using the attribute of the Macedonian shell armor when military appearance was required (Kropp 2013). Compared with the neighboring provinces such as Asia Minor, Egypt, Creta et Cyrenaica, and Africa Proconsularis, the Roman Near East proves to be astonishingly poor in both official and private portraits. While the western Anatolian and North African realm produced hundreds of standard draped portrait figures in the *togati* type, along the Levantine coast and its hinterlands hardly more than a dozen of these popular portrait statues can be identified (e.g., Gadara / Umm Qais: Weber 2002, 408–9; Gerash: Weber 2002, 490–91; Palmyra: Colledge 1976, 91–2; SRS 2, Sid-114, Gada 19, Gera 17–20, Palmy 17–19). The same scarcity can be observed in the case of official Roman portraiture: a torso of a cuirassed statue from Samaria-Sebaste

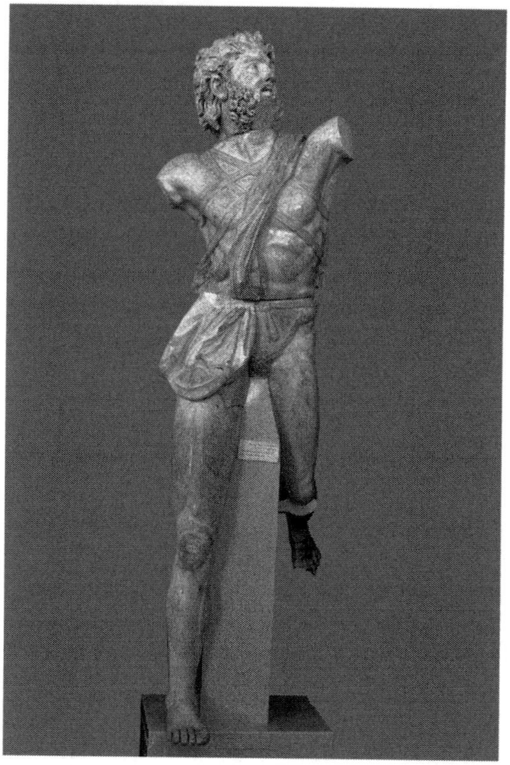

FIGURE 5.7.2 Marble statue of flying Daidalos found at the southeastern slope of the Philadelphia citadel. Amman, Jordan Archaeological Museum, inv. no. J.933.

may be an Augustus or Agrippa (Weber 2008, 261–2, figs. 8–11); another headless statue of the same type from the theater at Philadelphia / Amman (Friedland and Tykot 2010, 178–9; SRS 2, Phila 9) must have represented Hadrian for typological reasons (type Agora S166); only two preserved Julio-Claudian marble portraits found at Berytus, probably the representation of Germanicus (figure 5.7.3; Skupińska-Løvset 1999, 47) and a fragmented head of Musa, mother and wife of the Parthian King Phraates V, from Bytyllion Hometerion/al-Mina (SRS 2, Byty-1) are known today, and epigraphic evidence (e.g., Palmyra) does not point to the existence of many more. Not a single portrait of the Flavian emperors survives, nor one of the founder of the Arabian province, Trajan. It was first Hadrian (Skupińska-Løvset 1999, 61–3; SRS 2, Anti 50b, Seleu 12, Bery 30–31), followed by his successors of the second and third centuries AD (Antoninus Pius: Skupińska-Løvset 1999, 64–5; SRS 2, Laod 16; Marcus Aurelius: Albertson 1988; Skupińska-Løvset 1999, 68–70; Albertson 2004; Lucius Verus: Skupińska-Løvset 1999, 70–72; SRS 2, Antar 4; Aelius Caesar or Lucius Verus: Kreikenbom and Weber 2002; Fittschen 2011; Septimius Severus: Skupińska-Løvset 1999, 106–7; Commodus: SRS 2, Bery 33; Philippus Arabs: Skupińska-Løvset 1999, 108–111; SRS 2, Phili-1), who left official Roman portraiture in the region. An outstanding piece of this category is the splendid marble bust of Antinous from Syrian Balaneai Claudia Leucas/Banias (private collection; Friedland 2012b, 159–60, fig. 95; SRS 2, Bala-5). This imperial

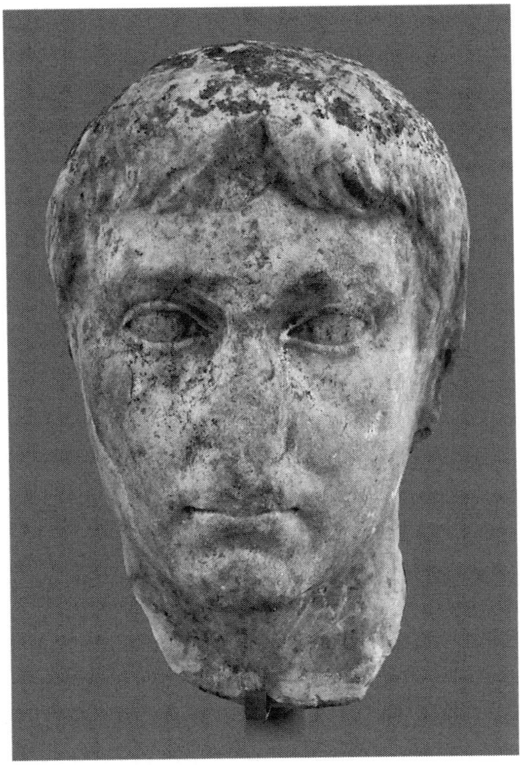

FIGURE 5.7.3 Marble portrait of a Julio-Claudian prince, probably Germanicus, from Berytus, acquired from Iskandar Farrah. H 31.5 cm. Beirut, American University of Beirut, Museum, inv. no. 32.33. Courtesy of Dr. L. Bader, Beirut.

portrait of Hadrian's favorite is outstanding not only in respect to its high quality but also because of its unique Greek inscription, the only one associated with a sculpted portrait that specifically names Antinous.

What was the impact of these western Graeco-Roman imports on the Near Eastern production of sculpture? It has variously been observed that some imports, above all portrait statues, arrived in a semi-finished condition. Research of the recent decades tried further to classify the specifics of an Oriental or "Eastern" style within the classical schools in order to understand the differences between imported and locally fabricated pieces (Friedland 2012a). Such knowledge is essential to comprehend the transfer of images from the central Mediterranean and their reconfiguration in Near Eastern environments.

An instructive example to illustrate the process of adaptation of Greek models by local artists is a marble figurine depicting a flying Nike/Victory in Vienna (SRS 2, Laod-11) from Ladhakiya, ancient Laodikeia ad Mare on the northwestern Syrian coast (figure 5.7.4). Missing are the head, the arms, and both lower legs. The goddess is clad in a sleeveless, overfolded Doric *peplos*, held together on both shoulders by *fibulae* and girded underneath the breasts. The fabric splits over the thigh and displays the naked skin of the forward right leg. A headwind makes the drapery cling tightly

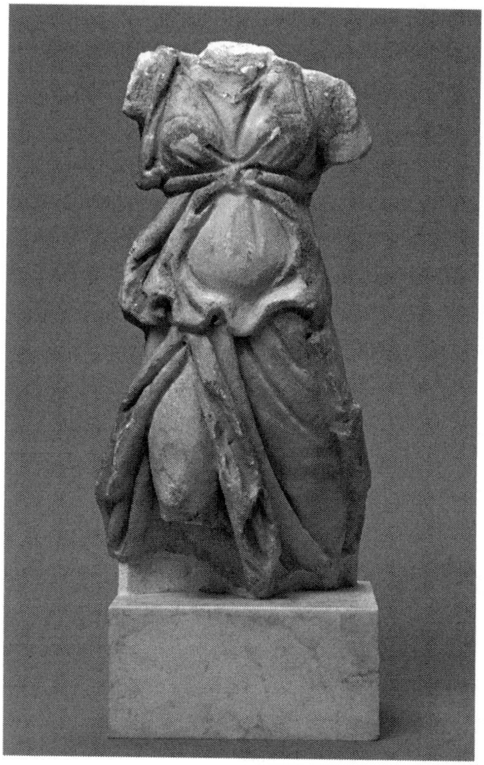

FIGURE 5.7.4 Marble figurine of a gliding Nike/Victory from Ladhakiya, Syrian Laodikeia ad Mare. Second to third centuries AD. Height: 48 cm. Vienna, Kunsthistorisches Museum, inv. no. I 648 (formerly collection of Georg Ritter Millosicz).

to the abdomen, with small waves around the edges, while the lateral folds whip backward in sickle-shapes. The scale of the preserved torso suggests an original size for the entire figure of about one meter. The reconstruction depicts the youthful goddess with a parted coiffure, gathering the hair into a bun in the nape of the neck, in the motion of gliding from a high position, suggesting a view from below for the spectator. The missing right arm must have been raised once holding a wreath, while the lowered left hand presumably grasped a palm leaf or a cornucopia. The restored figure depicted the goddess of Victory in an elevated position, flying and crowning a god or a mortal.

The iconography goes back to a famous late classical archetype, the Nike by Paionios, displayed on a high pillar of triangular cross-section as a triumphal monument in the Panhellenic sanctuary at Olympia. Already in early Hellenistic times this statue type had arrived at the Levantine coast where it served as acroteria of architectural pediments at sites as Enhydra/Tall Ghamqa (north of modern Tartus, Syria; SRS 2, Enyd-1) or Doris / Dor (in modern Israel). The distinct Syrian element of the Laodikeia example, however, manifests in its somewhat geometric and inorganic style of the drapery that resembles woodcarving, making the abdominal area into an oval, convex field framed by a swelling hem and long curved lateral folds along the lower body. The example from Laodikeia

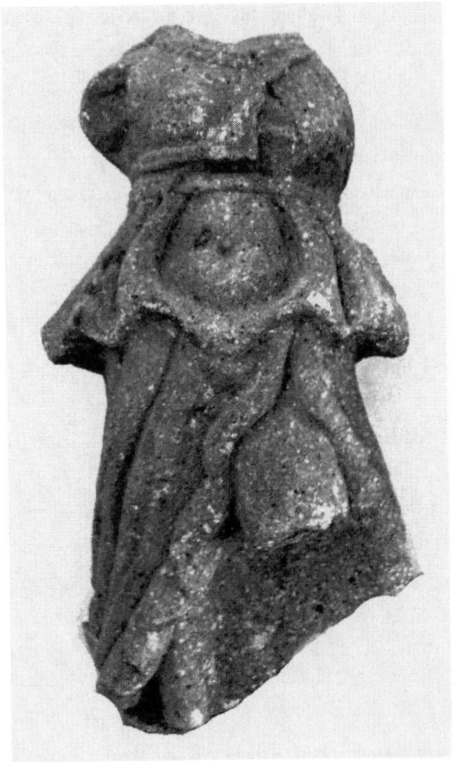

FIGURE 5.7.5 Basalt statue of a gliding Nike/Victory from Philippopolis. Second to third centuries AD. H 68 cm. Shahba, Museum, no inv. no. Courtesy of the Département des Antiquités et des Musées de la Syrie.

may have been a training piece of a local sculptor in a Levantine atelier working with imported marble. This iconographic type has been translated by many other indigenous artists into the traditional rocks of their homelands: basalt, limestone, and sandstone. Countless Victories carved out of the dark blue volcanic basalt (figure 5.7.5) populate the sculptural landscape, especially of the southern Syrian realm where the material originates. There are convincing reasons to assume that these Victories, placed on columns or pillars, accompanied sculptural groups of gods, local heroes, personifications, or mortal rulers in order to emphasize their triumphal attitudes (Weber 2009, 19–21, figs 10–12; 60–64, figs 91–103; 72, fig. 120).

Sculpture in Local Stone

Typical Near Eastern rocks are basalt and limestone, the latter especially in the eastern periphery in crystalline variants that are close to marble or alabaster. Those areas poorly supplied with Mediterranean marble imports manufactured freestanding and architectural sculpture in local materials. The regions fostering the most distinctive genres of local sculpture in the Roman Near East were the inland cities comprising the southern Syrian volcanic zone, the desert oasis of Palmyra, and the eastern frontier girdle along the Euphrates valley (Parlasca 1982). In the south, Nabataean sculpture carved predominantly in sandstone incorporates a conglomerate of Graeco-Roman, Alexandrian, Parthian, and Arabian influences (Wenning 2014). The present overview must confine itself to two distinctive Syrian art centers using such local rocks: the Hauran and the oasis of Palmyra.

Basalt Sculpture of the Hauran

The southern Syrian basalt zone encompassed the subregions of the mountainous Hauranitis (modern Djebel al-Arab), the remote Trachonitis (modern Ledja), and the fertile Batanea plain (modern Nuqra) to the Gaulanitis (Golan Heights). In these areas flying Victories served not only as acroteria or central figures for pediments, but also were frequently placed as three-dimensional sculptures at the four corners of square podia, where they were erected on pillars to flank groups of divine chariots or horse parades of local dynasts of the late first century AD (Weber 2009). Even though mixed with Near Eastern elements, these sculptures follow distinctly Graeco-Roman models.

In contrast, some of the basalt sculptures of southern Syria lack such obvious connections to the Graeco-Roman world (Bolelli 1986). Various busts and reliefs, today preserved in the museums at Suweida, Damascus, and Princeton University, as well as at the Louvre, come from the sanctuary of Baal Shamin at Seeia/Si', well dated by the dedicatory inscriptions to the period between 32–31 and 1 BC. For example, the base of an honorific statue for a local notable named Galis, adorned with garlands between corner lion heads, was erected in the years AD 29–30 (Weber and al-Muhammed 2006, 110, fig. 40; Weber 2009, 27–8, figs. 27–32). From the 80s AD comes an altar with the mask of Heracles, dedicated by Lucius Obulinus, an officer serving in the Herodian army of Agrippa I. A last chronological fixed point is gained by the basalt tombstone of Obbē, daughter of Sachamelos, buried in AD 143 (Weber 2010).

The most significant monuments come from the older part of the Si' sanctuary (Weber and al-Muhammed 2006, 109–114, cat. nos. 91–6, pls. 72–4). The figural depictions of men, to be identified with the local founders of the shrine, encapsulate recurrent elements of early Hauranite basalt sculpture that follow older local traditions. These sculptures are composed of compact elements and even though they display fluently modeled transitions, the style may best be described as additive, with each facial view, lateral as well as frontal, having its own sculptural values (Wenning 2001). A century later, in the Flavian-Trajanic period, the sculptures from Sahr al-Ledja develop a style still dominated by additive compositional structures, but executed in a precise elegance that recalls metalwork, similar to the Heracles mask of the Lucius Obulinus *ara* of AD 80–90 (Weber 2009, 69–70, figs. 114–18). As the tomb stone of Obbē testifies, this stylistic treatment of the black volcanic rock continues well into the first half of the second century AD with a tendency toward hybridization of single elements such as the rendering of drapery or the alignment of the eyes. Unfortunately, without additional fixed chronological points, the further stylistic development of Syrian basalt sculpture resists analysis.

Limestone Sculpture of Palmyra

Though our knowledge of the southern Syrian sculpture wanes around the mid-second century AD, the limestone art of the central Syrian desert fills this lacuna. The heyday of this Syrian substyle climaxed in the reign of Odeinathus and Zenobia in the third quarter of the third century AD, when Palmyra, the caravan station in the most important oasis of the central Syrian desert, reached the summit of political power—dangerous at that time to the Roman predominance in the area. In contrast to the sculpture from the Hauran, quite a large number of Palmyrene funerary busts and votive reliefs can be precisely dated by their Semitic inscriptions (Ploug 1995, 35–66, nos. 1–9; Sardurska 1972, 57–60, nos. 59–61, pls. 46, 3–4, 48; Parlasca 1985, 355, with note 75, pl. 152; Tanabe 1986, 148, no. 115). Sculptures in the round seem to have rarely been erected in the oasis, but some examples from northern Syria related to the Palmyrene style show the enthroned deceased, such as the statue of Barsemias, dated to January 11, AD 123 (Baratte 1991, 22–7, figs. 5–12) or Paulina of AD 157 (Skupińska-Løvset 2003, 592–4, fig. 7a–b). Despite the careful representation of embroidered clothing and jewelry, few of these portraits show individualizing physiognomic details, but instead use standardized formulae such as the snail-shell-shaped curls of male coiffures.

At Palmyra, a similar winged Victory to those from the Hauran appears in limestone at various public and funerary monuments, such as the temples of Bel and Baalshamin (Tanabe 1986, nos. 65–6, 74–9, pls. 105–6, 113–18). The critical location of this oasis on a trade route made it an interface of cultural exchange between the Graeco-Roman realm of the Mediterranean and the Parthian world of Mesopotamia.

Conclusion

The sculpture of the Roman Near East, in all its variety, bears much further investigation. Avenues for new research abound, first and foremost in the documentation and initial publication of hitherto unstudied or unpublished material (e.g., SRS 2; SRS 3). In addition, studies of origins and implications of imported materials are only a recent phenomenon. Close analyses of hybrid iconography and style are proving fruitful in better understanding of the cultural, social, and religious realms of the Roman Near East (e.g., Kropp 2011). Others are exploring the role of statuary in negotiating identity under Roman rule (e.g., Heyn 2010; Friedland 2012b). In short, the sculptural environment of the Roman Near East has much to contribute to our continued understanding of Roman provincial life.

Abbreviations

SRS 2: Koçak, M., D. Kreikenbom, K.-U. Mahler, and T. M. Weber, eds. In progress. *Marble Statuary in the Bilad ash-Sham*. Sculptures from Roman Syria 2. Worms: Wernersche Verlagsgesellschaft.

SRS 3: Seigne, J., and T. M. Weber. In progress. *Metal Statuary in the Oriental Provinces: Remnants of Sculptural Works and Casting Atelier Installations*. Sculptures from Roman Syria 3. Worms: Wernersche Verlagsgesellschaft.

Bibliography

Albertson, F. C. 1988. "A Portrait of Marcus Aurelius from Syro-Palestine." *DM* 3: 1–9.

Albertson, F. C. 2004. "The Creation and Dissemination of Roman Imperial Portrait Types: The Case of Marcus Aurelius Type IV." *JdI* 119: 259–306.

Al-Ghabban, A. I., B. André-Salvini, and F. Demargne. 2010. *Routes d'Arabie: Archéologie et Histoire du Royaume d'Arabie Saoudite*. Paris: Louvre.

Balty, J.-C. 2004. "La sculpture en Syrie, en Pannonie, dans le Norique et en Afrique du Nord." In *Lokale Identitäten in den Randgebieten des Römischen Reiches: Akten des internationalen Symposiums in Wiener Neustadt, 24.–26. April 2003*, edited by A. Schmidt-Colinet, 11–35. Vienna: Phoibos.

Baratte, F. 1991. "Villes et campagnes dans l'Orient romain: Sculptures funéraires au Louvre." *RLouvre* 41(5–6): 22–8.

Bernard, P. 1990. "Vicissitudes au gré de l'histoire d'une statue en bronze d'Heracles entre Seleucie du Tigre et la Mesene." *JSav* (1990): 3–68.

Bolelli, G. 1986. "La ronde-bosse de caractère indigène." *Hauran* 1.2, edited by J.-M. Dentzer, 311–72. Bibliothèque Archéologique et Historique 124. Paris: Paul Geuthner.

Butcher, K. 2003. *Roman Syria and the Near East*. Los Angeles: J. Paul Getty Publications.

Casson, L., trans. 1989. *The Periplus maris Erythraei*. Princeton: Princeton University Press.

Colledge, M. A. R. 1976. *The Art of Palmyra*. London: Thames and Hudson.

Fischer, M. L. 1998. *Marble Studies: Roman Palestine and the Marble Trade*. Konstanz: Universitätsverlag Konstanz.

———. 2009. "Sculpture in Roman Palestine: Import and Local Production, an Overview," In Gaggadis-Robin et al. 2009, 401–415.

Fittschen, K. 2011. "Lesefrüchte III." *Boreas* 34: 165–84.

Fleischer, R. 2012. *Figurale Bronzen ägyptischer und griechisch-römischer Art vom Jabal al-'Awd, Jemen*. Archäologische Berichte aus dem Yemen 13. Wiesbaden: Reichert.

Friedland, E. A. 2012a. "Marble sculpture in the Roman Near East: Remarks on Import, Production, and Impact." In *Ateliers and Artisans in Roman Art and Archaeology*, edited by T. M. Kristensen and B. Poulson, 55–73. JRA Supplement 92. Portsmouth, RI: Journal of Roman Archaeology.

———. 2012b. *The Roman Marble Sculptures from the Sanctuary of Pan at Caesarea Philippi/Panias (Israel)*. Archaeological Report Series 17. Boston: American Schools of Oriental Research.

Friedland, E. A., and R. H. Tykot. 2010. "The Quarry Origins of Nine Roman Marble Sculptures from Amman/Philadelphia and Gadara/Umm Qays," *Annual of the Department of Antiquities of Jordan* 54: 177–88.

Gaggadis-Robin, V., A. Hermary, M. Reddé, and C. Sintes, eds. 2009. *Les ateliers de sculpture régionaux: Techniques, styles et iconographie*. Aix-en-Provence: Centre Camille Jullian; Arles: Musée départemental d'Arles antique.

Gergel, R. A. 1991. "The Tel Shalem Hadrian Reconsidered." *AJA* 95(2): 231–51.

Gersht, R. 1996. "Roman Copies Discovered in the Land of Israel." In *Classical Studies in Honor of David Sohlberg*, edited by R. Katzoff, 433–50. Ramat-Gan: Bar-Ilan University.

Gogräfe, R. 2001. "Der Apollon von Seriana-Isriye: Datierung und Funktion." In *Antike Bronzen: Werkstattkreise und Geräte*, edited by R. Thomas, 57–70. Berlin: Mann.

Hannestad, N. 2001. "The Marble Group of Daidalos: Hellenism in Late Antique Amman." *Studies in the History and Archaeology of Jordan* 7: 13–519.

Heyn, M. K. 2010. "Gesture and Identity in the Funerary Art of Palmyra." *AJA* 114(4): 631–61.

Khalil, L. A., J. Seigne, and T. M Weber, eds. 2013. *Metal Casting in Roman Gerasa: Preliminary Reports on the Jordanian-European Conservation Program at Jerash in 2012*. Amman: DAAD and L'Institut Français du Proche-Orient.

Kreikenbom, D., and T. M. Weber. 2002. "Un nouveau portrait d'Aelius Caesar à Pétra." *Syria* 79: 195–206.

Kropp, A. 2011. "Anatomy of a Phoenician Goddess: The Tyche of Berytus and Her Acolytes." *JRA* 24(1): 389–407.

———. 2013. "Kings in Cuirass: Some Overlooked Full-Length Portraits of Herodian and Nabataean Dynasts." *Levant* 45: 45–56.

Mussche, H. F. 1957. "De greco-romeinse plastiek in westelik Syrie en Libanon van Alexander te Grote tot Keizer Konstantijn." PhD diss., Ghent University.

Parlasca, K. 1982. *Syrische Grabreliefs hellenistischer und römischer Zeit: Fundgruppen und Probleme*. Mainz: Philipp von Zabern.

———. 1985. "Das Verhältnis der palmyrenischen Grabplastik zur römischen Porträtkunst." *RM* 92: 343–56.

Pensabene, P. 1997. "Marmi d'importazione, pietre locali e committenza nella decorazione architettonica di eta severiana in alcuni centri delle province Syria et Palestina e Arabia." *ArchCl* 49: 275–422.

Ploug, G. 1995. *Catalogue of the Palmyrene Sculptures, Ny Carlsberg Glyptotek*. Copenhagen: Ny Carlsberg Glyptotek.

Romano, I. B., and M. L. Fischer. 2009. "Roman Marble and Limestone Sculpture from Beth Shean, Israel." In Gaggadis-Robin et al. 2009, 391–400.

Sabeh, A. 1950. "La Sculpture ancienne du Haurân et du Gebel ed-Druz." PhD diss., Yale University.

Sardurska, A. 1972. *Les Portraits Romains dans les Collections Polonaises*. CSIR Pologne 1. Warsaw: Editions scientifiques de Pologne.

Skupińska-Løvset, I. 1983. *Funerary Portraiture of Roman Palestine: An Analysis of Production in its Culture-Historical Context*. Studies in Mediterranean Archaeology 21. Gøthenborg: Paul Åstrøm.

———. 1999. *Portraiture in Roman Syria: A Study in Social and Regional Differentiation within the Art of Portraiture*. Łódź: Wydawn Uniwersytetu Łódzkiego.

———. 2003. "Private Portraits of Roman Syria and Palestine: Summing up Twenty Years of Study" In *Romanisation und Resistenz in Plastik, Architektur und Inschriften der Provinzen des Imperium Romanum*, edited by P. Noelke, F. Naumann-Steckner, and B. Schneider, 587–99. Mainz: Philipp von Zabern.

Tanabe, K. 1986. *Sculptures of Palmyra*. Memoirs of the Ancient Orient Museum 1. Tokyo: Ancient Orient Museum.

Weber, T. M. 2002. *Gadara—Umm Qēs: Ausgrabungen des Deutschen Evangelischen Instituts für Altertumswissenschaft des Heiligen Landes und des Deutschen Archäologischen Instituts*. Vol. 1, *Gadara Decapolitana: Untersuchungen zur Topographie, Geschichte, Architektur und der Bildenden Kunst einer "Polis Hellenis" im Ostjordanland*. Abhandlungen des Deutschen Palästina-Vereins 30. Wiesbaden: Harrassowitz.

———. 2008. "Der beste Freund des Kaisers: Herodes der Große und statuarische Repräsentationsformen in orientalischen Heiligtümern der frühen Kaiserzeit." *Augustus, Der Blick von außen: Die Wahrnehmung des Kaisers in den Provinzen des Reiches und in den Nachbarsaaten*, edited by D. Kreikenbom, K.-U. Mahler, et al., 249–69. Wiesbaden: Harrassowitz.

———. 2009. *Die Skulpturen aus Sahr und die Statuendenkmäler der römischen Kaiserzeit in südsyrischen Heiligtümern. Sahr al-Ledja: Recherches Syro-Européennes 1998–2008*, vol. 2, edited by J.-M. Dentzer and T. M. Weber. Hauran 4.2. Bibliothèque Archéologique et Historique 184. Beirut: Institut Français du Proche-Orient.

———. 2010. "Die Basaltplastik des Hauran: Ein Forschungüberblick." In *La Syrie du Sud du Néolithique à l'antiquité tardive, recherches récentes*, edited by M. Al-Maqdissi and J. Dentzer-Feydy, 1: 425–33. Hauran 5. Bibliothèque Archéologique et Historique 191. Beirut: Institut Français du Proche-Orient.

Weber, T. M., and Q. al-Muhammed. 2006. *Sculptures from Roman Syria in the Syrian National Museum at Damascus from Cities and Villages in central and southern Syria*. Sculptures from Roman Syria 1. Worms: Wernersche.

Weidemann, K. 1983. *Könige aus dem Yemen: Zwei spätantike Bronzestatuen*. Mainz: Römisch-Germanisches Zentralmuseum.

Wenning, R. 2001. "Hauranite Sculpture." In *Roman Sculpture in the Art Museum, Princeton University*, edited by J. M. Padgett, 312–47. Princeton: Princeton University Press.

———. 2014. "The Sculptures of Petra." In *With Trowel and Hightech: German Archaeological Projects in Jordan*, edited by F. Kenkel and D. Vieweger, 43. Wuppertal: Wiechern.

Wielgosz, D. 2008. "Marbles Sculptures from the Archaeological Museum of Bosra." *Marmora* 4: 57–64.

Will, E. 1965. "La Syrie romaine entre l'Occident gréco-romain et l'Orient parthe." In *Le rayonnement des civilisations grecques et romaines sur les cultures péripheriques*, 511–26. Paris: Paul Geuthner.

PART VI

VIEWING AND RECEPTION

CHAPTER 6.1

AESTHETICS AND LATIN LITERARY RECEPTION

MICHAEL SQUIRE

Introduction

FIGURE 6.1.1 envisions one "aesthetics" of Roman sculpture (see color insert). Sir Lawrence Alma-Tadema's 1867 painting brings together some of the most famous classical statues, displaying them in a make-believe Roman home (Swanson 1990, 144, no. 89): a bronze portrait of Sophocles stares out at us from the foreground (modeled after a marble sculpture in Rome's Museo Laterano), with other sculptures clustered close behind (a sarcophagus from the Musei Capitolini, the Laocoön, the Vatican Penelope, the Capitoline Helena, and a seated Poseidippos). To the left of the bronze Sophocles, a bearded elder—with the portrait features of Alma-Tadema himself—points to what he deems most admirable in the image (his outstretched hand playfully intersecting with Laocoön's own entangled arms), while a young servant obligingly rotates the statue on its pedestal. The rest of the assembled audience gazes on in awed silence.

Whatever else we make of Roman "museum analogs" (see essay 6.3, Shaya), Alma-Tadema's makeshift gallery strikes me as decidedly more modern than ancient in inspiration. For all its historical trappings (inspired by Pompeian interiors in particular), *A Dealer in Statues* imposes back onto antiquity much later ideas about sculpture and its proper artistic appreciation (Tanner 2006, 1–3; Squire 2010, 133–6): just as the painting transforms ancient Romans into Victorian museum-goers, so too it decks out modern-day audiences in togate fancy dress. Everything here smacks of willful anachronism—even the colorful floor resembles the familiar trappings of a Victorian home, more like a woven carpet than a Roman mosaic. Pictured within the painting is a resoundingly modern view not only of Roman sculpture, but also of its artistic appreciation.

Perhaps most anachronistic of all is the assumption that statues called for this sort of intent, silent contemplation in the first place. From a historical perspective, such ideas have more to do with Victorian traditions of "art for art's sake" (Prettejohn 2007) than with Roman critical frameworks. Something similar might be said for the "aesthetics" of my essay-title. Despite its ancient etymology (from the Greek verb *aisthanesthai*, "to perceive"), the term "aesthetics" is relatively recent, coined by Alexander Gottlieb Baumgarten in the 1750s; as the counterpart to philosophies of logic and reason, aesthetics refers to the philosophical study of the senses—and, by extension, to critical reflections about beauty, taste, and artistic appreciation. The difficulty, however, is that ancient Graeco-Roman writers knew of no such equivalent, self-standing category through which to theorize what we call "the arts," still less sculpture specifically. By projecting his own aesthetic framework back onto antiquity, Alma-Tadema arguably aligns Roman ideas about sculpture with his own contemporary critical assumptions about the modern artwork at hand: as viewers of the painting, we too are invited to look on and wonder—to contemplate both the sculpted bronze portrait (specially turned around for us to see) and the painted figures in turn contemplating it.

Alma-Tadema's picture therefore illustrates a dilemma at the heart of any handbook on Roman sculpture: to what extent did Roman statues function like "art" as we understand it today? Much has been written about this question (Stewart 2003, 224–31; Tanner 2006, 1–30; Platt and Squire 2010). Positions range from those emphasizing a radical difference between ancient and modern traditions (especially traditions that arose in the eighteenth-century Enlightenment: Kristeller 1990, 163–227; Shiner 2001; 2009), to those proposing a more continuous or essential tradition (Porter 2009; 2010, 405–450): on one side are those who stress the conceptual gap between our languages of art and ancient critical terminologies (Kristeller 1990, 170–71; Shiner 2001, 22–4); on the other, those who cite ancient parallels for the sorts of critical reflections enshrined in Alma-Tadema's painting—Pliny the Elder's throwaway comment, for example, that artistic "appreciation [*admiratio*] requires leisure and deep silence in our surroundings" (*HN* 36.27; Neudecker 1998, 77–8; Carey 2000, 4).

Rather than rehearse scholarly debates about art in Graeco-Roman antiquity, this essay surveys some of the historical ways in which sculpture came to be conceptualized in the Roman world. How did Roman viewers go about making sense of sculpture and its display? What sorts of social, cultural, and intellectual frameworks governed their evaluation of sculptural subjects and styles? And in what ways were these ideas both like and unlike our own at the beginning of the twenty-first century (or indeed Alma-Tadema's toward the end of the nineteenth)? In line with this section's interest in viewing and reception, the essay will address these issues from the perspective of sculptural consumption rather than production. Where others in this volume have advanced some tentative conclusions from a materialist standpoint, my particular remit here will be with literary sources: what can Greek and Latin writers themselves tell us about the evaluative frameworks in which sculpture was theorized in the Roman world?

What is arguably most striking about Roman writings on statuary is their sheer diversity of analytical responses (at least as multifarious as our own ideas about art today). To demonstrate that diversity, this essay concentrates on three interconnecting evaluative modes, each one structured around a particular Latin author. We begin with the selection of appropriate sculptural subjects for particular spaces—the idea, encapsulated in a number of Cicero's letters, that statues should define, and in turn be defined by, their contexts of display. I then turn to Pliny the Elder's reflections on sculpture amid the final books of his *Natural History*, written in the 70s AD: Pliny's emphasis on history and agency enshrines a rather different evaluative framework for conceptualizing sculpture, emphasizing the place of a given work within a larger history of both media and makers. This leads, in the final section, to Roman rhetorical traditions of criticism, and to Quintilian's *Education of an Orator* in particular. Quintilian compares the expressive qualities of sculpture with those of both painting and verbal language; in doing so, Quintilian shows how different sculptural styles could be associated with different abstract values.

Appropriating What is Appropriate: Cicero's *Letters*

I begin with a series of letters penned by Cicero and addressed to T. Pomponius Atticus in the early 60s BC (the most pertinent passages come in the first book: *Att.* 1.1.5, 1.3.2, 1.4.3, 1.5.7, 1.6.2, 1.7, 1.8.2, 1.9.2, 1.10.3–4, 1.11.3; for the extracted texts and an English translation, see Marvin 1993, 180–83). The passages have attracted a substantial bibliography (e.g., Carcopino 1951, 1.70–75; Desmouliez 1976, 266–316; Neudecker 1988, 8–18; Bounia 2004, 290–306; Bravi 2012, 21–7; Rutledge 2012, 59–64). For our purposes, however, the letters demonstrate how an aristocratic Roman public figure like Cicero went about choosing, evaluating, and critiquing sculpture in the first century BC.

The recurrent theme of these letters is the adornment of Cicero's Tusculan villa, where the author purportedly "rests from all troubles and toils" (*Att.* 1.5.7). Cicero had commissioned Atticus to select sculptures for the villa, and the letters chart the author's various responses, interventions, and requests. Although Cicero also talks about a colonnade and "little hall" (*Att.* 1.8.2, 1.10.3), his foremost concern is to find statues for a self-declared "gymnasium" and "academy." Exactly what the letters mean here is decidedly ambiguous: some have supposed Cicero to refer to two separate peristyle gardens, associated respectively with the Academy and Lyceum where Plato and Aristotle taught in Athens (Marvin 1993, 162–4). For Cicero, at any rate, the Greek associations of these two places dictate the choice of sculptural themes: Atticus must select subjects that align not only with the cultural ethos of the villa, but also with its differently zoned spaces. Cicero was particularly delighted with a Hermathena (a two-sided composite bust of Hermes and Athena), for example, deeming it an appropriate emblem for his self-styled academy: "Hermes is the common ornament of all such spaces," he writes, "and Minerva [the Latin name for Athena] is special to that particular gymnasium" (*Att.* 1.4.3).

Underlying Cicero's rhetoric here are two interconnected ideas: the first concerns the select appropriation of Greek art in Roman homes (see essay 4.3, Gazda); the second the appropriate selection of sculptural subjects for a given architectural space. Though Cicero was at times eager to distance himself from the perceived *luxuria* of Greek art (Weis 2003; Miles 2008, 105), he nonetheless strove to decorate this villa *à la grecque*. Indeed, Cicero even bestows its various spaces with Greek-sounding names (referring in Greek to *ornamenta* γυμνασιώδη—"ornaments suitable for a gymnasium": *Att.* 1.6.2, 1.9.2); likewise, he refers to "Megarian statues" and "Pentelic herms," defining statues around a Greek geography as much as by their subjects (*Att.* 1.8.2, 1.9.2).

At the same time as he appropriated Greek materials, Cicero sought seemly assemblages for each segregated space. Atticus (whose Attic name connotes his Athenian credentials) is charged with finding commoditized subjects that suit (*convenire*) different locations—to select "anything of the same sort which you think worthy of the Academy" (*Att.* 1.9.2). The underlying rhetoric of appropriateness seems to have been drawn from debates about selecting subjects and forms suitable for a given speech or occasion (Desmouliez 1976, 266–85; Leen 1991, 236–8); Cicero also uses a Greek rhetorical term to describe his interest in whatever is topographically "fitting" (οἰκεῖον, 1.10.3). In these rhetorically crafted letters, however, such terminology is applied to the rationale of visual display: "Cicero tells Atticus what to buy," as Miranda Marvin puts it, "by describing the location where the works are to be placed" (1993, 165).

It is a later letter penned to a subsequent agent—one who *mis*construes Cicero's ideology of display—that provides our most poignant insight into the underlying principle (*Fam.* 7.23). Cicero chastises a certain M. Fadius Gallus for being "unacquainted with my practice" (*ignarus instituti mei*, 7.23.2). Authorized (like Atticus) to purchase sculptures on Cicero's behalf, Gallus is said to have procured the wrong sorts of statues: not only had he bought sculptures at a hugely inflated price ("one I consider excessive for all statues everywhere"), he had also chosen Bacchant subjects to adorn Cicero's library. Gallus seems to have explained his decision by comparing those statues to "Metellus's Muses"—a comparison which sends Cicero into a carefully staged rhetorical rage: "at least the Muses would have been suitable for a library and in keeping with my literary pursuits!" (*Fam.* 7.23.2). A statue of Mars is declared no less inappropriate: "what good is that to me, the advocate of peace?" Cicero quips. Such comments make it clear that, while sculptural collections should align with their intended setting, they could also reflect something about their collector. Gallus needed only to ask himself: was the bellicose Mars *really* a suitable emblem for a man championing republican peace? The studied self-displays of sculpture here mirror the lettered assemblages of the *Letters* as a literary collection: if sculptural choices actively define different domestic spaces, their evocation also sculpts a figurative portrait of Cicero himself (cf. Henderson 2002, albeit in a different context).

Cicero was not the only Latin author to talk about sculpture in such terms (Perry 2005, 31–48). Indeed, one of the most intriguing aspects of Cicero's critical framework is its apparent applicability across different modes of visual display (Pollitt 1974, 68–70, 343–7). So it is, for example, that Vitruvius lists *decor* (appropriateness) as one of the six basic concerns of the architect in the late first century BC (*De arch.* 1.2.1), defining it as the "faultless appearance of a work composed from the right parts with authority"

(1.2.5). Similar principles underlie Vitruvius's much-discussed diatribe about contemporary wall-painting, which—at least according to Vitruvius—pays insufficient attention to "rational knowledge of what is appropriate" (*ratione decoris*, 7.5.4; Elsner 1995, 51–8). Discussing the decorous display of paintings at a small theater at Tralles, Vitruvius explicitly draws a parallel with the proper display of public sculpture (*De arch.* 7.5.5–6; Marvin 1993, 168–70; Perry 2002, 156–7). Just as Cicero had ridiculed the prospect of installing Bacchants in his library, Vitruvius criticizes the people of Alabanda for failing to consider which sculptural themes were appropriate for specific topographic settings: "in the gymnasium the statues are all pleading cases, whereas in the forum they are throwing a discus, running, or playing ball" (*De arch.* 7.5.6; see essay 4.1, Longfellow).

Archaeology cannot substantiate Vitruvius's claims about Alabanda, nor can we know about the reality of Cicero's own sculptural installations. But material evidence does corroborate the underlying rationale in the late Republic and empire (Lafon 1981; Neudecker 1988; Bartman 1991; Bravi 2012). Consider the sculptural assemblages in the luxurious Villa of the Papyri, situated just outside Herculaneum on the Bay of Naples (see essays 2.4, Mattusch; and 3.3, Anguissola). The villa's sculptures have various chronologies, stretching back almost 200 years prior to the AD 79 Vesuvian eruption that preserved the site. But part of the collection seems to have been amassed at precisely the time when Cicero was writing. As in Cicero's *Letters*, moreover, the villa's sculptures appear to have been selected both on the basis of their suitability to different domestic spaces, and for what they conveyed about the villa's proprietor (Neudecker 1988, 105–114, 147–57; Stewart 2003, 252–9; Tanner 2006, 273–4; Welch 2006, 123–4).

Following the first excavations of the villa in the mid-eighteenth century, some eighty-five bronze and marble sculptures have been discovered (Mattusch 2005). Around half of these were found in the atrium and adjoining small peristyle, the rest amid a larger, elongated peristyle to the northwest of the complex. Various attempts have been made to reconstruct the supposed "programs" at work (Wojcik 1986; Warden and Romano 1994). Although the eclectic collection defies any single programmatic interpretation, there can be no doubting the considerable attention to issues of arrangement, always with an eye to different media, scales, and poses: this explains the mass of marble herms after Greek and Roman philosophical and political figures set up in parallel rows along the rectangular peristyle; it also explains the display of larger bronze statues set at one end (including runners, a satyr, and a Hermes). The sculptural displays seem to follow the spirit (if not the letter) of Cicero's concerns about *decorum*: like Cicero, the owner of the villa evidently appropriated Greek subjects to summon up an air of *otium* (leisure); in this particular case, it also seems likely that the choice of portrait-herms was intended to resonate with the Epicurean interests of the villa's eponymous library of papyrus scrolls (Mattusch 2005, 12–23).

A similar interest in aligning statues with spatial settings can be found in other Roman scenarios (Vermeule 1977, 45–81; Neudecker 1988, 130–247). With each case study, we must assume that the thinking worked both ways: just as Cicero considers context to be the defining variable for choosing sculptural themes, so too could sculpture actively influence responses to a given space. By this logic, the elaborate program of ancestral sculptures set up in the two exedras of the Forum of Augustus become spaces for contemplating the eponymous *princeps*'s ancestry (stretching back to the mythical exploits of Romulus and Aeneas: Spannagel 1999; Bravi 2012, 141–50; see essay 6.3, Shaya); similarly, the sculptural installations in the Baths of Caracalla bestowed viewers with a series of different body types in the context of their own physical exercise (Marvin 1983; see essay 4.1, Longfellow). The same can be said of the second-century imperial villa at Tivoli, where different sculptural subjects and styles helped conjure up the different lands over which Hadrian held sway (Macdonald and Pinto 1995; see essay 3.7, Swetnam-Burland); one might also compare the sculptural groups installed in the Sperlonga grotto, which transform an unprepossessing natural cave into a sort of Homeric theme-park (with potentially sinister connotations for those dining there: Squire 2009, 209–221). In each scenario, Cicero's literary *Letters* help to pinpoint an underlying critical idea: for Roman *literati*, making sense of sculptural subjects evidently meant considering them in light of their particular spatial settings.

The Art of Naming: Pliny the Elder's *Natural History*

From a modern perspective, perhaps most striking about Cicero's *Letters* is the lack of concern with artists' names. In stark contrast to modern scholarly attitudes toward Roman *Idealplastik* (see essay 3.3, Anguissola), Cicero's foremost interest lies not in Greek "masterworks," but rather in finding appropriate sculptural themes for specific sites and areas. To say that "Cicero raves about [his statues] with his eyes shut" (Carcopino 1951, 1.73) would be to express the point too strongly. Yet the fact remains that Cicero's letters make no mention of wanting a Praxiteles, Polyclitus, or Lysippus, nor do they distinguish between (or indeed make reference to) originals and copies.

Where Cicero's letters downplay sculptural origins and history, other late republican and early imperial authors certainly did champion these factors, associating different sculptors with different qualities, and assessing the relative authority (*auctoritas*) of each (Robert 1995). To demonstrate the point, the second part of this essay turns to Pliny the Elder's *Natural History*. As we shall see, Pliny's connoisseurial interest in names and makers counterbalances Cicero's concern with sculptural themes alone: in this sense, the *Natural History* reflects (and in turn constructs) a different Roman critical framework for approaching sculpture—one that is interested not only in *what* a statue depicts, but also in *how* it represents its subject.

Much has been written about Pliny as a prototypical art historian (Tanner 2006, 235–46), and about Pliny's influence on subsequent paradigms of Western art history (especially in relation to Giorgio Vasari's 1550 *Lives of the Artists*: Becatti 1972; Cheney 2007, 23–33; Marvin 2008, 16–25). It is therefore worth emphasizing from the outset that Pliny conceptualized his project rather differently (Carey 2003, 14–15; De Angelis 2008). For one thing, Pliny frames his discussion of "art" around Stoic concerns with nature and mankind's relationship to it (Isager 1991; Naas 2002, 95–104; Carey 2003, 102–137; Tanner 2006, 236–9). At the same time, the *Natural History*'s titular interest in nature goes hand in hand with a distinctly imperialist ideology, subsuming and ordering knowledge within his archetypal Roman "encyclopedia" (Rouveret 1995; Naas 2002, 416–32; Murphy 2004, 1–25; Naas 2011).

This agenda helps to explain how the *Natural History* structures its discussion of visual materials, and its analysis of sculpture in particular. Despite the extraction of relevant passages into self-contained "chapters on the history of Greek art" (Jex-Blake and Sellers 1896), Pliny's discussions are segregated across five books, relating respectively to metals (book 33), metal compounds (book 34), pigments and organic matter (book 35), stones and rocks (book 36), and gems (book 37). In each book, Pliny derived much of his information from earlier Hellenistic treatises (Pollitt 1974, 73–81; Rouveret 1995, 51–3, 58–9). Yet Pliny's analytical frame was decidedly his own. When it comes to sculpture, for example, Pliny deliberately scatters his analysis across several books: although the longest account comes in the context of bronze-working (34.15–93), statues also recur in Pliny's discussions of gold (33.82–3), silver (33.147, 151), iron (34.120–21), and not least marble (35.9–46).

Pliny's concern with materials is important: the very structure of the *Natural History* privileges the semantics of medium, underlining the aesthetic significance of different sculptural materials above all else. But there are nonetheless connections between Pliny's disparate discussions. Early on in his discussion of bronze statues, for example, Pliny mentions Italian terracotta sculptures (34.34) before alluding to his later analysis of marble statues (34.35); likewise, in discussing Praxiteles's marble works (36.20), Pliny refers back to his earlier analysis of Praxiteles's bronze statues (34.69). The *Natural History* also assumes a fundamental parallel between responses to sculpture and painting: some of the sculptors Pliny mentions are also said to have worked as painters (e.g., Protogenes: 35.91, Callimachus: 35.92), just as different metals lend themselves to works in both sculpture and painting alike (33.117, 158–64). The dividing lines between natural media are never as clear-cut as Pliny might have us believe.

So what did Pliny deem important when evaluating sculpture specifically? Perhaps most striking is his broad spectrum of taxonomic approaches. Take the discussion of bronze sculpture in the thirty-fourth book. Pliny begins by stressing the impossibility of any totalizing account: "who among mortal men could recapitulate them all—and what would be the value understood in such knowledge?" (34.37). He then offers a variety of critical frames—structured around size (4.39–42), for example, or else different types of motif or context (represented on horseback, foot, or displayed on columns: 34.15–34).

If Pliny testifies to a plurality of ways of cataloging bronze sculpture, the ensuing discussion nonetheless privileges two critical concerns: first, an emphasis on historical development (hence his opening chronology of sculptors according to different

Olympiads: 34.49–52); and second, through a series of lists, an interest in relating different sculptures to different sculptors. After laying out in historical order the "ages of the most famous" sculptors (34.53), Pliny analyses the more celebrated artists of the fifth and fourth centuries BC in greater detail (including Pheidias, Polyclitus, Myron, Lysippus, and Praxiteles: 34.53–71). The discussion subsequently proceeds to an alphabetical register of lesser known sculptors (arranged from Alcamenes to Xenocrates: 34.72–83), which in turn gives rise to at least three additional catalogues, each one again arranged in approximate alphabetical order: the first names bronze sculptors of "the same distinction but with no outstanding excellence for any of their single works" (34.85), a second provides an inventory of those "who have made works of the same class" (34.86–9), and a third specifies those famous for their sculptures of athletes (34.91).

We will return in the following section to Pliny's underlying rhetoric of sculptural styles here—his rationale in comparing the works of Pheidias with those of Polyclitus (34.56), for example, or else in pitching the *veritas* ("truthfulness") of Myron's statues against the art of Polyclitus (34.58). For now, I want instead to highlight Pliny's systematic emphasis on names. The *Natural History* assumes that anyone interested in statues must necessarily be interested in their makers. At the same time, Pliny privileges a particular canon of fifth- and fourth-century BC sculptors: underlying Pliny's rhetoric is a certain idea of cultural distance or remove—a sense of the "pastness" of sculpture and painting (or at least its best traditions), associated with masters long since dead (*HN* 34.52; Settis 1995, 27–30, 45–6; Tanner 2006, 242–4).

There are numerous literary comparanda for Pliny's obsession with artists here (cf. Neudecker 1988, 91–104; cf. Squire 2013a). Wherever we look among extant literary sources, moreover, we find the same "A-list" of canonical fifth- and fourth-century BC authorities. In a first-century AD poem dedicated to evoking Pollius Felix's villa at Sorrento, for example, Statius waxes lyrical about paintings and statues likened to the works of Apelles, Pheidias, Myron, and Polyclitus (*Silv.* 2.63–72; Tanner 2006, 274–5); later, in the second century AD, the Greek writer Lucian has a character tell of the house of Eucrates, adorned with all manner of famous sculptures, each one delineated according to their celebrated artists—Myron, Kritios and Nesiotes, Polykleitos (*Philops.* 18; Neudecker 1988, 63, 94; Tanner 2006, 205; Anguissola 2012, 129–31). In both passages, discussion centers on a recurrent canon of sculptors and sculptures—what Pasiteles had earlier called "masterworks" (*nobilia opera*) in a lost first-century BC treatise (Plin. *HN* 36.39). It is assumed that learned viewers—or, in these two cases, learned *readers*—might recognize and comment upon the different fifth- and fourth-century artistic hands. Given this Roman obsession with such a small handful of Greek artists, it is perhaps unsurprising that some latter-day artists occasionally turned to forgery. The Augustan poet Phaedrus grumbles about this practice in one of his *Fables* (5.pref.4–9), and archaeological evidence would seem to corroborate the phenomenon (Fuchs 1999, 44–52; Anguissola 2012, 146–50; Squire 2013a, 378–402; see essay 2.4, Mattusch).

Styling a Response: Quintilian's *Education of an Orator*

If Cicero made sense of statues on the grounds of their subjects and spatial context, and if Pliny the Elder theorized the history of sculpture through the lens of those who made it, how might Roman viewers have evaluated different visual forms? To begin answering that question, my third and final section explores some of the ways in which Roman rhetoricians approached sculptural styles specifically. In particular, I turn to Quintilian's *Education of an Orator* (written soon after Pliny's *Natural History*, at the end of the first century AD), exploring Quintilian's fundamental analogy between the different "hands" of sculptors and painters on the one hand, and different authorial "voices" on the other.

For all his rhetorical interest in the education of the orator, sculptural comparisons loom large in Quintilian (cf. Becatti 1951, 178–91): Quintilian associates statues with various educational roles—among other things, as visual prompts for remembering the order of a speech (*Inst.* 11.2.20; Rouveret 1989, 303–379). In one famous passage, however, he analyses sculpture in an effort to explain differences in oratorical voice (*Inst.* 12.10; Austin 1946; Pollitt 1974, 81–4; Neumeister 1990, 439–42; Perry 2002, 161–2). In order to evaluate divergent "types of speaking" (*genera orationis*), Quintilian argues, one might profitably compare similar differences in painterly (12.10.3–6) and sculptural (12.10.7–9) styles.

The subsequent commentary reveals much about both Roman tastes and critical standards. Quintilian's essential argument is that different works (*opera*)—whether works of painting, sculpture, or oratory—express themselves differently and therefore attract different sorts of responses. From this perspective, there is no single answer as to whose painted, sculptural, or oratorical styles are qualitatively best. Regardless of whether one's medium is sculpture, painting, or indeed words, judgment will always come down to subjective preference: "The reason why the perfect orator does not yet exist (and perhaps also no perfect art) is not only because different qualities predominate in different individuals, but also because no single form has pleased everyone; this is partly due to the conditions of different times and places, and partly because of the tastes and aims of each individual" (12.10.2). Although such talk is in some sense a far cry from the aesthetics of Immanuel Kant's *Critique of Judgment* (*Kritik der Urteilskraft*, 1790), it is perhaps worth noting the shared interest in subjective, individual preference: for all his evaluative critical discussions, Quintilian ultimately supposes that "beauty" lies in the eye of the beholder.

To demonstrate this larger point, Quintilian launches into a history of different painterly styles from the early fifth to the late fourth centuries BC, declaring that "there are similar differences in statuary" (12.10.7). His discussion then proceeds to a chronologically structured account of sculptural practitioners: he begins with (what we call) early archaic sculptors and ends with the late classical period (12.10.7–9). Where early sculptural styles (those of Callon and Hegesias) are said to be "rather hard" (*duriora*), those of Callias are "less rigid" (*minus rigida*), and those of Myron are in turn yet "softer" still (*molliora*). As he proceeds through the period styles of fifth-century sculptors, Quintilian describes how Polyclitus's work is distinctive for its "craftsmanship and grace" (*diligentia ac decor*), just as the works of Pheidias and Alcamenes possess something that Polyclitus's sculptures lack. In the fourth century, Lysippus and Praxiteles are said to have achieved the best approximation of reality (*ad veritatem... accessisse optime adfirmant*), whereas Demetrius is criticized for being "more enamored with likeness than with beauty" (*similitudinis quam pulchritudinis amantior*).

What might this passage mean for approaching Roman evaluative responses to sculpture? Two points seem particularly important. The first concerns Quintilian's explicit parallel between the critical appreciation of painting and sculpture: where Pliny the Elder's "natural historical" focus drew a distinction between the two, Quintilian posits a *shared* evaluative framework. Second, and no less important, is the analogy between different visual styles of painting and sculpture on the one hand, and the verbal styles of oratory on the other. Quintilian establishes the parallel right from the outset, when he likens differences between Tuscan and Greek statues to differences between Asiatic and Attic oratory (12.10.2). Applying ideas of literary authorship and agency to the visual arts, Quintilian argues that paintings, sculptures, and speeches have comparable sorts of authors (*auctores*; 12.10.2). The subsequent analysis teases out that underlying point, interweaving the technical languages of rhetorical and artistic criticism (*diligentia, pondus, veritas, auctoritas, facilitas*, etc.).

Despite (or perhaps because of) its brevity, Quintilian's discussion offers an important insight into Roman, rhetorically based ideas about sculpture and its critical evaluation. If nothing else, Quintilian presupposes a viewer who is acutely sensitive not only to different artists, but also to the connotations of divergent styles. In the same way that different orators employ different modulations of language, different sculptors are retrospectively associated with different virtues and vices. As Tonio Hölscher has argued, Quintilian's account might suggest a certain "codification" of sculptural styles: particular sculptural forms carry particular cultural connotations, which can be appropriated at will (hence Hölscher's talk of the semantic *Bildsprache*, or "pictorial language," of Roman sculpture: [1987] 2004, esp. 86–102). Of course, we should not assume that *all* viewers were as sensitive to differences in sculptural style (Elsner 2006; Welch 2006, 159–60n160), nor that evaluations of style were ever uniform (this, rather, is precisely Quintilian's point). What Quintilian makes clear, rather, is that educated viewers might be attentive to such issues—moreover, that consideration of fifth- and fourth-century BC sculptural styles could form part and parcel of an orator's education (Preisshofen and Zanker 1970–71).

To understand Quintilian's evaluative framework in practice, consider the so-called San Ildefonso Group of the late first century BC (figure 6.1.2; Zanker 1974, 28–30, no. 26, 42–3; Tanner 2006, 289–92). We know relatively little about the statue's original context, apparently in Rome's Sallustian Gardens; scholars have likewise failed to reach any consensus about its precise subjects (might the funerary torch suggest Castor and Pollux, Orestes and Pylades, or Hypnos and Thanatos?). While

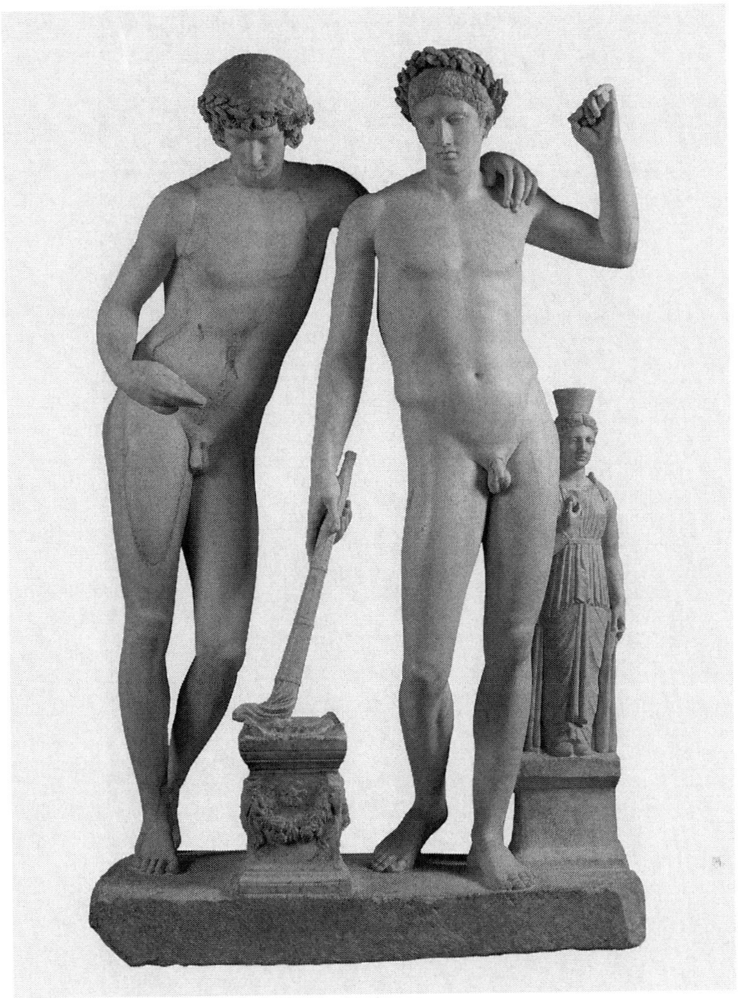

FIGURE 6.1.2 Marble San Ildefonso Group, late first century BC. Madrid, Museo Nacional del Prado, inv. no. E28, 161 × 106 × 56 cm.

we cannot reconstruct the topographical appropriateness of the theme, nor say very much about its makers (the piece is unsigned), the statue clearly combines an eclectic mix of sculptural styles (see essays 1.1, Bartman; and 3.6, Touchette). Although the head of the left-hand figure appears to be a second-century AD addition (the recognizable features are those of Antinous, thereby updating the group's allusive games), his elongated body looks decidedly Praxitelean: the sinuous curve is particularly distinctive, and the pose recalls that of Praxiteles's *Apollo Sauroctonos* in particular (figure 6.1.3). By contrast, the more athletic figure to the right seems modeled after statues by Polyclitus: it combines the young body of a softened Westmacott athlete with the head and coiffure of the Doryphoros (see essay 3.3, Anguissola, figure 3.3.1). The miniature—and playfully statuesque—female figure to the right, situated on its own

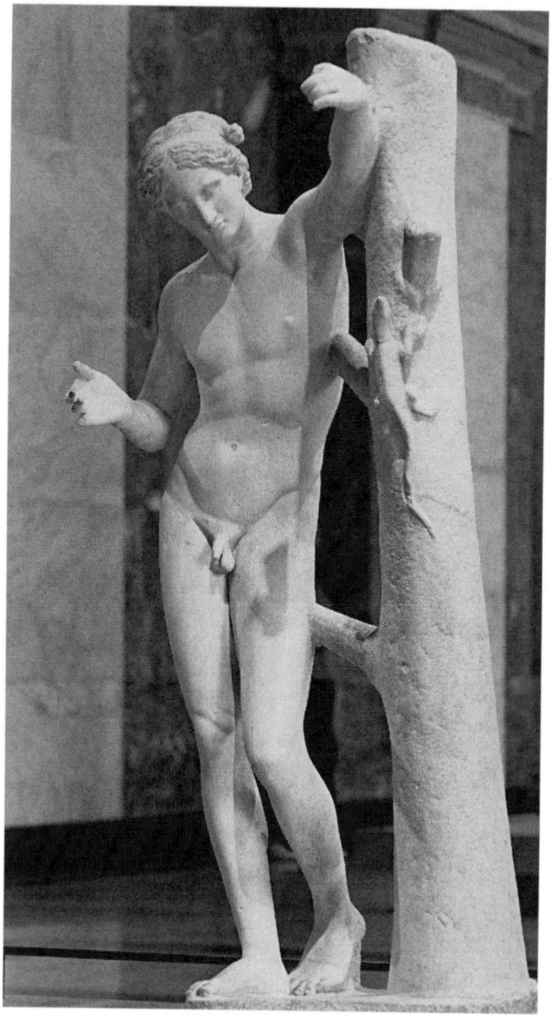

FIGURE 6.1.3 Roman first- or second-century AD marble version of Praxiteles's Apollo Sauroctonos (original, mid-fourth century BC), H c. 149 cm. Paris, Louvre Museum, inv. MA441.

pedestal, delivers a further classicizing allusion, reproducing the sorts of caryatids that Augustus emulated in his eponymous forum at Rome (see essays 2.2, Claridge; 3.3, Anguissola; 6.3, Shaya; and 6.4, Moormann).

Quintilian's *Education of an Orator* provides one insight into how rhetorically-trained viewers might have approached such diverse stylistic languages. As we have observed, Quintilian explicitly praises the "craftsmanship and grace" of Polyclitus (*diligentia et decor*, 12.10.7), but criticizes him for his lack of "weight" (*pondus*), highlighting Polyclitus's preference for young male subjects; by contrast, Praxiteles is said to have come closest to the sculptural approximation of "reality" (*veritatem*, 12.10.9)—something which Demetrius in turn took too far. The San Ildefonso

Group might be said to literalize the highly rhetorical art of "comparative judgment" (*synkrisis* / *comparatio*) which underlies Quintilian's account: thanks to the statue's staged stylistic prompts, viewers are invited to recognize different stylistic models, pitching its Polyclitan qualities against those of Praxiteles (and vice versa).

Much has recently been written about the appropriation of period styles in Roman sculpture (see essay 3.1, Fullerton). But Quintilian allows us to see the *rhetorical* grounding of such responses (Perry 2002, 161–3). Other texts corroborate Quintilian's sensitivity to the expressive values of different sculptural styles (Tanner 2006, 288–9): the anonymous first-century BC *Ad Herennium*, for example, likens the construction of speech to the image of a statue formed from a "Myronian head, Praxitelean arms and a Polyclitan chest" (4.9; see Preisshofen and Zanker 1970–71, 100–108; see essay 3.6, Touchette); some two centuries later, and writing in Greek, Lucian likewise has two characters style an image of the empress' consort by comparing her different bodily parts to the celebrated models of different artworks, each one defined through its sculptor (*Imagines* 1; Preisshofen and Zanker 1970–71, 108–110; Cistaro 2009, 113–47). Passages like these point to elite, rhetorically rooted cultures of viewing that paid close attention not only to different sculptural styles, but also to how different styles worked differently (cf. Squire 2013b).

Conclusion

This essay has examined just three elite Roman literary frameworks for evaluating sculpture. In each case, we have found different authors privileging different critical ideas—whether the subjects of sculpture, their makers, or their styles. In each case, moreover, these critical discussions have pivoted around Greek canonical standards: ultimately, it seems impossible to delineate *Roman* evaluative frameworks without reference to *Greek* sculptural paradigms (see essays 3.3, Anguissola; and 3.6, Touchette).

From our own twenty-first-century perspectives, some of these interpretive frames will strike us as inherently familiar (no surprise, perhaps, given the influence of ancient discourses on all subsequent Western art history). But other Roman responses to sculpture will strike us as markedly more strange. A historicist "aesthetics" of sculpture in the Roman world must wrestle with both the familiar and the unfamiliar aspects in turn: stories about statues coming to life (cf. Elsner 2007, 113–31, on Pygmalion's statue of Galatea, as described in Ov. *Met.* 10.148–739; see essay 6.4, Moormann), moments of iconoclasm (see essays 2.3, Varner; and 6.6, Kristensen), and not least anecdotes about "facing the gods" through their imagery (Platt 2011; see essay 6.5, Perry).

Such issues of cultural similarity and difference return us full circle to the aesthetics of our essay title, and not least to the Alma-Tadema painting with which we began. For all the differences between ancient and modern standards of beauty, taste, and artistic appreciation—and despite the diversity of both those ancient and modern traditions—to what extent might we project a Cicero, Pliny, or Quintilian into Alma-Tadema's picture?

There is no easy answer to that question: as Alma-Tadema's painting so conspicuously demonstrates, responses are necessarily colored by our own modern views. What this essay has ultimately demonstrated, though, is the importance of using literary sources alongside archaeological materials (and vice versa). Contemporary texts can help us to reconstruct at least some of the collective and individual ways in which Roman viewers conceptualized sculpture; just as importantly, they illuminate the finite parameters of our own aestheticizing horizons.

Bibliography

Anguissola, A. 2012. *"Difficillima imitatio": Immagine e lessico delle copie tra Grecia e Roma*. Rome: "L'Erma" di Bretschneider.

Austin, R. G. 1946. "Quintilian on Painting and Statuary." *CQ* 38: 17–26.

Bartman, E. 1991. "Sculptural Collecting and Display in the Private Realm." In *Roman Art in the Private Sphere: New Perspectives on the Architecture and Decor of the Domus, Villa, and Insula*, edited by E. K. Gazda, 71–88. Ann Arbor: University of Michigan Press.

Becatti, G. 1951. *Arte e gusto negli scrittori latini*. Florence: Sansouni.

———. 1972. "Plinio e Vasari." In *Studi di storia dell'arte in onore di Valerio Mariani*, 173–82. Naples: Libreria Scientifica Editrice.

Bounia, A. 2004. *The Nature of Classical Collecting: Collectors and Collections, 100 BCE–100 CE*. Aldershot: Ashgate.

Bravi, A. 2012. *"Ornamenta Urbis": Opere d'arte greche negli spazi romani*. Bari: Edipuglia.

Carcopino, J. 1951. *Cicero: The Secrets of His Correspondence*. 2 vols. London: Routledge.

Carey, S. 2000. "The Problems of Totality: Collecting Greek Art, Wonders, and Luxury in Pliny the Elder's *Natural History*." *Journal of the History of Collections* 12(1): 1–13.

———. 2003. *Pliny's Catalogue of Culture: Art and Empire in the Natural History*. Oxford: Oxford University Press.

Cheney, L. de G. 2007. *Giorgio Vasari's Teachers: Sacred and Profane Art*. New York: Peter Lang.

Cistaro, M. 2009. *Sotto il velo di Pantea: "Imagines" e "Pro Imaginibus" di Luciano*. Messina: Università degli Studi di Messina.

De Angelis, F. 2008. "Pliny the Elder and the Identity of Roman Art." *RES: Anthropology and Aesthetics* 53–4: 79–92.

Desmouliez, A. 1976. *Cicéron et son gout: Essai sur une définition d'une esthétique romaine à la fin de la république*. Brussels: Latomus.

Elsner, J. 1995. *Art and the Roman Viewer: The Transformation of Art from the Pagan World to Christianity*. Cambridge: Cambridge University Press.

———. 2006. "Classicism in Roman Art." In *Classical Pasts: The Classical Traditions of Greece and Rome*, edited by J. I. Porter, 270–97. Princeton: Princeton University Press.

———. 2007. *Roman Eyes: Visuality and Subjectivity in Art and Text*. Princeton: Princeton University Press.

Fuchs, M. 1999. *"In hoc etiam genere Graeciae nihil cedamus": Studien zur Romanisierung der späthellenistischen Kunst im 1. Jh. v. Chr.* Mainz: Philipp von Zabern.

Henderson, J. 2002. *Pliny's Statue: The "Letters," Self-Portraiture and Classical Art*. Exeter: University of Exeter Press.

Hölscher, T. (1987) 2004. *The Language of Images in Roman Art*. Translated by A. Snodgrass and A. M. Künzl-Snodgrass. Cambridge: Cambridge University Press. Originally published as *Römische Bildsprache als semantisches System*.

Isager, J. 1991. *Pliny on Art and Society: The Elder Pliny's Chapters on the History of Art*. London: Routledge.

Jex-Blake, K., and E. Sellers, eds. 1896. *The Elder Pliny's Chapters on the History of Art*. London: Macmillan.

Kristeller, P. O. 1990. *Renaissance Thought and the Arts*. Princeton: Princeton University Press.

Lafon, X. 1981. "À propos des '*villae*' republicaines: Quelques notes sur les programmes décoratifs et les commanditaires." In *L'art décoratif à Rome à la fin de la République et au début du Principat*, edited by X. Lafon and G. Sauron, 151–72. Rome: École Française de Rome.

Leen, A. 1991. "Cicero and the Rhetoric of Art." *AJP* 112: 229–45.

MacDonald, W. L., and J. A. Pinto. 1995. *Hadrian's Villa and its Legacy*. New Haven: Yale University Press.

Marvin, M. 1983. "Freestanding Sculptures from the Baths of Caracalla." *AJA* 87: 347–84.

———. 1993. "Copying in Roman Sculpture: The Replica Series." In *Roman Art in Context: An Anthology*, edited by E. D'Ambra, 161–88. Englewood Cliffs: Prentice-Hall.

———. 2008. *The Language of the Muses: The Dialogue between Roman and Greek Sculpture*. Los Angeles: J. Paul Getty Museum.

Mattusch, C. C. 2005. *The Villa dei Papiri: Life and Afterlife of a Sculptural Collection*. Los Angeles: J. Paul Getty Museum.

Miles, M. M. 2008. *Art as Plunder: The Ancient Origins of Debate about Cultural Property*. Cambridge: Cambridge University Press.

Murphy, T. M. 2004. *Pliny the Elder's Natural History: The Empire in the Encyclopedia*. Oxford: Oxford University Press.

Naas, V. 2002. *Le projet encyclopédique de Pline l'Ancien*. Rome: École Française de Rome.

———. 2011. "Imperialism, *Mirabilia*, and Knowledge: Some Paradoxes in the *Naturalis Historia*." In *Pliny the Elder: Themes and Contexts*, edited by R. K. Gibson and R. Morello, 57–70. Leiden: Brill.

Neudecker, R. 1988. *Die Skulpturenausstattung römischer Villen in Italien*. Mainz: Philipp von Zabern.

———. 1998. "The Roman Villa as a Locus for Art Collections." In *The Roman Villa: Villa Urbana*, edited by A. Frazer, 77–91. Philadelphia: University of Pennsylvania Press.

Neumeister, C. 1990. "Polyklet in der römischen Literatur." In *Polyklet: Der Bildhauer der griechischen Klassik*, edited by H. Beck, P. C. Bol, and M. Bückling, 428–49. Mainz: Philipp von Zabern.

Perry, E. 2002. "Rhetoric, Literary Criticism, and the Roman Aesthetics of Artistic Imitation." In *The Ancient Art of Emulation: Studies in Artistic Originality and Tradition from the Present to Classical Antiquity*, edited by E. K. Gazda, 153–71. Ann Arbor: University of Michigan Press.

———. 2005. *The Aesthetics of Emulation in the Visual Arts of Ancient Rome*. Cambridge: Cambridge University Press.

Platt, V. J. 2011. *Facing the Gods: Epiphany and Representation in Graeco-Roman Art, Literature and Religion*. Cambridge: Cambridge University Press.

Platt, V. J., and M. J. Squire, eds. 2010. "The Art of Art History in Greco-Roman Antiquity." Special issue, *Arethusa* 43(2).

Pollitt, J. J. 1974. *The Ancient View of Greek Art: Criticism, History and Terminology*. New Haven: Yale University Press.

Porter, J. I. 2009. "Is Art Modern? Kristeller's 'Modern System of the Arts' Reconsidered." *British Journal of Aesthetics* 49: 1–24, 171–8.

———. 2010. *The Origins of Aesthetic Thought in Ancient Greece: Matter, Sensation and Experience*. Cambridge: Cambridge University Press.

Preisshofen, F., and P. Zanker. 1970–71. "Reflex einer eklektischen Kunstanschauung beim Auctor *Ad Herennium*." *DialArch* 4–5: 100–119.

Prettejohn, E. 2007. *Art for Art's Sake: Aestheticism in Victorian Painting*. New Haven: Yale University Press.

Robert, R. 1995. "*Immensa potentia artis*: Prestige et statut des œuvres d'art à Rome, à la fin de la république et au début de l'Empire." *RA* 1995: 291–305.

Rouveret, A. 1989. *Histoire et imaginaire de la peinture ancienne (Ve siècle av. J.-C–Ier siècle ap. J.-C.)*. Paris: École Française de Rome.

———. 1995. "Artistes, collectionneurs et antiquaires: L'histoire de l'art dans l'encyclopédie plinienne." In *Histoire de l'histoire de l'art: De l'antiquité au XVIIIe siècle*, edited by É. Pommier, 49–64. Paris: Klincksieck.

Rutledge, S. H. 2012. *Ancient Rome as a Museum: Power, Identity, and the Culture of Collecting*. Oxford: Oxford University Press.

Settis, S. 1995. "Did the Ancients Have an Antiquity? The Idea of Renaissance in the History of Classical Art." In *Language and Images of Renaissance Italy*, edited by A. Brown, 27–50. Oxford: Oxford University Press.

Shiner, L. 2001. *The Invention of Art: A Cultural History*. Chicago: Chicago University Press.

———. 2009. "Continuity and Discontinuity in the Concept of Art." *British Journal of Aesthetics* 49: 159–69.

Spannagel, M. 1999. *Exemplaria Principis: Untersuchungen zu Entstehung und Ausstattung des Augustusforums*. Heidelberg: Archäologie und Geschichte.

Squire, M. J. 2009. *Image and Text in Graeco-Roman Antiquity*. Cambridge: Cambridge University Press.

———. 2010. "Introduction: The Art of Art History in Greco-Roman Antiquity." In Platt and Squire 2010, 133–63.

———. 2013a. "*Ars* in their I's: Authority and Authorship in Graeco-Roman Visual Culture." In *The Author's Voice in Classical and Late Antiquity*, edited by A. Marmodoro and J. Hill, 357–414. Oxford: Oxford University Press.

———. 2013b. "Embodied Ambiguities on the Prima Porta Augustus." *Art History* 36: 242–79.

Stewart, P. 2003. *Statues in Roman Society: Representation and Response*. Oxford: Oxford University Press.

Swanson, V. G. 1990. *The Biography and Catalogue Raisonné of the Paintings of Sir Lawrence Alma-Tadema*. London: Garton.

Tanner, J. 2006. *The Invention of Art History in Ancient Greece: Religion, Society and Artistic Rationalisation*. Cambridge: Cambridge University Press.

Vermeule, C. C. 1977. *Greek Sculpture and Roman Taste: The Purpose and Setting of Graeco-Roman Art in Italy and the Greek Imperial East*. Ann Arbor: University of Michigan Press.

Warden, P. G., and D. G. Romano. 1994. "The Course of Glory: Greek Art in a Roman Context at the Villa of the Papyri at Herculaneum." *Art History* 17: 228–54.

Weis, A. 2003. "Gaius Verres and the Roman Art Market: Consumption and Connoisseurship in Late Republican Rome." In *O tempora, O mores*, edited by A. Haltenhoff, A. Heil, and F.-H. Mutschler, 355–400. Munich: Saur.

Welch, K. E. 2006. "*Domi Militiaeque*: Roman Domestic Aesthetics and War Booty in the Republic." In *Representations of War in Ancient Rome*, edited by S. Dillon and K. E. Welch, 91–161. Cambridge: Cambridge University Press.
Wojcik, M. R. 1986. *La Villa dei Papiri ad Ercolano*. Rome: "L'Erma" di Bretschneider.
Zanker, P. 1974. *Klassizistische Statuen: Studien zur Veränderung des Kunstgeschmacks in der römischen Zeit*. Mainz: Philipp von Zabern.

CHAPTER 6.2

RECEPTION THEORY

JENNIFER TRIMBLE

Introduction

How did people in the Roman world see, understand, and respond to sculpture? And how can we know these things? This essay considers four approaches to Roman viewing and reception and the ways in which they relate to recent studies of Roman sculpture: historical reception as represented by Hans Robert Jauss; reception aesthetics as formulated by Wolfgang Iser; social historical studies; and approaches that concentrate on the power of images and viewers' responses to that power. In organizing the material in this way, I have three goals. First, the study of Roman sculpture is rarely explicit about its theoretical underpinnings, so it is useful to highlight some ways in which different approaches entail different research questions, forms of evidence explored, methods employed, and results obtained. Second, a pragmatic focus on methods helps show how these abstract theories can be applied in practice. In many cases cited below, studies of Roman sculpture do not draw explicitly on reception theory, but there are productive echoes and analogies in the ways they think about the material. Third, this essay is in part a response to R. R. R. Smith's 2002 essay on the state of Roman art history and his eloquent formulation of the contributions made by the historical and contextual turn in Roman art in the 1970s and 1980s. That approach continues to dominate the field, but productive alternatives have also emerged. In this essay I try to show where these various approaches originate, how they interact, and where the field stands now methodologically.

What Did Viewers Expect to See?

It is useful to begin with two fundamental theorists of reception, Hans Robert Jauss and Wolfgang Iser, perhaps the best-known members of the "Constance School," a group of literary scholars exploring reception theory at the University of Constance in Germany in the late 1960s and 1970s (Holub 1984; Holly 2002). Above all, they shifted the interpretive focus from the text itself to how it was read and received. This idea is powerfully applicable to visual art and to Roman sculpture: the work and the viewer together constitute what is seen. Jauss and Iser theorized reception in different ways, Jauss paying more attention to the empirical and actual conditions of reading, and Iser primarily interested in the role of the work in structuring its own reading. In this key difference, they became leading figures for, respectively, historical reception and reception aesthetics.

Jauss was committed to returning a dynamic historical dimension to the study of literature, avoiding nationalistic or essentialist approaches and anachronistic modern judgments. For Jauss, art could be transformative, having "the characteristic that it can lead men beyond the stabilized images and prejudices of their historical situation toward a new perception of the world or an anticipated reality" (Jauss 1982, 14). In these premises, his work resonates strongly with the contextual and historical turn that transformed Roman art and archaeology in the 1970s and 1980s (Smith 2002). With this new perspective, scholars sought to understand works of Roman art not through the lens of modern aesthetic preferences, anachronistic classifications, or evolutionary schemes of art, but in relation to the world in which they were made and to the people who made and saw them.

A key concept for Jauss was the *Erwartungshorizont*, the audience's "horizon of expectations," defined as follows: "the objectifiable system of expectations that arises for each work in the historical moment of its appearance, from a pre-understanding of the genre, from the form and themes of already familiar works, and from the opposition between poetical and practical language" (Jauss 1982, 22). Analysis could accordingly focus on the existing literary landscape and how any new work related to readers' expectations at the time. For visual art, the key question becomes: what were viewers' expectations in relation to a work of Roman sculpture in that historical moment? How did the new work confirm, confound, or otherwise play with those expectations? Drawing on Jauss's three-part definition, we might consider how a given work related to viewers' "pre-understanding of the genre," to "the form and themes of already familiar works," and to "the opposition between poetic and practical language." As this horizon of expectations shifted over time, so would viewers' reception of that work.

Generic expectations included, for example, the visual conventions of Roman portrait statuary (see essay 3.4, Wood). Viewers expected an individualized head to be combined with a generic body. That body—for example, togate, cuirassed, nude, clothed as a respectable matron—was not expected to represent the person's actual body but instead expressed collective social and symbolic values (Trimble 2011). For example, the famous "Tivoli General," made in the middle decades of the first century BC, juxtaposes a highly individualized male portrait head, carved with the wrinkles, sagging skin, and receding hairline of middle age, with the idealized physique of a nearly nude, well-muscled adult man (figure 6.2.1). This juxtaposition is jarring to modern expectations of unity between head and body, but it worked very well in relation to ancient visual expectations. In this statue, and in similar ones made in the late republican period, the heroic connotations of Greek nudity were appropriated for representations of important Roman men (Hallett 2005, 1–4, 102–158; see essays 3.6,

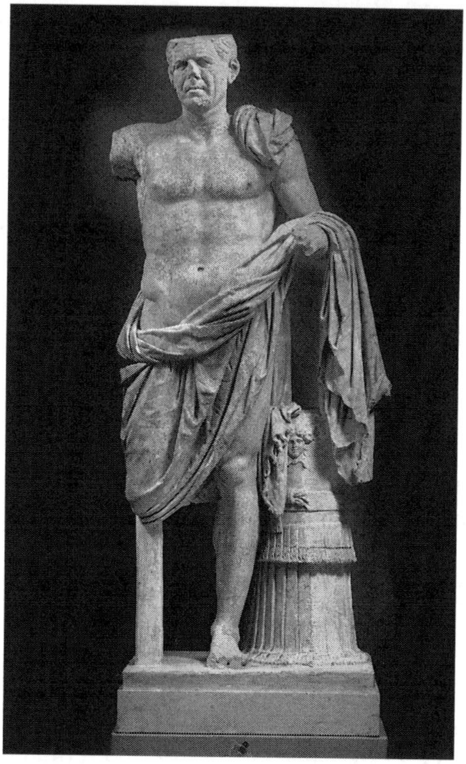

FIGURE 6.2.1 The Tivoli General. Portrait of a man in heroic nudity from the sanctuary of Hercules at Tivoli. Marble. First century BC. Rome, Museo Nazionale Romano, Palazzo Massimo alle Terme, inv. no. 106513.

Touchette; and 4.8, D'Ambra and Tronchin). Viewers also had expectations about physical setting and viewing conditions. Certain kinds of sculpture (e.g., honorific portrait statues, state monuments) were expected in public and sacred spaces and were viewed accordingly (see essay 4.1, Longfellow). Others belonged to the funerary realm (e.g., sarcophagi; see essay 4.4, Ewald) or domestic religion (e.g., statuettes of the Lares; see essay 4.3, Gazda).

For Roman sculpture, "the forms and themes of already familiar works" included their iconography. Viewers must have easily recognized Hercules's lion skin and club, Athena's aegis, the male citizen's marker of the toga, the ruling emperor's portrait features. The Tivoli General's cloak and the breastplate depicted next to his left leg told the viewer that this was a high-ranking military man (figure 6.2.1). The early second-century AD Circus Relief in the Vatican Museums (figure 6.2.2) depicts a scene familiar to tens of thousands of people: chariot-racing in the Circus Maximus, with recognizable details like a four-horse chariot, a palm of victory, and the obelisk that stood on the central barrier (Sinn 1991, cat 14, 37–9, figs. 35–9).

This familiarity extended to visual conventions of gesture, movement, scale, and style. Sculptures depicted high-status people gesturing and moving in restrained ways (figure 6.2.1). Vigorous efforts of the body were reserved for battling soldiers, entertainers and athletes (figure 6.2.2), slaves and other workers, and mythological scenes (figure 6.2.3).

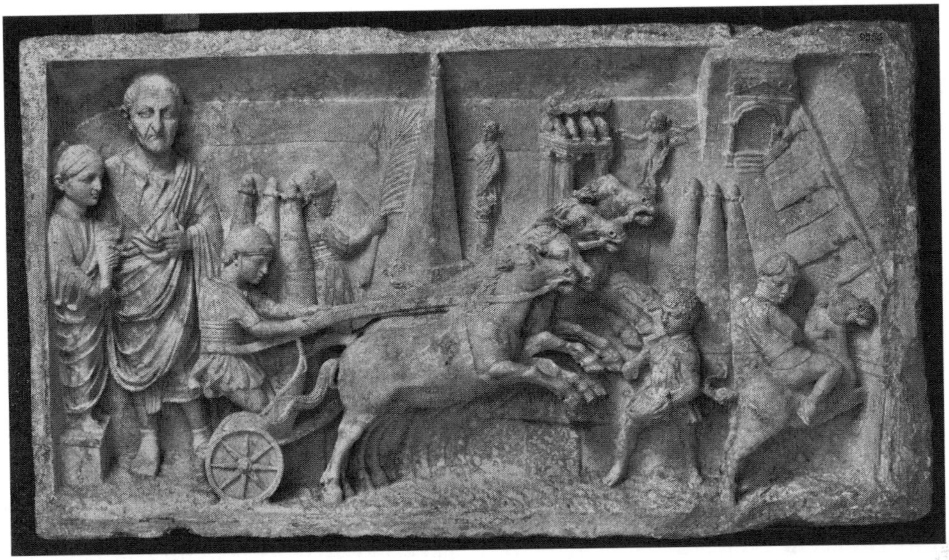

FIGURE 6.2.2 Relief, probably funerary, depicting chariot racing, provenance unknown (probably from Rome). Marble. Early second century AD. Vatican City, Musei Vaticani: Museo Gregoriano Profano, inv. no. 9556.

Equally relevant to viewers' expectations was the style chosen for the work, which had consistent semantic meanings (Hölscher [1987] 2004; see essays 3.1, Fullerton; 3.3, Anguissola; 3.6, Touchette; 4.7, Petersen; and 6.1, Squire). The classicizing arrangement of figures on the processional reliefs of the Ara Pacis Augustae connoted high state ceremonial; by contrast, the chariot-racing scene illustrated in figure 6.2.2 employs a combination of bird's-eye and head-on perspective to depict crucial details of action in space.

Jauss's "opposition between poetic and practical language" is at first sight more difficult to apply directly to the study of visual material. Here, Jauss was rejecting Formalist analyses of literature, which in his view focused too much on stylistic devices, defining art as everything that was *not* everyday language. By contrast, Jauss stressed the simultaneous presence of both poetic and practical language, and the importance of their interactions (Jauss 1982, 16, 24). Productive analogies for Roman sculpture might include the ways in which a given sculpture heightened, distilled, or allegorized a known reality. In this sense, the Tivoli General worked on viewers through its combination of traditional Roman verism and Greek visual ideals; it appeared to faithfully depict an actual man while linking him to symbolic meanings and cultural values. Similarly, later imperial reliefs often worked allegorically (see essay 3.5, Sobocinski and Wolfram Thill). Representations of the ruling emperor sacrificing, charging into battle, or showing mercy to defeated enemies expressed his identity and role in relation to imperial virtues of *pietas*, *virtus*, and *clementia*.

An important point is that this horizon of expectations changed over time. The same object could be perceived quite differently in a changed visual landscape. For example, veristic portraiture was seen in one way in the late Republic, as noted above for the Tivoli

General (figure 6.2.1). Augustus's portraiture famously broke with those expectations by combining veristic details like large eyes and protruding ears with classicizing features like smooth skin and unchanging youth (Zanker 1988, 98–100). By the late first century AD, viewers' expectations had shifted again and were now shaped by the conventions of Julio-Claudian portraiture. In this climate, the verism employed for Vespasian's portraits (including deep forehead lines, drooping eyelids, and other signs of age) helped signal the new ruler's distance from his notorious predecessor, Nero.

Jauss's approach asks us to consider what viewers knew and expected in looking at Roman sculptures. It situates analysis firmly within the visual circumstances of the time; it also provides a way to substantiate any claims we make about ancient viewing and reception. At the same time, working with viewers' expectations depends on the existence of well-established patterns in ancient art. It will be less helpful for the study of an unusual image for which good comparanda do not exist, and it may not allow for nuances specific to a single work. Another problem is that this approach assumes that there is no real difference between ancient and modern viewers: the modern scholar can reconstruct and even participate in the visual expectations of a given time. This kind of immersive reconstruction, however, is very difficult to do and risks erasing profound historical differences between ancient and modern viewers. A related problem is the model of a widely shared and largely uniform visual literacy, the assumption that all or most viewers' expectations were largely similar at any given time. To some extent, this assumption must be true. People living in Roman cities were surrounded by images and participated in collective rituals and other mechanisms that fostered a widely shared knowledge of visual culture. But not all viewers had the same level of knowledge or responded to a given sculpture in the same way; Jauss does not help us with differentiated receptions.

How Did Roman Sculpture Prestructure Its Own Viewing?

By contrast to Jauss's emphasis on actual audiences, Wolfgang Iser focused much more on the work itself and the way it prestructures its own reception (Iser 1974; 1978). A crucial concept for Iser was the implied reader: "this term incorporates both the prestructuring of the potential meaning by the text, and the reader's actualization of this potential through the reading process" (Iser 1974, xii; 1978, 27–38). Any work is created in relation to an imagined reader but the reader also brings his or her own predispositions and decisions to this encounter. Reading is an active process, and so the reception of the text changes from one person to the next, as well as over time. Methodologically, the crucial question is: what part of reception does the work itself prestructure, and what part is left open for the audience's imagination?

We rarely have specific evidence for the actual viewers of Roman sculpture, so the possibility of understanding reception by analyzing the artworks themselves is very appealing.

Wolfgang Kemp has explored most fully what Iser's ideas mean for visual art (Kemp 1992; 1998). For any artwork, the implied viewer should refer both to the way the work prestructures its own viewing and to the viewer's active looking, which actualizes the work's potential even as it differs from one person to the next. Viewing thus becomes an active process of recognizing, decoding, and interpreting. An artwork can attempt to channel, structure, or otherwise try to shape how it is seen, but it cannot fully predetermine what its viewers see.

Iser describes several ways in which a work of art can prestructure its own reception. He begins from the work's historical context, purposes, and intended audience (Iser 1974, 1 and *passim*; cf. Kemp 1998, 185–6). For Roman sculpture, a large and eclectic body of material, it is crucial to ask: what kind of sculpture was this, and for what purpose and audience was it made? These questions have been enormously productive for Roman art independently of Iser's writings, illuminating, for example, late republican portraiture as an expression of aristocratic ideology (Giuliani 1986), or the way that considerations of audience shaped the iconography on the coins Antony minted to pay his troops (Hölscher 1984). Sculpture in a public setting (Boschung 2002) was received very differently from sculpture seen inside a tomb in connection with a family's grief and commemoration rituals (Bielfeldt 2003; Zanker and Ewald 2012).

An important next question for Iser is then: What does the work demand of its audience? He was particularly interested in how texts engaged their readers through direct address, shifts of perspective, narrative structure, and so on. Similarly, a work of visual art can involve the viewer through internal compositional features like the arrangement of figures in space, shifts of perspective, narrative structure, or a figure's gestures or gaze at the viewer (Kemp 1998, 187; Riegl 1902 is an important antecedent). In this approach, there is little discussion of the artist or patron—not because the image maker is deemed unimportant, or because the image is thought to have independent agency of its own, but because the focus is on the finished work and the reader's (or viewer's) encounter with that work. For example, on the Circus Relief in the Vatican (figure 6.2.2), the togate man at the far left is the largest figure in the scene and the only one to look directly out at the viewer; these details suggest that he is the most important figure, the deceased and commemorated subject.

We can also consider what moment in a story is depicted, what knowledge the viewer is expected to bring, and how the image maker plays with the viewer's expectations (Iser 1974; Brilliant 1984). Ruth Bielfeldt draws on Iser's ideas to explore ancient receptions of the Orestes Sarcophagus from the Tomba della Medusa in Rome (Bielfeldt 2003). The viewer must know the story of Orestes to understand the image (figure 6.2.3). At center, two young men brandish swords while a man and a woman lie dead below; two female figures with snakes rush in from the viewer's right. The young men are Orestes and Pylades; Orestes has just killed his mother Clytemnestra and her lover Aigisthus, and the avenging Furies are already in pursuit. At far right, a nude, armed young man steps

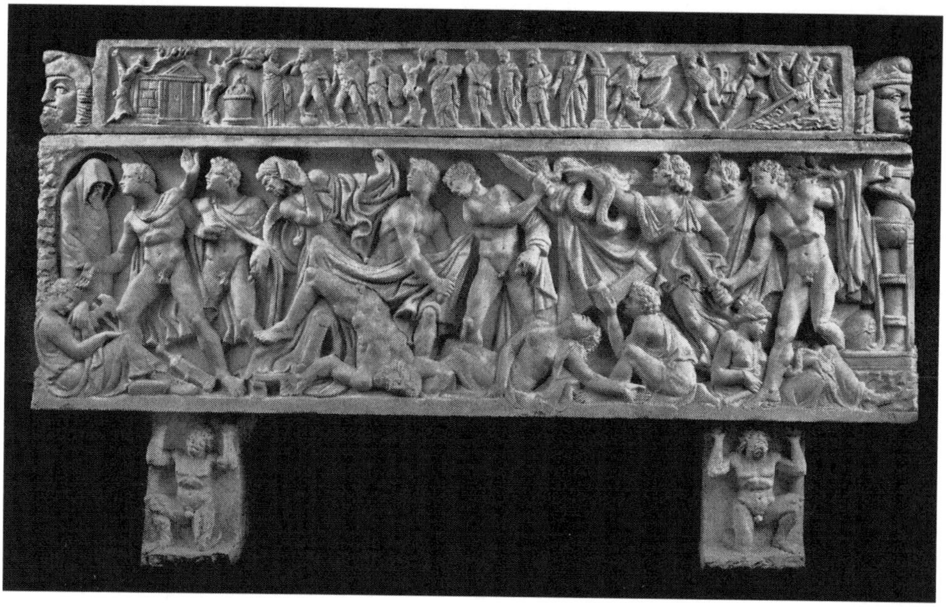

FIGURE 6.2.3 Sarcophagus depicting the revenge of Orestes from the Tomba della Medusa in Rome. Marble. 130s AD. Vatican City, Musei Vaticani: Museo Gregoriano Profano, inv. no. 10450.

away from a tripod; this is the young hero Orestes leaving Delphi. Bielfeldt argues that on this sarcophagus, unusual ways of depicting figures and actions nudged the viewer's interpretation down particular pathways. At the far left, for example, the two young men encounter a dead man's shade in front of a tomb; this scene is not attested in other versions of the myth, but it must depict Agamemnon, sanctioning his son's deed.

External, contextual features of a composition also played important roles in prestructuring reception, including visual interactions with other images in the same space, any associated inscriptions, the surrounding architecture, and viewers' access or exclusion (Elsner 1995; Clarke 2003; Fejfer 2008; Trimble 2011). In the Tomba della Medusa, the Orestes sarcophagus was one of three figured sarcophagi that together faced any member of the bereaved family who entered the tomb. A garland sarcophagus with Medusa heads stood opposite the entrance, with the Orestes sarcophagus on the viewer's right and a sarcophagus depicting the dying Niobids on the left. Juxtaposed, the latter two thematize the terrible violence of death and loss within the family (Bielfeldt 2003).

One of Iser's key contributions was the concept of "gaps," the distances between the audience's expectations and what actually happens in the work; these are the spaces left open that a reader must fill in from his own imagination (Iser 1974, 40; 1978, 166–70). For example, a text's ironic tone signals that the literal meaning of the words is not meant, but it does not say what the meaning should be instead; that part is left up to the reader. In this way, the text depends in crucial ways on imaginative contributions from the audience. Drawing on these ideas for Roman sculpture, we might look for "gaps" in a work's particular emphases or duplications, what expected figures are absent or unexpected figures are present, or other discontinuities that require the reader to fill in the blank. On the Circus Relief in the Vatican (figure 6.2.2), the togate male figure and the woman next to him clasp hands in a *dextrarum iunctio*, indicating that they were married. But the woman is shown standing on a pedestal, statue-like; this discontinuity, or "gap," suggests that she had previously died and was depicted here as a figure of commemoration.

A more difficult Iserian gap lies between this couple and the chariot-racing scene that fills the remainder of the relief. Here, the figures and perspective change abruptly. The two parts of the relief are clearly interrelated, as signaled by their careful compression into the same sculptural panel, but the image does not tell the viewer exactly *how* they are related; that is left to his or her imagination. Additional images or inscriptions belonging to the original ensemble may once have provided clues, but none survive. Modern scholars have proposed various interpretations to fill this gap, including that the togate man may have been a charioteer himself or an official of the races (Sinn 1991, 38). Iser's concept of gaps is helpful here in two ways. First, it suggests that, by definition, there can be no single or correct interpretation of this relief (or any work of Roman sculpture), since reception differed to some degree from viewer to viewer. Second, it makes clear that modern scholarly viewers have to fill in the same gaps, but with less knowledge than most ancient viewers would have had.

By contrast to Jauss's *Erwartungshorizont*, Iser's approach focuses on implied rather than actual viewers; it shifts the perspective to the ways in which a work prestructures its own reception. For ancient and modern receptions alike, Iser valuably helps us see what part of viewing the relief prestructures and what portion its viewers must supply. This approach can be extended to multiple works at a time (Zanker 1988; Boschung 2002; Bielfeldt 2003) or even to works that impair their own viewing (Trimble 2007). Iser's ideas also pose challenges for Roman art. This approach implies that a work's prestructuring is stable over time, that is, that we will see the same gaps, emphases, or visual cross-references that ancient viewers did, but that may not be the case. And Iser presupposes an individual male reader, a construct that belongs to Western, post-Enlightenment ideas of the autonomous individual; it is anachronistic for ancient Roman viewing situations (Zanker 1997). We still have no access to differentiated viewings, either; like Jauss, Iser insists that different audiences will have responded differently, without saying much about how to discover those differences.

These distinctions between Jauss and Iser help explain a tension in the current scholarship on Roman art between contextual/historical approaches on the one hand and aesthetic/interpretive ways of analyzing the material on the other. Very different assumptions and methods underlie these ways of engaging with the material. To some extent, this contrast boils down to the difference between historical reception and reception aesthetics, that is, whether we give interpretive priority to the surrounding historical and contextual situation or to the formal makeup of the work itself, to the evidence of actual viewers and receptions or to a wider range of implied viewings and interpretive possibilities (see, for example, the very different approaches taken by Smith 2002 and Squire 2009). This opposition is by no means cut and dried; many studies of Roman sculpture examine both the work itself and its contextual situation. For example, most current scholarship takes into account historical and contextual circumstances; however, focusing on those aspects alone limits our ability to understand the full visual and expressive power of Roman sculpture.

In the second half of this essay, I accordingly address two further questions. First, if reception changes from viewer to viewer, how can we analyze those differences? Second, the analytical approaches seen so far do not account for being awed, enraged, or otherwise powerfully affected by viewing; how can we engage with the more multifaceted power of images? I move now to two further approaches to viewing and reception, one of them interested primarily in the social historical situations of viewers and the other focused on the power of images and how viewers engaged with and responded to that power.

Who Was the Viewer?

Social historical approaches to viewing and reception have been fundamental in recent work on Roman sculpture, as in art history more broadly (e.g., Clarke 2003; Smith et al. 2006; Fejfer 2008; Stewart 2008). Strongly shaped by analyses of power and social relations, from Foucault to feminist theory to postcolonialism, a major theme has been the analysis of subjectivity and its interactions with visual imagery. For our purposes, the fundamental idea is that people who are differently positioned in society will see and experience images very differently: who the viewer is (socially speaking) will shape viewing and reception. In the study of Roman sculpture, this has been explored in two main directions: studies of the role of the patron and studies of different social positions and responses among viewers (see essays 4.5, Tuck; 4.6, Kellum; 4.7, Petersen; and 4.8, D'Ambra and Tronchin). Methods and results take shape accordingly.

The patron is a crucial figure because the work itself provides direct evidence of what at least this one viewer intended and paid for. To put it another way, once we attribute the selection and appearance of a piece of sculpture to the person who commissioned it, we can see what the patron desired, found important, and was pleased with. It follows that other viewers also understood that work as an expression of the patron's intentions and agency. In this view, the sculptor is much less important, his role reduced to carrying out the wishes of the patron. So, for example, the installations of sculpture in luxurious villas tell us a great deal about the world of cultivated *otium* that the owners wished to inhabit and the artful ways in which they manipulated images, nature, and seeing (Bergmann 2002; see essays 3.3, Anguissola; 4.3, Gazda; and 6.1, Squire). The emperor was the most powerful of patrons, and so the sculptural program of the Forum of Augustus and its Temple of Mars Ultor can be understood to express the ideological program and symbolism important to the first *princeps*; these ideological programs played a crucial role in legitimizing the new order (Zanker 1988; see essays 3.3, Anguissola; 6.1, Squire; and 6.3, Shaya). Portrait commissions and installations at Aphrodisias provide a wealth of information about civic values, local politics, and cultural negotiations between the city and the larger world (Smith et al. 2006; see essays 4.6, Kellum; and 5.5, Ng).

Textual sources play a greater role in this scholarship than in the approaches seen above, because they provide the information necessary to reconstruct patrons' social positions and preoccupations. A strikingly productive area of research has been the self-representation of freedpeople (Zanker 1975; Petersen 2006). Ancient texts explain freedmen's legal status and rights, including the right of legal marriage, control over their own money and commercial ventures, and the fully free status of any children born after the manumission of the mother (Mouritsen 2011). Freedmen's funerary monuments seem to emphasize exactly these themes (see essay 4.7, Petersen). On the relief of the Servilii, for example, we see portrait busts of a man and a woman at right (figure 6.2.4). He wears a citizen's toga; she wears the drapery of a respectable Roman woman. At left is a boy portrayed with the large, rounded forehead and soft facial features of a very young child; he, too, wears a toga, and the *bulla* hanging on a strap around his neck marks him as freeborn (Sinn 1991, cat. 8, 29–30, figs. 14–18).

The inscriptions below are an equally important part of the composition (*CIL* 6.26410). Underneath the bust of the man, we read that this is Quintus Servilius Hilarus, freedman of Quintus Servilius; the woman is Sempronia Eune, previously owned by Caius Sempronius. By contrast, the boy at left is described as Publius Servilius Globulus, son of Quintus; that is, he is designated freeborn in both text and image, a double emphasis. The final word or abbreviation describes family relationships: Hilarus is the father (*pater*); Eune is his wife (*uxor*); Globulus is their son (*f*[*ilius*]). It is probable that they had a powerful hand in designing their own permanent commemoration, and here we gain insight into ex-slaves' priorities and values as viewers of their own lives: this monument emphasizes the adults' freed status, their legal marriage, and the freeborn status of their son. It also emphasizes Eune's transformed gender possibilities. Slave women had no legal control over their bodies, sexually, reproductively, or otherwise.

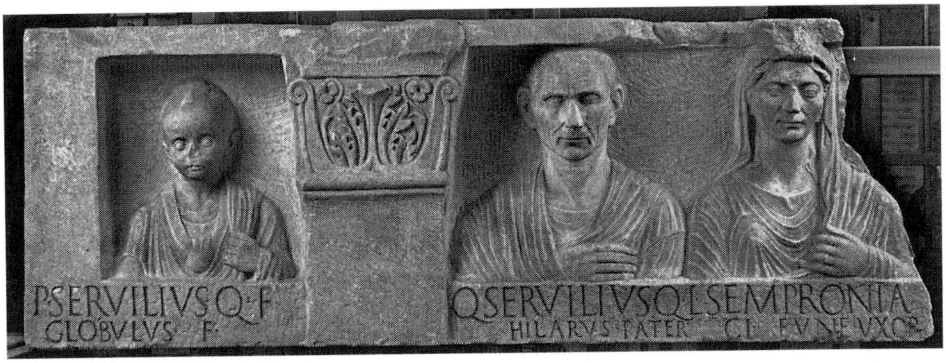

FIGURE 6.2.4 Funerary relief of the Servilii from Rome (exact provenance unknown). Marble. End of the first century BC. Vatican City, Musei Vaticani: Museo Gregoriano Profano, inv. no. 10491.

Eune's respectable matron's clothing and the term *uxor* signal her new ability to participate in the norms of (free) Roman femininity, including sexual modesty and sexual fidelity to her husband.

At the same time, deep ambivalence and grief are woven through the monument. The past remains present; the promising future is bereft. For former slaves, it was only the next generation that could obtain full freedom with all its privileges. The freeborn Globulus might have fulfilled these hopes, but he is separated from his parents by a carved pilaster. This visual device creates two different architectural spaces within the relief, symbolically distinguishing the son's place from the parents'. The device of the pilaster recalls another wife's statue base in the Circus Relief (figure 6.2.2) and other examples in Roman funerary art; these visual devices created differentiated focuses of grief and memory (Koortbojian 2005). On the relief of the Servilii, the dividing pilaster suggests that the son died very young. The grieving parents could reconstitute their family only through this act of visual memory and commemoration.

What about responses of viewers other than the patron? This is an important but more difficult question, and less work has been done on this aspect of viewing and reception in Roman art. John Clarke has explored it most fully (Clarke 2003). His method involves reconstructing viewing based on what we know about viewers' diverse historical and social situations. This can heighten our sensitivity to the ways in which sculptures could resonate differently for differently positioned viewers. A relief on the Arch of Titus depicts the golden Menorah from the Temple in Jerusalem being carried in triumph at Rome (Kleiner 1992, 183–91, 203). This powerful image surely resonated in multiple ways. For the Flavian dynasty, it symbolized the Roman army's suppression of the Jewish Revolt and the legitimacy of Vespasian and his sons' claim to rule. For other viewers, the carved menorah may have been seen as an exotic piece of loot among many such treasures in a long history of conquests, materializing Roman victory in a spectacular and specific way. For members of the Jewish communities in Rome, this triumphal scene dislocated and reframed a sacred religious object, creating a permanent visual reminder in Rome of the destruction of the Temple in Jerusalem in AD 70. For other diaspora communities, this image may have sparked memories of their own people's experiences of Roman military conquest, and so on.

The great advantage of the social historical approaches is their attention to the range of experiences that shaped viewing and reception in the ancient world. These approaches can illuminate the lives, experiences, hopes, and emotions of people long gone. Challenges arise as well. The patron-centered approach depends on assigning the patron control over a sculpture's appearance, but it is unlikely that a patron could determine everything about how a work looked or that every aspect of a sculpture expressed a particular desire of the patron. In exploring differentiated receptions, the risk is that viewing can be made identical with social position: a woman necessarily saw artworks in one way, a slave saw them in another way, and so on. Viewing was surely more variegated than this; we also do not know whether our categories of meaningful social position were the ones that mattered most for ancient viewers and viewing.

Interestingly, and by contrast to Jaussian and Iserian approaches, social historical methods highlight the great differences between ancient viewers and modern commentators; by definition, we are not in the same subject position as any ancient viewer. But this truth raises a new question. If viewing and reception depend on the viewer's historical and social position, and by definition we do not share the position of any ancient viewer, then how can we reconstruct ancient receptions, much less verify them? The immersive capacities of digital technology can potentially tell us a great deal about the physical and sensory experiences of ancient viewers (see essay 1.5, Frischer), but much less about viewers' social constraints and cultural conditioning. Another way forward is to exploit the social historical approach's insights into difference and multiplicity, rather than trying to describe just one possible perspective. Importantly, these observations continue to unsettle the possibility that there is a single or correct interpretation of a work of sculpture. The immediate question becomes: "correct" for whom?

How Were Roman Sculptures Seen as Powerful?

This final section offers a fourth group of approaches to reception and viewing, which focus on the emotional, irrational, sensory, or physical interactions between image and viewers, people's frame of mind in the moment of viewing, and the multifaceted power of images (see essay 6.5, Perry). A shared theme, by contrast to some of the approaches discussed above, is a rejection of linguistic models for the understanding of visual art. W. J. T. Mitchell has characterized this rejection as a broader "pictorial turn" in the arts and in media (Mitchell 1994, 16), which raises new questions about the nature and power of images, and the interactions of image and text, seeing and experience. Those relationships are at stake here.

David Freedberg's work remains important as a provocative antithesis to the serene, analytical approaches seen so far. He set out instead to explore a far wider range of human responses to images (Freedberg 1989, xix). Equally startling was his cross-cultural perspective; he considered specific historical situations but was most interested in deep-seated, recurring patterns in human response: erotic and sexual reactions to images, religious veneration of images treated as embodying the divine, magic and witchcraft, iconoclasm and censorship, and so on. Freedberg did not develop a specific theory or a set of methods we can employ in the study of Roman sculpture, but this approach has enormous implications for viewing and reception.

First, this way of thinking enlarges the scope of viewing and reception far beyond the decipherment of a work's *meaning* to include all the things that images *do* in relation to the many ways in which people respond to them. This can include erotic, devotional, bereaved, destructive, and other responses to Roman sculpture (Stewart 2003, 261–99), as in the organized attacks of *damnatio memoriae* (Varner 2004; Boschung 2002, 168–71;

see essays 2.3, Varner; and 6.6, Kristensen). Second, this focus on response implicitly expands the range of objects that count as "Roman sculpture" well beyond the most impressive works and the standard corpora. The (lost) statue group of Aeneas carrying his father and leading his son by the hand, originally installed in a hemicycle of the Forum of Augustus, is important for thinking about viewing and reception, but so are its repetitions in other sizes and media (see essay 6.4, Moormann), including the satirical version with animal heads and tails painted onto a wall at Stabiae. Finally, this kind of work offers new ways of engaging with ancient textual sources to understand viewing and reception.

For Roman art, Jaś Elsner has contributed perhaps the fullest exploration of different ways of viewing, suggesting both Freedberg's commitment to powerful responses and Iser's implied viewer. One way of viewing is associated with naturalist forms of depiction, the other with symbolic and sacred approaches to the image (Elsner 1995; 2007, 1–26). To develop these ideas, Elsner explores textual sources previously untapped for the study of art, such as the *Tabula* of Cebes. Naturalism was not merely a visual style or way of depicting things; its viewing was interwoven with ideas about desire, fantasy, mimesis, and visuality. By contrast, sacred viewing was associated with ritual and the experience of the divine, constructed, for example, by the frontality and direct gaze of an image of the deity or by the progression through ritual and space that culminated in this visual encounter with the divine (see essays 4.2, McCarty; and 6.5, Perry). And in fact, religion has been an especially productive area for recent work on Roman viewing, as politics and social relations were for the earlier approaches discussed above (Platt 2011).

But *how* do images have power over people? If some scholars have focused on the viewer's frame of mind, others look at how images create these powerful effects. Alfred Gell's *Art and Agency* has been the most influential anthropological study of this problem (Gell 1998). Gell's theory hinges on the ways in which images can act as secondary agents (for people or other social actors, e.g., the gods), and on the ways in which viewers abduct (or infer) that agency. Gell further describes the ways in which artworks and other objects can extend and distribute social agency. For Roman sculpture, this distributed agency is a helpful way to think, for example, about the extraordinary proliferation around the empire of portraits of the emperor (see essays 4.5, Tuck; and 4.6, Kellum).

Gell is perhaps most useful in insisting that we be explicit about the mechanisms of agency and abduction we are inferring for an image and in providing a clear way to articulate and diagram those (Osborne and Tanner 2007). Using a very few conceptual building blocks (prototype, artist, index, recipient), Gell is able to show that the abduction of agency can work in multiple directions and at multiple levels, depending on who or what is thought to be acting on whom or what. For example, in sorcery—as in *damnatio memoriae*—the index (or artwork) is thought to act on its own prototype. That is, attacking the representation of a person is thought to cause harm to that person. But the reverse happens as well (as do many other permutations). In the case of an emperor's portrait statue, which can offer asylum or guarantee an oath (Boschung 2002, 168–71), it is the prototype—the emperor himself—who is treated as acting directly on the image and on viewers.

These more broadly aesthetic and anthropological approaches are still relatively new for the study of Roman sculpture, but they offer stimulating challenges to the historical/contextual approach that has dominated the field since the 1970s and 1980s. The specific context and formal structure of the work remain essential, but interpretive lines have opened up more widely, allowing for more complex interactions of image and viewer, as well as image and text. These approaches also offer questions, methods, and outcomes that are different from those of the strictly historical/contextual approach, and for this reason are probably best evaluated not by the latter criteria but by how fully the material opens up in response, and how much new insight we gain into the complex interactions of Roman sculptures and their viewers.

Conclusion

There is a great deal of overlap in these various ways of thinking about viewing and reception, including recurring themes and shared challenges. Emphasizing the differences in research questions, methods, and kinds of results obtained does not mean we can work within only a single approach. The study of viewing and reception is in part a cumulative enterprise; even in the newest approaches, iconography remains fundamental; the works themselves continue to prestructure what is seen and what can be said about them; the social, historical, and physical circumstances must be taken into account in trying to understand the power of images. This makes for a hopeful outlook. The study of viewing and reception in Roman sculpture currently includes a rich mix of existing frameworks and open directions for research, rigorous methods together with new possibilities for combining and developing them.

Bibliography

Bergmann, B. 2002. "Art and Nature in the Villa at Oplontis." In *Pompeian Brothels, Pompeii's Ancient History, Mirrors and Mysteries, Art and Nature at Oplontis, and the Herculaneum "Basilica"*, by T. McGinn, P. Carafa, N. de Grummond, B. Bergmann, and T. Najbjerg, 87–120. JRA Supplement 47. Portsmouth, RI: Journal of Roman Archaeology.

Bielfeldt, R. 2003. "Orest im Medusengrab: Ein Versuch zum Betrachter." *RM* 110: 117–50.

Boschung, D. 2002. *Gens Augusta: Untersuchungen zu Aufstellung, Wirkung und Bedeutung der Statuengruppen des julisch-claudischen Kaiserhauses*. Monumenta Artis Romanae 32. Mainz: Philipp von Zabern.

Brilliant, R. 1984. *Visual Narratives: Storytelling in Etruscan and Roman Art*. Ithaca: Cornell University Press.

Clarke, J. R. 2003. *Art in the Lives of Ordinary Romans: Visual Representation and Non-Elite Viewers in Italy, 100 B.C.–A.D. 315*. Berkeley: University of California Press.

Elsner, J. 1995. *Art and the Roman Viewer: The Transformation of Art from the Pagan World to Christianity*. Cambridge: Cambridge University Press.

Elsner, J. 2007. *Roman Eyes: Visuality and Subjectivity in Art and Text.* Princeton: Princeton University Press.

Fejfer, J. 2008. *Roman Portraits in Context.* Berlin: Walter de Gruyter.

Freedberg, D. 1989. *The Power of Images: Studies in the History and Theory of Response.* Chicago: University of Chicago Press.

Gell, A. 1998. *Art and Agency: An Anthropological Theory.* Oxford: Oxford University Press.

Giuliani, L. 1986. *Bildnis und Botschaft: Hermeneutische Untersuchungen zur Bildniskunst der römischen Republik.* Frankfurt: Suhrkamp.

Hallett, C. H. 2005. *The Roman Nude: Heroic Portrait Statuary, 200 BC–AD 300.* Oxford: Oxford University Press.

Holly, M. A. 2002. "Reciprocity and Reception Theory." In *A Companion to Art Theory*, edited by P. Smith and C. Wilde, 448–57. Oxford: Blackwell.

Holub, R. C. 1984. *Reception Theory: A Critical Introduction.* New York: Methuen.

Hölscher, T. 1984. *Staatsdenkmal und Publikum: Vom Untergang der Republik bis zur Festigung des Kaisertums in Rom.* Xenia 9. Constance: Universitätsverlag Konstanz.

———. (1987) 2004. *The Language of Images in Roman Art.* Translated by A. Snodgrass and A. Künzl-Snodgrass. Cambridge: Cambridge University Press. Originally published as *Römische Bildsprache als semantisches System.*

Iser, W. 1974. *The Implied Reader: Patterns of Communication in Prose Fiction from Bunyan to Beckett.* Baltimore: Johns Hopkins University Press.

———. 1978. *The Act of Reading: A Theory of Aesthetic Response.* Baltimore: Johns Hopkins University Press.

Jauss, H. R. 1982. *Toward an Aesthetic of Reception.* Translated by T. Bahti. Minneapolis: University of Minnesota Press.

Kemp, W. 1992. *Der Betrachter ist im Bild.* Berlin: Dietrich Reimer Verlag.

———. 1998. "The Work of Art and Its Beholder: The Methodology of the Aesthetic of Reception." In *The Subjects of Art History: Historical Objects in Contemporary Perspectives*, edited by M. A. Cheetham, M. A. Holly, and K. Moxey, 180–96. Cambridge: Cambridge University Press.

Kleiner, D. E. E. 1992. *Roman Sculpture.* New Haven: Yale University Press.

Koortbojian, M. 2005. "Mimesis or *Phantasia*? Two Representational Modes in Roman Commemorative Art." *ClAnt* 24(2): 285–306.

Mitchell, W. J. T. 1994. *Picture Theory: Essays on Verbal and Visual Representation.* Chicago: University of Chicago Press.

Mouritsen, H. 2011. *The Freedman in the Roman World.* Cambridge: Cambridge University Press.

Osborne, R., and J. Tanner, eds. 2007. *Art's Agency and Art History.* Blackwell.

Petersen, L. H. 2006. *The Freedman in Roman Art and Art History.* Cambridge: Cambridge University Press.

Platt, V. J. 2011. *Facing the Gods: Epiphany and Representation in Graeco-Roman Art, Literature, and Religion.* Cambridge: Cambridge University Press.

Riegl, A. 1902. "Das holländische Gruppenporträt." *Jahrbuch der Kunstsammlungen des Allerhöchsten Kaiserhauses* 23: 71–278.

Sinn, F. 1991. *Die Grabdenkmäler.* Vol. 1, *Reliefs, Altäre, Urnen.* Vatikanische Museen, Museo Gregoriano Profano ex Lateranense, Katalog der Skulpturen 1.1. Monumenta Artis Romanae 17. Mainz: Philipp von Zabern.

Smith, R. R. R. 2002. "The Use of Images: Visual History and Ancient History." In *Classics in Progress: Essays on Ancient Greece and Rome*, edited by T. P. Wiseman, 59–102. Oxford: Oxford University Press.

Smith, R. R. R., with S. Dillon, C. H. Hallett, J. Lenaghan, and J. Van Voorhis. 2006. *Aphrodisias II: Roman Portrait Statuary from Aphrodisias*. Mainz: Philipp von Zabern.

Squire, M. J. 2009. *Image and Text in Graeco-Roman Antiquity*. Cambridge: Cambridge University Press.

Stewart, P. 2003. *Statues in Roman Society: Representation and Response*. Oxford: Oxford University Press.

———. 2008. *The Social History of Roman Art*. Cambridge: Cambridge University Press.

Trimble, J. 2007. "Visibility and Viewing on the Severan Marble Plan." In *Severan Culture*, edited by S. Swain, S. Harrison, and J. Elsner, 368–84. Cambridge: Cambridge University Press.

———. 2011. *Women and Visual Replication in Roman Imperial Art and Culture*. Cambridge: Cambridge University Press.

Varner, E. R. 2004. *Mutilation and Transformation: "Damnatio Memoriae" and Roman Imperial Portraiture*. Leiden: Brill.

Zanker, P. 1975. "Grabreliefs römischer Freigelassener." *JdI* 90: 267–315.

———. 1988. *The Power of Images in the Age of Augustus*. Translated by A. Shapiro. Ann Arbor: University of Michigan Press.

———. 1997. "In Search of the Roman Viewer." In *The Interpretation of Architectural Sculpture in Greece and Rome*, edited by D. Buitron-Oliver, 179–91. Studies in the History of Art 49. Washington, DC: National Gallery of Art.

Zanker, P., and B. C. Ewald. 2012. *Living with Myths: The Imagery of Roman Sarcophagi*. Translated by J. Slater. Oxford: Oxford University Press.

CHAPTER 6.3

ANCIENT ANALOGS OF MUSEUMS

JOSEPHINE SHAYA

INTRODUCTION

THE term museum comes from the Greek *mouseion*, a place connected to the Muses and their arts. The most famous of antiquity was the Mouseion at Alexandria, a royally funded cult center of learning, well known not because of any collections of objects but because of its scholars and its connection to the Library of Alexandria (El-Abbadi 1992; MacLeod 2000, 1–15). The ancient *mouseion* was something quite different from the modern museum (Findlen 1989; Lee 1997). But ancient analogs of the modern museum—public and private efforts to collect, organize, and display works of art and cultural artifacts—did exist and had important social functions. More to the point, modern museum studies offer new ways of thinking about Roman art and cultural patrimony. This essay lays out recent insights in museum studies and looks at directions for applying them to ancient Rome.

ANCIENT MUSEUMS?

Over forty years ago, Donald Strong compared the spoils and historical memorabilia collected in Rome's public and religious buildings to objects collected in museums. Strong argued that while Romans did not have museums in a modern sense, "museums" of a kind did exist. Republican generals and later emperors displayed collections of cultural artifacts together with historical memorabilia in temples, porticoes, and triumphal monuments. Strong used the analogy with museums to highlight the role that these buildings played as repositories of wealth, spoils, and historical relics (Strong 1973).

Strong was not alone; many before and after him have drawn similar analogies (e.g. Lehmann 1945; Beaujeu 1982). Quasi-museums included public displays of loot in temples, porticos, theaters, and baths, as well as private collections in villas and palaces. Moved by ancient descriptions of spoils and historical memorabilia, researchers have complied lists of noteworthy objects that accumulated in ancient Rome. The Porticus Octaviae, for instance, contained renowned sculptures, including Praxiteles's Eros of Thespiae, an Eros with a Thunderbolt, two statues of breezes, four satyrs, an Artemis and Asclepius by Kephisodotos (Praxiteles's son), three statues of Aphrodite (one by Pheidias), a Pan and Olympus by Heliodoros, an ivory statue of Jupiter, Lysippos's Granikos monument, and a bronze seated statue of Cornelia, the mother of the Gracchi (*LTUR* 4: 141–5). Other well-known public collections were found in the Porticus Metelli, the Porticus Liviae, the Porticus Pompeiana, the temple of Capitoline Jupiter, and the Templum Pacis, just to name a few.

But we would be mistaken to see ancient analogs as modern museums in embryo. Roman collections rivaled modern ones in their acts of cultural possession and appropriation, but their intellectual frameworks and intentional purposes differed. Temples, for example, accumulated votive offerings (both newly commissioned and dedicated spoils) that framed rituals involving animal sacrifice, incense burning, and the oiling and bedecking of statues. Nevertheless, the museum is a potent analogy for antiquity. While the Romans did not have museums, practices of collecting and display were fully developed in Rome.

The History of Collecting

In the 1980s, a wave of studies on the history of museums changed the way that scholars think not only about museums but about collecting and display more broadly. The literature quickly branched out to include research into all sorts of collections and today museums and collecting are central topics in art history and cultural studies (Alsop 1982; Bourdieu 1984; Stewart 1984; Clifford 1988; Pomian 1990; Karp and Lavine 1991; Hooper-Greenhill 1992; Elsner and Cardinal 1994; Kaplan 1994; Pearce 1994; Bennett 1995; Duncan 1995; Preziosi and Farago 2004). While ancient collecting is one of the least-studied areas in this literature, it is clear that various practices of collecting and display existed in the ancient Near East, Egypt, Greece, and Rome (Harper 1992; Pearce and Bounia 2000; Shaya 2005; Thomason 2005; Tanner 2006, 219–34; Prioux 2008; Rutledge 2012).

Recent work on museums and the history of collecting offers a set of analytic tools and methods with which to approach ancient analogs of museums. This literature points us to the complex arguments and messages constructed in material form by collections. In sum, the accumulation, selection, organization, and description of objects express ways in which cultures make sense of the world: to know a collection and its hierarchies is to know a way of thinking (Foucault 1970; Elsner 1996; Bounia 2004, 7–14; Starn 2005). Today, debates about the acquisition, ownership, and display of cultural property are at the forefront of museum studies and on the front pages of newspapers. The literature emphasizes the value that some objects acquire as tangible expressions of cultural, religious, or personal identity. Possessed by others and displayed in new spaces, objects take on new meanings, often loaded with moral and political significance. A related insight is that collections radically transform the meaning of the objects that have been collected. Collected objects come to have different meanings from those that their makers intended, meanings created not only by their movement from one context to another, but also by the ways in which they are displayed and by the narratives in which they are framed. Viewers, furthermore, selectively see and interpret objects based upon their own knowledge and experience. Politics, ideas of ownership and authority, cultural and religious beliefs, education, gender, and more all play a role in the interpretation of objects.

In recent years, Roman art historians and archaeologists have drawn on such thinking not to suggest an equivalency between Roman collections and modern museums, but to better explore how ancient collections worked, what was at stake in their creation, and how they were viewed. Much of their research has focused on the significance of collections in the private sphere (Neudecker 1988; Bartman 1991; Mattusch 2005; Stirling 2005; Dillon 2006, 39–57), but some have looked at public collections or the broader phenomenon of Roman collecting in general (Pollitt 1978; Bryson 1994; Kuttner 1999; Carey 2003; Bounia 2004; Isager 2006; Miles 2008; Rutledge 2012). This scholarship explores questions of viewing, debates over what we call cultural property, and the role of collections in the construction of personal and imperial identities.

Acquisition

As noted above, debates over the acquisition and ownership of cultural property are at the forefront of museum studies today (Renfrew 2000; Skeates 2000). Do cultural artifacts have a fixed location where they rightly belong? What should be the fate of cultural property in times of war or unrest? Should local populations have control over their cultural patrimony?

Such questions have prompted new thinking about the Roman booty taken from South Italy, Sicily, Greece, Asia Minor, and elsewhere (Gruen 1992, 84–130; Beard 2007; Östenberg 2009). For centuries Roman writers described with awe and fascination wagonloads of loot paraded in triumphs through the city and subsequently showcased in its monuments. We get a sense for the way Romans imagined the scale of the spoils from descriptions like those of Livy, who recounted the 515 bronze and marble statues that Fulvius Nobilior paraded through Rome after the sack of Ambracia in 187 BC (Livy 39.5.16). While other ancient cities had collections of captured cultural artifacts, Rome was exceptional in the extent and the celebration of them.

Romans were much more concerned with the question of the impact of loot on the character of Rome than on its absence from the peoples from whom they took it. Over generations,

Roman writers repeated the topos that Rome, once lacking in luxury, conquered the East and was seduced and corrupted by its abundance (Livy 25.40.1–3; Plin. *HN* 33.148, 37.12–14; Plut. *Vit. Marc.* 21.5; August. *De civ. D.* 3.21). Cato famously likened the statues brought back from Syracuse to "an enemy horde" let into the city (quoted in Livy 34.4.3–4).

This trope did not stop Roman elites from appropriating Greek art (see essays 3.3, Anguissola; and 3.6, Touchette). Hellenization was a fundamental feature of Roman aristocratic culture from the city's beginnings, and it only accelerated in the second century BC when the voracious Roman appetite for things Greek fueled a revolution in Roman art and literature. Through the aggressive absorption of Greek language, ideas, and arts, the Romans shaped their own literary and artistic traditions (Feeney 1998; Wallace-Hadrill 2008, 3–35). In the process, Romans projected their anxieties over imperial expansion onto its profits. The very ideas of loot and luxury became touchstones in cultural debates about the meaning of Rome's absorption of materials and ideas from the East (Gruen 1992, 55–83, 223–71). The key context for the discussion of Roman collecting is the cultural appropriation of Greece.

Along with conquest, many objects came to Rome through extortion. Cicero's attack on Verres, the notorious Roman praetor who was brought to trial in 70 BC for exploiting the province of Sicily, illustrates its scale and rapaciousness. The often violent tactics that Verres had used to seize ancient votive offerings, cult statues, and privately owned works of art only added to Cicero's larger picture of his brutal exploitation. In his defense, Verres might have argued that his behavior was no different from that of many Roman governors. The existence of the extortion court, Cicero's line of argument that the court should not protect its own, and evidence for other Romans charged with extortion (some of whom Cicero defended) point to widespread practices.

While Cicero and the court had no qualms about taking art from enemies, plundering Rome's allies or provinces for one's own private enrichment was, at least in public, reprehensible. Along with illustrating the violence of Roman extortion and the fundamental yet frequently ignored principle that one did not purloin art for one's private advantage but for the adornment of the temples and the city (Cic. *Verr.* 2.1.54–5), Cicero's prosecution also speaks to the role that loot played in larger debates about Rome's relationship to its provinces. The statues that Verres displayed in the forum and the Comitium from Asia and Achaea, Cicero asserted, were "magnificent to the eye, but bitter and grievous to the heart and mind" for to plunder Rome's allies was to plunder Rome itself (Cic. *Verr.* 2.1.58). Their display, however, also shows that the statues, together with countless other Greek works in the city, delighted many (like Verres).

Margaret Miles has argued that Cicero's remarks signal the very beginning of the close of the era of looting the Greek world (Miles 2008, 251). With the consolidation of power in the hands of Augustus and the gradual extension of the idea of Rome to include the provinces, the attitudes heralded by Cicero gained ground. While the plundering did not suddenly cease, Miles argues, it was drawing to an end. In the *Res Gestae*, for instance, Augustus boasted that he had returned to the cities of Asia the temple dedications that Antony had seized for his own private use (*RG* 24.1). The political expediency of such remarks points to an evolving attitude toward plunder that later imperial writers echoed when they illustrated the deviant characters of emperors like Caligula and Nero with indignant stories of art theft. But these stories, too, suggest that appropriations continued. And while Augustus failed to mention in the *Res Gestae* his own appropriations of statues from those on the losing side of the war, he was careful to record the scale of his dedications: "I consecrated gifts from spoils in the Capitoline temple and the temple of Divine Julius and the temple of Apollo and the temple of Vesta and the temple of Mars Ultor, which cost me around 100,000,000 sesterces" (*RG* 21.2; Scheer 1995).

Logic

Recent studies in the theory of collecting emphasize that collections have a logic; in the eyes of collectors, collected objects belong together. Governed by rules for what to include and what to exclude, collections communicate something greater than their parts: they might tell a story, witness an event, represent an idea, or demonstrate a particular view. One way to access this knowledge is to investigate the ideas of classification and order within a collection (Hooper-Greenhill 1992, 4–9). Studies of how collectors classify, describe, and exhibit objects bring the stories that collections tell to light.

The Lindian temple chronicle—a remarkable inscription erected in 99 BC that cataloged treasures from a Rhodian temple as well as miracles of the goddess Athena—offers a compelling ancient example to which we can apply this mode of analysis. About thirty years before Cicero's prosecution of Verres and during a time of increasing Roman hegemony in the East, the Lindians erected the stele to commemorate the legendary possessions of their temple, including an inscribed bronze cauldron from Kadmos, a silver drinking cup from Minos, bracelets of Helen, statues called Daidaleia, weapons from Alexander the Great, and much more. A decree tells how the inscription came to be made: because time had destroyed the ancient offerings, the Lindians commissioned two local scholars to draw up a record of the objects together with a list of testimonials to them, followed by accounts of Athena's epiphanies.

A deep antiquarian spirit runs through the record. Arranged in chronological order, each entry begins with the donor's name followed by a description of the gift, its material, its inscription, and references to literary works, letters, and temple archives that attested to it. The catalog demonstrated who the Lindians had been and how they reached their present. The impressive scholarly apparatus, with 103 citations from at least twenty-five different sources, celebrated the offerings' fame, testified to their authenticity, and glorified Athena to whom they had been given. The epiphany stories that close the record attest to just what the treasure demonstrated, namely the renown and power of Athena, her long devotion to Lindos, and the history of her temple (Higbie 2003; Shaya 2005; Platt 2010).

Roman temples, like those in Greece, housed treasures that belonged to and evoked the gods—offerings (including spoils) that witnessed the manifest power of divinities worshipped for generations and images that embodied the gods. What made Rome different was the larger geopolitical situation of the treasures. If the Lindos stele sold a heroic vision of Lindos to locals and visitors, Roman collections attested to Rome's mastery of the world.

One of the best-known collections from Rome was created for the porticoes that framed the Forum of Augustus and the temple to Mars Ultor (see essays 3.3, Anguissola; 4.6, Kellum; 6.1, Squire; and 6.4, Moormann). Its logic was seductively straightforward. More than one hundred larger-than-life-sized statues of Rome's leaders, ranging from Aeneas to Drusus (stepson of Augustus) represented the advancement of the Roman Empire. Each image was labeled with a grand title, below which a longer inscription set forth the leader's most noteworthy accomplishments. Together, the statues and inscriptions told a story of the growth of the empire. For 500 years, Rome's leaders held the same offices and priesthoods. What changed were Rome's size and enemies; the inscribed lives resounded with the names of armies defeated, places conquered, and peoples and kings paraded in triumph.

As many scholars have shown, the collection traced a simple unity of purpose from the city's foundation to its present and placed the continuity of this purpose in the trust of Augustus, whose self-aggrandizing equestrian statue stood in the center of the forum and tied the whole thing together (Spannagel 1999, 259–62; Rutledge 2012, 250–57). With the consolidation of power in the hands of Augustus, the past was reimagined as a time in which Rome's leaders undertook a long, unified, and great imperial project—the very building of Rome.

Such a programmatic reading of the collection, however, is only part of the story, for it assumes an audience that fully understood the intentions of Augustus. While the collection had a logic, viewers also came to their own understandings of it. Some of the statues, for instance, served as meeting points for litigants appearing before the courts of the urban *praetor* and the *praetor peregrinus*. Litigants used them in their negotiations of the court system (Bablitz 2007; Shaya 2013). The reception of the collection also would have changed over time as more objects were added: relics, imperial memorabilia, spoils, honorary statues, and images of emperors and gods. The collection that had originally told a story about the building of Rome became the core of an even larger collection that spoke to the achievements of Rome and its emperors with the support of its gods.

Context

The relationship between objects and context is a central concern in studies of collecting. How objects communicate depends on their context and how they are displayed within that context (Newhouse 2005, 8). The appropriation, movement, and display of objects speak to relationships of power between previous owners, current possessors, and viewers. The spatial and architectural placement of objects also cues certain types of viewing: display engenders interest by setting objects apart from the ordinary and encouraging viewers to attend to them closely (Alpers 1991; Greenblatt 1991).

Torn from their original ritual and civic settings, objects that were carted off from conquered cities were at first displayed as symbols of victories in wars that took place in faraway lands. Greek art became a medium through which generals demonstrated claims to power. Our earliest sources for such displays are republican statue bases inscribed with the names of generals and places conquered: "Marcus Claudius, son of Marcus, consul, took [this] from Henna" (a Sicilian town captured in 214 BC; *CIL* 6.1281); "Lucius Quinctius, son of Lucius, took [this] from Leukas" (an Akarnanian city sacked in 197 BC; *CIL* 1.613); "Marcus Acilius, son of Gaius, consul, took [this] from Scarphea" (a city in near Thermopylae sacked in 191 BC; *CIL* 1.2926). As Tonio Hölscher (2006) argues, through such displays, generals and their descendants reaped the profits of their victories in the form of increased status and authority.

Years later, literary references to statues and paintings displayed in Rome's temples and porticos echoed these inscriptions, noting who captured what from where. Pliny the Elder, for instance, observed that Aemilius Paullus, famed for his triumph over Macedon (168 BC), had dedicated an Athena by Pheidias in the Temple of Today's Fortune (Plin. *HN* 34.54). The statue perpetuated Paulus's second-century BC victory well into the first century AD.

The places such objects were displayed were long-living memorials of the prowess of Rome's generals and the backing of the gods (Beard 2007, 21, 263; Bravi 2012). An entire fifth century BC pediment depicting an Amazonomachia, perhaps taken from the Temple of Apollo Daphnephoros at Eretria in Euboea, crowned the entrance to the Temple of Apollo Sosianus (figure 6.3.1; La Rocca 1985). A triumphal procession (figure 6.3.2) parading around the interior frieze and embracing the temple's contents—an ancient cedar-wood image of Apollo from Seleucia (Plin. *HN* 13.53), Niobids by Scopas or Praxiteles (Plin. *HN* 36.28), an Apollo by Philiscus of Rhodes, a Latona, a Diana, nine Muses, a nude Apollo, and

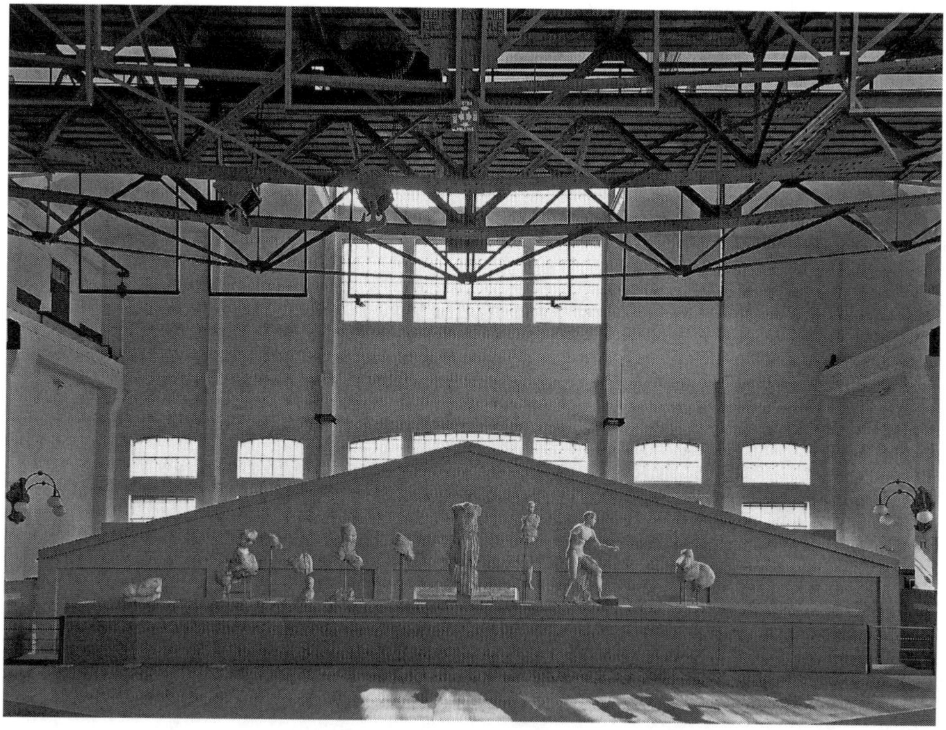

FIGURE 6.3.1 Fifth-century BC pediment from Temple of Apollo Sosianus. Rome, Musei Capitolini, Centrale Montemartini.

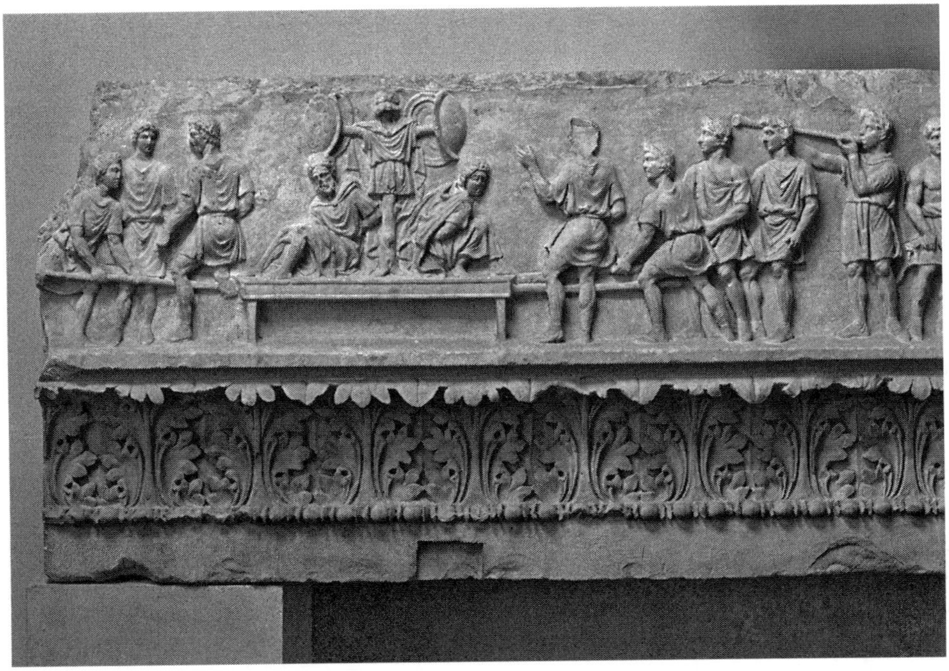

FIGURE 6.3.2 Interior frieze from Temple of Apollo Sosianus, late first century BC. Rome, Musei Capitolini, Centrale Montemartini.

another image of the god with his lyre by Timarchides (Plin. *HN* 36.35)—made the connection between Apollo's possessions and triumph clear. Such displays played an important role in fixing conquests in public memory; years later Pliny observed that it was Sosianus who had brought the ancient cedar-wood Apollo to Rome (Plin. *HN* 13.53).

One of the remarkable things about plunder in Rome is that it ended up in so many contexts: in temples certainly, but also in porticos, theaters, bath buildings, fora, palaces, and villas. The powerful—cults, emperors, generals, and the rich—displayed spectacular objects that made clear the reach of their power. Pliny recounted that the theater of Scaurus, built in 58 BC, was "made up of things collected from all over the world," including 3,000 bronze statues (Plin. *HN* 36.115; see essay 4.1, Longfellow). In 55 BC, Pompey filled his theater complex not just with paintings, tapestries, and statues, but even with living trees transported from Asia and Africa that brought a conquered landscape home to Rome (Kuttner 1999, 345–50).

Viewers brought their own perceptions, understandings, and agendas to these displays. Spoils that commemorated victories meant something very different to the defeated who poured into Rome as slaves, immigrants, and envoys (Edwards 2003, 57–9; see essay 6.2, Trimble). Ambassadors from Asia and Achaea, Cicero wrote, stood in the forum with tears in their eyes as they gazed upon images of their gods stolen from their sanctuaries (Cic. *Verr.* 2.1.59). The second-century BC Greek historian Polybius condemned the Romans for adorning their city with the possessions of others rather than with their own virtues. When a victor collects around himself stolen treasures, Polybius wrote, the treasures almost invite those who were robbed to come and inspect them. For the defeated, he continued, not only jealousy, but a sort of passionate hatred for the victors flares up, for memories awakened of their own disaster enhance their hatred of its authors (Polyb. 9.10.10; Williams 2012).

Art

Collecting and display have played a key role in the construction of images as works of art and in the creation of the discipline of art history (see essays 1.1, Bartman; 1.3, Mallampati Gleason; and 3.3, Anguissola). Roman collecting played no small part in turning the category of art into what Jeremy Tanner has aptly called an "autonomous province of meaning" (Tanner 2006, 220). Here, in the making of art to be viewed, studied, and discussed, analogies with the museum are again useful.

The treasures in the Templum Pacis demonstrated Rome's centrality both in geopolitical terms and as heir to the world's artistic heritage (La Rocca 2001, 195–207; Noreña 2003, 79–92; see essay 4.6, Kellum). Vespasian filled the forum with famous Greek sculptures looted by Nero to furnish his Golden House and other marvels, such as an Egyptian greywacke figure of the Nile, a renowned painting of Ialysus by the fourth-century Rhodian Protogenes, a Scylla painted by the fourth-century Theban Nicomachus, a battle of Issos painted by Helena, the bronze cow of Myron, a statue of the Olympic victor Cheimon by Naukydes, a statue by Pheidias, and another by Lysippos (*LTUR* 4: 67–70). According to Josephus, who defected to the Roman side in the First Jewish Revolt and traveled the elite circles of Flavian Rome, the forum was the conclusion to Vespasian's conquest of Judaea. Like the triumph, it laid the treasures of the Jews at Rome's feet. The spoils were added to the precinct where "all those works that people had travelled over the whole world to see were collected and deposited" (Joseph. *BJ* 7.158). The forum was both a victory monument and a public art gallery where Romans could view masterpieces whose significance transcended cultural boundaries.

The epigraphic framing of images from the Tempum Pacis echoes Josephus's reading of the spoils. Among the objects discovered in its excavations were bases that once carried statues by the Athenian sculptors Polykleitos, Leochares, Praxiteles, Kephisodotos, and Parthenokles (La Rocca 2001, 197–201). The Greek inscriptions are to the point: "The Athenian Leochares's Ganymede"; "The Argive Polykleitos's Pentathlete Pythokles of Elis" (figure 6.3.3). They celebrate the artist and his subject, not the general or emperor who brought the work to Rome. Rather than "art as plunder" (Miles 2008), here we have plunder as art.

The appropriation of statues and paintings and the valorization of them as art were complementary processes. As Tanner observes, the theft and purchase of renowned statues and paintings gave rise to writings on art and the creation of new ways of exhibiting and viewing it; the appreciation of art, in turn, motivated further collecting (Tanner 2006, 220). The roots of this kind of aesthetic viewing (and appropriation) lay in the

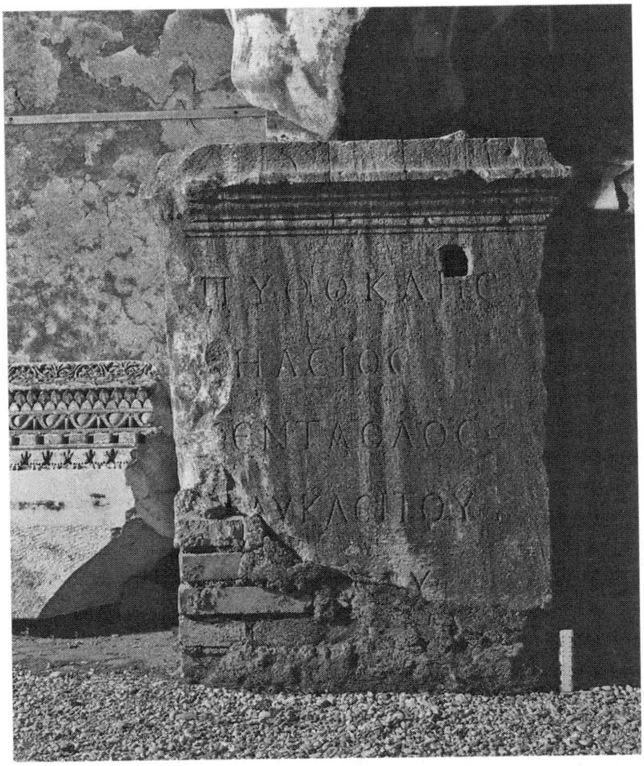

FIGURE 6.3.3 Base for statue of the athlete Pythokles by Polykleitos, originally from Olympia. Rome, Templum Pacis, first century AD. Rome, Museo Capitolini.

collecting practices of Hellenistic kings, who poured immense resources into the acquisition and display of old and new works of art (Kuttner 2005; Calandra 2011). A series of statue bases dedicated in the temple of Athena Nikephoros in Pergamon and inscribed with the names of ancient artists and the cities from which the statues were taken attests to the appropriation of works of art by Attalos I (r. 241–197 BC) and the subsequent valorization of them as masterpieces (Tanner 2006, 222–8). Literary evidence adds detail: following the sack of Corinth, Attalos II (r. 160–138 BC) is said by Pliny to have paid 600,000 denarii for a painting by the fourth-century Aristeides (Plin. *HN* 35.24; Howard 1986). By creating art collections, building libraries, and maintaining court poets and philosophers, the Attalids laid claim to Hellenic culture (Gruen 2000). Here, culture itself was something to be possessed.

This aesthetic way of viewing only grew stronger with the Romans among whom knowledge of art as its own domain became a marker of cultural distinction. The valorization of art was closely connected with looting and expropriation, as well as with the art market, copying, art historical writing, and travel to see works of art that "must be seen." Many sources—Varro, Quintilian, Cicero, Pliny, Statius, Martial, Petronius, and more—show how cultivated persons viewed art: they brought to it a sophisticated aesthetic vocabulary, a conversance with its history, a knowledge of ancient artists' names, a familiarity with iconography, an understanding of Greek myths, and an appreciation of materials. We see such learning on display in Pliny's "art historical" pages, which place statuary and painting within a larger chronological history of art, while identifying personal styles, recounting anecdotes about artists and their works, and discussing the properties of artistic materials (Isager 1991; see essay 6.1, Squire).

Along with becoming a hallmark of elite taste and distinction, art also became a realm through which one could be morally educated. Temples, porticoes, and villas were spaces for learned discussions about deep allegorical meanings of images. Such conversations occur in many texts (e.g., *Tabula Cebes*), where they follow a familiar pattern: typically a viewer does not understand an image; an interpreter appears—a philosopher/teacher type—who promises enlightenment (Elsner 2007, 189); through careful exegesis, the interpreter reveals the allegorical meaning of the image for the viewer (and the reader), offering insight, even salvation, couched in moral or philosophical terms.

Identity

Studies in the history of collecting have long recognized the role that collections play in the materialization of cultural and personal identities. Public collections bear on larger questions of what constitutes the community, the past, the truth, and who exercises the power to articulate and define this knowledge (Kaplan 1994, 2; Bennett 1995, 148–9). Private collections, too, express the self, communicating such values as the status, power, and education of their owners (Clifford 1985, 237–8; Pomian 1990, 165).

The wealthy filled their villas with artworks that were expressions not only of their power and prestige but also their intellectual pursuits and pleasures (see essay 4.3, Gazda). Cicero aimed to create spaces in his villa—an Academy (*Att.* 1.4.3), Lyceum (*Div.* 1.5.8), Amaltheam (*Att.* 1.16.18), gymnasium (*Att.* 1.6.2) and *palaestra* (*Fam.* 1.8.2)—that evoked the Greece of his reading, imagination, and travels (Neudecker 1988, 8–18; Bergmann 2001; see essay 6.1, Squire). Owners of well-appointed villas lived among images of Greek philosophers, poets, leaders, athletes, gods, nymphs, and heroes, together with portraits of their own ancestors, honorific statues, and even tombs, as the vast sculpture collection from the Villa of the Papyri near Herculaneum demonstrates (see essays 2.4, Mattusch; 3.3, Anguissola; 3.6, Touchette; and 6.1, Squire). As John Bodel aptly put it, the villa was "an extension of the man" (Bodel 1997, 5). Its decoration played a key role in constructing and communicating its owner's identity (Wiseman 1987; Tronchin 2012). In the second half of the first century AD, perhaps in response to restrictions on elite self-commemoration in Rome's public spaces, poets began to praise their patrons through descriptions of their villas and artworks. As Pliny the Younger's elaborate "villa letters" show, rich patrons, too, shaped their own reputations through loving descriptions of their estates.

In the emperors' hands, villas and collections took on epic dimensions. A well-known passage from the fourth-century *Historia Augusta* stated that Hadrian had inscribed upon his Tiburtine villa "the names of the most famous provinces and places; for example, he called one the Lyceum, another the Academy, the Prytaneum, the Canopus, the Stoa Poikile and [the Vale of] Tempe. And, so that he would not omit anything, he even made an Underworld" (SHA *Hadr.* 26.5). The villa reflected Hadrian's travels both in the empire and in his mind. Its collection of sites and statues made up an eclectic assortment of references to the Mediterranean past that reached back a thousand years. Several hundred sculptures survive scattered among many modern museums including replicas of the Caryatids from the Erechtheion, a Knidian Aphrodite, Amazons by Pheidias, Tiber and Nile gods, as well as imperial portraits, and images of Hadrian's favorite, Antinous (see essay 3.7, Swetnam-Burland). Embracing this vast collection, the villa itself embodied Hadrian's Rome as the culmination and steward of Mediterranean culture and history (MacDonald and Pinto 1995, 146).

A telling foil to Hadrian's Villa and its engagements with Greece and Egypt is Pausanias's *Guide to Greece*. As Hadrian collected monuments and arts of empire, Pausanias, too, collected (in his text at least) the "things most worth knowing" of Greece (Paus. 1.39.3). While other Greek travel books were rooted in particular places, describing a city, sanctuary, or even a monument, Pausanias set out to portray the whole of Greece and articulate its cultural importance. As Jaś Elsner has shown, this Greece was a fantasy (Elsner 2001, 18). Pausanias shepherded his reader through an imaginary world—a textual museum of sorts—in which a selected past revealed Pausanias's political and religious identity. But there was also a physical world behind the text, with monuments transformed by the ravages of time and a history of warfare and looting. Thefts were remembered for generations; well over a century after the event, Pausanias noted that Augustus had taken the ancient Tegean statue of Alean Athena to Rome (Paus. 8.46.5). It is in such absences, in the memory of them, and in Pausanias's valorization of Greece that we find ourselves on the other side of Rome's "museums."

Conclusion

While Romans did not have museums, they did collect. What difference does it make to look to museum studies when thinking about their collecting practices? Today most of us encounter Roman art in museums. Those institutions shape to a great degree the ways in which we see and engage with antiquities. Museum studies have much to say about our practices of viewing and the history of our field (see essays in part I, Collecting, Conservation, and Display). At the same time, this field opens up meanings of objects that are constituted by forces not visible in the objects themselves.

While the Romans did not have museums, there are important historical links between Roman collections and our own museums. Much of the history of Roman art from antiquity to the present lies in the collection, imitation, appropriation, adaptation, and display of cultural artifacts. Roman collecting played a key role in creating aesthetic viewing practices and in the invention of art history. To a remarkable degree, it has shaped our knowledge of Greek art. The wider frames around the educated viewing of such works are those of acquisition, spoils, loot. It is here—with the creation of art, with the rise of educated viewing, with antiquarianism, with the appropriation of cultural patrimony, and with ideas of a universal artistic heritage—rather than with the *mouseion* at Alexandria that we find the roots of the modern museum.

Bibliography

Alcock, S. E., J. F. Cherry, and J. Elsner, eds. 2001. *Pausanias: Travel and Memory in Roman Greece*. New York: Oxford University Press.

Alpers, S. 1991. "The Museum as a Way of Seeing." In *Exhibiting Cultures: The Poetics and Politics of Museum Display*, edited by I. Karp and S. Lavine, 25–32. Washington, DC: Smithsonian Institution Press.

Alsop, J. 1982. *The Rare Art Traditions: The History of Art Collecting and Its Linked Phenomena Wherever These Have Appeared*. New York: Harper and Row.

Bablitz, L. 2007. *Actors and Audience in the Roman Courtroom*. London: Routledge.

Bartman, E. 1991. "Sculptural Collecting and Display in the Private Realm." In *Roman Art in the Private Sphere: New Perspectives on the Architecture and Decor of the Domus, Villa, and Insula*, edited by E. K. Gazda, 71–88. Ann Arbor: University of Michigan Press.

Beard, M. 2007. *The Roman Triumph*. Cambridge, MA: Belknap.

Beaujeu, J. M. 1982. "A-t-il existe une direction des musées dans la Rome imperial?" *CRAI* 126(4): 671–88.

Bennett, T. 1995. *The Birth of the Museum: History, Theory, Politics*. London: Routledge.

Bergmann, B. 2001. "Meanwhile, Back in Italy. . . Creating Landscapes of Allusion." In Alcock, Cherry, and Elsner 2001, 154–66.

Bodel, J. 1997. "Monumental Villas and Villa Monuments." *JRA* 10: 5–35.

Bounia, A. 2004. *The Nature of Classical Collecting: Collectors and Collections, 100 BCE–100 CE*. Aldershot: Ashgate.

Bourdieu, P. 1984. *Distinction: A Social Critique of the Judgement of Taste*. Translated by R. Nice. Cambridge, MA: Harvard University Press.

Bravi, A. 2012. *"Ornamenta Urbis": Opere d'arte greche negli spazi romani*. Bari: Edipuglia.

Bryson, N. 1994. "Philostratus and the Imaginary Museum." In *Art and Text in Ancient Greek Culture*, edited by S. Goldhill and R. Osborne, 255–83. New York: Cambridge University Press.

Calandra, E. 2011. *The Ephemeral and the Eternal: The Pavilion of Ptolemy Philadelphos in the Court of Alexandria*. Athens: Scuola Archeologica Italiana di Atene.

Carey, S. 2003. *Pliny's Catalogue of Culture: Art and Empire in the Natural History*. New York: Oxford University Press.

Clifford, J. 1985. "Objects and Selves—an Afterword." In *Objects and Others: Essays on Museums and Material Culture*, edited by G. W. Stocking, 236–46. Madison: University of Wisconsin Press.

———. 1988. *The Predicament of Culture: Twentieth-Century Ethnography, Literature, and Art*. Cambridge, MA: Harvard University Press.

Dillon, S. 2006. *Ancient Greek Portrait Sculpture: Contexts, Subjects, and Styles*. Cambridge: Cambridge University Press.

Duncan, C. 1995. *Civilizing Rituals: Inside Public Art Museums*. New York: Routledge.

Edwards, C. 2003. "Incorporating the Alien: The Art of Conquest." In *Rome the Cosmopolis*, edited by C. Edwards and G. Woolf, 44–70. Cambridge: Cambridge University Press.

El-Abbadi, M. 1992. *The Life and Fate of the Ancient Library of Alexandria*. Paris: UNESCO/UNDP.

Elsner, J. 1996. "The New Museology and Classical Art." *AJA* 100(4): 769–73.

———. 2001. "Structuring 'Greece.' Pausanias's Periegesis as a Literary Construct." In Alcock, Cherry, and Elsner 2001, 3–20.

———. 2007. "Viewing and Decadence: Petronius' Picture Gallery." In *Roman Eyes: Visuality and Subjectivity in Art and Text*, 67–112. Princeton: Princeton University Press.

Elsner, J., and R. Cardinal, eds. 1994. *The Cultures of Collecting*. London: Reaktion Books.

Feeney, D. 1998. *Literature and Religion at Rome: Cultures, Contexts, and Beliefs*. Cambridge: Cambridge University Press.

Findlen, P. 1989. "The Museum: Its Classical Etymology and Renaissance Genealogy." *Journal of the History of Collections* 1989 (1): 59–78.

Foucault, M. 1970. *The Order of Things: An Archaeology of the Human Sciences*. New York: Random House.

Greenblatt, S. 1991. "Resonance and Wonder." In *Exhibiting Cultures: The Poetics and Politics of Museum Display*, edited by I. Karp and S. Lavine, 42–56. Washington, DC: Smithsonian Institution Press.

Gruen, E. S. 1992. *Culture and National Identity in Republican Rome*. Ithaca: Cornell University Press.

———. 2000. "Culture as Policy: The Attalids of Pergamon." In *From Pergamon to Sperlonga: Sculpture and Context*, edited by N. de Grummond and B. Ridgway, 17–31. Berkeley: University of California Press.

Harper, P. 1992. "Mesopotamian Monuments Found at Susa." In *The Royal City of Susa: Ancient Near Eastern Treasures in the Louvre*, edited by P. Harper, J. Aruz, and F. Tallon, 159–62. New York: Metropolitan Museum of Art.

Higbie, C. 2003. *The Lindian Chronicle and the Greek Creation of Their Past*. Oxford: Oxford University Press.

Hölscher, T. 2006. "The Transformation of Victory into Power: From Event to Structure." In *Representations of War in Ancient Rome*, edited by S. Dillon and K. E. Welch, 27–48. Cambridge: Cambridge University Press.

Hooper-Greenhill, E. 1992. *Museums and the Shaping of Knowledge*. New York: Routledge.

Howard, S. 1986. "Pergamene Art Collecting and its Aftermath." *Akten des XXV Internationalen Kongresses für Kunstgeschichte* 4: 25–36.

Isager, J. 1991. *Pliny on Art and Society: The Elder Pliny's Chapters on the History of Art*. London: Routledge.

———. 2006. "The Whole World Gathered in One Place. Pliny's Vision of Rome as a Museum." *ActaAArtHist* 20: 65–78.

Kaplan, F., ed. 1994. *Museums and the Making of "Ourselves": The Role of Objects in National Identity*. London: Leicester University Press.

Karp, I. and S. Lavine, ed. 1991. *Exhibiting Cultures: The Poetics and Politics of Museum Display*. Washington, DC: Smithsonian Institution Press.

Kuttner, A. 1999. "Culture and History at Pompey's Museum." *TAPA* 129: 343–73.

———. 2005. "Cabinet Fit for a Queen: The *Λιθικά* as Posidippus' Gem Museum." In *The New Posidippus: A Hellenistic Poetry Book*, edited by K. Gutzwiller, 141–63. New York: Oxford University Press.

La Rocca, E. 1985. *Amazzonomachia: Le sculture frontonali del tempio di Apollo Sosiano*. Rome: De Luca.

———. 2001. "La nuova imagine dei fori imperiali: Appunti in margine agli scavi." *RM* 108: 171–231.

Lee, P. Y. 1997. "The Musaeum of Alexandria and the Formation of the Museum in Eighteenth-Century France." *ArtB* 79(3): 385–412.

Lehmann, K. 1945. "A Roman Poet Visits a Museum." *Hesperia* 14: 259–69.

MacDonald, W. L., and J. A. Pinto. 1995. *Hadrian's Villa and its Legacy*. New Haven: Yale University Press.

MacLeod, R., ed. 2000. *The Library of Alexandria: Centre of Learning in the Ancient World*. London: I. B. Tauris.

Mattusch, C. C. 2005. *The Villa dei Papiri at Herculaneum: Life and Afterlife of a Sculpture Collection*. Los Angeles: J. Paul Getty Museum.

Miles, M. M. 2008. *Art as Plunder: The Ancient Origins of Debate about Cultural Property*. Cambridge: Cambridge University Press.

Neudecker, R. 1988. *Die Skulpturenausstattung römischer Villen in Italien*. Mainz: Philipp von Zabern.

Newhouse, V. 2005. *Art and the Power of Placement*. New York: Monacelli.

Noreña, C. F. 2003. "Medium and Message in Vespasian's Templum Pacis." *MAAR* 48: 25–43.

Östenberg, I. 2009. *Staging the World: Spoils, Captives, and Representations in the Roman Triumphal Procession*. Oxford: Oxford University Press.

Pearce, S., ed. 1994. *Interpreting Objects and Collections*. New York: Routledge.

Pearce, S., and A. Bounia, ed. 2000. *The Collector's Voice: Critical Readings in the Practice of Collecting*. Vol. 1. Burlington, VT: Ashgate.

Platt, V. 2010. "Art History in the Temple." *Arethusa* 43(2): 197–213.

Pollitt, J. J. 1978. "The Impact of Greek Art on Rome." *TAPA* 108: 155–74.

Pomian, K. 1990. *Collectors and Curiosities: Paris and Venice 1500–1800*. Cambridge, MA: Basil Blackwell.

Preziosi, D., and C. J. Farago, ed. 2004. *Grasping the World: The Idea of the Museum*. Burlington, VT: Ashgate.

Prioux, É. 2008. *Petits musées en vers: Épigrammes et discours sur les collections antiques*. Paris: CTHS Editions.

Renfrew, C. 2000. *Loot, Legitimacy, and Ownership: The Ethical Crisis in Archaeology*. London: Duckworth.

Rutledge, S. H. 2012. *Ancient Rome as a Museum: Power, Identity, and the Culture of Collecting*. Oxford: Oxford University Press.

Scheer, T. S. 1995. "Res Gestae Divi Augusti 24: Die Restituierung göttlichen Eigentums in Kleinasien durch Augustus." In *Rom und der griechische Osten: Festschrift für Hatto H. Schmitt zum 65. Geburtstag*, 209–223. Stuttgart: Franz Steiner.

Shaya, J. 2005. "The Greek Temple as Museum: The Case of the Legendary Treasure of Athena from Lindos." *AJA* 109: 423–42.

———. 2013. "The Public Life of Monuments: The *Summi Viri* of the Forum of Augustus." *AJA* 117: 83–110.

Skeates, R. 2000. *Debating the Archaeological Heritage*. London: Duckworth.

Spannagel, M. 1999. *Exemplaria Principis: Untersuchungen zu Entstehung und Ausstattung des Augustusforums*. Heidelberg: Archäologie und Geschichte.

Starn, R. 2005. "A Historian's Brief Guide to New Museum Studies." *AHR* 100(1): 68–98.

Stewart, S. 1984. *On Longing: Narratives of the Miniature, the Gigantic, the Souvenir, the Collection*. Baltimore: John Hopkins University Press.

Stirling, L. M. 2005. *The Learned Collector: Mythological Statuettes and Classical Taste in Late Antique Gaul*. Ann Arbor: University of Michigan Press.

Strong, D. 1973. "Roman Museums." In *Archaeological Theory and Practice*, edited by Donald Strong, 247–64. London: Seminar Press.

Tanner, J. 2006. *The Invention of Art History in Ancient Greece: Religion, Society and Artistic Rationalisation*. Cambridge: Cambridge University Press.

Thomason, A. K. 2005. *Luxury and Legitimation: Royal Collecting in Ancient Mesopotamia*. Burlington, VT: Ashgate.

Tronchin, F. 2012. "Introduction: Collecting the Eclectic in Roman Houses." *Arethusa* 45(3): 261–82.

Wallace-Hadrill, A. 2008. *Rome's Cultural Revolution*. Cambridge: Cambridge University Press.

Williams, J. 2012. "From Polybius to the Parthenon: Religion, Art, and Plunder." In *Imperialism, Cultural Politics and Polybius*, edited by C. Smith and L. Yarrow, 278–97. Oxford: Oxford University Press.

Wiseman, T. P. 1987. "*Conspicui Postes Tectaque Digna Deo*: The Public Image of Aristocratic and Imperial Houses in the Late Republic and Early Principate." In *L'Urbs: Espace urbain et histoire (Ier siècle av. J.-C.–IIIe siècle ap. J.-C.)*, 393–413. Rome: École Française de Rome.

CHAPTER 6.4

IMAGES OF STATUES IN OTHER MEDIA

ERIC M. MOORMANN

Introduction

Representations of statues were often included in other artistic media such as mural paintings, glyptic art, coins, mosaics, and tableware. While these representations do not constitute precise reproductions of statues and, therefore, cannot be seen as fully trustworthy sources for the reconstruction of lost works, they provide valuable sources for the study of sculpture and can inform us about the use of statuary types, lost monuments, style, and taste. It is important to note at the outset that it is not possible to equate real and depicted statuary by asking the same degree and sort of information. Representations of statues never convey the essence of real sculpture, which is their volume, demand of space, tangibility, and materiality: two-dimensionality strongly contrasts with three-dimensionality, and we lack the spatial environment on the flat surface. In addition, the viewer sees a depicted statue from one side only, as in the case of a photograph, which implies a limited degree of information. Moreover, the artist manipulates a reproduced work in a certain way by depicting his own view of the figure, in which process he is not necessarily rendering the essence of the sculpted object. On the other hand, there are numerous advantages to having these two-dimensional depictions of statuary. For example, colored representations may give us a certain insight into the use of materials and polychromy (see essay 2.6, Abbe), which preserved sculptures often can no longer transmit. Another facet of two-dimensional art that provides fascinating insights is the lack of statics: in two-dimensional realms a statue can stand on one toe or float on a surface without offending the principles of gravity. As a result, a depicted statue's attitude can be much freer and more vivacious than that of a real statue. If that effect is enhanced by the application of natural colors, the resulting representation is ambiguous, and we encounter the blurred line between depictions of humans as statues and so-called "living statues," a phenomenon that fascinated the ancients and is enshrined in the famous story of Pygmalion (Ov. *Met.* 10.243; see also essay 6.5, Perry).

This essay will begin with a brief survey of the types of representations of statues found in two-dimensions and the range of media in which they occur. Following this survey, I will discuss what images of statues in other media can contribute to our understanding of Roman sculpture including the study of lost sculptural monuments, new insights into the Roman relationship to Greek sculpture, the recreation of aspects of the sculptural landscape, the longevity and political uses of sculptural types and individual, renowned statues, and the ancient interest in "living statues."

Media and Contexts

The most important source of images of statuary is mural painting, followed by coins and glyptic art, as well as mosaics, tableware (both ceramics and metal), and other media. In these, various categories of statuary are represented, the most important of which are freestanding figures and figures engaged in or forming parts of architectural settings (like caryatids, acroteria, consoles, and cornices). Images of freestanding sculptures mainly occur in figural scenes representing myths, histories, genre, still-lives, landscapes, and gardens. Wall paintings contain the full array of possibilities, from isolated figures and freestanding groups, such as sculptures placed in fictitious settings, to sculptures integrated into architectural facades. While most surviving examples come from the Vesuvian cities and villas between c. 70 BC and AD 79, murals with statuary motifs as parts of wall and ceiling decoration are found throughout the entire Roman period and empire. Stucco reliefs on walls and ceilings can be considered a subgenre of mural paintings and as a rule allow for the same observations as for paintings (Moormann 1988). Floor and wall mosaics also include sculptures as part of figural scenes and in some cases as elements in architectural schemes. In both paintings and mosaics the figures can have various sizes, depending on their position within the whole. Interestingly, no painted or mosaic images of statues illustrate real, original, historical settings of sculptures; for those we must turn to coins and monumental reliefs (see essay 3.5, Sobocinski and Wolfram Thill).

In what follows, I provide a brief survey of representations of statues in mural painting, stucco reliefs, mosaics, and stone reliefs, as well as on coins, gems, and intaglio, presenting examples of the most popular categories, that is sculptural motifs presented as architectural elements and freestanding statues. First, though, it should be noted that ancient artists employed various means to denote that the two-dimensional figures included in their paintings, mosaics, coins, and other media were representations of statues. One way of identifying a statue was its placement on a base, in a shrine, next to an altar, and so forth. Other ways of marking images as statues include crowning heads with a pillar, cornice, or console, and similar techniques are used to depict living persons made into statues (Moormann 2008, 214–16). Color is another distinctive marker, since (mainly monochrome) white, yellow, red, and green figures are obviously made of, respectively, marble, gilded bronze, and bronze, with various patinas (Moormann 1988, 71–5). Paintings and mosaics most often convey this information, whereas other media lack polychromy. For example, statues inserted into garden representations of the first century AD contrast with plants and trees thanks to their dominating white tones.

Roman wall paintings containing architectural elements are full of sculptural motifs and show a bewildering array of caryatids, Atlases, acroteria, and figural consoles (as do wall mosaics and stucco reliefs, but to a lesser degree). For instance, in a fourth-style painting in the Villa of Ariadne in Stabiae, a large Triton serves as a huge acroterion (figure 6.4.1, see color insert; now Museo Archeologico Nazionale di Napoli, inv. no. 8860: Moormann 1988, 98–9 cat. 010/3; Allroggen-Bedel 1999; Bragantini and Sampaolo 2009, 452–3 cat. 242). The eponymous mosaic from the House of the Tragic Poet at Pompeii shows the master with his actors in a luxurious room adorned with a colonnade on top of which runs a low second floor, supported by two pilasters, a column, and two brown herms of men carrying an object in their extended left hands (Museo Archeologico Nazionale di Napoli, inv. no. 9986: Pugliese Carratelli and Baldassarre 1990–, 4: 546–7; Andreae 2003, 235–6, figs. 231–3). They stress the lavish setting in the same way as the painted herms in oecus 22 of the House of the Cryptoporticus at Pompeii from the middle of the first century BC (Moormann 1988, 58–9, 143–4, cat. 148/1; Pugliese Carratelli and Baldassarre 1990–, 1: 260–69). Both sets show seemingly living figures actively engaged with their environment, although those in the mosaic are monochrome with delineated torsos (so-called "hip herms").

A few floor mosaics represent caryatids or Atlases. At Avenches, in a work probably dated to AD 260, sturdy Atlases kneeling on small podia support a circle representing the celestial globe and surrounded by the zodiac (Von Gonzenbach 1961, 43–5, 297, pl. 79). A mid-fourth-century mosaic in the villa of Horkstow (Lincolnshire, Great Britain; Neal and Cosh 2002, 148–57, cat. 53) shows four anguipede giants supporting a circular panel filled with various scenes and subdivided as if it were a wheel with spokes, perhaps reflecting a dome. On a fourth-century mosaic from the Augustinerhof in Trier (Hoffmann, Hupe, and Goethert 1999, 88–9, cat. 6, pl. 6), swimming tritons support the circle. The Hellenistic mosaic of a dog sitting next to an empty wine jar found on the spot of the modern Bibliotheca Alexandrina (Andreae 2003, 38–9) has grayish heads around the tondo that seem to support it as if they were marble consoles and formed architectural elements.

In most of these depictions of caryatids, Atlases, acroteria, and figural consoles, no relationship with known prototypes in architecture can be established, and in fact some of the most frequently repeated architectural caryatids, the Korai or caryatids of the Erechtheum in Athens, copied in the attics of the porticoes of the Forum Augustum in Rome and elsewhere, do not occur in painted or stuccoed wall decorations. Likewise, structures known to have been replete with such sculpted architectural elements, like the Façade of the Captives in Corinth (recently dated to the Julio-Claudian period; Strocka 2010) or Las Incantadas from Thessaloniki (now in Paris, Musée du Louvre), have no painted or mosaic counterparts either.

Figures standing on pedestals or consoles within rectangular panels occur in mural paintings and stucco decorations. They may form galleries of statues, and all belong to few frequently adopted themes, particularly Muses, nude athletes, and warriors. The Muses, sometimes combined with Apollo, form a substitute of the Helicon or Parnassus within the walls of a domestic room that might have served as a library or shrine like the Musaeum in Alexandria (see essay 6.3, Shaya), although we have no certainty about that equation in a private context (Moormann 2012, 208–210). The athletes show the classical *contrapposto* and fifth-century Polycletan proportions popular in neoclassical sculpture of the Roman era (Moormann 1988, 30–31; cf. Zanker 1974; Koortbojian 2002). A good example is a set of stucco figures in the Suburban Baths in Herculaneum who aptly illustrate the health effects of good sports and bathing. They date to the Neronian or Flavian era and have been seen as images of Greek statues robbed in Greece and brought to Rome by Nero (Strocka 2002; though some scholars believe that these do not represent statues at all: Bohne 2011, 30, 279—*contra* Mielsch 1975, 47; cf. Moormann 2008, 199n6).

Depictions of freestanding statues are often included in two-dimensional media to adorn the setting of a story or form the object of veneration. For example, in paintings, depictions of statues frequently appear in images of landscapes, a genre that is well known never to represent pristine nature (the so-called *paysage pur*), but is always marked by the presence of manmade objects symbolizing the domination of nature by man. Most of these painted statues are summarily rendered, and in few cases only a god or goddess is easily recognizable (most frequently depicted are Priapus, Dionysus, Artemis, and Poseidon, near waterfronts). Still lives can contain statues as part of the arrangement. One excellent example is a set of offerings to Dionysus, including the head of a ram and a cantharus next to a statuette of Dionysus himself in a small square scene from the House of the Stags at Herculaneum (now Museo Archeologico Nazionale di Napoli, inv. no. 8615; Moormann 1988, 109, cat. 029/2). These objects populate a rocky space and the red statuette might be a cheap terracotta figurine. In a late Second-Style landscape from Portici a woman brings a votive offering to the bronze statue of Dionysus (now Museo Archeologico Nazionale di Napoli, inv. no. 8593; Moormann 1988, 226–7, cat. 308). In the Sacrifice of Iphigenia from the House of the Tragic Poet at Pompeii, the protagonists are gathered on the beach of Aulis, next to a bronze statue of Artemis standing on a pillar. This archaistic figure holds torches in her outstretched hands and is flanked by two stags, which identify her as a *potnia theron*, a mistress of nature (now Museo Archeologico Nazionale di Napoli, inv. no. 9112; Moormann 1988, 172, cat. 198/2; Pugliese Carratelli and Baldassarre 1990–, 4: 551–3; Bragantini and Sampaolo 2009, 332–3, cat. 142).

Scenes showing the interior of houses, often banquets, but also other motifs, contain utensils in the shape of statues like lamp stands or servant's statues. On a banquet scene formerly interpreted as Sophonisba and Massinissa from the House of Joseph II in Pompeii, dating to the first half of the first century AD (figure 6.4.2, see color insert), statues of a bearded old Dionysus holding a wine cup and a nude young Apollo with an olive branch, bow, and quiver form the appropriate adornment of the luxurious banqueting room (now Museo Archeologico Nazionale di Napoli, inv. no. 8968; Moormann 1988, 207, cat. 269/3; Pugliese Carratelli and Baldassarre 1990–, 8: 354–6; Bragantini and

Sampaolo 2009, 248, cat. 87). Their monochrome color scheme—yellow and white, respectively—betray the materials they are made of: gilded bronze and silver. Four Fourth-Style banquet scenes from the House of Marcus Lucretius contain statues behind feasting and drinking Erotes. One shows a bearded Dionysus with a thyrsus, more or less imitating the Sardanapallos type; the other has a Psyche, Hermes or Apollo, and Heracles, following the type of Heracles Farnese (now Museo Archeologico Nazionale di Napoli, inv. no. 9207, 9208, 9193, 9255; Moormann 1988, 213, cat. 282/7; Pugliese Carratelli and Baldassarre 1990–, 9: 267). As in the "Sophonisba" (figure 6.4.2), the statues are movable objects, brought to the place to enhance the atmosphere. The gods are appropriate patrons of the luxury or *tryphe* that should stimulate the visitors of the room.

Various hunting scenes are also enlivened with freestanding statues. For example, in three mosaic scenes from Pompeii, Capua, and Antium, in which groups of Erotes are attacking a huge single lion (Andreae 2003, 192–201), statues of a bearded Dionysus bearing a thyrsus and a cantharus are conspicuous elements. The mosaics from the House of the Centaur in Pompeii (now Museo Archeologico Nazionale di Napoli, inv. no. 10019; Pugliese Carratelli and Baldassarre 1990–, 4: 855–7) and from Capua (now London, British Museum, 1856,1213.5) show fully clad Dionysi, while in that from Antium (now Rome, Antiquarium Comunale, inv. no. Stuart Jones 271.5) the god of wine wears only a long brown skirt over the lower part of his body. In all these, drinking vessels are lying around and the lion seems to have interrupted a fine rustic gathering in which Dionysus is present, since the god is represented in full color and seems to be a living figure, though he is not paying attention to the struggle in front of him. In a hunting scene from a villa near Antioch, hunters bring an offering to a similar gilded statue of Artemis (now Paris, Musée du Louvre, inv. no. MA 3444; Baratte 1978, 112–13, fig. 120). On the "Small hunt" in the Villa of Piazza Armerina in the center of Sicily, dated to the second quarter of the fourth century, the party is offering some game to a statue of Diana sporting a quiver and bow and probably representing a small rustic sanctuary of the goddess of hunt (Dunbabin 2003, 147–8, fig. 86).

Relief sculpture also provides important examples of two-dimensional depictions of statues. For example, several stone altars with reliefs depicting open-air ceremonies like the Altar of the Vicomagistri and the "Belvedere Altar," both in the Vatican Museums (figure 6.4.3), show participants carrying small statues in their hands, which in some cases replicate the now-entirely lost large cult statues of the venerated gods. A few of these are Lares, which are similar to the many bronze statuettes of these tutelary divinities found in private shrines in Pompeii and elsewhere (Madigan 2013, 1–35). The second story of the north building of the Sebasteion in Aphrodisias, dated to the second quarter of the first century AD, contained some fifty relief representations of geographical personifications. The female figures, worked almost in the round, stand on bases bearing their names, and act like a "line of statues in a colonnade" (Smith 2013, 86, fig. 45, pls. 26–44). The women are clad in classicistic dress and stand in a tranquil, really statuesque pose. Reliefs that depict temples and other buildings often include their sculptural embellishment as well.

Miniature depictions of statues from coins, gems, and intaglios tend to feature ideal models from Greek statuary as well as Roman statues (Horster 1970). For example, on gems we find representations of the Ephesian Amazons by Polyclitus, Phidias,

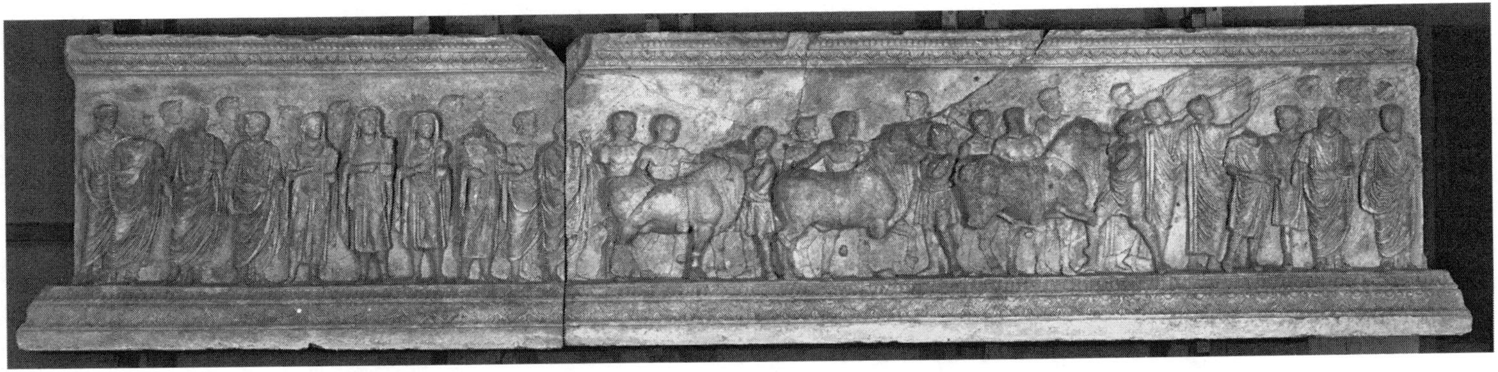

FIGURE 6.4.3 Altar of the Vicomagistri. Vatican City, Vatican Museums, Museo Pio Clementino inv. no. 1156, 1157.

and Cresilas (Beck, Bol, and Bückling 1990, 575–8, nos. 95–8a–c, 581–4, nos. 101a–b) and Scopas's Lansdowne Heracles (Platz-Horster 2013), and on both gems and coins Eutychides's Tyche from Antioch (Meyer 2006).

The examples noted above are merely a handful of the numerous instances of depictions of statuary in a wide range of two-dimensional media. All of these, in one way are another, provide important insights regarding three-dimensional Roman sculpture, including study of now-lost sculptural monuments, Roman interests in Greek sculpture, the profusion and placement of statuary in the urban landscape, the longevity of sculptural types and their various roles in society, and the ancient fascination with "living statues."

Study of Lost Sculptural Monuments

As noted above, it is not always productive to mine two-dimensional depictions of statues for information about the specifics of now-lost, real statuary. Nevertheless, depictions of statuary in two-dimensional form can be used to study some aspects of no-longer-extant sculptures, including general aspects of their iconography, their placement in the urban landscape, further substantiation of literary testimony to their existence, and even aspects of their transport. For example, the *Plutei Traianei* or *Anaglypha Traiani* from the Roman Forum, now on display in the Curia, show Trajan annulling debts of citizens to the state as he sits in front of the Basilica Iulia, next to which is visible the statue of Marsyas and the old fig tree, the *ficus Ruminalis*, the site where the she-wolf had once offered her breast to Romulus and Remus (Torelli 1982, 89–118, pls. IV.1–14; *LTUR* 4: 95–6; Kemkes 1999; https://vimeo.com/15808133 at time code 03:07–03:59; see essay 3.5, Sobocinski and Wolfram Thill). Because the statue of Marsyas no longer exists, this Trajanic relief and its pendant, coins of a member of the Censorinus family from the early first century BC (figure 6.4.4), and contemporary gems all provide important visual sources for its shape and iconography (Coarelli 1985, 36–8, 91–100, 104–123; *LIMC* 5: 375, nos. 68–71; 377; *LTUR* 4: 364–5; Schertz 2005, 26–7, 131–6). It is important to note, though, that Marsyas's presence on the relief is justified by its theme of the annulment of debts and freeing citizens, not by the logic of the setting, since the statue would not have been visible from the position of the onlooker if he were in the forum itself.

Other examples provide links to otherwise unknown, now-lost objects. The Arch of Constantine has tondi dating to the Hadrianic time showing offerings to four gods in the open and mostly rustic air: Silvanus, Apollo, Diana, and Hercules, all standing on square bases and not imitating specific models, while the speaking platform in the late-antique relief below, of Constantine addressing the citizens of Rome, is adorned with two large seated statues of Hadrian and Marcus Aurelius, *exempla* for the reigning emperor (L'Orange and Von Gerkan 1939; Koeppel 1990).

Another relief transmitting a lost statue is that of the *haruspex* Gaius Fulvius Salvis from Ostia, which shows a huge Hercules Victor standing next to an altar. At the right, in an independent but unframed section, a statue of the same god is being drawn from the sea by two triples of fishermen with a gigantic net (Becatti [1939] 1987). Looking at the

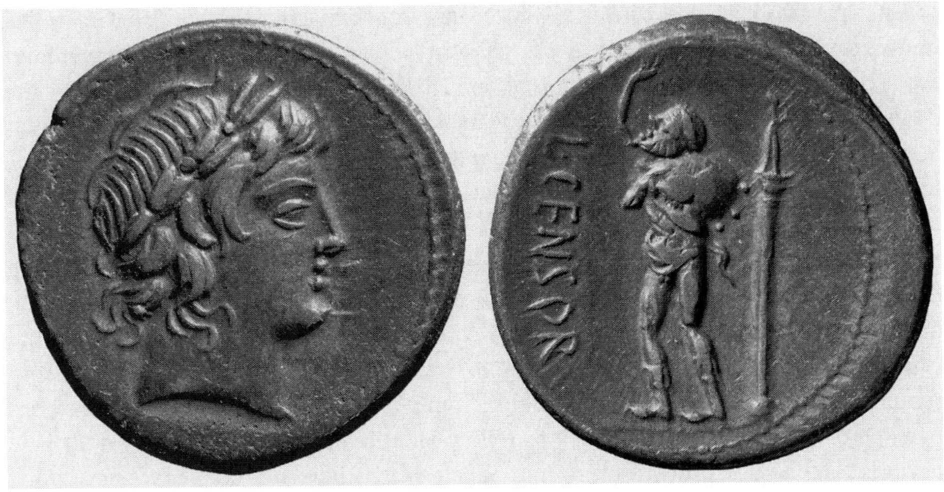

FIGURE 6.4.4 Denarius struck under L. Censorinus in 82 BC, showing on the reverse the Marsyas statue in the Forum Romanum. Collection De Nederlandsche Bank, Amsterdam.

shape, it must be an over-life-size bronze in the attitude of the Zeus or Poseidon from Cape Artemision or the large bronze being assembled on the outside of the famous titular cup of the Foundry Painter in Berlin (Beck, Bol, and Bückling 1990, 82, 84, 90, 92, figs. 15a–c). The figure is executed in the late archaic or severe style, which makes it an excellent image of the venerable god from the sea, bringing richness to the Ostians in the form of salt. It has been proposed that the statue in the net might show a Spartan style and iconography from c. 490 BC (Becatti [1939] 1987), which supports the hypothesis that the sculptor really copied an old cult statue, imported from Laconia or Magna Graecia, lost at sea, and recovered by fishermen, though this relief is the only evidence for such a statue and event.

Though they are generally unable to render detailed characteristics, depictions of statues on tiny coins still provide useful information. A clear example is that of the Venus Genetrix of the Forum Iulium. As we know from written sources, the famous cult statue was apparently Arcesilaus's reworking of Callimachus's Aphrodite of the late fifth century BC (*Künstlerlexikon der Antike* [2004], s.v. "Arkesilaos IV"). Ancient coins labeled "Venus Genetrix" on the reverse allow us to identify the statue's general stance, overall drapery configuration and attributes, and visually substantiate the literary sources (*LTUR* 2: 306–7, fig. 143; *LIMC* 8: 197, with reserve about the prototype).

Roman Interest in Greek Sculpture

Two-dimensional representations tell us a great deal about the Roman interest in Greek sculpture, since *opera nobilia* (famous works of art of Greek origin, Plin. *HN* 36.39) are the most frequently adopted motif in two-dimensional art, and Roman themes are absent, apart from specific categories like bronze *lararium* figurines, honorific portraits, images of equestrian statues and *quadrigae*, and architectural sculpture (cf. Bergemann 1990; Sehlmeyer 1999 for honorific statues; Kleiner 1985 for a reconstruction of the Arch of Nero and its sculptures; Madigan 2013 for portable statue(tte)s; essay 3.5, Sobocinski and Wolfram Thill, for relief depictions of architectural sculpture). For this reason, the images pertaining to the topic of this paper tell more about the interest of the Romans in Greek and Hellenistic sculpture than about Roman sculpture and its appreciation. These evocations can be realized in two ways, that is, either as living figures modeled after sculptural types according to their stance, or as statues standing on bases and more or less thoroughly reflecting ancient statuary. In general, Roman two-dimensional art adopted classical and Hellenistic types that we also know from sculptural reproductions and adaptations. Even if models are lacking or not yet recognized, most statues in two dimensions follow schemes and styles of these two artistic periods. Archaic sculpture rarely occurs, except when cult statues or venerable antique pieces are meant to be reproduced, which may happen more frequently in coinage and on Campana plaques than in other media (see essay 3.6, Touchette). In the case of Campana plaques, "archaic" should be read as "in an archaic or archaistic way" (cf. Fullerton 1990).

Recreating the Sculptural Landscape

Several reliefs from Rome representing buildings include images of their sculptural decoration and thus provide important evidence for the profusion of statuary on public display, common types of display contexts and manners of display, and even some cases where the buildings and sculptural displays represented seem to be truly informative about reality. One example of a relief that provides important information about the quantity of statuary and varied displayed contexts in the urban landscape is the "Sacra Via" relief from the funerary monument of the Haterii, now in the Vatican Museums (figure 4.1.1; Sinn and Freyberger 1996, 63–76, pls. 20–24). This relief depicts several constructions connected with the building company of this family and date, like the relief itself, to the late first century AD. At the left is the *Arcus ad Isis*, with statues occupying the three passages under the arches: they represent Anubis, Minerva, and Isis. The adjacent Colosseum contains statues of male divinities and its entrance is crowned by a *quadriga*. A relatively small arch contains a statue of Magna Mater and is also topped by a *quadriga*, now with a triumphing general. Also depicted is a third arch, called *arcus in sacra via summa*, whose exact identity is still debated. It is enriched by a statue of Mars in the center and small statues in the lateral intercolumniations. Finally, there is a temple front with a nude Jupiter standing on a base. The latter has been connected with various temples dedicated to this god (*Stator, Custos*, or *Tonans*). While the exact interpretations of these figures and buildings remain contested, and even though the renderings of the statues themselves are more impressionistic than detailed, the relief successfully transmits the abundance and location of statuary on temples, arches, and the amphitheater (see essay 4.1, Longfellow).

In other instances, sculptures depicted on a building image in relief seem truly informative. For example, several reliefs and coins of varying date provide convergent evidence regarding the general iconography of the pedimental group and cult statue of the Temple of Fortuna Redux in Rome (Sobocinski 2009). Other well-known examples include the Aurelian relief illustrating the pediment and acroteria of the Temple of Jupiter Optimus Maximus, which shows the Capitoline triad seated in the pediment (Sobocinski 2014). Whether or not images of buildings are identifiable topographically, the frequent depictions of their sculptural decoration are richly informative about the varied compositions and iconographies deemed suitable for adorning buildings and temple pediments in particular.

The Longevity and Political Uses of Sculptural Types and Individual, Renowned Statues

Two-dimensional representations of statuary also demonstrate that some sculptural types endured well beyond their original historical and artistic periods and were used by individuals or groups for various political and social ends. This phenomenon is most common with coins, since they tended to represent the issuer, whether individual or city, and because they circulated widely. It is important to note, though, that the makers of the coins representing statues did not necessarily know or work from the original (Lacroix 1949, 8–15; Flashar 1998–9, 227–8; Herzog 1996; Burnett 1999; Stewart 2003, 208–214), since they could use a sculptural copy or an image in another medium as a source. Also, while style, perspective, and position of attributes are difficult to convey on coin images, the best coins combine data to show a figure as clearly as possible (Flashar 1998–9, 232). These numismatic images acquire a signification of their own, even transforming the original bearing and iconology into a new one fitting the occasion of issuing the coin. The meaning of representations of statues on coins often depends on the reason for issue and the historical moment at which the coin was struck. For example, people who represent old monuments on their coins may refer to the erection of the monument by an ancestor, as is the case with the aforementioned coin of 83 BC (figure 6.4.4), with the statue of Marsyas as a reference to the censor C. Marcius Rutilus Censorinus (the *nomen gentilicium* Marcius was even supposed to derive from Marsyas).

One of the most famous examples of the longevity and civic use of a two-dimensional representation of statue is the Aphrodite from Aphrodisias, communicated in the form of numismatic and other images (Bianchi 1996). These represent a case of local pride expressed by means of reproducing this specific cult statue. In some cases, we have evidence that two-dimensional images of actual statues achieve a surprising degree of likeness. One example involves the colossal cult statues in the Temple of Apollo at Clarus. Because we possess fragments of the original cult statues, coin images from nearby Colophon can be compared with the originals (Flashar 1998–9, pls. 11, 13). The close resemblance between coins and originals is no wonder, since Clarus's sanctuary was located within the area of the polis. Here also the coins seem to have been a means of remembering for the inhabitants and branding Apollo's oracle at Clarus outwards.

Living Statues

Depictions of statues in two-dimensions can also offer a window onto the ancients' fascination with "the animated image" or living statues (Stewart 2003; Hersey 2009; Bussels 2013). Especially in paintings, the line between inanimate objects and live figures is often blurred, such that the distinction between living figures and statues can be difficult to assess, if we refrain from rigorously applying the "rules" noted earlier for signifying that a two-dimensional figure is actually a statue (base, engagement within architecture, and the like). In some examples, even figures really meant as sculptures by means of such features can function as living people of flesh and blood rather than statues (Moormann 2008, 209–211). For example, a man or woman functioning as pillar really becomes a mythical caryatid or Atlas who had to bear the weight of heaven.

Some scholars have viewed the megalographies of the Villa of the Mysteries at Pompeii and of the Villa of P. Fannius Synistor at Boscoreale in this light, considering these large paintings of the 70s to 50s BC as reproductions of ephemeral statues carried around in lavish processions organized by Ptolemy II Philadelphus in Alexandria (Wesenberg 1991; Barbet and Verbanck-Piérard 2013; on the *pompe*, Rice 1983) or as a "gallery of sculptural models" (Grimaldi 2011, 549–52).

In two-dimensional images of sculptural groups, we see examples in which the iconography and composition match those of known sculptural groups of earlier date, but the figures are treated as living within the two-dimensional world in which they are included. Examples include the Chiron teaching Achilles playing the oboe, known from the Augusteum at Herculaneum and the House of Wounded Adonis (Allroggen-Bedel 1999, pl. 103.2; Moormann 2011, 127–8, fig. 58); the famous sexual struggle of a satyr and a Hermaphrodite, known from many sculptures and some paintings; and the Three Graces, found in numerous paintings of the first century AD (House of T. Dentatius Panthera, in a landscape, now Museo Archeologico Nazionale di Napoli, inv. no. 9236: Moormann 1988, 210, cat. 279/3; Pugliese Carratelli and Baldassarre 1990–, 9:35; same depiction from Insula Occidentalis, Masseria Cuomo, now Museo Archeologico Nazionale di Napoli, inv. no. 9207: Moormann 1988, 189, cat. 227; mural mosaic from the House of Apollo in Pompeii, now Museo Archeologico Nazionale di Napoli, inv. no. 10004: Sear 1977, 33, 71, cat. 31, pl. 16.2; Pugliese Carratelli and Baldassarre

1990–, 4: 511; note though that the source of this sculptural group is not known at all, as Pausanias observed in his *Periegesis* 9.35.6; on this old debate: Moormann 1988, 54; *LIMC* 3: 203–210, esp. 203). While corresponding with sculptural groups known from either three-dimensional statues or descriptions in literary sources, these two-dimensional mythical figures are represented as living figures, in flesh and blood.

In some cases, the two-dimensional figures seem to be treated as living, but their coloration suggests that they are statues. For example, a mosaic in the vault of Nymphaeum 45 of Nero's Golden House in Rome shows a bronze-colored group of Odysseus and Polyphemus, which has been seen as a parallel for the marble groups of the first century AD in various imperial villas (Sear 1977, 90–92, cat. 90, pls. 35–6; Meyboom and Moormann 2013, 174, fig. 45.6). The play with three-dimensional representations is enhanced by the use of dark- and bright-yellowish mosaic tesserae that resemble bronze.

In other instances, we have literary sources that describe a sculptural group, and though no three-dimensional version of the group remains, the statue has been recognized in representations on coinage, though without the historical reference, we would not have known that the two-dimensional depiction referred to a specific sculptural group, as the figure on the coin appears to be living. For example, the cow and the four heifers of Myron, exposed in the Templum Pacis by Vespasian in the 70s, were eternized on urban coins of that time and praised in the famous epigram 66 of Posidippus (Hill 1987, 51–2, pl. 8.1; *LTUR* 4: 67–70, esp. 68; Corso 1994; Moormann 2008, 212–13; Rutledge 2012, 272–84, esp. 274 and note 127). The images on coins show only the cow striding to the right, without a base or architectural framework, and the connection with the other famous animals from the Acropolis in Athens of the late fifth century BC could only be made on the basis of our historical knowledge of the setting of the works of art in the Templum Pacis (and better, that of the users of the coins in those years). As is shown by these examples, two-dimensional representations of statues and sculptural groups offer valuable evidence to those scholars interested in the phenomenon of living statues or animated images in the Roman world.

Conclusion

Images of statues are quite common in two-dimensional art. Statues can enliven all genres of figural scenes, façades of monuments, and underline the specific meaning of an image. Moreover, they serve as architectural elements within façades and complicated architectural structures such as caryatids and acroteria. This category very seldom reflects built structures we know in three dimensions but instead reflects fantastic renderings. Nevertheless, these images of statues give an idea of populated built structures. Coins depicting the Colosseum, for instance, illustrate the multitude of statuary displayed in this class of luxurious and prestigious buildings. The *Anaglypha Traiani* showing Marsyas on the Forum Romanum is unique as a source of information: it confirms the existence of an old statue still standing after hundreds of years on its original spot.

We should not demand exactitude of these images of statues. In some cases they reflect well-known statue types, but even in these imitations the student of copies and their original forerunners cannot take into account the two-dimensional images, unless as proofs of the reception of these types in the Roman era. The image makers did not aspire to create images of photographic precision, if I may use this anachronism, and ignored the mimesis theories used for the quite realistic artistic expressions of Hellenism (cf. on that concept Sobocinski 2014; cf. Moormann 2008, 209–214). The essentials should be recognizable, but reliability regarding the copying of an original apparently was no urgent issue in Roman art. This is true for the images discussed here, but also for major art works like ideal statues modeled after (lost) Greek originals (cf. Zanker 1974).

Painters, coin makers, and other artists of two-dimensional objects containing statues could play with statuary motifs. They were able to represent living persons functioning as statues or bearing heavy burdens, balancing in impossible poses (even for acrobats) and painted in strong and colorful contrasts and, conversely, statues with a high degree of being living creatures. This play reflects the ecphrasis of realistic sculpture in literature and the trope of representing men and animals as living creatures that might deceive the onlookers as if they were there in real time.

Bibliography

Allroggen-Bedel, A. 1999. "Hellenistische Gruppen in der römischen Wandmalerei." In *Hellenistische Gruppen: Gedenkschrift für Andreas Linfert*, 352–64. Mainz: Philipp von Zabern.

Andreae, B. 2003. *Antike Bildmosaiken*. Mainz: Philipp von Zabern.

Baratte, F. 1978. *Catalogue des mosaïques romaines et paléochrétiennes du musée du Louvre*. Paris: Réunion des musées nationaux.

Barbet, A., and A. Verbanck-Piérard, eds. 2013. *La villa romaine de Boscoreale et ses fresques*. Paris: Editions Errance/Actes Sud.

Becatti, G. (1939) 1987. "Il culto di Ercole ad Ostia ed un nuovo rilievo votivo." In *Kosmos: Studi sul mondo antico*, 641–65. Rome: "L'Erma" di Bretschneider.

Beck, H., P. C. Bol, and M. Bückling, eds. 1990. *Polyklet: Der Bildhauer der griechischen Klassik*. Mainz: Philipp von Zabern.

Bergemann, J. 1990. *Römische Reiterstatuen*. Mainz: Philipp von Zabern.

Bianchi, L. 1996. "Il simulacro dell'Afrodite di Afrodisia nelle rappresentazioni su monete." In *Ricerche sui materiali e studi tipologici*, edited by F. Panvini Rosati, 87–111. Rome: Giorgio Bretschneider.

Bohne, A. 2011. *Bilder vom Sport: Untersuchungen zur Ikonographie römischer Athleten-Darstellungen*. Hildesheim: Weidmannsche.

Bragantini, I., and V. Sampaolo. 2009. *La pittura pompeiana*. Milan: Mondadori Electa.

Burnett, A. 1999. "Buildings and Monuments on Roman Coins." In *Roman Coins and Public Life under the Empire: E. Togo Salmon Papers II*, edited by G. Paul and M. Ierardi, 137–64. Ann Arbor: University of Michigan Press.

Bussels, S. 2013. *The Animated Image: Roman Theory on Naturalism, Vividness and Divine Power*. Chicago: University of Chicago Press.

Coarelli, F. 1985. *Il foro romano*. Vol. 2, *Periodo repubblicano e augusteo*. Rome: Quasar.
Corso, A. 1994. "La vacca di Mirone." *NumAntCl* 23: 49–91.
Dunbabin, K. M. D. 2003. *The Roman Banquet: Images of Conviviality*. Cambridge: Cambridge University Press.
Flashar, M. 1998–9. "Die Bedeutung der kaiserzeitlichen Münzprägung von Kolophon für die Kultbildgruppe von Klaros." *Boreas* 21–2: 227–39.
Fullerton, M. D. 1990. *Archaistic Style in Roman Statuary*. Mnemosyne Supplement 110. Leiden: Brill.
Grimaldi, M. 2011. "Alcuni esempi di riflessi nella grande scultura ellenistica nella pittura romano-campana." In *Pittura ellenistica in Italia e in Sicilia: Linguaggi e tradizioni*, edited by G. F. La Torre and M. Torelli, 547–60. Rome: Giorgio Bretschneider.
Hersey, G. L. 2009. *Falling in Love with Statues: Artificial Humans from Pygmalion to the Present*. Chicago: University of Chicago Press.
Herzog, H. 1996. *Untersuchungen zur Darstellung von Statuen auf Athener Silbermünzen des Neuen Stils*. Hamburg: Kovač.
Hill, P. V. 1987. "Buildings and Monuments of Rome as Coin-Types: Addenda." *NC* 147: 51–64.
Hoffmann, P., H.-J. Hupe, and K. Goethert. 1999. *Katalog der römischen Mosaiken aus Trier und dem Umland*. Trier: Rheinisches Landesmuseum.
Horster, G. 1970. *Statuen auf Gemmen*. Bonn: Habelt.
Kemkes, M. 1999. "Politische Propaganda zur Zeit des Trajans im Spiegel der Münzen und historischen Reliefs." In *Trajan in Germanien—Trajan im Reich*, edited by E. Schallmayer, 127–36. Bad Homburg: Saalburgmuseum.
Kleiner, F. 1985. *The Arch of Nero in Rome*. Rome: Giorgio Bretschneider.
Koeppel, G. M. 1990. "Die historischen Reliefs der römischen Kaiserzeit VII: Der Bogen des Septimius Severus, die Decennalienbasis und der Konstantinsbogen." *BJb* 190: 1–64.
Koortbojian, M. 2002. "Forms of Attention: Four Notes on Replication and Variation." In *The Ancient Art of Emulation: Studies in Artistic Originality and Tradition from the Present to Classical Antiquity*, edited by E. K. Gazda, 173–204. Ann Arbor: University of Michigan Press.
Lacroix, L. 1949. *Les reproductions de statues sur les monnaies grecques: La statuaire archaïque et classique*. Liège: Faculté de Philosophie et de Lettres.
L'Orange, H. P., and A. Von Gerkan. 1939. *Der spätantike Bildschmuck des Konstantinsbogens*. Berlin: Walter de Gruyter.
Madigan, B. 2013. *The Ceremonial Sculptures of the Roman Gods*. Monumenta Graeca et Romana 20. Leiden: Brill.
Meyboom, P. G. P., and E. M. Moormann. 2013. *Le decorazioni dipinte e marmoree della Domus Aurea di Nerone a Roma*. BABesch Supplement 20. Leuven: Peeters.
Meyer, M. 2006. *Die Personifikation der Stadt Antiocheia: Ein neues Bild für eine neue Gottheit*. JdI Ergänzungsheft 33. Berlin: Walter de Gruyter.
Mielsch, H. 1975. *Römische Stuckreliefs*. RM Ergänzungsheft 21. Heidelberg: Kerle.
Moormann, E. M. 1988. *La pittura parietale romana come fonte di conoscenza per la scultura antica*. Assen: Van Gorcum.
———. 2008. "Statues on the Wall: The Representation of Statuary in Roman Wall Painting." In *The Sculptural Environment of the Roman Near East: Reflections on Culture, Ideology, and Power*, edited by Y. Z. Eliav, E. A. Friedland, and S. Herbert, 197–224. Leuven: Peeters.
———. 2011. *Divine Interiors: Mural Paintings in Greek and Roman Sanctuaries*. Amsterdam: Amsterdam University Press.

———. 2012. "Musen. C. Bildliche Darstellungen. I. Nichtchristlich. " In *Reallexikon für Antike und Christentum* 25: 201–212.

Neal, D. S., and S. R. Cosh. 2002. *Roman Mosaics of Britain*. Vol. 1, *Northern Britain*. London: Illuminata.

Platz-Horster, G. 2013. "Herakles in Brabant: Die Amethyst-Gemme aus Sint-Oedenrode." *BABesch* 88: 191–203.

Pugliese Carratelli, G., and I. Baldassarre, eds. 1990–. *Pompei: Pitture e mosaici*. Rome: Treccani.

Rice, E. E. 1983. *The Grand Procession of Ptolemy Philadelphus*. Oxford: Oxford University Press.

Rutledge, S. H. 2012. *Ancient Rome as a Museum: Power, Identity, and the Culture of Collecting*. Oxford: Oxford University Press.

Sear, F. B. 1977. *Roman Wall and Vault Mosaics*. Heidelberg: F. H. Kerle.

Sehlmeyer, M. 1999. *Stadtrömische Ehrenstatuen der republikanischen Zeit: Historizität und Kontext von Symbolen nobilitären Standesbewusstseins*. Historia Einzelschriften 130. Stuttgart: Franz Steiner.

Schertz, P. J. M. 2005. "Seer or Victim? The Figure of Marsyas in Roman Art, Religion, and Politics." PhD diss., University of Southern California.

Sinn, F., and K. S. Freyberger. 1996. *Die Ausstattung des Hateriergrabes*. Part 2 of *Die Grabdenkmäler*, Vol. 1 of *Katalog der Skulpturen, Vatikanische Museen, Museo Gregoriano Profano ex Lateranense*. Monumenta Artis Romanae 24. Mainz: Philipp von Zabern.

Smith, R. R. R. 2013. *The Marble Reliefs from the Julio-Claudian Sebasteion*. Aphrodisias 6. Darmstadt: Philipp von Zabern.

Sobocinski, M. G. 2009. "Porta Triumphalis and Fortuna Redux: Reconsidering the Evidence." *MAAR* 54: 135–64.

———. 2014. "Visualizing Architecture Then and Now: Mimesis and the Capitoline Temple of Jupiter Optimus Maximus." In *A Companion to Roman Architecture*, edited by R. Ulrich and C. Quenemoen, 446–61. Chichester, UK, and Malden, MA: Wiley-Blackwell.

Stewart, P. 2003. *Statues in Roman Society: Representation and Response*. Oxford: Oxford University Press.

Strocka, V. M. 2002. "Neros Statuenraub für die Domus Aurea: Zeitgenössische Reflexe." In *Neroniana VI: Rome à l'époque néronienne*, edited by J.-M. Croisille and Y. Perrin, 35–45. Bruxelles: Editions Latomus.

———. 2010. *Die Gefangenenfassade an der Agora von Korinth: Ihr Ort in der römischen Kunstgeschichte*. Regensburg: Schnell and Steiner.

Torelli, M. 1982. *Typology and Structure of Roman Historical Reliefs*. Ann Arbor: University of Michigan Press.

Von Gonzenbach, V. 1961. *Die römischen Mosaiken der Schweiz*. Basel: Birkhäuser.

Wesenberg, B. 1991. "Zur Bildvorstellung im großen Fries der Mysterienvilla." *KölnJb* 24: 67–72.

Zanker, P. 1974. *Klassizistische Statuen: Studien zur Veränderung des Kunstgeschmacks in der römischen Zeit*. Frankfurt: Philipp von Zabern.

CHAPTER 6.5

HUMAN INTERACTIONS WITH STATUES

ELLEN E. PERRY

INTRODUCTION

> People are sexually aroused by pictures and sculptures; they break pictures and sculptures; they mutilate them, kiss them, cry before them, and go on journeys to them; they are calmed by them, stirred by them and incited to revolt. They give thanks by means of them, expect to be elevated by them, and are moved to the highest levels of empathy and fear. They have always responded in these ways; they still do.
>
> Freedberg 1989, 1

THE subject matter referred to by my title requires some limitation. After all, most things that can happen to a statue necessarily involve some kind of human interaction, including the statue's commission, manufacture, and dedication (if the statue is religious or honorific), as well as its viewing, its deployment and reception as propaganda, its restoration history, and, indeed, any history the statue might have enjoyed after antiquity. These, however, have been traditional topics of investigation. A more recent line of inquiry investigates the various social functions of the image and does not limit itself to the answer that images served to convey propaganda or ideology (Freedberg 1989; Tanner 2000; Stewart 2003; Mylonopoulos 2010). In this essay, therefore, human interactions are taken to mean all of the many things that Romans did to and with a statue after a workshop had put the finishing touches to it—that is, all of the things the Romans did in addition to viewing. These sorts of interactions often, but not always, involved touching, though they rarely leave a trace on the statues themselves. Obvious exceptions include recarving, mutilation, and destruction, topics addressed elsewhere in this volume (see essays 2.3, Varner; and 6.6, Kristensen). Because human interactions with statues generally did not alter those statues, most of our evidence for the phenomenon necessarily comes from literary sources. Inscriptions, relief depictions, and the statues themselves offer occasional information, but to a much lesser degree.

Even given these limitations, the topic is vast, and this essay can consider only some of its most salient features. The ubiquity of statues in Roman society meant that people interacted with them a great deal more than we interact with statues today. Images of the gods, for example, might be bathed, clothed, fed, carried in procession, or crowned with flowers. When the statues themselves behaved in an extraordinary fashion—for example, by sweating or speaking, falling or being struck by lightning—at least a part of the population felt it necessary to do something, and often what they did, they did with or to the statue itself. In addition, we have some evidence for individuals using statuettes as protective talismans: Sulla, for example, is said to have owned a golden statuette of Apollo that he always carried into battle (Plut. *Vit. Sull.* 29; Plut. *Vit. Cic.* 31; Amm. Marc. 22.13; Apul. *Apol.* 63.2; Kaufmann-Heinimann 2007, 200).

There were, nevertheless, boundaries to human interactions with statues. Not all statues were available or subject to touching at all times, and disrespectful or abnormal interactions were noticed and sometimes punished (Stewart 2003, 262–3). In addition, we can presume that not all statues attracted enough interest to elicit some sort of interaction.

Statues might be touched as part of a regularly celebrated ritual or in the expiation of a prodigy, and occasionally a particular statue might attract frequent devotional touching. Cicero, for example, reports that the mouth and chin of a bronze statue of Hercules at Agrigentum were worn down by the kisses of worshippers (Cic. *Verr.* 2.4.94). It is clear from the context, however, that this case is exceptional: the physical evidence of frequent kissing serves for Cicero as a sign of how important this particular statue was to the people of Agrigentum, and therefore how appalling it was for Verres, the governor of Sicily, to steal it. In other words, we are expected to understand that this sort of thing did not happen to many statues. For the most part, then, interactions with statues took place under regulated circumstances.

Rituals of Bathing, Clothing, and Feeding

An inscription dating to the second century AD from Misenum outlines one man's testamentary arrangements for the cleaning and anointing of two statues representing the Genius of the Town and the Protective Goddess of the Fleet (D'Arms 2000, 136; see essay 4.5, Tuck). In general, however, regular, even ritual, washing and bathing of divine statues probably occurred, even though ancient authors rarely noted the practice. A Campana relief appears to depict attendants in the process of washing a herm with a sponge (figure 6.5.1; Paris, Louvre, inv. no. CP 4038; Weddle 2010, no. 211). We cannot know whether these attendants were simply providing proper care for the object or engaging in ritual, but it seems possible that they were doing both at once. Other acts of washing sculpture are more obviously rituals. We learn from Plutarch, for example, that even in his day (μέχρι νῦν) the archon of Plataea annually washed and perfumed the funerary steles of those who had died at the Battle of Plataea (Plut. *Vit. Arist.* 21).

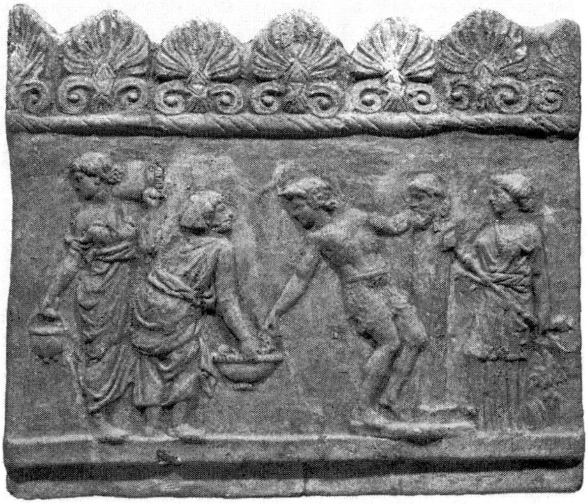

FIGURE 6.5.1 Plaque of a cult scene with maenads and a satyr bathing a herm. Terracotta. Second half of the first century BC to first half of the first century AD. Paris, Louvre, inv. no. 4038.

There were, however, a number of rituals in which statues were actually carried to another location—often to the banks of a river or to the seashore—and bathed there. Such rituals of bathing, perfuming, and adornment appear to have been largely, though not exclusively, reserved for goddesses (Kahil 1994, 218–23). The cult of Venus Verticordia was founded around 220 BC, and Ovid informs us that thereafter at her festival Roman mothers and brides (*matres nurusque*) removed her golden necklaces in order to bathe her. They then replaced the jewelry, decorated her further with flowers, and bathed themselves (Ov. *Fast.* 4.133–9).

This informative passage draws our attention to an important feature of statue bathing, namely, that it might require the removal of adornment as well as its subsequent replacement after the bathing. We must remind ourselves to envision human caregivers or worshippers adorning statues with jewelry, garlands, clothing, and crowns in the same way that we repeatedly remind ourselves to envision color (see essay 2.6, Abbe). For example, a statue of Hercules in the Forum Boarium was dressed in triumphal garb on the occasion of triumphal processions (Plin. *HN* 34.33). Such adornments are no longer extant or are not easily identified, because for the most part they were made of materials that were either precious or perishable and because, like the Hercules Triumphalis, statues often received their adornments only on special occasions.

That bathing and adornment often occurred together also explains, to some extent, the many goddesses who enjoyed such rituals and the frequent mention in our sources of female attendants. For a Roman, these actions were *cultus*, a word whose semantic range included not only regular acts of religious devotion but also care of the body. In the mortal sphere, *cultus* might call for attractive and, depending on the period, even luxurious clothing, an orderly or elaborate coiffure, and other signs of meticulous personal grooming. As such, *cultus* had both gender and class connotations: it was primarily the concern of aristocratic women (Wyke 1994; Taylor 2008, 32–4). Indeed, on funerary reliefs, adornment scenes generally indicate the high social rank of the women depicted (Wyke 1994, 141–2). The bathing, grooming, and adornment of statues of goddesses will, therefore, have resonated with daily rituals of aristocratic women, and female religious attendants were reminiscent of the servants who helped their ladies with these rituals.

Statues of the Gods in Procession

A relief from Amiternum in Italy, traditionally assigned to the Claudian period, depicts statues of the gods Jupiter and (perhaps) Juno carried in procession on *fercula* (biers). One of the inscriptions found with the relief mentions a *triumvir Augustalis*, an alternate, local term for the *sevir Augustalis*. Because one of the duties of the *seviri* was to give games in honor of the deified emperor, and because another noncontiguous fragment from the same findspot depicts gladiators, this relief is generally understood to depict a procession before an otherwise unknown celebration of gladiatorial games (Fornari 1917, 336–9; Bates 1919, 80; Ryberg 1955, 98–100). At the far right of the preserved relief is a figure of the goddess Victoria (not a statue) in a chariot or *biga*, leading the procession. Various figures follow her on foot; then, after another *biga*, four men are seen carrying a *ferculum* that supports a standing statue of Jupiter, his left arm raised to hold a scepter, his right arm lowered to hold a thunderbolt. A little farther back in the procession we see two litter bearers carrying a female statue. The relief breaks off to the left (rear) of these figures; the two litter bearers to the rear are no longer preserved.

This representation of statues on *fercula* directs our attention to the practicalities of carrying statues in procession. If only four men carried a *ferculum*, then their collective strength will have limited the weight and size of the statues that could be carried in such rituals (Long 1987, 242). Even if this relief is an abbreviation—and it may well be—even if more than four men might be assigned to a *ferculum*, the statues still had to be light enough that they would not damage the *fercula* on which they were carried, a requirement that limited both the size and the materials of such statues (i.e., excluding life-size or larger sculptures in bronze or marble; see essay 2.7, Russell). Duncan Fishwick suggests that the wheeled vehicles in this relief were carrying larger statues, while the smaller ones were carried "on shoulder" (1990, 554).

One of the best-known religious processions in which statuary was carried was the *pompa circensis*. This parade from the Capitoline Hill to the Circus Maximus preceded important religious games celebrated there, including the *Ludi Romani* in September and the *Ludi Plebei* in November (Livy 23.30; Latte 1960, 248; Gabba 1991, 134). Dionysius of Halicarnassus provides us with a thorough description (which he credits to an earlier source, Q. Fabius Pictor) of a procession that included young men on horseback and foot, chariots, competitors in the games, dancers, a chorus dressed as satyrs, musicians, and men carrying sacred vessels. Then, "last of all came the images of the gods carried on the shoulders of men, having similar forms to those made by the Greeks in dress, attributes and gifts which each is traditionally credited with discovering and giving to men" (Dion. Hal. *Ant. Rom.* 7.72.13; trans. Long 1987, 100). While Caesar was still alive, an ivory statue of him was carried in at least two processions, along with the statues of the gods (Cass. Dio 43.45.2; Cic. *Att.* 13.28, 13.44; Suet. *Iul.* 76), an honor which Suetonius lists among those Caesar received that were beyond human (*ampliora humano fastigio*) and that led to his assassination.

Feeding the Gods: Sacrifice and *Lectisternium*

Oddly, although sacrifice was the quintessential religious act of ancient Rome, the degree to which animal sacrifice was a form of interaction with statues of the gods is unclear. Weddle has pointed out that Dionysius of Halicarnassus, who provides "the only full ethnographic description" of a Roman animal sacrifice, dwells on the animals and the altars, omitting any mention of the cult statue (Weddle 2010, 202). In reality, however, both the columns of the temple and the depth of its cella must often have made it impossible for the image of the god to "see" a sacrifice in progress, even if the doors were opened. Particular statues might be included in the ritual when offerings were left on tables near them or even in their hands or laps. Generally speaking, however, it would seem that public sacrifice involved far less interaction with the statues than we might have expected (Weddle 2010, 202–215).

The Romans did arrange couches for their gods in order to regale them at the religious banquets known as *lectisternia*. Some *lectisternia* were irregular events, prompted by plague or some other threat to the well-being of the Roman people. The first of these extraordinary events took place in 399 BC, in the wake of a freak snowstorm that dumped many feet of snow on the region and destroyed orchards and houses. This storm was followed by a plague, which prompted the *duumviri*, the priests whose job it was to address extraordinary state crises, to consult the Sibylline Books. These books prescribed a *lectisternium* and specified that there should be three couches, one for Apollo and Latona, one for Hercules and Diana, and the last for Mercury and Neptune. For seven days, the Romans offered sacrifices to the gods. A parallel domestic celebration took place throughout the city: citizens opened their doors for those seven days and set out food for friends and strangers alike (Livy 5.13; Dion. Hal. *Ant. Rom.* 12.8–9).

Expiatory *lectisternia* appear to have been particularly popular in the fourth and third centuries BC, at least to judge from Livy, who lists a string of them from this period (Livy 7.2. 7.27, 8.25, 21.62; Nouilhan 1989). Thereafter, our evidence for banquets tails off. Tacitus does mention that after Nero's great fire of AD 64, the married women of Rome celebrated *sellisternia*, banquets that employed thrones rather than couches, and Mattingly argues that there is numismatic evidence for *lectisternia* (or *sellisternia*) after the eruption of Vesuvius in AD 79 and after Rome's great fire of AD 80 (Tac. *Ann.* 15.44; Mattingly 1930, lxxii–lxxiii, lxxxv; *contra* Taylor 1935).

A second type of *lectisternium* was part of the cult of various Roman gods and so was more regularly celebrated. The most famous of these was the *epulum Iovis*, which ultimately came to be celebrated in September as part of the *Ludi Romani* and again in November as part of the *Ludi Plebeii*. Valerius Maximus informs us that at the *epulum Iovis* Jupiter was given a little couch (*lectuculum*), while Juno and Minerva sat on chairs—an obsolete practice for the actual Roman women of his day (Val. Max. 2.1.2).

For the purposes of this inquiry, it is crucial to address the question of whether and to what degree the gods at *lectisternia* took the form of statues or were in any way depicted anthropomorphically. It is, put simply, difficult to imagine the exact mechanics of laying a full-length bronze or marble statue on a couch. The images that we think of as standing or sitting in temple cellas might well have been difficult to lay out on a *pulvinar*, as if they were going to dine; but we do not possess unambiguous examples of divine statues that were designed both to stand and to recline, in the way that some medieval figures of Christ on the crucifix possess moveable arms and heads that once enabled them to participate in liturgical dramas (Taubert and Taubert 1969; Freedberg 1989, 286–7).

We also possess no divine images that were carved, cast, or modeled already in the reclining position as if for a dining couch. In other words, we possess no sculptures of gods in the round that look like the anthropomorphic figures on the lids of Etruscan cinerary urns or Roman sarcophagi. There is, moreover, little evidence of anthropomorphic images at the earliest celebrations of the *lectisternium*. It is possible that the gods were simply considered to have been present in spirit.

Livy does, however, report that during the *lectisternium* at the *Ludi Romani* of 179 BC, there was an earthquake and that the gods were seen to turn their heads away from the offerings. This fact, combined with the disturbing discovery that mice had tasted the offerings intended for the gods, actually necessitated a repetition of the games (Livy 40.59). This is the only extant source on *lectisternium* that might suggest images of the gods were employed in the ritual, but scholarly interpretations of it diverge (Long 1987; Weddle 2010, 221). Long argues that the gods at *lectisternia* took the form of human heads and not full-length statues (238). Since Livy's history is full of statues that bleed, sweat, and cry, statues that turn their heads might seem plausible. Nevertheless, placing a head on a couch does not pose the same mechanical problems as reclining a full-length statue would.

Talking Statues and Talking to Statues

Following a thwarted attack on the city of Rome, narrowly averted by a group of Roman women in 493 BC, the Senate voted to dedicate, at public expense, a temple and cult statue of Fortuna Muliebris, Women's Good Fortune, outside the city. In response, the women of Rome, extraordinarily, collected money on their own and set up a second statue of Fortuna. Both statues were consecrated at the same time, on the dedication day of the temple itself, a fact that probably rendered both statues sacred and inalienable from the temple estate. By contrast, objects dedicated later, *ornamenta*, might be rendered profane and eventually cleared out or sold (Estienne 2010, 261–6). As the story goes, a number of witnesses were present when the second statue, the one dedicated by the women, was heard to speak loud and clear the words, "Women, you have given me in accordance with the holy law of the city" (Dion. Hal. *Ant. Rom.* 8.55–6; a variant of the story is found in Plutarch, *Life of Coriolanus* 37–8). Later, the statue repeated the very same words. In response, the women of Rome—and, it is interesting to note, *not* the Senate in consultation with the pontiffs—decided that only women who had been married just once might crown the statue or touch it.

This story is, of course, at its heart aetiological. It provides an origin for the cult of Fortuna Muliebris and offers an explanation for the cult's most peculiar features, including the fact that two statues of the same goddess received ritual in the same sanctuary and seemingly on equal terms. Our two sources for this legend, Dionysius of Halicarnassus and Plutarch, though they are far removed in time both from one another and from the events they describe, agree that the story of the talking statue would likely meet with skepticism from some of their contemporaries and with belief from others. Both seem to feel that the detail of the statue speaking a second time—Plutarch says to a larger and more attentive crowd—would be reassuring to the believers. Dionysius sides firmly with the believers, asserting that the story was recorded in the "books of the pontiffs" and that it would encourage those who received their notions of the spiritual from their ancestors. Plutarch is more skeptical.

Plutarch's is a particularly interesting stance, since he served as a priest of the oracle of Delphi and so must have had well-considered notions about whether and how gods might communicate with mortals. He does not reject the notion of a speaking statue altogether; rather, he rationalizes it. He seems to believe that there was probably some sort of divine agency at play—that perhaps what occurred was a sort of collective hallucination, something analogous to a dream in which we see and hear things that are not, in reality, either visible or audible. According to this reading, the goddess did communicate with the women in the sanctuary, even if she did not literally speak out.

A similar middle-ground skepticism is evident when Plutarch recounts the famous legend of the *evocatio* or "calling out" of the statue of Juno after the defeat of Veii at the beginning of the fourth century BC. Some versions of the story circulating in antiquity indicated that the statue had spoken to indicate her assent to a new home in Rome. Aware that this detail is likely to meet with skepticism, Plutarch points to the many accounts, past and present, of statues sweating, groaning, turning away, and closing their eyes; and he cautions his readers against being either too credulous or too distrusting of such stories (Plut. *Vit. Cam.* 6).

Livy's version of the same *evocatio* makes it clear that he does not believe the statue spoke. He dismisses this detail as a mere tale, a *fabula*, that attached itself to the story after the fact. However, he does report that before the move, the statue was approached by its movers with a scrupulous attention to ritual detail: the particular young men who were selected for the job were washed thoroughly and dressed in white. As was the case with the statue of Fortuna Muliebris, there had been traditional restrictions—in this case, quite narrowly tailored restrictions—as to who might touch the statue, and these occasioned a certain amount of anxiety among the movers. The direct address to the statue, asking if she wanted to go to Rome, and its supposed nodding (or speaking) response worked together to defuse this anxiety.

Statue Prodigies and Expiations

While the legend of the speaking statue of Fortuna Muliebris is recorded as a miracle, it does share an important narrative element with the many statues, especially during the Republic, that offered admonitory prodigies, unusual occurrences that served as a sign, omen, or warning: such events often prompted further interaction with the statues. Statue prodigies included bleeding (Livy 22.1, 46.33, 46.43), sweating (Cic. *Div.* 1.74, 1.98, 1.99; Cass. Dio 48.50.4), crying (Cass. Dio 46.33), and turning around (Cass. Dio 46.33; Tac. *Ann.* 14.32), among other human behaviors.

Occasionally statues toppled over (Cass. Dio 48.43, 4–6), fell from the sky (Julius Obsequens, *De Prodigiis* 23), were blown over by the wind (Julius Obsequens, *De Prodigiis* 18) or struck by lightning (Cic. *Div.* 1.16, 1.19, 2.46–7; Julius Obsequens, *De Prodigiis* 38). All of these events were taken to indicate the displeasure of the gods. For much of the Republic, statues that demonstrated divine disapprobation were of interest to the state and prompted an official reaction. Like all prodigies, they were reported to the consuls, who then referred them to the Senate for decisions about expiation.

Such expiation often took the form of further attention to the statue. When statues were struck by lightning, the official response was sometimes to move them to a different location (Gell. 4.5; MacBain 1982, 50–51). In an unusual instance in 278 BC, however, lightning knocked the head off a clay image of Summanus (an Etruscan god of nocturnal lightning) that was perched on top of the Capitoline Temple. Etruscan *haruspices* were brought to Rome for the purpose of finding the missing head. The head was, in fact, discovered in the Tiber River, some thousand feet away (Cic. *Div.* 1.16; MacBain 1982, 46–77). Sometimes statue prodigies were handled in other ways: in 38 BC, for example, when a statue of Virtus fell down, the Sibylline Books called for it to be taken down to the sea and bathed (Cass. Dio 48.43, 4–6).

By the early first century BC, there are clear signs of skepticism concerning the relevance of certain prodigies to the well-being of the *res publica*, and there appears to be less official interest in expiating them (Cic. *Div. passim*; Drews 1988, 297–9). Cicero, whose *De Divinatione* is a lengthy expression of such skepticism, nevertheless made rhetorical use of prodigies when it proved convenient. He seems, however, to have done this more often with a popular audience than with an elite one, perhaps an indication of who might be more likely to believe such stories (Beard 1986; Schofield 1986; Wardle 2006, 5–6, 10–14).

Under the empire, we still encounter statue prodigies, but official expiation is rarely recorded. Thus, during the uprising of Boudicca in AD 60, a statue of Victory that had been erected in the Roman colony of Camulodunum (Colchester) reportedly fell and turned its back to the enemy as if in flight. Tacitus remarks that this event sent the women of Camulodunum into a *furor* and caused them to foretell destruction for the Romans. He also indicates that this and accompanying portentous events were considered by the Briton rebels to be good omens and by the Roman veterans of Camulodunum to be bad omens. Still, Tacitus records no evidence of any attempt to expiate these prodigies. Indeed, the veterans had a difficult time even getting troop reinforcements to face the very real threat posed by the uprising. In the end, Camulodunum was in fact destroyed (Tac. *Ann.* 14.32).

Portraits and Politics

During the Republic, the portraits of mortals did not require or receive the *cultus* or care that we associate with statues of gods. Interactions with portraits were therefore more overtly political in nature. They were installed in particular locations in order to produce some intended effect, or removed from their situations in order diminish their impact. They were also treated as stand-ins for politicians and so were received with approval by their adherents and with disapproval by their opponents.

The people in assembly and the Senate of Rome decreed honorific statues for prominent citizens and decided their location. Others might attempt to dedicate honorific statues in public places, but their right to do so was openly contested, as in 158 BC, when the censors removed unofficial honorific statues (Plin. *HN* 34.30; Tanner 2000, 25). Under these circumstances, the location of a statue in a particularly prominent spot often served to indicate the degree of honor bestowed upon the recipient (Tanner 2000, 24). Similarly, wealthy provincial patrons during both the late Republic and the empire would receive portraits of themselves to be displayed in exchange for their patronage, for their construction of city gates, theaters, and urban fountains (see essays 4.1, Longfellow; 4.5, Tuck; and 4.6, Kellum).

"Interaction" under these circumstances might be an accident or an epiphenomenon of other business: a walk to the Roman Forum or, in the provinces, to a vital urban fountain, would introduce an inhabitant or visitor to honorific statues whose very location conveyed something about the importance of the recipient. Both types of honorific statue—those granted by the Roman Senate and those granted prominent locations in provincial cities—served, no doubt, to enhance the benevolence and patriotism of the man or woman depicted.

Publicly displayed portraits sometimes attracted a political following or opposition. In such instances, statues served as symbolic stand-ins for their subjects, just as today when a crowd burns some political figure in effigy. We know of a number of episodes in which the portraits of controversial figures either attracted a following or prompted official anxiety that they might do so. One has to do with the *imagines* of Brutus and Cassius during the reign of Augustus. Because portraits could indicate political allegiance, the funeral of Iunia Tertulla, who was Brutus's sister and Cassius's wife, included neither the *imagines* of the Cassii nor those of the Iunii Bruti (Tac. *Ann.* 16.7.3).

Imagines (wax ancestor masks) were not statues in any traditional sense of the word (see essay 3.4, Wood). However, what we know of their function in Roman society helps us to understand something about how people might have acted around and reacted to the portraits of famous figures in any medium. The *locus classicus* for understanding the functions of *imagines* is of course Polybius's description of an aristocratic Roman funeral (Polyb. 6.53), in which we learn that the masks were decorated during public sacrifices and then brought out for the funerals of prominent family members. Actors or family members would don the masks of each prominent ancestor and would also put on garb associated with the highest political office achieved by each. A son or some other relative of the deceased gave a funeral speech at the rostra in the Forum and the "prominent ancestors" sat behind him on ivory chairs as he not only praised the deceased but also detailed the deeds of all the ancestors present. Polybius makes clear that the effect of this spectacle on the audience, particularly the young listeners, was intended to be an inspirational one. The ancestors, in other words, were presented as *exempla*.

An elderly Galba may have been deliberately parodying this ritual when he mounted a tribunal in AD 68 to be proclaimed *imperator* (Suet. *Galb.* 10.1). Galba, who subsequently supported his own dynastic claims through appeals to his distinguished ancestry, stood on the tribunal that day and spoke to his troops with the *imagines* of Nero's victims lined up behind him. While Suetonius provides only a very general idea of the content of that speech, the likelihood is that it included a laundry list of Nero's atrocities. If so, Galba's speech will have inverted the traditional funeral eulogy: merely by displaying the *imagines* of Nero's victims instead of his ancestors and by listing his atrocities instead of his illustrious achievements, Galba had branded Nero as a negative *exemplum*. He may also have been implying that the emperor was as good as dead.

The exclusion of portraits from locations or events where they might normally be expected seems to have served sometimes as a strategy for averting political strife. Appian tells us that Caesar included images and colorful paintings of the various participants in the civil war in his triumphal procession of 46 BC, but that he decided to exclude the portrait of Pompey. This was, he said, because Pompey had died only a year and a half earlier and "everyone still yearned for him exceedingly" (App. *B Civ* 2.101). Many decades later, Augustus's funeral procession included not only the *imagines* of the emperor's ancestors, but also those of the great men of Roman history, and for this occasion a portrait of Pompey was included in the funeral procession (Cass. Dio 56.34). In effect, this inclusion signified that Pompey had received posthumously the sort of *clementia* Caesar had wanted to offer him in life.

At times, the adherents of well-known political figures might demonstrate their allegiance through their reactions not to the portraits, but to statues of their divine proxies. Sextus Pompey had declared himself a "son of Neptune" and had even taken to dressing the part (Pease 1943, 75–6). After Antony and Octavian excluded Sextus from the Treaty of Brundisium, the people of Rome showed their approval for him, and for peace, by vigorously applauding the statue of Neptune during the *pompa circensis*. When Neptune's statue subsequently failed to appear in the procession, they threw stones at Octavian and Antony and toppled their portraits. Dio suggests that this violent behavior and its consequences forced Octavian and Antony eventually to approach Sextus and negotiate with him (Cass. Dio 48.31; Hadas 1930, 89–90).

Imperial Statues

Statues of the emperor possessed a very real and particular power: the right of asylum. While desperate people of all classes might seek refuge at an imperial statue, slaves in particular seem to have done so with some regularity (Plin. *Ep.* 10.74. Philostr. *V A* 1.15; Price 1984, 192–3). During the Republic, slaves who fled abusive masters had little recourse (Naiden 2006, 255n215). By the reign of Tiberius, however, asylum appears to have been an accepted function of imperial statues. In the second century AD, the *Institutes* of Gaius even record a decision by Antoninus Pius that if slaves fled to the temples of the gods or to the statues of the emperor (*ad fana deorum vel ad statuas principum confugiunt*), and their masters were subsequently found to have been unbearably cruel, the masters might be forced to sell them (Gai. *Inst.* 1.53).

At times, the protective authority of imperial statues seemed, at least to those in power, open to abuse. In AD 21 a senator named C. Cestius complained that criminals were taking advantage of this protection, since he himself had had to endure a verbal attack outside the Senate House by Annia Rufilla, a woman whom he had recently accused in court of fraud. Annia is said to have clung to an image of the emperor while she insulted and even threatened Cestius (Tac. *Ann.* 3.30). Drusus, the son of Tiberius, went ahead and prosecuted her, presumably for *iniuria*, and sentenced her to prison—a sequence of events that is interesting, because it shows us something of the limits of the refuge offered by the emperor's portrait. Criminal charges could, at least sometimes, still be brought against somebody claiming asylum at the emperor's statue (Naiden 2006, 254–5).

Both officials and private citizens had to be extremely careful how they interacted with statues of the emperor. Even actions that fell far short of actual damage, destruction, or recarving might nevertheless be considered *maiestas*, a violation of the dignity of the state, and, as such, a form of treason. Such actions therefore sometimes earned severe sanctions, even capital punishment. They might include manifestly disrespectful treatment, like urinating near or on imperial portraits, but also less obviously insulting actions, like removing the garlands from an imperial portrait or placing the new emperor's portrait head on a statue of a previous emperor (SHA *M. Ant.* 5.7; Tac. *Ann.* 1.74). Suetonius asserts that beating a slave and even changing one's clothes near a statue of Augustus became a capital offense during the reign of Tiberius (Suet. *Tib.* 58). Likewise, Dio reports that a man nearly lost his life simply for selling a statue of Tiberius along with his house; it was only the vote of Tiberius himself that saved him (Suet. *Tib.* 58; Cass. Dio 57.24).

Even the simple removal of an imperial portrait from display could be dangerous. An edict of Augustus dating to 7/6 BC and preserved on an inscription from Cyrene informs us that an envoy named Aulus Stlaccius Maximus was detained in Rome pending the emperor's review of an accusation that he had removed a likeness of the emperor from public view (*SEG* 9.8; Bauman 1967, 290–91). Whatever punishment Stlaccius may have endured or escaped, the inscription itself must have served as a form of public shaming.

Conclusion

The sanctity of the imperial image was such an accepted feature of Roman imperial life that in the fourth century AD the emperor Julian is supposed to have placed painted images of the gods beside his own, so that people might honor the gods under cover of honoring him (Gregory of Nazianzus, *Orations* 4.81; Sozomen, *Historia ecclesiastica* 5.17). However, this clever deployment of the imperial image also indicates the increasing danger—to humans and artworks alike—of certain interactions with divine statues. Depictions of traditional gods that could be defended as works of art might survive and be appreciated, but if they were too clearly objects of ritual attention, they risked destruction. In Palestine this distinction—between art object and object of worship—went back many centuries and was rooted in the encounter between the Roman sculptural habit and the biblical prohibition against idolatry (Eliav 2002, 423–7). By the fourth century AD, however, the distinction obtained throughout the empire and at the highest levels (Perry 2008). A law of AD 382 recorded in the Theodosian Code permits the governor of Osrhoene to keep open a temple in which the *imagines* were considered to have great artistic value, but the permission was valid only if the *imagines* were not honored for their divinity (*Cod. Theod.* 16.10.8). People continued to interact with statues, of course: they always have and they always will, but by late antiquity, statues of traditional gods could no longer safely receive the various attentions described at the beginning of this essay.

Addendum: Several relevant essays appear in Borgeaud and Fabiano 2013, which came to my attention while this volume was in press.

Bibliography

Bates, W. N. 1919. "Archaeological News." *AJA* 23(1): 75–100.

Bauman, R. A. 1967. *The Crimen Maiestatis in the Roman Republic and Augustan Principate.* Johannesburg: Witwatersrand University Press.

Beard, M. 1986. "Cicero and Divination: The Formation of a Latin Discourse." *JRS* 76: 33–46.

Bourgeaud, P., and D. Fabiano, eds. 2013. *Perception et construction du divin dans l'Antiquité: Recherches et rencontres.* Geneva: Librairie Droz.

D'Arms, J. H. 2000. "Memory, Money, and Status at Misenum: Three New Inscriptions from the *Collegium* of the Augustales." *JRS* 90: 126–44.

Drews, R. 1988. "Pontiffs, Prodigies and the Disappearance of the 'Annales Maximi.'" *CP* 83(4): 289–99.

Eliav, Y. 2002. "Viewing the Sculptural Environment; Shaping the Second Commandment." In *The Talmud Yerushalmi and Graeco-Roman Culture III*, edited by P. Schäfer, 411–33. Texte und Studien zum Antiken Judentum 93. Tübingen: Mohr Siebeck.

Estienne, S. 2010. "*Simulacra Deorum* versus *Ornamenta Aedium*: The Status of Divine Images in the Temples of Ancient Rome." In Mylonopoulos 2010, 257–71.

Fishwick, D. 1990. *The Imperial Cult in the Latin West: Studies in the Ruler Cult of the Western Provinces of the Roman Empire*. Vol. 2, pt. 1. Leiden: Brill.

Fornari, F. 1917. "Regione IV (Samnium et Sabina): S. Vittorino (Amiternum)." *NSc* 14: 332–41.

Freedberg, D. 1989. *The Power of Images: Studies in the History and Theory of Response*. Chicago: University of Chicago Press.

Gabba, E. 1991. *Dionysius and the History of Archaic Rome*. Berkeley: University of California Press.

Hadas, M. 1930. *Sextus Pompey*. New York: Columbia University Press.

Kahil, L. 1994. "Bains de Statues et de Divinités." In *L'Eau, La Santé et la Maladie dans le Monde Grec*, edited by R. Ginouvès, A. Guimier-Sorbets, J. Jouanna, and L. Villard, 217–23. Athens: École Française d'Athènes.

Kaufmann-Heinimann, A. 2007. "Religion in the House." In *A Companion to Roman Religion*, edited by J. Rüpke, 188–202. Malden, MA: Blackwell.

Latte, K. 1960. *Römische Religionsgeschichte*. Munich: C. H. Beck.

Long, C. R. 1987. *The Twelve Gods of Greece and Rome*. Leiden: Brill.

MacBain, B. 1982. *Prodigy and Expiation: A Study in Religion and Politics in Republican Rome*. Brussels: Latomus.

Mattingly, H. 1930. *Coins of the Roman Empire in the British Museum*. Vol. 2, *Vespasian to Domitian*. London: Trustees of the British Museum.

Mylonopoulos, J., ed. 2010. *Divine Images and Human Imaginations in Ancient Greece and Rome*. Leiden: Brill.

Naiden, F. S. 2006. *Ancient Supplication*. Oxford: Oxford University Press.

Nouilhan, M. 1989. "Les lectisternes républicains." In *Entre Hommes et Dieux: Le convive, le héros, le prophète*, edited by A.-F. Laurens, 27–41. Paris: Les Belles Lettres.

Pease, A S. 1943. "The Son of Neptune." *HSCP* 54: 69–82.

Perry, E. E. 2008. "Divine Statues in the Works of Libanius of Antioch: The Actual and Rhetorical Desacralization of Pagan Cult Furniture in the Late Fourth Century C.E." In *The Sculptural Environment of the Roman Near East*, edited by Y. Eliav, E. Friedland and S. Herbert, 437–48. Leuven: Peeters.

Price, S. R. F. 1984. *Rituals and Power: The Roman Imperial Cult in Asia Minor*. Cambridge: Cambridge University Press.

Ryberg, I. S. 1955. *Rites of the State Religion in Roman Art*. MAAR 22. Rome: American Academy in Rome.

Schofield, M. 1986. "Cicero for and against Divination." *JRS* 76: 47–65.

Stewart, P. 2003. *Statues in Roman Society: Representation and Response*. Oxford: Oxford University Press.

Tanner, J. 2000. "Portraits, Power, and Patronage in the Late Roman Republic." *JRS* 90: 18–50.

Taubert, G., and J. Taubert. 1969. "Mittelalterliche Kruzifixe mit schwenkbaren Armen: Ein Beitrag zur Verwendung von bildwerken in der Liturgie." *Zeitschrift des Deutschen Vereins für Kunstwissenschaft* 23: 79–121.

Taylor, L. R. 1935. "The Sellisternium and the Theatrical *Pompa*." *CP* 30(2): 122–30.

Taylor, R. 2008. *The Moral Mirror of Roman Art*. Cambridge: Cambridge University Press.

Wardle, D. 2006. "Introduction." In *Cicero on Divination, Book 1*, translated by D. Wardle, 1–44. Oxford: Clarendon Press.

Weddle, P. 2010. "Touching the Gods: Physical Interaction with Cult Statues in the Roman World." PhD diss., Durham University.

Wyke, M. 1994. "Woman in the Mirror: The Rhetoric of Adornment in the Roman World." In *Women in Ancient Societies: "An Illusion of the Night"*, edited by L. Archer, S. Fischler and M. Wyke, 134–51. New York: Routledge.

CHAPTER 6.6

ICONOCLASM

TROELS MYRUP KRISTENSEN

Introduction

The Roman world experienced several episodes of iconoclasm in which sculpture that had been on display in public or religious contexts was intentionally broken, mutilated, and subsequently buried, reused, or disposed of in secondary contexts. The recurrence of this phenomenon is a telling sign of the important role that sculpture played in Roman society in general and, more specifically, how it was perceived in contemporary cultural and religious practices. Iconoclasm itself is a Latinizing term, combining two Greek words (*eikon*, image or likeness, and *klan*, to break), but one that did not become widely used until the sixteenth century. The term originally refers to Byzantine debates about the nature of divine representation that raged during the eighth and ninth centuries (Brubaker 2012). Because of the loaded genealogy of the term and the very particular meanings that it held in later periods, not only in Byzantium but also during the Protestant Reformation as well as in an altogether broader sense during and after the French Revolution, its application in the study of Roman sculpture is not self-explanatory (Bremmer 2008). The term "iconoclasm" is consequently used here only in its most general meaning to describe the practice of breaking sculpture with both political and religious objectives in mind. In the Roman context, when used with careful consideration of potential anachronisms, the term has the great advantage of facilitating the study of the phenomenon of statue-breaking as a recurrent feature of Roman society, which can be explained by reference to various social factors and which has also been studied in many other periods (earlier as well as later) from the perspectives of history, art history, sociology, and anthropology, providing us with important theoretical and methodological frameworks for further cultural analysis (e.g., Freedberg 1989; Camille 1991; Gamboni 1997; Latour and Weibel 2002; Koerner 2004; Graves 2008; Wells 2008). While the terminology may then be relatively modern, the practice itself is very old. As such, iconoclasm constitutes an important term for understanding both the sociopolitical and theological importance of Roman sculpture as well as its role in Roman social history more generally. This essay aims to outline briefly some of the historical contexts in which cases of Roman iconoclasm have been identified and then to review some of the apparent problems that we face when trying to interpret this material and place it within its social, political, and religious frameworks. Lastly, it proposes some areas for future exploration.

Approaching Iconoclasm

Roman statues frequently survive today only in a headless, mutilated, or otherwise fragmentary state that poses important questions about their changing roles and ultimate fate. Recent years have witnessed the publication of several monographs as well as numerous articles that present case studies of particular ancient acts of violence that have been inflicted on statues in different contexts (see bibliography). The sociohistorical approach to art (Stewart 2003; 2008) that inspired many of these studies aims to shed light on issues such as the consumption, use, and even the abuse of images (see essay 6.2, Trimble). Many studies of viewer response have taken as their starting point the textual sources (e.g., Gregory 1994 on responses to Roman portraits including violence, inspired by Freedberg 1989), although a tendency to work also from the archaeological sources is becoming apparent in recent years. As we will see below, both sources present methodological challenges for the student of Roman sculpture.

More specifically, the interest in Roman iconoclasm can be seen as a consequence of dramatic events during the 2000s, most notoriously the Taliban's destruction of the Bamiyan Buddhas in Afghanistan as well as the events of September 11, 2001, and their aftermath, not least the toppling and subsequent abuse of colossal portraits of Saddam Hussein after the fall of his regime in Iraq in 2003 that was broadcast worldwide. Such striking images and the seeming relevance of the phenomenon in the contemporary world that struggles with its own problems of religious violence have resulted in scholars investing much energy in the study of the ways that different kinds of Roman sculpture were defaced or destroyed in acts of iconoclasm, in particular as part of the phenomenon of *damnatio memoriae* (see essay 2.3, Varner). These connections with the contemporary world are not merely coincidental, but point to the immense rhetorical and theological powers that have been invested in the visual culture of representation throughout history, including in the Roman world.

An equally important catalyst for recent studies of Roman iconoclasm has been the growing interest across the social sciences in cultural memory, an interdisciplinary field that has produced a number of influential works (Connerton 1989; Assmann 2011). These studies have investigated the role of memory as well as the use and manipulation of the past in various historical settings. Several scholars working on Roman iconoclasm have explicitly drawn on this field of social theory in their own analyses (Hedrick 2000; Kristensen 2010). Recent work by the anthropologist Paul Connerton has focused on the concept of forgetting (Connerton 2009), a function that acts of iconoclasm arguably intend to serve through the deliberate erasure of statues and the removal of monuments from public view, but in a manner that is far from always straightforward. In reality, iconoclastic events were rarely completely effective in their execution, and forgetting was a complex (and altogether necessary) social practice in Roman society that is worthy of further analysis (Levene 2012). Iconoclasm has also been studied from the perspective of religious visual culture, another emergent field of scholarship, particularly as an aspect of the sacred gaze and the way in which religious identities are maintained or usurped by other traditions (Morgan 2005, 115–46). As in many other historical contexts, Roman episodes of iconoclasm are bound up with the concept of "Othering" and the ways in which religious and social boundaries are established between groups.

Iconoclasm frequently encompassed ritualized violence and belonged to a number of closely linked contexts in the Roman world: sociopolitical, during more or less spontaneous statue riots (as part of uprisings against civic and imperial authorities) or the somewhat more closely controlled practice of *damnatio memoriae* (orchestrated, at least to a certain extent, by a central authority); and religious, as a result of conflict or competition between different religious groups (such as pagans and Christians) or because of state-sanctioned persecution of particular cults.

Iconoclasm, Memory, and the Politics of Representation

Damnatio memoriae, a modern term first attested in the seventeenth century, is used by scholars of Roman history as a catch-all phrase to describe a group of diverse punishments that served the collective purpose of condemning the memory of an individual who had fallen from grace. In particular, it is often used to refer to the sanction and negation of the memory of dishonored members of the imperial family. Particularly influential for modern definitions of the term in the Roman context was the groundbreaking work by the German historian Friedrich Vittinghoff, who focused on the legal aspects of the practice (1936, esp. 13–18). *Damnatio memoriae* incorporates a wide range of different memory sanctions, some of which targeted portraits in the round and other sculpted images (such as reliefs, wax masks, and numismatic likenesses) that represented the condemned person in the public sphere (Stewart 2003, 267–78). Public inscriptions naming individuals who were subjected to this punishment were also frequently erased or altered (Hedrick 2000; Flower 2006). The Senate, who would declare the victim a *hostis*, enemy of the state, was most often responsible for allotting these punishments. Pliny the Younger gives a powerful and metaphorically rich presentation of one such case of Roman *damnatio memoriae*, the destruction of the images of Domitian after his death in AD 96 (*Pan.* 52.4), providing us with a potent example of the deeply rhetorical power of iconoclasm as well as how it could be exploited for political purposes in panegyric. The kind of memory sanctions that these punishments bear witness to were not unique to Rome but have also been observed within the contexts of Pharaonic Egypt and to a lesser extent in archaic, classical, and Hellenistic Greece (Varner 2004, 1–20; Flower 2006, 17–41).

Taken together, the practices of *damnatio memoriae* can be understood as a reversal of the considerable honors that were invested in the erection of a public statue in Roman culture (Fejfer 2008, 17–20; see essays 3.8, Witschel; and 4.5, Tuck) as well as the rituals of *consecratio* in which a deceased emperor was deified and worshipped after death (Varner 2004, 6; De Jong and Hekster 2008). They have generally received broad interest because of the widespread popular appeal of "bad emperors," although the abuse of portraits of "good" emperors has also been discussed from the perspective of *damnatio memoriae* (see Arce 2007 on Constantine's portraits on his arch in Rome). Today the term is used to refer very broadly to a wide range of acts that served to erase the memory of individuals or groups in the Roman world, and it is thus applied in ways that extend beyond the strictly legal definitions laid out by Vittinghoff and other early work.

Expansion of the scholarly study of *damnatio memoriae* to include the archaeological evidence of mutilated and recarved imperial portraits received particular impetus as a result of the publication of Marianne Bergmann and Paul Zanker's seminal 1981 article on Nero and Domitian, a later volume for an exhibition that toured American museums (Varner 2000), and the subsequent publication of Eric Varner's dissertation that presents a catalogue of first- to early fourth-century examples (2004). Other recent studies have focused more explicitly on individual cases of *damnatio memoriae*. For example, several studies have looked at the evidence for the erasure in textual, epigraphic, and visual media of Geta, who was murdered by his brother and co-emperor Caracalla (Hillert 2003–4; Krüpe 2011). On some Carian coins originally depicting Caracalla and Geta, the image of Geta has been thoroughly erased, which seemingly would have allowed the coin to continue to circulate, although the resulting empty space clearly would have signified his absence to those who held the coin in their hands. Geta's image was also removed from, among other places, the Arch of the Argentarii in the Forum Boarium at Rome, an honorary arch in Leptis Magna, and a famous painted *tondo* from Egypt that is now in Berlin. These cases of partial erasure from different parts of the empire attest to a particular function of *damnatio memoriae*, reminding viewers that they should "remember to forget" the disgraced emperor or at least maintain a very particular kind of memory of the individuals subjected to this punishment through what has been coined "discernible destruction" (Vout 2008, 153; Elsner 2003). An alternative to outright destruction and disposal in these imperial cases of *damnatio memoriae* was the recarving of a portrait, a practice which appears from recent assessments to have been relatively widespread (see essay 2.3, Varner) and which in some cases would have been recognizable to people on the street, at least according to Jerome, writing in the late fourth/early fifth century (*Commentarius in Abacuc* 2.3.14–16).

An example of a sculptural portrait that was not simply removed from view or recarved into an effigy of another emperor, but instead clearly mutilated as part of the practices of *damnatio memoriae*, is a bronze statuette of Caligula now in Basel (figure 6.6.1; Varner 2004, cat. 1.3). Caligula was assassinated on 24 January AD 41, and shortly after *de facto* subjected to *damnatio memoriae*. Unfortunately, the bust comes without a known

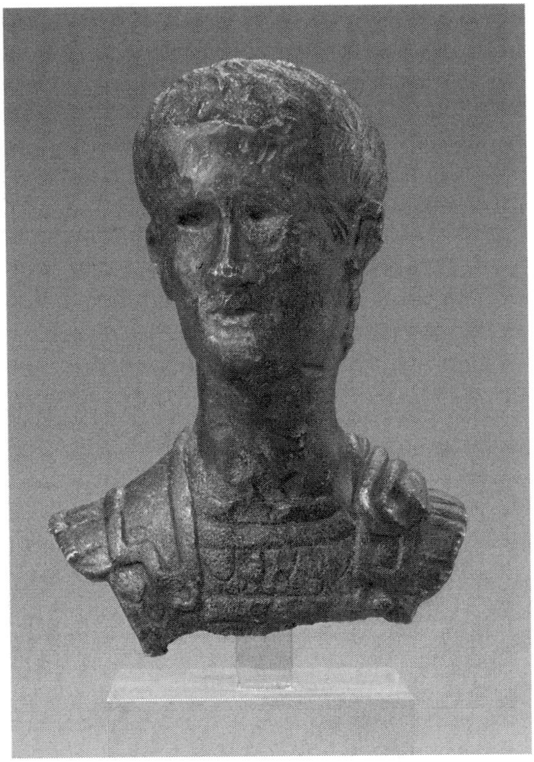

FIGURE 6.6.1 Mutilated bronze statuette of Caligula. Antikenmuseum Basel und Sammlung Ludwig, inv. no. BS 547.

archaeological provenience. It shows clear signs of deliberate mutilation, in particular in the area above the mouth and around the eyes, which have been thoroughly disfigured, and it has been struck numerous times with a sharp instrument. Intriguingly, whereas several of Caligula's portraits were recarved into other likenesses, few mutilated portraits have been identified (Varner 2004, 23–4). This likely reflects the difficult situation that Claudius found himself in after Caligula's death, as he had to negotiate a delicate balance between distancing himself from his deposed predecessor, while at the same time avoiding negation of the memory of the Julio-Claudian family *en masse* (Flower 2006, 148–59). His portraits were therefore quietly removed at night rather than in full daylight (Cass. Dio 60.4.5). Indeed, a marble portrait of Caligula, removed from a full-size statue body that could be reused, was uncovered from the bottom of the Tiber (and is now in the Yale University Art Gallery). This treatment provides evidence of another way of handling the defamed emperor's images that more effectively erased Caligula's memory from history: it drew on earlier traditions of disposing bodies of criminals and defeated enemies in Rome's river, thus at the same time both dishonoring and cleansing them from impurities (Kyle 1998, 213–41). In fact, close to half of the bronze statuettes of Caligula that are known today have been found in the Tiber, giving us some indication of the scale of the practice (Pollini 2006, 593). The disposal of representational media in the Tiber is furthermore a tradition that can be demonstrated to have had remarkable longevity in Rome, continuing into the medieval period (Sprenger 2012).

Identifying examples of statuary that have been defaced in episodes of *damnatio memoriae* requires careful assessment of how and when a particular portrait was mutilated. In the case of a late Severan bronze portrait of a female member of the imperial household found on the acropolis of Sparta, both date and context of mutilation have been debated (Riccardi 1998; Stewart 2008, 128). Only the face of this statue was smashed in, a particularly pointed response, given that a bronze statue easily could have been melted down and reused, and they rarely survive. This particular statue has been interpreted either as a case of *damnatio memoriae*, which seems more likely, or as a victim of Christian iconoclasm (see below). In many other cases, archaeological documentation is lacking or insubstantial, but it remains crucial to discuss the physical state in which statues were found, as well as the context in which they were deposited, in order to understand more closely their contribution to social history.

Furthermore, not all instances of *damnatio memoriae* are archaeologically visible. For example, Suetonius notes that placards with abusive inscriptions were placed on images on Nero (*Ner.* 45.2; Gregory 1994, 93). The ways in which particular images were subjected to mockery and abuse (see essay 6.5, Perry) or "warehousing" mostly remains invisible to us, but may account for the chronological gap that separates some examples of recarving from their initial production date (e.g., a portrait of Caligula that was recarved into one of Claudius Gothicus in the late 260s, more than 200 years after the former's death; Varner 2004, fig. 25).

The memory sanctions of *damnatio memoriae*, as they were observed within the upper echelons of society and within the imperial family, rubbed off on similar practices in other strata of Roman society. In the funerary sphere, inscriptions and portraits were destroyed or altered to suit new social circumstances or changes to the family structure (Carroll 2011). Furthermore, such examples attest to the social importance and representational power invested in funerary monuments and their decoration. Similar practices of erasure may also have been used as a way to punish troops who had rebelled against the emperor and participated in usurpations, as in the case of more than a hundred tombstones belonging to legionaries found at Chester in northwest England that had been reused in a defensive wall (Clay 2004).

Urban riots and revolts in which crowds pulled down statues as part of popular uprisings and social upheaval were another important context for political and social iconoclasm in the Roman world. The best-known of these "statue riots" took place in Antioch in late February 387 seemingly in response to the introduction of a new tax by the emperor Theodosius (Van Dam 2008). During these riots, imperial portraits in both stone and bronze were torn down, mutilated, and then dragged through the streets. The reasons for such social unrest were always complex and can be very difficult to reconstruct today, but what remains important here is once again the central role of statuary as a locus for response to imperial power. The punishment for such attacks was consequently dire (rumors circulated that entire cities would be laid waste) and long-lasting harm to a city's standing might ensue. During the fifth and sixth centuries, statues increasingly became victims of urban riots, which may have contributed to the extinction of the tradition of displaying statues in the round (see essay 3.8, Witschel). It is likely that many such riots have been lost to history, but archaeology may shed some light on their occurrence and impact on the urban environment. At least one group in the empire, the Jews, employed the latent threat of iconoclasm against imperial portraiture and sanctuaries of the imperial cult as a key part of their resistance to Roman rule (Von Ehrenkrook 2011).

Peoples from outside the empire could also be the agents of iconoclasm. In the early twentieth century, a famous bronze head of Augustus, now in the British Museum, was excavated south of the Egyptian border at Meroë, buried underneath a temple, strongly suggesting that the imperial portrait had been captured in a raid or campaign within the Roman borders, and then brought back as a trophy that was believed to have ritual significance (see essay 5.6, Riggs). Numerous interpretations have furthermore been presented concerning the fate of Jupiter columns in the Northwestern provinces, sometimes attributing their destruction and deposition to iconoclastic, barbarian incursions (Sauer 2003, 55–6; Noelke 2006; see essay 5.1, Cassibry). Such columns have in several cases been found dismembered and dumped in wells, strongly suggesting that they met a violent end.

The phenomenon of *damnatio memoriae* and the various other memory sanctions that fed off it attest to the central importance of statuary in several aspects of Roman society and are particularly informative about the role of the portrait as a vehicle for the public image not only of emperors, empresses, and high-ranking officials, but also of members of lower social strata who invested considerable parts of their income in funerary monuments in order to be remembered in perpetuity. The destruction of funerary images fed off the representational power of Roman portraits and offers as such powerful testimony to their agency and inherent presence (Stewart 2006). The archaeological evidence of mutilated portraits furthermore gives us insights into what has been termed "inscribed memory politics" (Rowlands 1993); textual descriptions of episodes of *damnatio memoriae*, on the other hand, allow us to flesh out some of the incorporated memory politics, such as verbal abuse and other rituals of desecration, which remain invisible from an archaeological perspective. Both attest to sculpture's crucial role in constructing and maintaining social memory as a political medium of representation.

Iconoclasm and Religious Conflict

Statues were also destroyed or desecrated as a result of religious conflicts in the Roman world. Persecution of foreign cults is already attested during the republican period (i.e., well before the Christian era). Notably, the Senate targeted the cult of Bacchus (infamous for its orgiastic rituals) in 186 BC, leading to the destruction of at least some Bacchic temples and their cult images (Beard, North, and Price 1998, 91–6). The Egyptian cult of Isis, including its altars and cult statues, was persecuted between 59 and 48 BC and again during the reign of Tiberius (Moehring 1959). Such episodes cannot be explained solely by reference to religious conservatism on behalf of the Roman elite. They were also the result of specific responses to political crises, internal pressures, or the threat of foreign wars.

In late antiquity, the process of Christianization slowly brought with it new attitudes toward images of the pagan gods that were now framed as idols by Christian authors and church authorities and sometimes regarded as potentially dangerous demonic presences. Christian apologists took their cues from and continued centuries-old discussions concerning *superstitio* and the status of images in religion to frame arguments that sculptures were only lifeless matter, formed by men (Nasrallah 2010). Later legislation from both the fourth and fifth centuries, preserved in the Theodosian Code, explicitly prohibited the worship of pagan images (Stirling 2005, 158–63). These edicts deal exclusively with statues that had been at the center of sacrificial rituals in temples (see essay 6.5, Perry); as such, they did not discuss all of the religious statuary that was on display in private houses or in the city streets and which clearly in many cases did not pose major problems to Christian viewers (on their fate, see Jacobs 2010; Lavan 2011).

Some trustworthy sources describe the destruction of pagan sculptures, such as a letter by Jerome, dated to 403, which tells of a city prefect of Rome, Furius Maecius Gracchus, who destroyed a group of Mithraic images in 376–7, following his conversion to Christianity (Jer. *Ep.* 107; Coates-Stephens 2007, 173–4). In accounts like this one, in which a recent convert destroyed idols, the act of iconoclasm functioned as a kind of purifying ritual.

However, many genres of Christian literature present us with narratives of iconoclasm in which cult images and altars in both religious and urban settings were verbally scorned and also physically attacked, whether by man (fire) or god (lightening; Caseau 2011, 479–85). An uneasy and altogether questionable relationship between rhetoric and reality is at work in many of these sources, and they often rely heavily on conventional topoi drawn from the Bible or earlier writings (e.g., Dijkstra 2008 on Egypt). Etiological stories of the foundation of Christian communities often claim that the place of congregation replaced a pagan sanctuary. Iconoclastic narratives, often interlaced with accounts of conversion, explained to their readers the treacherous relationship between pagan past and Christian present in terms of both continuity and change. Iconoclasm was furthermore a common trope among the standard repertoire of saints, martyrs, and other holy men in the genre of hagiography, where pagan cult statues and sanctuaries offered an appropriate religious battleground for their heroic and miraculous deeds. In spite of the questionable nature of many of the textual accounts of late antique Christian iconoclasm, archaeological studies of the topic have confirmed that such destructions were more than isolated anecdotes. Eberhard Sauer gives a "maximalist" account of Christian iconoclasm in a volume that explores archaeological evidence from the northwestern provinces in particular, but also Egypt and Italy (Sauer 2003). Evidence points to episodes of large-scale destruction, such as cult statues of Serapis and Cybele from Sarsina in northern Italy that were found in several hundred fragments, suggestive of a particularly hard-line Christian response, even if this episode cannot be precisely dated or placed within its proper social context. John Pollini presents a similarly maximizing view of Christian intolerance toward pagan sculpture in the Parthenon during its conversion to a church (2007) and toward the portraits of imperial priests in late antiquity (2008). Elsewhere, I discuss episodes of Christian destruction (both strictly rhetorical constructions and accounts of real acts of iconoclasm), analyzing this evidence for visual culture within a framework of viewer-object engagements and ontologies of the image (Kristensen 2009; 2013). In cases where they were marked with Christian crosses or words, as a sign of their purification or "conversion," pagan statues could also be appropriated for new uses (Kristensen 2012).

Extracting Christian responses to cult statues from the archaeological record is complicated by the difficulty not only of dating, but also of attributing damage to particular groups. In Cyrene, the centerpiece of the monumental Temple of Zeus was an enthroned colossal statue of the divinity, modeled on the Pheidian cult image at Olympia and epigraphically dated to 185–92 (Goodchild, Reynolds, and Herington 1958). The excavators reassembled more than a hundred fragments of the marble head of the statue, which had been deliberately and thoroughly shattered by human hands (figure 6.6.2). The other body parts to survive are similarly pulverized, and the statue's supporting base bears

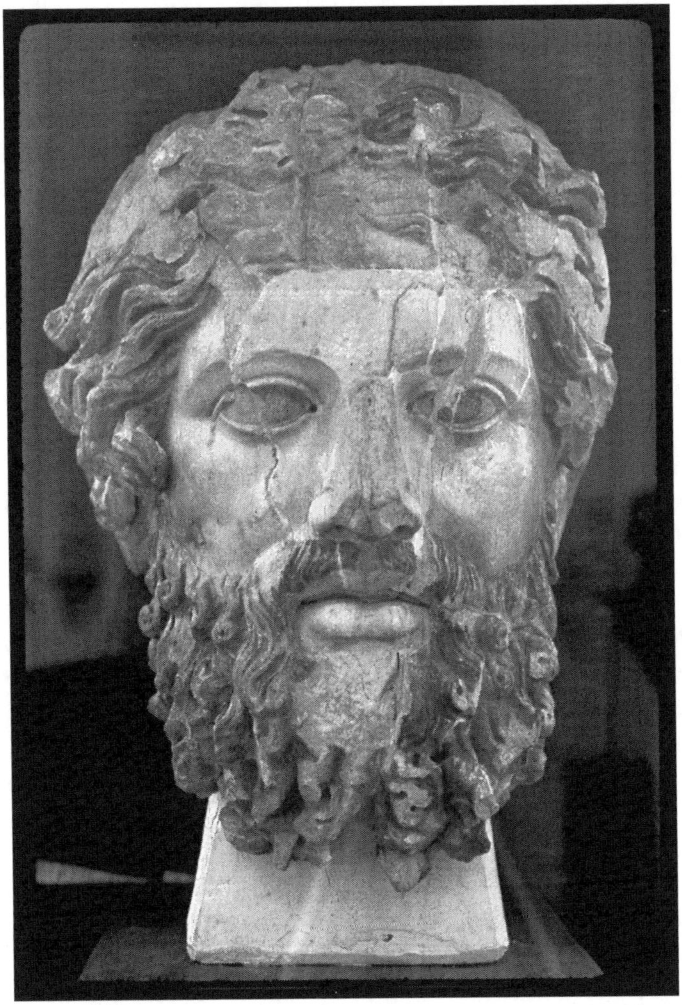

FIGURE 6.6.2 Reconstructed head of the cult statue of Zeus from Cyrene.

clear traces of burning. The meticulous destruction of the cult statue, which originally would have stood at a height of some 12 m, has been dated to the late fourth century and is testimony to a highly volatile religious environment, which can be compared with other known episodes of religious conflict in North African cities in late antiquity. At Rhamnous in Attica the base that supported the cult image of Nemesis was similarly shattered into thousands of fragments that were left behind in the temple (Pétracos 1981). In other contexts, much more targeted and selective destruction of particularly offensive parts of images can be observed. For example, in the Sebasteion at Aphrodisias, mostly representations of cult statues and scenes of sacrifice were objectionable and thus singled out for defacement (Smith 2012). Many cases of selective destruction have also been observed in Egypt; during late antiquity damage was inflicted particularly on those body parts that were believed to hold ritual potency or that had discrete symbolic meanings within local systems of representation (Frankfurter 2008; Kristensen 2009; 2013, 107–95). Such responses can also be discerned in other regions where vital parts of the body were mutilated. Another sculpture from Cyrene, a high-quality Pentelic marble statue of a nude athlete, demonstrates this well (Paribeni 1959, 48, cat. no. 81; Kristensen 2013, 105, fig. 1.27). Its nose has been completely removed, whereas the rest of the body is relatively unscathed. Various depositions of pagan statuary are furthermore suggestive of Christian desecration and disposal of pagan statues (Caseau 2011, 494). At Mamre in Palestine, a collection of mutilated statuary was reused in the foundations of the Constantinian church (Mader 1957, 136). Episodes of iconoclasm, therefore, could have diverse meanings depending on the context. Taken together, Christian responses to pagan sculpture took part in a negotiation of the role of divine images in religious practices and thus allow us to study theological aspects of Roman sculpture as well as how such images were perceived within a newly Christianized society. Some responses can be linked to demonology, the ways in which late antique Christians imagined demons and ritually expunged them from society. Destruction by fire furthermore appears to have had particular resonance in Christian iconoclasm, as it mirrored Biblical episodes of iconoclasm.

Conclusion: Interpreting Iconoclasm

As mentioned above, it can be difficult enough to identify and date specific damage to sculpture that often comes with little or no archaeological context and to work with textual sources that suffer from heavy triumphal rhetoric and repeated use of topoi. Yet perhaps more important than identifying further examples of iconoclasm is the still larger task of understanding the underlying practices that drove such cases of image violence and their representation in various media, notably text. Several scholars have pointed out that iconoclasm produces as much meaning as it destroys. For that reason, it is important to try to interpret what particular iconoclastic practices reveal about the modus operandi of the attackers (Stewart 2003, 278–90). Arguably, iconoclasm is part of the larger spectrum of human engagements with statues that appeal not only to sight, but also to touch and the senses (see essay 6.5, Perry). How then did iconoclasts conceptualize the power of the image they were attacking? Why was it worthwhile to destroy particular images in particular ways? When trying to answer these questions, we address the central issue that is at stake in cases of iconoclasm, namely the nature of representation, both divine and imperial, in the Roman world. We should also frame discussions of iconoclasm as related to agency, even if it can be difficult to disentangle the rhetorical nature of many textual sources and address the role of individual participants. In cases of *damnatio memoriae*, for example, what was the role of the army, of the people on the streets, of others?

Roman iconoclasm is thus not only about forgetting, erasure, or outright destruction; it also opens up a window to understanding particular conceptions of visual culture as well as the political and religious uses of images. As noted, the semantics of Roman iconoclasm were sometimes dependent on earlier traditions and practices relating to the ritual use and abuse of images (see, e.g., Aldhouse-Green 2004, 18–20, on the ritual destruction of images in the northwestern provinces, and Croxford 2003 on structured deposits in Britain). Additionally, the ritual killing of images, whether through decapitation or mutilation, rested on the notion that a stone body should be treated in ways similar to a flesh-and-blood body (see Varner 2001 and 2005 on treatment of images that mirrored contemporary corporal punishment). This seemingly basic point is essential. Decapitation, pointing to the immense importance of the head, is a well-established aspect of iconoclasm in a variety of contexts. For example, a headless statue was found in a third- to fifth-century dump at Puteoli (Cozzolino 1999, 25–31). A series of philosopher portraits from Aphrodisias (Smith 1990), and a portrait bust of Germanicus in the British Museum (Kristensen 2009, 229–32), all appear to have been targeted by Christian iconoclasts in a similar fashion. In such cases, there lies a particular challenge in understanding the specific form of the response and revealing its cultural significance.

The exploration of iconoclasm constitutes an important component of the social history of Roman sculpture and provides an important contribution to the growing field of memory studies. More publications that fully document the physical state of statuary and properly record the archaeological context in which sculptures have been found, including the provision of high-quality photographs are needed. Still, much evidence from older excavations has yet to be analyzed and could potentially answer many questions of a sociohistorical nature (Ward-Perkins 2011). The expanding literature on memory studies will no doubt provide continued inspiration for scholars interested in engaging with the entire life histories of statuary, particularly their destruction.

Bibliography

Aldhouse-Green, M. J. 2004. *An Archaeology of Images: Iconology and Cosmology in Iron Age and Roman Europe*. London: Routledge.

Arce, J. 2007. "*Damnatio memoriae* sur l'arc de Constantin à Rome." In *Mémoire et histoire: Les procédures de condamnation dans l'Antiquité romaine*, edited by S. Benoist, 131–6. Metz: Centre Régional Universitaire Lorrain d'Histoire.

Assmann, J. 2011. *Cultural Memory and Early Civilization: Writing, Remembrance, and Political Imagination.* Cambridge: Cambridge University Press.

Beard, M., J. North, and S. R. F. Price. 1998. *Religions of Rome.* 2 vols. Cambridge: Cambridge University Press.

Benoist, S., and A. Daguet-Gagey, eds. 2008. *Un discours en images de la condamnation de mémoire.* Metz: Centre Régional Universitaire Lorrain d'Histoire.

Bergmann, M., and P. Zanker. 1981. "'Damnatio Memoriae': Umgearbeitete Nero- und Domitiansporträts; Zur Ikonographie der flavischen Kaiser und des Nerva." *JdI* 96: 317–412.

Bremmer, J. N. 2008. "Iconoclast, Iconoclastic, and Iconoclasm: Notes Towards a Genealogy." *Church History and Religious Culture* 88: 1–17.

Brubaker, L. 2012. *Inventing Byzantine Iconoclasm.* London: Bristol Classical Press.

Camille, M. 1991. *The Gothic Idol: Ideology and Image-Making in Medieval Art.* Cambridge: Cambridge University Press.

Carroll, M. 2011. "*Memoria* and *Damnatio Memoriae*: Preserving and Erasing Identities in Roman Funerary Commemoration." In *Living through the Dead: Burial and Commemoration in the Ancient World*, edited by M. Carroll and J. Rempel, 65–90. Oxford: Oxbow.

Caseau, B. 2011. "Religious Intolerance and Pagan Statuary." In Lavan and Mulryan 2011, 479–502.

Clay, C. 2004. "Iconoclasm in Roman Chester: The Significance of the Mutilated Tombstones from the North Wall." *Journal of the British Archaeological Association* 157: 1–16.

Coates-Stephens, R. 2007. "The Reuse of Ancient Statuary in Late Antique Rome and the End of the Statue Habit." In *Statuen in der Spätantike*, edited by F. A. Bauer and C. Witschel, 171–88. Wiesbaden: Reichert.

Connerton, P. 1989. *How Societies Remember.* Cambridge: Cambridge University Press.

———. 2009. *How Modernity Forgets.* Cambridge: Cambridge University Press.

Cozzolino, C. 1999. "Recent Discoveries in Campania." In *Egyptological Studies for Claudio Barocas*, edited by R. Pirelli, 21–36. Naples: Istituto Universitario Orientale.

Croxford, B. 2003. "Iconoclasm in Roman Britain?" *Britannia* 34: 81–95.

De Jong, J., and O. Hekster. 2008. "Damnation, Deification, Commemoration." In Benoist and Daguet-Gagey 2008, 79–96.

Dignas, B., and R. R. R. Smith, eds. 2012. *Historical and Religious Memory in the Ancient World.* Oxford: Oxford University Press.

Dijkstra, J. H. F. 2008. *Philae and the End of Ancient Egyptian: A Regional Study of Religious Transformation (298–642 CE).* Leuven: Peeters.

Eliav, Y. Z., E. A. Friedland, and S. Herbert, eds. 2008. *The Sculptural Environment of the Roman Near East: Reflections on Culture, Ideology, and Power.* Leuven: Peeters.

Elsner, J. 2003. "Iconoclasm and the Preservation of Memory." In *Monuments and Memory, Made and Unmade*, edited by R. S. Nelson and M. Olin, 209–232. Chicago: University of Chicago Press.

Fejfer, J. 2008. *Roman Portraits in Context.* Berlin: Walter de Gruyter.

Flower, H. I. 2006. *The Art of Forgetting: Disgrace and Oblivion in Roman Political Culture.* Chapel Hill: University of North Carolina Press.

Frankfurter, D. 2008. "Iconoclasm and Christianization in Late Antique Egypt: Christian Treatments of Space and Image." In *From Temple to Church*, edited by J. Hahn, S. Emmel, and U. Gotter, 135–60. Leiden: Brill.

Freedberg, D. 1989. *The Power of Images: Studies in the History and Theory of Response.* Chicago: University of Chicago Press.
Gamboni, D. 1997. *The Destruction of Art. Iconoclasm and Vandalism since the French Revolution.* London: Reaktion.
Goodchild, R. G., J. M. Reynolds, and C. J. Herington. 1958. "The Temple of Zeus in Cyrene: Studies and Discoveries in 1954–1957." *PBSR* 26: 30–62.
Graves, C. P. 2008. "From an Archaeology of Iconoclasm to an Anthropology of the Body: Images, Punishment, and Personhood in England, 1500–1600." *CurrAnthr* 49(1): 35–57.
Gregory, A. P. 1994. "'Powerful Images': Responses to Portraits and the Political Uses of Images in Rome." *JRA* 7: 80–99.
Hedrick, C. W., Jr. 2000. *History and Silence: Purge and Rehabilitation of Memory in Late Antiquity.* Austin: University of Texas Press.
Hillert, A. 2003–4. "Die ermordete Silberbüste eines römischen Prinzen: Ein aus der Krone eines Kaiserpriesters entsorgtes Geta-Bildnis?" *Hephaistos* 21–2: 119–43.
Jacobs, I. 2010. "From Production to Destruction? Pagan and Mythological Sculpture in Asia Minor." *AJA* 114(2): 267–303.
Koerner, J. 2004. *The Reformation of the Image.* London: Reaktion.
Kristensen, T. M. 2009. "Embodied Images: Christian Response and Destruction in Late Antique Egypt." *Journal of Late Antiquity* 2(2): 224–50.
———. 2010. "The Display of Statues in the Late Antique Cities of the Eastern Mediterranean: Reflections on Memory, Meaning, and Aesthetics." In *Debating Urbanism: Within and Beyond the Walls A.D. 300–700*, edited by D. Sami and G. Speed, 265–87. Leicester: University of Leicester.
———. 2012. "Miraculous Bodies: Christian Viewers and the Transformation of Pagan Sculpture in Late Antiquity." In *Patrons and Viewers in Late Antiquity*, edited by S. Birk and B. Poulsen, 31–66. Aarhus: Aarhus University Press.
———. 2013. *Making and Breaking the Gods: Christian Responses to Pagan Sculpture in Late Antiquity.* Aarhus: Aarhus University Press.
Krüpe, F. 2011. *Die "Damnatio memoriae": Über die Vernichtung von Erinnerung; Eine Fallstudie zu Publius Septimius Geta (189–211 n.Chr.).* Gutenberg: Computus.
Kyle, D. 1998. *Spectacles of Death in Ancient Rome.* London: Routledge.
Latour, B., and P. Weibel, eds. 2002. *Iconoclash.* Cambridge, MA: MIT Press.
Lavan, L. 2011. "Political Talismans? Residual 'Pagan' Statues in Late Antique Public Space." In Lavan and Mulryan 2011, 439–77.
Lavan, L., and M. Mulryan, eds. 2011. *The Archaeology of Late Antique "Paganism."* Leiden: Brill.
Levene, D. S. 2012. "'You Shall Blot out the Memory of Amalek': Roman Historians on Remembering to Forget." In Dignas and Smith 2012, 217–39.
Mader, E. 1957. *Mambre: Die Ergebnisse der Ausgrabungen im heiligen Bezirk Râmet el-Halîl in Südpälastina, 1926–1928.* Freiburg im Breisgau: Erich Wewel.
Moehring, H. R. 1959. "The Persecution of the Jews and the Adherents of the Isis Cult at Rome A.D. 19." *Novum Testamentum* 3(4): 293–304.
Morgan, D. 2005. *The Sacred Gaze.* Berkeley: University of California Press.
Nasrallah, L. S. 2010. *Christian Responses to Roman Art and Architecture: The Second-Century Church Amid the Spaces of Empire.* Cambridge: Cambridge University Press.
Noelke, P. 2006. "Bildersturm und Wiederverwendung am Beispiel der Iuppitersäulen in den germanischen Provinzen des Imperium Romanum." *BerRGK* 87: 272–386.

Paribeni, E. 1959. *Catalogo delle sculture di Cirene: Statue e rilievi di carattere religioso*. Rome: "L'Erma" di Bretschneider.

Pétracos, B. 1981. "La base de la Némésis d'Agoracrite." *BCH* 105: 228–53.

Pollini, J. 2006. Review of Varner 2004. *ArtB* 88(3): 590–97.

———. 2007. "Christian Desecration and Mutilation of the Parthenon." *AM* 122: 207–228.

———. 2008. "Gods and Emperors in the East: Images of Power and the Power of Intolerance." In Eliav, Friedland, and Herbert 2008, 165–94.

Riccardi, L. A. 1998. "The Mutilation of the Bronze Portrait of a Severan Empress from Sparta: 'Damnatio Memoriae' or Christian Iconoclasm?" *AM* 113: 259–69.

Rowlands, M. 1993. "The Role of Memory in the Transmission of Culture." *WorldArch* 25(2): 141–51.

Sauer, E. 2003. *The Archaeology of Religious Hatred in the Roman and Early Medieval World*. Stroud: Tempus.

Smith, R. R. R. 1990. "Late Roman Philosopher Portraits from Aphrodisias." *JRS* 80: 127–55.

———. 2012. "Defacing the Gods at Aphrodisias." In Dignas and Smith 2012, 283–326.

Sprenger, K.-M. 2012. "The Tiara in the Tiber: An Essay on the *damnatio* in *memoria* of Clement III (1084–1100) and Rome's River as a Place of Oblivion and Memory." *Reti Medievali Rivista* 13(1): 153–74.

Stewart, P. 2003. *Statues in Roman Society: Representation and Response*. Oxford: Oxford University Press.

———. 2006. "The Image of the Roman Emperor." In *Presence: The Inherence of the Prototype within Images and Other Objects*, edited by R. Maniura and R. Shepherd, 243–58. Aldershot: Ashgate.

———. 2008. *The Social History of Roman Art*. Cambridge: Cambridge University Press.

Stirling, L. M. 2005. *The Learned Collector: Mythological Statuettes and Classical Taste in Late Antique Gaul*. Ann Arbor: University of Michigan Press.

Van Dam, R. 2008. "Imagining an Eastern Roman Empire: A Riot at Antioch in 387 C.E." In Eliav, Friedland, and Herbert 2008, 451–81.

Varner, E. R., ed. 2000. *From Caligula to Constantine: Tyranny and Transformation in Roman Portraiture*. Atlanta: Michael C. Carlos Museum.

———. 2001. "Punishment after Death: Mutilation of Images and Corpse Abuse in Ancient Rome." *Mortality* 6(1): 45–64.

———. 2004. *Mutilation and Transformation: "Damnatio Memoriae" and Roman Imperial Portraiture*. Leiden: Brill.

———. 2005. "Execution in Effigy: Severed Heads and Decapitated Statues in Imperial Rome." In *Roman Bodies: Antiquity to the Eighteenth Century*, edited by A. Hopkins and M. Wyke, 67–82. London: British School at Rome.

Vittinghoff, F. 1936. *Der Staatsfeind in der römischen Kaiserzeit: Untersuchungen zur "damnatio memoriae."* Berlin: Junker und Dünnhaupt.

Von Ehrenkrook, J. 2011. *Sculpting Idolatry in Flavian Rome: (An)Iconic Rhetoric in the Writings of Flavius Josephus*. Atlanta: Society of Biblical Literature.

Vout, C. 2008. "The Art of 'Damnatio Memoriae.'" In Benoist and Daguet-Gagey 2008, 153–72.

Ward-Perkins, B. 2011. "The End of the Temples: An Archaeological Problem." In *Spätantiker Staat und religiöser Konflikt: Imperiale und lokale Verwaltung und die Gewalt gegen Heiligtümer*, edited by J. Hahn, 187–99. Berlin: Walter de Gruyter.

Wells, P. S. 2008. *Image and Response in Early Europe*. London: Duckworth.

Art Credits

FIGURE 1.1.1 Drawing of the hanging garden of Cardinal Andrea della Valle, attributed to Maartin Van Heemskerck. Photograph: Bibliothèque nationale de France, Paris, Estampes et Photographie, Réserve B-2 (3).

FIGURE 1.1.2 Drawing of the Laocoön in Belvedere Courtyard by Francesco de Hollande. Photograph: Library, Escorial, Madrid; © Patrimonio Nacional.

FIGURE 1.1.3 Carracci Gallery, Palazzo Farnese, Rome, Italy. Photograph: © Gianni Dagli Orti/The Art Archive at Art Resource, New York.

FIGURE 1.1.4 Engraving from *Galleria Givstiniana del marchese Vincenzo Givstiniani*. Photograph: Art & Architecture Collection, Miriam and Ira D. Wallach Division of Art, Prints and Photographs, The New York Public Library, Astor, Lenox and Tilden Foundations.

FIGURE 1.1.5 Child's sarcophagus from Museum Kircheranum. Rome, Museo Nazionale Romano, Terme di Diocleziano. Photograph: Singer, Detail of Neg. D-DAI-ROM 73.1784.

FIGURE 1.1.6 View of the Roman portrait gallery, Ny Carlsberg Glyptotek, Copenhagen. Photograph: Ny Carlsberg Glyptotek, Copenhagen.

FIGURE 1.2.1 Engraving of a statue of a god restored as Alexander the Great, 1704, Robert van Audenaerde (Belgian, 1663–1743), Maffei and de Rossi 1704. Digital image courtesy of the Getty's Open Content Program, The Getty Research Institute, 93-B5694.

FIGURE 1.2.2 Engraving of a statue of a god restored as Alexander the Great, 1804, after Schubert (German, active 1700s), Becker 1804, pl. 18. Digital image courtesy of the Getty's Open Content Program, The Getty Research Institute, 89-B16556.

FIGURE 1.2.3 Photograph of Antinous as Bacchus, 1885–8, by Hermann Krone. Courtesy of the Skulpturensammlung, Staatliche Kunstsammlungen Dresden.

FIGURE 1.2.4 Photograph of the re-restoration carried out between 1888 and 1894 on statue of a god. Skulpturensammlung, Staatliche Kunstsammlungen Dresden. Courtesy of the J. Paul Getty Museum.

FIGURE 1.2.5 Statue of a god (Roman, AD 100–200). Skulpturensammlung, Staatliche Kunstsammlungen Dresden. Courtesy of the J. Paul Getty Museum.

FIGURE 1.3.1 Cast Gallery in the Old Library at the University of Michigan. Photograph: Bentley Historical Library, University of Michigan. Collection Name UM Photographs, Folder UBImus C450-79, Filename HS11775.

FIGURE 1.3.2 Court of Classical Casts, Museum of Fine Arts, Boston. Photograph: Trustees of the Boston Public Library. File no. 08_02_002766.

FIGURE 1.4.1 View of "Women and Children in Antiquity" gallery of the Getty Villa, Malibu. Photograph: Tahnee Cracchiola; courtesy of the J. Paul Getty Museum.

FIGURE 1.4.2 Roman gallery, San Antonio Museum of Art. Photograph: Peggy Tenison, courtesy of the San Antonio Museum of Art.

FIGURE 1.4.3 Installation of Roman torsos of Athena, Ny Carlsberg Glyptotek, Copenhagen. Photograph: author; reproduced with permission of the Ny Carlsberg Glyptotek.

FIGURE 1.5.1 3DDM of the Amazon Sciarra from the Canopus of Hadrian's Villa. Sponsored by NSF grant # 1018512. Copyright 2012 by The Board of Visitors of the University of Virginia. All rights reserved.

FIGURE 1.5.2 3DDM of the Laocoön. Copyright 2009 by The Vatican Museums. All rights reserved.

FIGURE 1.5.3 Detail of 3DDM of Pan-Nymph in the Dresden State Museums. Copyright 2009 by the Dresden State Museums. All rights reserved.

FIGURE 1.5.4 3DDM of the lower rotunda of Roccabruna. Hadrian's Villa. Sponsored by NSF grant # 1018512. Copyright 2012 by The Board of Visitors of the University of Virginia. All rights reserved.

FIGURE 2.1.1 Map of the principal quarries of white marbles in the Roman Empire. Map: Eleonora Gasparini.

FIGURE 2.1.2 Quarry of white marble at Aliki. Thasos, Greece. Photograph: Patrizio Pensabene.

FIGURE 2.1.3 Excavations of the harbor along the Tiber in the nineteenth century. Rome. Photograph: Patrizio Pensabene.

FIGURE 2.1.4 So-called Bagni di Livia, a part of Nero's imperial palace. Rome. Photograph: Patrizio Pensabene.

FIGURE 2.2.1 Unfinished statue of a Dacian prisoner. Vatican Museums, Museo Gregoriano Profano ex Lateranense. Photograph: author.

FIGURE 2.2.2 Apprentice training piece. Rome, Palazzo della Cancelleria, S. Lorenzo in Damaso excavation storerooms. Photograph: author.

FIGURE 2.2.3 Cast in EUR, Museo della Civiltà Romana, of sculptor Amabilis at work on his own funerary monument. Photograph: author.

FIGURE 2.2.4 Signature of the sculptor Zenon, son of Attinas, of Aphrodisias, on a fold of drapery beside knee of a seated togate statue, c. AD 110. Rome, Palazzo Altemps, inv. no. 8641. Photograph: author.

FIGURE 2.3.1 Caligula/Claudius. Grosseto Museo Archeologico e d'Arte della Maremma. Photograph: author.

FIGURE 2.3.2 Posidippus / late republican portrait. Rome, Musei Vaticani, Galleria delle Statue. Photograph: author.

FIGURE 2.3.3 Late republican female portrait. Rome, Centrale Montemartini. Photograph: author.

FIGURE 2.3.4 Hadrianic/Severan female portrait. Rome, Museo Capitolino, Stanza degli Imperatori. Photograph: author.

FIGURE 2.3.5 Constantius II or Constans (?). Rome, Palazzo dei Conservatori, Sala dei Fasti Moderni. Photograph: author.

FIGURE 2.4.1 Roman bronze bust of a youth. Museo Archeologico Nazionale di Napoli. Photograph: H. Lie.

FIGURE 2.4.2 Indirect lost-wax process for casting a bronze statue. Drawing: Séan Hemingway.

FIGURE 2.4.3 Bronze portrait of a man. Museo Archeologico Nazionale di Napoli. Photograph: H. Lie.

FIGURE 2.4.4 Mahdia herm (left): Bardo National Museum, Tunis; photograph: H. Lilienthal, courtesy of Rheinisches Landesmuseum. Getty herm (right): J. Paul Getty Museum, Malibu; photograph: Digital image courtesy of the Getty's Open Content Program.

FIGURE 2.5.1 Terracotta model of uterus from Italy. British Museum. Photograph: © The Trustees of the British Museum.

FIGURE 2.5.2 Terracotta of a woman seated in a wicker chair and holding a baby. British Museum. Photograph: © The Trustees of the British Museum.

FIGURE 2.5.3 Terracotta from Myrina depicting Aphrodite. British Museum. Photograph: © The Trustees of the British Museum.

FIGURE 2.5.4 Two terracottas from Beit Nattif, Israel. Photograph: Israel Antiquities Authority.

FIGURE 2.5.5 Terracotta of Harpocrates from Egypt. Photograph: © The National Maritime Museum, Haifa.

FIGURE 2.6.1 Impression of intaglio ring stone with Greek artisan painting a portrait of a Roman woman. Metropolitan Museum of Art. Photograph: Art Resource, New York.

FIGURE 2.6.2 So-called Treu Head. British Museum. Photograph: © Trustees of the British Museum.

FIGURE 2.6.3 So-called Venus Lovatelli. Museo Archeologico Nazionale di Napoli. Photograph: © www.pedicinimages.com, courtesy of the Museo Archeologico Nazionale di Napoli.

FIGURE 2.6.4 Bronze statue of child Dionysos. Saint Louis Art Museum. Photograph: © Saint Louis Art Museum.

FIGURE 2.7.1 Colossal marble statue from the Şile shipwreck. Photograph: author, courtesy of İstanbul Arkeoloji Müzeleri/Istanbul Archaeological Museums.

FIGURE 2.7.2 Marble bust of Aphrodite from the Mahdia shipwreck. Musée National du Bardo, Tunis. Photograph: Koppermann, Neg. D-DAI-ROM 61.476.

FIGURE 2.7.3 Bronze bust of a man from the Antikythera shipwreck. National Archaeological Museum, Athens. Photograph: Hellner, Neg. D–DAI–ATH–NM 6065.

FIGURE 2.7.4 Plan of the cargo of the Torre Sgarrata shipwreck off Puglia (after Throckmorton 1972, 13). Plan: courtesy of Thames and Hudson and the Institute of Nautical Archaeology.

FIGURE 3.1.1 Gemma Augustea. Vienna, Kunsthistorisches Museum. Photograph: E. Lessing / Art Resource, New York.

FIGURE 3.2.1 Tomb group from Fontecucchiaia (Clusium). Copenhagen, National Museum. Photograph: Courtesy of the National Museum of Denmark.

FIGURE 3.2.2 Hercules and Minerva, acroteria from the sacred area of Sant'Omobono, Rome. Drawing: Renata Spooner Za for N. Winter.

FIGURE 3.2.3 Tinia, bronze statuette of unknown provenance. Heidelberg University. Photograph: Archäologisches Institut der Universität Heidelberg, N.S. 867.

FIGURE 3.2.4 The Orator from area of Lake Trasimeno. Florence, Museo Archeologico Nazionale. Photograph: By permission of the Soprintendenza per i Beni Archeologici della Toscana—Firenze.

FIGURE 3.2.5 Stone sarcophagus from the Tomba Campanari, Tuscania. The British Museum. Photograph: Sir Percival David Collection /© The Trustees of the British Museum.

FIGURE 3.3.1 Bust of the head of the Doryphoros by Polykleitos from the Villa of the Papyri, Herculaneum. Museo Archeologico Nazionale di Napoli. Photograph: Koppermann, Neg. D-DAI-ROM 64-1804.

FIGURE 3.3.2 So-called Stephanos Athlete. Rome, Museo di Villa Albani. Photograph: Alinari/Art Resource, New York.

FIGURE 3.3.3 Copy of the Diskobolos by Myron found on the Esquiline. Rome, Museo Nazionale Romano. Photograph: courtesy of Ministero per i Beni e le Attività Culturali e del Turismo—Soprintendenza Speciale per i Beni Archeologici di Roma.

FIGURE 3.3.4 Fragment of a plaster cast used to produce copies of the statue of Aristogeiton. Baiae, Museo Archeologico dei Campi Flegrei. Photograph: Hellner, Neg. D-DAI-ROM 78.1857.

FIGURE 3.4.1 Portrait herm of Lucius Caecilius Iucundus from Pompeii. Museo Archeologico Nazionale di Napoli. Photograph: Werner Forman/Art Resource, New York.

FIGURE 3.4.2 Colossal portrait head of Gallienus. Copenhagen, Ny Carlsberg Glyptotek. Photograph: Album/Art Resource, New York.

FIGURE 3.4.3 Portrait statue of Augustus from the Via Labicana. Rome, Museo Nazionale Romano, Palazzo Massimo. Photograph: Album/Art Resource, New York.

FIGURE 3.4.4 Portrait statue of Faustina the Elder. Photograph: Digital image courtesy of the Getty's Open Content Program, The J. Paul Getty Museum, Villa Collection, Malibu, California.

FIGURE 3.5.1 Chariot Relief, Arch of Titus, Rome. Photograph: Elizabeth Wolfram Thill.

FIGURE 3.5.2 Detail of the relief from the Monument of Philopappus, Athens. Photograph: Elizabeth Wolfram Thill.

FIGURE 3.5.3 Detail of the arch from the Spoils Relief, Arch of Titus, Rome. Photograph: Melanie Grunow Sobocinski.

FIGURE 3.6.1 Archaistic female herm from the Horti Maecenatiani. Rome, Musei Capitolini. Photograph: Neg. D-DAI-ROM 4472.

FIGURE 3.6.2 Archaistic female herm from the Horti Maecenatiani. Rome, Musei Capitolini. Photograph: K. Anger, Neg. D-DAI-ROM 2001.1936.

FIGURE 3.6.3 Orestes and Electra. Rome, Museo Nazionale Romano. Photograph: Courtesy of Ministero dei beni e delle attività culturali e del turismo—Soprintendenza Speciale per il Colosseo, il Museo Nazionale Romano e l'Area Archeologica di Roma.

FIGURE 3.6.4 Head of a male, life-size terracotta sculpture from the Domus Tiberiana, Palatine Hill, Rome. Rome, Museo Nazionale Romano. Photograph: Courtesy of Ministero dei beni e delle attività culturali e del turismo—Soprintendenza Speciale per il Colosseo, il Museo Nazionale Romano e l'Area Archeologica di Roma.

FIGURE 3.7.1 Apis bull, c. second century BC, discovered on the Esquiline Hill in 1886. Photograph: Gianni Dagli Orti/Art Resource, New York.

FIGURE 3.7.2 Drawing of *aediculum* on the Esquiline with Isis and assemblage, c. AD 300. After Visconti 1885, Tav. IV.

FIGURE 3.7.3 Relief of an Isiac ceremony, imperial period, found in a burial in Arriccia. Photograph: Vanni Archive/Art Resource, New York.

FIGURE 3.7.4 Antinous in Egyptian dress, after AD 130, from Hadrian's Villa. Photograph: Scala/Art Resource, New York.

FIGURE 3.8.1 Restored elevation of the Monument of Theodosius (I or II) from Aphrodisias. Drawing: K. Görkay; courtesy of R. R. R. Smith (2001, fig. 34).

FIGURE 3.8.2 Portrait of a Tetrarch (Galerius?) from Gamzigrad/Romuliana. Zaječar, National Museum. Photograph: C. Witschel.

FIGURE 3.8.3 Statue of a high-ranking late antique magistrate (Stephanos?) wearing a toga, from Ephesos. Efes Müzesi Selçuk. Photograph: Courtesy of Österreichisches Archäologisches Institut.

FIGURE 3.8.4 Statuette of Diana from the villa of Saint Georges de Montagne. Bordeaux, Musée d'Aquitaine. Photograph: Lysiane Gauthier, mairie de Bordeaux.

FIGURE 3.8.5 Portrait of Augustus with an incised cross on the forehead from Ephesos. Efes Müzesi Selçuk. Photograph: Courtesy of Österreichisches Archäologisches Institut.

FIGURE 4.1.1 Relief from the Tomb of the Haterii on the Via Labicana, Rome. Vatican Museums, Lateran Collection. Photograph: Scala/Art Resource, New York.

FIGURE 4.1.2 Hercules from the Baths of Caracalla, Rome. Museo Archeologico Nazionale di Napoli. Photograph: Scala/Art Resource, New York.

FIGURE 4.1.3 Roman theater in Colonia Augusta Emerita (Mérida, Spain). Photograph: Manuel Cohen/The Art Archive at Art Resource, New York.

FIGURE 4.2.1 Statue of Mercury (proposed reconstruction), from the Sanctuary of Mercury, West Hill, Uley, Gloucestershire. Drawing: Joanna Richards.

FIGURE 4.2.2 Altar with Mercury, from the Sanctuary of Mercury, West Hill, Uley. London, British Museum. Photograph: author.

FIGURE 4.2.3 Severus's confession stela, probably from northeast Lydia. Private collection. Photograph: courtesy of J. Nollé.

FIGURE 4.2.4 Statuette of Saturn, from Sanctuary of Saturn, Haïdra. Photograph: Courtesy of *Revue Archéologique*, originally published in F. Baratte and Z. Benzina Ben Abdallah, "Le sanctuaire de Saturne à Ammaedara: Nouveaux documents," *RA* 2000, fig. 6b–c.

FIGURE 4.3.1 Diagram of sculptural display at Villa A, Oplontis. Drawing: Victoria I and Mary Todd. Courtesy of Bettina Bergmann and the *Journal of Roman Archaeology*.

FIGURE 4.3.2 Reconstruction of the sculptural display at Punta Epitaffio, Baiae. Drawing: Lorene Sterner; reproduced by permission of the author.

FIGURE 4.3.3 Pendants from *domus*, Via Cavour, Rome. Drawing: Shelly Smith Kellam; reproduced by permission of Elizabeth Bartman.

FIGURE 4.3.4 Niche in house C119, Karanis, Egypt. Photograph: KM Negative # 816, Kelsey Museum of Archaeology, University of Michigan.

FIGURE 4.4.1 Funerary relief of the Vettii. Rome, Via Po. Photograph: Singer, Neg. D-DAI-ROM 72.2938.

FIGURE 4.4.2 Funerary altar of Carienius Venustus. Toronto, Royal Ontario Museum. Photograph: With permission of the Royal Ontario Museum © ROM.

FIGURE 4.4.3 Funerary urn of Claudius Chryseros, Iulia Theonoe, and Claudia Dorcas from Rome, Via Appia, Vigna Codini, Tomb III. Rome, Museo Nazionale Romano. Photograph: Rossa, Neg. D-DAI-ROM 74.245.

FIGURE 4.4.4 *Kline* monument depicting a woman holding a garland. Rome, Museo Nazionale Romano. Photograph: Schwanke, Neg. D-DAI-ROM 80.2707.

FIGURE 4.4.5 Sarcophagus with Amazonomachy. Toronto, Royal Ontario Museum. Photograph: With permission of the Royal Ontario Museum © ROM.

FIGURE 4.5.1 Dedicatory inscription below niche in the north passageway of the amphitheater of Pompeii. Photograph: author.

FIGURE 4.5.2 Dedication of Mazaeus from market gate at Ephesus. Photograph: author.

FIGURE 4.5.3 Three of the four *tituli* on the large base dedicated by the *aenatores* at Rome. Photograph: author.

FIGURE 4.5.4 Statue base for L. Licinius Primitivus from the Sacellum of the Augustales, Misenum. Photograph: author.

FIGURE 4.7.1 Statue of Bacchus, from workshop VII.12.17/21, Pompeii. Museo Archeologico Nazionale di Napoli. Photograph: Alinari/Art Resource, New York.

FIGURE 4.7.2 Front of the altar of the Vicus Aesculeti. Rome. Photograph: Koppermann, Neg. D-DAI-Rom 60.1472.

FIGURE 4.7.3 Lar figure on the right side of the altar of the Vicus Aesculeti. Rome. Photograph: Michael Larvey.

FIGURE 4.7.4 Cast of reliefs from the Monument of Eurysaces. Museo della Civiltà Romana, Rome. Photograph: Singer, Neg. D-DAI-Rom 72.3819.

FIGURE 4.7.5 Funerary stele of a shoemaker. Rome. Photograph: Rossa, Neg. D-DAI-Rom 77.1705.

FIGURE 4.8.1 Greengrocer's Relief. Ostia, Museo Ostiense. Photograph: Eve D'Ambra.

FIGURE 4.8.2 Relief from the Basilica Aemilia, Punishment of Tarpeia. Rome, Antiquarium of the Roman Forum. Photograph: Eve D'Ambra.

FIGURE 4.8.3 Doll of Crepereia Tryphaena. Rome, Musei Capitolini, Centrale Montemartini. Photograph: © Roma, Sovrintendenza Capitolina ai Beni Culturali.

FIGURE 4.8.4 Sleeping Hermaphrodite. Pompeii, Ufficio Scavi. Photograph: Francesca Tronchin.

FIGURE 4.8.5 Warren Cup. British Museum. Photograph: © The Trustees of the British Museum.

FIGURE 5.1.1 Detail of Cernunnos, Pillar of the Sailors. Paris, Musée National du Moyen Age—Musée de Cluny. Photograph: author.

FIGURE 5.1.2 Cast of a Jupiter Column. Ladenburg, Lobdengau-Museum Ladenburg. Photograph: author.

FIGURE 5.1.3 Tombstone of Insus the Treveran. Lancaster, Lancaster City Museum. Photograph: author.

FIGURE 5.1.4 Tombstones of Victor and Regina. South Shields, Arbeia Roman Fort and Museum. Photograph: author.

FIGURE 5.2.1 Minerva. Tarragona. Photograph: Carmen García Bueno.

FIGURE 5.2.2 Warrior. Osuna. Photograph: Peter Whitte, Deutsches Archäologisches Institut, Abt. Madrid, D-DAI-MAD-WIT-R-052-93-01.

FIGURE 5.2.3 Silver male portrait from Vaison. Photograph: Courtesy of the Musée archéologique Théo Desplans. Vaison-la-Romaine, France. Réference J. Sautel 2220.

FIGURE 5.2.4 Aeneas group. Mérida. Drawing and Photographs: Courtesy of Trinidad Nogales.

FIGURE 5.2.5 Stela from Adai. Photograph: Courtesy of Museo Provincial de Lugo.

FIGURE 5.3.1 Saturn/Caelus from Hadrumetum. Photograph: Nathalie de Chaisemartin.

FIGURE 5.3.2 Center of the pediment of the Temple of Genius Civitatis of Oea depicting turreted Fortune between Apollo and Minerva. Tripoli, Libya. Photograph: Nathalie de Chaisemartin.

FIGURE 5.3.3 Portrait of Gordion I. Tunis, Musée du Bardo. Photograph: François Baratte.

FIGURE 5.3.4 Portrait of a hunter from Sidi Ghrib. Carthage, Musée de Carthage. Photograph: François Baratte.

FIGURE 5.3.5 Stela of Maghrawa (called Ghorfa). Tunis, Musée du Bardo. Photograph: François Baratte.

FIGURE 5.4.1 The Epidauros Aphrodite. Athens, National Museum. Photograph: Walter Hege, Neg. D-DAI-ATH-Hege 1100.

FIGURE 5.4.2 Attic Sarcophagus with Calydonian Boar Hunt. Patras. Athens, National Museum. Photograph: Neg. D-DAI-ATH-NM 450.

FIGURE 5.4.3 Late antique portrait of prominent woman. Archaeological Museum of Thessaloniki. Photograph: Makis Skiadaressis. Photoarchive ΑΓΜΕ: Museum of Casts of the University of Thessaloniki, no. 87A.

FIGURE 5.4.4 Late antique portrait of prominent man. Archaeological Museum of Thessaloniki. Photograph: Makis Skiadaressis. Photoarchive ΑΓΜΕ: Museum of Casts of the University of Thessaloniki, no. 133A.

FIGURE 5.6.1 Statue of the Egyptian god Horus. London, British Museum. Photograph: © Trustees of the British Museum.

FIGURE 5.6.2 Seated statue of Tesenuphis. Cairo, Egyptian Museum Photograph: After Graindor 1937, pl. lxi.a.

FIGURE 5.6.3 Statue of a woman found at Asyut. Alexandria, Graeco-Roman Museum. Photograph: After Graindor 1937, pl. lv.

FIGURE 5.6.4 Bronze head with glass inlaid eyes. Alexandria, Graeco-Roman Museum. Photograph: After Graindor 1937, pl. x.

FIGURE 5.7.1 Distribution of Graeco-Roman marble sculpture in the Near East. Map: © Karl-Uwe Mahler, Mainz.

FIGURE 5.7.2 Marble statue of flying Daidalos from the slope of the citadel in Philadelphia/Amman. Amman, Jordan Archaeological Museum. Photograph: © Dr. Mustafa Koçak, Mainz.

FIGURE 5.7.3 Marble portrait of a Julio-Claudian prince, probably Germanicus, from Berytus. Courtesy of Dr. L. Bader, Beirut. Photograph: © Dr. Karl-Uwe Mahler, Mainz.

FIGURE 5.7.4 Marble figurine of a gliding Nike/Victory from Ladhakiya, Syrian Laodikeia ad Mare. Vienna, Kunsthistorisches Museum. Photograph: © Kunsthistorisches Museum Vienna.

FIGURE 5.7.5 Basalt statue of a gliding Nike/Victory from Philippopolis. Shahba, Museum. Photograph: © Thomas M. Weber.

FIGURE 6.1.1 Lawrence Alma-Tadema, A Dealer in Statues / A Sculpture Gallery in Rome at the Time of Augustus (Opus XLIX). The Montreal Museum of Fine Arts, purchase, the

Horsley and Annie Townsend Bequest. Photograph: The Montreal Museum of Fine Arts, Denis Farley.

FIGURE 6.1.2 Marble San Ildefonso Group. Madrid, Museo Nacional del Prado. Photograph: Museo Nacional del Prado/Art Resource, New York.

FIGURE 6.1.3 Roman version of Praxiteles's Apollo Sauroctonos. Paris, Louvre Museum. Photograph: author.

FIGURE 6.2.1 The Tivoli General. Rome, Museo Nazionale Romano, Palazzo Massimo alle Terme. Photograph: Faraglia, D-DAI-ROM 32.412.

FIGURE 6.2.2 Relief, probably funerary, depicting chariot racing. Probably from Rome. Vatican City, Musei Vaticani: Museo Gregoriano Profano. Photograph: FA2208-02, www.arachne.uni-koeln.de.

FIGURE 6.2.3 Sarcophagus depicting the revenge of Orestes. Tomba della Medusa, Rome. Vatican City, Musei Vaticani: Museo Gregoriano Profano. Photograph: FA S5709-01, www.arachne.uni-koeln.de.

FIGURE 6.2.4 Funerary relief of the Servilii. Rome. Vatican City, Musei Vaticani: Museo Gregoriano Profano. Photograph: FA-S5722-01, www.arachne.uni-koeln.de.

FIGURE 6.3.1 Pediment from Temple of Apollo Sosianus. Rome, Musei Capitolini, Centrale Montemartini. Photograph: Archivio Fotografico dei Musei Capitolini, © Roma, Sovrintendenza Capitolina ai Beni Culturali.

FIGURE 6.3.2 Interior frieze from Temple of Apollo Sosianus. Rome, Musei Capitolini, Centrale Montemartini. Photograph: Singer, D-DAI-ROM 71.45.

FIGURE 6.3.3 Base for statue of the athlete Pythokles by Polykleitos. Originally from Olympia; found in Templum Pacis, Rome. Museo Capitolini. Photograph: Archivio Fotografico dei Musei Capitolini, © Roma, Sovrintendenza Capitolina ai Beni Culturali.

FIGURE 6.4.1 Wall painting. Villa of Ariadne, Castellammare di Stabia. Museo Archeologico Nazionale di Napoli. Photograph: Ministero dei Beni e delle Attività Culturali e del Turismo—Museo Archeologico Nazionale di Napoli. © Luigi Spina.

FIGURE 6.4.2 Wall painting. House of Joseph II in Pompeii. Museo Archeologico Nazionale di Napoli. Photograph: Ministero dei Beni e delle Attività Culturali e del Turismo—Museo Archeologico Nazionale di Napoli. © Luigi Spina.

FIGURE 6.4.3 Altar of the Vicomagistri. Vatican City, Vatican Museums, Museo Pio Clementino. Photograph: Vatican Museums.

FIGURE 6.4.4 Denarius of L. Censorinus. 82 BC. Photograph: Courtesy of Collection De Nederlandsche Bank, Amsterdam.

FIGURE 6.5.1 Terracotta plaque of a cult scene with maenads and a satyr bathing a herm. Paris, Louvre. Photograph: © RMN-Grand Palais/Christian Larrieu/Art Resource, New York.

FIGURE 6.6.1 Mutilated bronze statuette of Caligula. Antikenmuseum Basel und Sammlung Ludwig. Photograph: A. Voegelin.

FIGURE 6.6.2 Reconstructed head of the cult statue of Zeus from Cyrene. Photograph: Courtesy of Donald White.

Index

Printed and bound by CPI Group (UK) Ltd, Croydon, CR0 4YY